HOLT SCIENCE & TECHNOLOGY

Life Science

HOLT, RINEHART AND WINSTON
A Harcourt Education Company
Orlando • Austin • New York • San Diego • Toronto • London

Acknowledgments

Contributing Authors

Katy Z. Allen
Science Writer
Wayland, Massachusetts

Linda Ruth Berg, Ph.D.
Adjunct Professor
Natural Sciences
St. Petersburg College
St. Petersburg, Florida

Barbara Christopher
Science Writer and Editor
Austin, Texas

Jennie Dusheck
Science Writer
Santa Cruz, California

Mark F. Taylor, Ph.D.
Associate Professor of Biology
Biology Department
Baylor University
Waco, Texas

Inclusion Specialist

Ellen McPeek Glisan
Special Needs Consultant
San Antonio, Texas

Safety Reviewer

Jack Gerlovich, Ph.D.
Associate Professor
School of Education
Drake University
Des Moines, Iowa

Academic Reviewers

Glenn Adelson
Instructor
Biology Undergraduate Program
Harvard University
Cambridge, Massachusetts

Christopher B. Boyko, Ph.D.
Research Associate
Division of Invertebrate Zoology
American Museum of Natural History
New York, New York

John Brockhaus, Ph.D.
Professor of Geospatial Information Science and Director of Geospatial Information Science Program
Department of Geography and Environmental Engineering
United States Military Academy
West Point, New York

Ruth E. Buskirk, Ph.D.
Senior Lecturer
Biological Sciences
The University of Texas at Austin
Austin, Texas

Michael Carleton, Ph.D.
Curator of Mammals
Smithsonian Museum of Natural History
Washington, D.C.

Joe W. Crim, Ph.D.
Professor and Head of Cellular Biology
Department of Cellular Biology
University of Georgia
Athens, Georgia

Jim Denbow, Ph.D.
Associate Professor of Archaeology
Department of Anthropology and Archaeology
The University of Texas at Austin
Austin, Texas

William E. Dunscombe
Chairman
Biology Department
Union County College
Cranford, New Jersey

William Grisham, Ph.D.
Lecturer
Psychology Department
University of California, Los Angeles
Los Angeles, California

David Haig, Ph.D.
Professor of Biology
Organismic and Evolutionary Biology
Harvard University
Cambridge, Massachusetts

David Hershey, Ph.D.
Education Consultant
Hyattsville, Maryland

Ping H. Johnson, M.D., Ph.D., CHES
Assistant Professor of Health Education
Department of Health, Physical Education and Sport Science
Kennesaw State University
Kennesaw, Georgia

Linda Jones
Program Manager
Texas Department of Public Health
Austin, Texas

Jamie Kneitel, Ph.D.
Postdoctoral Associate
Department of Biology
Washington University
St. Louis, Missouri

John Krenz, Ph.D.
Associate Professor
Biological Sciences
Minnesota State University
Mankato, Minnesota

Nancy L. McQueen, Ph.D.
Professor of Microbiology
Department of Biological Sciences
California State University, Los Angeles
Los Angeles, California

Gerald J. Niemi, Ph.D.
Professor and Center Director
Biology and Center for Water and the Environment
Natural Resources Research Institute
University of Minnesota
Duluth, Minnesota

Acknowledgments
continued on page 874

Printed in the United States of America

ISBN 0-03-066476-4

3 4 5 6 7 048 08 07 06 05 04

Contents in Brief

Contents

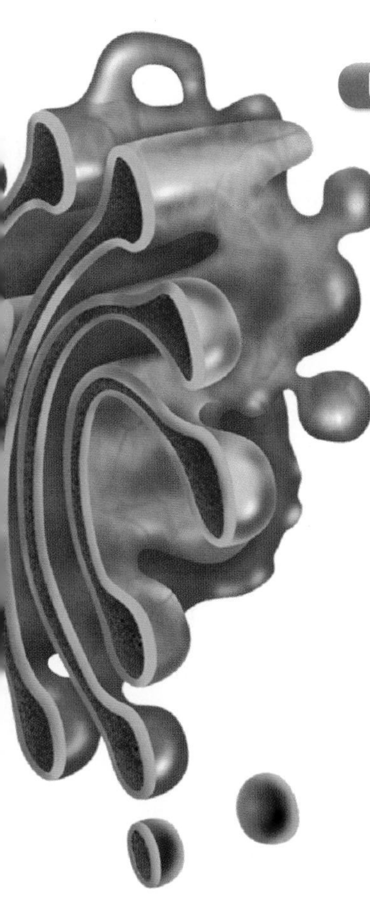

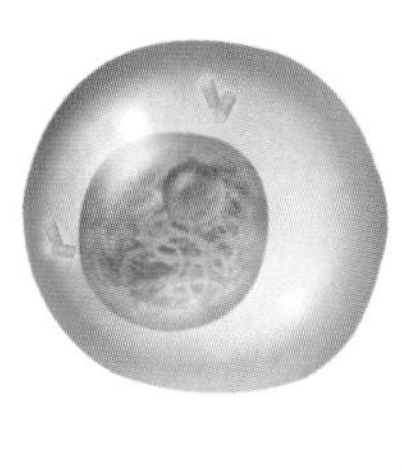
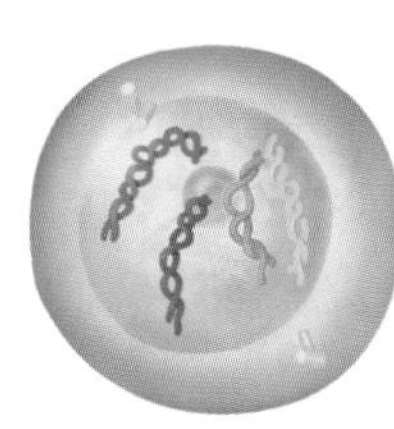

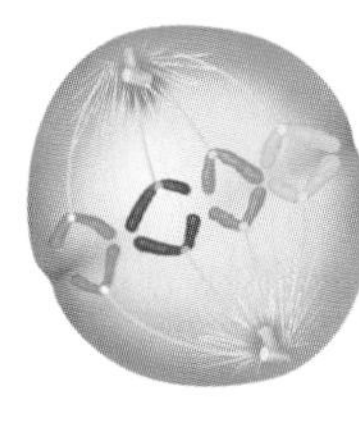
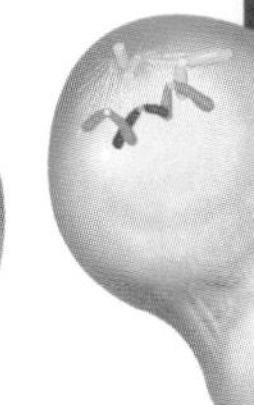

UNIT 3 Heredity, Evolution, and Classification

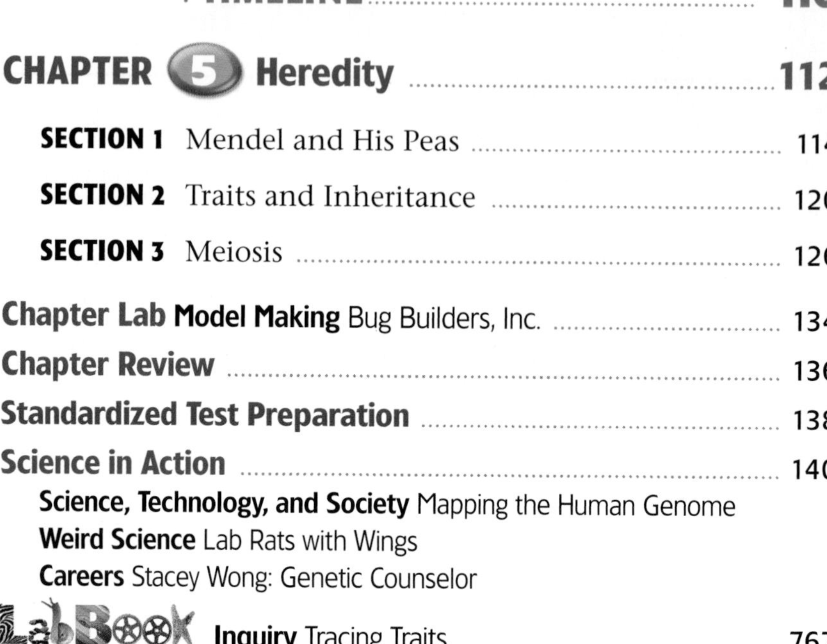

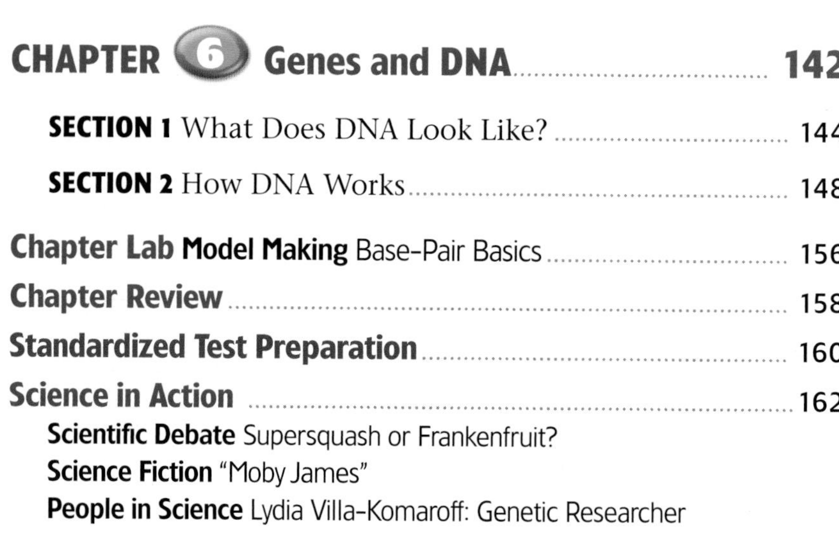

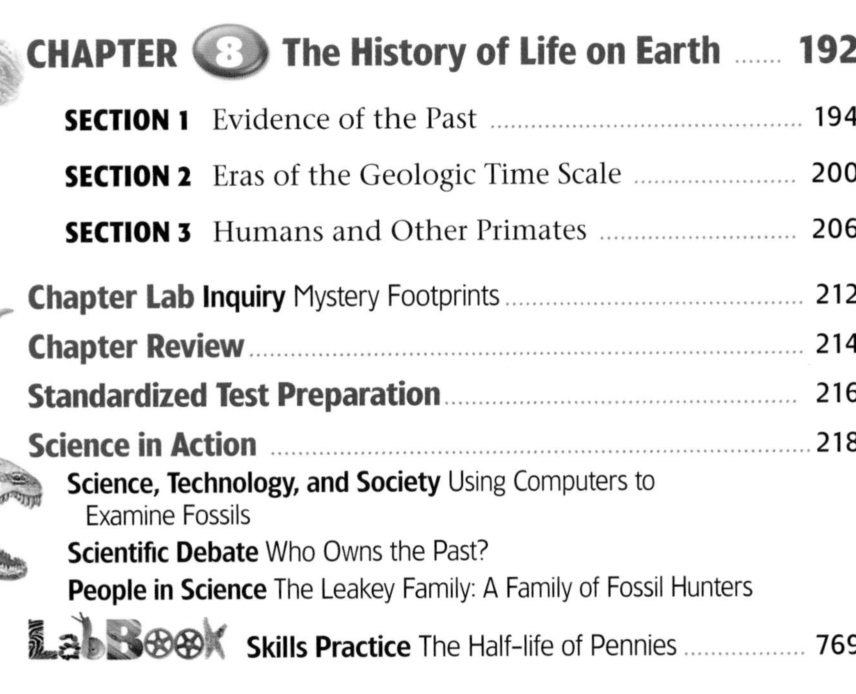

UNIT 4 Simple Organisms, Fungi, and Plants

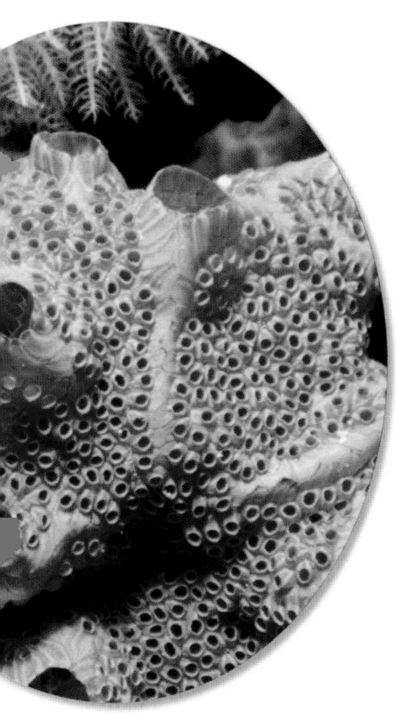

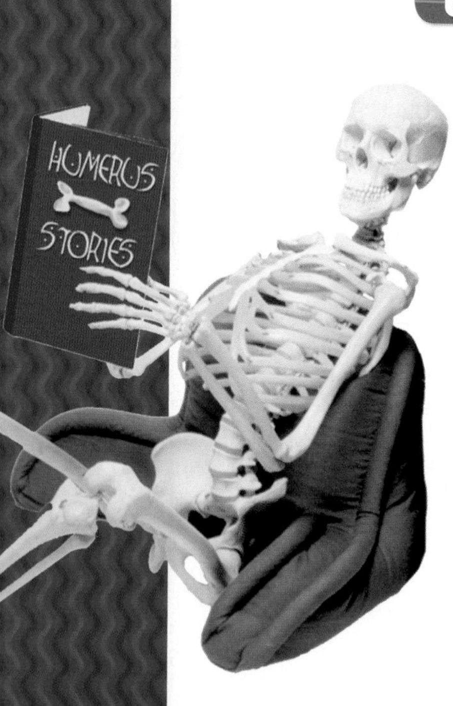
HUMERUS
STORIES

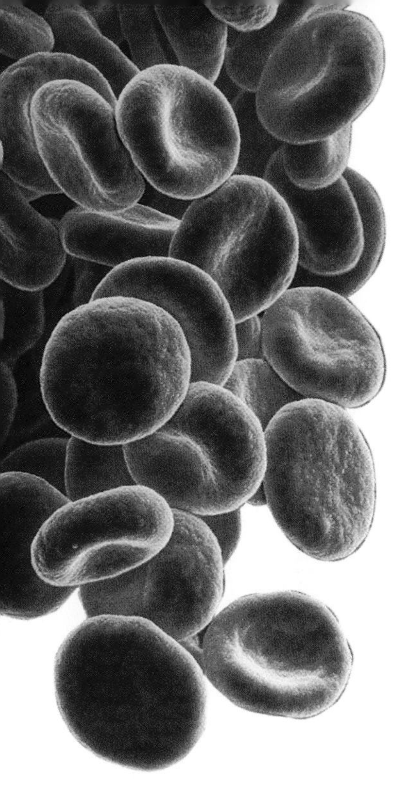

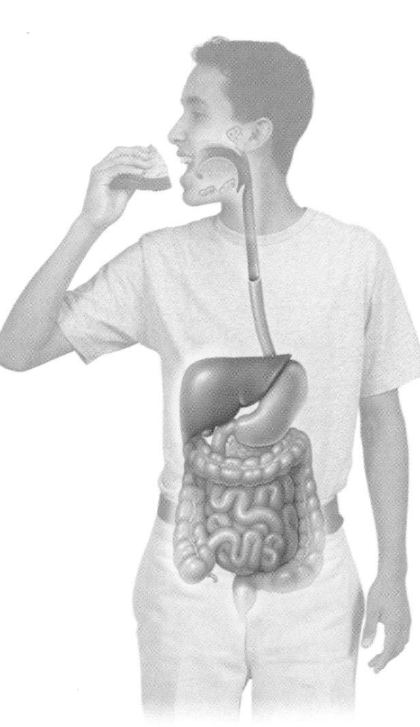

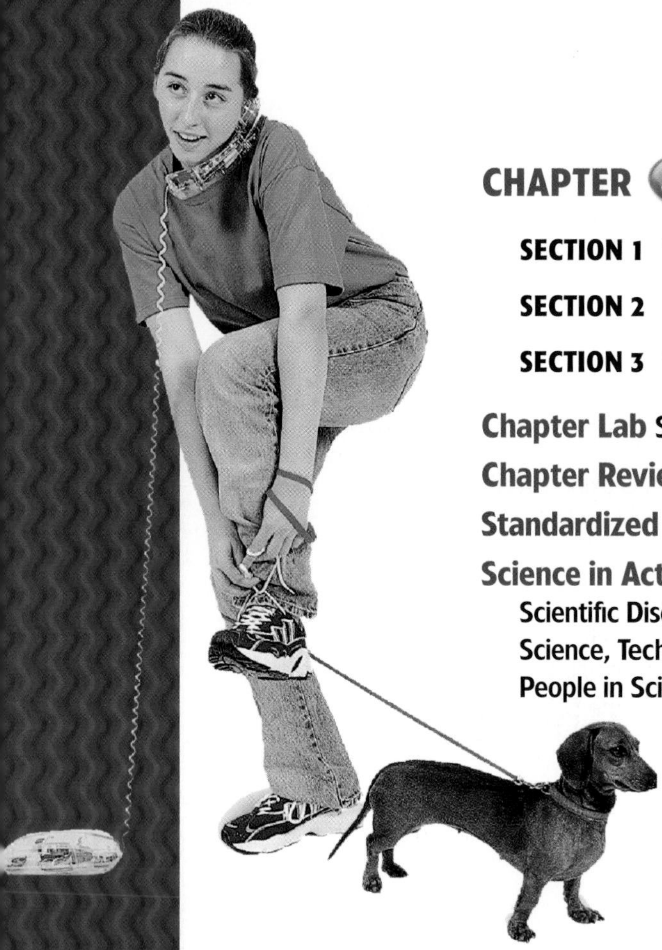

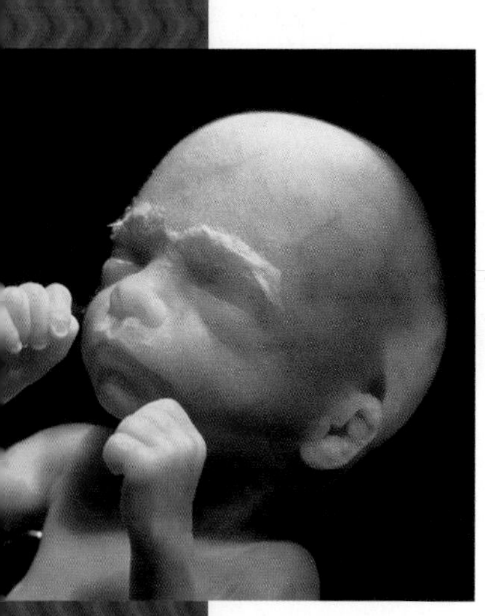

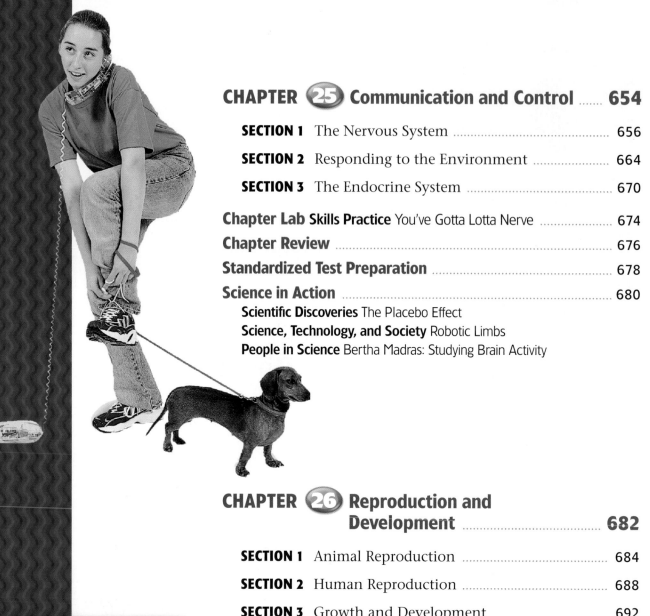

Chapter Labs and LabBook

The more labs, the better!

Take a minute to browse the variety of exciting **labs** in this textbook. Labs appear within the chapters and in a special LabBook in the back of the textbook. All labs are designed to help you experience science firsthand. But please don't forget to be safe. Read the Safety First! section before starting any of the labs.

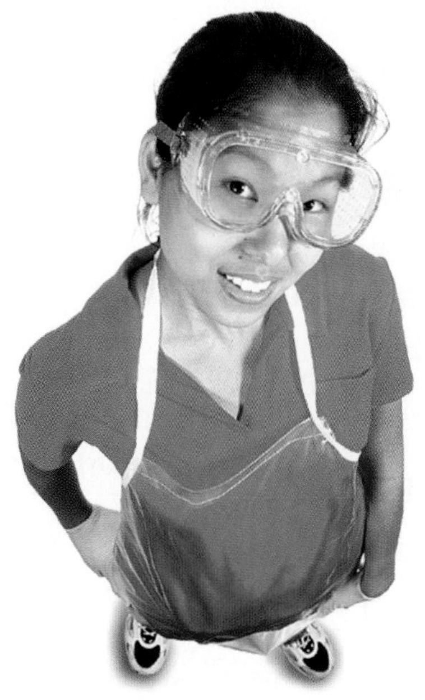

Start your engines with an activity!

Get motivated to learn by doing the two activities at the beginning of each chapter. The **Pre-Reading Activity** helps you organize information as you read the chapter. The **Start-up Activity** helps you gain scientific understanding of the topic through hands-on experience.

FOLDNOTES

Graphic Organizer

START-UP ACTIVITY

READING STRATEGY

Remembering what you read doesn't have to be hard!

A **Reading Strategy** at the beginning of every section provides tips to help you remember and/or organize the information covered in the section.

Quick Lab

School to Home Activity

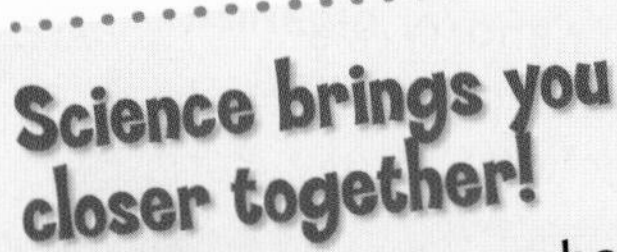

Science brings you closer together!

Bring science into your home by doing **School-to-Home Activities** with a parent or another adult in your household.

Internet Activity

Get caught in the Web!

Go to **go.hrw.com** for **Internet Activities** related to each chapter. To find the Internet Activity for a particular chapter, just type in the keyword listed below.

Math Practice

Math Focus

Science and math go hand in hand.

The **Math Focus** and **Math Practice** items show you many ways that math applies directly to science and vice versa.

Connection to . . .

One subject leads to another.

You may not realize it at first, but different subjects are related to each other in many ways. Each **Connection** explores a topic from the viewpoint of another discipline. In this way, all of the subjects you learn about in school merge to improve your understanding of the world around you.

Science in Action

Science moves beyond the classroom!

Read **Science in Action** articles to learn more about science in the real world. These articles will give you an idea of how interesting, strange, helpful, and action packed science is. At the end of each chapter, you will find three short articles. And if your thirst is still not quenched, go to **go.hrw.com** for in-depth coverage.

Science Fiction

Science, Technology, and Society

Scientific Debate

Scientific Discoveries

Weird Science

Careers

People in Science

How to Use Your Textbook

Your Roadmap for Success with Holt Science and Technology

Reading Warm-Up

A Reading Warm-Up at the beginning of every section provides you with the section's objectives and key terms. The objectives tell you what you'll need to know after you finish reading the section.

Key terms are listed for each section. Learn the definitions of these terms because you will most likely be tested on them. Each key term is highlighted in the text and is defined at point of use and in the margin. You can also use the glossary to locate definitions quickly.

STUDY TIP Reread the objectives and the definitions to the key terms when studying for a test to be sure you know the material.

SECTION 2

How DNA Works

Almost every cell in your body contains 1.5 m of DNA. How does all of the DNA fit in a cell? And how does the DNA hold a code that affects your traits?

DNA is found in the cells of all organisms, including bacteria, mosquitoes, and humans. Each organism has a unique set of DNA. But DNA functions the same way in all organisms.

READING WARM-UP

Objectives

- Explain the relationship between DNA, genes, and proteins.
- Outline the basic steps in making a protein.
- Describe three types of mutations, and provide an example of a gene mutation.
- Describe two examples of uses of genetic knowledge.

Terms to Learn

RNA
ribosome
mutation

READING STRATEGY

Reading Organizer As you read this section, make a flowchart of the steps of how DNA codes for proteins.

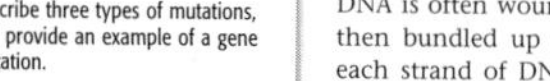

Unraveling DNA

DNA is often wound around proteins, coiled into strands, and then bundled up even more. In a cell that lacks a nucleus, each strand of DNA forms a loose loop within the cell. In a cell that has a nucleus, the strands of DNA and proteins are bundled into chromosomes, as shown in **Figure 1.**

The structure of DNA allows DNA to hold information. The order of the bases on one side of the molecule is a code that carries information. A *gene* consists of a string of nucleotides that give the cell information about how to make a specific trait. There is an enormous amount of DNA, so there can be a large variety of genes. Humans have at least 30,000 genes.

Reading Check What makes up a gene? *(See the Appendix for answers to Reading Checks.)*

Figure 1 Unraveling DNA

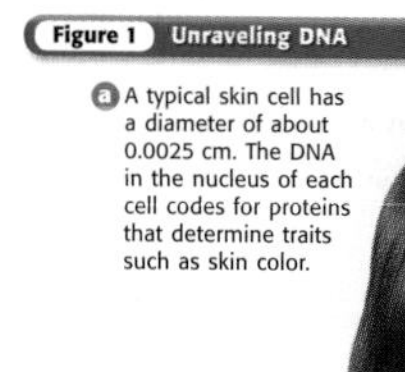

a) A typical skin cell has a diameter of about 0.0025 cm. The DNA in the nucleus of each cell codes for proteins that determine traits such as skin color.

b) The DNA in the nucleus is part of a material called *chromatin*. Long strands of chromatin are usually bundled loosely within the nucleus.

148 Chapter 6

Get Organized

A Reading Strategy at the beginning of every section provides tips to help you organize and remember the information covered in the section. Keep a science notebook so that you are ready to take notes when your teacher reviews the material in class. Keep your assignments in this notebook so that you can review them when studying for the chapter test.

Be Resourceful — Use the Web

SCILINKS

Internet Connect boxes in your textbook take you to resources that you can use for science projects, reports, and research papers. Go to scilinks.org, and type in the SciLinks code to get information on a topic.

go.hrw.com

Visit go.hrw.com

Find worksheets, **Current Science®** magazine articles online, and other materials that go with your textbook at **go.hrw.com.** Click on the textbook icon and the table of contents to see all of the resources for each chapter.

An Example of a Substitution

A mutation, such as a substitution, can be harmful because it may cause a gene to produce the wrong protein. Consider the DNA sequence GAA. When copied as mRNA, this sequence gives the instructions to place the amino acid glutamic acid into the growing protein. If a mistake happens and the original DNA sequence is changed to GTA, the sequence will code for the amino acid valine instead.

This simple change in an amino acid can cause the disease *sickle cell anemia*. Sickle cell anemia affects red blood cells. When valine is substituted for glutamic acid in a blood protein, as shown in **Figure 4,** the red blood cells are changed into a sickle shape.

The sickle cells are not as good at carrying oxygen as normal red blood cells are. Sickle cells are also likely to get stuck in blood vessels and cause painful and dangerous clots.

Reading Check What causes sickle cell anemia?

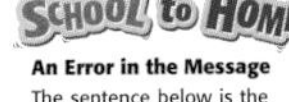

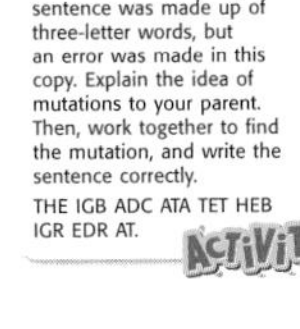

An Error in the Message

The sentence below is the result of an error similar to a DNA mutation. The original sentence was made up of three-letter words, but an error was made in this copy. Explain the idea of mutations to your parent. Then, work together to find the mutation, and write the sentence correctly.

THE IGB ADC ATA TET HEB IGR EDR AT.

ACTIVITY

Figure 4 How Sickle Cell Anemia Results from a Mutation

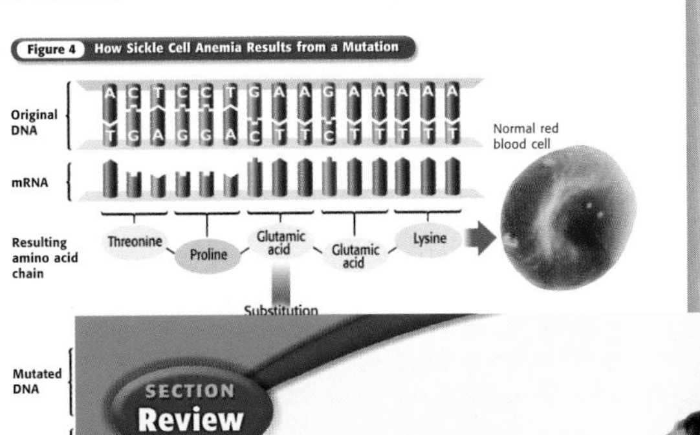

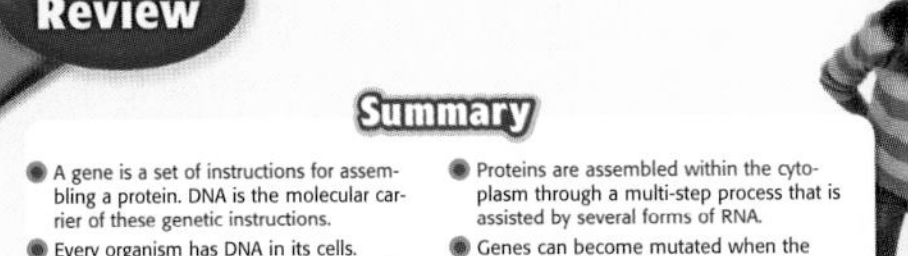

SECTION **Review**

Summary

- A gene is a set of instructions for assembling a protein. DNA is the molecular carrier of these genetic instructions.
- Every organism has DNA in its cells. Humans have 1.5 m of DNA in each cell. This DNA makes up over 30,000 genes.
- Within a gene, each group of three bases codes for one amino acid. A sequence of amino acids is linked to make a protein.
- Proteins are fundamental to the function of cells and the expression of traits.
- Proteins are assembled within the cytoplasm through a multi-step process that is assisted by several forms of RNA.
- Genes can become mutated when the order of the bases is changed. Three main types of mutations are possible: insertion, deletion, and substitution.
- Genetic knowledge has many practical uses. Some applications of genetic knowledge are controversial.

Using Key Terms

1. Use each of the following terms in the same sentence: *ribosome* and *RNA*.
2. In your own words, write a definition for the term *mutation*.

Understanding Key Ideas

3. Explain the relationship between genes and proteins.
4. List three possible types of mutations.
5. Which type of mutation causes sickle cell anemia?
   a. substitution c. deletion
   b. insertion d. mutagen

Math Skills

6. A set of 23 chromosomes in a human cell contains 3.2 billion pairs of DNA bases in sequence. On average, about how many pairs of bases are in each chromosome?

Critical Thinking

7. **Applying Concepts** In which cell type might a mutation be passed from generation to generation? Explain.
8. **Making Comparisons** How is genetic engineering different from natural reproduction?

Interpreting Graphics

The illustration below shows a sequence of bases on one strand of a DNA molecule. Use the illustration below to answer the questions that follow.

9. How many amino acids are coded for by the sequence on one side (A) of this DNA strand?
10. What is the order of bases on the complementary side of the strand (B), from left to right?
11. If a G were inserted as the first base on the top side (A), what would the order of bases be on the complementary side (B)?

SciLINKS
NSTA
Developed and maintained by the National Science Teachers Association
For a variety of links related to this chapter, go to www.scilinks.org
Topic: Genetic Engineering
SciLinks code: HSM0654

155

Use the Illustrations and Photos

Art shows complex ideas and processes. Learn to analyze the art so that you better understand the material you read in the text.

Tables and graphs display important information in an organized way to help you see relationships.

A picture is worth a thousand words. Look at the photographs to see relevant examples of science concepts that you are reading about.

Answer the Section Reviews

Section Reviews test your knowledge of the main points of the section. Critical Thinking items challenge you to think about the material in greater depth and to find connections that you infer from the text.

STUDY TIP When you can't answer a question, reread the section. The answer is usually there.

Do Your Homework

Your teacher may assign worksheets to help you understand and remember the material in the chapter.

STUDY TIP Don't try to answer the questions without reading the text and reviewing your class notes. A little preparation up front will make your homework assignments a lot easier. Answering the items in the Chapter Review will help prepare you for the chapter test.

Holt Online Learning

Visit Holt Online Learning

If your teacher gives you a special password to log onto the Holt Online Learning site, you'll find your complete textbook on the Web. In addition, you'll find some great learning tools and practice quizzes. You'll be able to see how well you know the material from your textbook.

CNN Student News™

Visit CNN Student News

You'll find up-to-date events in science at **cnnstudentnews.com.**

Exploring, inventing, and investigating are essential to the study of science. However, these activities can also be dangerous. To make sure that your experiments and explorations are safe, you must be aware of a variety of safety guidelines. You have probably heard of the saying, "It is better to be safe than sorry." This is particularly true in a science classroom where experiments and explorations are being performed. Being uninformed and careless can result in serious injuries. Don't take chances with your own safety or with anyone else's.

The following pages describe important guidelines for staying safe in the science classroom. Your teacher may also have safety guidelines and tips that are specific to your classroom and laboratory. Take the time to be safe.

Safety Rules!

Start Out Right

Always get your teacher's permission before attempting any laboratory exploration. Read the procedures carefully, and pay particular attention to safety information and caution statements. If you are unsure about what a safety symbol means, look it up or ask your teacher. You cannot be too careful when it comes to safety. If an accident does occur, inform your teacher immediately regardless of how minor you think the accident is.

If you are instructed to note the odor of a substance, wave the fumes toward your nose with your hand. Never put your nose close to the source.

Safety Symbols

All of the experiments and investigations in this book and their related worksheets include important safety symbols to alert you to particular safety concerns. Become familiar with these symbols so that when you see them, you will know what they mean and what to do. It is important that you read this entire safety section to learn about specific dangers in the laboratory.

Eye protection

Clothing protection

Hand safety

Heating safety

Electric safety

Chemical safety

Animal safety

Sharp object

Plant safety

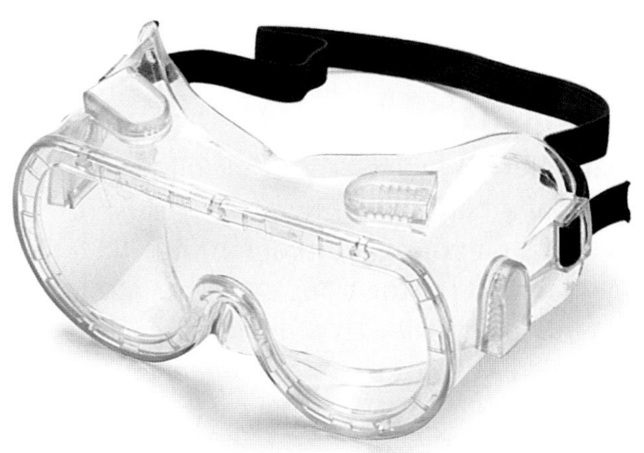

Eye Safety

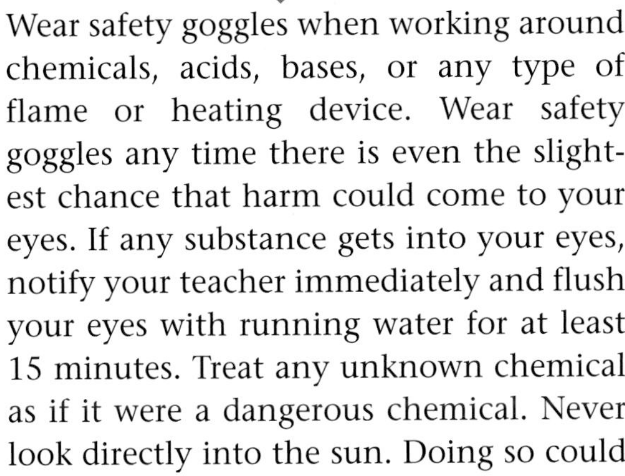

Wear safety goggles when working around chemicals, acids, bases, or any type of flame or heating device. Wear safety goggles any time there is even the slightest chance that harm could come to your eyes. If any substance gets into your eyes, notify your teacher immediately and flush your eyes with running water for at least 15 minutes. Treat any unknown chemical as if it were a dangerous chemical. Never look directly into the sun. Doing so could cause permanent blindness.

Avoid wearing contact lenses in a laboratory situation. Even if you are wearing safety goggles, chemicals can get between the contact lenses and your eyes. If your doctor requires that you wear contact lenses instead of glasses, wear eye-cup safety goggles in the lab.

Safety Equipment

Know the locations of the nearest fire alarms and any other safety equipment, such as fire blankets and eyewash fountains, as identified by your teacher, and know the procedures for using the equipment.

Neatness

Keep your work area free of all unnecessary books and papers. Tie back long hair, and secure loose sleeves or other loose articles of clothing, such as ties and bows. Remove dangling jewelry. Don't wear open-toed shoes or sandals in the laboratory. Never eat, drink, or apply cosmetics in a laboratory setting. Food, drink, and cosmetics can easily become contaminated with dangerous materials.

Certain hair products (such as aerosol hair spray) are flammable and should not be worn while working near an open flame. Avoid wearing hair spray or hair gel on lab days.

Sharp/Pointed Objects

Use knives and other sharp instruments with extreme care. Never cut objects while holding them in your hands. Place objects on a suitable work surface for cutting.

Be extra careful when using any glassware. When adding a heavy object to a graduated cylinder, tilt the cylinder so the object slides slowly to the bottom.

Chemicals    

Wear safety goggles when handling any potentially dangerous chemicals, acids, or bases. If a chemical is unknown, handle it as you would a dangerous chemical. Wear an apron and protective gloves when you work with acids or bases or whenever you are told to do so. If a spill gets on your skin or clothing, rinse it off immediately with water for at least 5 minutes while calling to your teacher.

Never mix chemicals unless your teacher tells you to do so. Never taste, touch, or smell chemicals unless you are specifically directed to do so. Before working with a flammable liquid or gas, check for the presence of any source of flame, spark, or heat.

Heat

Wear safety goggles when using a heating device or a flame. Whenever possible, use an electric hot plate as a heat source instead of using an open flame. When heating materials in a test tube, always angle the test tube away from yourself and others. To avoid burns, wear heat-resistant gloves whenever instructed to do so.

Electricity

Be careful with electrical cords. When using a microscope with a lamp, do not place the cord where it could trip someone. Do not let cords hang over a table edge in a way that could cause equipment to fall if the cord is accidentally pulled. Do not use equipment with damaged cords. Be sure that your hands are dry and that the electrical equipment is in the "off" position before plugging it in. Turn off and unplug electrical equipment when you are finished.

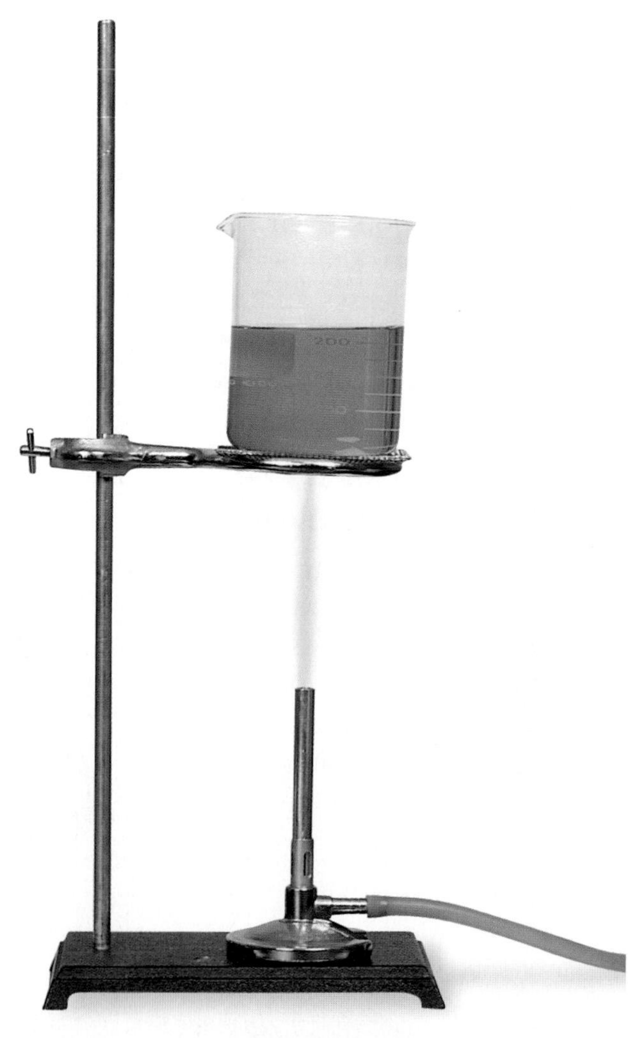

Animal Safety

Always obtain your teacher's permission before bringing any animal into the school building. Handle animals only as your teacher directs. Always treat animals carefully and respectfully. Wash your hands thoroughly after handling any animal.

Plant Safety 

Do not eat any part of a plant or plant seed used in the laboratory. Wash your hands thoroughly after handling any part of a plant. When in nature, do not pick any wild plants unless your teacher instructs you to do so.

Glassware

Examine all glassware before use. Be sure that glassware is clean and free of chips and cracks. Report damaged glassware to your teacher. Glass containers used for heating should be made of heat-resistant glass.

TIMELINE

The Study of Living Things

Life science is the study of living things—from the tiniest bacterium to the largest tree! In this unit, you will discover the similarities of all living things. You will learn about the tools that life scientists use, and you'll learn to ask your own questions about the living world around you.

People have always searched for answers about life. This timeline includes a few of the many people who have studied living things and a few events that have shaped the history of life science. And there's always more to be learned, so keep your eyes open.

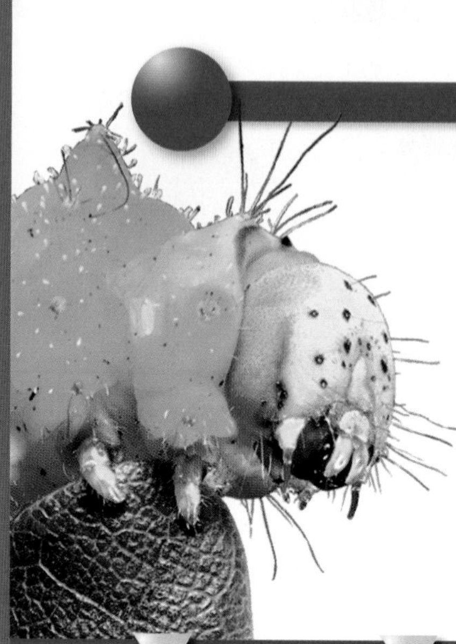

Around 2700 BCE

Si Ling-Chi, empress of China, observes silkworms in her garden and develops a process to cultivate them and make silk.

1931

The first electron microscope is developed.

1934

Dorothy Crowfoot Hodgkin uses X-ray techniques to determine the protein structure of insulin.

1970

Floppy disks for computer data storage are introduced.

1983

Dian Fossey writes *Gorillas in the Mist*, a book about her research on mountain gorillas in Africa and her efforts to save them from poachers.

Around 1000
Arab mathematician and physicist Ibn al Haytham discovers that vision is caused by the reflection of light from objects into the eye.

1684
Improvements to microscopes allow the first observation of red blood cells.

1914
His studies on agriculture and soil conservation lead George Washington Carver to perform research on peanuts.

1944
Oswald T. Avery demonstrates that **DNA** is the material that carries genetic properties in living organisms.

1946
ENIAC, the first entirely electronic computer, is built. It weighs 30 tons.

1967
Dr. Christiaan Barnard performs the first successful human heart transplant.

1984
A process known as **DNA** fingerprinting is developed by Alec Jeffreys.

1998
In China, scientists discover a fossil of a dinosaur that had feathers.

2001
A team of scientists led by Philippa Uwins announces that tiny nanobes that are 20 to 150 nanometers wide have been found in Australia. Scientists debate whether these particles are living.

1

The World of Life Science

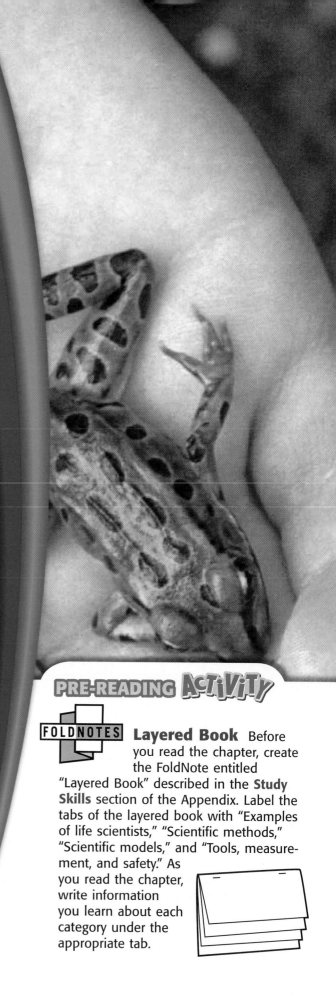

What happened to the legs of these frogs? Life science can help answer this question. Deformed frogs, such as the ones in this photo, have been found in the northern United States and southern Canada. Scientists and students like you have been using life science to find out how frogs can develop deformities.

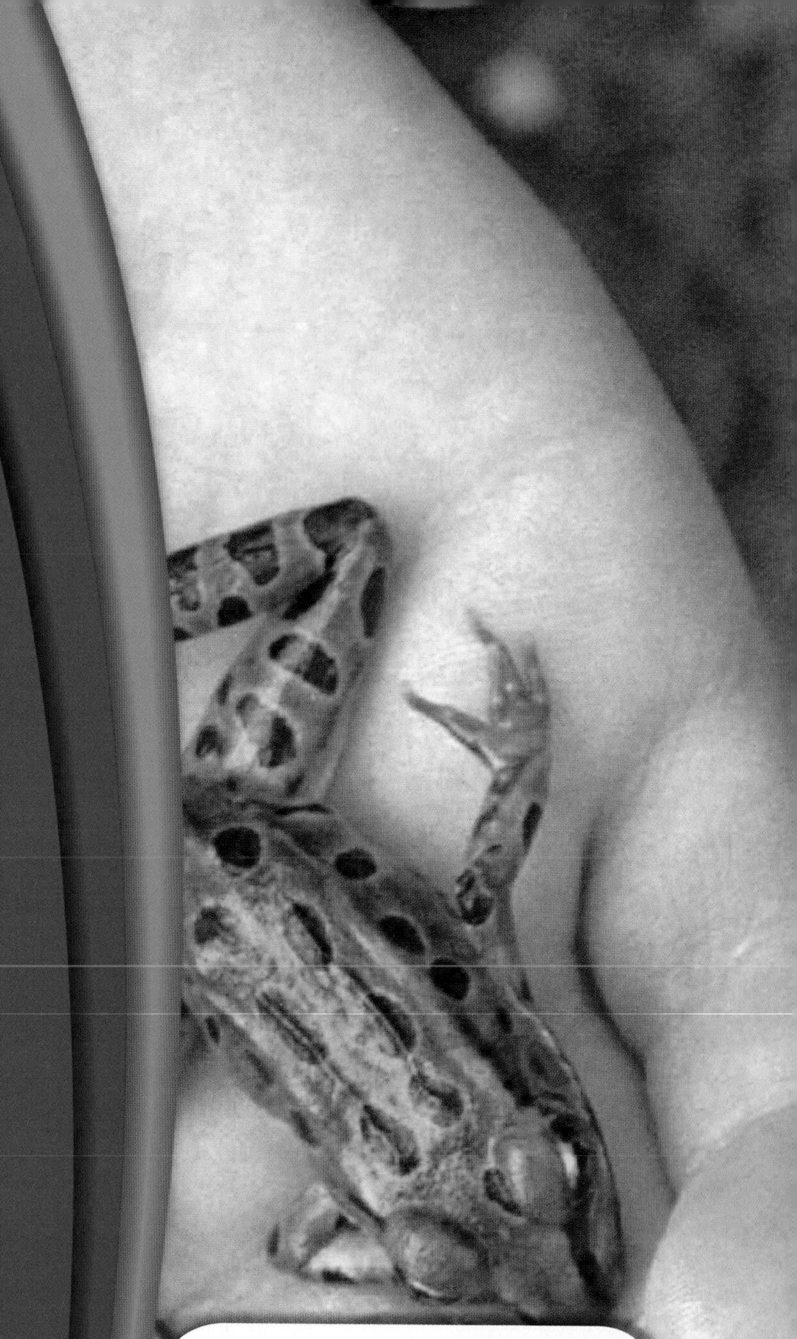

PRE-READING ACTIVITY

FOLDNOTES **Layered Book** Before you read the chapter, create the FoldNote entitled "Layered Book" described in the **Study Skills** section of the Appendix. Label the tabs of the layered book with "Examples of life scientists," "Scientific methods," "Scientific models," and "Tools, measurement, and safety." As you read the chapter, write information you learn about each category under the appropriate tab.

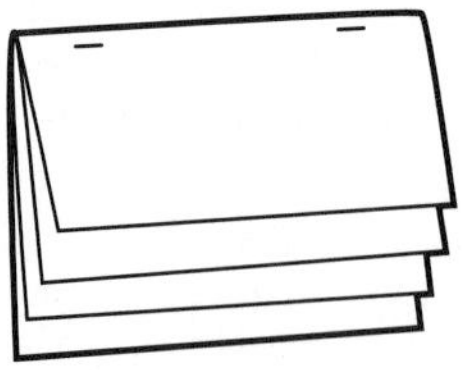

START-UP ACTIVITY

A Little Bit of Science

In this activity, you'll find out that you can learn about the unknown without having to see it.

Procedure

1. Your teacher will give you a **coffee can** to which a **sock** has been attached. Do not look into the can.
2. Reach through the opening in the sock. You will feel **several objects** inside the can.
3. Record observations you make about the objects by feeling them, shaking the can, and so on.
4. What do you think is in the can? List your guesses. State some reasons for your guesses.
5. Pour the contents of the can onto your desk. Compare your list with what was in the can.

Analysis

1. Did you guess the contents of the can correctly? What might have caused you to guess wrongly?
2. What observations did you make about each of the objects while they were in the can? Which of your senses did you use?

SECTION 1

Asking About Life

READING WARM-UP

Objectives

- Explain the importance of asking questions in life science.
- State examples of life scientists at work.
- List three ways life science is beneficial to living things.

Terms to Learn

life science

READING STRATEGY

Paired Summarizing Read this section silently. In pairs, take turns summarizing the material. Stop to discuss ideas that seem confusing.

Imagine that it's summer. You are lying in the grass at the park, casually looking around. Three dogs are playing on your left. A few bumblebees are visiting nearby flowers. And an ant is carrying a crumb away from your sandwich.

Suddenly, a question pops into your head: How do ants find food? Then, you think of another question: Why do the bees visit the yellow flowers but not the red ones? Congratulations! You have just taken the first steps toward becoming a life scientist. How did you do it? You observed the living world around you. You were curious, and you asked questions about your observations. Those steps are what science is all about. **Life science** is the study of living things.

Reading Check **What is life science?** (*See the Appendix for answers to Reading Checks.*)

life science the study of living things

It All Starts with a Question

The world around you is full of an amazing diversity of life. Single-celled algae float unseen in ponds. Giant redwood trees seem to touch the sky. And 40-ton whales swim through the oceans. For every living thing, or organism, that has ever lived, you could ask many questions. Those questions could include (1) How does the organism get its food? (2) Where does it live? and (3) Why does it behave in a particular way?

In Your Own Backyard

Questions are easy to think of. Take a look around your room, your home, and your neighborhood. What questions about life science come to mind? The student in **Figure 1** has questions about some very familiar organisms. Do you know the answer to any of his questions?

Touring the World

The questions you can ask about your neighborhood are just a sample of all the questions you could ask about the world. The world is made up of many different places to live, such as deserts, forests, coral reefs, and tide pools. Just about anywhere you go, you will find some kind of living organism. If you observe these organisms, you can easily think of questions to ask about them.

Why do leaves change color in the fall?
Why did the dinosaurs die out?
How do birds know where to go when they migrate?

Figure 1 *Part of science is asking questions about the world around you.*

Irene Duhart Long asks, "How does the human body respond to space travel?"

Geerat Vermeij asks, "How have shells changed over time?"

Irene Pepperberg asks, "Are parrots smart enough to learn human language?"

Figure 2 *Life scientists ask many different kinds of questions about living things.*

Life Scientists

Close your eyes for a moment, and imagine a life scientist. What do you see? Do you see someone who is in a laboratory and peering into a microscope? Which of the people in **Figure 2** do you think are life scientists?

Anyone

If you guessed that all of the people in **Figure 2** are life scientists, then you are right. Anyone can investigate the world around us. Women and men from any cultural or ethnic background can become life scientists.

Anywhere

Making investigations in a laboratory is an important part of life science, but life science can be studied in many other places, too. Life scientists carry out investigations on farms, in forests, on the ocean floor—even in space. They work for businesses, hospitals, government agencies, and universities. Many are also teachers.

Anything

What a life scientist studies is determined by one thing—his or her curiosity. Life scientists specialize in many different areas of life science. They may study how organisms function and behave. Or they may study how organisms interact with each other and with their environment. Some life scientists explore how organisms reproduce and pass traits from one generation to the next. Some life scientists investigate the ancient origins of organisms and the ways in which organisms have changed over time.

WRITING SKILL **Profile of a Life Scientist** Research some of the life scientists named in this chapter. Choose the scientist who interests you the most. In your **science journal,** write a short biography, career feature, or informational piece about your chosen scientist and the work he or she does. Style the article as a newspaper or magazine article.

Why Ask Questions?

What is the point of asking all these questions? Life scientists might find some interesting answers, but do any of the answers really matter? Will the answers affect *your* life? Absolutely! As you study life science, you will see how the investigations of life science affect you and all the living things around you.

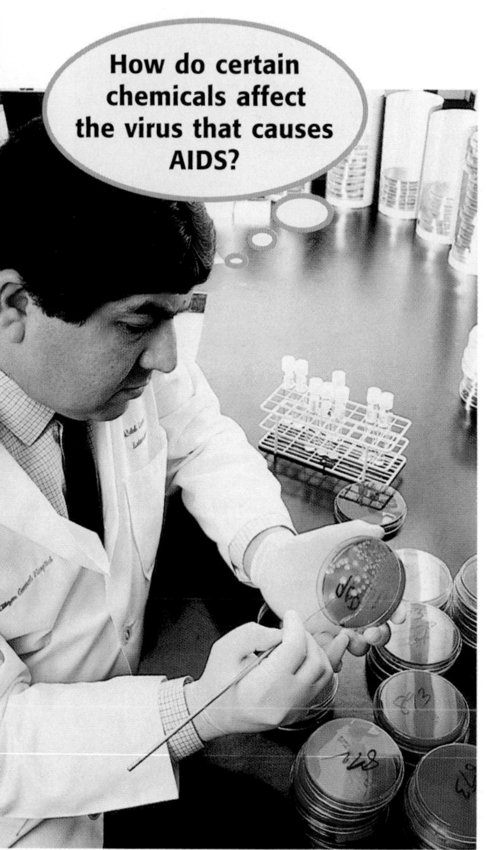

How do certain chemicals affect the virus that causes AIDS?

Figure 3 *Abdul Lakhani studies AIDS to try to find a cure for the disease.*

Fighting Diseases

Polio is a disease that causes paralysis by affecting the brain and nerves. Do you know anyone who has had polio? Probably not. The polio virus has been eliminated from most of the world. But at one time, it was much more common. In 1952, before life scientists discovered ways to prevent the spread of the polio virus, it infected 58,000 Americans.

Today, life scientists continue to search for ways to fight diseases. Acquired immune deficiency syndrome (AIDS) is a disease that kills millions of people every year. The scientist in **Figure 3** is trying to learn more about AIDS. Life scientists have discovered how the virus that causes AIDS is carried from one person to another. Scientists have also learned about how the virus affects the body. By learning more about the virus, scientists may find a cure for this deadly disease.

Understanding Inherited Diseases

Some diseases, such as cystic fibrosis, are inherited. They are passed from parents to children. Most of the information that controls an organism's cells is inherited as coded information. Changes in small parts of this information may cause the organism to be born with or to develop certain diseases. The scientist in **Figure 4** is one of the many scientists worldwide who are studying the way humans inherit the code that controls their cells. By learning about this code, scientists hope to find ways to cure or prevent inherited diseases.

Which part of a person's inherited information is responsible for certain inherited diseases?

Figure 4 *Susumu Tonegawa's work may help in the battle to fight inherited diseases.*

Protecting the Environment

Life scientists also study environmental problems on Earth. Many environmental problems are caused by people's misuse of natural resources. Understanding how we affect the world around us is the first step in finding solutions to problems such as pollution and the extinction of wildlife.

Why should we try to decrease pollution? Pollution can harm our health and the health of other organisms. Water pollution may be a cause of frog deformities seen in Minnesota and other states. Pollution in oceans kills marine mammals, birds, and fish. By finding ways to produce less pollution, we can help make the world a healthier place.

When we cut down trees to clear land for crops or for lumber, we change and sometimes destroy habitats. The man in **Figure 5** is part of a team of Russian and American scientists studying the Siberian tiger. Hunting and loss of forests have caused the tigers to become almost extinct. By learning about the tigers' food and habitat needs, the scientists hope to develop a plan that will ensure their survival.

How much space does a tiger need in order to survive?

Figure 5 *To learn how much land area is used by an individual Siberian tiger, Dale Miquelle puts radio-transmitting collars on the tigers.*

Reading Check **Give an example of a pollution problem.**

SECTION Review

Summary

- Science is a process of gathering knowledge about the natural world. Science includes making observations and asking questions about those observations. Life science is the study of living things.
- A variety of people may become life scientists for a variety of reasons.
- Life science can help solve problems such as disease or pollution, and it can be applied to help living things survive.

Using Key Terms

1. In your own words, write a definition for the term *life science*.

Understanding Key Ideas

2. Life scientists may study any of the following EXCEPT
   - **a.** things that were once living.
   - **b.** environmental problems.
   - **c.** stars in outer space.
   - **d.** diseases that are not inherited by humans.
3. What is the importance of asking questions in life science?
4. Where do life scientists work? What do life scientists study?

Math Skills

5. Students in a science class collected 50 frogs from a pond and found that 15 of these frogs had deformities. What percentage of the frogs had deformities?

Critical Thinking

6. **Identifying Relationships** Make a list of five things you do or deal with daily. Give an example of how life science might relate to each of these things.
7. **Applying Concepts** Look at **Figure 5.** Propose five questions about what you see. Share one of your questions with your classmates.

SCILINKS.
NSTA
Developed and maintained by the National Science Teachers Association
For a variety of links related to this chapter, go to www.scilinks.org
Topic: Careers in Life Science
SciLinks code: HSM0244

SECTION 2

Scientific Methods

Imagine that your class is on a field trip to a wildlife refuge. You discover several deformed frogs. You wonder what could be causing the frogs' deformities.

A group of students from Le Sueur, Minnesota, actually made this discovery! By making observations and asking questions about the observations, the students used scientific methods.

READING WARM-UP

Objectives

- Describe scientific methods.
- Determine the appropriate design of a controlled experiment.
- Use information in tables and graphs to analyze experimental results.
- Explain how scientific knowledge can change.

Terms to Learn

scientific methods
hypothesis
controlled experiment
variable

READING STRATEGY

Reading Organizer As you read this section, make a flowchart of the possible steps in scientific methods.

What Are Scientific Methods?

When scientists observe the natural world, they often think of a question or problem. But scientists don't just guess at answers. They use scientific methods. **Scientific methods** are the ways in which scientists follow steps to answer questions and solve problems. The steps used for all investigations are the same. But the order in which the steps are followed may vary, as shown in **Figure 1.** Scientists may use all of the steps or just some of the steps during an investigation. They may even repeat some of the steps. The order depends on what works best to answer their question. No matter where life scientists work or what questions they try to answer, all life scientists have two things in common. They are curious about the natural world, and they use similar methods to investigate it.

Reading Check What are scientific methods? (*See the Appendix for answers to Reading Checks.*)

scientific methods a series of steps followed to solve problems

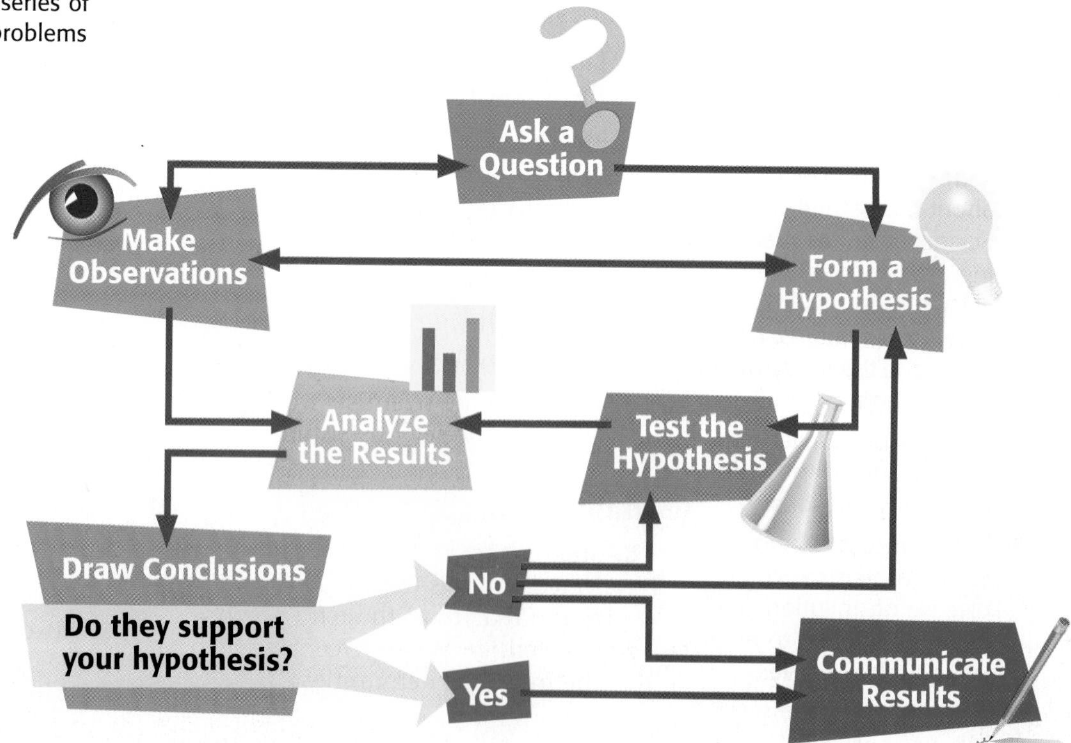

Figure 1 *Scientific methods often include the same steps, but the steps are not always used in the same order.*

Ask a Question

Have you ever observed something out of the ordinary or difficult to explain? Such an observation usually raises questions. For example, you might ask, "Could something in the water be causing the frog deformities?" Looking for answers may include making more observations.

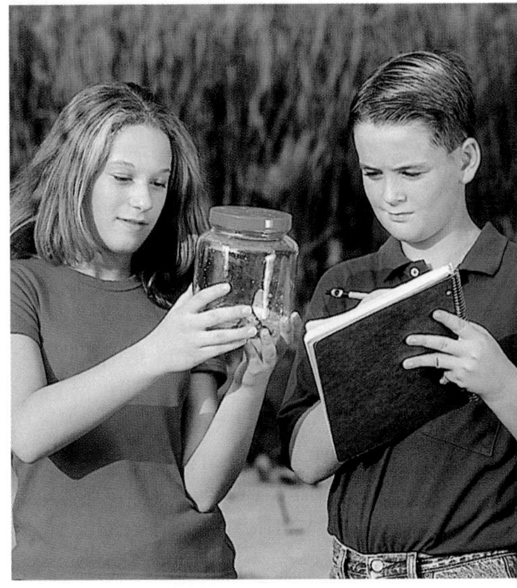

Figure 2 *Making careful observations is often the first step in an investigation.*

Make Observations

After the students from Minnesota realized something was wrong with the frogs, they decided to make additional, careful observations, as shown in **Figure 2.** They counted the number of deformed frogs and the number of normal frogs they caught. The students also photographed the frogs, took measurements, and wrote a thorough description of each frog.

In addition, the students collected data on other organisms living in the pond. They also conducted many tests on the pond water, measuring things such as the level of acidity. The students carefully recorded their data and observations.

Accurate Observations

Any information you gather through your senses is an observation. Observations can take many forms. They may be measurements of length, volume, time, or speed or of how loud or soft a sound is. They may describe the color or shape of an organism. Or they may record the behavior of organisms in an area. The range of observations a scientist can make is endless. But no matter what observations reveal, they are useful only if they are accurately made and recorded. Scientists use many standard tools and methods to make and record observations. Examples of these tools are shown in **Figure 3.**

Figure 3 *Microscopes, rulers, and thermometers are some of the many tools scientists use to collect information. Scientists also record their observations carefully.*

Form a Hypothesis

After asking questions and making observations, scientists may form a hypothesis. A **hypothesis** (hie PAHTH uh sis) is a possible explanation or answer to a question. A good hypothesis is based on observation and can be tested. When scientists form hypotheses, they think logically and creatively and consider what they already know.

To be useful, a hypothesis must be testable. A hypothesis is testable if an experiment can be designed to test the hypothesis. Yet, if a hypothesis is not testable, it is not always wrong. An untestable hypothesis is simply one that cannot be supported or disproved. Sometimes, it may be impossible to gather enough observations to test a hypothesis.

Scientists may form different hypotheses for the same problem. In the case of the Minnesota frogs, scientists formed the hypotheses shown in **Figure 4.** Were any of these explanations correct? To find out, each hypothesis had to be tested.

Reading Check What makes a hypothesis testable?

CONNECTION TO Environmental Science

WRITING SKILL Vanishing Amphibians

Since the 1980s, scientists have been concerned about a steady worldwide decline in the number of amphibians, such as frogs and salamanders. Scientists have studied several possible causes, including UV radiation, chemical pollutants, parasites, and skin fungi. Find a recent news article about one such study, and write a short summary of the article.

hypothesis an explanation that is based on prior scientific research or observations and that can be tested

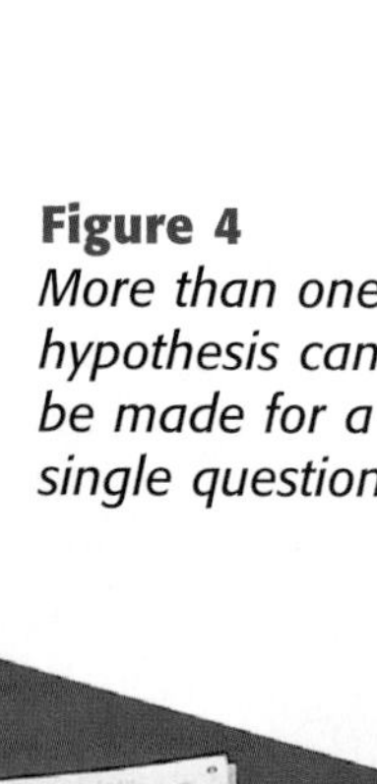

Hypothesis 1:
The deformities were caused by one or more chemical pollutants in the water.
Hypothesis 2:
The deformities were caused by attacks from parasites or other frogs.
Hypothesis 3:
The deformities were caused by an increase in exposure to ultraviolet light from the sun.

Figure 4 *More than one hypothesis can be made for a single question.*

Predictions

Before scientists can test a hypothesis, they must first make predictions. A prediction is a statement of cause and effect that can be used to set up a test for a hypothesis. Predictions are usually stated in an if-then format, as shown in **Figure 5.**

More than one prediction may be made for each hypothesis. For each of the hypotheses on the previous page, the predictions shown in **Figure 5** were made. After predictions are made, scientists can conduct experiments to see which predictions, if any, prove to be true and support the hypotheses.

Figure 5 *More than one prediction may be made for a single hypothesis.*

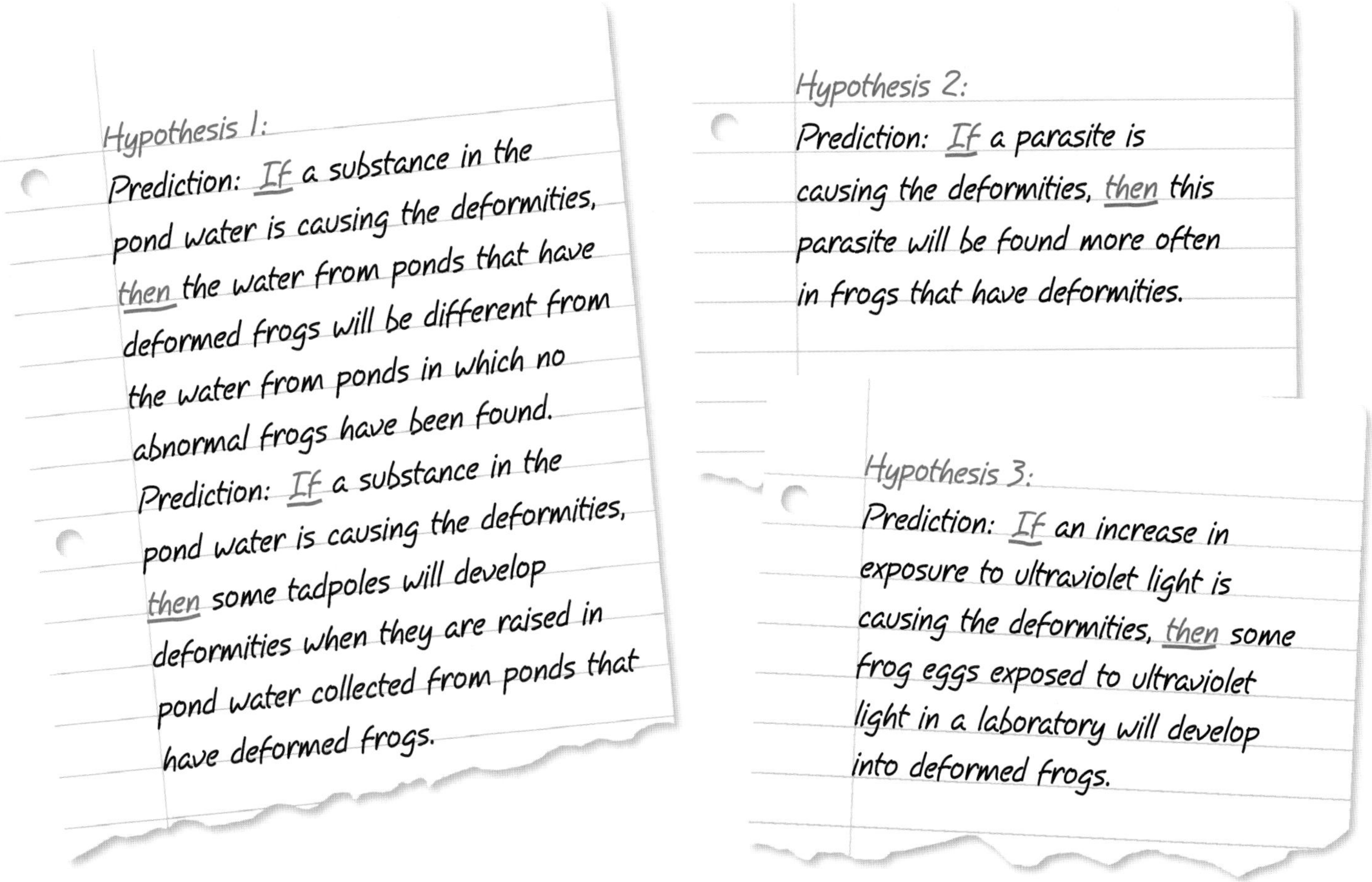

Hypothesis 1:
Prediction: If a substance in the pond water is causing the deformities, then the water from ponds that have deformed frogs will be different from the water from ponds in which no abnormal frogs have been found.
Prediction: If a substance in the pond water is causing the deformities, then some tadpoles will develop deformities when they are raised in pond water collected from ponds that have deformed frogs.

Hypothesis 2:
Prediction: If a parasite is causing the deformities, then this parasite will be found more often in frogs that have deformities.

Hypothesis 3:
Prediction: If an increase in exposure to ultraviolet light is causing the deformities, then some frog eggs exposed to ultraviolet light in a laboratory will develop into deformed frogs.

CONNECTION TO Language Arts

WRITING SKILL **Have Aliens Landed?** Suppose that you and a friend are walking through a heavily wooded park. Suddenly, you come upon a small cluster of trees lying on the ground. What caused them to fall over? Your friend thinks that extraterrestrials knocked the trees down. Write a dialogue of the debate you might have with your friend about whether this hypothesis is testable.

Figure 6 *Many factors affect this tadpole in the wild. These factors include chemicals, light, temperature, and parasites.*

Test the Hypothesis

After scientists make a prediction, they test the hypothesis. Scientists try to design experiments that will clearly show whether a particular factor caused an observed outcome. A *factor* is anything in an experiment that can influence the experiment's outcome. Factors can be anything from temperature to the type of organism being studied.

Under Control

Scientists studying the frogs in Minnesota observed many factors that affect the development of frogs in the wild, as shown in **Figure 6.** But it was hard to tell which factor could be causing the deformities. To sort factors out, scientists perform controlled experiments. A **controlled experiment** tests only one factor at a time and consists of a control group and one or more experimental groups. All of the factors for the control group and the experimental groups are the same except for one. The one factor that differs is called the **variable.** Because only the variable differs between the control group and the experimental groups, any differences observed in the outcome of the experiment are probably caused by the variable.

Reading Check How many factors should an experiment test?

controlled experiment an experiment that tests only one factor at a time by using a comparison of a control group with an experimental group

variable a factor that changes in an experiment in order to test a hypothesis

Designing an Experiment

Designing a good experiment requires planning. Every factor should be considered. Examine the prediction for Hypothesis 3: *If an increase in exposure to ultraviolet light is causing the deformities, then some frog eggs exposed to ultraviolet light in a laboratory will develop into deformed frogs.* An experiment to test this hypothesis is summarized in **Table 1.** In this case, the variable is the length of time the eggs are exposed to ultraviolet (UV) light. All other factors, such as the temperature of the water, are the same in the control group and in the experimental groups.

Table 1 **Experiment to Test Effect of UV Light on Frogs**

	Control factors			Variable
Group	**Kind of frog**	**Number of Eggs**	**Temperature of water**	**UV light exposure**
#1 (control)	leopard frog	100	25°C	0 days
#2 (experimental)	leopard frog	100	25°C	15 days
#3 (experimental)	leopard frog	100	25°C	24 days

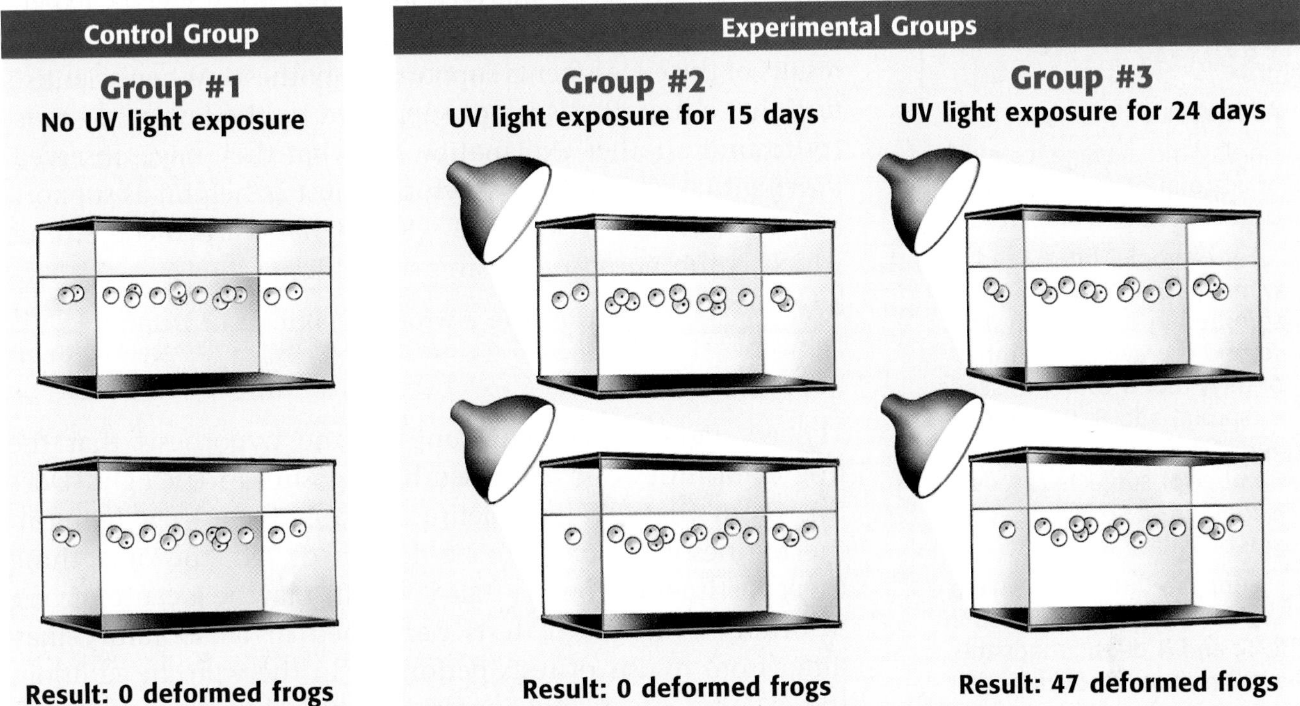

Collecting Data

As **Table 1** shows, each group in the experiment contains 100 eggs. Scientists always try to test many individuals. The more organisms tested, the more certain scientists can be of the data they collect in an experiment. They want to be certain that differences between control and experimental groups are actually caused by differences in the variable and not by any differences among the individuals. Scientists also support their conclusions by repeating their experiments. If an experiment produces the same results again and again, scientists can be more certain about the effect the variable has on the outcome of the experiment. The experimental setup to test Hypothesis 3 is illustrated in **Figure 7.** The results are also shown.

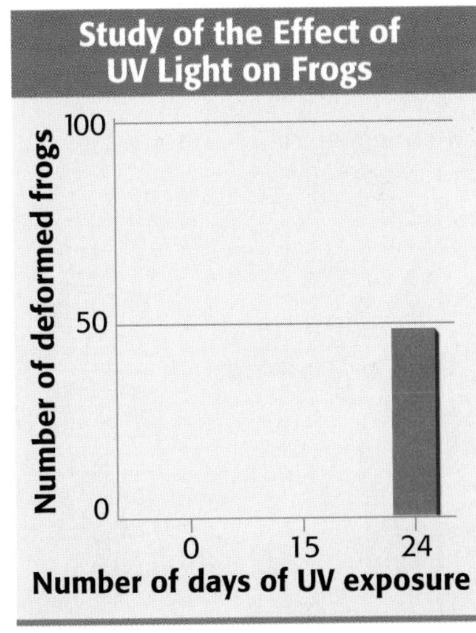

Figure 8 *This graph shows that 24 days of UV exposure had an effect on frog deformities, while less exposure had no effect.*

Analyze the Results

A scientist's work does not end when an experiment is finished. After scientists finish their tests, they must analyze the results. Scientists must organize the data so that they can be analyzed. For example, scientists may organize the data in a table or a graph. The data collected from the UV light experiment are shown in the bar graph in **Figure 8.** Analyzing results helps scientists explain and focus on the effect of the variable. For example, the graph shows that the length of UV exposure has an effect on the development of frog deformities.

Averages

Finding the average, or mean, of a group of numbers is a common way to analyze data.

For example, three seeds were kept at 25°C and sprouted in 8, 8, and 5 days. To find the average number of days that it took the seeds to sprout, add 8, 8, and 5 and divide the sum by 3, the number of subjects (seeds). It took these seeds an average of 7 days to sprout.

Suppose three seeds were kept at 30°C and sprouted in 6, 5, and 4 days. What's the average number of days that it took these seeds to sprout?

Draw Conclusions

After scientists have analyzed the data from several experiments, they can draw conclusions. They decide whether the results of the experiments support a hypothesis. When scientists find that a hypothesis is not supported by the tests, they must try to find another explanation for what they have observed. Proving that a hypothesis is wrong is just as helpful as supporting it. Why? Either way, the scientist has learned something, which is the purpose of using scientific methods.

Reading Check **How can a wrong hypothesis be helpful?**

Is It the Answer?

The UV light experiment supports the hypothesis that the frog deformities can be caused by exposure to UV light. Does this mean that UV light definitely caused the frogs living in the Minnesota wetland to be deformed? No, the only thing this experiment shows is that UV light may be a cause of frog deformities. Results of tests performed in a laboratory may differ from results of tests performed in the wild. In addition, the experiment did not investigate the effects of parasites or some other substance on the frogs. In fact, many scientists now think that more than one factor could be causing the deformities.

Puzzles as complex as the deformed-frog mystery are rarely solved with a single experiment. The quest for a solution may continue for years. Finding an answer doesn't always end an investigation. Often, that answer begins another investigation. In this way, scientists continue to build knowledge.

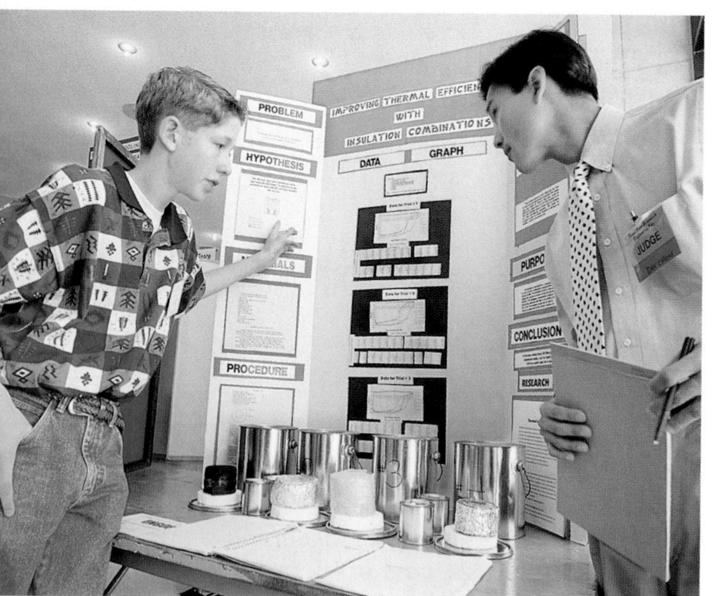

Figure 9 *This student scientist is communicating the results of his investigation at a science fair.*

Communicate Results

Scientists form a global community. After scientists complete their investigations, they communicate their results to other scientists. The student in **Figure 9** is explaining the results of a science project.

There are several reasons scientists regularly share their results. First, other scientists may then repeat the experiments to see if they get the same results. Second, the information can be considered by other scientists with similar interests. The scientists can then compare hypotheses and form consistent explanations. New data may strengthen existing hypotheses or show that the hypotheses need to be altered. There are many paths from observations and questions to communicating results.

SECTION Review

Summary

- Scientific methods are the ways in which scientists follow steps to answer questions and solve problems.
- Any information you gather through your senses is an observation. Observations often lead to the formation of questions and hypotheses.
- A hypothesis is a possible explanation or answer to a question. A well-formed hypothesis is testable by experiment.
- A controlled experiment tests only one factor at a time and consists of a control group and one or more experimental groups.
- After testing a hypothesis, scientists analyze the results and draw conclusions about whether the hypothesis is supported.
- Communicating results allows others to check the results, add to their knowledge, and design new experiments.

Using Key Terms

1. Use the following terms in the same sentence: *hypothesis, controlled experiment,* and *variable.*

Understanding Key Ideas

2. The steps of scientific methods
   a. are exactly the same in every investigation.
   b. must always be used in the same order.
   c. are not always used in the same order.
   d. always end with a conclusion.
3. What are the essential parts of a controlled experiment?
4. What causes scientific knowledge to change?

Math Skills

5. Calculate the average of the following values: 4, 5, 6, 6, 9.

Critical Thinking

6. **Analyzing Methods** Why was UV light chosen to be the variable in the frog experiment?
7. **Analyzing Processes** Why are there many ways to follow the steps of scientific methods?
8. **Making Inferences** Why might two scientists working on the same problem draw different conclusions?
9. **Identifying Bias** Investigations often begin with observation. How does observation limit what scientists can study?

Interpreting Graphics

10. The table below shows how long it takes for one bacterium to divide and become two bacteria. Plot this information on a graph, with temperature on the *x*-axis and the time to double on the *y*-axis. Do not graph values for which there is no growth. What temperature allows the bacteria to multiply most quickly?

Temperature (°C)	Time to double (min)
10	130
20	60
25	40
30	29
37	17
40	19
45	32
50	no growth

SCILINKS.
NSTA
Developed and maintained by the National Science Teachers Association
For a variety of links related to this chapter, go to www.scilinks.org
Topic: Scientific Methods; Deformed Frogs
SciLinks code: HSM1359; HSM0383

SECTION 3

Scientific Models

How can you see the parts of a cell? Unless you had superhuman eyesight, you couldn't see inside most cells without a microscope.

How do you learn about the parts of the cell if you don't have a microscope? You can look at a model of a cell. A model can help you understand what the parts of a cell look like.

READING WARM-UP

Objectives

- Give examples of three types of models.
- Identify the benefits and limitations of models.
- Compare the ways that scientists use hypotheses, theories, and laws.

Terms to Learn

model
theory
law

READING STRATEGY

Reading Organizer As you read this section, create an outline of the section. Use the headings from the section in your outline.

Types of Scientific Models

A **model** is a representation of an object or a system. Models are used in science to help explain how something works or to describe how something is structured. Models can also be used to make predictions or to explain observations. However, models have limitations. A model is never exactly like the real thing—if it were, it would no longer be a model. There are many kinds of scientific models. Some examples are physical models, mathematical models, and conceptual models.

model a pattern, plan, representation, or description designed to show the structure or workings of an object, system, or concept

Physical Models

A toy rocket and a plastic skeleton are examples of physical models. Many physical models, such as the model of a human body in **Figure 1,** look like the thing they model. However, a limitation of the model of a body is that it is not alive and doesn't act exactly like a human body. But the model is useful for understanding how the body works. Other physical models may look and act more like or less like the thing they represent than the model in **Figure 1** does. Scientists often use the model that is simplest to use but that still serves their purpose.

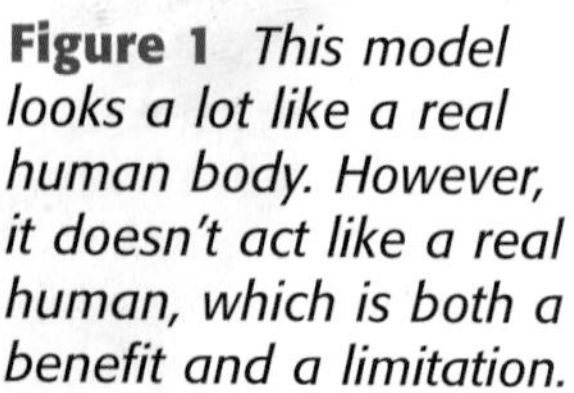

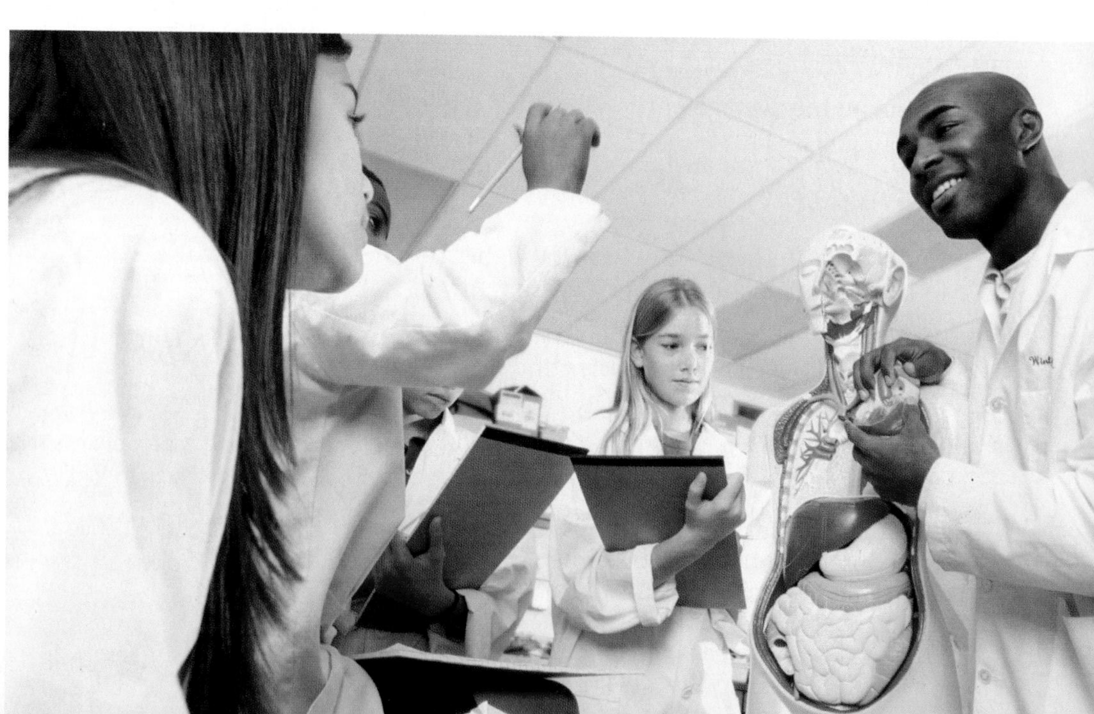

Figure 1 *This model looks a lot like a real human body. However, it doesn't act like a real human, which is both a benefit and a limitation.*

Figure 2 Mathematical Model: A Punnett Square

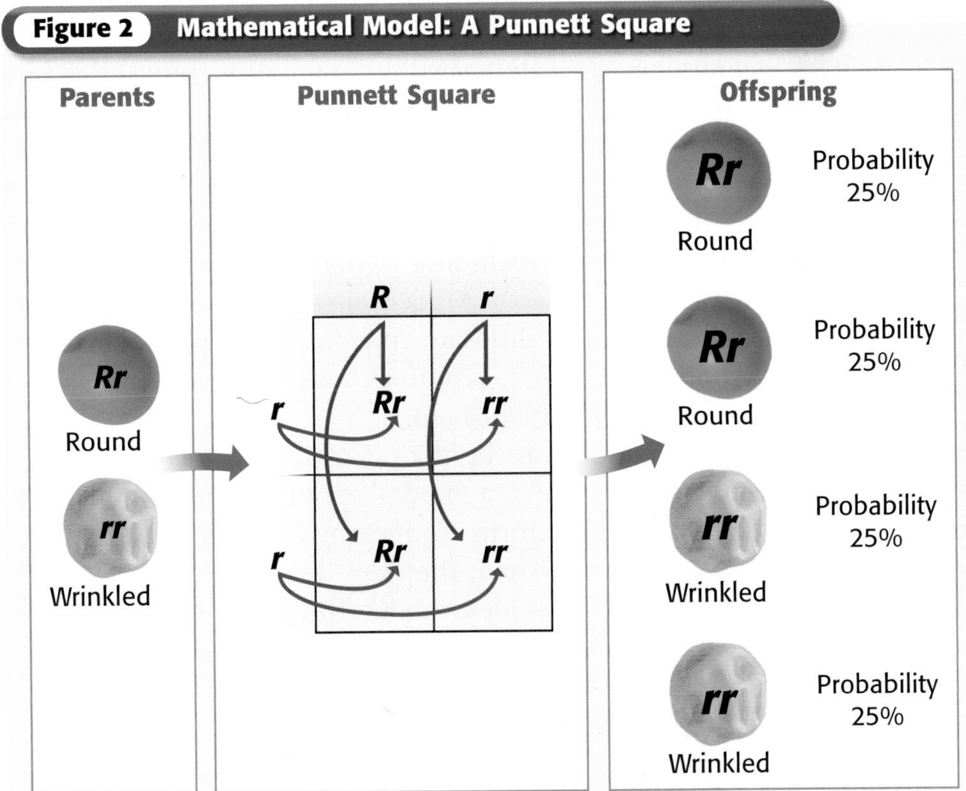

Mathematical Models

A mathematical model may be made up of numbers, equations, or other forms of data. Some mathematical models are simple and can be used easily. The Punnett square shown in **Figure 2** is a model of how traits may be passed from parents to offspring. Using this model, scientists can predict how often certain traits will appear in the offspring of certain parents.

Computers are very useful for creating and manipulating mathematical models. They make fewer mistakes and can keep track of more variables than a human can. But a computer model can be incorrect in many ways. The more complex a model is, the more carefully scientists must build the model.

Reading Check **What type of model is a Punnett square?** (*See the Appendix for answers to Reading Checks.*)

Conceptual Models

The third type of model is the conceptual model. Some conceptual models represent systems of ideas. Others compare unfamiliar things with familiar things. These comparisons help explain unfamiliar ideas. The idea that life originated from chemicals is a conceptual model. Scientists also use conceptual models to classify behaviors of animals. Scientists can then predict how an animal might respond to a certain action based on the behaviors that have already been observed.

CONNECTION TO Social Studies

Gregor Mendel About 150 years ago, Gregor Mendel studied the passing of traits in pea plants. After studying biology at a university, Mendel entered a monastery. His work with peas in the monastery garden started the field of life science called *genetics*.

Use the library or the Internet to research Gregor Mendel. Also, research the time and place where he lived. Discuss the following questions with your classmates: What made Mendel unique in his time? In what ways was Mendel a great life scientist?

ACTIVITY

Figure 3 *This computer-generated model doesn't just look like a dinosaur. This model includes the movement of bones and muscles.*

Benefits of Models

Models are often used to represent things that are very small or very large. Models may also represent things that are very complicated or things that no longer exist. For example, **Figure 3** is a model of a dinosaur. Such computer models have been used for many things, including to make movies about prehistoric life on Earth. Models are used, of course, because filming a real dinosaur in action is impossible. But in building models, scientists may discover things they hadn't thought of before.

A model can be a kind of hypothesis and can be tested. To build a model of an organism, scientists must gather information learned from fossils and other observations. Then, they can test whether their model fits with their ideas about how an organism might have moved or what it might have eaten.

Building Scientific Knowledge

Sometimes, scientists may draw different conclusions from the same data. Other times, new results show that old conclusions are wrong. Sometimes, more information is needed. Life scientists are always asking new questions or looking at old questions from a new angle. As they find new answers, scientific knowledge continues to grow and change.

Scientific Theories

theory an explanation that ties together many hypotheses and observations

law a summary of many experimental results and observations; a law tells how things work

For every hypothesis, more than one prediction can be made. Each time another prediction is proven true, the hypothesis gains more support. Over time, scientists try to tie together all they have learned. An explanation that ties together many related facts, observations, and tested hypotheses is called a **theory.** Theories are conceptual models that help to organize scientific thinking. Theories are used to explain observations and also to predict what might happen in the future.

Reading Check How do scientists use theories?

Scientific Laws

The one kind of scientific idea that rarely changes is called a *scientific law*. In science, a **law** is a summary of many experimental results and observations. Unlike traffic laws, scientific laws are not based on what people may want to happen. Instead, scientific laws are statements of what *will* happen in a specific situation. And unlike theories, scientific laws tell you only what happens, not why it happens.

Combining Scientific Ideas

Scientific laws are at work around you every day. For example, the law of gravity is at work when we see a leaf fall to the ground. The law of gravity tells us that objects always fall toward the center of the Earth. Many laws of chemistry are at work inside your cells. However, living organisms are very complex. So, there are very few laws within life science. But some theories are very important in life science and are widely accepted. An example is the theory that all living things are made up of cells.

Scientific Change

History shows that new scientific ideas take time to develop into theories or to become accepted as facts or laws. Scientists should be open to new ideas, but they should always test those ideas with scientific methods. And if new evidence contradicts an accepted idea, scientists must be willing to re-examine the evidence and re-evaluate their reasoning. The process of building scientific knowledge never ends.

CONNECTION TO Physics

The Laws of Physics Part of understanding a scientific law is knowing the conditions under which it is true. Many of the laws of physics deal with a simple set of conditions. For example, Newton's laws of motion are used to predict how objects, such as planets, will move through space. The same laws apply on Earth, but predicting the motion of objects on Earth is more complex. Look up Newton's laws, and then brainstorm ways in which the conditions in space differ from the conditions on Earth.

ACTIVITY

SECTION Review

Summary

- A model is a representation of an object or system. Models often use familiar things to represent unfamiliar things. Three main types of models are physical, mathematical, and conceptual. Models have limitations but are useful and can be changed based on new evidence.
- Scientific knowledge is built as scientists form and revise scientific hypotheses, models, theories, and laws.

Using Key Terms

In each of the following sentences, replace the incorrect term with the correct term from the word bank.

theory law

1. A conclusion is an explanation that matches many hypotheses but may still change.
2. A model tells you exactly what to expect in certain situations.

Understanding Key Ideas

3. A limitation of models is that
   a. they are large enough to see.
   b. they do not act exactly like the things that they model.
   c. they are smaller than the things that they model.
   d. they model unfamiliar things.
4. What are three types of models? Give an example of each type.
5. Compare how scientists use theories with how they use laws.

Math Skills

6. If Jerry is 2.1 m tall, how tall is a scale model of Jerry that is 10% of his size?

Critical Thinking

7. **Applying Concepts** You are making a three-dimensional model of an extinct plant. Describe some of the potential uses for your model. What are some limitations of your model?

SCILINKS
NSTA
Developed and maintained by the National Science Teachers Association
For a variety of links related to this chapter, go to www.scilinks.org
Topic: Using Models
SciLinks code: HSM1588

SECTION 4

Tools, Measurement, and Safety

READING WARM-UP

Objectives

- Give three examples of how life scientists use computers and technology.
- Describe three tools life scientists use to observe organisms.
- Explain the importance of the International System of Units, and give four examples of SI units.

Terms to Learn

technology
compound light microscope
electron microscope
area
volume
mass
temperature

READING STRATEGY

Reading Organizer As you read this section, make a concept map by using the terms above.

Would you use a hammer to tighten a bolt on a bicycle? You probably wouldn't. To be successful in many tasks, you need the correct tools.

Life scientists use various tools to help them in their work. These tools are used to make observations and to gather, store, and analyze information. Choosing and using tools properly are important parts of scientific work.

Computers and Technology

The application of science for practical purposes is called **technology.** By using technology, life scientists are able to find information and solve problems in new ways. New technology allows scientists to get information that wasn't available previously.

technology the application of science for practical purposes; the use of tools, machines, materials, and processes to meet human needs

Since the first electronic computer was built in 1946, improvements in technology have made computers more powerful and easier to use. Computers can be used to create graphs, solve complex equations, and analyze data. Computers also help scientists share data and ideas with each other and publish reports about their research.

Tools for Seeing

It's difficult to make accurate observations of things that cannot be seen. When the first microscopes were invented, scientists were able to see into a whole new world. Today, the workings of tiny cells and organisms are well understood. New tools and technologies allow us to see inside organisms in new ways. For example, the images shown in **Figure 1** were created by sending electromagnetic waves through human bodies.

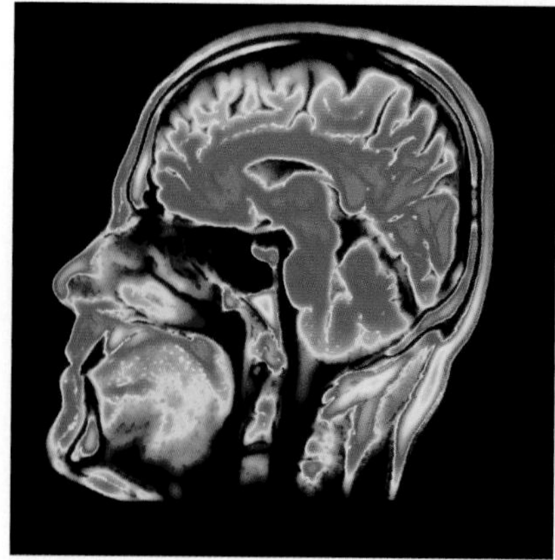

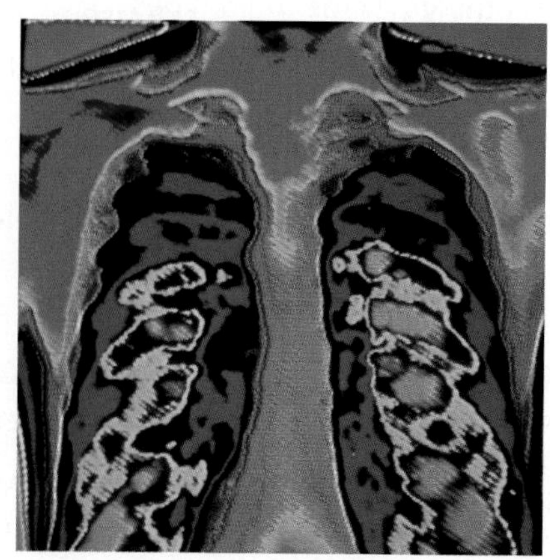

Figure 1 *The image on the left is a computerized axial tomography scan (CAT scan). The image on the right was made with magnetic resonance imagery (MRI).*

Figure 2 Types of Microscopes

Compound Light Microscope Light passes through the specimen and produces a flat image.

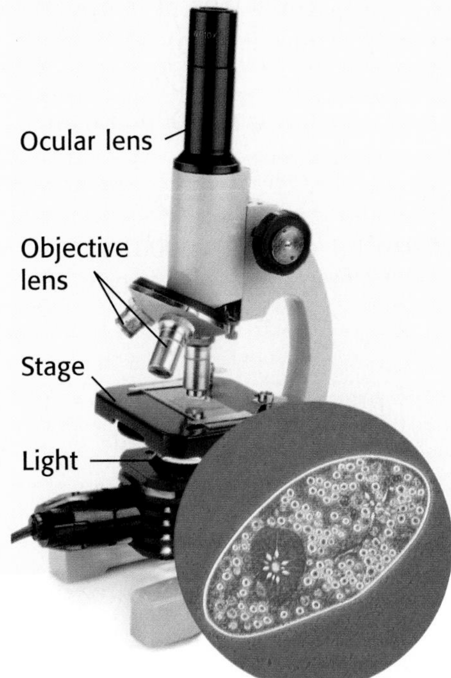

Transmission Electron Microscope Electrons pass through the specimen and produce a flat image.

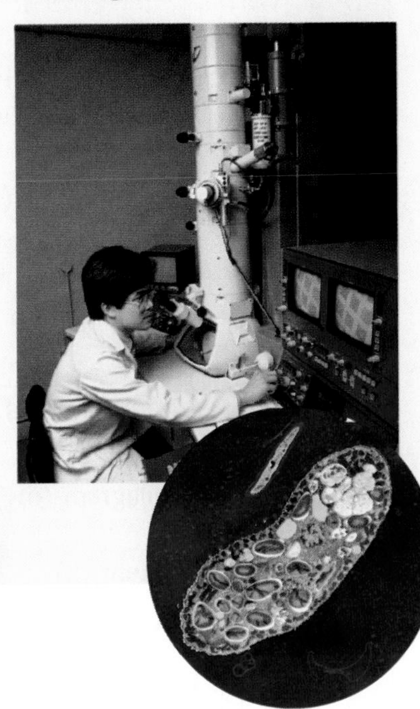

Scanning Electron Microscope Electrons bounce off the surface of the specimen and produce a three-dimensional (3-D) image.

Compound Light Microscope

The compound light microscope is a common tool in a life science laboratory. A **compound light microscope** is an instrument that magnifies small objects so that they can be seen easily. It has three main parts—a tube with two or more lenses, a stage, and a light. Items viewed through a compound microscope may be colored with special dyes to make them more visible. Items are placed on the stage so that the light passes through them. The lenses at each end of the tube magnify the image.

compound light microscope an instrument that magnifies small objects so that they can be seen easily by using two or more lenses

electron microscope a microscope that focuses a beam of electrons to magnify objects

Electron Microscopes

Not all microscopes use light. In **electron microscopes,** tiny particles called *electrons* are used to produce magnified images. The images produced are clearer and more detailed than those made by light microscopes. However, living things cannot be viewed with electron microscopes because the preparation process kills them. There are two kinds of electron microscopes used in life science—the transmission electron microscope (TEM) and the scanning electron microscope (SEM). **Figure 2** shows each kind of microscope, describes the specialized purpose of each, and shows an example of the images each can produce.

Reading Check How are SEMs different from TEMs? (*See the Appendix for answers to Reading Checks.*)

Table 1 Common SI Units and Conversions		
Length	**meter (m)**	
	kilometer (km)	1 km = 1,000 m
	decimeter (dm)	1 dm = 0.1 m
	centimeter (cm)	1 cm = 0.01 m
	millimeter (mm)	1 mm = 0.001 m
	micrometer (µm)	1 µm = 0.000001 m
	nanometer (nm)	1 nm = 0.000000001 m
Volume	**cubic meter (m^3)**	
	cubic centimeter (cm^3)	1 cm^3 = 0.000001 m^3
	liter (L)	1 L = 1 dm^3 = 0.001 m^3
	milliliter (mL)	1 mL = 0.001 L = 1 cm^3
Mass	**kilogram (kg)**	
	gram (g)	1 g = 0.001 kg
	milligram (mg)	1 mg = 0.000001 kg
Temperature	**kelvin (K)**	
	Celsius (°C)	0°C = 273 K
		100°C = 373 K

How You Measure Matters

Measure the length and width of a desk or table, but do not use a ruler. Pick a common object to use as your unit of measurement. It could be a pencil, your hand, or anything else. Use that unit to determine the area of the desk or table.

To calculate the area of a rectangle, first measure the length and width. Then, use the following equation:

area = *length* × *width*

Ask your parent or sibling to do this activity on their own. When they are finished, compare your area calculation with theirs.

ACTIVITY

Measurement

The ability to make reliable measurements is an important skill in science. But different standards of measurement have developed throughout the world. Ancient measurement units were based on parts of the body, such as the foot, or on objects, such as grains of wheat. Such systems were not very reliable. Even as better standards were developed, they varied from country to country.

The International System of Units

In the late 1700s, the French Academy of Sciences began to form a global measurement system now known as the *International System of Units* (also called *SI,* or *Système International d'Unités*). Today, most scientists and almost all countries use this system. One advantage of using SI measurements is that it helps scientists share and compare their observations and results.

Another advantage of SI units is that almost all units are based on the number 10, which makes conversions from one unit to another easier. **Table 1** contains commonly used SI units for length, volume, mass, and temperature. Notice how the prefix of each SI unit relates to a base unit.

Length

How long is an ant? A life scientist would probably use millimeters (mm) to describe an ant's length. If you divide 1 m into 1,000 parts, each part equals 1 mm. So, 1 mm is one-thousandth of a meter. Although millimeters seem small, some organisms and structures are so tiny that even smaller units—micrometers (µm) or nanometers (nm)—must be used.

Area

How much paper would you need to cover your desktop? To answer this question, you must find the area of the desk. **Area** is a measure of how much surface an object has. Area can be calculated from measurements such as length and width. Area is stated in square units, such as square meters (m^2), square centimeters (cm^2), and square kilometers (km^2).

area a measure of the size of a surface or a region

volume a measure of the size of a body or region in three-dimensional space

Reading Check **What kinds of units describe area?**

Volume

How many books will fit into a backpack? The answer depends on the volume of the backpack and the volume of each book. **Volume** is a measure of the size of something in three-dimensional space.

The volume of a liquid is most often described in liters (L). Liters are based on the meter. A cubic meter (1 m^3) is equal to 1,000 L. So 1,000 L will fit into a box measuring 1 m on each side. A milliliter (mL) will fit into a box that is 1 cm on each side. So, 1 mL = 1 cm^3. Graduated cylinders are used to measure the volume of liquids, as shown in **Figure 3.**

The volume of a solid object is given in cubic units, such as cubic meters (m^3), cubic centimeters (cm^3), or cubic millimeters (mm^3). To find the volume of a box-shaped object, multiply the object's length by its width and height. As **Figure 3** shows, the volume of an irregularly shaped object is found by measuring the volume of liquid that the object displaces.

Figure 3 *A rock added to a graduated cylinder raised the level of water from 70 mL to 80 mL of water. Because the rock displaced 10 mL of water and because 1 mL = 1 cm^3, the volume of the rock is 10 cm^3.*

Measure Up!

1. For each of the following tasks, find a different item to measure. With permission from your teacher or parent, you may choose items within your classroom, school, or home.
   a. Measure length with a **meterstick.**
   b. Measure length with a **metric ruler.**
   c. Measure and calculate area in square meters.
   d. Measure volume with a **graduated cylinder.**
   e. Measure and calculate volume in cubic meters.
   f. Measure mass with a **balance.**
   g. Measure temperature with a **thermometer.**
2. Make a **poster** to present your measurements. Include drawings showing how you measured each item and tips stating how to use the measurement tools properly.

mass a measure of the amount of matter in an object

temperature a measure of how hot (or cold) something is

Mass

How much matter is in an apple? **Mass** is a measure of the amount of matter in an object. The kilogram (kg) is the basic unit for mass. The mass of a very large object is described in kilograms or metric tons. A metric ton equals 1,000 kg. The mass of a small object may be described in grams (g). A kilogram equals 1,000 g; therefore, a gram is one-thousandth of a kilogram. A medium-sized apple has a mass of about 100 g. Mass can be measured by using a balance.

Temperature

How much should food be heated to kill any bacteria in the food? To answer this question, a life scientist would measure the temperature at which bacteria die. **Temperature** is a measure of how hot or cold something is. Temperature is actually an indication of the amount of energy within matter. You are probably used to describing temperature in degrees Fahrenheit (°F). Scientists commonly use degrees Celsius (°C), although the kelvin (K) is the official SI base unit for temperature. You will use degrees Celsius in this book. The thermometer in **Figure 4** shows how two of these scales compare.

Reading Check What does temperature indicate about matter?

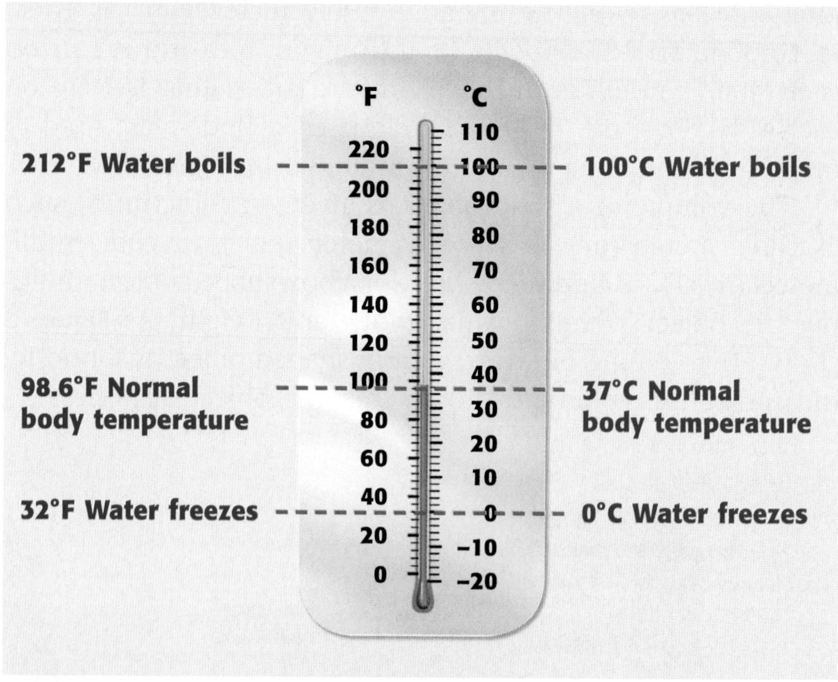

Figure 4 *Water freezes at 0°C and boils at 100°C. Your normal body temperature is 37°C, which is equal to 98.6°F.*

Safety Rules!

Life science is exciting and fun, but it can also be dangerous. So, don't take any chances! Always follow your teacher's instructions, and don't take shortcuts—even when you think there is no danger in doing so. Before starting an experiment, get your teacher's permission, and read the lab procedures carefully. Pay particular attention to safety information and caution statements. **Figure 5** shows the safety symbols used in this book. Get to know these symbols and their meanings by reading the safety information in the front of this book. **This is important!** If you are still unsure about what a safety symbol means, ask your teacher.

Figure 5 **Safety Symbols**

Eye protection	Clothing protection	Hand safety
Heating safety	Electric safety	Sharp object
Chemical safety	Animal safety	Plant safety

SECTION Review

Summary

- Life scientists use computers to collect, store, organize, analyze, and share data.
- Life scientists commonly use light microscopes and electron microscopes to make observations of things that are too small to be seen without help. Electromagnetic waves are also used in other ways to create images.
- The International System of Units (SI) is a simple and reliable system of measurement that is used by most scientists.

Using Key Terms

Complete each of the following sentences by choosing the correct term from the word bank.

mass	area
volume	temperature

1. The measure of the surface of an object is called ___.
2. Life scientists use kilograms when measuring an object's ___.
3. The ___ of a liquid is usually described in liters.

Understanding Key Ideas

4. SI units are
   a. always based on standardized measurements of body parts.
   b. almost always based on the number 10.
   c. used only to measure length.
   d. used only in France.
5. How is temperature related to energy?
6. If you were going to measure the mass of a fly, which SI unit would be most appropriate?

Math Skills

7. Convert 3.0 L into cubic centimeters.
8. Calculate the volume of a textbook that is 28.5 cm long, 22 cm wide, and 3.5 cm thick.

Critical Thinking

9. **Making Inferences** The mite shown below is about 500 μm long in real life. What tool was probably used to produce this image? How can you tell?

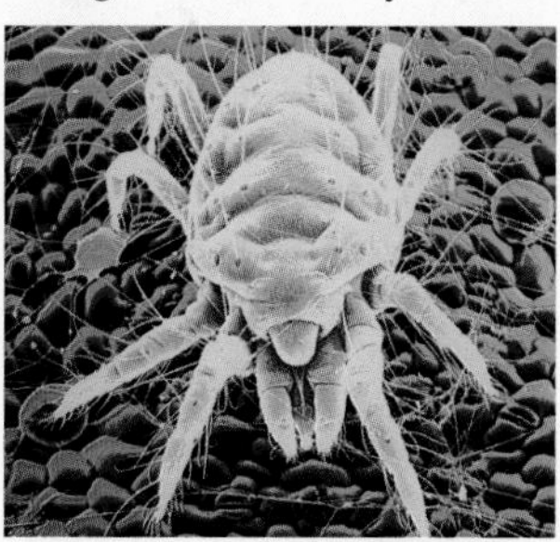

10. **Applying Concepts** Give an example of what could happen if you do not follow safety rules.

SCI LINKS.
NSTA
Developed and maintained by the National Science Teachers Association
For a variety of links related to this chapter, go to www.scilinks.org
Topic: Tools of Science; SI Units
SciLinks code: HSM1535; HSM1390

Using Scientific Methods

Skills Practice Lab

Does It All Add Up?

OBJECTIVES

Apply scientific methods to predict, measure, and observe the mixing of two unknown liquids.

MATERIALS

- beakers, 100 mL (2)
- Celsius thermometer
- glass-labeling marker
- graduated cylinders, 50 mL (3)
- liquid A, 75 mL
- liquid B, 75 mL
- protective gloves

SAFETY

Your math teacher won't tell you this, but did you know that sometimes 2 + 2 does not appear to equal 4?! In this experiment, you will use scientific methods to predict, measure, and observe the mixing of two unknown liquids. You will learn that a scientist does not set out to prove a hypothesis but to test it and that sometimes the results just don't seem to add up!

Make Observations

1. Put on your safety goggles, gloves, and lab apron. Examine the beakers of liquids A and B provided by your teacher. Write down as many observations as you can about each liquid. **Caution:** Do not taste, touch, or smell the liquids.

2. Pour exactly 25 mL of liquid A from the beaker into each of two 50 mL graduated cylinders. Combine these samples in one of the graduated cylinders. Record the final volume. Pour the liquid back into the beaker of liquid A. Rinse the graduated cylinders. Repeat this step for liquid B.

Form a Hypothesis

3. Based on your observations and on prior experience, formulate a testable hypothesis that states what you expect the volume to be when you combine 25 mL of liquid A with 25 mL of liquid B.

4. Make a prediction based on your hypothesis. Use an if-then format. Explain why you made your prediction.

Data Table				
	Contents of cylinder A	Contents of cylinder B	Mixing results: predictions	Mixing results: observations
Volume				
Appearance				
Temperature				

Test the Hypothesis

5. Make a data table like the one above.
6. Mark one graduated cylinder "A." Carefully pour exactly 25 mL of liquid A into this cylinder. In your data table, record its volume, appearance, and temperature.
7. Mark another graduated cylinder "B." Carefully pour exactly 25 mL of liquid B into this cylinder. Record its volume, appearance, and temperature in your data table.
8. Mark the empty third cylinder "A + B."
9. In the "Mixing results: predictions" column in your table, record the prediction you made earlier. Each classmate may have made a different prediction.
10. Carefully pour the contents of both cylinders into the third graduated cylinder.
11. Observe and record the total volume, appearance, and temperature in the "Mixing results: observations" column of your table.

Analyze the Results

1. **Analyzing Data** Discuss your predictions as a class. How many different predictions were there? Which predictions were supported by testing? Did any measurements surprise you?

Draw Conclusions

2. **Drawing Conclusions** Was your hypothesis supported or disproven? Either way, explain your thinking. Describe everything that you think you learned from this experiment.
3. **Analyzing Methods** Explain the value of incorrect predictions.

Chapter Review

USING KEY TERMS

1. Use the following terms in the same sentence: *life science* and *scientific methods*.

2. Use the following terms in the same sentence: *controlled experiment* and *variable*.

For each pair of terms, explain how the meanings of the terms differ.

3. *theory* and *hypothesis*

4. *compound light microscope* and *electron microscope*

5. *area* and *volume*

UNDERSTANDING KEY IDEAS

Multiple Choice

6. The steps of scientific methods
   - **a.** must all be used in every scientific investigation.
   - **b.** must always be used in the same order.
   - **c.** often start with a question.
   - **d.** always result in the development of a theory.

7. In a controlled experiment,
   - **a.** a control group is compared with one or more experimental groups.
   - **b.** there are at least two variables.
   - **c.** all factors should be different.
   - **d.** a variable is not needed.

8. Which of the following tools is best for measuring 100 mL of water?
   - **a.** 10 mL graduated cylinder
   - **b.** 150 mL graduated cylinder
   - **c.** 250 mL beaker
   - **d.** 500 mL beaker

9. Which of the following is NOT an SI unit?
   - **a.** meter
   - **b.** foot
   - **c.** liter
   - **d.** kilogram

10. A pencil is 14 cm long. How many millimeters long is it?
    - **a.** 1.4 mm
    - **b.** 140 mm
    - **c.** 1,400 mm
    - **d.** 1,400,000 mm

11. The directions for a lab include the safety icons shown below. These icons mean that

    - **a.** you should be careful.
    - **b.** you are going into the laboratory.
    - **c.** you should wash your hands first.
    - **d.** you should wear safety goggles, a lab apron, and gloves during the lab.

Short Answer

12. List three ways that science is beneficial to living things.

13. Why do hypotheses need to be testable?

14. Give an example of how a life scientist might use computers and technology.

15. List three types of models, and give an example of each.

16. What are some advantages and limitations of models?

17. Which SI units can be used to describe the volume of an object? Which SI units can be used to describe the mass of an object?

18. In a controlled experiment, why should there be several individuals in the control group and in each of the experimental groups?

CRITICAL THINKING

19. **Concept Mapping** Use the following terms to create a concept map: *observations, predictions, questions, controlled experiments, variable,* and *hypothesis.*

20. **Making Inferences** Investigations often begin with observation. What limits are there to the observations that scientists can make?

21. **Forming Hypotheses** A scientist who studies mice observes that on the day the mice are fed vitamins with their meals, they perform better in mazes. What hypothesis would you form to explain this phenomenon? Write a testable prediction based on your hypothesis.

INTERPRETING GRAPHICS

The pictures below show how an egg can be measured by using a beaker and water. Use the pictures to answer the questions that follow.

Before: 125 mL After: 200 mL

22. What kind of measurement is being taken?
    a. area
    b. length
    c. mass
    d. volume

23. Which of the following is an accurate measurement of the egg in the picture?
    a. 75 cm^3
    b. 125 cm^3
    c. 125 mL
    d. 200 mL

24. Make a double line graph from the data in the following table.

Number of Frogs		
Date	Normal	Deformed
1995	25	0
1996	21	0
1997	19	1
1998	20	2
1999	17	3
2000	20	5

Standardized Test Preparation

READING

Read each of the passages below. Then, answer the questions that follow the passage.

Passage 1 Zoology is the study of animals. Zoology dates back more than 2,300 years, to ancient Greece. There, the philosopher Aristotle observed and theorized about animal behavior. About 200 years later, Galen, a Greek physician, began dissecting and experimenting with animals. However, there were few advances in zoology until the 1700s and 1800s. During this period, the Swedish naturalist Carolus Linnaeus developed a classification system for plants and animals, and British naturalist Charles Darwin published his theory of evolution by natural selection.

1. According to the passage, when did major advances in Zoology begin?

A About 2,300 years ago
B About 2,100 years ago
C During the 1700s and 1800s
D Only during recent history

2. Which of the following is a possible meaning of the word *naturalist,* as used in the passage?

F a scientist who studies plants and animals
G a scientist who studies animals
H a scientist who studies theory
I a scientist who studies animal behavior

3. Which of the following is the **best** title for this passage?

A Greek Zoology
B Modern Zoology
C The Origins of Zoology
D Zoology in the 1700s and 1800s

Passage 2 When looking for answers to a problem, scientists build on existing knowledge. For example, scientists have wondered if there is some relationship between Earth's core and Earth's magnetic field. To form a hypothesis, scientists started with what they knew: Earth has a dense, solid inner core and a molten outer core. Scientists then created a computer model to simulate how Earth's magnetic field might be generated.

They tried different things with their model until the model produced a magnetic field that matched that of the real Earth. The model predicted that Earth's inner core spins in the same direction as the rest of the Earth, but the inner core spins slightly faster than Earth's surface. If the hypothesis is correct, it might explain how Earth's magnetic field is produced. Although scientists cannot reach the Earth's core to examine it directly, they can test whether other observations match what is predicted by their hypothesis.

1. What does the word *model* refer to in this passage?

A a giant plastic globe
B a representation of the Earth created on a computer
C a computer terminal
D a technology used to drill into the Earth's core

2. Which of the following is the **best** summary of the passage?

F Scientists can use models to help them answer difficult and complex questions.
G Scientists have discovered the source of Earth's magnetic field.
H The spinning of Earth's molten inner core causes Earth's magnetic field.
I Scientists make a model of a problem and then ask questions about the problem.

INTERPRETING GRAPHICS

The table below shows the plans for an experiment in which bees will be observed visiting flowers. Use the table to answer the questions that follow.

Bee Experiment				
Group	Type of bee	Time of day	Type of plant	Flower color
#1	Honey-bee	9:00 A.M.–10:00 A.M.	Portland rose	red
#2	Honey-bee	9:00 A.M.–10:00 A.M.	Portland rose	yellow
#3	Honey-bee	9:00 A.M.–10:00 A.M.	Portland rose	white
#4	Honey-bee	9:00 A.M.–10:00 A.M.	Portland rose	pink

1. Which factor is the variable in this experiment?

A the type of bee
B the time of day
C the type of plant
D the color of the flowers

2. Which of the following hypotheses could be tested by this experiment?

F Honeybees prefer to visit rose plants.
G Honeybees prefer to visit red flowers.
H Honeybees prefer to visit flowers in the morning.
I Honey bees prefer to visit Portland rose flowers between 9 and 10 A.M.

3. Which of the following is the **best** reason why the Portland rose plant is included in all of the groups to be studied?

A The type of plant is a control factor; any type of flowering plant could be used as long as all plants were of the same type.
B The experiment will test whether bees prefer the Portland rose over other flowers.
C An experiment should always have more than one variable.
D The Portland rose is a very common plant.

MATH

Read each question below, and choose the best answer.

1. A survey of students was conducted to find out how many people were in each student's family. The replies from five students were as follows: 3, 3, 4, 4, and 6. What was the average family size?

A 3
B 3.5
C 4
D 5

2. In the survey above, if one more student were surveyed, which reply would make the average lower?

F 3
G 4
H 5
I 6

3. If an object that is 5 µm long were magnified by 1,000, how long would that object then appear?

A 5 µm
B 5 mm
C 1,000 µm
D 5,000 mm

4. How many meters are in 50 km?

F 50 m
G 500 m
H 5,000 m
I 50,000 m

5. What is the area of a square whose sides measure 4 m each?

A 16 m
B 16 m^2
C 32 m
D 32 m^2

Science in Action

Scientific Debate

Should We Stop All Forest Fires?

Since 1972, the policy of the National Park Service has been to manage the national parks as naturally as possible. Because fire is a natural event in forests, this policy includes allowing most fires caused by lightning to burn. The only lightning-caused fires that are put out are those that threaten lives, property, uniquely scenic areas, or endangered species. All human-caused fires are put out. However, this policy has caused some controversy. Some people want this policy followed in all public forests and even grasslands. Others think that all fires should be put out.

Social Studies ACTIVITY

WRITING SKILL Research a location where there is a debate about controlling forest fires. You might look into national forests or parks. Write a newspaper article about the issue. Be sure to present all sides of the debate.

Science Fiction

"The Homesick Chicken" by Edward D. Hoch

Why did the chicken cross the road? You think you know the answer to this old riddle, don't you? But "The Homesick Chicken," by Edward D. Hoch, may surprise you. That old chicken may not be exactly what it seems.

You see, one of the chickens at the high-tech Tangaway Research Farms has escaped. Then, it was found in a vacant lot across the highway from Tangaway, pecking away contentedly. Why did it bother to escape? Barnabus Rex, a specialist in solving scientific riddles, is called in to work on this mystery. As he investigates, he finds clues and forms a hypothesis. Read the story, and see if you can explain the mystery before Mr. Rex does.

Language Arts ACTIVITY

WRITING SKILL Write your own short story about a chicken crossing a road for a mysterious reason. Give clues (evidence) to the reader about the mysterious reason but do not reveal the truth until the end of the story. Be sure the story makes sense scientifically.

People in Science

Yvonne Cagle

Flight Surgeon and Astronaut Most doctors practice medicine with both feet on the ground. But Dr. Yvonne Cagle found a way to fly with her medical career. Cagle became a flight surgeon for the United States Air Force and an astronaut for the National Aeronautics and Space Administration (NASA).

Cagle's interest in both medicine and space flight began early. As a little girl, Cagle spent hours staring at X rays in her father's medical library. Those images sparked an early interest in science. Cagle also remembers watching Neil Armstrong walk on the moon when she was five years old. As she tried to imagine the view of Earth from space, Cagle decided she wanted to see it for herself.

Becoming an Air Force flight surgeon was a good first step toward becoming an astronaut. As a flight surgeon, Cagle learned about the special medical challenges humans face when they are launched high above the Earth. Being a flight surgeon had the extra benefits of working with some of the best pilots and getting to fly in the latest jets.

It wasn't long before Cagle worked as an occupational physician for NASA at the Johnson Space Center. Two years later, she was chosen to begin astronaut training. Cagle is looking forward to her first flight into space. Her first mission will likely take her to the *International Space Station,* where she can monitor astronaut health and perform scientific experiments.

Math Activity

In space flight, astronauts experience changes in gravity that affect their bodies in several ways. Because of gravity, a person who has a mass of 50 kg weighs 110 pounds on Earth. But on the moon, the same person weighs about 17% of his or her weight on Earth. How much does the same person weigh on the moon?

To learn more about these Science in Action topics, visit go.hrw.com and type in the keyword **HL5LIVF.**

Current Science

Check out Current Science® articles related to this chapter by visiting go.hrw.com. Just type in the keyword HL5CS01.

2

It's Alive!! Or Is It?

About the PHOTO

What does it mean to say something is *alive*? Machines have some of the characteristics of living things, but machines do not have all of these characteristics. This amazing robot insect can respond to changes in its environment. It can walk over obstacles. It can perform some tasks. But it is still not alive. How is it like and unlike a living insect?

PRE-READING ACTIVITY

Graphic Organizer

Concept Map Before you read the chapter, create the graphic organizer entitled "Concept Map" described in the **Study Skills** section of the Appendix. As you read the chapter, fill in the concept map with details about the characteristics of living things.

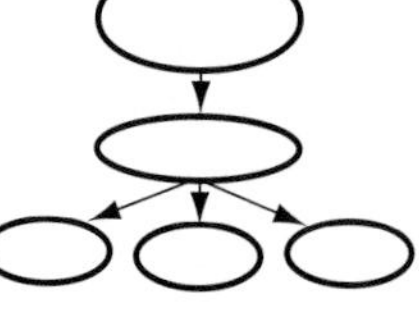

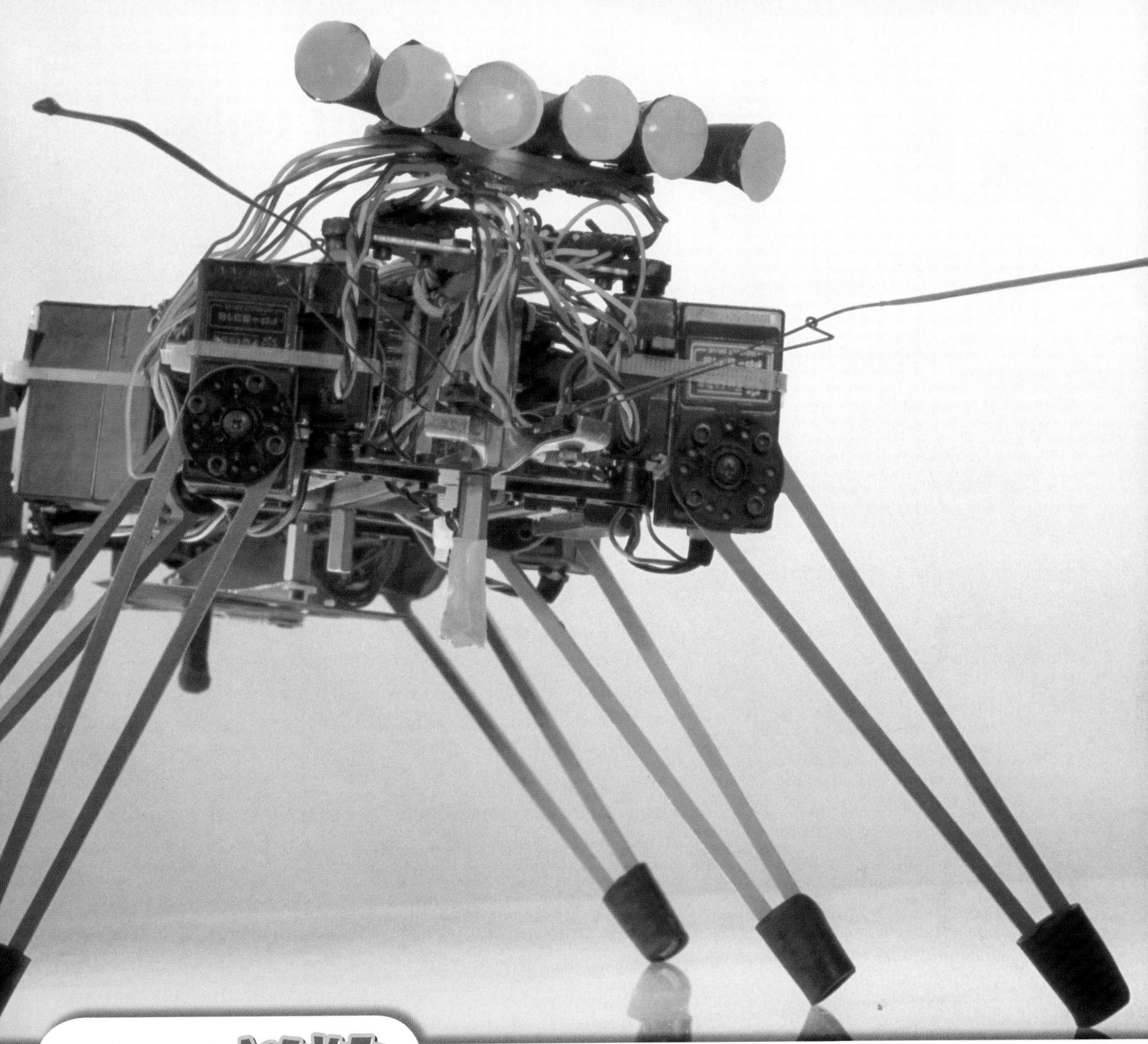

START-UP ACTIVITY

Lights On!

In this activity, you will work with a partner to see how eyes react to changes in light.

Procedure

1. Observe a classmate's eyes in a lighted room. Note the size of your partner's pupils.
2. Have your partner keep both eyes open. Ask him or her to cover each one with a cupped hand. Wait about one minute.
3. Instruct your partner to pull away both hands quickly. Immediately, look at your partner's pupils. Record what happens.
4. Now, briefly shine a **flashlight** into your partner's eyes. Record how this affects your partner's pupils. **Caution:** Do not use the sun as the source of the light.
5. Change places with your partner, and repeat steps 1–4 so that your partner can observe your eyes.

Analysis

1. How did your partner's eyes respond to changes in the level of light?
2. How did changes in the size of your pupils affect your vision? What does this tell you about why pupils change size?

SECTION 1

Characteristics of Living Things

While outside one day, you notice something strange in the grass. It's slimy, bright yellow, and about the size of a dime. You have no idea what it is. Is it a plant part that fell from a tree? Is it alive? How can you tell?

READING WARM-UP

Objectives

- Describe the six characteristics of living things.
- Describe how organisms maintain stable internal conditions.
- Explain how asexual reproduction differs from sexual reproduction.

Terms to Learn

cell
stimulus
homeostasis
sexual reproduction
asexual reproduction
heredity
metabolism

READING STRATEGY

Prediction Guide Before reading this section, write the title of each heading in this section. Next, under each heading, write what you think you will learn.

An amazing variety of living things exists on Earth. But living things are all alike in several ways. What does a dog have in common with a bacterium? What does a fish have in common with a mushroom? And what do *you* have in common with a slimy, yellow blob, known as a *slime mold*? Read on to find out about the six characteristics that all organisms share.

Living Things Have Cells

All living things, such as those in **Figure 1,** are composed of one or more cells. A **cell** is a membrane-covered structure that contains all of the materials necessary for life. The membrane that surrounds a cell separates the contents of the cell from the cell's environment. Most cells are too small to be seen with the naked eye.

cell the smallest unit that can perform all life processes; cells are covered by a membrane and have DNA and cytoplasm

Some organisms are made up of trillions of cells. In an organism with many cells, different kinds of cells perform specialized functions. For example, your nerve cells transport signals, and your muscle cells are specialized for movement.

In an organism made up of only one cell, different parts of the cell perform different functions. For example, a one-celled paramecium needs to eat. So, some parts of the cell take in food. Other parts of the cell break down the food. Still other parts of the cell excrete wastes.

Figure 1 *Some organisms, such as the protists on the right, are made of one cell or a few cells. The monkeys on the left are made up of trillions of cells.*

Figure 2 *The touch of an insect triggers the Venus' flytrap to close its leaves quickly.*

Living Things Sense and Respond to Change

All organisms have the ability to sense change in their environment and to respond to that change. When your pupils are exposed to light, they respond by becoming smaller. A change that affects the activity of the organism is called a **stimulus** (plural, *stimuli*).

Stimuli can be chemicals, gravity, light, sounds, hunger, or anything that causes organisms to respond in some way. A gentle touch causes a response in the plant shown in **Figure 2.**

stimulus anything that causes a reaction or change in an organism or any part of an organism

homeostasis the maintenance of a constant internal state in a changing environment

Homeostasis

Even though an organism's outside environment may change, conditions inside an organism's body must stay the same. Many chemical reactions keep an organism alive. These reactions can take place only when conditions are exactly right, so an organism must maintain stable internal conditions to survive. The maintenance of a stable internal environment is called **homeostasis** (HOH mee OH STAY sis).

Responding to External Changes

Your body maintains a temperature of about 37°C. When you get hot, your body responds by sweating. When you get cold, your muscles twitch in an attempt to warm you up. This twitching is called *shivering*. Whether you are sweating or shivering, your body is trying to return itself to normal.

Other animals also need to have stable internal conditions. But many cannot respond the way you do. They have to control their body temperature by moving from one environment to another. If they get too warm, they move to the shade. If they get too cool, they move out into the sunlight.

Reading Check How do some animals maintain homeostasis? (*See the Appendix for answers to Reading Checks.*)

CONNECTION TO Physics

Temperature Regulation
Your body temperature does not change very much throughout the day. When you exercise, you sweat. Sweating helps keep your body temperature stable. As your sweat evaporates, your skin cools. Given this information, why do you think you feel cooler faster when you stand in front of a fan?

Figure 3 *Like most animals, bears produce offspring by sexual reproduction.*

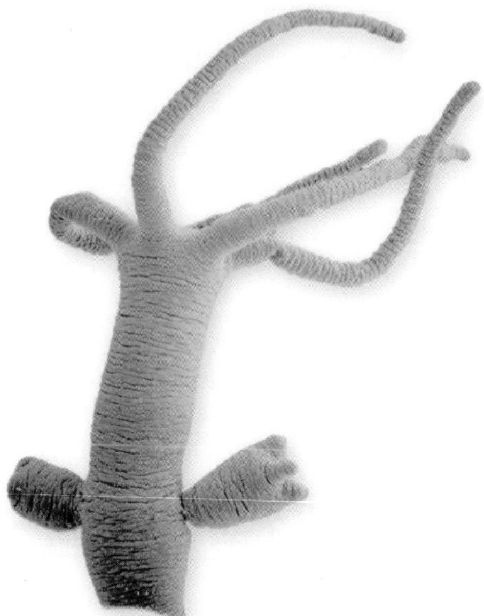

Figure 4 *The hydra can reproduce asexually by forming buds that break off and grow into new individuals.*

Living Things Reproduce

Organisms make other organisms similar to themselves. They do so in one of two ways: by sexual reproduction or by asexual reproduction. In **sexual reproduction,** two parents produce offspring that will share characteristics of both parents. Most animals and plants reproduce in this way. The bear cubs in **Figure 3** were produced sexually by their parents.

In **asexual reproduction,** a single parent produces offspring that are identical to the parent. **Figure 4** shows an organism that reproduces asexually. Most single-celled organisms reproduce in this way.

Living Things Have DNA

The cells of all living things contain the molecule **d**eoxyribo**n**ucleic (dee AHKS uh RIE boh noo KLEE ik) **a**cid, or DNA. *DNA* controls the structure and function of cells. When organisms reproduce, they pass copies of their DNA to their offspring. Passing DNA ensures that offspring resemble parents. The passing of traits from one generation to the next is called **heredity.**

Living Things Use Energy

Organisms use energy to carry out the activities of life. These activities include such things as making food, breaking down food, moving materials into and out of cells, and building cells. An organism's **metabolism** (muh TAB uh LIZ uhm) is the total of all of the chemical activities that the organism performs.

Reading Check **Name four chemical activities in living things that require energy.**

sexual reproduction reproduction in which the sex cells from two parents unite, producing offspring that share traits from both parents

asexual reproduction reproduction that does not involve the union of sex cells and in which one parent produces offspring identical to itself

heredity the passing of genetic traits from parent to offspring

metabolism the sum of all chemical processes that occur in an organism

Living Things Grow and Develop

All living things, whether they are made of one cell or many cells, grow during periods of their lives. In a single-celled organism, the cell gets larger and divides, making other organisms. In organisms made of many cells, the number of cells gets larger, and the organism gets bigger.

In addition to getting larger, living things may develop and change as they grow. Just like the organisms in **Figure 5,** you will pass through different stages in your life as you develop into an adult.

Figure 5 *Over time, acorns develop into oak seedlings, which become oak trees.*

SECTION Review

Summary

- Organisms are made of one or more cells.
- Organisms detect and respond to stimuli.
- Organisms make more organisms like themselves by reproducing either asexually or sexually.
- Organisms have DNA.
- Organisms use energy to carry out the chemical activities of life.
- Organisms grow and develop.

Using Key Terms

Complete each of the following sentences by choosing the correct term from the word bank.

cells | stimulus
homeostasis | metabolism

1. Sunlight can be a ___.
2. Living things are made of ___.

Understanding Key Ideas

3. Homeostasis means maintaining
   a. stable internal conditions.
   b. varied internal conditions.
   c. similar offspring.
   d. varied offspring.
4. Explain the difference between asexual and sexual reproduction.
5. Describe the six characteristics of living things.

Math Skills

6. Bacteria double every generation. One bacterium is in the first generation. How many are in the sixth generation?

Critical Thinking

7. **Applying Concepts** How do you respond to some stimuli in your environment?
8. **Identifying Relationships** What does the fur coat of a bear have to do with homeostasis?

For a variety of links related to this chapter, go to www.scilinks.org

Topic: Characteristics of Living Things
SciLinks code: HSM0258

SECTION 2

The Necessities of Life

Would it surprise you to learn that you have the same basic needs as a tree, a frog, and a fly?

READING WARM-UP

Objectives

- Explain why organisms need food, water, air, and living space.
- Describe the chemical building blocks of cells.

Terms to Learn

producer
consumer
decomposer
protein
carbohydrate
lipid
phospholipid
ATP
nucleic acid

READING STRATEGY

Discussion Read this section silently. Write down questions that you have about this section. Discuss your questions in a small group.

In fact, almost every organism has the same basic needs: water, air, a place to live, and food.

Water

You may know that your body is made mostly of water. In fact, your cells and the cells of almost all living organisms are approximately 70% water. Most of the chemical reactions involved in metabolism require water.

Organisms differ greatly in terms of how much water they need and how they get it. You could survive for only about three days without water. You get water from the fluids you drink and the food you eat. The desert-dwelling kangaroo rat never drinks. It gets all of its water from its food.

Air

Air is a mixture of several different gases, including oxygen and carbon dioxide. Most living things use oxygen in the chemical process that releases energy from food. Organisms living on land get oxygen from the air. Organisms living in water either take in dissolved oxygen from the water or come to the water's surface to get oxygen from the air. The European diving spider in **Figure 1** goes to great lengths to get oxygen.

Green plants, algae, and some bacteria need carbon dioxide gas in addition to oxygen. These organisms produce food and oxygen by using photosynthesis (FOHT oh SIN thuh sis). In *photosynthesis*, green organisms convert the energy in sunlight to energy stored in food.

Reading Check **What process do plants use to make food?** (*See the Appendix for answers to Reading Checks.*)

Figure 1 *This spider surrounds itself with an air bubble that provides the spider with a source of oxygen underwater.*

Figure 2 *A warbler's song is more than just a pretty tune. The warbler is protecting its home by telling other warblers to stay out of its territory.*

A Place to Live

All organisms need a place to live that contains all of the things they need to survive. Some organisms, such as elephants, require a large amount of space. Other organisms may live their entire life in one place.

Space on Earth is limited. So, organisms often compete with each other for food, water, and other necessities. Many animals, including the warbler in **Figure 2,** will claim a particular space. After claiming a space, they try to keep other animals away.

Food

All living things need food. Food gives organisms energy and the raw materials needed to carry on life processes. Organisms use nutrients from food to replace cells and build body parts. But not all organisms get food in the same way. In fact, organisms can be grouped into three different groups based on how they get their food.

producer an organism that can make its own food by using energy from its surroundings

consumer an organism that eats other organisms or organic matter

decomposer an organism that gets energy by breaking down the remains of dead organisms or animal wastes and consuming or absorbing the nutrients

Making Food

Some organisms, such as plants, are called producers. **Producers** can make their own food. Like most producers, plants use energy from the sun to make food from water and carbon dioxide. Some producers get energy and food from the chemicals in their environment.

Taking Food

Other organisms are called **consumers** because they must eat (consume) other organisms to get food. The frog in **Figure 3** is an example of a consumer. It gets the energy it needs by eating insects and other organisms.

Some consumers are decomposers. **Decomposers** are organisms that get their food by breaking down the nutrients in dead organisms or animal wastes. The mushroom in **Figure 3** is a decomposer.

Figure 3 *The frog is a consumer. The mushroom is a decomposer. The green plants are producers.*

Pen a Menu

WRITING SKILL With a parent, write a menu for a favorite meal. Using Nutrition Facts labels, find out which items on your menu include proteins, carbohydrates, and fats. Try making the meal.

ACTIVITY

Putting It All Together

Some organisms make their own food. Some organisms get food from eating other organisms. But all organisms need to break down that food in order to use the nutrients in it.

Nutrients are made up of molecules. A *molecule* is a substance made when two or more atoms combine. Molecules made of different kinds of atoms are *compounds*. Molecules found in living things are usually made of different combinations of six elements: carbon, hydrogen, nitrogen, oxygen, phosphorus, and sulfur. These elements combine to form proteins, carbohydrates, lipids, ATP, and nucleic acids.

Proteins

Almost all of the life processes of a cell involve proteins. **Proteins** are large molecules that are made up of smaller molecules called *amino acids*.

protein a molecule that is made up of amino acids and that is needed to build and repair body structures and to regulate processes in the body

Making Proteins

Organisms break down the proteins in food to supply their cells with amino acids. These amino acids are then linked together to form new proteins. Some proteins are made up of only a few amino acids, but others contain more than 10,000 amino acids.

Proteins in Action

Proteins have many different functions. Some proteins form structures that are easy to see, such as those in **Figure 4.** Other proteins are very small and help cells do their jobs. Inside red blood cells, the protein hemoglobin (HEE moh GLOH bin) binds to oxygen to deliver and release oxygen throughout the body. Some proteins protect cells. Other proteins, called *enzymes* (EN ZIEMZ), start or speed up chemical reactions in cells.

Figure 4 *Spider webs, hair, horns, and feathers are all made from proteins.*

Figure 5 *The extra sugar in a potato plant is stored in the potato as starch, a complex carbohydrate.*

Carbohydrates

Molecules made of sugars are called **carbohydrates.** Cells use carbohydrates as a source of energy and for energy storage. An organism's cells break down carbohydrates to release the energy stored in them. There are two kinds of carbohydrates—simple carbohydrates and complex carbohydrates.

carbohydrate a class of energy-giving nutrients that includes sugars, starches, and fiber; contains carbon, hydrogen, and oxygen

Simple Carbohydrates

Simple carbohydrates are made up of one sugar molecule or a few sugar molecules linked together. Table sugar and the sugar in fruits are examples of simple carbohydrates.

Complex Carbohydrates

When an organism has more sugar than it needs, its extra sugar may be stored as complex carbohydrates. *Complex carbohydrates* are made of hundreds of sugar molecules linked together. Plants, such as the potato plant in **Figure 5,** store extra sugar as starch. When you eat mashed potatoes, you are eating a potato plant's stored starch. Your body then breaks down this complex carbohydrate to release the energy stored in the potato.

Reading Check **What is the difference between simple carbohydrates and complex carbohydrates?**

How Much Oxygen?

Each red blood cell carries about 250 million molecules of hemoglobin. How many molecules of oxygen could a single red blood cell deliver throughout the body if every hemoglobin molecule attached to four oxygen molecules?

Starch Search

1. Obtain several **food samples** from your teacher.
2. Put **a few drops of iodine** on each sample. Record your observations. **Caution:** Iodine can stain clothing.
3. When iodine comes into contact with starch, a black substance appears. Which samples contain starch?

Figure 6 **Phospholipid Membranes**

The head of a phospholipid molecule is attracted to water, but the tail is not.

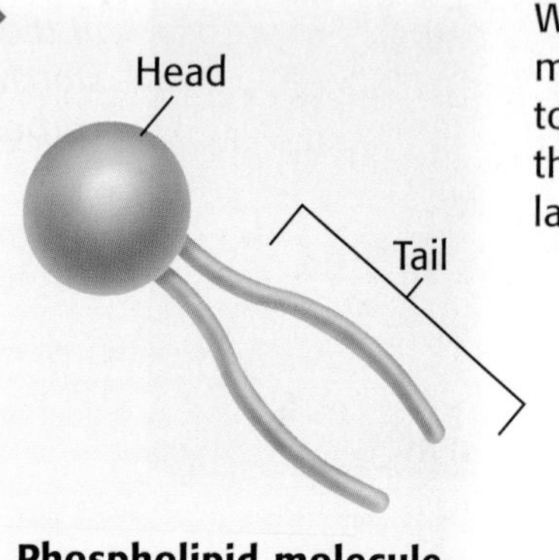

Phospholipid molecule

When phospholipid molecules come together in water, they form two layers.

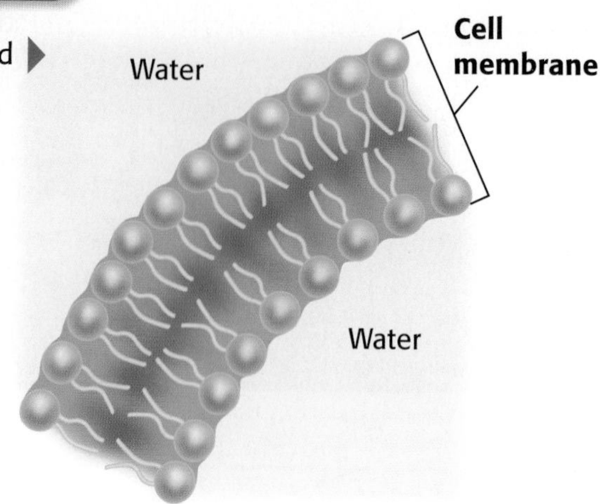

lipid a type of biochemical that does not dissolve in water; fats and steroids are lipids

phospholipid a lipid that contains phosphorus and that is a structural component in cell membranes

ATP **a**denosine **tri**p**h**osphate, a molecule that acts as the main energy source for cell processes

Lipids

Lipids are compounds that cannot mix with water. Lipids have many important jobs in the cell. Like carbohydrates, some lipids store energy. Other lipids form the membranes of cells.

Phospholipids

All cells are surrounded by a cell membrane. The cell membrane helps protect the cell and keep the internal conditions of the cell stable. **Phospholipids** (FAHS foh LIP idz) are the molecules that form much of the cell membrane. The head of a phospholipid molecule is attracted to water. The tail is not. Cells are mostly water. When phospholipids are in water, the tails come together, and the heads face out into the water. **Figure 6** shows how phospholipid molecules form two layers in water.

Fats and Oils

Fats and oils are lipids that store energy. When an organism has used up most of its carbohydrates, it can get energy from these lipids. The structures of fats and oils are almost the same, but at room temperature, most fats are solid, and most oils are liquid. Most of the lipids stored in plants are oils. Most of the lipids stored in animals are fats.

Reading Check **What is one difference between oils and fats?**

CONNECTION TO Social Studies

Whaling In the 1900s, whales were hunted and killed for their oil. Whale oil was often used as fuel for oil lamps. Most of the oil taken from whales was taken from their fat, or *blubber*. Some whales had blubber over 18 in. thick, producing over 40 barrels of oil per whale. Research whether anyone still hunts whales or uses whale oil. Make a presentation to the class on your findings.

ATP

Adenosine **trip**hosphate (uh DEN uh SEEN trie FAHS FAYT), also called ATP, is another important molecule. **ATP** is the major energy-carrying molecule in the cell. The energy in carbohydrates and lipids must be transferred to ATP, which then provides fuel for cellular activities.

Nucleic Acids

Nucleic acids are sometimes called the blueprints of life because they have all the information needed for a cell to make proteins. **Nucleic acids** are large molecules made up of molecules called *nucleotides* (NOO klee oh TIEDZ). A nucleic acid may have thousands of nucleotides. The order of those nucleotides stores information. DNA is a nucleic acid. A DNA molecule is like a recipe book entitled *How to Make Proteins.* When a cell needs to make a certain protein, the cell gets information from the order of the nucleotides in DNA. This order of nucleotides tells the cell the order of the amino acids that are linked together to make that protein.

nucleic acid a molecule made up of subunits called *nucleotides*

SECTION Review

Summary

- Organisms need water for cellular processes.
- Organisms need oxygen to release the energy contained in their food.
- Organisms must have a place to live.
- Cells store energy in carbohydrates, which are made of sugars.
- Proteins are made up of amino acids. Some proteins are enzymes.
- Fats and oils store energy and make up cell membranes.
- Cells use molecules of ATP to fuel their activities.
- Nucleic acids, such as DNA, are made up of nucleotides.

Using Key Terms

For each pair of terms, explain how the meanings of the terms differ.

1. *producer* and *consumer*
2. *lipid* and *phospholipid*

Understanding Key Ideas

3. Plants store extra sugar as
   a. proteins.
   b. starch.
   c. nucleic acids.
   d. phospholipids.
4. Explain why organisms need food, water, air, and living space.
5. Describe the chemical building blocks of cells.
6. Why are decomposers categorized as consumers? How do they differ from producers?
7. What are the subunits of proteins?

Math Skills

8. Protein A is a chain of 660 amino acids. Protein B is a chain of 11 amino acids. How many times more amino acids does protein A have than protein B?

Critical Thinking

9. **Making Inferences** Could life as we know it exist on Earth if air contained only oxygen? Explain.
10. **Identifying Relationships** How might a cave, an ant, and a lake each meet the needs of an organism?
11. **Predicting Consequences** What would happen to the supply of ATP in your cells if you did not eat enough carbohydrates? How would this affect your cells?
12. **Applying Concepts** Which resource do you think is most important to your survival: water, air, a place to live, or food? Explain your answer.

SCILINKS
NSTA
Developed and maintained by the National Science Teachers Association
For a variety of links related to this chapter, go to www.scilinks.org
Topic: The Necessities of Life
SciLinks code: HSM1018

Using Scientific Methods

Inquiry Lab

Roly-Poly Races

OBJECTIVES

Observe responses to stimuli.

Analyze responses to stimuli.

MATERIALS

- chalk (1 stick)
- container, plastic, small, with lid
- gloves, protective
- isopod (4)
- potato, raw (1 small slice)
- ruler, metric
- soil (8 oz)
- stopwatch

SAFETY

Have you ever watched a bug run? Did you wonder why it was running? The bug you saw running was probably reacting to a stimulus. In other words, something happened to make the bug run! One characteristic of living things is that they respond to stimuli. In this activity, you will study the movement of roly-polies. Roly-polies are also called *pill bugs*. But they are not really bugs; they are land-dwelling animals called *isopods*. Isopods live in dark, moist areas under rocks or wood. You will provide stimuli to determine how fast your isopod can move and what affects its speed and direction. Remember that isopods are living things and must be treated gently and respectfully.

Ask a Question

1. Ask a question such as, "Which stimuli cause pill bugs to run?"

Form a Hypothesis

2. Using your question as a guide, form a hypothesis. For example, you could form the following hypothesis: "Light, sound, and touch stimulate pill bugs to run."

Test the Hypothesis

3. Choose a partner, and decide together how you will run your roly-poly race. Discuss some gentle ways to stimulate your isopods to move. Choose five or six things that might cause movement, such as a gentle nudge or a change in temperature, sound, or light. Check your choices with your teacher.

4. Make a data table similar to the table below. Label the columns with the stimuli that you've chosen. Label the rows "Isopod 1," "Isopod 2," "Isopod 3," and "Isopod 4."

Isopod Responses			
	Stimulus 1	Stimulus 2	Stimulus 3
Isopod 1			
Isopod 2			
Isopod 3			
Isopod 4			

DO NOT WRITE IN BOOK

5. Place a layer of soil that is 1 cm or 2 cm deep in a small plastic container. Add a small slice of potato and a piece of chalk. Your isopods will eat these items.

6. Place four isopods in your container. Observe them for a minute or two before you perform your tests. Record your observations.

7. Decide which stimulus you want to test first. Carefully arrange the isopods at the "starting line." The starting line can be an imaginary line at one end of the container.

8. Gently stimulate each isopod at the same time and in the same way. In your data table, record the isopods' responses to the stimulus. Be sure to record the distance that each isopod travels. Don't forget to time the race.

9. Repeat steps 7–8 for each stimulus. Be sure to wait at least 2 min between trials.

Analyze the Results

1. **Describing Events** Describe the way that isopods move. Do their legs move together?

2. **Analyzing Results** Did your isopods move before or between the trials? Did the movement seem to have a purpose, or were the isopods responding to a stimulus? Explain.

Draw Conclusions

3. **Interpreting Information** Did any of the stimuli make the isopods move faster or go farther? Explain.

Applying Your Data

Like isopods and all other living things, humans react to stimuli. Describe three stimuli that might cause humans to run.

Chapter Review

USING KEY TERMS

Complete each of the following sentences by choosing the correct term from the word bank.

lipid	carbohydrate
consumer	heredity
homeostasis	producer

1. The process of maintaining a stable internal environment is known as ___.

2. Offspring resemble their parents because of ___.

3. A ___ obtains food by eating other organisms.

4. Starch is a ___ and is made up of sugars.

5. Fat is a ___ that stores energy for an organism.

UNDERSTANDING KEY IDEAS

Multiple Choice

6. Which of the following statements about cells is true?
   - **a.** Cells are the structures that contain all of the materials necessary for life.
   - **b.** Cells are found in all organisms.
   - **c.** Cells are sometimes specialized for particular functions.
   - **d.** All of the above

7. Which of the following statements about all living things is true?
   - **a.** All living things reproduce sexually.
   - **b.** All living things have one or more cells.
   - **c.** All living things must make their own food.
   - **d.** All living things reproduce asexually.

8. Organisms must have food because
   - **a.** food is a source of energy.
   - **b.** food supplies cells with oxygen.
   - **c.** organisms never make their own food.
   - **d.** All of the above

9. A change in an organism's environment that affects the organism's activities is a
   - **a.** response.
   - **b.** stimulus.
   - **c.** metabolism.
   - **d.** producer.

10. Organisms store energy in
    - **a.** nucleic acids.
    - **b.** phospholipids.
    - **c.** lipids.
    - **d.** water.

11. The molecule that contains the information about how to make proteins is
    - **a.** ATP.
    - **b.** a carbohydrate.
    - **c.** DNA.
    - **d.** a phospholipid.

12. The subunits of nucleic acids are
    - **a.** nucleotides.
    - **b.** oils.
    - **c.** sugars.
    - **d.** amino acids.

Short Answer

13. What is the difference between asexual reproduction and sexual reproduction?

14. In one or two sentences, explain why living things must have air.

15. What is ATP, and why is it important to a cell?

CRITICAL THINKING

16. **Concept Mapping** Use the following terms to create a concept map: *cell, carbohydrates, protein, enzymes, DNA, sugars, lipids, nucleotides, amino acids,* and *nucleic acid.*

17. **Analyzing Ideas** A flame can move, grow larger, and give off heat. Is a flame alive? Explain.

18. **Applying Concepts** Based on what you know about carbohydrates, lipids, and proteins, why is it important for you to eat a balanced diet?

19. **Evaluating Hypotheses** Your friend tells you that the stimulus of music makes his goldfish swim faster. How would you design a controlled experiment to test your friend's claim?

INTERPRETING GRAPHICS

The pictures below show the same plant over a period of 3 days. Use the pictures below to answer the questions that follow.

20. What is the plant doing?

21. What characteristic(s) of living things is the plant exhibiting?

Standardized Test Preparation

READING

Read each of the passages below. Then, answer the questions that follow each passage.

Passage 1 Organisms make other organisms similar to themselves. They do so in one of two ways: by sexual reproduction or by asexual reproduction. In sexual reproduction, two parents produce offspring that will share characteristics of both parents. Most animals and plants reproduce in this way. In asexual reproduction, a single parent produces offspring that are identical to the parent. Most single-celled organisms reproduce in this way.

1. In the passage, what does the term *asexual reproduction* mean?

A A single parent produces offspring.
B Two parents make identical offspring.
C Plants make offspring.
D Animals make offspring.

2. What is characteristic of offspring produced by sexual reproduction?

F They are identical to both parents.
G They share the traits of both parents.
H They are identical to one parent.
I They are identical to each other.

3. What is characteristic of offspring produced by asexual reproduction?

A They are identical to both parents.
B They share the traits of both parents.
C They are identical to one parent.
D They are usually plants.

4. What is the difference between sexual and asexual reproduction?

F the number of offspring produced
G the number of parents needed to produce offspring
H the number of traits produced
I the number of offspring that survive

Passage 2 In 1996, a group of researchers led by NASA scientists studied a 3.8-billion-year-old meteorite named ALH84001. These scientists agree that ALH84001 is a potato-sized piece of the planet Mars. They also agree that it fell to Earth about 13,000 years ago. It was discovered in Antarctica in 1984. According to the NASA team, ALH84001 brought with it evidence that life once existed on Mars.

Scientists found certain kinds of organic molecules (molecules containing carbon) on the surface of ALH84001. These molecules are similar to those left behind when living things break down substances for food. When these scientists examined the interior of the meteorite, they found the same organic molecules throughout. Because these molecules were spread throughout the meteorite, scientists concluded that the molecules were not contamination from Earth. The NASA team believes that these organic compounds are strong evidence that tiny organisms similar to bacteria lived, ate, and died on Mars millions of years ago.

1. How old is the meteorite named ALH84001?

A 13,000 years old
B millions of years old
C 3.8 billion years old
D 3.8 trillion years old

2. Which of the following would best support a claim that life might have existed on Mars?

F remains of organisms
G water
H meteorite temperatures similar to Earth temperatures
I oxygen

INTERPRETING GRAPHICS

The graph below shows an ill person's body temperature. Use the graph below to answer the questions that follow.

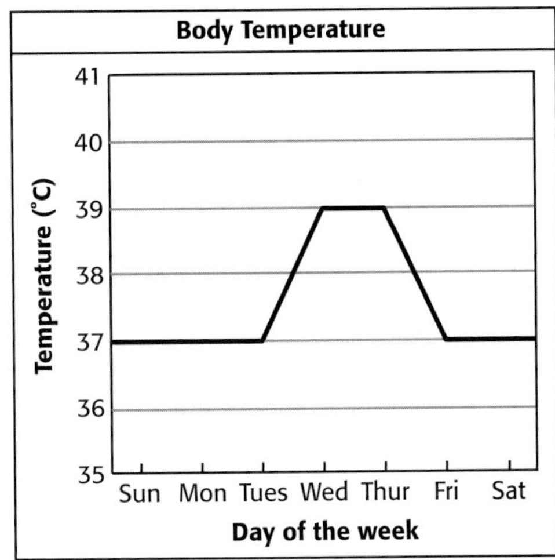

1. A fever is a spike in temperature. On which day does this person have a fever?

A Sunday
B Monday
C Wednesday
D Saturday

2. A body with a fever is often fighting an infection. Fevers help eliminate the pathogens that cause the infection. According to the chart, when does this person probably have the highest fever?

F Sunday
G Monday
H Wednesday
I Saturday

3. What is the highest temperature that this fever reaches?

A 37°C
B 38°C
C 39°C
D 40°C

4. What is probably this person's normal body temperature?

F 37°C
G 38°C
H 39°C
I 40°C

MATH

Read each question below, and choose the best answer.

1. An aquarium is a place where fish can live. What is the volume of the aquarium shown below?

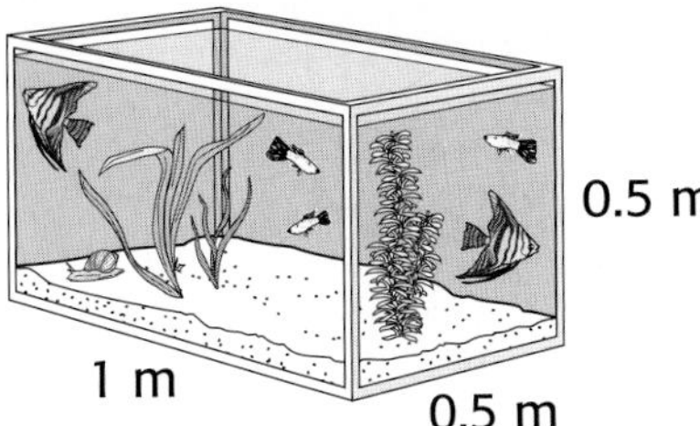

A 0.25 m
B 0.25 m^2
C 0.25 m^3
D 0.52 m^3

2. The cost of admission to a natural history museum is $7 per adult. What is the total cost of admission for a group of five adults?

F $25
G $35
H $45
I $55

3. Lee biked 25.3 km on Monday, 20.7 km on Tuesday, and 15.6 km on Wednesday. How many kilometers did Lee bike during those three days?

A 66.1 km
B 61.6 km
C 51.6 km
D 16.6 km

4. Laura collected 24 leaves. One-third of the leaves were oak leaves. How many oak leaves did Laura collect?

F 6
G 8
H 12
I 24

Science in Action

Science, Technology, and Society

Chess-Playing Computers

Computers can help us explore how humans think. One way to explore how humans think is to study how people and computers play chess against each other.

A computer's approach to chess is straightforward. By calculating each piece's possible board position for the next few moves, a computer creates what is called a *position tree.* A position tree shows how each move can lead to other moves. This way of playing requires millions of calculations.

Human chess champions play differently. Humans calculate only three or four moves every minute. Even so, human champions are still a match for computer opponents. By studying the ways that people and computers play chess, scientists are learning how people think and make choices.

Math ACTIVITY

A chess-playing computer needs to evaluate 3 million positions before a move. If you could evaluate two positions in 1 min, how long would it take you to evaluate 3 million possible positions?

Science Fiction

"They're Made Out of Meat" by Terry Bisson

Two space explorers millions of light-years from home are visiting an uncharted sector of the universe to find signs of life. Their mission is to contact, welcome, and log any and all beings in this part of the universe.

During their mission, they encounter a life-form quite unlike anything they have ever seen before. It looked too strange and, well, disgusting. The explorers have very strong doubts about adding this new organism to the list. But the explorers' official duty is to contact and welcome all life-forms no matter how ugly they are. Can the explorers bring themselves to perform their duty?

You'll find out by reading "They're Made Out of Meat," a short story by Terry Bisson. This story is in the *Holt Anthology of Science Fiction.*

Language Arts ACTIVITY

WRITING SKILL Write a story about what happens when the explorers next meet the creatures on the star in G445 zone.

People in Science

Janis Davis-Street

NASA Nutritionist Do astronauts eat shrimp cocktail in space? Yes, they do! Shrimp cocktail is nutritious and tastes so good that it is one of the most popular foods in the space program. And eating a proper diet helps astronauts stay healthy while they are in space.

But who figures out what astronauts need to eat? Janis Davis-Street is a nutritionist and laboratory supervisor for the Nutritional Biochemistry Laboratory at the Johnson Space Center in Houston, Texas. She was born in Georgetown, Guyana, on the north-eastern coast of South America. She was educated in Canada.

Davis-Street is part of a team that uses their knowledge of nutrition, biology, and chemistry to figure out the nutritional requirements for spaceflight. For example, they determine how many calories and other nutrients each astronaut needs per day during spaceflight.

The Nutritional Biochemistry Laboratory's work on the space shuttle missions and *Mir* space station developed into tests that allow NASA to help ensure astronaut health before, during, and after flight. These tests are important for understanding how the human body adapts to long space missions, and for determining whether treatments for preventing bone and muscle loss during spaceflight are working.

Social Studies ACTIVITY

Scientists from more than 30 countries have been on space missions. Research which countries have provided astronauts or cosmonauts for space missions. Using a map, place self-stick notes on countries that have provided scientists for space missions. Write the names of the appropriate scientists on the self-stick notes.

To learn more about these Science in Action topics, visit go.hrw.com and type in the keyword HL5ALVF.

Current Science

Check out Current Science® articles related to this chapter by visiting go.hrw.com. Just type in the keyword HL5CS02.

TIMELINE

Cells

Cells are everywhere. Even though most cells can't be seen with the naked eye, they make up every living thing. Your body alone contains trillions of cells.

In this unit, you will learn about cells. You will learn the difference between animal cells, plant cells, and bacterial cells. You will learn about the parts of a cell and will see how they work together.

Since cells were discovered in 1665, we have learned a lot about cells and the way they work. This timeline shows some of the discoveries that have been made along the way, but there is still a lot to learn about the fascinating world of cells!

1620
The Pilgrims settle Plymouth Colony.

1665
Robert Hooke discovers cells after observing a thin piece of cork under a microscope.

1861
The American Civil War begins.

1952
Martha Chase and Alfred Hershey demonstrate that DNA is the hereditary material.

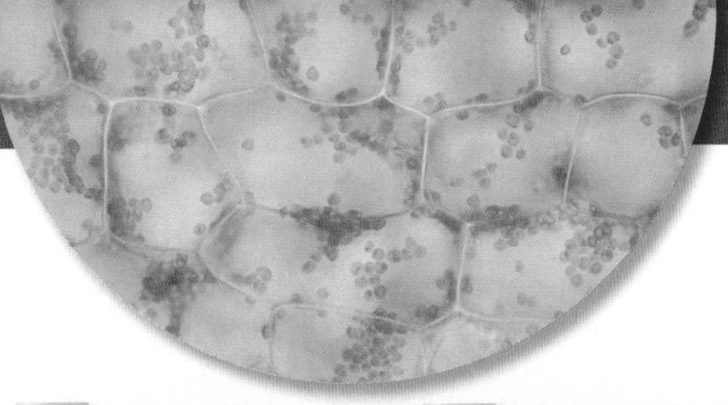

1831

Robert Brown discovers the nucleus in a plant cell.

1838

Matthias Schleiden discovers that all plant tissue is made up of cells.

1839

Theodor Schwann shows that all animal tissue is made up of cells.

1858

Rudolf Virchow determines that all cells are produced from cells.

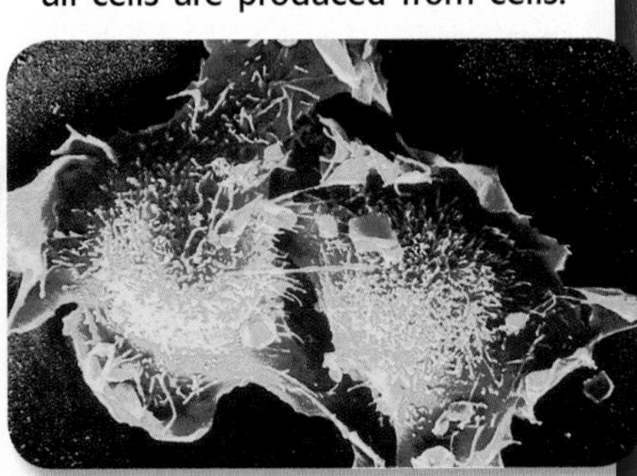

1873

Anton Schneider observes and accurately describes mitosis.

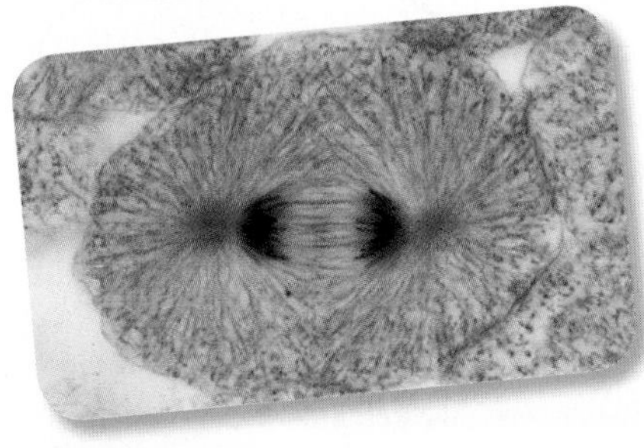

1937

The Golden Gate Bridge opens in San Francisco.

1941

George Beadle and Edward Tatum discover that genes control the chemical reactions in cells by directing protein production.

1956

The manufacture of protein in the cell is found to occur in ribosomes.

1971

Lynn Margulis proposes the endosymbiotic theory of the origin of cell organelles.

1997

A sheep named Dolly becomes the first animal to be cloned from a single body cell.

2002

Scientists test a cancer vaccine that can be given orally. Tests on mice lead scientists to be hopeful that the vaccine can be tested on humans.

Cells: The Basic Units of Life

About the PHOTO

Harmful bacteria may invade your body and make you sick. But wait—your white blood cells come to the rescue! In this image, a white blood cell (the large, yellowish cell) reaches out its pseudopod to destroy bacteria (the purple cells). The red discs are red blood cells.

PRE-READING ACTIVITY

FOLDNOTES **Key-Term Fold** Before you read the chapter, create the FoldNote entitled "Key-Term Fold" described in the **Study Skills** section of the Appendix. Write a key term from the chapter on each tab of the key-term fold. Under each tab, write the definition of the key term.

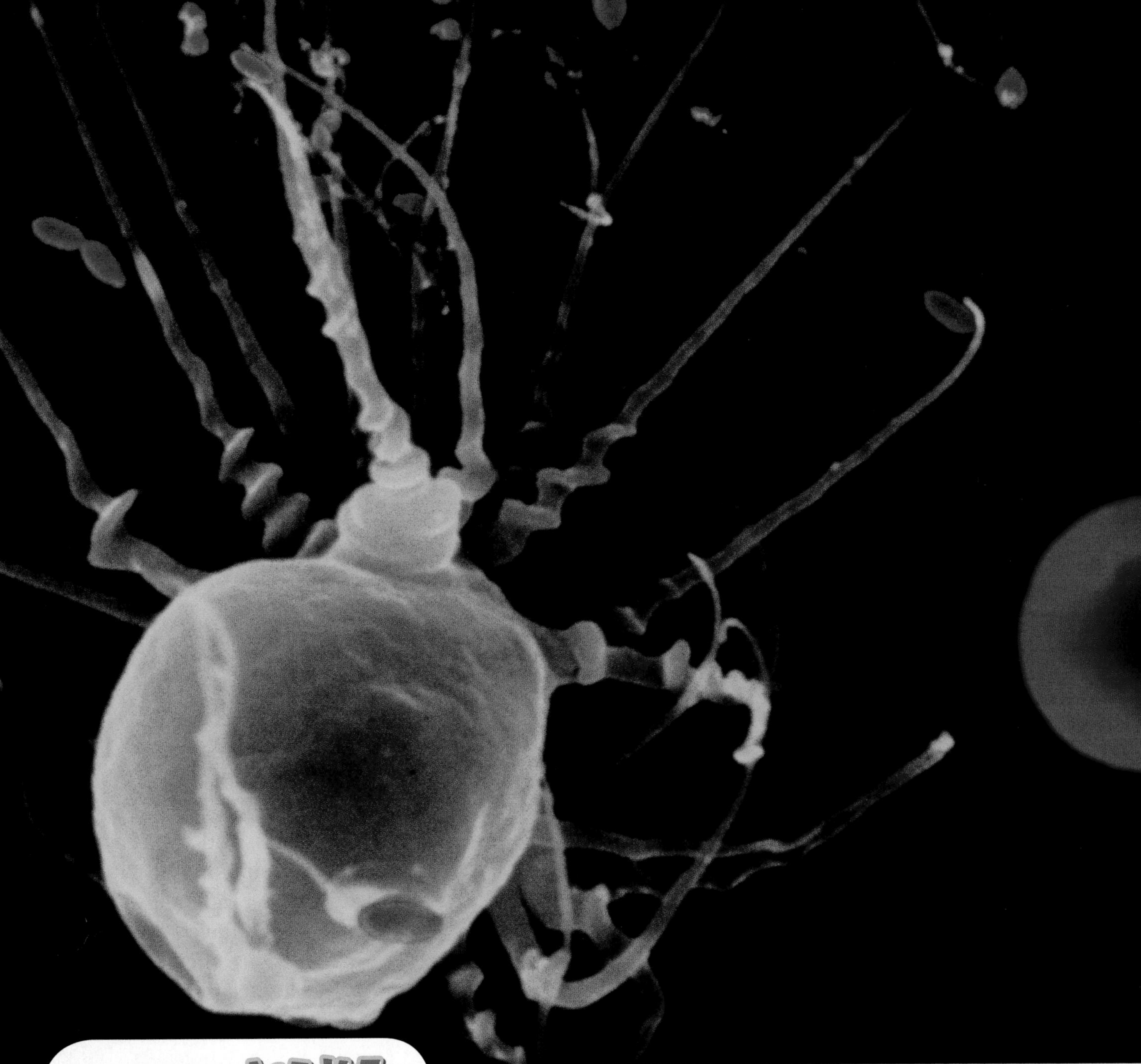

START-UP ACTIVITY

What Are Plants Made Of?

All living things, including plants, are made of cells. What do plant cells look like? Do this activity to find out.

Procedure

1. Tear off a **small leaf** from near the tip of an **Elodea sprig.**
2. Using **forceps,** place the whole leaf in a **drop of water** on a **microscope slide.**
3. Place a **coverslip** on top of the water drop by putting one edge of the coverslip on the slide near the water drop. Next, lower the coverslip slowly so that the coverslip does not trap air bubbles.
4. Place the slide on your **microscope.**
5. Using the lowest-powered lens first, find the plant cells. When you can see the cells under the lower-powered lens, switch to a higher-powered lens.
6. Draw a picture of what you see.

Analysis

1. Describe the shape of the *Elodea* cells. Are all of the cells in the *Elodea* the same?
2. Do you think human cells look like *Elodea* cells? How do you think they are different? How might they be similar?

SECTION 1

The Diversity of Cells

Most cells are so small they can't be seen by the naked eye. So how did scientists find cells? By accident, that's how! The first person to see cells wasn't even looking for them.

All living things are made of tiny structures called cells. A **cell** is the smallest unit that can perform all the processes necessary for life. Because of their size, cells weren't discovered until microscopes were invented in the mid-1600s.

Cells and the Cell Theory

Robert Hooke was the first person to describe cells. In 1665, he built a microscope to look at tiny objects. One day, he looked at a thin slice of cork. Cork is found in the bark of cork trees. The cork looked like it was made of little boxes. Hooke named these boxes *cells,* which means "little rooms" in Latin. Hooke's cells were really the outer layers of dead cork cells. Hooke's microscope and his drawing of the cork cells are shown in **Figure 1.**

Hooke also looked at thin slices of living plants. He saw that they too were made of cells. Some cells were even filled with "juice." The "juicy" cells were living cells.

Hooke also looked at feathers, fish scales, and the eyes of houseflies. But he spent most of his time looking at plants and fungi. The cells of plants and fungi have cell walls. This makes them easy to see. Animal cells do not have cell walls. This absence of cell walls makes it harder to see the outline of animal cells. Because Hooke couldn't see their cells, he thought that animals weren't made of cells.

READING WARM-UP

Objectives

- State the parts of the cell theory.
- Explain why cells are so small.
- Describe the parts of a cell.
- Describe how eubacteria are different from archaebacteria.
- Explain the difference between prokaryotic cells and eukaryotic cells.

Terms to Learn

cell, cell membrane, organelle, nucleus, prokaryote, eukaryote

READING STRATEGY

Reading Organizer As you read this section, create an outline of the section. Use the headings from the section in your outline.

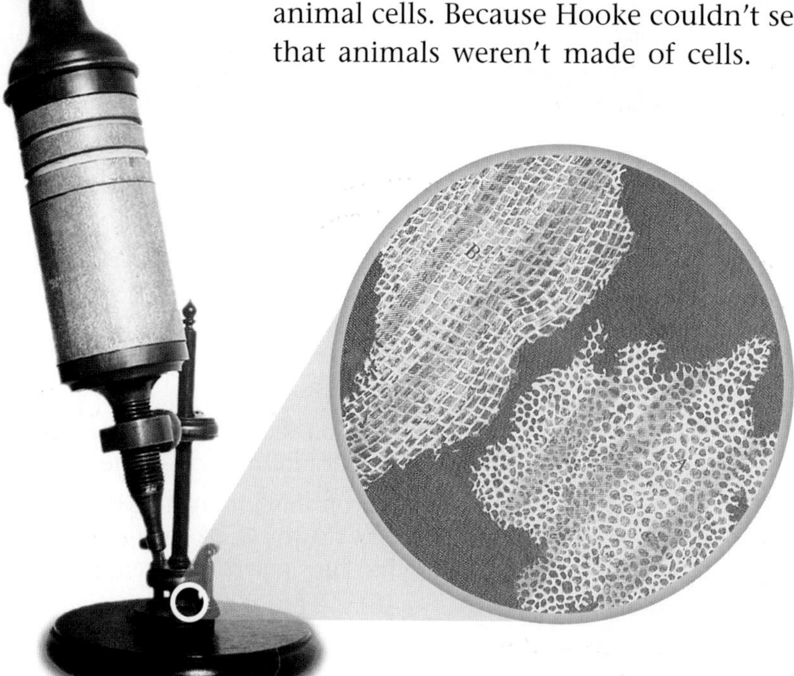

Figure 1 *Hooke discovered cells using this microscope. Hooke's drawing of cork cells is shown to the right of his microscope.*

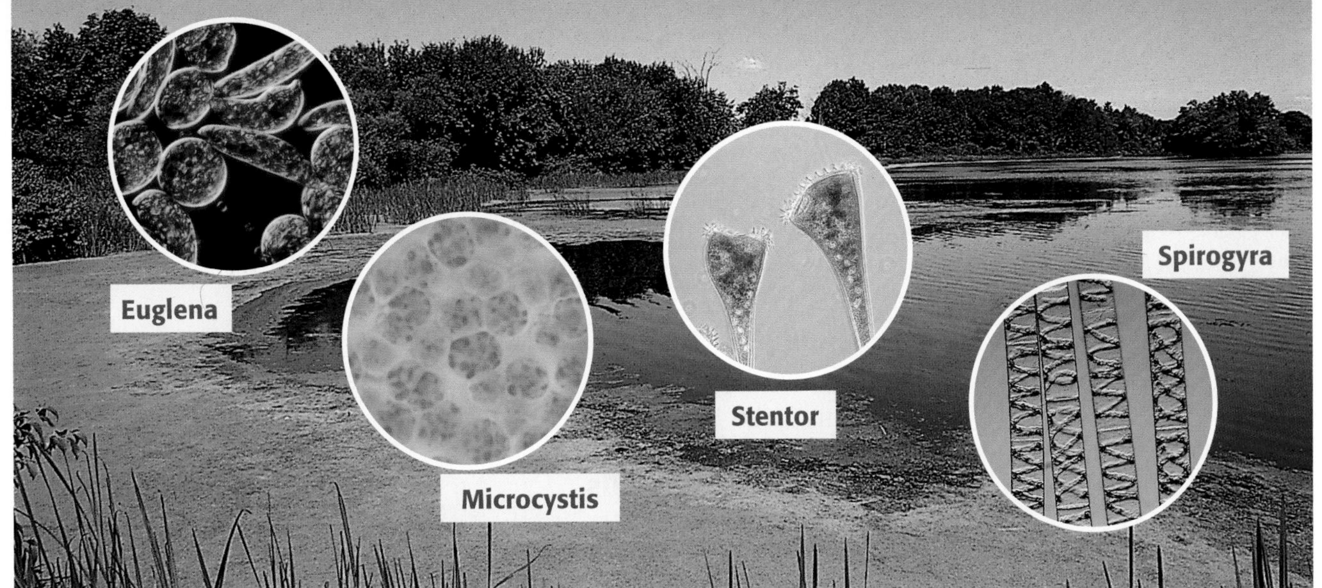

Figure 2 *The green area at the edge of the pond is a layer of pond scum. This pond scum contains organisms called* protists, *such as those shown above.*

Finding Cells in Other Organisms

In 1673, Anton van Leeuwenhoek (LAY vuhn HOOK), a Dutch merchant, made his own microscopes. Leeuwenhoek used one of his microscopes to look at pond scum. Leeuwenhoek saw small organisms in the water. He named these organisms *animalcules,* which means "little animals." Today, we call these single-celled organisms protists (PROH tists). Pond scum and some of the protists it contains are shown in **Figure 2.**

Leeuwenhoek also looked at animal blood. He saw differences in blood cells from different kinds of animals. For example, blood cells in fish, birds, and frogs are oval. Blood cells in humans and dogs are round and flat. Leeuwenhoek was also the first person to see bacteria. And he discovered that yeasts that make bread dough rise are single-celled organisms.

cell in biology, the smallest unit that can perform all life processes; cells are covered by a membrane and have DNA and cytoplasm

The Cell Theory

Almost 200 years passed before scientists concluded that cells are present in all living things. Scientist Matthias Schleiden (mah THEE uhs SHLIE duhn) studied plants. In 1838, he concluded that all plant parts were made of cells. Theodor Schwann (TAY oh dohr SHVAHN) studied animals. In 1839, Schwann concluded that all animal tissues were made of cells. Soon after that, Schwann wrote the first two parts of what is now known as the *cell theory*.

- All organisms are made of one or more cells.
- The cell is the basic unit of all living things.

Later, in 1858, Rudolf Virchow (ROO dawlf FIR koh), a doctor, stated that all cells could form only from other cells. Virchow then added the third part of the cell theory.

- All cells come from existing cells.

Reading Check What are the three parts of the cell theory? (*See the Appendix for answers to Reading Checks.*)

CONNECTION TO Physics

Microscopes The microscope Hooke used to study cells was much different from microscopes today. Research different kinds of microscopes, such as light microscopes, scanning electron microscopes (SEMs), and transmission electron microscopes (TEMs). Select one type of microscope. Make a poster or other presentation to show to the class. Describe how the microscope works and how it is used. Be sure to include images.

ACTIVITY

Cell Size

Most cells are too small to be seen without a microscope. It would take 50 human cells to cover the dot on this letter *i*.

A Few Large Cells

Most cells are small. A few, however, are big. The yolk of a chicken egg, shown in **Figure 3,** is one big cell. The egg can be this large because it does not have to take in more nutrients.

Figure 3 *The white and yolk of this chicken egg provide nutrients for the development of a chick.*

Many Small Cells

There is a physical reason why most cells are so small. Cells take in food and get rid of wastes through their outer surface. As a cell gets larger, it needs more food and produces more waste. Therefore, more materials pass through its outer surface.

As the cell's volume increases, its surface area grows too. But the cell's volume grows faster than its surface area. If a cell gets too large, the cell's surface area will not be large enough to take in enough nutrients or pump out enough wastes. So, the area of a cell's surface—compared with the cell's volume—limits the cell's size. The ratio of the cell's outer surface area to the cell's volume is called the *surface area–to-volume ratio,* which can be calculated by using the following equation:

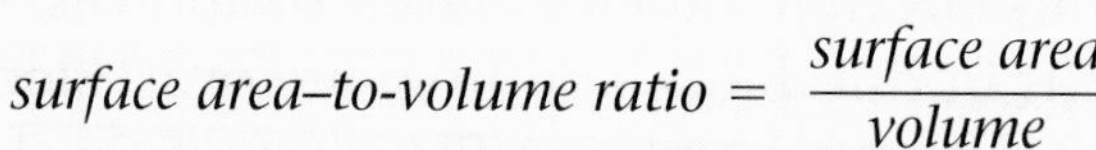

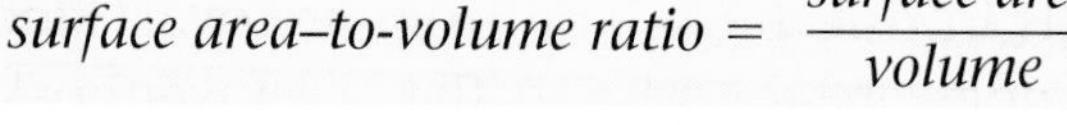

$$\textit{surface area–to-volume ratio} = \frac{\textit{surface area}}{\textit{volume}}$$

Reading Check Why are most cells small?

MATH FOCUS

Surface Area-to-Volume Ratio Calculate the surface area–to-volume ratio of a cube whose sides measure 2 cm.

Step 1: Calculate the surface area.

$$\textit{surface area of cube} = \textit{number of sides} \times \textit{area of side}$$

$$\textit{surface area of cube} = 6 \times (2 \text{ cm} \times 2 \text{ cm})$$

$$\textit{surface area of cube} = 24 \text{ cm}^2$$

Step 2: Calculate the volume.

$$\textit{volume of cube} = \textit{side} \times \textit{side} \times \textit{side}$$

$$\textit{volume of cube} = 2 \text{ cm} \times 2 \text{ cm} \times 2 \text{ cm}$$

$$\textit{volume of cube} = 8 \text{ cm}^3$$

Step 3: Calculate the surface area–to-volume ratio.

$$\textit{surface area–to-volume ratio} = \frac{\textit{surface area}}{\textit{volume}} = \frac{24}{8} = \frac{3}{1}$$

Now It's Your Turn

1. Calculate the surface area–to-volume ratio of a cube whose sides are 3 cm long.
2. Calculate the surface area–to-volume ratio of a cube whose sides are 4 cm long.
3. Of the cubes from questions 1 and 2, which has the greater surface area–to-volume ratio?
4. What is the relationship between the length of a side and the surface area–to-volume ratio of a cell?

Parts of a Cell

Cells come in many shapes and sizes. Cells have many different functions. But all cells have the following parts in common.

The Cell Membrane and Cytoplasm

All cells are surrounded by a cell membrane. The **cell membrane** is a protective layer that covers the cell's surface and acts as a barrier. It separates the cell's contents from its environment. The cell membrane also controls materials going into and out of the cell. Inside the cell is a fluid. This fluid and almost all of its contents are called the *cytoplasm* (SIET oh PLAZ uhm).

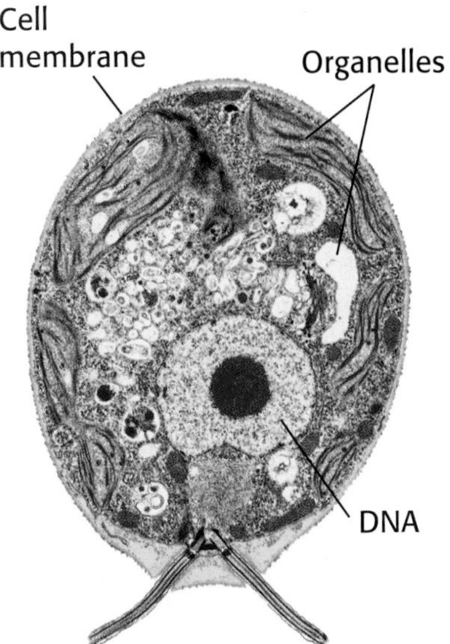

Figure 4 *This green alga has organelles. The organelles and the fluid surrounding them make up the cytoplasm.*

Organelles

Cells have organelles that carry out various life processes. **Organelles** are structures that perform specific functions within the cell. Different types of cells have different organelles. Most organelles are surrounded by membranes. For example, the algal cell in **Figure 4** has membrane-bound organelles. Some organelles float in the cytoplasm. Other organelles are attached to membranes or other organelles.

Reading Check What are organelles?

Genetic Material

All cells contain DNA (**d**eoxyribo**n**ucleic **a**cid) at some point in their life. *DNA* is the genetic material that carries information needed to make new cells and new organisms. DNA is passed on from parent cells to new cells and controls the activities of a cell. **Figure 5** shows the DNA of a bacterium.

In some cells, the DNA is enclosed inside an organelle called the **nucleus.** For example, your cells have a nucleus. In contrast, bacterial cells do not have a nucleus.

In humans, mature red blood cells lose their DNA. Red blood cells are made inside bones. When red blood cells are first made, they have a nucleus with DNA. But before they enter the bloodstream, red blood cells lose their nucleus and DNA. They survive with no new instructions from their DNA.

cell membrane a phospholipid layer that covers a cell's surface; acts as a barrier between the inside of a cell and the cell's environment

organelle one of the small bodies in a cell's cytoplasm that are specialized to perform a specific function

nucleus in a eukaryotic cell, a membrane-bound organelle that contains the cell's DNA and that has a role in processes such as growth, metabolism, and reproduction

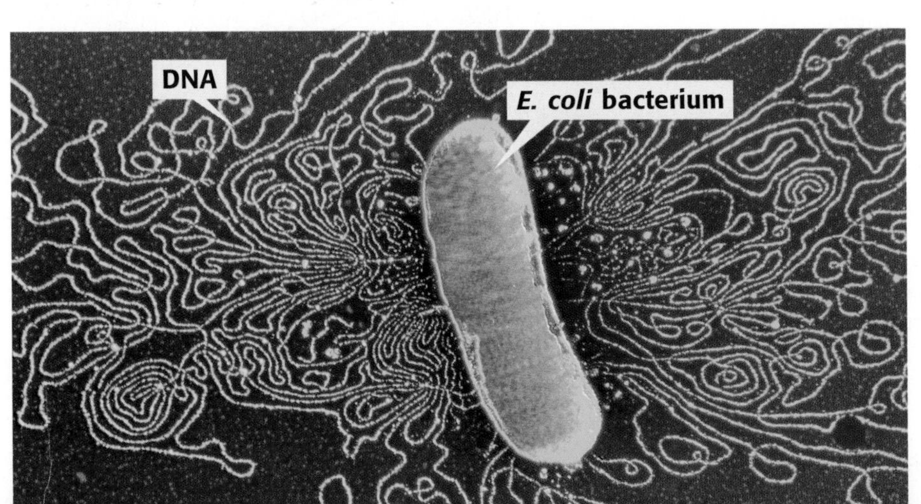

Figure 5 *This photo shows an* Escherichia coli *bacterium. The bacterium's cell membrane has been treated so that the cell's DNA is released.*

Bacteria in Your Lunch?

Most of the time, you don't want bacteria in your food. Many bacteria make toxins that will make you sick. However, some foods—such as yogurt—are supposed to have bacteria in them! The bacteria in these foods are not dangerous.

In yogurt, masses of rod-shaped bacteria feed on the sugar (lactose) in milk. The bacteria convert the sugar into lactic acid. Lactic acid causes milk to thicken. This thickened milk makes yogurt.

1. Using a **cotton swab,** put a **small dot of yogurt** on a **microscope slide.**
2. Add a **drop of water.** Use the cotton swab to stir.
3. Add a **coverslip.**
4. Use a **microscope** to examine the slide. Draw what you observe.

Two Kinds of Cells

All cells have cell membranes, organelles, cytoplasm, and DNA in common. But there are two basic types of cells—cells without a nucleus and cells with a nucleus. Cells with no nucleus are *prokaryotic* (proh KAR ee AHT ik) *cells.* Cells that have a nucleus are *eukaryotic* (yoo KAR ee AHT ik) *cells.* Prokaryotic cells are further classified into two groups: *eubacteria* (yoo bak TIR ee uh) and *archaebacteria* (AHR kee bak TIR ee uh).

Prokaryotes: Eubacteria and Archaebacteria

Eubacteria and archaebacteria are prokaryotes (pro KAR ee OHTS). **Prokaryotes** are single-celled organisms that do not have a nucleus or membrane-bound organelles.

prokaryote an organism that consists of a single cell that does not have a nucleus

Eubacteria

The most common prokaryotes are eubacteria (or just *bacteria*). Bacteria are the world's smallest cells. These tiny organisms live almost everywhere. Bacteria do not have a nucleus, but they do have DNA. A bacteria's DNA is a long, circular molecule, shaped sort of like a rubber band. Bacteria have no membrane-covered organelles. But they do have ribosomes. *Ribosomes* are tiny, round organelles made of protein and other material.

Bacteria also have a strong, weblike exterior cell wall. This wall helps the cell retain its shape. A bacterium's cell membrane is just inside the cell wall. Together, the cell wall and cell membrane allow materials into and out of the cell.

Some bacteria live in the soil and water. Others live in, or on, other organisms. For example, you have bacteria living on your skin and teeth. You also have bacteria living in your digestive system. These bacteria help the process of digestion. A typical bacterial cell is shown in **Figure 6.**

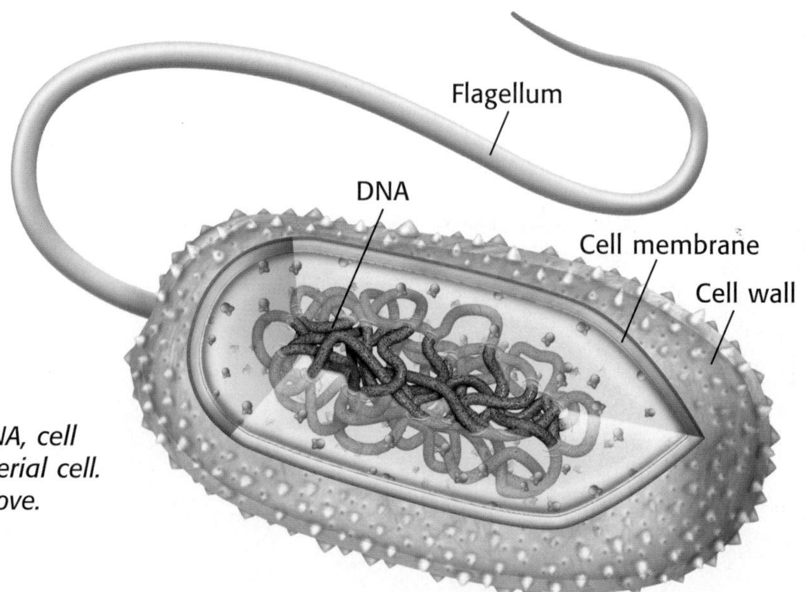

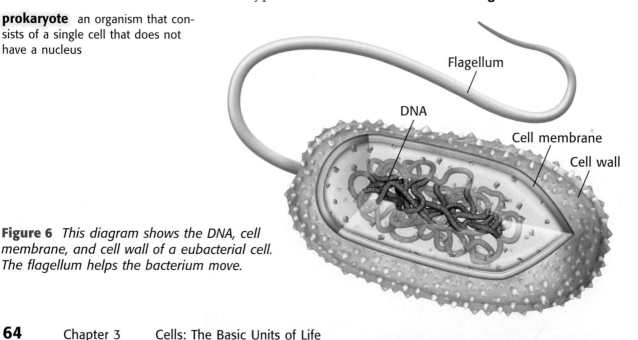

Figure 6 *This diagram shows the DNA, cell membrane, and cell wall of a eubacterial cell. The flagellum helps the bacterium move.*

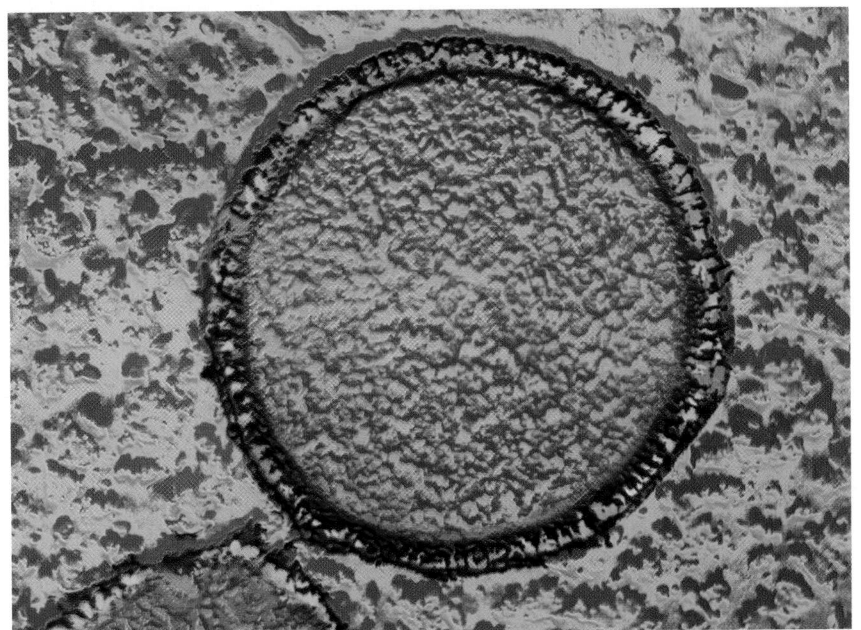

Figure 7 *This photograph, taken with an electron microscope, is of an archaebacterium that lives in the very high temperatures of deep-sea volcanic vents. The photograph has been colored so that the cell wall is green and the cell contents are pink.*

Archaebacteria

The second kind of prokaryote are the archaebacteria. These organisms are also called *archaea* (ahr KEE uh). Archaebacteria are similar to bacteria in some ways. For example, both are single-celled organisms. Both have ribosomes, a cell membrane, and circular DNA. And both lack a nucleus and membrane-bound organelles. But archaebacteria are different from bacteria. For example, archaebacterial ribosomes are different from eubacterial ribosomes.

Archaebacteria are similar to eukaryotic cells in some ways, too. For example, archaebacterial ribosomes are more like the ribosomes of eukaryotic cells. But archaebacteria also have some features that no other cells have. For example, the cell wall and cell membranes of archaebacteria are different from the cell walls of other organisms. And some archaebacteria live in places where no other organisms could live.

Three types of archaebacteria are *heat-loving, salt-loving,* and *methane-making.* Methane is a kind of gas frequently found in swamps. Heat-loving and salt-lovng archaebacteria are sometimes called extremophiles. *Extremophiles* live in places where conditions are extreme. They live in very hot water, such as in hot springs, or where the water is extremely salty. **Figure 7** shows one kind of methane-making archaebacteria that lives deep in the ocean near volcanic vents. The temperature of the water from those vents is extreme: it is above the boiling point of water at sea level.

Reading Check **What is one difference between eubacteria and archaebacteria?**

CONNECTION TO Social Studies

Where Do They Live? While most archaebacteria live in extreme environments, scientists have found that archaebacteria live almost everywhere. Do research about archaebacteria. Select one kind of archaebacteria. Create a poster showing the geographical location where the organism lives, describing its physical environment, and explaining how it survives in its environment.

ACTIVITY

Eukaryotic Cells and Eukaryotes

eukaryote an organism made up of cells that have a nucleus enclosed by a membrane; eukaryotes include animals, plants, and fungi, but not archaebacteria or eubacteria

Eukaryotic cells are the largest cells. Most eukaryotic cells are still microscopic, but they are about 10 times larger than most bacterial cells. A typical eukaryotic cell is shown in **Figure 8.**

Unlike bacteria and archaebacteria, eukaryotic cells have a nucleus. The nucleus is one kind of membrane-bound organelle. A cell's nucleus holds the cell's DNA. Eukaryotic cells have other membrane-bound organelles as well. Organelles are like the different organs in your body. Each kind of organelle has a specific job in the cell. Together, organelles, such as the ones shown in **Figure 8,** perform all the processes necessary for life.

All living things that are not bacteria or archaebacteria are made of one or more eukaryotic cells. Organisms made of eukaryotic cells are called **eukaryotes.** Many eukaryotes are multicellular. *Multicellular* means "many cells." Multicellular organisms are usually larger than single-cell organisms. So, most organisms you see with your naked eye are eukaryotes. There are many types of eukaryotes. Animals, including humans, are eukaryotes. So are plants. Some protists, such as amoebas, are single-celled eukaryotes. Other protists, including some types of green algae, are multicellular eukaryotes. Fungi are organisms such as mushrooms or yeasts. Mushrooms are multicellular eukaryotes. Yeasts are single-celled eukaryotes.

Reading Check How are eukaryotes different from prokaryotes?

Figure 8 Organelles in a Typical Eukaryotic Cell

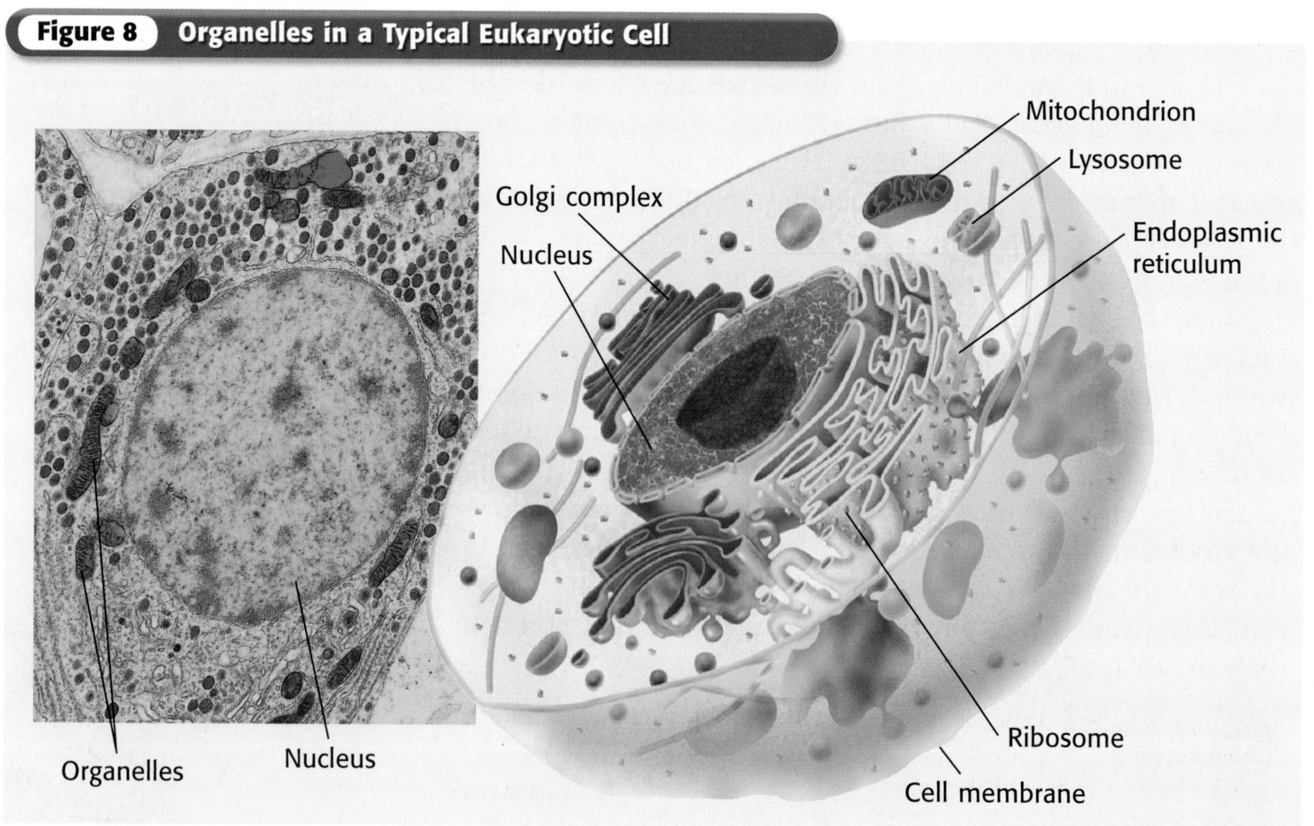

SECTION Review

Summary

- Cells were not discovered until microscopes were invented in the 1600s.
- Cell theory states that all organisms are made of cells, the cell is the basic unit of all living things, and all cells come from other cells.
- All cells have a cell membrane, cytoplasm, and DNA.
- Most cells are too small to be seen with the naked eye. A cell's surface area–to-volume ratio limits the size of a cell.
- The two basic kinds of cells are prokaryotic cells and eukaryotic cells. Eukaryotic cells have a nucleus and membrane-bound organelles. Prokaryotic cells do not.
- Prokaryotes are classified as archaebacteria and eubacteria.
- Archaebacterial cell walls and ribosomes are different from the cell walls and ribosomes of other organisms.
- Eukaryotes can be single-celled or multicellular.

Using Key Terms

1. In your own words, write a definition for the term *organelle.*
2. Use the following terms in the same sentence: *prokaryotic, nucleus,* and *eukaryotic.*

Understanding Key Ideas

3. Cell size is limited by the
   a. thickness of the cell wall.
   b. size of the cell's nucleus.
   c. cell's surface area–to-volume ratio.
   d. amount of cytoplasm in the cell.
4. What are the three parts of the cell theory?
5. Name three structures that every cell has.
6. Give two ways in which archaebacteria are different from bacteria.

Critical Thinking

7. **Applying Concepts** You have discovered a new single-celled organism. It has a cell wall, ribosomes, and long, circular DNA. Is it a eukaryote or a prokaryote cell? Explain.
8. **Identifying Relationships** One of your students brings you a cell about the size of the period at the end of this sentence. It is a single cell, but it also forms chains. What characteristics would this cell have if the organism is a eukaryote? If it is a prokaryote? What would you look for first?

Interpreting Graphics

The picture below shows a particular organism. Use the picture to answer the questions that follow.

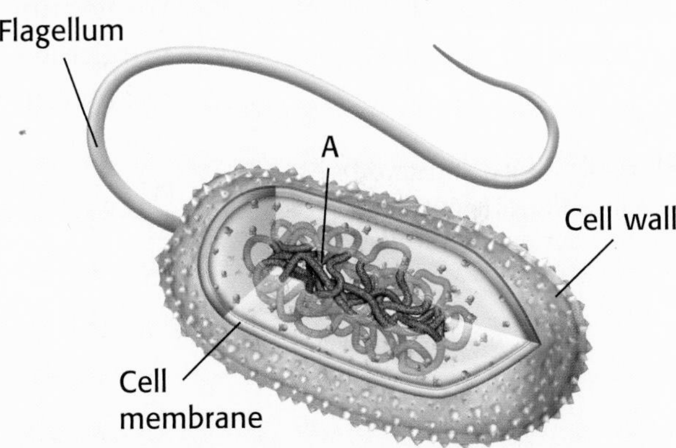

9. What type of organism does the picture represent? How do you know?
10. Which structure helps the organism move?
11. What part of the organism does the letter *A* represent?

SCILINKS.
NSTA
Developed and maintained by the National Science Teachers Association
For a variety of links related to this chapter, go to www.scilinks.org
Topic: Prokaryotic Cells
SciLinks code: HSM1225

SECTION 2

Eukaryotic Cells

Most eukaryotic cells are small. For a long time after cells were discovered, scientists could not see what was going on inside cells. They did not know how complex cells are.

Now, scientists know a lot about eukaryotic cells. These cells have many parts that work together and keep the cell alive.

READING WARM-UP

Objectives

- Identify the different parts of a eukaryotic cell.
- Explain the function of each part of a eukaryotic cell.

Terms to Learn

cell wall	mitochondrion
ribosome	Golgi complex
endoplasmic reticulum	vesicle
	lysosome

READING STRATEGY

Reading Organizer As you read this section, make a table comparing plant cells and animal cells.

Cell Wall

Some eukaryotic cells have cell walls. A **cell wall** is a rigid structure that gives support to a cell. The cell wall is the outermost structure of a cell. Plants and algae have cell walls made of cellulose (SEL yoo LOHS) and other materials. *Cellulose* is a complex sugar that most animals can't digest.

The cell walls of plant cells allow plants to stand upright. In some plants, the cells must take in water for the cell walls to keep their shape. When such plants lack water, the cell walls collapse and the plant droops. **Figure 1** shows a cross section of a plant cell and a close-up of the cell wall.

Fungi, including yeasts and mushrooms, also have cell walls. Some fungi have cell walls made of *chitin* (KIE tin). Other fungi have cell walls made from a chemical similar to chitin. Eubacteria and archaebacteria also have cell walls, but those walls are different from plant or fungal cell walls.

cell wall a rigid structure that surrounds the cell membrane and provides support to the cell

Reading Check What types of cells have cell walls? (*See the Appendix for answers to Reading Checks.*)

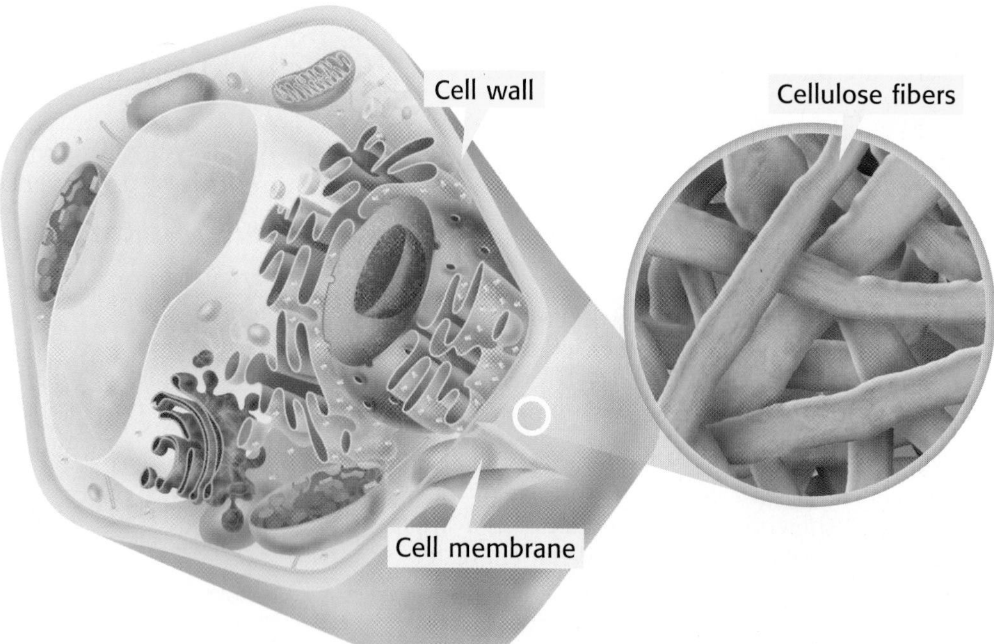

Figure 1 *The cell walls of plant cells help plants retain their shape. Plant cell walls are made of cellulose.*

Cell Membrane

All cells have a cell membrane. The *cell membrane* is a protective barrier that encloses a cell. It separates the cell's contents from the cell's environment. The cell membrane is the outermost structure in cells that lack a cell wall. In cells that have a cell wall, the cell membrane lies just inside the cell wall.

The cell membrane contains proteins, lipids, and phospholipids. *Lipids,* which include fats and cholesterol, are a group of compounds that do not dissolve in water. The cell membrane has two layers of phospholipids (FAHS foh LIP idz), shown in **Figure 2.** A *phospholipid* is a lipid that contains phosphorus. Lipids are "water fearing," or *hydrophobic.* Lipid ends of phospholipids form the inner part of the membrane. Phosphorus-containing ends of the phospholipids are "water loving," or *hydrophilic.* These ends form the outer part of the membrane.

Some of the proteins and lipids control the movement of materials into and out of the cell. Some of the proteins form passageways. Nutrients and water move into the cell, and wastes move out of the cell, through these protein passageways.

Reading Check What are two functions of a cell membrane?

CONNECTION TO Language Arts

WRITING SKILL **The Great Barrier** In your **science journal,** write a science fiction story about tiny travelers inside a person's body. These little explorers need to find a way into or out of a cell to solve a problem. You may need to do research to find out more about how the cell membrane works. Illustrate your story.

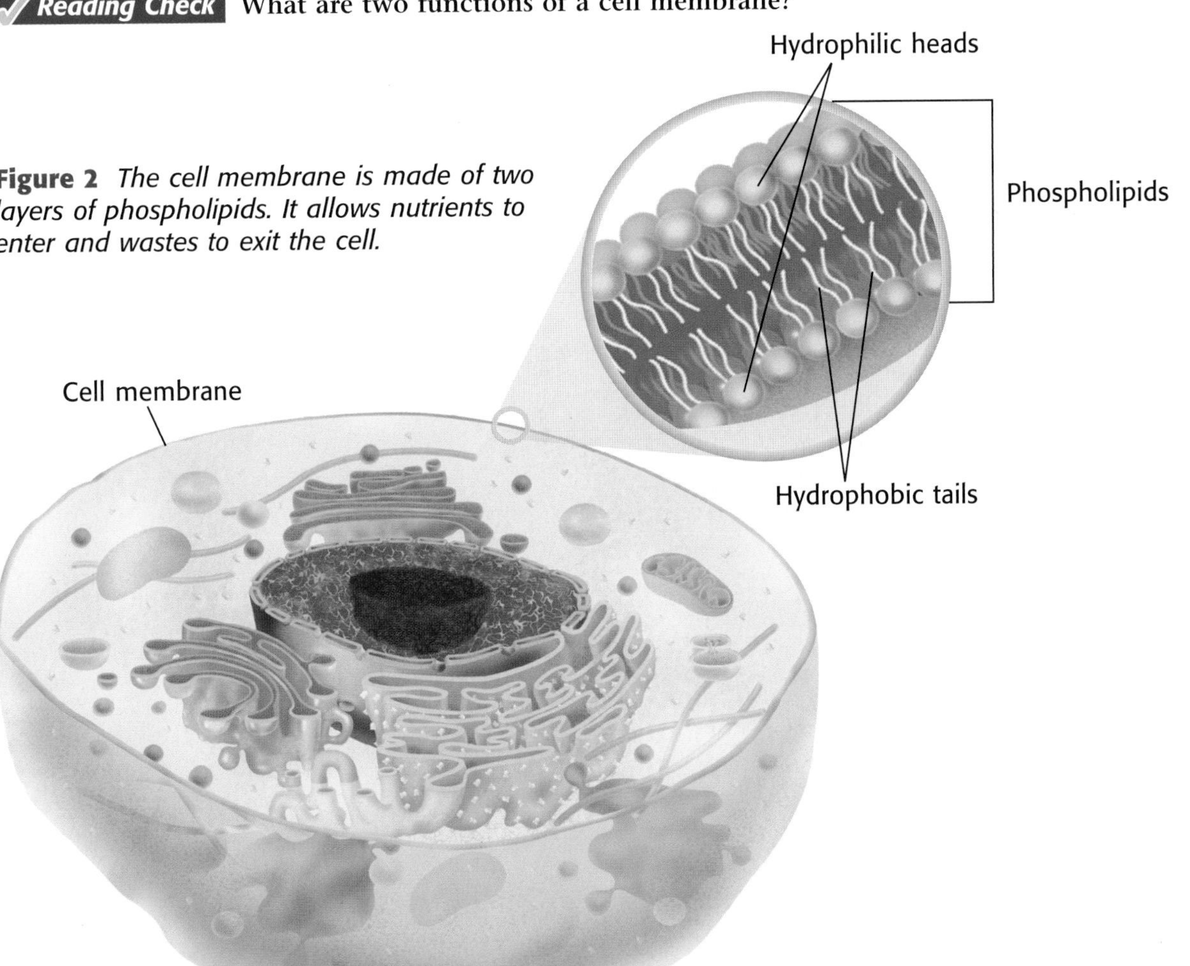

Figure 2 *The cell membrane is made of two layers of phospholipids. It allows nutrients to enter and wastes to exit the cell.*

Cytoskeleton

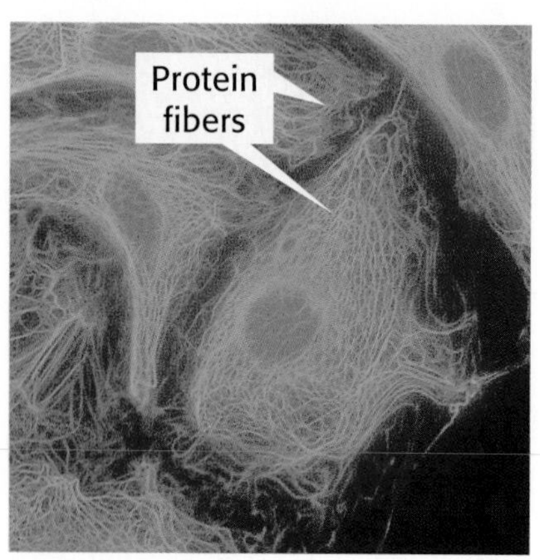

Figure 3 *The cytoskeleton, made of protein fibers, helps a cell retain its shape, move in its environment, and move its organelles.*

The *cytoskeleton* (SIET oh SKEL uh tuhn) is a web of proteins in the cytoplasm. The cytoskeleton, shown in **Figure 3,** acts as both a muscle and a skeleton. It keeps the cell's membranes from collapsing. The cytoskeleton also helps some cells move.

The cytoskeleton is made of three types of protein. One protein is a hollow tube. The other two are long, stringy fibers. One of the stringy proteins is also found in muscle cells.

Reading Check **What is the cytoskeleton?**

Nucleus

All eukaryotic cells have the same basic membrane-bound organelles, starting with the nucleus. The *nucleus* is a large organelle in a eukaryotic cell. It contains the cell's DNA, or genetic material. DNA contains the information on how to make a cell's proteins. Proteins control the chemical reactions in a cell. They also provide structural support for cells and tissues. But proteins are not made in the nucleus. Messages for how to make proteins are copied from the DNA. These messages are then sent out of the nucleus through the membranes.

The nucleus is covered by two membranes. Materials cross this double membrane by passing through pores. **Figure 4** shows a nucleus and nuclear pores. The nucleus of many cells has a dark area called the nucleolus (noo KLEE uh luhs). The *nucleolus* is where a cell begins to make its ribosomes.

Figure 4 *The nucleus contains the cell's DNA. Pores allow materials to move between the nucleus and the cytoplasm.*

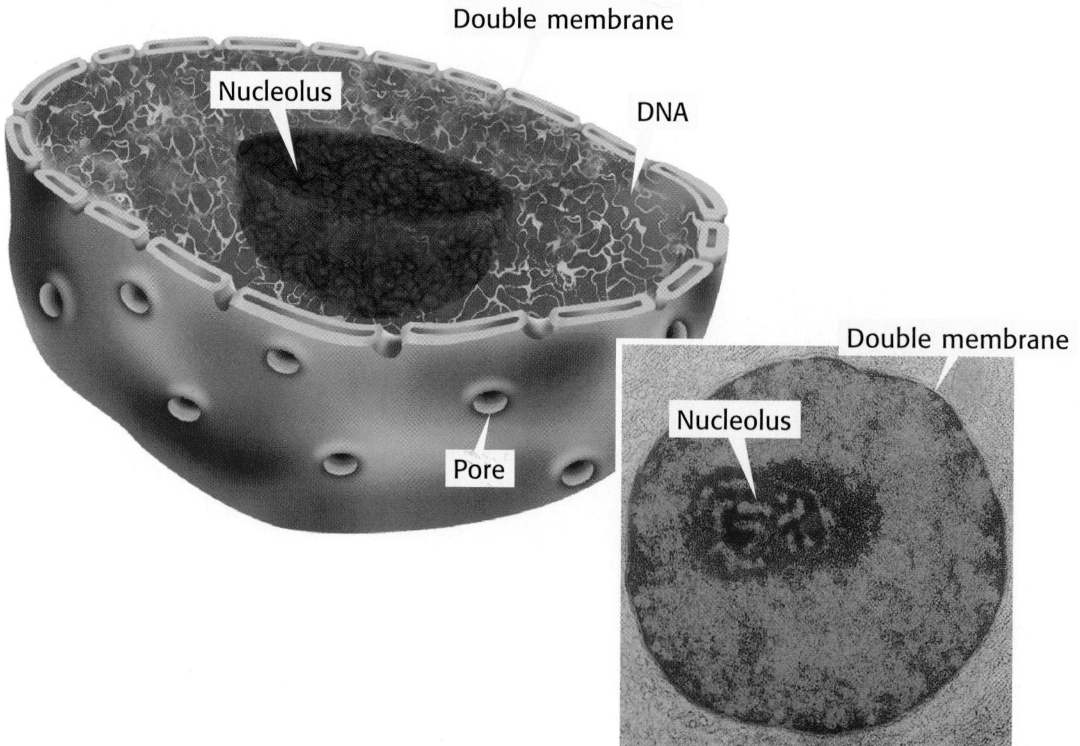

Ribosomes

Organelles that make proteins are called **ribosomes.** Ribosomes are the smallest of all organelles. And there are more ribosomes in a cell than there are any other organelles. Some ribosomes float freely in the cytoplasm. Others are attached to membranes or the cytoskeleton. Unlike most organelles, ribosomes are not covered by a membrane.

Proteins are made within the ribosomes. Proteins are made of amino acids. An *amino acid* is any one of about 20 different organic molecules that are used to make proteins. All cells need proteins to live. All cells have ribosomes.

ribosome cell organelle composed of RNA and protein; the site of protein synthesis

endoplasmic reticulum a system of membranes that is found in a cell's cytoplasm and that assists in the production, processing, and transport of proteins and in the production of lipids

Endoplasmic Reticulum

Many chemical reactions take place in a cell. Many of these reactions happen on or in the endoplasmic reticulum (EN doh PLAZ mik ri TIK yuh luhm). The **endoplasmic reticulum,** or ER, is a system of folded membranes in which proteins, lipids, and other materials are made. The ER is shown in **Figure 5.**

The ER is part of the internal delivery system of the cell. Its folded membrane contains many tubes and passageways. Substances move through the ER to different places in the cell.

Endoplasmic reticulum is either rough ER or smooth ER. The part of the ER covered in ribosomes is rough ER. Rough ER is usually found near the nucleus. Ribosomes on rough ER make many of the cell's proteins. The ER delivers these proteins throughout the cell. ER that lacks ribosomes is smooth ER. The functions of smooth ER include making lipids and breaking down toxic materials that could damage the cell.

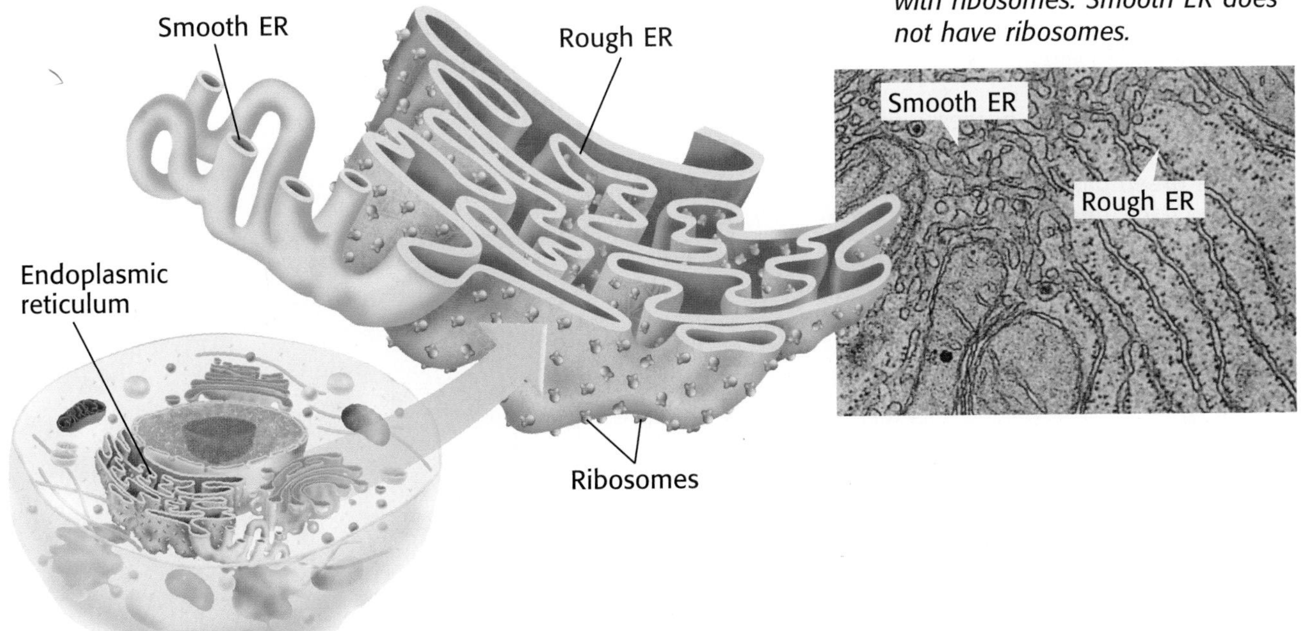

Figure 5 *The endoplasmic reticulum (ER) is a system of membranes. Rough ER is covered with ribosomes. Smooth ER does not have ribosomes.*

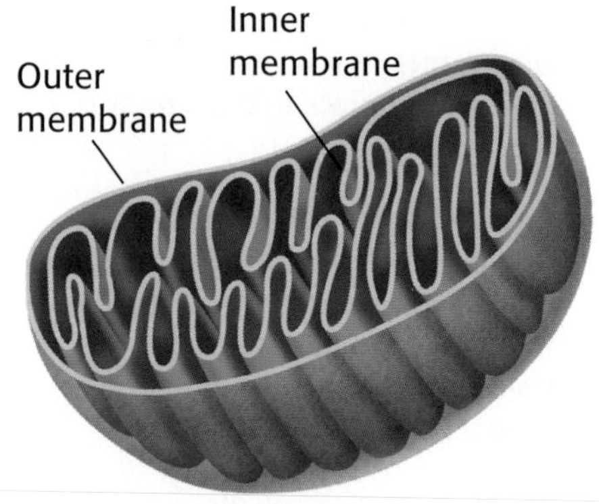

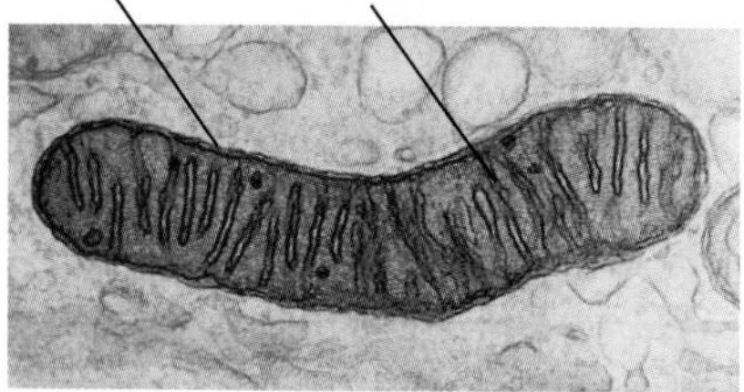

Figure 6 *Mitochondria break down sugar and make ATP. ATP is produced on the inner membrane.*

Mitochondria

A mitochondrion (MIET oh KAHN dree uhn) is the main power source of a cell. A **mitochondrion** is the organelle in which sugar is broken down to produce energy. Mitochondria are covered by two membranes, as shown in **Figure 6.** Energy released by mitochondria is stored in a substance called *ATP* (**a**denosine **tri**phosphate). The cell then uses ATP to do work. ATP can be made at several places in a cell. But most of a cell's ATP is made in the inner membrane of the cell's mitochondria.

Most eukaryotic cells have mitochondria. Mitochondria are the size of some bacteria. Like bacteria, mitochondria have their own DNA, and mitochondria can divide within a cell.

Reading Check **Where is most of a cell's ATP made?**

mitochondrion in eukaryotic cells, the cell organelle that is surrounded by two membranes and that is the site of cellular respiration

Chloroplasts

Animal cells cannot make their own food. Plants and algae are different. They have chloroplasts (KLAWR uh PLASTS) in some of their cells. *Chloroplasts* are organelles in plant and algae cells in which photosynthesis takes place. Like mitochondria, chloroplasts have two membranes and their own DNA. A chloroplast is shown in **Figure 7.** *Photosynthesis* is the process by which plants and algae use sunlight, carbon dioxide, and water to make sugar and oxygen.

Chloroplasts are green because they contain *chlorophyll,* a green pigment. Chlorophyll is found inside the inner membrane of a chloroplast. Chlorophyll traps the energy of sunlight, which is used to make sugar. The sugar produced by photosynthesis is then used by mitochondria to make ATP.

Figure 7 *Chloroplasts harness and use the energy of the sun to make sugar. A green pigment—chlorophyll—traps the sun's energy.*

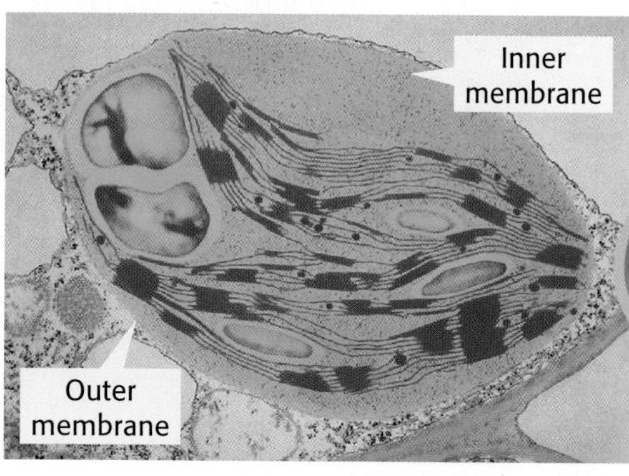

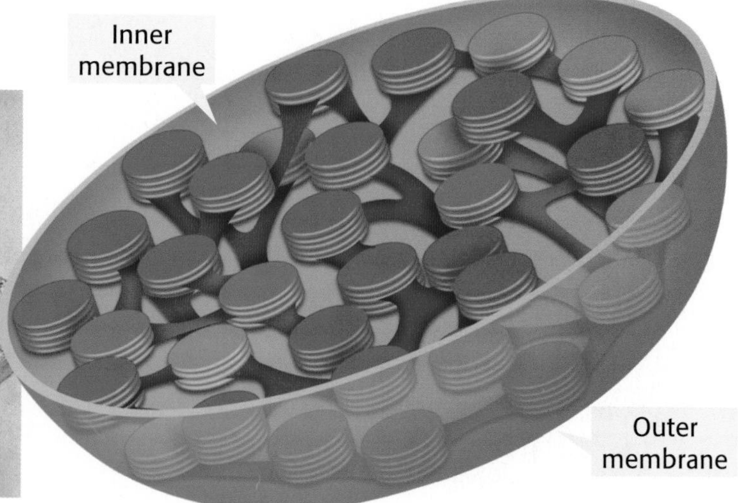

Golgi Complex

The organelle that packages and distributes proteins is called the **Golgi complex** (GOHL jee KAHM PLEKS). It is named after Camillo Golgi, the Italian scientist who first identified the organelle.

The Golgi complex looks like smooth ER, as shown in **Figure 8.** Lipids and proteins from the ER are delivered to the Golgi complex. There, the lipids and proteins may be modified to do different jobs. The final products are enclosed in a piece of the Golgi complex's membrane. This membrane pinches off to form a small bubble. The bubble transports its contents to other parts of the cell or out of the cell.

Golgi complex cell organelle that helps make and package materials to be transported out of the cell

vesicle a small cavity or sac that contains materials in a eukaryotic cell

Cell Compartments

The bubble that forms from the Golgi complex's membrane is a vesicle. A **vesicle** (VES i kuhl) is a small sac that surrounds material to be moved into or out of a cell. All eukaryotic cells have vesicles. Vesicles also move material within a cell. For example, vesicles carry new protein from the ER to the Golgi complex. Other vesicles distribute material from the Golgi complex to other parts of the cell. Some vesicles form when part of the cell membrane surrounds an object outside the cell.

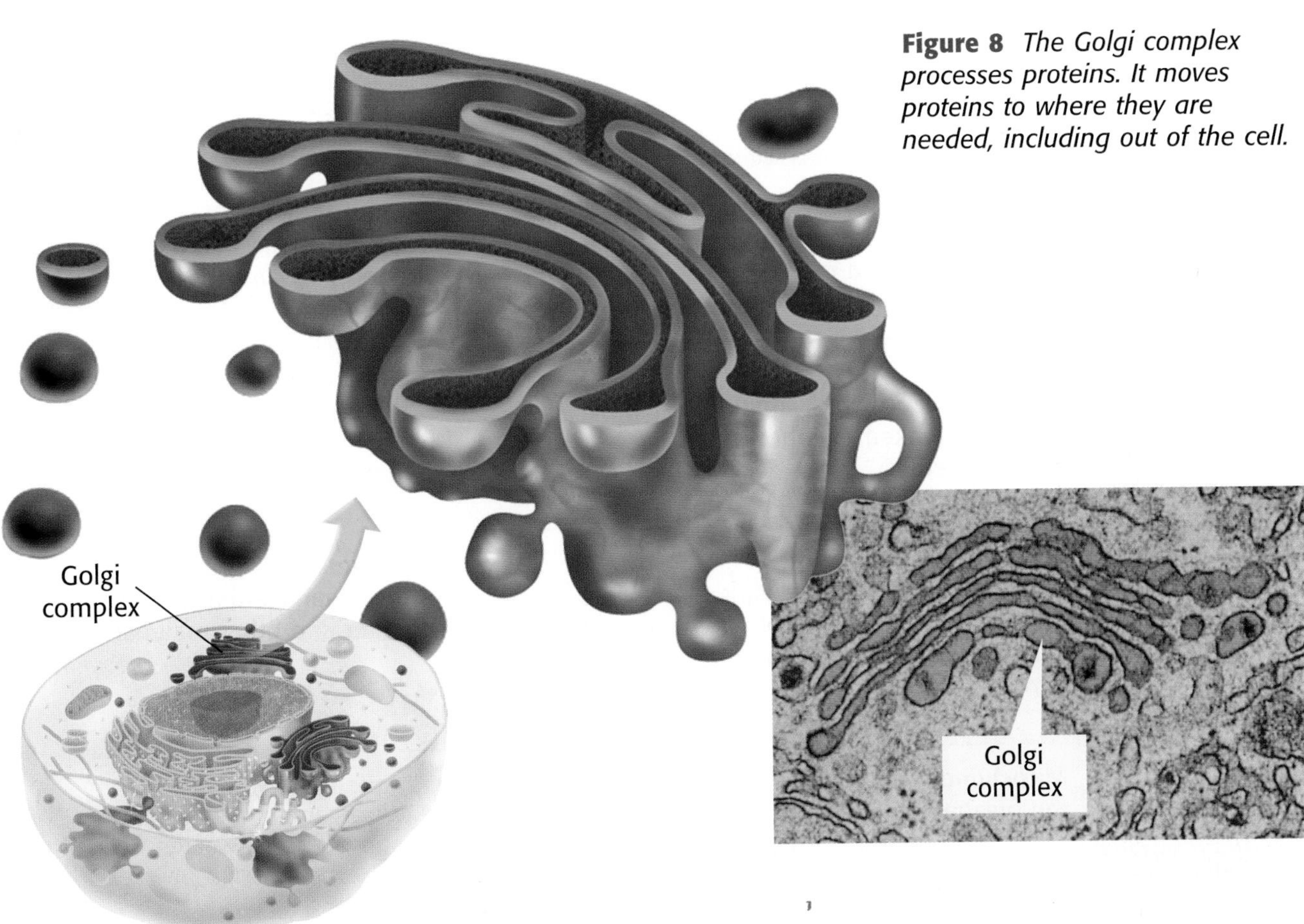

Figure 8 *The Golgi complex processes proteins. It moves proteins to where they are needed, including out of the cell.*

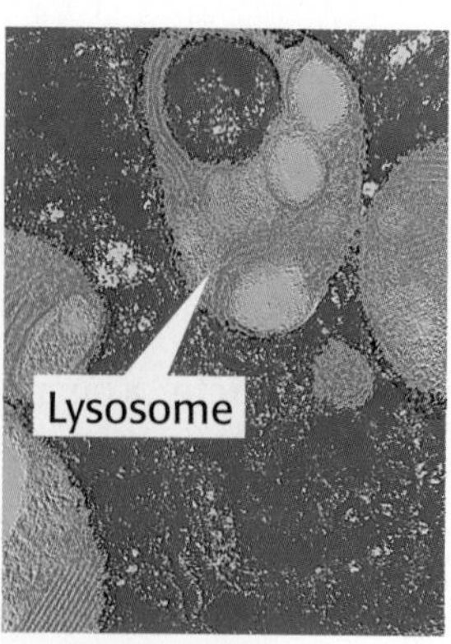

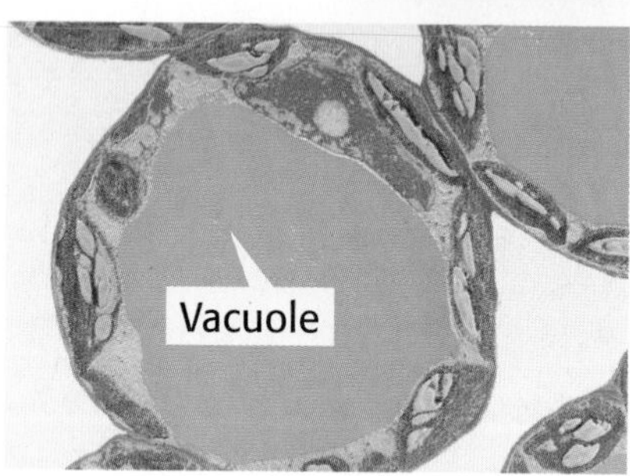

Figure 9 *Lysosomes digest materials inside a cell. In plant and fungal cells, vacuoles often perform the same function.*

Cellular Digestion

Lysosomes (LIE suh SOHMZ) are vesicles that are responsible for digestion inside a cell. **Lysosomes** are organelles that contain digestive enzymes. They destroy worn-out or damaged organelles, get rid of waste materials, and protect the cell from foreign invaders. Lysosomes, which come in a wide variety of sizes and shapes, are shown in **Figure 9.**

Lysosomes are found mainly in animal cells. When eukaryotic cells engulf particles, they enclose the particles in vesicles. Lysosomes bump into these vesicles and pour enzymes into them. These enzymes digest the particles in the vesicles.

Reading Check Why are lysosomes important?

Vacuoles

A *vacuole* (VAK yoo OHL) is a large vesicle. In plant and fungal cells, some vacuoles act like large lysosomes. They store digestive enzymes and aid in digestion within the cell. Other vacuoles in plant cells store water and other liquids. Vacuoles that are full of water, such as the one in **Figure 9,** help support the cell. Some plants wilt when their vacuoles lose water. **Table 1** shows some organelles and their functions.

lysosome a cell organelle that contains digestive enzymes

Table 1 Organelles and Their Functions

Organelle	Function	Organelle	Function
Nucleus	the organelle that contains the cell's DNA and is the control center of the cell	**Chloroplast**	the organelle that uses the energy of sunlight to make food
Ribosome	the organelle in which amino acids are hooked together to make proteins	**Golgi complex**	the organelle that processes and transports proteins and other materials out of cell
Endoplasmic reticulum	the organelle that makes lipids, breaks down drugs and other substances, and packages proteins for Golgi complex	**Vacuole**	the organelle that stores water and other materials
Mitochondria	the organelle that breaks down food molecules to make ATP	**Lysosome**	the organelle that digests food particles, wastes, cell parts, and foreign invaders

SECTION Review

Summary

- Eukaryotic cells have organelles that perform functions that help cells remain alive.
- All cells have a cell membrane. Some cells have a cell wall. Some cells have a cytoskeleton.
- The nucleus of a eukaryotic cell contains the cell's genetic material, DNA.
- Ribosomes are the organelles that make proteins. Ribosomes are not covered by a membrane.
- The endoplasmic reticulum (ER) and the Golgi complex make and process proteins before the proteins are transported to other parts of the cell or out of the cell.
- Mitochondria and chloroplasts are energy-producing organelles.
- Lysosomes are organelles responsible for digestion within a cell. In plant cells, organelles called *vacuoles* store cell materials and sometimes act like large lysosomes.

Using Key Terms

1. In your own words, write a definition for each of the following terms: *ribosome, lysosome,* and *cell wall.*

Understanding Key Ideas

2. Which of the following are found mainly in animal cells?
   a. mitochondria
   b. lysosomes
   c. ribosomes
   d. Golgi complexes
3. What is the function of a Golgi complex? What is the function of the endoplasmic reticulum?

Critical Thinking

4. **Making Comparisons** Describe three ways in which plant cells differ from animal cells.
5. **Applying Concepts** Every cell needs ribosomes. Explain why.
6. **Predicting Consequences** A certain virus attacks the mitochondria in cells. What would happen to a cell if all of its mitochondria were destroyed?
7. **Expressing Opinions** Do you think that having chloroplasts gives plant cells an advantage over animal cells? Support your opinion.

Interpreting Graphics

Use the diagram below to answer the questions that follow.

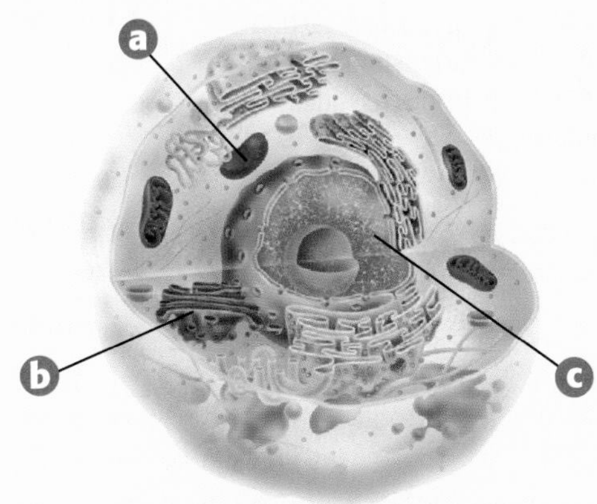
a
b
c

8. Is this a diagram of a plant cell or an animal cell? Explain how you know.
9. What organelle does the letter *b* refer to?

SCILINKS
NSTA
Developed and maintained by the National Science Teachers Association
For a variety of links related to this chapter, go to www.scilinks.org
Topic: Eukaryotic Cells
SciLinks code: HSM0541

SECTION 3

The Organization of Living Things

READING WARM-UP

Objectives

- List three advantages of being multicellular.
- Describe the four levels of organization in living things.
- Explain the relationship between the structure and function of a part of an organism.

Terms to Learn

tissue	organism
organ	structure
organ system	function

READING STRATEGY

Paired Summarizing Read this section silently. In pairs, take turns summarizing the material. Stop to discuss ideas that seem confusing.

In some ways, organisms are like machines. Some machines have just one part. But most machines have many parts. Some organisms exist as a single cell. Other organisms have many—even trillions—of cells.

Most cells are smaller than the period that ends this sentence. Yet, every cell in every organism performs all the processes of life. So, are there any advantages to having many cells?

The Benefits of Being Multicellular

You are a *multicellular organism.* This means that you are made of many cells. Multicellular organisms grow by making more small cells, not by making their cells larger. For example, an elephant is bigger than you are, but its cells are about the same size as yours. An elephant just has more cells than you do. Some benefits of being multicellular are the following:

- **Larger Size** Many multicellular organisms are small. But they are usually larger than single-celled organisms. Larger organisms are prey for fewer predators. Larger predators can eat a wider variety of prey.
- **Longer Life** The life span of a multicellular organism is not limited to the life span of any single cell.
- **Specialization** Each type of cell has a particular job. Specialization makes the organism more efficient. For example, the cardiac muscle cell in **Figure 1** is a specialized muscle cell. Heart muscle cells contract and make the heart pump blood.

Reading Check **List three advantages of being multicellular.** *(See the Appendix for answers to Reading Checks.)*

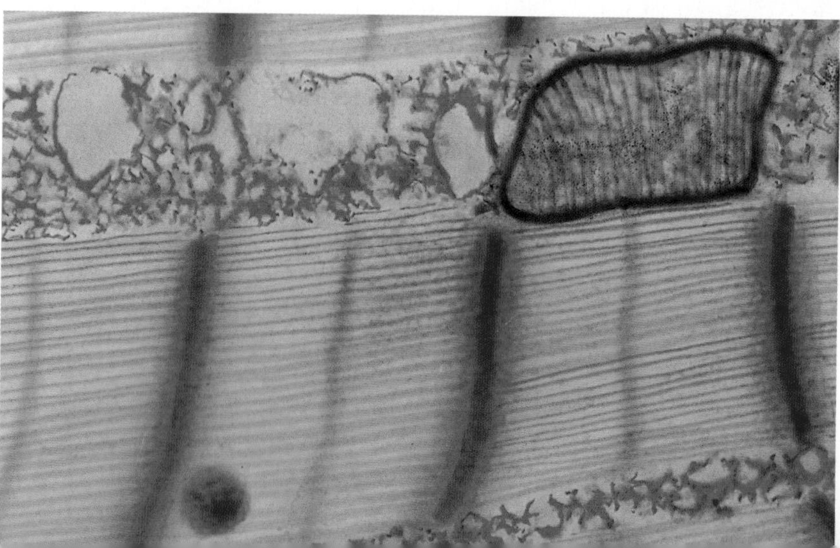

Figure 1 *This photomicrograph shows a small part of one heart muscle cell. The green line surrounds one of many mitochondria, the powerhouses of the cell. The pink areas are muscle filaments.*

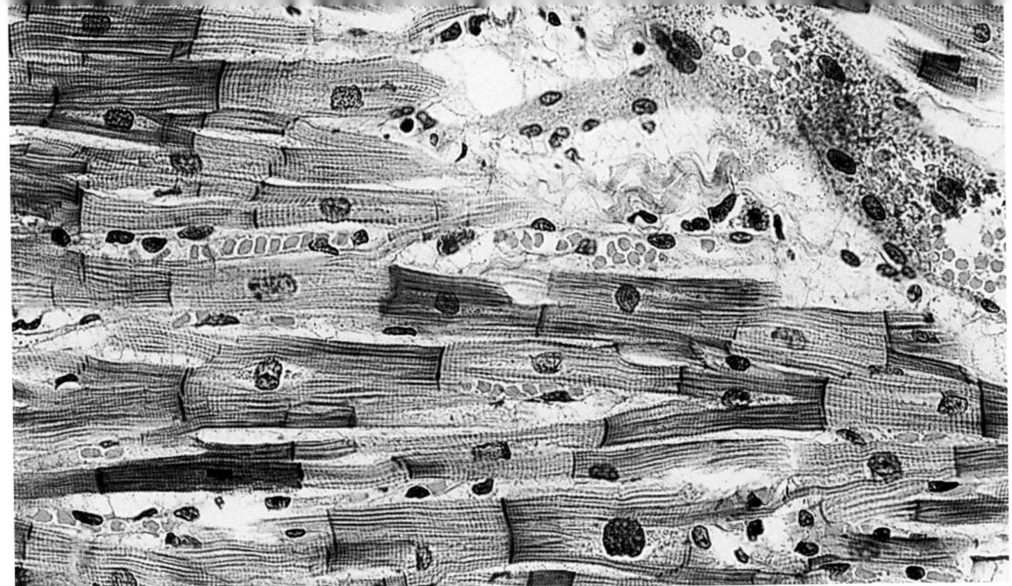

Figure 2 *This photomicrograph shows cardiac muscle tissue. Cardiac muscle tissue is made up of many cardiac cells.*

Cells Working Together

A **tissue** is a group of cells that work together to perform a specific job. The material around and between the cells is also part of the tissue. The cardiac muscle tissue, shown in **Figure 2,** is made of many cardiac muscle cells. Cardiac muscle tissue is just one type of tissue in a heart.

Animals have four basic types of tissues: nerve tissue, muscle tissue, connective tissue, and protective tissue. In contrast, plants have three types of tissues: transport tissue, protective tissue, and ground tissue. Transport tissue moves water and nutrients through a plant. Protective tissue covers the plant. It helps the plant retain water and protects the plant against damage. Photosynthesis takes place in ground tissue.

tissue a group of similar cells that perform a common function

organ a collection of tissues that carry out a specialized function of the body

Tissues Working Together

A structure that is made up of two or more tissues working together to perform a specific function is called an **organ.** For example, your heart is an organ. It is made mostly of cardiac muscle tissue. But your heart also has nerve tissue and tissues of the blood vessels that all work together to make your heart the powerful pump that it is.

Another organ is your stomach. It also has several kinds of tissue. In the stomach, muscle tissue makes food move in and through the stomach. Special tissues make chemicals that help digest your food. Connective tissue holds the stomach together, and nervous tissue carries messages back and forth between the stomach and the brain. Other organs include the intestines, brain, and lungs.

Plants also have different kinds of tissues that work together as organs. A leaf is a plant organ that contains tissue that traps light energy to make food. Other examples of plant organs are stems and roots.

Reading Check What is an organ?

A Pet Protist

Imagine that you have a tiny box-shaped protist for a pet. To care for your pet protist properly, you have to figure out how much to feed it. The dimensions of your protist are roughly 25 µm × 20 µm × 2 µm. If seven food particles per second can enter through each square micrometer of surface area, how many particles can your protist eat in 1 min?

organ system a group of organs that work together to perform body functions

organism a living thing; anything that can carry out life processes independently

structure the arrangement of parts in an organism

function the special, normal, or proper activity of an organ or part

Organs Working Together

A group of organs working together to perform a particular function is called an **organ system.** Each organ system has a specific job to do in the body.

For example, the digestive system is made up of several organs, including the stomach and intestines. The digestive system's job is to break down food into small particles. Other parts of the body then use these small particles as fuel. In turn, the digestive system depends on the respiratory and cardiovascular systems for oxygen. The cardiovascular system, shown in **Figure 3,** includes organs and tissues such as the heart and blood vessels. Plants also have organ systems. They include leaf systems, root systems, and stem systems.

Reading Check List the levels of organization in living things.

Organisms

Anything that can perform life processes by itself is an **organism.** An organism made of a single cell is called a *unicellular organism.* Bacteria, most protists, and some kinds of fungi are unicellular. Although some of these organisms live in colonies, they are still unicellular. They are unicellular organisms living together, and all of the cells in the colony are the same. Each cell must carry out all life processes in order for that cell to survive. In contrast, even the simplest multicellular organism has specialized cells that depend on each other for the organism to survive.

Figure 3 **Levels of Organization in the Cardiovascular System**

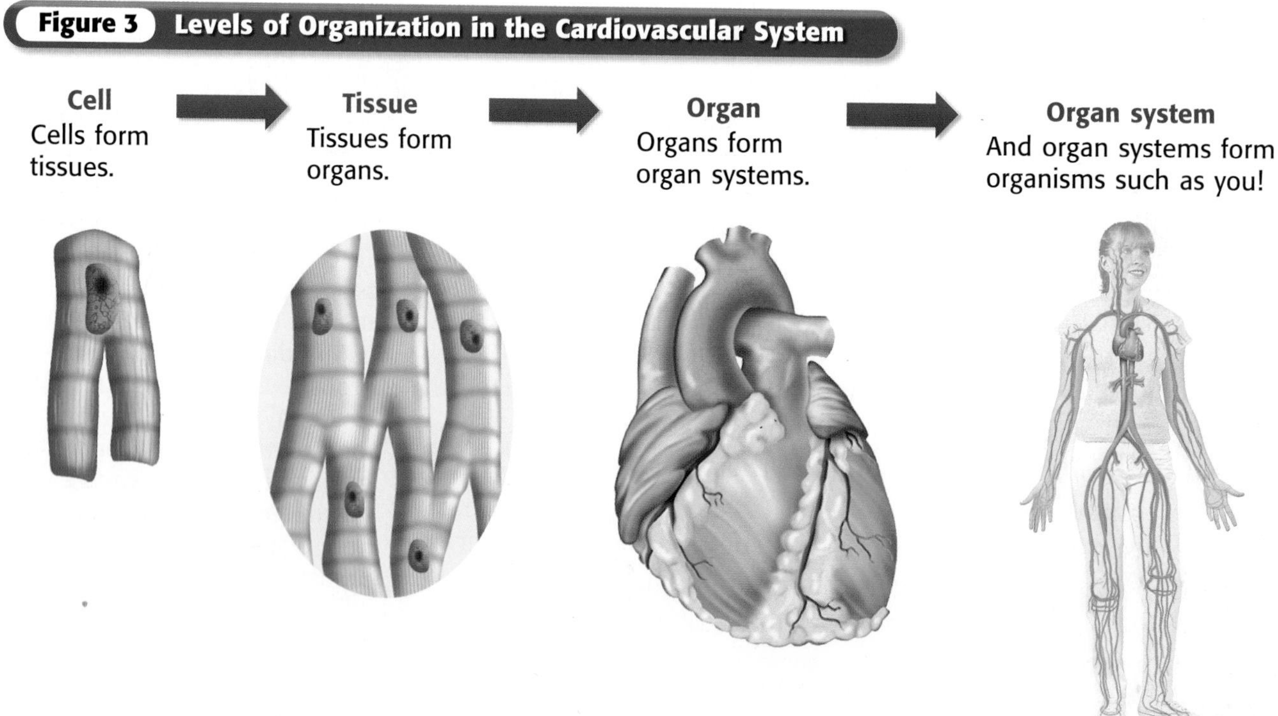
Cell
Cells form tissues.
Tissue
Tissues form organs.
Organ
Organs form organ systems.
Organ system
And organ systems form organisms such as you!

Structure and Function

In organisms, structure and function are related. **Structure** is the arrangement of parts in an organism. It includes the shape of a part and the material of which the part is made. **Function** is the job the part does. For example, the structure of the lungs is a large, spongy sac. In the lungs, there are millions of tiny air sacs called *alveoli*. Blood vessels wrap around the alveoli, as shown in **Figure 4.** Oxygen from air in the alveoli enters the blood. Blood then brings oxygen to body tissues. Also, in the alveoli, carbon dioxide leaves the blood and is exhaled.

The structures of alveoli and blood vessels enable them to perform a function. Together, they bring oxygen to the body and get rid of its carbon dioxide.

Figure 4 The Structure and Function of Alveoli

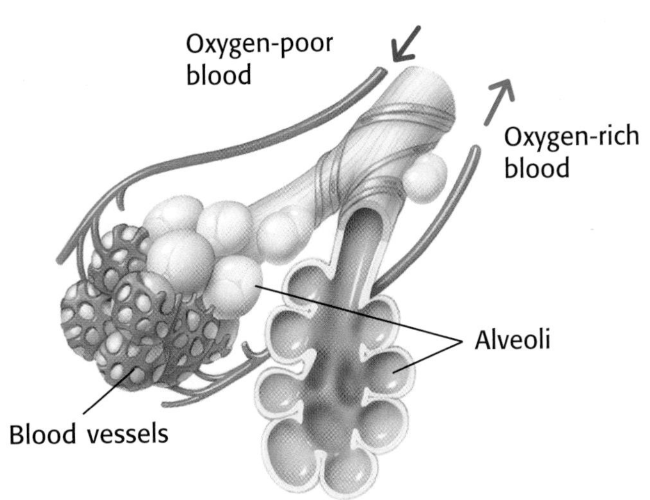

SECTION Review

Summary

- Advantages of being multicellular are larger size, longer life, and cell specialization.
- Four levels of organization are cell, tissue, organ, and organ system.
- A *tissue* is a group of cells working together. An *organ* is two or more tissues working together. An *organ system* is two or more organs working together.
- In organisms, a part's structure and function are related.

Using Key Terms

1. Use each of the following terms in a separate sentence: *tissue, organ,* and *function.*

Understanding Key Ideas

2. What are the four levels of organization in living things?
   a. cell, multicellular, organ, organ system
   b. single cell, multicellular, tissue, organ
   c. larger size, longer life, specialized cells, organs
   d. cell, tissue, organ, organ system

Math Skills

3. One multicellular organism is a cube. Each of its sides is 3 cm long. Each of its cells is 1 cm^3. How many cells does it have? If each side doubles in length, how many cells will it then have?

Critical Thinking

4. **Applying Concepts** Explain the relationship between structure and function. Use alveoli as an example. Be sure to include more than one level of organization.

5. **Making Inferences** Why can multicellular organisms be more complex than unicellular organisms? Use the three advantages of being multicellular to help explain your answer.

For a variety of links related to this chapter, go to www.scilinks.org

Topic: Organization of Life
SciLinks code: HSM1080

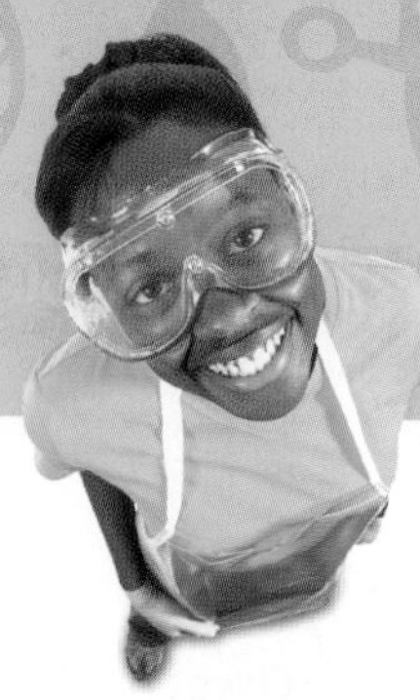

Model-Making Lab

Elephant-Sized Amoebas?

An amoeba is a single-celled organism. Like most cells, amoebas are microscopic. Why can't amoebas grow as large as elephants? If an amoeba grew to the size of a quarter, the amoeba would starve to death. To understand how this can be true, build a model of a cell and see for yourself.

OBJECTIVES

Explore why a single-celled organism cannot grow to the size of an elephant.

Create a model of a cell to illustrate the concept of surface area–to-volume ratio.

MATERIALS

- calculator (optional)
- cubic cell patterns
- heavy paper or poster board
- sand, fine
- scale or balance
- scissors
- tape, transparent

SAFETY

Procedure

1. Use heavy paper or poster board to make four cube-shaped cell models from the patterns supplied by your teacher. Cut out each cell model, fold the sides to make a cube, and tape the tabs on the sides. The smallest cell model has sides that are each one unit long. The next larger cell has sides of two units. The next cell has sides of three units, and the largest cell has sides of four units. These paper models represent the cell membrane, the part of a cell's exterior through which food and wastes pass.

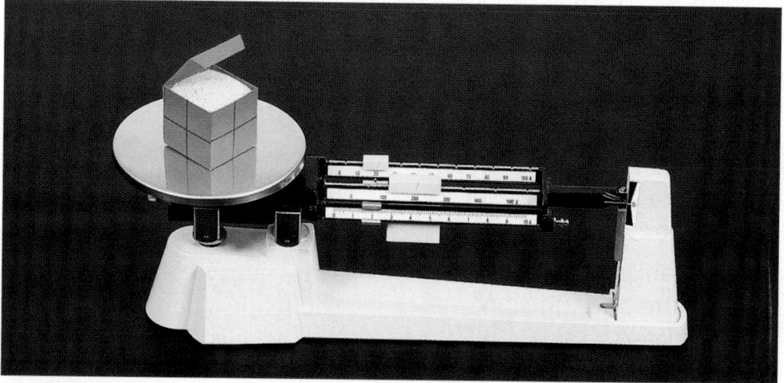

Data Table for Measurements				
Length of side	Area of one side (A = S × S)	Total surface area of cube cell (TA = S × S × 6)	Volume of cube cell (V = S × S × S)	Mass of filled cube cell
1 unit	1 $unit^2$	6 $unit^2$	1 $unit^3$	
2 unit				
3 unit				
4 unit				

DO NOT WRITE IN BOOK

Key to Formula Symbols

S = the length of one side

A = area

6 = number of sides

V = volume

TA = total area

2. Copy the data table shown above. Use each formula to calculate the data about your cell models. Record your calculations in the table. Calculations for the smallest cell have been done for you.

3. Carefully fill each model with fine sand until the sand is level with the top edge of the model. Find the mass of the filled models by using a scale or a balance. What does the sand in your model represent?

4. Record the mass of each filled cell model in your Data Table for Measurements. (Always remember to use the appropriate mass unit.)

Analyze the Results

1. **Constructing Tables** Make a data table like the one shown at right.

2. **Organizing Data** Use the data from your Data Table for Measurements to find the ratios for each of your cell models. For each of the cell models, fill in the Data Table for Ratios .

Draw Conclusions

3. **Interpreting Information** As a cell grows larger, does the ratio of total surface area to volume increase, decrease, or stay the same?

4. **Interpreting Information** As a cell grows larger, does the total surface area–to-mass ratio increase, decrease, or stay the same?

5. **Drawing Conclusions** Which is better able to supply food to all the cytoplasm of the cell: the cell membrane of a small cell or the cell membrane of a large cell? Explain your answer.

6. **Evaluating Data** In the experiment, which is better able to feed all of the cytoplasm of the cell: the cell membrane of a cell that has high mass or the cell membrane of a cell that has low mass? You may explain your answer in a verbal presentation to the class, or you may choose to write a report and illustrate it with drawings of your models.

Data Table for Ratios		
Length of side	Ratio of total surface area to volume	Ratio of total surface area to mass
1 unit		
2 unit		
3 unit		
4 unit		

DO NOT WRITE IN BOOK

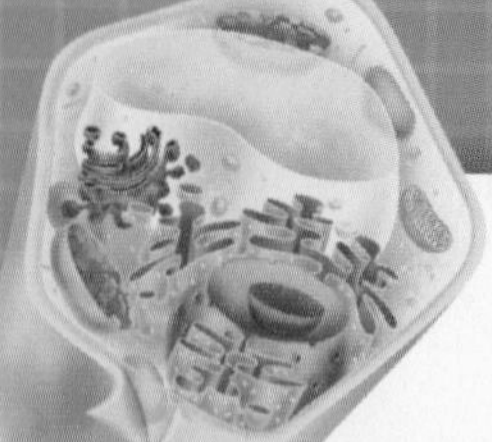

Chapter Review

USING KEY TERMS

Complete each of the following sentences by choosing the correct term from the word bank.

cell	organ
cell membrane	prokaryote
organelles	eukaryote
cell wall	tissue
structure	function

1. A(n) ___ is the most basic unit of all living things.

2. The job that an organ does is the ___ of that organ.

3. Ribosomes and mitochondria are types of ___.

4. A(n) ___ is an organism whose cells have a nucleus.

5. A group of cells working together to perform a specific function is a(n) ___.

6. Only plant cells have a(n) ___.

UNDERSTANDING KEY IDEAS

Multiple Choice

7. Which of the following best describes an organ?
   a. a group of cells that work together to perform a specific job
   b. a group of tissues that belong to different systems
   c. a group of tissues that work together to perform a specific job
   d. a body structure, such as muscles or lungs

8. The benefits of being multicellular include
   a. small size, long life, and cell specialization.
   b. generalized cells, longer life, and ability to prey on small animals.
   c. larger size, more enemies, and specialized cells.
   d. longer life, larger size, and specialized cells.

9. In eukaryotic cells, which organelle contains the DNA?
   a. nucleus
   b. Golgi complex
   c. smooth ER
   d. vacuole

10. Which of the following statements is part of the cell theory?
    a. All cells suddenly appear by themselves.
    b. All cells come from other cells.
    c. All organisms are multicellular.
    d. All cells have identical parts.

11. The surface area–to-volume ratio of a cell limits
    a. the number of organelles that the cell has.
    b. the size of the cell.
    c. where the cell lives.
    d. the types of nutrients that a cell needs.

12. Two types of organisms whose cells do not have a nucleus are
    a. prokaryotes and eukaryotes.
    b. plants and animals.
    c. eubacteria and archaebacteria.
    d. single-celled and multicellular organisms.

Short Answer

13. Explain why most cells are small.

14. Describe the four levels of organization in living things.

15. What is the difference between the structure of an organ and the function of the organ?

16. Name two functions of a cell membrane.

17. What are the structure and function of the cytoskeleton in a cell?

CRITICAL THINKING

18. **Concept Mapping** Use the following terms to create a concept map: *cells, organisms, Golgi complex, organ systems, organs, nucleus, organelle,* and *tissues.*

19. **Making Comparisons** Compare and contrast the functions of the endoplasmic reticulum and the Golgi complex.

20. **Identifying Relationships** Explain how the structure and function of an organism's parts are related. Give an example.

21. **Evaluating Hypotheses** One of your classmates states a hypothesis that all organisms must have organ systems. Is your classmate's hypothesis valid? Explain your answer.

22. **Predicting Consequences** What would happen if all of the ribosomes in your cells disappeared?

23. **Expressing Opinions** Scientists think that millions of years ago the surface of the Earth was very hot and that the atmosphere contained a lot of methane. In your opinion, which type of organism, a eubacterium or an archaebacterium, is the older form of life? Explain your reasoning.

INTERPRETING GRAPHICS

Use the diagram below to answer the questions that follow.

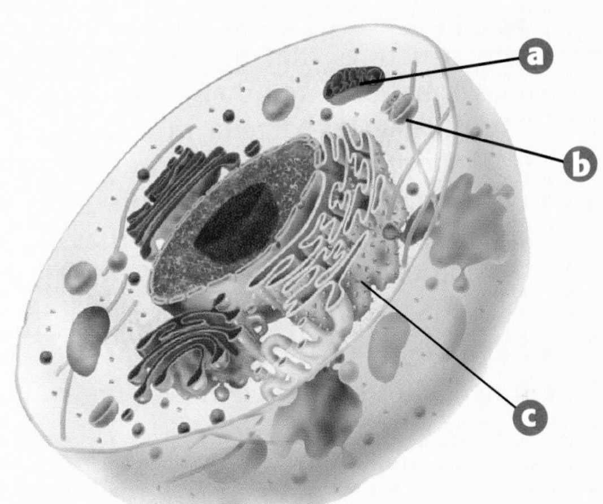

24. What is the name of the structure identified by the letter *a*?

25. Which letter identifies the structure that digests food particles and foreign invaders?

26. Which letter identifies the structure that makes proteins, lipids, and other materials and that contains tubes and passageways that enable substances to move to different places in the cell?

Standardized Test Preparation

READING

Read each of the passages below. Then, answer the questions that follow each passage.

Passage 1 Exploring caves can be dangerous but can also lead to interesting discoveries. For example, deep in the darkness of Cueva de Villa Luz, a cave in Mexico, are slippery formations called *snottites*. They were named snottites because they look just like a two-year-old's runny nose. If you use an electron microscope to look at them, you see that snottites are bacteria; thick, sticky fluids; and small amounts of minerals produced by the bacteria. As tiny as they are, these bacteria can build up snottite structures that may eventually turn into rock. Formations in other caves look like hardened snottites. The bacteria in snottites are acidophiles. Acidophiles live in environments that are highly acidic. Snottite bacteria produce sulfuric acid and live in an environment that is similar to the inside of a car battery.

1. Which statement best describes snottites?

A Snottites are bacteria that live in car batteries.

B Snottites are rock formations found in caves.

C Snottites were named for a cave in Mexico.

D Snottites are made of bacteria, sticky fluids, and minerals.

2. Based on this passage, which conclusion about snottites is most likely to be correct?

F Snottites are found in caves everywhere.

G Snottite bacteria do not need sunlight.

H You could grow snottites in a greenhouse.

I Snottites create other bacteria in caves.

3. What is the main idea of this passage?

A Acidophiles are unusual organisms.

B Snottites are strange formations.

C Exploring caves is dangerous.

D Snottites are large, slippery bacteria.

Passage 2 The world's smallest mammal may be a bat about the size of a jelly bean. The scientific name for this tiny animal, which was unknown until 1974, is *Craseonycteris thonglongyai*. It is so small that it is sometimes called the *bumblebee bat*. Another name for this animal is the *hog-nosed bat*. Hog-nosed bats were given their name because one of their distinctive features is a piglike muzzle. Hog-nosed bats differ from other bats in another way: they do not have a tail. But, like other bats, hog-nosed bats do eat insects that they catch in mid-air. Scientists think that the bats eat small insects that live on the leaves at the tops of trees. Hog-nosed bats live deep in limestone caves and have been found in only one country, Thailand.

1. According to the passage, which statement about hog-nosed bats is most accurate?

A They are the world's smallest animal.

B They are about the size of a bumblebee.

C They eat leaves at the tops of trees.

D They live in hives near caves in Thailand.

2. Which of the following statements describes distinctive features of hog-nosed bats?

F The bats are very small and eat leaves.

G The bats live in caves and have a tail.

H The bats live in Thailand and are birds.

I The bats have a piglike muzzle and no tail.

3. From the information in this passage, which conclusion is most likely to be correct?

A Hog-nosed bats are similar to other bats.

B Hog-nosed bats are probably rare.

C Hog-nosed bats can sting like a bumblebee.

D Hog-nosed bats probably eat fruit.

INTERPRETING GRAPHICS

The diagrams below show two kinds of cells. Use these cell diagrams to answer the questions that follow.

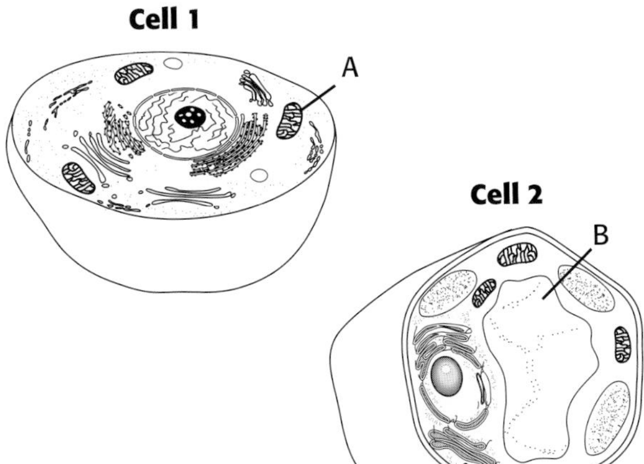

1. What is the name of the organelle labeled *A* in Cell 1?
   A endoplasmic reticulum
   B mitochondrion
   C vacuole
   D nucleus

2. What type of cell is Cell 1?
   F a bacterial cell
   G a plant cell
   H an animal cell
   I a prokaryotic cell

3. What is the name and function of the organelle labeled *B* in Cell 2?
   A The organelle is a vacuole, and it stores water and other materials.
   B The organelle is the nucleus, and it contains the DNA.
   C The organelle is the cell wall, and it gives shape to the cell.
   D The organelle is a ribosome, where proteins are put together.

4. What type of cell is Cell 2? How do you know?
   F prokaryotic; because it does not have a nucleus
   G eukaryotic; because it does not have a nucleus
   H prokaryotic; because it has a nucleus
   I eukaryotic; because it has a nucleus

MATH

Read each question below, and choose the best answer.

1. What is the surface area–to-volume ratio of the rectangular solid shown in the diagram below?

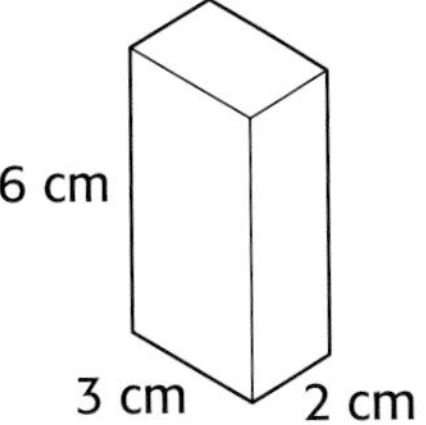

   A 0.5:1
   B 2:1
   C 36:1
   D 72:1

2. Look at the diagram of the cell below. Three molecules of food per cubic unit of volume per minute are required for the cell to survive. One molecule of food can enter through each square unit of surface area per minute. What will happen to this cell?

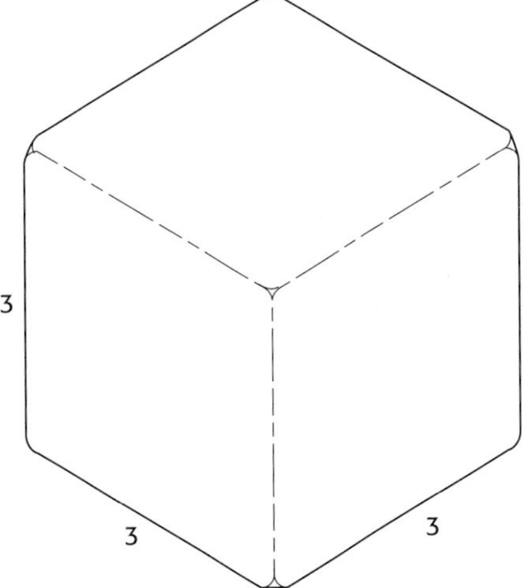

   F The cell is too small, and it will starve.
   G The cell is too large, and it will starve.
   H The cell is at a size that will allow it to survive.
   I There is not enough information to determine the answer.

Science in Action

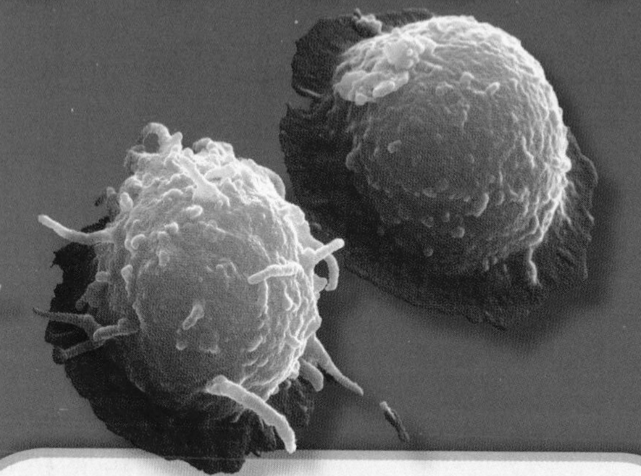

Scientific Discoveries

Discovery of the Stem Cell

What do Parkinson's disease, diabetes, aplastic anemia, and Alzheimer's disease have in common? All of these diseases are diseases for which stem cells may provide treatment or a cure. Stem cells are unspecialized cells from which all other kinds of cells can grow. And research on stem cells has been going on almost since microscopes were invented. But scientists have been able to culture, or grow, stem cells in laboratories for only about the last 20 years. Research during these 20 years has shown scientists that stem cells can be useful in treating—and possibly curing—a variety of diseases.

Language Arts ACTIVITY

WRITING SKILL Imagine that you are a doctor who treats diseases such as Parkinson's disease. Design and create a pamphlet or brochure that you could use to explain what stem cells are. Include in your pamphlet a description of how stem cells might be used to treat one of your patients who has Parkinson's disease. Be sure to include information about Parkinson's disease.

Weird Science

Extremophiles

Are there organisms on Earth that can give scientists clues about possible life elsewhere? Yes, there are! These organisms are called *extremophiles,* and they live where the environment is extreme. For example, some extremophiles live in the hot volcanic thermal vents deep in the ocean. Other extremophiles live in the extreme cold of Antarctica. But these organisms do not live only in extreme environments. Research shows that extremophiles may be abundant in plankton in the ocean. And not all extremophiles are archaebacteria; some extremophiles are eubacteria.

Social Studies ACTIVITY

Choose one of the four types of extremophiles. Do some research about the organism you have chosen and make a poster showing what you learned about it, including where it can be found, under what conditions it lives, how it survives, and how it is used.

People in Science

Caroline Schooley

Microscopist Imagine that your assignment is the following: Go outside. Look at 1 ft^2 of the ground for 30 min. Make notes about what you observe. Be prepared to describe what you see. If you look at the ground with just your naked eyes, you may quickly run out of things to see. But what would happen if you used a microscope to look? How much more would you be able to see? And how much more would you have to talk about? Caroline Schooley could tell you.

Caroline Schooley joined a science club in middle school. That's when her interest in looking at things through a microscope began. Since then, Schooley has spent many years studying life through a microscope. She is a microscopist. A *microscopist* is someone who uses a microscope to look at small things. Microscopists use their tools to explore the world of small things that cannot be seen by the naked eye. And with today's powerful electron microscopes, microscopists can study things we could never see before, things as small as atoms.

Math Activity

An average bacterium is about 0.000002 m long. A pencil point is about 0.001 m wide. Approximately how many bacteria would fit on a pencil point?

To learn more about these Science in Action topics, visit go.hrw.com and type in the keyword HL5CELF.

Current Science

Check out Current Science® articles related to this chapter by visiting go.hrw.com. Just type in the keyword HL5CS03.

The Cell in Action

About the PHOTO

This adult katydid is emerging from its last immature, or nymph, stage. As the katydid changed from a nymph to an adult, every structure of its body changed. To grow and change, an organism must produce new cells. When a cell divides, it makes a copy of its genetic material.

PRE-READING ACTIVITY

FOLDNOTES **Tri-Fold** Before you read the chapter, create the FoldNote entitled "Tri-Fold" described in the **Study Skills** section of the Appendix. Write what you know about the actions of cells in the column labeled "Know." Then, write what you want to know in the column labeled "Want." As you read the chapter, write what you learn about the actions of cells in the column labeled "Learn."

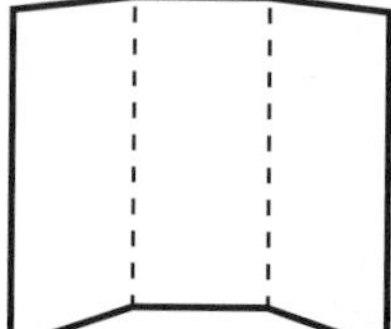

START-UP ACTIVITY

Cells in Action

Yeast are single-celled fungi that are an important ingredient in bread. Yeast cells break down sugar molecules to release energy. In the process, carbon dioxide gas is produced, which causes bread dough to rise.

Procedure

1. Add **4 mL of a sugar solution** to **10 mL of a yeast-and-water mixture**. Use a **stirring rod** to thoroughly mix the two liquids.
2. Pour the stirred mixture into a small test tube.
3. Place a slightly **larger test tube** over the **small test tube.** The top of the small test tube should touch the bottom of the larger test tube.
4. Hold the test tubes together, and quickly turn both test tubes over. Place the test tubes in a test-tube rack.
5. Use a **ruler** to measure the height of the fluid in the large test tube. Wait 20 min, and then measure the height of the liquid again.

Analysis

1. What is the difference between the first height measurement and the second height measurement?
2. What do you think caused the change in the fluid's height?

SECTION 1

Exchange with the Environment

READING WARM-UP

Objectives

- Explain the process of diffusion.
- Describe how osmosis occurs.
- Compare passive transport with active transport.
- Explain how large particles get into and out of cells.

Terms to Learn

diffusion
osmosis
passive transport
active transport
endocytosis
exocytosis

READING STRATEGY

Reading Organizer As you read this section, make a table comparing active transport and passive transport.

What would happen to a factory if its power were shut off or its supply of raw materials never arrived? What would happen if the factory couldn't get rid of its garbage?

Like a factory, an organism must be able to obtain energy and raw materials and get rid of wastes. An organism's cells perform all of these functions. These functions keep cells healthy so that they can divide. Cell division allows organisms to grow and repair injuries.

The exchange of materials between a cell and its environment takes place at the cell's membrane. To understand how materials move into and out of the cell, you need to know about diffusion.

What Is Diffusion?

What happens if you pour dye on top of a layer of gelatin? At first, it is easy to see where the dye ends and the gelatin begins. But over time, the line between the two layers will blur, as shown in **Figure 1.** Why? Everything, including the gelatin and the dye, is made up of tiny moving particles. Particles travel from where they are crowded to where they are less crowded. This movement from areas of high concentration (crowded) to areas of low concentration (less crowded) is called **diffusion** (di FYOO zhuhn). Dye particles diffuse from where they are crowded (near the top of the glass) to where they are less crowded (in the gelatin). Diffusion also happens within and between living cells. Cells do not need to use energy for diffusion.

diffusion the movement of particles from regions of higher density to regions of lower density

Figure 1 *The particles of the dye and the gelatin slowly mix by diffusion.*

Figure 2 **Osmosis**

1. The side that holds only pure water has the higher concentration of water particles.

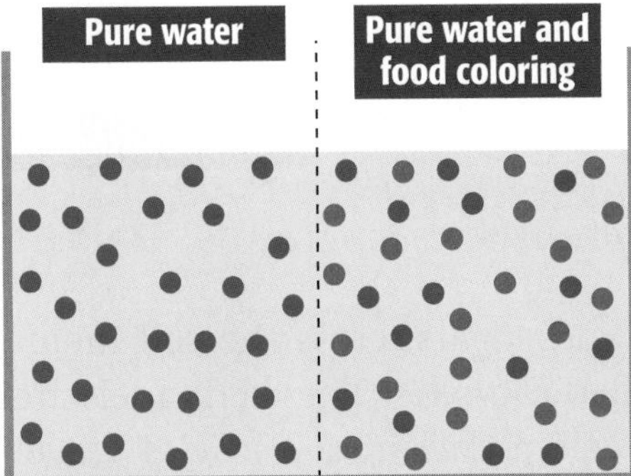

2. During osmosis, water particles move to where they are less concentrated.

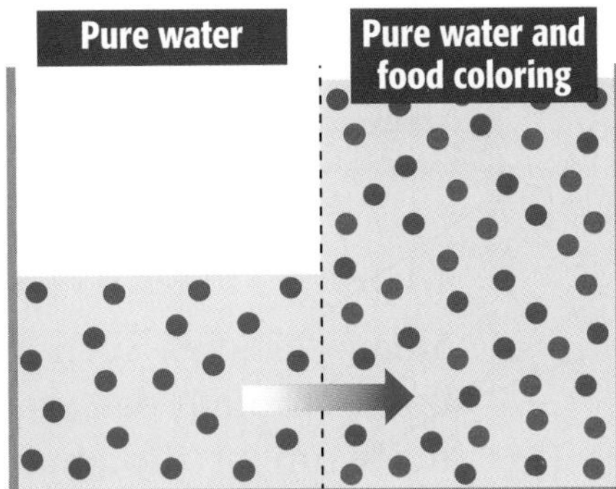

Diffusion of Water

The cells of organisms are surrounded by and filled with fluids that are made mostly of water. The diffusion of water through cell membranes is so important to life processes that it has been given a special name—**osmosis** (ahs MOH sis).

osmosis the diffusion of water through a semipermeable membrane

Water is made up of particles, called *molecules*. Pure water has the highest concentration of water molecules. When you mix something, such as food coloring, sugar, or salt, with water, you lower the concentration of water molecules. **Figure 2** shows how water molecules move through a membrane that is semipermeable (SEM i PUHR mee uh buhl). *Semipermeable* means that only certain substances can pass through. The picture on the left in **Figure 2** shows liquids that have different concentrations of water. Over time, the water molecules move from the liquid with the high concentration of water molecules to the liquid with the lower concentration of water molecules.

The Cell and Osmosis

Osmosis is important to cell functions. For example, red blood cells are surrounded by plasma. Plasma is made up of water, salts, sugars, and other particles. The concentration of these particles is kept in balance by osmosis. If red blood cells were in pure water, water molecules would flood into the cells and cause them to burst. When red blood cells are put into a salty solution, the concentration of water molecules inside the cell is higher than the concentration of water outside. This difference makes water move out of the cells, and the cells shrivel up. Osmosis also occurs in plant cells. When a wilted plant is watered, osmosis makes the plant firm again.

Reading Check **Why would red blood cells burst if you placed them in pure water?** *(See the Appendix for answers to Reading Checks.)*

Bead Diffusion

1. Put three groups of **colored beads** on the bottom of a **plastic bowl.** Each group should be made up of five beads of the same color.
2. Stretch some **clear plastic wrap** tightly over the top of the bowl. Gently shake the bowl for 10 seconds while watching the beads.
3. How is the scattering of the beads like the diffusion of particles? How is it different from the diffusion of particles?

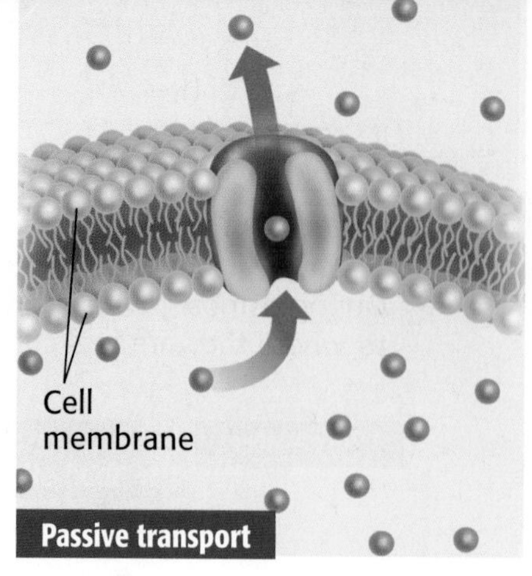

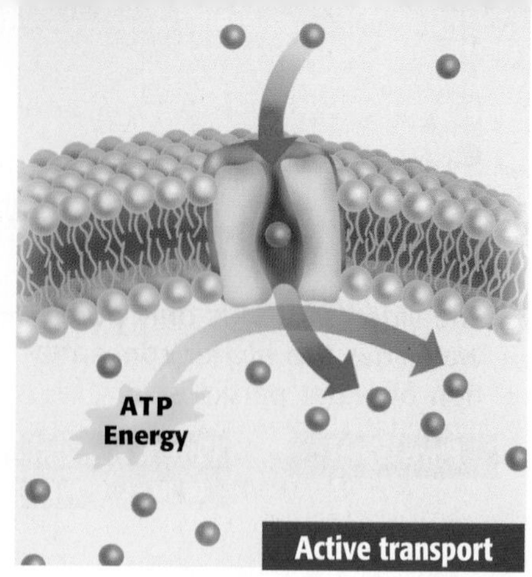

Figure 3 *In passive transport, particles travel through proteins to areas of lower concentration. In active transport, cells use energy to move particles, usually to areas of higher concentration.*

Moving Small Particles

Small particles, such as water and sugars, cross the cell membrane through passageways called *channels.* These channels are made up of proteins in the cell membrane. Particles travel through these channels by either passive or active transport. The movement of particles across a cell membrane without the use of energy by the cell is called **passive transport**, and is shown in **Figure 3.** During passive transport, particles move from an area of high concentration to an area of low concentration. Diffusion and osmosis are examples of passive transport.

A process of transporting particles that requires the cell to use energy is called **active transport.** Active transport usually involves the movement of particles from an area of low concentration to an area of high concentration.

passive transport the movement of substances across a cell membrane without the use of energy by the cell

active transport the movement of substances across the cell membrane that requires the cell to use energy

endocytosis the process by which a cell membrane surrounds a particle and encloses the particle in a vesicle to bring the particle into the cell

Moving Large Particles

Small particles cross the cell membrane by diffusion, passive transport, and active transport. Large particles move into and out of the cell by processes called *endocytosis* and *exocytosis.*

Endocytosis

The active-transport process by which a cell surrounds a large particle, such as a large protein, and encloses the particle in a vesicle to bring the particle into the cell is called **endocytosis** (EN doh sie TOH sis). *Vesicles* are sacs formed from pieces of cell membrane. **Figure 4** shows endocytosis.

Figure 4 Endocytosis

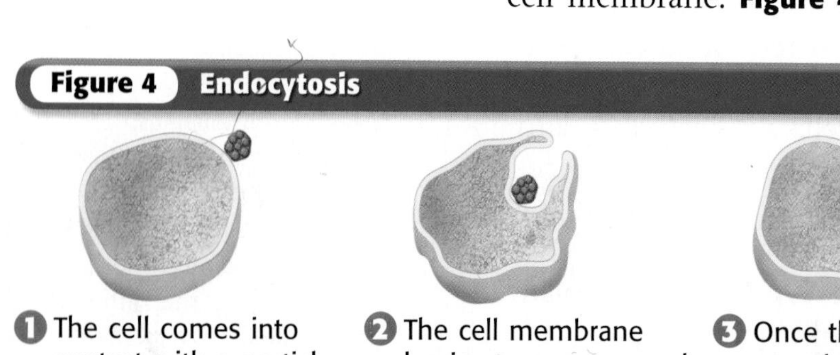

1. The cell comes into contact with a particle.
2. The cell membrane begins to wrap around the particle.
3. Once the particle is completely surrounded, a vesicle pinches off.

This photo shows the end of *endocytosis,* which means "within the cell."

Figure 5 Exocytosis

1. Large particles that must leave the cell are packaged in vesicles.

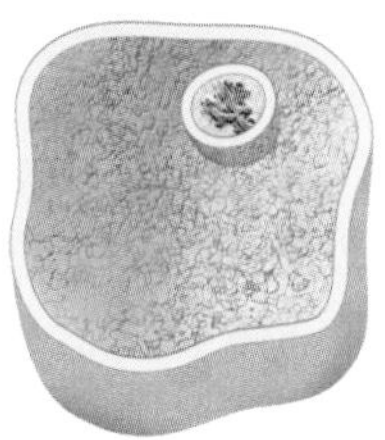

2. The vesicle travels to the cell membrane and fuses with it.

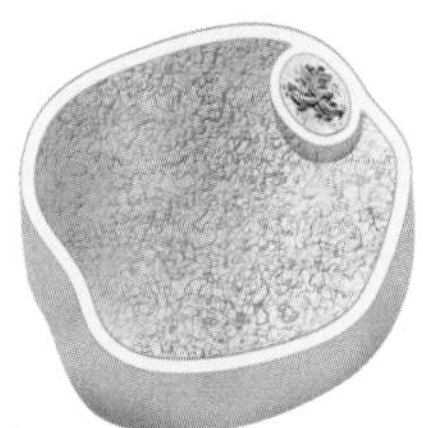

3. The cell releases the particle to the outside of the cell.

Exocytosis means "outside the cell."

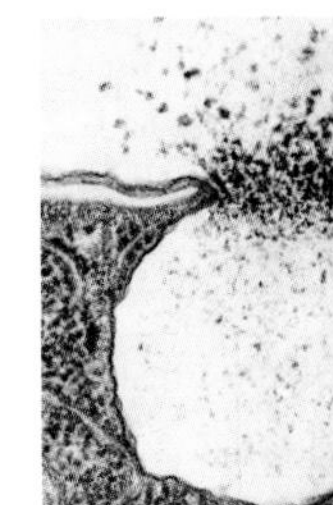

Exocytosis

When large particles, such as wastes, leave the cell, the cell uses an active-transport process called **exocytosis** (EK soh sie TOH sis). During exocytosis, a vesicle forms around a large particle within the cell. The vesicle carries the particle to the cell membrane. The vesicle fuses with the cell membrane and releases the particle to the outside of the cell. **Figure 5** shows exocytosis.

exocytosis the process in which a cell releases a particle by enclosing the particle in a vesicle that then moves to the cell surface and fuses with the cell membrane

Reading Check What is exocytosis?

SECTION Review

Summary

- Diffusion is the movement of particles from an area of high concentration to an area of low concentration.
- Osmosis is the diffusion of water through a semipermeable membrane.
- Cells move small particles by diffusion, which is an example of passive transport, and by active transport.
- Large particles enter the cell by endocytosis, and exit the cell by exocytosis.

Using Key Terms

For each pair of terms, explain how the meanings of the terms differ.

1. *diffusion* and *osmosis*
2. *active transport* and *passive transport*
3. *endocytosis* and *exocytosis*

Understanding Key Ideas

4. The movement of particles from a less crowded area to a more crowded area requires
   a. sunlight.
   b. energy.
   c. a membrane.
   d. osmosis.
5. What structures allow small particles to cross cell membranes?

Math Skills

6. The area of particle 1 is $2.5\ mm^2$. The area of particle 2 is $0.5\ mm^2$. The area of particle 1 is how many times as big as the area of particle 2?

Critical Thinking

7. **Predicting Consequences** What would happen to a cell if its channel proteins were damaged and unable to transport particles? What would happen to the organism if many of its cells were damaged in this way? Explain your answer.
8. **Analyzing Ideas** Why does active transport require energy?

SCILINKS
NSTA
Developed and maintained by the National Science Teachers Association
For a variety of links related to this chapter, go to www.scilinks.org
Topics: Diffusion; Osmosis
SciLinks code: HSM0406; HSM1090

SECTION 2

Cell Energy

Why do you get hungry? Feeling hungry is your body's way of telling you that your cells need energy.

All cells need energy to live, grow, and reproduce. Plant cells get their energy from the sun. Many animal cells get the energy they need from food.

READING WARM-UP

Objectives

- Describe photosynthesis and cellular respiration.
- Compare cellular respiration with fermentation.

Terms to Learn

photosynthesis
cellular respiration
fermentation

READING STRATEGY

Discussion Read this section silently. Write down questions that you have about this section. Discuss your questions in a small group.

From Sun to Cell

Nearly all of the energy that fuels life comes from the sun. Plants capture energy from the sun and change it into food through a process called **photosynthesis.** The food that plants make supplies them with energy. This food also becomes a source of energy for the organisms that eat the plants.

Photosynthesis

Plant cells have molecules that absorb light energy. These molecules are called *pigments*. Chlorophyll (KLAWR uh FIL), the main pigment used in photosynthesis, gives plants their green color. Chlorophyll is found in chloroplasts.

Plants use the energy captured by chlorophyll to change carbon dioxide and water into food. The food is in the form of the simple sugar glucose. Glucose is a carbohydrate. When plants make glucose, they convert the sun's energy into a form of energy that can be stored. The energy in glucose is used by the plant's cells. Photosynthesis also produces oxygen. Photosynthesis is summarized in **Figure 1.**

photosynthesis the process by which plants, algae, and some bacteria use sunlight, carbon dioxide, and water to make food

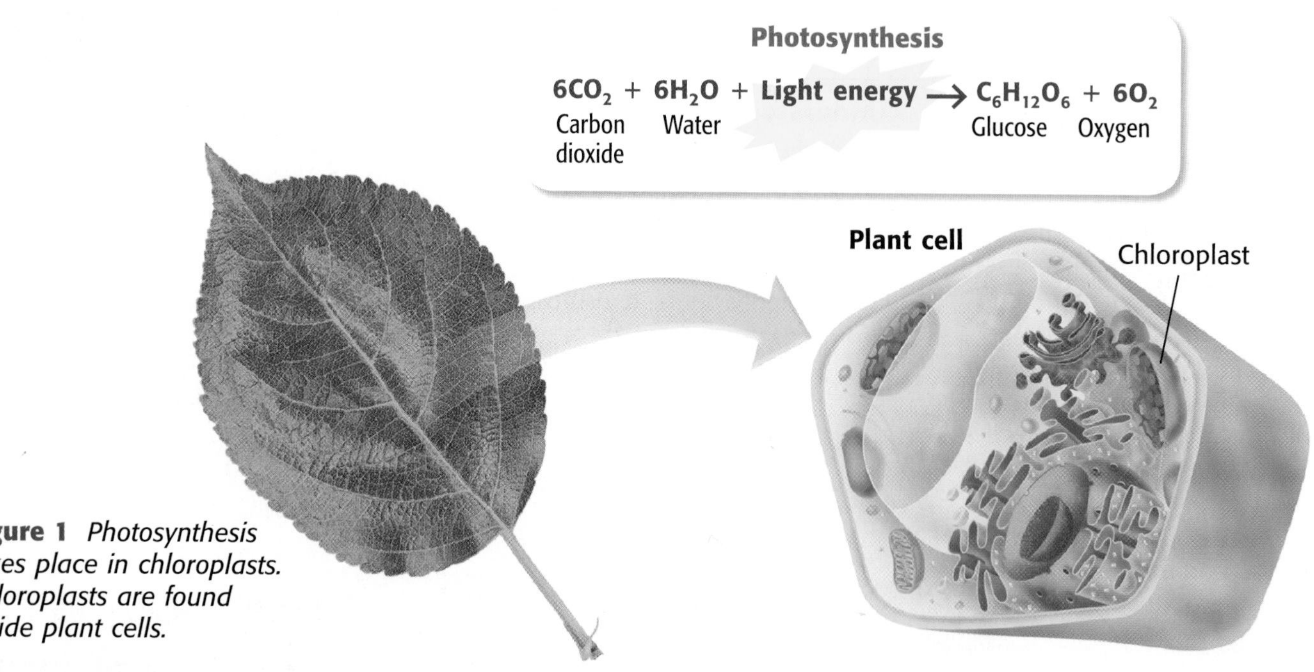

Figure 1 *Photosynthesis takes place in chloroplasts. Chloroplasts are found inside plant cells.*

Getting Energy from Food

Animal cells have different ways of getting energy from food. One way, called **cellular respiration,** uses oxygen to break down food. Many cells can get energy without using oxygen through a process called **fermentation.** Cellular respiration will release more energy from a given food than fermentation will.

Cellular Respiration

The word *respiration* means "breathing," but cellular respiration is different from breathing. Breathing supplies the oxygen needed for cellular respiration. Breathing also removes carbon dioxide, which is a waste product of cellular respiration. But cellular respiration is a chemical process that occurs in cells.

Most complex organisms, such as the cow in **Figure 2,** obtain energy through cellular respiration. During cellular respiration, food (such as glucose) is broken down into CO_2 and H_2O, and energy is released. Most of the energy released maintains body temperature. Some of the energy is used to form adenosine triphosphate (ATP). ATP supplies energy that fuels cell activities.

Most of the process of cellular respiration takes place in the cell membrane of prokaryotic cells. But in the cells of eukaryotes, cellular respiration takes place mostly in the mitochondria. The process of cellular respiration is summarized in **Figure 2.** Does the equation in the figure remind you of the equation for photosynthesis? **Figure 3** on the next page shows how photosynthesis and respiration are related.

Reading Check **What is the difference between cellular respiration and breathing?** (*See the Appendix for answers to Reading Checks.*)

CONNECTION TO Chemistry

Earth's Early Atmosphere

Scientists think that Earth's early atmosphere lacked oxygen. Because of this lack of oxygen, early organisms used fermentation to get energy from food. When organisms began to photosynthesize, the oxygen they produced entered the atmosphere. How do you think this oxygen changed how other organisms got energy?

cellular respiration the process by which cells use oxygen to produce energy from food

fermentation the breakdown of food without the use of oxygen

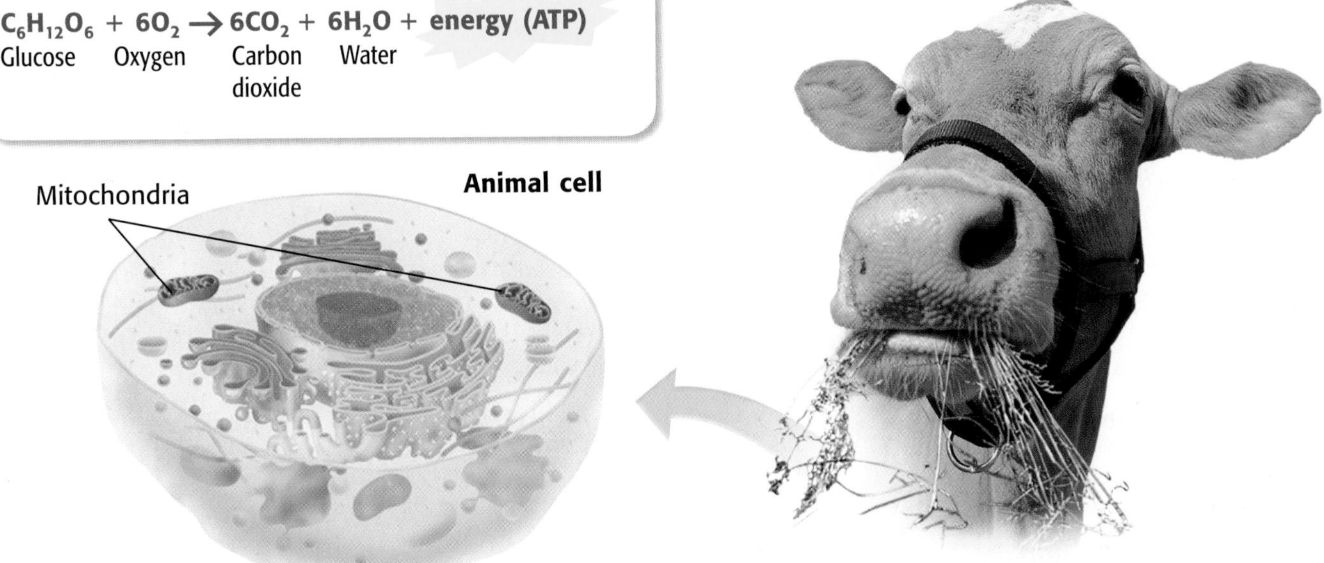

Figure 2 *The mitochondria in the cells of this cow will use cellular respiration to release the energy stored in the grass.*

Figure 3 **The Connection Between Photosynthesis and Respiration**

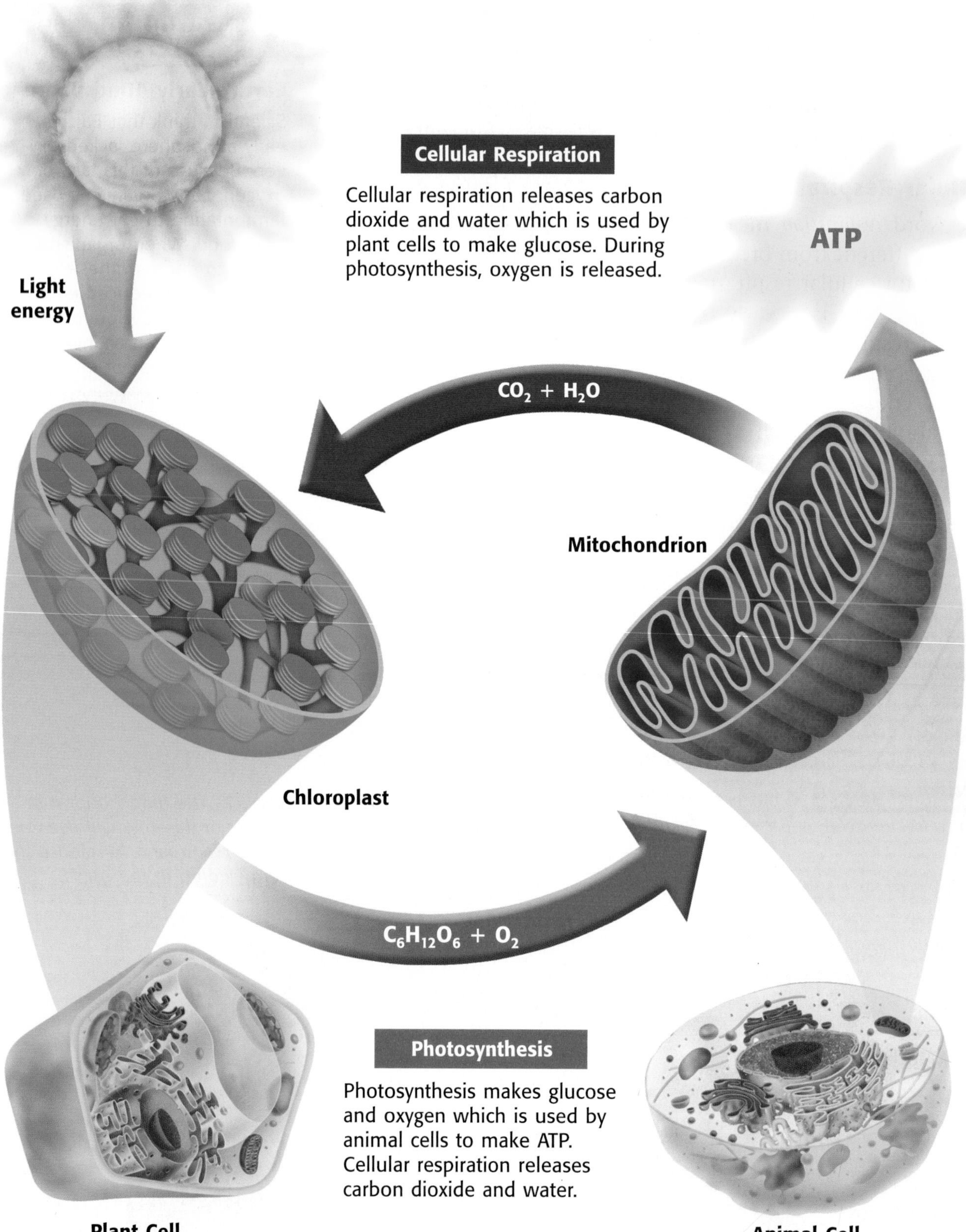

Cellular Respiration
Cellular respiration releases carbon dioxide and water which is used by plant cells to make glucose. During photosynthesis, oxygen is released.
ATP
Light energy
$CO_2 + H_2O$
Mitochondrion
Chloroplast
$C_6H_{12}O_6 + O_2$
Photosynthesis
Photosynthesis makes glucose and oxygen which is used by animal cells to make ATP. Cellular respiration releases carbon dioxide and water.
Plant Cell
Animal Cell

Connection Between Photosynthesis and Respiration

As shown in **Figure 3,** photosynthesis transforms energy from the sun into glucose. During photosynthesis, cells use CO_2 to make glucose, and the cells release O_2. During cellular respiration, cells use O_2 to break down glucose and release energy and CO_2. Each process makes the materials that are needed for the other process to occur elsewhere.

Figure 4 *Yeast forms carbon dioxide during fermentation. The bubbles of CO_2 gas cause the dough to rise and leave small holes in bread after it is baked.*

Fermentation

Have you ever felt a burning sensation in your leg muscles while you were running? When muscle cells can't get the oxygen needed for cellular respiration, they use the process of fermentation to get energy. One kind of fermentation happens in your muscles and produces lactic acid. The buildup of lactic acid contributes to muscle fatigue and causes a burning sensation. This kind of fermentation also happens in the muscle cells of other animals and in some fungi and bacteria. Another type of fermentation occurs in some types of bacteria and in yeast as described in **Figure 4.**

Reading Check What are two kinds of fermentation?

SECTION Review

Summary

- Most of the energy that fuels life processes comes from the sun.
- The sun's energy is converted into food by the process of photosynthesis.
- Cellular respiration breaks down glucose into water, carbon dioxide, and energy.
- Fermentation is a way that cells get energy from their food without using oxygen.

Using Key Terms

1. In your own words, write a definition for the term *fermentation.*

Understanding Key Ideas

2. O_2 is released during
   a. cellular respiration.
   b. photosynthesis.
   c. breathing.
   d. fermentation.
3. How are photosynthesis and cellular respiration related?
4. How are respiration and fermentation similar? How are they different?

Math Skills

5. Cells of plant A make 120 molecules of glucose an hour. Cells of plant B make half as much glucose as plant A does. How much glucose does plant B make every minute?

Critical Thinking

6. **Analyzing Relationships** Why are plants important to the survival of all other organisms?
7. **Applying Concepts** You have been given the job of restoring life to a barren island. What types of organisms would you put on the island? If you want to have animals on the island, what other organisms must you bring? Explain your answer.

SCILINKS
NSTA
Developed and maintained by the National Science Teachers Association
For a variety of links related to this chapter, go to www.scilinks.org
Topic: Cell Energy; Photosynthesis
SciLinks code: HSM0237; HSM1140

SECTION 3

The Cell Cycle

In the time that it takes you to read this sentence, your body will have made millions of new cells! Making new cells allows you to grow and replace cells that have died.

READING WARM-UP

Objectives

- Explain how cells produce more cells.
- Describe the process of mitosis.
- Explain how cell division differs in animals and plants.

Terms to Learn

cell cycle
chromosome
homologous chromosomes
mitosis
cytokinesis

READING STRATEGY

Paired Summarizing Read this section silently. In pairs, take turns summarizing the material. Stop to discuss ideas that seem confusing.

The environment in your stomach is so acidic that the cells lining your stomach must be replaced every few days. Other cells are replaced less often, but your body is constantly making new cells.

The Life of a Cell

As you grow, you pass through different stages in life. Your cells also pass through different stages in their life cycle. The life cycle of a cell is called the **cell cycle.**

The cell cycle begins when the cell is formed and ends when the cell divides and forms new cells. Before a cell divides, it must make a copy of its deoxyribonucleic acid (DNA). DNA is the hereditary material that controls all cell activities, including the making of new cells. The DNA of a cell is organized into structures called **chromosomes.** Copying chromosomes ensures that each new cell will be an exact copy of its parent cell. How does a cell make more cells? It depends on whether the cell is prokaryotic (with no nucleus) or eukaryotic (with a nucleus).

cell cycle the life cycle of a cell

chromosome in a eukaryotic cell, one of the structures in the nucleus that are made up of DNA and protein; in a prokaryotic cell, the main ring of DNA

Making More Prokaryotic Cells

Prokaryotic cells are less complex than eukaryotic cells are. Bacteria, which are prokaryotes, have ribosomes and a single, circular DNA molecule but don't have membrane-enclosed organelles. Cell division in bacteria is called *binary fission,* which means "splitting into two parts." Binary fission results in two cells that each contain one copy of the circle of DNA. A few of the bacteria in **Figure 1** are undergoing binary fission.

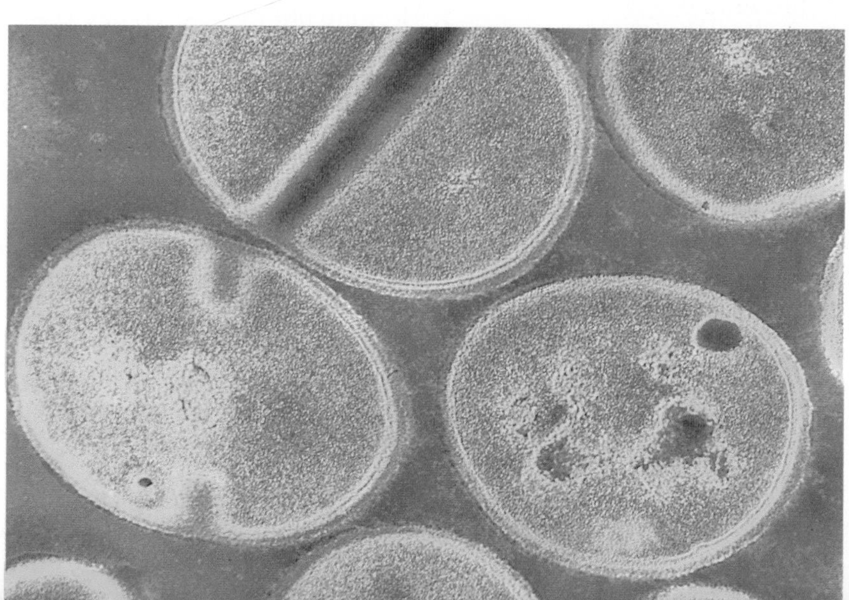

Figure 1 *Bacteria reproduce by binary fission.*

Eukaryotic Cells and Their DNA

Eukaryotic cells are more complex than prokaryotic cells are. The chromosomes of eukaryotic cells contain more DNA than those of prokaryotic cells do. Different kinds of eukaryotes have different numbers of chromosomes. More-complex eukaryotes do not necessarily have more chromosomes than simpler eukaryotes do. For example, fruit flies have 8 chromosomes, potatoes have 48, and humans have 46. **Figure 2** shows the 46 chromosomes of a human body cell lined up in pairs. These pairs are made up of similar chromosomes known as **homologous chromosomes** (hoh MAHL uh guhs KROH muh SOHMZ).

Reading Check **Do more-complex organisms always have more chromosomes than simpler organisms do?** (*See the Appendix for answers to Reading Checks.*)

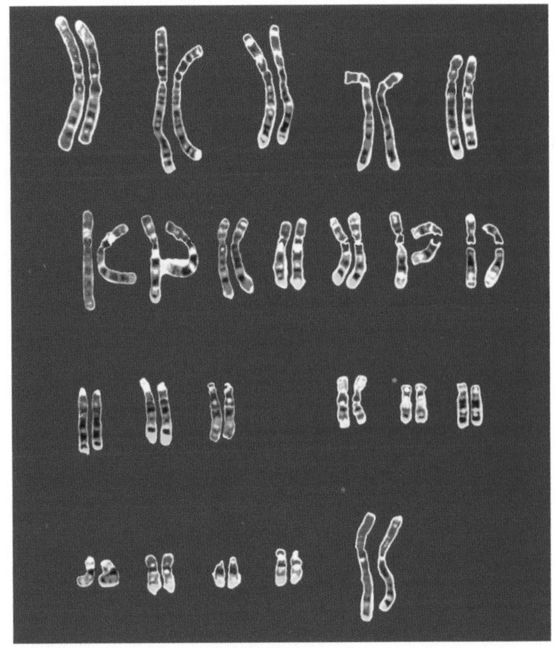

Figure 2 *Human body cells have 46 chromosomes, or 23 pairs of chromosomes.*

Making More Eukaryotic Cells

The eukaryotic cell cycle includes three stages. In the first stage, called *interphase,* the cell grows and copies its organelles and chromosomes. After each chromosome is duplicated, the two copies are called *chromatids*. Chromatids are held together at a region called the *centromere*. The joined chromatids twist and coil and condense into an X shape, as shown in **Figure 3.** After this step, the cell enters the second stage of the cell cycle.

In the second stage, the chromatids separate. The complicated process of chromosome separation is called **mitosis.** Mitosis ensures that each new cell receives a copy of each chromosome. Mitosis is divided into four phases, as shown on the following pages.

In the third stage, the cell splits into two cells. These cells are identical to each other and to the original cell.

homologous chromosomes chromosomes that have the same sequence of genes and the same structure

mitosis in eukaryotic cells, a process of cell division that forms two new nuclei, each of which has the same number of chromosomes

Figure 3 *This duplicated chromosome consists of two chromatids. The chromatids are joined at the centromere.*

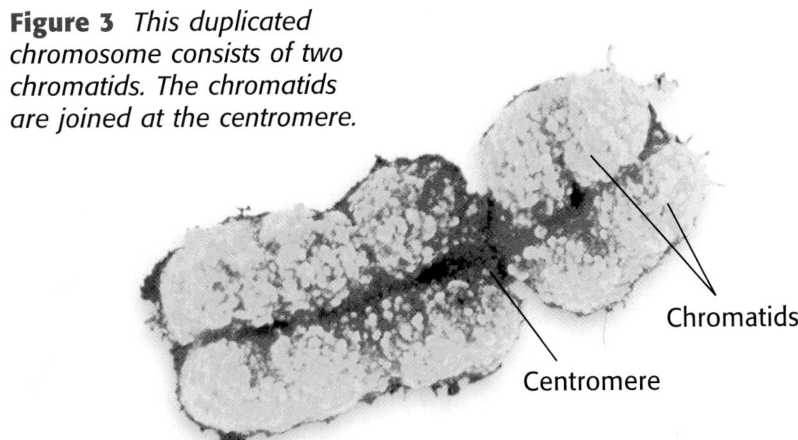

CONNECTION TO Language Arts

Picking Apart Vocabulary

Brainstorm what words are similar to the parts of the term *homologous chromosome*. What can you guess about the meaning of the term's root words? Look up the roots of the words, and explain how they help describe the concept. **ACTIVITY**

Figure 4 **The Cell Cycle**

Copying DNA (Interphase)

Before mitosis begins, chromosomes are copied. Each chromosome is then two chromatids.

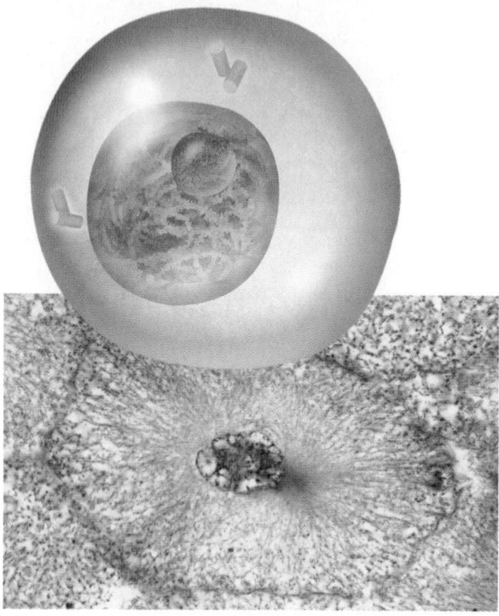

Mitosis Phase 1 (Prophase)

Mitosis begins. The nuclear membrane dissolves. Chromosomes condense into rodlike structures.

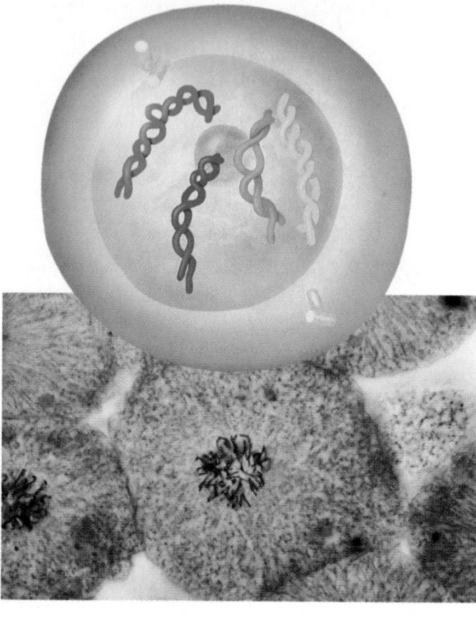

Mitosis Phase 2 (Metaphase)

The chromosomes line up along the equator of the cell. Homologous chromosomes pair up.

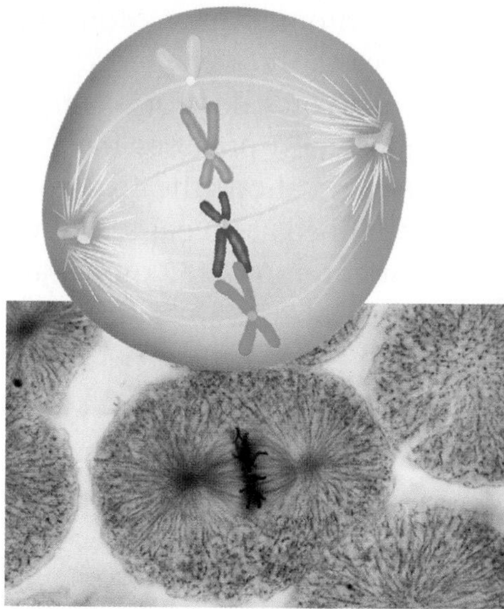

Mitosis and the Cell Cycle

cytokinesis the division of the cytoplasm of a cell

Figure 4 shows the cell cycle and the phases of mitosis in an animal cell. Mitosis has four phases that are shown and described above. This diagram shows only four chromosomes to make it easy to see what's happening inside the cell.

Cytokinesis

In animal cells and other eukaryotes that do not have cell walls, division of the cytoplasm begins at the cell membrane. The cell membrane begins to pinch inward to form a groove, which eventually pinches all the way through the cell, and two daughter cells form. The division of cytoplasm is called **cytokinesis** and is shown at the last step of **Figure 4.**

Eukaryotic cells that have a cell wall, such as the cells of plants, algae, and fungi, reproduce differently. In these cells, a *cell plate* forms in the middle of the cell. The cell plate contains the materials for the new cell membranes and the new cell walls that will separate the new cells. After the cell splits into two, a new cell wall forms where the cell plate was. The cell plate and a late stage of cytokinesis in a plant cell are shown in **Figure 5.**

Cell plate

Figure 5 *When a plant cell divides, a cell plate forms and the cell splits into two cells.*

Reading Check **What is the difference between cytokinesis in an animal cell and cytokinesis in a plant cell?**

Mitosis Phase 3 (Anaphase)

The chromatids separate and move to opposite sides of the cell.

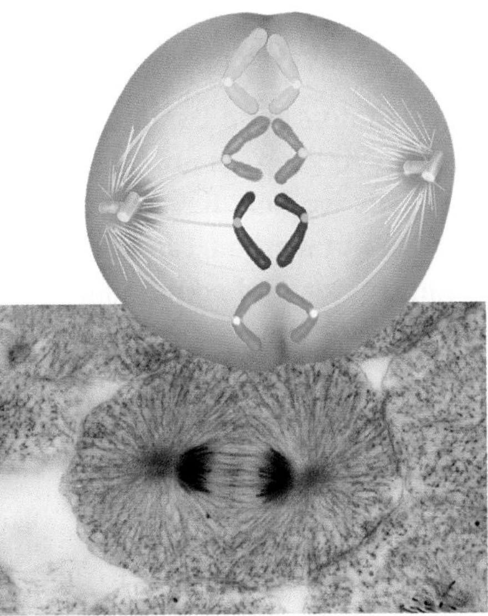

Mitosis Phase 4 (Telophase)

A nuclear membrane forms around each set of chromosomes, and the chromosomes unwind. Mitosis is complete.

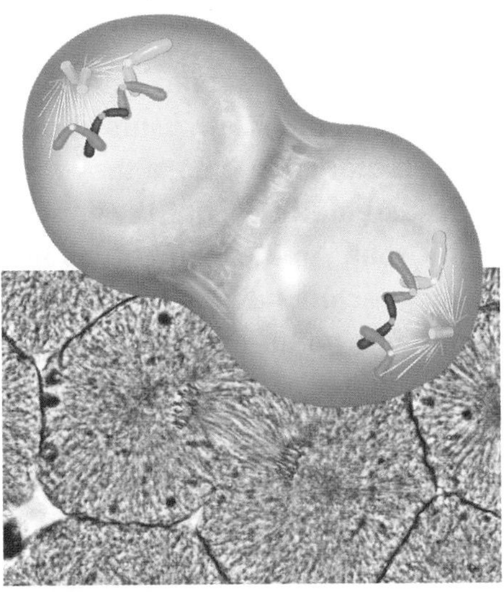

Cytokinesis

In cells that lack a cell wall, the cell pinches in two. In cells that have a cell wall, a cell plate forms between the two new cells.

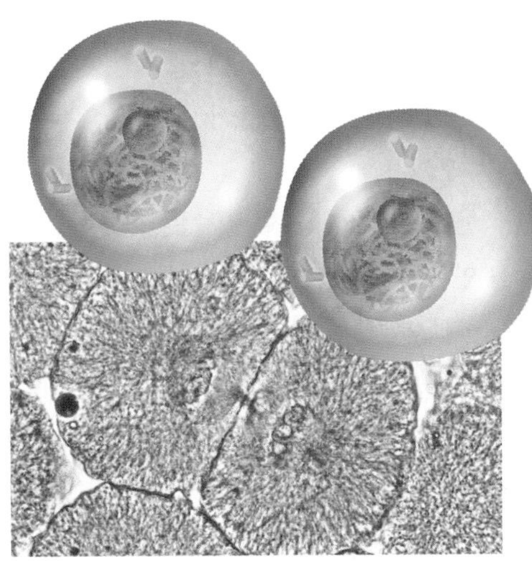

SECTION Review

Summary

- A cell produces more cells by first copying its DNA.
- Eukaryotic cells produce more cells through the four phases of mitosis.
- Mitosis produces two cells that have the same number of chromosomes as the parent cell.
- At the end of mitosis, a cell divides the cytoplasm by cytokinesis.
- In plant cells, a cell plate forms between the two new cells during cytokinesis.

Using Key Terms

1. In your own words, write a definition for each of the following terms: *cell cycle* and *cytokinesis.*

Understanding Key Ideas

2. Eukaryotic cells
   - **a.** do not divide.
   - **b.** undergo binary fission.
   - **c.** undergo mitosis.
   - **d.** have cell walls.
3. Why is it important for chromosomes to be copied before cell division?
4. Describe mitosis.

Math Skills

5. Cell A takes 6 h to complete division. Cell B takes 8 h to complete division. After 24 h, how many more copies of cell A would there be than cell B?

Critical Thinking

6. **Predicting Consequences** What would happen if cytokinesis occurred without mitosis?
7. **Applying Concepts** How does mitosis ensure that a new cell is just like its parent cell?
8. **Making Comparisons** Compare the processes that animal cells and plant cells use to make new cells. How are the processes different?

SCILINKS.
NSTA
Developed and maintained by the National Science Teachers Association
For a variety of links related to this chapter, go to www.scilinks.org
Topic: Cell Cycle
SciLinks code: HSM0235

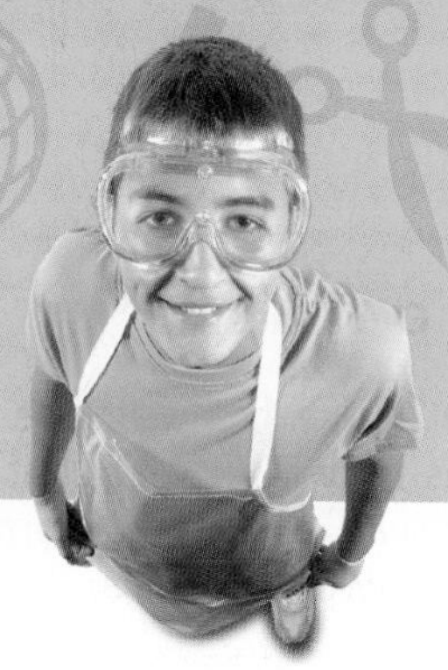

Using Scientific Methods

Inquiry Lab

The Perfect Taters Mystery

OBJECTIVES

Examine osmosis in potato cells.

Design a procedure that will give the best results.

MATERIALS

- cups, clear plastic, small
- potato pieces, freshly cut
- potato samples (A, B, and C)
- salt
- water, distilled

SAFETY

You are the chief food detective at Perfect Taters Food Company. The boss, Mr. Fries, wants you to find a way to keep his potatoes fresh and crisp before they are cooked. His workers have tried several methods, but these methods have not worked. Workers in Group A put the potatoes in very salty water, and something unexpected happened to the potatoes. Workers in Group B put the potatoes in water that did not contain any salt, and something else happened! Workers in Group C didn't put the potatoes in any water, and that didn't work either. Now, you must design an experiment to find out what can be done to make the potatoes stay crisp and fresh.

- Before you plan your experiment, review what you know. You know that potatoes are made of cells. Plant cells contain a large amount of water. Cells have membranes that hold water and other materials inside and keep some things out. Water and other materials must travel across cell membranes to get into and out of the cell.
- Mr. Fries has told you that you can obtain as many samples as you need from the workers in Groups A, B, and C. Your teacher will have these samples ready for you to observe.
- Make a data table like the one below. List your observations in the data table. Make as many observations as you can about the potatoes tested by workers in Groups A, B, and C.

Observations	
Group A	
Group B	
Group C	

Ask a Question

1. Now that you have made your observations, state Mr. Fries's problem in the form of a question that can be answered by your experiment.

Form a Hypothesis

2. Form a hypothesis based on your observations and your questions. The hypothesis should be a statement about what causes the potatoes not to be crisp and fresh. Based on your hypothesis, make a prediction about the outcome of your experiment. State your prediction in an if-then format.

Test the Hypothesis

3. Once you have made a prediction, design your investigation. Check your experimental design with your teacher before you begin. Mr. Fries will give you potato pieces, water, salt, and no more than six containers.

4. Keep very accurate records. Write your plan and procedure. Make data tables. To be sure your data is accurate, measure all materials carefully and make drawings of the potato pieces before and after the experiment.

Analyze the Results

1. **Explaining Events** Explain what happened to the potato cells in Groups A, B, and C in your experiment. Include a discussion of the cell membrane and the process of osmosis.

Draw Conclusions

2. **Analyzing Results** Write a letter to Mr. Fries that explains your experimental method, results, and conclusion. Then, make a recommendation about how he should handle the potatoes so that they will stay fresh and crisp.

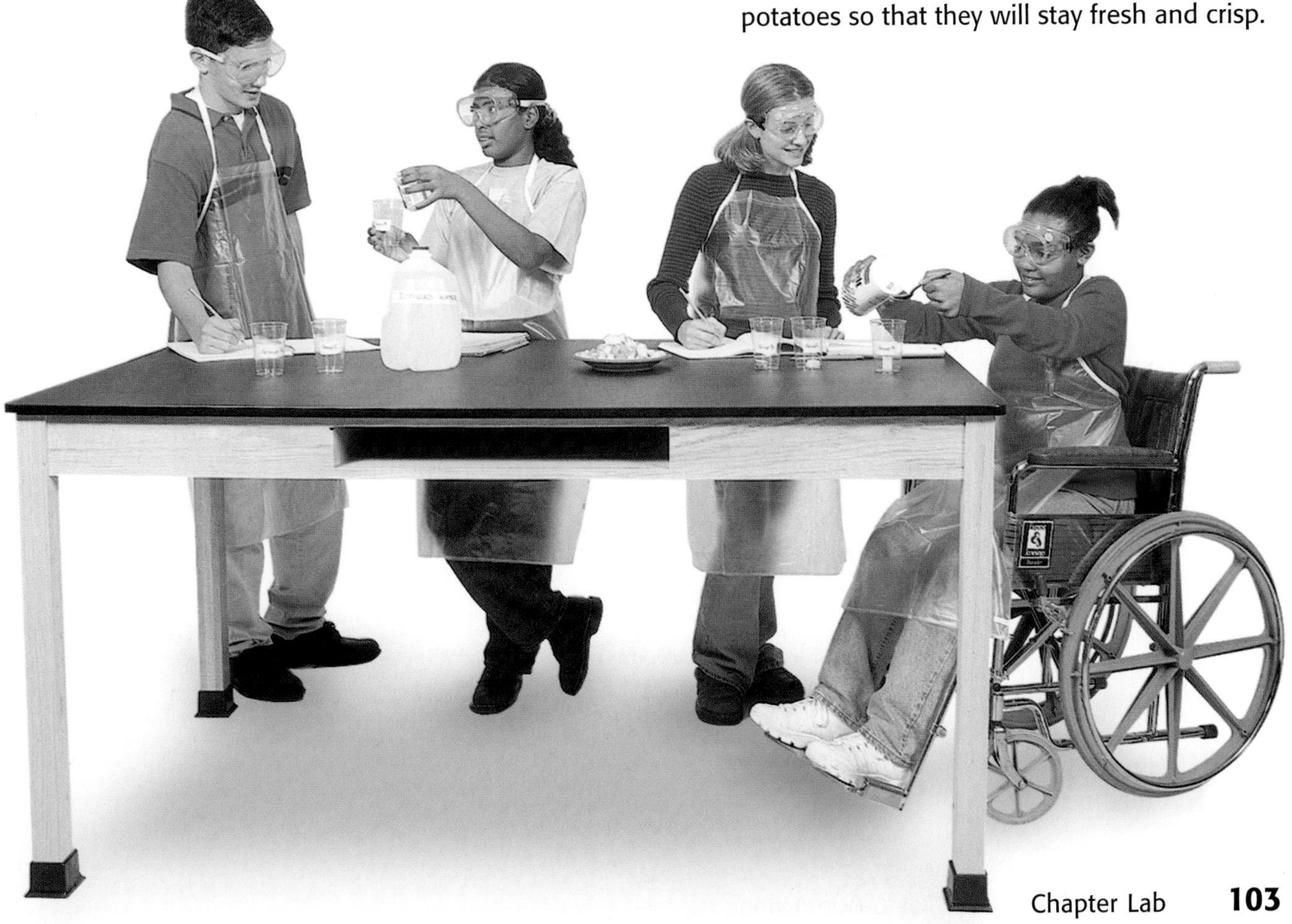

Chapter Review

USING KEY TERMS

1. Use the following terms in the same sentence: *diffusion* and *osmosis*.

2. In your own words, write a definition for each of the following terms: *exocytosis* and *endocytosis*.

Complete each of the following sentences by choosing the correct term from the word bank.

cellular respiration
photosynthesis
fermentation

3. Plants use ___ to make glucose.

4. During ___, oxygen is used to break down food molecules releasing large amounts of energy.

For each pair of terms, explain how the meanings of the terms differ.

5. *cytokinesis* and *mitosis*

6. *active transport* and *passive transport*

7. *cellular respiration* and *fermentation*

UNDERSTANDING KEY IDEAS

Multiple Choice

8. The process in which particles move through a membrane from a region of low concentration to a region of high concentration is
   a. diffusion.
   b. passive transport.
   c. active transport.
   d. fermentation.

9. What is the result of mitosis and cytokinesis?
   a. two identical cells
   b. two nuclei
   c. chloroplasts
   d. two different cells

10. Before the energy in food can be used by a cell, the energy must first be transferred to molecules of
   a. proteins.
   b. carbohydrates.
   c. DNA.
   d. ATP.

11. Which of the following cells would form a cell plate during the cell cycle?
   a. a human cell
   b. a prokaryotic cell
   c. a plant cell
   d. All of the above

Short Answer

12. Are exocytosis and endocytosis examples of active or passive transport? Explain your answer.

13. Name the cell structures that are needed for photosynthesis and the cell structures that are needed for cellular respiration.

14. Describe the three stages of the cell cycle of a eukaryotic cell.

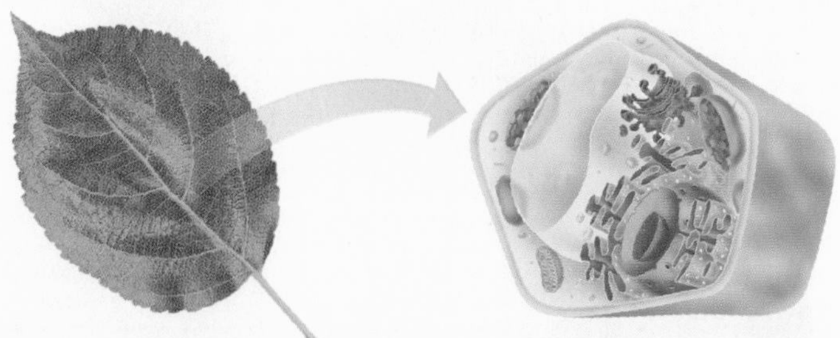

CRITICAL THINKING

15 **Concept Mapping** Use the following terms to create a concept map: *chromosome duplication, cytokinesis, prokaryote, mitosis, cell cycle, binary fission,* and *eukaryote.*

16 **Making Inferences** Which one of the plants pictured below was given water mixed with salt, and which one was given pure water? Explain how you know, and be sure to use the word *osmosis* in your answer.

17 **Identifying Relationships** Why would your muscle cells need to be supplied with more food when there is a lack of oxygen than when there is plenty of oxygen present?

18 **Applying Concepts** A parent cell has 10 chromosomes.

a. Will the cell go through binary fission or mitosis and cytokinesis to produce new cells?

b. How many chromosomes will each new cell have after the parent cell divides?

INTERPRETING GRAPHICS

The picture below shows a cell. Use the picture below to answer the questions that follow.

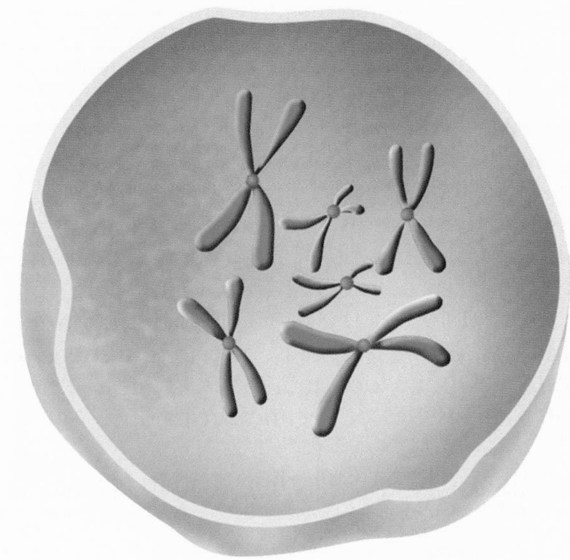

19 Is the cell prokaryotic or eukaryotic?

20 Which stage of the cell cycle is this cell in?

21 How many chromatids are present? How many pairs of homologous chromosomes are present?

22 How many chromosomes will be present in each of the new cells after the cell divides?

Standardized Test Preparation

READING

Read each of the passages below. Then, answer the questions that follow each passage.

Passage 1 Perhaps you have heard that jogging or some other kind of exercise "burns" a lot of Calories. The word *burn* is often used to describe what happens when your cells release stored energy from food. The burning of food in living cells is not the same as the burning of logs in a campfire. When logs burn, the energy stored in wood is released as thermal energy and light in a single reaction. But this kind of reaction is not the kind that happens in cells. Instead, the energy that cells get from food molecules is released at each step of a series of chemical reactions.

1. According to the passage, how do cells release energy from food?

A in a single reaction
B as thermal energy and light
C in a series of reactions
D by burning

2. Which of the following statements is a fact in the passage?

F Wood burns better than food does.
G Both food and wood have stored energy.
H Food has more stored energy than wood does.
I When it is burned, wood releases only thermal energy.

3. According to the passage, why might people be confused between what happens in a living cell and what happens in a campfire?

A The word *burn* may describe both processes.
B Thermal energy is released during both processes.
C Wood can be burned and broken down by living cells.
D Jogging and other exercises use energy.

Passage 2 The word *respiration* means "breathing," but cellular respiration is different from breathing. Breathing supplies your cells with the oxygen that they need for cellular respiration. Breathing also rids your body of carbon dioxide, which is a waste product of cellular respiration. Cellular respiration is the chemical process that releases energy from food. Most organisms obtain energy from food through cellular respiration. During cellular respiration, oxygen is used to break down food (glucose) into CO_2 and H_2O, and energy is released. In humans, most of the energy released is used to maintain body temperature.

1. According to the passage, what is glucose?

A a type of chemical process
B a type of waste product
C a type of organism
D a type of food

2. According to the passage, how does cellular respiration differ from breathing?

F Breathing releases carbon dioxide, but cellular respiration releases oxygen.
G Cellular respiration is a chemical process that uses oxygen to release energy from food, but breathing supplies cells with oxygen.
H Cellular respiration requires oxygen, but breathing does not.
I Breathing rids your body of waste products, but cellular respiration stores wastes.

3. According to the passage, how do humans use most of the energy released?

A to break down food
B to obtain oxygen
C to maintain body temperature
D to get rid of carbon dioxide

INTERPRETING GRAPHICS

The graph below shows the cell cycle. Use this graph to answer the questions that follow.

The Cell Cycle

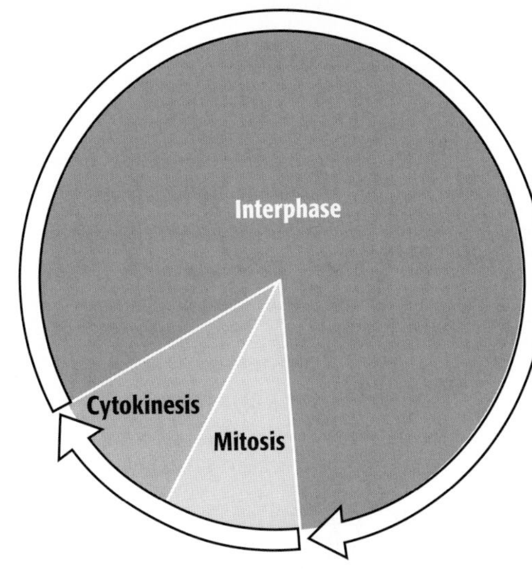

1. Which part of the cell cycle lasts longest?
   - **A** interphase
   - **B** mitosis
   - **C** cytokinesis
   - **D** There is not enough information to determine the answer.

2. Which of the following lists the parts of the cell cycle in the proper order?
   - **F** mitosis, cytokinesis, mitosis
   - **G** interphase, cytokinesis, mitosis
   - **H** interphase, mitosis, interphase
   - **I** mitosis, cytokinesis, interphase

3. Which part of the cell cycle is the briefest?
   - **A** interphase
   - **B** cell division
   - **C** cytokinesis
   - **D** There is not enough information to determine the answer.

4. Why is the cell cycle represented by a circle?
   - **F** The cell cycle is a continuous process that begins again after it finishes.
   - **G** The cell cycle happens only in cells that are round.
   - **H** The cell cycle is a linear process.
   - **I** The cell is in interphase for more than half of the cell cycle.

MATH

Read each question below, and choose the best answer.

1. A normal cell spends 90% of its time in interphase. How is 90% expressed as a fraction?
   - **A** 3/4
   - **B** 4/5
   - **C** 85/100
   - **D** 9/10

2. If a cell lived for 3 weeks and 4 days, how many days did it live?
   - **F** 7
   - **G** 11
   - **H** 21
   - **I** 25

3. How is $2 \times 3 \times 3 \times 3 \times 3$ expressed in exponential notation?
   - **A** 3×2^4
   - **B** 2×3^3
   - **C** 3^4
   - **D** 2×3^4

4. Cell A has 3 times as many chromosomes as cell B has. After cell B's chromosomes double during mitosis, cell B has 6 chromosomes. How many chromosomes does cell A have?
   - **F** 3
   - **G** 6
   - **H** 9
   - **I** 18

5. If $x + 2 = 3$, what does $x + 1$ equal?
   - **A** 4
   - **B** 3
   - **C** 2
   - **D** 1

6. If $3x + 2 = 26$, what does $x + 1$ equal?
   - **F** 7
   - **G** 8
   - **H** 9
   - **I** 10

Science in Action

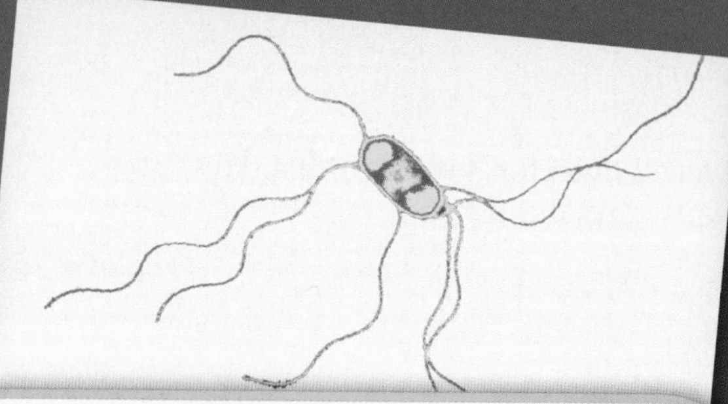

Scientific Discoveries

Electrifying News About Microbes

Your car is out of fuel, and there isn't a service station in sight. This is not a problem! Your car's motor runs on electricity supplied by trillions of microorganisms. Some chemists think that "living" batteries will someday operate everything from watches to entire cities. A group of scientists at King's College in London have demonstrated that microorganisms can convert food into usable electrical energy. The microorganisms convert foods such as table sugar and molasses most efficiently. An efficient microorganisms can convert more than 90% of its food into compounds that will fuel an electric reaction. A less efficient microbe will only convert 50% of its food into these types of compounds.

Math ACTIVITY

An efficient microorganism converts 90% of its food into fuel compounds, and an inefficient microorganism converts only 50%. If the inefficient microorganism makes 60 g of fuel out of a possible 120 g of food, how much fuel would an efficient microorganism make out of the same amount of food?

Science Fiction

"Contagion" by Katherine MacLean

A quarter mile from their spaceship, the *Explorer,* a team of doctors walk carefully along a narrow forest trail. Around them, the forest looks like a forest on Earth in the fall—the leaves are green, copper, purple, and fiery red. But it isn't fall. And the team is not on Earth.

Minos is enough like Earth to be the home of another colony of humans. But Minos might also be home to unknown organisms that could cause severe illness or death among the crew of *Explorer*. These diseases might be enough like diseases on Earth to be contagious, but they might be different enough to be very difficult to treat.

Something large moves among the shadows—it looks like a man. What happens next? Read Katherine's MacLean's "Contagion" in the *Holt Anthology of Science Fiction* to find out.

Language Arts ACTIVITY

WRITING SKILL Write two to three paragraphs that describe what you think might happen next in the story.

Careers

Jerry Yakel

Neuroscientist Jerry Yakel credits a sea slug for making him a neuroscientist. In a college class studying neurons, or nerve cells, Yakel got to see firsthand how ions move across the cell membrane of *Aplysia californica,* also known as a sea hare. He says, "I was totally hooked. I knew that I wanted to be a neurophysiologist then and there. I haven't wavered since."

Today, Yakel is a senior investigator for the National Institutes of Environmental Health Sciences, which is part of the U.S. government's National Institutes of Health. "We try to understand how the normal brain works," says Yakel of his team. "Then, when we look at a diseased brain, we train to understand where the deficits are. Eventually, someone will have an idea about a drug that will tweak the system in this or that way."

Yakel studies the ways in which nicotine affects the human brain. "It is one of the most prevalent and potent neurotoxins in the environment," says Yakel. "I'm amazed that it isn't higher on the list of worries for the general public."

Social Studies ACTIVITY

WRITING SKILL Research a famous or historical figure in science. Write a short report that outlines how he or she became interested in science.

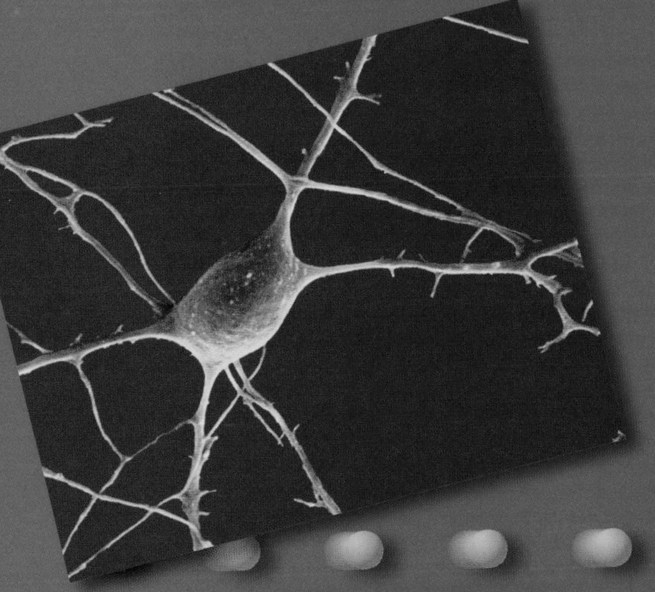

To learn more about these Science in Action topics, visit go.hrw.com and type in the keyword **HL5ACTF.**

Current Science

Check out Current Science® articles related to this chapter by visiting go.hrw.com. Just type in the keyword HL5CS04.

TIMELINE

Heredity, Evolution, and Classification

The differences and similarities between living things are the subject of this unit. You will learn how characteristics are passed from one generation to another, how living things are classified based on their characteristics, and how these characteristics help living things survive.

Scientists have not always understood these topics, and there is still much to be learned. This timeline will give you an idea of some things that have been learned so far.

1753
Carolus Linnaeus publishes the first of two volumes containing the classification of all known species.

1905
Nettie Stevens describes how human gender is determined by the X and Y chromosomes.

1930
The planet Pluto is discovered.

1969
Apollo 11 lands on the moon. Neil Armstrong becomes the first person to walk on the lunar surface.

1859
Charles Darwin suggests that natural selection is a mechanism of evolution.

1860
Abraham Lincoln is elected the 16th president of the United States.

1865
Gregor Mendel publishes the results of his studies of genetic inheritance in pea plants.

1951
Rosalind Franklin photographs DNA.

1953
James Watson and Francis Crick figure out the structure of DNA.

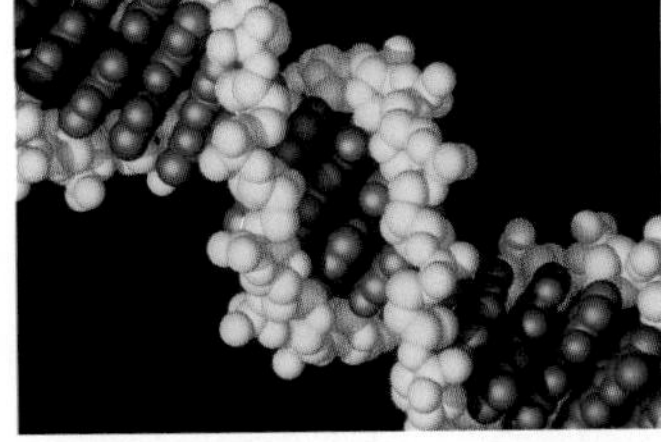

1960
Mary and Jonathan Leakey discover fossil bones of the human ancestor *Homo habilis* in Olduvai Gorge, Tanzania.

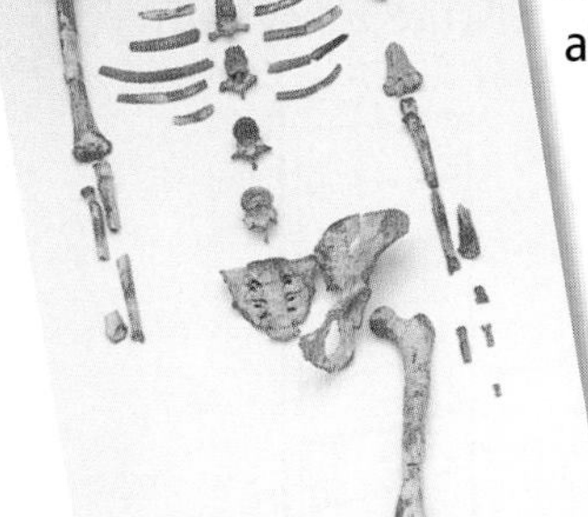

1974
Donald Johanson discovers a fossilized skeleton of one of the first hominids, *Australopithecus afarensis,* also called "Lucy."

1990
Ashanti DeSilva's white blood cells are genetically engineered to treat her immune deficiency disease.

2003
The Human Genome Project is completed. Scientists spent 13 years mapping out the 3 billion DNA subunits of chromosomes.

5

Heredity

About the PHOTO

The guinea pig in the middle has dark fur, and the other two have light orange fur. The guinea pig on the right has longer hair than the other two. Why do these guinea pigs look different from one another? The length and color of their fur was determined before they were born. These are just two of the many traits determined by genetic information. Genetic information is passed on from parents to their offspring.

PRE-READING ACTIVITY

FOLDNOTES **Key-Term Fold** Before you read the chapter, create the FoldNote entitled "Key-Term Fold" described in the **Study Skills** section of the Appendix. Write a key term from the chapter on each tab of the key-term fold. Under each tab, write the definition of the key term.

START-UP ACTIVITY

Clothing Combos

How do the same parents have children with many different traits?

Procedure

1. Gather **three boxes**. Put **five hats** in the first box, **five gloves** in the second, and **five scarves** in the third.
2. Without looking in the boxes, select one item from each box. Repeat this process, five students at a time, until the entire class has picked "an outfit." Record what outfit each student chooses.

Analysis

1. Were any two outfits exactly alike? Did you see all possible combinations? Explain your answer.
2. Choose a partner. Using your outfits, how many different combinations could you make by giving a third person one hat, one glove, and one scarf? How is this process like parents passing traits to their children?
3. After completing this activity, why do you think parents often have children who look very different from each other?

SECTION 1

Mendel and His Peas

Why don't you look like a rhinoceros? The answer to this question seems simple: Neither of your parents is a rhinoceros. But there is more to this answer than meets the eye.

READING WARM-UP

Objectives

- Explain the relationship between traits and heredity.
- Describe the experiments of Gregor Mendel.
- Explain the difference between dominant and recessive traits.

Terms to Learn

heredity
dominant trait
recessive trait

READING STRATEGY

Brainstorming The key idea of this section is heredity. Brainstorm words and phrases related to heredity.

As it turns out, **heredity,** or the passing of traits from parents to offspring, is more complicated than you might think. For example, you might have curly hair, while both of your parents have straight hair. You might have blue eyes even though both of your parents have brown eyes. How does this happen? People have investigated this question for a long time. About 150 years ago, Gregor Mendel performed important experiments. His discoveries helped scientists begin to find some answers to these questions.

Reading Check **What is heredity?** (*See the Appendix for answers to Reading Checks.*)

heredity the passing of genetic traits from parent to offspring

Who Was Gregor Mendel?

Gregor Mendel, shown in **Figure 1,** was born in 1822 in Heinzendorf, Austria. Mendel grew up on a farm and learned a lot about flowers and fruit trees.

When he was 21 years old, Mendel entered a monastery. The monks taught science and performed many scientific experiments. From there, Mendel was sent to Vienna where he could receive training in teaching. However, Mendel had trouble taking tests. Although he did well in school, he was unable to pass the final exam. He returned to the monastery and put most of his energy into research. Mendel discovered the principles of heredity in the monastery garden.

Figure 1 *Gregor Mendel discovered the principles of heredity while studying pea plants.*

Unraveling the Mystery

From working with plants, Mendel knew that the patterns of inheritance were not always clear. For example, sometimes a trait that appeared in one generation (parents) was not present in the next generation (offspring). In the generation after that, though, the trait showed up again. Mendel noticed these kinds of patterns in several other living things, too. Mendel wanted to learn more about what caused these patterns.

To keep his investigation simple, Mendel decided to study only one kind of organism. Because he had studied garden pea plants before, they seemed like a good choice.

Self-Pollinating Peas

In fact, garden peas were a good choice for several reasons. Pea plants grow quickly, and there are many different kinds available. They are also able to self-pollinate. A *self-pollinating plant* has both male and female reproductive structures. So, pollen from one flower can fertilize the ovule of the same flower or the ovule of another flower on the same plant. The flower on the right side of **Figure 2** is self-pollinating.

Why is it important that pea plants can self-pollinate? Because eggs (in an ovule) and sperm (in pollen) from the same plant combine to make a new plant, Mendel was able to grow true-breeding plants. When a *true-breeding plant* self-pollinates, all of its offspring will have the same trait as the parent. For example, a true-breeding plant with purple flowers will always have offspring with purple flowers.

Pea plants can also cross-pollinate. In *cross-pollination,* pollen from one plant fertilizes the ovule of a flower on a different plant. There are several ways that this can happen. Pollen may be carried by insects to a flower on a different plant. Pollen can also be carried by the wind from one flower to another. The left side of **Figure 2** shows these kinds of cross-pollination.

Describing Traits

How would you describe yourself? Would you say that you are tall or short, have curly hair or straight hair? Make a list of some of your physical traits. Make a second list of traits that you were not born with, such as "caring" or "good at soccer." Talk to your family about your lists. Do they agree with your descriptions?

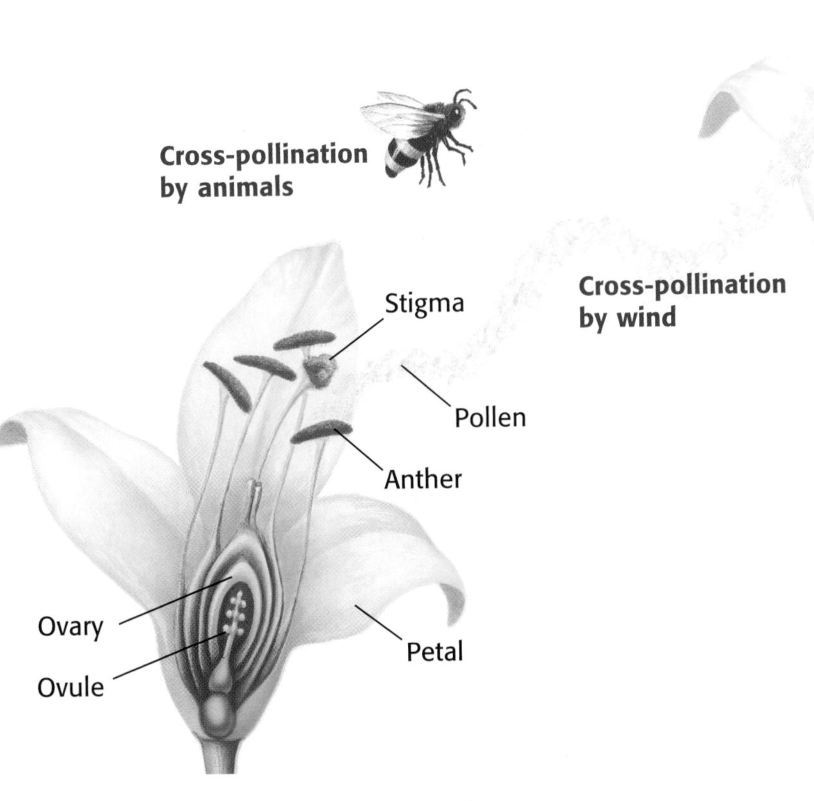

Figure 2 *During pollination, pollen from the anthers (male) is transferred to the stigma (female). Fertilization occurs when a sperm from the pollen travels through the stigma and enters the egg in an ovule.*

Characteristics

Mendel studied only one characteristic at a time. A *characteristic* is a feature that has different forms in a population. For example, hair color is a characteristic in humans. The different forms, such as brown or red hair, are called *traits*. Mendel used plants that had different traits for each of the characteristics he studied. For instance, for the characteristic of flower color, he chose plants that had purple flowers and plants that had white flowers. Three of the characteristics Mendel studied are shown in **Figure 3.**

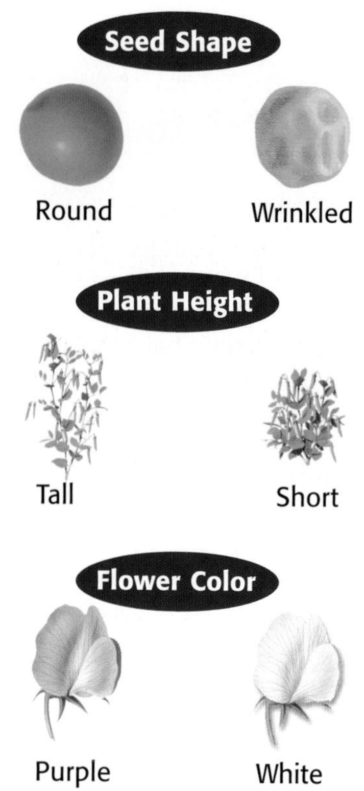

Figure 3 *These are some of the plant characteristics that Mendel studied.*

Mix and Match

Mendel was careful to use plants that were true breeding for each of the traits he was studying. By doing so, he would know what to expect if his plants were to self-pollinate. He decided to find out what would happen if he bred, or crossed, two plants that had different traits of a single characteristic. To be sure the plants cross-pollinated, he removed the anthers of one plant so that the plant could not self-pollinate. Then, he used pollen from another plant to fertilize the plant, as shown in **Figure 4.** This step allowed Mendel to select which plants would be crossed to produce offspring.

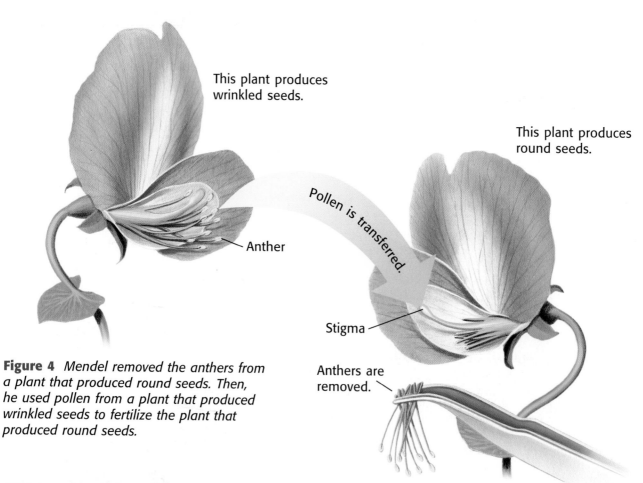

Figure 4 *Mendel removed the anthers from a plant that produced round seeds. Then, he used pollen from a plant that produced wrinkled seeds to fertilize the plant that produced round seeds.*

Mendel's First Experiments

In his first experiments, Mendel crossed pea plants to study seven different characteristics. In each cross, Mendel used plants that were true breeding for different traits for each characteristic. For example, he crossed plants that had purple flowers with plants that had white flowers. This cross is shown in the first part of **Figure 5.** The offspring from such a cross are called *first-generation plants.* All of the first-generation plants in this cross had purple flowers. Are you surprised by the results? What happened to the trait for white flowers?

Mendel got similar results for each cross. One trait was always present in the first generation, and the other trait seemed to disappear. Mendel chose to call the trait that appeared the **dominant trait.** Because the other trait seemed to fade into the background, Mendel called it the **recessive trait.** (To *recede* means "to go away or back off.") To find out what might have happened to the recessive trait, Mendel decided to do another set of experiments.

dominant trait the trait observed in the first generation when parents that have different traits are bred

recessive trait a trait that reappears in the second generation after disappearing in the first generation when parents with different traits are bred

Mendel's Second Experiments

Mendel allowed the first-generation plants to self-pollinate. **Figure 5** also shows what happened when a first-generation plant with purple flowers was allowed to self-pollinate. As you can see, the recessive trait for white flowers reappeared in the second generation.

Mendel did this same experiment on each of the seven characteristics. In each case, some of the second-generation plants had the recessive trait.

Reading Check Describe Mendel's second set of experiments.

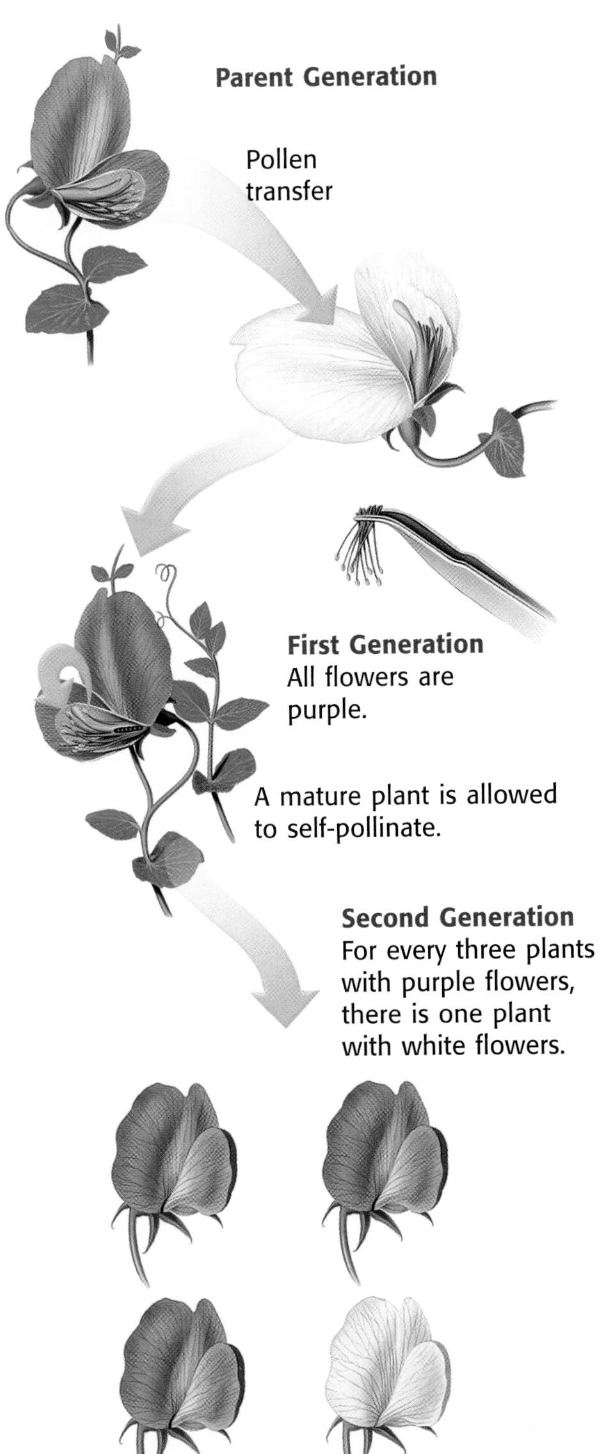
Parent Generation
Pollen transfer
First Generation
All flowers are purple.
A mature plant is allowed to self-pollinate.
Second Generation
For every three plants with purple flowers, there is one plant with white flowers.

Figure 5 *Mendel used the pollen from a plant with purple flowers to fertilize a plant with white flowers. Then, he allowed the offspring to self-pollinate.*

Understanding Ratios

A ratio is a way to compare two numbers. Look at **Table 1.** The ratio of plants with purple flowers to plants with white flowers can be written as 705 to 224 or 705:224. This ratio can be reduced, or simplified, by dividing the first number by the second as follows:

$$\frac{705}{224} = \frac{3.15}{1}$$

which is the same thing as a ratio of 3.15:1.

For every 3 plants with purple flowers, there will be roughly 1 plant with white flowers. Try this problem:

In a box of chocolates, there are 18 nougat-filled chocolates and 6 caramel-filled chocolates. What is the ratio of nougat-filled chocolates to caramel-filled chocolates?

Ratios in Mendel's Experiments

Mendel then decided to count the number of plants with each trait that turned up in the second generation. He hoped that this might help him explain his results. Take a look at Mendel's results, shown in **Table 1.**

As you can see, the recessive trait did not show up as often as the dominant trait. Mendel decided to figure out the ratio of dominant traits to recessive traits. A *ratio* is a relationship between two different numbers that is often expressed as a fraction. Calculate the dominant-to-recessive ratio for each characteristic. (If you need help, look at the Math Practice at left.) Do you notice anything interesting about the ratios? Round to the nearest whole number. Are the ratios all the same, or are they different?

Reading Check What is a ratio?

Table 1 Mendel's Results

Characteristic	Dominant traits	Recessive traits	Ratio
Flower color	705 purple	224 white	3.15:1
Seed color	6,002 yellow	2,001 green	?
Seed shape	5,474 round	1,850 wrinkled	?
Pod color	428 green	152 yellow	?
Pod shape	882 smooth	299 bumpy	?
Flower position	651 along stem	207 at tip	?
Plant height	787 tall	277 short	?

Gregor Mendel—Gone but Not Forgotten

Mendel realized that his results could be explained only if each plant had two sets of instructions for each characteristic. Each parent would then donate one set of instructions. In 1865, Mendel published his findings. But good ideas are sometimes overlooked or misunderstood at first. It wasn't until after his death, more than 30 years later, that Mendel's work was widely recognized. Once Mendel's ideas were rediscovered and understood, the door was opened to modern genetics. Genetic research, as shown in **Figure 6,** is one of the fastest changing fields in science today.

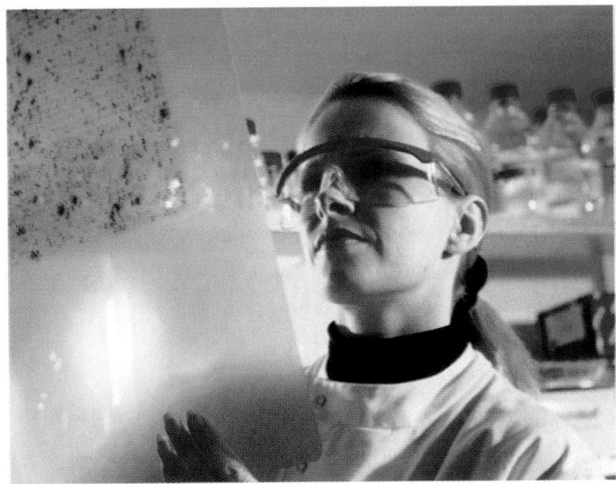

Figure 6 *This researcher is continuing the work started by Gregor Mendel more than 100 years ago.*

SECTION Review

Summary

- Heredity is the passing of traits from parents to offspring.
- Gregor Mendel made carefully planned experiments using pea plants that could self-pollinate.
- When parents with different traits are bred, dominant traits are always present in the first generation. Recessive traits are not visible in the first generation but reappear in the second generation.
- Mendel found a 3:1 ratio of dominant-to-recessive traits in the second generation.

Using Key Terms

1. Use each of the following terms in a separate sentence: *heredity, dominant trait,* and *recessive trait.*

Understanding Key Ideas

2. A plant that has both male and female reproductive structures is able to
   a. self-replicate.
   b. self-pollinate.
   c. change colors.
   d. None of the above
3. Explain the difference between self-pollination and cross-pollination.
4. What is the difference between a trait and a characteristic? Give one example of each.
5. Describe Mendel's first set of experiments.
6. Describe Mendel's second set of experiments.

Math Skills

7. In a bag of chocolate candies, there are 21 brown candies and 6 green candies. What is the ratio of brown to green? What is the ratio of green to brown?

Critical Thinking

8. **Predicting Consequences** Gregor Mendel used only true-breeding plants. If he had used plants that were not true breeding, do you think he would have discovered dominant and recessive traits? Explain.
9. **Applying Concepts** In cats, there are two types of ears: normal and curly. A curly-eared cat mated with a normal-eared cat, and all of the kittens had curly ears. Are curly ears a dominant or recessive trait? Explain.
10. **Identifying Relationships** List three other fields of study that use ratios.

SCiLINKS®
NSTA
Developed and maintained by the National Science Teachers Association
For a variety of links related to this chapter, go to www.scilinks.org
Topic: Heredity; Dominant and Recessive Traits
SciLinks code: HSM0738; HSM0423

SECTION 2

Traits and Inheritance

Mendel calculated the ratio of dominant traits to recessive traits. He found a ratio of 3:1. What did this tell him about how traits are passed from parents to offspring?

READING WARM-UP

Objectives

- Explain how genes and alleles are related to genotype and phenotype.
- Use the information in a Punnett square.
- Explain how probability can be used to predict possible genotypes in offspring.
- Describe three exceptions to Mendel's observations.

Terms to Learn

gene
allele
phenotype
genotype
probability

READING STRATEGY

Paired Summarizing Read this section silently. In pairs, take turns summarizing the material. Stop to discuss ideas that seem confusing.

A Great Idea

Mendel knew from his experiments with pea plants that there must be two sets of instructions for each characteristic. The first-generation plants carried the instructions for both the dominant trait and the recessive trait. Scientists now call these instructions for an inherited trait **genes.** Each parent gives one set of genes to the offspring. The offspring then has two forms of the same gene for every characteristic—one from each parent. The different forms (often dominant and recessive) of a gene are known as **alleles** (uh LEELZ). Dominant alleles are shown with a capital letter. Recessive alleles are shown with a lowercase letter.

Reading Check **What is the difference between a gene and an allele?** (*See the Appendix for answers to Reading Checks.*)

Phenotype

Genes affect the traits of offspring. An organism's appearance is known as its **phenotype** (FEE noh TIEP). In pea plants, possible phenotypes for the characteristic of flower color would be purple flowers or white flowers. For seed color, yellow and green seeds are the different phenotypes.

Phenotypes of humans are much more complicated than those of peas. Look at **Figure 1** below. The man has an inherited condition called *albinism* (AL buh NIZ uhm). Albinism prevents hair, skin, and eyes from having normal coloring.

gene one set of instructions for an inherited trait

allele one of the alternative forms of a gene that governs a characteristic, such as hair color

phenotype an organism's appearance or other detectable characteristic

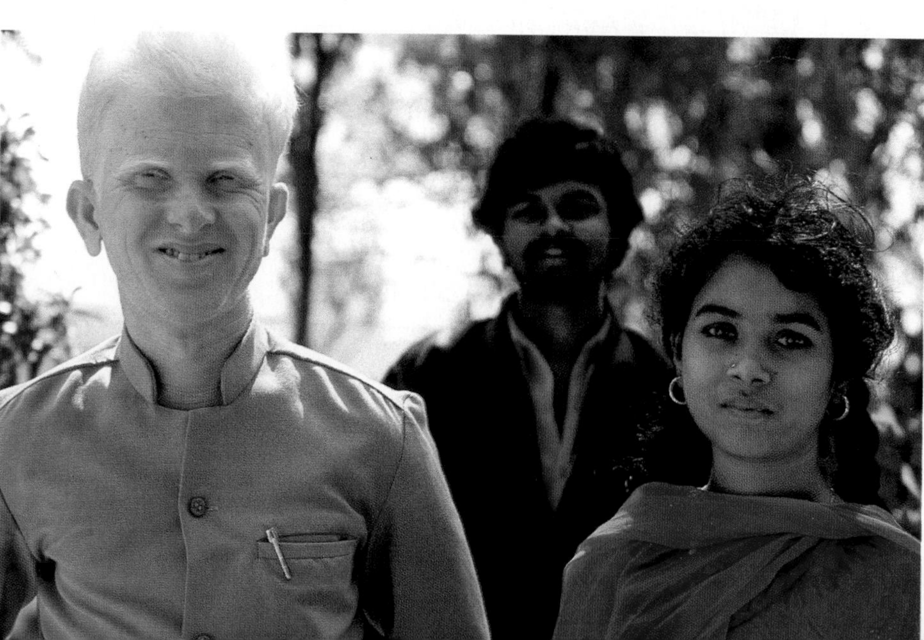

Figure 1 *Albinism is an inherited disorder that affects a person's phenotype in many ways.*

Genotype

Both inherited alleles together form an organism's **genotype.** Because the allele for purple flowers (*P*) is dominant, only one *P* allele is needed for the plant to have purple flowers. A plant with two dominant or two recessive alleles is said to be *homozygous* (HOH moh ZIE guhs). A plant that has the genotype *Pp* is said to be *heterozygous* (HET uhr OH ZIE guhs).

Punnett Squares

A Punnett square is used to organize all the possible combinations of offspring from particular parents. The alleles for a true-breeding, purple-flowered plant are written as *PP.* The alleles for a true-breeding, white-flowered plant are written as *pp.* The Punnett square for this cross is shown in **Figure 2.** All of the offspring have the same genotype: *Pp*. The dominant allele, *P,* in each genotype ensures that all of the offspring will be purple-flowered plants. The recessive allele, *p,* may be passed on to the next generation. This Punnett square shows the results of Mendel's first experiments.

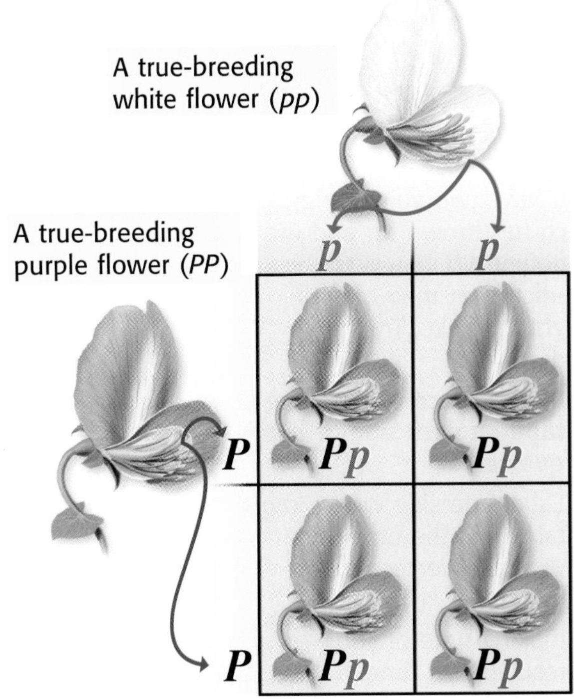

Figure 2 *All of the offspring for this cross have the same genotype—*Pp.

genotype the entire genetic makeup of an organism; also the combination of genes for one or more specific traits

Making a Punnett Square

1. Draw a square, and divide it into four sections.
2. Write the letters that represent alleles from one parent along the top of the box.
3. Write the letters that represent alleles from the other parent along the side of the box.
4. The cross shown at right is between two plants that produce round seeds. The genotype for each is *Rr*. Round seeds are dominant, and wrinkled seeds are recessive. Follow the arrows to see how the inside of the box was filled. The resulting alleles inside the box show all the possible genotypes for the offspring from this cross. What would the phenotypes for these offspring be?

Taking Your Chances

You have two guinea pigs. Each has brown fur and the genotype *Bb*. You want to predict what their offspring might look like. Try this to find out.

1. Stick a **piece of masking tape** on each side of **two quarters.**
2. Label one side with a capital *B* and the other side with a lowercase *b*.
3. Toss both coins 10 times, making note of your results each time.
4. How many times did you get the *bb* combination?
5. What is the probability that the next toss will result in *bb*?
6. What are the chances that the guinea pigs' offspring will have white fur (with the genotype *bb*)?

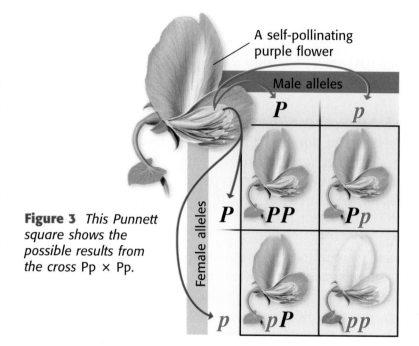

Figure 3 *This Punnett square shows the possible results from the cross* Pp × Pp.

More Evidence for Inheritance

In Mendel's second experiments, he allowed the first generation plants to self-pollinate. **Figure 3** shows a self-pollination cross of a plant with the genotype *Pp*. What are the possible genotypes of the offspring?

Notice that one square shows the genotype *Pp,* while another shows *pP*. These are exactly the same genotype. The other possible genotypes of the offspring are *PP* and *pp*. The combinations *PP, Pp,* and *pP* have the same phenotype—purple flowers. This is because each contains at least one dominant allele (*P*).

Only one combination, *pp,* produces plants that have white flowers. The ratio of dominant to recessive is 3:1, just as Mendel calculated from his data.

What Are the Chances?

Each parent has two alleles for each gene. When these alleles are different, as in *Pp,* offspring are equally likely to receive either allele. Think of a coin toss. There is a 50% chance you'll get heads and a 50% chance you'll get tails. The chance of receiving one allele or another is as random as a coin toss.

Probability

probability the likelihood that a possible future event will occur in any given instance of the event

The mathematical chance that something will happen is known as **probability.** Probability is most often written as a fraction or percentage. If you toss a coin, the probability of tossing tails is 1/2—you will get tails half the time.

Reading Check **What is probability?**

Probability If you roll a pair of dice, what is the probability that you will roll 2 threes?

Step 1: Count the number of faces on a single die. Put this number in the denominator: 6.

Step 2: Count how many ways you can roll a three with one die. Put this number in the numerator: 1/6.

Step 3: To find the probability that you will throw 2 threes, multiply the probability of throwing the first three by the probability of throwing the second three: $1/6 \times 1/6 = 1/36$.

Now It's Your Turn

If you roll a single die, what is the probability that you will roll an even number?

Calculating Probabilities

To find the probability that you will toss two heads in a row, multiply the probability of tossing the first head (1/2) by the probability of tossing the second head (1/2). The probability of tossing two heads in a row is 1/4.

Genotype Probability

To have white flowers, a pea plant must receive a *p* allele from each parent. Each offspring of a $Pp \times Pp$ cross has a 50% chance of receiving either allele from either parent. So, the probability of inheriting two *p* alleles is $1/2 \times 1/2$, which equals 1/4, or 25%. Traits in pea plants are easy to predict because there are only two choices for each trait, such as purple or white flowers and round or wrinkled seeds. Look at **Figure 4.** Do you see only two distinct choices for fur color?

Figure 4 *These kittens inherited one allele from their mother for each trait.*

CONNECTION TO Chemistry

Round and Wrinkled Round seeds may look better, but wrinkled seeds taste sweeter. The dominant allele for seed shape, *R*, causes sugar to be changed into starch (which is a storage molecule for sugar). This change makes the seed round. Seeds with the genotype *rr* do not make or store this starch. Because the sugar has not been changed into starch, the seed tastes sweeter. If you had a pea plant with round seeds (*Rr*), what would you cross it with to get some offspring with wrinkled seeds? Draw a Punnett square showing your cross.

ACTIVITY

More About Traits

As you may have already discovered, things are often more complicated than they first appear to be. Gregor Mendel uncovered the basic principles of how genes are passed from one generation to the next. But as scientists learned more about heredity, they began to find exceptions to Mendel's principles. A few of these exceptions are explained below.

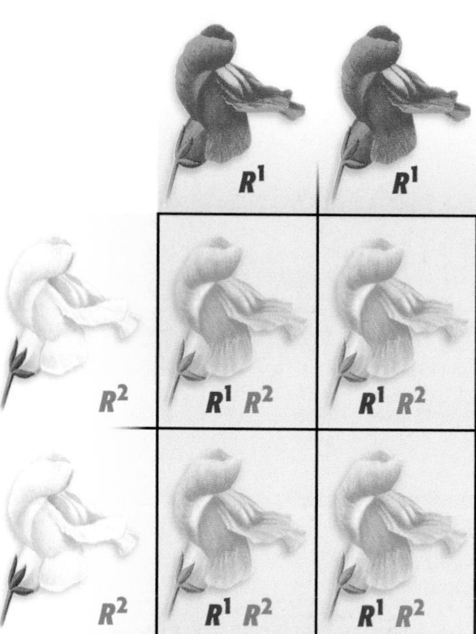

Figure 5 *Cross-breeding two true-breeding snapdragons provides a good example of incomplete dominance.*

Incomplete Dominance

Since Mendel's discoveries, researchers have found that sometimes one trait is not completely dominant over another. These traits do not blend together, but each allele has its own degree of influence. This is known as *incomplete dominance.*

One example of incomplete dominance is found in the snapdragon flower. **Figure 5** shows a cross between a true-breeding red snapdragon (R^1R^1) and a true-breeding white snapdragon (R^2R^2). As you can see, all of the possible phenotypes for their offspring are pink because both alleles of the gene have some degree of influence.

Reading Check What is incomplete dominance?

One Gene, Many Traits

Sometimes one gene influences more than one trait. An example of this phenomenon is shown by the white tiger in **Figure 6.** The white fur is caused by a single gene, but this gene influences more than just fur color. Do you see anything else unusual about the tiger? If you look closely, you'll see that the tiger has blue eyes. Here, the gene that controls fur color also influences eye color.

Figure 6 *The gene that gave this tiger white fur also influenced its eye color.*

Many Genes, One Trait

Some traits, such as the color of your skin, hair, and eyes, are the result of several genes acting together. Therefore, it's difficult to tell if some traits are the result of a dominant or a recessive gene. Different combinations of alleles result in different eye-color shades, as shown in **Figure 7.**

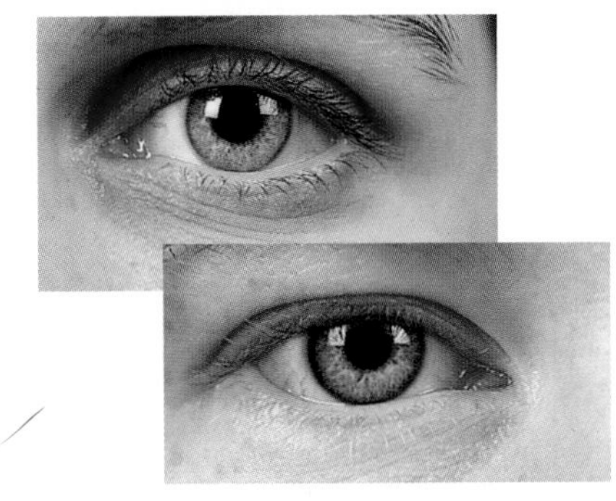

Figure 7 *At least two genes determine human eye color. That's why many shades of a single color are possible.*

The Importance of Environment

Genes aren't the only influences on traits. A guinea pig could have the genes for long fur, but its fur could be cut. In the same way, your environment influences how you grow. Your genes may make it possible that you will grow to be tall, but you need a healthy diet to reach your full potential height.

SECTION Review

Summary

- Instructions for an inherited trait are called *genes*. For each gene, there are two alleles, one inherited from each parent. Both alleles make up an organism's genotype. Phenotype is an organism's appearance.
- Punnett squares show all possible offspring genotypes.
- Probability can be used to describe possible outcomes in offspring and the likelihood of each outcome.
- Incomplete dominance occurs when one allele is not completely dominant over the other allele.
- Some genes influence more than one trait.

Using Key Terms

1. Use the following terms in the same sentence: *gene* and *allele.*
2. In your own words, write a definition for each of the following terms: *genotype* and *phenotype.*

Understanding Key Ideas

3. Use a Punnett square to determine the possible genotypes of the offspring of a *BB* × *Bb* cross.
   a. all *BB* **c.** *BB, Bb, bb*
   b. *BB, Bb* **d.** all *bb*
4. How are genes and alleles related to genotype and phenotype?
5. Describe three exceptions to Mendel's observations.

Math Skills

6. What is the probability of rolling a five on one die three times in a row?

Critical Thinking

7. **Applying Concepts** The allele for a cleft chin, *C*, is dominant among humans. What are the results of a cross between parents with genotypes *Cc* and *cc*?

Interpreting Graphics

The Punnett square below shows the alleles for fur color in rabbits. Black fur, *B*, is dominant over white fur, *b*.

?
?
?
Bb
Bb
?
Bb
Bb

8. Given the combinations shown, what are the genotypes of the parents?
9. If black fur had incomplete dominance over white fur, what color would the offspring be?

SCILINKS
NSTA
Developed and maintained by the National Science Teachers Association
For a variety of links related to this chapter, go to www.scilinks.org
Topic: Genotypes; Phenotypes
SciLinks code: HSM0664; HSM1135

SECTION 3

Meiosis

Where are genes located, and how do they pass information? Understanding reproduction is the first step to finding the answers.

READING WARM-UP

Objectives

- Explain the difference between mitosis and meiosis.
- Describe how chromosomes determine sex.
- Explain why sex-linked disorders occur in one sex more often than in the other.
- Interpret a pedigree.

Terms to Learn

homologous chromosomes
meiosis
sex chromosome
pedigree

READING STRATEGY

Reading Organizer As you read this section, make a flowchart of the steps of meiosis.

There are two kinds of reproduction: asexual and sexual. Asexual reproduction results in offspring with genotypes that are exact copies of their parent's genotype. Sexual reproduction produces offspring that share traits with their parents but are not exactly like either parent.

Asexual Reproduction

In *asexual reproduction,* only one parent cell is needed. The structures inside the cell are copied, and then the parent cell divides, making two exact copies. This type of cell reproduction is known as *mitosis*. Most of the cells in your body and most single-celled organisms reproduce in this way.

Sexual Reproduction

In sexual reproduction, two parent cells join together to form offspring that are different from both parents. The parent cells are called *sex cells*. Sex cells are different from ordinary body cells. Human body cells have 46, or 23 pairs of, chromosomes. One set of human chromosomes is shown in **Figure 1.** Chromosomes that carry the same sets of genes are called **homologous** (hoh MAHL uh guhs) **chromosomes.** Imagine a pair of shoes. Each shoe is like a homologous chromosome. The pair represents a homologous pair of chromosomes. But human sex cells are different. They have 23 chromosomes—half the usual number. Each sex cell has only one of the chromosomes from each homologous pair. Sex cells have only one "shoe."

homologous chromosomes chromosomes that have the same sequence of genes and the same structure

meiosis a process in cell division during which the number of chromosomes decreases to half the original number by two divisions of the nucleus, which results in the production of sex cells

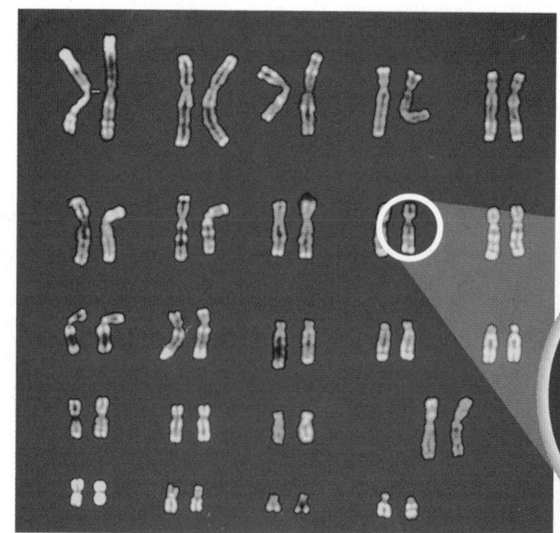

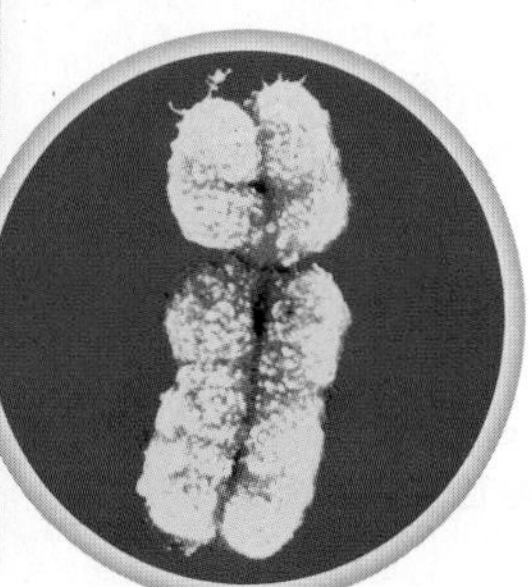

Figure 1 *Human body cells have 23 pairs of chromosomes. One member of a pair of homologous chromosomes is shown below.*

Meiosis

Sex cells are made during meiosis (mie OH sis). **Meiosis** is a copying process that produces cells with half the usual number of chromosomes. Each sex cell receives one-half of each homologous pair. For example, a human egg cell has 23 chromosomes, and a sperm cell has 23 chromosomes. The new cell that forms when an egg cell and a sperm cell join has 46 chromosomes.

Reading Check **How many chromosomes does a human egg cell have?** *(See the Appendix for answers to Reading Checks.)*

Genes and Chromosomes

What does all of this have to do with the location of genes? Not long after Mendel's work was rediscovered, a graduate student named Walter Sutton made an important observation. Sutton was studying sperm cells in grasshoppers. Sutton knew of Mendel's studies, which showed that the egg and sperm must each contribute the same amount of information to the offspring. That was the only way the 3:1 ratio found in the second generation could be explained. Sutton also knew from his own studies that although eggs and sperm were different, they did have something in common: Their chromosomes were located inside a nucleus. Using his observations of meiosis, his understanding of Mendel's work, and some creative thinking, Sutton proposed something very important:

Genes are located on chromosomes!

Understanding meiosis was critical to finding the location of genes. Before you learn about meiosis, review mitosis, shown in **Figure 2.** Meiosis is outlined in **Figure 3** on the next two pages.

CONNECTION TO Language Arts

Greek Roots The word *mitosis* is related to a Greek word that means "threads." Threadlike spindles are visible during mitosis. The word *meiosis* comes from a Greek word that means "to make smaller." How do you think meiosis got its name?

Figure 2 **Mitosis Revisited**

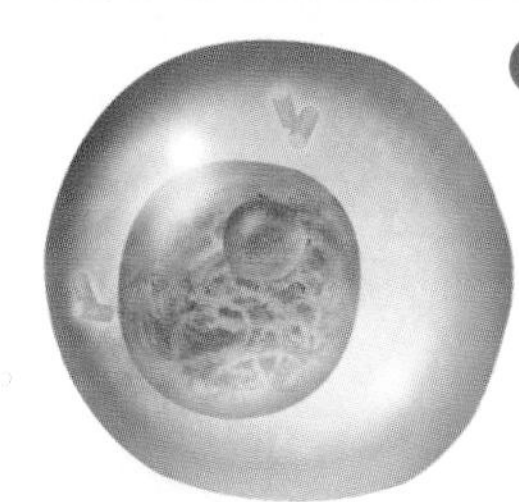

1 Each chromosome is copied.

2 The chromosomes thicken and shorten. Each chromosome consists of two identical copies, called *chromatids.*

3 The nuclear membrane dissolves. The chromatids line up along the equator (center) of the cell.

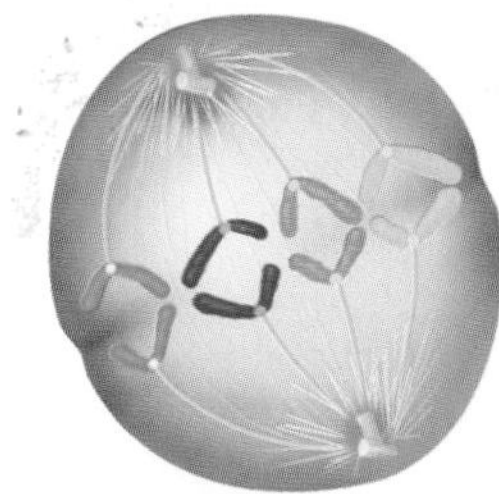

4 The chromatids pull apart.

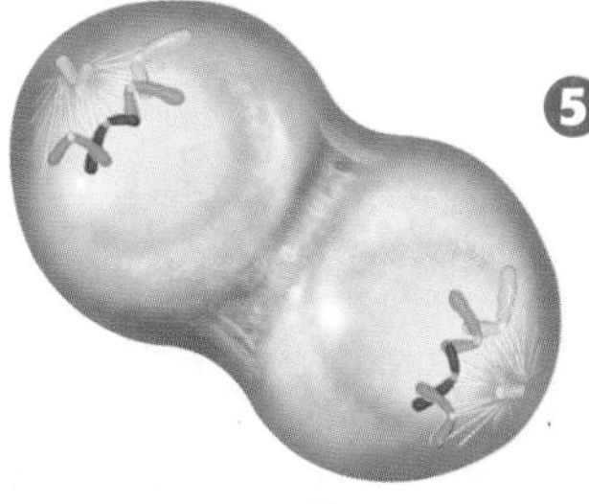

5 The nuclear membrane forms around the separated chromatids. The chromosomes unwind, and the cell divides.

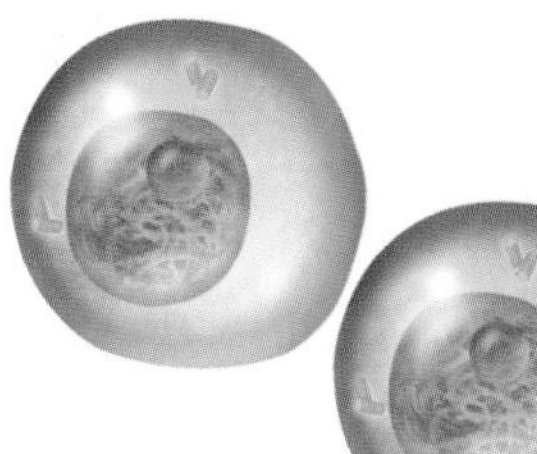

6 The result is two identical copies of the original cell.

The Steps of Meiosis

During mitosis, chromosomes are copied once, and then the nucleus divides once. During meiosis, chromosomes are copied once, and then the nucleus divides twice. The resulting sperm and eggs have half the number of chromosomes of a normal body cell. **Figure 3** shows all eight steps of meiosis. Read about each step as you look at the figure. Different types of living things have different numbers of chromosomes. In this illustration, only four chromosomes are shown.

Reading Check **How many cells are made from one parent cell during meiosis?**

Figure 3 **Steps of Meiosis**

Read about each step as you look at the diagram. Different types of living things have different numbers of chromosomes. In this diagram, only four chromosomes are shown.

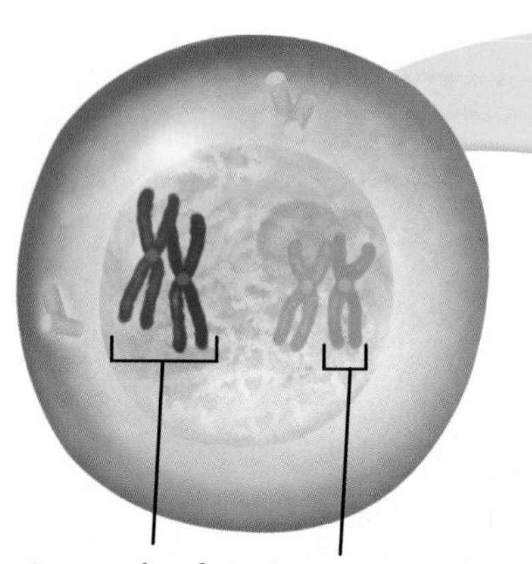

One pair of homologous chromosomes

Two chromatids

1 Before meiosis begins, the chromosomes are in a threadlike form. Each chromosome makes an exact copy of itself, forming two halves called *chromatids*. The chromosomes then thicken and shorten into a form that is visible under a microscope. The nuclear membrane disappears.

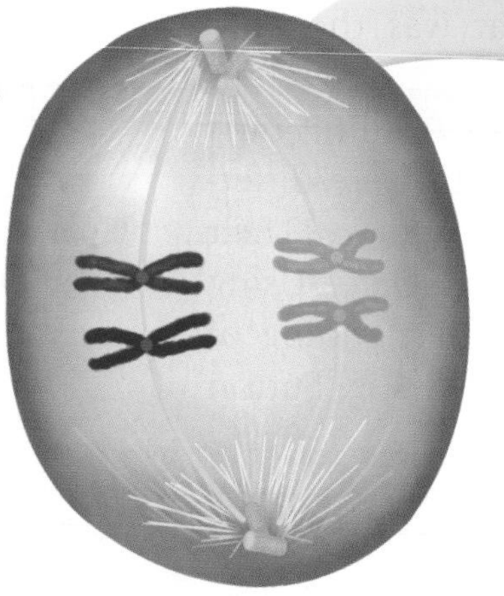

2 Each chromosome is now made up of two identical chromatids. Similar chromosomes pair with one another, and the paired homologous chromosomes line up at the equator of the cell.

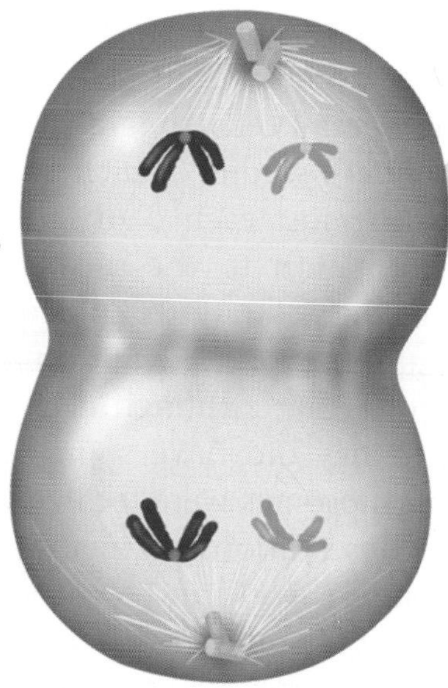

3 The chromosomes separate from their homologous partners and then move to opposite ends of the cell.

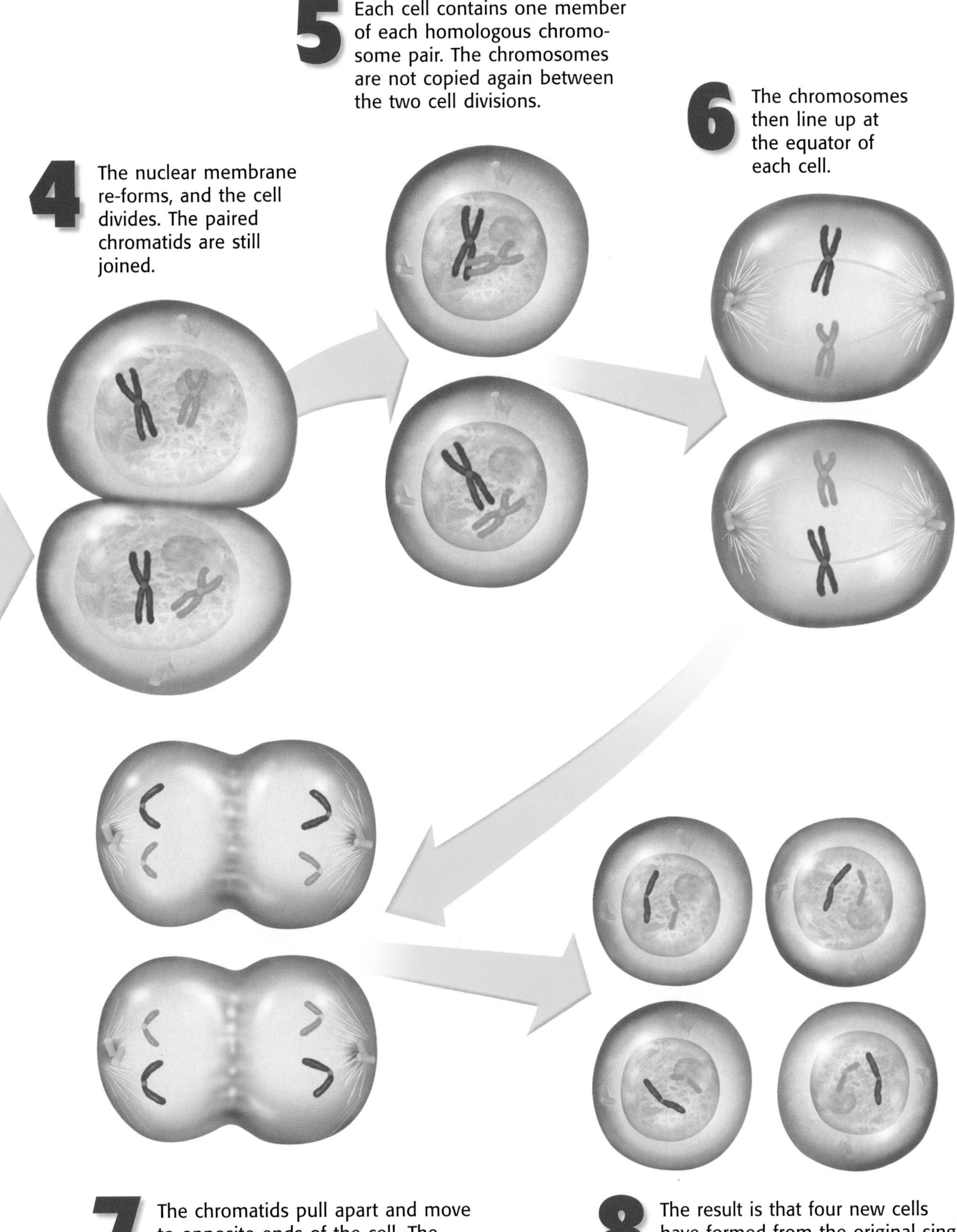

5
Each cell contains one member of each homologous chromosome pair. The chromosomes are not copied again between the two cell divisions.
6
The chromosomes then line up at the equator of each cell.
4
The nuclear membrane re-forms, and the cell divides. The paired chromatids are still joined.
7
The chromatids pull apart and move to opposite ends of the cell. The nuclear membrane forms around the separated chromosomes, and the cells divide.
8
The result is that four new cells have formed from the original single cell. Each new cell has half the number of chromosomes present in the original cell.

Meiosis and Mendel

As Walter Sutton figured out, the steps in meiosis explained Mendel's results. **Figure 4** shows what happens to a pair of homologous chromosomes during meiosis and fertilization. The cross shown is between a plant that is true breeding for round seeds and a plant that is true breeding for wrinkled seeds.

Each fertilized egg in the first generation had one dominant allele and one recessive allele for seed shape. Only one genotype was possible because all sperm formed by the male parent during meiosis had the wrinkled-seed allele, and all of the female parent's eggs had the round-seed allele. Meiosis also helped explain other inherited characteristics.

Figure 4 **Meiosis and Dominance**

Male Parent In the plant-cell nucleus below, each homologous chromosome has an allele for seed shape, and each allele carries the same instructions: to make wrinkled seeds.

Female Parent In the plant-cell nucleus below, each homologous chromosome has an allele for seed shape, and each allele carries the same instructions: to make round seeds.

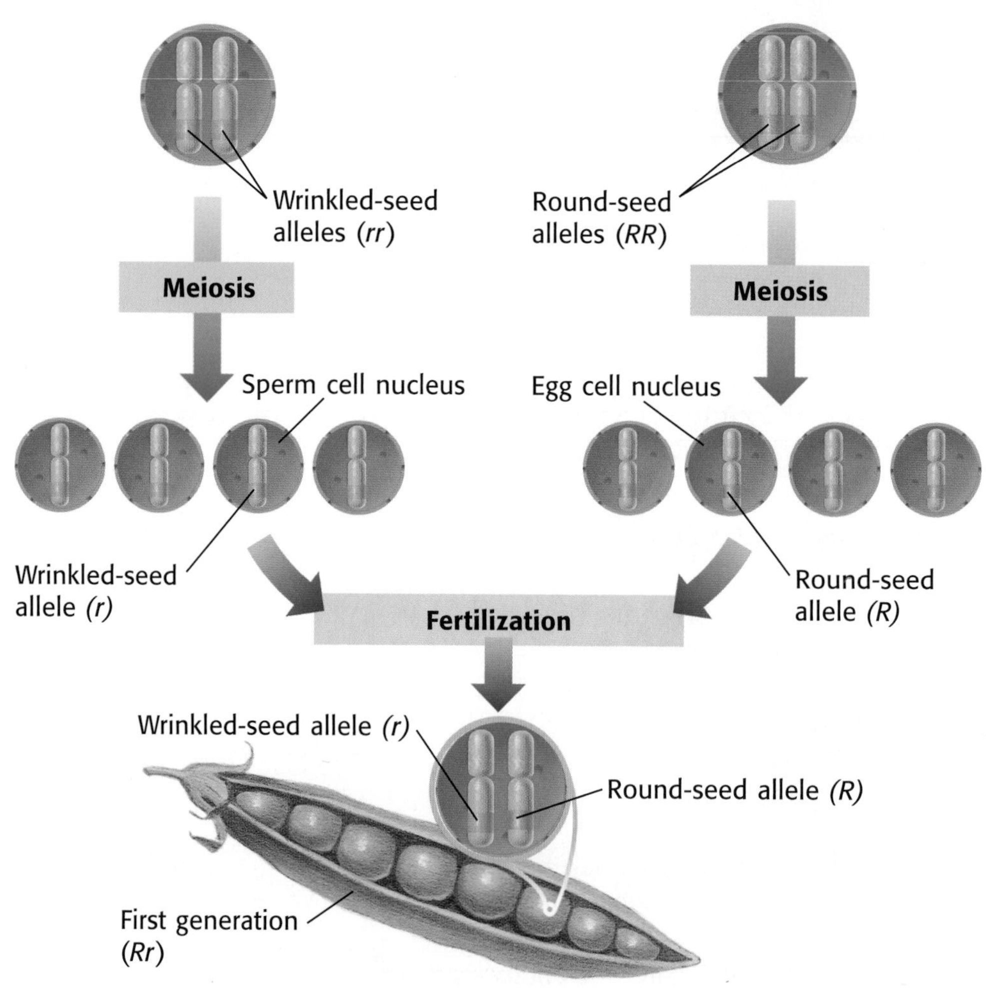

a Following **meiosis,** each sperm cell has a recessive allele for wrinkled seeds, and each egg cell has a dominant allele for round seeds.

b **Fertilization** of any egg by any sperm results in the same genotype (*Rr*) and the same phenotype (round). This result is exactly what Mendel found in his studies.

Sex Chromosomes

Information contained on chromosomes determines many of our traits. **Sex chromosomes** carry genes that determine sex. In humans, females have two X chromosomes. But human males have one X chromosome and one Y chromosome.

During meiosis, one of each of the chromosome pairs ends up in a sex cell. Females have two X chromosomes in each body cell. When meiosis produces the egg cells, each egg gets one X chromosome. Males have both an X chromosome and a Y chromosome in each body cell. Meiosis produces sperm with either an X or a Y chromosome. An egg fertilized by a sperm with an X chromosome will produce a female. If the sperm contains a Y chromosome, the offspring will be male, as shown in **Figure 5.**

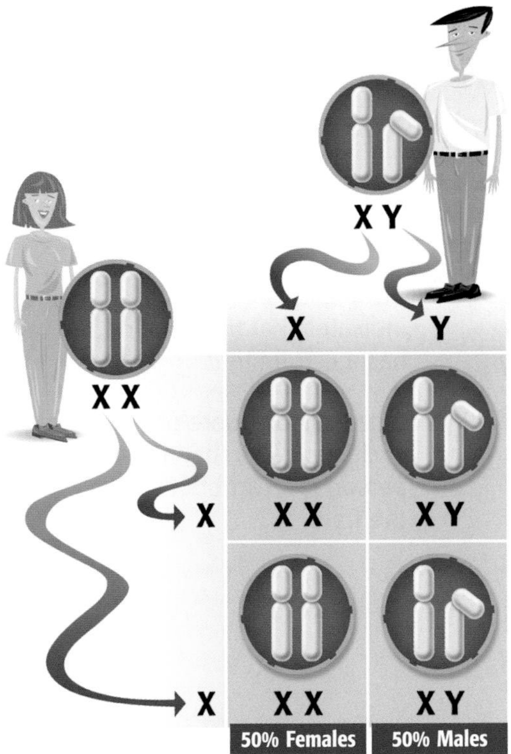

Figure 5 *Egg and sperm combine to form either the XX or XY combination.*

sex chromosome one of the pair of chromosomes that determine the sex of an individual

Sex-Linked Disorders

The Y chromosome does not carry all of the genes of an X chromosome. Females have two X chromosomes, so they carry two copies of each gene found on the X chromosome. This makes a backup gene available if one becomes damaged. Males have only one copy of each gene on their one X chromosome. The genes for certain disorders, such as colorblindness, are carried on the X chromosome. These disorders are called *sex-linked disorders.* Because the gene for such disorders is recessive, men are more likely to have sex-linked disorders.

People who are colorblind can have trouble distinguishing between shades of red and green. To help the colorblind, some cities have added shapes to their street lights, as shown in **Figure 6.** Hemophilia (HEE moh FIL ee uh) is another sex-linked disorder. Hemophilia prevents blood from clotting, and people with hemophilia bleed for a long time after small cuts. Hemophilia can be fatal.

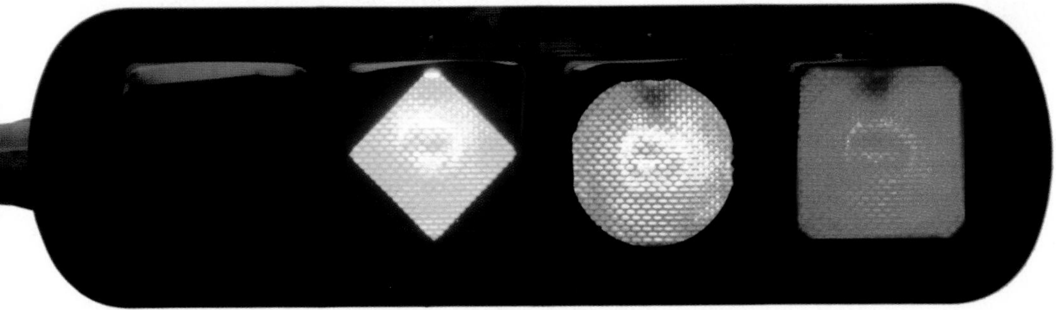

Figure 6 *This stoplight in Canada is designed to help the colorblind see signals easily. This photograph was taken over a few minutes to show all three shapes.*

Figure 7 **Pedigree for a Recessive Disease**

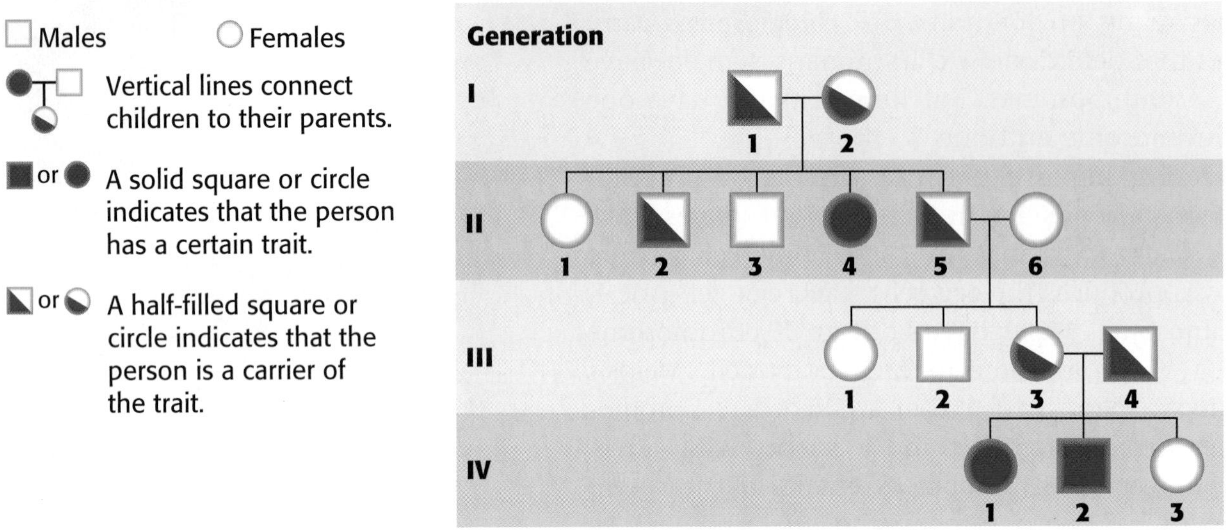

Males Females

Vertical lines connect children to their parents.

or A solid square or circle indicates that the person has a certain trait.

or A half-filled square or circle indicates that the person is a carrier of the trait.

Generation

I 1 2

II 1 2 3 4 5 6

III 1 2 3 4

IV 1 2 3

Genetic Counseling

Hemophilia and other genetic disorders can be traced through a family tree. If people are worried that they might pass a disease to their children, they may consult a genetic counselor. These counselors often make use of a diagram known as a **pedigree,** which is a tool for tracing a trait through generations of a family. By making a pedigree, a counselor can often predict whether a person is a carrier of a hereditary disease. The pedigree shown in **Figure 7** traces a disease called *cystic fibrosis* (SIS tik FIE broh sis). Cystic fibrosis causes serious lung problems. People with this disease have inherited two recessive alleles. Both parents need to be carriers of the gene for the disease to show up in their children.

pedigree a diagram that shows the occurrence of a genetic trait in several generations of a family

Pedigrees can be drawn up to trace any trait through a family tree. You could even draw a pedigree that would show how you inherited your hair color. Many different pedigrees could be drawn for a typical family.

Selective Breeding

For thousands of years, humans have seen the benefits of the careful breeding of plants and animals. In *selective breeding,* organisms with desirable characteristics are mated. You have probably enjoyed the benefits of selective breeding, although you may not have realized it. For example, you have probably eaten an egg from a chicken that was bred to produce more eggs. Your pet dog may be a result of selective breeding. Roses, like the one shown in **Figure 8,** have been selectively bred to produce large flowers. Wild roses are much smaller and have fewer petals than roses that you could buy at a nursery.

Figure 8 *Roses have been selectively bred to create large, bright flowers.*

SECTION Review

- In mitosis, chromosomes are copied once, and then the nucleus divides once. In meiosis, chromosomes are copied once, and then the nucleus divides twice.
- The process of meiosis produces sex cells, which have half the number of chromosomes. These two halves combine during reproduction.
- In humans, females have two X chromosomes. So, each egg contains one X chromosome. Males have both an X and a Y chromosome. So, each sperm cell contains either an X or a Y chromosome.
- Sex-linked disorders occur in males more often than in females. Colorblindness and hemophilia are examples of sex-linked disorders.
- A pedigree is a diagram used to trace a trait through many generations of a family.

Using Key Terms

1. Use each of the following terms in the same sentence: *meiosis* and *sex chromosomes*.

In each of the following sentences, replace the incorrect term with the correct term from the word bank.

pedigree	homologous chromosomes
meiosis	mitosis

2. During fertilization, chromosomes are copied, and then the nucleus divides twice.
3. A Punnett square is used to show how inherited traits move through a family.
4. During meiosis, sex cells line up in the middle of the cell.

Understanding Key Ideas

5. Genes are found on
   a. chromosomes.
   b. proteins.
   c. alleles.
   d. sex cells.
6. If there are 14 chromosomes in pea plant cells, how many chromosomes are present in a sex cell of a pea plant?
7. Draw the eight steps of meiosis. Label one chromosome, and show its position in each step.

Interpreting Graphics

Use this pedigree to answer the question below.

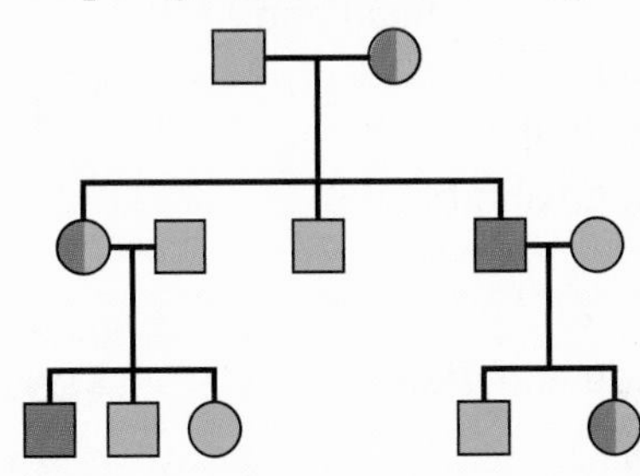

8. Is this disorder sex linked? Explain your reasoning.

Critical Thinking

9. **Identifying Relationships** Put the following in order of smallest to largest: chromosome, gene, and cell.
10. **Applying Concepts** A pea plant has purple flowers. What alleles for flower color could the sex cells carry?

SCILINKS.
NSTA
Developed and maintained by the National Science Teachers Association
For a variety of links related to this chapter, go to www.scilinks.org
Topic: Meiosis; Genetic Diseases, Screening, Counseling
SciLinks code: HSM0935; HSM0651

Using Scientific Methods

Model-Making Lab

Bug Builders, Inc.

Imagine that you are a designer for a toy company that makes toy alien bugs. The president of Bug Builders, Inc., wants new versions of the wildly popular Space Bugs, but he wants to use the bug parts that are already in the warehouse. It's your job to come up with a new bug design. You have studied how traits are passed from one generation to another. You will use this knowledge to come up with new combinations of traits and assemble the bug parts in new ways. Model A and Model B, shown below, will act as the "parent" bugs.

OBJECTIVES

Build models to further your understanding of inheritance.

Examine the traits of a population of offspring.

MATERIALS

- allele sacks (14) (supplied by your teacher)
- gumdrops, green and black (feet)
- map pins (eyes)
- marshmallows, large (head and body segments)
- pipe cleaners (tails)
- pushpins, green and blue (noses)
- scissors
- toothpicks, red and green (antennae)

SAFETY

Ask a Question

1. If there are two forms of each of the seven traits, then how many possible combinations are there?

Form a Hypothesis

2. Write a hypothesis that is a possible answer to the question above. Explain your reasoning.

Test the Hypothesis

3. Your teacher will display 14 allele sacks. The sacks will contain slips of paper with capital or lowercase letters on them. Take one piece of paper from each sack. (Remember: Capital letters represent dominant alleles, and lowercase letters represent recessive alleles.) One allele is from "Mom," and one allele is from "Dad." After you have recorded the alleles you have drawn, place the slips of paper back into the sack.

Model A ("Mom")
- red antennae
- 3 body segments
- curly tail
- 2 pairs of legs
- green nose
- black feet
- 3 eyes

Model B ("Dad")
- green antennae
- 2 body segments
- straight tail
- 3 pairs of legs
- blue nose
- green feet
- 2 eyes

Bug Family Traits				
Trait	**Model A "Mom" allele**	**Model B "Dad" allele**	**New model "Baby" genotype**	**New model "Baby" phenotype**
Antennae color				
Number of body segments				
Tail shape				
Number of leg pairs				
Nose color				
Foot color				
Number of eyes				

4. Create a table like the one above. Fill in the first two columns with the alleles that you selected from the sacks. Next, fill in the third column with the genotype of the new model ("Baby").

5. Use the information below to fill in the last column of the table.

Genotypes and Phenotypes	
RR or *Rr*—red antennae	*rr*—green antennae
SS or *Ss*—3 body segments	*ss*—2 body segments
CC or *Cc*—curly tail	*cc*—straight tail
LL or *Ll*—3 pairs of legs	*ll*—2 pairs of legs
BB or *Bb*—blue nose	*bb*—green nose
GG or *Gg*—green feet	*gg*—black feet
EE or *Ee*—2 eyes	*ee*—3 eyes

6. Now that you have filled out your table, you are ready to pick the parts you need to assemble your bug. (Toothpicks can be used to hold the head and body segments together and as legs to attach the feet to the body.)

Analyze the Results

1. **Organizing Data** Take a poll of the traits of the offspring. What are the ratios for each trait?

2. **Examining Data** Do any of the new models look exactly like the parents? Explain.

Draw Conclusions

3. **Interpreting Information** What are the possible genotypes of the parent bugs?

4. **Making Predictions** How many different genotypes are possible in the offspring?

Applying Your Data

Find a mate for your "Baby" bug. What are the possible genotypes and phenotypes of the offspring from this match?

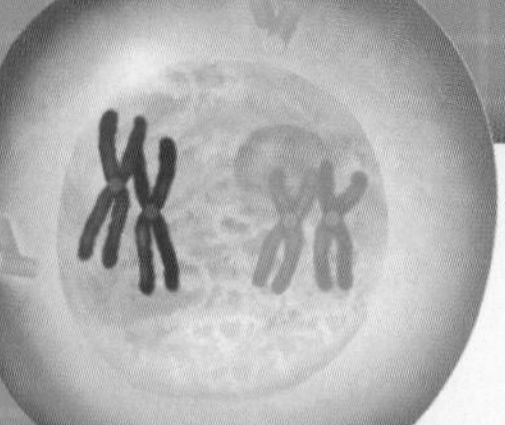

Chapter Review

USING KEY TERMS

Complete each of the following sentences by choosing the correct term from the word bank.

sex cells	genotype
sex chromosomes	alleles
phenotype	meiosis

1. Sperm and eggs are known as ____.

2. The ____ is the expression of a trait and is determined by the combination of alleles called the ____.

3. ____ produces cells with half the normal number of chromosomes.

4. Different versions of the same genes are called ____.

UNDERSTANDING KEY IDEAS

Multiple Choice

5. Genes carry information that determines
   - **a.** alleles.
   - **b.** ribosomes.
   - **c.** chromosomes.
   - **d.** traits.

6. The process that produces sex cells is
   - **a.** mitosis.
   - **b.** photosynthesis.
   - **c.** meiosis.
   - **d.** probability.

7. The passing of traits from parents to offspring is called
   - **a.** probability.
   - **b.** heredity.
   - **c.** recessive.
   - **d.** meiosis.

8. If you cross a white flower with the genotype *pp* with a purple flower with the genotype *PP*, the possible genotypes in the offspring are
   - **a.** *PP* and *pp*.
   - **b.** all *Pp*.
   - **c.** all *PP*.
   - **d.** all *pp*.

9. For the cross in item 8, what would the phenotypes be?
   - **a.** all white
   - **b.** 3 purple and 1 white
   - **c.** all purple
   - **d.** half white, half purple

10. In meiosis,
    - **a.** chromosomes are copied twice.
    - **b.** the nucleus divides once.
    - **c.** four cells are produced from a single cell.
    - **d.** two cells are produced from a single cell.

11. When one trait is not completely dominant over another, it is called
    - **a.** recessive.
    - **b.** incomplete dominance.
    - **c.** environmental factors.
    - **d.** uncertain dominance.

Short Answer

12 Which sex chromosomes do females have? Which do males have?

13 In one or two sentences, define the term *recessive trait* in your own words.

14 How are sex cells different from other body cells?

15 What is a sex-linked disorder? Give one example of a sex-linked disorder that is found in humans.

CRITICAL THINKING

16 **Concept Mapping** Use the following terms to create a concept map: *meiosis, eggs, cell division, X chromosome, mitosis, Y chromosome, sperm,* and *sex cells.*

17 **Identifying Relationships** If you were a carrier of one allele for a certain recessive disorder, how could genetic counseling help you prepare for the future?

18 **Applying Concepts** If a child has blond hair and both of her parents have brown hair, what does that tell you about the allele for blond hair? Explain.

19 **Applying Concepts** What is the genotype of a pea plant that is true-breeding for purple flowers?

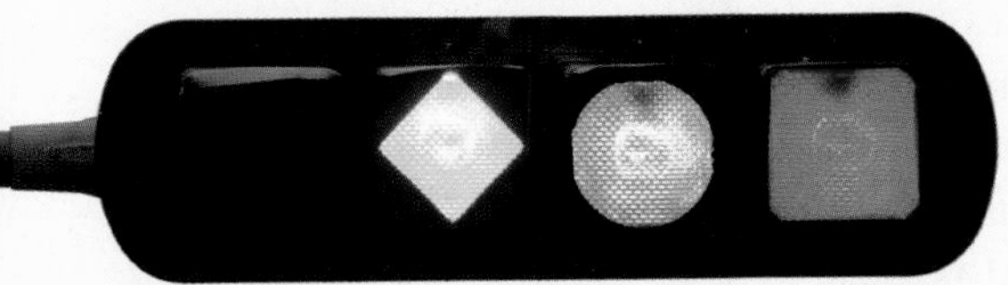

INTERPRETING GRAPHICS

Use the Punnett square below to answer the questions that follow.

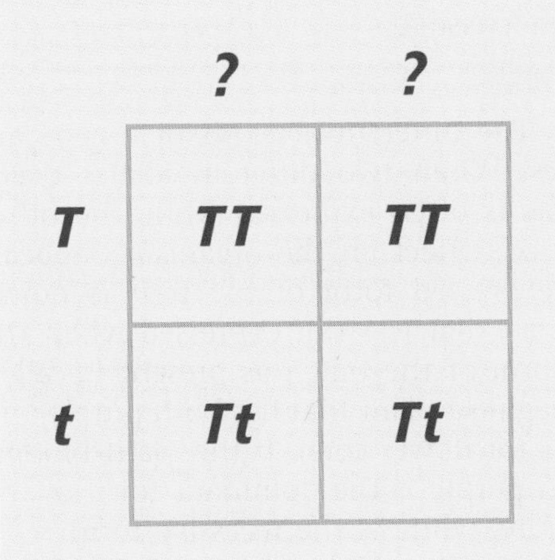

20 What is the unknown genotype?

21 If *T* represents the allele for tall pea plants and *t* represents the allele for short pea plants, what is the phenotype of each parent and of the offspring?

22 If each of the offspring were allowed to self-fertilize, what are the possible genotypes in the next generation?

23 What is the probability of each genotype in item 22?

Standardized Test Preparation

READING

Read the passages below. Then, answer the questions that follow each passage.

Passage 1 The different versions of a gene are called *alleles*. When two different alleles occur together, one is often expressed while the other has no obvious effect on the organism's appearance. The expressed form of the trait is dominant. The trait that was not expressed when the dominant form of the trait was present is called *recessive*. Imagine a plant that has both purple and white alleles for flower color. If the plant blooms purple, then purple is the dominant form of the trait. Therefore, white is the recessive form.

1. According to the passage, which of the following statements is true?

A All alleles are expressed all of the time.
B All traits for flower color are dominant.
C When two alleles are present, the expressed form of the trait is dominant.
D A recessive form of a trait is always expressed.

2. According to the passage, a trait that is not expressed when the dominant form is present is called

F recessive.
G an allele.
H heredity.
I a gene.

3. According to the passage, which allele for flower color is dominant?

A white
B pink
C purple
D yellow

Passage 2 Sickle cell anemia is a recessive genetic disorder. People inherit this disorder only when they inherit the disease-causing recessive allele from both parents. The disease causes the body to make red blood cells that bend into a sickle (or crescent moon) shape. The sickle-shaped red blood cells break apart easily. Therefore, the blood of a person with sickle cell anemia carries less oxygen. Sickle-shaped blood cells also tend to get stuck in blood vessels. When a blood vessel is blocked, the blood supply to organs can be cut off. But the sickle-shaped blood cells can also protect a person from malaria. Malaria is a disease caused by an organism that invades red blood cells.

1. According to the passage, sickle cell anemia is a

A recessive genetic disorder.
B dominant genetic disorder.
C disease caused by an organism that invades red blood cells.
D disease also called *malaria*.

2. According to the passage, sickle cell anemia can help protect a person from

F blocked blood vessels.
G genetic disorders.
H malaria.
I low oxygen levels.

3. Which of the following is a fact in the passage?

A When blood vessels are blocked, vital organs lose their blood supply.
B When blood vessels are blocked, it causes the red blood cells to bend into sickle shapes.
C The blood of a person with sickle cell anemia carries more oxygen.
D Healthy red blood cells never get stuck in blood vessels.

INTERPRETING GRAPHICS

The Punnett square below shows a cross between two flowering plants. Use this Punnett square to answer the questions that follow.

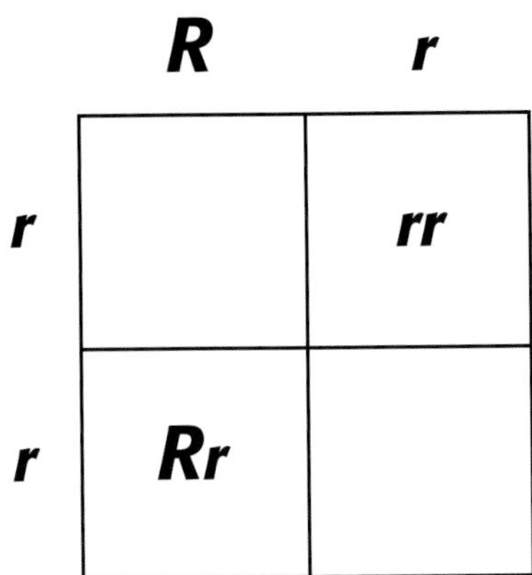

1. What is the genotype of the offspring represented in the upper left-hand box of the Punnett square?
   - **A** *RR*
   - **B** *Rr*
   - **C** *rr*
   - **D** *rrr*

2. What is the genotype of the offspring represented in the lower right-hand box of the Punnett square?
   - **F** *RR*
   - **G** *Rr*
   - **H** *rr*
   - **I** *rrr*

3. What is the ratio of *Rr* (purple-flowered plants) to *rr* (white-flowered plants) in the offspring?
   - **A** 1:3
   - **B** 2:2
   - **C** 3:1
   - **D** 4:0

MATH

Read each question below, and choose the best answer.

1. What is another way to write $4 \times 4 \times 4$?
   - **A** 4^2
   - **B** 4^3
   - **C** 3^3
   - **D** 3^4

2. Jane was making a design on top of her desk with pennies. She put 4 pennies in the first row, 7 pennies in the second row, and 13 pennies in the third row. If Jane continues this pattern, how many pennies will she put in the sixth row?
   - **F** 25
   - **G** 49
   - **H** 97
   - **I** 193

3. In which of the following lists are the numbers in order from smallest to greatest?
   - **A** 0.012, 0.120, 0.123, 1.012
   - **B** 1.012, 0.123, 0.120, 0.012
   - **C** 0.123, 0.120, 0.012, 1.012
   - **D** 0.123, 1.012, 0.120, 0.012

4. In which of the following lists are the numbers in order from smallest to greatest?
   - **F** −12.0, −15.5, 2.2, 4.0
   - **G** −15.5, −12.0, 2.2, 4.0
   - **H** −12.0, −15.5, 4.0, 2.2
   - **I** 2.2, 4.0, −12.0, −15.5

5. Which of the following is equal to −11?
   - **A** $7 + 4$
   - **B** $-4 + 7$
   - **C** $-7 + 4$
   - **D** $-7 + -4$

6. Catherine earned $75 for working 8.5 h. How much did she earn per hour?
   - **F** $10.12
   - **G** $9.75
   - **H** $8.82
   - **I** $8.01

Science in Action

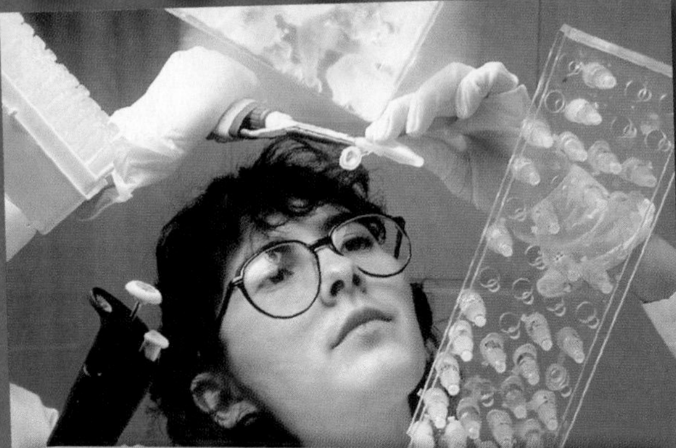

Science, Technology, and Society

Mapping the Human Genome

In 2003, scientists finished one of the most ambitious research projects ever. Researchers with the Human Genome Project (HGP) mapped the human body's complete set of genetic instructions, which is called the *genome*. You might be wondering whose genome the scientists are decoding. Actually, it doesn't matter—only 0.1% of each person's genetic material is unique. The researchers' goals are to identify how tiny differences in that 0.1% make each of us who we are and to begin to understand how some differences can cause disease. Scientists are already using the map to think of new ways to treat genetic diseases, such as asthma, diabetes, and kidney disease.

Social Studies ACTIVITY

WRITING SKILL Research DNA fingerprinting. Write a short report describing how DNA fingerprinting has affected the way criminals are caught.

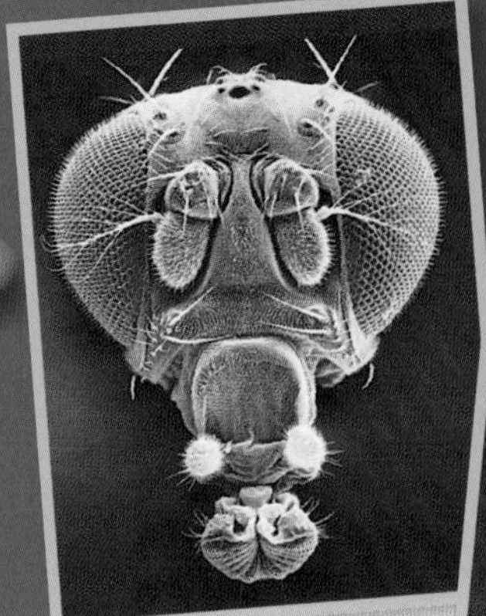

This is a normal fruit fly under a scanning electron microscope.

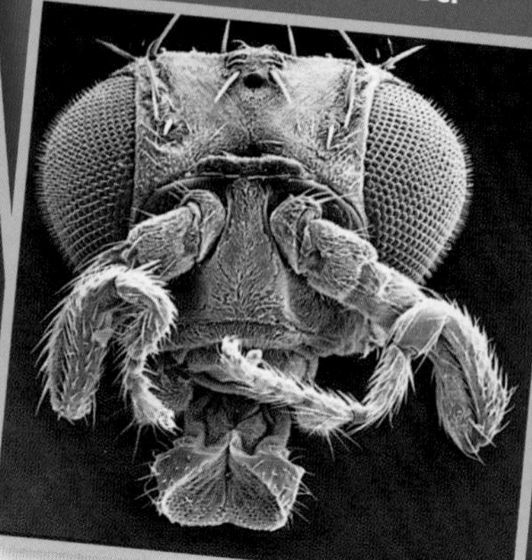

This fruit fly has legs growing where its antennae should be.

Weird Science

Lab Rats with Wings

Drosophila melanogaster (droh SAHF i luh muh LAN uh GAS tuhr) is the scientific name for the fruit fly. This tiny insect has played a big role in helping scientists understand many illnesses. Because fruit flies reproduce every 2 weeks, scientists can alter a fruit fly gene and see the results of the experiment very quickly. Another important reason for using these "lab rats with wings" is that their genetic code is simple and well understood. Fruit flies have 12,000 genes, but humans have more than 25,000. Scientists use fruit flies to find out about diseases like cancer, Alzheimer's, and muscular dystrophy.

Language Arts ACTIVITY

WRITING SKILL The mythical creature called the *Chimera* (kie MIR uh) was said to be part lion, part goat, and part serpent. According to legend, the Chimera terrorized people for years until it was killed by a brave hero. The word *chimera* now refers to any organism that has parts from many organisms. Write a short story about the Chimera that describes what it looks like and how it came to be.

Careers

Stacey Wong

Genetic Counselor If your family had a history of a particular disease, what would you do? Would you eat healthier foods, get more exercise, or visit your doctor regularly? All of those are good ideas, but Stacey Wong went a step farther. Her family's history of cancer helped her decide to become a genetic counselor. "Genetic counselors are usually part of a team of health professionals," she says, which can include physicians, nurses, dieticians, social workers, laboratory personnel, and others. "If a diagnosis is made by the geneticist," says Wong, "then I provide genetic counseling." When a patient visits a genetic counselor, the counselor asks many questions and builds a family medical history. Although counseling involves discussing what it means to have a genetic condition, Wong says "the most important part is to get to know the patient or family we are working with, listen to their concerns, gain an understanding of their values, help them to make decisions, and be their advocate."

Math Activity

The probability of inheriting genetic disease *A* is 1/10,000. The probability of inheriting genetic disease *B* is also 1/10,000. What is the probability that one person would inherit both genetic diseases *A* and *B*?

To learn more about these Science in Action topics, visit go.hrw.com and type in the keyword **HL5HERF.**

Current Science

Check out Current Science® articles related to this chapter by visiting go.hrw.com. Just type in the keyword HL5CS05.

Genes and DNA

About the PHOTO

These adult mice have no hair—not because their hair was shaved off but because these mice do not grow hair. In cells of these mice, the genes that normally cause hair to grow are not working. The genes were "turned off" by scientists who have learned to control the function of some genes. Scientists changed the genes of these mice to research medical problems such as cancer.

PRE-READING ACTIVITY

Graphic Organizer

Concept Map Before you read the chapter, create the graphic organizer entitled "Concept Map" described in the **Study Skills** section of the Appendix. As you read the chapter, fill in the concept map with details about DNA.

START-UP ACTIVITY

Fingerprint Your Friends

One way to identify people is by taking their fingerprints. Does it really work? Are everyone's fingerprints unique? Try this activity to find out.

Procedure

1. Rub the tip of a **pencil** back and forth across a **piece of tracing paper.** Make a large, dark mark.
2. Rub the tip of one of your fingers on the pencil mark. Then place a small **piece of transparent tape** over the darkened area on your finger.
3. Remove the tape, and stick it on **a piece of white paper.** Repeat steps 1–3 for the rest of your fingers.
4. Look at the fingerprints with a **magnifying lens.** What patterns do you see? Is the pattern the same on every finger?

Analysis

1. Compare your fingerprints with those of your classmates. Do any two people in your class have the same prints? Try to explain your findings.

SECTION 1

What Does DNA Look Like?

For many years, the structure of a DNA molecule was a puzzle to scientists. In the 1950s, two scientists deduced the structure while experimenting with chemical models. They later won a Nobel Prize for helping solve this puzzle!

READING WARM-UP

Objectives

- List three important events that led to understanding the structure of DNA.
- Describe the basic structure of a DNA molecule.
- Explain how DNA molecules can be copied.

Terms to Learn

DNA
nucleotide

READING STRATEGY

Prediction Guide Before reading this section, write the title of each heading in this section. Next, under each heading, write what you think you will learn.

Inherited characteristics are determined by genes, and genes are passed from one generation to the next. Genes are parts of chromosomes, which are structures in the nucleus of most cells. Chromosomes are made of protein and DNA. **DNA** stands for *d*eoxyribo*n*ucleic *a*cid (dee AHKS ee RIE boh noo KLEE ik AS id). DNA is the genetic material—the material that determines inherited characteristics. But what does DNA look like?

The Pieces of the Puzzle

Scientists knew that the material that makes up genes must be able to do two things. First, it must be able to give instructions for building and maintaining cells. Second, it must be able to be copied each time a cell divides, so that each cell contains identical genes. Scientists thought that these things could be done only by complex molecules, such as proteins. They were surprised to learn how much the DNA molecule could do.

Nucleotides: The Subunits of DNA

DNA is made of subunits called nucleotides. A **nucleotide** consists of a sugar, a phosphate, and a base. The nucleotides are identical except for the base. The four bases are *adenine, thymine, guanine,* and *cytosine.* Each base has a different shape. Scientists often refer to a base by the first letter of the base, *A, T, G,* and *C.* **Figure 1** shows models of the four nucleotides.

DNA **d**eoxyribo**n**ucleic **a**cid, a molecule that is present in all living cells and that contains the information that determines the traits that a living thing inherits and needs to live

nucleotide in a nucleic-acid chain, a subunit that consists of a sugar, a phosphate, and a nitrogenous base

Figure 1 The Four Nucleotides of DNA

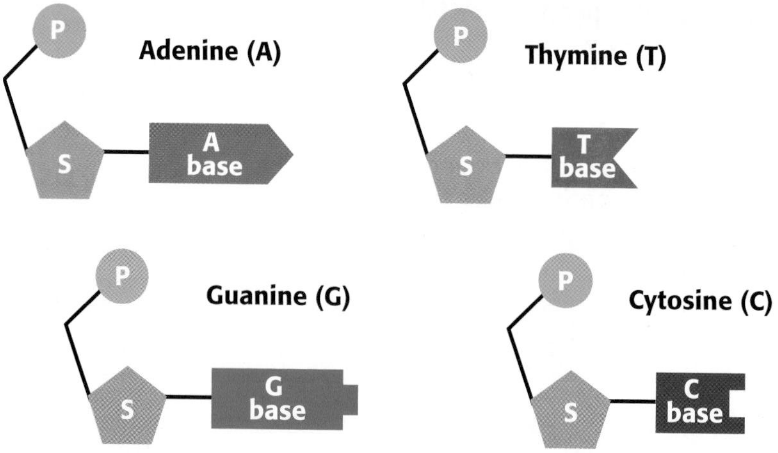

Chargaff's Rules

In the 1950s, a biochemist named Erwin Chargaff found that the amount of adenine in DNA always equals the amount of thymine. And he found that the amount of guanine always equals the amount of cytosine. His findings are known as *Chargaff's rules*. At the time of his discovery, no one knew the importance of these findings. But Chargaff's rules later helped scientists understand the structure of DNA.

Reading Check **Summarize Chargaff's rules.** *(See the Appendix for answers to Reading Checks.)*

CONNECTION TO Chemistry

WRITING SKILL **Linus Pauling** Many scientists contributed to the discovery of DNA's structure. In fact, some scientists competed to be the first to make the discovery. One of these competitors was a chemist named Linus Pauling. Research and write a paragraph about how Pauling's work helped Watson and Crick.

Franklin's Discovery

More clues about the structure of DNA came from scientists in Britain. There, chemist Rosalind Franklin, shown in **Figure 2,** was able to make images of DNA molecules. She used a process known as *X-ray diffraction* to make these images. In this process, X rays are aimed at the DNA molecule. When an X ray hits a part of the molecule, the ray bounces off. The pattern made by the bouncing rays is captured on film. Franklin's images suggested that DNA has a spiral shape.

Figure 2 *Rosalind Franklin used X-ray diffraction to make images of DNA that helped reveal the structure of DNA.*

Watson and Crick's Model

At about the same time, two other scientists were also trying to solve the mystery of DNA's structure. They were James Watson and Francis Crick, shown in **Figure 3.** After seeing Franklin's X-ray images, Watson and Crick concluded that DNA must look like a long, twisted ladder. They were then able to build a model of DNA by using simple materials from their laboratory. Their model perfectly fit with both Chargaff's and Franklin's findings. The model eventually helped explain how DNA is copied and how it functions in the cell.

Figure 3 *This photo shows James Watson (left) and Francis Crick (right) with their model of DNA.*

DNA's Double Structure

The shape of DNA is shown in **Figure 4.** As you can see, a strand of DNA looks like a twisted ladder. This shape is known as a *double helix* (DUB uhl HEE LIKS). The two sides of the ladder are made of alternating sugar parts and phosphate parts. The rungs of the ladder are made of a pair of bases. Adenine on one side of a rung always pairs with thymine on the other side. Guanine always pairs with cytosine.

Notice how the double helix structure matches Chargaff's observations. When Chargaff separated the parts of a sample of DNA, he found that the matching bases were always present in equal amounts. To model how the bases pair, Watson and Crick tried to match Chargaff's observations. They also used information from chemists about the size and shape of each of the nucleotides. As it turned out, the width of the DNA ladder matches the combined width of the matching bases. Only the correct pairs of bases fit within the ladder's width.

Making a Model of DNA

1. Gather assorted simple materials that you could use to build a basic model of DNA. You might use **clay, string, toothpicks, paper, tape, plastic foam,** or **pieces of food.**
2. Work with a partner or a small team to build your model. Use your book and other resources to check the details of your model.
3. Show your model to your classmates. Give your classmates feedback about the scientific aspects of their models.

Making Copies of DNA

The pairing of bases allows the cell to *replicate*, or make copies of, DNA. Each base always bonds with only one other base. Thus, pairs of bases are *complementary* to each other, and both sides of a DNA molecule are complementary. For example, the sequence CGAC will bond to the sequence GCTG.

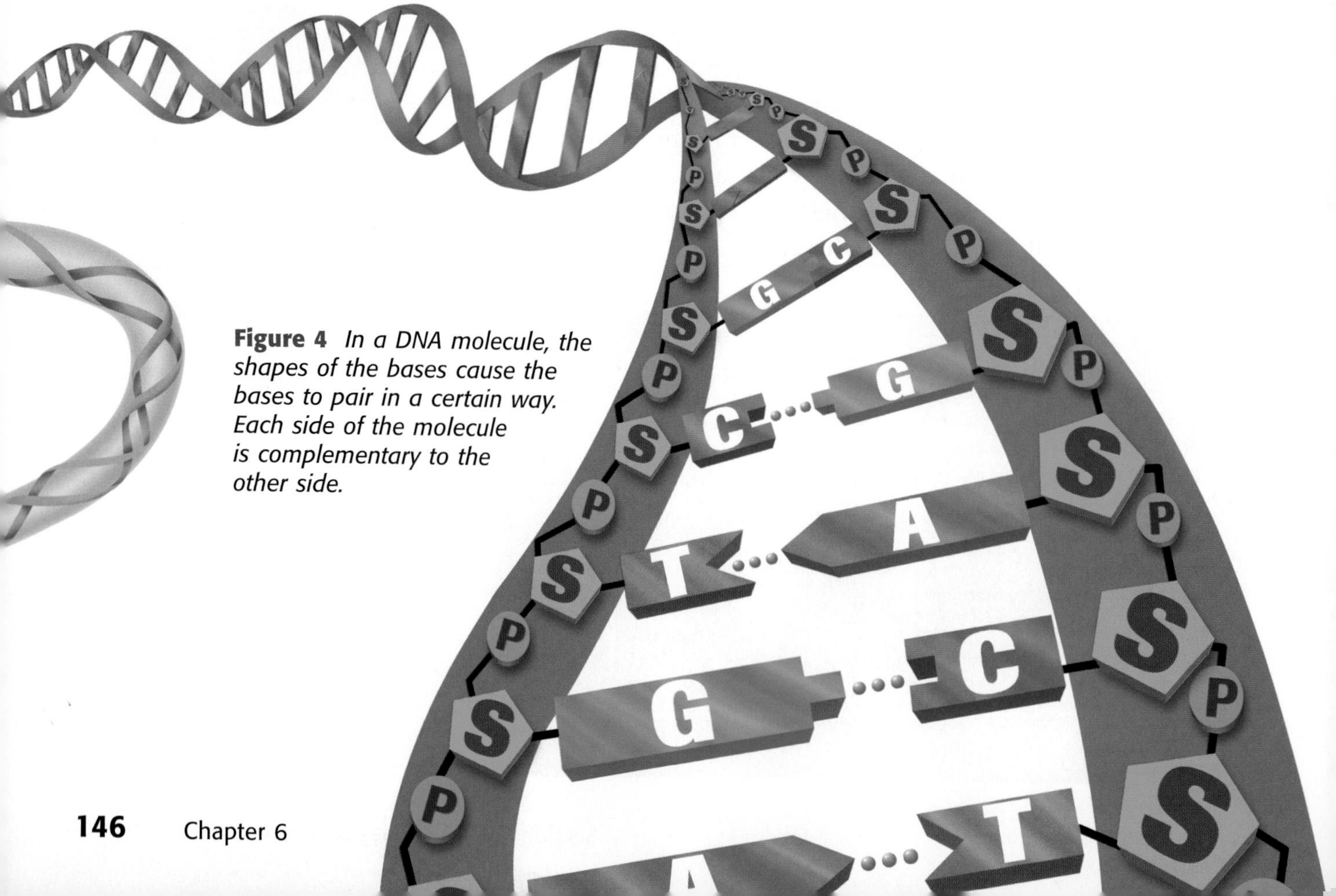

Figure 4 *In a DNA molecule, the shapes of the bases cause the bases to pair in a certain way. Each side of the molecule is complementary to the other side.*

How Copies Are Made

During replication, as shown in **Figure 5,** a DNA molecule is split down the middle, where the bases meet. The bases on each side of the molecule are used as a pattern for a new strand. As the bases on the original molecule are exposed, complementary nucleotides are added to each side of the ladder. Two DNA molecules are formed. Half of each of the molecules is old DNA, and half is new DNA.

When Copies Are Made

DNA is copied every time a cell divides. Each new cell gets a complete copy of all the DNA. The job of unwinding, copying, and re-winding the DNA is done by proteins within the cell. So, DNA is usually found with several kinds of proteins. Other proteins help with the process of carrying out the instructions written in the code of the DNA.

Reading Check How often is DNA copied?

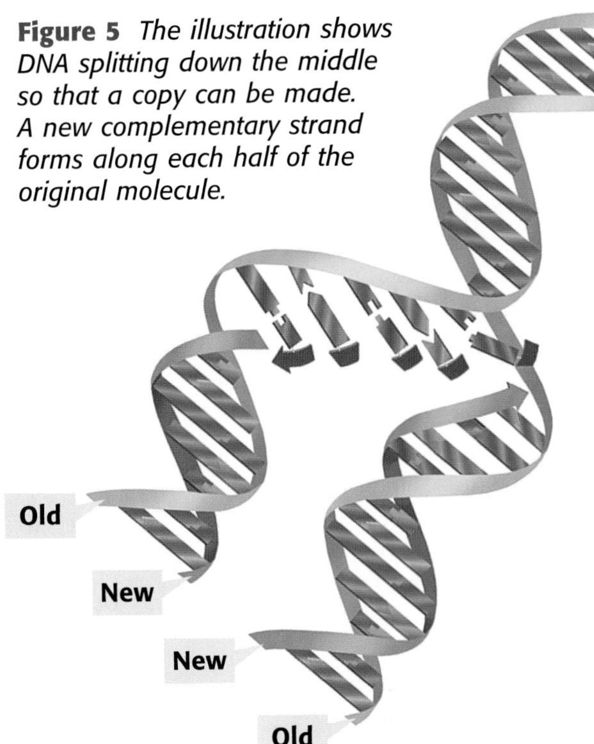

Figure 5 *The illustration shows DNA splitting down the middle so that a copy can be made. A new complementary strand forms along each half of the original molecule.*

SECTION Review

Summary

- DNA is the material that makes up genes. It carries coded information that is copied in each new cell.
- The DNA molecule looks like a twisted ladder. The two halves are long strings of nucleotides. The rungs are complementary pairs of bases.
- Because each base has a complementary base, DNA can be replicated accurately.

Using Key Terms

1. Use the term *DNA* in a sentence.
2. In your own words, write a definition for the term *nucleotide*.

Understanding Key Ideas

3. List three important events that led to understanding the structure of DNA.
4. Which of the following is NOT part of a nucleotide?
   a. base
   b. sugar
   c. fat
   d. phosphate

Math Skills

5. If a sample of DNA contained 20% cytosine, what percentage of guanine would be in this sample? What percentage of adenine would be in the sample? Explain.

Critical Thinking

6. **Making Inferences** Explain what is meant by the statement "DNA unites all organisms."
7. **Applying Concepts** What would the complementary strand of DNA be for the sequence of bases below?

   C T T A G G C T T A C C A

8. **Analyzing Processes** How are copies of DNA made? Draw a picture as part of your answer.

SCILINKS
NSTA
Developed and maintained by the National Science Teachers Association
For a variety of links related to this chapter, go to www.scilinks.org
Topic: DNA; Genes and Traits
SciLinks code: HSM0418; HSM0647

SECTION 2

How DNA Works

Almost every cell in your body contains about 2 m of DNA. How does all of the DNA fit in a cell? And how does the DNA hold a code that affects your traits?

READING WARM-UP

Objectives

- Explain the relationship between DNA, genes, and proteins.
- Outline the basic steps in making a protein.
- Describe three types of mutations, and provide an example of a gene mutation.
- Describe two examples of uses of genetic knowledge.

Terms to Learn

RNA
ribosome
mutation

READING STRATEGY

Reading Organizer As you read this section, make a flowchart of the steps of how DNA codes for proteins.

DNA is found in the cells of all organisms, including bacteria, mosquitoes, and humans. Each organism has a unique set of DNA. But DNA functions the same way in all organisms.

Unraveling DNA

DNA is often wound around proteins, coiled into strands, and then bundled up even more. In a cell that lacks a nucleus, each strand of DNA forms a loose loop within the cell. In a cell that has a nucleus, the strands of DNA and proteins are bundled into chromosomes, as shown in **Figure 1.**

The structure of DNA allows DNA to hold information. The order of the bases on one side of the molecule is a code that carries information. A *gene* consists of a string of nucleotides that give the cell information about how to make a specific trait. There is an enormous amount of DNA, so there can be a large variety of genes.

Reading Check **What makes up a gene?** (*See the Appendix for answers to Reading Checks.*)

Figure 1 **Unraveling DNA**

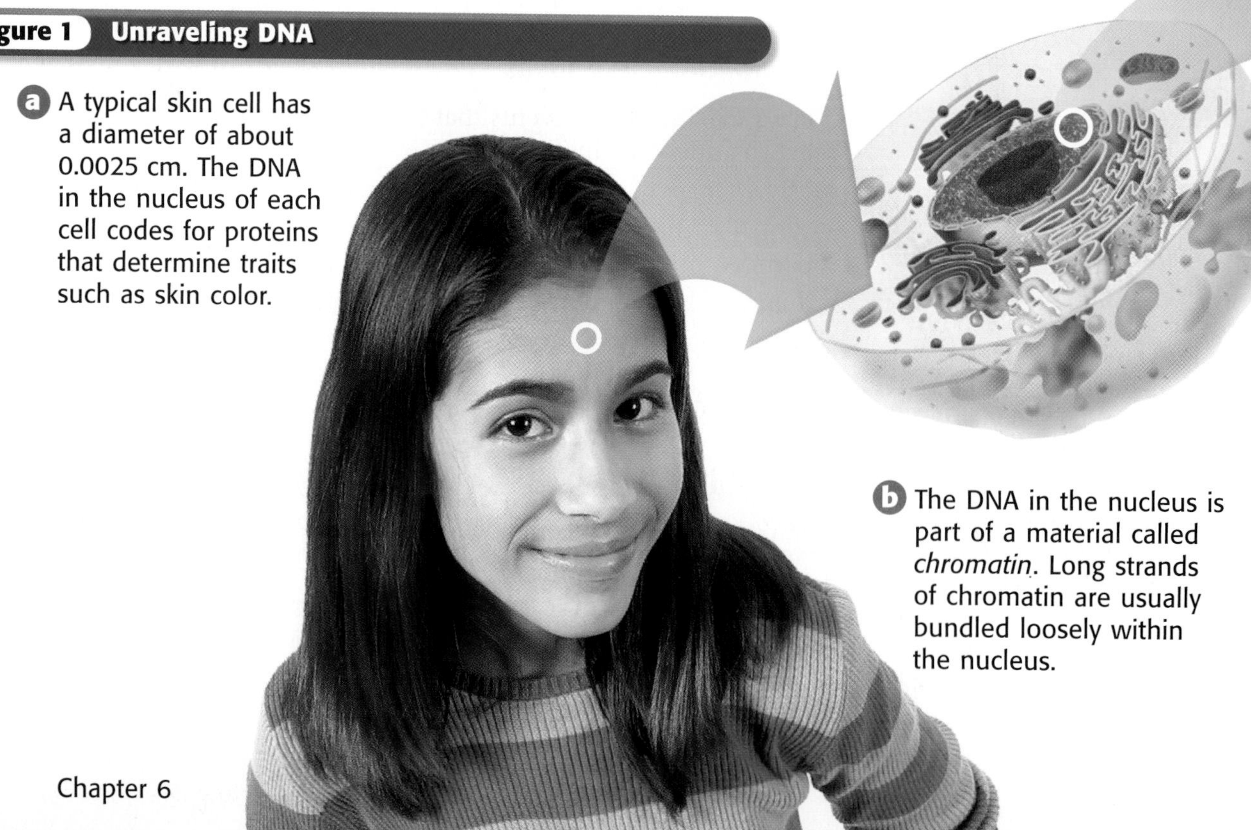

a A typical skin cell has a diameter of about 0.0025 cm. The DNA in the nucleus of each cell codes for proteins that determine traits such as skin color.

b The DNA in the nucleus is part of a material called *chromatin*. Long strands of chromatin are usually bundled loosely within the nucleus.

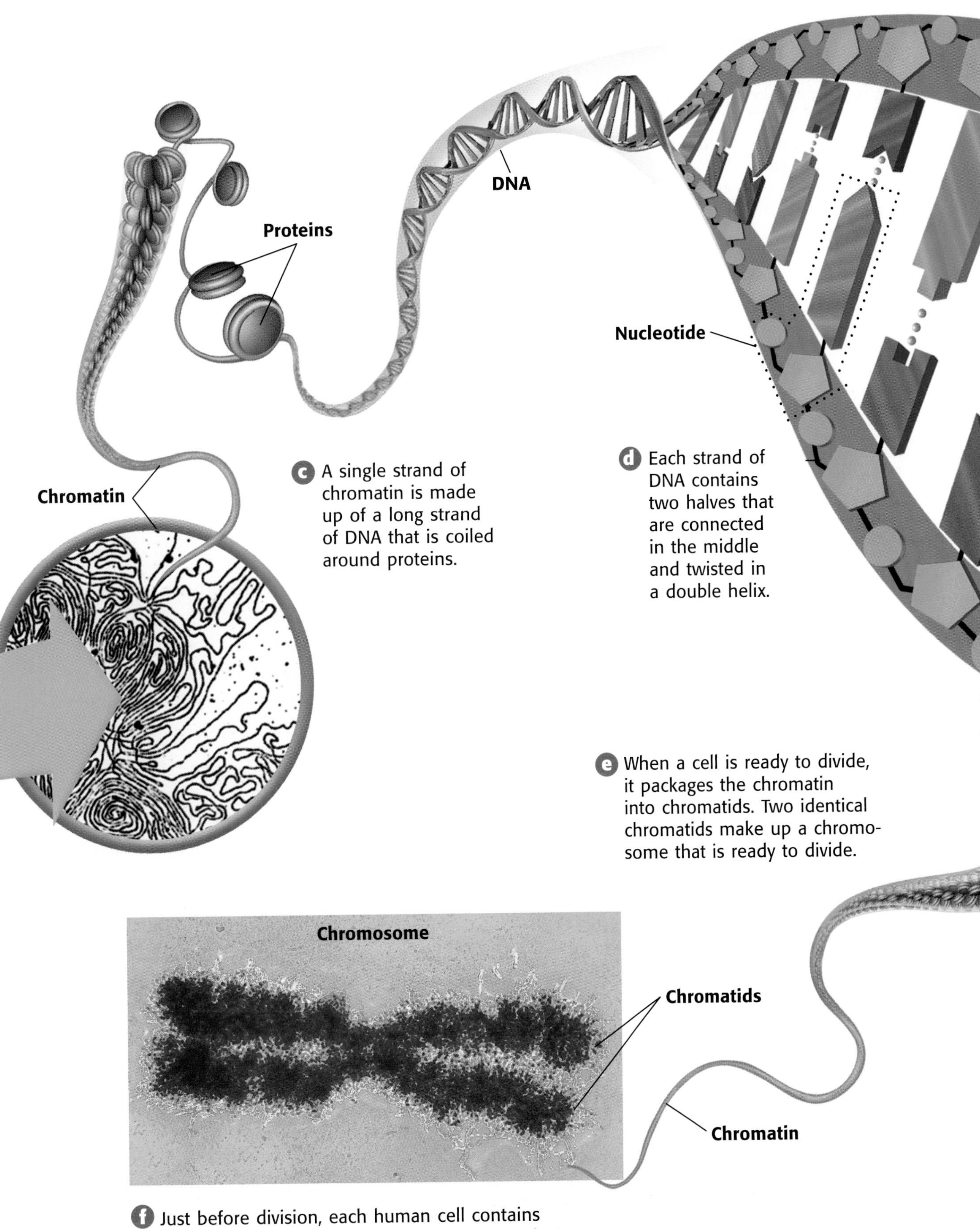

c A single strand of chromatin is made up of a long strand of DNA that is coiled around proteins.

d Each strand of DNA contains two halves that are connected in the middle and twisted in a double helix.

e When a cell is ready to divide, it packages the chromatin into chromatids. Two identical chromatids make up a chromosome that is ready to divide.

f Just before division, each human cell contains 46 chromosomes. These chromosomes contain two identical copies of all of the cell's genetic material.

For another activity related to this chapter, go to **go.hrw.com** and type in the keyword **HL5DNAW.**

Genes and Proteins

The DNA code is read like a book—from one end to the other and in one direction. The bases form the alphabet of the code. Groups of three bases are the codes for specific amino acids. For example, the three bases CCA form the code for the amino acid proline. The bases AGC form the code for the amino acid serine. A long string of amino acids forms a protein. Thus, each gene is usually a set of instructions for making a protein.

Proteins and Traits

How are proteins related to traits? Proteins are found throughout cells and cause most of the differences that you can see among organisms. Proteins act as chemical triggers and messengers for many of the processes within cells. Proteins help determine how tall you grow, what colors you can see, and whether your hair is curly or straight. Proteins exist in an almost limitless variety. A single organism may have thousands of genes that code for thousands of proteins.

RNA **r**ibo**n**ucleic **a**cid, a molecule that is present in all living cells and that plays a role in protein production

Help from RNA

Another type of molecule that helps make proteins is called **RNA,** or *ribonucleic acid* (RIE boh noo KLEE ik AS id). RNA is so similar to DNA that RNA can serve as a temporary copy of a DNA sequence. Several forms of RNA help in the process of changing the DNA code into proteins, as shown in **Figure 2.**

Figure 2 *Proteins are built in the cytoplasm by using RNA copies of a segment of DNA. The order of the bases on the RNA determines the order of amino acids that are assembled at the ribosome.*

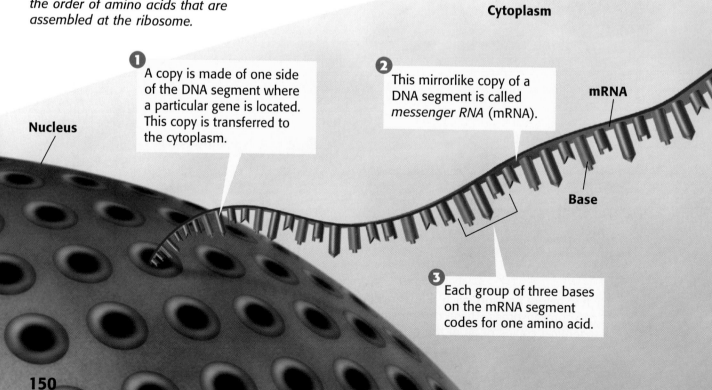

The Making of a Protein

The first step in making a protein is to copy one side of the segment of DNA containing a gene. A mirrorlike copy of the DNA segment is made out of RNA. This copy of the DNA segment is called *messenger RNA* (mRNA). It moves out of the nucleus and into the cytoplasm of the cell.

In the cytoplasm, the messenger RNA is fed through a protein assembly line. The "factory" that runs this assembly line is known as a ribosome. A **ribosome** is a cell organelle composed of RNA and protein. The messenger RNA is fed through the ribosome three bases at a time. Then, molecules of *transfer RNA* (tRNA) translate the RNA message. Each transfer RNA molecule picks up a specific amino acid from the cytoplasm. Inside the ribosome, bases on the transfer RNA match up with bases on the messenger RNA like pieces of a puzzle. The transfer RNA molecules then release their amino acids. The amino acids become linked in a growing chain. As the entire segment of messenger RNA passes through the ribosome, the growing chain of amino acids folds up into a new protein molecule.

Reading Check **What do the transfer RNA molecules transfer?**

Code Combinations

A given sequence of three bases codes for one amino acid. For example, AGT is one possible sequence. How many different sequences of the four DNA base types are possible? (Hint: Make a list.)

ribosome a cell organelle composed of RNA and protein; the site of protein synthesis

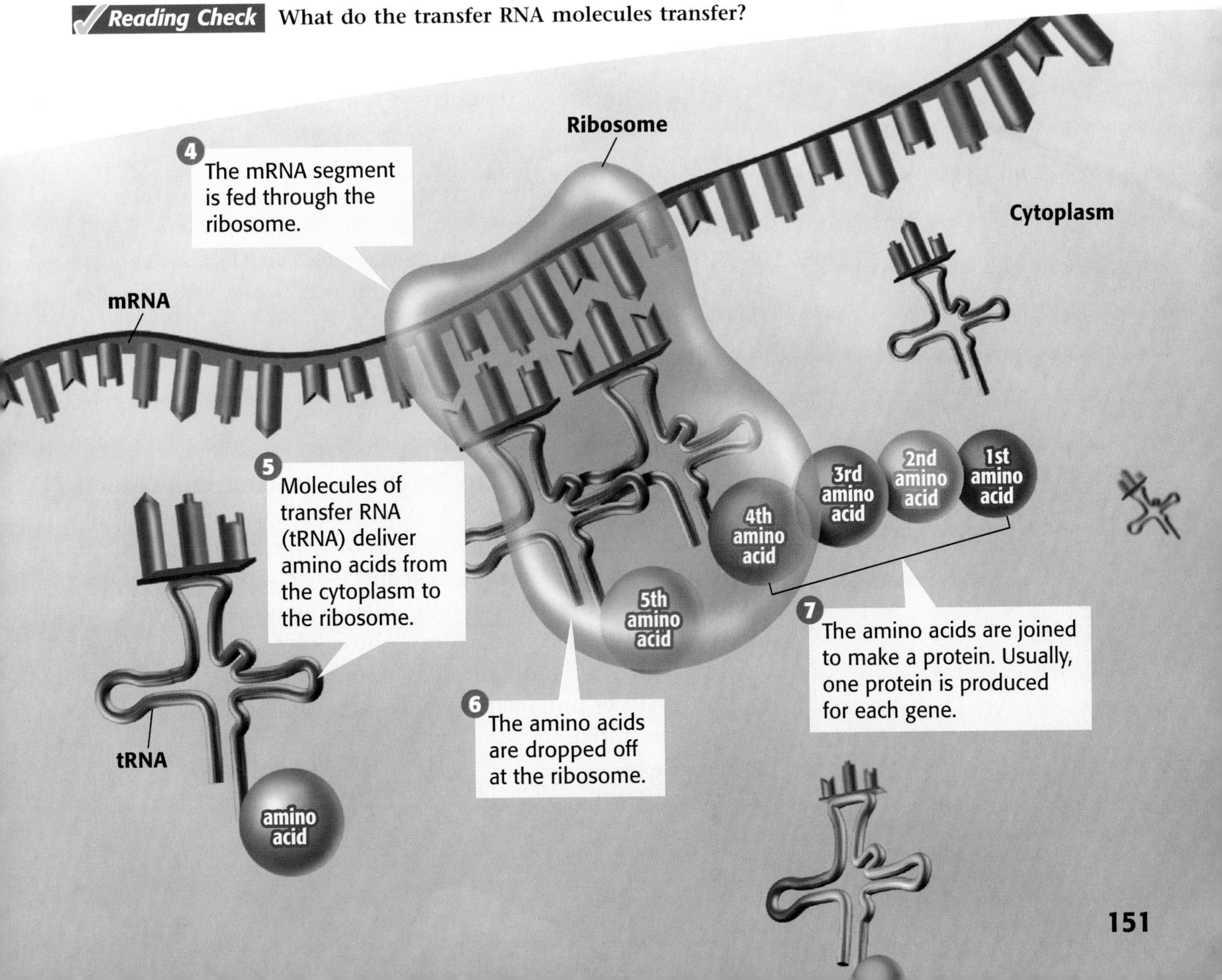

Ribosome

Cytoplasm

mRNA

tRNA

4 The mRNA segment is fed through the ribosome.

5 Molecules of transfer RNA (tRNA) deliver amino acids from the cytoplasm to the ribosome.

6 The amino acids are dropped off at the ribosome.

7 The amino acids are joined to make a protein. Usually, one protein is produced for each gene.

1st amino acid

2nd amino acid

3rd amino acid

4th amino acid

5th amino acid

amino acid

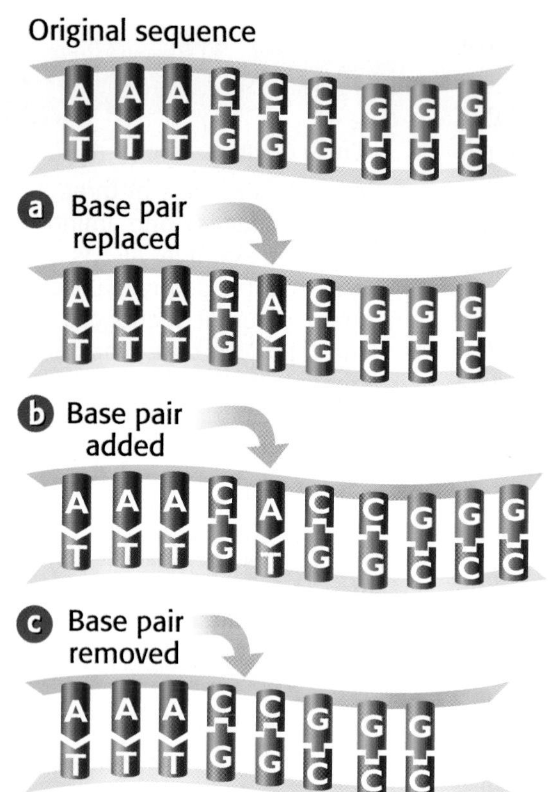

Figure 3 *The original base sequence on the top has been changed to illustrate (a) a substitution, (b) an insertion, and (c) a deletion.*

Changes in Genes

Imagine that you have been invited to ride on a new roller coaster at the state fair. Before you climb into the front car, you are told that some of the metal parts on the coaster have been replaced by parts made of a different substance. Would you still want to ride this roller coaster? Perhaps a strong metal was used as a substitute. Or perhaps a material that is not strong enough was used. Imagine what would happen if cardboard were used instead of metal!

Mutations

Substitutions like the ones in the roller coaster can accidentally happen in DNA. Changes in the number, type, or order of bases on a piece of DNA are known as **mutations.** Sometimes, a base is left out. This kind of change is known as a *deletion.* Or an extra base might be added. This kind of change is known as an *insertion.* The most common change happens when the wrong base is used. This kind of change is known as a *substitution.* **Figure 3** illustrates these three types of mutations.

Do Mutations Matter?

There are three possible consequences to changes in DNA: an improved trait, no change, or a harmful trait. Fortunately, cells make some proteins that can detect errors in DNA. When an error is found, it is usually fixed. But occasionally the repairs are not accurate, and the mistakes become part of the genetic message. If the mutation occurs in the sex cells, the changed gene can be passed from one generation to the next.

How Do Mutations Happen?

mutation a change in the nucleotide-base sequence of a gene or DNA molecule

Mutations happen regularly because of random errors when DNA is copied. In addition, damage to DNA can be caused by abnormal things that happen to cells. Any physical or chemical agent that can cause a mutation in DNA is called a *mutagen.* Examples of mutagens include high-energy radiation from X rays and ultraviolet radiation. Ultraviolet radiation is one type of energy in sunlight. It is responsible for suntans and sunburns. Other mutagens include asbestos and the chemicals in cigarette smoke.

Reading Check What is a mutagen?

An Example of a Substitution

A mutation, such as a substitution, can be harmful because it may cause a gene to produce the wrong protein. Consider the DNA sequence GAA. When copied as mRNA, this sequence gives the instructions to place the amino acid glutamic acid into the growing protein. If a mistake happens and the original DNA sequence is changed to GTA, the sequence will code for the amino acid valine instead.

This simple change in an amino acid can cause the disease *sickle cell disease*. Sickle cell disease affects red blood cells. When valine is substituted for glutamic acid in a blood protein, as shown in **Figure 4,** the red blood cells are changed into a sickle shape.

The sickle cells are not as good at carrying oxygen as normal red blood cells are. Sickle cells are also likely to get stuck in blood vessels and cause painful and dangerous clots.

Reading Check What causes sickle cell disease?

An Error in the Message

The sentence below is the result of an error similar to a DNA mutation. The original sentence was made up of three-letter words, but an error was made in this copy. Explain the idea of mutations to your parent. Then, work together to find the mutation, and write the sentence correctly.

THE IGB ADC ATA TET HEB IGR EDR AT.

ACTIVITY

Figure 4 How Sickle Cell Disease Results from a Mutation

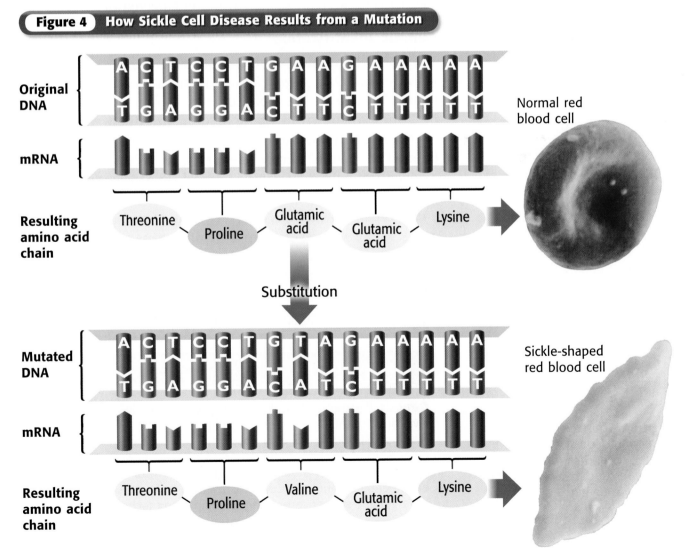

Original DNA: A C T C C T G A A G A A A A A / T G A G G A C T T C T T T T T

mRNA

Resulting amino acid chain: Threonine — Proline — Glutamic acid — Glutamic acid — Lysine

Normal red blood cell

Substitution

Mutated DNA: A C T C C T G T A G A A A A A / T G A G G A C A T C T T T T T

mRNA

Resulting amino acid chain: Threonine — Proline — Valine — Glutamic acid — Lysine

Sickle-shaped red blood cell

Uses of Genetic Knowledge

In the years since Watson and Crick made their model, scientists have learned a lot about genetics. This knowledge is often used in ways that benefit humans. But some uses of genetic knowledge also cause ethical and scientific debates.

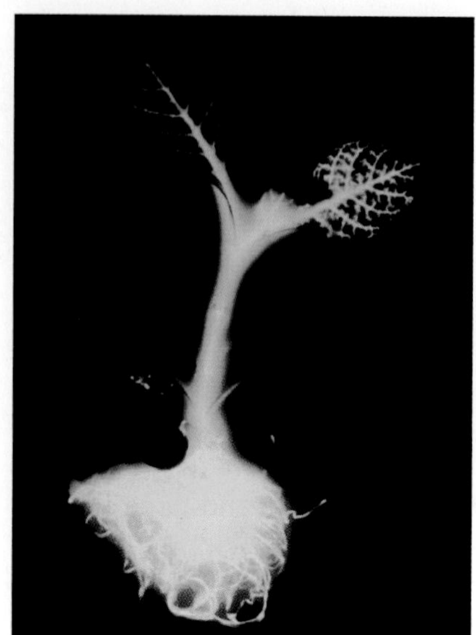

Figure 5 *This genetically engineered tobacco plant contains firefly genes.*

Genetic Engineering

Scientists can manipulate individual genes within organisms. This kind of manipulation is called *genetic engineering*. In some cases, genes may be transferred from one type of organism to another. An example of a genetically engineered plant is shown in **Figure 5.** Scientists added a gene from fireflies to this plant. The gene produces a protein that causes the plant to glow.

Scientists may use genetic engineering to create new products, such as drugs, foods, or fabrics. For example, bacteria may be used to make the proteins found in spider's silk. Or cows may be used to produce human proteins. In some cases, this practice could produce a protein that is needed by a person who has a genetic disease. However, some scientists worry about the dangers of creating genetically engineered organisms.

Genetic Identification

Your DNA is unique, so it can be used like a fingerprint to identify you. *DNA fingerprinting* identifies the unique patterns in an individual's DNA. DNA samples are now used as evidence in crimes, as shown in **Figure 6.** Similarities between people's DNA can reveal other information, too. For example, DNA can be used to identify family relations or hereditary diseases.

Identical twins have truly identical DNA. Scientists are now able to create something like a twin, called a clone. A *clone* is a new organism that has an exact copy of another organism's genes. Clones of several types of organisms, including some mammals, have been developed by scientists. However, the possibility of cloning humans is still being debated among both scientists and politicians.

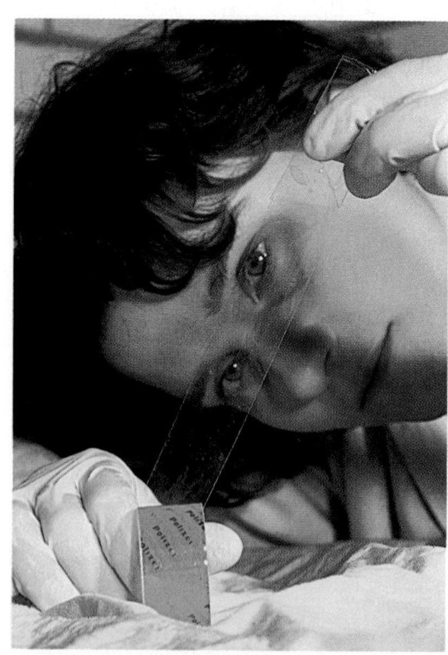

Figure 6 *This scientist is gathering dead skin cells from a crime scene. DNA from the cells could be used as evidence of a criminal's identity.*

Reading Check **What is a clone?**

CONNECTION TO Social Studies

Genetic Property Could you sell your DNA code? Using current laws and technology, someone could sell genetic information like authors sell books. It is also possible to file a patent to establish ownership of the information used to make a product. Thus, a patent can be filed for a unique sequence of DNA or for new genetic engineering technology. Conduct research to find an existing patent on a genetic sequence or genetic engineering technology.

SECTION Review

Summary

- A gene is a set of instructions for assembling a protein. DNA is the molecular carrier of these genetic instructions.
- Every organism has DNA in its cells. Humans have about 2 m of DNA in each cell.
- Within a gene, each group of three bases codes for one amino acid. A sequence of amino acids is linked to make a protein.
- Proteins are fundamental to the function of cells and the expression of traits.
- Proteins are assembled within the cytoplasm through a multi-step process that is assisted by several forms of RNA.
- Genes can become mutated when the order of the bases is changed. Three main types of mutations are possible: insertion, deletion, and substitution.
- Genetic knowledge has many practical uses. Some applications of genetic knowledge are controversial.

Using Key Terms

1. Use each of the following terms in the same sentence: *ribosome* and *RNA*.
2. In your own words, write a definition for the term *mutation*.

Understanding Key Ideas

3. Explain the relationship between genes and proteins.
4. List three possible types of mutations.
5. Which type of mutation causes sickle cell anemia?
   a. substitution
   b. insertion
   c. deletion
   d. mutagen

Math Skills

6. A set of 23 chromosomes in a human cell contains 3.2 billion pairs of DNA bases in sequence. On average, about how many pairs of bases are in each chromosome?

Critical Thinking

7. **Applying Concepts** In which cell type might a mutation be passed from generation to generation? Explain.
8. **Making Comparisons** How is genetic engineering different from natural reproduction?

Interpreting Graphics

The illustration below shows a sequence of bases on one strand of a DNA molecule. Use the illustration below to answer the questions that follow.

9. How many amino acids are coded for by the sequence on one side (A) of this DNA strand?
10. What is the order of bases on the complementary side of the strand (B), from left to right?
11. If a G were inserted as the first base on the top side (A), what would the order of bases be on the complementary side (B)?

SCILINKS
NSTA
Developed and maintained by the National Science Teachers Association
For a variety of links related to this chapter, go to www.scilinks.org
Topic: Genetic Engineering
SciLinks code: HSM0654

Model-Making Lab

Base-Pair Basics

You have learned that DNA is shaped something like a twisted ladder. The side rails of the ladder are made of sugar parts and phosphate parts. The two side rails are connected to each other by parts called *bases*. The bases join in pairs to form the rungs of the ladder. Within DNA, each base can pair with only one other base. Each of these pairs is called a *base pair*. When DNA replicates, enzymes separate the base pairs, which breaks the rungs of the ladder in half. Then, each half of the DNA ladder can be used as a template for building a new half. In this activity, you will construct a paper model of DNA and use it to model the replication process.

OBJECTIVES

Construct a model of a DNA strand.

Model the process of DNA replication.

MATERIALS

- bag, large paper
- paper, colored (4 colors)
- paper, white
- scissors

SAFETY

Procedure

1. Trace the models of nucleotides below onto white paper. Label the pieces "A" (**a**denine), "T" (**t**hymine), "C" (**c**ytosine), and "G" (**g**uanine). Draw the pieces again on colored paper. Use a different color for each type of base. Draw the pieces as large as you want, and draw as many of the white pieces and as many of the colored pieces as time will allow.
2. Carefully cut out all of the pieces.
3. Put all of the colored pieces in the classroom into a large paper bag. Spread all of the white pieces in the classroom onto a large table.
4. Remove nine colored pieces from the bag. Arrange the colored pieces in any order in a straight column so that the letters *A, T, C,* and *G* are right side up. Be sure to fit the sugar notches to the phosphate tabs. Draw this arrangement.
5. Find the white bases that correctly pair with the nine colored bases. Remember the base-pairing rules, and pair the bases according to those rules.
6. Pair the pieces by fitting tabs to notches. The letters on the white pieces should be upside down. You now have a model of a double-stranded piece of DNA. The strand contains nine pairs of complementary nucleotides. Draw your model.

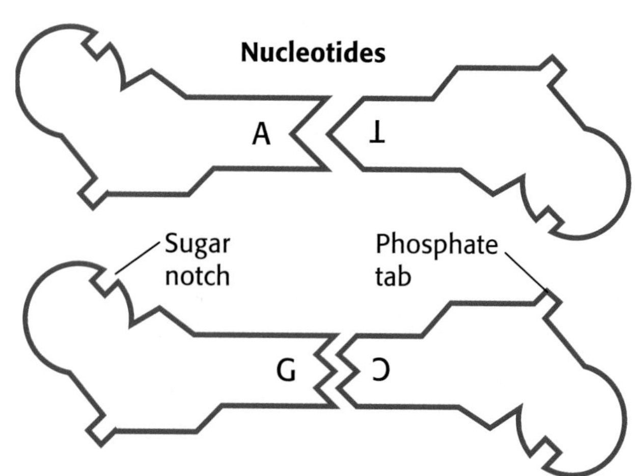

Analyze the Results

1. **Identifying Patterns** Now, separate the two halves of your DNA strand along the middle of the base pair rungs of the ladder. Keep the side rails together by keeping the sugar notches fitted to the phosphate tabs. Draw this arrangement.

2. **Recognizing Patterns** Look at the drawing made in the previous step. Along each strand in the drawing, write the letters of the bases that complement the bases in that strand.

3. **Examining Data** Find all of the bases that you need to complete replication. Find white pieces to pair with the bases on the left, and find colored pieces to pair with the bases on the right. Be sure that the tabs and notches fit and the sides are straight. You have now replicated your model of DNA. Are the two models identical? Draw your results.

Draw Conclusions

4. **Interpreting Information** State the correct base-pairing rules. How do these rules make DNA replication possible?

5. **Evaluating Models** What happens when you attempt to pair thymine with guanine? Do they fit together? Are the sides straight? Do all of the tabs and notches fit? Explain.

Applying Your Data

Construct a 3-D model of a DNA molecule that shows DNA's twisted-ladder structure. Use your imagination and creativity to select materials. You may want to use licorice, gum balls, and toothpicks or pipe cleaners and paper clips.

1. Display your model in your classroom.
2. Take a vote to decide which models are the most accurate and the most creative.

Chapter Review

USING KEY TERMS

1. Use the following terms in the same sentence: *mutation* and *mutagen*.

The statements below are false. For each statement, replace the underlined term to make a true statement.

2. The information in DNA is coded in the order of <u>amino acids</u> along one side of the DNA molecule.

3. The "factory" that assembles proteins based on the DNA code is called a <u>gene</u>.

UNDERSTANDING KEY IDEAS

Multiple Choice

4. James Watson and Francis Crick
   - **a.** took X-ray pictures of DNA.
   - **b.** discovered that genes are in chromosomes.
   - **c.** bred pea plants to study heredity.
   - **d.** made models to figure out DNA's shape.

5. In a DNA molecule, which of the following bases pair together?
   - **a.** adenine and cytosine
   - **b.** thymine and adenine
   - **c.** thymine and guanine
   - **d.** cytosine and thymine

6. A gene can be all of the following EXCEPT
   - **a.** a set of instructions for a trait.
   - **b.** a complete chromosome.
   - **c.** instructions for making a protein.
   - **d.** a portion of a strand of DNA.

7. Which of the following statements about DNA is NOT true?
   - **a.** DNA is found in all organisms.
   - **b.** DNA is made up of five subunits.
   - **c.** DNA has a structure like a twisted ladder.
   - **d.** Mistakes can be made when DNA is copied.

8. Within the cell, where are proteins assembled?
   - **a.** the cytoplasm
   - **b.** the nucleus
   - **c.** the amino acids
   - **d.** the chromosomes

9. Changes in the type or order of the bases in DNA are called
   - **a.** nucleotides.
   - **b.** mutations.
   - **c.** RNA.
   - **d.** genes.

Short Answer

10. What would be the complementary strand of DNA for the following sequence of bases?

    C T T A G G C T T A C C A

11. If the DNA sequence TGAGCCATGA is changed to TGAGCACATGA, what kind of mutation has occurred?

12. Explain how the DNA in genes relates to the traits of an organism.

13. Why is DNA frequently found associated with proteins inside of cells?

14. What is the difference between DNA and RNA?

CRITICAL THINKING

15 **Concept Mapping** Use the following terms to create a concept map: *bases, adenine, thymine, nucleotides, guanine, DNA,* and *cytosine.*

16 **Analyzing Processes** Draw and label a picture that explains how DNA is copied.

17 **Analyzing Processes** Draw and label a picture that explains how proteins are made.

18 **Applying Concepts** The following DNA sequence codes for how many amino acids?

T C A G C C A C C T A T G G A

19 **Making Inferences** Why does the government make laws about the use of chemicals that are known to be mutagens?

INTERPRETING GRAPHICS

The illustration below shows the process of replication of a DNA strand. Use this illustration to answer the questions that follow.

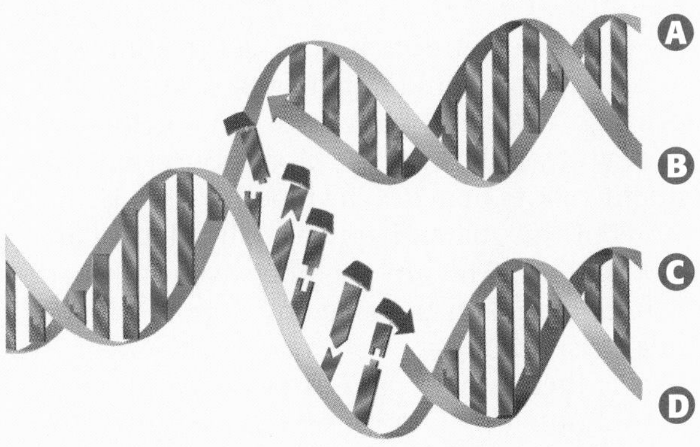

20 Which strands are part of the original molecule?

a. A and B
b. A and C
c. A and D
d. None of the above

21 Which strands are new?

a. A and B
b. B and C
c. C and D
d. None of the above

22 Which strands are complementary?

a. A and C
b. B and C
c. All of the strands
d. None of the strands

Standardized Test Preparation

READING

Read each of the passages below. Then, answer the questions that follow each passage.

Passage 1 The tension in the courtroom was so thick that you could cut it with a knife. The prosecuting attorney presented this evidence: "DNA analysis indicates that blood found on the defendant's shoes matches the blood of the victim. The odds of this match happening by chance are 1 in 20 million." The jury members were stunned by these figures. Can there be any doubt that the defendant is guilty?

DNA is increasingly used as evidence in court cases. Traditional fingerprinting has been used for more than 100 years, and it has been an extremely important identification tool. Recently, DNA fingerprinting, also called *DNA profiling,* has started to replace traditional techniques. DNA profiling has been used to clear thousands of wrongly accused or convicted individuals. However, there is some controversy over whether DNA evidence should be used to prove a suspect's guilt.

1. What does the first sentence in this passage describe?

- **A** the air pollution in a particular place
- **B** the feeling that a person might experience during an event
- **C** the motion of an object
- **D** the reason that a person was probably guilty of a crime

2. Which of the following best describes the main idea of the second paragraph of this passage?

- **F** A defendant was proven guilty by DNA analysis.
- **G** Court battles involving DNA fingerprinting are very exciting.
- **H** The technique of DNA profiling is increasingly used in court cases.
- **I** The technique of DNA profiling is controversial.

Passage 2 Most of the <u>biochemicals</u> found in living things are proteins. In fact, other than water, proteins are the most abundant molecules in your cells. Proteins have many functions, including regulating chemical activities, transporting and storing materials, and providing structural support.

Every protein is composed of small "building blocks" called *amino acids*. Amino acids are molecules that are composed of carbon, hydrogen, oxygen, and nitrogen atoms. Some amino acids also include sulfur atoms. Amino acids chemically bond to form proteins of many shapes and sizes.

The function of a protein depends on the shape of the bonded amino acids. If even a single amino acid is missing or out of place, the protein may not function correctly or may not function. Foods such as meat, fish, cheese, and beans contain proteins, which are broken down into amino acids as the foods are digested. Your body can then use these amino acids to make new proteins.

1. In the passage, what does *biochemical* mean?

- **A** a chemical found in nonliving things
- **B** a chemical found in living things
- **C** a pair of chemicals
- **D** a protein

2. According to the passage, which of the following statements is true?

- **F** Amino acids contain carbon dioxide.
- **G** Amino acids contain proteins.
- **H** Proteins are made of living things.
- **I** Proteins are made of amino acids.

INTERPRETING GRAPHICS

The diagram below shows an original sequence of DNA and three possible mutations. Use the diagram to answer the questions that follow.

Original sequence

Mutation A

Mutation B

Mutation C

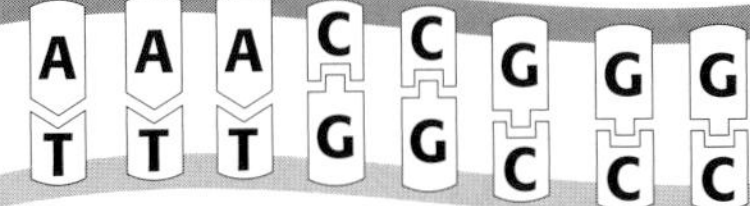

1. In which mutation was an original base pair replaced?

A Mutation A
B Mutation B
C Mutation C
D There is not enough information to determine the answer.

2. In which mutation was a new base pair added?

F Mutation A
G Mutation B
H Mutation C
I There is not enough information to determine the answer.

3. In which mutation was an original base pair removed?

A Mutation A
B Mutation B
C Mutation C
D There is not enough information to determine the answer.

MATH

Read each question below, and choose the best answer.

1. Mary was making a design on top of her desk with marbles. She put 3 marbles in the first row, 7 marbles in the second row, 15 marbles in the third row, and 31 marbles in the fourth row. If Mary continues this pattern, how many marbles will she put in the seventh row?

A 46
B 63
C 127
D 255

2. Bobby walked 3 1/2 km on Saturday, 2 1/3 km on Sunday, and 1 km on Monday. How many kilometers did Bobby walk on those 3 days?

F 5 1/6
G 5 5/6
H 6 1/6
I 6 5/6

3. Marie bought a new aquarium for her goldfish. The aquarium is 60 cm long, 20 cm wide, and 30 cm high. Which equation could be used to find the volume of water needed to fill the aquarium to 25 cm deep?

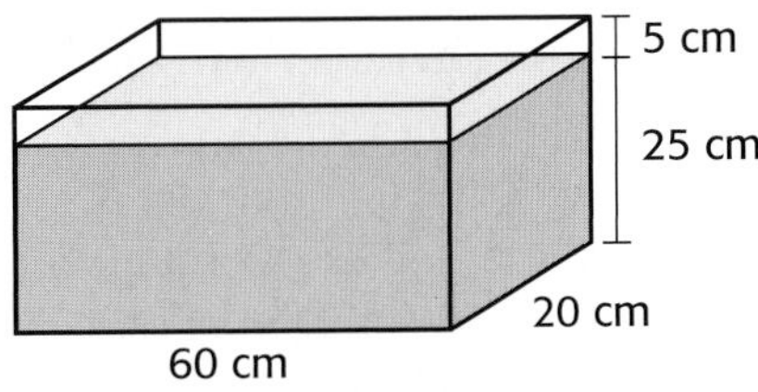

A $V = 30 \times 60 \times 20$
B $V = 25 \times 60 \times 20$
C $V = 30 \times 60 \times 20 - 5$
D $V = 30 \times 60 \times 25$

4. How is the product of $6 \times 6 \times 6 \times 4 \times 4 \times 4$ expressed in scientific notation?

F $6^4 \times 3^6$
G $6^3 \times 4^3$
H $3^6 \times 3^4$
I 24^6

Standardized Test Preparation

Science in Action

Scientific Debate

Supersquash or Frankenfruit?

Some food that you buy may have been developed in a new way. Food producers may use genetic engineering to make food crops easier to grow or sell, more nutritious, or resistant to pests and disease. More than half of the packaged foods sold in the United States are likely to contain ingredients from genetically modified organisms.

The U.S. government has stated that research shows that these foods are safe. But some scientists are concerned that genes introduced into crop plants could cause new environmental or health problems. For example, people who are allergic to peanuts might also be allergic to tomato plants that contain peanut genes.

Math ACTIVITY

Write a survey about genetically altered foods. Ask your teacher to approve your questions. Ask at least 15 people to answer your survey. Create graphs to summarize your results.

Science Fiction

"Moby James" by Patricia A. McKillip

Rob Trask and his family live on a space station. Rob thinks that his real brother was sent back to Earth. The person who claims to be his brother, James, is really either some sort of mutated plant or a mutant pair of dirty sweat socks.

Now, Rob has another problem—his class is reading Herman Melville's novel *Moby Dick*. As he reads the novel, Rob becomes convinced that his brother is a great white mutant whale—Moby James. To see how Rob solves his problems, read "Moby James" in the *Holt Anthology of Science Fiction*.

Language Arts ACTIVITY

WRITING SKILL Read "Moby James" by Patricia A. McKillip. Then, write your own short science-fiction story about a mutant organism. Be sure to incorporate some science into your science fiction.

People in Science

Lydia Villa-Komaroff

Genetic Researcher When Lydia Villa-Komaroff was young, science represented "a kind of refuge" for her. She grew up in a very large family that lived in a very small house. "I always wanted to find things out. I was one of those kids who took things apart."

In college, Villa-Komaroff became very interested in the process of embryonic development—how a simple egg grows into a complex animal. This interest led her to study genes and the way that genes code for proteins. For example, insulin is a protein that is normally produced by the human body. Often, people who suffer from diabetes lack the insulin gene, so their bodies can't make insulin. These people may need to inject insulin into their blood as a drug treatment.

Before the research by Villa-Komaroff's team was done, insulin was difficult to produce. Villa-Komaroff's team isolated the human gene that codes for insulin. Then, the scientists inserted the normal human insulin gene into the DNA of bacteria. This inserted gene caused the bacteria to produce insulin. This technique was a new and more efficient way to produce insulin. Now, most of the insulin used for diabetes treatment is made in this way. Many genetic researchers dream of making breakthroughs like the one that Villa-Komaroff made in her work with insulin.

Social Studies ACTIVITY

WRITING SKILL Do some research about several women, such as Marie Curie, Barbara McClintock, or Maxine Frank Singer, who have done important scientific research. Write a short biography about one of these women.

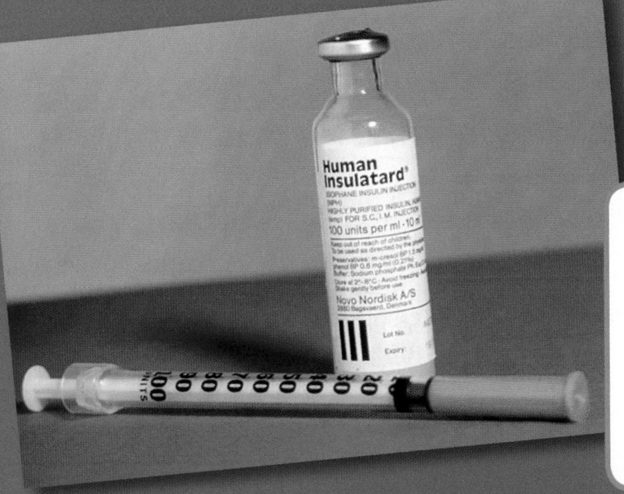

To learn more about these Science in Action topics, visit go.hrw.com and type in the keyword HL5DNAF.

Current Science

Check out Current Science® articles related to this chapter by visiting go.hrw.com. Just type in the keyword HL5CS06.

The Evolution of Living Things

About the 

What happened to this fish's face? This flounder wasn't born this way, but it did develop naturally. When young, a flounder looks and swims as most fish do. But as it becomes an adult, one of its eyes moves to the other side of its head, and the flounder begins to swim sideways. An adult flounder is adapted to swim and hide along the sandy bottom of coastal areas.

PRE-READING ACTIVITY

Graphic Organizer

Concept Map Before you read the chapter, create the graphic organizer entitled "Concept Map" described in the **Study Skills** section of the Appendix. As you read the chapter, fill in the concept map with details about evolution and natural selection.

START-UP ACTIVITY

Out of Sight, Out of Mind

In this activity, you will see how traits can affect the success of an organism in a particular environment.

Procedure

1. Count out **25 colored marshmallows** and **25 white marshmallows.**
2. Ask your partner to look away while you spread the marshmallows out on a **white cloth.** Do not make a pattern with the marshmallows. Now, ask your partner to turn around and pick the first marshmallow that he or she sees.
3. Repeat step 2 ten times.

Analysis

1. How many white marshmallows did your partner pick? How many colored marshmallows did he or she pick?
2. What did the marshmallows and the cloth represent in your investigation? What effect did the color of the cloth have?
3. When an organism blends into its environment, the organism is *camouflaged*. How does this activity model camouflaged organisms in the wild? What are some weaknesses of this model?

SECTION 1

Change over Time

If someone asked you to describe a frog, you might say that a frog has long hind legs, has bulging eyes, and croaks. But what color skin would you say that a frog has?

READING WARM-UP

Objectives

- Identify two kinds of evidence that show that organisms have evolved.
- Describe one pathway through which a modern whale could have evolved from an ancient mammal.
- Explain how comparing organisms can provide evidence that they have ancestors in common.

Terms to Learn

adaptation
species
evolution
fossil
fossil record

READING STRATEGY

Paired Summarizing Read this section silently. In pairs, take turns summarizing the material. Stop to discuss ideas that seem confusing.

Once you start to think about frogs, you realize that frogs differ in many ways. These differences set one kind of frog apart from another. The frogs in **Figures 1, 2,** and **3** look different from each other, yet they may live in the same areas.

Differences Among Organisms

As you can see, each frog has a different characteristic that might help the frog survive. A characteristic that helps an organism survive and reproduce in its environment is called an **adaptation.** Adaptations may be physical, such as a long neck or striped fur. Or adaptations may be behaviors that help an organism find food, protect itself, or reproduce.

Living things that have the same characteristics may be members of the same species. A **species** is a group of organisms that can mate with one another to produce fertile offspring. For example, all strawberry poison arrow frogs are members of the same species and can mate with each other to produce more strawberry poison arrow frogs. Groups of individuals of the same species living in the same place make up a *population.*

Reading Check **How can you tell that organisms are members of the same species?** (*See the Appendix for answers to Reading Checks.*)

Figure 1 The red-eyed tree frog hides among a tree's leaves during the day and comes out at night.

Figure 2 The bright coloring of the strawberry poison arrow frog warns predators that the frog is poisonous.

Figure 3 The smoky jungle frog blends into the forest floor.

Do Species Change over Time?

In a single square mile of rain forest, there may be dozens of species of frogs. Across the Earth, there are millions of different species of organisms. The species that live on Earth today range from single-celled bacteria, which lack cell nuclei, to multicellular fungi, plants, and animals. Have these species always existed on Earth?

Scientists think that Earth has changed a great deal during its history, and that living things have changed, too. Scientists estimate that the planet is 4.6 billion years old. Since life first appeared on Earth, many species have died out, and many new species have appeared. **Figure 4** shows some of the species that have existed during Earth's history.

Scientists observe that species have changed over time. They also observe that the inherited characteristics in populations change over time. Scientists think that as populations change over time, new species form. Thus, newer species descend from older species. The process in which populations gradually change over time is called **evolution.** Scientists continue to develop theories to explain exactly how evolution happens.

adaptation a characteristic that improves an individual's ability to survive and reproduce in a particular environment

species a group of organisms that are closely related and can mate to produce fertile offspring

evolution the process in which inherited characteristics within a population change over generations such that new species sometimes arise

Figure 4 *This diagram shows some of the many kinds of organisms that have lived on Earth since the planet formed 4.6 billion years ago.*

Figure 5 *The fossil on the left is of a trilobite, an ancient aquatic animal. The fossils on the right are of seed ferns.*

Evidence of Changes over Time

Evidence that evolution has happened is buried within Earth. Earth's crust is arranged in layers. These layers are made up of different kinds of rock and soil stacked on top of each other. These layers form when *sediments,* particles of sand, dust, or soil, are carried by wind and water and are deposited in an orderly fashion. Older layers are deposited before newer layers and are buried deeper within Earth.

Fossils

fossil the remains or physical evidence of an organism preserved by geological processes

fossil record a historical sequence of life indicated by fossils found in layers of the Earth's crust

Sometimes, the remains or imprints of once-living organisms are found in the layers of rock. These remains are called **fossils.** Examples of fossils are shown in **Figure 5.** Fossils can be complete organisms, parts of organisms, or just a set of footprints. Fossils usually form when a dead organism is covered by a layer of sediment. Over time, more sediment settles on top of the organism. Minerals in the sediment may seep into the organism and gradually replace the organism with stone. If the organism rots away completely after being covered, it may leave an imprint of itself in the rock.

The Fossil Record

By studying fossils, scientists have made a timeline of life that is known as the **fossil record.** The fossil record organizes fossils by their estimated ages and physical similarities. Fossils found in newer layers of Earth's crust tend to be similar to present-day organisms. This similarity indicates that the fossilized organisms were close relatives of present-day organisms. Fossils from older layers are less similar to present-day organisms than fossils from newer layers are. The older fossils are of earlier life-forms, which may not exist anymore.

Reading Check How does the fossil record organize fossils?

Evidence of Ancestry

The fossil record provides evidence about the order in which species have existed. Scientists observe that all living organisms have characteristics in common and inherit characteristics in similar ways. So, scientists think that all living species descended from common ancestors. Evidence of common ancestors can be found in fossils and in living organisms.

Sedimentary Rock Fossils are most often found in sedimentary rock. *Sedimentary rock* usually forms when rock is broken into sediment by wind, water, and other means. The wind and water move the sediment around and deposit it. Over time, layers of sediment pile up. Lower layers are compressed and changed into rock. Find out if your area has any sedimentary rocks that contain fossils. Mark the location of such rocks on a copy of a local map. ACTIVITY

Drawing Connections

Scientists examine the fossil record to figure out the relationships between extinct and living organisms. They draw models, such as the one shown in **Figure 6,** that illustrate their hypotheses. The short horizontal line at the top left in the diagram represents a species that lived in the past. Each branch in the diagram represents a group of organisms that descended from that species.

As shown in **Figure 6,** scientists think that whales and some types of hoofed mammals have a common ancestor. This ancestor was probably a mammal that lived on land between 50 million and 70 million years ago. During this time period, the dinosaurs died out and a variety of mammals appeared in the fossil record. The first ocean-dwelling mammals appeared about 50 million years ago. Scientists think that all mammal species alive today evolved from common ancestors.

Scientists have named and described hundreds of thousands of living and ancient species. Scientists use information about these species to sketch out a "tree of life" that includes all known organisms. But scientists know that their information is incomplete. For example, parts of Earth's history lack a fossil record. In fact, fossils are rare because specific conditions are necessary for fossils to form.

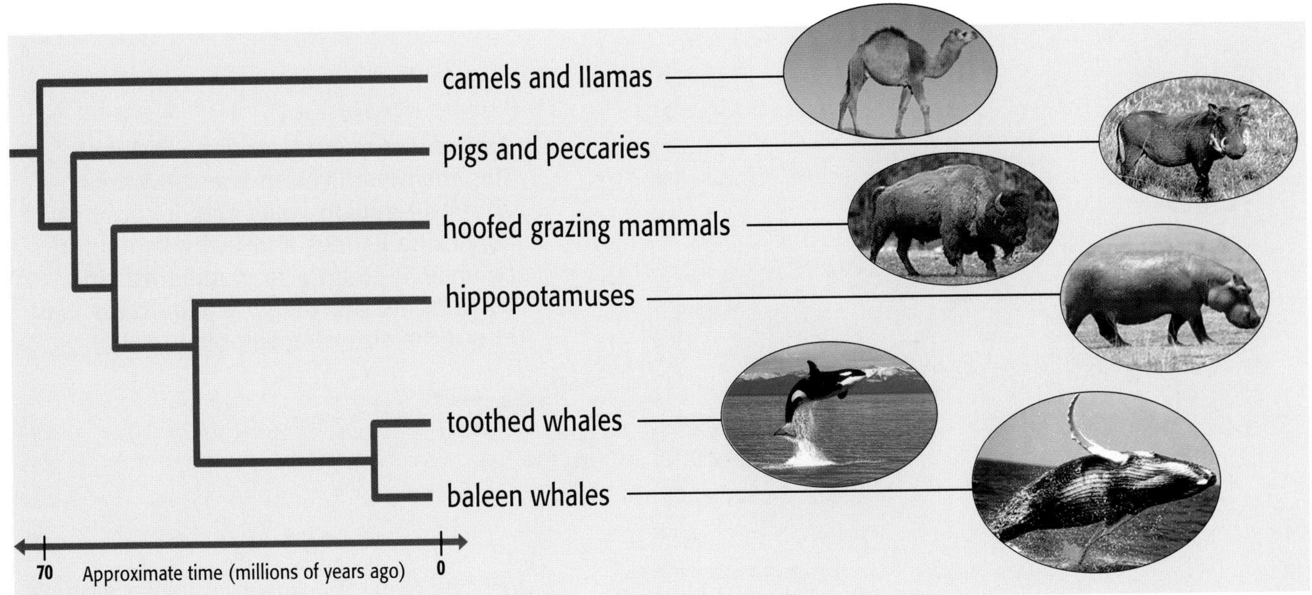

Figure 6 *This diagram is a model of the proposed relationships between ancient and modern mammals that have characteristics similar to whales.*

Examining Organisms

Examining an organism carefully can give scientists clues about its ancestors. For example, whales seem similar to fish. But unlike fish, whales breathe air, give birth to live young, and produce milk. These traits show that whales are *mammals*. Thus, scientists think that whales evolved from ancient mammals.

Case Study: Evolution of the Whale

Scientists think that the ancient ancestor of whales was probably a mammal that lived on land and that could run on four legs. A more recent ancestor was probably a mammal that spent time both on land and in water. Comparisons of modern whales and a large number of fossils have supported this hypothesis. **Figure 7** illustrates some of this evidence.

Reading Check **What kind of organism do scientists think was an ancient ancestor of whales?**

Figure 7 **Evidence of Whale Evolution**

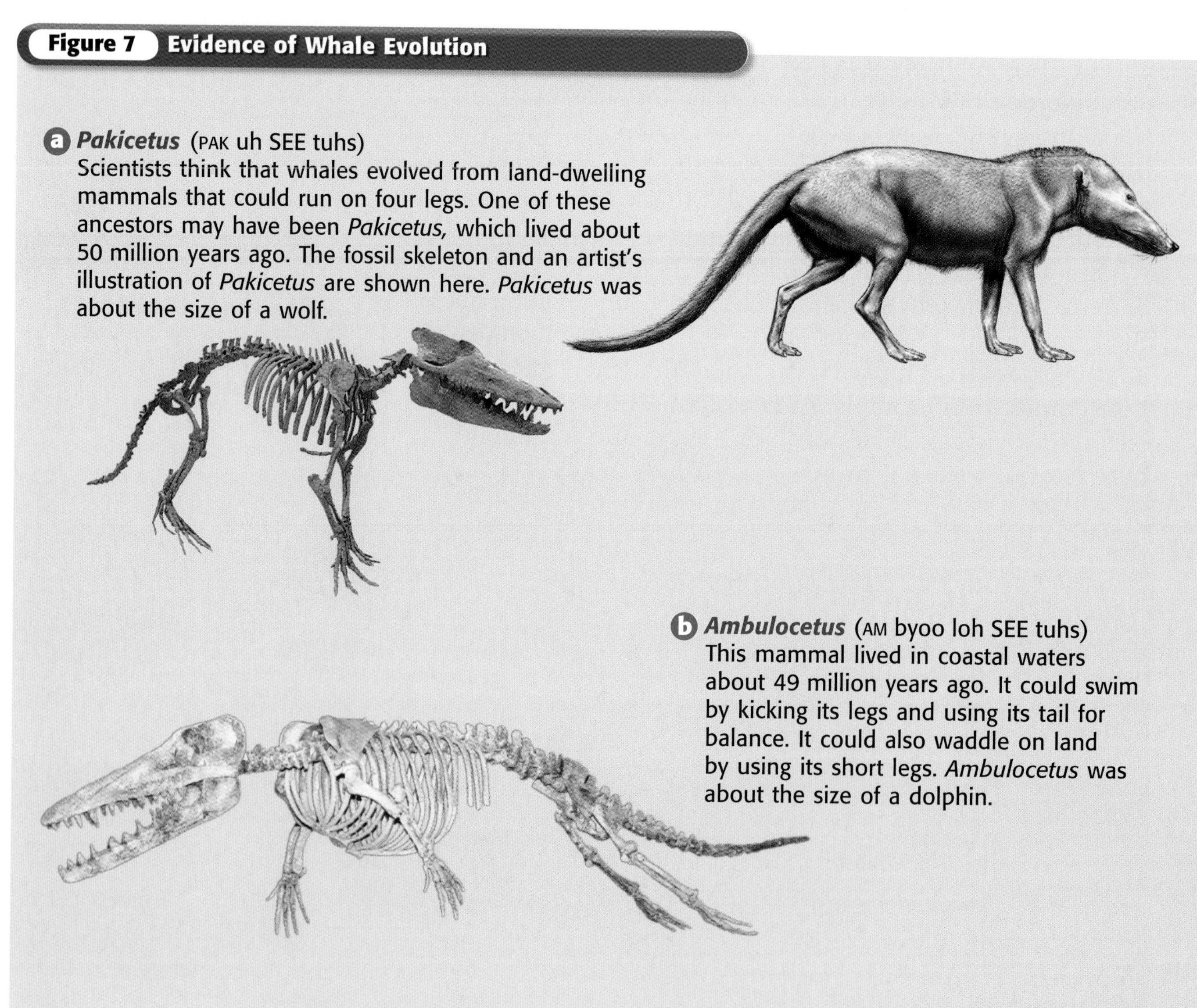

a ***Pakicetus*** (PAK uh SEE tuhs)
Scientists think that whales evolved from land-dwelling mammals that could run on four legs. One of these ancestors may have been *Pakicetus,* which lived about 50 million years ago. The fossil skeleton and an artist's illustration of *Pakicetus* are shown here. *Pakicetus* was about the size of a wolf.

b ***Ambulocetus*** (AM byoo loh SEE tuhs)
This mammal lived in coastal waters about 49 million years ago. It could swim by kicking its legs and using its tail for balance. It could also waddle on land by using its short legs. *Ambulocetus* was about the size of a dolphin.

Walking Whales

The organisms in **Figure 7** form a sequence between ancient four-legged mammals and modern whales. Several pieces of evidence indicate that these species are related by ancestry. Each species shared some traits with an earlier species. However, some species had new traits that were shared with later species. Yet, each species had traits that allowed it to survive in a particular time and place in Earth's history.

Further evidence can be found inside the bodies of living whales. For example, although modern whales do not have hind limbs, inside their bodies are tiny hip bones, as shown in **Figure 7.** Scientists think that these hip bones were inherited from the whales' four-legged ancestors. Scientists often look at this kind of evidence when they want to determine the relationships between organisms.

The Weight of Whales

Whales are the largest animals ever known on Earth. One reason whales can grow so large is that they live in water, which supports their weight in a way that their bones could not. The blue whale—the largest type of whale in existence—is about 24 m long and has a mass of about 99,800 kg. Convert these measurements into feet and pounds, and round to whole numbers.

c ***Dorudon*** (DOH roo DON)
This mammal lived in the oceans about 40 million years ago. It resembled a giant dolphin and propelled itself with its massive tail. *Dorudon* had tiny hind limbs that it could not use for walking or swimming.

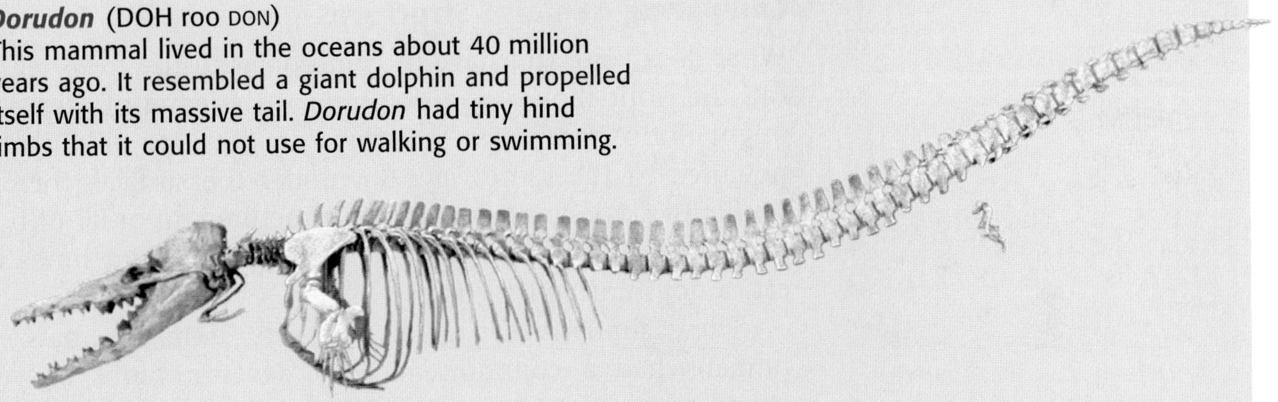

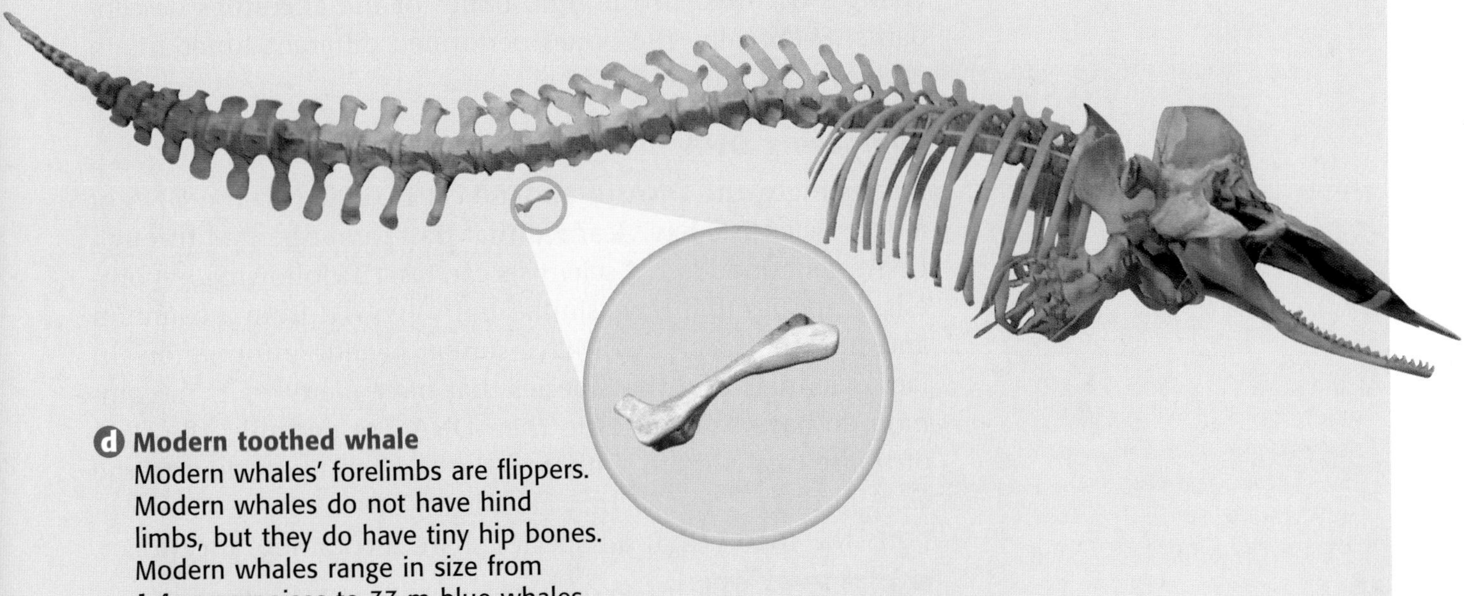

d **Modern toothed whale**
Modern whales' forelimbs are flippers. Modern whales do not have hind limbs, but they do have tiny hip bones. Modern whales range in size from 1.4 m porpoises to 33 m blue whales.

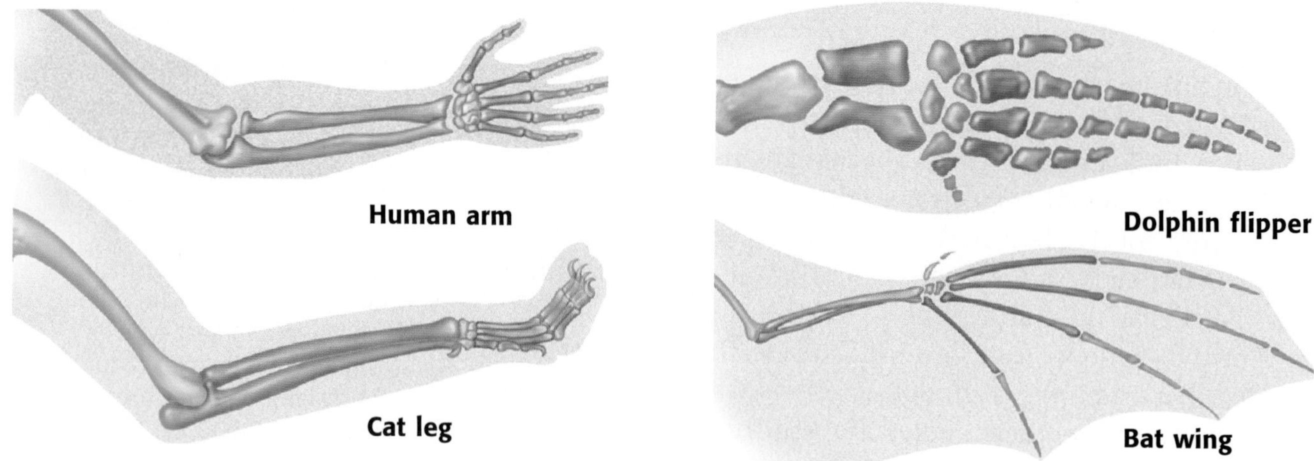

Figure 8 *The bones in the front limbs of these animals are similar. Similar bones are shown in the same color. These limbs are different sizes in life.*

Comparing Organisms

Evidence that groups of organisms have common ancestry can be found by comparing the groups' DNA. Because every organism inherits DNA, every organism inherits the traits determined by DNA. Organisms contain evidence that populations and species undergo changes in traits and DNA over time.

Comparing Skeletal Structures

What does your arm have in common with the front leg of a cat, the front flipper of a dolphin, or the wing of a bat? You might notice that these structures do not look alike and are not used in the same way. But under the surface, there are similarities. Look at **Figure 8.** The structure and order of bones of a human arm are similar to those of the front limbs of a cat, a dolphin, and a bat.

These similarities suggest that cats, dolphins, bats, and humans had a common ancestor. Over millions of years, changes occurred in the limb bones of the ancestor's descendants. Eventually, the bones performed different functions in each type of animal.

Comparing DNA

Interestingly, the DNA of a house cat is similar to the DNA of a tiger. Scientists have learned that traits are inherited through DNA's genetic code. So, scientists can test the following hypothesis: If species that have similar traits evolved from a common ancestor, the species will have similar genetic information. In fact, scientists find that species that have many traits in common do have similarities in their DNA. For example, the DNA of house cats is more similar to the DNA of tigers than to the DNA of dogs. The fact that all existing species have DNA supports the theory that all species share a common ancestor.

Reading Check **If two species have similar DNA, what hypothesis is supported?**

SECTION
Review

Summary

- Evolution is the process in which inherited characteristics within a population change over generations, sometimes giving rise to new species. Scientists continue to develop theories to explain how evolution happens.
- Evidence that organisms evolve can be found by comparing living organisms to each other and to the fossil record. Such comparisons provide evidence of common ancestry.
- Scientists think that modern whales evolved from an ancient, land-dwelling mammal ancestor. Fossil organisms that support this hypothesis have been found.
- Evidence of common ancestry among living organisms is provided by comparing DNA and inherited traits. Species that have a common ancestor will have traits and DNA that are more similar to each other than to those of distantly related species.

Using Key Terms

Complete each of the following sentences by choosing the correct term from the word bank.

adaptation	species
fossil	evolution

1. Members of the same ___ can mate with one another to produce offspring.
2. A(n) ___ helps an organism survive.
3. When populations change over time, ___ has occurred.

Understanding Key Ideas

4. A human's arm, a cat's front leg, a dolphin's front flipper, and a bat's wing
   - **a.** have similar kinds of bones.
   - **b.** are used in similar ways.
   - **c.** are very similar to insect wings and jellyfish tentacles.
   - **d.** have nothing in common.
5. How does the fossil record show that species have changed over time?
6. What evidence do fossils provide about the ancestors of whales?

Critical Thinking

7. **Making Comparisons** Other than the examples provided in the text, how are whales different from fishes?
8. **Forming Hypotheses** Is a person's DNA likely to be more similar to the DNA of his or her biological parents or to the DNA of one of his or her cousins? Explain your answer.

Interpreting Graphics

9. The photograph below shows the layers of sedimentary rock exposed during the construction of a road. Imagine that a species that lived 200 million years ago is found in layer **b.** Would the species' ancestor, which lived 250 million years ago, most likely be found in layer **a** or in layer **c**? Explain your answer.

SCILINKS.
NSTA
Developed and maintained by the National Science Teachers Association
For a variety of links related to this chapter, go to www.scilinks.org
Topic: Species and Adaptation; Fossil Record
SciLinks code: HSM1433; HSM0615

SECTION 2

How Does Evolution Happen?

Imagine that you are a scientist in the 1800s. Fossils of some very strange animals have been found. And some familiar fossils have been found where you would least expect them. How did seashells end up on the tops of mountains?

READING WARM-UP

Objectives

- List four sources of Charles Darwin's ideas about evolution.
- Describe the four parts of Darwin's theory of evolution by natural selection.
- Relate genetics to evolution.

Terms to Learn

trait
selective breeding
natural selection

READING STRATEGY

Brainstorming The key idea of this section is natural selection. Brainstorm words and phrases related to natural selection.

In the 1800s, geologists began to realize that the Earth is much older than anyone had previously thought. Evidence showed that gradual processes had changed the Earth's surface over millions of years. Some scientists saw evidence of evolution in the fossil record. However, no one had been able to explain *how* evolution happens—until Charles Darwin.

Charles Darwin

In 1831, 21-year-old Charles Darwin, shown in **Figure 1,** graduated from college. Like many young people just out of college, Darwin didn't know what he wanted to do with his life. His father wanted him to become a doctor, but seeing blood made Darwin sick. Although he eventually earned a degree in theology, Darwin was most interested in the study of plants and animals.

So, Darwin signed on for a five-year voyage around the world. He served as the *naturalist*—a scientist who studies nature—on the British ship the HMS *Beagle,* similar to the ship in **Figure 2.** During the trip, Darwin made observations that helped him form a theory about how evolution happens.

Figure 1 *Charles Darwin wanted to understand the natural world.*

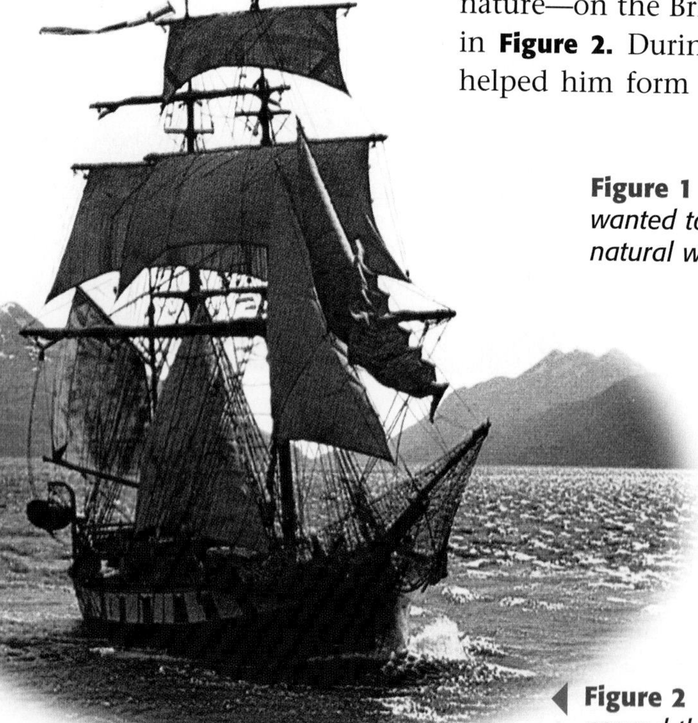

Figure 2 *Darwin sailed around the world on a ship similar to this one.*

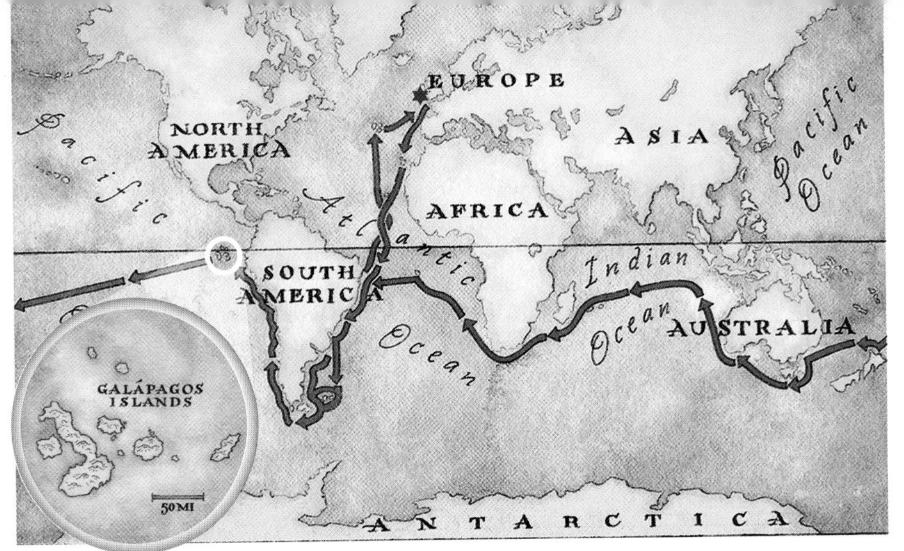

Figure 3 *The course of the HMS* Beagle *is shown by the red line. The journey began and ended in England.*

Darwin's Excellent Adventure

The *Beagle*'s journey is charted in **Figure 3.** Along the way, Darwin collected thousands of plant and animal samples. He kept careful notes of his observations. One interesting place that the ship visited was the Galápagos Islands. These islands are found 965 km (600 mi) west of Ecuador, a country in South America.

Reading Check **Where are the Galápagos Islands?** *(See the Appendix for answers to Reading Checks.)*

Darwin's Finches

Darwin noticed that the animals and plants on the Galápagos Islands were a lot like those in Ecuador. However, they were not exactly the same. The finches of the Galápagos Islands, for example, were a little different from the finches in Ecuador. And the finches on each island differed from the finches on the other islands. As **Figure 4** shows, the beak of each finch is adapted to the way the bird usually gets food.

Figure 4 **Some Finches of the Galápagos Islands**

The **large ground finch** has a wide, strong beak that it uses to crack open big, hard seeds. This beak works like a nutcracker.

The **cactus finch** has a tough beak that it uses for eating cactus parts and insects. This beak works like a pair of needle-nose pliers.

The **warbler finch** has a small, narrow beak that it uses to catch small insects. This beak works like a pair of tweezers.

Darwin's Thinking

After returning to England, Darwin puzzled over the animals of the Galápagos Islands. He tried to explain why the animals seemed so similar to each other yet had so many different adaptations. For example, Darwin hypothesized that the island finches were descended from South American finches. The first finches on the islands may have been blown from South America by a storm. Over many generations, the finches may have adapted to different ways of life on the islands.

During the course of his travels, Darwin came up with many new ideas. Before sharing these ideas, he spent several years analyzing his evidence. He also gathered ideas from many other people.

Ideas About Breeding

trait a genetically determined characteristic

selective breeding the human practice of breeding animals or plants that have certain desired characteristics

In Darwin's time, farmers and breeders had produced many kinds of farm animals and plants. These plants and animals had traits that were desired by the farmers and breeders. **Traits** are specific characteristics that can be passed from parent to offspring through genes. The process in which humans select which plants or animals to reproduce based on certain desired traits is called **selective breeding.** Most pets, such as the dogs in **Figure 5,** have been bred for various desired traits.

You can see the results of selective breeding in many kinds of organisms. For example, people have bred horses that are particularly fast or strong. And farmers have bred crops that produce large fruit or that grow in specific climates.

Figure 5 *Over the past 12,000 years, dogs have been selectively bred to produce more than 150 breeds.*

Population Growth Versus Food Supply

1. Get an **egg carton** and a **bag of rice.** Use a **marker** to label one row of the carton "Food supply." Then, label the second row "Human population."
2. In the row labeled "Food supply," place one grain of rice in the first cup. Place two grains of rice in the second cup, and place three grains of rice in the third cup. In each subsequent cup, place one more grain than you placed in the previous cup. Imagine that each grain represents enough food for one person's lifetime.
3. In the row labeled "Human population," place one grain of rice in the first cup. Place two grains in the second cup, and place four grains in the third cup. In each subsequent cup, place twice as many grains as you placed in the previous cup. This rice represents people.
4. How many units of food are in the sixth cup? How many "people" are in the sixth cup? If this pattern continued, what would happen?
5. Describe how the patterns in the food supply and in the human population differ. Explain how the patterns relate to Malthus's hypothesis.

Ideas About Population

During Darwin's time, Thomas Malthus wrote a famous book entitled *An Essay on the Principle of Population*. Malthus noted that humans have the potential to reproduce rapidly. He warned that food supplies could not support unlimited population growth. **Figure 6** illustrates this relationship. However, Malthus pointed out that human populations are limited by choices that humans make or by problems such as starvation and disease.

After reading Malthus's work, Darwin realized that any species can produce many offspring. He also knew that the populations of all species are limited by starvation, disease, competition, and predation. Only a limited number of individuals survive to reproduce. Thus, there is something special about the survivors. Darwin reasoned that the offspring of the survivors inherit traits that help the offspring survive in their environment.

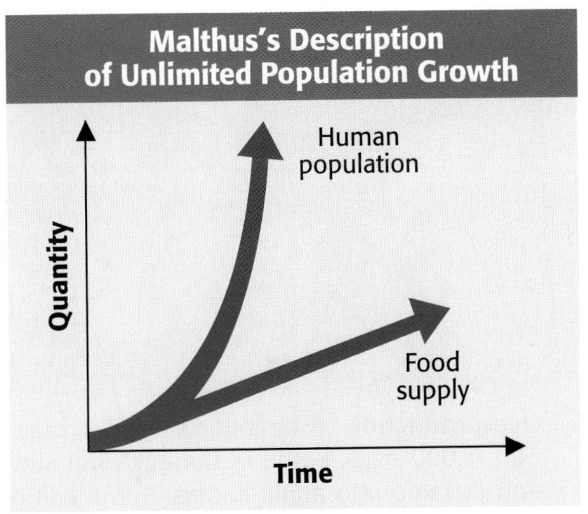

Figure 6 *Malthus thought that the human population could increase more quickly than the food supply, with the result that there would not be enough food for everyone.*

Ideas About Earth's History

Darwin had begun to think that species could evolve over time. But most geologists at the time did not think that Earth was old enough to allow for slow changes. Darwin learned new ideas from *Principles of Geology,* a book by Charles Lyell. This book presented evidence that Earth had formed by natural processes over a long period of time. It became clear to Darwin that Earth was much older than anyone had imagined.

Reading Check What did Darwin learn from Charles Lyell?

Darwin's Theory of Natural Selection

natural selection the process by which individuals that are better adapted to their environment survive and reproduce more successfully than less well adapted individuals do; a theory to explain the mechanism of evolution

After he returned from his voyage on the HMS *Beagle,* Darwin privately struggled with his ideas for about 20 years. Then, in 1858, Darwin received a letter from a fellow naturalist named Alfred Russel Wallace. Wallace had arrived at the same ideas about evolution that Darwin had. Darwin grew more and more motivated to present his ideas. In 1859, Darwin published a famous book called *On the Origin of Species by Means of Natural Selection.* In his book, Darwin proposed the theory that evolution happens through a process that he called **natural selection.** This process, explained in **Figure 7,** has four parts.

Reading Check What is the title of Darwin's famous book?

Figure 7 **Four Parts of Natural Selection**

1 Overproduction A tarantula's egg sac may hold 500–1,000 eggs. Some of the eggs will survive and develop into adult spiders. Some will not.

2 Inherited Variation Every individual has its own combination of traits. Each tarantula is similar to, but not identical to, its parents.

3 Struggle to Survive Some tarantulas may be caught by predators, such as this wasp. Other tarantulas may starve or get a disease. Only some of the tarantulas will survive to adulthood.

4 Successful Reproduction The tarantulas that are best adapted to their environment are likely to have many offspring that survive.

Genetics and Evolution

Darwin lacked evidence for parts of his theory. For example, he knew that organisms inherit traits, but not *how* they inherit traits. He knew that there is great variation among organisms, but not *how* that variation occurs. Today, scientists have found most of the evidence that Darwin lacked. They know that variation happens as a result of differences in genes. Changes in genes may happen whenever organisms produce offspring. Some genes make an organism more likely to survive to reproduce. The process called *selection* happens when only organisms that carry these genes can survive to reproduce. New fossil discoveries and new information about genes add to scientists' understanding of natural selection and evolution.

SECTION Review

Summary

- Darwin explained that evolution occurs through natural selection. His theory has four parts:
  1. Each species produces more offspring than will survive to reproduce.
  2. Individuals within a population have slightly different traits.
  3. Individuals within a population compete with each other for limited resources.
  4. Individuals that are better equipped to live in an environment are more likely to survive to reproduce.
- Modern genetics helps explain the theory of natural selection.

Using Key Terms

1. In your own words, write a definition for the term *trait.*
2. Use the following terms in the same sentence: *selective breeding* and *natural selection.*

Understanding Key Ideas

3. Modern scientific explanations of evolution
   a. have replaced Darwin's theory.
   b. rely on genetics instead of natural selection.
   c. fail to explain how traits are inherited.
   d. combine the principles of natural selection and genetic inheritance.
4. Describe the observations that Darwin made about the species on the Galápagos Islands.
5. Summarize the ideas that Darwin developed from books by Malthus and Lyell.
6. Describe the four parts of Darwin's theory of evolution by natural selection.
7. What knowledge did Darwin lack that modern scientists now use to explain evolution?

Math Skills

8. In a sample of 80 beetles, 50 beetles had 4 spots each, and the rest had 6 spots each. What was the average number of spots per beetle?

Critical Thinking

9. **Making Comparisons** In selective breeding, humans influence the course of evolution. What determines the course of evolution in natural selection?
10. **Predicting Consequences** Suppose that an island in the Pacific Ocean was just formed by a volcano. Over the next million years, how might species evolve on this island?

SCILINKS
NSTA
Developed and maintained by the National Science Teachers Association
For a variety of links related to this chapter, go to www.scilinks.org
Topic: Galápagos Islands; Darwin and Natural Selection
SciLinks code: HSM0631; HSM0378

SECTION 3

Natural Selection in Action

Have you ever had to take an antibiotic? Antibiotics are supposed to kill bacteria. But sometimes, bacteria are not killed by the medicine. Do you know why?

READING WARM-UP

Objectives

- Give three examples of natural selection in action.
- Outline the process of speciation.

Terms to Learn

generation time
speciation

READING STRATEGY

Prediction Guide Before reading this section, write the title of each heading in this section. Next, under each heading, write what you think you will learn.

A population of bacteria might develop an adaptation through natural selection. Most bacteria are killed by the chemicals in antibiotics. But in some cases, a few bacteria are naturally *resistant* to the chemicals, so they are not killed. These survivors are then able to pass this adaptation to their offspring. This situation is an example of how natural selection works.

Changes in Populations

The theory of natural selection explains how a population changes in response to its environment. If natural selection is always taking place, a population will tend to be well adapted to its environment. But not all individuals are the same. The individuals that are likely to survive and reproduce are those that are best adapted at the time.

Adaptation to Hunting

Changes in populations are sometimes observed when a new force affects the survival of individuals. In Uganda, scientists think that hunting is affecting the elephant population. In 1930, about 99% of the male elephants in one area had tusks. Only 1% of the elephants were born without tusks. Today, as few as 85% of the male elephants in that area have tusks. What happened?

A male African elephant that has tusks is shown in **Figure 1.** The ivory of an elephant's tusks is very valuable. People hunt the elephants for their tusks. As a result, fewer of the elephants that have tusks survive to reproduce, and more of the tuskless elephants survive. When the tuskless elephants reproduce, they pass the tuskless trait to their offspring.

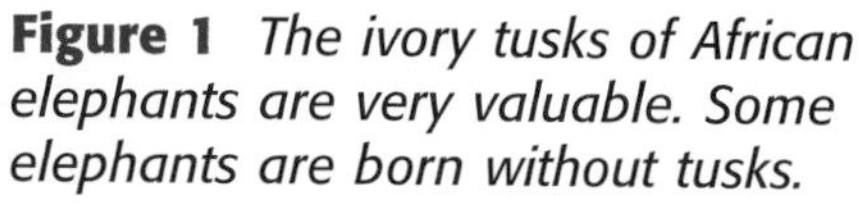

Figure 1 *The ivory tusks of African elephants are very valuable. Some elephants are born without tusks.*

Figure 2 Natural Selection of Insecticide Resistance

1 An insecticide will kill most insects, but a few may survive. These survivors have genes that make them resistant to the insecticide.

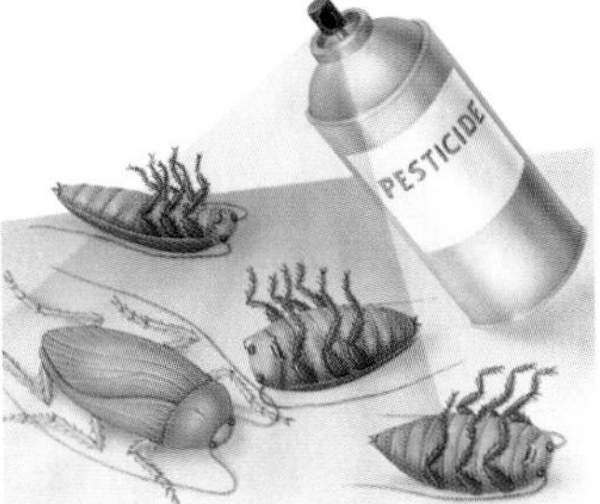

2 The survivors then reproduce, passing the insecticide-resistance genes to their offspring.

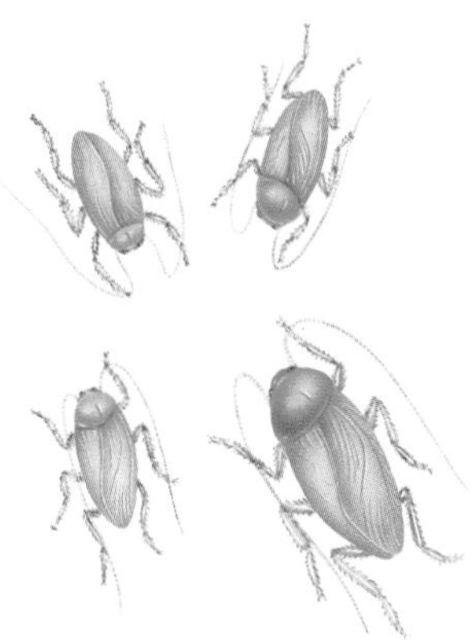

3 In time, the replacement population of insects is made up mostly of individuals that have the insecticide-resistance genes.

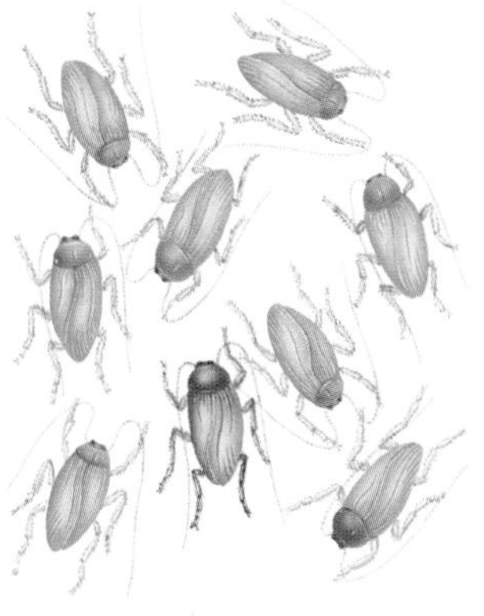

4 When the same kind of insecticide is used on the insects, only a few are killed because most of them are resistant to that insecticide.

Insecticide Resistance

People have always wanted to control the insect populations around their homes and farms. Many insecticides are used to kill insects. But some chemicals that used to work well do not work as well anymore. Some individual insects within the population are resistant to certain insecticides. **Figure 2** shows how a population of insects might become resistant to common insecticides.

More than 500 kinds of insects are now resistant to certain insecticides. Insects can quickly develop resistance because they often produce many offspring and have short generation times. **Generation time** is the average time between one generation of offspring and the next.

generation time the period between the birth of one generation and the birth of the next generation

Reading Check **Why do insects quickly develop resistance to insecticides?** (*See the Appendix for answers to Reading Checks.*)

Competition for Mates

In the process of evolution, survival is simply not enough. Natural selection is at work when individuals reproduce. In organisms that reproduce sexually, finding a mate is part of the struggle to reproduce. Many species have so much competition for mates that interesting adaptations result. For example, the females of many bird species prefer to mate with males that have certain types of colorful feathers.

Forming a New Species

Sometimes, drastic changes that can form a new species take place. In the animal kingdom, a *species* is a group of organisms that can mate with each other to produce fertile offspring. A new species may form after a group becomes separated from the original population. This group forms a new population. Over time, the two populations adapt to their different environments. Eventually, the populations can become so different that they can't mate anymore. Each population may then be considered a new species. The formation of a new species as a result of evolution is called **speciation** (SPEE shee AY shuhn). **Figure 3** shows how new species of Galápagos finches may have formed. Speciation may happen in other ways as well.

speciation the formation of new species as a result of evolution

Separation

Speciation often begins when a part of a population becomes separated from the rest. The process of separation can happen in several ways. For example, a newly formed canyon, mountain range, or lake can divide the members of a population.

Reading Check How can parts of a population become separated?

Figure 3 The Evolution of Galápagos Finch Species

1. Some finches left the mainland and reached one of the islands (separation).

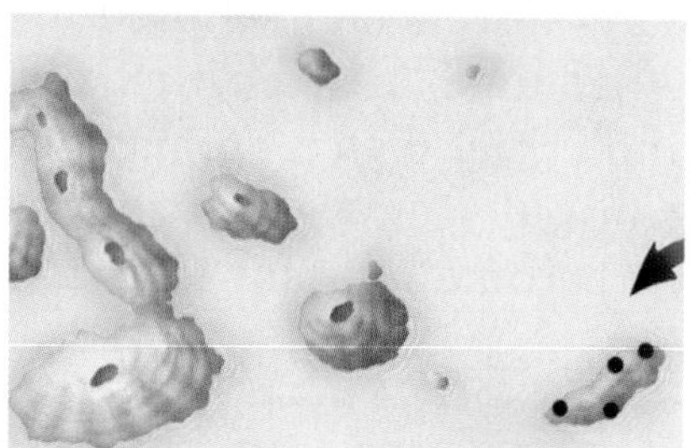

2. The finches reproduced and adapted to the environment (adaptation).

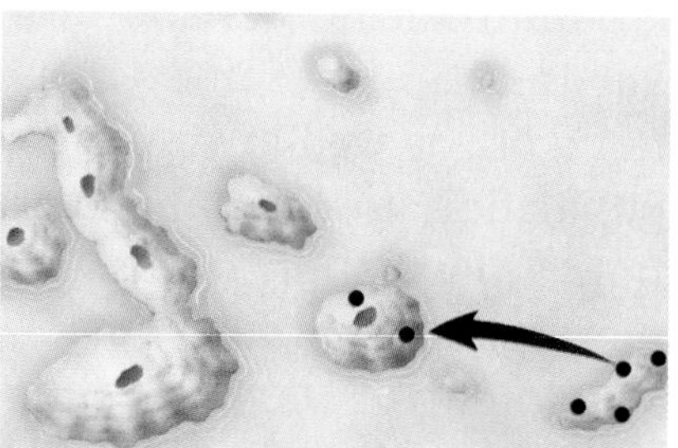

3. Some finches flew to a second island (separation).

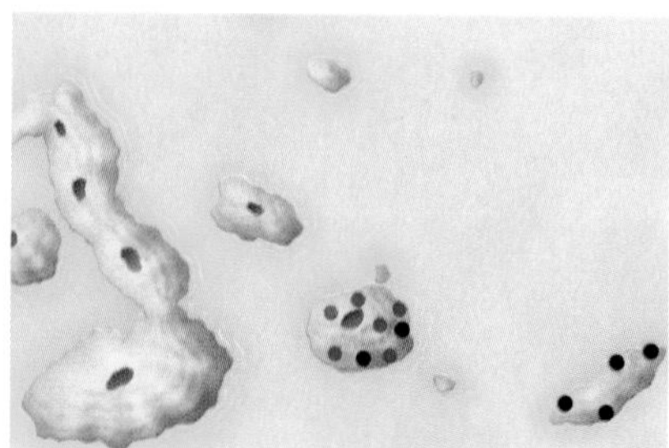

4. The finches reproduced and adapted to the different environment (adaptation).

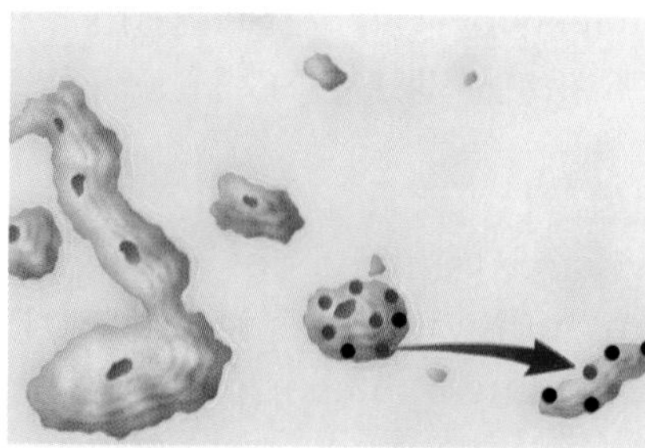

5. Some finches flew back to the first island but could no longer interbreed with the finches there (division).

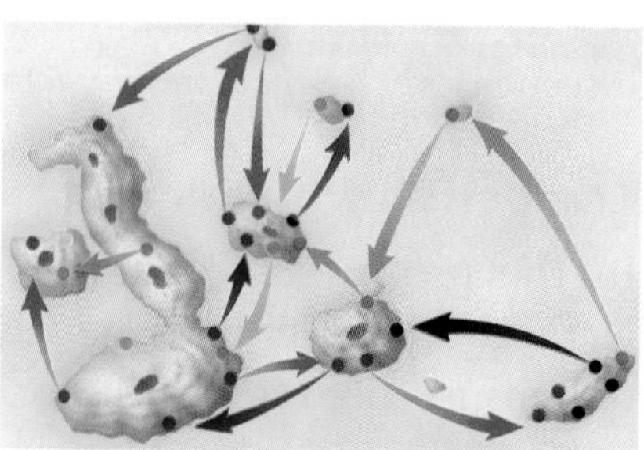

6. This process may have occurred over and over again as the finches flew to the other islands.

Adaptation

Populations constantly undergo natural selection. After two groups have separated, natural selection may act on each group in different ways. Over many generations, the separated groups may evolve different sets of traits. If the environmental conditions for each group differ, the adaptations in the groups will also differ.

Division

Over many generations, two separated groups of a population may become very different. Even if a geographical barrier is removed, the groups may not be able to interbreed anymore. At this point, the two groups are no longer the same species.

Figure 4 shows another way that populations may stop interbreeding. Leopard frogs and pickerel frogs probably had the same ancestor species. Then, at some point, some of these frogs began to mate at different times during the year.

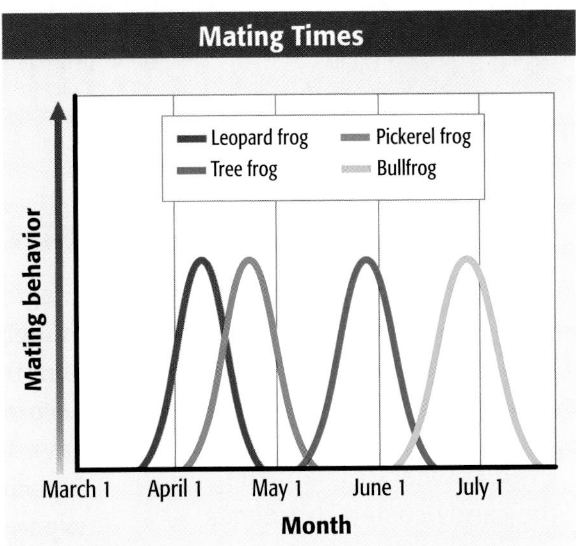

Figure 4 *The leopard frog and the pickerel frog are similar species. However, leopard frogs do not search for mates at the same time of year that pickerel frogs do.*

SECTION Review

Summary

- Natural selection explains how populations adapt to changes in their environment. A variety of examples of such adaptations can be found.
- Natural selection also explains how one species may evolve into another. Speciation occurs as populations undergo separation, adaptation, and division.

Using Key Terms

1. In your own words, write a definition for the term *speciation*.

Understanding Key Ideas

2. Two populations have evolved into two species when
   a. the populations are separated.
   b. the populations look different.
   c. the populations can no longer interbreed.
   d. the populations adapt.
3. Explain why the number of tuskless elephants in Uganda may be increasing.

Math Skills

4. A female cockroach can produce 80 offspring at a time. If half of the offspring produced by a certain female are female and each female produces 80 offspring, how many cockroaches are there in the third generation?

Critical Thinking

5. **Forming Hypotheses** Most kinds of cactus have leaves that grow in the form of spines. The stems or trunks become thick, juicy pads or barrels. Explain how these cactus parts might have evolved.
6. **Making Comparisons** Suggest an organism other than an insect that might evolve an adaptation to human activities.

SCILINKS
NSTA
Developed and maintained by the National Science Teachers Association
For a variety of links related to this chapter, go to www.scilinks.org
Topic: Species and Adaptation
SciLinks code: HSM1433

Using Scientific Methods

Inquiry Lab

Survival of the Chocolates

OBJECTIVES

Form a hypothesis about the fate of the candy-coated chocolates.

Predict what will happen to the candy-coated chocolates.

Design and conduct an experiment to test your hypothesis.

MATERIALS

- chocolates, candy-coated, small, in a variety of colors (about 100)
- items to be determined by the students and approved by the teacher

SAFETY

Imagine a world populated with candy, and hold that delicious thought in your head for just a moment. Try to apply the idea of natural selection to a population of candy-coated chocolates. According to the theory of natural selection, individuals who have favorable adaptations are more likely to survive. In the "species" of candy-coated chocolates you will study in this experiment, the characteristics of individual chocolates may help them "survive." For example, shell strength (the strength of the candy coating) could be an adaptive advantage. Plan an experiment to find out which characteristics of the chocolates are favorable "adaptations."

Ask a Question

1. What might "survival" mean for a candy-coated chocolate? What are some ways you can test which chocolates are the "strongest" or "most fit" for their environment? Also, write down any other questions that you could ask about the "survival" of the chocolates.

Form a Hypothesis

2. Form a hypothesis, and make a prediction. For example, if you chose to study candy color, your prediction might be similar to this: If the ___ colored shell is the strongest, then fewer of the chocolates with this color of shell will ___ when ___.

Test the Hypothesis

3. Design a procedure to determine which type of candy-coated chocolate is most likely to survive. In your plan, be sure to include materials and tools you may need to complete this procedure.

4. Check your experimental design with your teacher before you begin. Your teacher will supply the candy and assist you in gathering materials and tools.

5. Record your results in a data table. Be sure to organize your data in a clear and understandable way.

Analyze the Results

1. **Describing Events** Write a report that describes your experiment. Be sure to include tables and graphs of the data you collected.

Draw Conclusions

2. **Evaluating Data** In your report, explain how your data either support or do not support your hypothesis. Include possible errors and ways to improve your procedure.

Applying Your Data

Can you think of another characteristic of the chocolates that can be tested to determine which type is best adapted to survive? Explain your idea, and describe how you might test it.

Chapter Review

USING KEY TERMS

Complete each of the following sentences by choosing the correct term from the word bank.

adaptation
evolution
generation time
species
speciation
fossil record
selective breeding
natural selection

1. When a single population evolves into two populations that cannot interbreed anymore, ___ has occurred.
2. Darwin's theory of ___ explained the process by which organisms become well-adapted to their environment.
3. A group of organisms that can mate with each other to produce offspring is known as a(n) ___.
4. The ___ provides information about organisms that have lived in the past.
5. In ___, humans select organisms with desirable traits that will be passed from one generation to another.
6. A(n) ___ helps an organism survive better in its environment.
7. Populations of insects and bacteria can evolve quickly because they usually have a short ___.

UNDERSTANDING KEY IDEAS

Multiple Choice

8. Fossils are commonly found in
   - **a.** sedimentary rock.
   - **b.** all kinds of rock.
   - **c.** granite.
   - **d.** loose sand.
9. The fact that all organisms have DNA as their genetic material is evidence that
   - **a.** all organisms undergo natural selection.
   - **b.** all organisms may have descended from a common ancestor.
   - **c.** selective breeding takes place every day.
   - **d.** genetic resistance rarely occurs.
10. Charles Darwin puzzled over differences in the ___ of the different species of Galápagos finches.
    - **a.** webbed feet
    - **b.** beaks
    - **c.** bone structure of the wings
    - **d.** eye color
11. Darwin observed variations among individuals within a population, but he did not realize that these variations were caused by
    - **a.** interbreeding.
    - **b.** differences in food.
    - **c.** differences in genes.
    - **d.** selective breeding.

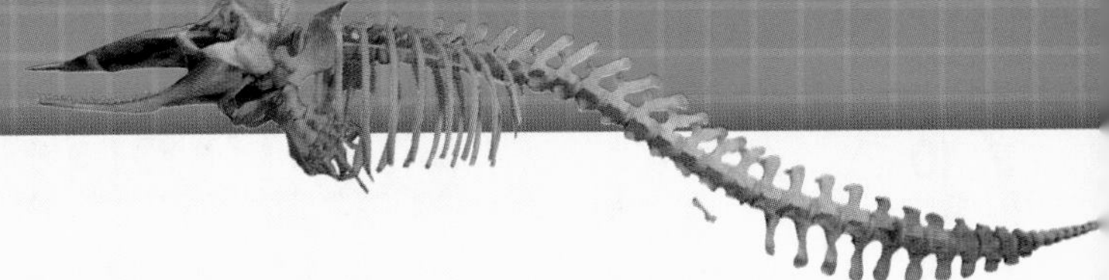

Short Answer

12 Identify two ways that organisms can be compared to provide evidence of evolution from a common ancestor.

13 Describe evidence that supports the hypothesis that whales evolved from land-dwelling mammals.

14 Why are some animals more likely to survive to adulthood than other animals are?

15 Explain how genetics is related to evolution.

16 Outline an example of the process of speciation.

CRITICAL THINKING

17 **Concept Mapping** Use the following terms to create a concept map: *struggle to survive, theory, genetic variation, Darwin, overpopulation, natural selection,* and *successful reproduction.*

18 **Making Inferences** How could natural selection affect the songs that birds sing?

19 **Forming Hypotheses** In Australia, many animals look like mammals from other parts of the world. But most of the mammals in Australia are marsupials, which carry their young in pouches after birth. Few kinds of marsupials are found anywhere else in the world. What is a possible explanation for the presence of so many of these unique mammals in Australia?

20 **Analyzing Relationships** Geologists have evidence that the continents were once a single giant continent. This giant landform eventually split apart, and the individual continents moved to their current positions. What role might this drifting of continents have played in evolution?

INTERPRETING GRAPHICS

The graphs below show information about the infants that are born and the infants that have died in a population. The weight of each infant was measured at birth. Use the graphs to answer the questions that follow.

Infant Births by Birth Weight

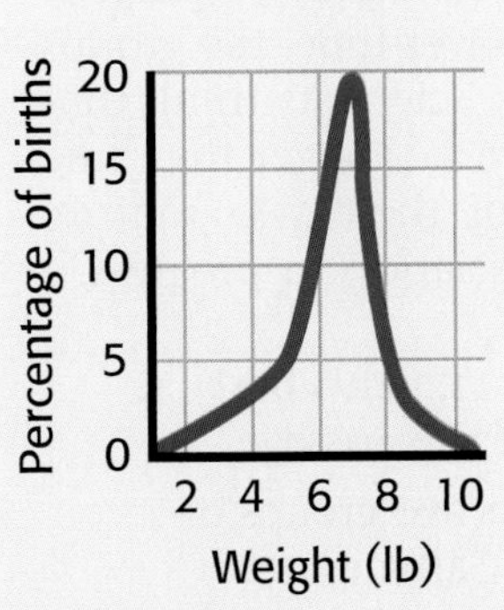

Infant Deaths by Birth Weight

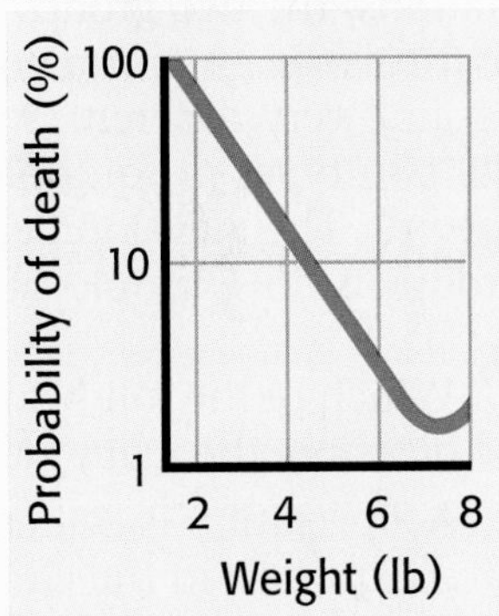

21 What is the most common birth weight?

22 At which birth weight is an infant most likely to survive?

23 How do the principles of natural selection help explain why there are more deaths among babies whose birth weights are low than among babies whose birth weights are average?

Standardized Test Preparation

READING

Read each of the passages below. Then, answer the questions that follow each passage.

Passage 1 When the Grand Canyon was forming, a single population of tassel-eared squirrels may have been separated into two groups. Today, descendants of the two groups live on opposite sides of the canyon. The two groups share many characteristics, but they do not look the same. For example, both groups have tasseled ears, but each group has a unique fur color pattern. An important difference between the groups is that the Abert squirrels live on the south rim of the canyon, and the Kaibab squirrels live on the north rim.

The environments on the two sides of the Grand Canyon are different. The north rim is about 370 m higher than the south rim. Almost twice as much precipitation falls on the north rim than on the south rim every year. Over many generations, the two groups of squirrels have adapted to their new environments. Over time, the groups became very different. Many scientists think that the two types of squirrels are no longer the same species. The development of these two squirrel groups is an example of speciation in progress.

1. Which of the following statements **best** describes the main idea of this passage?

- **A** Speciation is evident in two groups of squirrels in the Grand Canyon area.
- **B** Two groups of squirrels in the Grand Canyon area are closely related.
- **C** Two species can form from one species. This process is called *speciation*.
- **D** There are two groups of squirrels because the Grand Canyon has two sides.

2. Which of the following statements about the two types of squirrels is true?

- **F** They look the same.
- **G** They live in similar environments.
- **H** They have tasseled ears.
- **I** They can interbreed with each other.

Passage 2 You know from experience that individuals in a population are not exactly the same. If you look around the room, you will see a lot of differences among your classmates. You may have even noticed that no two dogs or two cats are exactly the same. No two individuals have exactly the same adaptations. For example, one cat may be better at catching mice, and another is better at running away from dogs. Observations such as these form the basis of the theory of natural selection. Because adaptations help organisms survive to reproduce, the individuals that are better adapted to their environment are more likely to pass their traits to future generations.

1. In the passage, what does *population* mean?

- **A** a school
- **B** some cats and dogs
- **C** a group of the same type of organism
- **D** a group of individuals that are the same

2. In this passage, which of the following are given as examples of adaptations?

- **F** differences among classmates
- **G** differences among cats
- **H** differences between cats and dogs
- **I** differences among environments

3. Which of the following statements about the individuals in a population that survive to reproduce is true?

- **A** They have the same adaptations.
- **B** They are likely to pass on adaptations to the next generation.
- **C** They form the basis of the theory of natural selection.
- **D** They are always better hunters.

INTERPRETING GRAPHICS

The graph below shows average beak sizes of a group of finches on one island over several years. Use the graph to answer the questions that follow.

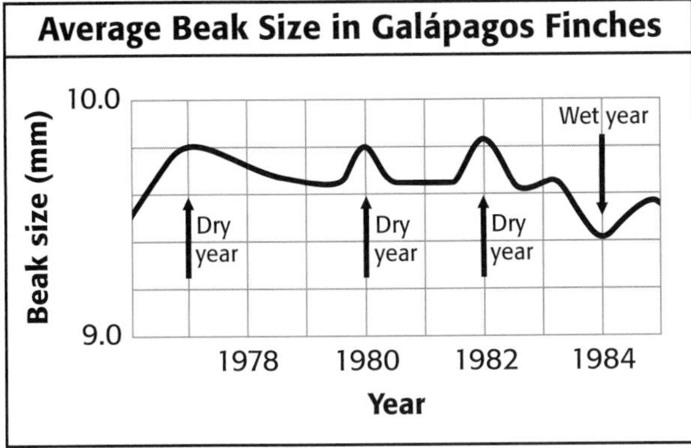

1. In which of the years studied was average beak size the largest?
   A 1977
   B 1980
   C 1982
   D 1984

2. If beak size in this group of birds is linked to the amount of rainfall, what can you infer about the year 1976 on this island?
   F The year 1976 was drier than 1977.
   G The year 1976 was drier than 1980.
   H The year 1976 was wetter than 1977.
   I The year 1976 was wetter than 1984.

3. During which year(s) was rainfall probably the lowest on the island?
   A 1978, 1980, and 1982
   B 1977, 1980, 1982, and 1984
   C 1982
   D 1984

4. Which of the following statements **best** summarizes this data?
   F Average beak size stayed about the same except during wet years.
   G Average beak size decreased during dry years and increased during wet years.
   H Average beak size increased during dry years and decreased during wet years.
   I Average beak size changed randomly.

MATH

Read each question below, and choose the best answer.

Average Beak Measurements of Birds of the Colores Islands

Island	Average beak length (mm)	Average beak width (mm)	Number of unique species
Verde	9.7	6.5	5
Azul	8.9	8.7	15
Rosa	5.2	8.0	10

1. What is the ratio of the number of species on Verde Island to the total number of species on all three of the Colores Islands?
   A 1:2
   B 1:5
   C 1:6
   D 5:15

2. What percentage of all bird species on the Colores Islands are on Rosa Island?
   F approximately 15%
   G approximately 30%
   H approximately 50%
   I approximately 80%

3. On which of the islands is the ratio of average beak length to average beak width closest to 1:1?
   A Verde Island
   B Azul Island
   C Rosa Island
   D There is not enough information to determine the answer.

4. On which island does the bird with the smallest beak length live?
   F Verde Island
   G Azul Island
   H Rosa Island
   I There is not enough information to determine the answer.

Science in Action

Science, Technology, and Society

Seed Banks

All over the world, scientists are making deposits in a special kind of bank. These banks are not for money, but for seeds. Why should seeds be saved? Saving seeds saves plants that may someday save human lives. These plants could provide food or medicine in the future. Throughout human history, many medicines have been developed from plants. And scientists keep searching for new chemicals among the incredible variety of plants in the world. But time is running out. Many plant species are becoming extinct before they have even been studied.

Math Activity

Many drugs were originally developed from plants. Suppose that 100 plants are used for medicines this year, but 5% of plant species become extinct each year. How many of the medicinal plants would be left after 1 year? after 10 years? Round your answers to whole numbers.

Science Fiction

"The Anatomy Lesson" by Scott Sanders

Do you know the feeling you get when you have an important test? A medical student faces a similar situation in this story. The student needs to learn the bones of the human body for an anatomy exam the next day. The student goes to the anatomy library to study. The librarian lets him check out a box of bones that are supposed to be from a human skeleton. But something is wrong. There are too many bones. They are the wrong shape. They don't fit together correctly. Somebody must be playing a joke! Find out what's going on and why the student and the librarian will never be the same after "The Anatomy Lesson." You can read it in the *Holt Anthology of Science Fiction*.

Language Arts Activity

WRITING SKILL Before you read this story, predict what you think will happen. Write a paragraph that "gives away" the ending that you predict. After you have read the story, listen to some of the predictions made by your classmates. Discuss your opinions about the possible endings.

People in Science

Raymond Pierotti

Canine Evolution Raymond Pierotti thinks that it's natural that he became an evolutionary biologist. He grew up exploring the desert around his home in New Mexico. He was fascinated by the abundant wildlife surviving in the bleak landscape. "One of my earliest memories is getting coyotes to sing with me from my backyard," he says.

Pierotti now studies the evolutionary relationships between wolves, coyotes, and domestic dogs. Some of his ideas come from the traditions of the Comanches. According to the Comanche creation story, humans came from wolves. Although Pierotti doesn't believe that humans evolved from wolves, he sees the creation story as a suggestion that humans and wolves have evolved together. "Wolves are very similar to humans in many ways," says Pierotti. "They live in family groups and hunt together. It is possible that wolves actually taught humans how to hunt in packs, and there are ancient stories of wolves and humans hunting together and sharing the food. I think it was this relationship that inspired the Comanche creation stories."

Social Studies ACTIVITY

WRITING SKILL Research a story of creation that comes from a Greek, Roman, or Native American civilization. Write a paragraph summarizing the myth, and share it with a classmate.

To learn more about these Science in Action topics, visit go.hrw.com and type in the keyword **HL5EVOF.**

Current Science

Check out Current Science® articles related to this chapter by visiting go.hrw.com. Just type in the keyword HL5CS07.

8

The History of Life on Earth

About the PHOTO

What is 23,000 years old and 9 ft tall? The partial remains of the woolly mammoth in this picture! The mammoth was found in the frozen ground in Siberia in 1999. Scientists think that several types of woolly mammoths roamed the northern hemisphere until about 4,000 years ago.

PRE-READING ACTIVITY

FOLDNOTES **Layered Book** Before you read the chapter, create the Foldnote entitled "Layered Book" described in the **Study Skills** section of the Appendix. Label the tabs of the layered book with "Precambrian time," "Paleozoic era," "Mesozoic era," and "Cenozoic era." As you read the chapter, write information you learn about each category under the appropriate tab.

START-UP ACTIVITY

Making a Fossil

In this activity, you will make a model of a fossil.

Procedure

1. Get a **paper plate,** some **modeling clay,** and a **leaf** or a **shell** from your teacher.
2. Flatten some of the modeling clay on the paper plate. Push the leaf or shell into the clay. Be sure that your leaf or shell has made a mark in the clay. Remove the leaf or shell carefully.
3. Ask your teacher to cover the clay with **plaster of Paris.** Allow the plaster to dry overnight.
4. Carefully remove the paper plate and the clay from the plaster the next day.

Analysis

1. Consider the following objects—a clam, a seed, a jellyfish, a crab, a leaf, and a mushroom. Which of the objects do you think would make good fossils? Explain your answers.
2. In nature, fossils form only under certain conditions. For example, fossils may form when a dead organism is covered by tiny bits of sand or dirt for a long period of time. The presence of oxygen can prevent fossils from forming. Considering these facts, what are some limitations of your model of how a fossil is formed?

SECTION 1

Evidence of the Past

READING WARM-UP

Objectives

- Explain how fossils can be formed and how their age can be estimated.
- Describe the geologic time scale and the way that scientists use it.
- Compare two ways that conditions for life on Earth have changed over time.

Terms to Learn

fossil
relative dating
absolute dating
geologic time scale
extinct
plate tectonics

READING STRATEGY

Reading Organizer As you read this section, make a concept map by using the terms above.

In 1995, scientist Paul Sereno found a dinosaur skull that was 1.5 m long in the Sahara, a desert in Africa. The dinosaur may have been the largest land predator that has ever existed!

Scientists such as Paul Sereno look for clues to help them reconstruct what happened in the past. These scientists, called *paleontologists* (PAY lee uhn TAHL uh jists), use fossils to reconstruct the history of life before humans existed. Fossils show us that life on Earth has changed a great deal. They also provide us clues about how those changes happened.

Fossils

Fossils are traces or imprints of living things—such as animals, plants, bacteria, and fungi—that are preserved in rock. Fossils sometimes form when a dead organism is covered by a layer of sediment. The sediment may later be pressed together to form sedimentary rock. **Figure 1** shows one way that fossils can form in sedimentary rock.

fossil the remains or physical evidence of an organism preserved by geological processes

Figure 1 One Way Fossils Can Form

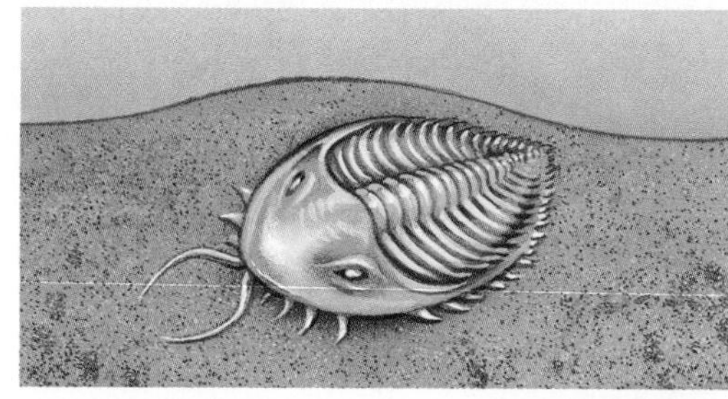

1. Fossils can form in several ways. The most common way is when an organism dies and becomes buried in sediment.

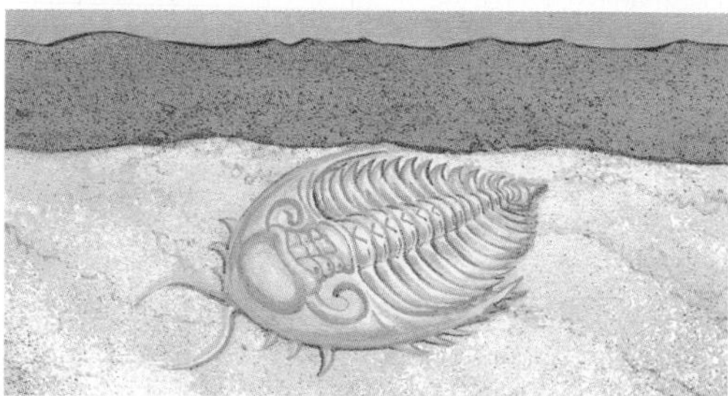

2. The organism gradually decomposes and leaves a hollow impression, or *mold*, in the sediment.

3. Over time, the mold fills with sediment, which forms a *cast* of the organism.

Figure 2 Using Half-Lives to Date Fossils

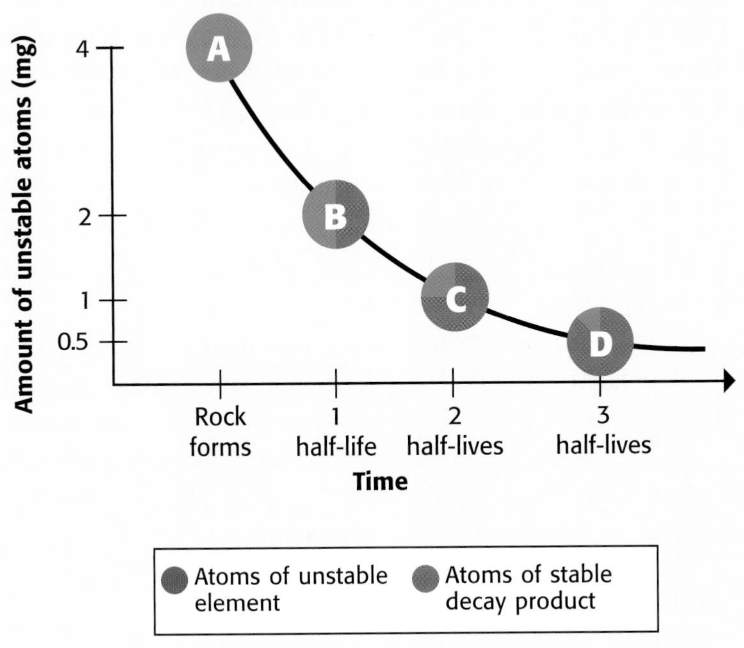

A The unstable atoms in this sample of rock have a half-life of 1.3 billion years. The sample contained 4 mg of unstable atoms when it formed.

B After 1.3 billion years, (one half-life for this type of unstable atom), 2 mg of the unstable atoms have decayed to become stable atoms, and 2 mg of unstable atoms remain.

C After 2.6 billion years (two half-lives for this sample), the rock sample contains 3 mg of stable decay atoms and 1 mg of unstable atoms.

D After three half-lives, only 0.5 mg of unstable atoms remain in the rock sample. This is equal to one-eighth of the original amount.

The Age of Fossils

Sedimentary rock has many layers. The oldest layers are usually on the bottom. The newest layers are usually on the top. The layers can tell a scientist the relative age of fossils. Fossils found in the bottom layers are usually older than the fossils in the top layers. So, scientists can determine whether a fossil is older or younger than other fossils based on its position in sedimentary rock. Estimating the age of rocks and fossils in this way is called **relative dating.**

In addition, scientists can determine the age of a fossil more precisely. **Absolute dating** is a method that measures the age of fossils or rocks in years. In one type of absolute dating, scientists examine atoms. *Atoms* are the particles that make up all matter. Atoms, in turn, are made of smaller particles. Some atoms are unstable and will decay by releasing energy, particles, or both. When an atom decays it becomes a different, and more stable, kind of atom. Each kind of unstable atom decays at its own rate. As shown in **Figure 2,** the time it takes for half of the unstable atoms in a sample to decay is the *half-life* of that type of unstable atom. By measuring the ratio of unstable atoms to stable atoms, scientists can determine the approximate age of a sample of rock.

Reading Check Which type of fossil dating is more precise? (*See the Appendix for answers to Reading Checks.*)

relative dating any method of determining whether an event or object is older or younger than other events or objects

absolute dating any method of measuring the age of an object or event in years

Fractions of Fractions

Find the answer to each of the following problems. Be sure to show your work. You may want to draw pictures.

1. 1/2 × 1/2 × 1/2 × 1/2
2. 1/2 × 1/8
3. 1/4 × 1/4

The Geologic Time Scale

Think about important events that have happened during your lifetime. You usually recall each event in terms of the day, month, or year in which it happened. These divisions of time make it easier to recall when you were born, when you kicked the winning soccer goal, or when you started the fifth grade. Scientists also use a type of calendar to divide the Earth's long history. The span of time from the formation of the Earth to now is very long. Therefore, the calendar is divided into very long units of time.

The calendar scientists use to outline the history of life on Earth is called the **geologic time scale,** shown in **Table 1.** After a fossil is dated, a paleontologist can place the fossil in chronological order with other fossils. This ordering forms a picture of the past that shows how organisms have changed over time.

Table 1 Geologic Time Scale

Era	Period	Time*
Cenozoic era	Quaternary	2
	Tertiary	65
Mesozoic era	Cretaceous	144
	Jurassic	206
	Triassic	248
Paleozoic era	Permian	290
	Carboniferous	345
	Devonian	408
	Silurian	439
	Ordovician	495
	Cambrian	543
Precambrian time		4,600

indicates how many millions of years ago the period began

Divisions in the Geologic Time Scale

Paleontologists have divided the geologic time scale into large blocks of time. Each block may be divided into smaller blocks of time as scientists continue to find more fossil information.

The divisions known as *era*s are characterized by the type of organism that dominated the Earth at the time. For instance, the Mesozoic era—dominated by dinosaurs and other reptiles—is referred to as the *Age of Reptiles.* Eras began with a change in the type of organism that was most dominant.

Paleontologists sometimes adjust and add details to the geologic time scale. For example, the early history of the Earth has been poorly understood. There is little evidence that life existed billions of years ago. So, the earliest part of the geologic time scale is not named as an era. But more evidence of life before the Paleozoic era is being gathered. Scientists have proposed using this evidence to name new eras before the Paleozoic era.

CONNECTION TO Social Studies

A Place in Time Most of the periods of the Paleozoic era were named by geologists for places where rocks from that period are found. Research the name of each period of the Paleozoic era listed in **Table 1.** On a copy of a world map, label the locations related to each name.

ACTIVITY

Figure 3 *Scientists think that a meteorite hit Earth about 65 million years ago and caused major climate changes.*

Mass Extinctions

Some of the important divisions in the geologic time scale mark times when rapid changes happened on Earth. During these times, many species died out completely, or became **extinct**. When a species is extinct, it does not reappear. At certain points in the Earth's history, a large number of species disappeared from the fossil record. These periods when many species suddenly become extinct are called *mass extinctions*.

Scientists are not sure what caused each of the mass extinctions. Most scientists think that the extinction of the dinosaurs happened because of extreme changes in the climate on Earth. These changes could have resulted from a giant meteorite hitting the Earth, as shown in **Figure 3.** Or, forces within the Earth could have caused many volcanoes and earthquakes.

Reading Check What are mass extinctions?

geologic time scale the standard method used to divide the Earth's long natural history into manageable parts

extinct describes a species that has died out completely

Making a Geologic Timeline

1. Use a **metric ruler** to mark 10 cm sections on a **strip of paper** that is 46 cm long.
2. Label each 10 cm section in order from top to bottom as follows: 1 bya (billion years ago), 2 bya, etc. The timeline begins at 4.6 bya.
3. Divide each 10 cm section into 10 equal subsections. Divide the top 1 cm into 10 subsections. Calculate the number of years that are represented by 1 mm on this scale.
4. On your timeline, label the following events:
   a. Earth forms. (4.6 billion years ago)
   b. First animals appear. (600 million years ago)
   c. Dinosaurs appear. (251 million years ago)
   d. Dinosaurs are extinct. (65 million years ago)
   e. Humans appear. (160,000 years ago)
5. Label other events from the chapter.
6. Describe what most of the timeline looks like.
7. Compare the length of time dinosaurs existed with the length of time humans have existed.

Figure 4 *The continents have been slowly moving throughout the history of Earth. The colored areas show the location of the continents 245 million years ago, and blue outlines show where the continents are today.*

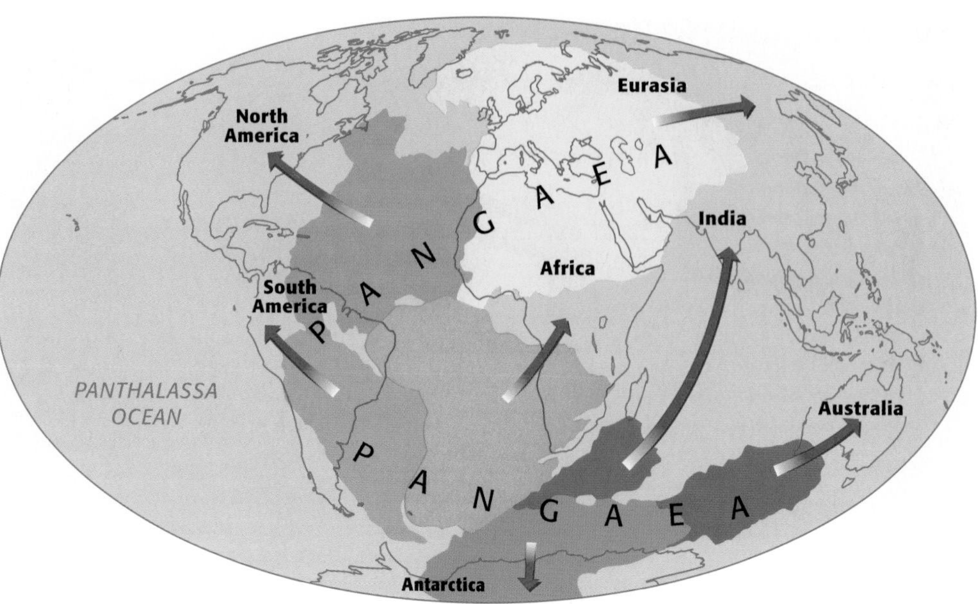

The Changing Earth

Did you know that fossils of tropical plants have been found in Antarctica? Antarctica, now frozen, must have once had a warm climate to support these plants. The fossils provide evidence that Antarctica was once located near the equator!

plate tectonics the theory that explains how large pieces of the Earth's outermost layer, called *tectonic plates,* move and change shape

Pangaea

Have you ever noticed that the continents look like pieces of a puzzle? German scientist Alfred Wegener had a similar thought in the early 1900s. He proposed that long ago the continents formed one landmass surrounded by a gigantic ocean. Wegener called that single landmass *Pangaea* (pan JEE uh), which means "all Earth." **Figure 4** shows how the continents may have formed from Pangaea.

Reading Check **What idea did Alfred Wegener propose?**

Do the Continents Move?

In the mid-1960s, J. Tuzo Wilson of Canada came up with the idea that the continents were not moving by themselves. Wilson thought that huge pieces of the Earth's crust were pushed around by forces within the planet. Each huge piece of crust is called a *tectonic plate.* Wilson's theory of how these huge pieces of crust move around the Earth is called **plate tectonics.**

According to Wilson, the outer crust of the Earth is broken into seven large, rigid plates and several smaller ones. The continents and oceans ride on top of these plates. The motion of the plates causes the continents to move. For example, the plates that carry South America and Africa are slowly moving apart, as shown in **Figure 5.**

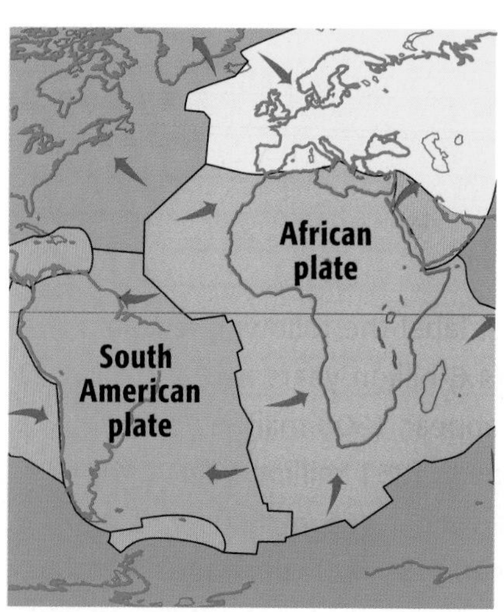

Figure 5 *The continents ride on tectonic plates, outlined here in black. The plates are still moving about 1 to 10 cm per year.*

Adaptation to Slow Changes

When conditions on the Earth change, organisms may become extinct. A rapid change, such as a meteorite impact, may cause a mass extinction. But slow changes, such as moving continents, allow time for adaptation.

Anywhere on Earth, you are able to see living things that are well adapted to the location where they live. Yet in the same location, you may find evidence of organisms that lived there in the past that were very different. For example, the animals currently living in Antarctica are able to survive very cold temperatures. But under the frozen surface of Antarctica are the remains of tropical forests. Conditions on Earth have changed many times in history, and life has changed, too.

Mid-Atlantic Ridge In 1947, scientists examined rock from a ridge that runs down the middle of the Atlantic Ocean, between Africa and the Americas. They found that this rock was much younger than the rock on the continents. Explain what this finding indicates about the tectonic plates.

SECTION Review

Summary

- Fossils are formed most often in sedimentary rock. The age of a fossil can be determined using relative dating and absolute dating.
- The geologic time scale is a timeline that is used by scientists to outline the history of Earth and life on Earth.
- Conditions for life on Earth have changed many times. Rapid changes, such as a meteorite impact, might have caused mass extinctions. But many groups of organisms have adapted to changes such as the movement of tectonic plates.

Using Key Terms

1. Use the following terms in the same sentence: *fossil* and *extinct.*
2. In your own words, write a definition for the term *plate tectonics.*

Understanding Key Ideas

3. Explain how a fossil forms in sedimentary rock.
4. What kind of information does the geologic time scale show?
5. About how many years of Earth's history was Precambrian time?
6. What are two possible causes of mass extinctions?

Math Skills

7. The Earth formed 4.6 billion years ago. Modern humans have existed for about 160,000 years. Simple worms have existed for at least 500 million years. For what fraction of the history of Earth have humans existed? have worms existed?

Critical Thinking

8. **Identifying Relationships** Why are both absolute dating and relative dating used to determine the age of fossils?
9. **Making Inferences** Fossils of *Mesosaurus,* the small aquatic reptile shown below, have been found only in Africa and South America. Using what you know about plate tectonics, how would you explain this finding?

For a variety of links related to this chapter, go to www.scilinks.org

Topic: Evidence of the Past
SciLinks code: HSM0545

SECTION 2

Eras of the Geologic Time Scale

The walls of the Grand Canyon are layered with different kinds and colors of rocks. The deeper down into the canyon you go, the older the layers of rocks. Try to imagine a time when the bottom layer was the only layer that existed.

READING WARM-UP

Objectives

- Outline the major developments that allowed life to exist on Earth.
- Describe the types of organisms that arose during the four major divisions of the geologic time scale.

Terms to Learn

Precambrian time
Paleozoic era
Mesozoic era
Cenozoic era

READING STRATEGY

Mnemonics As you read this section, create a mnemonic device to help you remember the eras of geologic time.

Each layer of rock tells a story about what was happening on Earth when that layer was on top. The rocks and fossils in each layer tell the story. Scientists have compared the stories told by fossils and rocks all over the Earth. From these stories, scientists have divided geologic history into four major parts. These divisions are Precambrian time, the Paleozoic era, the Mesozoic era, and the Cenozoic era.

Precambrian Time

The layers at the bottom of the Grand Canyon are from the oldest part of the geologic time scale. **Precambrian time** (pree KAM bree UHN TIEM) is the time from the formation of Earth 4.6 billion years ago to about 543 million years ago. Life on Earth began during this time.

Scientists think that the early Earth was very different than it is today. The atmosphere was made of gases such as water vapor, carbon dioxide, and nitrogen. Also, the early Earth was a place of great turmoil, as illustrated in **Figure 1.** Volcanic eruptions, meteorite impacts, and violent storms were common. Intense radiation from the sun bombarded Earth's surface.

Precambrian time the period in the geologic time scale from the formation of the Earth to the beginning of the Paleozoic era, from about 4.6 billion to 543 million years ago

Reading Check **Describe the early Earth.** (*See the Appendix for answers to Reading Checks.*)

Figure 1 *This illustration shows the conditions under which the first life on Earth may have formed.*

How Did Life Begin?

Scientists think that life developed from simple chemicals in the oceans and in the atmosphere. Energy from radiation and storms could have caused these chemicals to react. Some of these reactions formed the complex molecules that made life possible. Eventually, these molecules may have joined to form structures such as cells.

The early atmosphere of the Earth did not contain oxygen gas. The first organisms did not need oxygen to survive. These organisms were *prokaryotes* (proh KAR ee OHTS), or single-celled organisms that lack a nucleus.

For another activity related to this chapter, go to **go.hrw.com** and type in the keyword **HL5HISW.**

Photosynthesis and Oxygen

There is evidence that *cyanobacteria,* a new kind of prokaryotic organism, appeared more than 3 billion years ago. Some cyanobacteria are shown in **Figure 2.** Cyanobacteria use sunlight to produce their own food. Along with doing other things, this process releases oxygen. The first cyanobacteria began to release oxygen gas into the oceans and air.

Eventually, some of the oxygen formed a new layer of gas in the upper atmosphere. This gas, called *ozone,* absorbs harmful radiation from the sun, as shown in **Figure 3.** Before ozone formed, life existed only in the oceans and underground. The new ozone layer reduced the radiation on Earth's surface.

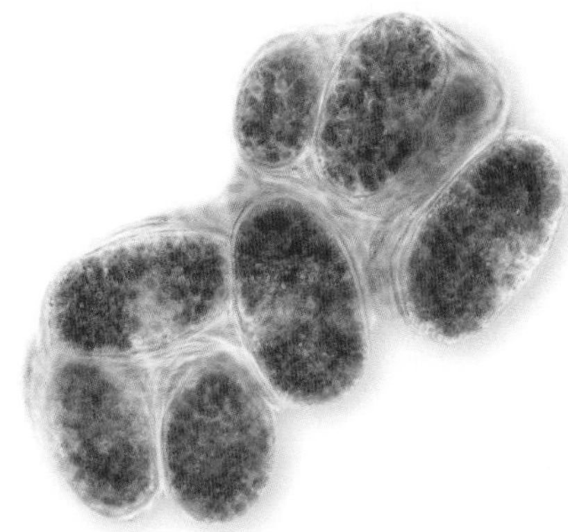

Figure 2 *Cyanobacteria are the simplest living organisms that use the sun's energy to produce their own food.*

Multicellular Organisms

After about 1 billion years, organisms that were larger and more complex than prokaryotes appeared in the fossil record. These organisms, known as *eukaryotes* (yoo KAR ee OHTS), contain a nucleus and other complex structures in their cells. Eventually, eukaryotic cells may have evolved into organisms that are composed of many cells.

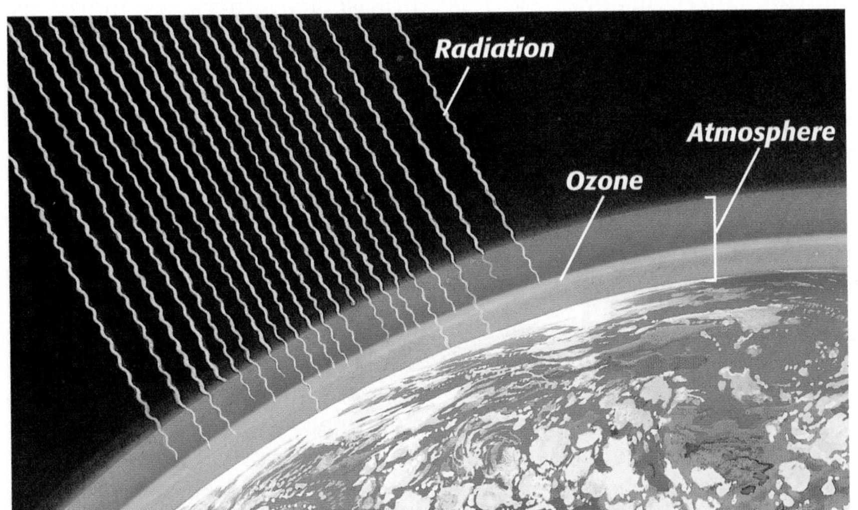

Figure 3 *Oxygen in the atmosphere formed a layer of ozone, which helps to absorb harmful radiation from the sun.*

Figure 4 *Organisms that first appeared in the Paleozoic era include reptiles, amphibians, fishes, worms, and ferns.*

The Paleozoic Era

The **Paleozoic era** (PAY lee OH ZOH ik ER uh) began about 543 million years ago and ended about 248 million years ago. Considering the length of Precambrian time, you can see that the Paleozoic era was relatively recent. Rocks from the Paleozoic era are rich in fossils of animals such as sponges, corals, snails, clams, squids, and trilobites. Fishes, the earliest animals with backbones, appeared during this era, and sharks became abundant. **Figure 4** shows an artist's depiction of life in the Paleozoic era.

The word *Paleozoic* comes from Greek words that mean "ancient life." When scientists first named this era, they thought it held the earliest forms of life. Scientists now think that earlier forms of life existed, but less is known about those life-forms. Before the Paleozoic era, most organisms lived in the oceans and left few fossils.

Life on Land

During the 300 million years of the Paleozoic era, plants, fungi, and air-breathing animals slowly colonized land. By the end of the era, forests of giant ferns, club mosses, horsetails, and conifers covered much of the Earth. All major plant groups except for flowering plants appeared during this era. These plants provided food and shelter for animals.

Fossils indicate that crawling insects were some of the first animals to live on land. They were followed by large salamander-like animals. Near the end of the Paleozoic era, reptiles and winged insects appeared.

The largest mass extinction known took place at the end of the Paleozoic era. By 248 million years ago, as many as 90% of all Paleozoic species had become extinct. The mass extinction wiped out entire groups of marine organisms, such as trilobites. The oceans were completely changed.

Paleozoic era the geologic era that followed Precambrian time and that lasted from 543 million to 248 million years ago

CONNECTION TO Oceanography

Prehistoric Marine Organisms Find a variety of pictures and descriptions of marine organisms from the Cambrian period of the Paleozoic era. Choose three organisms that you find interesting. Draw or write a description of each organism. Find out whether scientists think the organism is related to any living group of organisms, and add this information to your description.

The Mesozoic Era

The **Mesozoic era** (MES oh ZOH ik ER uh) began about 248 million years ago and lasted about 183 million years. *Mesozoic* comes from Greek words that mean "middle life." Scientists think that the surviving reptiles evolved into many different species after the Paleozoic era. Therefore, the Mesozoic era is commonly called the *Age of Reptiles*.

Life in the Mesozoic Era

Dinosaurs are the most well known reptiles that evolved during the Mesozoic era. Dinosaurs dominated the Earth for about 150 million years. A great variety of dinosaurs lived on Earth. Some had unique adaptations, such as ducklike bills for feeding or large spines on their bodies for defense. In addition to dinosaurs roaming the land, giant marine lizards swam in the ocean. The first birds also appeared during the Mesozoic era. In fact, scientists think that some of the dinosaurs became the ancestors of birds.

The most important plants during the early part of the Mesozoic era were conifers, which formed large forests. Flowering plants appeared later in the Mesozoic era. Some of the organisms of the Mesozoic era are illustrated in **Figure 5.**

Figure 5 *The Mesozoic era was dominated by dinosaurs. The era ended with the mass extinction of many species.*

The Extinction of Dinosaurs

At the end of the Mesozoic era, 65 million years ago, dinosaurs and many other animal and plant species became extinct. What happened to the dinosaurs? According to one hypothesis, a large meteorite hit the Earth and generated giant dust clouds and enough heat to cause worldwide fires. The dust and smoke from these fires blocked out much of the sunlight and caused many plants to die out. Without enough plants to eat, the plant-eating dinosaurs died out. And the meat-eating dinosaurs that fed on the plant-eating dinosaurs died. Global temperatures may have dropped for many years. However, some mammals and birds survived.

Reading Check What kind of event happened at the end of both the Paleozoic and Mesozoic eras?

Mesozoic era the geologic era that lasted from 248 million to 65 million years ago; also called the *Age of Reptiles*

Figure 6 *Many types of mammals evolved during the Cenozoic era.*

The Cenozoic Era

The **Cenozoic era** (SEN uh ZOH ik ER uh) began about 65 million years ago and continues today. *Cenozoic* comes from Greek words that mean "recent life." Scientists have more information about the Cenozoic era than about any of the previous eras. Fossils from the Cenozoic era formed recently in geologic time, so they are found in rock layers closer to the Earth's surface. The closer the fossils are to the surface, the easier they are to find.

During the Cenozoic era, many kinds of mammals, birds, insects, and flowering plants appeared. Some organisms that appeared in the Cenozoic era are shown in **Figure 6.**

Reading Check What does *Cenozoic* mean?

The Age of Mammals

The Cenozoic era is sometimes called the *Age of Mammals*. Mammals have dominated the Cenozoic era the way reptiles dominated the Mesozoic era. Early Cenozoic mammals were small, forest dwellers. Larger mammals appeared later in the era. Some of these larger mammals had long legs for running, teeth that were specialized for eating different kinds of food, and large brains. Cenozoic mammals have included mastodons, saber-toothed cats, camels, giant ground sloths, and small horses.

MATH FOCUS

Relative Scale It's hard to imagine 4.6 billion years. One way is to use a *relative scale*. For example, we can represent all of Earth's history by using the 12 h shown on a clock. The scale would begin at noon, representing 4.6 billion years ago, and end at midnight, representing the present. Because 12 h represent 4.6 billion years, 1 h represents about 383 million years. (Hint: 4.6 billion ÷ 12 = 383 million) So, what time on the clock represents the beginning of the Paleozoic era, 543 million years ago?

Step 1: Write the ratio.

$$\frac{x}{543{,}000{,}000 \text{ years}} = \frac{1 \text{ h}}{383{,}000{,}000 \text{ years}}$$

Step 2: Solve for *x*.

$$x = \frac{543{,}000{,}000 \text{ years} \times 1 \text{ h}}{383{,}000{,}000 \text{ years}} = 1.42 \text{ h}$$

Step 3: Convert the answer to the clock scale.

$$1.42 \text{ h} = 1 \text{ h} + (0.42 \times 60 \text{ min/h})$$

$$1.42 \text{ h} = 1 \text{ h } 25 \text{ min}$$

So, the Paleozoic era began 1 h 25 min before midnight, at about 10:35.

Now It's Your Turn

1. Use this method to calculate the relative times at which the Mesozoic and Cenozoic eras began.

The Cenozoic Era Today

We are currently living in the Cenozoic era. Modern humans appeared during this era. The environment and landscapes that we see around us today are part of this era.

However, the climate has changed many times during the Cenozoic era. Earth's history includes some periods called *ice ages,* during which the climate was very cold. During the ice ages, ice sheets and glaciers extended from the Earth's poles. To survive, many organisms migrated toward the equator. Other organisms adapted to the cold or became extinct.

When will the Cenozoic era end? No one knows. In the future, geologists might draw the line at a time when life on Earth again undergoes major changes.

Cenozoic era the most recent geologic era, beginning 65 million years ago; also called the *Age of Mammals*

SECTION Review

Summary

- The Earth is about 4.6 billion years old. Life formed from nonliving matter long ago.
- Precambrian time includes the formation of the Earth and the appearance of simple organisms.
- The first cells did not need oxygen. Later, photosynthetic cells evolved and released oxygen into the atmosphere.
- During the Paleozoic era, animals appeared in the oceans and on land, and plants grew on land.
- Dinosaurs dominated the Earth during the Mesozoic era.
- Mammals have dominated the Cenozoic era. This era continues today.

Using Key Terms

1. Use each of the following terms in a separate sentence: *Precambrian time, Paleozoic era, Mesozoic era,* and *Cenozoic era.*

Understanding Key Ideas

2. Unlike the atmosphere today, the atmosphere 3.5 billion years ago did not contain
   a. carbon dioxide.
   b. nitrogen.
   c. gases.
   d. ozone.
3. How do prokaryotic cells and eukaryotic cells differ?
4. Explain why cyanobacteria were important to the development of life on Earth.
5. Place in chronological order the following events on Earth:
   a. The first cells appeared that could make their own food from sunlight.
   b. The ozone layer formed.
   c. Simple chemicals reacted to form the molecules of life.
   d. Animals appeared.
   e. The first organisms appeared.
   f. Humans appeared.
   g. The Earth formed.

Math Skills

6. Calculate the total number of years that each of the geologic eras lasted, rounding to the nearest 100 million. Then, calculate each of these values as a percentage of the total 4.6 billion years of Earth's history. Round your answer to the units place.

Critical Thinking

7. **Making Inferences** Which chemicals probably made up the first cells on Earth?
8. **Forming Hypotheses** Think of your own hypothesis to explain the disappearance of the dinosaurs. Explain your hypothesis.

SCILINKS.
NSTA
Developed and maintained by the National Science Teachers Association
For a variety of links related to this chapter, go to www.scilinks.org
Topic: Geologic Time Scale
SciLinks code: HSM0669

SECTION 3

Humans and Other Primates

READING WARM-UP

Objectives

- Describe two characteristics that all primates share.
- Describe three major groups of hominids.

Terms to Learn

primate
hominid
Homo sapiens

READING STRATEGY

Discussion Read this section silently. Write down questions that you have about this section. Discuss your questions in a small group.

Have you ever heard someone say that humans descended from monkeys or apes? Well, scientists would not exactly say that. The scientific theory is that humans, apes, and monkeys share a common ancestor. This common ancestor probably lived more than 45 million years ago.

Most scientists agree that there is enough evidence to support this theory. Many fossils of organisms have been found that show traits of both humans and apes. Also, comparisons of modern humans and apes support this theory.

Primates

What characteristics make us human? Humans are classified as primates. **Primates** are a group of mammals that includes humans, apes, monkeys, and lemurs. Primates have the characteristics illustrated in **Figure 1.**

primate a type of mammal characterized by opposable thumbs and binocular vision

The First Primates

The ancestors of primates may have co-existed with the dinosaurs. These ancestors were probably mouselike mammals that were active at night, lived in trees, and ate insects. The first primates did not exist until after the dinosaurs died out. About 45 million years ago, primates that had larger brains appeared. These were the first primates that had traits similar to monkeys, apes, and humans.

Figure 1 **Characteristics of Primates**

Both eyes are located at the front of the head, and they provide binocular, or three-dimensional, vision.

Almost all primates, such as these orangutans, have five flexible fingers—four fingers and an opposable thumb. This thumb enables primates to grip objects. Most primates besides humans also have opposable big toes.

Apes and Chimpanzees

Scientists think that the chimpanzee, a type of ape, is the closest living relative of humans. This theory does not mean humans descended from chimpanzees. It means that humans and chimpanzees share a common ancestor. Sometime between 5 million and 30 million years ago, the ancestors of humans, chimpanzees, and other apes began to evolve along different lines.

Hominids

Humans are in a family separate from other primates. This family, called **hominids,** includes only humans and their human-like ancestors. The main characteristic that separates hominids from other primates is bipedalism. *Bipedalism* means "walking primarily upright on two feet." Evidence of bipedalism can be seen in a primate's skeletal structure. **Figure 2** shows a comparison of the skeletal features of apes and hominids.

hominid a type of primate characterized by bipedalism, relatively long lower limbs, and lack of a tail

Reading Check **In which family are humans classified?**
(See the Appendix for answers to Reading Checks.)

Figure 2 Comparison of Primate Skeletons

The bones of gorillas (a type of ape) and humans (a type of hominid) have a very similar form, but the human skeleton is adapted for walking upright.

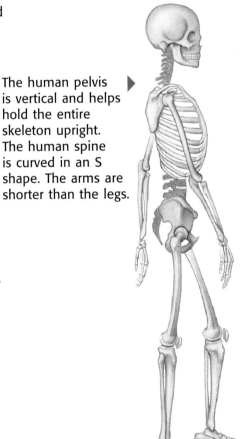

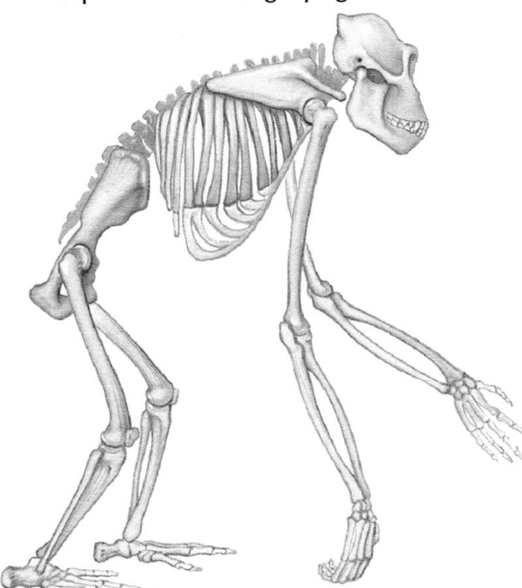

▲ The gorilla pelvis tilts the ape's large rib cage and heavy neck and head forward. The gorilla spine is curved in a C shape. The arms are long to provide balance on the ground.

The human pelvis is vertical and helps hold the entire skeleton upright. The human spine is curved in an S shape. The arms are shorter than the legs. ▶

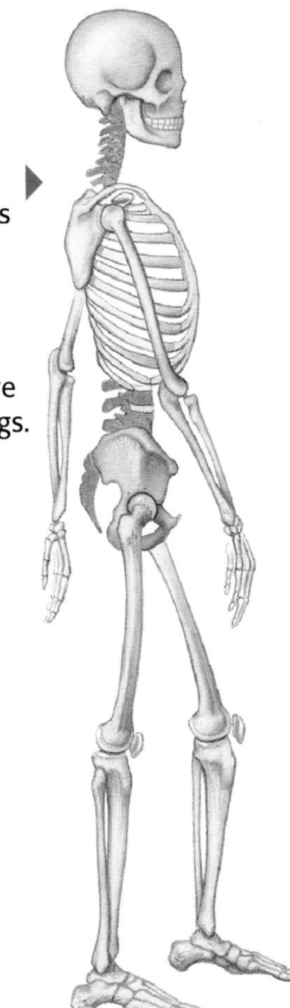

Hominids Through Time

Figure 3 *This skull was found in the Sahel desert in Chad, Africa. The skull is estimated to be 6 million to 7 million years old.*

Scientists are constantly filling in pieces of the hominid family picture. They have found many different fossils of ancient hominids and have named at least 18 types of hominids. However, scientists do not agree on the classification of every fossil. Fossils are classified as hominids when they share some of the characteristics of modern humans. But each type of hominid was unique in terms of size, the way it walked, the shape of its skull, and other characteristics.

The Earliest Hominids

The earliest hominids had traits that were more humanlike than apelike. These traits include the ability to walk upright as well as smaller teeth, flatter faces, and larger brains than earlier primates. The oldest hominid fossils have been found in Africa. So, scientists think hominid evolution began in Africa. **Figure 3** shows a fossil that may be from one of the earliest hominids. It is 6 million to 7 million years old.

Where are the earliest hominid fossils found?

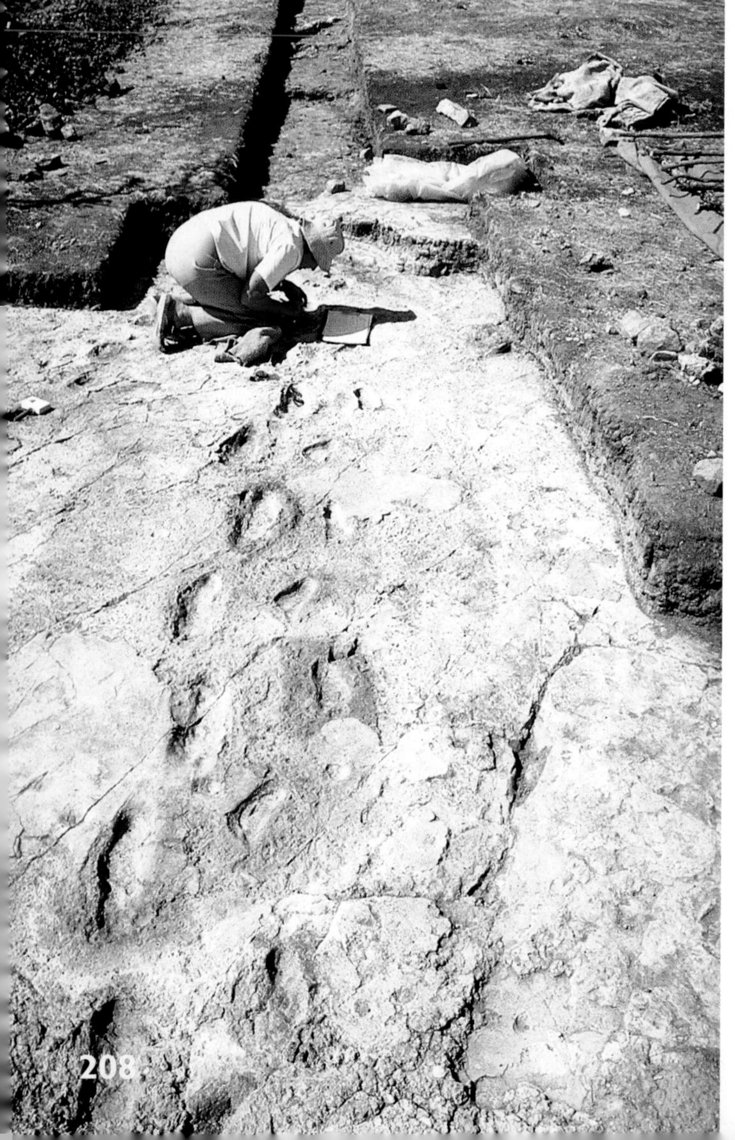

Australopithecines

Many early hominids are classified as *australopithecines* (AW struh LOH PITH uh SEENS). Members of this group were similar to apes but were different from apes in several ways. For example, their brains were slightly larger than the brains of apes. Some of them may have used stone tools. They climbed trees but also walked on two legs.

Fossil evidence of australopithecines has been found in several places in Africa. The fossilized footprints in **Figure 4** were probably made by a member of this group over 3 million years ago. Some skeletons of australopithecines have been found near what appear to be simple tools.

Figure 4 *Anthropologist Mary Leakey discovered these 3.6 million year old footprints in Tanzania, Africa.*

A Variety of Early Hominids

Many australopithecines and other types of hominids lived at the same time. Some australopithecines had slender bodies. They had humanlike jaws and teeth but had small, apelike skulls. They probably lived in forests and grasslands and ate a vegetarian diet. Scientists think that some of these types of hominids may have been the ancestors of modern humans.

Some early hominids had large bodies and massive teeth and jaws. They had a unique skull structure and relatively small brains. Most of these types of hominids lived in tropical forests and probably ate tough plant material, such as roots. Scientists do not think that these large-bodied hominids are the ancestors of modern humans.

Thumb Through This

1. Keep your thumbs from moving by attaching them to the sides of your hands with **tape.**
2. Attempt each of the following tasks: using a **pencil sharpener,** using **scissors,** tying your **shoelaces,** buttoning **buttons.**
3. After each attempt, answer the following questions:
   a. Is the task more difficult with an opposable thumb or without one?
   b. Do you think you would carry out this task on a regular basis if you did not have an opposable thumb?

ACTIVITY

Global Hominids

About 2.3 million years ago, a new group of hominids appeared. These hominids were similar to the slender australopithecines but were more humanlike. These new hominids had larger and more complex brains, rounder skulls, and flatter faces than early hominids. They showed advanced tool-making abilities and walked upright.

These new hominids were members of the group *Homo,* which includes modern humans. Fossil evidence indicates that several members of the *Homo* group existed at the same time and on several continents. Members of this group were probably scavengers that ate a variety of foods. Some of these hominids may have adapted to climate change by migrating and changing the way they lived.

An early member of this new group was *Homo habilis* (HOH moh HAB uh luhs), which lived about 2 million years ago. In another million years, a hominid called *Homo erectus* (HOH moh i REK tuhs) appeared. This type of hominid could grow as tall as modern humans do. A museum creation of a member of *Homo erectus* is shown in **Figure 5.** No one knows what early hominids looked like. Scientists construct models based on skulls and other evidence.

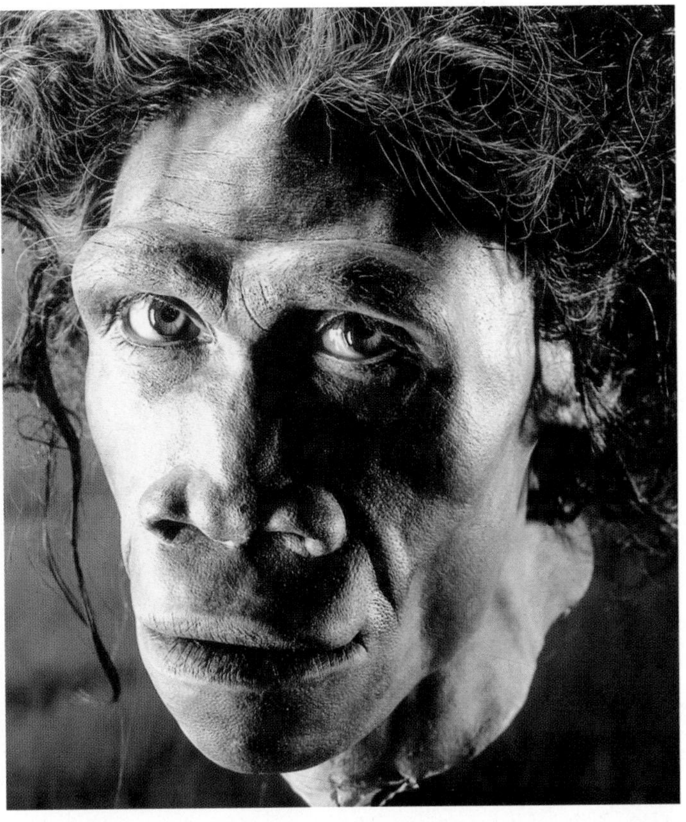

Figure 5 *Fossils of a hominid known as* Homo erectus *have been found in Africa, Europe, and Asia.*

Recent Hominids

As recently as 30,000 years ago, two types of hominids may have lived in the same areas at the same time. Both had the largest brains of any hominids and made advanced tools, clothing, and art. Scientists think that modern humans may have descended from one of these two types of hominids.

Neanderthals

One recent hominid is known as *Neanderthal* (nee AN duhr TAWL). Neanderthals lived in Europe and western Asia. They may have lived as early as 400,000 years ago. They hunted large animals, made fires, and wore clothing. They also may have cared for the sick and elderly and buried their dead with cultural rituals. About 30,000 years ago, Neanderthals disappeared. No one knows what caused their extinction.

Homo sapiens the species of hominids that includes modern humans and their closest ancestors and that first appeared about 100,000 to 160,000 years ago

Early and Modern Humans

Modern humans are classified as the species ***Homo sapiens*** (HOH moh SAY pee UHNZ). The earliest *Homo sapiens* existed in Africa 100,000 to 160,000 years ago. The group migrated out of Africa sometime between 40,000 and 100,000 years ago. Compared with Neanderthals, *Homo sapiens* has a smaller and flatter face, and has a skull that is more rounded. Of all known hominids, only *Homo sapiens* still exists.

Homo sapiens seems to be the first to create art. Early humans produced sculptures, carvings, paintings, and clothing such as that shown in **Figure 6.** The preserved villages and burial grounds of early humans show that they had an organized and complex society.

Figure 6 *These photos show museum recreations of early* Homo sapiens.

Drawing the Hominid Family Tree

Scientists review their hypotheses when they learn something new about a group of organisms and their related fossils. As more hominid fossils are discovered, there are more features to compare. Sometimes, scientists add details to the relationships they see between each group. Sometimes, new groups of hominids are recognized. Human evolution was once thought to be a line of descent from ancient primates to modern humans. But scientists now speak of a "tree" or even a "bush" to describe the evolution of various hominids in the fossil record.

Reading Check **What is likely to happen when a new hominid fossil is discovered?**

SECTION Review

Summary

- Humans, apes, and monkeys are primates. Almost all primates have opposable thumbs and binocular vision.
- Hominids, a subgroup of primates, include humans and their humanlike ancestors. The oldest known hominid fossils may be 7 million years old.
- Early hominids included australopithecines and the *Homo* group.
- Early *Homo sapiens* did not differ very much from present-day humans. *Homo sapiens* is the only type of hominid living today.

Using Key Terms

1. Use each of the following words in the same sentence: *primate, hominid,* and *Homo sapiens.*

Understanding Key Ideas

2. The unique characteristics of primates are
   a. bipedalism and thumbs.
   b. opposable thumbs.
   c. opposable thumbs and binocular vision.
   d. opposable toes and thumbs.
3. Describe the major evolutionary developments from early hominids to modern humans.
4. Compare members of the *Homo* group with australopithecines.

Critical Thinking

5. **Forming Hypotheses** Suggest some reasons why Neanderthals might have become extinct.
6. **Making Inferences** Imagine you are a scientist excavating an ancient campsite. What might you infer about the people who used the site if you found the charred bones of large animals and various stone blades among human fossils?

Interpreting Graphics

The figure below shows a possible ancestral relationships between humans and some modern apes. Use this figure to answer the questions that follow.

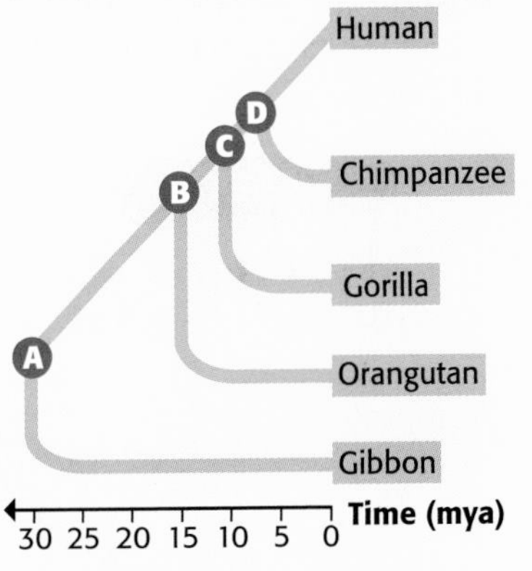

7. Which letter represents the ancestor of all the apes?
8. To which living ape are gorillas most closely related?

SCILINKS.
NSTA
Developed and maintained by the National Science Teachers Association
For a variety of links related to this chapter, go to www.scilinks.org
Topic: Human Evolution
SciLinks code: HSM0769

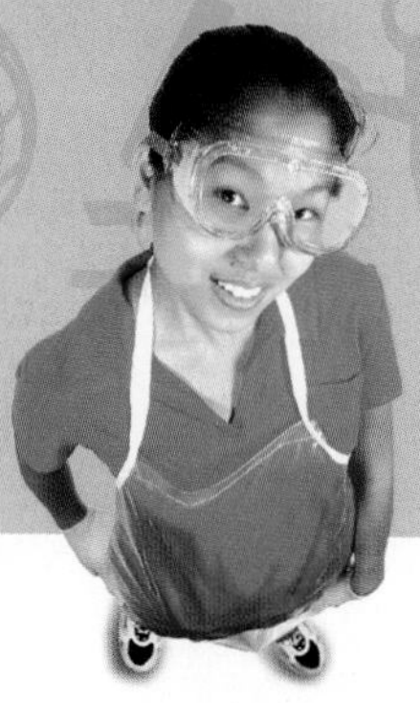

Using Scientific Methods

Inquiry Lab

Mystery Footprints

Sometimes, scientists find clues preserved in rocks that are evidence of the activities of organisms that lived thousands of years ago. Evidence such as preserved footprints can provide important information about an organism. Imagine that your class has been asked by a group of scientists to help study some human footprints. These footprints were found embedded in rocks in an area just outside of town.

OBJECTIVES

Form a hypothesis to explain observations of traces left by other organisms.

Design and **conduct** an experiment to test one of these hypotheses.

Analyze and **communicate** the results in a scientific way.

MATERIALS

- ruler, metric or meterstick
- sand, slightly damp
- large box, at least 1 m^2 or large enough to contain 3 or 4 footprints

SAFETY

Ask a Question

1. Your teacher will give you some mystery footprints in sand. Examine the mystery footprints. Brainstorm what you might learn about the people who walked on this patch of sand.

Form a Hypothesis

2. As a class, formulate several testable hypotheses about the people who left the footprints. Form groups of three people, and choose one hypothesis for your group to investigate.

Test the Hypothesis

3. Draw a table for recording your data. For example, if you have two sets of mystery footprints, your table might look similar to the one below.

Mystery Footprints

	Footprint set 1	Footprint set 2
Length		
Width		
Depth of toe	DO NOT WRITE IN BOOK	
Depth of heel		
Length of stride		

4. With the help of your group, you may first want to analyze your own footprints to help you draw conclusions about the mystery footprints. For example, use a meterstick to measure your stride when you are running. Is your stride different when you are walking? What part of your foot touches the ground first when you are running? When you are running, which part of your footprint is deeper?
5. Make a list of the kind of footprint each different activity produces. For example, you might write, "When I am running, my footprints are deep near the toe area and 110 cm apart."

Analyze the Results

1. **Classifying** Compare the data from your footprints with the data from the mystery footprints. How are the footprints alike? How are they different?
2. **Identifying Patterns** How many people do you think made the mystery footprints? Explain your interpretation.
3. **Analyzing Data** Can you tell if the mystery footprints were made by men, women, children, or a combination? Can you tell if they were standing still, walking, or running? Explain your interpretation.

Draw Conclusions

4. **Drawing Conclusions** Do your data support your hypothesis? Explain.
5. **Evaluating Methods** How could you improve your experiment?

Communicating Your Data

WRITING SKILL Summarize your group's conclusions in a report for the scientists who asked for your help. Begin by stating your hypothesis. Then, summarize the methods you used to study the footprints. Include the comparisons you made between your footprints and the mystery footprints. Add pictures if you wish. State your conclusions. Finally, offer some suggestions about how you could improve your investigation.

Chapter Review

USING KEY TERMS

Complete each of the following sentences by choosing the correct term from the word bank.

Precambrian time	Paleozoic era
Mesozoic era	Cenozoic era

1. During ___, life is thought to have originated from nonliving matter.
2. The Age of Mammals refers to the ___.
3. The Age of Reptiles refers to the ___.
4. Plants colonized land during the ___.

For each pair of terms, explain how the meanings of the terms differ.

5. *relative dating* and *absolute dating*
6. *primates* and *hominids*

UNDERSTANDING KEY IDEAS

Multiple Choice

7. If the half-life of an unstable element is 5,000 years, what percentage of the parent material will be left after 10,000 years?
   - **a.** 100%
   - **b.** 75%
   - **c.** 50%
   - **d.** 25%
8. The first cells on Earth appeared in
   - **a.** Precambrian time.
   - **b.** the Paleozoic era.
   - **c.** the Mesozoic era.
   - **d.** the Cenozoic era.
9. In which era are we currently living?
   - **a.** Precambrian time
   - **b.** Paleozoic era
   - **c.** Mesozoic era
   - **d.** Cenozoic era
10. Scientists think that the closest living relatives of humans are
    - **a.** lemurs.
    - **b.** monkeys.
    - **c.** gorillas.
    - **d.** chimpanzees.

Short Answer

11. Describe how plant and animal remains can become fossils.
12. What information do fossils provide about the history of life?
13. List three important steps in the early development of life on Earth.
14. List two important groups of organisms that appeared during each of the three most recent geologic eras.
15. Describe the event that scientists think caused the mass extinction at the end of the Mesozoic era.

16 From which geologic era are fossils most commonly found?

17 Describe two characteristics that are shared by all primates.

18 Which hominid species is alive today?

CRITICAL THINKING

19 **Concept Mapping** Use the following terms to create a concept map: *Earth's history, humans, Paleozoic era, dinosaurs, Precambrian time, land plants, Mesozoic era, cyanobacteria,* and *Cenozoic era.*

20 **Applying Concepts** Can footprints be fossils? Explain your answer.

21 **Making Inferences** If you find rock layers containing fish fossils in a desert, what can you infer about the history of the desert?

22 **Applying Concepts** Explain how an environmental change can threaten the survival of a species. Give two examples.

23 **Analyzing Ideas** Why do scientists think the first cells did not need oxygen to survive?

24 **Identifying Relationships** How does the extinction that occurred at the end of the Mesozoic era relate to the Age of Mammals?

25 **Making Comparisons** Make a table listing the similarities and differences between australopithecines, early members of the group *Homo*, and modern members of the species *Homo sapiens*.

INTERPRETING GRAPHICS

The graph below shows data about fossilized teeth that were found within a series of rock layers. Use this graph to answer the questions that follow.

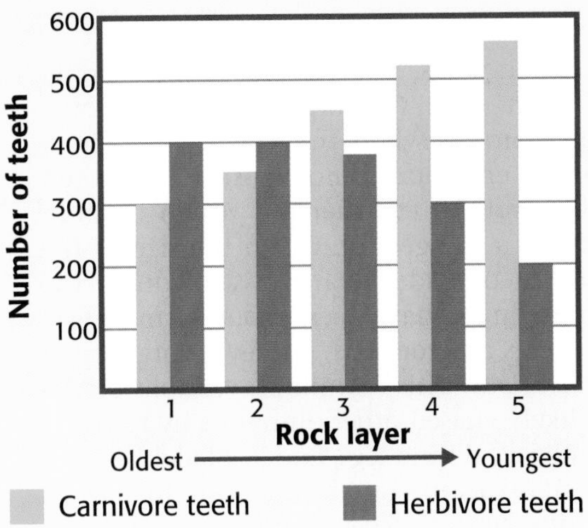

26 Which of the following statements best describes the information presented in the graph?

a. Over time, the number of carnivores decreased and the number of herbivores increased.

b. Over time, the number of carnivores increased and the number of herbivores increased.

c. Over time, the number of carnivores and herbivores remained the same.

d. Over time, the number of carnivores increased and the number of herbivores decreased.

27 At what point did carnivore teeth begin to outnumber herbivore teeth?

a. between layer 1 and layer 2

b. between layer 2 and layer 3

c. between layer 3 and layer 4

d. between layer 4 and layer 5

Standardized Test Preparation

READING

Read each of the passages below. Then, answer the questions that follow each passage. Decide which is the best answer to each question.

Passage 1 In 1995, paleontologist Paul Sereno and his team were working in an unexplored region of Morocco when they made an incredible find—an enormous dinosaur skull! The skull measured about 1.6 m in length, which is about the height of a refrigerator. Given the size of the skull, Sereno concluded that the skeleton of the entire animal must have been about 14 m long—about as big as a school bus, and even larger than *Tyrannosaurus rex*. This 90-million-year-old predator most likely chased other dinosaurs by running on large, powerful hind legs, and its bladelike teeth meant certain death for its prey. Sereno named his new discovery *Carcharodontosaurus saharicus*, which means "shark-toothed reptile from the Sahara."

1. Paul Sereno estimated the total size of this *Carcharodontosaurus* based on

A the size of *Tyrannosaurus rex*.
B the fact that it was a predator.
C the fact that it had bladelike teeth.
D the fact that its skull was 1.6 m long.

2. Which of the following is evidence that the *Carcharodontosaurus* was a predator?

F It had bladelike teeth.
G It had a large skeleton.
H It was found with the bones of a smaller animal nearby.
I It is 90 million years old.

3. Which of the following is a fact in the passage?

A *Carcharodontosaurus* was the largest predator that ever existed.
B *Carcharodontosaurus* had bladelike teeth.
C *Carcharodontosaurus* was as large as *Tyrannosaurus rex*.
D *Carcharodontosaurus* was a shark-like reptile.

Passage 2 In 1912, Alfred Wegener proposed a hypothesis called *continental drift*. At the time, many scientists laughed at his idea. Yet Wegener's idea jolted the very foundations of geology.

Wegener used rock, fossil, and glacial evidence from opposite sides of the Atlantic Ocean to support the idea that continents can "drift." For example, Wegener recognized similar rocks and rock structures in the Appalachian Mountains and the Scottish Highlands, as well as similarities between rock layers in South Africa and Brazil. He thought that these striking similarities could be explained only if these geologic features were once part of the same continent. Wegener proposed that because continents are less dense, they float on top of the denser rock of the ocean floor.

Although continental drift explained many of Wegener's observations, he could not find evidence to explain exactly how continents move. But by the 1960s, this evidence was found and continental drift was well understood. However, Wegener's contributions went unrecognized until years after his death.

1. Which of the following did Wegener use as evidence to support his hypothesis?

A similarities between nearby rock layers
B similarities between rock layers in different parts of the world
C a hypothesis that continents float
D an explanation of how continents move

2. Which of the following statements is supported by the above passage?

F A hypothesis is never proven.
G A new hypothesis may take many years to be accepted by scientists.
H The hypothesis of continental drift was not supported by evidence.
I Wegener's hypothesis was proven wrong.

INTERPRETING GRAPHICS

The map below shows the areas where fossils of certain organisms have been found. Use the map below to answer the questions that follow.

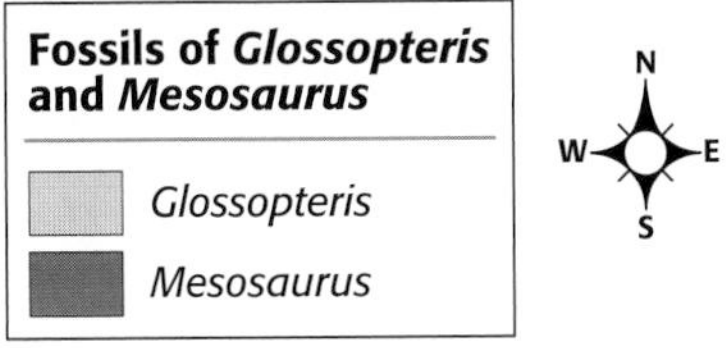

1. *Mesosaurus* was a small, aquatic reptile and *Glossopteris* was an ancient plant species. What do these two have in common?

A Their fossils have been found on several continents.

B Their fossils are found in exactly the same places.

C Their fossils have been found only in North America.

D Their fossils have only been found near oceans.

2. Which of the following statements is best supported by these findings?

F All of the continents were once connected to each other.

G South America was once connected to Africa.

H *Glossopteris* is adapted to life at the South Pole.

I *Mesosaurus* could swim.

3. The map provides evidence that the following continents were once connected to each other, with the exception of

A North America.

B Africa.

C Antarctica.

D South America.

MATH

Read each question below, and choose the best answer.

1. Four students are sharing a birthday cake. The first student takes half of the cake. The second student take half of what remains of the cake. Then, the third student takes half of what remains of the cake. What fraction of the cake is left for the fourth student?

A 1/2

B 1/4

C 1/8

D 1/16

2. One sixteenth is equal to what percentage?

F 6.25%

G 12.5%

H 25%

I 50%

3. What is one-half of one-fourth?

A 1/2

B 1/4

C 1/8

D 1/16

4. Half-life is the time it takes for one-half of the radioactive atoms in a rock sample to decay, or change into different atoms. Carbon-14 is a radioactive isotope with a half-life of 5,730 years. In a sample that is 11,460 years old, what percentage of carbon-14 from the original sample would remain?

F 100%

G 50%

H 25%

I 12.5%

5. If a sample contains an isotope with a half-life of 10,000 years, how old would the sample be if 1/8 of the original isotope remained in the sample?

A 5,000 years

B 10,000 years

C 20,000 years

D 30,000 years

Science in Action

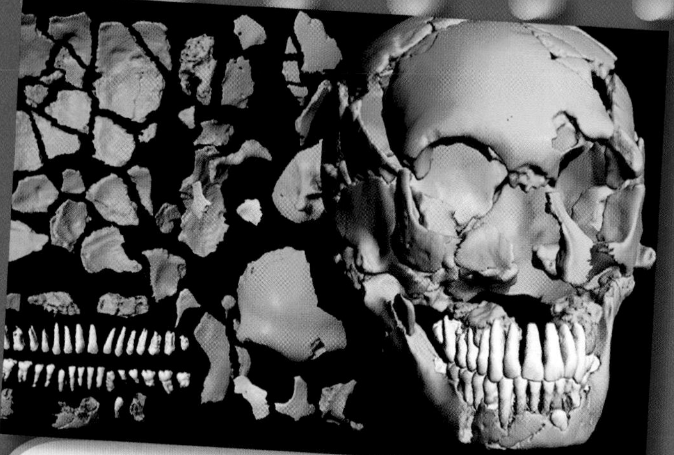

Residents of this neighborhood in Jerusalem, Israel, objected when anthropologists started to dig in the area.

Science, Technology, and Society

Using Computers to Examine Fossils

Paleontologists want to examine fossils without taking apart or damaging the fossils. Fortunately, they can now use a technology called *computerized axial tomography*, or *CAT scanning,* which provides views inside objects without touching the objects. A CAT scan is a series of cross-section pictures of an object. A computer can assemble these "slices" to create a three-dimensional picture of the entire object. Computer graphic programs can also be used to move pictures of fossil pieces around to see how the pieces fit together. The fossil skull above was reconstructed using CAT scans and computers.

Math ACTIVITY

The average volume of a Neanderthal adult's brain was about 1,400 cm^3, while that of an adult gorilla is about 400 cm^3. Calculate how much larger a Neanderthal brain was than a gorilla brain. Express your answer as a percentage.

Scientific Debate

Who Owns the Past?

Does a piece of land include all the layers below it? If you start digging, you may find evidence of past life. In areas that have been inhabited by human ancestors, you may find artifacts that they left behind. But who has the right to dig up these "leftovers" from the past? And who owns them?

In areas that contain many remains of the past, digging up land often leads to conflicts. Landowners may want to build on their own land. But when remains of ancient human cultures are found, living relatives of those cultures may lay claim to the remains. Scientists are often caught in the middle, because they want to study and preserve evidence of past life.

Social Studies ACTIVITY

WRITING SKILL Research an area where there is a debate over what to do with fossils or remains of human ancestors. Write a newspaper article about the issue. Be sure to present all sides of the debate.

People in Science

The Leakey Family

A Family of Fossil Hunters In some families, a business is passed down from one generation to the next. For the Leakey's, the family business is paleoanthropology (PAY lee OH AN thruh PAWL uh jee)—the study of the origin of humans. The first famous Leakey was Dr. Louis Leakey, who was known for his hominid fossil discoveries in Africa in the 1950s. Louis formed many important hypotheses about human evolution. Louis' wife, Mary, made some of the most-important hominid fossil finds of her day.

Louis and Mary's son, Richard, carried on the family tradition of fossil hunting. He found his first fossil, which was of an extinct pig, when he was six years old. As a young man, he went on safari expeditions in which he collected photographs and specimens of African wildlife. Later, he met and married a zoologist named Meave. The photo at right shows Richard (right), Meave (left), and their daughter Louise (middle) Each of the Leakeys has contributed important finds to the study of ancient hominids.

Language Arts ACTIVITY

WRITING SKILL Visit the library and look for a book by or about the Leakey family and other scientists who have worked with them. Write a short book review to encourage your classmates to read the book.

To learn more about these Science in Action topics, visit go.hrw.com and type in the keyword HL5HISF.

Current Science

Check out Current Science® articles related to this chapter by visiting go.hrw.com. Just type in the keyword HL5CS08.

9

Classification

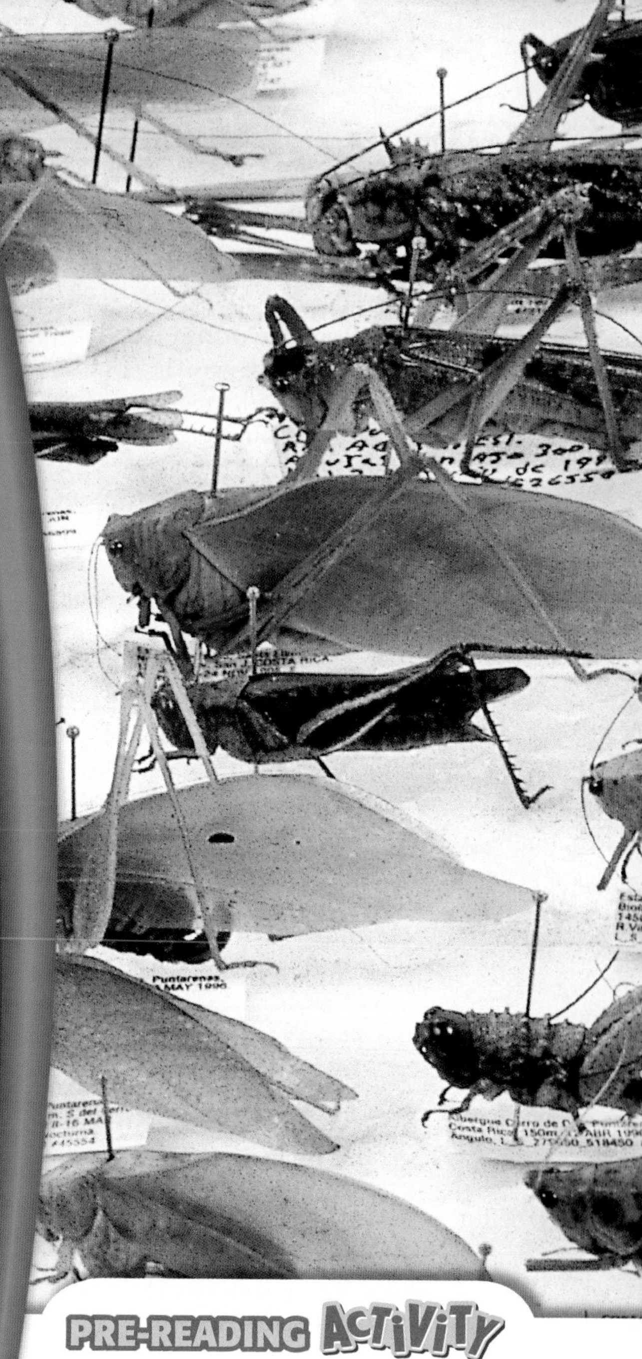

About the PHOTO

Look at the katydids, grasshoppers, and mantids in the photo. A scientist is classifying these insects. Every insect has a label describing the insect. These descriptions will be used to help the scientist know if each insect has already been discovered and named. When scientists discover a new insect or other organism, they have to give the organism a name. The name chosen is unique and should help other scientists understand some basic facts about the organism.

PRE-READING ACTIVITY

FOLDNOTES **Booklet** Before you read the chapter, create the FoldNote entitled "Booklet" described in the **Study Skills** section of the Appendix. Label each page of the booklet with a main idea from the chapter. As you read the chapter, write what you learn about each main idea on the appropriate page of the booklet.

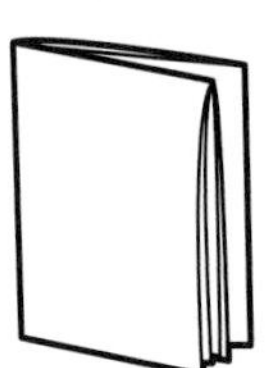

START-UP ACTIVITY

Classifying Shoes

In this group activity, each group will develop a system of classification for shoes.

Procedure

1. Gather **10 shoes.** Number pieces of **masking tape** from 1 to 10. Label the sole of each shoe with a numbered piece of tape.
2. Make a list of shoe features. Make a table that has a column for each feature. Complete the table by describing each shoe.
3. Use the data in the table to make a shoe identification key.
4. The key should be a list of steps. Each step should have two contrasting statements about the shoes. The statements will lead you either to the next step or to a specific shoe.
5. If your shoe is not identified in one step, go on to the next step or steps until the shoe is identified.
6. Trade keys with another group. How did the other group's key help you identify the shoes?

Analysis

1. How was listing the shoe features before making the key helpful?
2. Were you able to identify the shoes using another group's key? Explain.

SECTION 1

Sorting It All Out

Imagine that you live in a tropical rain forest and must get your own food, shelter, and clothing from the forest. What do you need to know to survive in the forest?

READING WARM-UP

Objectives

- Explain how to classify organisms.
- List the seven levels of classification.
- Explain scientific names.
- Describe how dichotomous keys help in identifying organisms.

Terms to Learn

classification
taxonomy
dichotomous key

READING STRATEGY

Reading Organizer As you read this section, create an outline of the section. Use the headings from the section in your outline.

To survive in the rain forest, you need to know which plants are safe to eat and which are not. You need to know which animals you can eat and which might eat you. In other words, you need to study the living things around you and organize them into categories, or classify them. **Classification** is putting things into orderly groups based on similar characteristics.

classification the division of organisms into groups, or classes, based on specific characteristics

Why Classify?

For thousands of years, humans have classified living things based on usefulness. The Chácabo people of Bolivia know of 360 types of plants that grow in the forest where they live. Of these 360 plant types, 305 are useful to the Chácabo.

Some biologists, such as those shown in **Figure 1,** classify living and extinct organisms. Scientists classify organisms to help make sense and order of the many kinds of living things in the world. Biologists use a system to classify living things. This system groups organisms according to the characteristics they share. The classification of living things makes it easier for biologists to answer many important questions, such as the following:

- How many known species are there?
- What are the defining characteristics of each species?
- What are the relationships between these species?

Reading Check **What are three questions that classifying organisms can help answer?** (*See the Appendix for answers to Reading Checks.*)

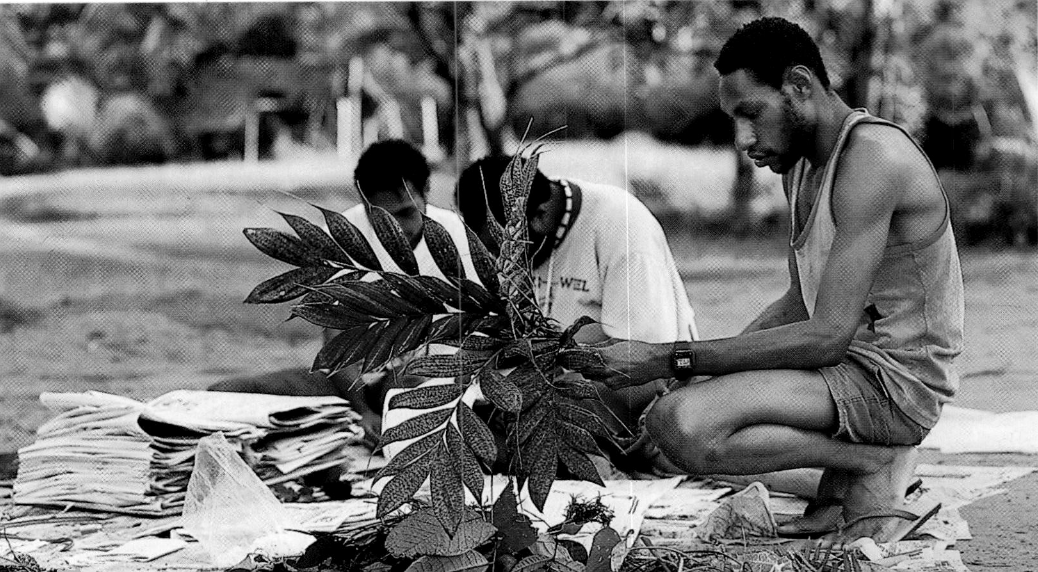

Figure 1 *These biologists are sorting rain-forest plant material.*

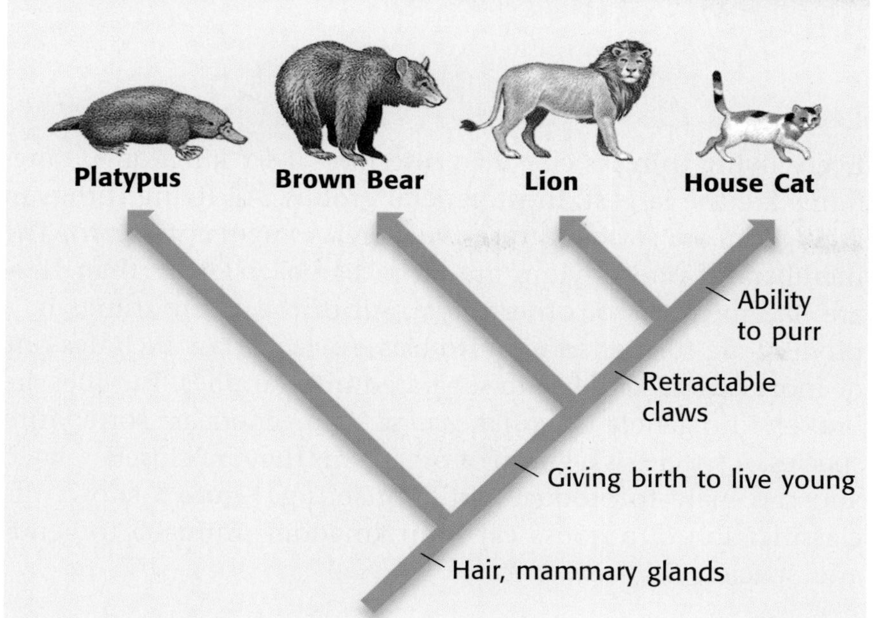

Figure 2 *This branching diagram shows the similarities and differences between four mammals.*

How Do Scientists Classify Organisms?

Before the 1600s, many scientists divided organisms into two groups: plants and animals. But, as more organisms were discovered, some organisms did not fit into either group. In the 1700s, a Swedish scientist named Carolus Linnaeus (KAR uh luhs li NAY uhs) founded modern taxonomy. **Taxonomy** (taks AHN uh mee) is the science of describing, classifying, and naming living things. Linnaeus tried to classify all living things based on their shape and structure. He described a seven-level system of classification, which is still used today.

taxonomy the science of describing, naming, and classifying organisms

Classification Today

Taxonomists use the seven-level system to classify living things based on shared characteristics. Scientists also use shared characteristics to hypothesize how closely related living things are. The more characteristics the organisms share, the more closely related the organisms may be. For example, the platypus, brown bear, lion, and house cat are thought to be related because they share many characteristics. These animals have hair and mammary glands, so they are grouped together as mammals. But they can be further classified into more-specific groups.

Branching Diagrams

Look at the branching diagram in **Figure 2.** Several characteristics are listed along the line that points to the right. Each characteristic is shared by the animals to the right of it. All of the animals shown have hair and mammary glands. But only the bear, lion, and house cat give birth to live young. The lion and the house cat have retractable claws, but the other animals do not. Thus, the lion and the house cat are more closely related to each other than to the other animals.

A Branching Diagram

1. Construct a diagram similar to the one in **Figure 2.**
2. Use a frog, a snake, a kangaroo, and a rabbit in your diagram.
3. Think of one major change that happened before the frog evolved.
4. For the last three organisms, think of a change that happened between one of these organisms and the other two. Write all of these changes in your diagram.

Levels of Classification

Every living thing is classified into one of six kingdoms. Kingdoms are the largest, most general groups. All living things in a kingdom are sorted into several phyla (singular, *phylum*). The members of one phylum are more like each other than they are like members of other phyla. All of the living things in a phylum are further sorted into classes. Each class includes one or more orders. Orders are separated into families. Families are broken into genera (singular, *genus*). And genera are sorted into species. A species is a group of organisms that are closely related and can mate to produce fertile offspring. **Figure 3** shows the classification of a house cat from kingdom Animalia to genus and species, *Felis domesticus.*

INTERNET ACTIVITY

For another activity related to this chapter, go to **go.hrw.com** and type in the keyword **HL5CLSW.**

Scientific Names

By classifying organisms, biologists are able to give organisms scientific names. A scientific name is always the same for a specific kind of organism no matter how many common names there might be. Before Linnaeus's time, scholars used names that were as long as 12 words to identify species. The names were hard to work with because they were so long. And different scientists named organisms differently, so an organism could have more than one name.

Figure 3 *The seven levels of classification are kingdom, phylum, class, order, family, genus, and species.*

Kingdom Animalia	Phylum Chordata	Class Mammalia	Order Carnivora
All animals are in the **kingdom Animalia.**	All animals in the **phylum Chordata** have a hollow nerve cord. Most have a backbone.	Animals in the **class Mammalia** have a backbone. They also nurse their young.	Animals in the **order Carnivora** have a backbone and nurse their young. They also have special teeth for tearing meat.

Two-Part Names

Linnaeus simplified the naming of living things by giving each species a two-part scientific name. For example, the scientific name for the Asian elephant is *Elephas maximus* (EL uh fuhs MAK suh muhs). The first part of the name, *Elephas,* is the genus name. The second part, *maximus,* is the species name. No other species has both this genus name and this species name. Naming rules help scientists communicate clearly about living things.

All genus names begin with a capital letter. All species names begin with a lowercase letter. Usually, both words are underlined or italicized. But if the surrounding text is italicized, the genus and species names are not italicized, as shown in **Figure 4.** These printing styles show a reader which names are genus and species names.

Scientific names, which are usually in Latin or Greek, contain information about an organism. The name of the animal shown in **Figure 4** is *Tyrannosaurus rex. Tyrannosaurus* is a combination of two Greek words and means "tyrant lizard." The word *rex* is Latin for "king." The name tells you that this animal was probably not a passive grass eater! Sometimes, *Tyrannosaurus rex* is referred to as *T. rex*. The species name is not correct without the genus name or its abbreviation.

Figure 4 *You would never call* Tyrannosaurus rex *just* rex*!*

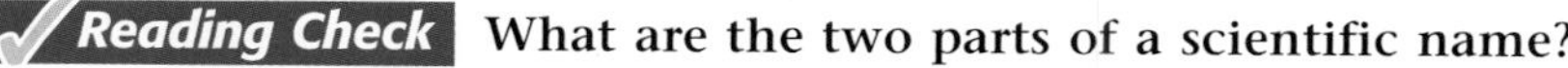

What are the two parts of a scientific name?

Family Felidae	Genus *Felis*	Species *Felis domesticus*
Animals in the **family Felidae** are cats. They have a backbone, nurse their young, have special teeth for tearing meat, and have retractable claws.	Animals in the **genus *Felis*** have traits of other animals in the same family. However, these cats cannot roar; they can only purr.	The **species *Felis domesticus*** is the common house cat. The house cat shares traits with all of the organisms in the levels above the species level, but it also has unique traits.

Dichotomous Keys

dichotomous key an aid that is used to identify organisms and that consists of the answers to a series of questions

You might someday turn over a rock and find an organism that you don't recognize. How would you identify the organism? Taxonomists have developed special guides to help scientists identify organisms. A **dichotomous key** (die KAHT uh muhs KEE) is an identification aid that uses sequential pairs of descriptive statements. There are only two alternative responses for each statement. From each pair of statements, the person trying to identify the organism chooses the statement that describes the organism. Either the chosen statement identifies the organism or the person is directed to another pair of statements. By working through the statements in the key in order, the person can eventually identify the organism. Using the simple dichotomous key in **Figure 5,** try to identify the two animals shown.

Reading Check **What is a dichotomous key?**

Figure 5 *A dichotomous key can help you identify organisms.*

Dichotomous Key to 10 Common Mammals in the Eastern United States

1. a. This mammal flies. Its "hand" forms a wing. **b.** This mammal does not fly. It's "hand" does not form a wing.	**little brown bat** **Go to step 2.**
2. a. This mammal has no hair on its tail. **b.** This mammal has hair on its tail.	**Go to step 3.** **Go to step 4.**
3. a. This mammal has a short, naked tail. **b.** This mammal has a long, naked tail.	**eastern mole** **Go to step 5.**
4. a. This mammal has a black mask across its face. **b.** This mammal does not have a black mask across its face.	**raccoon** **Go to step 6.**
5. a. This mammal has a tail that is flat and paddle shaped. **b.** This mammal has a tail that is not flat or paddle shaped.	**beaver** **opossum**
6. a. This mammal is brown and has a white underbelly. **b.** This mammal is not brown and does not have a white underbelly.	**Go to step 7.** **Go to step 8.**
7. a. This mammal has a long, furry tail that is black on the tip. **b.** This mammal has a long tail that has little fur.	**longtail weasel** **white-footed mouse**
8. a. This mammal is black and has a narrow white stripe on its forehead and broad white stripes on its back. **b.** This mammal is not black and does not have white stripes.	**striped skunk** **Go to step 9.**
9. a. This mammal has long ears and a short, cottony tail. **b.** This mammal has short ears and a medium-length tail.	**eastern cottontail** **woodchuck**

A Growing System

You may think that all of the organisms on Earth have already been classified. But people are still discovering and classifying organisms. Some newly discovered organisms fit into existing categories. But sometimes, someone discovers new evidence or an organism that is so different from other organisms that it does not fit existing categories. For example, in 1995, scientists studied an organism named *Symbion pandora* (SIM bee AHN pan DAWR uh). Scientists found *S. pandora* living on lobster lips! Scientists learned that *S. pandora* had some characteristics that no other known organism had. In fact, scientists trying to classify *S. pandora* found that it didn't fit in any existing phylum. So, taxonomists created a new phylum for *S. pandora*.

SECTION Review

Summary

- Classification refers to the arrangement of living things into orderly groups based on their similarities.
- Today's living things are classified by using a seven-level system of organization. The seven levels are kingdom, phylum, class, order, family, genus, and species.
- An organism has only one correct scientific name.
- Dichotomous keys are tools for identifying organisms.

Using Key Terms

1. In your own words, write a definition for each of the following terms: *classification* and *taxonomy*.

Understanding Key Ideas

2. The two parts of a scientific name are the names of the genus and the
   - **a.** species.
   - **b.** phylum.
   - **c.** family.
   - **d.** order.
3. Why do scientists use scientific names for organisms?
4. List the seven levels of classification.
5. Describe how a dichotomous key helps scientists identify organisms.

Critical Thinking

6. **Analyzing Processes** Biologists think that millions of species are not classified yet. Why do you think so many species have not been classified yet?
7. **Applying Concepts** Both dolphins and sharks have a tail and fins. How can you determine if dolphins and sharks are closely related?

Interpreting Graphics

Use the figure below to answer the questions that follow.

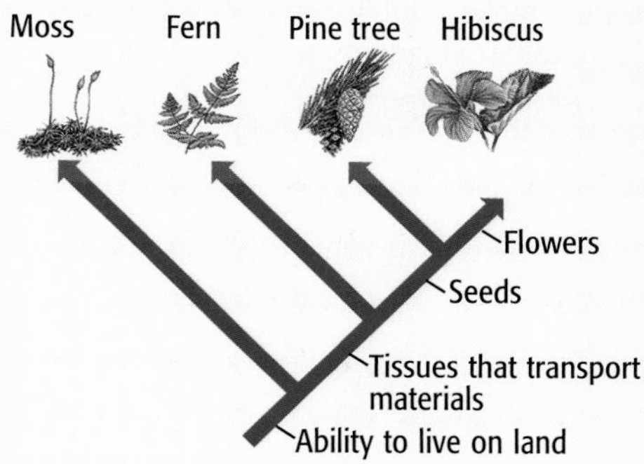

8. Which plant is most similar to the hibiscus?
9. Which plant is least similar to the hibiscus?

SCILINKS.
NSTA
Developed and maintained by the National Science Teachers Association
For a variety of links related to this chapter, go to www.scilinks.org
Topic: Basis for Classification; Levels of Classification
SciLinks code: HSM0138; HSM0870

SECTION 2

The Six Kingdoms

What do you call an organism that is green, makes its own food, lives in pond water, and moves? Is it a plant, an animal, or something in between?

READING WARM-UP

Objectives

- Explain how classification schemes for kingdoms developed as greater numbers of different organisms became known.
- Describe each of the six kingdoms.

Terms to Learn

Archaebacteria
Eubacteria
Protista
Fungi
Plantae
Animalia

READING STRATEGY

Reading Organizer As you read this section, make a table comparing the six classification kingdoms to each other.

For hundreds of years, all living things were classified as either plants or animals. But over time, scientists discovered species that did not fit easily into these two kingdoms. For example, an organism of the genus *Euglena,* such as the one shown in **Figure 1,** has characteristics of both plants and animals. How would you classify such an organism?

What Is It?

Organisms are classified by their characteristics. For example, organisms of the genus *Euglena* are

- single celled and live in pond water
- green and make their own food through photosynthesis

These two characteristics might lead you to conclude that the genus of *Euglena* are plants. However, you should consider the following other characteristics before you form your conclusion:

- Members of the genus *Euglena* move by whipping their "tails," which are called *flagella*.
- *Euglena* can feed on other organisms.

Plants don't move themselves around and usually do not eat other organisms. So, are organisms of the genus *Euglena* animals? As you can see, *Euglena* does not fit into the category of plants or animals. Scientists solved this classification problem by adding another kingdom, the kingdom Protista, to classify organisms such as *Euglena*.

As scientists continued to learn about living things, they added kingdoms that account for the characteristics of different organisms. Currently, most scientists agree that the six-kingdom classification system works best. However, scientists will continue to adjust the system as they learn more.

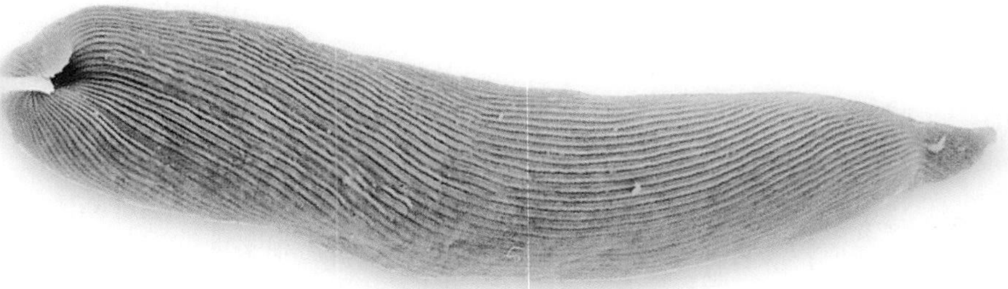

Figure 1 *How would you classify this organism? This member of the genus* Euglena, *which is shown here highly magnified, has characteristics of both plants and animals.*

Figure 2 *The Grand Prismatic Spring in Yellowstone National Park contains water that is about 90°C (194°F). The spring is home to archaebacteria that thrive in its hot water.*

Archaebacteria a kingdom made up of bacteria that live in extreme environments

Eubacteria a kingdom that contains all prokaryotes except archaebacteria

The Two Kingdoms of Bacteria

Bacteria are extremely small, single-celled organisms that differ from all other living things. Bacteria are *prokaryotes* (proh KAYR ee OHTS), organisms that lack nuclei. Many biologists divide bacteria into two kingdoms: Archaebacteria (AHR kee bak TEER ee uh) and Eubacteria (YOO bak TEER ee uh).

Archaebacteria

Prokaryotes that can live in extreme environments are in the kingdom **Archaebacteria.** The prefix *archae-* comes from a Greek word meaning "ancient." Today, most archaebacteria can be found living in places where most organisms could not survive. **Figure 2** shows a hot spring in Yellowstone National Park. The yellow and orange rings around the edge of the hot spring are made up of the billions of archaebacteria that live there.

Eubacteria

Bacteria that are not in the kingdom Archaebacteria are in the kingdom **Eubacteria.** Eubacteria are prokaryotes that live in the soil, in water, and even on and inside the human body! For example, *Escherichia coli,* pictured in **Figure 3,** is present in large numbers in human intestines, where it produces vitamin K. One kind of eubacterium converts milk into yogurt. Another kind of eubacterium causes pneumonia.

Reading Check **Name a type of eubacterium that lives in your body.** (*See the Appendix for answers to Reading Checks.*)

Figure 3 *Specimens of* E. coli *are shown on the point of a pin under a scanning electron microscope. These eubacteria live in the intestines of animals and decompose undigested food.*

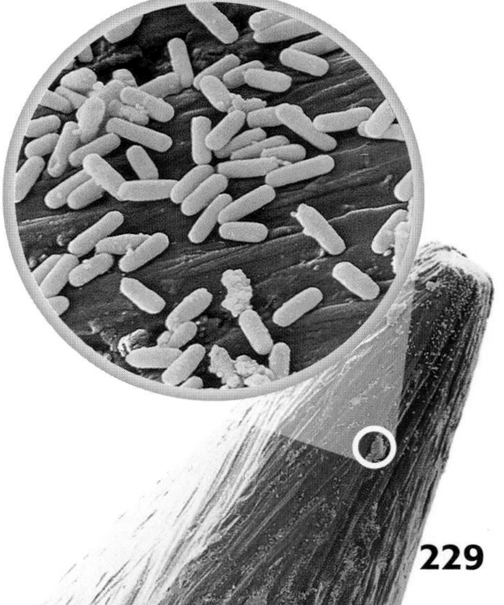

Kingdom Protista

Figure 4 *This slime mold is a protist.*

Members of the kingdom **Protista** (proh TIST uh), commonly called *protists* (PROH tists), are single-celled or simple multicellular organisms that don't fit into any other kingdom. Unlike bacteria, protists are *eukaryotes,* organisms whose cells have a nucleus and membrane-bound organelles. The kingdom Protista contains all eukaryotes that are not plants, animals, or fungi. Scientists think the first protists evolved from ancient bacteria about 2 billion years ago. Much later, protists gave rise to plants, fungi, and animals as well as to modern protists.

The kingdom Protista contains many kinds of organisms. Animal-like protists are called *protozoans.* Plantlike protists are called *algae.* Slime molds, such as the one shown in **Figure 4,** and water molds are fungus-like protists. Members of *Euglena* are also members of the kingdom Protista.

Kingdom Fungi

Molds and mushrooms are examples of the complex multicellular members of the kingdom Fungi (FUHN JIE). Unlike plants, fungi do not perform photosynthesis, and unlike animals, fungi do not eat food. Instead, members of the kingdom **Fungi** absorb nutrients from substances in their surroundings. Fungi use digestive juices to break down the substances. **Figure 5** shows a very poisonous fungus. Never eat wild fungi.

Protista a kingdom of mostly one-celled eukaryotic organisms that are different from plants, animals, bacteria, and fungi

Fungi a kingdom made up of nongreen, eukaryotic organisms that have no means of movement, reproduce by using spores, and get food by breaking down substances in their surroundings and absorbing the nutrients

Figure 5 *This beautiful fungus of the genus* Amanita *is poisonous.*

Figure 6 *Giant sequoias can measure 30 m around at the base and can grow to more than 91.5 m tall.*

Figure 7 *Plants such as these are common in the Tropics.*

Kingdom Plantae

Although plants vary remarkably in size and form, most people easily recognize the members of the kingdom Plantae. **Plantae** consists of organisms that are eukaryotic, have cell walls, and make food through photosynthesis. For photosynthesis to occur, plants must be exposed to sunlight. Plants can therefore be found on land and in water that light can penetrate.

The food that plants make is important not only for the plants but also for all of the organisms that get nutrients from plants. Most life on Earth is dependent on plants. For example, some members of the kingdoms Fungi, Protista, and Eubacteria consume plants. When these organisms digest the plant material, they get energy and nutrients made by the plants.

Plants also provide habitat for other organisms. The giant sequoias in **Figure 6** and the flowering plants in **Figure 7** provide birds, insects, and other animals with a place to live.

Reading Check How do members of the kingdom Plantae provide energy and nutrients to members of other kingdoms?

Plantae a kingdom made up of complex, multicellular organisms that are usually green, have cell walls made of cellulose, cannot move around, and use the sun's energy to make sugar by photosynthesis

Ring-Around-the-Sequoia

How many students would have to join hands to form a human chain around a giant sequoia that is 30 m in circumference? Assume for this calculation that the average student can extend his or her arms about 1.3 m.

Animalia a kingdom made up of complex, multicellular organisms that lack cell walls, can usually move around, and quickly respond to their environment

Kingdom Animalia

The kingdom **Animalia** contains complex, multicellular organisms that don't have cell walls, are usually able to move around, and have specialized sense organs. These sense organs help most animals quickly respond to their environment. Organisms in the kingdom Animalia are commonly called *animals*. You probably recognize many of the organisms in the kingdom Animalia. All of the organisms in **Figure 8** are animals.

Animals depend on the organisms from other kingdoms. For example, animals depend on plants for food. Animals also depend on bacteria and fungi to recycle the nutrients found in dead organisms.

Figure 8 *The kingdom Animalia contains many different organisms, such as eagles, tortoises, and beetles.*

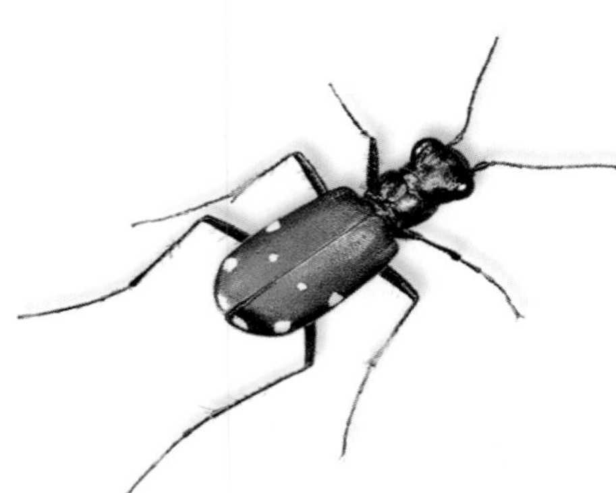

CONNECTION TO Social Studies

WRITING SKILL **Animals That Help** Humans have depended on animals for thousands of years. Many people around the world still use oxen to farm. Camels, horses, donkeys, goats, and llamas are all still used as pack animals. Dogs still help herd sheep, protect property, and help people hunt. Scientists are even discovering new ways that animals can help us. For example, scientists are training bees to help find buried land mines. Using the library or the Internet, research an animal that helps people. Make a poster describing the animal and the animal's scientific name. The poster should show who uses the animal, how the animal is used, and how long people have depended on the animal. Find or draw pictures to put on your poster.

ACTIVITY

Simple Animals

When you think of an animal, what do you imagine? You may think of a dog, a cat, or a parrot. All of those organisms are animals. But the animal kingdom also includes some members that might surprise you, such as worms, insects, and corals.

The red cup sponge shown in **Figure 9** is also an animal. Sponges are usually thought of as the simplest animals. They don't have sense organs. Most sponges cannot move. Sponges used to be considered plants. But sponges cannot make food. They must eat other organisms to get nutrients, which is one reason that sponges are classified as animals.

Reading Check Why were sponges once thought to be plants?

Figure 9 *This red cup sponge is a simple animal.*

SECTION Review

Summary

- Most biologists recognize six kingdoms: Archaebacteria, Eubacteria, Protista, Fungi, Plantae, and Animalia.
- Archaebacteria live in extreme environments. Eubacteria live almost everywhere else.
- Plants, animals, fungi, and protists are eukaryotic organisms. Plants perform photosynthesis. Animals eat food and digest it inside their body. Fungi absorb nutrients from material that they break down outside of their body. Protists are organisms that don't fit in other kingdoms.

Using Key Terms

For each pair of terms, explain how the meanings of the terms differ.

1. *Archaebacteria* and *Eubacteria*
2. *Plantae* and *Fungi*

Understanding Key Ideas

3. Biological classification schemes change
   a. as new evidence and more kinds of organisms are discovered.
   b. every 100 years.
   c. when scientists disagree.
   d. only once.
4. Explain the different ways in which plants, fungi, and animals obtain nutrients.
5. Why are protists placed in their own kingdom?
6. Describe the six kingdoms.

Math Skills

7. A certain eubacterium can divide every 30 min. If you begin with 1 eubacterium, when will you have more than 1,000 eubacteria?

Critical Thinking

8. **Identifying Relationships** How are bacteria similar to fungi? How are fungi similar to animals?
9. **Analyzing Methods** Why do you think Linnaeus did not include classification kingdoms for categories of bacteria?
10. **Applying Concepts** The Venus' flytrap does not move around. It can make its own food by using photosynthesis. It can also trap insects and digest the insects to get nutrients. The flytrap also has a cell wall. Into which kingdom would you place the Venus' flytrap? What makes this organism unusual in the kingdom you chose?

SCILINKS
NSTA
Developed and maintained by the National Science Teachers Association
For a variety of links related to this chapter, go to www.scilinks.org
Topic: The Six Kingdoms
SciLinks code: HSM1397

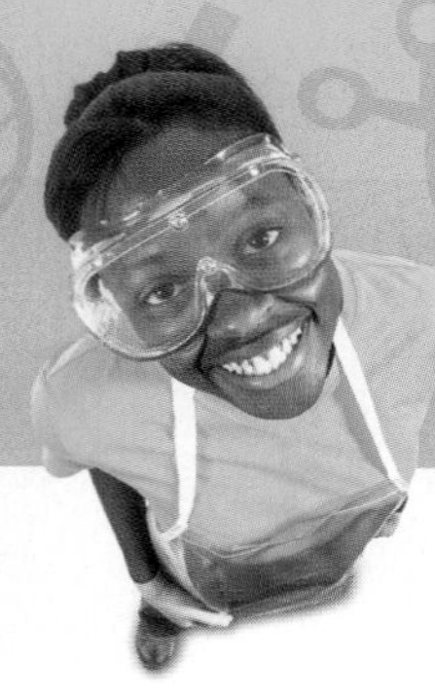

Skills Practice Lab

Shape Island

OBJECTIVES

Classify organisms.

Name organisms.

You are a biologist exploring uncharted parts of the world to look for new animal species. You sailed for days across the ocean and finally found Shape Island hundreds of miles south of Hawaii. Shape Island has some very unusual organisms. The shape of each organism is a variation of a geometric shape. You have spent more than a year collecting and classifying specimens. You have been able to assign a two-part scientific name to most of the species that you have collected. Now, you must assign a two-part scientific name to each of the last 12 specimens collected before you begin your journey home.

Procedure

1. Draw each of the organisms pictured on the facing page. Beside each organism, draw a line for its name, as shown on the top left of the following page. The first organism pictured has already been named, but you must name the remaining 12. Use the glossary of Greek and Latin prefixes, suffixes, and root words in the table to help you name the organisms.

Greek and Latin roots, prefixes, and suffixes	Meaning
ankylos	angle
antennae	external sense organs
bi-	two
cyclo-	circular
macro-	large
micro-	small
mono-	one
peri-	around
-plast	body
-pod	foot
quad-	four
stoma	mouth
tri-	three
uro-	tail

Analyze Results

1. **Analyzing Results** If you gave species 1 a common name, such as *round-face-no-nose,* would any other scientist know which of the newly discovered organisms you were referring to? Explain. How many others have a round face and no nose?

2. **Organizing Data** Describe two characteristics that are shared by all of your newly discovered specimens.

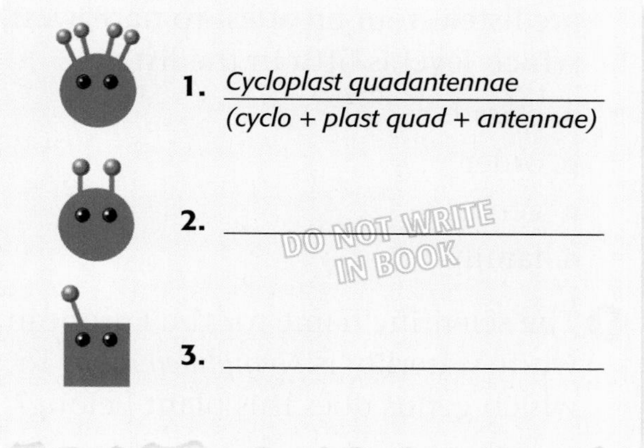

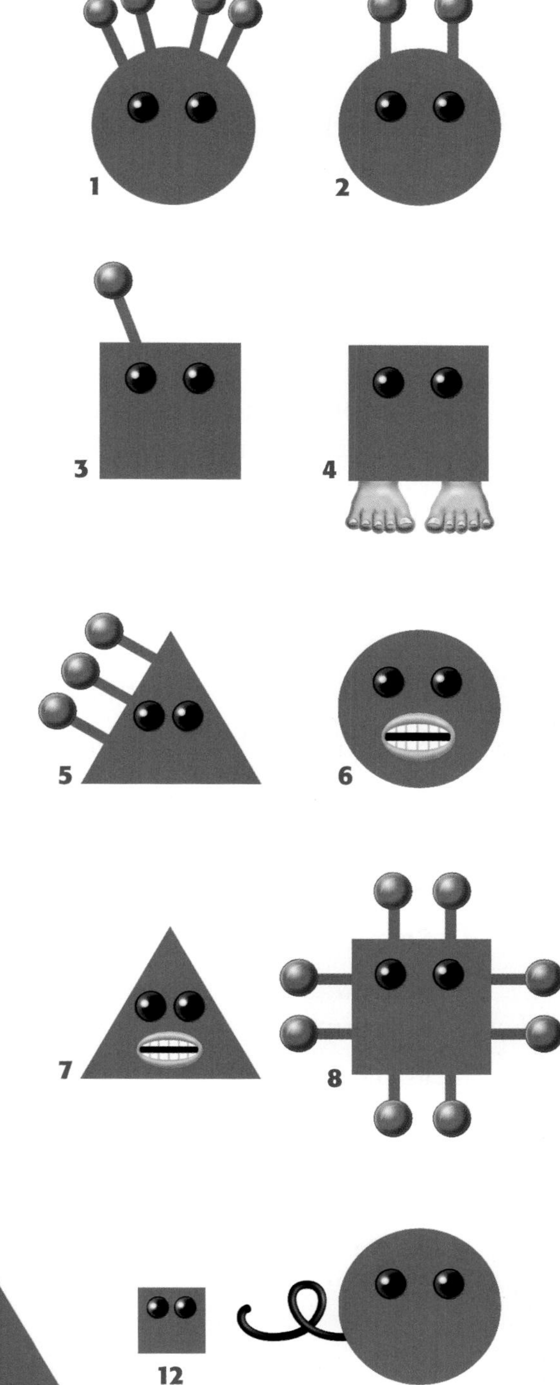

Draw Conclusions

3 **Applying Conclusions** One more organism exists on Shape Island, but you have not been able to capture it. However, your supplies are running out, and you must start sailing for home. You have had a good look at the unusual animal and can draw it in detail. Draw an animal that is different from all of the others, and give it a two-part scientific name.

Applying Your Data

Look up the scientific names *Mertensia virginica* and *Porcellio scaber.* Answer the following questions as they apply to each organism: Is the organism a plant or an animal? How many common names does the organism have? How many scientific names does it have?

Think of the name of your favorite fruit or vegetable. Find out if it has other common names, and find out its two-part scientific name.

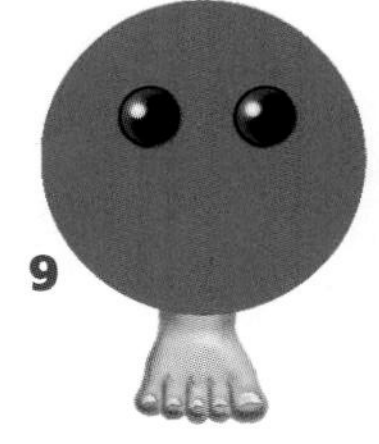

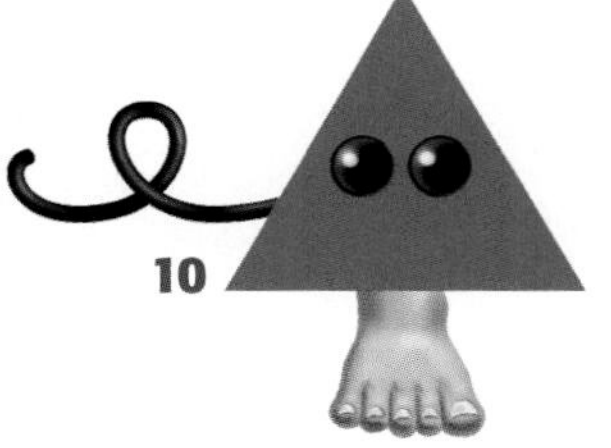

Chapter Review

USING KEY TERMS

Complete each of the following sentences by choosing the correct term from the word bank.

Animalia	Protista
Eubacteria	Plantae
Archaebacteria	classification
taxonomy	

1. Linnaeus founded the science of ___.
2. Bacteria that live in extreme environments are in the kingdom ___.
3. Complex multicellular organisms that can usually move around and respond to their environment are in the kingdom ___.
4. A system of ___ can help group animals into categories.
5. Prokaryotes that are not archaebacteria are in the kingdom ___.

UNDERSTANDING KEY IDEAS

Multiple Choice

6. Scientists classify organisms by
   - **a.** arranging the organisms in orderly groups.
   - **b.** giving the organisms many common names.
   - **c.** deciding whether the organisms are useful.
   - **d.** using only existing categories of classification.

7. When the seven levels of classification are listed from broadest to narrowest, which level is fifth in the list?
   - **a.** class
   - **b.** order
   - **c.** genus
   - **d.** family

8. The scientific name for the European white waterlily is *Nymphaea alba*. To which genus does this plant belong?
   - **a.** *Nymphaea*
   - **b.** *alba*
   - **c.** water lily
   - **d.** alba lily

9. *Animalia, Protista, Fungi, Archaebacteria, Eubacteria,* and *Plantae* are the
   - **a.** scientific names of different organisms.
   - **b.** names of kingdoms.
   - **c.** levels of classification.
   - **d.** scientists who organized taxonomy.

10. Bacteria that live in your intestines are classified in the kingdom
    - **a.** Protista.
    - **b.** Eubacteria.
    - **c.** Archaebacteria.
    - **d.** Fungi.

11. What kind of organism thrives in hot springs and other extreme environments?
    - **a.** fungus
    - **b.** eubacterium
    - **c.** archaebacterium
    - **d.** protist

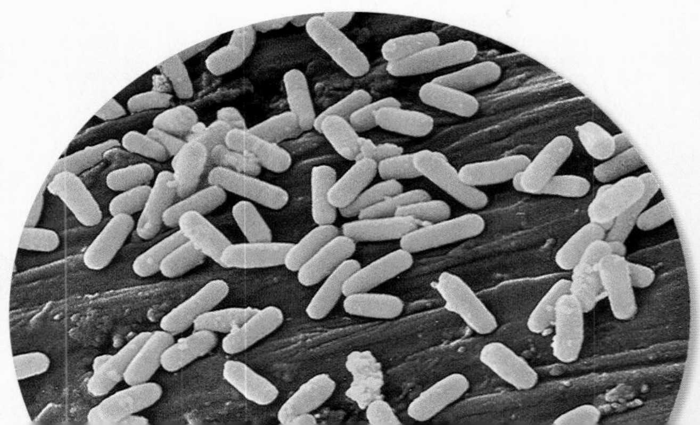

Short Answer

12. Why is the use of scientific names important in biology?

13. What kind of evidence is used by modern taxonomists to classify organisms based on evolutionary relationships?

14. Is a eubacterium a type of eukaryote? Explain your answer.

15. Scientists used to classify organisms as either plants or animals. Why doesn't that classification system work?

CRITICAL THINKING

16. **Concept Mapping** Use the following terms to create a concept map: *kingdom, fern, lizard, Animalia, Fungi, algae, Protista, Plantae,* and *mushroom.*

17. **Analyzing Methods** Explain how the levels of classification depend on the similarities and differences between organisms.

18. **Making Inferences** Explain why two species that belong to the same genus, such as white oak (*Quercus alba*) and cork oak (*Quercus suber*), also belong to the same family.

19. **Identifying Relationships** What characteristic do the members of all six kingdoms have in common?

INTERPRETING GRAPHICS

Use the branching diagram of selected primates below to answer the questions that follow.

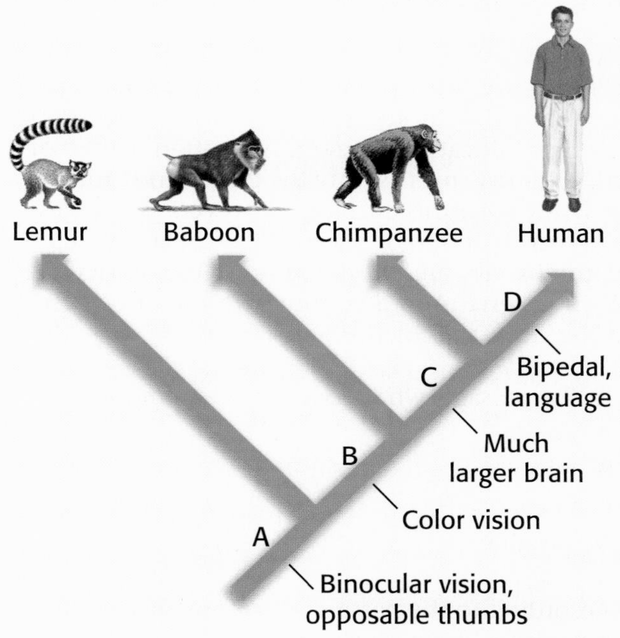

20. Which primate is the closest relative to the common ancestor of all primates?

21. Which primate shares the most traits with humans?

22. Do both lemurs and humans have the characteristics listed at point D? Explain your answer.

23. What characteristic do baboons have that lemurs do not have? Explain your answer.

Standardized Test Preparation

READING

Read each of the passages below. Then, answer the questions that follow each passage.

Passage 1 When organizing life on Earth into categories, we must remember that organisms are not equally distributed throughout the categories of our classification system. We often think of Earth's living things as only the plants and animals that live on Earth's surface. However, the largest kingdoms in terms of the number of individuals and total mass are the kingdoms Archaebacteria and Eubacteria. And a common home of bacteria may be deep within the Earth's crust.

1. In the passage, what does *distributed* mean?
- **A** divided
- **B** important
- **C** visible
- **D** variable

2. According to the passage, what are most of the organisms living on Earth?
- **F** plants
- **G** animals
- **H** fungi
- **I** bacteria

3. Which of the following statements is a fact according to the passage?
- **A** All organisms are equally distributed over Earth's surface.
- **B** Plants are the most important organisms on Earth.
- **C** Many bacteria may live deep within Earth's crust.
- **D** Bacteria are equally distributed over Earth's surface.

Passage 2 When you think of an animal, what do you imagine? You may think of a dog, a cat, or a parrot. All of those organisms are animals. But the animal kingdom also includes some members that might surprise you, such as worms, insects, corals, and sponges.

1. In the passage, what is coral?
- **A** a kind of animal
- **B** a kind of insect
- **C** a color similar to pink
- **D** an organism found in lakes and streams

2. What can you infer from the passage?
- **F** All members of the animal kingdom are visible.
- **G** Parrots make good pets.
- **H** Not all members of the animal kingdom have DNA.
- **I** Members of the animal kingdom come in many shapes and sizes.

3. Which of the following can you infer from the passage?
- **A** Worms and corals make good pets.
- **B** Corals and cats have some traits in common.
- **C** All organisms are animals.
- **D** Worms, corals, insects, and sponges are in the same family.

4. In the passage, what does *members* mean?
- **F** teammates
- **G** limbs
- **H** individuals admitted to a club
- **I** components

INTERPRETING GRAPHICS

The Venn diagrams below show two classification systems. Use the diagrams to answer the questions that follow.

Classification system A

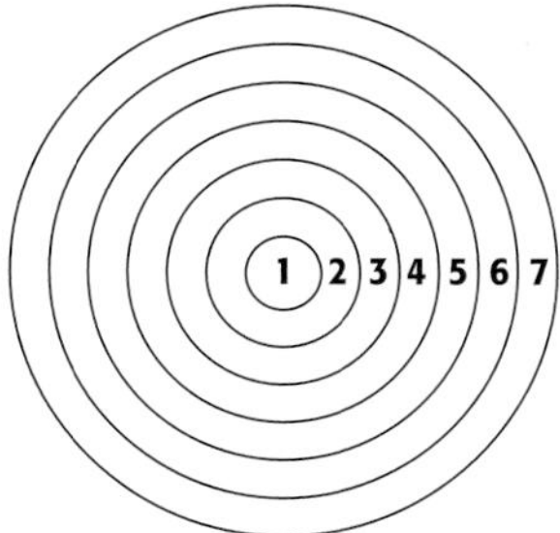

Classification system B

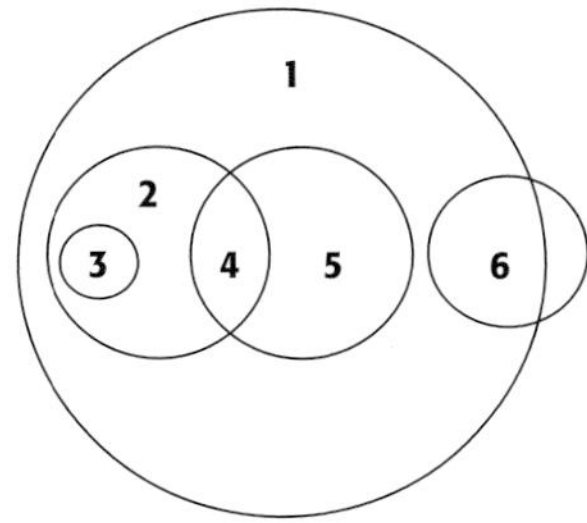

1. For Classification system A, which of the following statements is true?

A All organisms in group 6 are in group 7.
B All organisms in group 5 are in group 4.
C All organisms in group 6 are in group 1.
D All organisms in group 2 are in group 1.

2. For Classification system A, which of the following statements is true?

F All organisms in group 3 are in group 2.
G All organisms in group 3 are in group 4.
H All organisms in group 3 are in group 1.
I All organisms in group 3 are in every other group.

3. For Classification system B, which of the following statements is true?

A All organisms in group 1 are in group 6.
B All organisms in group 6 are in group 1.
C All organisms in group 3 are in group 1.
D All organisms in group 2 are in group 5.

4. For Classification system B, which of the following statements is true?

F All organisms in group 4 are in group 1, 2, and 5.
G All organisms in group 4 are in groups 3 and 5.
H All organisms in group 4 are in groups 5 and 6.
I All organisms in group 4 are in groups 1, 5, and 6.

5. In Classification system B, which group contains organisms that are not in group 1?

A 2
B 4
C 5
D 6

MATH

Read each question below, and choose the best answer.

1. Scientists estimate that millions of species have not yet been discovered and classified. About 1.8 million species have been discovered and classified. If scientists think that this 1.8 million makes up only 10% of the total number of species on Earth, how many species do scientists think exist on Earth?

A 180 million
B 18 million
C 1.8 million
D 180,000

2. Sequoia trees can grow to more than 90 m in height. There are 3.28 feet in 1 meter. How many feet are in 90 m?

F 27.4 ft
G 95.2 ft
H 270 ft
I 295.2 ft

Science in Action

Scientific Debate

Birds and Dinosaurs

Did birds evolve from dinosaurs? Some scientists think that birds evolved from small, carnivorous dinosaurs such as *Velociraptor* about 115 million to 150 million years ago. This idea is based on similarities of modern birds and these small dinosaurs. These similarities include the size, shape, and number of toes and "fingers," the location and shape of the breastbone and shoulder, and the presence of a hollow bone structure. Many scientists find this evidence convincing.

However, some scientists think that birds developed 100 million years before *Velociraptor* and its relatives did. These scientists point out that *Velociraptor* and its relatives were ground dwellers and were the wrong shape and size for flying.

Math ACTIVITY

Velociraptor lived between 115 million and 150 million years ago. Find the average of these two numbers. Use that average to answer the following questions: How many weeks ago did *Velociraptor* live on Earth? How many days ago did *Velociraptor* live on Earth?

Scientific Discovery

A New Insect Order

In 2001, Oliver Zompro was studying a fossil insect preserved in amber. Although the fossil insect resembled a grasshopper or a walking stick, it was unique and could not be classified in the same group as either one. Zompro wondered if he might be seeing a new type of insect or an insect that was now thought to be extinct. The fossil insect was less than 4 cm long. Its spiny appearance earned the insect the nickname "gladiator." The gladiator bug that Zompro discovered is so unusual that it cannot be classified in any of the 30 existing orders of insects. Instead, the gladiator bug constitutes its own new order, which has been named *Mantophasmatodea*.

Language Arts ACTIVITY

WRITING SKILL Give the gladiator bug a new nickname. Write a short essay about why you chose that particular name for the insect.

People in Science

Michael Fay

Crossing Africa Finding and classifying wild animals takes a great deal of perseverance. Just ask Michael Fay, who spent 15 months crossing 2,000 miles of uninhabited rain forest in the Congo River Basin of West Africa. He used video, photography, and old-fashioned note taking to record the types of animals and vegetation that he encountered along the way.

To find and classify wild animals, Fay often had to think like an animal. When coming across a group of monkeys swinging high above him in the emerald green canopy, Fay would greet the monkeys with his imitation of the crowned eagle's high-pitched, whistling cry. When the monkeys responded with their own distinctive call, Fay could identify exactly what species they were and would jot it down in one of his 87 waterproof notebooks. Fay also learned other tricks, such as staying downwind of an elephant to get as close to the elephant as possible. He could then identify its size, its age, and the length of its tusks.

Social Studies ACTIVITY

WRITING SKILL Many organizations around the world are committed to helping preserve biodiversity. Conduct some Internet and library research to find out about an organization that works to keep species safe from extinction. Create a poster that describes the organization and some of the species that the organization protects.

To learn more about these Science in Action topics, visit go.hrw.com and type in the keyword HL5CLSF.

Current Science

Check out Current Science® articles related to this chapter by visiting go.hrw.com. Just type in the keyword HL5CS09.

UNIT 4

TIMELINE

Simple Organisms, Fungi, and Plants

Do you know how important plants are? Plants provide oxygen and food for other living things.

Throughout history, people have been trying to understand plants. In this unit, you will join them. You'll also learn about, some other fascinating organisms—bacteria, protists, and fungi. Some of these organisms cause disease, but others provide food and medicines. Read on, and be amazed!

Around 250

Mayan farmers build terraces to control the flow of water to crops.

1864

Louis Pasteur uses heat to eliminate microbes. This process is later called *pasteurization*.

1897

Beatrix Potter, the author of *The Tale of Peter Rabbit*, completes her collection of 270 watercolors of fungi. Today, she is considered an expert in mycology, the study of fungi.

1971

Ananda Chakrabarty uses genetics to design bacteria that can break down oil in oil spills.

1580

Prospero Alpini discovers that plants have both male structures and female structures.

1683

Anton van Leeuwenhoek is the first person to describe bacteria.

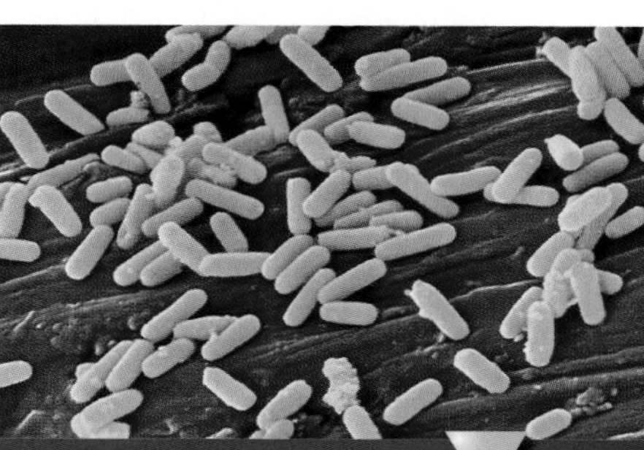

E. coli under an electron microscope

1763

Joseph Kolreuter studies orchid pollination and discovers that both parent plants contribute traits to the offspring.

1898

Martinus Beijerinck gives the name *virus* to infectious material that is smaller than a bacterium.

1928

Alexander Fleming observes that certain molds can eliminate bacterial growth, and he discovers penicillin.

1955

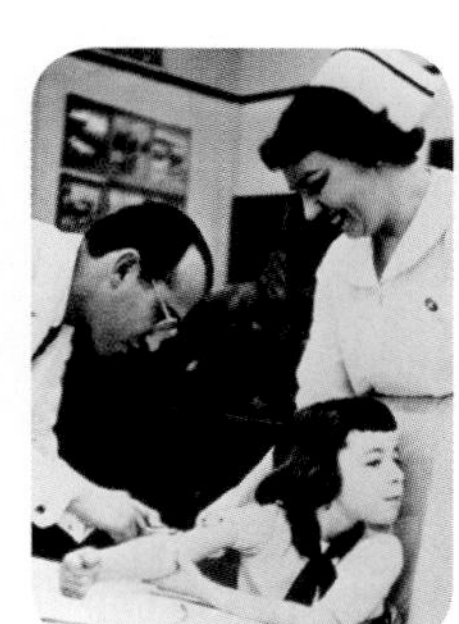

A vaccine for the polio virus developed by Dr. Jonas Salk becomes widely used.

1983

HIV, the virus responsible for AIDS, is isolated.

1995

An outbreak of the deadly Ebola virus occurs in Zaire.

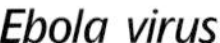

Ebola virus

2002

An international team decodes the DNA sequences for both the protist that causes malaria and the mosquito that carries this protist. As a result, the door to more-effective antimalaria drugs is opened.

10

Bacteria and Viruses

About the PHOTO

Bacteria are everywhere. Some provide us with medicines, and some make foods we eat. Others, such as the one pictured here, can cause illness. This bacterium is a kind of *Salmonella,* and it can cause food poisoning. *Salmonella* can live inside chickens and other birds. Cooking eggs and chicken properly helps make sure that you don't get sick from *Salmonella.*

PRE-READING ACTIVITY

FOLDNOTES **Double Door** Before you read the chapter, create the FoldNote entitled "Double Door" described in the **Study Skills** section of the Appendix. Write "Bacteria" on one flap of the double door and "Viruses" on the other flap. As you read the chapter, compare the two topics, and write characteristics of each on the inside of the appropriate flap.

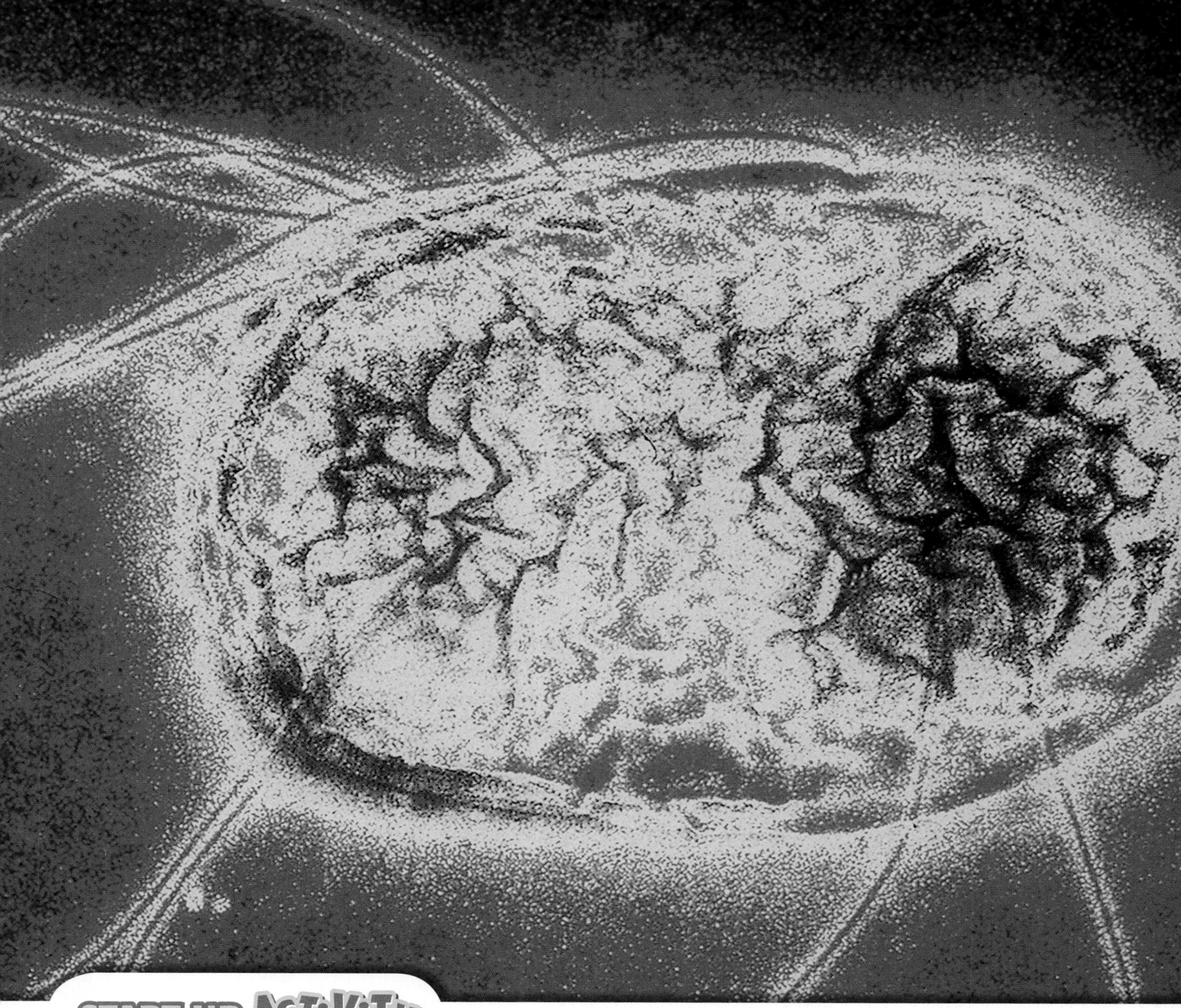

START-UP ACTIVITY

Our Constant Companions

Bacteria are in the soil, in the air, and even inside your body. When grown in a laboratory, microscopic bacteria form colonies that you can see. In this activity, you will observe some of the bacteria that share your world.

Procedure

1. Get **three plastic Petri dishes containing nutrient agar** from your teacher. Label one dish "Hand," another "Breath," and another "Soil."
2. Wipe your finger across the agar in the dish labeled "Hand." Breathe into the dish labeled "Breath." Place a **small amount of soil** in the dish labeled "Soil."
3. Secure the Petri dish lids with **transparent tape.** Wash your hands. Keep the dishes upside down in a warm, dark place for about one week. **Caution:** Do not open the Petri dishes after they are sealed.
4. Observe the Petri dishes each day. What do you see? Record your observations.

Analysis

1. How does the appearance of the colonies growing on the agar in each dish differ? What do bacterial colonies look like?
2. Which source caused the most bacterial growth—your hand, your breath, or the soil? Why do you think this source caused the most growth?

SECTION 1

Bacteria

How many bacteria are in a handful of soil? Would you believe that a single gram of soil—which is about the mass of a pencil eraser—may have more than 2.5 billion bacteria? A handful of soil may contain trillions of bacteria!

READING WARM-UP

Objectives

- Describe the characteristics of bacteria.
- Explain how bacteria reproduce.
- Compare and contrast eubacteria and archaebacteria.

Terms to Learn

prokaryote
binary fission
endospore

READING STRATEGY

Prediction Guide Before reading this section, predict whether each of the following statements is true or false:

- There are only a few kinds of bacteria.
- Most bacteria are too small to see.

There are more types of bacteria on Earth than all other living things combined. Most bacteria are too small to be seen without a microscope. But not all bacteria are the same size. In fact, the largest known bacteria are 1,000 times larger than the average bacterium. One of these giant bacteria was first found inside a surgeonfish and is shown in **Figure 1.**

Characteristics of Bacteria

All living things fit into one of six kingdoms: Protista, Plantae, Fungi, Animalia, Eubacteria, or Archaebacteria. Bacteria make up the kingdoms Eubacteria (YOO bak TIR ee uh) and Archaebacteria (AHR kee bak TIR ee uh). These two kingdoms contain the oldest forms of life on Earth. All bacteria are single-celled organisms. Bacteria are usually one of three main shapes: bacilli, cocci, or spirilla.

Reading Check **What two kingdoms are made up of bacteria?** *(See the Appendix for answers to Reading Checks.)*

Figure 1 *The giant bacteria inside this fish are 0.6 mm long, which is big enough to see without a microscope.*

Figure 2 The Most Common Shapes of Bacteria

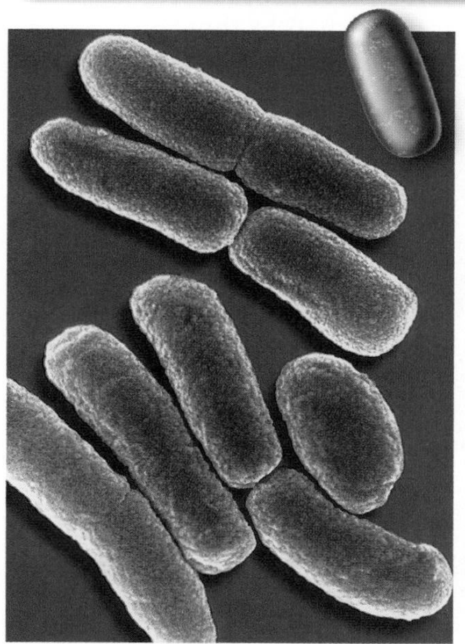

Bacilli (buh SIL IE) are rod shaped. They have a large surface area, which helps them take in nutrients. But a large surface area can cause them to dry out easily.

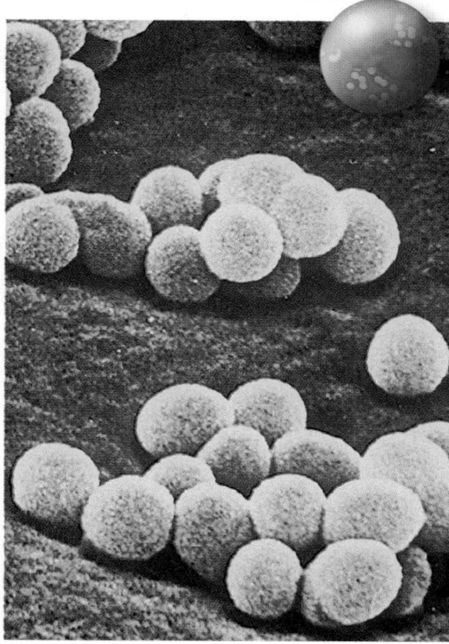

Cocci (KAHK SIE) are spherical. They do not dry out as quickly as rod-shaped bacteria.

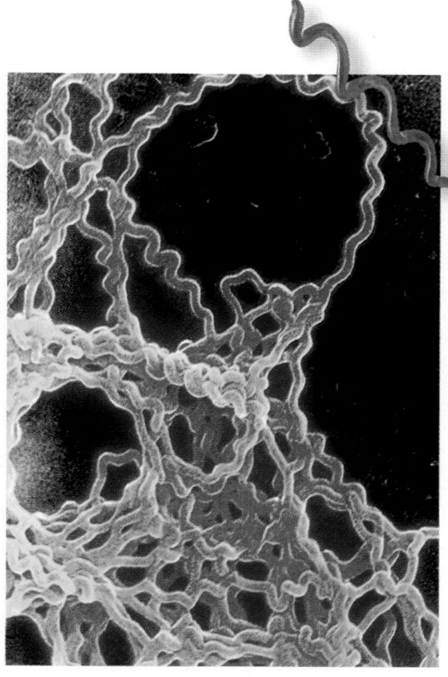

Spirilla (spie RIL uh) are long and spiral shaped. They use flagella at both ends to move like a corkscrew.

The Shape of Bacteria

Most bacteria have a rigid cell wall that gives them their shape. **Figure 2** shows the three most common shapes of bacteria. Bacilli (buh SIL IE) are rod shaped. Cocci (KAHK SIE) are spherical. Spirilla (spie RIL uh) are long and spiral shaped. Each shape helps bacteria in a different way.

Some bacteria have hairlike parts called *flagella* (fluh JEL uh) that help them move around. Flagella spin to push a bacterium through water or other liquids.

prokaryote an organism that consists of a single cell that does not have a nucleus

No Nucleus!

All bacteria are single-celled organisms that do not have a nucleus. An organism that does not have a nucleus is called a **prokaryote** (proh KAR ee OHT). A prokaryote is able to move, get energy, and reproduce like cells that have a nucleus, which are called *eukaryotes* (yoo KAR ee OHTZ).

Prokaryotes function as independent organisms. Some bacteria stick together to form strands or films, but each bacterium is still functioning as a single organism. Most prokaryotes are much simpler and smaller than eukaryotes. Prokaryotes also reproduce differently than eukaryotes do.

Spying on Spirilla

1. Using a **microscope,** observe prepared **slides of bacteria.** Draw each type of bacteria you see.
2. What different shapes do you see? What are these shapes called?

Figure 3 **Binary Fission**

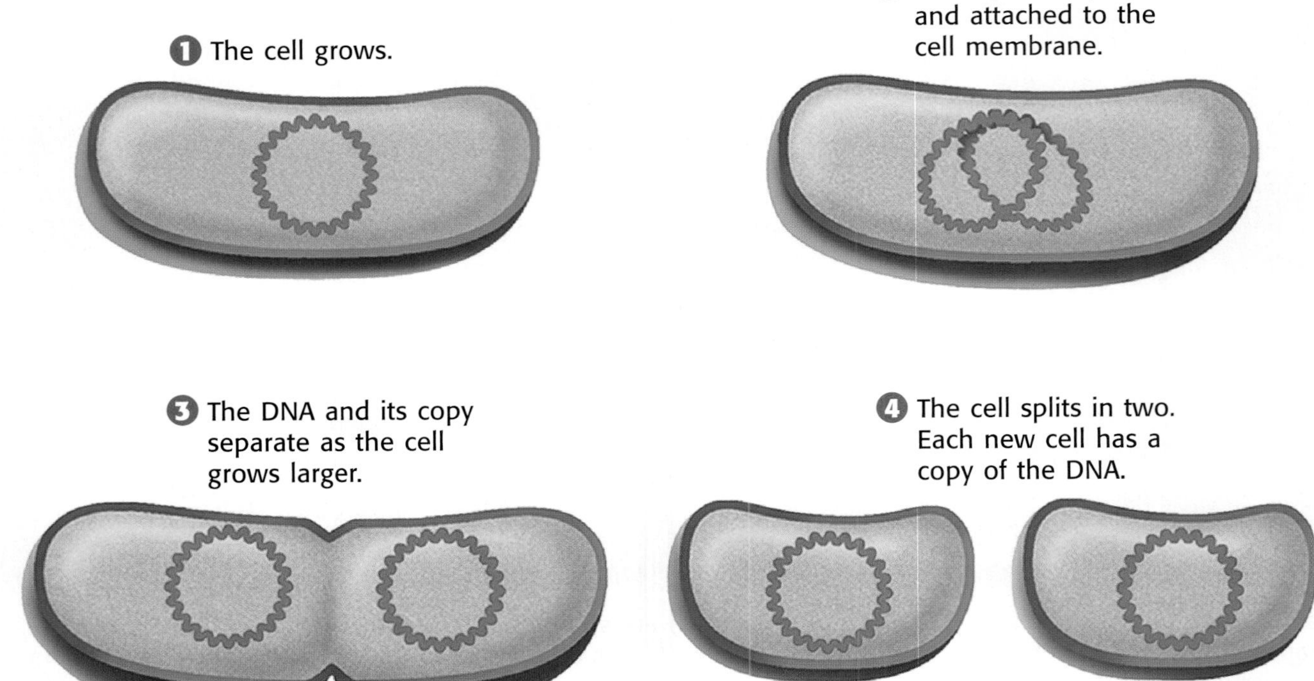

1 The cell grows.
2 The DNA is copied and attached to the cell membrane.
3 The DNA and its copy separate as the cell grows larger.
4 The cell splits in two. Each new cell has a copy of the DNA.

Bacterial Reproduction

binary fission a form of asexual reproduction in single-celled organisms by which one cell divides into two cells of the same size

Bacteria reproduce by the process shown in **Figure 3.** This process is called binary fission (BIE nuh ree FISH uhn). **Binary fission** is reproduction in which one single-celled organism splits into two single-celled organisms.

Prokaryotes have no nucleus, so their DNA is not surrounded by a membrane. The DNA of bacteria is in circular loops. In the first step of binary fission, the cell's DNA is copied. The DNA and its copy then bind to different places on the inside of the cell membrane. As the cell and its membrane grow bigger, the loops of DNA separate. Finally, when the cell is about double its original size, the membrane pinches inward as shown in **Figure 4.** A new cell wall forms and separates the two new cells. Each new cell has one exact copy of the parent cell's DNA.

Reading Check What is binary fission?

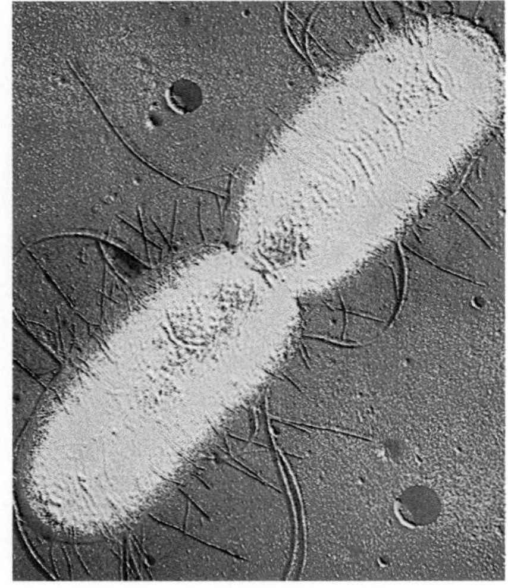

Figure 4 *This bacterium is about to complete binary fission.*

Endospores

Most species of bacteria do well in warm, moist places. In dry or cold surroundings, some species of bacteria will die. In these conditions, other bacteria become inactive and form endospores (EN doh SPAWRZ). An **endospore** contains genetic material and proteins and is covered by a thick, protective coat. Many endospores can survive in hot, cold, and very dry places. When conditions improve, the endospores break open, and the bacteria become active again. Scientists found endospores inside an insect that was preserved in amber for 30 million years. When the endospores were moistened in a laboratory, bacteria began to grow! A similar piece of amber can be seen in **Figure 5.**

Figure 5 *Endospores found in a preserved insect like this one showed scientists that bacteria can survive for millions of years.*

Kingdom Eubacteria

Most bacteria are eubacteria. The kingdom Eubacteria has more individuals than all of the other five kingdoms combined. Scientists think that eubacteria have lived on Earth for more than 3.5 billion years.

Eubacteria Classification

Eubacteria are classified by the way they get food. Most eubacteria, such as those breaking down the leaf in **Figure 6,** are consumers. Consumers get their food by eating other organisms. Many bacteria are decomposers, which feed on dead organisms. Other consumer bacteria live in or on the body of another organism. Eubacteria that make their own food are called *producers*. Like plants, producer bacteria use the energy from sunlight to make food. These bacteria are often green.

endospore a thick-walled protective spore that forms inside a bacterial cell and resists harsh conditions

Figure 6 *Decomposers, such as the ones helping to decay this leaf, return nutrients to the soil for other living things to use.*

Cyanobacteria

Cyanobacteria (SIE uh noh bak TIR ee uh) are producers. Cyanobacteria usually live in water. These bacteria contain the green pigment chlorophyll. Chlorophyll is important to photosynthesis (the process of making food from the energy in sunlight). Many cyanobacteria have other pigments as well. Some have a blue pigment that helps in photosynthesis. This pigment gives those cyanobacteria a blue tint. Other cyanobacteria have red pigment. Flamingos get their pink color from eating red cyanobacteria.

Some scientists think that billions of years ago, bacteria similar to cyanobacteria began to live inside larger cells. According to this theory, the bacteria made food, and the cells provided protection. This combination may have given rise to the first plants on Earth.

CONNECTION TO Language Arts

Colorful Names *Cyanobacteria* means "blue bacteria." Many other names also refer to colors. You might not recognize these colors because the words for the colors are in another language. Look at the list of Greek color words below. Write down two English words that have one of the color roots in them. (Hint: Many words have the color as the first part of the word.)

melano = black
chloro = green
erythro = red
leuko = white

Kingdom Archaebacteria

The three main types of archaebacteria are *heat lovers, salt lovers,* and *methane makers*. Heat lovers live in ocean vents and hot springs. They live in very hot water, usually from 60°C to 80°C, but they can survive temperatures of more than 250°C. Salt lovers live in environments that have high levels of salt, such as the Dead Sea and Great Salt Lake. Methane makers give off methane gas and live in swamps and animal intestines. **Figure 7** shows one type of methane maker found in the mud of swamps.

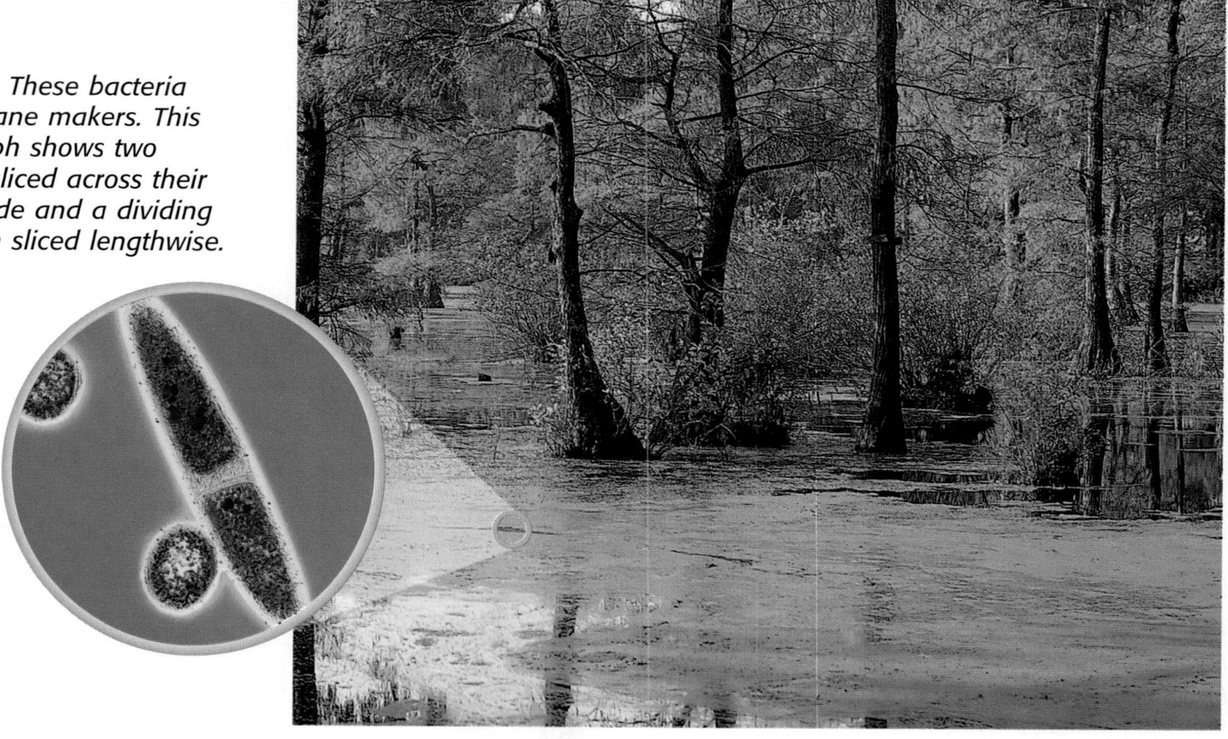

Figure 7 *These bacteria are methane makers. This micrograph shows two bacteria sliced across their narrow side and a dividing bacterium sliced lengthwise.*

Harsh Environments

Archaebacteria often live where nothing else can. Most archaebacteria prefer environments where there is little or no oxygen. Scientists have found them in the hot springs at Yellowstone National Park and beneath 430 m of ice in Antarctica. Archaebacteria have even been found living 8 km below the Earth's surface! Even though they are often found in these harsh environments, many archaebacteria can also be found in moderate environments in Earth's oceans.

Archaebacteria are very different from eubacteria. Not all archaebacteria have cell walls. When they do have them, the cell walls are chemically different from those of eubacteria.

SECTION Review

Summary

- Bacteria are single-celled organisms that are the smallest and simplest living things on Earth.
- Most bacteria have a rigid cell wall that gives them their shape. The main shapes of bacteria are rod shaped (bacilli), spherical (cocci), and spiral shaped (spirilla).
- Bacteria reproduce by binary fission. In binary fission, one cell divides into two cells.
- Eubacteria have cell walls and are either producers (bacteria that make their own food) or consumers (bacteria that get food from other organisms).
- Archaebacteria often live in harsh environments.

Using Key Terms

The statements below are false. For each statement, replace the underlined term to make a true statement.

1. Bacteria are eukaryotes.
2. Bacteria reproduce by primary fission.

Understanding Key Ideas

3. The structure that helps some bacteria survive harsh conditions is called a(n)
   a. endospore. **c.** exospore.
   b. shell. **d.** exoskeleton.
4. How are eubacteria and archaebacteria different?
5. Draw and label the four stages of binary fission.
6. Describe one advantage of each shape of bacteria.
7. What two things do producer bacteria and plants have in common?

Math Skills

8. An ounce (oz) is equal to about 28 g. If 1 g of soil contains 2.5 billion bacteria, how many bacteria are in 1 oz of soil?

Critical Thinking

9. **Applying Concepts** Many bacteria cannot reproduce in cooler temperatures and are destroyed at high temperatures. How do humans take advantage of this fact when preparing and storing food?
10. **Making Comparisons** Scientists are studying cold and dry environments on Earth that are like the environment on Mars. What kind of bacteria do you think they might find in these environments on Earth? Explain.
11. **Forming Hypotheses** You are studying a lake and the bacteria that live in it. What conditions of the lake would you measure to form a hypothesis about what kind of bacteria may live there?

SCILINKS.
NSTA
Developed and maintained by the National Science Teachers Association
For a variety of links related to this chapter, go to www.scilinks.org
Topic: Bacteria; Archaebacteria
SciLinks code: HSM0133; HSM0091

SECTION 2

Bacteria's Role in the World

Have you ever had strep throat or a cavity in your tooth? Did you know that both are caused by bacteria?

READING WARM-UP

Objectives

- Explain how life on Earth depends on bacteria.
- List three ways bacteria are useful to people.
- Describe two ways in which bacteria can be harmful to people.

Terms to Learn

bioremediation
antibiotic
pathogenic bacteria

READING STRATEGY

Reading Organizer As you read this section, create an outline of the section. Use the headings from the section in your outline.

Bacteria live in our water, our food, and our bodies. Much of what we know about bacteria was learned by scientists fighting bacterial diseases. But of the thousands of types of bacteria, only a few hundred cause disease. Many bacteria do things that are important and even helpful to us.

Good for the Environment

Life as we know it could not exist without bacteria. Bacteria are very important to the health of Earth. They help recycle dead animals and plants. Bacteria also play an important role in the nitrogen cycle.

Nitrogen Fixation

Most living things depend on plants. Plants need nitrogen to grow. Nitrogen gas makes up about 78% of the air, but most plants cannot use nitrogen directly from the air. They need to take in a different form of nitrogen. Nitrogen-fixing bacteria take in nitrogen from the air and change it to a form that plants can use. This process, called *nitrogen fixation,* is described in **Figure 1.**

Reading Check **What is nitrogen fixation?** (*See the Appendix for answers to Reading Checks.*)

Figure 1 **Bacteria's Role in the Nitrogen Cycle**

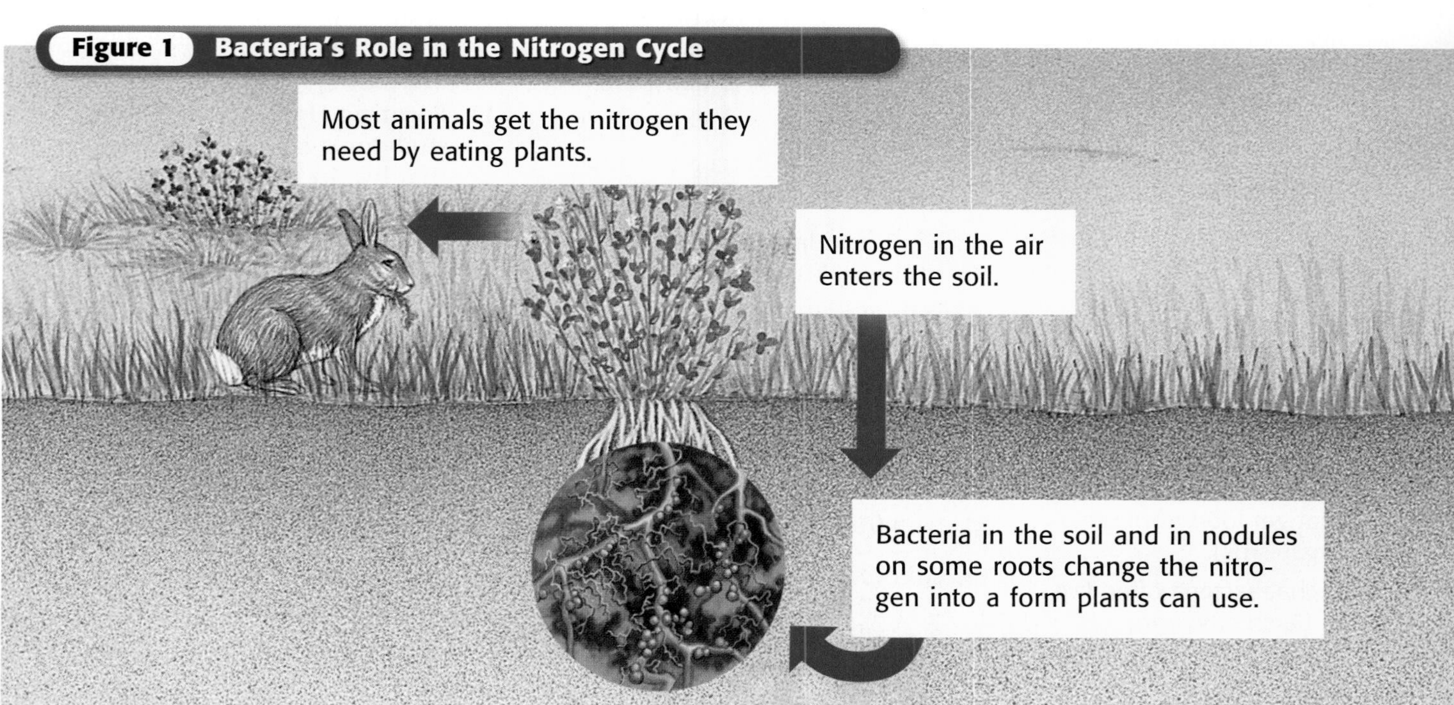

Most animals get the nitrogen they need by eating plants.
Nitrogen in the air enters the soil.
Bacteria in the soil and in nodules on some roots change the nitrogen into a form plants can use.

Recycling

Have you ever seen dead leaves and twigs on a forest floor? These leaves and twigs are recycled over time with the help of bacteria. Decomposer bacteria break down dead plant and animal matter. Breaking down dead matter makes nutrients available to other living things.

Cleaning Up

Bacteria and other microorganisms are also used to fight pollution. **Bioremediation** (BIE oh ri MEE dee AY shuhn) means using microorganisms to change harmful chemicals into harmless ones. Bioremediation is used to clean up hazardous waste from industries, farms, and cities. It is also used to clean up oil spills. The workers in **Figure 2** are using bacteria to remove pollutants from the soil.

Figure 2 *Bioremediating bacteria are added to soil to eat pollutants. The bacteria then release the pollutants as harmless waste.*

Good for People

Bacteria do much more than help keep our environment clean. Bacteria also help produce many of the foods we eat every day. They even help make important medicines.

bioremediation the biological treatment of hazardous waste by living organisms

Bacteria in Your Food

Believe it or not, people raise bacteria for food! Every time you eat cheese, yogurt, buttermilk, or sour cream, you are also eating bacteria. Lactic acid-producing bacteria break down the sugar in milk, which is called *lactose*. In the process, the bacteria change lactose into lactic acid. Lactic acid preserves and adds flavor to the food. All of the foods shown in **Figure 3** were made with the help of bacteria.

Make a Meal Plan

With a parent, create a week's meal plan without any foods made with bacteria. What would your diet be like without bacteria?

ACTIVITY

Figure 3 *Bacteria are used to make many kinds of foods.*

Figure 4 *Genes from the* Xenopus *frog were used to produce the first genetically engineered bacteria.*

Making Medicines

What's the best way to fight disease-causing bacteria? Would you believe that the answer is to use other bacteria? **Antibiotics** are medicines used to kill bacteria and other microorganisms. Many antibiotics are made by bacteria.

antibiotic medicine used to kill bacteria and other microorganisms

pathogenic bacteria bacteria that cause disease

Insulin

The human body needs insulin to break down and use sugar and carbohydrates. People who have diabetes do not make enough insulin. In the 1970s, scientists discovered how to put genes into bacteria so that the bacteria would make human insulin. The insulin can then be separated from the bacteria and given to people who have diabetes.

Genetic Engineering

When scientists change the genes of bacteria, or any other living thing, the process is called *genetic engineering*. Scientists have been genetically engineering bacteria since 1973. In that year, researchers put genes from a frog like the one in **Figure 4** into the bacterium *Escherichia coli* (ESH uh RIK ee uh KOH LIE). The bacterium then started making copies of the frog genes. Scientists can now engineer bacteria to make many products, such as insecticides, cleansers, and adhesives.

Reading Check What is genetic engineering?

Harmful Bacteria

Humans couldn't live without bacteria, but bacteria can also cause harm. Scientists learned in the 1800s that some bacteria are pathogenic (PATH uh JEN ik). **Pathogenic bacteria** are bacteria that cause disease. Pathogenic bacteria get inside a host organism and take nutrients from the host's cells. In the process, they harm the host. Today, we are protected from many bacterial diseases by vaccination, as shown in **Figure 5.** Many bacterial diseases can also be treated with antibiotics.

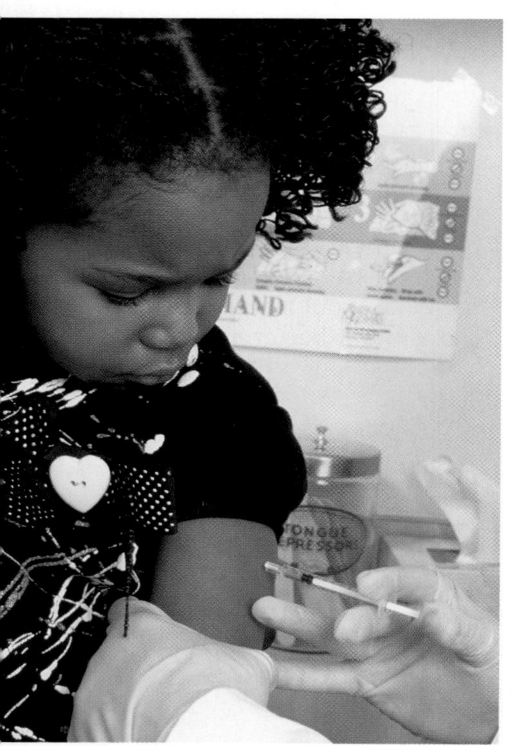

Figure 5 *Vaccines can protect you from bacterial diseases such as tetanus and diptheria.*

Diseases in Other Organisms

Bacteria cause diseases in other organisms as well as in people. Have you ever seen a plant with odd-colored spots or soft rot? If so, you've seen bacterial damage to plants. Pathogenic bacteria attack plants, animals, protists, fungi, and even other bacteria. They can cause damage to grain, fruit, and vegetable crops. The branch of the pear tree in **Figure 6** shows the effects of pathogenic bacteria. Plants are sometimes treated with antibiotics. Scientists have also genetically engineered certain plants to be resistant to disease-causing bacteria.

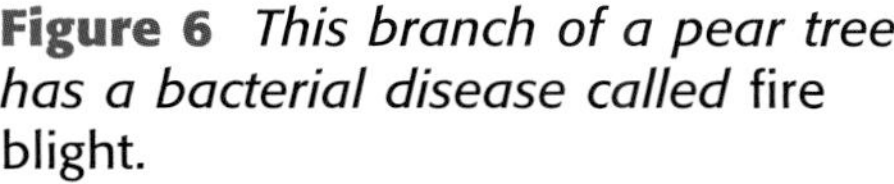

Figure 6 *This branch of a pear tree has a bacterial disease called* fire blight.

SECTION Review

Summary

- Bacteria are important to life on Earth because they fix nitrogen and decompose dead matter.
- Bacteria are useful to people because they help make foods and medicines.
- Scientists have genetically engineered bacteria to make medicines.
- Pathogenic bacteria are harmful to people. Bacteria can also harm the crops we grow for food.

Using Key Terms

1. In your own words, write a definition for the term *bioremediation*.
2. Use the following terms in the same sentence: *pathogenic bacteria* and *antibiotic*.

Understanding Key Ideas

3. What are two ways that bacteria affect plants?
4. How can bacteria both cause and cure diseases?
5. Explain two ways in which bacteria are crucial to life on Earth.
6. Describe two ways your life was affected by bacteria today.

Math Skills

7. Nitrogen makes up about 78% of air. If you have 2 L of air, how many liters of nitrogen are in the air?

Critical Thinking

8. **Identifying Relationships** Legumes, which include peas and beans, are efficient nitrogen fixers. Legumes are also a good source of amino acids. What chemical element would you expect to find in amino acids?
9. **Applying Concepts** Design a bacterium that will be genetically engineered. What do you want it to do? How would it help people or the environment?

SCILINKS
NSTA
Developed and maintained by the National Science Teachers Association
For a variety of links related to this chapter, go to www.scilinks.org
Topic: Antibiotics; Genetic Engineering
SciLinks code: HSM0082; HSM0654

SECTION 3

Viruses

One day, you discover red spots on your skin. More and more spots appear, and they begin turning into itchy blisters. What do you have?

READING WARM-UP

Objectives

- Explain how viruses are similar to and different from living things.
- List the four major virus shapes.
- Describe the two kinds of viral reproduction.

Terms to Learn

virus
host

READING STRATEGY

Discussion Read this section silently. Write down questions that you have about this section. Discuss your questions in a small group.

The spots could be chickenpox. Chickenpox is a disease caused by a virus. A **virus** is a microscopic particle that gets inside a cell and often destroys the cell. Many viruses cause diseases, such as the common cold, flu, and acquired immune deficiency syndrome (AIDS).

It's a Small World

Viruses are tiny. They are smaller than the smallest bacteria. About 5 billion virus particles could fit in a single drop of blood. Viruses can change rapidly. So, a virus's effect on living things can also change. Because viruses are so small and change so often, scientists don't know exactly how many types exist. These properties also make them difficult to fight.

Are Viruses Living?

Like living things, viruses contain protein and genetic material. But viruses, such as the ones shown in **Figure 1,** don't act like living things. They can't eat, grow, break down food, or use oxygen. In fact, a virus cannot function on its own. A virus can reproduce only inside a living cell that serves as a host. A **host** is a living thing that a virus or parasite lives on or in. Using a host's cell as a tiny factory, the virus forces the host to make viruses rather than healthy new cells.

virus a microscopic particle that gets inside a cell and often destroys the cell

host an organism from which a parasite takes food or shelter

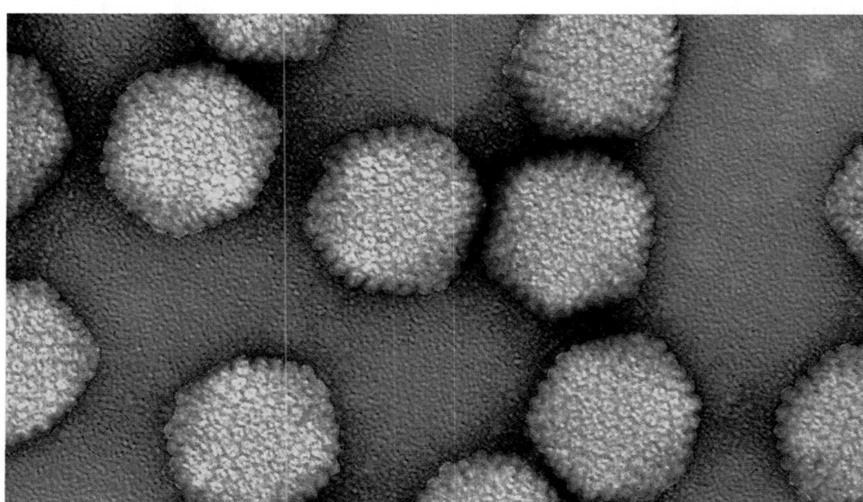

Figure 1 *Viruses are not cells. They do not have cytoplasm or organelles.*

Figure 2 **The Basic Shapes of Viruses**

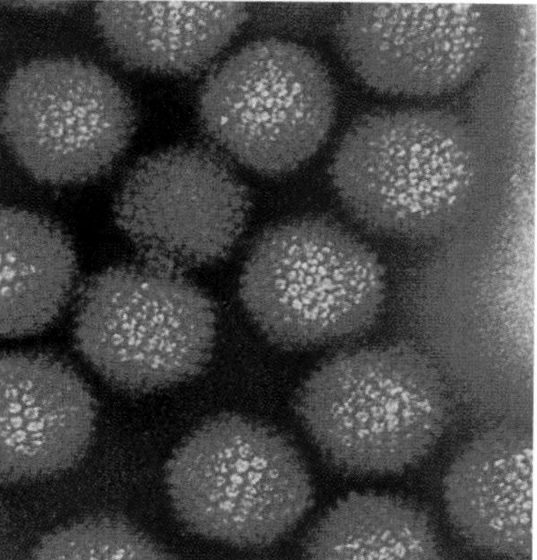

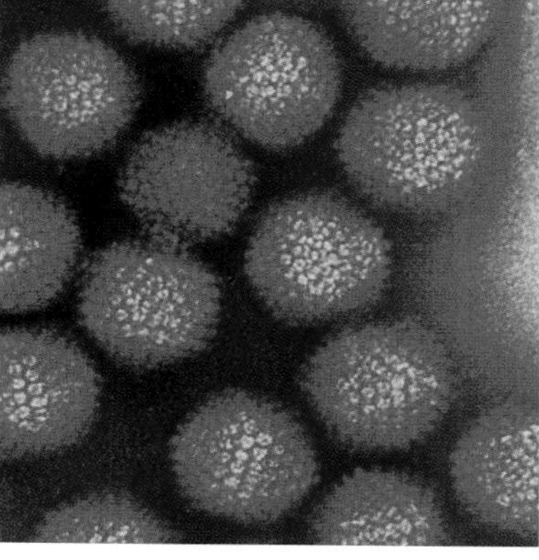

Crystals
The polio virus is shaped like the crystals shown here.

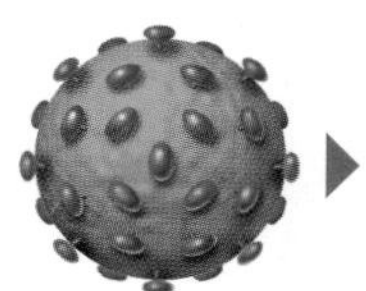

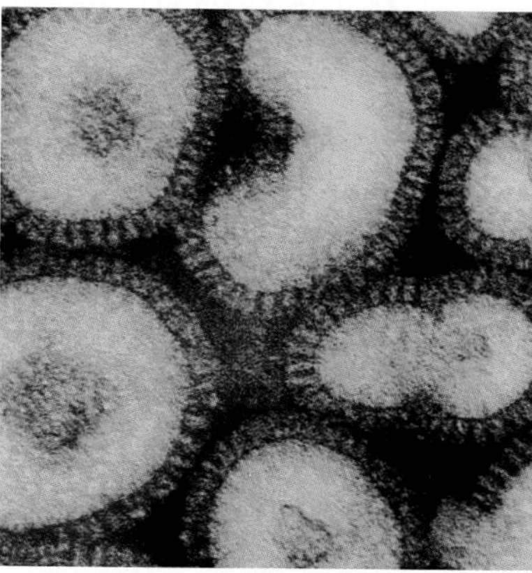

Spheres
Influenza viruses look like spheres. HIV is another virus that has this structure.

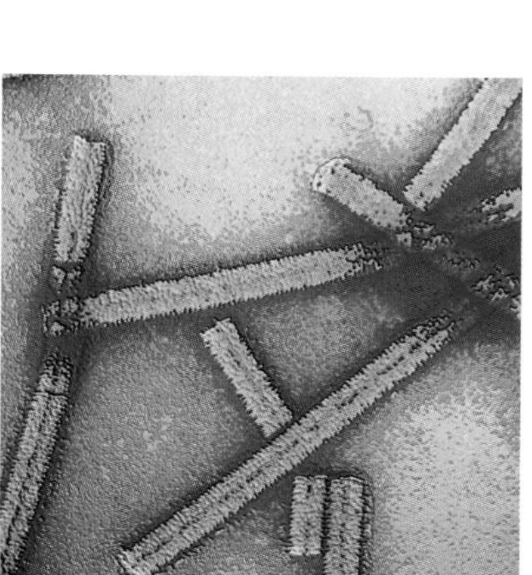

Cylinders
The tobacco mosaic virus is shaped like a cylinder and attacks tobacco plants.

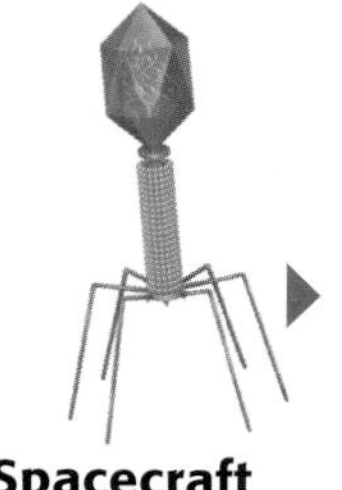

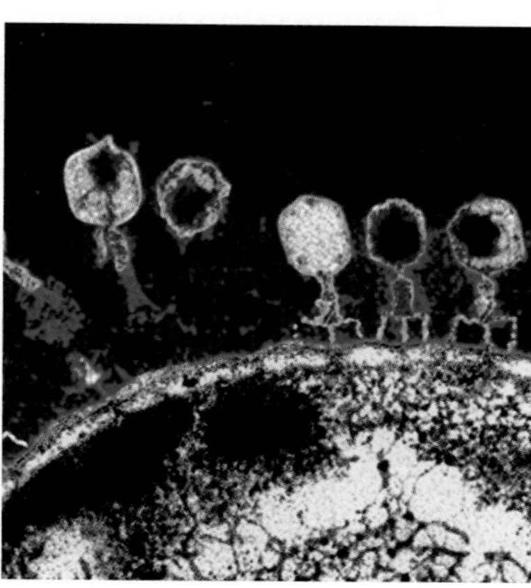

Spacecraft
One group of viruses attacks only bacteria. Many of these look almost like spacecraft.

Classifying Viruses

Viruses can be grouped by their shape, the type of disease they cause, their life cycle, or the kind of genetic material they contain. The four main shapes of viruses are shown in **Figure 2.** Every virus is made up of genetic material inside a protein coat. The protein coat protects the genetic material and helps a virus enter a host cell. Many viruses have a protein coat that matches characteristics of their specific host.

The genetic material in viruses is either DNA or RNA. Most RNA is made up of one strand of nucleotides. Most DNA is made up of two strands of nucleotides. Both DNA and RNA contain information for making proteins. The viruses that cause warts and chickenpox contain DNA. The viruses that cause colds and the flu contain RNA. The virus that causes AIDS, which is called the *human immunodeficiency virus* (HIV), also contains RNA.

Reading Check **What are two ways in which viruses can be classified?** (*See the Appendix for answers to Reading Checks.*)

Sizing Up a Virus

If you enlarged an average virus 600,000 times, it would be about the size of a small pea. How tall would you be if you were enlarged 600,000 times?

Figure 3 **The Lytic Cycle**

❶ The virus finds and joins itself to a host cell.

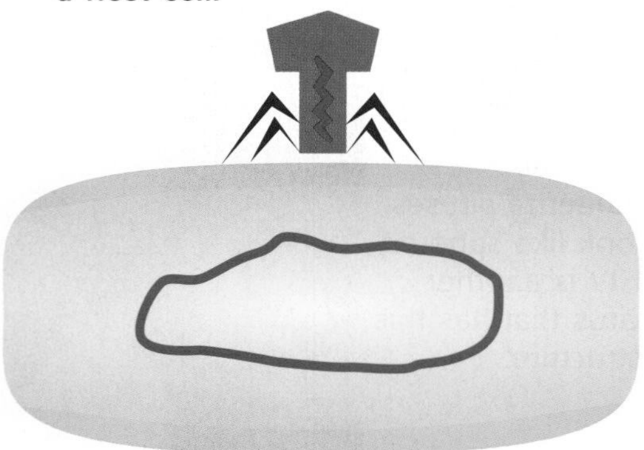

❷ The virus enters the cell, or the virus's genetic material is injected into the cell.

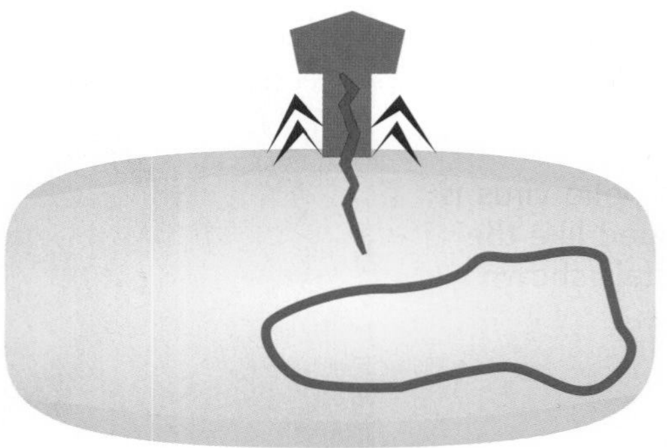

❸ Once the virus's genes are inside, they take over the direction of the host cell and turn it into a virus factory.

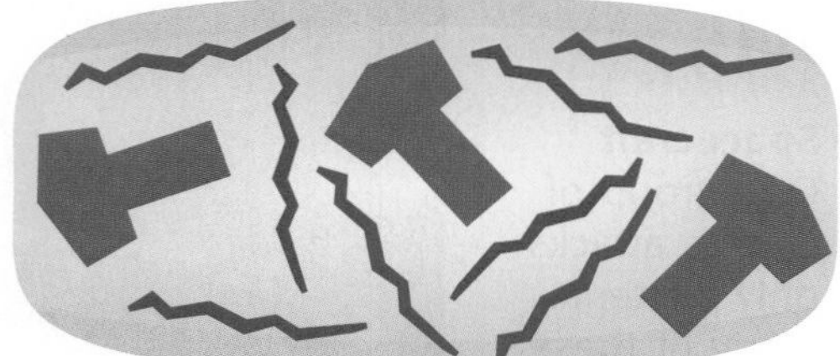

❹ The new viruses break out of the host cell, which kills the host cell. The cycle begins again.

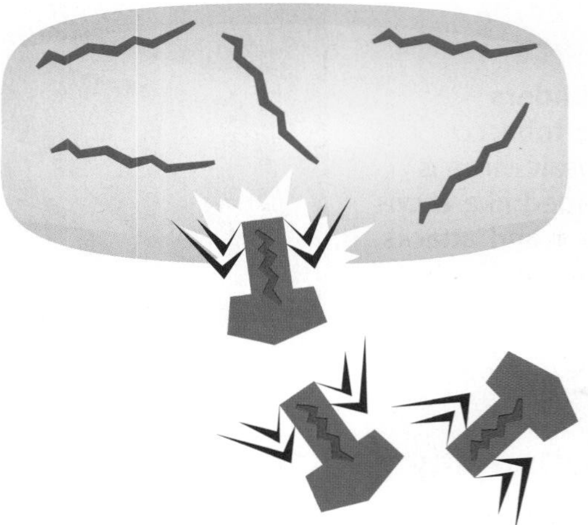

A Destructive House Guest

The one thing that viruses do that living things also do is make more of themselves. Viruses attack living cells and turn them into virus factories. This cycle is called the *lytic cycle* (LIT ik SIE kuhl), and it is shown in **Figure 3.**

Reading Check What is the lytic cycle?

CONNECTION TO Chemistry

Viral Crystals Many viruses can form into crystals. Scientists can study X rays of these crystals to learn about the structure of viruses. Why do you think scientists want to learn more about viruses?

A Time Bomb

Some viruses don't go straight into the lytic cycle. These viruses also put their genetic material into the host cell. But new viruses are not made right away. In the lysogenic (LIE soh JEN ik) cycle, each new cell gets a copy of the virus's genes when the host cell divides. The genes can stay inactive for a long time. When the genes do become active, they begin the lytic cycle and make copies of the virus.

Treating a Virus

Antibiotics do not kill viruses. But scientists have recently developed antiviral (AN tie VIE ruhl) medications. Many of these medicines stop viruses from reproducing. Because many viral diseases do not have cures, it is best to prevent a viral infection from happening in the first place. Childhood vaccinations give your immune system a head start in fighting off viruses. Having current vaccinations can prevent you from getting a viral infection. It is also a good practice to wash your hands often and never to touch wild animals. If you do get sick from a virus, like the boy in **Figure 4,** it is often best to rest and drink extra fluids. As with any sickness, you should tell your parents or a doctor.

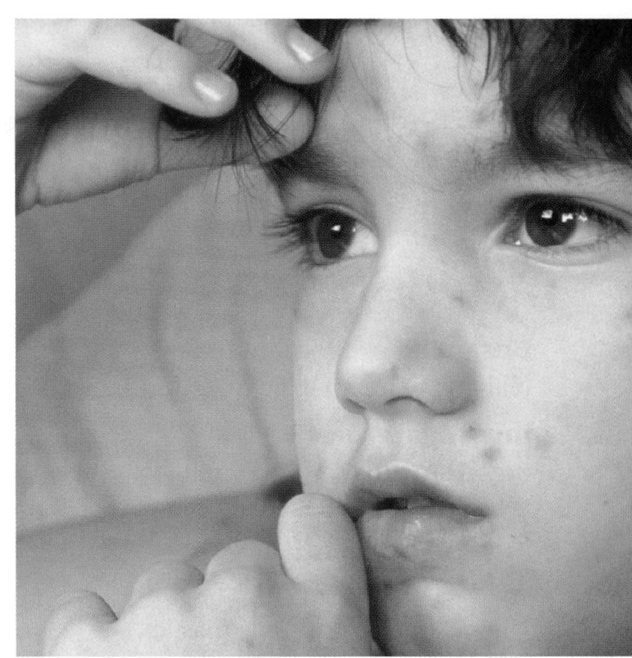

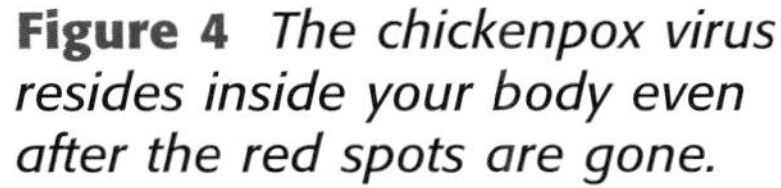

Figure 4 *The chickenpox virus resides inside your body even after the red spots are gone.*

SECTION Review

Summary

- Viruses have characteristics of living and nonliving things. They reproduce in living cells.
- Viruses may be classified by their shape, the kind of disease they cause, or their life cycle.
- To reproduce, a virus must enter a cell, reproduce itself, and then break open the cell. This is called the lytic cycle.
- In the lysogenic cycle, the genes of a virus are incorporated into the genes of the host cell.

Using Key Terms

1. Use the following terms in the same sentence: *virus* and *host.*

Understanding Key Ideas

2. One characteristic viruses have in common with living things is that they
   a. eat. **b.** reproduce. **c.** sleep. **d.** grow.
3. Describe the four steps in the lytic cycle.
4. Explain how the lytic cycle and the lysogenic cycle are different.

Math Skills

5. A bacterial cell infected by a virus divides every 20 min. After 10,000 divisions, the new viruses are released from their host cell. About how many weeks will this process take?

Critical Thinking

6. **Making Inferences** Do you think modern transportation has had an effect on the way viruses spread? Explain.
7. **Identifying Relationships** What characteristics of viruses do you think have made finding drugs to attack them difficult?
8. **Expressing Opinions** Do you think that vaccinations are important even in areas where a virus is not found?

SCILINKS
NSTA
Developed and maintained by the National Science Teachers Association
For a variety of links related to this chapter, go to www.scilinks.org
Topic: Viruses
SciLinks code: HSM1607

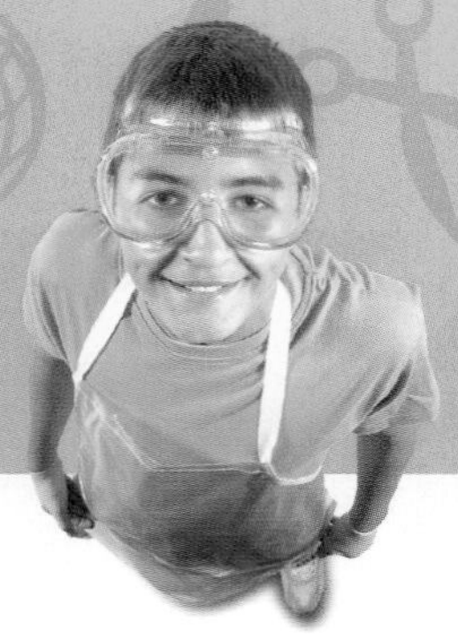

Using Scientific Methods

Inquiry Lab

Aunt Flossie and the Intruder

OBJECTIVES

Design an experiment that will answer a specific question.

Investigate what kind of organisms make food spoil.

MATERIALS

- gloves, protective
- items, such as sealable plastic bags, food samples, a scale, or a thermometer, to be determined by the students and approved by the teacher as needed for each experiment

SAFETY

Aunt Flossie is a really bad housekeeper! She never cleans the refrigerator, and things get really gross in there. Last week she pulled out a plastic bag that looked like it was going to explode! The bag was full of gas that she did not put there! Aunt Flossie remembered from her school days that gases are released from living things as waste products. Something had to be alive in the bag!

Aunt Flossie became very upset that there was an intruder in her refrigerator. She refuses to bake another cookie until you determine the nature of the intruder.

Ask a Question

1. How did gas get into Aunt Flossie's bag?

Form a Hypothesis

2. Write a hypothesis which answers the question above. Explain your reasoning.

Test the Hypothesis

3. Design an experiment that will determine how gas got into Aunt Flossie's bag. Make a list of the materials you will need, and prepare all the data tables you will need for recording your observations.
4. Get your teacher's approval of your experimental design and your list of materials before you begin.
5. Dispose of your materials according to your teacher's instructions at the end of your experiment. **Caution:** Do not open any bags of spoiled food or allow any of the contents to escape.

Ask a Question

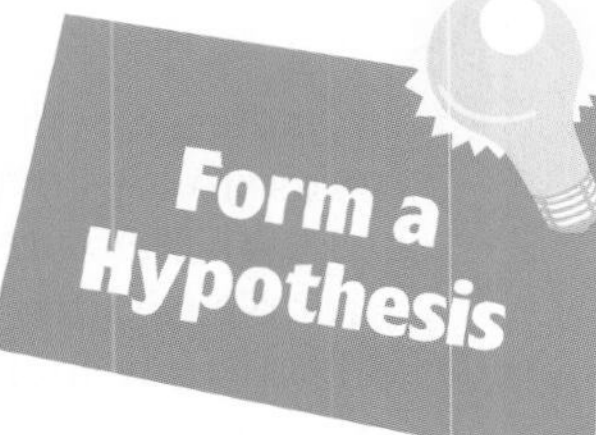

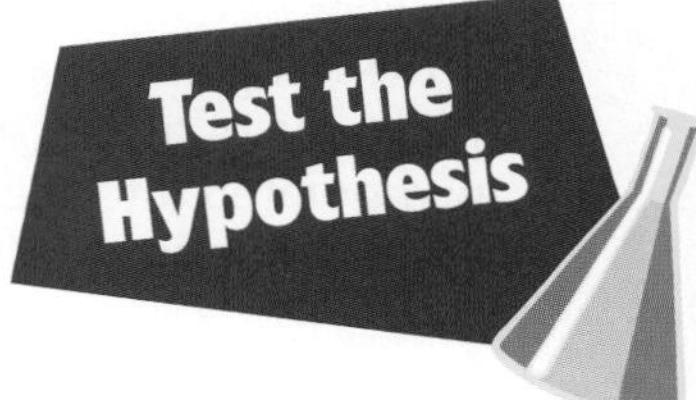

Analyze the Results

1. **Organizing Data** What data did you collect from your experiment?

Draw Conclusions

2. **Drawing Conclusions** What conclusions can you draw from your investigation? Where did the gas come from?

3. **Evaluating Methods** If you were going to perform another investigation, what would you change in the experiment to give better results? Explain your answer.

Communicating Your Data

WRITING SKILL Write a letter to Aunt Flossie describing your experiment. Explain what produced the gas in the bag and your recommendations for preventing these intruders in her refrigerator in the future.

Analyze the Results

Draw Conclusions

Do they support your hypothesis?

No

Yes

Chapter Review

USING KEY TERMS

1. In your own words, write a definition for the term *pathogenic bacteria.*

Complete each of the following sentences by choosing the correct term from the word bank.

binary fission	endospore
antibiotic	bioremediation
virus	bacteria

2. Most bacteria reproduce by ___.
3. Bacterial infections can be treated with ___.
4. A(n) ___ needs a host to reproduce.

UNDERSTANDING KEY IDEAS

Multiple Choice

5. Bacteria are used for all of the following EXCEPT
   a. making certain foods.
   b. making antibiotics.
   c. cleaning up oil spills.
   d. preserving fruit.

6. In the lytic cycle, the host cell
   a. is destroyed.
   b. destroys the virus.
   c. becomes a virus.
   d. undergoes cell division.

7. A bacterial cell
   a. is an endospore.
   b. has a loop of DNA.
   c. has a distinct nucleus.
   d. is a eukaryote.

8. Eubacteria
   a. include methane makers.
   b. include decomposers.
   c. all have chlorophyll.
   d. are rod-shaped.

9. Cyanobacteria
   a. are consumers.
   b. are parasites.
   c. contain chlorophyll.
   d. are decomposers.

10. Archaebacteria
    a. are a special type of eubacteria.
    b. live only in places without oxygen.
    c. are lactic acid-producing bacteria.
    d. can live in hostile environments.

11. Viruses
    a. are about the same size as bacteria.
    b. have nuclei.
    c. can reproduce only within a host cell.
    d. do not infect plants.

12. Bacteria are important to the planet as
    a. decomposers of dead organic matter.
    b. processors of nitrogen.
    c. makers of medicine.
    d. All of the above

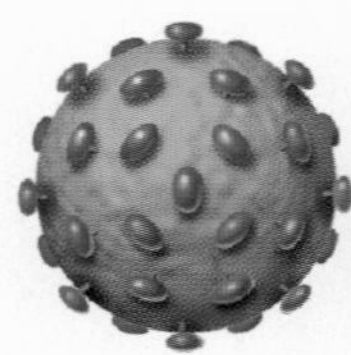

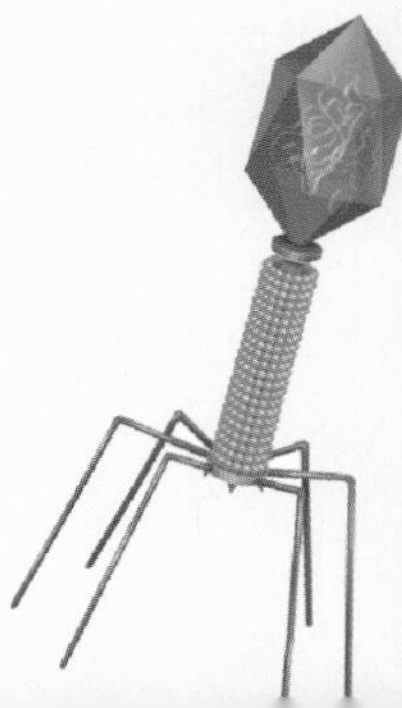

Short Answer

13. How are the functions of nitrogen-fixing bacteria and decomposers similar?

14. Which cycle takes more time, the lytic cycle or the lysogenic cycle?

15. Describe two ways in which viruses do not act like living things.

16. What is bioremediation?

17. Describe how doctors can treat a viral infection.

CRITICAL THINKING

18. **Concept Mapping** Use the following terms to create a concept map: *eubacteria, bacilli, cocci, spirilla, consumers, producers,* and *cyanobacteria.*

19. **Predicting Consequences** Describe some of the problems you think bacteria might face if there were no humans.

20. **Applying Concepts** Many modern soaps contain chemicals that kill bacteria. Describe one good outcome and one bad outcome of the use of antibacterial soaps.

21. **Identifying Relationships** Some people have digestive problems after they take a course of antibiotics. Why do you think these problems happen?

INTERPRETING GRAPHICS

The diagram below illustrates the stages of binary fission. Match each statement with the correct stage.

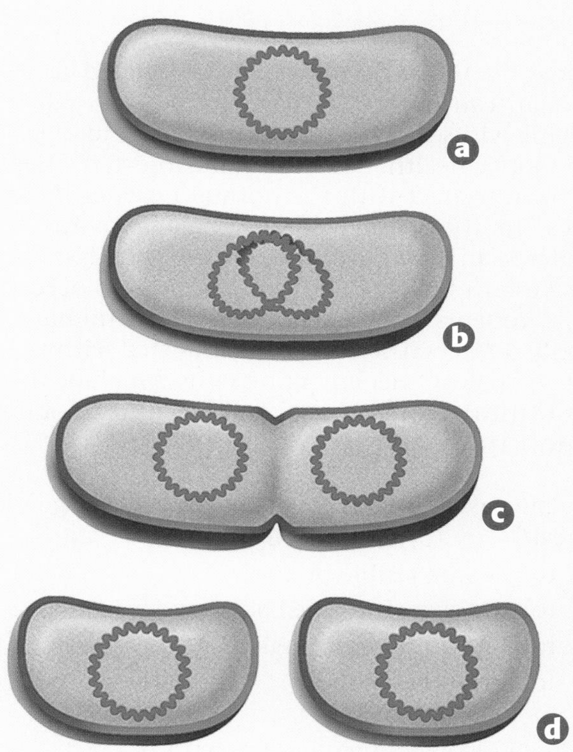

22. The DNA loops separate.

23. The DNA loop replicates.

24. The parent cell starts to expand.

25. The DNA attaches to the cell membrane.

Standardized Test Preparation

READING

Read each of the passages below. Then, answer the questions that follow each passage.

Passage 1 Viruses that evolve in isolated areas and that can infect human beings are called emerging viruses. These new viruses are dangerous to public health. People become infected when they have contact with the normal hosts of these viruses. In the United States, the hantavirus is considered an emerging virus. First detected in the southwestern United States, the hantavirus occurs in wild rodents and can infect and kill humans. Roughly 40% to 50% of humans infected with the hantavirus die. Other emerging viruses include the Ebola (Africa), Lassa (Africa), and Machupo (South America) viruses.

1. In the passage, what does the word *emerging* mean?
   - **A** to become visible or known
   - **B** to fade away into the background
   - **C** to melt from two things into one
   - **D** to become urgent

2. Which of the following statements is a fact from the passage?
   - **F** Hantavirus causes death in more than 40% of its victims.
   - **G** Hantavirus causes death in more than 50% of its victims.
   - **H** Hantavirus causes death in fewer than 30% of its victims.
   - **I** Hantavirus causes death in fewer than 40% of its victims.

3. Which of the following is an emergent virus in South America?
   - **A** Ebola virus
   - **B** Lassa virus
   - **C** SARS virus
   - **D** Machupo virus

Passage 2 Less than 100 years ago, people had no way to treat bacterial infections. But in 1928, a Scottish scientist named Alexander Fleming discovered the first antibiotic, or bacteria-killing drug. This first antibiotic was called *penicillin*. The discovery of antibiotics improved healthcare dramatically. However, scientists are now realizing that many bacteria are becoming resistant to existing antibiotics. Scientists are hoping that a particular type of virus called a bacteriophage (bak TIR ee uh FAHJ) might hold the key to fighting bacteria in the future. Bacteriophages destroy bacteria cells. Each kind of bacteriophage can infect only a particular species of bacteria.

1. In what year was penicillin discovered?
   - **A** 1905
   - **B** 1928
   - **C** 1969
   - **D** 1974

2. According to the passage, what might be the key to fighting bacteria in the future?
   - **F** antibiotics
   - **G** bacteriophages
   - **H** penicillin
   - **I** antibiotic-resistant bacteria

3. According to the passage, what can each kind of bacteriophage infect?
   - **A** viruses that cause disease
   - **B** only antibiotic-resistant bacteria
   - **C** all kinds of bacteria
   - **D** only a particular species of bacteria

INTERPRETING GRAPHICS

The images below show the four main shapes of viruses. Use these pictures to answer the questions that follow.

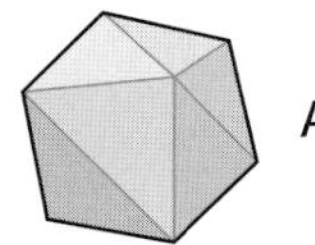

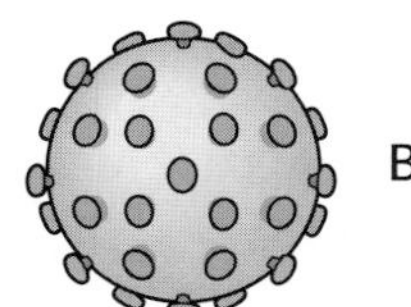

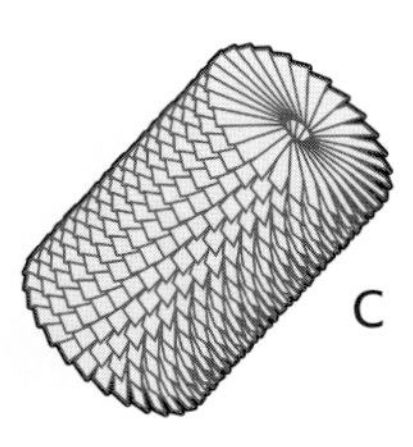

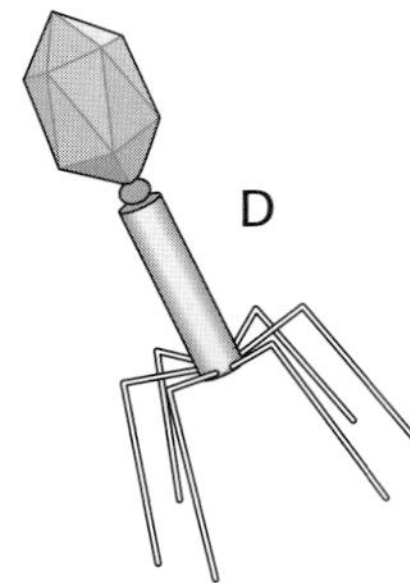

1. Which viral shape attacks only bacteria?

A virus A
B virus B
C virus C
D virus D

2. Which viral shape is the cylinder?

F virus A
G virus B
H virus C
I virus D

3. Which viral shape would you expect to have the largest surface area–to-volume ratio?

A virus A
B virus B
C virus C
D virus D

MATH

Read each question below, and choose the best answer.

1. Reagan spent \$26 for four equally priced CDs. Which of the following equations could be used to find how much each CD costs?

A $4 \times \$26 = n$
B $n = \$26 - 4$
C $4 \times n = \$26$
D $n \times \$26 = 4$

2. What is $5 + (-8)$ equal to?

F -13
G -3
H 3
I 13

3. What is $-9 - 2$ equal to?

A -11
B -7
C -4
D 7

4. What is the solution to $45 \div 0.009$?

F 5,000
G 500
H 50
I 5

5. What is $-9 + 2$ equal to?

A -11
B -7
C -4
D 7

6. Jennifer, Beth, and Sienna live 8 km, 2.2 km, and 7.4 km from the school. Which of the following is a reasonable estimate of the average distance these friends live from the school?

F 6 km
G 7.4 km
H 9 km
I 18 km

Science in Action

Science, Technology, and Society

Edible Vaccines

Vaccines protect you from life-threatening diseases. But vaccinations are expensive, and the people who give them must go through extensive training. These and other factors often prevent people in developing countries from getting vaccinations. But help may be on the way. Scientists are developing edible vaccines. Imagine eating a banana and getting the same protection you would from several painful injections. These vaccines are made from DNA that encodes a protein in the disease-causing particles. This DNA can then be inserted into the banana's genes. Researchers are still working on safe and effective edible vaccines.

Language Arts ACTIVITY

WRITING SKILL Write an advertisement for an edible vaccine. Be sure to describe the benefits of vaccinations.

Scientific Discoveries

Spanish Flu and the Flu Cycle

In 1918, a version of the influenza (the flu) virus killed millions of people worldwide. This disease, mistakenly called the Spanish Flu (it probably started in China), was one of the worst epidemics in history. Doctors and scientists realized that the large movement of people during the First World War probably made it easier for the Spanish Flu to spread. But the question of how this common disease could become so deadly remained unknown. One important factor is that the influenza virus is constantly changing. Many scientists now think that the influenza virus mutates into a more deadly form about every 30 years. There were flu epidemics in 1918, 1957, and 1968, which leads some scientists to believe that we are overdue for another flu epidemic.

Social Studies ACTIVITY

WRITING SKILL Conduct an interview with an older member of your family. Ask them how the flu, smallpox, tuberculosis, or polio has affected their lives. Write a report that includes information on how doctors deal with the disease today.

People in Science

Laytonville Middle School

Composting Project In 1973, Mary Appelhof tried an experiment. She knew that bacteria can help break down dead organic matter. In her basement, she set up a bin with worms and dumped her food scraps in there. Her basement didn't smell like garbage because her worms were eating the food scraps! Composting uses heat, bacteria, and, sometimes, worms to break down food wastes. Composting turns these wastes into fertilizer.

Binet Payne, a teacher at the Laytonville Middle School in California, decided to try Appelhof's composting system. Ms. Payne asked her students to separate their school cafeteria's trash into different categories: veggie wastes (worm food), protein foods (meat, milk, and cheese), bottles, cans, bags (to be recycled), and "yucky trash" (napkins and other nonrecyclables). The veggie waste was placed into the worm bins, and the protein foods were used to feed a local farm's chickens and pigs. In the first year, the Garden Project saved the school $6,000, which otherwise would have been used to dump the garbage into a landfill.

Math Activity

If the school saved $6,000 the first year, how much money did the school save each day of the year?

To learn more about these Science in Action topics, visit go.hrw.com and type in the keyword HL5VIRF.

Current Science

Check out Current Science® articles related to this chapter by visiting go.hrw.com. Just type in the keyword HL5CS10.

Protists and Fungi

About the PHOTO

These glowing disks may look like spaceships, but they are mushrooms! Some fungi—and some protists—glow with bioluminescence (BIE oh LOO muh NES uhns), just as fireflies do. Bioluminescence is the production of light from chemical reactions in an organism. The function of bioluminescence in fungi is not known. Some scientists think that the glow attracts insects that help spread the fungi's spores. Other scientists think that the light is just a way to release energy.

PRE-READING ACTIVITY

FOLDNOTES **Booklet** Before you read the chapter, create the FoldNote entitled "Booklet" described in the **Study Skills** section of the Appendix. Label each page of the booklet with a main idea from the chapter. As you read the chapter, write what you learn about each main idea on the appropriate page of the booklet.

START-UP ACTIVITY

A Microscopic World

In this activity, you will find some common protists in pond water or in a solution called a *hay infusion*.

Procedure

1. Use a **plastic eyedropper** to place **one drop of pond water or hay infusion** onto a **microscope slide.**
2. Add a **drop of ProtoSlo™** to the slide.
3. Add a **plastic coverslip** by putting one edge on the slide and then slowly lowering the coverslip over the drop to prevent air bubbles.
4. Observe the slide under low power of a **microscope.**
5. Find an organism in the liquid on the slide.
6. Observe the organism under high power to get a closer look.
7. Sketch the organism as you see it under high power. Then, return the microscope to low power, and find other organisms to sketch. Return the microscope to high power, and sketch the new organisms.

Analysis

1. How many kinds of organisms do you see?
2. Are the organisms alive? Support your answer with evidence.
3. How many cells does each organism appear to have?

SECTION 1

Protists

Some are so tiny that they cannot be seen without a microscope. Others grow many meters long. Some are poisonous. And some provide food for people.

READING WARM-UP

Objectives

- Describe the characteristics of protists.
- Describe four ways that protists get food.
- Describe three ways that protists reproduce.

Terms to Learn

protist
heterotroph
parasite
host

READING STRATEGY

Discussion Read this section silently. Write down questions that you have about this section. Discuss your questions in a small group.

What are they? The organisms described above are protists. A **protist** is a member of the kingdom Protista. Protists differ from other living things in many ways. Look at **Figure 1** to see a variety of protists.

protist an organism that belongs to the kingdom Protista

General Characteristics

Protists are very diverse and have few traits in common. Most protists are single-celled organisms, but some are made of many cells, and others live in colonies. Some protists produce their own food, and some eat other organisms or decaying matter. Some protists can control their own movement, and others cannot. However, protists do share a few characteristics. For example, all protists are *eukaryotic* (yoo KAR ee AHT ik), which means that their cells each have a nucleus.

Members of the kingdom Protista are related more by how they differ from members of other kingdoms than by how they are similar to other protists. Protists are less complex than other eukaryotic organisms are. For example, protists do not have specialized tissues. Fungi, plants, and animals have specialized tissues that have specific functions. Most scientists agree that fungi, plants, and animals evolved from early protists.

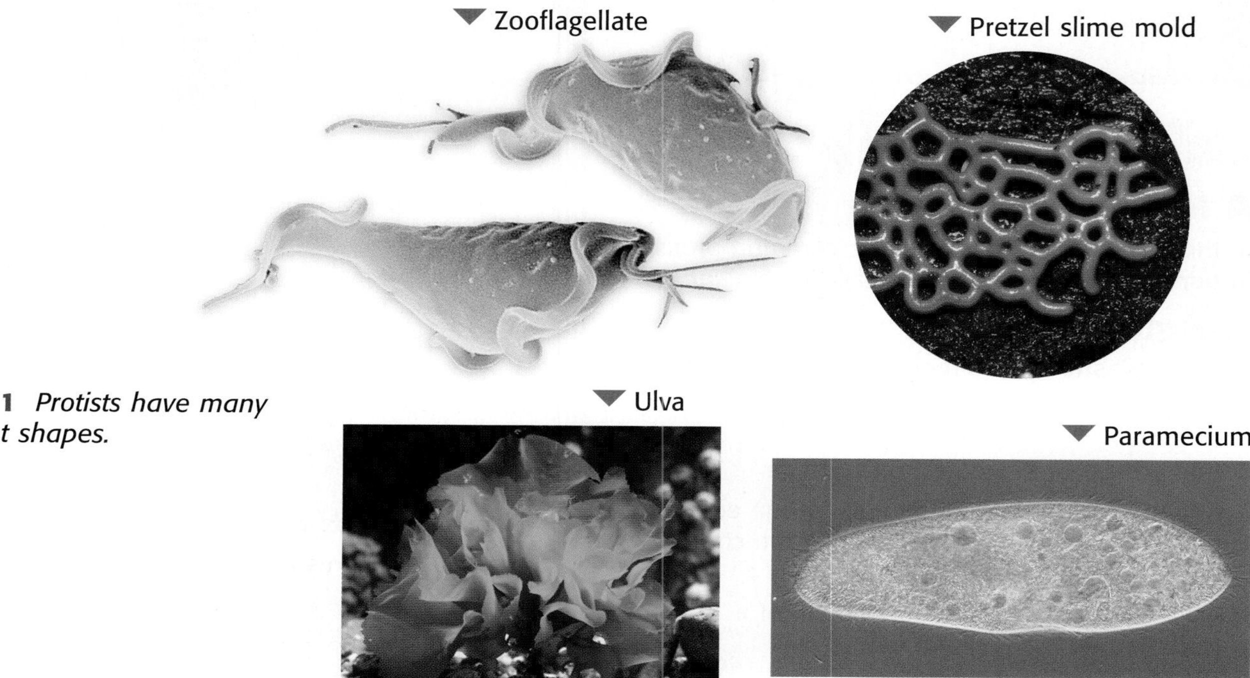

Figure 1 *Protists have many different shapes.*

Protists and Food

Protists get food in many ways. Some protists can make their own food. Other protists eat other organisms, parts or products of other organisms, or the remains of other organisms. Some protists use more than one method of getting food.

Producing Food

Some protists are *producers.* Like green plants, these protists make their own food. Protist producers have special structures called *chloroplasts* (KLAWR uh PLASTS) in their cells. These structures capture energy from the sun. Protists use this energy to produce food in a process called *photosynthesis* (FOHT oh SIN thuh sis). Plants use this same process to make their own food.

Reading Check **How do protist producers get their food?** (*See the Appendix for answers to Reading Checks.*)

Food for Thought

With your family, review how producers, consumers, decomposers, and parasites get energy. Think of organisms that live near your home and that get their food in these different ways. Then, make a poster to display your examples. Be sure that the poster describes each way of getting food.

ACTIVITY

Finding Food

Some protists must get food from their environment. These protists are heterotrophs (HET uhr oh TROHFS). **Heterotrophs** are organisms that cannot make their own food. These organisms eat other organisms, parts or products of other organisms, or the remains of other organisms.

Many protist heterotrophs eat small living organisms, such as bacteria, yeast, or other protists. The way that these heterotrophs get food is similar to how many animals get food. Some protist heterotrophs are decomposers. *Decomposers* get energy by breaking down dead organic matter. Some protists get energy in more than one way. For example, slime molds, such as the one in **Figure 2,** get energy by engulfing both small organisms and particles of organic matter.

Some protist heterotrophs are parasites. A **parasite** invades another organism to get the nutrients that it needs. An organism that a parasite invades is called a **host.** Parasites cause harm to their host. Parasitic protists may invade fungi, plants, or animals. During the mid-1800s, a parasitic protist wiped out most of the potatoes in Ireland. Without potatoes to eat, many people died of starvation. Today, people know how to protect crops from many such protists.

heterotroph an organism that gets food by eating other organisms or their byproducts and that cannot make organic compounds from inorganic materials

parasite an organism that feeds on an organism of another species (the host) and that usually harms the host; the host never benefits from the presence of the parasite

host an organism from which a parasite takes food or shelter

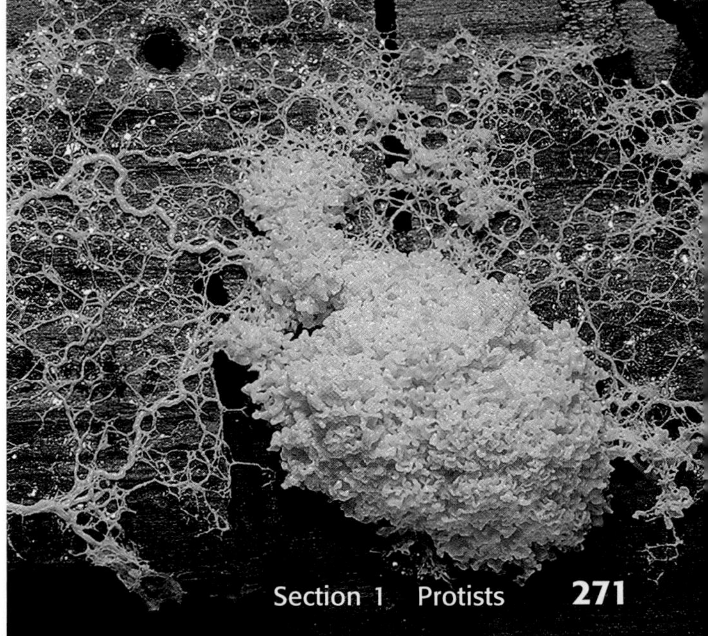

Figure 2 *Slime molds get energy from small organisms and particles of organic matter.*

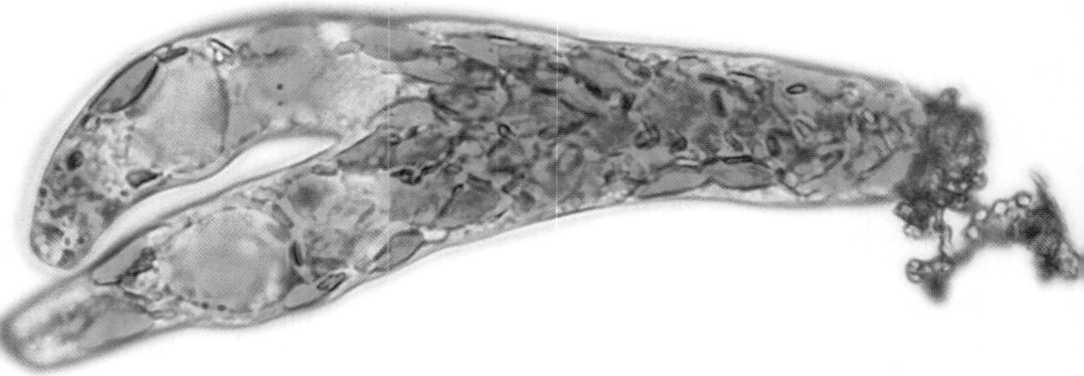

Figure 3 *Members of the genus* Euglena *reproduce by dividing lengthwise during fission.*

Producing More Protists

Like all living things, protists reproduce. Protists reproduce in several ways. Some protists reproduce asexually, and some reproduce sexually. Some protists even reproduce asexually at one stage in their life cycle and sexually at another stage.

Asexual Reproduction

Most protists reproduce asexually. In asexual reproduction, the offspring come from just one parent. These offspring are identical to the parent. **Figure 3** shows a member of the genus *Euglena* reproducing asexually by fission. In *binary fission,* a single-celled protist divides into two cells. In some cases, single-celled protists use *multiple fission* to make more than two offspring from one parent. Each new cell is a single-celled protist.

Reading Check **What are two ways that protists can reproduce asexually by fission?**

MATH PRACTICE

Pairs of Paramecia

Suppose that three pairs of protists from the genus *Paramecium* are conjugating at one time. Each pair successfully results in four protists that have new combinations of genetic material. Then, the new individuals pair up for another successful round of conjugation. How many protists will there be after this round of conjugation?

Sexual Reproduction

Some protists can reproduce sexually. Sexual reproduction requires two parents. Members of the genus *Paramecium* (PAR uh MEE see uhm) sometimes reproduce sexually by a process called *conjugation*. During conjugation, two individuals join together and exchange genetic material by using a small, second nucleus. Then, they divide to produce four protists that have new combinations of genetic material. **Figure 4** shows two paramecia in the process of conjugation.

Many protists can reproduce asexually and sexually. In some protist producers, the kind of reproduction alternates by generation. For example, a parent will reproduce asexually, and its offspring will reproduce sexually. Other protists reproduce asexually until environmental conditions become stressful, such as when there is little food or water. When conditions are stressful, these protists will use sexual reproduction until conditions improve.

Figure 4 *Members of the genus* Paramecium *can reproduce by conjugation, a type of sexual reproduction.*

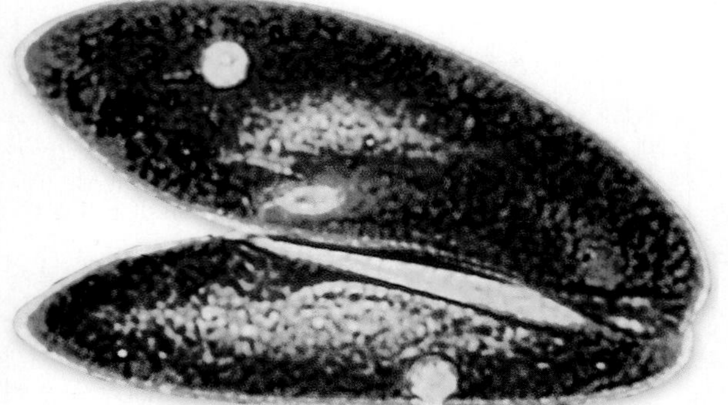

Reproductive Cycles

Some protists have complex reproductive cycles. These protists may change forms many times. **Figure 5** shows the life cycle of *Plasmodium vivax* (plaz MOH dee uhm VIE vaks), the protist that causes the disease malaria. *P. vivax* depends on both humans and mosquitoes to reproduce.

Figure 5 P. vivax *infects both humans and mosquitoes as it reproduces.*

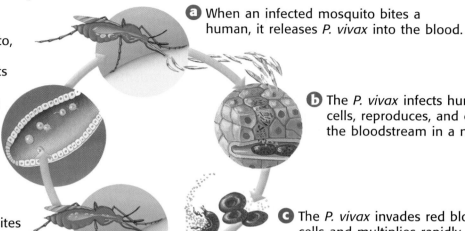

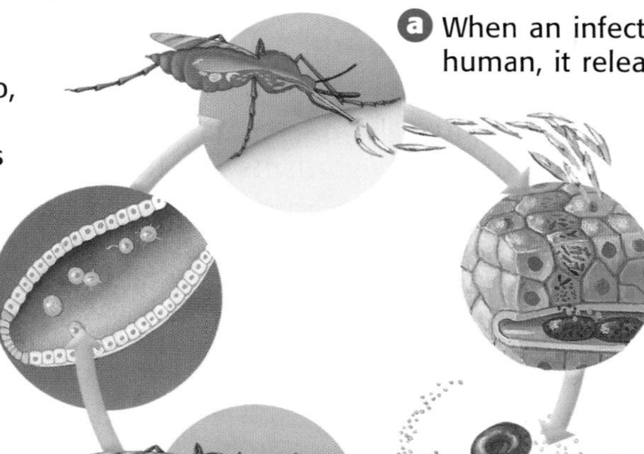

a When an infected mosquito bites a human, it releases *P. vivax* into the blood.
b The *P. vivax* infects human liver cells, reproduces, and enters the bloodstream in a new form.
c The *P. vivax* invades red blood cells and multiplies rapidly. The red blood cells burst open with *P. vivax* in another new form.
d A mosquito bites a human and picks up *P. vivax.*
e In the mosquito, the *P. vivax* matures into its original form. The cycle then repeats.

SECTION Review

Summary

- Protists are a diverse group of single-celled and many-celled organisms.
- Protists are grouped in their own kingdom because they differ from other organisms in many ways.
- Protists get food by producing it or by getting it from their environment.
- Some protists reproduce asexually, some reproduce sexually, and some reproduce both asexually and sexually.

Using Key Terms

1. Use the following terms in the same sentence: *parasite* and *host.*
2. In your own words, write a definition for each of the following terms: *protist* and *heterotroph.*

Understanding Key Ideas

3. What is one way that protists differ from plants and animals?
   a. Protists are eukaryotic.
   b. All protists have many cells.
   c. Protists do not have specialized tissues.
   d. Protists are not eukaryotic.
4. Name a characteristic shared by all protists.
5. Name three ways that protists can differ from each other.
6. Describe four ways that protists get food.
7. Describe three ways that protists reproduce.

Math Skills

8. If seven individuals of the genus *Euglena* reproduce at one time, how many individuals result?

Critical Thinking

9. **Identifying Relationships** How is conjugation similar to fission?
10. **Applying Concepts** The spread of malaria depends on both human and mosquito hosts. Use this fact to think of a way to stop the spread of malaria.

SCILINKS.
NSTA
Developed and maintained by the National Science Teachers Association
For a variety of links related to this chapter, go to www.scilinks.org
Topic: Protists
SciLinks code: HSM1245

SECTION 2

Kinds of Protists

Would you believe that there is an organism that lives in the forest and looks like a pile of scrambled eggs? This organism exists, and it's a protist.

READING WARM-UP

Objectives

- Describe how protists can be organized into three groups based on their shared traits.
- List an example for each group of protists.

Terms to Learn

algae
phytoplankton

READING STRATEGY

Reading Organizer As you read this section, make a table comparing protist producers, heterotrophs that can move, and heterotrophs that can't move.

Slimy masses of protists can look like spilled food. Smears of protists on the walls of a fish tank may look like dirt. Few of the many kinds of protists look alike.

These unique organisms are hard to classify. Scientists are always learning more about protist relationships. So, organizing protists into groups is not easy. One way that protists are grouped is based on shared traits. Using this method, scientists can place protists into three groups: producers, heterotrophs that can move, and heterotrophs that can't move. These groups do not show how protists are related to each other. But these groups do help us understand how protists can differ.

Protist Producers

Many protists are producers. Like plants, protist producers use the sun's energy to make food through photosynthesis. These protist producers are known as **algae** (AL JEE). All algae (singular, *alga*) have the green pigment chlorophyll, which is used for making food. But most algae also have other pigments that give them a color. Almost all algae live in water.

Some algae are made of many cells, as shown in **Figure 1.** Many-celled algae generally live in shallow water along the shore. You may know these algae as *seaweeds*. Some of these algae can grow to many meters in length.

Free-floating single-celled algae are called **phytoplankton** (FIET oh PLANGK tuhn). These algae cannot be seen without a microscope. They usually float near the water's surface. Phytoplankton provide food for most other organisms in the water. They also produce much of the world's oxygen.

algae eukaryotic organisms that convert the sun's energy into food through photosynthesis but that do not have roots, stems, or leaves (singular, *alga*)

phytoplankton the microscopic, photosynthetic organisms that float near the surface of marine or fresh water

Figure 1 *Some kinds of algae, such as this giant kelp, can grow to be many meters in length.*

Figure 2 *This* Sebdenia *(seb DEE nee uh) is a red alga.*

Red Algae

Most of the world's seaweeds are red algae. Most red algae live in tropical oceans, attached to rocks or to other algae. Red algae are usually less than 1 m in length. Their cells contain chlorophyll, but a red pigment gives them their color. Their red pigment allows them to absorb the light that filters deep into the clear water of the Tropics. Red algae can grow as deep as 260 m below the surface of the water. An example of a red alga can be seen in **Figure 2.**

Reading Check **If red algae have chlorophyll in their cells, why aren't they green?** (*See the Appendix for answers to Reading Checks.*)

Green Algae

The green algae are the most diverse group of protist producers. They are green because chlorophyll is the main pigment in their cells. Most live in water or moist soil. But others live in melting snow, on tree trunks, and inside other organisms.

Many green algae are single-celled organisms. Others are made of many cells. These many-celled species may grow to be 8 m long. Individual cells of some species of green algae live in groups called *colonies*. **Figure 3** shows colonies of *Volvox*.

Figure 3 Volvox *is a green alga that grows in round colonies.*

Brown Algae

Most of the seaweeds found in cool climates are brown algae. They attach to rocks or form large floating beds in ocean waters. Brown algae have chlorophyll and a yellow-brown pigment. Many are very large. Some grow 60 m—as long as about 20 cars—in just one season! Only the tops of these gigantic algae are exposed to sunlight. These parts of the algae make food through photosynthesis. This food is transported to parts of the algae that are too deep in the water to receive sunlight.

Diatoms

Diatoms (DIE e TAHMZ) are single celled. They are found in both salt water and fresh water. Diatoms get their energy from photosynthesis. They make up a large percentage of phytoplankton. **Figure 4** shows some diatoms' many unusual shapes. The cell walls of diatoms contain a glasslike substance called *silica*. The cells of diatoms are enclosed in a two-part shell.

Figure 4 *Although most diatoms are free floating, some cling to plants, shellfish, sea turtles, and whales.*

Dinoflagellates

Most dinoflagellates (DIE noh FLAJ uh lits) are single celled. Most live in salt water, but a few species live in fresh water. Some dinoflagellates even live in snow. Dinoflagellates have two whiplike strands called *flagella* (singular, *flagellum*). The beating of these flagella causes the cells to spin through the water. Most dinoflagellates get their energy from photosynthesis, but a few are consumers, decomposers, or parasites.

Reading Check **Name three places where dinoflagellates live.**

Euglenoids

Euglenoids (yoo GLEE NOYDZ) are single-celled protists. Most euglenoids live in fresh water. They use their flagella to move through the water. Many euglenoids are producers and so make their own food. But when there is not enough light to make food, these euglenoids can get food as heterotrophs. Other euglenoids do not contain chlorophyll and cannot make food. These euglenoids are full-time consumers or decomposers. Because euglenoids can get food in several ways, they do not fit well into any one protist group. **Figure 5** shows the structure of a euglenoid.

Figure 5 **The Structure of Euglenoids**

Photosynthesis takes place in **chloroplasts.** These structures contain the green pigment chlorophyll.

Most euglenoids have two **flagella,** one long and one short. Euglenoids use flagella to move through water.

Euglenoids can't see, but they have **eyespots** that sense light.

A special structure called a **contractile vacuole** holds excess water and removes it from the cell.

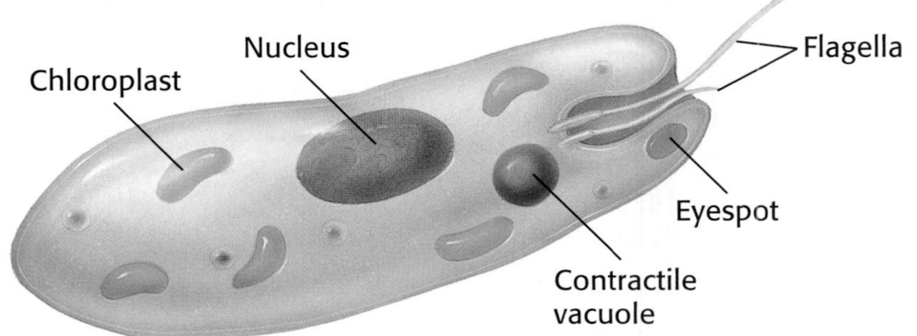

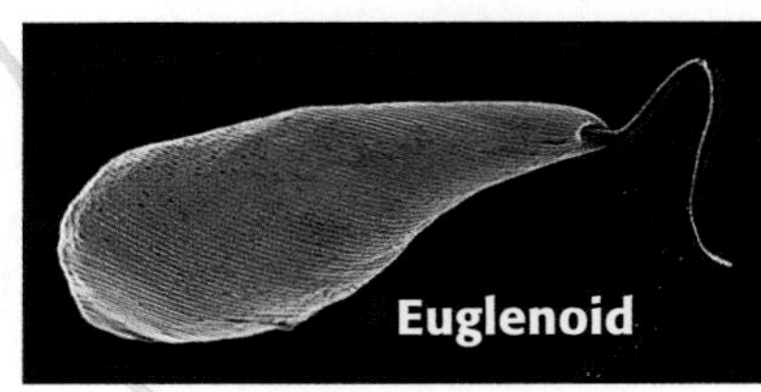

Figure 6 **Amoebic Movement**

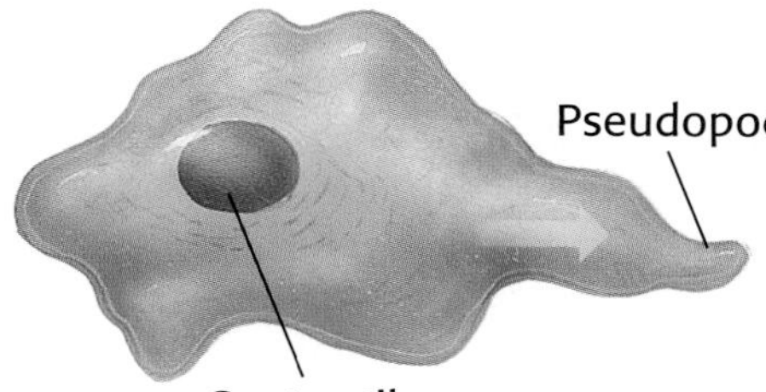

1 An amoeba extends a new pseudopod from part of its cell.
Pseudopod
Contractile vacuole

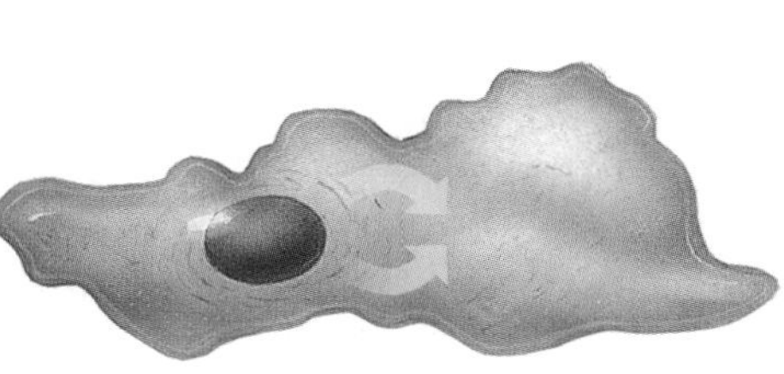

2 The rest of the cell flows into the new pseudopod.

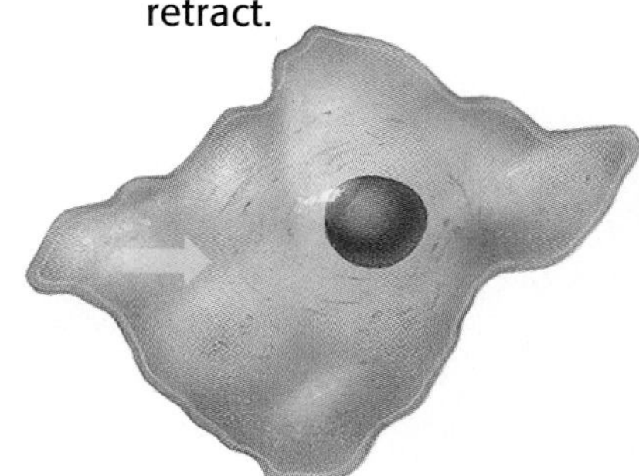

3 Other pseudopodia retract.

Heterotrophs That Can Move

Some heterotrophic protists have special traits that allow them to move. Other heterotrophic protists cannot move on their own. Those that can move are usually single-celled consumers or parasites. These mobile protists are sometimes called *protozoans* (PROHT oh ZOH uhnz).

Amoebas

Amoebas (uh MEE buhs) and similar amoeba-like protists are soft, jellylike protozoans. They are found in both fresh and salt water, in soil, and as parasites in animals. Although amoebas look shapeless, they are highly structured cells. Amoebas have contractile vacuoles to get rid of excess water. Many amoebas eat bacteria and small protists. But some amoebas are parasites that get food by invading other organisms. Certain parasitic amoebas live in human intestines and cause amoebic dysentery (uh MEE bik DIS uhn TER ee). This painful disease causes internal bleeding.

Amoebic Movement

Amoebas and amoeba-like protists move with pseudopodia (SOO doh POH dee uh). *Pseudopodia* means "false feet." To move, an amoeba stretches a pseudopod out from the cell. The cell then flows into the pseudopod. **Figure 6** shows how an amoeba uses pseudopodia to move.

Amoebas and amoeba-like protists use pseudopodia to catch food, too. When an amoeba senses a food source, it moves toward the food. The amoeba surrounds the food with its pseudopodia. This action forms a *food vacuole*. Enzymes move into the vacuole to digest the food, and the digested food passes into the amoeba. **Figure 7** shows an amoeba catching food. To get rid of wastes, an amoeba reverses the process. A waste-filled vacuole is moved to the edge of the cell and is released.

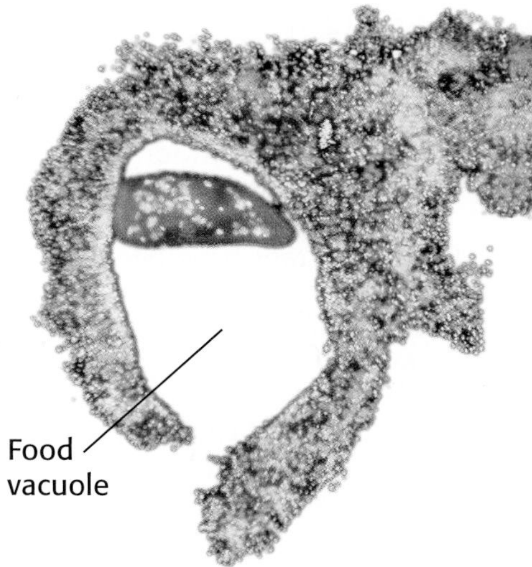

Figure 7 *An amoeba engulfs its prey with its pseudopodia.*

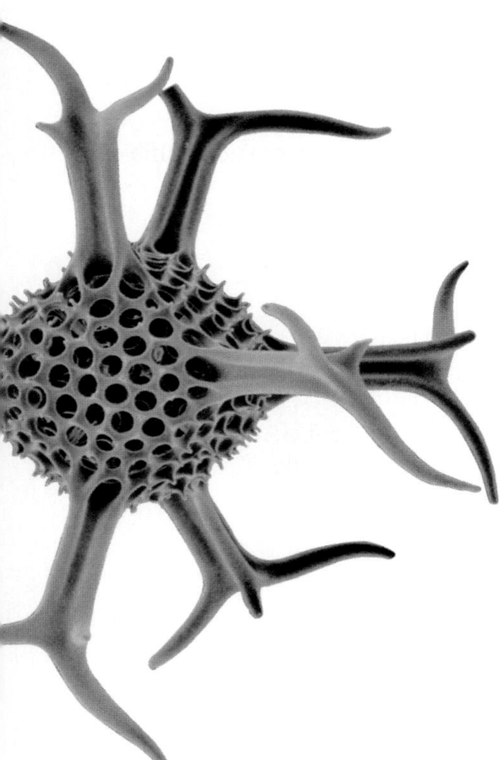

Figure 8 *Radiolarians are amoeba-like protists that have shells.*

Shelled Amoeba-Like Protists

Not all amoeba-like protists look shapeless. Some have an outer shell. *Radiolarian* (RAY dee oh LER ee uhn) shells look like glass ornaments, as shown in **Figure 8.** *Foraminiferans* (fuh RAM uh NIF uhr uhnz) have snail-like shells. These protists move by poking pseudopodia out of pores in the shells.

Reading Check **Name two shelled, amoeba-like protists.**

Zooflagellates

Zooflagellates (ZOH uh FLAJ uh LAYTS) are protists that wave flagella back and forth to move. Some zooflagellates live in water. Others live in the bodies of other organisms.

Some zooflagellates are parasites that cause disease. The parasite *Giardia lamblia* (jee AWR dee uh LAM blee uh) can live in the digestive tract of many vertebrates. One form of *G. lamblia* lives part of its life in water. People who drink water infected with *G. lamblia* can get severe stomach cramps.

Some zooflagellates live in mutualism with other organisms. In *mutualism,* one organism lives closely with another organism. Each organism helps the other live. The zooflagellate in **Figure 9** lives in the gut of termites. This zooflagellate digests the cell walls of the wood that the termites eat. Both organisms benefit from the arrangement. The protist helps the termite digest wood. The termite gives the protist food and a place to live.

Figure 9 The Structure of Flagellates

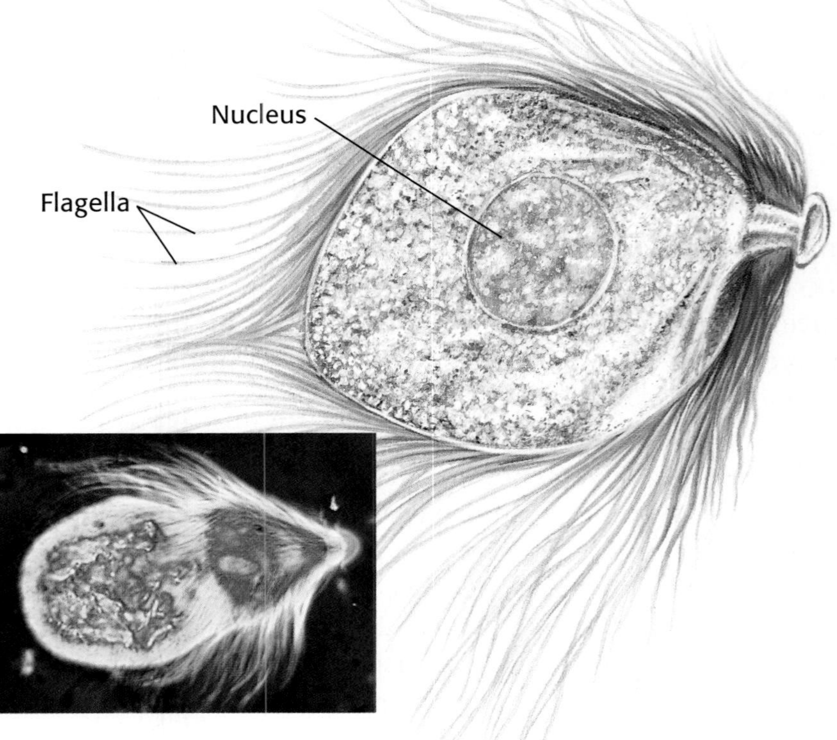

CONNECTION TO Geology

Shell Deposits Foraminiferans have existed for more than 600 million years. During this time, shells of dead foraminiferans have been sinking to the bottom of the ocean. Millions of years ago, foraminiferan shells formed a thick layer of sediment of limestone and chalk deposits. The chalk deposits in England that are known as the White Cliffs of Dover formed in this way. Use geology books to find examples of sedimentary rocks formed from protist shells. Make a poster that explains the process by which shells become sedimentary rock.

ACTIVITY

Figure 10 **The Structure of a Paramecium**

Members of the genus *Paramecium* eat by using cilia to sweep food into a **food passageway.**

Food enters a **food vacuole,** where enzymes digest the food.

Food waste is removed from the cell through the **anal pore.**

A **contractile vacuole** pumps out excess water.

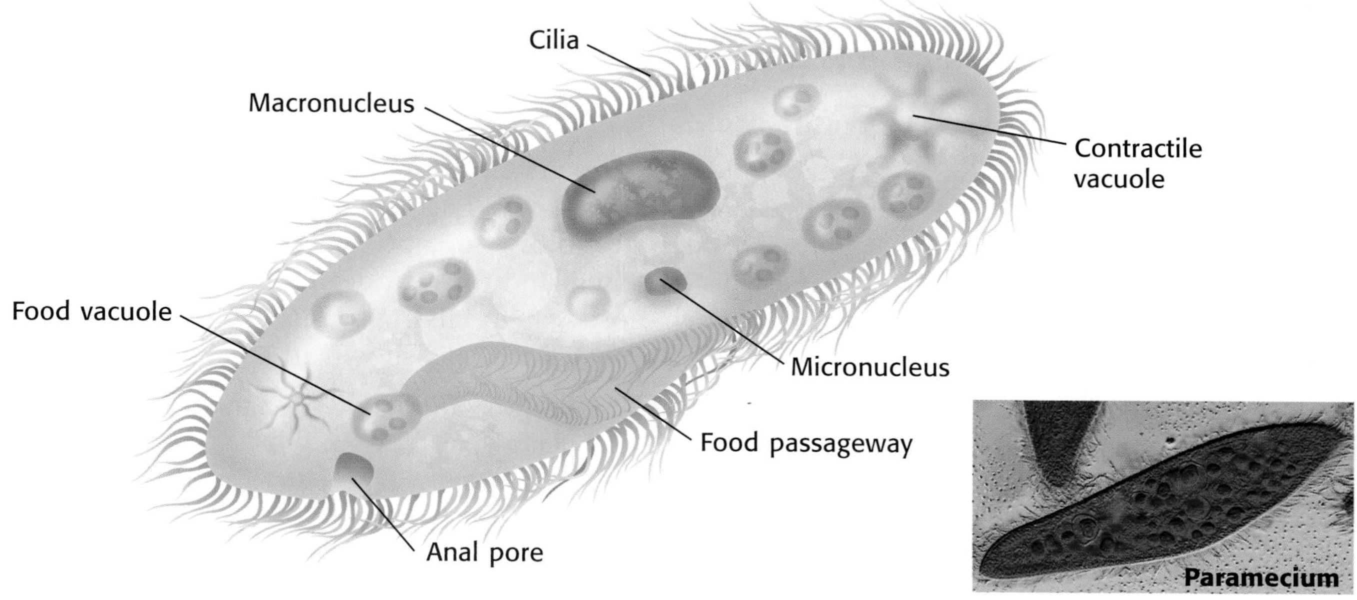

Ciliates

Ciliates (SIL ee its) are complex protists. They have hundreds of tiny, hairlike structures known as *cilia.* The cilia move a protist forward by beating back and forth. Cilia can beat up to 60 times a second! Ciliates also use their cilia for feeding. The cilia sweep food toward the protist's food passageway. The best-known genus of ciliates is *Paramecium,* shown in **Figure 10.**

The cell of a paramecium has two kinds of nuclei. A large nucleus called a *macronucleus* controls the functions of the cell. A smaller nucleus, the *micronucleus,* passes genes to another paramecium during sexual reproduction.

Heterotrophs That Can't Move

Not all protist heterotrophs have features that help them move. Some of these protists are parasites that do not move about. Others can move only at certain phases in their life cycle.

Spore-Forming Protists

Many spore-forming protists are parasites. They absorb nutrients from their hosts. They have no cilia or flagella, and they cannot move on their own. Spore-forming protists have complicated life cycles that usually include two or more hosts. For example, the spore-forming protist that causes malaria uses both mosquitoes and humans as hosts.

CONNECTION TO Social Studies

Malaria *Plasmodium vivax* is a spore-forming protist that causes malaria. People get malaria in tropical areas when they are bitten by mosquitoes carrying *P. vivax.* Malaria can be treated with drugs, but many people do not have access to these drugs. Millions of people die from malaria each year. Research malaria rates in different parts of the world, and give a presentation of your findings to the class.

ACTIVITY

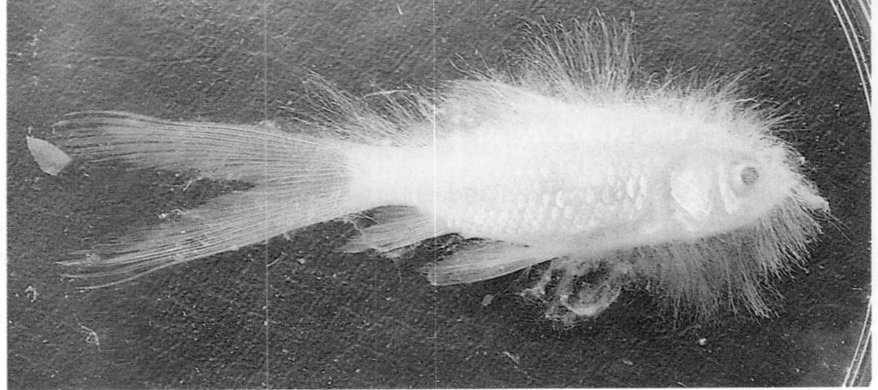

Figure 11 *Parasitic water molds attack various organisms, including fish.*

Water Molds

Water molds are also heterotrophic protists that can't move. Most water molds are small, single-celled organisms. Water molds live in water, moist soil, or other organisms. Some of them are decomposers and thus eat dead matter. But many are parasites. Their hosts can be living plants, animals, algae, or fungi. A parasitic water mold is shown in **Figure 11.**

For another activity related to this chapter, go to **go.hrw.com** and type in the keyword **HL5PROW.**

Reading Check **Name two ways that water molds get food.**

Slime Molds

Slime molds are heterotrophic protists that can move only at certain phases of their life cycle. They look like thin, colorful, shapeless globs of slime. Slime molds live in cool, moist places in the woods. They use pseudopodia to move and to eat bacteria and yeast. They also decompose small bits of rotting organic matter by surrounding small pieces of the matter and then digesting them.

Some slime molds live as a giant cell that has many nuclei and a single cytoplasm at one stage of life. As long as food and water are available, the cell will continue to grow. One cell may be more than 1 m across! Other slime molds live as single-celled individuals that can come together as a group when food or water is hard to find.

When environmental conditions are stressful, slime molds grow stalklike structures with rounded knobs at the top, as shown in **Figure 12.** The knobs contain spores. *Spores* are small reproductive cells covered by a thick cell wall. The spores can survive for a long time without water or nutrients. As spores, slime molds cannot move. When conditions improve, the spores will develop into new slime molds.

Figure 12 *The spore-containing knobs of a slime mold are called* sporangia *(spoh RAN jee uh).*

SECTION Review

Summary

- Protists can be organized into the following groups: producers, heterotrophs that can move, and heterotrophs that cannot move.
- Protist producers make their own food through photosynthesis. They are known as *algae,* and most live in water. Free-floating single-celled algae are phytoplankton.
- Red algae, green algae, brown algae, diatoms, dinoflagellates, and some euglenoids are producers.
- Heterotrophic protists cannot make their own food. They are consumers, decomposers, or parasites. Those that can move are sometimes called *protozoans.*
- Amoeba-like protists, shelled amoeba-like protists, flagellates, and ciliates are heterotrophs that can move.
- Spore-forming protists, water molds, and slime molds are protists that cannot move or can move only in certain phases of their life cycle.

Using Key Terms

1. Use the following terms in the same sentence: *phytoplankton* and *algae.*

Understanding Key Ideas

2. Which of the following kinds of protists are producers?
   a. diatoms
   b. amoebas
   c. slime molds
   d. ciliates
3. How do many amoeba-like protists eat?
   a. They secrete digestive juices onto food.
   b. They produce food from sunlight.
   c. They engulf food with pseudopodia.
   d. They use cilia to sweep food toward them.
4. Give an example of one protist from each of the three groups of protists.
5. Explain why it makes sense to group protists based on shared traits rather than by how they are related to each other.

Critical Thinking

6. **Making Comparisons** How do protist producers, heterotrophs that can move, and heterotrophs that can't move differ?
7. **Making Inferences** You learned how shelled amoeba-like protists move. How do you think they get food into their shells in order to eat?

Interpreting Graphics

Use the photo below to answer the questions that follow.

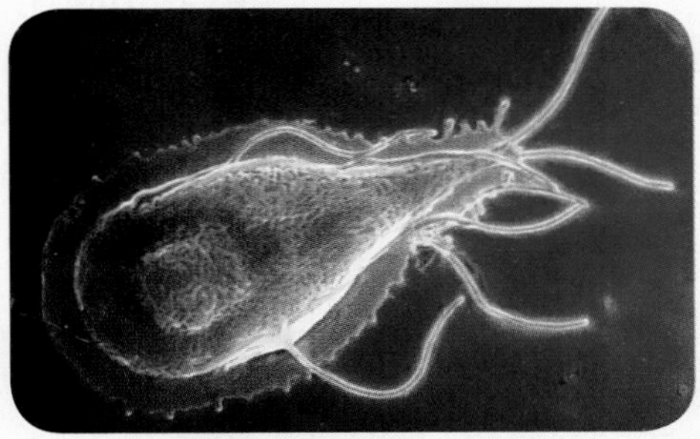

8. How does this protist move?
9. Identify what kind of protist is shown. To do so, first make a list of the kinds of protists that this organism could not be.

SCILINKS.
NSTA
Developed and maintained by the National Science Teachers Association
For a variety of links related to this chapter, go to www.scilinks.org
Topic: Algae; Protozoans
SciLinks code: HSM0042; HSM1247

SECTION 3

Fungi

How are cheese, bread, and soy sauce related to fungi? A fungus can help make each of these foods.

Fungi (singular, *fungus*) are everywhere. The mushrooms on pizza are a type of fungus. The yeast used to make bread is a fungus. And if you've ever had athlete's foot, you can thank a fungus for that, too.

READING WARM-UP

Objectives

- Describe the characteristics of fungi.
- Distinguish between the four main groups of fungi.
- Explain how lichens affect their environment.

Terms to Learn

fungus	spore
hypha	mold
mycelium	lichen

READING STRATEGY

Paired Summarizing Read this section silently. In pairs, take turns summarizing the material. Stop to discuss ideas that seem confusing.

Characteristics of Fungi

Fungi are eukaryotic heterotrophs that have rigid cell walls and no chlorophyll. They are so different from other organisms that they are placed in their own kingdom. As you can see in **Figure 1,** fungi come in a variety of shapes, sizes, and colors.

fungus an organism whose cells have nuclei, rigid cell walls, and no chlorophyll and that belongs to the kingdom Fungi

Food for Fungi

Fungi are heterotrophs, but they cannot catch or surround food. Fungi must live on or near their food supply. Most fungi are consumers. These fungi get nutrients by secreting digestive juices onto a food source and then absorbing the dissolved food. Many fungi are decomposers, which feed on dead plant or animal matter. Other fungi are parasites.

Some fungi live in mutualism with other organisms. For example, many types of fungi grow on or in the roots of a plant. The plant provides nutrients to the fungus. The fungus helps the root absorb minerals and protects the plant from some disease-causing organisms. This relationship between a plant and a fungus is called a *mycorrhiza* (MIE koh RIE zuh).

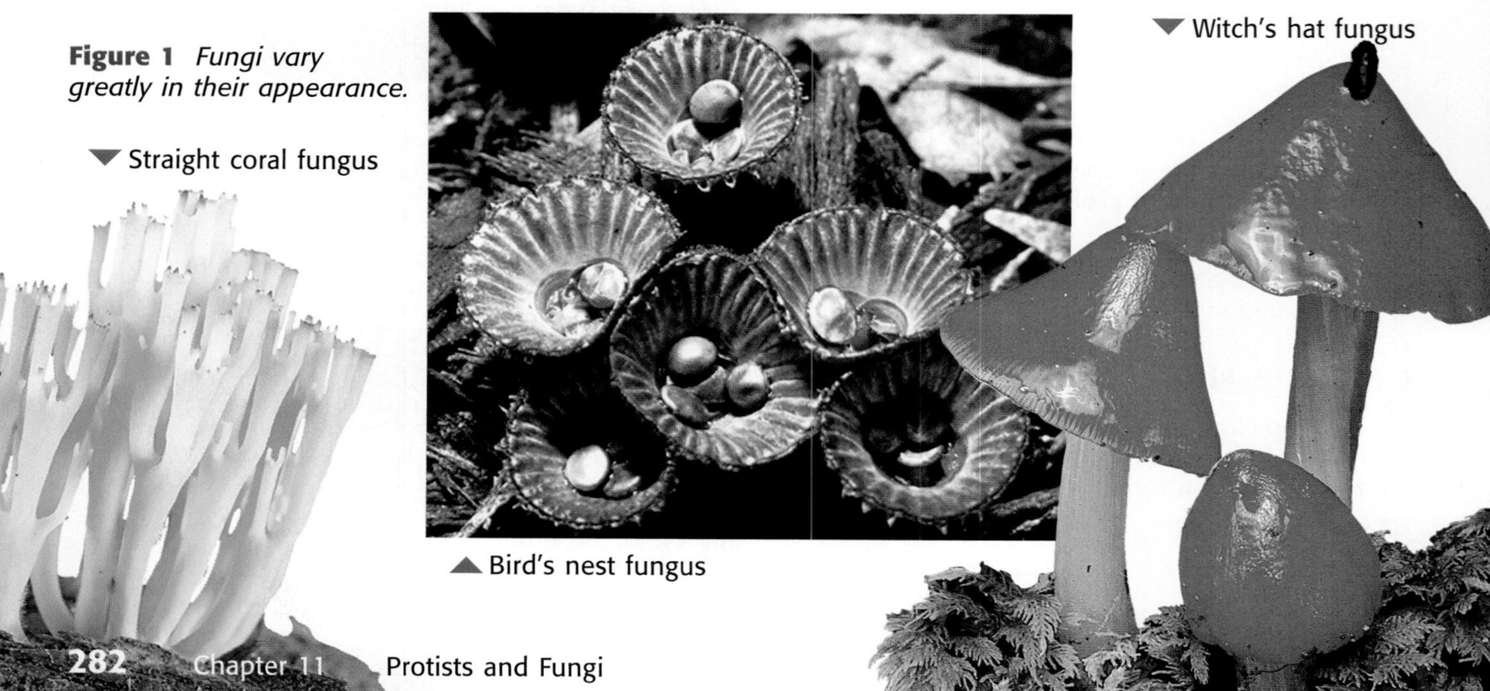

Figure 1 *Fungi vary greatly in their appearance.*

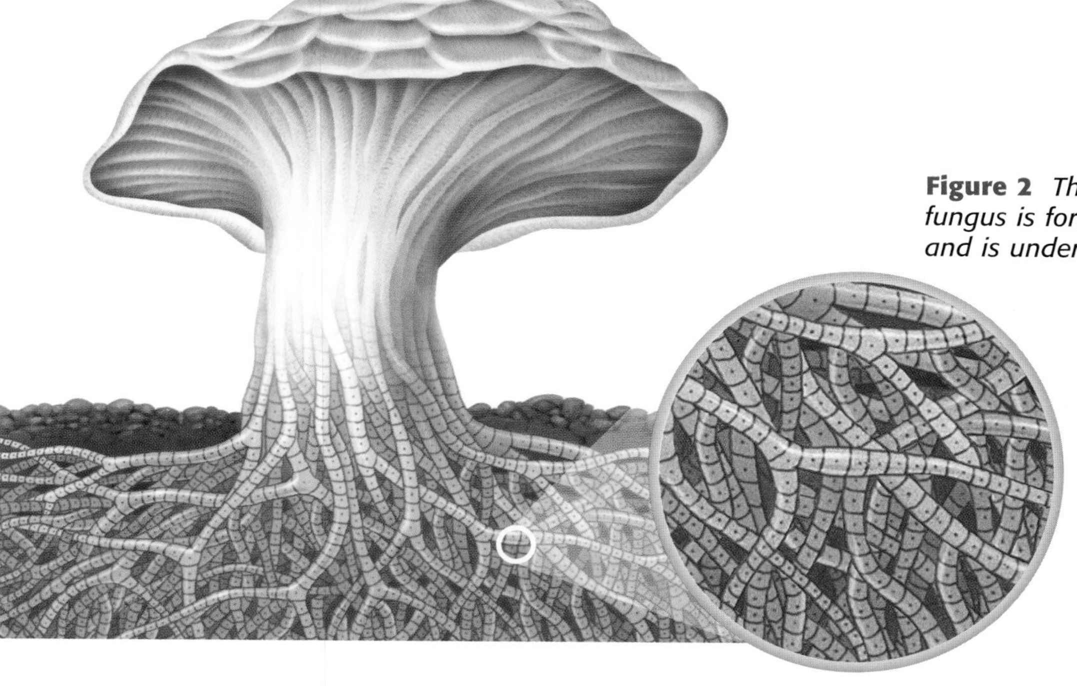

Figure 2 *The mycelium of a fungus is formed by hyphae and is underground.*

Hidden from View

All fungi are made of eukaryotic cells, which have nuclei. Some fungi are single celled, but most fungi are made of many cells. These many-celled fungi are made up of chains of cells called hyphae (HIE fee). **Hyphae** (singular, *hypha*) are threadlike fungal filaments. These filaments are made of cells that have openings in their cell walls. These openings allow cytoplasm to move freely between the cells.

Most of the hyphae that make up a fungus grow together to form a twisted mass called the **mycelium** (mie SEE lee uhm). The mycelium makes up the major part of the fungus. However, this mass is hidden from view underneath the ground. **Figure 2** shows the hyphae of a fungus.

hypha a nonreproductive filament of a fungus

mycelium the mass of fungal filaments, or hyphae, that forms the body of a fungus

spore a reproductive cell or multicellular structure that is resistant to stressful environmental conditions and that can develop into an adult without fusing with another cell

Making More Fungi

Reproduction in fungi may be either asexual or sexual. Asexual reproduction in fungi occurs in two ways. In one type of asexual reproduction, the hyphae break apart, and each new piece becomes a new fungus. Asexual reproduction can also take place by the production of spores. **Spores** are small reproductive cells that are protected by a thick cell wall. Spores are light and easily spread by wind. When the growing conditions where a spore lands are right, the spore will grow into a new fungus.

Sexual reproduction in fungi happens when special structures form to make sex cells. The sex cells join to produce sexual spores that grow into a new fungus. **Figure 3** shows a fungus releasing sexual spores into the air.

Reading Check **What are two ways that fungi can reproduce asexually?** (*See the Appendix for answers to Reading Checks.*)

Figure 3 *This puffball is releasing sexual spores that can produce new fungi.*

Kinds of Fungi

Fungi are classified based on their shape and the way that they reproduce. There are four main groups of fungi. Most species of fungi fit into one of these groups. These groups are threadlike fungi, sac fungi, club fungi, and imperfect fungi.

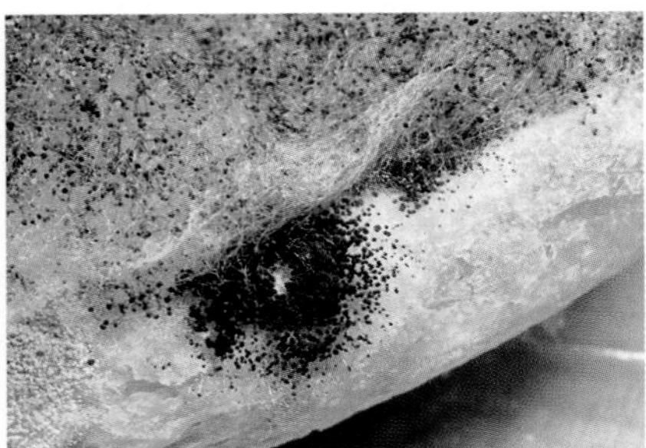

Figure 4 *Black bread mold is a soft, cottony mass that grows on bread and fruit.*

Threadlike Fungi

Have you ever seen fuzzy mold growing on bread? A **mold** is a shapeless, fuzzy fungus. **Figure 4** shows a black bread mold. This particular mold belongs to a group of fungi called *threadlike fungi*. Most of the fungi in this group live in the soil and are decomposers. However, some threadlike fungi are parasites.

mold a fungus that looks like wool or cotton

Threadlike fungi can reproduce asexually. Parts of the hyphae grow into the air and form round spore cases at the tips. These spore cases are called *sporangia* (spoh RAN jee uh). **Figure 5** shows some magnified sporangia. When the sporangia break open, many tiny spores are released into the air. New fungi will develop from these spores if they land in an area with good growing conditions.

Threadlike fungi can also reproduce sexually. Threadlike fungi reproduce sexually when a hypha from one individual joins with a hypha from another individual. The hyphae grow into specialized sporangia that can survive times of cold or little water. When conditions improve, these specialized sporangia release spores that can grow into new fungi.

Reading Check **Describe two ways that threadlike fungi can reproduce.**

Moldy Bread

1. Dampen a **slice of bread** with a **few drops of water,** and then seal it in a **plastic bag** for 1 week.
2. Draw a picture of the bread in the plastic bag.
3. Predict what you think will happen during the week. Will the bread get moldy?
4. After the week has passed, check on the bread in the plastic bag. Compare it with your original drawing. What happened? Were your predictions correct?
5. With a partner, discuss where you think mold spores come from and how they grow.

Figure 5 *Each of the round sporangia contains thousands of spores.*

Figure 6 *Morels are only part of a larger fungus. They are the sexual reproductive part of a fungus that lives under the soil.*

Sac Fungi

Sac fungi are the largest group of fungi. Sac fungi include yeasts, powdery mildews, truffles, and morels. Some morels are shown in **Figure 6.**

Sac fungi can reproduce both asexually and sexually during their life cycles. Most of the time, they use asexual reproduction. When they reproduce sexually, they form a sac called an *ascus*. This sac gives the sac fungi their name. Sexually produced spores develop within the ascus.

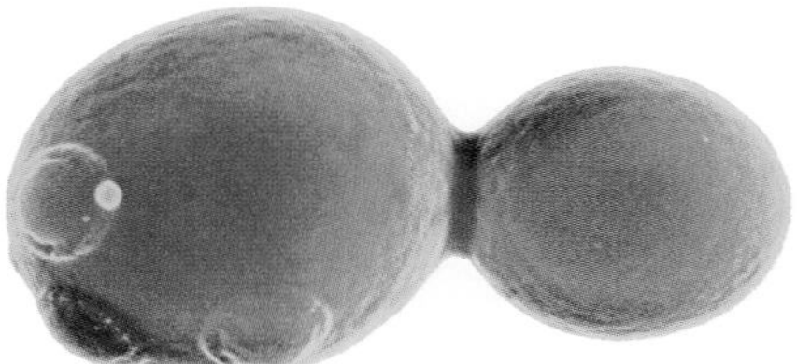

Figure 7 *Yeasts reproduce by budding. A round scar forms where a bud breaks off from a parent cell.*

Most sac fungi are made of many cells. However, *yeasts* are single-celled sac fungi. When yeasts reproduce asexually, they use a process called *budding*. In budding, a new cell pinches off from an existing cell. **Figure 7** shows a yeast that is budding. Yeasts are the only fungi that reproduce by budding.

Some sac fungi are very useful to humans. For example, yeasts are used in making bread and alcohol. Yeasts use sugar as food and produce carbon dioxide gas and alcohol as waste. Trapped bubbles of carbon dioxide cause bread dough to rise. This process is what makes bread light and fluffy. Other sac fungi are sources of antibiotics and vitamins. And some sac fungi, such as truffles and morels, are prized as human foods.

Not all sac fungi are helpful. In fact, many sac fungi are parasites. Some cause plant diseases, such as chestnut blight and Dutch elm disease. The effects of Dutch elm disease are shown in **Figure 8.**

Figure 8 *Dutch elm disease is a fungal disease that has killed millions of elm trees.*

Figure 9 *A ring of mushrooms can appear overnight. In European folk legends, these were known as "fairy rings."*

Club Fungi

The umbrella-shaped mushrooms are the most familiar fungi. Mushrooms belong to a group of fungi called *club fungi*. This group gets its name from structures that the fungi grow during reproduction. Club fungi reproduce sexually. During reproduction, they grow special hyphae that form clublike structures. These structures are called *basidia* (buh SID ee uh), the Greek word for "clubs." Sexual spores develop on the basidia.

When you think of a mushroom, you probably picture only the spore-producing, above-ground part of the organism. But most of the organism is underground. The mass of hyphae from which mushrooms are produced may grow 35 m across. That's about as long as 18 adults lying head to toe! Mushrooms usually grow at the edges of the mass of hyphae. As a result, mushrooms often appear in circles, as shown in **Figure 9.**

The most familiar mushrooms are known as *gill fungi*. The basidia of these mushrooms develop in structures called *gills,* under the mushroom cap. Some varieties are grown commercially and sold in supermarkets. However, not all gill fungi are edible. For example, the white destroying angel is a very poisonous fungus. Simply a taste of this mushroom can be fatal. See if you can pick out the poisonous fungus in **Figure 10.**

Reading Check What part of a club fungus grows above the ground?

Observe a Mushroom

1. Identify the stalk, cap, and gills on a **mushroom** that your teacher has provided.
2. Carefully twist or cut off the cap, and cut it open with a **plastic knife.** Use a **magnifying lens** to observe the gills. Look for spores.
3. Use the magnifying lens to observe the other parts of the mushroom. The mycelium begins at the bottom of the stalk. Try to find individual hyphae.
4. Sketch the mushroom, and label the parts.

Figure 10 *Many poisonous mushrooms look just like edible ones. Never eat a mushroom from the wild unless a professional identifies it in person.*

Figure 11 *Bracket fungi look like shelves on trees. The underside of the bracket contains spores.*

Figure 12 *This corn is infected with a club fungus called* smut.

Nonmushroom Club Fungi

Mushrooms are not the only club fungi. Bracket fungi, puffballs, smuts, and rusts are also club fungi. Bracket fungi grow outward from wood and form small shelves or brackets, as shown in **Figure 11.** Smuts and rusts are common plant parasites. They often attack crops such as corn and wheat. The corn in **Figure 12** has been infected with a smut.

Imperfect Fungi

The *imperfect fungi* group includes all of the species of fungi that do not quite fit in the other groups. These fungi do not reproduce sexually. Most are parasites that cause diseases in plants and animals. One common human disease caused by these fungi is athlete's foot, a skin disease. Another fungus from this group produces a poison called *aflatoxin* (AF luh TAHKS in), which can cause cancer.

Some imperfect fungi are useful. *Penicillium,* shown in **Figure 13,** is the source of the antibiotic penicillin. Other imperfect fungi are also used to produce medicines. Some imperfect fungi are used to produce cheeses, soy sauce, and the citric acid used in cola drinks.

Figure 13 *The fungus* Penicillium *produces a substance that kills certain bacteria.*

CONNECTION TO Language Arts

Beatrix Potter Beatrix Potter (1866–1943) is best known for writing children's stories, such as *The Tale of Peter Rabbit* and *The Tale of Two Bad Mice*. Potter lived and worked in England and had a scholarly interest in fungi. She was a shy person, and she was not taken seriously by fungi scholars of her time. But today, she is widely respected as a mycologist (a scientist who studies fungi). She wrote many valuable papers about fungi and made detailed drawings of more than 270 fungi. Research Potter's life, and present a report to your class.

ACTIVITY

▲ Wolf lichen

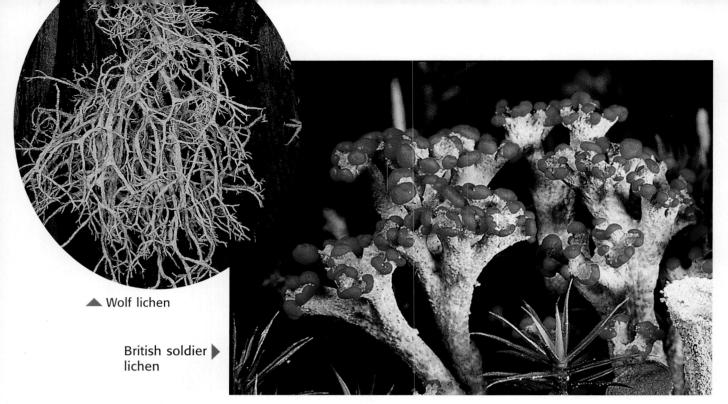

British soldier lichen ▶

▼ Christmas lichen

Figure 14 *These are some of the many types of lichens.*

Lichens

A **lichen** (LIE kuhn) is a combination of a fungus and an alga that grow together. The alga actually lives inside the protective walls of the fungus. The resulting organism is different from either organism growing alone. The lichen is a result of a mutualistic relationship. But the merging of the two organisms to form a lichen is so complete that scientists give lichens their own scientific names. **Figure 14** shows some examples of lichens.

Unlike fungi, lichens are producers. The algae in the lichens produce food through photosynthesis. And unlike algae, lichens can keep from drying out. The protective walls of the fungi keep water inside the lichens. Lichens are found in almost every type of land environment. They can even grow in dry environments, such as deserts, and cold environments, such as the Arctic.

Because lichens need only air, light, and minerals to grow, they can grow on rocks. As lichens grow, the changes that they make to their surroundings allow other organisms to live there, too. For example, lichens make acids that break down rocks and cause cracks. When bits of rock and dead lichens fill the cracks, soil is made. Other organisms then grow in this soil.

Lichens absorb water and minerals from the air. As a result, lichens are easily affected by air pollution. So, the presence or absence of lichens can be a good measure of air quality in an area.

lichen a mass of fungal and algal cells that grow together in a symbiotic relationship and that are usually found on rocks or trees

Reading Check **How can lichens affect rocks?**

SECTION Review

Summary

- Fungi can be consumers, decomposers, or parasites, or they can live in mutualistic relationships with other organisms.
- Most fungi are made up of chains of cells called *hyphae*. Many hyphae join together to form a mycelium.
- The four main groups of fungi are threadlike fungi, sac fungi, club fungi, and imperfect fungi.
- Threadlike fungi are primarily decomposers that form sporangia containing spores.
- During sexual reproduction, sac fungi form little sacs in which sexual spores develop.
- Club fungi form structures called *basidia* during sexual reproduction.
- The imperfect fungi include all of the species that do not quite fit in the other groups. Many are parasites that reproduce only by asexual reproduction.
- A lichen is a combination of a specific fungus and a specific alga. The lichen is different from either organism growing alone.

Using Key Terms

1. In your own words, write a definition for each of the following terms: *spore* and *mold.*

For each pair of terms, explain how the meanings of the terms differ.

2. *fungus* and *lichen*

3. *hyphae* and *mycelium*

Understanding Key Ideas

4. Which of the following statements about fungi is true?

a. All fungi are eukaryotic.
b. All fungi are decomposers.
c. All fungi reproduce by sexual reproduction.
d. All fungi are producers.

5. What are the four main groups of fungi? Give a characteristic of each group.

6. How are fungi able to withstand periods of cold or drought?

Critical Thinking

7. Analyzing Processes Many fungi are decomposers. Imagine what would happen to the natural world if decomposers no longer existed. Write a description of how a lack of decomposers might affect the processes of nature.

8. Identifying Relationships Explain how two organisms make up a lichen.

Interpreting Graphics

Use the photo below to answer the questions that follow.

9. To which group of fungi does this organism belong? How can you be sure?

10. What part of the organism is shown in this photo? What part is not shown? Explain.

SCLINKS®
NSTA
Developed and maintained by the National Science Teachers Association
For a variety of links related to this chapter, go to www.scilinks.org
Topics: Fungi; Lichens
SciLinks codes: HSM0628; HSM0871

Skills Practice Lab

There's a Fungus Among Us!

OBJECTIVES

Examine the parts of a mushroom.

Describe your observations of the mushroom.

MATERIALS

- gloves, protective
- incubator
- microscope or magnifying lens
- mushroom
- paper, white (2 sheets)
- Petri dish with fruit-juice agar plate
- tape, masking
- tape, transparent
- tweezers

SAFETY

Fungi share many characteristics with plants. For example, most fungi live on land and cannot move from place to place. But fungi have several unique features that suggest that they are not closely related to any other kingdom of organisms. In this activity, you will observe some of the unique structures of a mushroom, a member of the kingdom Fungi.

Procedure

1. Put on your safety goggles and gloves. Get a mushroom from your teacher. Carefully pull the cap of the mushroom from the stem.
2. Using tweezers, remove one of the gills from the underside of the cap. Place the gill on a sheet of white paper.
3. Place the mushroom cap gill-side down on the other sheet of paper. Use masking tape to keep the mushroom cap in place. Place the paper aside for at least 24 hours.
4. Use tweezers to take several 1 cm pieces from the stem, and place these pieces in your Petri dish. Record the appearance of the plate by drawing the plate in a notebook. Cover the Petri dish, and incubate it overnight.
5. Use tweezers to gently pull the remaining mushroom stem apart lengthwise. The individual fibers or strings that you see are the hyphae, which form the structure of the fungus. Place a thin strand on the same piece of paper on which you placed the gill that you removed from the cap.
6. Use a magnifying lens or microscope to observe the gill and the stem hyphae.
7. After at least 24 hours, record any changes that occurred in the Petri dish.
8. Carefully remove the mushroom cap from the paper. Place a piece of transparent tape over the print left behind on the paper. Record your observations.

Analyze the Results

1. **Describing Events** Describe the structures that you saw on the gill and hyphae.
2. **Explaining Events** What makes up the print that was left on the white paper?
3. **Examining Data** Describe the structures on the mushroom gill. Explain how these structures are connected to the print.
4. **Analyzing Data** Compare your original drawing of the Petri dish to your observations of the dish after leaving it for 24 hours.

Draw Conclusions

5. **Evaluating Results** Explain how the changes that occurred in your Petri dish are related to methods of fungal reproduction.

Applying Your Data

Fungi such as mushrooms and yeast are used in cooking and baking in many parts of the world. Bread is a staple food in many cultures. There are thousands of kinds of bread. Conduct library and Internet research on how yeast makes bread rise. Find a bread recipe, and show how the recipe involves the care and feeding of yeast. Ask an adult to help you bake a loaf of bread to share with your class during your presentation.

Chapter Review

USING KEY TERMS

1. In your own words, write a definition for each of the following terms: *mycelium, lichen,* and *heterotroph.*

2. Use the following terms in the same sentence: *protists, algae,* and *phytoplankton.*

3. Use the following terms in the same sentence: *spore* and *mold.*

For each pair of terms, explain how the meanings of the terms differ.

4. *fungus* and *hypha*

5. *parasite* and *host*

UNDERSTANDING KEY IDEAS

Multiple Choice

6. Protist producers include
   - **a.** euglenoids and ciliates.
   - **b.** lichens and zooflagellates.
   - **c.** spore-forming protists and smuts.
   - **d.** dinoflagellates and diatoms.

7. Protists can be
   - **a.** parasites or decomposers.
   - **b.** made of chains of cells called *hyphae.*
   - **c.** divided into four major groups.
   - **d.** only parasites.

8. A euglenoid has
   - **a.** a micronucleus.
   - **b.** pseudopodia.
   - **c.** two flagella.
   - **d.** cilia.

9. Which statement about fungi is true?
   - **a.** Fungi are producers.
   - **b.** Fungi cannot eat or engulf food.
   - **c.** Fungi are found only in the soil.
   - **d.** Fungi are primarily single celled.

10. A lichen is made up of
    - **a.** a fungus and a funguslike protist that live together.
    - **b.** an alga and a fungus that live together.
    - **c.** two kinds of fungi that live together.
    - **d.** an alga and a funguslike protist that live together.

11. Heterotrophic protists that can move
    - **a.** are also known as *protozoans.*
    - **b.** include amoebas and paramecia.
    - **c.** may be either free living or parasitic.
    - **d.** All of the above

Short Answer

12. How are fungi helpful to humans?

13. What is the function of cilia in a paramecium?

14. How are fungi different from protists that get food as decomposers?

15. How are slime molds and amoebas similar?

16. What is a contractile vacuole?

17. Compare how *Paramecium, Plasmodium vivax,* and *Euglena* reproduce.

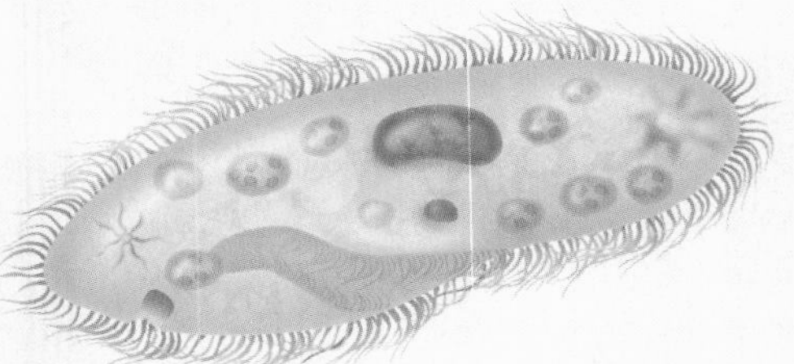

18. Compare how phytoplankton, amoebas, and *Giardia lamblia* get food.

19. Explain how protists differ from other organisms.

20. Give an example of where you might find each of the following fungi: threadlike fungi, sac fungi, club fungi, and imperfect fungi.

CRITICAL THINKING

21. **Concept Mapping** Use the following terms to create a concept map: *yeast, basidia, threadlike fungi, mushrooms, fungi, bread mold, ascus,* and *club fungi.*

22. **Applying Concepts** Why do you think bread turns moldy less quickly when it is kept in a refrigerator than when it is kept at room temperature?

23. **Making Inferences** Some protozoans, such as radiolarians and foraminiferans, have shells around their bodies. How might these shells be helpful to the protists that live in them?

24. **Predicting Consequences** Suppose a forest where many threadlike fungi live goes through a very dry summer and fall and then a very cold winter. How could this extreme weather affect the reproductive patterns of these fungi?

INTERPRETING GRAPHICS

Use the pictures of fungi below to answer the questions that follow.

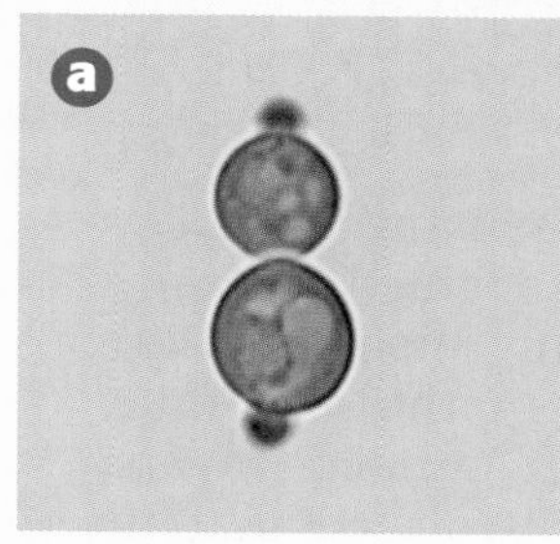

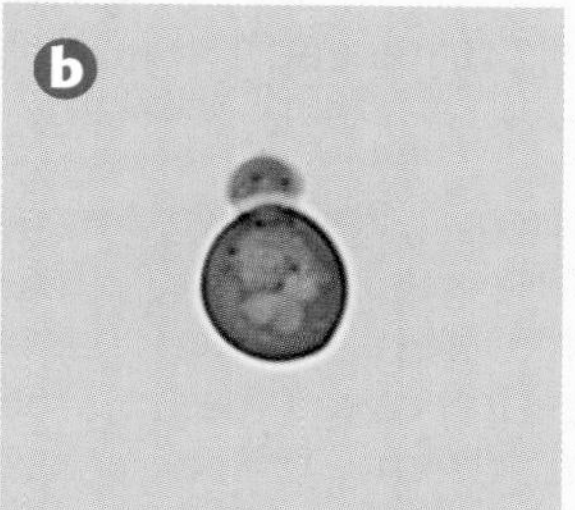

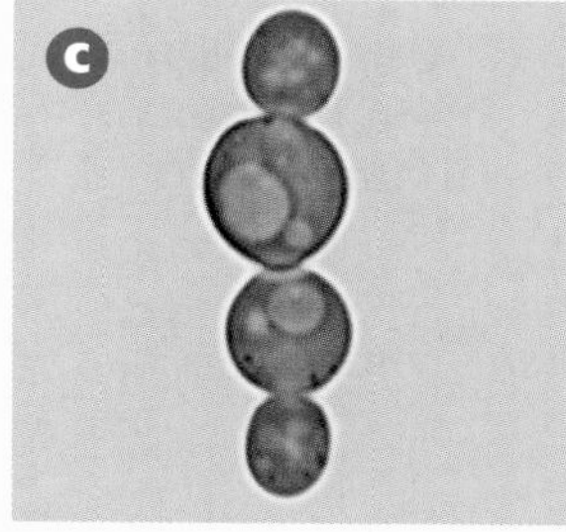

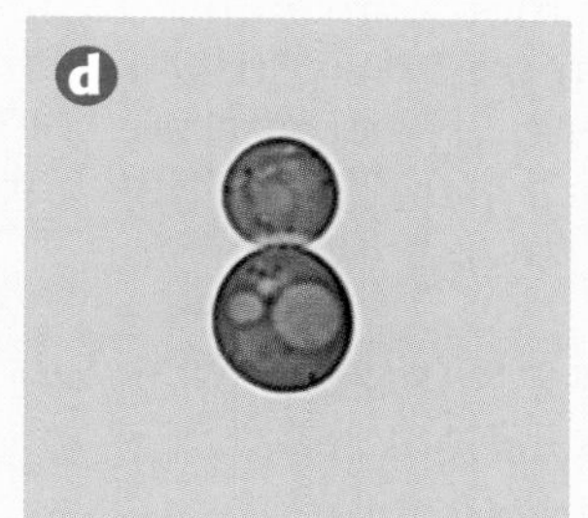

25. What kind of fungus is shown here?

26. What cellular process is shown in these pictures?

27. Which picture was taken first? Which was taken last? Arrange the pictures in order.

28. Which is the original parent cell? How do you know?

Standardized Test Preparation

READING

Read each of the passages below. Then, answer the questions that follow each passage.

Passage 1 For centuries, people living near Cueva de Villa Luz (the Cave of the Lighted House) in Mexico have walked past slimy globs that drip from the cave's ceiling without thinking much about them. When scientists decided to analyze these slime balls, they discovered that the formations are home to billions of microscopic organisms! Scientists nicknamed these colonies "snot-tites" because the colonies <u>resemble</u> mucus. Actually, the "snot-tites" are a mixture of fungi and bacteria.

1. In the passage, what does *resemble* mean?

A to look like
B to feel like
C to smell like
D to sound like

2. Which of the following statements is a fact according to the passage?

F Many kinds of organisms live in Cueva de Villa Luz.
G The people of Mexico ignore the snot-tites.
H Scientists found no explanation for the slime balls that are in Cueva de Villa Luz.
I Cueva de Villa Luz's ceiling is dripping with microscopic organisms.

3. The microscopic organisms discovered by scientists

A are fungi.
B are bacteria.
C are a mixture of fungi and bacteria.
D are a mixture of protists and fungi.

Passage 2 Between 1845 and 1852, Ireland lost one-third of its population. In 1846, a disease swept through the potato fields of Ireland. In just a few weeks, it destroyed almost the entire crop of potatoes. Because the Irish depended on potatoes for food, people were dying of starvation each day. About 2 million people fled the country to find a place to live where they could find enough food. The cause of all of these deaths and this devastation was a simple organism. The disease was caused by a water mold, which is a kind of protist.

1. What caused the population of Ireland to decline between 1845 and 1852?

A a fungus
B a water mold
C a potato
D poisonous potatoes

2. According to the passage, why did the population of Ireland decline?

F A disease swept through the people of Ireland.
G Some people died of starvation, and others fled the country.
H A simple organism infected the people of Ireland.
I When people ate potatoes, they became sick.

3. Which of the following statements is a fact according to the passage?

A People in Ireland have always depended on potatoes for food.
B Protists are parasitic and cause disease.
C About 2 million people fled Ireland between 1845 and 1852.
D Food is more readily available in the United States than it is in Ireland.

INTERPRETING GRAPHICS

The table below shows the number of species in different phyla of protists. Use this table to answer the questions that follow.

Protist Phyla	
Phylum	**Number of Species**
Rhizopoda	300
Foraminifera	300
Chlorophyta	7,000
Rhodophyta	4,000
Phaeophyta	1,500
Bacillariophyta	11,500
Dinoflagellata	2,100
Euglenophyta	1,000
Kinetoplastida	3,000
Ciliophora	8,000
Acrasiomycota	70
Myxomycota	800
Oomycota	580
Apicomplexa	3,900

1. Which phylum has the largest number of species?

A Rhizopoda
B Bacillariophyta
C Ciliophora
D Euglenophyta

2. Which phylum has the smallest number of species?

F Acrasiomycota
G Rhizopoda
H Chlorophyta
I Bacillariophyta

3. If the total number of species of protists is 43,000, what percentage of species are in the phylum Bacillariophyta?

A 0.27%
B 3.7%
C 27%
D 374%

4. If the total number of species of protists is 43,000, what percentage of species are in the phylum Rhizopoda?

F 0.7%
G 1.4%
H 7%
I 143%

MATH

Read each question below, and choose the best answer.

1. Beth had $300 in her savings account when she started her summer job as an assistant to a commercial mushroom grower. If she put $25 into her savings account each month, which equation could be used to find n, the number of months it took Beth to increase her savings to $1,000?

A $1,000 = 300 + n$
B $1,000 = 25n$
C $1,000 = 25n + 300$
D $1,000 = 300n + 25$

2. If you want to determine whether a polygon-shaped protist has the shape of a pentagon, which of the following pieces of information do you need to know?

F the area
G the length of the diagonal
H the number of sides
I the number of faces

3. Marcus had an average score of 90% on two biology tests about protists. If his first test score was 96%, which score did he receive on the second test?

A 45%
B 84%
C 90%
D 102%

Science in Action

Science, Technology, and Society

Algae Ice Cream

If someone offered you a bowl of algae ice cream, would you eat it? Would you eat algae pudding? These foods may not sound appetizing, but algae are a central ingredient in these foods. You eat many kinds of algae every day. Parts of brown algae help thicken ice cream and other dairy products. Red algae help keep breads and pastries from drying out. They are also used in chocolate, milk, eggnog, ice cream, sherbet, instant pudding, and frosting. Green algae contain a pigment that is used as yellow and orange food coloring. Algae are all around you!

Social Studies ACTIVITY

Food products are not the only products that use protist producers. In groups, research how people take advantage of the shiny shells of diatoms. Then, present your findings to the class.

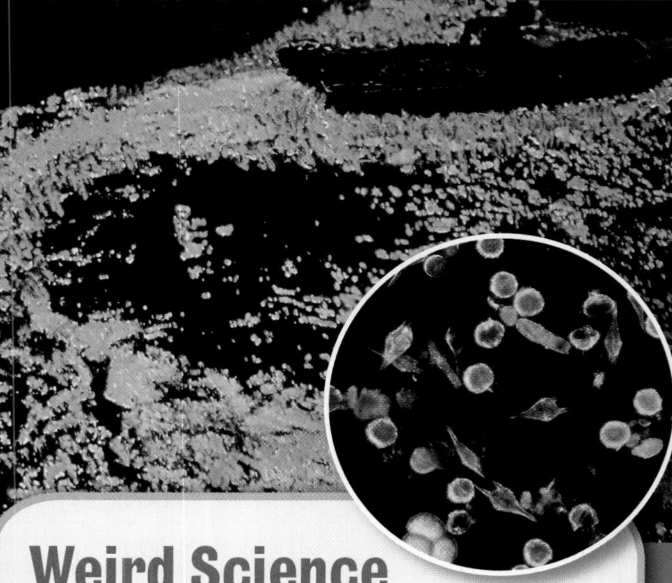

Weird Science

Glowing Protists

As your kayak drifts silently through the night, it leaves a trail of swirling green light in the water behind it. You jump in the water to swim, and your hands turn into glowing underwater comets, which leave sparkling trails that slowly fade away. This may sound like a dream, but it happens every night for swimmers at Mosquito Bay on the island of Vieques in Puerto Rico. The source of this green glow is a protist. The waters of this bay contain millions of dinoflagellates that glow when the water around them is disturbed.

The species of dinoflagellates in Mosquito Bay is *Pyrodinium bahamense,* which means "whirling fire." These spherical single-celled protists are covered by armored plates. Each individual has two flagella that spin it through the water. The light is produced by a chemical reaction that is similar to the reaction in fireflies.

Math ACTIVITY

Living in every gallon of water in Mosquito Bay are 750,000 dinoflagellates. Suppose you took a gallon of water from this bay and dumped it into a bathtub full of 6 gal of fresh water that didn't contain any dinoflagellates. Then, you mixed up the water and turned out the lights to see if the bathtub would glow in the dark. How many dinoflagellates would be in each gallon of water in the bathtub after you mixed up the water?

People in Science

Terrie Taylor

Fighting Malaria Malaria claims about 2 million victims each year. A person gets malaria when the blood is infected by protists from the genus *Plasmodium*. Dr. Terrie Taylor of Michigan State University's College of Osteopathic Medicine has devoted her life to malaria research. Since 1987, Dr. Taylor has spent six months of every year in Malawi, a small African country in which malaria is widespread.

When Dr. Taylor first traveled to Malawi, she did not have a particular interest in malaria. However, she quickly started to realize that the majority of her patients were infected with the deadly disease. The patients who were suffering the most were children. For every 100 children infected with malaria and treated by Dr. Taylor, between 20 and 25 would die from a malaria-induced coma. When a malaria coma starts, the patient becomes confused and sleepy. The patient then falls into a coma, which may lead to death. Dr. Taylor worked with other doctors at the hospital to develop a coma scale so that doctors could have a standardized way to assess patients moving toward coma. This scale is now used around the world.

Dr. Taylor wanted to find out why malaria victims fell into a coma. She took blood samples from malaria patients. She realized that severe malaria often led to a rapid fall in the patient's blood-sugar level. Dr. Taylor hypothesizes that the drop in blood sugar is related to the fact that the protists that cause malaria primarily infect a person's liver. The liver is the organ responsible for releasing sugar into the blood. Dr. Taylor has used this information to create a new treatment. Whenever she treats children who have a severe case of malaria, she gives them glucose, the type of sugar that is found in the bloodstream. This simple treatment has already saved hundreds of lives!

Language Arts Activity

The word *malaria* is a combination of two words. *Mala* means "bad," and *aria* means "air." Why do you think that people would use these words to describe the disease? Note that people did not realize that malaria was transmitted to people by mosquitoes until about 1899.

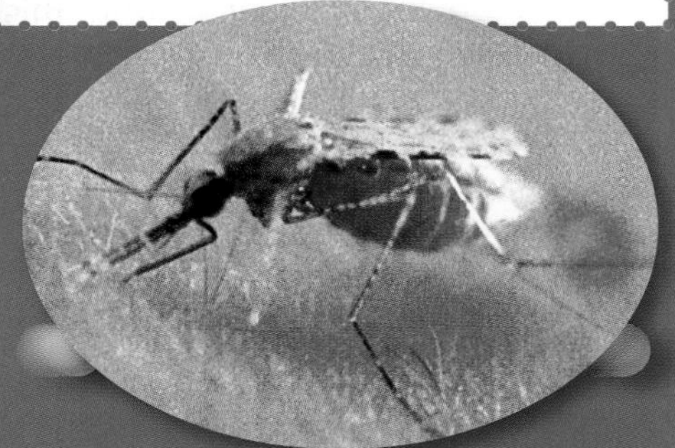

To learn more about these Science in Action topics, visit go.hrw.com and type in the keyword HL5PROF.

Current Science

Check out Current Science® articles related to this chapter by visiting go.hrw.com. Just type in the keyword HL5CS11.

12

Introduction to Plants

About the PHOTO

In Costa Rica's Monteverde Cloud Forest Preserve, a green coil begins to unfold. It is hidden from all but the most careful observer. The coil looks alien, but it is very much of this Earth. The coil is the leaf of a fern, a plant that grows in moist areas. Soon, the coil will unfold into a lacy, delicate frond.

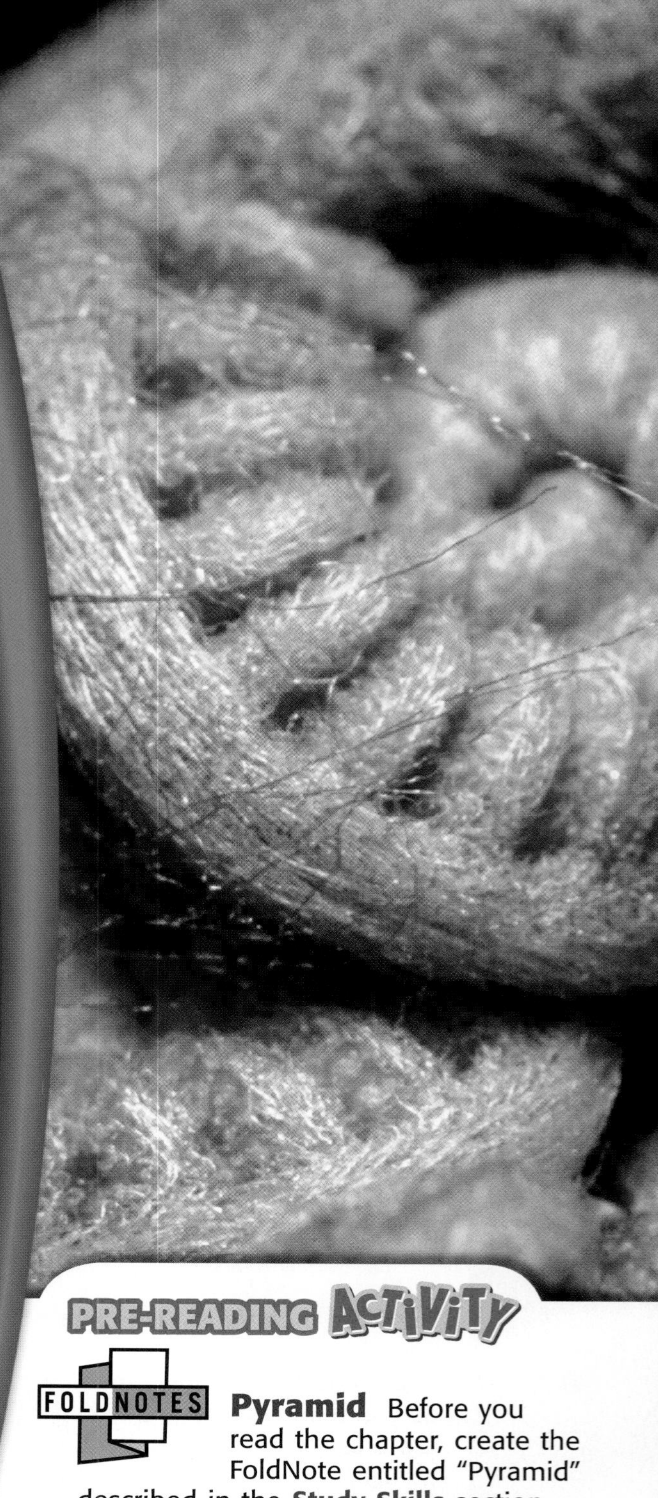

PRE-READING ACTIVITY

FOLDNOTES **Pyramid** Before you read the chapter, create the FoldNote entitled "Pyramid" described in the **Study Skills** section of the Appendix. Label the sides of the pyramid with "Nonvascular plants," "Seedless vascular plants," and "Seed plants." As you read the chapter, define each kind of plant, and write characteristics of each kind of plant on the appropriate pyramid side.

START-UP ACTIVITY

Observing Plant Growth

When planting a garden, you bury seeds and water them. What happens to the seeds below the soil? How do seeds grow into plants?

Procedure

1. Fill a clear **2 L soda bottle** to within 8 cm of the top with **moist potting soil.** Your teacher will have already cut off the neck of the bottle.
2. Press **three or four bean seeds** into the soil and against the wall of the bottle. Add enough additional potting soil to increase the depth by 5 cm.
3. Cover the sides of the bottle with **aluminum foil** to keep out light. Leave the top of the bottle uncovered.
4. Water the seeds with about **60 mL of water,** or water them until the soil is moist. Add more water when the soil dries out.
5. Place the bottle in an area that receives sunshine. Check on your seeds each day, and record your observations.

Analysis

1. How many seeds grew?
2. How long did the seeds take to start growing?
3. From where did the seeds most likely get the energy to grow?

SECTION 1

What Is a Plant?

Imagine spending a day without plants. What would you eat? It would be impossible to make chocolate chip cookies and many other foods.

Without plants, you couldn't eat much. Almost all food is made from plants or from animals that eat plants. Life would be very different without plants!

READING WARM-UP

Objectives

- Identify four characteristics that all plants share.
- Describe the four main groups of plants.
- Explain the origin of plants.

Terms to Learn

nonvascular plant
vascular plant
gymnosperm
angiosperm

READING STRATEGY

Reading Organizer As you read this section, create an outline of the section. Use the headings from the section in your outline.

Plant Characteristics

Plants come in many different shapes and sizes. So, what do cactuses, water lilies, ferns, and all other plants have in common? One plant may seem very different from another. But most plants share certain characteristics.

Photosynthesis

Take a look at **Figure 1.** Do you know why this plant is green? Plant cells contain chlorophyll (KLAWR uh FIL). *Chlorophyll* is a green pigment that captures energy from sunlight. Chlorophyll is found in chloroplasts (KLAWR uh PLASTS). Chloroplasts are organelles found in many plant cells and some protists. Plants use energy from sunlight to make food from carbon dioxide and water. This process is called *photosynthesis* (FOHT oh SIN thuh sis). Because plants make their own food, they are called *producers*.

Figure 1 *Chlorophyll makes the leaves of this plant green. Chlorophyll helps plants make their own food by capturing energy from sunlight.*

Cuticles

Most plants live on dry land and need sunlight to live. But why don't plants dry out? Plants are protected by a cuticle. A *cuticle* is a waxy layer that coats most of the surfaces of plants that are exposed to air. The cuticle keeps plants from drying out.

Figure 2 Some Structures of a Photosynthetic Plant Cell

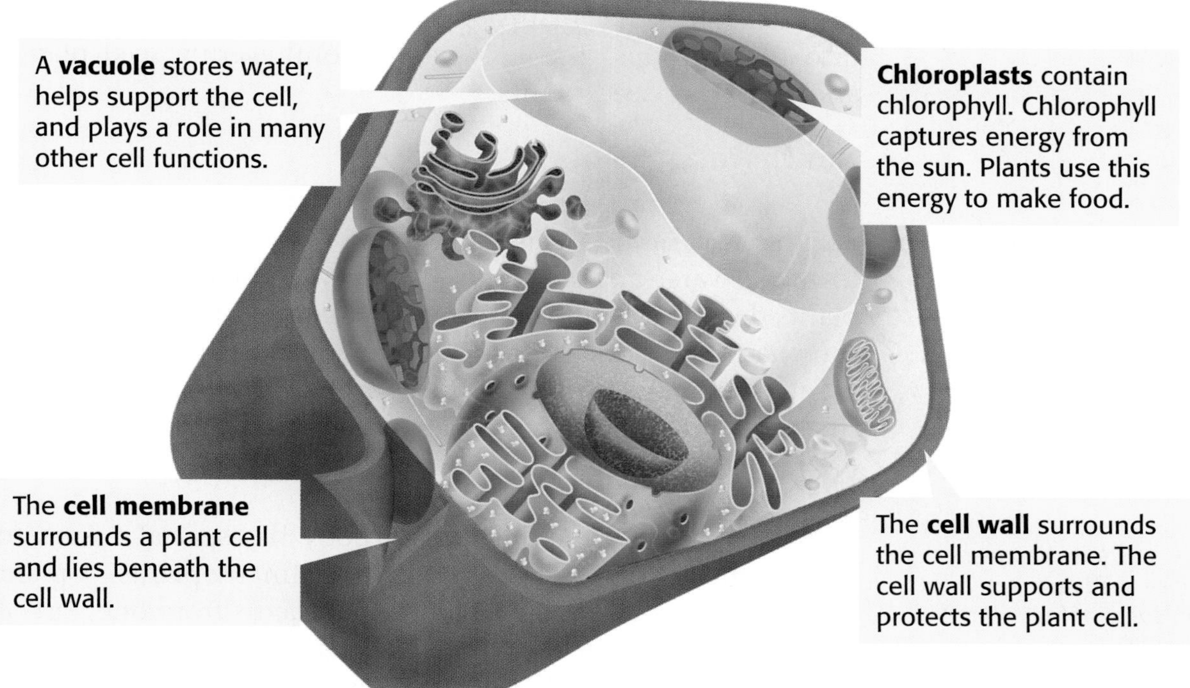

A **vacuole** stores water, helps support the cell, and plays a role in many other cell functions.
Chloroplasts contain chlorophyll. Chlorophyll captures energy from the sun. Plants use this energy to make food.
The **cell membrane** surrounds a plant cell and lies beneath the cell wall.
The **cell wall** surrounds the cell membrane. The cell wall supports and protects the plant cell.

Cell Walls

How do plants stay upright? They do not have skeletons like many animals do. Instead, plant cells are surrounded by a rigid cell wall. The cell wall lies outside the cell membrane, as shown in **Figure 2.** Carbohydrates and proteins in the cell wall form a hard material. Cell walls support and protect the plant cell. Some plant cells also have a secondary cell wall that forms after the cell is mature. When this wall has formed, a plant cell cannot grow larger.

Reproduction

Plants have two stages in their life cycle—the sporophyte (SPAWR uh FIET) stage and the gametophyte (guh MEET uh FIET) stage. In the sporophyte stage, plants make spores. In a suitable environment, such as damp soil, the spores of some plants grow. These new plants are called *gametophytes*.

During the gametophyte stage, female gametophytes produce eggs. Male gametophytes produce sperm. Eggs and sperm are sex cells. Sex cells cannot grow directly into new plants. Instead, a sperm must fertilize an egg. The fertilized egg grows into a sporophyte. The sporophyte makes more spores. So, the cycle starts again.

Reading Check **How do plants reproduce?** (*See the Appendix for answers to Reading Checks.*)

CONNECTION TO Social Studies

Countries and Crops Without plants, most life on land couldn't survive. But plants are important for more than the survival of living things. Many countries rely on plants for income. Identify five major food crops. Then, find out which countries are the main producers of these crops and how much the countries produce each year. Make a table to show your findings.

Plant Classification

Although all plants share basic characteristics, they can be classified into four groups. First, they are classified as nonvascular plants and vascular plants. Vascular plants are further divided into three groups—seedless plants, nonflowering seed plants, and flowering seed plants.

Nonvascular Plants

Mosses, liverworts, and hornworts are nonvascular plants. A **nonvascular plant** is a plant that doesn't have specialized tissues to move water and nutrients through the plant. Nonvascular plants depend on diffusion to move materials from one part of the plant to another. Diffusion is possible because nonvascular plants are small. If nonvascular plants were large, the cells of the plants would not get enough water and nutrients.

nonvascular plant the three groups of plants (liverworts, hornworts, and mosses) that lack specialized conducting tissues and true roots, stems, and leaves

vascular plant a plant that has specialized tissues that conduct materials from one part of the plant to another

gymnosperm a woody, vascular seed plant whose seeds are not enclosed by an ovary or fruit

angiosperm a flowering plant that produces seeds within a fruit

Vascular Plants

In the same way that the human body has special tissues to move materials through the body, so do many plants. A plant that has tissues to deliver water and nutrients from one part of the plant to another is called a **vascular plant.** These tissues are called *vascular tissues*. Vascular tissues can move water to any part of a plant. So, vascular plants can be almost any size.

Vascular plants are divided into three groups—seedless plants and two types of seed plants. Seedless vascular plants include ferns, horsetails, and club mosses. Nonflowering seed plants are called **gymnosperms** (JIM noh SPUHRMZ). Flowering seed plants are called **angiosperms** (AN jee oh SPUHRMZ). The four main groups of plants are shown in **Figure 3.**

Reading Check What are the four main groups of plants?

Figure 3 The Main Groups of Plants

Nonvascular plants
Mosses, liverworts, and hornworts
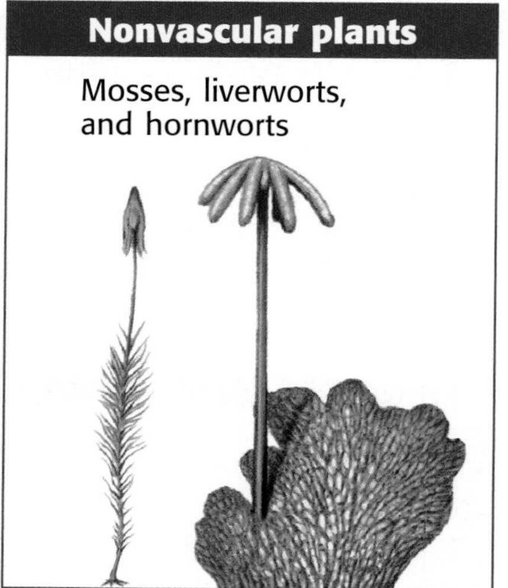

Vascular plants		
Seedless plants	Seed plants	
	Nonflowering	Flowering
Ferns, horsetails, and club mosses	Gymnosperms	Angiosperms

The Origin of Plants

Imagine that you traveled back in time about 440 million years. The Earth seems like a strange, bare, and unfriendly place. For one thing, no plants live on land. So, where did plants come from?

Take a look at **Figure 4.** The photo on the left shows a green alga. The photo on the right shows a fern. The green alga may look like a plant, such as a fern, but it isn't a plant. However, green algae and plants have many similarities. Green algae cells and plant cells have the same kind of chlorophyll. They have similar cell walls. Green algae and plants make their own food through photosynthesis. Both store energy in the form of starch. Like plants, green algae have a two-stage life cycle. Because of these similarities, some scientists think that green algae and plants share a common ancestor.

Reading Check **What are some characteristics that green algae and plants have in common?**

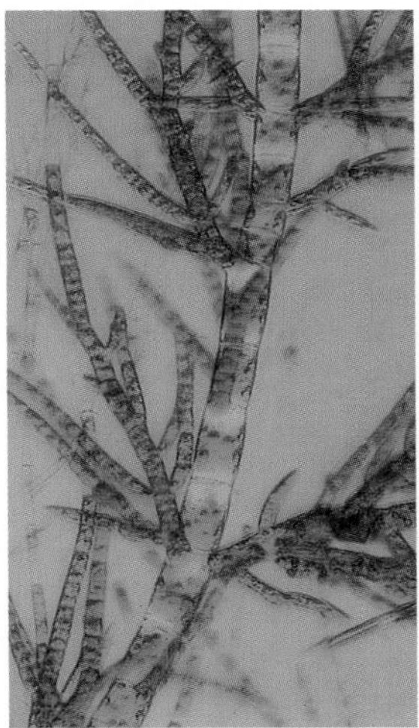

Figure 4 *The similarities between a modern green alga (left) and plants, such as ferns (right), suggest that both may have originated from an ancient species of green algae.*

SECTION Review

Summary

- All plants make their own food and have cuticles, cells walls, and a two-stage life cycle.
- Plants are first classified into two groups: nonvascular plants and vascular plants. Vascular plants are further divided into seedless plants, gymnosperms, and angiosperms.
- Similarities between green algae and plants suggest they may have a common ancestor.

Using Key Terms

For each pair of terms, explain how the meanings of the terms differ.

1. *nonvascular plants* and *vascular plants*
2. *gymnosperms* and *angiosperms*

Understanding Key Ideas

3. Which of the following plants is nonvascular?
   a. ferns
   b. mosses
   c. gymnosperms
   d. club mosses
4. What are four characteristics that all plants share?
5. What do green algae and plants have in common?
6. Describe the plant life cycle.

Math Skills

7. A plant produced 200,000 spores and one-third as many eggs. How many eggs did the plant produce?

Critical Thinking

8. **Making Inferences** One difference between green algae and plants is that green algae do not have a cuticle. Why don't green algae have a cuticle?
9. **Applying Concepts** Imagine an environment that is very dry and receives a lot of sunlight. Water is found deep below the soil. Which of the four groups of plants could survive in this environment? Explain your answer.

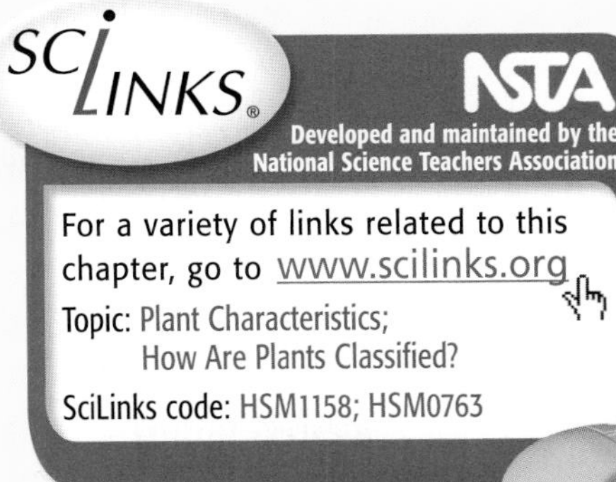

SCILINKS
NSTA
Developed and maintained by the National Science Teachers Association
For a variety of links related to this chapter, go to www.scilinks.org
Topic: Plant Characteristics; How Are Plants Classified?
SciLinks code: HSM1158; HSM0763

SECTION 2

Seedless Plants

When you think of plants, you probably think of plants, such as trees and flowers, that make seeds. But two groups of plants don't make seeds.

READING WARM-UP

Objectives

- List three nonvascular plants and three seedless vascular plants.
- Explain how seedless plants are important to the environment.
- Describe the relationship between seedless vascular plants and coal.

Terms to Learn

rhizoid
rhizome

READING STRATEGY

Paired Summarizing Read this section silently. In pairs, take turns summarizing the material. Stop to discuss ideas that seem confusing.

One group of seedless plants is the nonvascular plants—mosses, liverworts, and hornworts. The other group is seedless vascular plants—ferns, horsetails, and club mosses.

Nonvascular Plants

Mosses, liverworts, and hornworts are small. They grow on soil, the bark of trees, and rocks. These plants don't have vascular tissue. So, nonvascular plants usually live in places that are damp. Each cell of the plant must get water from the environment or from a nearby cell.

Mosses, liverworts, and hornworts don't have true stems, roots, or leaves. They do, however, have structures that carry out the activities of stems, roots, and leaves.

Mosses

Mosses often live together in large groups. They cover soil or rocks with a mat of tiny green plants. Mosses have leafy stalks and rhizoids (RIE ZOYDZ). A **rhizoid** is a rootlike structure that holds nonvascular plants in place. Rhizoids help the plants get water and nutrients. As you can see in **Figure 1,** mosses have two stages in their life cycle.

rhizoid a rootlike structure in nonvascular plants that holds the plants in place and helps plants get water and nutrients

Figure 1 Moss Life Cycle

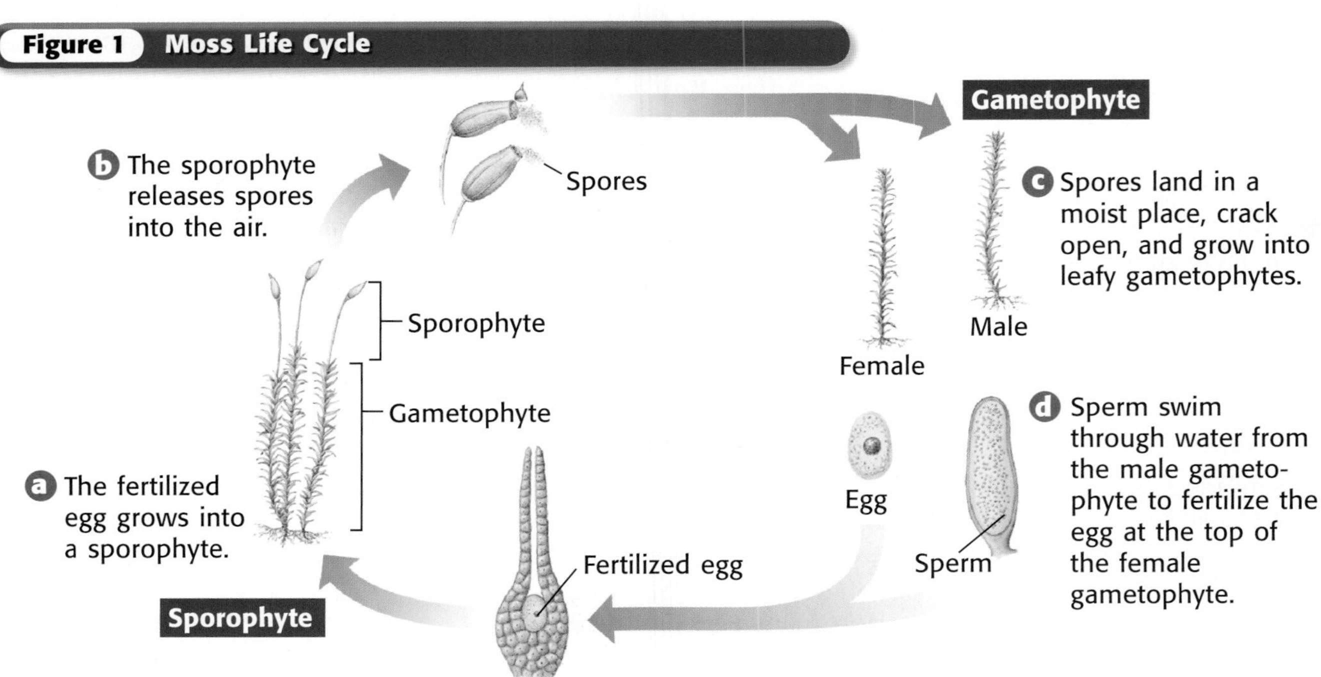
Gametophyte
b The sporophyte releases spores into the air.
Spores
c Spores land in a moist place, crack open, and grow into leafy gametophytes.
Sporophyte
Male
Female
Gametophyte
d Sperm swim through water from the male gametophyte to fertilize the egg at the top of the female gametophyte.
Egg
a The fertilized egg grows into a sporophyte.
Fertilized egg
Sperm
Sporophyte

Liverworts and Hornworts

Like mosses, liverworts and hornworts are small, nonvascular plants that usually live in damp places. The life cycles of liverworts and hornworts are similar to the life cycle of mosses. The gametophytes of liverworts can be leafy and mosslike or broad and flattened. Hornworts also have broad, flattened gametophytes. Both liverworts and hornworts have rhizoids.

The Importance of Nonvascular Plants

Nonvascular plants have an important role in the environment. They are usually the first plants to live in a new environment, such as newly exposed rock. When these nonvascular plants die, they form a thin layer of soil. New plants can grow in this soil. More nonvascular plants may grow and hold the soil in place. This reduces soil erosion. Some animals eat nonvascular plants. Other animals use these plants for nesting material.

Peat mosses are important to humans. Peat mosses grow in bogs and other wet places. In some places, dead peat mosses have built up over time. This peat can be dried and burned as a fuel. Peat mosses are also used in potting soil.

Reading Check **How are nonvascular plants important to the environment?** (*See the Appendix for answers to Reading Checks.*)

Seedless Vascular Plants

Ancient ferns, horsetails, and club mosses grew very tall. Club mosses grew to 40 m in ancient forests. Horsetails once grew to 18 m tall. Some ferns grew to 8 m tall. Today, ferns, horsetails, and club mosses are usually much smaller. But because they have vascular tissue, they are often larger than nonvascular plants. **Figure 2** shows club mosses and horsetails.

Moss Mass

1. Determine the mass of a small sample of **dry sphagnum moss.**
2. Observe what happens when you put a small piece of the moss in **water.** Predict what will happen if you put the entire sample in water.
3. Place the moss sample in a **large beaker of water** for 10 to 15 minutes.
4. Remove the wet moss from the beaker, and determine the mass of the moss.
5. How much mass did the moss gain? Compare your result with your prediction.
6. What could this plant be used for?

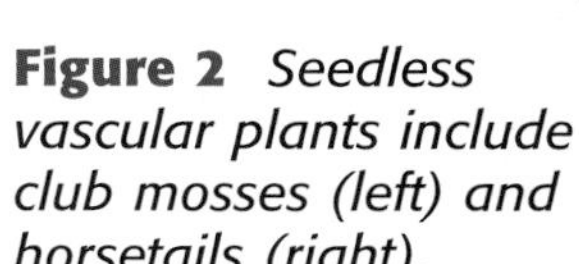

Figure 2 *Seedless vascular plants include club mosses (left) and horsetails (right).*

rhizome a horizontal, underground stem that produces new leaves, shoots, and roots

Ferns

Ferns grow in many places, from the cold Arctic to warm, humid tropical forests. Many ferns are small plants. But some tropical tree ferns grow as tall as 24 m. Most ferns have a rhizome. A **rhizome** is an underground stem from which new leaves and roots grow. At first, fern leaves, or fronds, are tightly coiled. These fronds look like the end of a violin, or fiddle. So, they are called *fiddleheads*. You are probably most familiar with the leafy fern sporophyte. The fern gametophyte is a tiny plant about half the size of one of your fingernails. The fern gametophyte is green and flat. It is usually shaped like a tiny heart. The life cycle of ferns is shown in **Figure 3.**

Horsetails and Club Mosses

Modern horsetails can be as tall as 8 m. But many horsetails are smaller. They usually grow in wet, marshy places. Their stems are hollow and contain silica. The silica gives horsetails a gritty texture. In fact, early American pioneers referred to horsetails as *scouring rushes*. They used horsetails to scrub pots and pans. Horsetails and ferns have similar life cycles.

Club mosses are often about 20 cm tall. They grow in woodlands. Club mosses are not actually mosses. Unlike mosses, club mosses have vascular tissue. The life cycle of club mosses is similar to the fern life cycle.

Figure 3 **Fern Life Cycle**

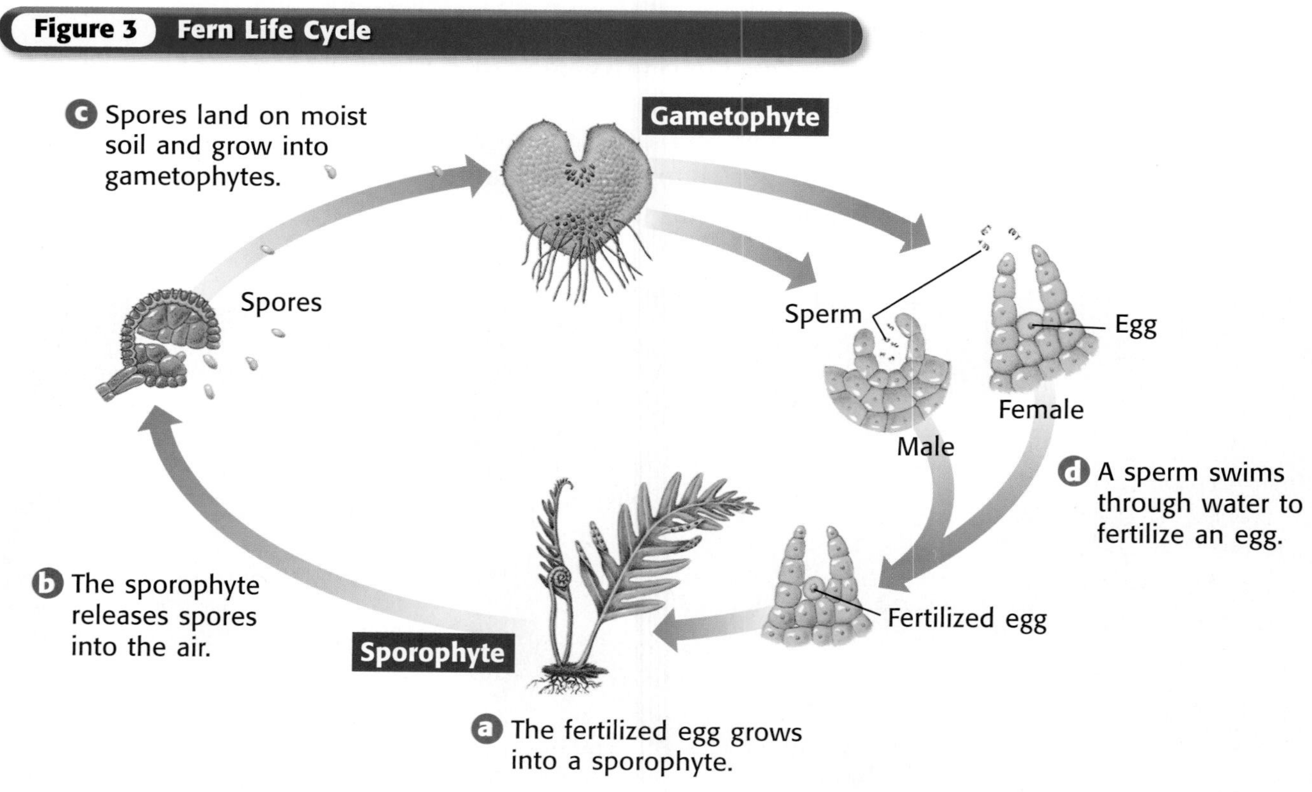

Gametophyte
c Spores land on moist soil and grow into gametophytes.
Spores
Sperm
Egg
Female
Male
d A sperm swims through water to fertilize an egg.
Fertilized egg
b The sporophyte releases spores into the air.
Sporophyte
a The fertilized egg grows into a sporophyte.

The Importance of Seedless Vascular Plants

Seedless vascular plants play important roles in the environment. Ferns, horsetails, and club mosses help form soil. They also help prevent soil erosion. In rocky areas, ferns can play a role in the formation of communities. After lichens and mosses create a layer of soil, ferns may take over. Ferns add to soil depth, which allows other plants to grow.

Ferns and some club mosses are popular houseplants. The fiddleheads of some ferns can be cooked and eaten. Young horsetail shoots and their roots are also edible. Horsetails are used in some dietary supplements, shampoos, and skin-care products.

Seedless vascular plants that lived and died about 300 million years ago are among the most important to humans. The remains of these ancient ferns, horsetails, and club mosses formed coal. Coal is a fossil fuel that humans mine from the Earth's crust. Humans rely on coal for energy.

Reading Check **How are seedless vascular plants important to the environment?**

CONNECTION TO Language Arts

WRITING SKILL **Selling Plants** Imagine that you work for an advertising agency. Your next assignment is to promote seedless vascular plants. Write an advertisement describing seedless vascular plants and ways people benefit from them. Your advertisement should be exciting and persuasive.

SECTION Review

Summary

- Nonvascular plants include mosses, liverworts, and hornworts.
- Seedless vascular plants include ferns, horsetails, and club mosses.
- The rhizoids and rhizomes of seedless plants prevent erosion by holding soil in place.
- The remains of seedless vascular plants that lived and died about 300 million years ago formed coal. Humans rely on coal for energy.

Using Key Terms

1. Use each of the following terms in a separate sentence: *rhizoid* and *rhizome.*

Understanding Key Ideas

2. Seedless plants
   a. help form communities.
   b. reduce soil erosion.
   c. add to soil depth.
   d. All of the above
3. Describe six kinds of seedless plants.
4. What is the relationship between coal and seedless vascular plants?

Math Skills

5. Club mosses once grew as tall as 40 m. Now, they grow no taller than 20 cm. What is the difference in height between ancient and modern club mosses?

Critical Thinking

6. **Making Inferences** Imagine a very damp area. Mosses cover the rocks and trees in this area. Liverworts and hornworts are also very abundant. What might happen if the area dries out? Explain your answer.
7. **Applying Concepts** Modern ferns, horsetails, and club mosses are smaller than they were millions of years ago. Why might these plants be smaller?

SCILINKS
NSTA
Developed and maintained by the National Science Teachers Association
For a variety of links related to this chapter, go to www.scilinks.org
Topic: Seedless Plants
SciLinks code: HSM1368

SECTION 3

Seed Plants

Think about the seed plants that you use during the day. You likely use dozens of seed plants, from the food you eat to the paper you write on.

READING WARM-UP

Objectives

- Describe three ways that seed plants differ from seedless plants.
- Describe the structure of seeds.
- Compare angiosperms and gymnosperms.
- Explain the economic and environmental importance of gymnosperms and angiosperms.

Terms to Learn

pollen
pollination

READING STRATEGY

Reading Organizer As you read this section, make a table comparing angiosperms and gymnosperms.

The two groups of vascular plants that produce seeds are gymnosperms and angiosperms. Gymnosperms are trees and shrubs that do not have flowers or fruit. Angiosperms have flowers and seeds that are protected by fruit.

Characteristics of Seed Plants

As with seedless plants, the life cycle of seed plants alternates between two stages. But seed plants, such as the plant in **Figure 1,** differ from seedless plants in the following ways:

- Seed plants produce seeds. Seeds nourish and protect young sporophytes.
- Unlike the gametophytes of seedless plants, the gametophytes of seed plants do not live independently of the sporophyte. The gametophytes of seed plants are tiny. The gametophytes form within the reproductive structures of the sporophyte.
- The sperm of seedless plants need water to swim to the eggs of female gametophytes. The sperm of seed plants do not need water to reach an egg. Sperm form inside tiny structures called **pollen.** Pollen can be transported by wind or by animals.

pollen the tiny granules that contain the male gametophyte of seed plants

These three characteristics of seed plants allow them to live just about anywhere. For this reason, seed plants are the most common plants on Earth today.

Reading Check **List three characteristics of seed plants.** (*See the Appendix for answers to Reading Checks.*)

Figure 1 *Dandelion fruits, which each contain a seed, are spread by wind.*

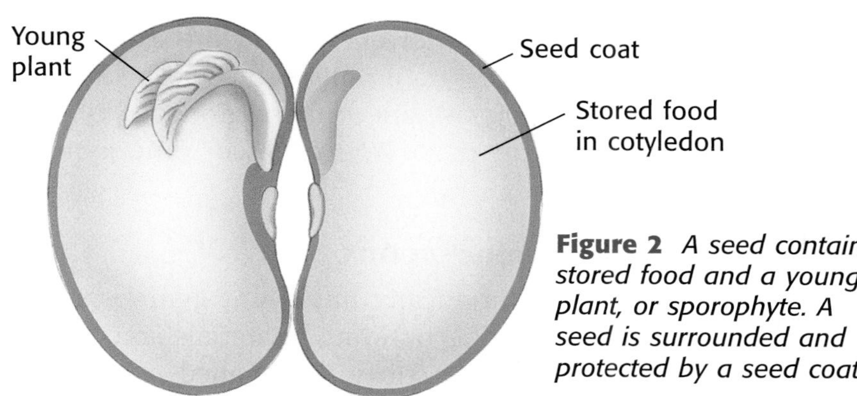

Figure 2 *A seed contains stored food and a young plant, or sporophyte. A seed is surrounded and protected by a seed coat.*

The Structure of Seeds

A seed forms after fertilization, when sperm and eggs are joined. A seed is made up of three parts, as shown in **Figure 2.** The first part is a young plant, or the sporophyte. The second part is stored food. It is often found in the cotyledons (KAHT uh LEED uhnz), or the seed leaves of the young plant. Finally, a seed coat surrounds and protects the young plant.

Seed plants have some advantages over seedless plants. For example, when a seed begins to grow, the young plant uses the food stored in the seed. The spores of seedless plants don't have stored food to help a new plant grow. Another advantage of seed plants is that seeds can be spread by animals. The spores of seedless plants are usually spread by wind. Animals spread seeds more efficiently than the wind spreads spores.

Reading Check Describe two advantages that seed plants have over seedless plants.

CONNECTION TO Environmental Science

WRITING SKILL **Animals That Help Plants** Animals need plants to live, but some plants benefit from animals, too. These plants produce seeds with tough seed coats. An animal's digestive system can wear down these seed coats and speed the growth of a seed. Identify a plant that animals help in this way. Then, find out how being eaten by animals makes it possible for seeds to grow. Write about your findings in your **science journal.**

Dissecting Seeds

1. Soak a **lima bean seed** in **water** overnight. Draw the seed before placing it in the water.
2. Remove the seed from the water. Draw what you see.
3. The seed will likely look wrinkly. This is the seed coat. Use a **toothpick** to gently remove the seed coat from the lima bean seed.
4. Gently separate the halves of the lima bean seed. Draw what you see.
5. What did you see after you split the lima bean seed in half?
6. What part of the seed do you think provides the lima bean plant with the energy to grow?

Gymnosperms

Seed plants that do not have flowers or fruit are called *gymnosperms*. Gymnosperm seeds are usually protected by a cone. The four groups of gymnosperms are conifers, ginkgoes, cycads, and gnetophytes (NEE toh FIETS). You can see some gymnosperms in **Figure 3.**

The Importance of Gymnosperms

Conifers are the most economically important gymnosperms. People use conifer wood for building materials and paper products. Pine trees produce a sticky fluid called *resin*. Resin is used to make soap, turpentine, paint, and ink. Some conifers produce an important anticancer drug. Some gnetophytes produce anti-allergy drugs. Conifers, cycads, and ginkgoes are popular in gardens and parks.

Figure 3 **Examples of Gymnosperms**

Conifers The conifers, such as this ponderosa pine, are the largest group of gymnosperms. There are about 550 species of conifers. Most conifers are evergreens that keep their needle-shaped leaves all year. Conifer seeds develop in cones.

Ginkgoes Today, there is only one living species of ginkgo, the ginkgo tree. Ginkgo seeds are not produced in cones. The seeds have fleshy seed coats and are attached directly to the branches of the tree.

Cycads The cycads were more common millions of years ago. Today, there are only about 140 species of cycads. These plants grow in the Tropics. Like conifer seeds, cycad seeds develop in cones.

Gnetophytes About 70 species of gnetophytes, such as this joint fir, exist today. Many gnetophytes are shrubs that grow in dry areas. The seeds of most gnetophytes develop in cones.

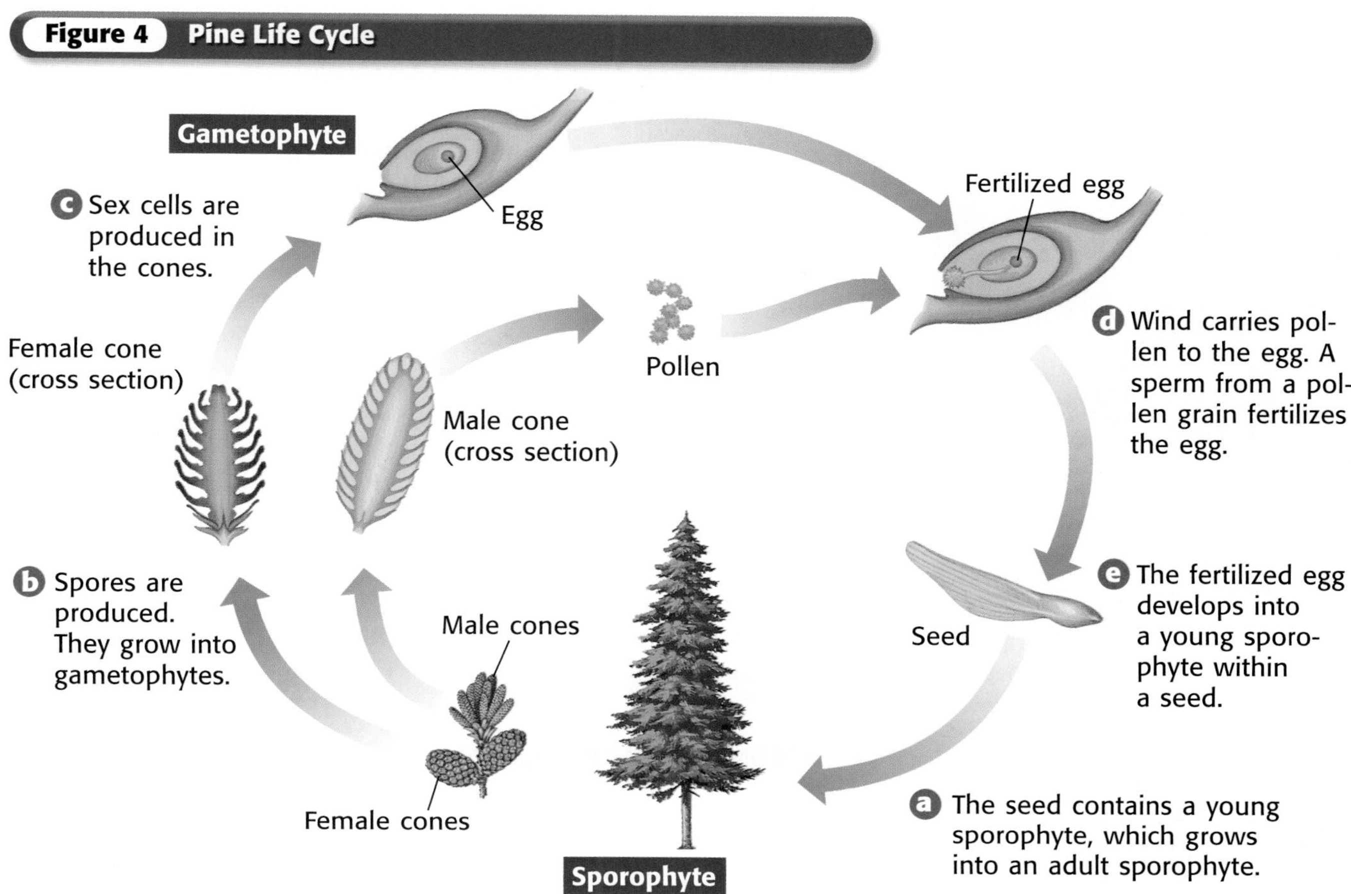
Gametophyte
c Sex cells are produced in the cones.
Egg
Fertilized egg
d Wind carries pollen to the egg. A sperm from a pollen grain fertilizes the egg.
Pollen
Female cone (cross section)
Male cone (cross section)
b Spores are produced. They grow into gametophytes.
Male cones
Seed
e The fertilized egg develops into a young sporophyte within a seed.
Female cones
a The seed contains a young sporophyte, which grows into an adult sporophyte.
Sporophyte

Figure 4 Pine Life Cycle

Gymnosperm Life Cycle

The gymnosperms that are most familiar to you are probably the conifers. The word *conifer* comes from two words that mean "cone-bearing." Conifers have two kinds of cones—male cones and female cones. The spores of each kind of cone become tiny gametophytes.

The male gametophytes of gymnosperms are found in pollen. Pollen contain sperm. The female gametophytes produce eggs. Wind carries pollen from the male cones to the female cones. This transfer of pollen from the male cones to the female cones is called **pollination.** The female cones can be on the same plant. Or, they can be on a different plant of the same species.

pollination the transfer of pollen from the male reproductive structures to the female structures of seed plants

Sperm from pollen fertilize the eggs of the female cone. A fertilized egg develops into a young sporophyte within the female cone. The sporophyte is surrounded by a seed. Eventually, the seed is released. Some cones release seeds right away. Other cones release seeds under special circumstances, such as after forest fires. If conditions are right, the seed will grow. The life cycle of a pine tree is shown in **Figure 4.**

Reading Check **Describe the gymnosperm life cycle.**

Angiosperms

Vascular plants that produce flowers and fruits are called *angiosperms*. Angiosperms are the most abundant plants today. There are at least 235,000 species of angiosperms. Angiosperms can be found in almost every land ecosystem.

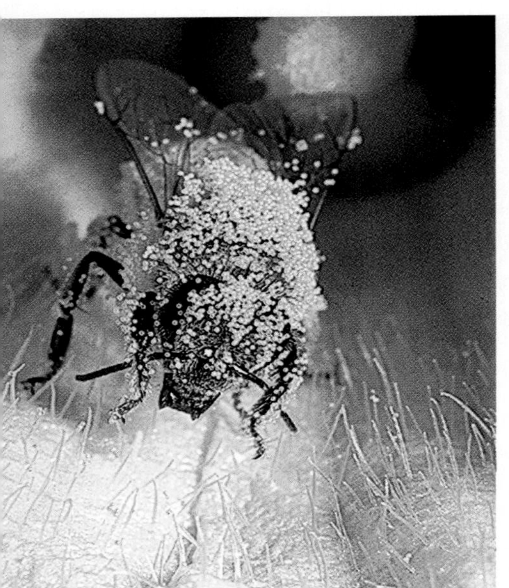

Figure 5 *This bee is on its way to another squash flower, where it will leave some of the pollen it is carrying.*

Angiosperm Reproduction

Flowers help angiosperms reproduce. Some angiosperms depend on the wind for pollination. But others have flowers that attract animals. As shown in **Figure 5,** when animals visit different flowers, the animals may carry pollen from flower to flower.

Fruits surround and protect seeds. Some fruits and seeds have structures that help the wind carry them short or long distances. Other fruits attract animals that eat the fruits. The animals discard the seeds away from the plant. Some fruits, such as burrs, are carried from place to place by sticking to the fur of animals.

Reading Check **Why do angiosperms have flowers and fruits?**

Two Kinds of Angiosperms

Angiosperms are divided into two classes—monocots and dicots. The two classes differ in the number of cotyledons, or seed leaves, their seeds have. Monocot seeds have one cotyledon. Grasses, orchids, onions, lilies, and palms are monocots. Dicot seeds have two cotyledons. Dicots include roses, cactuses, sunflowers, peanuts, and peas. Other differences between monocots and dicots are shown in **Figure 6.**

Figure 6 **Two Classes of Angiosperms**

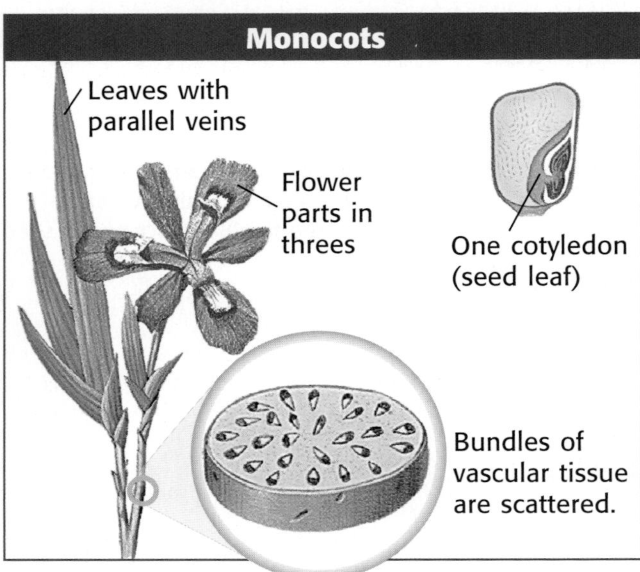

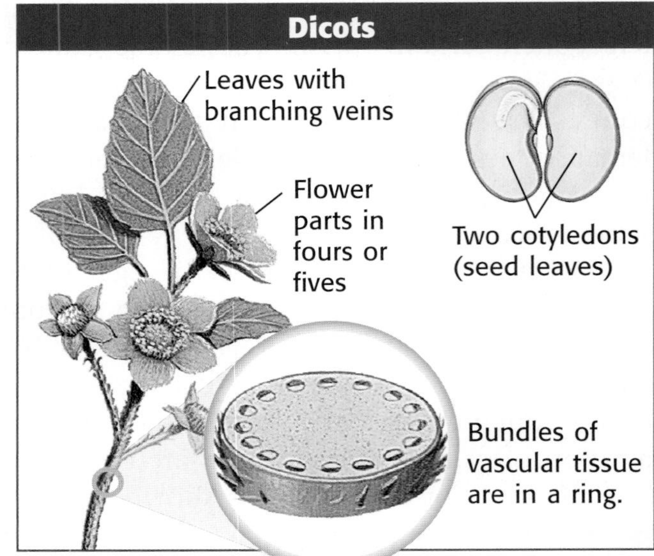

The Importance of Angiosperms

Flowering plants provide many land animals with the food they need to survive. A field mouse that eats seeds and berries is using flowering plants directly as food. An owl that eats a field mouse is using flowering plants indirectly as food.

People use flowering plants in many ways. Major food crops, such as corn, wheat, and rice, are flowering plants. Some flowering plants, such as oak trees, are used for building materials. Flowering plants, such as cotton and flax, are used to make clothing and rope. Flowering plants are also used to make medicines, rubber, and perfume oils.

Reading Check **How are flowering plants important to humans?**

SECTION Review

Summary

- Seeds nourish the young sporophyte of seed plants. Seed plant gametophytes rely on the sporophyte. Also, they do not need water for fertilization.
- Seeds nourish a young plant until it can make food by photosynthesis.
- Gymnosperms do not have flowers or fruits. Gymnosperm seeds are usually protected by cones. Gymnosperms are used for building materials, paper, resin, and medicines.
- Angiosperms have flowers and fruits. Angiosperms are used for food, medicines, fibers for clothing, rubber, and building materials.

Using Key Terms

1. In your own words, write a definition for each of the following terms: *pollen* and *pollination*.

Understanding Key Ideas

2. One advantage of seed plants is that
   a. seed plants grow in few places.
   b. they can begin photosynthesis as soon as they begin to grow.
   c. they need water for fertilization.
   d. young plants are nourished by food stored in the seed.
3. The gametophytes of seed plants
   a. live independently of the sporophytes.
   b. are very large.
   c. are protected in the reproductive structures of the sporophyte.
   d. None of the above
4. Describe the structure of seeds.
5. Briefly describe the four groups of gymnosperms. Which group is the largest and most economically important?
6. Compare angiosperms and gymnosperms.

Math Skills

7. More than 265,000 species of plants have been discovered. Approximately 235,000 of those species are angiosperms. What percentage of plants are NOT angiosperms?

Critical Thinking

8. **Making Inferences** In what ways are flowers and fruits adaptations that help angiosperms reproduce?
9. **Applying Concepts** An angiosperm lives in a dense rainforest, close to the ground. It receives little wind. Several herbivores live in this area of the rainforest. What are some ways the plant can ensure its seeds are carried throughout the forest?

SCILINKS®
NSTA
Developed and maintained by the National Science Teachers Association
For a variety of links related to this chapter, go to www.scilinks.org
Topic: Plants with Seeds
SciLinks code: HSM1168

SECTION 4

Structures of Seed Plants

You have different body systems that carry out many functions. Plants have systems too—a root system, a shoot system, and a reproductive system.

READING WARM-UP

Objectives

- List three functions of roots and three functions of stems.
- Describe the structure of a leaf.
- Identify the parts of a flower and their functions.

Terms to Learn

xylem
phloem
sepal
petal
stamen
pistil
ovary

READING STRATEGY

Mnemonics As you read this section, create a mnemonic device to help you remember the parts of a plant.

A plant's root system and shoot system supply the plant with what it needs to survive. The root system is made up of roots. The shoot system includes stems and leaves.

The vascular tissues of the root and shoot systems are connected. There are two kinds of vascular tissue—xylem (ZIE luhm) and phloem (FLOH EM). **Xylem** is vascular tissue that transports water and minerals through the plant. Xylem moves materials from the roots to the shoots. **Phloem** is vascular tissue that transports food molecules to all parts of a plant. Xylem and phloem are found in all parts of vascular plants.

xylem the type of tissue in vascular plants that provides support and conducts water and nutrients from the roots

phloem the tissue that conducts food in vascular plants

Roots

Most roots are underground, as shown in **Figure 1.** So, many people do not realize how extensive root systems can be. For example, a corn plant that is 2.5 m tall can have roots that grow 2.5 m deep and 1.2 m out and away from the stem!

Root Functions

The following are the three main functions of roots:

- Roots supply plants with water and dissolved minerals. These materials are absorbed from the soil. The water and minerals are transported to the shoots in the xylem.
- Roots hold plants securely in the soil.
- Roots store surplus food made during photosynthesis. The food is produced in the leaves. Then, it is transported in the phloem to the roots. In the roots, the surplus food is usually stored as sugar or starch.

Onion

Dandelion

Carrots

Figure 1 *The roots of these plants provide the plants with water and minerals.*

Root Structure

The structures of a root are shown in **Figure 2.** The layer of cells that covers the surface of roots is called the *epidermis.* Some cells of the epidermis extend from the root. These cells, or root hairs, increase the surface area of the root. This surface area helps the root absorb water and minerals. After water and minerals are absorbed by the epidermis, they diffuse into the center of the root, where the vascular tissue is located.

Roots grow longer at their tips. A group of cells called the *root cap* protects the tip of a root. The root cap produces a slimy substance. This substance makes it easier for the root to push through soil as it grows.

Root Systems

There are two kinds of root systems—taproot systems and fibrous root systems. A taproot system has one main root, or a taproot. The taproot grows downward. Many smaller roots branch from the taproot. Taproots can reach water deep underground. Dicots and gymnosperms usually have taproot systems.

A fibrous root system has several roots that spread out from the base of a plant's stem. The roots are usually the same size. Fibrous roots usually get water from close to the soil surface. Monocots usually have fibrous roots.

Reading Check **What are two types of root systems?** (*See the Appendix for answers to Reading Checks.*)

Practice with Percentages

The following table gives an estimate of the number of species in each plant group.

Plant Species

Plant group	Number of species
Mosses, liverworts, and hornworts	15,600
Ferns, horsetails, and club mosses	12,000
Gymnosperms	760
Angiosperms	235,000

What percentage of plants do not produce seeds?

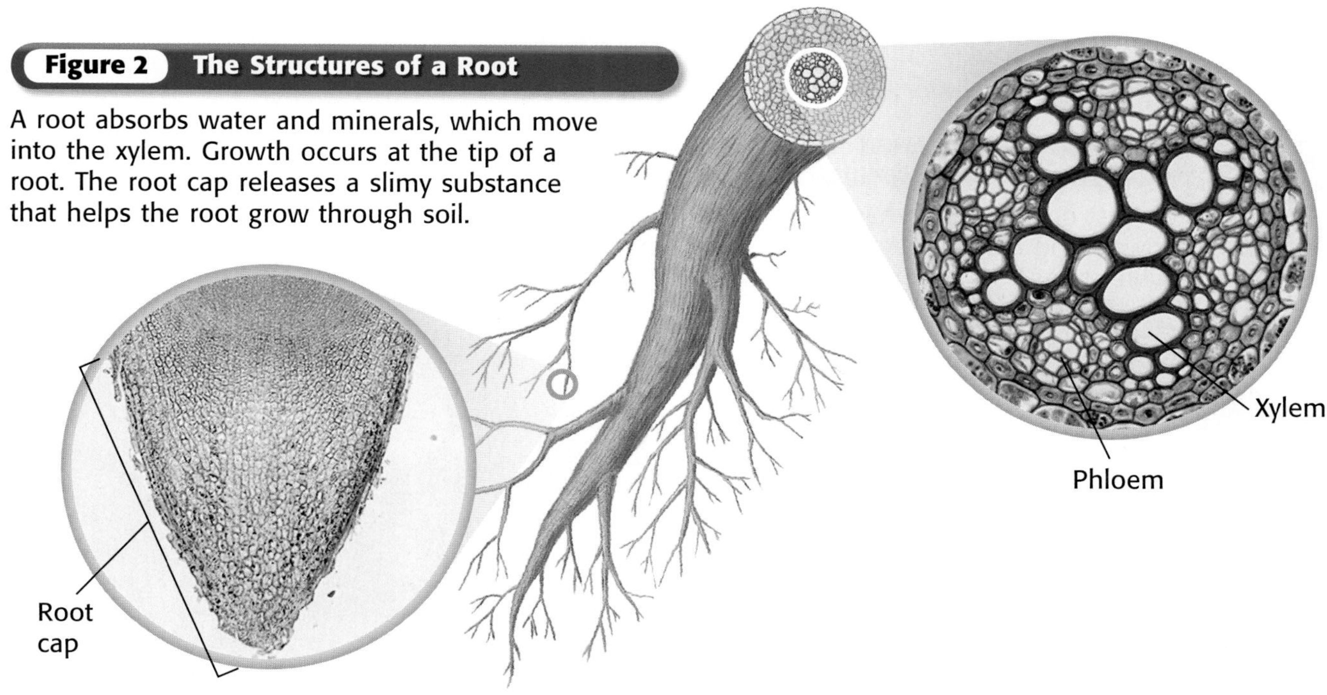

Figure 2 **The Structures of a Root**

A root absorbs water and minerals, which move into the xylem. Growth occurs at the tip of a root. The root cap releases a slimy substance that helps the root grow through soil.

Stems

Stems vary greatly in shape and size. Stems are usually located above ground. However, many plants have underground stems. The trunk of the valley oak in **Figure 3** is a stem.

Figure 3 *The stem, or trunk, of this valley oak keeps the tree upright, which helps leaves get sunlight for photosynthesis.*

Stem Functions

A stem connects a plant's roots to its leaves and flowers. A stem also has the following functions:

- Stems support the plant body. Leaves are arranged along stems or on the ends of stems. This arrangement helps leaves get sunlight for photosynthesis. Stems hold up flowers, which helps pollinators, such as bees, see the flowers.
- Stems transport materials between the root system and the shoot system. Xylem carries water and dissolved minerals from the roots to the leaves and other shoot parts. Phloem carries the food made during photosynthesis to roots and other parts of the plant.
- Some stems store materials. For example, the stems of cactuses and some trees are adapted for water storage.

Herbaceous Stems

Many plants have stems that are soft, thin, and flexible. These stems are called *herbaceous stems* (huhr BAY shuhs STEMZ). Examples of plants that have herbaceous stems include wildflowers, such as clovers and poppies. Many crops, such as beans, tomatoes, and corn, have herbaceous stems. A cross section of an herbaceous stem is shown in **Figure 4.**

Reading Check **What are herbaceous stems? Give an example of a plant that has an herbaceous stem.**

Figure 4 **Cross Section of an Herbaceous Stem**

Buttercups are just one plant that has herbaceous stems. Wildflowers and many vegetables have soft, thin, and flexible stems.

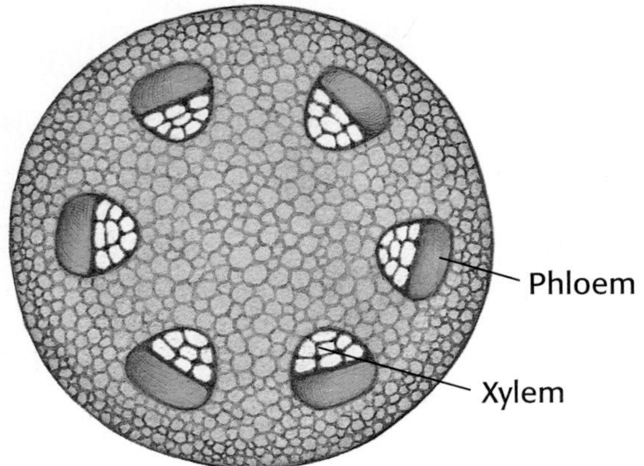

Figure 5 **Cross Section of a Woody Stem**

Some plants, such as these trees, have woody stems. Plants that have woody stems usually live for many years. People can use growth rings to estimate the age of a plant.

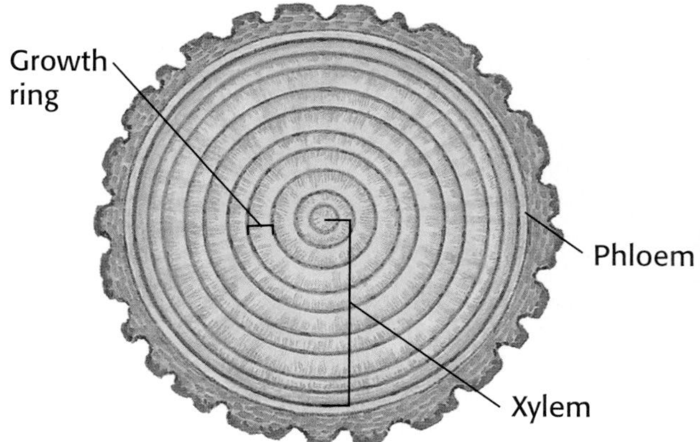

Woody Stems

Trees and shrubs have rigid stems made of wood and bark. These stems are called *woody stems*. **Figure 5** shows a cross section of a woody stem. Trees or shrubs that live in areas with cold winters have a growing period during the spring and summer. These plants have a dormant period during the winter. At the beginning of each growing period, large xylem cells are produced. As fall approaches, the plants produce smaller xylem cells, which appear darker. In the fall and winter, the plants stop producing new cells. The cycle begins again the next spring. A ring of dark cells surrounding a ring of light cells makes up a growth ring.

Leaves

Leaves vary greatly in shape. They may be round, narrow, heart-shaped, or fan-shaped. Leaves also vary in size. The raffia palm has leaves that may be six times longer than you are tall. The leaves of duckweed, a tiny aquatic plant, are so small that several of the leaves can fit on your fingernail. **Figure 6** shows a poison ivy leaf.

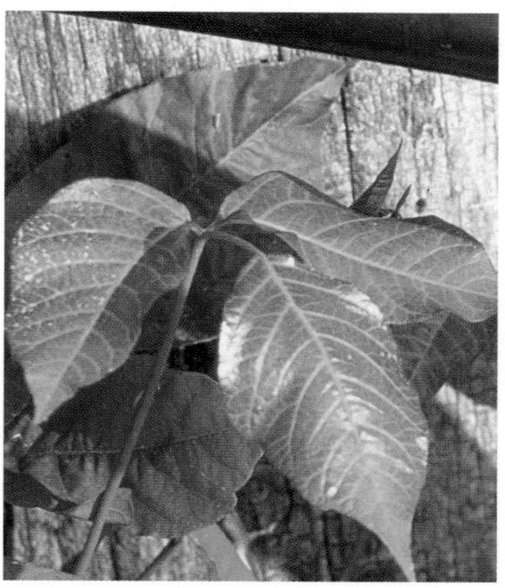

Figure 6 *The leaves of poison ivy are very distinctive. They make food to help the plant survive.*

Leaf Functions

The main function of leaves is to make food for the plant. Chloroplasts in the cells of leaves capture energy from sunlight. The leaves also absorb carbon dioxide from the air. The leaves use the captured energy to make food, or sugar, from carbon dioxide and water.

Figure 7 **The Structure of a Leaf**

Leaf cells are arranged in layers. These layers allow the leaf to work efficiently.

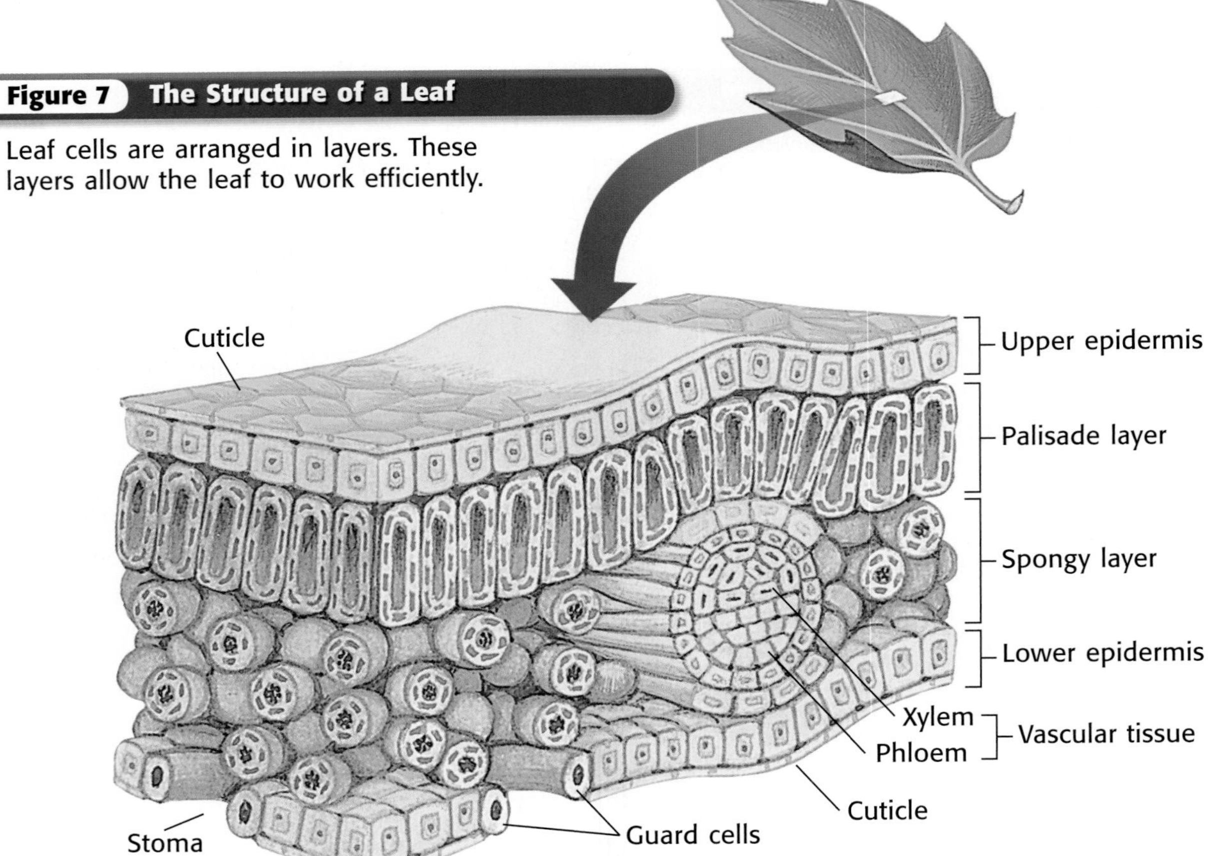

Leaf Structure

The structure of leaves, shown in **Figure 7,** is related to their main function—photosynthesis. The outer surfaces of a leaf are covered by a cuticle. The cuticle prevents water loss from the leaf. A single layer of cells, the epidermis, lies beneath the cuticle. Light passes through the epidermis. Tiny openings in the epidermis, called *stomata* (singular, *stoma*), let carbon dioxide enter the leaf. Guard cells open and close the stomata.

Most photosynthesis takes place in the middle of a leaf. This part of a leaf often has two layers. Cells in the upper layer, the palisade layer, contain many chloroplasts. Photosynthesis takes place in the chloroplasts. Carbon dioxide moves freely in the space between the cells of the second layer, the spongy layer. Xylem and phloem are also found in the spongy layer.

Reading Check What are the cell layers of a leaf?

Looking at Leaves

Leaves are many shapes and sizes. They are also arranged on a stem in many ways. Walk around your home. In your **science journal,** sketch the leaves of the plants you see. Notice how the leaves are arranged on the stem, the shapes of the leaves, and the veins in the leaves. Use a ruler to measure the size of the leaves.

ACTIVITY

Leaf Adaptations

Some leaves have functions other than photosynthesis. For example, the leaves of many cactuses are modified as spines. These spines keep animals from eating the cactuses. The leaves of another plant, the sundew, are modified to catch insects. Sundews grow in soil that does not contain enough nitrogen to meet the plants' needs. By catching and digesting insects, a sundew is able to get enough nitrogen.

Flowers

Most people admire the beauty of flowers, such as the wildflowers in **Figure 8.** But why do plants have flowers? Flowers are adaptations for sexual reproduction.

Flowers come in many shapes, colors, and fragrances. Brightly colored and fragrant flowers usually rely on animals for pollination. For example, some flowers look and smell like rotting meat. These flowers attract flies. The flies pollinate the flowers. Plants that lack brightly colored flowers and fragrances, such as grasses, depend on the wind to spread pollen.

Many flowers also produce nectar. Nectar is a fluid that contains sugar. Nectar attracts birds and insects. These animals move from flower to flower and drink the nectar. As they do so, they often carry pollen to the flowers.

sepal in a flower, one of the outermost rings of modified leaves that protect the flower bud

petal one of the ring or rings of the usually brightly colored, leaf-shaped parts of a flower

Sepals and Petals

Flowers usually have the following basic parts: sepals, petals, stamens, and one or more pistils. The flower parts are usually arranged in rings around the central pistil.

Sepals are modified leaves that make up the outermost ring of flower parts and protect the bud. Sepals are often green like other leaves. Sepals cover and protect the flower while it is a bud. As the blossom opens, the sepals fold back. Then, the petals can unfold and become visible. **Petals** are broad, flat, thin leaflike parts of a flower. Petals vary greatly in color and shape. Petals attract insects or other animals to the flower. These animals help plants reproduce by carrying pollen from flower to flower.

Figure 8 *Many flowers help the plants reproduce by attracting pollinators with bright petals and strong fragrances.*

Figure 9 **The Structure of a Flower**

The stamens, which produce pollen, and the pistil, which produces eggs, are surrounded by the petals and the sepals.

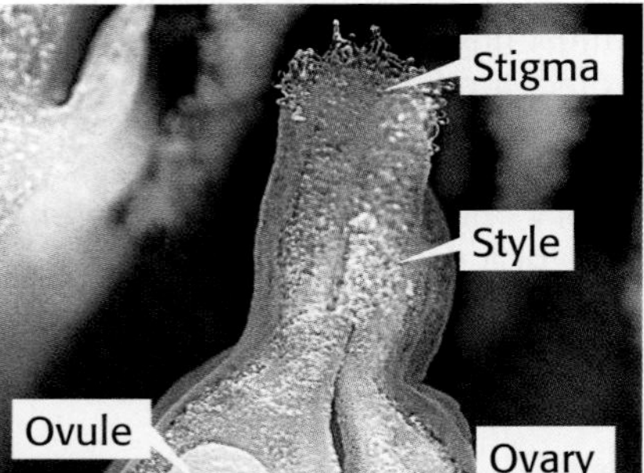

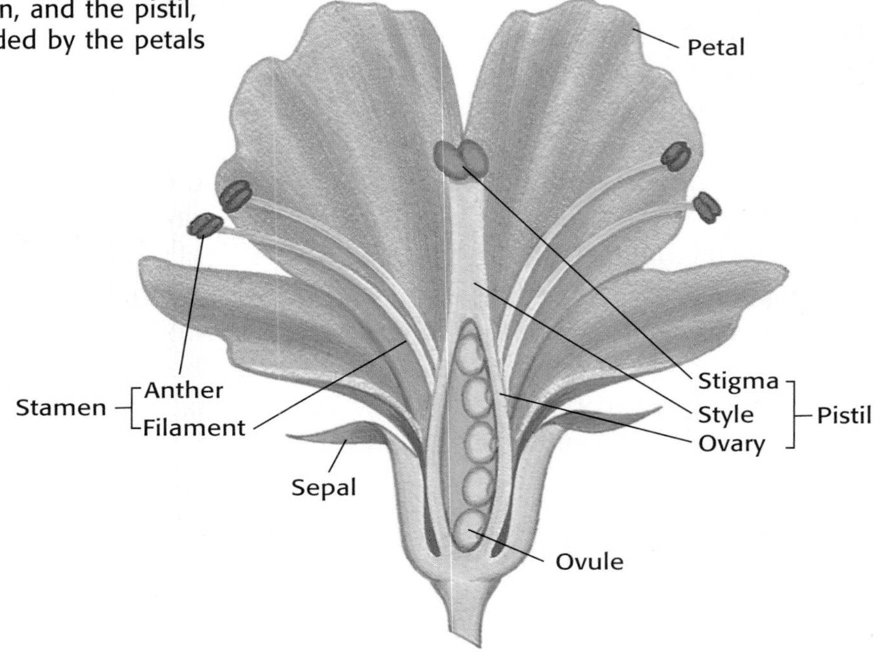

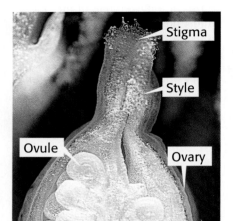

stamen the male reproductive structure of a flower that produces pollen and consists of an anther at the tip of a filament

pistil the female reproductive part of a flower that produces seeds and consists of an ovary, style, and stigma

ovary in flowering plants, the lower part of a pistil that produces eggs in ovules

Stamens and Pistils

As you can see in **Figure 9,** the stamens of flowers are usually found just above the petals. A **stamen** is a male reproductive structure of flowers. Each stamen has a thin stalk called a *filament*. The filament is topped by an anther. Anthers are saclike structures that produce pollen.

Found in the center of most flowers is one or more pistils. A **pistil** is the female reproductive structure of flowers. The tip of the pistil is called the *stigma*. Pollen grains collect on stigmas, which are often sticky or feathery. The long, slender part of the pistil is the style. The rounded base of a pistil that contains one or more ovules is called the **ovary.** Each ovule contains an egg. When the egg is fertilized, the ovule develops into a seed. The ovary develops into a fruit.

✓ Reading Check **Describe stamens and pistils. Which are the female parts of a flower? the male parts of a flower?**

The Importance of Flowers

Flowers help plants reproduce. Humans also use flowers for many things. Roses and many other flowers are used for floral arrangements. Some flowers, such as artichokes, broccoli, and cauliflower, can be eaten. Other flowers, such as hibiscus and chamomile flowers, are used to make tea. Flowers used as spices include cloves and saffron. Flowers are also used in perfumes, lotions, and shampoos.

SECTION
Review

Summary

- Roots supply plants with water and dissolved minerals. They support and anchor plants. Roots also store surplus food made during photosynthesis.
- Stems support the body of a plant. They allow transport of material between the root system and shoot system. Some stems store materials, such as water.
- A leaf has a thin epidermis on its upper and lower surfaces. The epidermis allows sunlight to pass through to the center of the leaf.
- Most photosynthesis takes place in the palisade layer of a leaf. The spongy layer of a leaf allows the movement of carbon dioxide and contains the xylem and phloem.
- The four main parts of a flower are the sepals, the petals, the stamens, and one or more pistils.
- Flowers are usually arranged around the pistil. The ovary of a pistil contains ovules. When the eggs are fertilized, ovules develop into seeds and the ovary becomes a fruit.

Using Key Terms

1. In your own words, write a definition for each of the following terms: *xylem, phloem, stamen,* and *pistil.*
2. Use each of the following terms in a separate sentence: *sepal, petal, pistil,* and *ovary.*

Understanding Key Ideas

3. Which of the following flower structures produces pollen?
   a. pistil
   b. filament
   c. anther
   d. stigma
4. The ___ of a leaf allows carbon dioxide to enter.
   a. stoma
   b. epidermis
   c. palisade layer
   d. spongy layer
5. Compare xylem and phloem.
6. Describe the internal structure of a leaf.
7. What are the functions of stems?
8. Identify the two types of stems, and briefly describe them.
9. How do people use flowers?

Critical Thinking

10. **Making Inferences** Describe two kinds of root systems. How does the structure of each system help the roots perform their three functions?
11. **Applying Concepts** Pampas grass flowers are found at the top of tall stems, are light-colored, and are unscented. Explain how pampas grass flowers are most likely pollinated.

Interpreting Graphics

Use the table below to answer the questions that follow.

Age of Trees in a Small Forest

Number of trees	Number of growth rings
5	71
1	73
3	68

12. How many trees are older than 70 years?
13. What is the average age of these trees, in years?

SCILINKS.
NSTA
Developed and maintained by the National Science Teachers Association
For a variety of links related to this chapter, go to www.scilinks.org
Topic: Structure of Seed Plants
SciLinks code: HSM1467

Model-Making Lab

Build a Flower

OBJECTIVES

Build a model of a flower.

Explain how the model represents an actual flower.

Describe the basic parts of a flower.

MATERIALS

- art materials such as colored paper, pipe cleaners, beads, and yarn
- card, index, 3 × 5 in.
- glue
- recycled items such as paper plates and cups, yogurt containers, wire, string, buttons, cardboard, and bottles
- scissors
- tape

SAFETY

Scientists often make models in the laboratory. Models help scientists understand processes and structures. Models are especially useful when scientists are trying to understand processes that are too small to be seen easily, such as pollination, or processes that are too large to be examined in a laboratory, such as the growth of a tree. Models also make it possible to examine the structures of objects, such as flowers.

In this activity, you will use your creativity and your understanding of the structure of a flower to make a model of a flower from recycled materials and art supplies.

Procedure

1. Draw a flower similar to the one shown in the figure below. This flower has both male and female parts. Not all flowers have this structure. The flowers of many species of plants have only male parts or only female parts, not both.

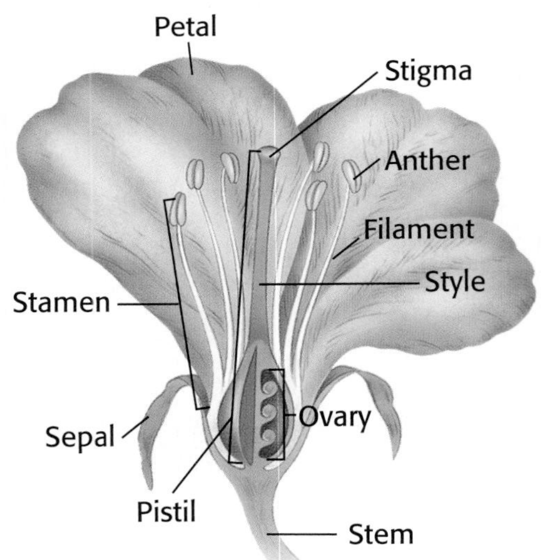

2. Decide which materials you will use to represent each flower part. Then, build a three-dimensional model of a flower that looks like one of the flowers shown on the next page. The model you build should contain each of the following parts: stem, sepals, petals, stamens (anther and filament), and pistil (stigma, style, and ovary).

Lily

Tulip

Hibiscus

3. After you build your model, draw a key for your flower model on an index card. Label each of the structures represented on your flower.

Analyze the Results

1. **Organizing Data** List the structures of a flower, and explain the function of each part.
2. **Identifying Patterns** What is the outermost part of your flower? the innermost part of your flower?
3. **Analyzing Data** How are your flower model and an actual flower alike? How are they different?

Draw Conclusions

4. **Drawing Conclusions** How might your flower attract pollinators? What modifications could you make to your flower to attract a greater number of pollinators?
5. **Evaluating Models** Is your model an accurate representation of a flower? Why or why not?
6. **Making Predictions** If you based your flower model on a plant species that had flowers that did not have both male and female parts, how would that model be different from your current model?

Applying Your Data

Research flowering plants whose flowers do not have both male and female reproductive parts. Build models of the male flower and the female flower for one of these flowering plants. Then, compare the new models to your original model, which includes both male and female reproductive parts.

Chapter Review

USING KEY TERMS

Complete each of the following sentences by choosing the correct term from the word bank.

pistil	rhizoid
vascular plant	rhizome
xylem	phloem
pollen	stamen
nonvascular plant	

1. A ___ is the male part of a flower.
2. ___ transports water and nutrients through a plant.
3. An underground stem that produces new leaves and roots is called a ___.
4. The male gametophytes of flowers are contained in structures called ___.
5. A ___ does not have specialized tissues for transporting water.
6. ___ transports food through a plant.

UNDERSTANDING KEY IDEAS

Multiple Choice

7. Which of the following statements about angiosperms is NOT true?
   a. Their seeds are protected by cones.
   b. They produce seeds.
   c. They provide animals with food.
   d. They have flowers.
8. Roots
   a. supply water and nutrients.
   b. anchor and support a plant.
   c. store surplus food.
   d. All of the above
9. Which of the following statements about plants and green algae is true?
   a. Plants and green algae may have a common ancestor.
   b. Green algae are plants.
   c. Plants and green algae have cuticles.
   d. None of the above
10. In which part of a leaf does most photosynthesis take place?
    a. palisade layer **c.** xylem
    b. phloem **d.** epidermis

Short Answer

11. List four characteristics that all plants share.
12. List the four main groups of plants.
13. Name three nonvascular plants and three seedless vascular plants.
14. Why do scientists think green algae and plants have a common ancestor?
15. How are seedless plants, gymnosperms, and angiosperms important to the environment?
16. What are two advantages that seeds have over spores?

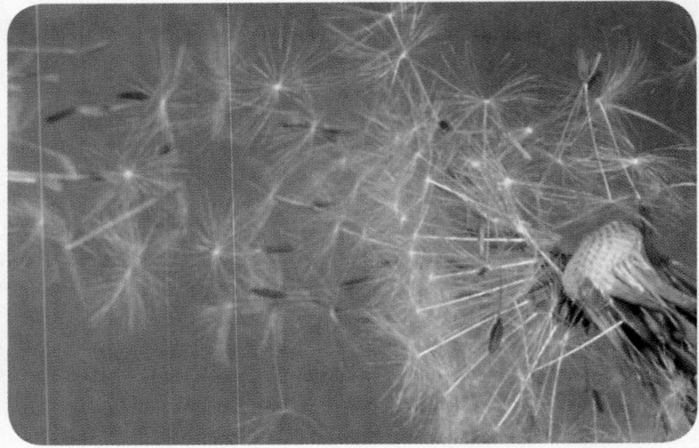

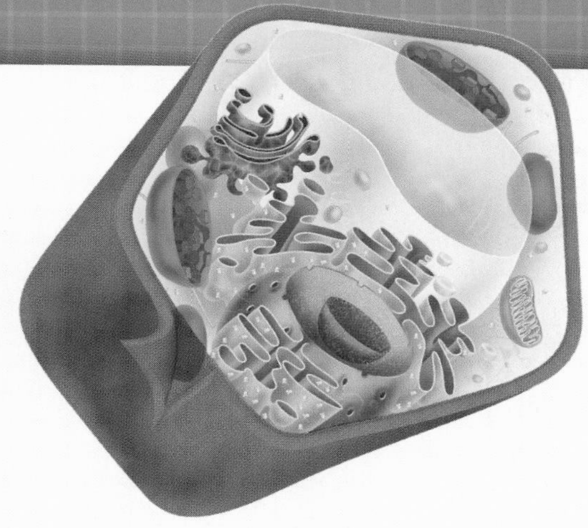

CRITICAL THINKING

17. **Concept Mapping** Use the following terms to create a concept map: *flowers, pollen, stamens, ovaries, pistils, stigmas, filaments, anthers, ovules, petals,* and *sepals.*

18. **Making Comparisons** Imagine that a seed and a spore are beginning to grow in a deep, dark crack in a rock. Which of the two is more likely to grow into an adult plant? Explain your answer.

19. **Identifying Relationships** Grass flowers do not have strong fragrances or bright colors. How might these characteristics be related to the way by which grass flowers are pollinated?

20. **Analyzing Ideas** Plants that are pollinated by wind produce more pollen than plants pollinated by animals do. Why might wind-pollinated plants produce more pollen?

21. **Applying Concepts** A scientist discovered a new plant. The plant has vascular tissue and produces seeds. It has brightly colored and strongly scented flowers. It also has sweet fruits. Based on this information, which of the four main types of plants did the scientist discover? How is the plant most likely pollinated? How does the plant most likely spread its seeds?

INTERPRETING GRAPHICS

22. Look at the cross section of a woody stem below. Use the diagram to determine the age of the tree.

Use the diagram of the flower below to answer the questions that follow.

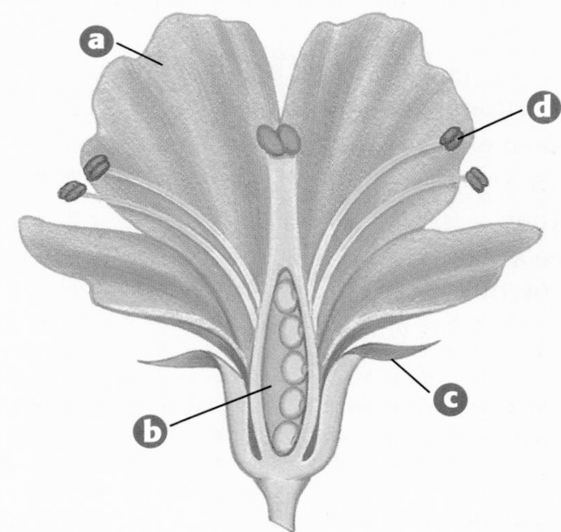

23. Which letter corresponds to the structure in which pollen is produced? What is the name of this structure?

24. Which letter corresponds to the structure that contains the ovules? What is the name of this structure?

25. Which letter corresponds to the structure that protects the flower bud? What is the name of this structure?

Standardized Test Preparation

READING

Read each of the passages below. Then, answer the questions that follow each passage.

Passage 1 Through genetic engineering, scientists are now able to duplicate one organism's DNA and place a certain gene from the DNA into the cells of another species of plant or animal. This technology enables scientists to give plants and animals a new trait that can then be passed on to future generations. There are two methods to introduce new DNA into plant cells. In one method, DNA is first placed inside a special bacterium, which carries the DNA into the plant cell. In the second method, microscopic particles of metal are coated with the new DNA and fired into the plant cells with a device called a *gene gun*.

1. Based on the passage, what does genetic engineering allow scientists to do?

A to breed better plants
B to move genes from one organism to another
C to see a very small object without a microscope
D to grow plants without soil

2. In the passage, what does the word *species* most likely mean?

F DNA
G future generations
H group of organisms
I genes

3. Based on the passage, what are the two most common ways genes are moved to plant cells?

A by bacteria and fungi
B by bacteria and a gene gun
C by fungi and a gene gun
D by particles of metal and a gene gun

Passage 2 The main function of leaves is photosynthesis, or the production of food. However, some leaves have functions other than photosynthesis. For example, the leaves on a cactus plant are modified as spines. These spines discourage animals from eating the cactus. The leaves of another plant, the sundew, are modified to catch insects. Sundews live in areas with nitrogen-poor soil. They don't get enough nitrogen from the soil to meet their needs. So, the plants use their modified leaves to catch insects. Then, the sundews digest the insects to get the nitrogen they need to survive.

1. Based on the passage, which of the following statements about photosynthesis is true?

A Photosynthesis produces modified leaves.
B Photosynthesis is how plants catch insects for food.
C Photosynthesis discourages animals from eating plants.
D Photosynthesis is how plants get food.

2. Based on the passage, what do the modified leaves of cactuses do?

F They discourage animals from eating them.
G They catch insects for nitrogen.
H They function mainly for photosynthesis.
I They help cactuses get enough nitrogen from the soil.

3. Based on the passage, what can be concluded about pitcher plants if they capture insects?

A They grow in areas with nitrogen-poor soil.
B They are trying to discourage animals from eating them.
C They don't need nitrogen from insects to survive.
D They have leaves that are modified as spines.

INTERPRETING GRAPHICS

The pie graph below shows the distribution of four types of plants. Use the pie graph below to answer the questions that follow.

Distribution of Plants

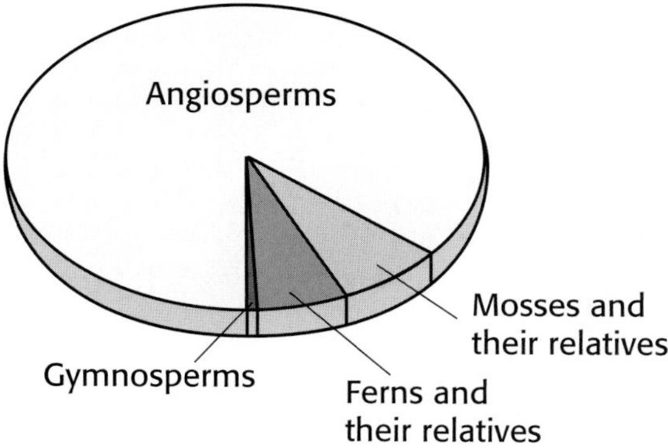

1. Which of the following types of plants is the least common?

A ferns and their relatives
B mosses and their relatives
C angiosperms
D gymnosperms

2. About what percentage of plants are angiosperms?

F 1%
G 10%
H 20%
I 80%

3. About what percentage of plants are mosses, ferns, and their relatives?

A 1%
B 10%
C 20%
D 80%

4. If there are about 265,000 species of plants, about how many of the species are mosses and relatives of mosses?

F 2,650 species
G 13,250 species
H 26,500 species
I 212,000 species

MATH

Read each question below, and choose the best answer.

1. Sophie wants to plant a garden. Her garden is 25 m wide. She puts a row of plants every half meter. Every fifth row is a row of flowers. If the rest of the rows are vegetables, about how many rows of vegetables are in the garden?

A 10 rows
B 25 rows
C 40 rows
D 50 rows

2. The area of a garden is 50 m^2. If the garden is 12 m long, which of the following equations expresses the value of *w*, the width of the garden?

F $w = 12 \times 50$
G $w = 50 \times 12$
H $w = 50 \div 12$
I $w = 12 \div 12$

3. There are 140 species of cycads. If 18% of gymnosperms are cycads, about how many gymnosperms are there?

A 25 gymnosperms
B 165 gymnosperms
C 775 gymnosperms
D 2,520 gymnosperms

4. A packet of cabbage seeds that contains enough seeds for two rows costs $2.00. A packet of carrots that contains enough seeds for three rows costs $2.25. If Katy wants to plant five rows of cabbage and seven rows of carrots, how much will the seeds cost?

F $12.75
G $12.00
H $8.50
I $6.00

Science in Action

Scientific Debate

Are Herbal Supplements Safe?

Humans have always used plants for food, for shelter, or for medicine. In fact, one of our most common medicines, aspirin, is similar to a chemical found in the bark of a willow tree. Today, many people still use natural plant products, such as pills or teas, as medicine. These products are often called *herbal supplements*. Echinacea, St. John's wort, and ma huang are just a few examples of the herbal supplements that people use to treat a variety of health problems. People spend billions of dollars on herbal supplements each year. But are herbal supplements safe to use?

Social Studies 

Make a poster illustrating a plant used for medicine by native cultures and the health problems the plant is used to treat.

Science, Technology, and Society

Plant Poachers

Imagine you're walking through a swamp. The swamp is full of life. You're surrounded by trees, vines, and water lilies. You can hear frogs singing and mosquitoes buzzing. Then, you notice a ghost orchid hanging from a tree branch. The flower of this orchid looks like a ghost or like a white frog leaping. For some people, this orchid is worth stealing. These people, called *plant poachers*, steal orchids and other plants from the wild. Many plant species and natural areas are threatened by plant theft.

Math ACTIVITY

A plant poacher stole 100 plants from a nature preserve. He planned on selling each plant for $50, but he was caught and was fined $300 for each plant he stole. What is the difference between the total fine and the total amount of money the plant poacher planned on selling the plants for?

Careers

Paul Cox

Ethnobotanist Paul Cox is an ethnobotanist. He travels to remote places to look for plants that can help treat diseases. He seeks the advice of native healers in his search. In Samoan cultures, the healer is one of the most valued members of the community. In 1984, Cox met a 78-year-old Samoan healer named Epenesa. Epenesa understood human anatomy, and she dispensed medicines with great accuracy.

After Cox spent months observing Epenesa, she gave him her treatment for yellow fever. Cox brought the yellow-fever remedy to the United States. In 1986, researchers at the National Cancer Institute found that the plant contains a virus-fighting chemical called *prostratin,* which may have potential as a treatment for AIDS.

When two of the Samoan healers that Cox observed died in 1993, generations of medical knowledge was lost with them. The healers' deaths show the urgency of recording this knowledge before all of the healers are gone. Cox and other ethnobotanists work hard to gather knowledge from healers before their knowledge is lost.

Language Arts ACTIVITY

WRITING SKILL Imagine that you are a healer. Write a letter to an ethnobotanist describing some of the plants you use to treat diseases.

To learn more about these Science in Action topics, visit go.hrw.com and type in the keyword HL5PL1F.

Current Science

Check out Current Science® articles related to this chapter by visiting go.hrw.com. Just type in the keyword HL5CS12.

Plant Processes

About the PHOTO

The plant in this photo is a Venus' flytrap. Those red and green spiny pads are its leaves. Like other plants, Venus' flytraps rely on photosynthesis to get energy. What is so unusual about the Venus' flytrap? Unlike most plants, the Venus' flytrap gets important nutrients, such as nitrogen, by capturing and digesting insects or other small animals.

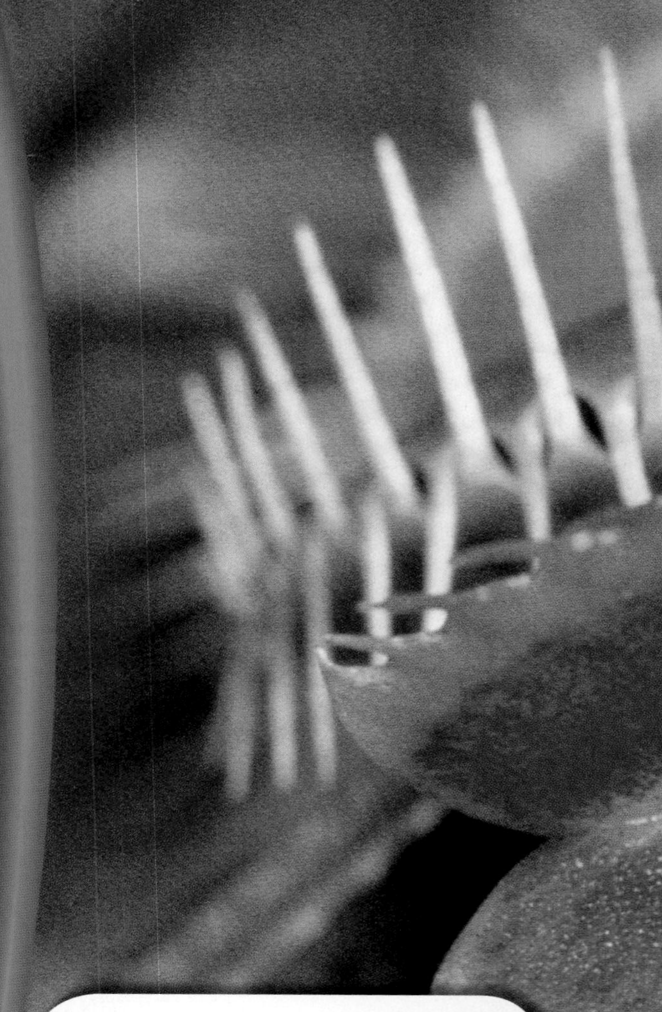

PRE-READING ACTIVITY

FOLDNOTES **Booklet** Before you read the chapter, create the FoldNote entitled "Booklet" described in the **Study Skills** section of the Appendix. Label each page of the booklet with a main idea from the chapter. As you read the chapter, write what you learn about each main idea on the appropriate page of the booklet.

START-UP ACTIVITY

Which End Is Up?

If you plant seeds with their "tops" facing in different directions, will their stems all grow upward? Do this activity to find out.

Procedure

1. Pack a **clear, medium-sized plastic cup** with slightly moistened **paper towels.**
2. Place **five or six corn seeds,** equally spaced, around the cup between the side of the cup and the paper towels. Point the tip of each seed in a different direction.
3. Using a **marker,** draw arrows on the outside of the cup to show the direction each seed tip points.
4. Place the cup in a well-lit location for 1 week. Keep the seeds moist by adding **water** to the paper towels as needed.
5. After 1 week, observe the seeds. Record the direction in which each shoot grew.

Analysis

1. In which direction did each of your shoots grow?
2. What might explain why your shoots grew the way they did?

SECTION 1

Photosynthesis

Plants don't have lungs. But like you, plants need air. Air contains oxygen, carbon dioxide, and other gases. Your body needs oxygen, and plants need oxygen. But what other gas is important to plants?

READING WARM-UP

Objectives

- Describe photosynthesis.
- Compare photosynthesis and cellular respiration.
- Describe how gas is exchanged in the leaves of plants.
- Describe two ways in which photosynthesis is important.

Terms to Learn

photosynthesis
chlorophyll
cellular respiration
stoma
transpiration

READING STRATEGY

Discussion Read this section silently. Write down questions that you have about this section. Discuss your questions in a small group.

If you guessed *carbon dioxide,* you are correct. Plants use carbon dioxide for photosynthesis (FOHT oh SIN thuh sis). **Photosynthesis** is the process by which plants make their own food. Plants capture energy from sunlight during photosynthesis. This energy is used to make the sugar glucose ($C_6H_{12}O_6$) from carbon dioxide (CO_2) and water (H_2O).

Capturing Light Energy

Plant cells have organelles called *chloroplasts* (KLAWR uh PLASTS), shown in **Figure 1.** Chloroplasts are surrounded by two membranes. Inside the chloroplast, another membrane forms stacks called *grana* (GRAY nuh). Grana contain a green pigment, called **chlorophyll** (KLAWR uh FIL), that absorbs light energy.

Sunlight is made up of many different wavelengths of light. Chlorophyll absorbs many of these wavelengths. But it reflects more wavelengths of green light than wavelengths of other colors of light. So, most plants look green.

Reading Check **Why are most plants green?** (*See the Appendix for answers to Reading Checks.*)

Figure 1 **Chloroplast Structure**

The grana found in chloroplasts contain chlorophyll, which captures energy from sunlight.

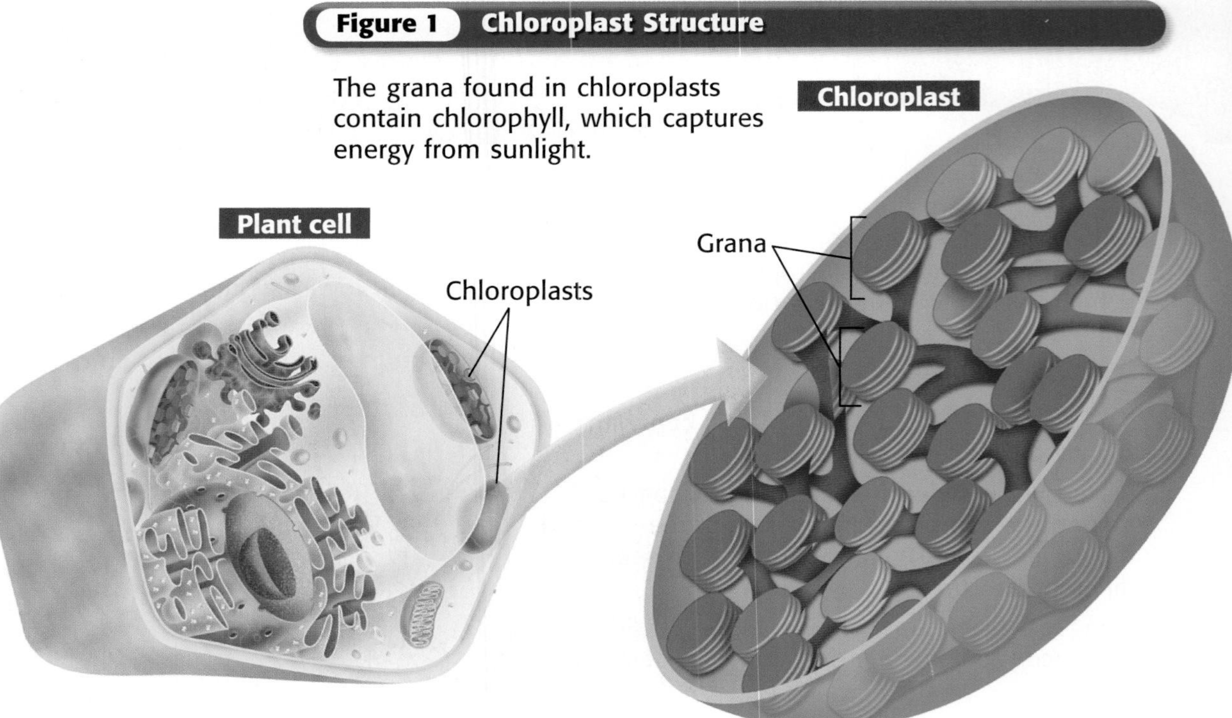

Making Sugar

The light energy captured by chlorophyll is used to help form glucose molecules. In turn, oxygen gas (O_2) is given off by plant cells. Photosynthesis is a complicated process made up of many steps. But photosynthesis can be summarized by the following chemical equation:

$$6CO_2 + 6H_2O \xrightarrow{\text{light energy}} C_6H_{12}O_6 + 6O_2$$

Six molecules of carbon dioxide and six molecules of water are needed to form one molecule of glucose and six molecules of oxygen. **Figure 2** shows where plants get the materials for photosynthesis.

Getting Energy from Sugar

Glucose molecules store energy. Plant cells use this energy for their life processes. To get energy, plant cells break down glucose and other food molecules in a process called **cellular respiration.** During this process, plant cells use oxygen. The cells give off carbon dioxide and water. Excess glucose is converted to another sugar called *sucrose* or stored as starch.

CONNECTION TO Social Studies

WRITING SKILL **Sugar** Some plants make and store large amounts of sucrose, or table sugar, during photosynthesis. People harvest these plants for sucrose. Identify a plant that produces large amounts of sucrose. Then, identify how people use the plant and which countries are major growers of the plant. Write an article about your findings in your **science journal.**

photosynthesis the process by which plants, algae, and some bacteria use sunlight, carbon dioxide, and water to make food

chlorophyll a green pigment that captures light energy for photosynthesis

cellular respiration the process by which cells use oxygen to produce energy from food

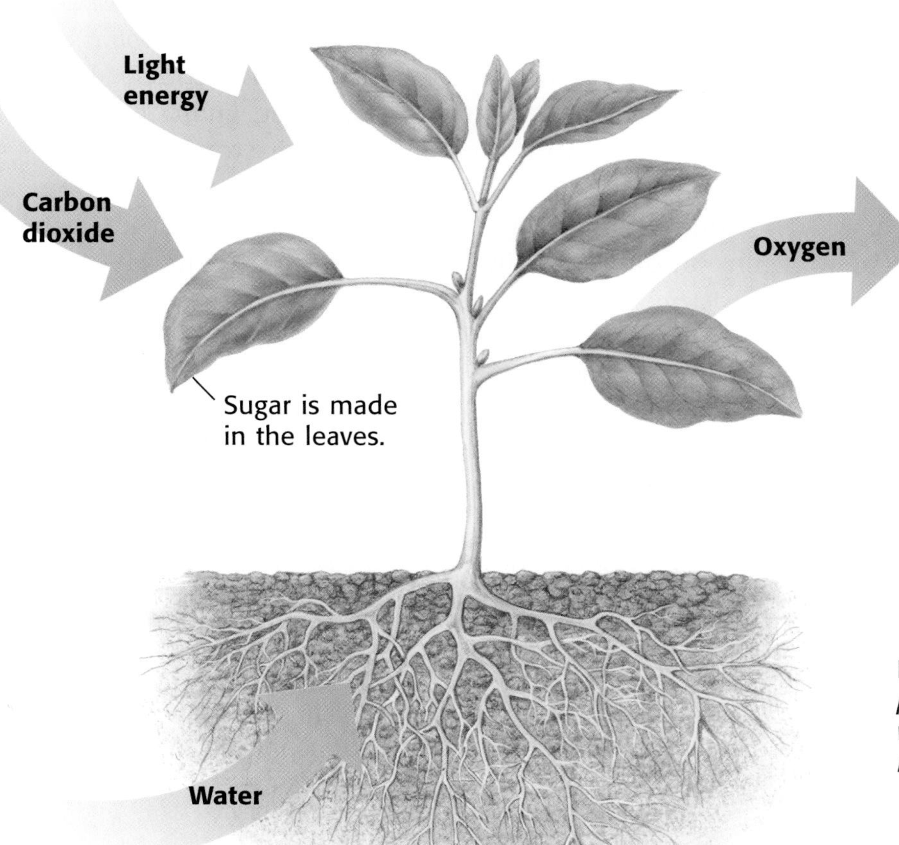

Figure 2 *During photosynthesis, plants take in carbon dioxide and water and absorb light energy. They make sugar and release oxygen.*

Figure 3 **Gas Exchange in Leaves**

When light is available for photosynthesis, the stomata are usually open. At nighttime, the stomata close to conserve water.

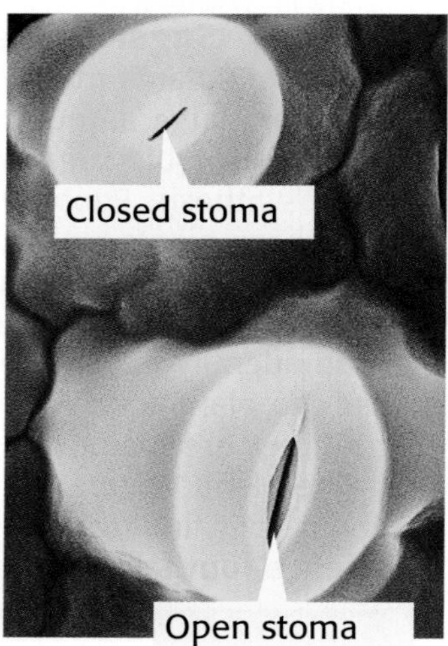

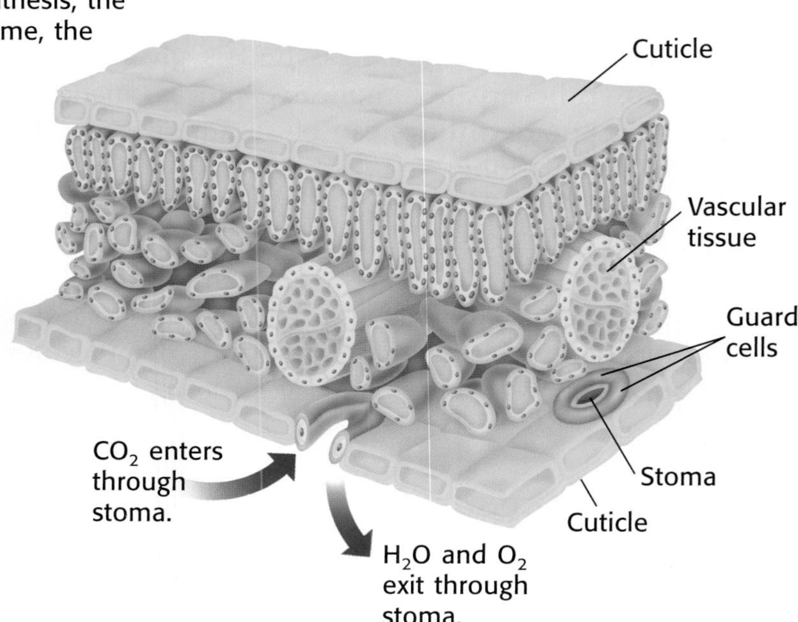

Gas Exchange

Many above-ground plant surfaces are covered by a waxy cuticle. The cuticle protects the plant from water loss. How does a plant get carbon dioxide through this barrier? Carbon dioxide enters the plant's leaves through stomata (singular, *stoma*). A **stoma** is an opening in the leaf's epidermis and cuticle. Each stoma is surrounded by two *guard cells*. The guard cells act like double doors, opening and closing the stoma. You can see stomata in **Figure 3.**

When stomata are open, carbon dioxide enters the leaf. The oxygen produced during photosynthesis exits the leaf through the stomata. Water vapor also exits the leaf in this way. The loss of water from leaves is called **transpiration.** Most of the water absorbed by a plant's roots replaces the water lost during transpiration. Sometimes, more water is lost through a plant's leaves than is absorbed by the plant's roots. When this happens, the plant wilts.

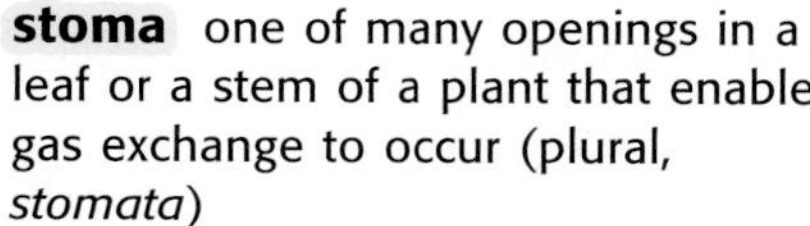

stoma one of many openings in a leaf or a stem of a plant that enable gas exchange to occur (plural, *stomata*)

transpiration the process by which plants release water vapor into the air through stomata

CONNECTION TO Chemistry

Transpiration Wrap a plastic bag around the branch of a tree or a portion of a potted plant. Secure the bag closed with a piece of tape or a rubber band, but be sure not to injure the plant. Record what happens over the next few days. What happened to the bag? How does this illustrate transpiration?

ACTIVITY

The Importance of Photosynthesis

Plants and other photosynthetic organisms, such as some bacteria and many protists, form the base of nearly all food chains on Earth. An example of one food chain is shown in **Figure 4.** During photosynthesis, plants store light energy as chemical energy. Some animals use this chemical energy when they eat plants. Other animals get energy from plants indirectly. These animals eat animals that eat plants. Most organisms could not survive without photosynthetic organisms.

Plants, animals, and most other organisms rely on cellular respiration to get energy. Cellular respiration requires oxygen. Oxygen is a byproduct of photosynthesis. So, photosynthesis provides the oxygen that animals and plants need for cellular respiration.

Reading Check **What are two ways in which photosynthesis is important?**

Figure 4 *Mice rely on plants for food. In turn, cats get energy from mice.*

SECTION Review

Summary

- During photosynthesis, plants use energy from sunlight, carbon dioxide, and water to make food.
- Plants get energy from food by cellular respiration, which uses oxygen and releases carbon dioxide and water.
- Transpiration, or the loss of water through the leaves, happens when stomata are open.
- Photosynthesis provides oxygen. Most animals rely on photosynthetic organisms for food.

Using Key Terms

1. In your own words, write a definition for each of the following terms: *photosynthesis*, *chlorophyll*, and *cellular respiration*.

Understanding Key Ideas

2. During photosynthesis, plants
   a. absorb energy from sunlight.
   b. use carbon dioxide and water.
   c. make food and oxygen.
   d. All of the above
3. How is cellular respiration related to photosynthesis?
4. Describe gas exchange in plants.

Math Skills

5. Plants use 6 carbon dioxide molecules and 6 water molecules to make 1 glucose molecule. How many carbon dioxide and water molecules would be needed to make 12 glucose molecules?

Critical Thinking

6. **Predicting Consequences** Predict what might happen if plants and other photosynthetic organisms disappeared.
7. **Applying Concepts** Light filters let through certain colors of light. Predict what would happen if you grew a plant under a green light filter.

For a variety of links related to this chapter, go to www.scilinks.org

Topic: Photosynthesis
SciLinks code: HSM1140

SECTION 2

Reproduction of Flowering Plants

READING WARM-UP

Objectives

- Describe pollination and fertilization in flowering plants.
- Explain how fruits and seeds are formed from flowers.
- List three reasons why a seed might be dormant.
- List three examples of asexual reproduction in plants.

Terms to Learn

dormant

READING STRATEGY

Reading Organizer As you read this section, make a table comparing sexual reproduction and asexual reproduction in plants.

Imagine you are standing in a field of wildflowers. You're surrounded by bright colors and sweet fragrances. You can hear bees buzzing from flower to flower.

Flowering plants are the largest and most diverse group of plants. Their success is partly due to their flowers. Flowers are adaptations for sexual reproduction. During sexual reproduction, an egg is fertilized by a sperm.

Fertilization

In flowering plants, fertilization takes place within flowers. *Pollination* happens when pollen is moved from anthers to stigmas. Usually, wind or animals move pollen from one flower to another flower. Pollen contains sperm. After pollen lands on the stigma, a tube grows from each pollen grain. The tube grows through the style to an ovule. Ovules are found inside the ovary. Each ovule contains an egg. Sperm from the pollen grain move down the pollen tube and into an ovule. Fertilization happens when a sperm fuses with the egg inside an ovule. **Figure 1** shows pollination and fertilization.

Figure 1 Pollination and Fertilization

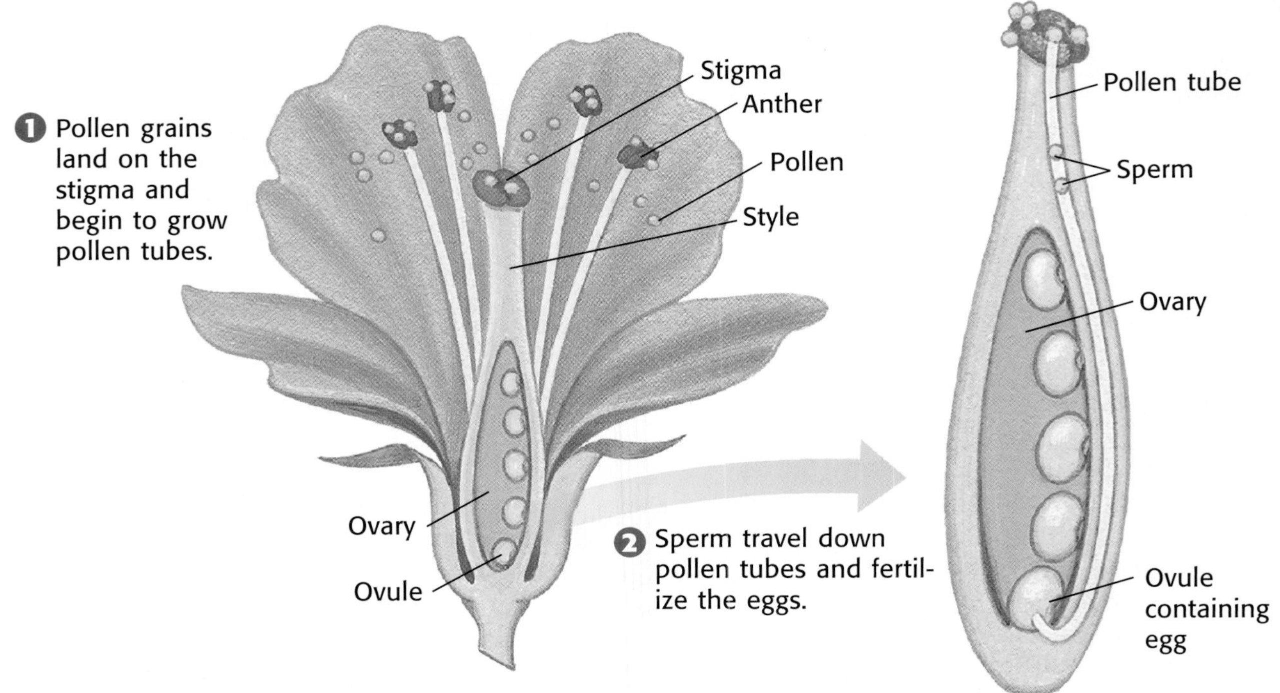

1 Pollen grains land on the stigma and begin to grow pollen tubes.
Stigma
Anther
Pollen
Style
Ovary
Ovule
2 Sperm travel down pollen tubes and fertilize the eggs.
Pollen tube
Sperm
Ovary
Ovule containing egg

Figure 2 Seed Production

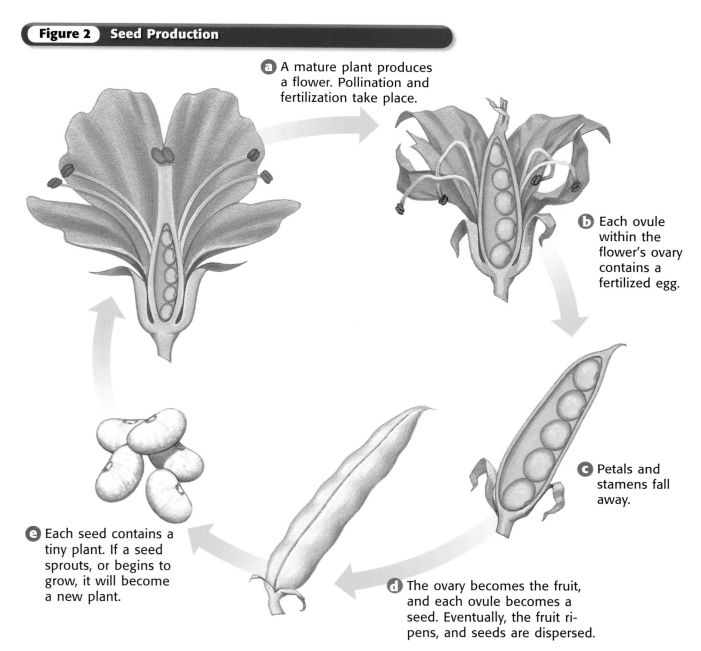

a A mature plant produces a flower. Pollination and fertilization take place.

b Each ovule within the flower's ovary contains a fertilized egg.

c Petals and stamens fall away.

d The ovary becomes the fruit, and each ovule becomes a seed. Eventually, the fruit ripens, and seeds are dispersed.

e Each seed contains a tiny plant. If a seed sprouts, or begins to grow, it will become a new plant.

From Flower to Fruit

After fertilization takes place, the ovule develops into a seed. The seed contains a tiny, undeveloped plant. The ovary surrounding the ovule becomes a fruit, as shown in **Figure 2.**

As a fruit swells and ripens, it protects the developing seeds. **Figure 3** shows a common fruit. Fruits often help a plant spread its seeds. Many fruits are edible. Animals may eat these fruits. Then, the animals discard the seeds away from the parent plant. Other fruits, such as burrs, get caught in an animal's fur. Some fruits are carried by the wind.

Reading Check **How do fruits help a plant spread its seeds?** (*See the Appendix for answers to Reading Checks.*)

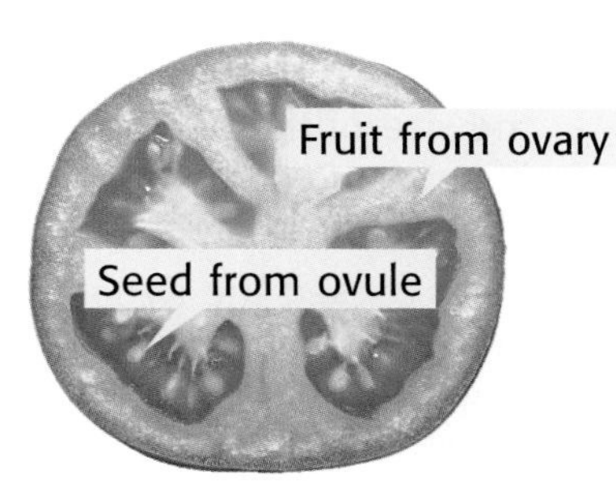

Figure 3 *Tomatoes develop from a flower's ovary and ovules.*

Figure 4 *Seeds grow into new plants. The roots begin to grow first. Then, the shoot grows up through the soil.*

From Seed to Plant

Once a seed is fully developed, the young plant inside the seed stops growing. The seed may become dormant. When seeds are **dormant,** they are inactive. Dormant seeds often survive long periods of drought or freezing temperatures. Some seeds need extreme conditions, such as cold winters or forest fires, to break their dormancy.

dormant describes the inactive state of a seed or other plant part when conditions are unfavorable to growth

When seeds are dropped or planted in a suitable environment, the seeds sprout. To sprout, most seeds need water, air, and warm temperatures. Each plant species has an ideal temperature at which most of its seeds will begin to grow. For many plants, the ideal temperature for growth is about 27°C (80.6°F). **Figure 4** shows the *germination* (JUHR muh NAY shuhn), or sprouting, of a bean seed.

Thirsty Seeds

1. Fill a **Petri dish** two-thirds full of **water,** and add **six dry bean seeds.** Using a **wax pencil,** label the dish "Water."
2. Add **six dry bean seeds** to a dry **Petri dish.** Label this dish "Control."
3. The next day, compare the size of the two sets of seeds. Record your observations.
4. What caused the size of the seeds to change? Why might this be important to the seed's survival?

Other Methods of Reproduction

Flowering plants may also reproduce asexually. For asexual reproduction, plants do not need flowers. Part of a plant, such as a stem or root, produces a new plant. The following are three structures plants use to reproduce asexually:

- **Plantlets** Tiny plants grow along the edges of a plant's leaves. These plantlets fall off and grow on their own.
- **Tubers** Underground stems, or tubers, can produce new plants after a dormant season.
- **Runners** Above-ground stems from which new plants can grow are called *runners.*

You can see an example of each kind of asexual reproduction in **Figure 5.**

Reading Check **What are three structures plants use to reproduce asexually?**

Figure 5 Three Structures for Asexual Reproduction

Kalanchoe plants produce **plantlets** along the edges of their leaves. The plantlets eventually fall off and root in the soil to grow on their own.

A potato is a **tuber,** or underground stem. The "eyes" of potatoes are buds that can grow into new plants.

The strawberry plant produces **runners,** or stems that grow horizontally along the ground. Buds along the runners take root and grow into new plants.

SECTION Review

Summary

- After pollination, a pollen tube forms from the stigma to an ovule. This tube allows a sperm to fertilize an egg.
- After fertilization, seeds and fruit form. The seeds are protected by fruit.
- A dormant seed can survive drought and freezing temperatures. Some seeds need extreme conditions to break their dormancy.
- Some plants use plantlets, tubers, or runners to reproduce asexually.

Using Key Terms

1. In your own words, write a definition for the term *dormant*.

Understanding Key Ideas

2. Pollination happens when
   a. a pollen tube forms.
   b. a sperm cell fuses with an egg.
   c. pollen is transferred from the anther to the stigma.
   d. None of the above
3. Which part of a flower develops into a fruit? into a seed?
4. Why do seeds become dormant?
5. Describe how plants reproduce asexually.

Math Skills

6. A seed sprouts when the temperature is 27°C. If the temperature is now 20°C and it rises 1.5°C per week, in how many weeks will the seed sprout?

Critical Thinking

7. **Making Inferences** What do flowers and runners have in common? How do they differ?
8. **Identifying Relationships** When might asexual reproduction be important for the survival of some flowering plants?
9. **Analyzing Ideas** Sexual reproduction produces more genetic variety than asexual reproduction. Why is variety important?

SCILINKS.
NSTA
Developed and maintained by the National Science Teachers Association
For a variety of links related to this chapter, go to www.scilinks.org
Topic: Reproduction of Plants
SciLinks code: HSM1295

SECTION 3

Plant Responses to the Environment

READING WARM-UP

Objectives

- Describe how plants may respond to light and gravity.
- Explain how some plants respond to night length.
- Describe how some plants respond to the changes of season.

Terms to Learn

tropism

READING STRATEGY

Discussion Read this section silently. Write down questions that you have about this section. Discuss your questions in a small group.

What happens when you get really cold? Do your teeth chatter? Or do you shiver? Anything that causes a reaction in your body is a stimulus *(plural,* stimuli*). But would a plant respond to a stimulus?*

Plants do respond to stimuli! For example, they respond to light, gravity, and changing seasons.

Plant Tropisms

Some plants respond to an environmental stimulus by growing in a particular direction. Growth in response to a stimulus is called a **tropism** (TROH PIZ uhm). Tropisms are either positive or negative. Plant growth toward a stimulus is a positive tropism. Plant growth away from a stimulus is a negative tropism.

tropism the growth of all or part of an organism in response to an external stimulus, such as light

Light

What happens if you place a houseplant so that it gets light from only one direction, such as from a window? The shoot tips probably bend toward the light. Bending toward the light is a positive tropism. A change in the direction a plant grows that is caused by light is called *phototropism* (FOH toh TROH PIZ uhm). The result of phototropism is shown in **Figure 1.** Shoots bend because cells on one side of the shoot grow longer than cells on the other side of the shoot.

Reading Check **What happens when a plant gets light from only one direction?** (*See the Appendix for answers to Reading Checks.*)

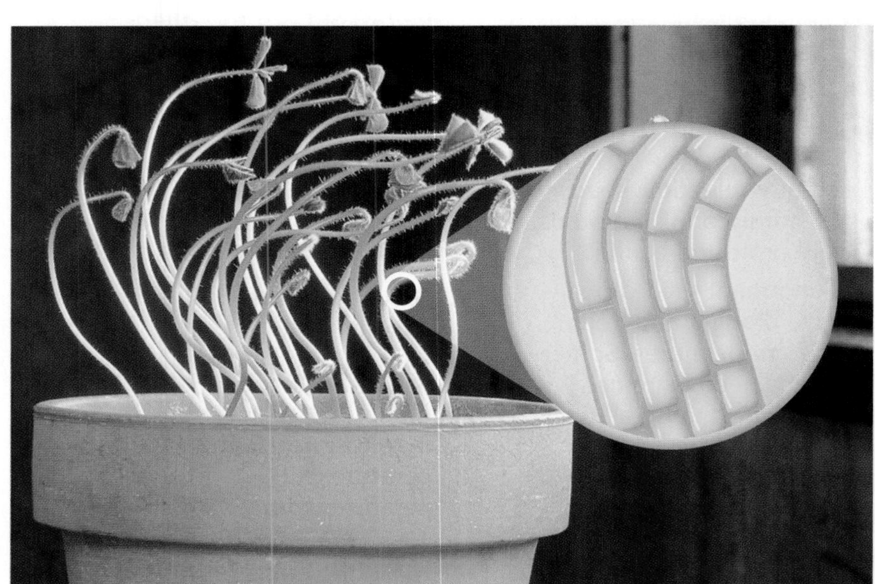

Figure 1 *The plant cells on the dark side of the shoot grow longer than the cells on the other side. So, the shoot bends toward the light.*

Figure 2 Gravitropism

To grow away from the pull of gravity, this plant has grown upward.

This plant has recently been upside down.

MATH PRACTICE

Bending by Degrees

Suppose a plant has a positive phototropism and bends toward light at a rate of 0.3° per minute. In how many hours will the plant bend 90°?

Gravity

Plant growth also changes in response to the direction of gravity. This change is called *gravitropism* (GRAV i TROH PIZ uhm). The effect of gravitropism is demonstrated by the plants in **Figure 2.** A few days after a plant is placed on its side or turned upside down, the roots and shoots change direction of growth. Most shoot tips have negative gravitropism. They grow upward, away from the center of the Earth. In contrast, most root tips have positive gravitropism. Roots grow downward, toward the center of the Earth.

Seasonal Responses

What would happen if a plant living in an area that has very cold winters flowered in December? Would the plant be able to successfully produce seeds and fruits? Probably not. The plant's flowers would likely freeze and die. So, the flowers would never produce mature seeds.

Plants living in regions with cold winters can detect the change in seasons. How do plants do this? As fall and winter approach, the days get shorter, and the nights get longer. The opposite happens when spring and summer approach. Plants respond to the change in the length of day.

For another activity related to this chapter, go to **go.hrw.com** and type in the keyword **HL5PL2W.**

Reading Check How do plants detect seasonal changes?

Figure 3 **Night Length and Flower Color**

Early summer

Night length

Day length

In the early summer, night length is short. At this time, poinsettia leaves are all green, and there are no flowers.

Late fall

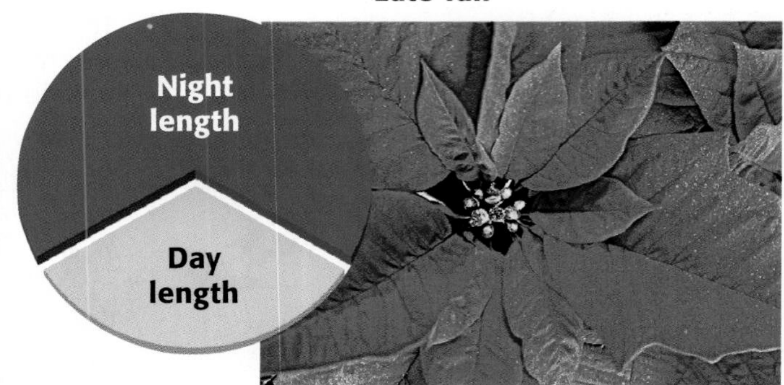

Poinsettias flower in the fall, when nights are longer. The leaves surrounding the flower clusters turn red. Professional growers use artificial lighting to control the timing of this color change.

Length of Day

The difference between day length and night length is an important environmental stimulus for many plants. This stimulus can cause plants to begin reproducing. For example, some plants flower in fall or winter. At this time, night length is long. These plants are called *short-day plants*. Poinsettias, such as those shown in **Figure 3,** are short-day plants. Chrysanthemums are also short-day plants. Other plants flower in spring or early summer, when night length is short. These plants are called *long-day plants*. Clover, spinach, and lettuce are examples of long-day plants.

Earth's Orbit and the Seasons

The seasons are caused by Earth's tilt and its orbit around the sun. Research how Earth's orbit determines the seasons. With a parent, make a model of the Earth's orbit around the sun to illustrate your findings.

ACTIVITY

Seasons and Leaf Loss

All trees lose their leaves. Some trees, such as pine and holly, shed some of their leaves year-round so that some leaves are always on the tree. These trees are called *evergreen trees*. Evergreen trees have leaves adapted to survive throughout the year. The leaves are often covered with a thick cuticle. This cuticle protects the leaves from cold and dry weather.

Other trees, such as maple, oak, and elm trees, are called *deciduous* (dee SIJ oo uhs) *trees*. These trees lose all of their leaves around the same time each year. In colder areas, deciduous trees usually lose their leaves before winter begins. In warmer climates that have wet and dry seasons, deciduous trees lose their leaves before the dry season. The loss of leaves helps plants survive low temperatures or long periods without rain.

Reading Check Compare evergreen trees and deciduous trees.

Figure 4 Amount of Pigment Based on Season

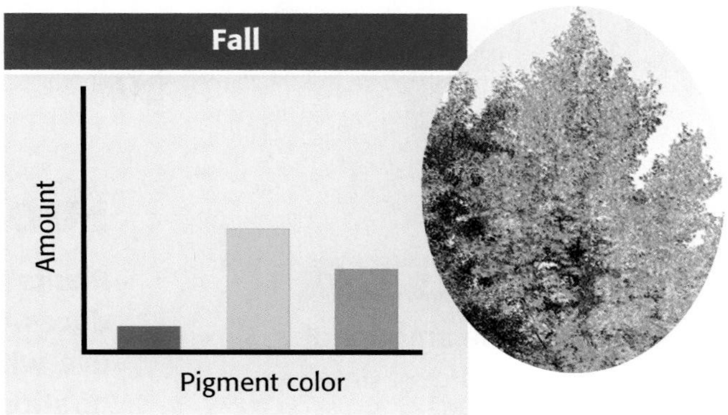

Seasons and Leaf Color

As shown in **Figure 4,** the leaves of deciduous trees may change color before they are lost. As fall approaches, green chlorophyll breaks down. Orange or yellow pigments in the leaves are then revealed. These pigments were always present in the leaves. But they were hidden by green chlorophyll.

SECTION Review

Summary

- Plant growth in response to a stimulus is called a tropism. Tropisms are positive or negative.
- Plants react to light, gravity, and changing seasons.
- Short-day plants flower when night length is long. Long-day plants flower when night length is short.
- Evergreen trees do not lose all their leaves at one time. Deciduous trees lose their leaves at the same time each year.

Using Key Terms

1. In your own words, write a definition for the term *tropism*.

Understanding Key Ideas

2. Deciduous trees lose their leaves
   a. to conserve water during the dry season.
   b. around the same time each year.
   c. to survive low winter temperatures.
   d. All of the above
3. How do light and gravity affect plants?
4. Describe how day length can affect the flowering of plants.

Math Skills

5. A certain plant won't bloom until it is dark for 70% of a 24 h period. How long is the day when the plant will bloom?

Critical Thinking

6. **Making Inferences** Many evergreen trees live in areas with long, cold winters. Why might these evergreen trees keep their leaves all year?
7. **Analyzing Ideas** Some short-day plants bloom during the winter. If cold weather reduces the chances that a plant will produce seeds, what might you conclude about where these short-day plants are found?

For a variety of links related to this chapter, go to www.scilinks.org

Topic: Plant Tropisms; Plant Growth
SciLinks code: HSM1166; HSM1159

Skills Practice Lab

Food Factory Waste

OBJECTIVES

Measure the amount of gas produced over time by photosynthesis.

Draw a graph of the amount of gas produced versus time.

MATERIALS

- baking-soda-and-water solution, 5% (500 mL)
- beaker (600 mL)
- *Elodea* sprigs, 20 cm long (2–3)
- funnel
- gloves, protective
- ruler, metric
- test tube

SAFETY

Plants use photosynthesis to make food. Photosynthesis produces oxygen gas. Humans and many other organisms cannot live without this oxygen. Oxygen is necessary for cellular respiration. In this activity, you will determine the rate of oxygen production for an *Elodea* plant.

Procedure

1. Add 450 mL of baking-soda-and-water solution to a beaker.
2. Put two or three sprigs of *Elodea* in the beaker. The baking soda will provide the *Elodea* with the carbon dioxide it needs for photosynthesis.
3. Place the wide end of the funnel over the *Elodea*. The small end of the funnel should be pointing up. The *Elodea* and the funnel should be completely under the solution.
4. Fill a test tube with the remaining baking-soda-and-water solution. Place your thumb over the end of the test tube, and turn the test tube upside down. Make sure no air enters the test tube. Hold the opening of the test tube under the solution. Place the test tube over the small end of the funnel. Try not to let any solution out of the test tube.

5. Place the beaker setup in a well-lit area.
6. Prepare a data table similar to the one below.

Amount of Gas Present in the Test Tube		
Days of exposure to light	Total amount of gas present (mm)	Amount of gas produced per day (mm)
0		
1		
2		
3		
4	DO NOT WRITE IN BOOK	
5		

7. If no air entered the test tube, record that there was 0 mm of gas in the test tube on day 0. If air got into the tube while you were placing it, measure the height of the column of air in the test tube in millimeters. Measure the gas in the test tube from the middle of the curve on the bottom of the upside-down test tube to the level of the solution. Record this number for day 0.
8. As described in the previous step, measure the amount of gas in the test tube each day for the next 5 days. Record your measurements in the second column of your data table.
9. Calculate the amount of gas produced each day. Subtract the amount of gas present on the previous day from the amount of gas present on the current day. Record these amounts in the third column of your data table.

Analyze the Results

1. **Constructing Graphs** Make a graph similar to the one below. Based on your measurements, your graph should show the amount of gas produced versus time.

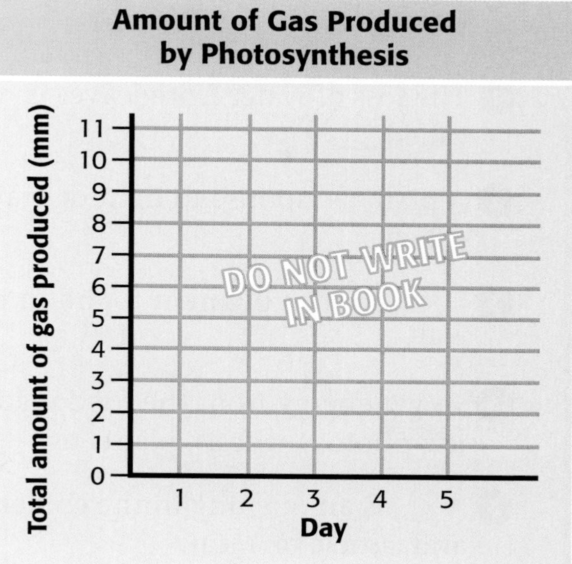

2. **Describing Events** Based on your graph, what happened to the amount of gas in the test tube?

Draw Conclusions

3. **Interpreting Information** Write the equation for photosynthesis. Then, relate each part of your experiment to the part of the equation it represents.

Applying Your Data

As you can see from your results, *Elodea* produces oxygen gas as a byproduct of photosynthesis. Research photosynthesis. Find out if there are factors that affect the rate of photosynthesis. Then, predict what would happen to the production of oxygen gas.

Chapter Review

USING KEY TERMS

Complete each of the following sentences by choosing the correct term from the word bank.

stoma	photosynthesis
dormant	cellular respiration
tropism	chlorophyll
transpiration	

1. The loss of water from leaves is called ___.
2. A plant's response to light or gravity is called a ___.
3. ___ is a green pigment found in plant cells.
4. To get energy from the food made during photosynthesis, plants use ___.
5. A ___ is an opening in the epidermis and cuticle of a leaf.
6. An inactive seed is ___.
7. ___ is the process by which plants make their own food.

UNDERSTANDING KEY IDEAS

Multiple Choice

8. During gas exchange in plants,
   a. carbon dioxide exits while oxygen and water enter the leaf.
   b. oxygen and water exit while carbon dioxide enters the leaf.
   c. carbon dioxide and water enter while oxygen exits the leaf.
   d. carbon dioxide and oxygen enter while water exits the leaf.

9. Plants often respond to light from one direction by
   a. bending away from the light.
   b. bending toward the light.
   c. wilting.
   d. None of the above

10. Which of the following is NOT a way that plants reproduce asexually?
    a. runners
    b. tubers
    c. flowers
    d. plantlets

Short Answer

11. Compare short-day plants and long-day plants.
12. How do potted plants respond to gravity if placed on their sides?
13. Describe the pollination and fertilization of flowering plants.
14. What three things do seeds need before they will sprout?
15. Explain how fruits and seeds form from flowers.
16. Compare photosynthesis and cellular respiration.
17. What are two ways in which photosynthesis is important?

CRITICAL THINKING

18 **Concept Mapping** Use the following terms to create a concept map: *plants, cellular respiration, light energy, photosynthesis, chemical energy, carbon dioxide,* and *oxygen.*

19 **Making Inferences** Many plants live in areas that have severe winters. Some of these plants have seeds that will not germinate unless the seeds have first been exposed to a long period of cold. How might this characteristic help new plants survive?

20 **Analyzing Ideas** Most plant shoots have positive phototropism. Plant roots have positive gravitropism. What might be the benefits of each of these characteristics?

21 **Applying Concepts** If you wanted to make poinsettias bloom and the leaves turn red in the summer, what would you have to do?

22 **Making Inferences** Imagine that someone discovered a new flowering plant. The plant has yellow flowers and underground stems. How might this plant reproduce asexually?

INTERPRETING GRAPHICS

The graph below shows seed germination rates for different seed companies. Use the graph below to answer the questions that follow.

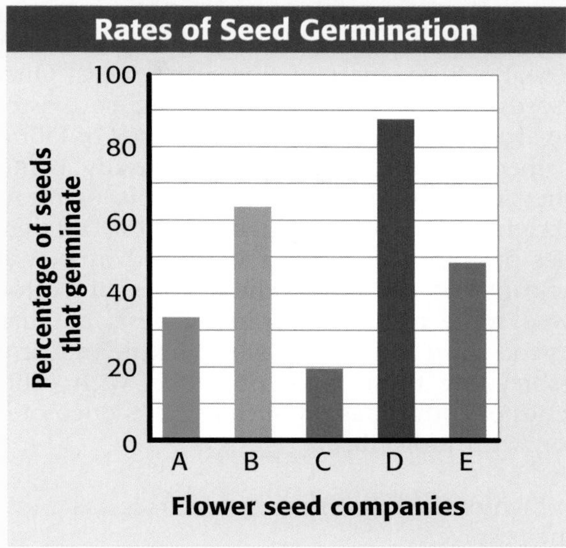

23 Which seed company had the highest rate of seed germination? the lowest rate of seed germination?

24 Which seed companies had seed germination rates higher than 50%?

25 If Elaine wanted to buy seeds that had a germination rate higher than 60%, which seed companies would she buy seeds from? Why might Elaine want to buy seeds with a higher germination rate?

Standardized Test Preparation

READING

Read each of the passages below. Then, answer the questions that follow each passage.

Passage 1 Cotton fibers are contained in the plant's seed pods, or bolls. Bolls open at maturity to reveal a fuzzy mass of fibers and seeds. Once the seeds are removed, the fibers can be twisted into yarn and used to make many kinds of fabric. The fibers in cotton plants are naturally white, so they must be dyed with chemicals to create the bright colors seen in many fabrics. Different shades of cotton have been harvested by Native Americans for centuries. These types of cotton showed some resistance to insect pests but had fibers too short to be used by the textile industry. Crossbreeding these types of cotton with other varieties of cotton has produced strains of colored cotton with long fibers.

1. Which of the following statements is a fact in the passage?

A Crossbreeding colored cotton has produced colored cotton with short fibers.
B Colored cotton is better than white cotton.
C Cotton fibers can be used to make fabrics.
D Native Americans harvested only white cotton.

2. Based on the passage, how are bright fabric colors produced?

F The cotton fibers are twisted into a yarn.
G Crossbreeding different varieties of cotton produces brightly colored fabrics.
H Cotton with long fibers is always brightly colored.
I Cotton must be dyed with chemicals.

3. Based on the passage, how has crossbreeding benefited the textile industry?

A It produced colored cotton with long fibers.
B It produced white cotton with long fibers.
C It produced cotton yarn.
D It produced brightly colored cotton.

Passage 2 Most above-ground plant surfaces are covered by a waxy <u>cuticle</u>. The cuticle protects the plant from water loss. Carbon dioxide enters the plant's leaves through stomata (singular, *stoma*). A stoma is an opening in the leaf's epidermis and cuticle. Each stoma is surrounded by two guard cells, which act like double doors, opening and closing the gap. When stomata are open, carbon dioxide enters the leaf. The oxygen produced during photosynthesis diffuses out of leaf cells and exits the leaf through the stomata. Water vapor also exits the leaf in this way. The loss of water from leaves is called *transpiration*.

1. In the passage, the word *cuticle* most likely means which of the following?

A protective covering
B double doors
C water vapor
D transpiration

2. Based on the passage, which of the following is true about stomata?

F Oxygen enters the leaf through the stomata.
G Stomata are always open.
H Stomata are surrounded by two guard cells.
I Carbon dioxide exits the leaf through the stomata.

3. Which of the following statements about water vapor is a fact in the passage?

A Water vapor enters the leaf through the stomata.
B Water vapor is produced during photosynthesis.
C Water vapor is lost through transpiration.
D Water vapor does not enter or exit the leaf.

INTERPRETING GRAPHICS

The graph below shows the pollen counts for three kinds of plants over a 5-day period. Use the graph below to answer the questions that follow.

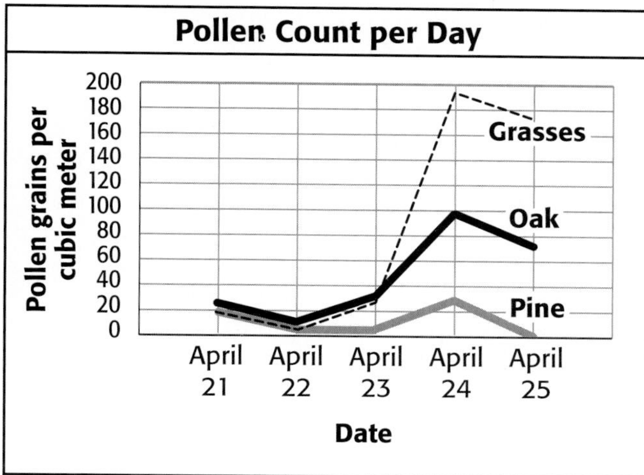

1. On which of the following days was grass pollen the most common type of pollen?

A April 21
B April 22
C April 23
D April 24

2. What was the total pollen count for April 24?

F 30 pollen grains per cubic meter
G 100 pollen grains per cubic meter
H 190 pollen grains per cubic meter
I 320 pollen grains per cubic meter

3. On what days were the total pollen counts lower than 100 pollen grains per cubic meter?

A April 21, April 22, and April 23
B April 22 and April 23
C April 23, April 24, and April 25
D April 24 and April 25

4. What was the pollen count for grasses on April 25?

F 0 pollen grains per cubic meter
G 75 pollen grains per cubic meter
H 175 pollen grains per cubic meter
I 250 pollen grains per cubic meter

MATH

Read each question below, and choose the best answer.

1. Choose the list in which the numbers are in order from smallest to greatest.

A 0.123, 0.132, 0.321, 0.231
B 0.321, 0.231, 0.132, 0.123
C 0.123, 0.132, 0.231, 0.321
D 0.123, 0.231, 0.132, 0.321

2. If a plant stem takes 6 h to bend 90° toward the light coming from a window, about how many degrees does the stem bend each minute?

F 0.07°
G 0.25°
H 4°
I 15°

3. If $50 = 3x + 20$, what is x?

A 10
B 23
C 73
D 90

4. In a swamp that is 20 km long and 15 km wide, there are 1,200 orchid plants. On average, how many orchids are there per square kilometer in this swamp?

F 4
G 35
H 60
I 80

5. A certain plant grows 0.12 cm per day. About how many meters will the plant grow in a year?

A 0.044 m
B 0.44 m
C 4.4 m
D 44 m

Science in Action

Weird Science

What's That Smell?

Imagine that you are walking through a tropical rain forest. You're surrounded by green—green leaves, green vines, and green trees. You can hear monkeys and birds calling to each other. When you touch the plants nearby, they are wet from a recent rain shower. But what's that horrible smell? You don't see any rotting garbage around, but you do see a huge flower spike. As you get closer, the smell gets stronger. Then, you realize the flower is what smells so bad! The flower is called a *corpse flower*. The corpse flower is just one plant that uses bad odors to attract pollinators.

Math ACTIVITY

A corpse flower sprouts and grows to a maximum height of 2.35 m in 28 days. In centimeters, what is the average growth of the corpse flower per day?

Scientific Debate

Are Exotic Species Helpful or Harmful?

Have you visited the coast of California? If so, you may have seen large eucalyptus trees. You may be surprised to know that those trees are an exotic species. An *exotic species* is an organism that makes a new home for itself in a new place. People brought eucalyptus trees to California to use them in their yards and gardens. Since then, eucalyptus trees have spread to other areas. Exotic species often take over areas. Exotic species may compete with native species. Sometimes, exotic species keep native species from surviving. But in urban areas, exotic species are sometimes the only plants that will grow. So, are exotic species helpful or harmful?

Social Studies ACTIVITY

Identify an exotic species that people imported to grow in their gardens. Find out where the exotic species came from and the effect it is having on the environment.

Careers

Nalini Nadkarni

Canopy Scientist As a child, Nalini Nadkarni loved to climb trees. She still does. Nadkarni is a biologist who studies the forest canopy. The canopy is the uppermost layer of the trees. It includes leaves, twigs, and branches and the air among them. Far above the ground, the canopy is home to many different plants, birds, insects, and other animals.

Canopy science was a new field of study when Nadkarni started her research 20 years ago. Because most canopies are tall, few scientists visited them. Most field biologists did their research with both feet planted firmly on the ground. Today, scientists know that the canopy is an important habitat for wildlife.

Nadkarni tells others about the importance of forests. As she puts it, "I can have a real impact in raising public awareness of the need to save forests." Nadkarni has invited artists and musicians to visit the canopy. "In my job, I try to understand the science of the canopy, but artists and musicians help capture the aesthetic value of the canopy."

Language Arts ACTIVITY

WRITING SKILL Imagine that you are a canopy scientist. Then, write a creative story about something that you would like to study in the canopy.

To learn more about these Science in Action topics, visit go.hrw.com and type in the keyword **HL5PL2F.**

Current Science

Check out Current Science® articles related to this chapter by visiting go.hrw.com. Just type in the keyword HL5CS13.

TIMELINE

Animals

Have you ever been to a zoo or watched a wild-animal program on TV? If so, you have some idea of how many types of animals—from tiny insects to massive whales—are found on Earth.

Animals are fascinating, in part because of their variety in appearance and behavior. They also teach us about ourselves because humans are also classified as animals.

In this unit, you will learn about many types of animals—maybe even some that you never knew existed. So, get ready for an animal adventure!

1610
Galileo Galilei uses a compound microscope to study insect anatomy.

1681
The Mauritius Dodo, a flightless bird, becomes extinct.

1827
John James Audubon publishes the first edition of *Birds of America.*

1839
The first bicycle is constructed.

1983
The U.S. Space Shuttle *Challenger* is launched. Sally Ride, the first American woman in space, is on board.

1987
The last wild California condor is captured in an effort to save the species from extinction.

1995
Fourteen Canadian gray wolves are reintroduced into Yellowstone National Park.

1693
John Ray correctly identifies whales as mammals.

1761
The first veterinary school is founded in Lyons, France.

1775
J. C. Fabricius develops a system for the classification of insects.

1882
Research on the ship *The Albatross* helps increase our knowledge of marine life.

1935
Francis B. Sumner studies the protective coloration of fish.

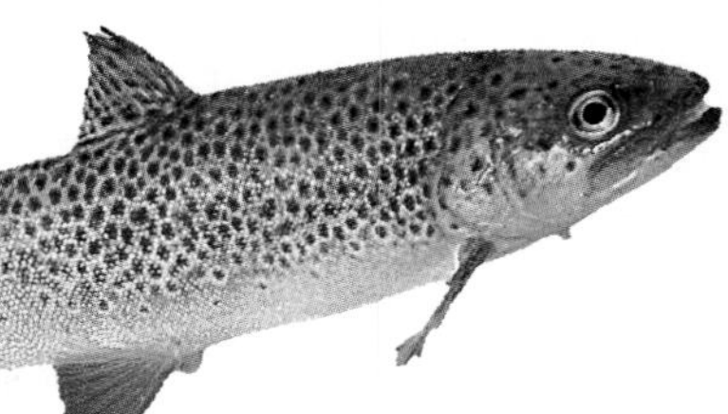

1960
Jane Goodall, an English zoologist, begins her research on chimpanzees in Tanzania.

1998
Keiko, the killer-whale star of the movie *Free Willy,* is taught to catch fish so that he can be released from captivity.

2003
Researchers find that individual cloned pigs behave in very different ways. This finding shows that environmental conditions affect behavior.

Animals and Behavior

About the PHOTO

This spider needs to eat in order to survive. On the other hand, this hover fly needs to avoid being eaten in order to survive. How do the spider, the fly, and other animals get what they need to live? Animals use many behaviors to compete with each other for survival.

PRE-READING ACTIVITY

Graphic Organizer

Spider Map Before you read the chapter, create the graphic organizer entitled "Spider Map" described in the **Study Skills** section of the Appendix. Label the circle "Animal Behavior." Create a leg for each type of animal behavior. As you read the chapter, fill in the map with details about each type of animal behavior.

START-UP ACTIVITY

Go on a Safari!

You don't have to travel far to see interesting animals. If you look closely, you can find many animals nearby. **Caution:** Always be careful around wild or unfamiliar animals, because they may bite or sting. Do not handle wild animals or any animals that are unfamiliar to you.

Procedure

1. Go outside, and find **two different kinds of animals** to observe.
2. Without disturbing the animals, watch them quietly for a few minutes from a distance. You may want to use **binoculars** or a **magnifying lens.**
3. Write down everything you notice about each animal. Do you know what kind of animal each is? Where did you find them? What do they look like? How big are they? What are they doing? You may want to draw a picture of them.

Analysis

1. Compare the two animals that you studied. Do they look alike? Do they have similar behaviors?
2. How do the animals move? Did you see them communicating with other animals or defending themselves?
3. Can you tell what each animal eats? What characteristics of each animal help it find or catch food?

SECTION 1

What Is an Animal?

What do you think of when you hear the word animal*? You may think of your dog or cat. You may think about giraffes or grizzly bears. But would you think of a sponge?*

READING WARM-UP

Objectives

- Describe the difference between vertebrates and invertebrates.
- Describe the five characteristics that all animals share.

Terms to Learn

embryo
consumer

READING STRATEGY

Prediction Guide Before reading this section, write the title of each heading in this section. Next, under each heading, write what you think you will learn.

The natural sponges that people use for washing are the remains of an animal. Animals come in many shapes and sizes. Some have four legs and fur, but most do not. Some are too small to be seen without a microscope, and others are bigger than a school bus. They are all part of the animal kingdom.

Animal Diversity

How many different kinds of animals do you see in **Figure 1**? You may be surprised to learn that feather stars and corals are animals. Spiders, fish, and birds are also animals. And slugs, kangaroos, and monkeys are animals, too. Scientists have named more than 1 million species of animals. Many species that exist have not yet been named. Some scientists estimate that more than 3 million species of animals live on the Earth.

Vertebrates

Most animals look nothing like humans. However, we share many characteristics with a group of animals called vertebrates (VUHR tuh brits). A *vertebrate* is an animal that has a backbone. Vertebrates include fishes, amphibians, reptiles, birds, and mammals. Humans are one of about 5,000 species of mammals.

Figure 1 *All of the living things in this picture are animals.*

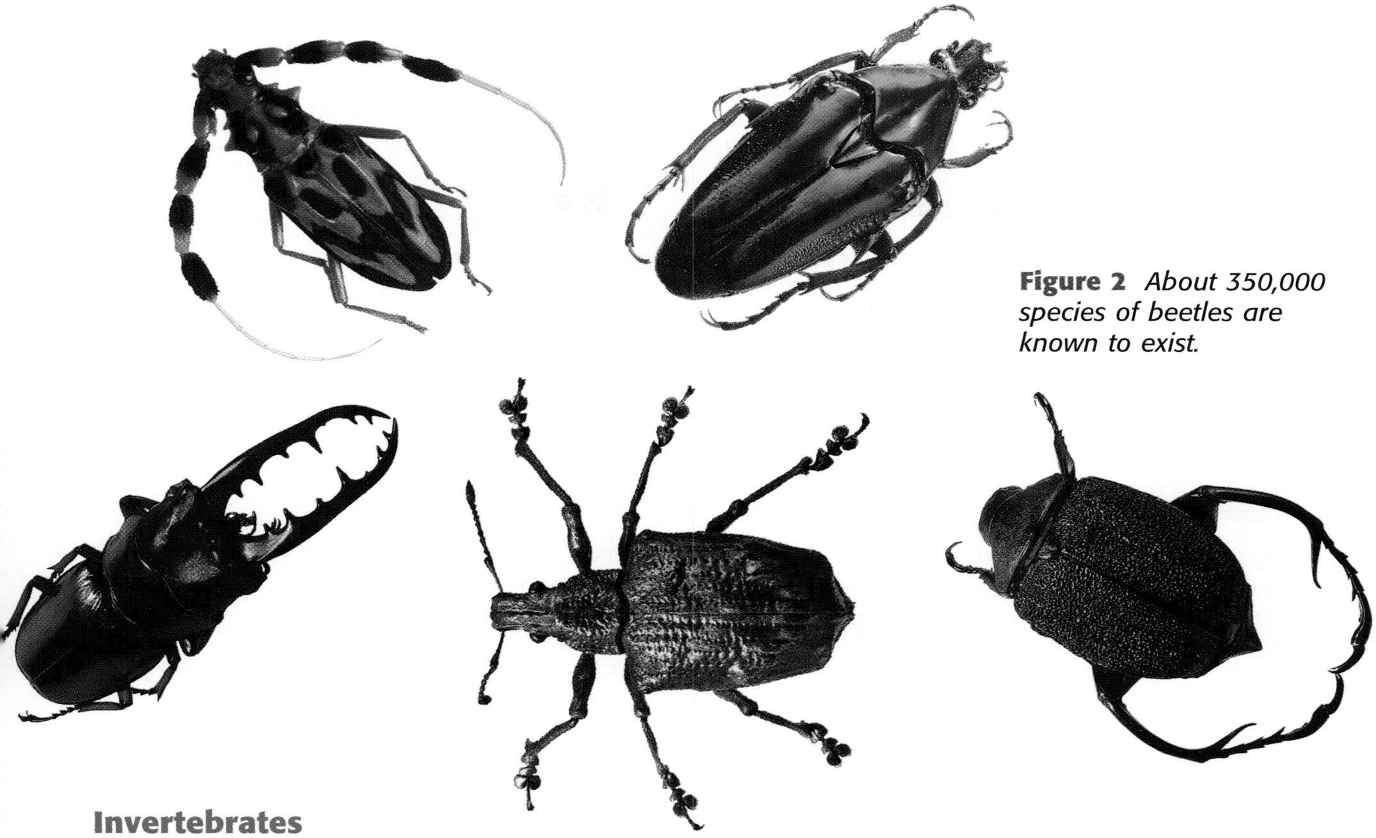

Figure 2 About 350,000 species of beetles are known to exist.

Invertebrates

You are probably more familiar with vertebrates than invertebrates, but vertebrates are definitely the minority among living things. Less than 5% of known animal species are vertebrates. Most animal species are insects, snails, jellyfish, worms, and other *invertebrates* (in VUHR tuh brits), or animals without backbones. In fact, beetles make up more than 30% of all animal species! **Figure 2** shows a few species of beetles.

Reading Check **Are people vertebrates or invertebrates?** (*See the Appendix for answers to Reading Checks.*)

Animal Characteristics

Sponges, worms, penguins, and lions are animals. But until about 200 years ago, most people thought sponges were plants. And worms don't look anything like penguins or lions. So why do we say all these things are animals? What determines whether a living thing is an animal, a plant, or something else? There is no single answer. But all animals share characteristics that set them apart from all other living things.

Multicellular Makeup

All animals are *multicellular,* which means they are made of many cells. Your own body has trillions of cells. Animal cells are *eukaryotic,* which means they have a nucleus. Unlike plant cells, animal cells do not have cell walls. Animal cells are surrounded by only cell membranes.

Explore Your Home

With your family, list all the animals that you find around your home. Do you have pets? Do any spiders spin webs outside your front door? Can you see any animals outside your window? Remember that cats, spiders, and birds are animals. When you have finished writing your list, make a poster about the animals you found.

ACTIVITY

Reproduction and Development

Almost all animals reproduce sexually. These animals make sex cells—eggs or sperm. When an egg and a sperm join during fertilization, they form the first cell of a new organism. This cell divides into many cells to form an embryo (EM bree OH). An **embryo** is an organism at an early stage of development. A mouse embryo is shown in **Figure 3.** Many stages of development follow the embryo stage as an animal grows.

A few animals can reproduce asexually. For example, hydras can reproduce by budding. In *budding,* part of an organism breaks off and develops as a new organism.

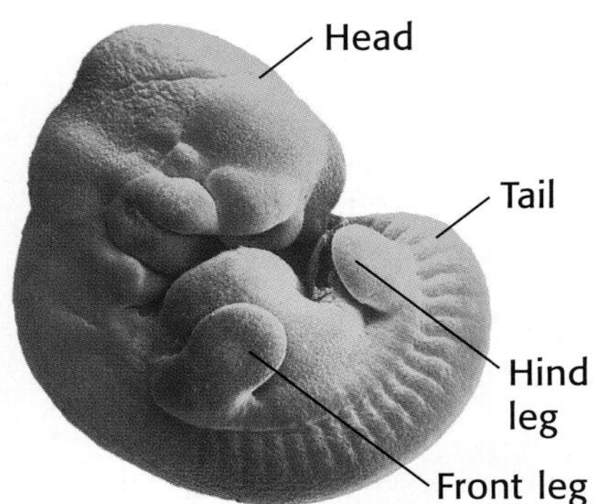

Figure 3 *Embryos are very small. When mouse embryos like this one are 10 days old, they are about 4.5 mm long.*

embryo a plant or animal at an early stage of development

Many Specialized Parts

An animal's body has distinct parts that do different things. When a fertilized egg cell divides into many cells to form an embryo, the cells become different from each other. Some of the cells may become skin cells. Other cells may become muscle cells, nerve cells, or bone cells. These different kinds of cells form *tissues,* which are collections of similar cells. For example, muscle cells form muscle tissue, and nerve cells form nerve tissue.

Most animals also have organs. An *organ* is a group of tissues that carry out a special function of the body. Your heart, lungs, and kidneys are all organs. Each organ in an animal's body has a unique job. The shark shown in **Figure 4** has organs that allow the shark to digest food, pump blood, and sense the environment.

Reading Check Name three organs that are inside your body.

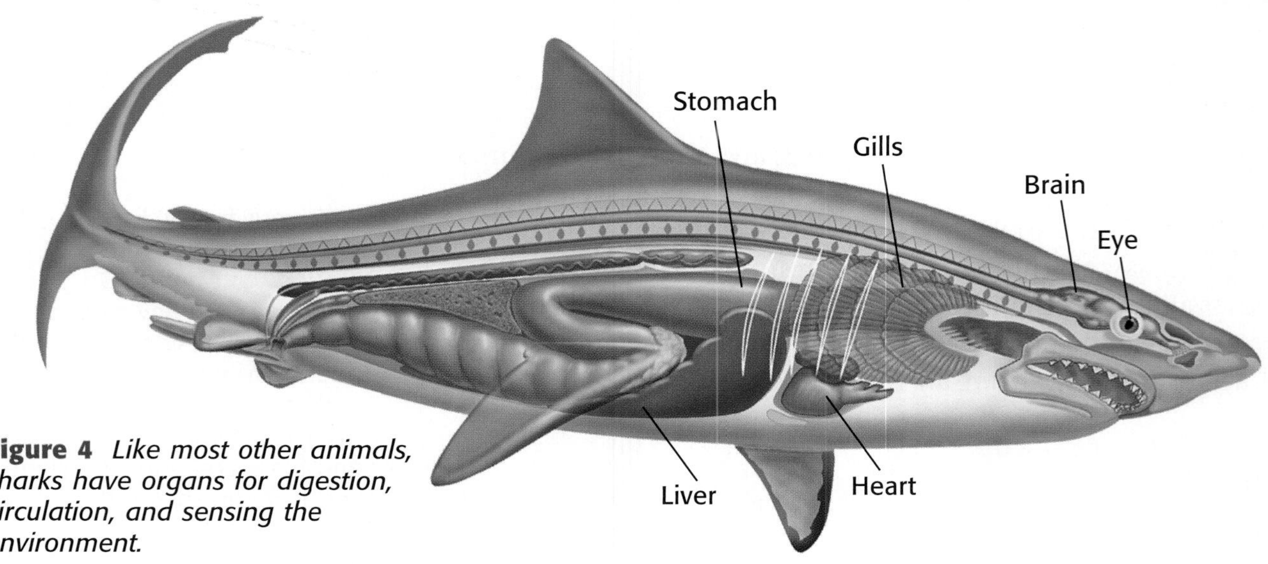

Figure 4 *Like most other animals, sharks have organs for digestion, circulation, and sensing the environment.*

Movement

Most animals can move from place to place. They may fly, run, swim, or jump. Nearly all animals use movement to search for food, shelter, or mates at some stage of life. However, some animals are less active at certain stages of life than at other stages. For example, young sea anemones swim through the ocean to find their food. But adult sea anemones attach to rocks or the ocean floor and wait for food to arrive.

Consuming

Animals cannot make their own food. All animals survive by eating other organisms or parts and products of other organisms. In other words, animals are consumers. A **consumer** is an organism that eats other organisms. This trait sets animals apart from plants. Though there are a few exceptions, most plants do not eat other organisms. Plants make their own food.

Animals eat a great variety of foods. As shown in **Figure 5,** pandas eat bamboo. Spiders eat other animals. Mosquitoes drink blood. Butterflies drink nectar from flowers. All animals need to eat to survive.

Figure 5 *Pandas eat about 30 pounds of bamboo every day.*

consumer an organism that eats other organisms or organic matter

SECTION Review

Summary

- Scientists have named over 1 million animal species. Humans are vertebrates, but most animals are invertebrates.
- Animals are multicellular, reproduce sexually (usually), have many specialized parts, are able to move, and consume other organisms. Only animals have all of these characteristics.

Using Key Terms

1. In your own words, write a definition for each of the following terms: *embryo* and *consumer*.

Understanding Key Ideas

2. Which of the following must be true if a sponge is an animal?
   a. Sponges eat other organisms.
   b. Sponges make their own food.
   c. Sponges move all of the time.
   d. Sponges have a backbone.
3. What five characteristics distinguish animals from other organisms?
4. How are vertebrates different from invertebrates?

Math Skills

5. If a fish can swim short distances at 48 km/h, how long would the fish take to reach a smaller fish that is 3 m away?

Critical Thinking

6. **Applying Concepts** Choose an animal that interests you. Explain how you know that this organism is an animal.
7. **Identifying Relationships** Suppose that a certain fish tank contains the following: water, chemicals, fish, snails, algae, plants, and gravel. Which of these items are alive? Which are animals? Why aren't some of the living organisms classified as animals?

SCILINKS
NSTA
Developed and maintained by the National Science Teachers Association
For a variety of links related to this chapter, go to www.scilinks.org
Topic: Vertebrates and Invertebrates
SciLinks code: HSM1603

SECTION 2

Animal Behavior

Suppose that you look out a window and see a bird flying away from a tree. Could the bird be leaving a nest in search of food? Or could the bird be escaping from danger?

Though the bird's purpose may not be clear, the bird is flying away for a specific reason. Animals run from enemies, search for food, battle for territory, and build homes. All of these activities are known as *behavior*.

READING WARM-UP

Objectives

- Explain the difference between learned and innate behavior.
- Describe five kinds of behaviors that help animals survive.
- Name three cycles that are influenced by biological clocks.

Terms to Learn

innate behavior
learned behavior
territory
hibernation
estivation
circadian rhythm

READING STRATEGY

Discussion Read this section silently. Write down questions that you have about this section. Discuss your questions in a small group.

Kinds of Behavior

How do animals know when a situation is dangerous? How do they know where to find food? Sometimes animals instinctively know how to behave, but sometimes they learn how.

Innate Behavior

Behavior that doesn't depend on learning or experience is known as **innate behavior.** Innate behaviors are inherited through genes. Puppies inherit the tendency to chew, and bees inherit the tendency to fly. The male bird in **Figure 1** inherited the tendency to collect colorful objects for its nest. Some innate behaviors are present at birth. Newborn whales have the innate ability to swim. Other innate behaviors develop months or years after birth. For example, walking is innate for humans. But we do not walk until we are about one year old.

Learned Behavior

Innate behaviors can be modified. Animals can use learning to change a behavior. **Learned behavior** is behavior that has been learned from experience or from observing other animals. Humans inherit the tendency to speak. But the language we use is not inherited. We might learn English, Spanish, or sign language. Humans are not the only animals that change behaviors through learning. All animals can learn.

Figure 1 *The male bowerbird collected colorful objects for its nest to attract the female bowerbird to be his mate.*

Figure 2 *Chimpanzees make and use tools to get ants and other food out of hard-to-reach places.*

Survival Behavior

Animals depend on their behaviors to survive. To stay alive, an animal has to do many things. It must avoid being eaten, and it must find food, water, and a place to live.

innate behavior an inherited behavior that does not depend on the environment or experience

learned behavior a behavior that has been learned from experience

territory an area that is occupied by one animal or a group of animals that do not allow other members of the species to enter

Finding Food

Animals find food in many ways. Bees fly from flower to flower collecting nectar. Koala bears climb trees to get eucalyptus leaves. Some animals, such as the chimpanzee shown in **Figure 2,** use tools to get food. Many animals hunt for their food. For example, owls hunt mice.

Animals that eat other animals are known as *predators*. The animal being eaten is the *prey*. Animals that are predators can also be the prey for another animal. For example, a frog eats insects. So the frog is a predator. But a frog may be eaten by a snake. In this case, the frog is the prey.

Reading Check **What is the relationship between a predator and its prey?** (*See the Appendix for answers to Reading Checks.*)

Marking Territory

Sometimes, members of the same species must compete for food and mates. Some animals claim territories to save energy by avoiding this competition. A **territory** is an area that is occupied by one animal or by a group of animals that do not allow other members of the species to enter. Some birds mark a territory by singing. The song lets other birds know not to enter the area. If other birds do enter the area, the first bird may chase them away. Animals use their territories for mating, raising young, and finding food.

For another activity related to this chapter, go to **go.hrw.com** and type in the keyword **HL5ANMW**.

Defensive Action

Defensive behavior allows animals to protect resources, including territories, from other animals. Animals defend food, mates, and offspring. Have you ever heard a pet dog growl when a person approached while it was eating? Many male animals, such as lions, fight violently to defend mates. Some birds use distraction to defend their young. When a predator is near, a mother killdeer may pretend to have a broken wing and move away from her young. This action distracts the predator's attention from the young so they will remain safe.

Defensive behavior also helps animals protect themselves from predators. One way animals avoid predators is to make themselves hard to see. For example, a rabbit often "freezes" so that its color blends into a background of shrubs or grass. But once a predator is aware of its prey, the prey needs another way to defend itself. Rabbits try to outrun predators. Bees, ants, and wasps inject a powerful acid into their attackers. As seen in **Figure 3,** skunks spray irritating chemicals at predators. Has an animal ever defended itself against you?

Reading Check What are two ways a rabbit can defend itself?

CONNECTION TO Social Studies

WRITING SKILL **Defensive Tools** People use tools to help defend their homes. Some people build homes on stilts to stay safe from floods. Others build smoky fires to force biting insects from their homes. Write a paragraph in your **science journal** about how houses in your area are built to defend people from animals or bad weather.

Courtship

Animals need to find mates to reproduce. Reproduction is essential for the survival of an individual's genes. Animals have special behaviors that help them find a mate. These behaviors are referred to as *courtship*. Some birds and fish build nests to attract a mate. Other animals use special movements and sounds to attract a mate. **Figure 4** shows two cranes performing a courtship display.

Figure 3 *Skunks spray irritating chemicals at attackers to protect themselves.*

Figure 4 *These Japanese ground cranes use an elaborate courtship dance to tell each other when they are ready to mate.*

Figure 5 *Adult killer whales teach their young how to hunt in the first years of life.*

Parenting

Some animals, such as caterpillars, begin life with the ability to take care of themselves. But many young animals depend on their parents for survival. Some adult birds bring food to their young because they cannot feed themselves at hatching. Other animals, such as the killer whales in **Figure 5,** spend years teaching their young how to hunt for food.

Migration Mapping

1. Pair up with a classmate to draw a map of your school. Include at least five landmarks.
2. Use a **compass** to label North, South, East, and West on your map.
3. Draw the path you would travel if you were migrating from north to south.
4. Use the landmarks and compass directions to describe the path of your migration.

Seasonal Behavior

Humans bundle up when it is cold outside. Many other animals have to deal with bitter cold during the winter, too. They may even face winter food shortages. Frogs hide from the cold by burrowing in mud. Squirrels store food to prepare for winter. Seasonal behaviors help animals adjust to the environment.

Migration

Many animals avoid cold weather by traveling to warmer places. These animals migrate to find food, water, or safe nesting grounds. To *migrate* is to travel from one place to another. Whales, salmon, bats, and even chimpanzees migrate. Each winter, the monarch butterflies shown in **Figure 6** migrate to central Mexico from all over North America. And each fall, birds in the Northern Hemisphere fly south thousands of kilometers. In the spring, they return north to nest.

If you were planning a trip, you would probably use a map. But how do animals know which way to go? For short trips, many animals use landmarks to find their way. *Landmarks* are fixed objects that an animal uses to find its way. Birds use landmarks such as mountain ranges, rivers, and coastlines to find their way.

Figure 6 *When monarch butterflies gather in Mexico for the winter, there can be as many as 4 million butterflies per acre!*

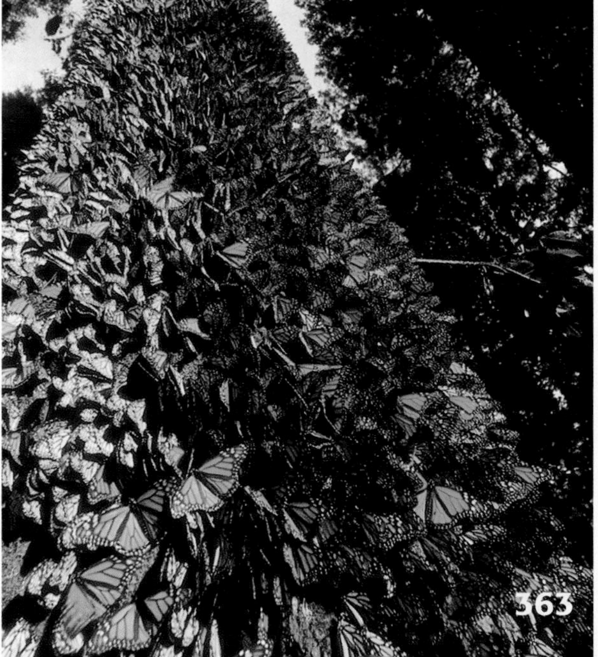

Figure 7 *Bears slow down for the winter, but they do not enter deep hibernation.*

hibernation a period of inactivity and lowered body temperature that some animals undergo in winter as a protection against cold weather and lack of food

estivation a period of inactivity and lowered body temperature that some animals undergo in summer as a protection against hot weather and lack of food

circadian rhythm a biological daily cycle

Slowing Down

Some animals deal with food and water shortages by hibernating. **Hibernation** is a period of inactivity and decreased body temperature that some animals experience in winter. Hibernating animals survive on stored body fat. Many animals hibernate, including mice, squirrels, and skunks. While an animal hibernates, its temperature, heart rate, and breathing rate drop. Some hibernating animals drop their body temperature to a few degrees above freezing and do not wake for weeks at a time. Other animals, such as the bear in **Figure 7,** slow down but do not enter deep hibernation. The bear's body temperature does not drop to just above freezing. Also, bears sleep for shorter periods of time than hibernating animals sleep.

Winter is not the only time that resources can be hard to find. Many desert squirrels and mice experience a similar internal slowdown in the hottest part of the summer, when they run low on water and food. This period of reduced activity in the summer is called **estivation.**

Reading Check **Name three animals that hibernate.**

A Biological Clock

Animals need to keep track of time so that they know when to store food and when to migrate. The internal control of an animal's natural cycles is called a *biological clock*. Animals may use clues such as the length of the day and the temperature to set their clocks.

Some biological clocks keep track of daily cycles. These daily cycles are called **circadian rhythms.** Most animals wake up and get sleepy at about the same time each day and night. This is an example of a circadian rhythm.

CONNECTION TO Environmental Science

Do Not Disturb Many bats avoid food shortages during winter by hibernating in caves. Visiting a cave of hibernating bats may sound like fun, but people can endanger the bats by visiting their caves. The bats sleep with a lowered heart rate that allows them to save their energy until food is available. When people visit the caves, the bats may wake up. Waking up requires a lot of energy and makes it harder for the bats to survive until spring to find more food. If the bats lose too much energy, they can die. Make a poster that explains how people can help bats survive winters by avoiding their caves.

ACTIVITY

Cycles of Change

Some biological clocks control long cycles. Seasonal cycles are nearly universal among animals. Many animals hibernate at certain times of the year and reproduce at other times. Reproducing during a particular season takes advantage of environmental conditions that help the young survive. Migration patterns are also controlled by seasonal cycles.

Biological clocks also control cycles of internal changes. For example, treehoppers, such as the one in **Figure 8,** go through several stages in life. They begin as an egg, then hatch as a nymph, and then develop into an adult. Finally, the adult emerges from the skin of its nymph form.

Figure 8 *The treehopper's biological clock signals the animal to shed the skin of its nymph form.*

SECTION Review

Summary

- Behavior may be classified as innate or learned. The potential for innate behavior is inherited. Learned behavior depends on experience.
- Behaviors that help animals survive include finding food, marking a territory, defensive action, courtship, and parenting.
- Animals have internal biological clocks that control daily, seasonal, and internal natural cycles.

Using Key Terms

1. Use each of the following terms in a separate sentence: *territory, innate behavior,* and *circadian rhythm.*
2. In your own words, write a definition for each of the following terms: *hibernation* and *estivation.*

Understanding Key Ideas

3. An animal that lives in a hot, dry environment might spend the summer
   a. hibernating.
   b. estivating.
   c. migrating to a warmer climate.
   d. None of the above
4. Biological clocks control
   a. seasonal cycles.
   b. circadian rhythms.
   c. internal cycles.
   d. All of the above
5. How do innate behaviors and learned behaviors differ?
6. Do bears hibernate? Explain your answer.
7. Name five behaviors that help animals survive.

Math Skills

8. Suppose that an animal's circadian rhythms tell it to eat a meal every 4 h. How many meals will the animal eat each day?

Critical Thinking

9. **Applying Concepts** People who travel to different time zones often suffer from *jet lag.* Jet lag makes people have trouble waking up and going to sleep at appropriate times. Why do you think people experience jet lag? Explain.
10. **Making Inferences** Many children are born with the tendency to make babbling sounds. But few adults make these sounds. How could you explain this change in an innate behavior?

SCILINKS®
NSTA
Developed and maintained by the National Science Teachers Association
For a variety of links related to this chapter, go to www.scilinks.org
Topic: Animal Behavior; Rhythms of Life
SciLinks code: HSM0069; HSM1311

SECTION 3

Social Relationships

Have you ever noticed a pair of squirrels chattering and chasing each other through the branches of a tree? Though it may not be clear why they behave this way, it is clear that they are interacting.

READING WARM-UP

Objectives

- Describe four ways that animals communicate.
- List the advantages and disadvantages of living in groups.

Terms to Learn

social behavior
communication
pheromone

READING STRATEGY

Paired Summarizing Read this section silently. In pairs, take turns summarizing the material. Stop to discuss ideas that seem confusing.

Animals often interact with each other—in groups and one on one. They may work together, or they may compete. All of this behavior is called social behavior. **Social behavior** is the interaction among animals of the same species. Animals depend on communication for their social interactions.

Communication

Imagine what life would be like if people could not talk or read. There would be no telephones, no books, and no Internet. The world would certainly be different! Language is an important way for humans to communicate. In **communication,** a signal must travel from one animal to another, and the receiver of the signal must respond in some way. Animals do not use a language with complex words and grammar, but they communicate in many ways.

Communication helps animals survive. Many animals, such as the wolves in **Figure 1,** communicate to defend a territory from other members of the species. Animals also communicate to find food, to warn others of danger, to identify family members, to frighten predators, and to find mates.

social behavior the interaction between animals of the same species

communication a transfer of a signal or message from one animal to another that results in some type of response

Reading Check **What are six reasons that animals communicate with each other?** *(See the Appendix for answers to Reading Checks.)*

Figure 1 *These wolves are howling to discourage neighboring wolves from invading their territory.*

Ways to Communicate

Animals communicate by signaling information to other animals through sound, touch, chemicals, and sight. Each of these methods can be used to convey specific information.

Sound

Many animals communicate by making noises. Wolves howl. Dolphins use whistles and complex clicking noises to communicate with other dolphins. Male birds may sing songs in the spring to claim their territory or to attract a mate.

Sound is a signal that can reach many animals over a large area. As described in **Figure 2,** elephants use low frequency rumbles to communicate with other elephants that are kilometers away. Humpback whales sing songs that can be heard for many kilometers. Both species use these sounds to convey information about their locations.

Figure 2 *Elephants communicate with low-pitched sounds that humans cannot hear. When an elephant is communicating this way, the skin on its forehead flutters.*

Touch

Animals may also use touch to communicate. For example, chimpanzees often groom each other. Grooming involves animals resting together while picking bits of skin from each other's fur. This activity is an important way for primates to communicate. Chimpanzees use grooming to calm and comfort one another. Through touch, they may communicate friendship or support.

pheromone a substance that is released by the body and that causes another individual of the same species to react in a predictable way

Chemicals

One way to communicate is through chemicals. The chemicals that animals use to communicate are called **pheromones** (FER uh MOHNZ). Ants and other insects secrete a variety of pheromones. For example, alarm chemicals can warn other ants of danger. Recognition chemicals announce which colony an ant is from to both friends and enemies.

Many animals use pheromones to find a mate. Amazingly, elephants and insects use some of the same pheromones to attract mates. Fire ants, such as the ones in **Figure 3,** use pheromones to control which colony members can reproduce.

Figure 3 *This fire ant queen can make pheromones that other ants in the colony cannot make.*

Figure 4 **The Dance of the Bees**

a A honeybee leader does a "waggle dance" to tell other bees where it has found food. Other worker bees—followers—gather closely around the dancing bee to learn the details about the food source.

Followers can tell what kind of food was found by smelling the pollen on the leader's body. Or the leader may spit out some nectar for the followers to smell.

b The leader dances a figure eight, beating its wings rapidly and waggling its abdomen. The wings make sounds that communicate information about the food's distance from the hive.

As the bee goes through the center, it waggles its abdomen. The number of waggles tells the other bees how far away the nectar is.

The direction of the center line of the figure eight tells the other bees the direction from the hive to the nectar.

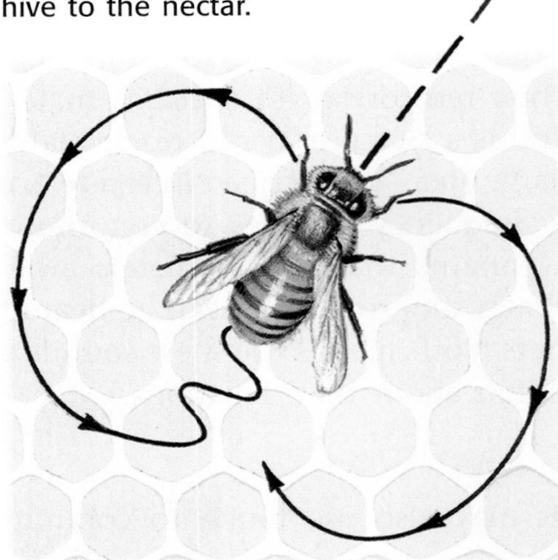

Sight

Animals also use visual communication. When we smile at a friend, we are sending a visual message with *body language*. As shown in **Figure 4,** bees use body language, along with other forms of communication, to spread news about food.

Body language can communicate many ideas. An animal that wants to scare another animal may ruffle its feathers to look bigger, or it may show its teeth as a threat. Visual displays are also used in courtship. For example, fireflies blink signals to attract each other. Animals also use body language when playing. The dog in **Figure 5** is play bowing to show that it wants to play.

Figure 5 *When dogs want to play, they drop down on their forelegs.*

Reading Check How do honeybees use body language?

Living Together

Tigers live alone. Except for the time a mother tiger spends with her cubs, a tiger meets other tigers rarely. Yet the tiger's closest relative, the lion, is rarely alone. Lions live in groups called *prides*. The members of a pride sleep together, hunt together, and raise their cubs together. Why do some animals live in groups, while others live apart?

The Benefits of Living in Groups

Living in groups can be safer than living alone. Large groups can spot a predator quickly because they have so many pairs of eyes watching for danger. As shown in **Figure 6,** one animal can warn many others of danger. Also, groups can work together to defend themselves. For example, threatened musk oxen will circle their young with their horns pointed outward.

Living together can also help animals find food. Animals that hunt alone can usually kill only animals that are smaller than themselves. In contrast, predators such as lions and wolves, which hunt in groups, can kill larger prey.

Figure 6 *A ground squirrel whistles a loud alarm to alert other ground squirrels that danger is near.*

The Downside of Living in Groups

Living in groups causes problems as well. Animals living in large groups must compete with each other for food and mates. An area that has enough food for one animal may not have enough food for a group of animals. In these cases, groups must move around in search of food. Also, animals in groups attract predators, so they must always be on the lookout. Living as a group can also help diseases spread.

SECTION Review

Summary

- Animals communicate with each other. Communication must include both a signal and a response.
- Animals communicate through chemicals, touch, sound, and sight.
- Animals that live in groups can spot both prey and predators more easily. But living in a group increases competition for food and mates and attracts the attention of predators.

Using Key Terms

1. Use each of the following terms in a separate sentence: *social behavior* and *communication.*
2. In your own words, write a definition for the following term: *pheromone.*

Understanding Key Ideas

3. Which of the following is NOT an example of social behavior?
   a. a wolf howling at distant wolves to protect its territory
   b. a rabbit hiding from a predator
   c. a ground squirrel calling to signal danger to other squirrels
   d. a group of lions working together to hunt prey
4. Describe four ways that animals communicate with each other. Give an example of each type of communication.
5. Compare the costs and benefits of living in a group of animals.

Math Skills

6. How fast could a bee that flies 6 km/h reach a flower that is 1.2 km from the hive?

Critical Thinking

7. **Applying Concepts** Why do you think humans live together?
8. **Identifying Relationships** Language is not the only way that humans communicate. Describe how we use sound, touch, chemicals, and sight to communicate.

SCI LINKS®
NSTA
Developed and maintained by the National Science Teachers Association
For a variety of links related to this chapter, go to www.scilinks.org
Topic: Communication in the Animal Kingdom
SciLinks code: HSM0320

Using Scientific Methods

Inquiry Lab

Aunt Flossie and the Bumblebee

OBJECTIVES

Plan a way to test bumblebee behavior.

Conduct your own experiment on bumblebees.

Describe materials that attract bumblebees.

MATERIALS

- items to be determined by the students and approved by the teacher

SAFETY

Last week Aunt Flossie came to watch the soccer game, and she was chased by a big, yellow-and-black bumblebee. Everyone tried not to laugh, but Aunt Flossie did look pretty funny. She was running and screaming, and she was wearing perfume and dressed in a bright floral dress, shiny jewelry, and a huge hat with a big purple bow. No one could understand why the bumblebee bugged Aunt Flossie and left everyone else alone. She told you that she would not come to another game until you figure out why the bee chased her.

Your job is to design and carry out an experiment that will determine why the bee was attracted to Aunt Flossie. You may simulate the situation by using objects that contain the same sensory clues that Aunt Flossie wore that day—bright, shiny colors and strong scents.

Ask a Question

1. Use the information in the story above to ask a question that would lead you to a hypothesis about the bee's behavior. For example, your question may be one of the following: What was Aunt Flossie wearing? What did she look like to a bumblebee? What scent was she wearing? Which characteristics may have affected the bee's behavior? What characteristic of Aunt Flossie affected the bee's behavior?

Form a Hypothesis

2. Form a testable hypothesis about insect behavior based on your observations of Aunt Flossie and the bumblebee at the soccer game. One possible hypothesis is the following: Insects are attracted to strong floral scents. Write out your own hypothesis.

Test the Hypothesis

3. Plan a procedure for your experiment. Be sure to follow the steps of the scientific methods. Design your procedure to answer specific questions. For example, if you want to know if insects are attracted to different colors, you might want to hang up pieces of paper of different colors.
4. Make a list of materials for your experiment. You may want to include colored paper, pictures from magazines, or strong perfumes as bait. You may not use living things as bait in your experiment. Your teacher must approve your experimental design before you begin.
5. Decide what safety procedures are necessary for your experiment. Add them to your written procedure.
6. Find a place to conduct your experiment. For example, you may want to place your materials in a box on the ground, or you may want to hang items from a tree branch.
7. Using graph paper or a computer, construct tables to organize your data. Be sure that your data tables fit your investigation.
8. Have your teacher approve your plans. Carry out your procedure using the materials and safety procedures that you selected. **Caution:** Be sure to remain at a safe distance from your experimental setup. Do not touch any insects. Have an adult help you release any insects that are trapped or collected.
9. When you are finished, clean and store your equipment. Recycle or dispose of all materials properly.

Analyze the Results

1. **Describing Events** Describe your experimental procedure. How did bumblebees and other insects behave in your experiment?
2. **Analyzing Results** Did your results support your original hypothesis? Explain.

Draw Conclusions

3. **Evaluating Results** Compare your results with those of your classmates. Which hypotheses were supported? What conclusions can you draw from the class results?
4. **Applying Conclusions** Write a letter to Aunt Flossie telling her what you have learned. Tell her what you think caused the bee attack. Invite her to attend another soccer game, and tell her what you think she should or should not wear!

Chapter Review

USING KEY TERMS

1. In your own words, write a definition for each of the following terms: *embryo, consumer,* and *pheromone.*

2. Use the following terms in the same sentence: *estivation, hibernation,* and *circadian rhythm.*

For each pair of terms, explain how the meanings of the terms differ.

3. *social behavior* and *communication*

4. *learned behavior* and *innate behavior*

UNDERSTANDING KEY IDEAS

Multiple Choice

5. Which of the following is a characteristic of all animals?
   - **a.** asexual reproduction
   - **b.** producing their own food
   - **c.** having many specialized parts
   - **d.** being unable to move

6. An innate behavior
   - **a.** cannot change.
   - **b.** must be learned from parents.
   - **c.** is always present from birth.
   - **d.** does not depend on learning or experience.

7. Migration
   - **a.** occurs only in birds.
   - **b.** helps animals escape cold and food shortages in winter.
   - **c.** always refers to moving southward for the winter.
   - **d.** is a way to defend against predators.

8. A biological clock controls
   - **a.** circadian rhythms.
   - **b.** defensive behavior.
   - **c.** learned behavior.
   - **d.** being a consumer.

9. For animals, living as part of a group
   - **a.** is always safer than living alone.
   - **b.** can attract attention from predators.
   - **c.** keeps them from killing large prey.
   - **d.** decreases competition for mates and food.

Short Answer

10. What is a territory? Give an example of a territory from your environment.

11. What landmarks help you find your way home from school?

12. What are five behaviors that animals may use to survive?

13. What do migration and hibernation have in common?

14. Describe the differences between vertebrates and invertebrates.

15. Describe four ways that an animal could communicate a message to other animals about where to find food.

CRITICAL THINKING

16. **Concept Mapping** Use the following terms to create a concept map: *animals, survival behavior, finding food, migration, defensive action, seasonal behavior, marking a territory, estivation, parenting, hibernation,* and *courtship.*

17. **Analyzing Processes** If you see a skunk raise its tail toward you while you are hiking and you turn around to take a different path, has the skunk communicated with you? Explain your answer.

18. **Making Inferences** Ants depend on pheromones and touch for communication, but birds depend more on sight and sound. Why might these two types of animals have different forms of communication?

19. **Making Comparisons** Dogs use visual communication in many situations. They may arch their back and raise their fur to look threatening. When they want to play, they may bow down on their front legs. How are these two visual signals different from each other? How do the different visual signals relate to the different information they are meant to communicate?

20. **Analyzing Ideas** People have internal biological clocks. However, people are used to keeping track of time by using clocks and calendars. Why do you think people use these tools if they have internal clocks?

21. **Applying Concepts** Imagine that you are taking care of a friend's cat for a few days but that the friend forgot to tell you where to find the cat food. When you arrive at the friend's house, the cat meows and runs to the door that leads to the garage. Where would you look for the cat food? What kind of communication led you to this conclusion?

INTERPRETING GRAPHICS

The diagram below shows some internal organs of a fish. Use the diagram below to answer the questions that follow.

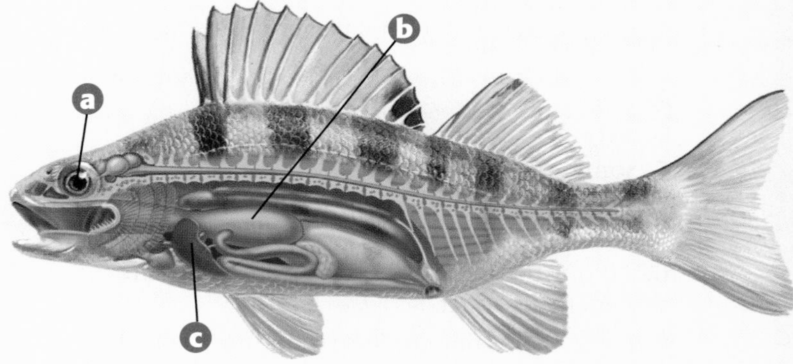

22. What characteristics suggest that this organism is an animal?

23. Which labels point to the animal's organs? Name any organs that you can recognize.

24. Do any labels point to the animal's tissues? Explain.

25. Is this animal a vertebrate or an invertebrate? Explain.

Standardized Test Preparation

READING

Read each of the passages below. Then, answer the questions that follow each passage.

Passage 1 Competing, surviving, and reproducing are all part of life. And in some species, cannibalism (eating members of one's own species) is part of life. But how does cannibalism relate to competing, surviving, and reproducing? It turns out that sometimes competition for survival can lead to cannibalism. Young tiger salamanders eat zooplankton, aquatic insect larvae, and sometimes tadpoles. But if conditions in their small pond include <u>intense</u> competition with members of their own species, certain larger salamanders may begin to eat other salamanders!

1. In the passage, what does the term *intense* mean?

A weak
B strong
C some
D furious

2. Based on the passage, which of the following statements is a fact?

F Large tiger salamanders sometimes eat other tiger salamanders.
G Animals often use cannibalism to help themselves survive.
H Female spiders sometimes eat male spiders.
I Tadpoles do not practice cannibalism.

3. What do young salamanders eat?

A other small salamanders
B large salamanders
C frogs and small fish
D zooplankton, aquatic insect larvae, and tadpoles

Passage 2 Unlike many birds, most bat species in the northern and central parts of the United States don't fly south for the winter. Instead of migrating, many bat species go into hibernation. Hibernation is usually a safe way to pass the cold winter. However, if their deep sleep is disturbed too often, the bats may die. People visiting bat caves sometimes force hibernating bats to wake up. When the bats wake up, they use up their stored fat too quickly. For example, each time a little brown bat wakes up, it consumes stored fat that would have lasted for 67 days of deep sleep. And because few insects live in the caves during the winter, the bats cannot build up fat <u>reserves</u> during the winter.

1. According to the passage, what is one reason that it is harmful for people to visit bat caves in the winter?

A Bats migrate south for the winter.
B People wake up the bats, which forces the bats to use much of their stored fat.
C People spread diseases to hibernating bats.
D People may scare insects away from the bat caves and leave the bats with no food.

2. In the passage, what does the term *reserve* mean?

F needs
G days
H supply
I weight

3. Why do many bats from the northern and central parts of the United States hibernate?

A to survive the winter
B to store fat
C to compete with birds
D to be near people that visit their caves

INTERPRETING GRAPHICS

The graphs below show the average high and low temperatures for 1 year at two locations. Use the graphs to answer the questions that follow.

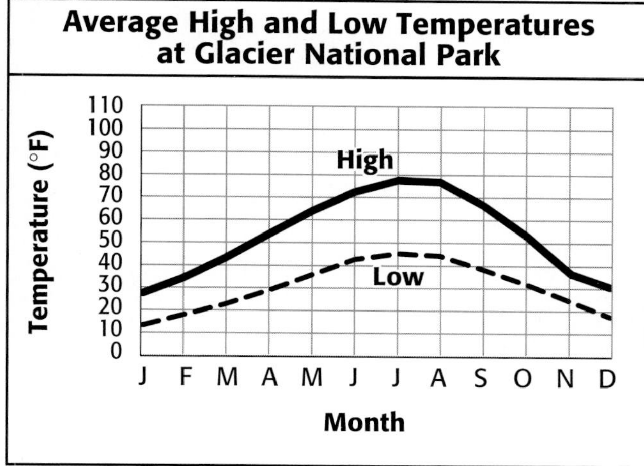

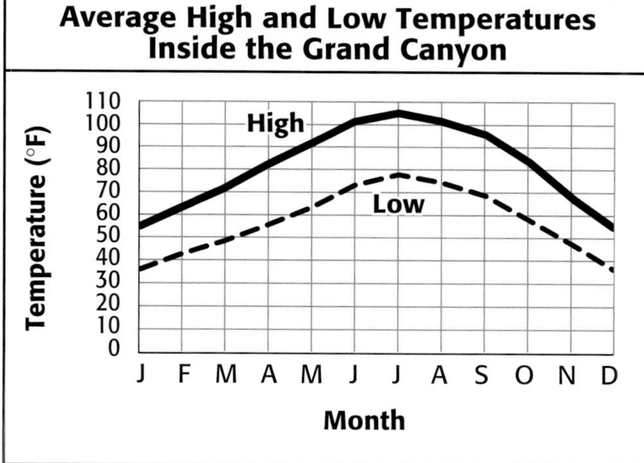

1. What is the average high temperature for each location in July?

A Glacier Park: 79°F; Grand Canyon: 106°F
B Glacier Park: 47°F; Grand Canyon: 78°F
C Glacier Park: 63°F; Grand Canyon: 92°F
D Glacier Park: 70°F; Grand Canyon: 100°F

2. What is the average low temperature for each location in January?

F Glacier Park: 15°F; Grand Canyon: 56°F
G Glacier Park: 30°F; Grand Canyon: 36°F
H Glacier Park: 15°F; Grand Canyon: 36°F
I Glacier Park: 22°F; Grand Canyon: 46°F

3. In which location would animals be more likely to estivate? to hibernate?

A Glacier Park; Grand Canyon
B Glacier Park; Glacier Park
C Grand Canyon; Grand Canyon
D Grand Canyon; Glacier Park

4. During which three months would animals be most likely to estivate?

F May, June, and July
G June, July, and August
H December, January, and February
I January, February, and March

MATH

Read each question below, and choose the best answer.

1. Manuel wants to build a fence so that he can let his pet dog out in the backyard without worrying about it wandering away from home. If he builds the fence to be 3 m long and 4.5 m wide, what will the size of the fenced area be?

A 7.5 m
B 7.5 m^2
C 13.5 m^2
D 135 m^2

2. A bird gathers insects for its three baby birds each day. If each baby eats three bugs per day, how do you express the number of bugs that the mother bird gathers for her babies over a period of 3 weeks in exponential notation?

F $3^3 \times 7^3$
G $3^3 + 7^1$
H $3^3 \times 7^1$
I $3^1 \times 7^3$

3. In which of the following lists are the numbers in order from smallest to largest?

A 0.027, 0.072, 0.270, 0.720
B 0.027, 0.072, 0.720, 0.270
C 0.072, 0.027, 0.270, 0.720
D 0.720, 0.270, 0.072, 0.027

Science in Action

Science, Technology, and Society

Kanzi

Did you know that some chimpanzees raised in captivity can learn to understand some parts of human language? These animals cannot vocally speak any human words. But researchers working with Kanzi, a bonobo chimp who has grown up in Georgia, have used technology to help him communicate. Kanzi uses a board that has more than 400 buttons with symbols on them that represent different words. Kanzi presses a button to communicate the word represented by that button. This board of buttons allows Kanzi to communicate with people.

Language Arts ACTIVITY

WRITING SKILL What would you ask Kanzi if you could speak to him? Think of a question that you would like to ask an animal. Imagine its response. Write this response in a creative essay. Write in the first person.

Weird Science

Guide Horses

You've probably heard of trained dogs guiding visually impaired people. But have you heard of guide horses? Guide horses are miniature—about 2 ft tall! They can learn to follow orders that help them guide people through streets, crowds, and escalators.

Guide horses are trained to stay calm in tough situations. Trainers take the horses to busy streets or malls so that the horses can learn to follow the trainer's lead and to focus in spite of distractions. The horses even learn to disobey orders that could be dangerous. This ability allows the horses to help people avoid dangers they can't see.

Social Studies

People around the world train animals to help people. For example, some people train camels to carry people. Research ways people in different cultures train animals, and present a poster to your class.

People in Science

George Archibald

Dancing with Cranes Imagine a man flapping his arms in a dance with a whooping crane. Does this sound funny? When Dr. George Archibald danced with a crane named Tex, he wasn't joking around. To help this endangered species survive, Archibald wanted cranes to mate in captivity so that he could release cranes into the wild. But the captive cranes wouldn't do their courtship dance. Archibald's cranes had imprinted on the humans that raised them. *Imprinting* is a process in which birds learn to recognize their species by looking at their parents. The birds saw humans as their own species, and could only reproduce if a human did the courtship dance. So, Archibald decided to dance. His plan worked! After some time, Tex hatched a baby crane.

After that, Archibald found a way to help the captive cranes imprint on other cranes. He and his staff now feed baby cranes with hand puppets that look like crane heads. They play recordings of real crane sounds for the young cranes. They even wear crane suits when they are near older birds. These cranes are happy to do their courtship dance with each other instead of with Archibald.

Math Activity

Suppose you want to drive a group of cranes from Madison, Wisconsin, to Orlando, Florida. Find and measure this distance on a map. If your truck goes 500 km per gas tank and a tank costs $30, how much would gas cost on your trip?

To learn more about these Science in Action topics, visit go.hrw.com and type in the keyword HL5ANMF.

Current Science

Check out Current Science® articles related to this chapter by visiting go.hrw.com. Just type in the keyword HL5CS14.

Invertebrates

About the PHOTO

No, this creature isn't an alien! It's a sea slug, a relative of garden slugs and snails. This sea slug lives in the cold Pacific Ocean, near the coast of California. Its bright coloring comes from the food that the slug eats. This animal doesn't breathe with lungs. Instead, it brings oxygen into its body through the orange clubs on its back. Like all invertebrates, sea slugs don't have a backbone.

PRE-READING ACTIVITY

Tri-Fold Before you read the chapter, create the FoldNote entitled "Tri-Fold" described in the **Study Skills** section of the Appendix. Write what you know about invertebrates in the column labeled "Know." Then, write what you want to know in the column labeled "Want." As you read the chapter, write what you learn about invertebrates in the column labeled "Learn."

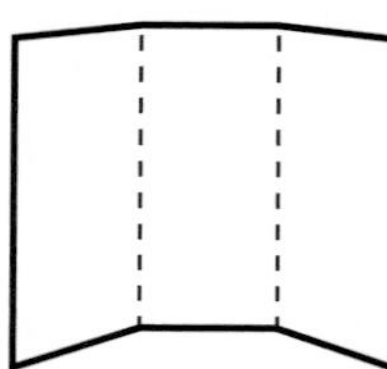

START-UP ACTIVITY

Classify It!

Animals are classified according to their different traits. In this activity, you will classify invertebrates.

Procedure

1. Look at the **pictures** that your teacher has provided. These animals do not have a backbone.
2. Which animals are the most alike? Organize them into groups according to their shared traits.
3. Decide which animals within each group are the most alike. Put these animals into smaller groups inside of their larger group.
4. Construct a table that organizes your classification groups.

Analysis

1. What features did you use to classify the animals into the larger groups? Explain why you think these features are the most important.
2. What features did you use to place the animals in smaller groups? Explain your reasoning.
3. Compare your table with those of your classmates. What similarities or differences do you find?

SECTION 1

Simple Invertebrates

Humans and snakes have them, but octopuses and butterflies don't. What are they? Backbones!

READING WARM-UP

Objectives

- Describe the body plans, nervous systems, and guts of invertebrates.
- Explain how sponges get food.
- Describe three cnidarian traits.
- Describe the three kinds of flatworms.
- Describe the body of a roundworm.

Terms to Learn

invertebrate
ganglion
gut
coelom

READING STRATEGY

Reading Organizer As you read this section, create an outline of the section. Use the headings from the section in your outline.

Animals that don't have backbones are called **invertebrates** (in VUHR tuh brits). They make up about 96% of all animal species. So far, more than 1 million invertebrates have been named. Most biologists think that millions more have not been identified yet.

Invertebrate Characteristics

Invertebrates come in many different shapes and sizes. Grasshoppers, clams, earthworms, and jellyfish are examples of invertebrates. They are all very different from each other. Some invertebrates have heads, and others do not. Some invertebrates eat food through their mouths. Others absorb food particles through their tissues. But all invertebrates are similar because they do not have backbones.

Invertebrates have three basic body plans, or types of *symmetry*. Symmetry can be bilateral (bie LAT uhr uhl) or radial (RAY dee uhl). Some animals have no symmetry at all. Animals that don't have symmetry are *asymmetrical* (AY suh MEH tri kuhl). Most animals have bilateral symmetry. **Figure 1** shows examples of each kind of symmetry.

Figure 1 Animal Body Plans

Bilateral Symmetry

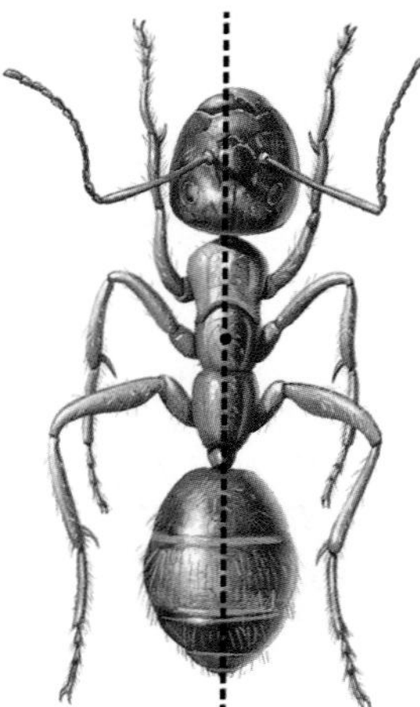

This ant has **bilateral symmetry.** The two sides of its body mirror each other. On each side of its body, the ant has one eye, one antenna, and three legs.

Radial Symmetry

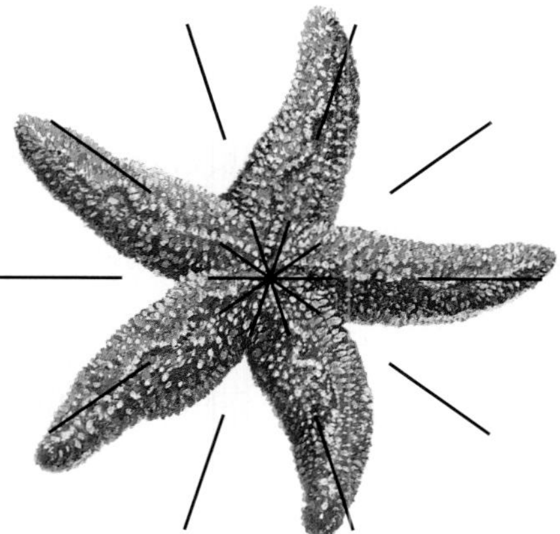

This sea star has **radial symmetry.** Its body is organized around the center, like spokes on a wheel.

Asymmetry

This sponge is **asymmetrical.** You cannot draw a straight line to divide its body into two or more equal parts. Its body is not organized around a center.

Neurons and Ganglia

All animals except sponges have special tissues that make fibers called *neurons*. Neurons allow animals to sense their environment. Neurons also carry messages around the body to control an animal's actions. Simple invertebrates have neurons arranged in networks or in nerve cords. *Nerve cords* are packs of neurons that carry messages along a single path.

In some invertebrates, many nerve cells come together as ganglia (singular, *ganglion*). A **ganglion** (GANG glee uhn) is a concentrated mass of nerve cells. Each ganglion controls different parts of the body. Ganglia are connected by nerve cords. In complex invertebrates, ganglia are controlled by a brain. The *brain* is an organ that controls nerves throughout the body.

invertebrate an animal that does not have a backbone

ganglion a mass of nerve cells

gut the digestive tract

coelom a body cavity that contains the internal organs

Guts

Almost all animals digest food in a gut. A **gut** is a pouch lined with cells that release chemicals that break down food into small particles. The cells in the gut then absorb the food particles. In complex animals, the gut is inside a coelom (SEE luhm). A **coelom** is the body cavity that surrounds the gut. The coelom contains many organs, such as the heart and lungs. But these organs are separated from the gut. This arrangement keeps gut movement from disturbing other body processes. **Figure 2** shows an earthworm's coelom.

Reading Check **How is the coelom related to the gut?** *(See the Appendix for answers to Reading Checks.)*

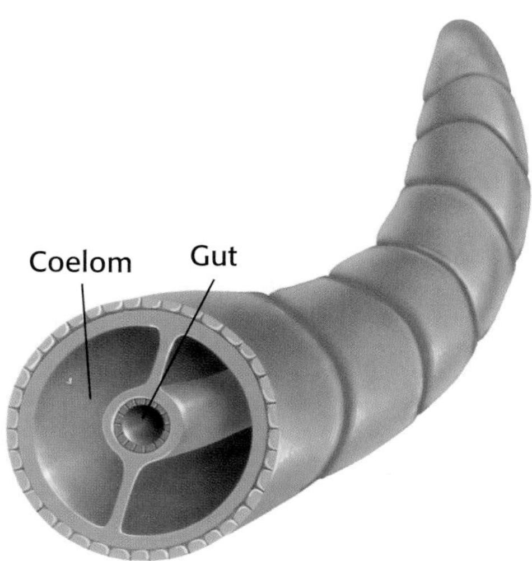

Figure 2 *Earthworms have a fluid-filled coelom that contains the gut.*

Sponges

Sponges are the simplest invertebrates. They are asymmetrical and have no tissues, gut, or neurons. Adult sponges move only millimeters per day—if they move at all. In fact, sponges were once thought to be plants! But sponges can't make their own food. That's one reason they are classified as animals. **Figure 3** shows a sponge.

Figure 3 *Some sponges are brightly colored.*

Figure 4 How Sponges Eat

Water carries food into the sponge through pores. Inside the sponge, collar cells remove food from the water. The water exits through an osculum.

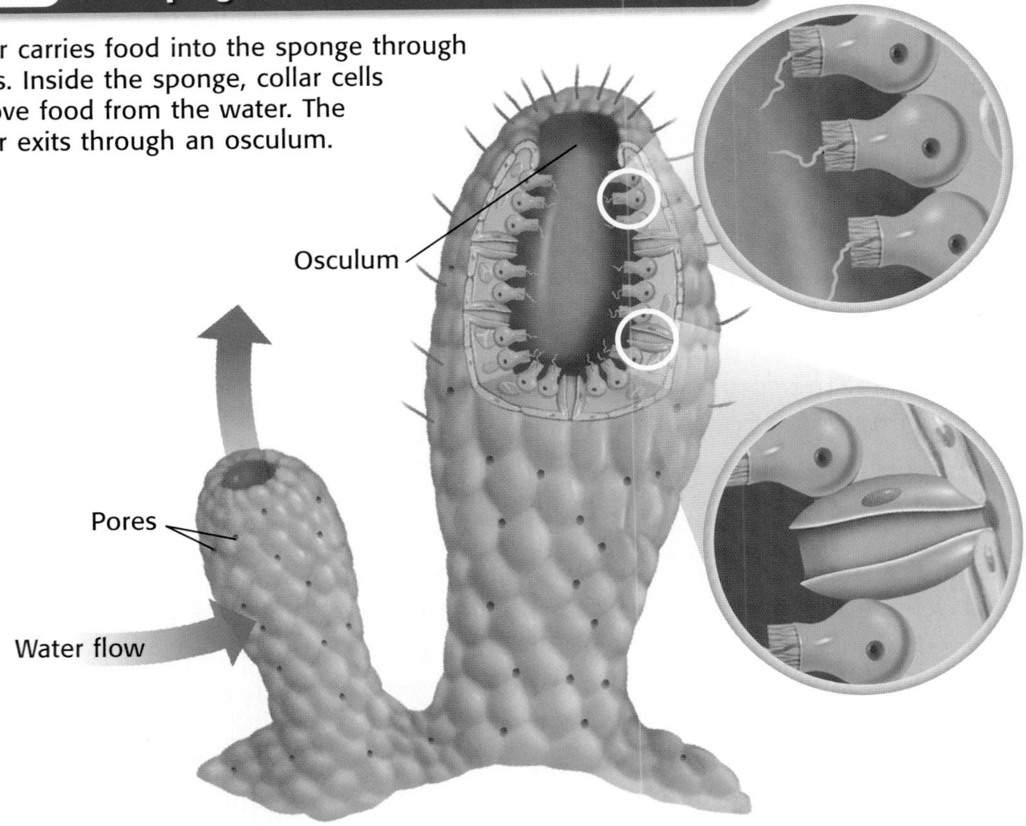

Osculum

Pores

Water flow

Collar cells line the central cavity of a sponge.

Pore cells have holes that let water flow into the sponge.

How Do Sponges Eat?

Sponges feed on tiny plants and animals. Because sponges cannot move in search of food and do not have a gut, they have a special way of getting food. A sponge sweeps water into its body through its pores. *Pores* are the holes on the outside of a sponge's body. Water flows into a cavity in the middle of the body, bringing oxygen and food. Special cells called *collar cells* line this cavity. Collar cells filter and digest food from the water that enters the body. Water leaves the body through a hole at the top of the sponge. This hole is called an *osculum* (AHS kyoo luhm). **Figure 4** shows this process.

Reading Check How does water enter a sponge's body?

Body Part Abilities

Sponges have some unusual abilities. If you forced a sponge's body through a strainer, the separated cells could come back together and re-form into a new sponge. If part of a sponge is broken off, the missing part can *regenerate,* or grow back. And if a sponge is broken into pieces, or fragmented, new sponges may form from each fragment. Though sponges can use regeneration as a form of reproduction, they also use sexual reproduction.

Several Sponges

Suppose that a big sponge breaks into seven pieces. Each piece begins to grow into a new sponge. Then, each new sponge breaks into five smaller pieces, and each of these new pieces forms a new sponge. How many sponges would you have?

Kinds of Sponges

All sponges live in water, and most live in the ocean. As shown in **Figure 5,** sponges come in many different shapes and sizes. Most sponges have a skeleton made of small, hard fibers called *spicules* (SPIK YOOLZ). Some spicules are straight, some are curved, and others have complex star shapes. A sponge's skeleton supports its body and helps protect it from predators. Sponges are divided into groups according to the kinds of skeletons they have.

Figure 5 *Sponges come in many shapes and sizes.*

Cnidarians

Do you know anyone who has been stung by a jellyfish? It is a very painful experience! Jellyfish are members of a group of invertebrates that have stinging cells. Animals in this group are called *cnidarians* (ni DER ee uhns).

Cnidarians are more complex than sponges. Cnidarians have complex tissues and a gut for digesting food. They also have a simple network of nerve cells. Most cnidarians can move more quickly than sponges can. But some cnidarians do share a special trait with sponges. If the body cells are separated, they can come back together to re-form the cnidarian.

Two Body Forms

A cnidarian body can have one of two forms—the *medusa* or the *polyp* form. These body forms are shown in **Figure 6.** Medusas swim through the water. Polyps usually attach to a surface. Some cnidarians change forms at different times in their lives. But many cnidarians are polyps for their whole lives.

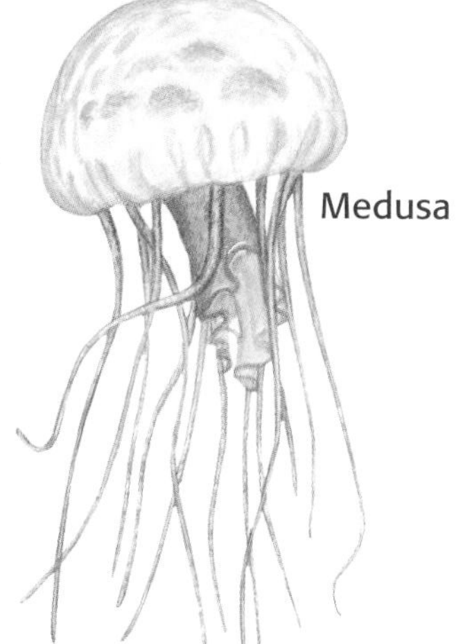

Polyp

Figure 6 *Both the medusa and the polyp forms of a jellyfish have radial symmetry.*

CONNECTION TO Environmental Science

Threatened Reefs Coral reefs are home to many beautiful cnidarians. But living coral reefs are threatened by overfishing, pollution, mining, coral harvesting, coastal development, and damage from swimmers and boats. Scientists are looking for ways to protect coral reefs. One solution is to teach people not to touch or collect living corals. Make a poster about how people can protect coral reefs by leaving them alone.

ACTIVITY

Figure 7 *Each stinging cell contains a tiny spear.*

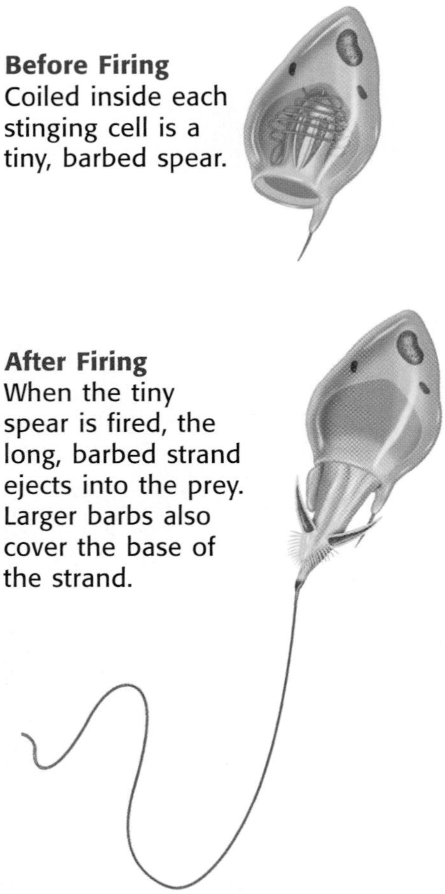

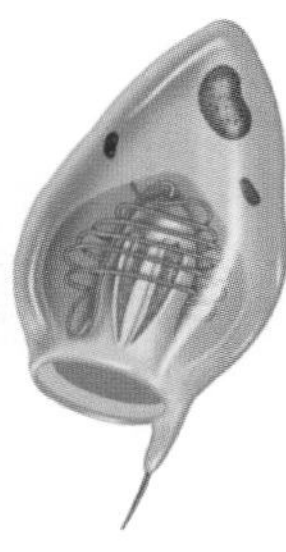

Before Firing Coiled inside each stinging cell is a tiny, barbed spear.

After Firing When the tiny spear is fired, the long, barbed strand ejects into the prey. Larger barbs also cover the base of the strand.

Stinging Cells

All cnidarians have tentacles covered with stinging cells. When an organism brushes against the tentacles, it activates hundreds of stinging cells. Each stinging cell uses water pressure to fire a tiny, barbed spear into the organism. **Figure 7** shows a stinging cell before and after firing. The tiny spears can release a painful—and sometimes paralyzing—poison into their targets. Cnidarians use their stinging cells to protect themselves and to catch food.

Kinds of Cnidarians

There are three major classes of cnidarians: hydrozoans (HIE dro ZOH uhn), jellyfish, and sea anemones and corals. **Figure 8** shows each kind of cnidarian. Hydrozoans are common cnidarians that live in both freshwater and marine environments. Most spend their entire lives as polyps. Jellyfish catch other invertebrates and fish in their tentacles. They spend most of their lives as medusas. Sea anemones and corals spend their lives as polyps. They are often brightly colored.

Most corals are small and live in colonies. The colonies build huge skeletons that are made of calcium carbonate. Each new generation of corals builds on top of the last generation. Over thousands of years, these tiny animals build massive underwater reefs. Coral reefs can be found in warm, tropical waters throughout the world.

Figure 8 **Kinds of Cnidarians**

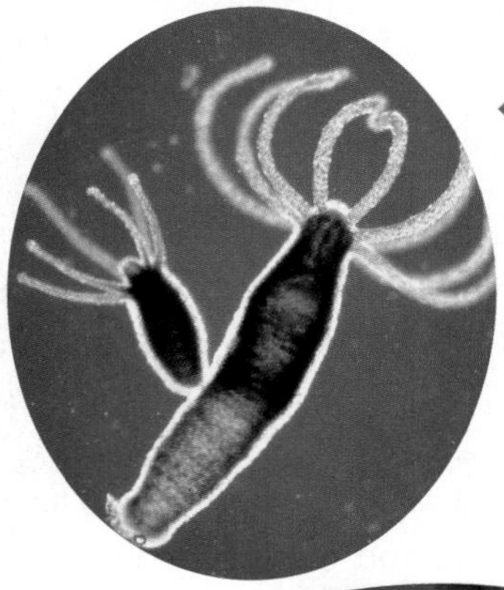

Hydrozoan

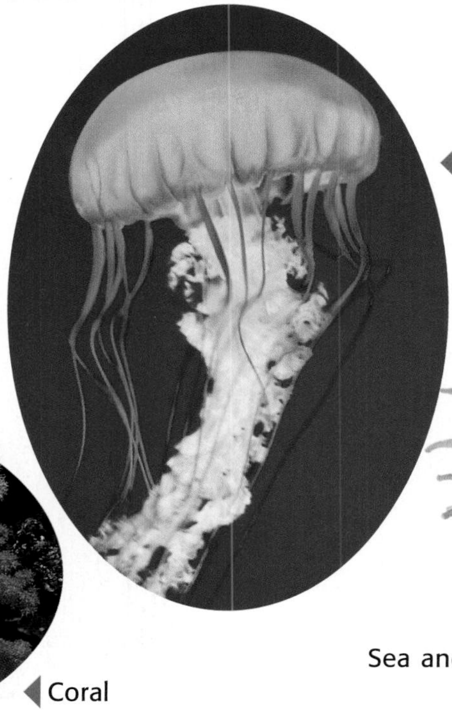

Jellyfish

Sea anemone

Coral

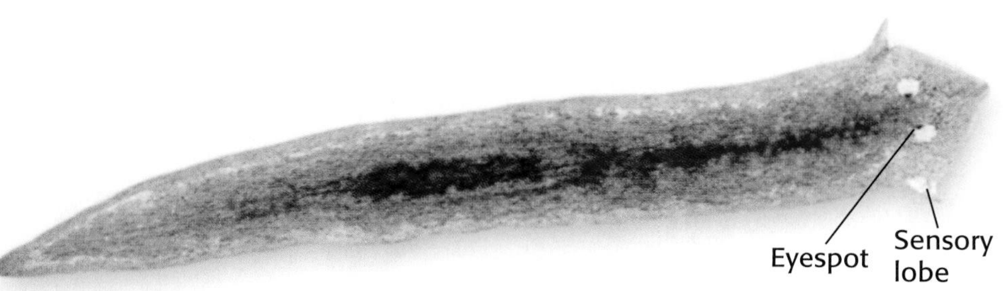

Figure 9 *This planarian has a head with eyespots and sensory lobes. Planarians are often about 15 mm long.*

Flatworms

When you think of worms, you probably think of earthworms. But there are many other kinds of worms. Many of them are too tiny to see without a microscope. The simplest worms are the flatworms. Flatworms are divided into three major classes: planarians (pluh NER ee uhnz) and marine flatworms, flukes, and tapeworms.

All flatworms have bilateral symmetry. Many flatworms also have a clearly defined head and two large eyespots. Even though the eyespots cannot focus, a flatworm knows the direction that light is coming from. Some flatworms also have a bump on each side of their head. These bumps are *sensory lobes*. Sensory lobes are used for detecting food. You can see these traits in the planarian shown in **Figure 9.**

Reading Check **What are the three major classes of flatworms?**

A Walk in the Park

With your family, take a walk around your neighborhood or a nearby park and make a list of all the invertebrates you find. If you can't recognize some of the invertebrates, draw them, and try to identify them later using a local guide to invertebrates.

ACTIVITY

Planarians

Planarians live in freshwater lakes and streams or on land in damp places. Most planarians are predators. They eat other animals or parts of other animals and digest food in a gut. They find food by using their sensory lobes. The planarian's head, eyespots, and sensory lobes are clues that it has a well-developed nervous system. Planarians even have a brain for processing information about their surroundings.

Flukes

Flukes are parasites. A *parasite* is an organism that invades and feeds on the body of another living organism that is called a *host*. Most flukes live and reproduce inside the bodies of other animals. A fluke's fertilized eggs pass out of the other animal's body with waste products. If these fertilized eggs infect drinking water or food, animals may eat them. The fertilized eggs will develop into new flukes inside the animals.

Flukes have tiny heads without eyespots or sensory lobes. They have special suckers and hooks for attaching to animals. **Figure 10** shows a fluke.

Figure 10 *Flukes use suckers to attach to their host. Most flukes are just a few millimeters long.*

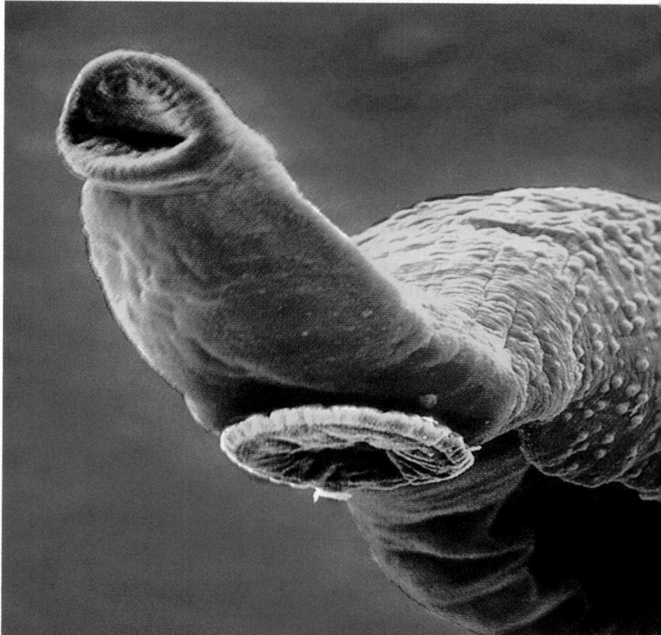

Figure 11 *Tapeworms can reach enormous sizes. Some can grow to be longer than a school bus!*

CONNECTION TO Social Studies

Tapeworms People and animals can become infected by tapeworms when they swallow something that contains tapeworm eggs or larvae. These eggs or larvae can come from unclean food, water, or surfaces. Animals can even get tapeworms by swallowing infected fleas. In a group, research one of the following topics: What are some different kinds of tapeworms? What are the effects of tapeworm infection? How can tapeworm infection be prevented? Then, present your research to the rest of the class.

ACTIVITY

Tapeworms

Tapeworms are similar to flukes. Like flukes, they have a small head with no eyespots or sensory lobes. They live and reproduce in other animals. They also feed on these animals as parasites. But tapeworms have a unique body that is very specialized for their internal environment. Tapeworms do not have a gut. These organisms simply attach to the intestines of another animal and absorb nutrients. The nutrients move directly through the tapeworm's tissues. **Figure 11** shows a tapeworm that can infect humans.

Roundworms

Roundworms have bodies that are long, slim, and round, like spaghetti. Like other worms, they have bilateral symmetry. Roundworms have a simple nervous system. A ring of ganglia forms a simple brain. Parallel nerve cords connect the two ends of their body. **Figure 12** shows one kind of roundworm.

Most species of roundworms are very small. A single rotten apple could contain 100,000 roundworms! These tiny worms break down the dead tissues of plants and animals. This process helps make soil rich and healthy.

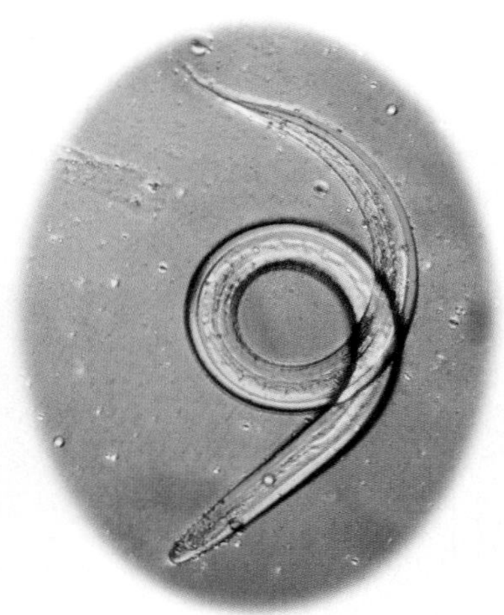

Figure 12 *This hookworm is a tiny larva. Even as an adult, it will be less than 15 mm long.*

Not all roundworms eat dead tissues. Many roundworms are parasites. Some of these roundworms, including pinworms and hookworms, infect humans. *Trichinella spiralis* (TRIK i NEL uh spuh RAL is) is a parasitic roundworm that is passed to people from infected pork. This roundworm causes the disease trichinosis (TRIK i NOH sis). This illness causes fever, fatigue, and digestive problems. Cooking pork thoroughly will kill any roundworms living in the meat.

Reading Check **Name three roundworms that are parasites and that can affect humans.**

SECTION Review

Summary

- Invertebrates are animals that do not have a backbone. Most invertebrates have neurons and a gut. The gut is surrounded by the coelom.
- Almost all animals have radial or bilateral symmetry. But some animals, including sponges, are asymmetrical.
- Sponges filter food from water with collar cells. Collar cells also digest food. Sponges can regenerate body parts. They are classified by the kinds of skeletons they have.
- Cnidarians have stinging cells and have two body forms: the medusa and the polyp. Hydrozoans, jellyfish, and sea anemones and corals are cnidarians.
- Planarians, flukes, and tapeworms are three classes of flatworms. Planarians have eyespots and sensory lobes. Flukes and tapeworms are parasites.
- Roundworms are tiny worms that break down dead plant and animal tissue. Some roundworms are parasites.

Using Key Terms

Complete each of the following sentences by choosing the correct term from the word bank.

invertebrate	gut
ganglion	coelom

1. A(n) ___ is a mass of nerve cells that controls an animal's actions.
2. A(n) ___ does not have a backbone.
3. The ___ is a special space in an animal's body that surrounds the ___ and other organs.

Understanding Key Ideas

4. Which of the following is a trait shared by all invertebrates?
   - **a.** having no backbone
   - **b.** having radial symmetry
   - **c.** having a brain
   - **d.** having a gut
5. What do sponges use to digest food?
   - **a.** an osculum
   - **b.** pores
   - **c.** collar cells
   - **d.** a gut
6. Describe cnidarian body forms and stinging cells.
7. How is a roundworm similar to a piece of spaghetti?

Interpreting Graphics

All invertebrate nervous systems are made up of some or all of the same basic parts. The drawing below shows the nervous system of a segmented worm. Use this drawing to answer the questions that follow.

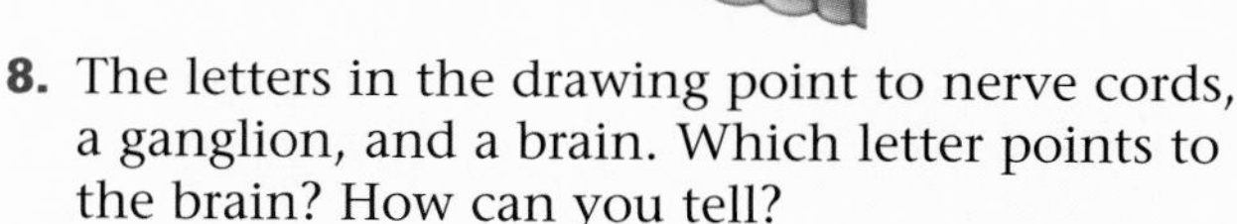

8. The letters in the drawing point to nerve cords, a ganglion, and a brain. Which letter points to the brain? How can you tell?
9. How is the brain connected to the ganglion?

Critical Thinking

10. **Making Inferences** Explain why it would be important for a parasite that its host survive.

SCILINKS.
NSTA
Developed and maintained by the National Science Teachers Association
For a variety of links related to this chapter, go to www.scilinks.org
Topic: Sponges; Roundworms
SciLinks code: HSM1443; HSM1332

SECTION 2

Mollusks and Annelid Worms

READING WARM-UP

Objectives

- Explain how mollusks eat, control body functions, and circulate blood.
- Describe the four body parts that most mollusks have in common.
- Describe three annelid worms.

Terms to Learn

open circulatory system
closed circulatory system
segment

READING STRATEGY

Discussion Read this section silently. Write down questions that you have about this section. Discuss your questions in a small group.

Have you ever eaten clams or calamari? Have you ever seen earthworms on the sidewalk after it rains?

If you have, then you already know a thing or two about mollusks and annelid worms. These animals are more complex than sponges, cnidarians, flatworms, and roundworms. For example, mollusks and annelid worms have a circulatory system that carries materials throughout their bodies.

Mollusks

Snails, slugs, clams, oysters, squids, and octopuses are all mollusks. Most of these animals live in the ocean. But some live in fresh water, and some live on land.

Most mollusks fit into three classes. The *gastropods* (GAS troh PAHDZ) include slugs and snails. The *bivalves* include clams and other shellfish that have two shells. *Cephalopods* (SEF uh loh PAHDZ) include squids and octopuses.

How Do Mollusks Eat?

Each kind of mollusk has its own way of eating. Snails and slugs eat with a ribbonlike organ—a tongue covered with curved teeth. This organ is called a *radula* (RAJ u luh). **Figure 1** shows a close-up of a slug's radula. Slugs and snails use the radula to scrape algae from rocks, chunks of tissue from seaweed, or pieces of leaves from plants. Clams and oysters attach to one place and use gills to filter tiny plants, bacteria, and other particles from the water. Octopuses and squids use tentacles to grab their food and to place it in their powerful jaws.

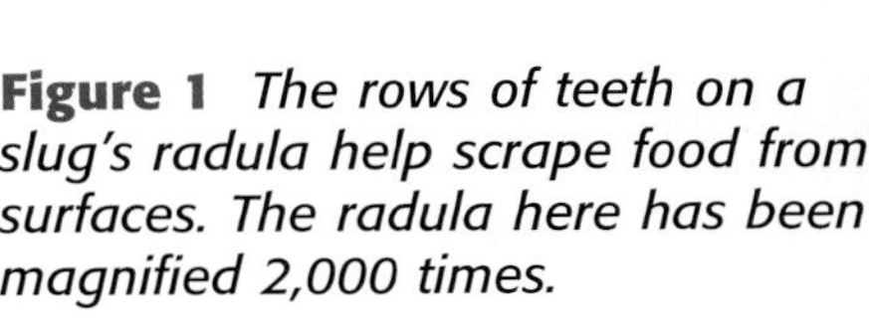

Figure 1 *The rows of teeth on a slug's radula help scrape food from surfaces. The radula here has been magnified 2,000 times.*

Ganglia and Brains

All mollusks have complex ganglia. They have special ganglia to control breathing, movement, and digestion. But octopuses and squids have the most advanced nervous system of all invertebrates. Cephalopods, such as the octopus in **Figure 2,** have large brains that connect all of their ganglia. Cephalopods are thought to be the smartest invertebrates.

Figure 2 *Octopuses are very smart. If they are given stones, they can build a cave to hide in.*

Pumping Blood

Unlike simple invertebrates, mollusks have a circulatory system. The circulatory system transports materials through the body in the blood. Most mollusks have an open circulatory system. In an **open circulatory system,** a simple heart pumps blood through blood vessels that empty into *sinuses*, or spaces in the animal's body. Squids and octopuses have a closed circulatory system. In a **closed circulatory system,** a heart pumps blood through a network of blood vessels that form a closed loop.

Reading Check **What is the difference between an open circulatory system and a closed circulatory system?** (*See the Appendix for answers to Reading Checks.*)

open circulatory system a circulatory system in which the circulatory fluid is not contained entirely within vessels

closed circulatory system a circulatory system in which the heart circulates blood through a network of blood vessels that form a closed loop

Mollusk Bodies

A snail, a clam, and a squid look quite different from one another. Yet if you look closely, you will see that their bodies all have similar structures. The body parts of mollusks are described in **Figure 3.**

Figure 3 **Body Parts of Mollusks**

Mollusks are known for their broad, muscular **foot.** The foot helps the animal move. In gastropods, the foot makes mucus that the animal slides along.

The gills, gut, and other organs form the **visceral mass** (VIS uhr uhl MAS). It lies in the center of a mollusk's body.

A layer of tissue called the **mantle** covers the visceral mass. The mantle protects the bodies of mollusks that do not have a shell.

In most mollusks, the outside of the mantle secretes a **shell.** The shell protects the mollusk from predators and keeps land mollusks from drying out.

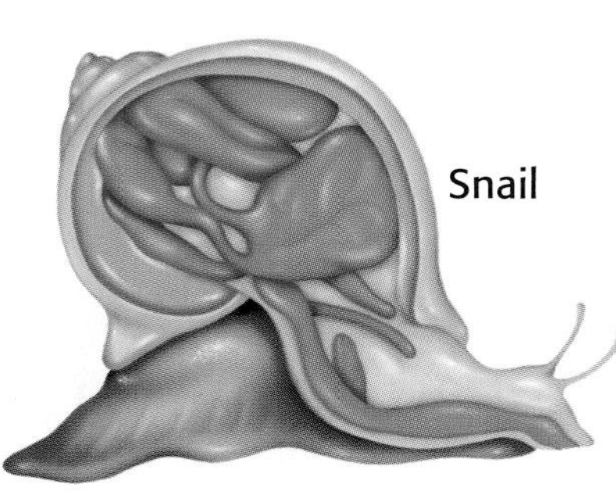

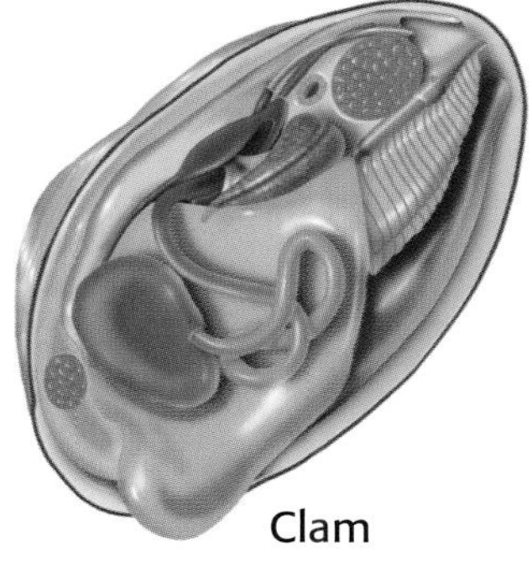

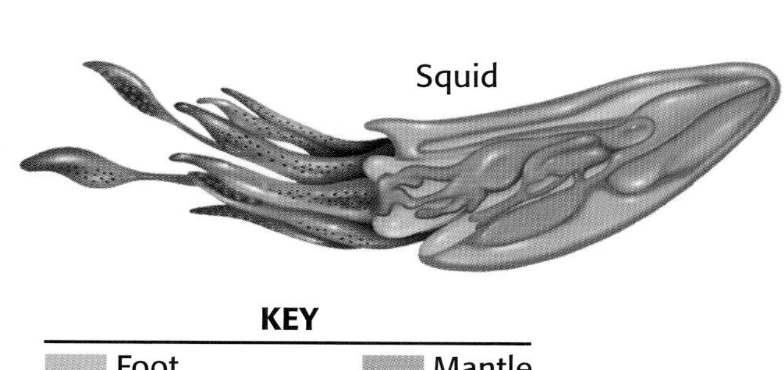

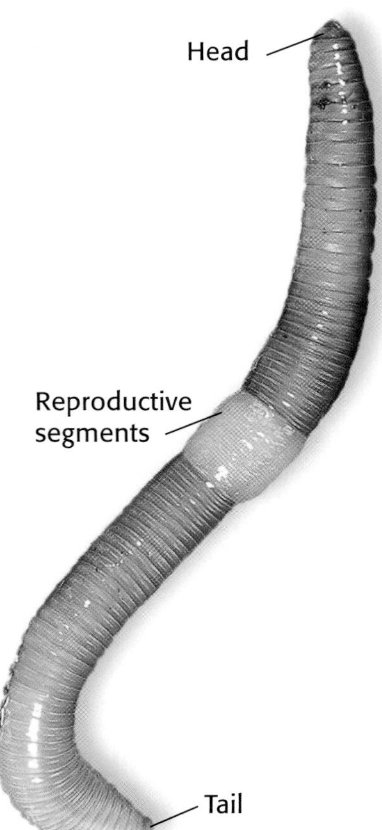

Figure 4 *Except for the head, tail, and reproductive segments, all of the segments of this earthworm are identical.*

Annelid Worms

Annelid worms are often called segmented worms because their bodies have segments. A **segment** is an identical, or almost identical, repeating body part. You can see the segments of an earthworm in **Figure 4.**

Like roundworms and flatworms, annelid worms have bilateral symmetry. But annelid worms are more complex than other worms. Annelid worms have a closed circulatory system. They also have a complex nervous system with a brain. A nerve cord connects the brain to a ganglion in each segment.

Annelid worms live in salt water, in fresh water, or on land. They eat plant material or animals. Three major groups of annelid worms are earthworms, marine worms, and leeches.

Earthworms

Earthworms are the most familiar annelid worms. Each earthworm has 100 to 175 segments. Most of these segments are identical, but some look different from the others. These segments have special jobs, such as eating or reproducing.

Earthworms eat material in the soil. They break down plant and animal matter in the soil and leave behind wastes called *castings*. Castings help gardens by making the soil richer. Earthworms also improve garden soil by digging tunnels. The tunnels allow air and water to reach deep into the soil.

To move, earthworms use stiff hairs, or bristles, on the outside of their body. The bristles hold the back part of the worm in place while the front part pushes through the soil.

segment any part of a larger structure, such as the body of an organism, that is set off by natural or arbitrary boundaries

Marine Worms

If there were a beauty contest for worms, marine worms would win. These worms are called *polychaetes* (PAHL ih KEETS), which means "many bristles." They are covered in bristles and come in many colors. **Figure 5** shows a marine worm. Most of these worms live in the ocean. Some eat mollusks and other small animals. Others filter small pieces of food from the water.

Figure 5 *This marine worm is a predator that eats small animals. Can you see the segments of this worm?*

Leeches

Leeches are known as parasites that suck other animals' blood. This is true of some leeches. But other leeches are not parasites. Some leeches are scavengers that eat dead animals. Others are predators that eat insects, slugs, and snails.

Leeches that suck blood can be useful in medicine. After surgery, doctors sometimes use leeches to prevent dangerous swelling near a wound. **Figure 6** shows two leeches being used for this purpose. Leeches also make a chemical that keeps blood thin so that it does not form clots. The leech uses the chemical to keep blood flowing from its host. Doctors use this chemical to prevent blood clots in people with circulation problems. This chemical can also help break down blood clots that already exist.

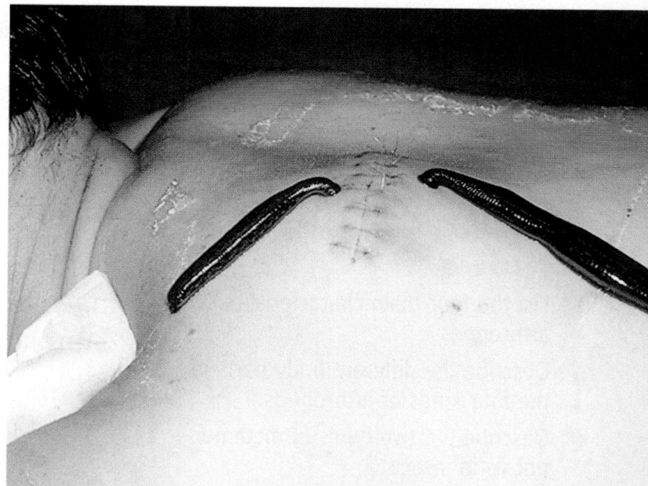

Figure 6 *Doctors sometimes use leeches to reduce swelling after surgery.*

Reading Check **What are two ways that doctors use leeches to help people?**

SECTION Review

Summary

- Mollusks get food with gills, a radula, or tentacles and jaws.
- Mollusks have a complex nervous system.
- Mollusks have either an open circulatory system or a closed circulatory system.
- All mollusks have a foot, a visceral mass, and a mantle. Most mollusks also have a shell.
- The three major groups of annelid worms are earthworms, marine worms, and leeches.

Using Key Terms

1. Use the following terms in the same sentence: *open circulatory system* and *closed circulatory system*.
2. In your own words, write a definition for the term *segment*.

Understanding Key Ideas

3. Some mollusks use a radula to
   a. scrape algae off rocks.
   b. filter food from water.
   c. grab food from water.
   d. place food in their jaws.
4. What trait do all mollusk nervous systems share? What is unique about squids' and octopuses' nervous systems?
5. What are the four main body parts of most mollusks?
6. Describe three different kinds of annelid worms.

Math Skills

7. If a squid swims at 30 km/h, how far can it swim in 1 min?

Critical Thinking

8. **Predicting Consequences** Clams use gills to filter food from water. How could water pollution affect clams?
9. **Analyzing Ideas** Cephalopods do not have shells. What other traits do they have to help make up for this lack of protection?

SCILINKS.
NSTA
Developed and maintained by the National Science Teachers Association
For a variety of links related to this chapter, go to www.scilinks.org
Topic: Mollusks and Annelid Worms
SciLinks code: HSM0986

SECTION 3

Arthropods

Have you ever explored a park or field, looking for living things? How many animals do you think can live on one acre of land? If you could find all the arthropods in that area, you could count more than a million animals!

READING WARM-UP

Objectives

- List the four main characteristics of arthropods.
- Describe the different body parts of the four kinds of arthropods.
- Describe the two types of metamorphosis in insects.

Terms to Learn

exoskeleton
antenna
compound eye
metamorphosis

READING STRATEGY

Prediction Guide Before reading this section, write the title of each heading in this section. Next, under each heading, write what you think you will learn.

Arthropods have lived for hundreds of millions of years. They have adapted to nearly every environment. You are probably familiar with many of them, such as insects, spiders, crabs, and centipedes. Arthropods are the largest group of animals on Earth. At least 75% of all animal species are arthropods.

Characteristics of Arthropods

All arthropods share four characteristics: a segmented body with specialized parts, jointed limbs, an exoskeleton, and a well-developed nervous system.

Segmented and Specialized

Like annelid worms, arthropods are segmented. In some arthropods, such as centipedes, nearly every segment is identical. Only the segments that make up the head and tail are different from the rest. But most species of arthropods have segments that include specialized structures, such as wings, antennae, gills, pincers, and claws. During an arthropod's development, some segments grow together. This process forms three main body parts. These body parts are the *head,* the *thorax,* and the *abdomen.* You can see these three body parts in **Figure 1.**

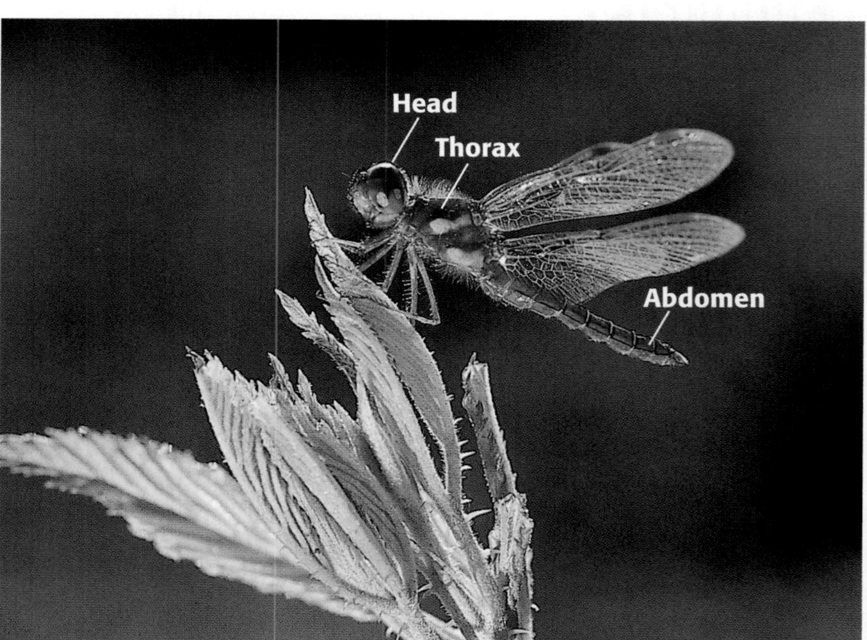

Figure 1 *Like most arthropods, this dragonfly has a head, a thorax, and an abdomen.*

Jointed Limbs

Jointed limbs give arthropods their name. *Arthro* means "joint," and *pod* means "foot." Jointed limbs are legs or other body parts that bend at the joints. Having jointed limbs makes it easier for arthropods to move.

Figure 2 *A ghost crab's exoskeleton protects its body from drying out on land.*

An External Skeleton

Arthropods have a hard outer covering. The hard, external structure that covers the outside of the body is an **exoskeleton.** You can see a crab's yellow and white exoskeleton in **Figure 2.** This structure is made of protein and a special substance called *chitin* (KIE tin). An exoskeleton does some of the same things that an internal skeleton does. Like your bones, it serves as a stiff frame that supports the body. It also allows the animal to move. An arthropod's muscles connect to different parts of the skeleton. When the muscles contract, they move the exoskeleton, which moves parts of the animal.

But the exoskeleton also does things that an internal skeleton doesn't do well. The exoskeleton acts like a suit of armor to protect organs inside the body. The exoskeleton also keeps water inside the animal's body. This feature allows arthropods to live on land without drying out.

exoskeleton a hard, external, supporting structure

compound eye an eye composed of many light detectors

Reading Check **How is an exoskeleton similar to an internal skeleton?** (*See the Appendix for answers to Reading Checks.*)

Sensing Surroundings

All arthropods have a head and a well-developed brain and nerve cord. The nervous system receives information from sense organs, including eyes and bristles. Some arthropods, such as the tarantula, use external bristles to sense their surroundings. The bristles detect motion, vibration, pressure, and chemicals.

Some arthropods have very simple eyes. These arthropods can detect light but cannot see images. But most arthropods have compound eyes. Arthropods that have compound eyes can see images. A **compound eye** is an eye that is made of many identical, light-sensitive units. The fruit fly in **Figure 3** has two compound eyes.

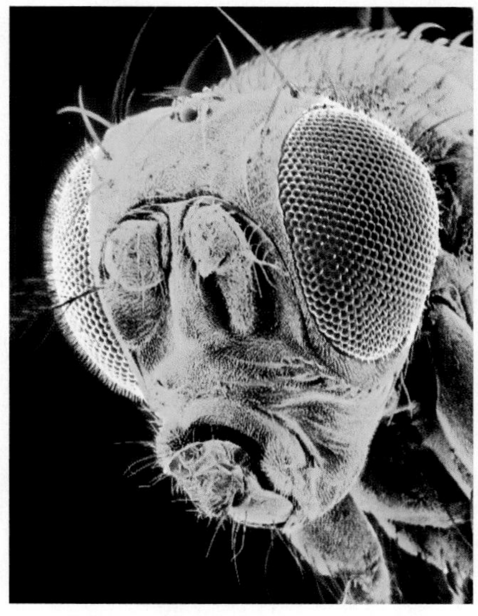

Figure 3 *Compound eyes are made of many identical, light-sensitive units that work together.*

Kinds of Arthropods

Arthropods are classified by the kinds of body parts they have. You can tell the difference between arthropods by looking at the number of legs, eyes, and antennae they have. An **antenna** is a feeler that senses touch, taste, or smell.

Figure 4 *Centipedes eat other animals. Millipedes eat plants.*

antenna a feeler that is on the head of an invertebrate, such as a crustacean or an insect, that senses touch, taste, or smell

Centipedes and Millipedes

Centipedes and millipedes have one pair of antennae, a hard head, and one pair of mandibles. *Mandibles* are mouthparts that can pierce and chew food. One way to tell these animals apart is to count the number of legs on each segment. Centipedes have one pair of legs on each segment. They can have 30 to 354 legs. Millipedes have two pairs of legs on each segment. The record number of legs on a millipede is 752! **Figure 4** shows a centipede and a millipede. How many legs can you count on each?

Crustaceans

Shrimps, barnacles, crabs, and lobsters are crustaceans. Most crustaceans live in water. They have gills for breathing in the water, mandibles for eating, and two compound eyes. Each eye is located on the end of an eyestalk. Unlike all other arthropods, crustaceans have two pairs of antennae. The crustaceans in **Figure 5** show some of these traits. The lobster's gills are located under the exoskeleton.

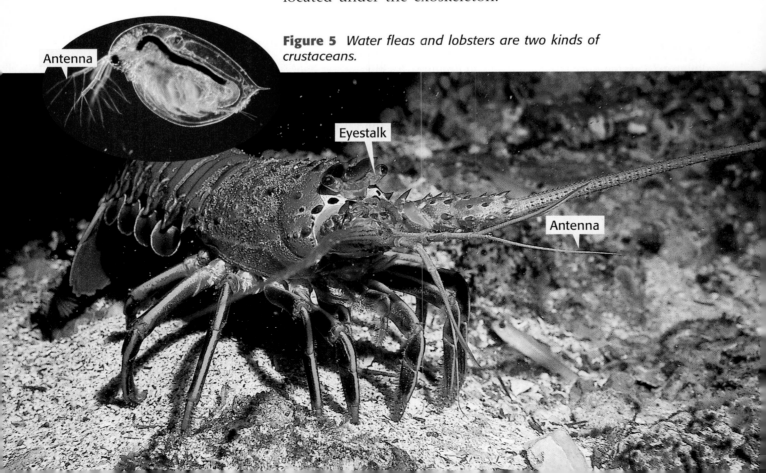

Figure 5 *Water fleas and lobsters are two kinds of crustaceans.*

Arachnids

Spiders, scorpions, mites, and ticks are arachnids (uh RAK nidz). **Figure 6** shows the two main body parts of an arachnid: the *cephalothorax* (SEF uh loh THAWR AKS) and the abdomen. The cephalothorax is made of both a head and a thorax. Most arachnids have four pairs of legs. They have no antennae. Instead of mandibles, they have a pair of clawlike mouthparts called *chelicerae* (kuh LIS uhr EE). And instead of compound eyes, they have simple eyes. The number of eyes varies—some spiders have eight eyes!

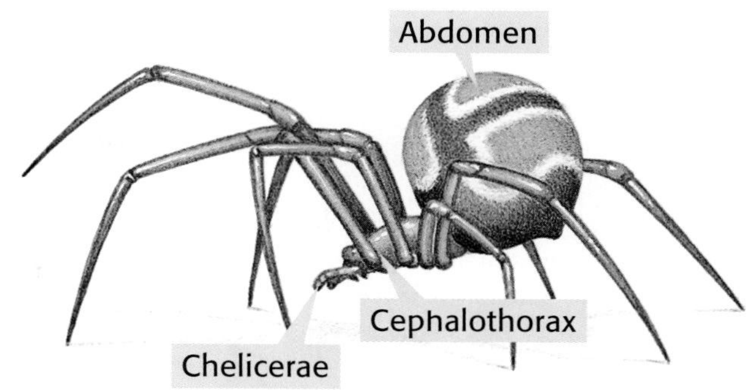

Figure 6 *Arachnids have two main body parts and special mouthparts called chelicerae.*

Though some people fear spiders, these arachnids are more helpful than harmful. A few kinds of spider bites do need medical treatment. But the chelicerae of many spiders cannot even pierce human skin. And spiders usually use their chelicerae to catch small insects. Spiders kill more insect pests than any other animal does.

Ticks live in forests, brushy areas, and even grassy lawns. Their bodies can be just a few millimeters long. The segments of these small bodies are joined as one part. Ticks are parasites that use chelicerae to slice into a host's skin. These parasites attach onto the host and feed on the host's blood. A few ticks that bite humans can carry diseases, such as Lyme disease. But most people who are bitten by ticks do not get sick.

Reading Check **How are spiders helpful to humans?**

Insects

Insects make up the largest group of arthropods. If you put all the insects in the world together, they would weigh more than all the other animals combined! **Figure 7** shows a few kinds of insects. Although they look different, they all have three main body parts, six legs, and two antennae.

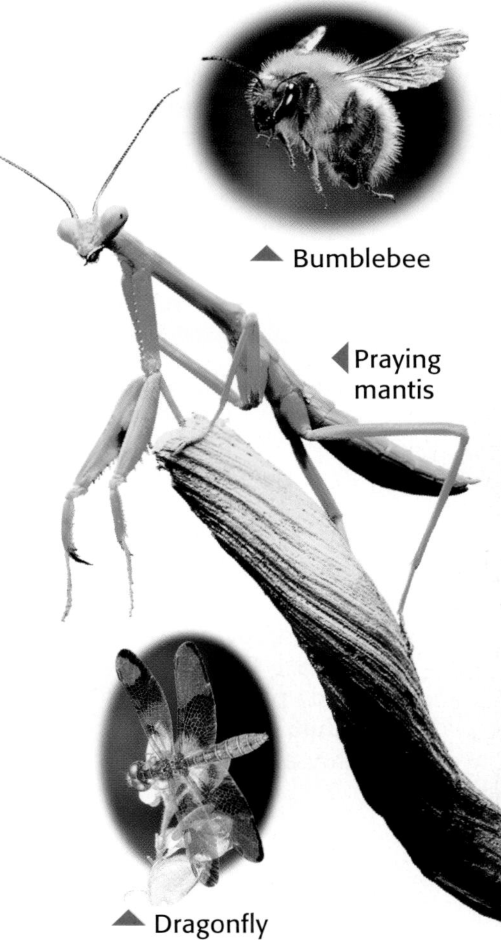

Figure 7 *These are just a few of the many different insects. Can you see any traits that they have in common?*

Sticky Webs

1. Place a **piece of tape** on your desk, sticky side up. The tape represents a web. Your fingers will represent an insect's legs, and then they will represent a spider's legs.
2. Holding the tape in place by the edges, "walk" your fingers across the tape. What happens?
3. Dip your fingers in **cooking oil,** and "walk" them across the tape again. What happens this time?
4. Use the results to explain why spiders don't get stuck in webs.

The World of Insects

The only place on Earth where insects do not live is in ocean water. They live on land, in fresh water, and near the sea in beach areas. Many insects are helpful. Most flowering plants depend on insects to carry pollen between plants. Farmers depend on insects to pollinate fruit crops. But some insects are pests that destroy crops or spread disease. And others, such as fleas, ticks, and mosquitoes, bite us and suck our blood.

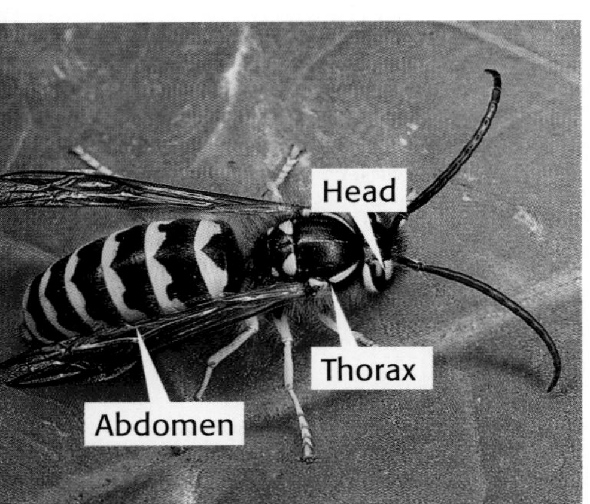

Figure 8 *All insect bodies have these three main parts.*

Insect Bodies

As shown in **Figure 8,** an insect's body has three parts: the head, the thorax, and the abdomen. On the head, insects have one pair of antennae, one pair of compound eyes, and mandibles. The thorax is made of three segments, each of which has one pair of legs. Some insects have no wings. Others may have one or two pairs of wings on the thorax.

Complete Metamorphosis

metamorphosis a phase in the life cycle of many animals during which a rapid change from the immature form of an organism to the adult form takes place

As an insect develops, it changes form. This process is called **metamorphosis** (MET uh MAWR fuh sis). Most insects go through a complex change called complete metamorphosis. As shown in **Figure 9,** complete metamorphosis has four main stages: egg, larva, pupa (PYOO puh), and adult. Butterflies, beetles, flies, bees, wasps, and ants go through this change.

Figure 9 **The Stages of Complete Metamorphosis**

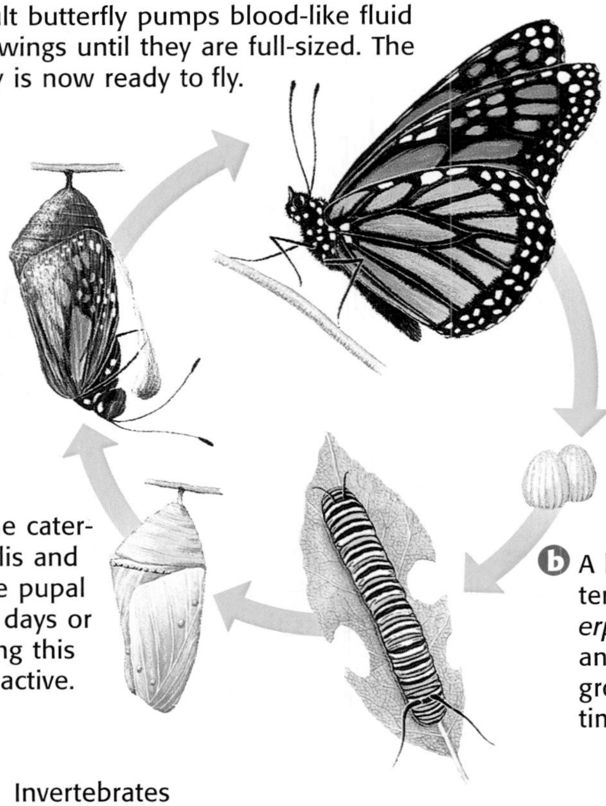

a. An adult lays **eggs.** An embryo forms inside each egg.

b. A **larva** hatches from the egg. Butterfly and moth larvae are called *caterpillars.* The caterpillar eats leaves and grows rapidly. As the caterpillar grows, it sheds its outer layer several times. This process is called *molting.*

c. After its final molt, the caterpillar makes a chrysalis and becomes a **pupa.** The pupal stage may last a few days or several months. During this stage, the insect is inactive.

d. Adult body parts replace the larval body parts. The **adult** splits its chrysalis.

e. The adult butterfly pumps blood-like fluid into its wings until they are full-sized. The butterfly is now ready to fly.

Incomplete Metamorphosis

Grasshoppers and cockroaches are some of the insects that go through incomplete metamorphosis. Incomplete metamorphosis is less complicated than complete metamorphosis. As shown in **Figure 10,** incomplete metamorphosis has three main stages: egg, nymph, and adult. Some nymphs shed their exoskeleton several times in a process called *molting.*

An insect in the nymph stage looks very much like an adult insect. But a nymph does not have wings and is very small. Through molting, it develops into an adult.

Reading Check What are the three stages of incomplete metamorphosis?

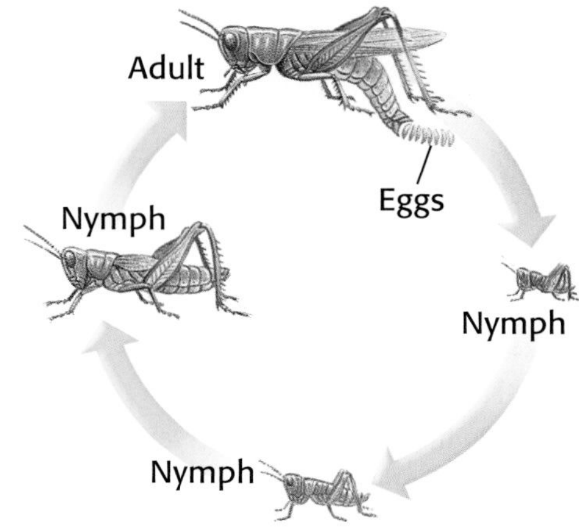

Figure 10 *The grasshopper nymphs look like smaller versions of the adult.*

SECTION Review

Summary

- At least 75% of all animal species are arthropods.
- The four main characteristics shared by arthropods are jointed limbs, a hard exoskeleton, body segments, and a well-developed nervous system.
- The four kinds of arthropods are centipedes and millipedes, crustaceans, arachnids, and insects. Insects are the largest group.
- Insects can go through complete or incomplete metamorphosis.

Using Key Terms

1. Use the following terms in the same sentence: *compound eye* and *antenna.*
2. In your own words, write a definition for each of the following terms: *exoskeleton* and *metamorphosis.*

Understanding Key Ideas

3. Which of the following is NOT a trait shared by all arthropods?
   - **a.** exoskeleton
   - **b.** body segments
   - **c.** antennae
   - **d.** jointed limbs
4. Which of the following arthropods is an arachnid?
   - **a.** butterfly
   - **b.** tick
   - **c.** centipede
   - **d.** lobster
5. What is the difference between complete metamorphosis and incomplete metamorphosis?
6. Name the four kinds of arthropods. How do their bodies differ?
7. Which arthropods have chelicerae? Which have mandibles?

Math Skills

8. How many segments does a millipede with 752 legs have? How many segments does a centipede with 354 legs have?

Critical Thinking

9. **Applying Concepts** Suppose that you find an arthropod in a swimming pool. The organism has compound eyes, antennae, and wings. Is it a crustacean? Why or why not?
10. **Forming Hypotheses** Suppose you have found several cocoons on a plant outside your school. Develop a hypothesis about what animal is inside the cocoon. How could you find out if your hypothesis is correct?

For a variety of links related to this chapter, go to www.scilinks.org

Topic: Arthropods

SciLinks code: HSM0098

SECTION 4

Echinoderms

READING WARM-UP

Objectives

- Describe the endoskeleton, nervous system, and water vascular system of echinoderms.
- Explain how an echinoderm's body symmetry changes with age.
- Describe five classes of echinoderms.

Terms to Learn

endoskeleton
water vascular system

READING STRATEGY

Paired Summarizing Read this section silently. In pairs, take turns summarizing the material. Stop to discuss ideas that seem confusing.

Would you touch an object that was covered in sharp spines? Probably not—the spines could hurt you! Some invertebrates are covered in spines that protect them from predators. The predators avoid spines, just like you do.

These spiny invertebrates are called *echinoderms* (ee KIE noh DUHRMZ). Sea stars (starfish), sea urchins, and sand dollars are some familiar members of this group. All echinoderms are marine animals. That means they live in the ocean. Echinoderms live on the sea floor in all parts of the world's oceans. Some of them eat shellfish, some eat dead plants and animals, and others eat algae that they scrape off rocks.

Spiny Skinned

The name *echinoderm* means "spiny skinned." But the animal's skin is not the spiny part. The spines are on the animal's skeleton. An echinoderm's internal skeleton is called an **endoskeleton** (EN doh SKEL uh tuhn). Endoskeletons can be hard and bony or stiff and flexible. The spines covering these skeletons can be long and sharp. They can also be short and bumpy. The animal's skin covers the endoskeleton.

endoskeleton an internal skeleton made of bone or cartilage

Bilateral or Radial?

Adult echinoderms have radial symmetry. But they develop from larvae that have bilateral symmetry. **Figure 1** shows a sea urchin larva and an adult sea urchin. Notice how the symmetry is different in the two forms.

Figure 1 *The sea urchin larva has bilateral symmetry. The adult sea urchin has radial symmetry.*

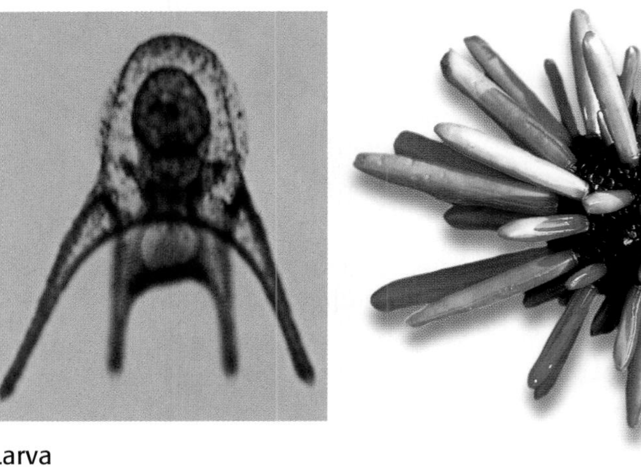

The Nervous System

All echinoderms have a simple nervous system similar to that of a jellyfish. Around the mouth is a circle of nerve fibers called the *nerve ring*. In sea stars, a *radial nerve* runs from the nerve ring to the tip of each arm, as shown in **Figure 2.** The radial nerves control the movements of the sea star's arms.

At the tip of each arm is a simple eye that senses light. The rest of the body is covered with cells that sense touch and chemical signals in the water.

Reading Check **How are the movements of a sea star's arms controlled?** (*See the Appendix for answers to Reading Checks.*)

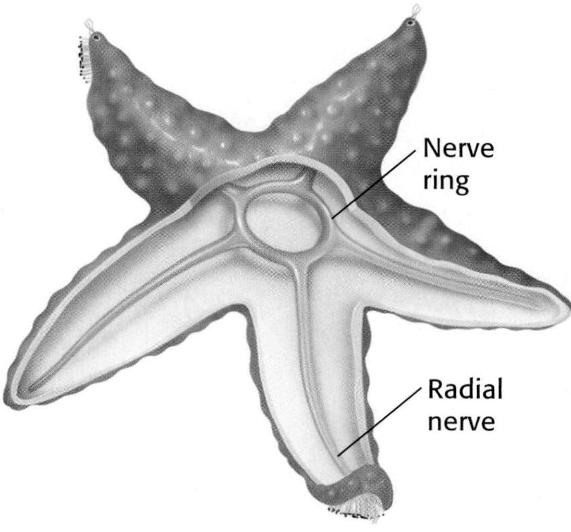

Figure 2 *Sea stars have a simple nervous system.*

Water Vascular System

One characteristic that is unique to echinoderms is the water vascular system. The **water vascular system** is a system of canals filled with fluid. It uses water pumps to help the animal move, eat, breathe, and sense its environment. **Figure 3** shows the water vascular system of a sea star. Notice how water pressure from the system is used for many functions.

water vascular system a system of canals filled with a watery fluid that circulates throughout the body of an echinoderm

Figure 3 **The Water Vascular System**

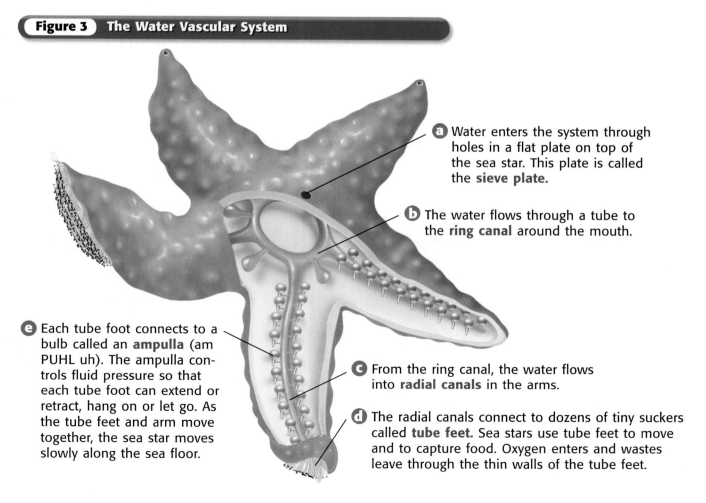

a Water enters the system through holes in a flat plate on top of the sea star. This plate is called the **sieve plate.**

b The water flows through a tube to the **ring canal** around the mouth.

c From the ring canal, the water flows into **radial canals** in the arms.

d The radial canals connect to dozens of tiny suckers called **tube feet.** Sea stars use tube feet to move and to capture food. Oxygen enters and wastes leave through the thin walls of the tube feet.

e Each tube foot connects to a bulb called an **ampulla** (am PUHL uh). The ampulla controls fluid pressure so that each tube foot can extend or retract, hang on or let go. As the tube feet and arm move together, the sea star moves slowly along the sea floor.

Figure 4 *Brittle stars and basket stars move around more than other echinoderms do.*

Kinds of Echinoderms

Scientists divide echinoderms into five major classes. Sea stars are the most familiar echinoderms, and they make up one class. But there are other classes of echinoderms that may not be as familiar to you.

Brittle Stars and Basket Stars

Brittle stars and basket stars look like their close relatives, sea stars. But these echinoderms have long, slim arms and are often smaller than sea stars. Also, they don't have suckers on their tube feet. **Figure 4** shows a brittle star and a basket star.

Sea Urchins and Sand Dollars

Sea urchins and sand dollars are round. Their endoskeletons form a solid, shell-like structure. As shown in **Figure 5,** they have no arms. But they use their tube feet to move in the same way that sea stars move. Some sea urchins can also walk on their spines. Sea urchins feed on algae they scrape from rocks and other objects. They chew the algae with special teeth. Sand dollars burrow into soft sand or mud. They eat tiny particles of food they find there.

Figure 5 *Sea urchins and sand dollars use their spines for defense and for movement.*

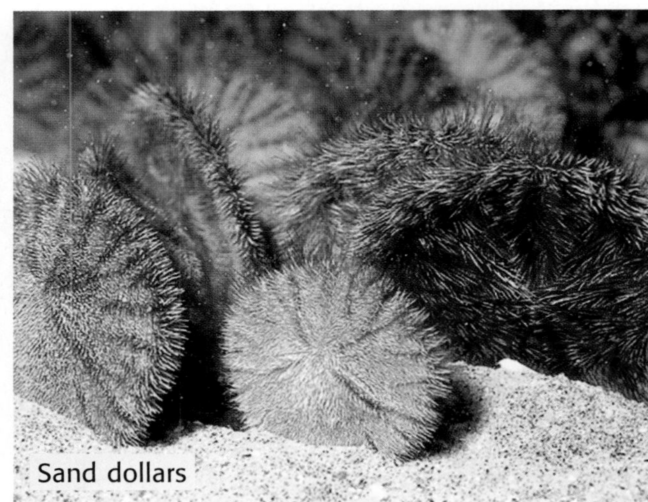

Sea Lilies and Feather Stars

Sea lilies and feather stars may have 5 to 200 feathery arms. Their arms stretch away from their body and trap small pieces of food. A sea lily's cup-shaped body sits on top of a long stalk, which sticks to a rock. Feather stars, such as the one shown in **Figure 6,** do not have a stalk.

Reading Check What is the difference between a feather star and a sea lily?

Figure 6 *Like sea stars, brittle stars, and basket stars, feather stars can regrow lost arms.*

Sea Cucumbers

Like sea urchins and sand dollars, sea cucumbers have no arms. A sea cucumber has a soft, leathery body. Unlike other echinoderms, sea cucumbers are long and have a wormlike shape. **Figure 7** shows a sea cucumber.

Figure 7 *Like other echinoderms, sea cucumbers move with tube feet.*

SECTION Review

Summary

- Echinoderms are marine animals that have an endoskeleton, a water vascular system, and a nerve ring with radial nerves.
- Echinoderms start life with bilateral symmetry and then develop radial symmetry.
- The different classes of echinoderms include sea stars, sea urchins and sand dollars, brittle stars and basket stars, feather stars and sea lilies, and sea cucumbers.

Using Key Terms

1. Use each of the following terms in a separate sentence: *endoskeleton* and *water vascular system.*

Understanding Key Ideas

2. Which of the following is NOT a trait found in echinoderms?
   a. an endoskeleton
   b. spiny skin
   c. a water vascular system
   d. a nerve ring
3. What is the path taken by water as it flows through the parts of the water vascular system?
4. How are sea cucumbers different from other echinoderms?
5. How does an echinoderm's body symmetry change with age?
6. Name five different classes of echinoderms. List at least one trait for each group.

Math Skills

7. A sea lily lost 12 of its 178 arms in a hurricane. What percentage of its arms were NOT damaged?

Critical Thinking

8. **Making Comparisons** How are echinoderms different from and similar to other invertebrates?
9. **Making Inferences** Suppose you found a sea star with four long arms and one short arm. What might explain the difference?

For a variety of links related to this chapter, go to www.scilinks.org

Topic: Echinoderms
SciLinks code: HSM0458

Using Scientific Methods

Skills Practice Lab

Soaking Sponges

Early biologists thought sponges were plants because sponges are like plants in some ways. In many species, the adults attach to a surface and stay there. They cannot chase their food. Instead, sponges absorb and filter a lot of water to get food. In this activity, you will observe the structure of a sponge. You will also consider how the size of the sponge's holes affects the amount of water the sponge can absorb.

OBJECTIVES

Observe the structure of a sponge.

Determine how the size of a sponge's holes affect the amount of water the sponge can absorb.

MATERIALS

- beaker
- bowl (large enough for sponge and water)
- calculator (optional)
- kitchen sponge
- natural sponge
- paper towel
- water

SAFETY

Ask a Question

1. Look at the natural sponge. Identify the pores on the outside of the sponge. See if you can find the sponge's central cavities and oscula.
2. Notice the size and shape of the sponge's holes. Look at the holes in the kitchen sponge and the paper towel. Think of a question about how the holes in each item affect its ability to absorb water.

Form a Hypothesis

3. Formulate a testable hypothesis to answer your question. Record your hypothesis.

Test the Hypothesis

4. Read steps 5–9. Design and draw a data table for the data that you will collect. Remember, you will collect data for the natural sponge, the kitchen sponge, and the paper towel.

5. Use a balance to measure the mass of the natural sponge. Record the mass.

6. Place the natural sponge in the bowl. Use the graduated cylinder to add water to the sponge, 10 mL at a time, until the sponge is completely soaked. Record the amount of water added.

7. Gently remove the sponge from the bowl. Measure the amount of water left in the bowl. How much water did the sponge absorb? Record your data.

8. Calculate how many milliliters of water your sponge holds per gram of dry sponge. For example, if your sponge's dry mass is 12 g and it holds 59.1 mL of water, then your sponge holds 4.9 mL of water per gram (59.1 mL ÷ 12 g = 4.9 mL/g).

9. Repeat steps 5–8 with the kitchen sponge and the paper towel.

Analyze the Results

1. **Analyzing Results** Compare your results from steps 5–9. Which item held the most water per gram of dry mass?

Draw Conclusions

2. **Evaluating Data** Did your results support your hypothesis? Explain your answer.

3. **Evaluating Results** Do you see a connection between the size of an item's holes and its ability to hold water?

4. **Analyzing Results** What can you conclude about how the size and shape of a sponge's holes affect its feeding ability?

Applying Your Data

WRITING SKILL Use the Internet to see if scientists have done research that backs up your ideas about how the size and shape of a sponge affect its feeding abilities. Write your findings in a report to present to the class.

Chapter Review

USING KEY TERMS

1. In your own words, write a definition for each of the following terms: *ganglion, water vascular system,* and *coelom.*

2. Use the following terms in the same sentence: *open circulatory system* and *invertebrate.*

Complete each of the following sentences by choosing the correct term from the word bank.

antennae	exoskeleton
coelom	gut
compound eyes	metamorphosis
endoskeleton	segments

3. Almost all invertebrates digest food in a(n) ___.

4. Repeating ___ make up the bodies of annelid worms and arthropods.

5. A crab's ___ keeps it from losing water.

6. Arthropods use ___ to see images.

7. Echinoderms have spines on their ___.

8. Arthropods use ___ to touch, taste, and smell.

9. Insects change form during ___.

UNDERSTANDING KEY IDEAS

Multiple Choice

10. No invertebrates have
    - **a.** a brain.
    - **b.** a gut.
    - **c.** ganglia.
    - **d.** a backbone.

11. Which animals have a nerve ring?
    - **a.** sponges
    - **b.** echinoderms
    - **c.** crustaceans
    - **d.** flatworms

12. Which of the following is NOT a flatworm?
    - **a.** a tapeworm
    - **b.** an earthworm
    - **c.** a planarian
    - **d.** a fluke

13. Which body part is NOT present in all mollusks?
    - **a.** foot
    - **b.** visceral mass
    - **c.** mantle
    - **d.** shell

Short Answer

14. Describe how a sponge eats.

15. What are the four main characteristics of arthropods?

16. Describe the body of a roundworm.

17. What are three ways that different mollusks eat?

18. Which insects go through complete metamorphosis? go through incomplete metamorphosis?

19. How is an adult echinoderm different from an echinoderm larva?

20. How are cephalopod nervous systems unique among mollusks?

CRITICAL THINKING

21 **Concept Mapping** Use the following terms to create a concept map: *segments, invertebrates, endoskeleton, antennae, exoskeleton, water vascular system, metamorphosis,* and *compound eyes.*

22 **Applying Concepts** You have discovered a new animal that has radial symmetry and tentacles with stinging cells. Can this animal be classified as a cnidarian? Explain.

23 **Making Inferences** Unlike other mollusks, cephalopods can move quickly. Based on what you know about the structure and function of mollusks, why do you think that cephalopods have this ability?

24 **Making Comparisons** Why don't roundworms, flatworms, and annelid worms belong to the same group of invertebrates?

25 **Analyzing Processes** Butterflies mate as adults and spend time eating and growing in their other stages. They have no wings during the larval or pupal stage of metamorphosis. Can you think of a reason that they would need wings in their adult form more than in the other stages of development? Explain your answer.

26 **Predicting Consequences** How do earthworms affect gardens? What do you think would happen to a garden if the gardener removed all the earthworms from it?

INTERPRETING GRAPHICS

The picture below shows an arthropod. Use the picture to answer the questions that follow.

27 Name the body segments labeled a, b, and c.

28 How many legs does this arthropod have?

29 To which segment are the arthropod's legs attached?

30 What kind of arthropod is this?

Standardized Test Preparation

READING

Read each of the passages below. Then, answer the questions that follow each passage.

Passage 1 Giant squids are very similar to their smaller relatives. They have a torpedo-shaped body, two tentacles, eight arms, a mantle, and a beak. All of their body parts are much larger, though. A giant squid's eye may be as large as a volleyball! Given the size of giant squids, it's hard to imagine that they have any enemies in the ocean, but they do.

Toothed sperm whales eat giant squids. How do we know this? Thousands of squid beaks have been found in the stomach of a single sperm whale. The hard beaks of giant squids are <u>indigestible</u>. Also, many whales bear ring marks on their forehead and fins that match the size of the suckers found on giant squids.

1. Based on the passage, what do you think the word *indigestible* describes?

- **A** something that cannot be digested
- **B** something that causes indigestion
- **C** something that one cannot dig out
- **D** something that one cannot guess

2. What can you infer from this passage?

- **F** Giant squids only imagine that they have enemies.
- **G** A toothed sperm whale can eat 10,000 giant squids in one meal.
- **H** Giant squids defend themselves against toothed sperm whales.
- **I** Giant squids and sperm whales compete with each other for food.

3. How are giant squids different from other kinds of squids?

- **A** Giant squids have a torpedo-shaped body, a mantle, and a beak.
- **B** Giant squids have enemies in the ocean.
- **C** Giant squids have larger body parts.
- **D** Giant squids are the size of a volleyball.

Passage 2 Water bears are microscopic invertebrates that are closely related to arthropods. Most water bears live on wet mosses and lichens. Some of them eat roundworms and other tiny animals, but most feed on mosses. What makes water bears unique is their ability to shut down their body processes. They do this when their environment becomes too hot, too cold, or too dry. Shutting down body processes means that the organism doesn't eat, move, or breathe. But it doesn't die, either. It just dries out. When conditions improve, the water bear returns to normal life. Scientists think that the water bear's cells become coated with sugar when its body shuts down. This sugar may keep the cells from breaking down while they are inactive.

1. How do scientists think sugar helps water bears survive while their body processes are shut down?

- **A** Sugar coats their cells, keeping the cells from breaking down.
- **B** Sugar coats their cells, trapping moisture inside the cells.
- **C** Sugar coats their cells, keeping moisture from entering the cells.
- **D** Sugar provides water bears with nutrients.

2. What do water bears eat?

- **F** sugar
- **G** mosses
- **H** lichens
- **I** arthropods

3. Which is a unique characteristic of water bears?

- **A** They are related to arthropods.
- **B** They often live on mosses or lichens.
- **C** They can live at the bottom of the ocean.
- **D** They can shut down their body processes without dying.

INTERPRETING GRAPHICS

The bar graph below shows the number of monarchs in a population from 1990 to 1994. Use the graph to answer the questions that follow.

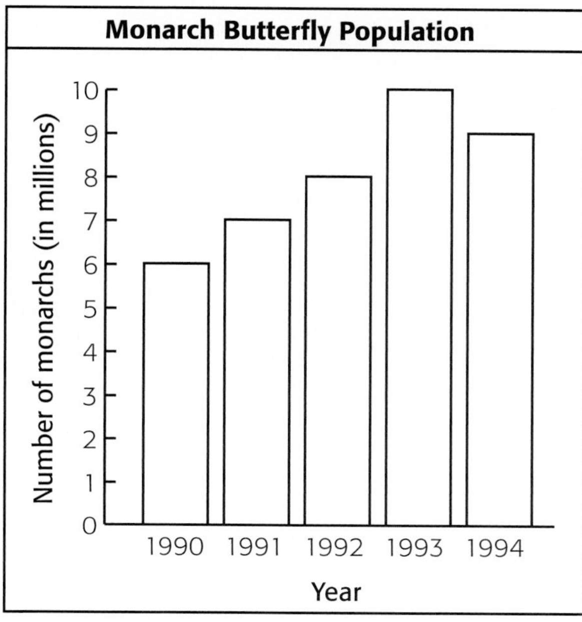

1. Compare the number of butterflies in the population during 1990, 1991, 1992, and 1993. Identify the statement that best describes how the population changed during those years.

A The population increased.
B The population remained the same.
C The population decreased.
D The population doubled yearly.

2. Why might butterfly scientists be surprised about the 1994 monarch population?

F The 1994 population was the first population of 9 million ever recorded.
G The 1994 population was the first decreased population recorded in 4 years.
H The 1994 population was the first increased population recorded in 4 years.
I The 1994 population was the first decreased population ever recorded.

3. What can you infer from the graph about how the monarch's environmental conditions changed between 1993 and 1994?

A Conditions were worse in 1994.
B Conditions did not change between 1993 and 1994.
C Conditions were better in 1994.
D This graph does not contain enough information to determine how conditions changed between 1993 and 1994.

4. What was the average population of monarchs during these 5 years?

F 7 million
G 8 million
H 9 million
I 40 million

MATH

Read each question below, and choose the best answer.

1. Raymond wanted to arrange his shell collection in order of size. Which group of shell lengths is listed in order from smallest to largest?

A 1.6 cm, 0.25 dm, 0.017 m, 5.0 cm
B 0.017 m, 0.25 dm, 1.6 cm, 5.0 cm
C 1.6 cm, 5.0 cm, 0.25 dm, 0.017 m
D 1.6 cm, 0.017 m, 0.25 dm, 5.0 cm

2. Raquelle wants to buy some earthworms to put in her garden. The earthworms are sold in containers that each hold 8 worms. How many containers will Raquelle need to buy if she wants 75 earthworms?

F 9 containers
G 10 containers
H 15 containers
I 83 containers

3. Maxwell found a huge basket star while he was scuba diving. The basket star had five arms, and each arm branched into three pieces. Each of these pieces branched into two more tips. How many tips did the basket star have?

A 2 tips
B 5 tips
C 15 tips
D 30 tips

Science in Action

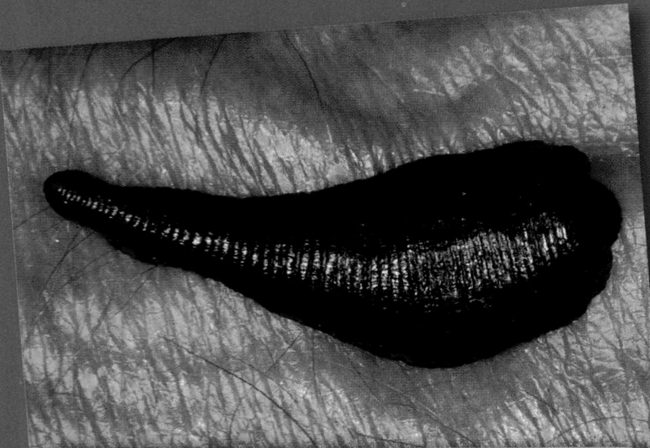

Science, Technology, and Society

Leeches to the Rescue

Bloodsucking leeches may sound scary, but they could save your toes! Leeches are used in operations to reattach lost limbs, fingers, or toes. During these operations, doctors can reconnect arteries, but not small veins, which are more delicate. As a result, blood flow in the limb, finger, or toe is impaired. The tissues may become full of loose blood. If this happens, the tissues of the reattached parts die. But if leeches suck the extra blood from the reattached part, the tissues can remain healthy until the veins grow back.

Math Activity

Measure the widest and narrowest parts of the leech in the photo. Calculate how many times wider the wide part is than the narrow part. Which end of the leech do you think is the head? Why do you think so?

Weird Science

A Powerful Punch

The mantis shrimp packs a powerful punch! This animal is nick-named "killer shrimp" and "thumb-splitter." These crustaceans can be divided into two groups: the *smashers* and the *spearers*. The smashers have large front limbs that they use to club their prey with great speed and power. They can easily smash through the shells of clams, snails, and crabs. Larger species have been known to break double-walled aquarium glass! The spearers have sharp spines on their front limbs, and lash out with incredible speed—at about 1,000 cm/sec. That is one of the fastest animal movements known!

Language Arts Activity

The words *crustacean* and *crust* both come from the same Latin root—*crusta*. Think of how crustaceans are similar to crusts, and then guess the meaning of the Latin root.

Careers

George Matsumoto

Marine Biologist Dr. George Matsumoto is a marine biologist at the Monterey Bay Aquarium in California. A seventh-grade snorkeling class first sparked his interest in ocean research. Since then, he's studied the deep seas by snorkeling, scuba diving, and using research vessels, remotely operated vehicles (ROVs), and deep-sea submersibles. On the Johnson Sea Link submersible, he traveled down to 1,000 m (3,281 ft) below sea level!

Marine biology is a field full of strange and wonderful creatures. Matsumoto focuses on marine invertebrates, particularly the delicate animals called comb jellies. These invertebrates are beautiful animals that have not been studied very much. Comb jellies are also called *ctenophores* (TEN uh FAWRZ), which means "comb-bearers." They have eight rows of cilia that look like the rows of a comb. These cilia help ctenophores move through the water. By studying ctenophores and similar marine invertebrates, Matsumoto and other marine scientists can learn about the ecology of ocean communities.

Social Studies ACTIVITY

WRITING SKILL One ctenophore from the United States took over both the Black Sea and the Sea of Azov by eating small fish and other food. This crowded out bigger fish, changing the ecosystem and ruining the fisheries. Write a paragraph about how Matsumoto's work as a marine biologist could help solve problems like this one.

To learn more about these Science in Action topics, visit go.hrw.com and type in the keyword HL5INVF.

Current Science

Check out Current Science® articles related to this chapter by visiting go.hrw.com. Just type in the keyword HL5CS15.

16

Fishes, Amphibians, and Reptiles

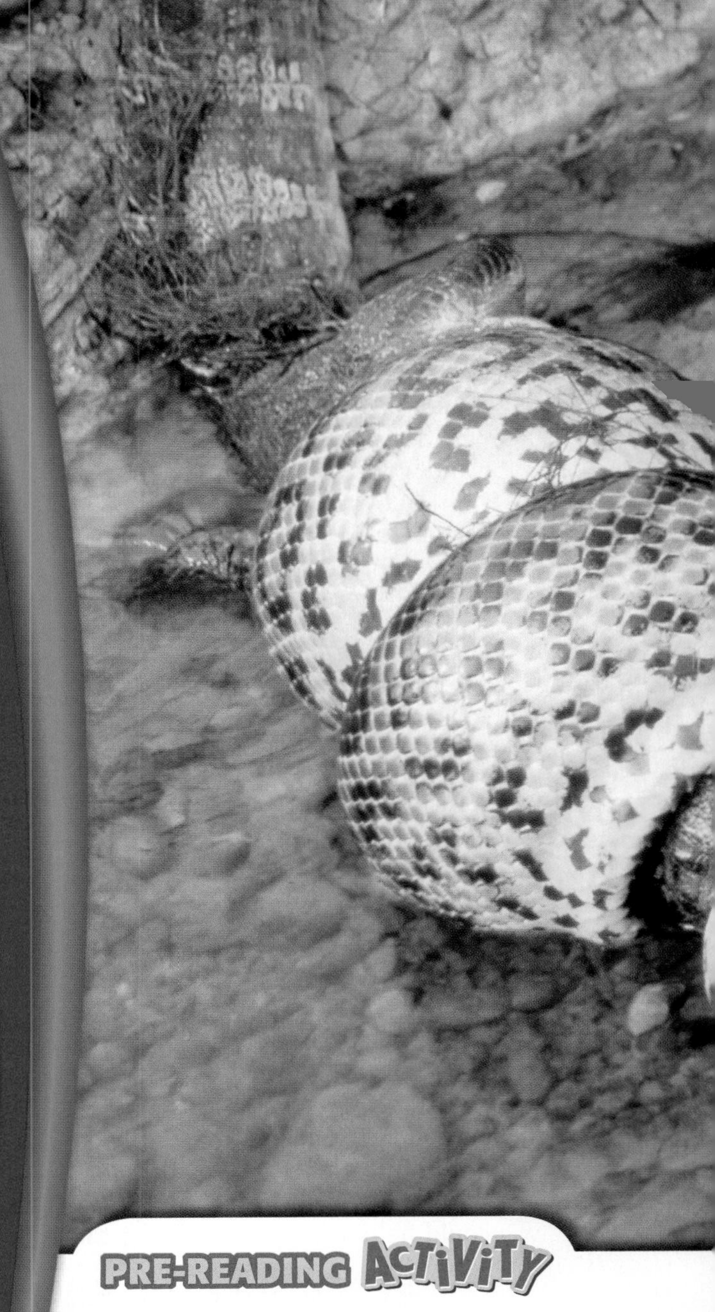

About the PHOTO

This unlucky caiman must have been quite a match for the snake. But somehow the snake's body strength overcame the caiman's muscular jaws. Each of these animals has a unique trait that makes the animal a strong predator. But as reptiles, these animals have many traits in common. For example, both animals are covered in thick skin, and both use lungs to breathe.

PRE-READING ACTIVITY

Graphic Organizer

Comparison Table Before you read the chapter, create the graphic organizer entitled "Comparison Table" described in the **Study Skills** section of the Appendix. Label the columns with "Fishes," "Amphibians," and "Reptiles." Label the rows with "Characteristics" and "Kinds." As you read the chapter, fill in the table with details about the characteristics and kinds of each animal.

START-UP ACTIVITY

Oil and Water

A shark stores a lot of oil in its liver. In this activity, you will build a model of an oily liver to see how an oily liver can help keep a shark from sinking.

Procedure

1. Use **two beakers** to measure equal amounts of **water** and **cooking oil.**
2. Use a **funnel** to fill **one balloon** with the water that you measured.
3. Using the funnel, fill a **second balloon** with the cooking oil.
4. Tie the balloons so that no air remains inside. Be careful not to squeeze the oil or water out of the balloons while tying them.
5. Put each balloon in a **fish tank** that is full of **water.** Observe what happens to each of the balloons.

Analysis

1. Compare where the two balloons come to rest in the tank of water.
2. A shark's oily liver helps keep the shark from sinking. How does the structure of the shark's oily liver help achieve this result?
3. Why do you think it was important to remove the air from the balloons before putting them in the water? What might have happened if you did not remove the air from the balloons?

SECTION 1

Fishes: The First Vertebrates

READING WARM-UP

Objectives

- List the four common body parts of chordates.
- Describe the two main characteristics of vertebrates.
- Explain the difference between an ectotherm and an endotherm.
- Describe four traits that fishes share.
- Describe the three classes of living fishes, and give an example of each.

Terms to Learn

vertebrate	lateral line
endotherm	gill
ectotherm	swim bladder

READING STRATEGY

Reading Organizer As you read this section, make a concept map by using the terms above.

You may have seen a dinosaur skeleton at a museum. And you've probably seen a lot of fish. Have you ever thought about what you might have in common with these animals or what they might have in common with each other?

The skeletons of humans and fish have many bones that are similar to dinosaur bones. Dinosaur bones are just bigger. For example, all of these skeletons have a backbone. Animals that have a backbone are called **vertebrates** (VUHR tuh brits).

Chordates

Vertebrates belong to the phylum Chordata. Members of this phylum are called *chordates* (KAWR DAYTS). Vertebrates make up the largest group of chordates. But there are two other groups of chordates—lancelets (LANS lits) and tunicates (TOO ni kits). These chordates are much simpler than vertebrates. They do not have a backbone or a well-developed head. **Figure 1** shows an example of each group of chordates.

The three groups of chordates share certain characteristics. All chordates have each of four particular body parts at some point in their life. These parts are shown in the lancelet in **Figure 2** on the next page.

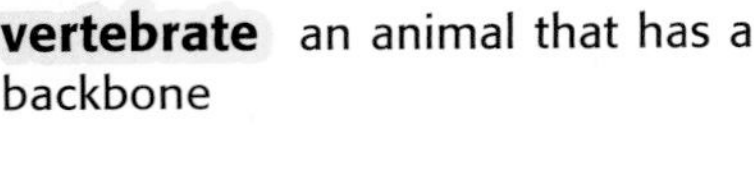
vertebrate an animal that has a backbone

Figure 1 *Tunicates (right), lancelets (lower right), and vertebrates, such as the fish (lower left), are chordates.*

Figure 2 **Chordate Body Parts**

Tail
Chordates have a tail that begins behind the anus. Some chordates have a tail only in the embryo stage.

Notochord
A stiff but flexible rod called a notochord (NOHT uh KAWRD) gives the body support. In most vertebrates, the embryo's notochord is replaced by a backbone.

Hollow Nerve Cord
A hollow nerve cord runs along the back and is full of fluid. In vertebrates, this nerve cord is called the *spinal cord.*

Pharyngeal Pouches
All chordate embryos have pharyngeal (fuh RIN jee uhl) pouches. These pouches develop into gills or other body parts as the embryo matures.

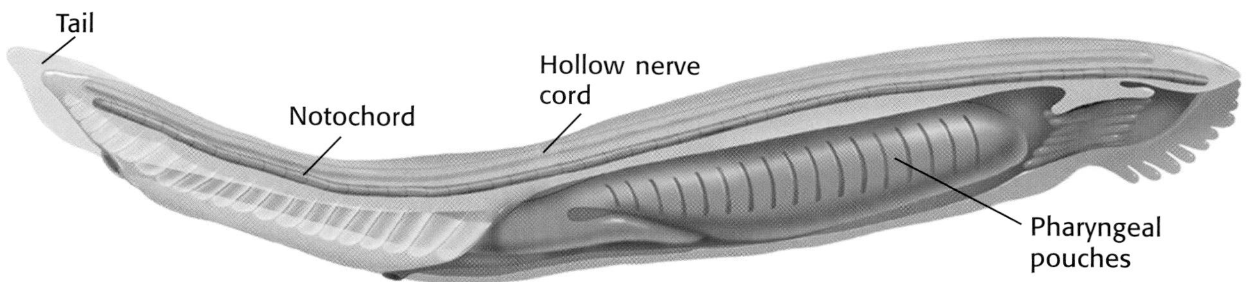

Vertebrate Characteristics

Fishes, amphibians, reptiles, birds, and mammals are vertebrates. Many things set vertebrates apart from lancelets and tunicates. One major difference is that only vertebrates have a backbone. The backbone is a strong but flexible column of bones that are called *vertebrae* (VUHR tuh BRAY). **Figure 3** shows the vertebrae of a human. The vertebrae surround and protect the spinal cord. They also help support the rest of the body.

Another difference between vertebrates and other chordates is the head. Vertebrates have a well-developed head protected by a skull. The skull is made of either cartilage or bone. *Cartilage* is the tough material that the flexible parts of our ears and nose are made of. The skeletons of all vertebrate embryos are made of cartilage. But as most vertebrates grow, the cartilage is replaced by bone. Bone is much harder than cartilage.

Because bone is so hard, it can be easily fossilized. Scientists have discovered many fossils of vertebrates. These fossils give scientists valuable clues about how organisms are related to each other. For example, fossil evidence indicates that fish appeared about 500 million years ago. These fossils show that fish were the first vertebrates on Earth.

Reading Check **What material makes up the skeleton of a human embryo?** (*See the Appendix for answers to Reading Checks.*)

Figure 3 *The vertebrae interlock to form the backbone.*

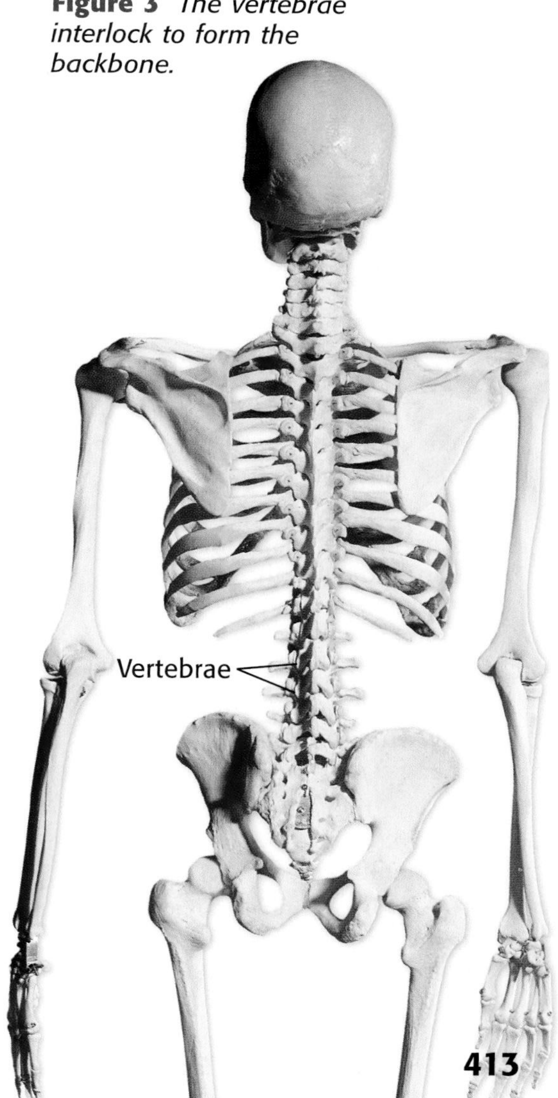

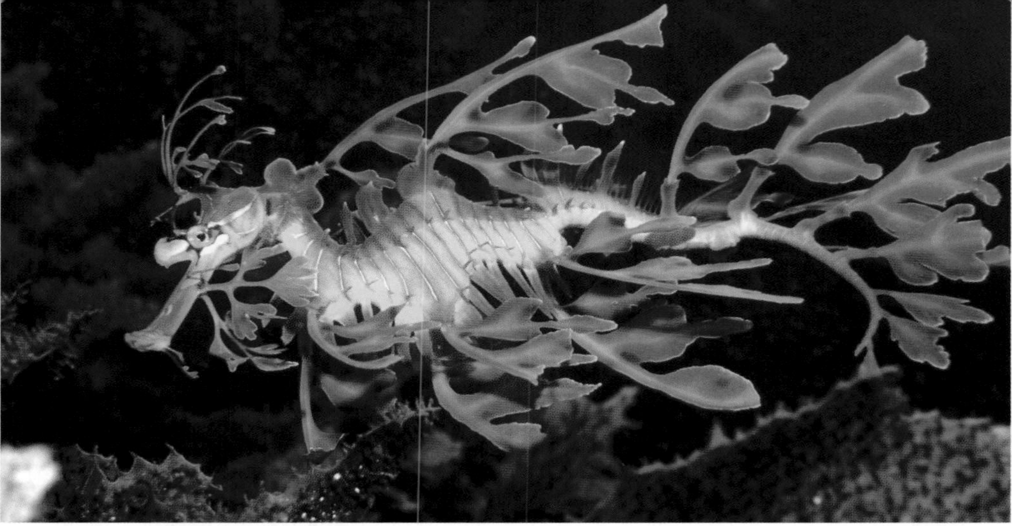

Figure 4 *Most fishes, including this leafy sea dragon, are ectotherms.*

Are Vertebrates Warm or Cold?

All vertebrates need to live at the proper temperature. An animal's cells work properly only at certain temperatures. If an animal's body temperature is too high or too low, its body cannot function well. Some animals heat their own bodies. Others depend on the environment to control their temperature.

endotherm an animal that can use body heat from chemical reactions in the body's cells to maintain a constant body temperature

ectotherm an organism that needs sources of heat outside of itself

Staying Warm

The body temperature of birds and mammals does not change much as the temperature of the environment changes. Birds and mammals use energy released by the chemical reactions in their cells to warm their bodies. Animals that have a stable body temperature are called **endotherms** (EN doh THUHRMZ). They are sometimes called *warmblooded animals*. Because of their stable temperature, endotherms can stay warm in cold weather.

Cold Blood?

Some animals depend on their surroundings to stay warm. Their body temperature changes as the temperature of the environment changes. Animals that do not control body temperature through activity in their cells are called **ectotherms** (EK toh THUHRMZ). They are sometimes called *coldblooded animals*. Nearly all amphibians and reptiles are ectotherms. Most fishes, such as the one in **Figure 4,** are also ectotherms. Being an ectotherm is one of many traits that most fishes share.

Reading Check **How would the body temperature of most fishes change if the temperature of the environment increased?**

Body Temperature

1. Use a **thermometer** to take your temperature every hour for 6 h.
2. Make a graph of your body temperature. Place the time of day on the *x*-axis and your temperature on the *y*-axis.
3. Does your temperature change throughout the day? How much does it change?
4. Do you think exercise changes your body temperature?
5. How do you think your results would be different if you were an ectotherm?

Fish Characteristics

Fishes come in many shapes, sizes, and colors. There are more than 25,000 species of fishes, and many look very different from each other. But all fishes share several characteristics. Some traits help fishes live in the water. Other traits, such as a strong body and a brain, help fishes catch or find food.

Born to Swim

Fishes have many body parts that help them swim. Strong muscles attached to the backbone allow many fishes to swim quickly after their prey. To steer, stop, and balance, fishes use *fins,* which are fan-shaped structures that help fishes move. And many fishes have bodies covered by bony structures called *scales*. Scales protect the body and lower friction as fishes swim through the water. **Figure 5** shows some body parts of a fish.

Making Sense of the World

Fishes have a brain that keeps track of information coming in from the senses. All fishes have the senses of vision, hearing, and smell. Most fishes also have a lateral line system. The **lateral line** is a row or rows of tiny sense organs that detect water vibrations, such as those caused by another fish swimming by. These organs are found along each side of the body and usually extend onto the head.

Underwater Breathing

Fishes use their gills to breathe. A **gill** is an organ that removes oxygen from the water. Oxygen in the water passes through the thin membrane of the gills to the blood. The blood then carries oxygen through the body. Gills are also used to remove carbon dioxide from the blood.

Making More Fish

Most fishes reproduce by *external fertilization*. The female lays unfertilized eggs in the water, and the male drops sperm on them. But some species of fish use *internal fertilization*. In this case, the male deposits sperm inside the female. Usually, the female then lays fertilized eggs that have embryos inside. But in some species, the embryos develop inside the female.

CONNECTION TO Physics

How Fish See the World You have to move a magnifying lens back and forth to bring an object into focus. Fish eyes focus on objects in the same way. Fish use muscles to change the position of the lenses in their eyes. By moving the eye lenses, fish can bring objects into focus. To understand how fish see the world, use a magnifying lens to look at objects in your classroom.

ACTIVITY

lateral line a faint line visible on both sides of a fish's body that runs the length of the body and marks the location of sense organs that detect vibrations in water

gill a respiratory organ in which oxygen from the water is exchanged with carbon dioxide from the blood

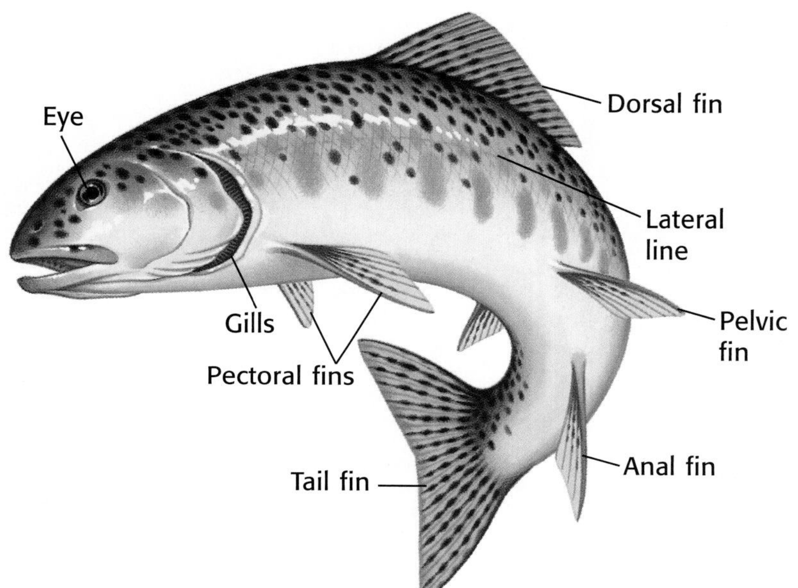

Figure 5 *Fishes have many shapes and sizes, but all fishes have gills, fins, and a tail.*

Kinds of Fishes

There are five very different classes of fishes. Two classes are now extinct. But scientists have been able to study the fossils of the extinct fishes. The three classes of fishes living today are *jawless fishes, cartilaginous* (KART'l AJ uh nuhs) *fishes,* and *bony fishes.*

INTERNET ACTIVITY

For another activity related to this chapter, go to **go.hrw.com** and type in the keyword **HL5VR1W.**

Jawless Fishes

The first fishes did not have jaws. You might think that having no jaws would make eating difficult and would lead to extinction. But the jawless fishes have thrived for half a billion years.

The two kinds of modern jawless fishes are hagfish and lampreys, as shown in **Figure 6.** These fishes are eel-like. They have smooth, slimy skin and a round, jawless mouth. Their skeleton is made of cartilage, and they have a notochord but no backbone. These fishes have a skull, a brain, and eyes.

Jawless fishes do not need jaws to eat. Hagfish eat dead fishes on the ocean floor. For this reason, they are sometimes called *vultures of the sea*. Lampreys suck other animals' blood and flesh. They have a suction cup–like mouth that has teeth. They don't need jaws because they don't bite or chew.

Reading Check Describe how jawless fishes eat.

Figure 6 **Jawless Fishes**

Hagfish can tie their flexible bodies into knots. They slide the knot from their tail end to their head to remove slime from their skin or to escape from predators.

Lampreys can live in salt water or fresh water, but they must reproduce in fresh water.

Figure 7 Cartilaginous Fishes

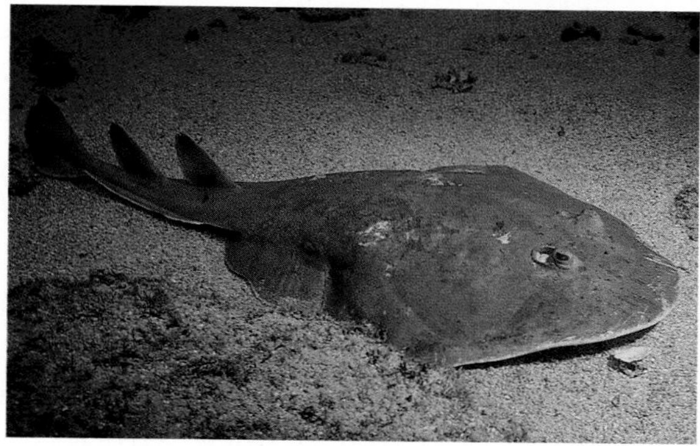

Unlike rays, **skates** have a small dorsal fin.

Rays, such as this **stingray,** feed on shellfish and worms on the sea floor. A ray swims by moving its fins up and down.

Sharks, such as this **hammerhead shark,** rarely prey on humans. They usually eat other fish.

Cartilaginous Fishes

Did you know that a shark is a fish? Sharks belong to a class of fishes called cartilaginous fishes. In most vertebrates, soft cartilage in the embryo is slowly replaced by bone. But in sharks, skates, and rays, the skeleton never changes to bone. So, they are called *cartilaginous fishes*.

Cartilaginous fishes have fully functional jaws. These fishes are strong swimmers and expert predators. Many have excellent senses of sight and smell, and they have a lateral line system. **Figure 7** shows some cartilaginous fishes.

To stay afloat, cartilaginous fishes store a lot of oil in their liver. The oil helps the fishes be more buoyant because the oil is less dense than water. But even with oily livers, these fishes are denser than water. They have to keep moving to stay afloat. When they stop swimming, they slowly sink.

Some cartilaginous fishes also swim to keep water moving over their gills. If these fishes stop swimming, they will suffocate. Other cartilaginous fishes do not have to swim. They can lie on the ocean floor and pump water across their gills.

Bony Fishes

When you hear the word *fish,* you probably think of a bony fish. Goldfish, tuna, trout, catfish, and cod are bony fishes. This class of fishes is the largest. Ninety-five percent of all fishes are bony fishes. They range in size from about 1 cm to 8.6 m long. Some bony fishes are shown in **Figure 8.**

Bony fishes are very different from other fishes. As their name suggests, bony fishes have a skeleton made of bone. Also, their bodies are covered by bony scales. Unlike other fishes, bony fishes can rest in one place without swimming. They have a swim bladder that keeps them from sinking. The **swim bladder** is a balloonlike organ that is filled with oxygen and other gases. These gases are lighter than water, so they help the fish be more buoyant. The swim bladder is sometimes called a *gas bladder.*

There are two main groups of bony fishes. Almost all bony fishes are *ray-finned fishes*. Ray-finned fishes have paired fins supported by thin rays of bone. Ray-finned fishes include many familiar fishes, such as eels, herrings, trout, minnows, and perch.

Lobe-finned fishes make up the second group of bony fishes. Lobe-finned fishes have fins that are muscular and thick. There are seven living species of lobe-finned fishes. Six of these species are lungfishes. Lungfishes have air sacs. Because air sacs can gulp air, they are like lungs. Scientists think that ancient fishes from this group were the ancestors of amphibians.

Reading Check **How do bony fishes differ from cartilaginous fishes?**

A Lot of Bones

If there are 30,000 species of fishes and 95% of all fishes are bony fishes, how many species of bony fishes are there?

swim bladder a gas-filled sac that is used to control buoyancy; also known as a *gas bladder*

Figure 8 **Bony Fishes**

Lungfishes live in shallow waters that often dry up in the summer.

Masked butterfly fish live in warm waters around coral reefs.

Pikes are fast predators that move in quick bursts of speed to catch fish and invertebrates.

SECTION Review

Summary

- Chordates include lancelets, tunicates, and vertebrates. At some point during their development, chordates have a notochord, a hollow nerve cord, pharyngeal pouches, and a tail.
- Most chordates are vertebrates. Vertebrates differ from other chordates in that they have a backbone composed of vertebrae.
- Endotherms control body temperature through the chemical reactions of their cells. Ectotherms do not.
- Fishes share many characteristics. Most have fins and scales to help them swim. Many have a lateral line system to sense water movement. Fishes breathe with gills.
- There are three groups of living fishes: jawless fishes, cartilaginous fishes, and bony fishes. Jawless fishes do not have a backbone. Cartilaginous fishes have an oily liver. Bony fishes have a swim bladder.
- The oily liver and the swim bladder both help fishes keep from sinking.

Using Key Terms

1. Use each of the following terms in a separate sentence: *vertebrate, lateral line system, gill,* and *swim bladder.*

2. In your own words, write a definition for each of the following terms: *endotherm* and *ectotherm.*

Understanding Key Ideas

3. At some point in its life, every chordate has each of the following EXCEPT
   - **a.** a tail.
   - **b.** a notochord.
   - **c.** a hollow nerve cord.
   - **d.** a backbone.

4. Which vertebrates are ectotherms?

5. What are four characteristics shared by most fishes?

6. What are the three classes of living fish? Give an example of each.

7. Most bony fishes reproduce by external fertilization. What does this mean?

Critical Thinking

8. **Analyzing Relationships** Describe the ways that cartilaginous fishes and bony fishes maintain buoyancy. Why do you think that jawless fishes do not use one of these methods?

9. **Applying Concepts** How could moving a fishbowl from a cold window sill to a warmer part of the house affect a pet fish?

Interpreting Graphics

Use the bar graph below to answer the questions that follow.

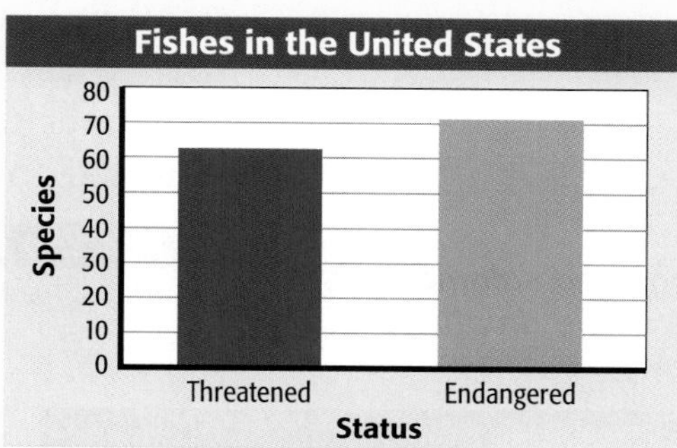

Source: U.S. Fish and Wildlife Services

10. How many fish species in the United States are threatened? How many are endangered?

11. What is the total number of threatened and endangered fish species in the United States?

For a variety of links related to this chapter, go to www.scilinks.org

Topic: Vertebrates; Fishes
SciLinks code: HSM1602; HSM0579

SECTION 2

Amphibians

Did you know that some animals are able to breathe through their skin? Do these animals live on land or in the water? Actually, they live both on land and in the water.

READING WARM-UP

Objectives

- Explain how amphibians breathe.
- Describe amphibian metamorphosis.
- Describe the three groups of amphibians, and give an example of each.
- Explain why amphibians are ecological indicators.

Terms to Learn

lung
tadpole
metamorphosis

READING STRATEGY

Reading Organizer As you read this section, create an outline of the section. Use the headings from the section in your outline.

About 350 million years ago, fishes lived wherever there was water. But no vertebrates lived on land. The land had many resources for vertebrates. It had plants and insects for vertebrates to eat, and there were few predators. But to live on land, vertebrates needed lungs for breathing and legs for walking.

Moving to Land

Amphibians (am FIB ee uhnz) are animals that can live in water and have lungs and legs. Scientists think that amphibians evolved from the ancestors of lungfish-like fishes. These ancient fishes developed lungs that got oxygen from the air. A **lung** is a saclike organ that takes oxygen from the air and delivers oxygen to the blood. These fishes also had strong fins that could have evolved into legs.

Most of today's amphibians are frogs or salamanders, such as those in **Figure 1.** But early amphibians looked different. Fossils show that the first amphibians looked like a cross between a fish and a salamander. Many were very large—up to 10 m long. Early amphibians could stay on dry land longer than today's amphibians can. But they still had to return to the water to keep from drying out or overheating. They also returned to the water to mate and to lay eggs.

Reading Check How do amphibians get oxygen from the air? (See the Appendix for answers to Reading Checks.)

Figure 1 *Frogs and salamanders are two kinds of the amphibians on Earth today.*

Characteristics of Amphibians

Amphibian means "double life." Most amphibians live part of their lives in water and part of their lives on land. Amphibian eggs do not have a shell or a membrane that prevents water loss. For this reason, embryos must develop in a wet environment. Most amphibians live in the water after hatching and then later develop into adults that can live on land.

But even adult amphibians are only partly adapted to life on land. Amphibians are ectotherms. So, their body temperature depends on the temperature of their environment. Water helps amphibians keep their bodies at a stable temperature. Also, water helps adults keep from losing too much moisture through their skin.

lung a respiratory organ in which oxygen from the air is exchanged with carbon dioxide from the blood

Thin Skin

Amphibian skin is thin, smooth, and moist. The skin is so thin that amphibians absorb water through it instead of drinking. But they can also lose water through their skin and easily become dehydrated. Their thin skin is one reason that most amphibians live in water or in damp habitats.

Amphibians can breathe by gulping air into their lungs. But many also absorb oxygen through their skin, which is full of blood vessels. In fact, a few amphibians, such as the salamander in **Figure 2,** breathe only through their skin.

Many amphibians also have brightly colored skin. The colors often warn predators that the skin contains poison glands. These poisons may simply be irritating, or they may be deadly. The skin of the poison arrow frog, shown in **Figure 3,** has one of the most deadly toxins known.

Figure 2 *The four-toed salamander has no lungs. It gets all of its oxygen through its skin.*

Figure 3 *The skin of this poison arrow frog is full of poison glands. Hunters in South America rub the tips of their arrows in the deadly toxin.*

CONNECTION TO Social Studies

WRITING SKILL **Troublesome Toads** In the 1930s, cane toads were shipped from Hawaii to Australia to eat cane grubs that were destroying sugar cane crops. But the toad populations grew out of control, and the toads did not eat the grubs. Native species that ate the toads were killed by the toads' poison glands. Research another animal that has caused disastrous effects in a new environment. In your **science journal,** write three paragraphs about this animal.

Figure 4 Amphibian Metamorphosis

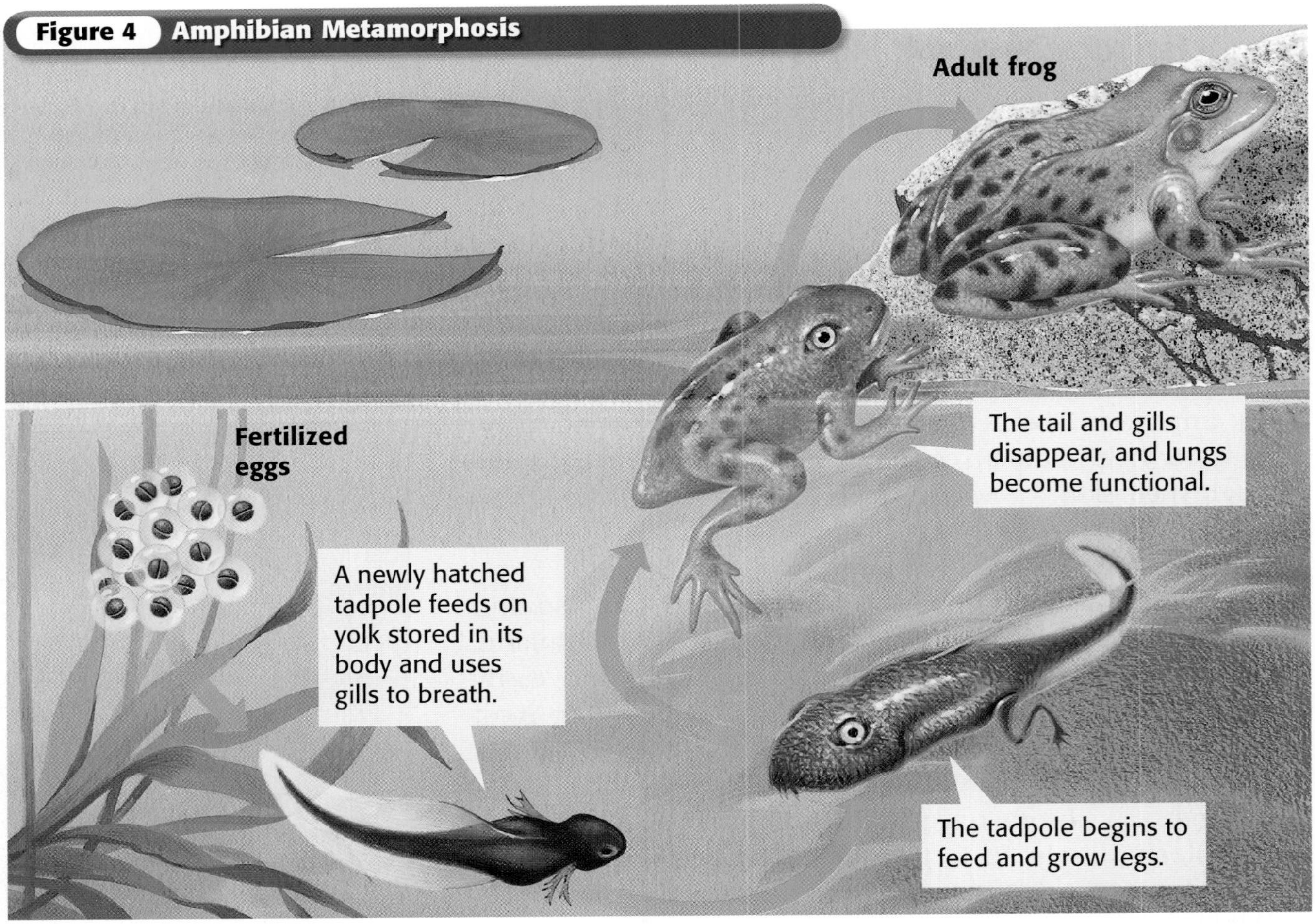

Adult frog

Fertilized eggs

A newly hatched tadpole feeds on yolk stored in its body and uses gills to breath.

The tadpole begins to feed and grow legs.

The tail and gills disappear, and lungs become functional.

tadpole the aquatic, fish-shaped larva of a frog or toad

metamorphosis a phase in the life cycle of many animals during which a rapid change from the immature form of an organism to the adult form takes place

Leading a Double Life

Most amphibians don't just get bigger as they grow into adults. They change form as they grow. After hatching, a frog or toad embryo becomes a tadpole. A **tadpole** is an immature frog or toad that must live in the water. It gets oxygen through gills and uses its long tail to swim. Later, the tadpole loses its gills and develops structures such as lungs and limbs that allow it to live on land. This change from an immature form to an adult form is called **metamorphosis** (MET uh MAWR fuh sis) and is shown in **Figure 4.** Most adult amphibians can live on land. However, they still need to keep their skin moist.

A few amphibians develop in other ways. Some do not go through full metamorphosis. They hatch as tiny versions of adults, but they have gills. Some develop on land in wet places. For example, Darwin's frogs lay eggs on moist ground. When an embryo begins to move, an adult male Darwin's frog takes it into his mouth and protects it inside his vocal sacs. When the embryo has finished developing, the adult opens his mouth and a tiny frog jumps out. **Figure 5** shows a Darwin's frog.

Figure 5 *Darwin's frogs live in Chile and Argentina. A male frog may carry 5 to 15 embryos in its vocal sacs.*

Kinds of Amphibians

More than 5,400 species of amphibians are alive today. They belong to three groups: caecilians (see SIL ee uhnz), salamanders, and frogs and toads.

Figure 6 *Caecilians do not have legs. They live in damp soil in the Tropics and eat small invertebrates in the soil.*

Caecilians

Most people are not familiar with caecilians. However, scientists have discovered more than 160 species of caecilians. These amphibians live in tropical areas of Asia, Africa, and South America. They look like earthworms or snakes, but they have the thin, moist skin of amphibians. Several traits distinguish caecilians from other amphibians. For example, caecilians do not have legs, as shown in **Figure 6.** And unlike other amphibians, some caecilians have bony scales in their skin.

Salamanders

There are about 500 known species of salamanders. As adults, most salamanders live under stones and logs in the woods of North America. Two salamanders are shown in **Figure 7.** Of modern amphibians, salamanders are the most like prehistoric amphibians in overall form. Although salamanders are much smaller than their ancestors, they have a similar body shape, a long tail, and four strong legs. They range in size from a few centimeters long to 1.5 m long.

Salamanders do not develop as tadpoles. But most of them do lose gills and grow lungs during their development. A few species, such as the axolotl (AK suh LAHT'l), never lose their gills. These species live their entire life in the water.

Reading Check **How does a salamander's body change during development?**

Looking for Locals

Talk with your family about whether amphibians might live near your home. Are there any ponds, streams, or lakes nearby? Do moist leaves cover the ground outside? Then, go outside to look for amphibians around your home. Be careful not to disturb any animals that you find. Were your predictions correct? Record your observations in your **science journal.**

Figure 7 Salamanders

The **marbled salamander** lives in damp places, such as under rocks or logs or among leaves.

This **axolotl** is an unusual salamander. It keeps its gills and never leaves the water.

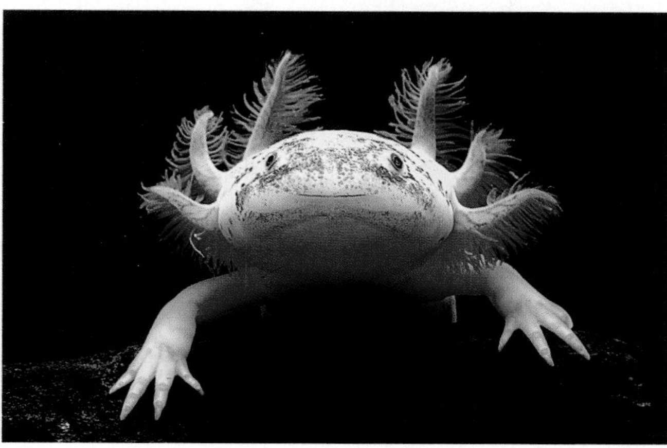

Figure 8 **Frogs and Toads**

Frogs, such as this **bull frog,** have smooth, moist skin.

Toads, such as this **Fowler's toad,** spend less time in water than frogs do. Their skin is drier and bumpier.

Frogs and Toads

About 90% of all amphibians are frogs or toads. Frogs and toads are very similar. In fact, toads are a type of frog. You can see a frog and a toad in **Figure 8.**

Frogs and toads live all over the world, except for very cold places. They are found in deserts and rain forests. They are highly adapted for life on land. Adults have strong leg muscles for jumping. They have well-developed ears for hearing and vocal cords for calling. They also have a long, sticky tongue. The tongue is attached to the front of the mouth so that it can be flipped out quickly to catch insects.

Figure 9 *Most frogs that sing are males. Their songs communicate messages to other frogs.*

Singing Frogs

Frogs are well known for their nighttime choruses, but many frogs sing in the daytime, too. Like humans, they force air from their lungs across vocal cords in the throat to make sounds. But frogs have something we lack. A thin-walled sac of skin called the *vocal sac* surrounds their vocal cords. When frogs sing, the sac inflates with vibrating air. The frog in **Figure 9** has an inflated vocal sac. The sac increases the volume of the song so that the song can be heard over long distances.

Frogs sing to communicate messages that help in attracting mates and marking territories. Usually, frogs sing songs that they know without having to learn the songs. But some frogs can change the notes they sing. For example, to make its voice louder, one frog uses a tree's acoustics. It sits in a hole in a tree trunk and tries many notes until it finds the loudest one. Then, it sings this note repeatedly to be as loud as possible.

Reading Check **How does a frog use its vocal sac?**

Amphibians as Ecological Indicators

Amphibians are often called *ecological indicators.* In other words, unhealthy amphibians can be an early sign of changes in an ecosystem. When large numbers of amphibians begin to die or show deformities, a problem with the environment may exist. For example, the disappearance of the golden toad, shown in **Figure 10,** caused concern about the toad's environment.

Amphibians are ecological indicators because they are very sensitive to changes in their environment. Their thin skin absorbs any chemicals in the water or air. And their lungs take in chemicals from the air. Climate change is another factor that may affect amphibians. As ectotherms, their body temperature depends on the temperature of their environment.

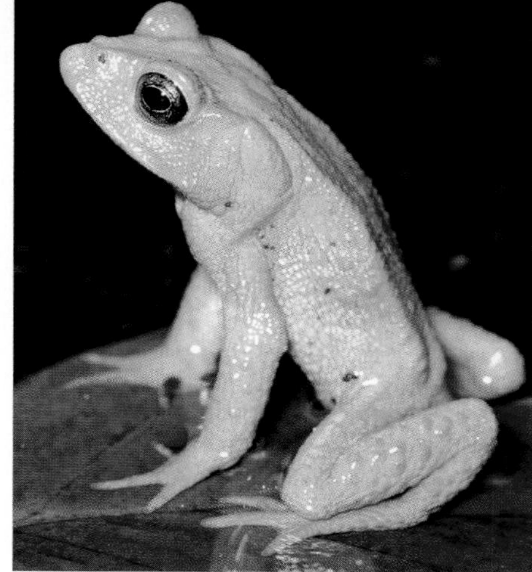

Figure 10 *Golden toads were seen regularly in Costa Rica until 1989. After that year, they disappeared.*

SECTION Review

Summary

- Amphibians were the first vertebrates to live on land.
- Amphibians breathe by gulping air into the lungs and by absorbing oxygen through the skin.
- Amphibians start life in water, where they use gills to breathe. During metamorphosis, they lose their gills and grow legs that allow them to live on land as adults.
- The three groups of amphibians are caecilians, salamanders, and frogs and toads.
- Because amphibians are very sensitive to environmental changes, they are sometimes called *ecological indicators*.

Using Vocabulary

1. Use each of the following terms in a separate sentence: *lung, tadpole,* and *metamorphosis.*

Understanding Key Ideas

2. The first vertebrates to live on land were
   - **a.** fish.
   - **b.** dinosaurs.
   - **c.** amphibians.
   - **d.** reptiles.
3. Many adult amphibians breathe by using
   - **a.** only their gills.
   - **b.** only their lungs.
   - **c.** only their skin.
   - **d.** their lungs and skin.
4. Describe metamorphosis in amphibians.
5. Why do adult amphibians have to live near water or in a very wet habitat?
6. Why are amphibians sometimes called *ecological indicators*?
7. Name the three types of amphibians. How are they similar? How are they different?
8. How are frogs and toads similar? How are they different?

Math Skills

9. A certain toad species spends 2 months of its life as a tadpole and 3 years of its life as an adult. What percentage of its life is spent in the water? What percentage is spent on land?

Critical Thinking

10. **Analyzing Relationships** Describe the relationship between lungfishes and amphibians. How are these animals alike? How are they different?
11. **Evaluating Conclusions** Scientists think that climate change may have caused the golden toad to become extinct. What other causes are possible, and how could scientists test these ideas?

SCILINKS®
NSTA
Developed and maintained by the National Science Teachers Association
For a variety of links related to this chapter, go to www.scilinks.org
Topic: Amphibians
SciLinks code: HSM0058

SECTION 3

Reptiles

How are reptiles different from amphibians? Amphibians need to spend part of their lives in or near the water. But most reptiles can spend their whole lives on land.

READING WARM-UP

Objectives

- Explain the traits that allow reptiles to live on land.
- Describe the characteristics of an amniotic egg.
- Name the four groups of modern reptiles, and give an example of each.

Terms to Learn

amniotic egg

READING STRATEGY

Brainstorming The key idea of this section is reptiles. Brainstorm words and phrases related to reptiles.

Living on Land

About 35 million years after amphibians moved onto land, some of them began to change. They grew thick, dry skin that reduced water loss. Their legs changed and grew stronger, so they could walk easily. They also laid eggs that did not dry out on dry land. They had become reptiles, the first animals to live out of the water.

Many reptiles are now extinct. Dinosaurs that lived on land are the most well known prehistoric reptiles. But there were many other ancient reptiles. Some could swim, others could fly, and many were similar to reptiles that are alive today. A few living reptiles are shown in **Figure 1.**

Figure 1 *These animals are just a few of the many kinds of reptiles on Earth today.*

▲ Crocodile

▼ South American emerald boa

▲ Giant tortoise

Characteristics of Reptiles

Reptiles are well adapted for life on land. For example, all reptiles—even reptiles that live in water—have lungs to breathe air. Reptiles also have thick skin, use their surroundings to control their temperature, and have a special kind of egg that is laid on land.

Figure 2 *Many people think snakes are slimy, but the skin of snakes and other reptiles is scaly and dry.*

Thick Skin

Thick, dry skin is a very important adaptation for life on land. This skin forms a watertight layer that keeps cells from losing water by evaporation. Unlike amphibians, most reptiles cannot breathe through their skin. Most reptiles, such as the snake in **Figure 2,** depend on only their lungs for oxygen.

Body Temperature

Nearly all reptiles are ectotherms. They cannot keep their bodies at a stable temperature. They are active when it is warm outside, and they slow down when it is cool. A few reptiles can get some heat from their own body cells. But most reptiles live in mild climates. They cannot handle the cold polar regions, where mammals and birds can thrive.

The Amazing Amniotic Egg

The most important adaptation to life on land is the amniotic (AM nee AHT ik) egg. An **amniotic egg** is an egg that holds fluid that protects the embryo. Reptiles, birds, and mammals have amniotic eggs. Reptiles' amniotic eggs have a shell, as shown in **Figure 3.** The amniotic eggs of birds and egg-laying mammals also have a shell. The shell protects the embryo and keeps the egg from drying out. A reptile's amniotic egg can be laid under rocks, in the ground, or even in the desert.

amniotic egg a type of egg that is surrounded by a membrane, the amnion, and that in reptiles, birds, and egg-laying mammals contains a large amount of yolk and is surrounded by a shell

Reading Check **Why don't reptile eggs dry out on land?** (*See the Appendix for answers to Reading Checks.*)

Figure 3 *Compare these amphibian and reptile eggs. The reptile eggs are amniotic, but the amphibian eggs are not.*

Figure 4 **An Amniotic Egg**

The amniotic egg of a bird shares important features with reptilian amniotic eggs.

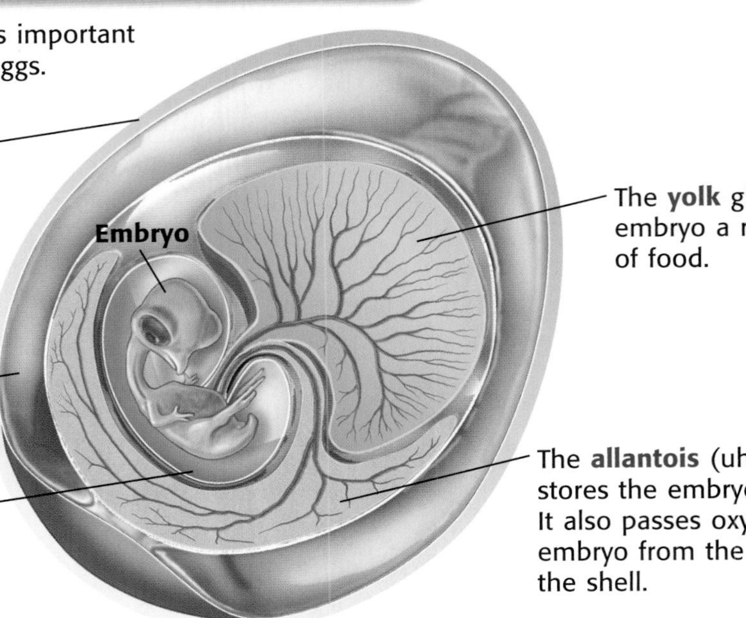
The **shell** protects the egg from damage and keeps the egg from drying out. The shell has small pores that allow oxygen to pass through to the growing embryo and allow carbon dioxide to be removed.
The **albumen** (al BYOO min) provides water and protein to the embryo.
The **amniotic sac** is filled with fluid. The amniotic fluid surrounds and protects the embryo.
Embryo
The **yolk** gives the embryo a rich supply of food.
The **allantois** (uh LAN toh is) stores the embryo's wastes. It also passes oxygen to the embryo from the pores in the shell.

Parts of the Amniotic Egg

The shell is just one important part of the amniotic egg of a reptile, bird, or egg-laying mammal. All of the parts of the amniotic egg are described in **Figure 4.** Together, these parts protect the embryo from predators, infections, and water loss.

Reptile Reproduction

Reptiles usually reproduce by internal fertilization. After the egg is fertilized inside the female, a shell forms around the egg. Then, the female lays the egg. Most reptiles lay their eggs in soil or sand. But a few reptiles do not lay their eggs. Instead, the embryos develop inside the mother, and the young are born live. In either case, the embryo develops into a tiny young reptile that looks like a small adult. Reptiles do not go through metamorphosis.

Figure 5 *This panther chameleon is a modern lizard.*

Kinds of Reptiles

The Age of Dinosaurs lasted from 300 million years ago until about 65 million years ago. During this time, most land vertebrates were reptiles. But today, about 8,000 species of living reptiles are known to exist. This number is much smaller than the number of reptile species that lived in the past. Turtles and tortoises, crocodiles and alligators, lizards and snakes, and tuataras are the four groups of reptiles that still live today. **Figure 5** shows one example of a modern reptile.

Reading Check What are the four groups of living reptiles?

Figure 6 **Turtles and Tortoises**

This **green sea turtle** has a streamlined shell that helps the turtle swim and turn rapidly.

The **Texas tortoise** is one of four living species of tortoises native to North America.

Turtles and Tortoises

Turtles and tortoises are distantly related to other living reptiles. Generally, tortoises live on land, and turtles spend all or much of their lives in the water. However, even sea turtles come on land to lay their eggs. **Figure 6** shows a turtle and a tortoise.

The trait that makes turtles and tortoises so unique is their shell. The shell makes them slow and inflexible, so outrunning predators is unlikely. But many turtles can draw their head and limbs into the armorlike shell to protect themselves.

Crocodiles and Alligators

Crocodiles and alligators spend most of their time in the water. Their eyes and nostrils are on the top of their flat head. So, they can watch their surroundings while most of their body is hidden underwater. Hiding in this way gives them a great advantage over their prey. Crocodiles and alligators are meat eaters. They eat invertebrates, fish, turtles, birds, and mammals. **Figure 7** shows how to tell the difference between an alligator and a crocodile.

Figure 7 **Crocodiles and Alligators**

A crocodile, such as this **American crocodile,** has a narrow head and a pointed snout.

An alligator, such as this **American alligator,** has a broad head and a rounded snout.

Snakes and Lizards

Today, the most common reptiles are snakes and lizards. Snakes are carnivores. They have special organs in the mouth that help them smell prey. When a snake flicks its tongue out, tiny molecules in the air stick to its tongue. The snake then touches its tongue to the organs in its mouth. The molecules on the tongue tell the snake what prey is nearby. Some snakes kill their prey by squeezing it until it suffocates. Other snakes have fangs for injecting venom. But no matter how snakes kill their prey, they eat it in the same way. Snakes can open their mouths very wide. So, snakes can eat animals and eggs by swallowing them whole. **Figure 8** shows two kinds of snakes.

Most lizards eat small insects and worms, but some lizards eat plants. One giant lizard—the Komodo dragon—eats deer, pigs, and goats! Lizards have a loosely connected lower jaw, but they do not swallow large prey whole. Lizards do have other eye-catching abilities, though. For example, many lizards can break their tails off to escape predators and then grow new tails. **Figure 9** shows two kinds of lizards.

Figure 8 **Snakes**

▼ **Cape cobras** are famous for their deadly venom. These aggressive snakes live in very dry areas.

▲ **Sinaloan milk snakes** are not poisonous, but they look a lot like poisonous coral snakes.

Figure 9 **Lizards**

The **frilled lizard** ▶ puffs out its frills to look threatening.

◀ The **thorny devil** is a harmless lizard that eats ants.

Tuataras

Tuataras (TOO uh TAH ruhs) live on only a few islands off the coast of New Zealand. **Figure 10** shows a tuatara in the wild. Tuataras look similar to lizards and can grow to be about 60 cm long.

Although tuataras look like lizards, the two reptiles are classified in different groups. Unlike many lizards, tuataras do not have visible ear openings on the outside of the body. Also, unlike many reptiles, tuataras are most active when the temperature is low. During the day, tuataras rest and absorb sunlight. At night, they search for food.

Reading Check Name two unique traits of tuataras.

Figure 10 *Tuataras have survived without changing for about 150 million years.*

SECTION Review

Summary

- Reptiles have thick, scaly skin that protects them from drying out. They also have lungs, and they depend on their surroundings to control their body temperature.
- A tough shell keeps the amniotic egg of a reptile from drying out and protects the embryo.
- Reptiles reproduce by internal fertilization.
- There are four groups of modern reptiles. The groups are: turtles and tortoises, crocodiles and alligators, lizards and snakes, and tuataras.

Using Vocabulary

1. In your own words, write a definition for the term *amniotic egg*.

Understanding Key Ideas

2. Reptiles are well adapted to living on land because they
   a. have thick, scaly skin.
   b. have lungs.
   c. lay amniotic eggs.
   d. All of the above
3. A reptile can lay its egg on land because
   a. the egg's shell prevents fertilization.
   b. the egg's shell keeps moisture inside the egg.
   c. the egg's shell keeps carbon dioxide inside the egg.
   d. the egg's shell allows water to leave the egg.
4. Name three ways that an amniotic egg protects reptile embryos.
5. Explain how most reptiles reproduce.
6. Name the four groups of modern reptiles, and give an example of each kind.
7. What special adaptations do snakes have for eating?

Math Skills

8. Suppose that a sea turtle lays 104 eggs. If 50% of the hatchlings reach the ocean alive and 25% of those survivors reach adulthood, how many adults result from the eggs?

Critical Thinking

9. **Applying Concepts** Mammals give birth to live young. The embryo develops inside the female's body. Which parts of a reptilian amniotic egg could a mammal do without? Explain.
10. **Analyzing Ideas** Rattlesnakes can't see well, but they can detect temperature changes of three-thousandths of a degree Celsius. How could this ability be useful to the snakes?

SCILINKS
NSTA
Developed and maintained by the National Science Teachers Association
For a variety of links related to this chapter, go to www.scilinks.org
Topic: Reptiles
SciLinks code: HSM1299

Using Scientific Methods

Model-Making Lab

Floating a Pipe Fish

Bony fishes control how deep or shallow they swim by using a special structure called a *swim bladder*. As gases are absorbed and released by the swim bladder, the fish's body rises or sinks in the water. In this activity, you will make a model of a fish that has a swim bladder. Your challenge will be to make the fish rest in one place, without rising or sinking, halfway between the top of the water and the bottom of the container. You will probably need to do several trials and a lot of observing and analyzing.

OBJECTIVES

Make a model of a fish that has a swim bladder.

Describe how swim bladders help fish maintain buoyancy.

MATERIALS

- balloon, slender
- container for water at least 15 cm deep
- cork, small
- PVC pipe, 12 cm in length, 3/4 in. diameter
- rubber band
- water

SAFETY

Ask a Question

1. Think of a question about the amount of gases needed to keep a pipe fish model resting halfway between the top of the water and the bottom of the container.

Form a Hypothesis

2. Formulate a testable hypothesis that answers your question. Estimate how much air you will need in the balloon so that your pipe fish will come to rest halfway between the top of the water and the bottom of the container. Will you need to inflate the balloon halfway, a small amount, or all the way?

Test the Hypothesis

3. Inflate your balloon. Hold the neck of the balloon so that no air escapes, and push the cork into the end of the balloon. If the cork is properly placed, no air should leak out when the balloon is held underwater.

4. Place your swim bladder inside the pipe, and place a rubber band along the pipe as shown. The rubber band will keep the swim bladder from coming out of either end of the pipe.

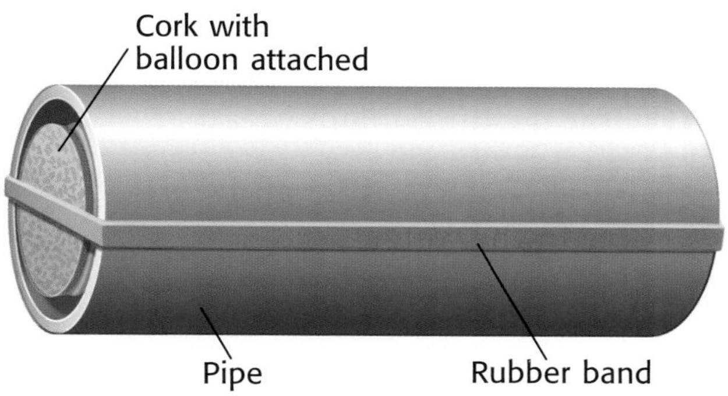

5. Place your pipe fish in the water, and note where the fish rests without sinking or rising. Record your observations.

6. If the pipe fish does not rest at the halfway point, take it out of the water, adjust the amount of air in the balloon, and try again.

7. You can release small amounts of air from the bladder by carefully lifting the neck of the balloon away from the cork. You can add more air by removing the cork and blowing more air into the balloon. Keep adjusting and testing until your fish rests, without sinking or rising, halfway between the bottom of the container and the top of the water.

Analyze the Results

1. **Analyzing Results** Was the estimate you made in your hypothesis the correct amount of air your balloon needed to rest at the halfway point? Explain your answer.

2. **Examining Data** Consider the length and volume of the entire pipe fish. How much air was needed to make the fish rest at the correct place? State your answer as a proportion or percentage. (Remember that the volume of a cylinder is equal to the height or length of the cylinder multiplied by the area of its base.)

3. **Evaluating Data** Analyze the information you gathered in this activity to explain how the structure of a fish's swim bladder complements its function. What are some limitations to your model?

Draw Conclusions

4. **Interpreting Information** Some fast-swimming fishes, such as sharks, and marine mammals, such as whales and dolphins, do not have a swim bladder. Do research at a library or on the Internet to find out how these animals keep from sinking to the bottom of the ocean. Can you find any reasons why a swim bladder would be helpful to them? How could a swim bladder cause problems for these animals?

Chapter Review

USING KEY TERMS

1. In your own words, write a definition for each of the following terms: *metamorphosis, amniotic egg,* and *vertebrate.*

2. Use the following terms in the same sentence: *lung, gills,* and *tadpole.*

For each pair of terms, explain how the meanings of the terms differ.

3. *endotherm* and *ectotherm*

4. *swim bladder* and *lateral line*

UNDERSTANDING KEY IDEAS

Multiple Choice

5. Which of the following structures is not present in some chordates?
   a. a tail
   b. a backbone
   c. a notochord
   d. a hollow nerve cord

6. Which fishes do not have jaws?
   a. sharks, skates, and rays
   b. hagfish and lampreys
   c. bony fishes
   d. None of the above

7. Both amphibians and reptiles
   a. have lungs.
   b. have gills.
   c. breathe only through their skin.
   d. have amniotic eggs.

8. Metamorphosis occurs in
   a. fishes and amphibians.
   b. amphibians.
   c. fishes, amphibians, and reptiles.
   d. amphibians and reptiles.

9. Both bony fishes and cartilaginous fishes have
   a. fins.
   b. an oily liver.
   c. a swim bladder.
   d. skeletons made of bone.

Short Answer

10. How do amphibians breathe?

11. What characteristics allow fishes to live in the water?

12. What characteristics allow reptiles to live on land?

13. How does a reptile embryo in an amniotic egg get oxygen?

14. Describe the stages of metamorphosis in a frog.

15. What two things are present in all vertebrates but not in some chordates?

16. Describe the three kinds of amphibians.

17. Explain why amphibians can be effective ecological indicators.

CRITICAL THINKING

18 **Concept Mapping** Use the following terms to create a concept map: *dinosaur, turtle, reptiles, amphibians, fishes, shark, salamander,* and *vertebrates.*

19 **Applying Concepts** If the air temperature outside is 43°C and the ideal body temperature of a lizard is 38°C, would you most likely find that lizard in the sun or in the shade? Explain your answer.

20 **Identifying Relationships** Describe three characteristics of amphibian skin. How do amphibians use their skin? How does the structure of amphibian skin relate to its function?

21 **Making Inferences** Suppose that you have found an animal that has a backbone and gills, but the animal does not seem to have a notochord. Is the animal a chordate? How can you be sure of your answer?

22 **Analyzing Processes** If you found a shark that lacks the muscles needed to pump water over its gills, what would that information tell you about how the shark lives?

23 **Forming Hypotheses** If you found a reptile that you did not recognize, what questions would you need to ask to determine which of the four reptile groups the reptile belongs to? Explain how you could form a hypothesis about the reptile's group based on the answers to these questions.

INTERPRETING GRAPHICS

The graph below shows body temperatures of two organisms and the ground temperature of their environment. Use the graph to answer the questions that follow.

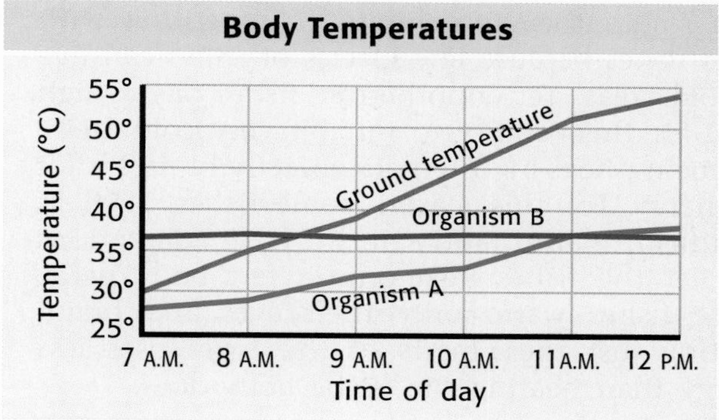

24 How do the body temperatures of organism A and organism B change as the ground temperature changes?

25 Which of these organisms is most likely an ectotherm? Explain your answer.

26 Which of these organisms is most likely an endotherm? Explain your answer.

Standardized Test Preparation

READING

Read each of the passages below. Then, answer the questions that follow each passage.

Passage 1 Only a few kinds of fishes are endotherms. These fishes depend on their environment for most of their body heat but can heat parts of their bodies by internal cell activity. Because they can produce heat within their bodies, endothermic fishes can hunt for prey in extremely chilly water. As a result, they face limited competition with other fishes because few species of fishes can live in cold areas. Yet endothermic fishes pay a high price for their ability to <u>inhabit</u> very cold areas. Producing heat by internal cell activity uses a lot of energy. For this reason, some fishes, such as swordfish, marlin, and sailfish, have adaptations that let the fishes heat only a few body parts. These fishes warm only their eyes and brain. Heating just these parts of the body uses less energy than heating the entire body does.

1. In this passage, what does *inhabit* mean?

A to use energy in
B to live in
C to heat up
D to eat in

2. Which of the following statements is a fact according to the passage?

F Tuna always live in very cold areas.
G Most prey live in extremely chilly water.
H Some fishes that heat parts of their body can hunt for prey in cold water.
I The eyes and the brain are the most important parts of a fish's body.

3. Which fishes can heat certain parts of their bodies and hunt in extremely cold waters?

A most fishes
B swordfish, marlin, and sailfish
C no fishes
D tropical fishes

Passage 2 Fishes are quicker and much more <u>maneuverable</u> than most ships and submarines. So, why aren't ships and submarines built more like fishes—with tails that flap back and forth? This question caught the attention of some scientists at MIT, and they decided to build a robot model of a bluefin tuna. This robot fish is 124 cm long. It contains six motors and has a skeleton made of aluminum ribs and hinges. These scientists think that if ships were designed more like the bodies of fishes, the ships would use much less energy than they currently use. If the new design does require less energy—and thus less fuel—the ships will save money.

1. According to the passage, what is one reason that scientists are designing a robot model of a fish?

A Designing ships to work more like fishes' bodies might save energy.
B Fishes' bodies do not use much energy.
C Bluefin tuna have tails that move back and forth.
D Designing ships to work more like fishes' bodies could reduce ocean pollution levels.

2. What does *maneuverable* probably mean?

F able to move easily
G able to move like a robot
H made of aluminum
I fuel efficient

3. Which of the following statements is a fact according to the passage?

A Fueling ships is very expensive.
B Some MIT scientists built a robot fish.
C Designing a ship that moves like a fish will save money.
D Fishes are 124 cm long.

INTERPRETING GRAPHICS

The chart below shows the kinds of amphibians that are threatened or endangered in the United States. Use the chart below to answer the questions that follow.

Threatened and Endangered Amphibian Species in the United States

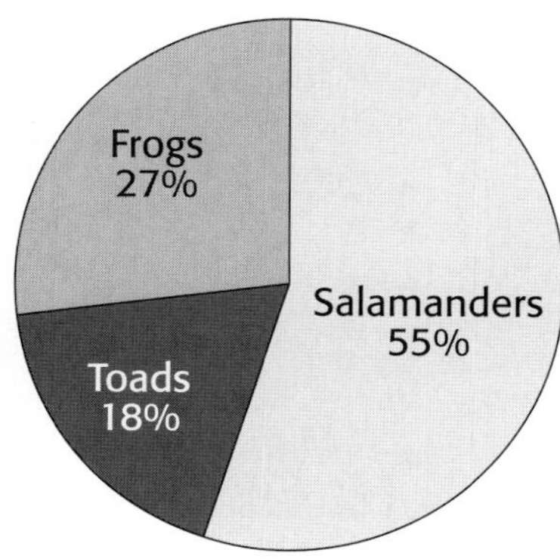

Source: U.S. Fish and Wildlife Service.

1. Which amphibian group has the most threatened and endangered species in the United States?

A frogs
B salamanders
C toads
D caecilians

2. If the total number of threatened and endangered amphibian species in the United States is 22, how many species of salamanders are threatened or endangered?

F 4
G 6
H 12
I 22

3. If the total number of threatened and endangered amphibian species in the United States is 22, how many more species of salamanders are threatened or endangered than species of frogs and toads?

A 12
B 10
C 6
D 2

4. Which of the following statements about the pie chart is true?

F The chart does not have any information about amphibians outside of the United States.
G The chart shows that amphibians outside of the United States are also endangered and threatened.
H The chart shows that frogs are more sensitive to environmental pollution than toads are.
I The chart shows that amphibians are ecological indicators.

MATH

Read each question below, and choose the best answer.

1. Suppose that a snake eats a mouse that has one-third more mass than the snake does. If the snake has a mass of 4.2 kg, what is the mass of the mouse?

A 1.4 kg
B 2.8 kg
C 4.2 kg
D 5.6 kg

2. One year, there were 2,000 salamanders in a state park. If the population decreased by 8% each year for 3 years, what would the salamander population be after the 3-year period?

F 1,520 salamanders
G 1,557 salamanders
H 1,840 salamanders
I 1,898 salamanders

3. What is the volume of a rectangular fish tank that is 1 m wide, 2 m long, and 1.5 m tall?

A 3 m^2
B 3 m^3
C 4.5 m
D 4.5 m^3

Science in Action

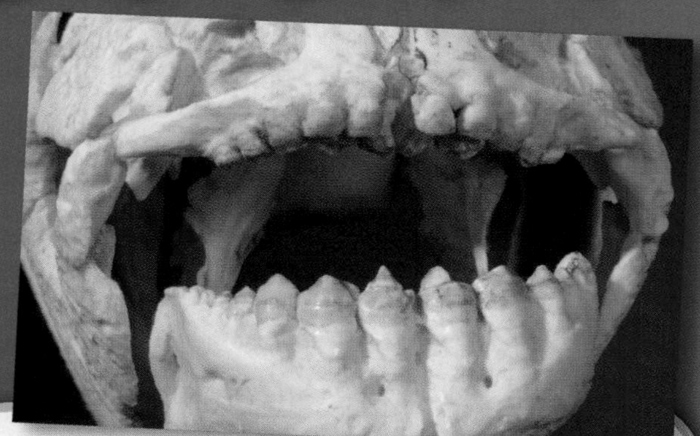

Weird Science

Fish That Eat Fruit

Have you ever thought about fish teeth? You probably know what shark teeth look like. So, you shouldn't be surprised that fish teeth are usually very different from your own teeth. But take a look at the fish shown above. This fish is *frugivorous* (froo JIV uh ruhs), which means that it eats fruit. Some frugivorous fishes live in the Amazon River in Brazil. Parts of the Amazon River basin flood for much of the year, which causes the water level to rise and spread under fruit trees. Fruit falls from the trees into the water, so these fishes have evolved to eat fruit. Eating fruit requires teeth that can bite and chew, just like human teeth. So, these fishes' teeth have evolved into a form that is similar to human teeth!

Math ACTIVITY

Suppose the water level in a river rose 8 m when it was flooded. At this time, 4 meters of a certain tree are above water. This tree is 16 m tall. What was the original depth of the river before it was flooded?

Scientific Discoveries

Giant Crocodiles

Have you ever watched a crocodile at a zoo or on TV? Even when crocodiles are resting and not moving, we instinctively know to be wary of them. Most crocodiles today are about 3.5 m long. But Paul Sereno recently discovered a fossil in the Sahara that shows how big crocodiles used to be. The fossil crocodile that Sereno found is 12 m—about the length of seven adult humans lying head to toe! This crocodile lived 110 million years ago. Sereno's find answered many questions raised by other crocodile fossils that had been found before. Now scientists can estimate the animal's huge size with accuracy.

Language Arts ACTIVITY

WRITING SKILL Imagine that you discovered an animal living today that was 4 times the size of an average organism of that species. For example, imagine discovering a rattlesnake that was 4 times the size of an average rattlesnake. Write a story about your discovery, and include your ideas about how size affected the life of the organism.

People in Science

Dagmar Werner

Raising Iguanas At the Carara Biological Preserve in Costa Rica, thousands of iguana eggs sit just below the surface of the Earth in sun-heated incubators. Why would anyone bother to incubate thousands of iguana eggs? Dr. Dagmar Werner leads this project in an attempt to restore an iguana population that has been severely reduced in the past several decades. The lizards have suffered from the effects of hunting, pollution, and habitat destruction by people who clear the rain forest for farming.

Dr. Werner combined her captive-breeding program at the preserve with an education program that shows farmers that there is more than one way to make a profit from the rain forest. She encourages local farmers to raise iguanas, which can be released into the wild or sold for food, instead of raising cattle (and cutting down the rain forest to do so). Known as the "chicken of the trees," the iguana has been a favored source of meat among native rain-forest inhabitants for thousands of years. Farmers not only profit from the sale of iguana meat but also produce iguana leather and other handicrafts.

According to Dr. Werner, "Many locals have never thought of wild animals as creatures that must be protected in order to survive. That's why so many go extinct." To get her message across, Dr. Werner has established an organization that sponsors festivals and education seminars in local communities. These activities promote the traditional appeal of the iguana, increase civic pride in the animal, and heighten awareness about the iguana's economic importance.

Social Studies ACTIVITY

WRITING SKILL Dr. Werner's project helps the iguanas because it takes hunting pressure off the iguana population. But it also helps farmers by increasing their income and preventing habitat destruction. Can you think of a project that could help both the people and the environment in your own community? Write a three-paragraph description of an environmental project that could work for your community.

go.hrw.com

To learn more about these Science in Action topics, visit go.hrw.com and type in the keyword HL5VR1F.

Current Science

Check out Current Science® articles related to this chapter by visiting go.hrw.com. Just type in the keyword HL5CS16.

Birds and Mammals

About the 

Why would an animal covered in stiff plates of armor jump up to 1.2 m (4 ft) high—straight up in the air? Armadillos jump when they are frightened. Jumping sometimes surprises and scares off predators, giving the armadillo a chance to run away. Armadillos are mammals.

PRE-READING ACTIVITY

FOLDNOTES

Table Fold Before you read the chapter, create the FoldNote entitled "Table Fold" described in the **Study Skills** section of the Appendix. Label the columns of the table fold with "Characteristics" and "Kinds." Label the rows with "Birds," "Placental mammals," and "Monotremes and marsupials." As you read the chapter, write examples of each topic under the appropriate column.

START-UP ACTIVITY

Let's Fly!

How do birds fly? This activity will give you a few hints.

Procedure

1. Carefully fold a **piece of paper** to make a paper airplane. Make the folds even and the creases sharp.
2. Throw the plane through the air very gently. What happened?
3. Take the same plane, and throw it more forcefully. Did anything change?
4. Reduce the size of the wings by folding them inward toward the center crease. Make sure the two wings are the same size and shape.
5. Throw the airplane two more times. Throw it gently at first, and then throw it with more force. What happened each time?

Analysis

1. Analyze what effect the force of your throw has on the paper airplane's flight. Do you think forces of different strengths affect bird flight in a similar way? Explain your answer.
2. What happened when the wings were made smaller? Why do you think this happened? Do you think wing size affects the way a bird flies? Explain your answer.
3. Based on your results, how would you design and throw the perfect paper airplane?

SECTION 1

Characteristics of Birds

What do a powerful eagle, a lumbering penguin, and a dainty finch have in common? They all have feathers, wings, and a beak, which means they are all birds.

READING WARM-UP

Objectives

- Describe two kinds of feathers.
- Describe how a bird's diet, breathing, muscles, and skeleton help it fly.
- Explain how lift works.
- Describe how birds raise their young.

Terms to Learn

preening, molting, down feather, contour feather, lift, brooding

READING STRATEGY

Prediction Guide Before reading this section, write the title of each heading in this section. Next, under each heading, write what you think you will learn.

Birds share many characteristics with reptiles. Like reptiles, birds are vertebrates. Birds' feet and legs are covered by thick scales like those that cover reptiles' bodies. Also, bird eggs have an amniotic sac and a shell, just as reptile eggs do.

Birds also have many unique characteristics. For example, bird eggs have harder shells than reptile eggs do. And as shown in **Figure 1,** birds have feathers and wings. They also have a horny beak instead of jaws with teeth. Also, birds can use heat from activity in their cells to maintain a constant body temperature.

Feathers

One familiar characteristic of birds is their feathers. Feathers help birds stay dry and warm, attract mates, and fly.

Preening and Molting

Birds take good care of their feathers. They use their beaks to spread oil on their feathers in a process called **preening.** The oil is made by a gland near the bird's tail. The oil helps waterproof the feathers and keeps them clean. When feathers wear out, birds replace them by molting. **Molting** is the process of shedding old feathers and growing new ones. Most birds shed their feathers at least once a year.

preening in birds, the act of grooming and maintaining their feathers

molting the shedding of an exoskeleton, skin, feathers, or hair to be replaced by new parts

Figure 1 *There are about 10,000 known species of birds on Earth today.*

Two Kinds of Feathers

Birds have two main kinds of feathers—down feathers and contour feathers. **Down feathers** are fluffy feathers that lie next to a bird's body. These feathers help birds stay warm. When a bird fluffs its down feathers, air is trapped close to the body. Trapping air keeps body heat near the body. **Contour feathers** are stiff feathers that cover a bird's body and wings. Their colors and shapes help some birds attract mates. Contour feathers have a stiff central shaft with many side branches, called *barbs*. The barbs link together to form a smooth surface, as shown in **Figure 2.** This streamlined surface helps birds fly.

Reading Check What is the function of a bird's down feathers? (*See the Appendix for answers to Reading Checks.*)

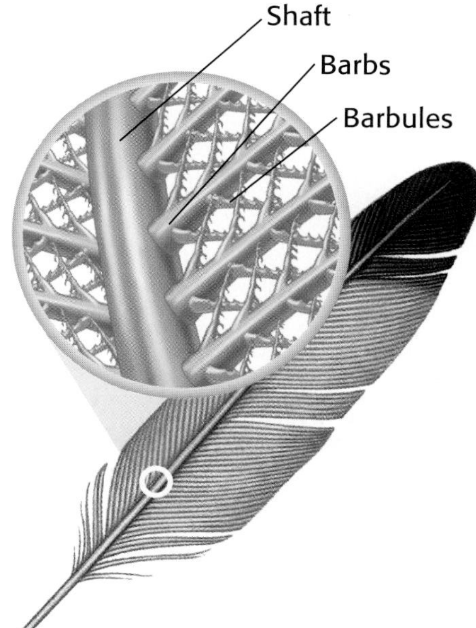

Figure 2 *The barbs of a contour feather have cross branches called* barbules. *Barbs and barbules give the feather strength and shape.*

High-Energy Animals

Birds need a lot of energy to fly. To get this energy, their bodies break down food quickly. This process generates a lot of body heat. In fact, the average body temperature of a bird is 40°C—three degrees warmer than yours. Birds cannot sweat to cool off if they get too hot. Instead, they lay their feathers flat and pant like dogs do.

Fast Digestion

Because birds need a lot of energy, they eat a lot. Hummingbirds need to eat almost constantly to get the energy they need! Most birds eat insects, nuts, seeds, or meat. These foods are high in protein and fat. A few birds, such as geese, eat grass, leaves, and other plants. Birds have a unique digestive system to help them get energy quickly. **Figure 3** shows this system. Modern birds don't have teeth, so they can't chew. Instead, food goes from the mouth to the crop. The *crop* stores food until it moves to the gizzard. Many *gizzards* have small stones inside. These stones grind up the food so that it can be easily digested in the intestine. This grinding action is similar to what happens when we chew our food.

down feather a soft feather that covers the body of young birds and provides insulation to adult birds

contour feather one of the most external feathers that cover a bird and that help determine its shape

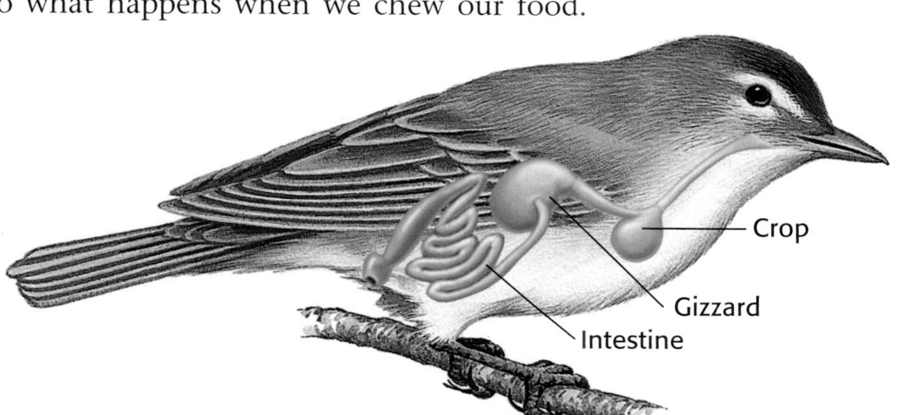

Figure 3 *A bird's digestive system helps the bird rapidly change food into usable energy.*

Flying

Most birds can fly. Even flightless birds, such as ostriches, have ancestors that could fly. So, it is not surprising that birds have many adaptations for flight. The most obvious characteristic related to flight is the wings. But birds also have lightweight bodies. And they have powerful flight muscles and a rapidly beating heart. The fast heart rate helps birds get plenty of oxygen-rich blood to the flight muscles. **Figure 4** describes many bird characteristics that are important for flight.

Reading Check **How does a bird's heart help the bird fly?**

Figure 4 **Flight Adaptations of Birds**

Most birds have **large eyes** and excellent eyesight. Large eyes allow birds to see objects and food from a distance. Some birds, such as hawks and eagles, can see 8 times better than humans can see!
Lung
Air sacs
Birds have a **rapidly beating heart.** The heart pumps a fast, steady stream of oxygen-rich blood to the flight muscles. In small birds, the heart beats almost 1,000 times a minute! (Your heart beats about 70 times a minute.)
Birds have special organs called **air sacs** attached to their lungs. The air sacs store air. Because of the stored air, a bird's lungs have a continuous supply of air—whether the bird is inhaling or exhaling.

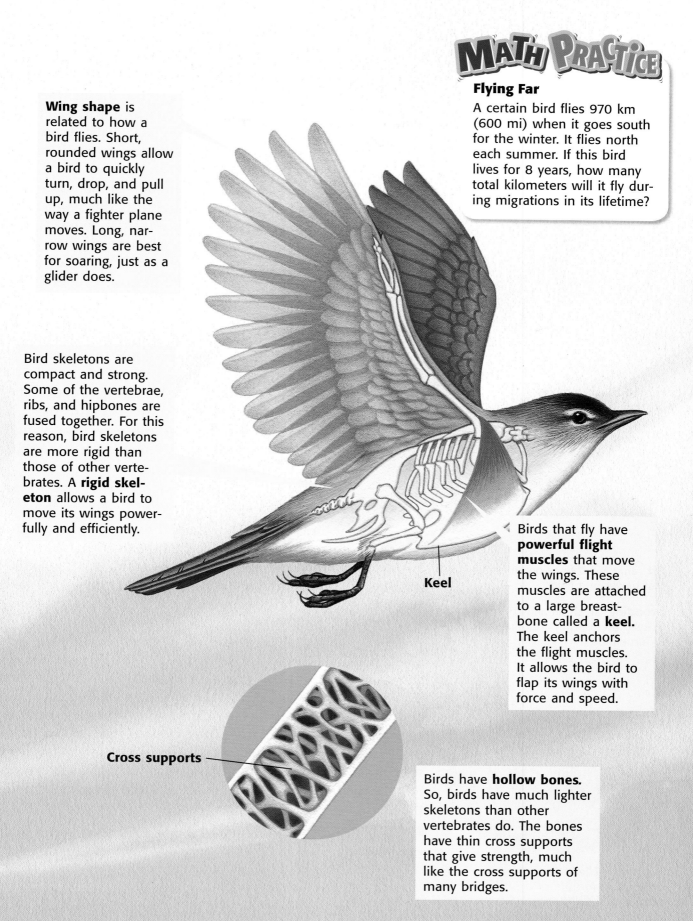

MATH PRACTICE
Flying Far
A certain bird flies 970 km (600 mi) when it goes south for the winter. It flies north each summer. If this bird lives for 8 years, how many total kilometers will it fly during migrations in its lifetime?
Wing shape is related to how a bird flies. Short, rounded wings allow a bird to quickly turn, drop, and pull up, much like the way a fighter plane moves. Long, narrow wings are best for soaring, just as a glider does.
Bird skeletons are compact and strong. Some of the vertebrae, ribs, and hipbones are fused together. For this reason, bird skeletons are more rigid than those of other vertebrates. A **rigid skeleton** allows a bird to move its wings powerfully and efficiently.
Keel
Birds that fly have **powerful flight muscles** that move the wings. These muscles are attached to a large breastbone called a **keel.** The keel anchors the flight muscles. It allows the bird to flap its wings with force and speed.
Cross supports
Birds have **hollow bones.** So, birds have much lighter skeletons than other vertebrates do. The bones have thin cross supports that give strength, much like the cross supports of many bridges.

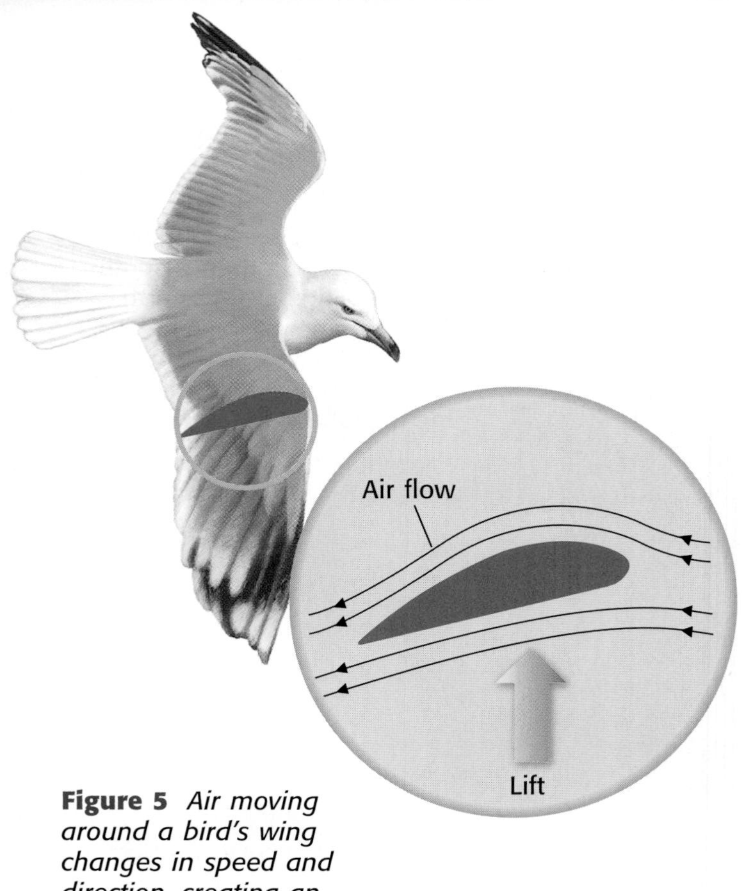

Figure 5 *Air moving around a bird's wing changes in speed and direction, creating an upward force that keeps a bird in the air.*

Getting off the Ground

How do birds overcome gravity to fly? Birds flap their wings to get into the air. They keep flapping to push themselves through the air. They are able to stay in the air because their wings cause lift. **Lift** is an upward force on a bird's wings.

As a bird flies through the air, some of the air is forced over the top of its wings. Some air is forced underneath the wings. **Figure 5** shows this airflow. A bird's wings are curved on top. The shape of the wings affects the air around them. As air flows over and under a bird's wings, the air's speed and direction change. These changes in the air's speed and direction affect the wings in a way that creates lift, the upward force that acts on the wings.

Lift is affected by flying speed and by wing shape. The faster a bird flies, the greater the lift. Also, the larger the wing is, the greater the lift. Birds with large wings can glide for long distances.

Raising Baby Birds

The way that birds reproduce is similar to the way that reptiles reproduce. Like reptiles, birds reproduce sexually by internal fertilization. Both birds and reptiles lay amniotic eggs in which there is a growing embryo. But unlike most reptiles, birds must keep their eggs warm for the embryos to live and grow.

lift an upward force on an object that moves in a fluid

brooding to sit on and cover eggs to keep them warm until they hatch; to incubate

Nests

Most birds build nests in which they lay their eggs. **Figure 6** shows a bird's nest with eggs in it. Birds keep their eggs warm by brooding. **Brooding** is the act of sitting on eggs and using body heat to keep them warm. Birds sit on their eggs until the eggs hatch. For some birds, such as gulls, the job of brooding is shared by both males and females. In many species of songbirds, the female broods the eggs, and the male brings food to the brooding female. In a few species, the male broods the eggs.

Reading Check How does the process of brooding keep a bird's eggs warm?

Figure 6 *This robin's nest is only one example of a bird's nest. Birds build nests of many different shapes and sizes.*

Precocial and Altricial

Some birds, such as chickens and ducks, are active soon after they hatch. These active chicks are *precocial* (pree KOH shuhl). Precocial chicks are covered with downy feathers. As soon as they can stand up, the chicks follow their parents around. These chicks depend on a mother for warmth and protection, but they can walk, swim, and feed themselves.

Some birds, such as hawks and songbirds, are weak and helpless for a while after hatching. These weak chicks are *altricial* (al TRISH uhl). When they hatch, they have no feathers and their eyes are closed. They cannot walk or fly. Their parents must keep them warm and feed them for several weeks. **Figure 7** shows a parent feeding its altricial chicks.

Figure 7 *Parents of altricial chicks bring food to the nest.*

SECTION Review

Summary

- Birds have feathers, a beak, wings, and a constant body temperature.
- Down feathers keep birds warm. Contour feathers help birds fly and attract mates.
- Birds must eat a high-energy diet to get energy for flying.
- Lightweight bodies and strong muscles help birds fly. Air sacs help them get enough oxygen to fly.
- Wings create lift as they cut through the air. Lift pushes the wings up to keep a bird in the air.
- Birds keep their eggs warm in a nest by brooding. When the chicks hatch, they are precocial or altricial.

Using Key Terms

1. Use each of the following terms in a separate sentence: *lift* and *brooding.*

For each pair of terms, explain how the meanings of the terms differ.

2. *down feather* and *contour feather*
3. *preening* and *molting*

Understanding Key Ideas

4. Which of the following is NOT a flight adaptation in birds?
   - **a.** hollow bones
   - **b.** air sacs
   - **c.** down feathers
   - **d.** rapidly beating heart
5. What do birds eat? Describe the path taken by a bird's food as it moves through the bird's digestive system.
6. How does the air around a bird's wings cause lift?
7. Explain the difference between precocial chicks and altricial chicks.
8. Name two ways that birds use their contour feathers. Name one way that birds use their down feathers.

Math Skills

9. Suppose that a bird that weighs 325 g loses 40% of its body weight during migration. What is the bird's weight when it reaches its destination?

Critical Thinking

10. **Analyzing Ideas** Why can't people fly without the help of technology? Name at least four human body characteristics that are poorly adapted for flight.
11. **Applying Concepts** Some people use the phrase "eats like a bird" to describe someone who does not eat very much. Does using the phrase in this way show an accurate understanding of a bird's eating habits? Why or why not?

SCILINKS®
NSTA
Developed and maintained by the National Science Teachers Association
For a variety of links related to this chapter, go to www.scilinks.org
Topic: Bird Characteristics
SciLinks code: HSM0167

SECTION 2

Kinds of Birds

There are about 10,000 species of birds on Earth. Birds vary in color, shape, and size. They range in mass from the 1.6 g bee hummingbird to the 125 kg North African ostrich. The ostrich is almost 80,000 times more massive than the hummingbird!

READING WARM-UP

Objectives

- Identify the differences between flightless birds, water birds, perching birds, and birds of prey.

READING STRATEGY

Discussion Read this section silently. Write down questions that you have about this section. Discuss your questions in a small group.

Scientists group living bird species into 28 different orders. Songbirds, such as robins or bluebirds, make up the largest order. This order includes about 60% of all bird species. But birds are often grouped into four nonscientific categories: flightless birds, water birds, perching birds, and birds of prey. These categories don't include all birds. But they do show how different birds can be.

Flightless Birds

Not all birds fly. Most flightless birds do not have the large keel that anchors birds' flight muscles. Instead of flying, some flightless birds run quickly to move around. Others are skilled swimmers. **Figure 1** shows three kinds of flightless birds.

Figure 1 Flightless Birds

Unlike other flightless birds, **penguins** have a large keel and very strong flight muscles. Their wings have changed over time to become flippers. They flap these wings to "fly" underwater.

The **ostrich** is the largest living bird. It can reach a height of 2.5 m and a mass of 125 kg. An ostrich's two-toed feet look almost like hoofs. These birds can run up to about 60 km/h.

The **kiwi** is a small, chicken-sized bird from New Zealand. Kiwis sleep during the day. At night, they hunt for worms, caterpillars, and berries.

Figure 2 **Water Birds**

The **blue-footed booby** is a tropical water bird. These birds have an elaborate courtship dance that includes raising their feet one at a time.

Male **wood ducks** have beautiful plumage to attract females. Like all ducks, they are strong swimmers and flyers.

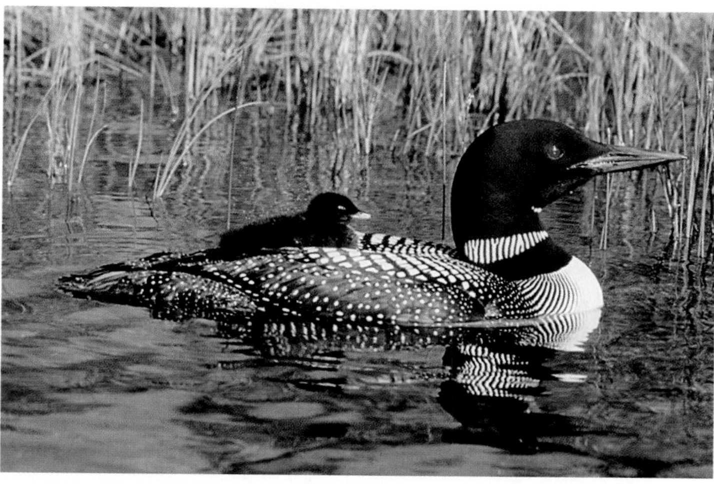

The **common loon** can make very deep dives and remain underwater for several minutes while searching for fish.

Water Birds

Many flying birds are also comfortable in the water. These water birds include cranes, ducks, geese, swans, pelicans, and loons. These birds usually have webbed feet for swimming or long legs for wading. **Figure 2** above shows three different water birds.

Water birds find food both in the water and on land. Many of these birds eat plants, invertebrates, or fish. Some water birds have a rounded, flat beak for eating plants or small invertebrates. Others have a long, sharp beak for catching fish.

Reading Check **What are the two kinds of beaks that are common in water birds?** (*See the Appendix for answers to Reading Checks.*)

For another activity related to this chapter, go to **go.hrw.com** and type in the keyword **HL5VR2W.**

Perching Birds

Perching birds have special adaptations for resting on branches. Songbirds, such as robins, warblers, and sparrows, make up a large part of this group of birds. When a perching bird lands in a tree, its feet automatically close around a branch. If the bird falls asleep while it is perching, its feet will stay closed. The sleeping bird will not fall off the branch. **Figure 3** shows three kinds of perching birds.

Reading Check **What happens to a perching bird that falls asleep while it is perching on a branch?**

Figure 3 **Perching Birds**

Parrots have special feet for perching and climbing. They open seeds and slice fruit with their strong, hooked beak.

Chickadees are lively, little birds that often visit garden feeders. They can dangle underneath a branch while hunting for insects, seeds, or fruits.

Most tanagers are tropical birds, but the **scarlet tanager** spends the summer in North America. The male is red, but the female is a yellow green color that blends into the trees.

Birds of Prey

Birds of prey hunt and eat other vertebrates. These birds may eat insects or other invertebrates in addition to mammals, fish, reptiles, and birds. Take a look at the birds in **Figure 4.** Birds of prey have sharp claws on their feet and a sharp, curved beak. These traits help the birds catch and eat their prey. Birds of prey also have very good vision. Most of them hunt during the day, as the osprey does. But most owls hunt at night.

Figure 4 **Birds of Prey**

Owls, such as this **northern spotted owl,** are the only birds of prey that hunt at night. They have a strong sense of hearing to help them find their prey in the dark.

Ospreys eat fish. They fly over the water and catch fish with their clawed feet.

SECTION Review

Summary

- Some flightless birds do not have a large keel as other birds do. Many flightless birds are fast runners or swimmers.
- Many water birds have webbed feet for swimming or long legs for wading.
- Perching birds have feet that automatically close around a branch.
- Birds of prey have a sharp beak and claws for catching and eating their prey.

Understanding Key Ideas

1. Which of the following groups of birds includes birds that do NOT have a large keel?
   a. flightless birds
   b. water birds
   c. perching birds
   d. birds of prey
2. Why do some water birds have long legs?
   a. for swimming
   b. for wading
   c. for running
   d. for flying
3. Most birds of prey have very good eyesight. Why do you think good vision is important for these birds?
4. To which group of birds do songbirds belong? Name three examples of songbirds.

Math Skills

5. How quickly could an ostrich, running at a speed of 60 km/h, run a 400 m track event?

Critical Thinking

6. **Predicting Consequences** Would it be helpful for a duck to have the feet of a perching bird? Explain why or why not.
7. **Making Inferences** How could being able to run 60 km/h be helpful for an ostrich?

SCILINKS.
NSTA
Developed and maintained by the National Science Teachers Association
For a variety of links related to this chapter, go to www.scilinks.org
Topic: Kinds of Birds
SciLinks code: HSM0831

SECTION 3

Characteristics of Mammals

What do you have in common with a bat, a donkey, a giraffe, and a whale? You're all mammals!

READING WARM-UP

Objectives

- Explain how early mammals lived.
- Describe seven common characteristics of mammals.

Terms to Learn

mammary gland
diaphragm

READING STRATEGY

Reading Organizer As you read this section, create an outline of the section. Use the headings from the section in your outline.

Mammals live in the coldest oceans, the hottest deserts, and almost every place in between. The tiniest bats weigh less than a cracker, and the blue whale can weigh more than twenty school buses. Though mammals vary in many ways, all of the approximately 5,000 modern species share certain characteristics. **Figure 1** shows a few of the many types of mammals.

The First Mammals

Fossil evidence indicates that about 280 million years ago, reptiles called *therapsids* (thuh RAP sihdz) existed. These animals had characteristics of both reptiles and mammals. True mammals appeared soon after. Mammals appeared in the fossil record more than 225 million years ago. They were about the size of mice. These animals were endotherms, so they were able to keep their body temperature constant. They did not depend on their surroundings to keep warm. This trait allowed them to look for food at night and to avoid being eaten by dinosaurs during the day.

When the dinosaurs died out, more land and food were available for the mammals. These resources allowed mammals to spread out and live in many different environments.

Figure 1 *Even though they look very different, all of these animals are mammals.*

▲ Mandrill baboon

▲ Rhinoceros

▼ Beluga whale

Figure 2 *Like all mammals, this calf drinks its mother's milk for its first meals.*

Common Characteristics

Dolphins, monkeys, and elephants have hair and specialized teeth, just as you do! Mammals share these and many other characteristics that make them unlike other animals.

mammary gland in a female mammal, a gland that secretes milk

diaphragm a dome-shaped muscle that is attached to the lower ribs and that functions as the main muscle in respiration

Making Milk

All mammals have mammary glands. No other animal has these glands. **Mammary glands** are structures that make milk. However, only mature females produce milk in their mammary glands. All female mammals feed their young with this milk. **Figure 2** shows a cow nursing her calf.

All milk is made of water, proteins, fats, and sugars. But the amount of each nutrient is different in different milk. For example, human milk has half the fat and twice the sugar of cow's milk.

Reading Check **What is milk made of?** (*See the Appendix for answers to Reading Checks.*)

Breathing Air

All animals need oxygen to get energy from their food. Like birds and reptiles, mammals use lungs to get oxygen from the air. But mammals have a muscle that helps them get air. The **diaphragm** (DIE uh FRAM) is a large muscle that helps bring air into the lungs. It lies at the bottom of the rib cage.

Endothermic

As oxygen helps to break down a mammal's food, energy is released. This energy keeps mammals warm. Has a dog or cat ever sat in your lap? If so, then you have felt how warm a mammal's body is. Like birds, mammals are endotherms. Their internal chemical changes keep their body temperature constant. The ability to stay warm helps them survive in cold areas and stay active when the weather is cool.

Diaphragm Demo

1. Place your hand under your rib cage to feel your abdominal muscles (which are indirectly connected to your diaphragm). Breathe in and out.
2. Write down what your hand feels as you breathe.
3. Place your hand under your rib cage again. Contract your abdominal muscles, and try breathing. Then, relax your abdominal muscles, and breathe.
4. Write down what happens.
5. Explain your observations. Then, draw a picture of how the diaphragm moves.

Hair

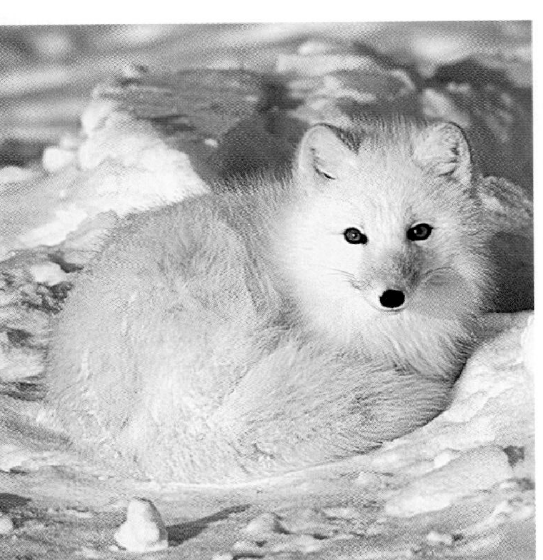

Figure 3 *The thick fur of this arctic fox helps its body stay warm in the coldest winters.*

Mammals have a few characteristics that keep them from losing their body heat. One way they stay warm is by having hair. Mammals are the only animals that have hair. All mammals—even whales—have hair. Mammals that live in cold climates, such as the fox in **Figure 3,** usually have thick coats of hair. These thick coats are called *fur*. Large mammals that live in warm climates, such as elephants, do not need warm fur. Humans have hair all over their bodies, as apes do. But human body hair is shorter and more fine than ape hair.

Most mammals also have a layer of fat under their skin to keep them warm. This fat helps trap heat in the body. Whales and other mammals that live in cold oceans have an especially thick layer of fat. This thick layer of fat is called *blubber*.

Specialized Teeth

Another unique mammal characteristic is specialized teeth. Modern birds don't have teeth. Fish and reptiles have teeth, but usually all of their teeth are identical. Mammals have teeth with different shapes and sizes for different jobs. Also, mammals replace their original baby teeth with a permanent set.

Your own mouth has three kinds of teeth. You have cutting teeth, called *incisors,* in the front of your mouth. Most people have four incisors on top and four on the bottom. Next to them are stabbing teeth, called *canines*. These help you grab and hold on to food. Your flat, grinding back teeth are *molars*.

Each kind of tooth helps mammals eat a certain kind of food. Meat-eating mammals have large canines to help them eat prey. Plant-eating mammals have larger incisors and molars to help them bite and grind plants. **Figure 4** shows the teeth of a meat-eating mammal and a plant-eating mammal.

Figure 4 *Mountain lions have sharp canine teeth for grabbing their prey. Horses have sharp incisors in front for cutting plants and flat molars in the back for grinding plants.*

Sexual Reproduction

All mammals reproduce sexually. Sperm fertilize eggs inside the female's body. Though there are a few exceptions, most mammals give birth to live young. Newborn mammals stay with at least one parent until they are grown. Mammal parents care for and protect their young during this time. **Figure 5** shows a brown bear with her young.

Reading Check **How long does a young mammal stay with at least one parent?**

Figure 5 *A mother bear will attack anything that threatens her cubs.*

Large Brains

A mammal's brain is much larger than that of most other animals that are the same size. This large brain allows mammals to learn and think quickly. It also allows mammals to respond quickly to events around them.

Mammals use vision, hearing, smell, touch, and taste to find out about the world around them. The importance of each sense often depends on a mammal's surroundings. For example, mammals that are active at night depend on their hearing more than on their vision.

SECTION Review

Summary

- Early mammals were small. Being endothermic helped them survive.
- Mammals have mammary glands, a diaphragm, and hair.
- All mammals are endotherms. Most have a layer of fat under their skin for extra warmth.
- Mammals have specialized teeth.
- Mammals reproduce sexually and raise young.
- Mammals have large brains and learn quickly.

Using Key Terms

1. Use each of the following terms in a separate sentence: *mammary gland* and *diaphragm.*

Understanding Key Ideas

2. Large brains help mammals survive by allowing them
   a. to think and learn quickly.
   b. to maintain their body temperature.
   c. to have hair all over their body.
   d. to depend on all of the senses equally.
3. What does a diaphragm do?
4. Name three characteristics that are unique to mammals.
5. Describe three characteristics that help mammals stay warm.
6. How are mammal teeth different from reptile and fish teeth?
7. How do mammals reproduce?

Math Skills

8. What is the mass of a 90,000 kg whale in grams? in milligrams?

Critical Thinking

9. **Making Inferences** Early endothermic mammals could be active at night. If this protected them from certain dinosaurs, were the dinosaurs endothermic? Explain.
10. **Applying Concepts** How could the teeth of a skull give you clues about a mammal's diet?

SCILINKS
NSTA
Developed and maintained by the National Science Teachers Association
For a variety of links related to this chapter, go to www.scilinks.org
Topic: Characteristics of Mammals
SciLinks code: HSM0259

SECTION 4

Placental Mammals

Both elephants and mice begin life by developing inside a mother. Elephants need up to 23 months to develop inside the mother. But mice need only a few weeks!

READING WARM-UP

Objectives

- Explain how placental mammals develop.
- Give an example of each type of placental mammal.

Terms to Learn

placental mammal
gestation period

READING STRATEGY

Brainstorming The key idea of this section is kinds of placental mammals. Brainstorm words and phrases related to placental mammals.

Mammals are divided into groups based on how they develop. The groups are placental mammals, monotremes, and marsupials. Most mammals are placental mammals. A **placental mammal** is a mammal whose embryos develop inside the mother's body. The embryos grow in an organ called the *uterus*. An organ called the *placenta* attaches the embryos to the uterus. The placenta carries food and oxygen from the mother's blood to the embryo and carries wastes away from the embryo.

The time in which an embryo develops within the mother is called a **gestation period** (jes TAY shuhn PIR ee uhd). This period lasts a different amount of time for each kind of placental mammal. In humans, this period lasts about 9 months.

Living placental mammals are divided into 18 orders. The most common orders are described on the following pages.

Anteaters, Armadillos, and Sloths

A few mammals have unique backbones that have special connections between the vertebrae. This group includes anteaters, armadillos, and sloths. These mammals are sometimes called "toothless mammals," but only anteaters have no teeth. The others have small teeth. Most mammals in this group eat insects they catch with their long, sticky tongues. **Figure 1** shows two mammals from this group.

Figure 1 **Anteaters, Armadillos, and Sloths**

▲ **Armadillos** eat insects, frogs, mushrooms, and roots. Threatened armadillos roll up into a ball, or they may jump to scare a predator. They are protected by their tough plates.

▼ **Giant anteaters** never destroy the nests of the insects they eat. They open a nest and eat a few insects. Then, they move on to another nest.

Figure 2 Insectivores

The **star-nosed mole** has sensitive feelers on its nose. These help the mole find earthworms to eat. Moles have poor vision.

Hedgehogs live throughout Europe, Asia, and Africa. Their spines keep them safe from most predators.

Insectivores

Insectivores make up another group of mammals that eat insects. This group includes moles, shrews, and hedgehogs. Most insectivores are small and have long, pointed noses that help them smell their food. They have small brains and simple teeth. Some eat worms, fish, frogs, lizards, and small mammals in addition to insects. **Figure 2** shows two insectivores.

Rodents

More than one-third of mammal species are rodents. Rodents live on every continent except Antarctica. They include squirrels, mice, rats, guinea pigs, porcupines, and chinchillas. Most rodents have sensitive whiskers. They all have one set of incisors in the upper jaw. Rodents gnaw and chew so much that these teeth wear down. But that doesn't stop their chewing—their incisors grow continuously! **Figure 3** shows two rodents.

placental mammal a mammal that nourishes its unborn offspring through a placenta inside its uterus

gestation period in mammals, the length of time between fertilization and birth

Reading Check **What do rodents do with their sharp incisors?** *(See the Appendix for answers to Reading Checks.)*

Figure 3 Rodents

Like all rodents, **porcupines** have gnawing teeth.

The **capybara** (KAP i BAH ruh) of South America is the largest rodent in the world. Females have a mass of up to 70 kg—as much as a grown man.

Figure 4 Rabbits, Hares, and Pikas

The large ears of this **black-tailed jack rabbit** help it hear well and keep cool. They also work with a sensitive nose and large eyes to detect predators.

Pikas are small animals that live high in the mountains. Pikas gather plants and pile them into "haystacks" to dry. In the winter, pikas use the dry plants for food and insulation.

Rabbits, Hares, and Pikas

Rodents are similar to a group of mammals that includes rabbits, hares, and pikas (PIE kuhz). **Figure 4** shows two members of this group. Like rodents, they have sharp gnawing teeth. But unlike rodents, they have two sets of incisors in their upper jaw. Also, their tails are shorter than rodents' tails.

Reading Check How are rabbits different from rodents?

Flying Mammals

Bats are the only mammals that fly. **Figure 5** shows two kinds of bats. Bats are active at night. They sleep in protected areas during the day. Most bats eat insects or other small animals. But some bats eat fruit or plant nectar. A few bats, called *vampire bats,* drink the blood of birds or mammals.

Most bats use echoes to find their food and their way. Using echoes to find things is called *echolocation.* Bats make clicking noises as they fly. The clicks echo off trees, rocks, and insects. Bats know what is around them by hearing these echoes.

Figure 5 Flying Mammals

Fruit bats, also called *flying foxes,* live in tropical regions. They pollinate plants as they go from one plant to another, eating fruit.

The **spotted bat** is found in parts of the American Southwest. Like most bats, it eats flying insects. It uses its large ears during echolocation.

Figure 6 **Carnivores**

Coyotes are members of the dog family. They live throughout North America and in parts of Central America.

Walruses, like all pinnipeds, eat in the ocean but sleep and mate on land. They use their huge canines in courtship displays, for defense, and to climb onto ice.

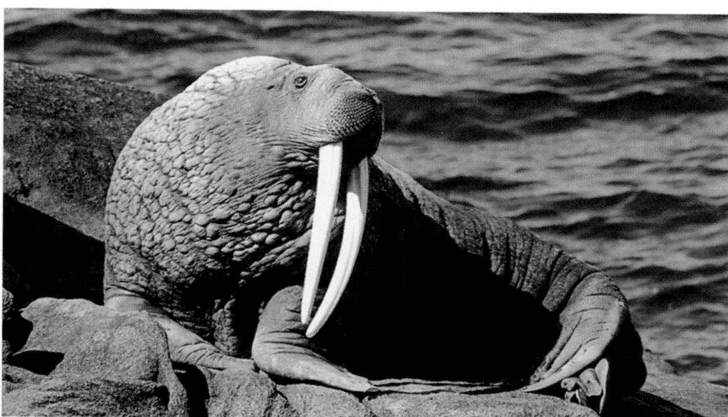

Carnivores

Mammals that have large canine teeth and special molar teeth for slicing meat are called *carnivores.* Many mammals in this group eat only meat. But some mammals in this group are omnivores or herbivores that eat plants. For example, black bears eat grass, nuts, and berries and rarely eat meat. The carnivore group includes cats, dogs, otters, bears, raccoons, and hyenas. *Pinnipeds,* a group of fish-eating ocean mammals, are also carnivores. Seals, sea lions, and walruses are pinnipeds. **Figure 6** shows two carnivores.

Trunk-Nosed Mammals

Elephants are the only living mammals that have a trunk. The trunk is a combination of an upper lip and a nose. An elephant uses its trunk in the same ways we use our hands, lips, and nose. An elephants uses its trunk to put food in its mouth. It also uses its trunk to spray water on its back to cool off. **Figure 7** shows two species of elephants.

Figure 7 **Trunk-Nosed Mammals**

Elephants are social. The females live in herds of mothers, daughters, and sisters. These elephants are **African elephants.**

These **Indian elephants** have smaller ears and tusks than African elephants do.

Hoofed Mammals

Horses, pigs, deer, and rhinoceroses are some of the many mammals that have thick hoofs. A *hoof* is a thick, hard pad that covers a mammal's toe. The hoof is similar to a toenail or a claw, but it covers the entire toe. Most hoofed mammals are fast runners. They also have large, flat molars. These teeth help hoofed mammals grind the plants that they eat.

Hoofed mammals include two orders—odd-toed and even-toed. Odd-toed hoofed mammals have one or three toes on each foot. Horses and zebras have one large, hoofed toe. Rhinoceroses have three toes. Even-toed hoofed mammals have two or four toes on each foot. Pigs, cattle, camels, deer, and giraffes are even-toed. **Figure 8** shows some hoofed mammals.

Figure 8 Hoofed Mammals

Tapirs are large, odd-toed mammals. They live in forests in Central America, South America, and Southeast Asia. Tapirs are active mostly at night.

Giraffes are the tallest living mammals. They have long necks and long legs and are even-toed. They eat leaves from tall trees.

Camels are even-toed mammals. The hump of a camel is a large lump of fat that provides energy for the camel when food is scarce. Camels can live without drinking water for a long time, so they can live in very dry places.

Figure 9 **Cetaceans**

Spinner dolphins spin like a football when they leap from the water. Like all dolphins, they are intelligent and highly social.

Humpback whales are toothless. Like all toothless whales, they strain sea water through special plates in their mouth. These plates are made of a substance called *baleen*. The baleen traps tiny sea life for the whale to eat.

Cetaceans

Cetaceans (suh TAY shuhnz) are a group of mammals made up of whales, dolphins, and porpoises. All cetaceans live in the water. **Figure 9** shows two kinds of cetaceans. At first glance, they may look more like fish than like mammals. But unlike fish, cetaceans have lungs and nurse their young.

Most of the largest whales are toothless. They strain tiny, shrimplike animals from sea water. However, dolphins, porpoises, sperm whales, and killer whales all have teeth to help them eat. Like bats, these animals use echolocation to find fish and other animals.

Manatees and Dugongs

The smallest group of mammals that live in the water are manatees (MAN uh TEEZ) and dugongs (DOO gawngz). This group includes three species of manatees and the dugong. Manatees and dugongs use their front flippers and a tail to swim slowly through the water. **Figure 10** shows a manatee.

Manatees and dugongs live along ocean coasts and in rivers. They are large animals that eat mostly seaweed and water plants. These animals spend all of their time in the water, but they lift their noses from the water to breathe air.

Figure 10 *Manatees are also called* sea cows.

Reading Check **How much of their time do dugongs and manatees spend in the water?**

Primates

Scientists classify prosimians, monkeys, apes, and humans as *primates.* These animals have five fingers on each hand and five toes on each foot. Most have flat fingernails instead of claws. Primates have a larger brain than most other mammals the same size have. They are considered highly intelligent mammals. Primates also have unique arrangements of body parts that help them do complicated things. For example, all primates have forward-facing eyes that can focus on a single point. And primates have opposable thumbs, which allow them to hold objects.

Many primates live in trees. They climb with their grasping hands and feet. Flexible shoulder joints allow them to swing between branches. They eat leaves and fruits, and some primates even hunt animals. **Figure 11** shows some primates.

Reading Check What traits help many primates live in trees?

CONNECTION TO Language Arts

WRITING SKILL **Funky Monkey** In many parts of the world, cities have taken over natural, nonhuman primate habitat. Some nonhuman primates have moved into the city and adopted new lifestyles. Macaques have been known to steal ice-cream cones from children or hop on a bus for a short ride! Write a story in your **science journal** about people living with monkeys in a city.

Figure 11 **Primates**

Orangutans and other apes often walk upright. Apes usually have larger brains and bodies than monkeys do.

Spider monkeys, like many monkeys, have grasping tails. Their long arms, legs, and tails help them move among the trees.

The **proboscis monkey** has an enormous nose! The males have larger noses than the females do. That difference makes some scientists wonder if the male's nose is used to attract females.

SECTION Review

Summary

- Placental mammals develop inside the mother during a gestation period. Placental mothers nurse their young after birth.
- Anteaters, armadillos, and sloths have unique backbones.
- Moles, shrews, and hedgehogs eat insects.
- Squirrels, rats, and porcupines are rodents.
- Rabbits, hares, and pikas are similar to rodents but have an extra pair of incisors.
- Bats are flying mammals.
- Cats, dogs, otters, bears, sea lions, and walruses are in the carnivore group.
- Horses, zebras, pigs, deer, rhinoceroses, and giraffes are hoofed mammals.
- Elephants are trunk-nosed mammals.
- Whales and porpoises are cetaceans.
- Manatees and dugongs are large, slow mammals that live in the water.
- Prosimians, monkeys, apes, and humans are primates.

Using Key Terms

1. Use the following terms in the same sentence: *placental mammal* and *gestation period*.

Understanding Key Ideas

2. Which mammals live entirely in the water?
   a. manatees, dugongs, cetaceans, and pinnipeds
   b. only manatees and dugongs
   c. only cetaceans
   d. manatees, dugongs, and cetaceans

3. A placental mammal's embryo
   a. develops in the uterus.
   b. develops in the placenta.
   c. develops in a pouch.
   d. develops in a leathery egg.

4. Could you tell a horse from a deer just by looking at their feet? Explain.

5. Give one example of each type of placental mammal described in the section.

Critical Thinking

6. Making Inferences What is a gestation period? Why do you think elephants have a longer gestation period than mice do?

7. Identifying Relationships Manatees may look a little like pinnipeds, but they are more closely related to elephants. In what ways is a manatee more like an elephant than like a pinniped?

Interpreting Graphics

Use the picture of the animal below to answer the questions that follow.

8. To which placental mammal group does this animal belong? How can you tell?

9. Why can't this animal be a rodent?

10. Why can't this animal be a primate?

For a variety of links related to this chapter, go to www.scilinks.org

Topic: Kinds of Mammals
SciLinks code: HSM0832

SECTION 5

Monotremes and Marsupials

Did you know that some mammals hatch from eggs and that others spend the first months of life in a mother's pouch? Only a few kinds of mammals develop this way.

READING WARM-UP

Objectives

- Describe the difference between monotremes and marsupials.
- Name the two kinds of monotremes.
- Give three examples of marsupials.
- Explain why many marsupials are endangered or extinct.

Terms to Learn

monotreme
marsupial

READING STRATEGY

Paired Summarizing Read this section silently. In pairs, take turns summarizing the material. Stop to discuss ideas that seem confusing.

Placental mammals are born as well-developed young. But monotremes hatch from eggs. And newborn marsupials still need months of development in a mother's pouch.

Monotremes

A **monotreme** (MAHN oh TREEM) is a mammal that lays eggs. Monotremes have all the traits of mammals, including mammary glands, a diaphragm, and hair. And like other mammals, they keep their body temperature constant.

A female monotreme lays eggs with thick, leathery shells. She uses her body's energy to keep the eggs warm. After the young hatch, the mother takes care of them and feeds them milk. Monotremes do not have nipples as other mammals do. Baby monotremes lick milk from the skin and hair around their mother's mammary glands.

monotreme a mammal that lays eggs

Echidnas

There are only three living species of monotremes. Two of these species are echidnas (ee KID nuhz). Echidnas are about the size of a house cat. Their large claws and long snouts help them dig ants and termites out of insect nests. **Figure 1** shows the two species of echidnas.

Figure 1 Echidnas

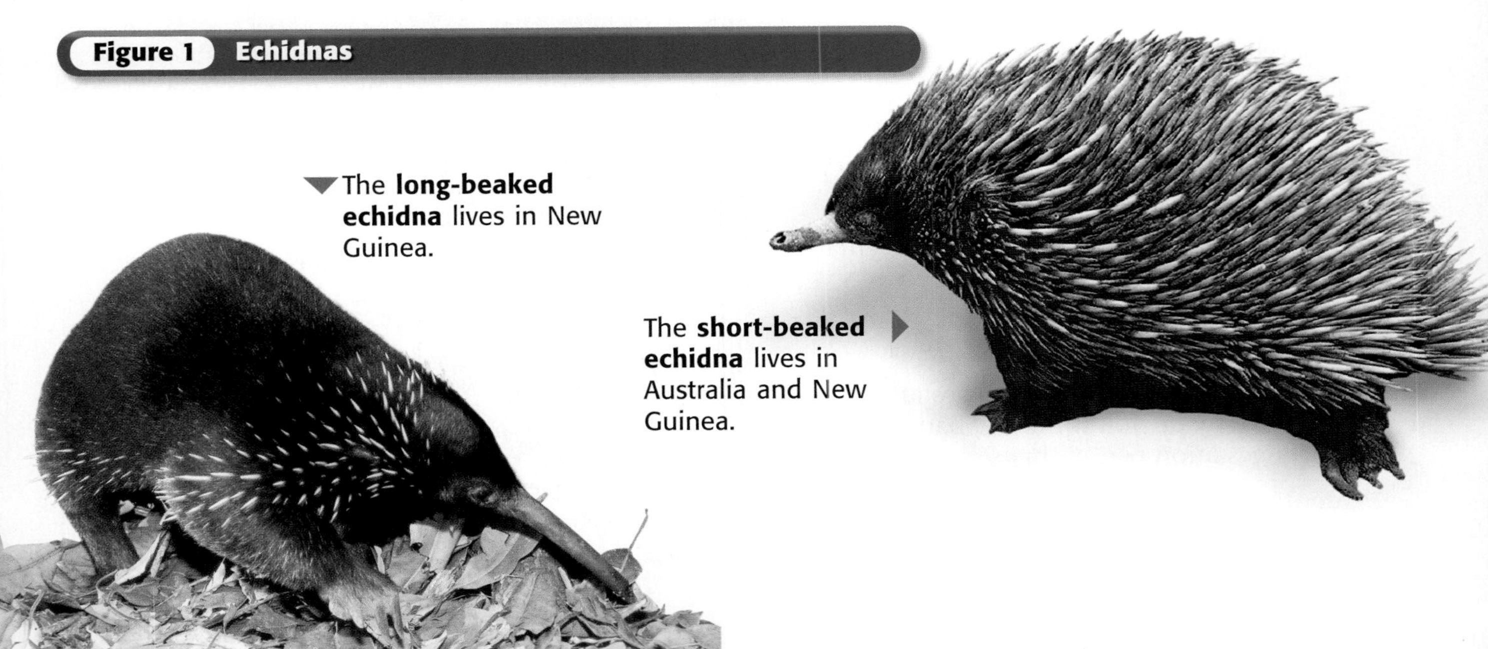

The **long-beaked echidna** lives in New Guinea.

The **short-beaked echidna** lives in Australia and New Guinea.

Figure 2 *When underwater, a duckbill platypus closes its eyes and ears. It uses its bill to find food.*

The Platypus

The only other living monotreme is the platypus. Only one species of platypus lives today. This animal lives in Australia. It looks very different from other mammals. In fact, when scientists outside Australia were first sent the remains of a platypus, they thought they were the victims of a practical joke. **Figure 2** shows a platypus.

The platypus is a swimming mammal that lives and feeds in rivers and ponds. It has webbed feet and a flat tail to help it move through the water. It uses its flat, rubbery bill to search for food. It uses its claws to dig tunnels in riverbanks. The platypus lays its eggs in these tunnels.

Reading Check **How does a platypus use its bill?** (*See Appendix for answers to Reading Checks.*)

Marsupials

You probably know that kangaroos carry their young in a pouch. Kangaroos and other mammals with pouches are **marsupials** (mahr SOO pee uhlz). Like all mammals, marsupials have mammary glands, hair, and specialized teeth. Unlike monotremes, marsupials give birth to live young. Marsupial development is unique because newborn marsupials continue their development in a mother's pouch. The newborns stay in the pouch for several months.

There are about 280 species of marsupials living today. Most of them live in Australia, New Guinea, and South America. The only living marsupial native to North America is the opossum (uh PAHS uhm).

CONNECTION TO Environmental Science

Pouches in Peril Australia's marsupials are in danger. Many other species have been artificially introduced into Australia's unique ecosystems. These new species are competing with native marsupials for food and living space. One way to stop the introduction of new species into Australia is to educate people about the dangers of species introduction. Make a poster that explains why people should be careful not to release pets or foreign animals into the wild.

ACTIVITY

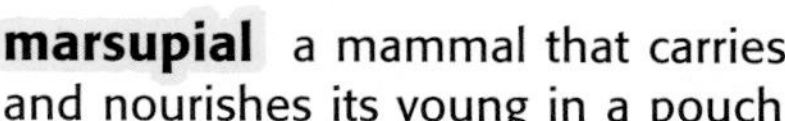

marsupial a mammal that carries and nourishes its young in a pouch

The Pouch

Figure 3 *This newborn kangaroo will stay in its mother's pouch for several months as it continues developing.*

Marsupials are born at an early stage of development. They are born just days or weeks after fertilization. At birth, kangaroos are as small as bumblebees. **Figure 3** shows a newborn kangaroo. Newborn marsupials are hairless, and only their front limbs are well developed. They use these limbs to drag themselves through their mother's fur to the pouch on her belly. Many do this without any help from their parents. Inside the pouch are mammary glands. The newborn climbs in, latches onto a nipple, and starts drinking milk. Young kangaroos, called *joeys,* stay in the mother's pouch for several months. When joeys first leave the pouch, they do so for only short periods of time.

Reading Check **How big is a newborn kangaroo?**

Kinds of Marsupials

You may be familiar with the well-known marsupials shown in **Figure 4.** But many marsupials are not as familiar. Have you heard of wallabies, bettongs, and numbats? Most marsupials live in and around Australia. Tasmanian devils, which are marsupials that eat other animals, live on the island of Tasmania. Tree kangaroos, which spend much of their time in trees, live in the rain forests of Queensland and New Guinea.

Figure 4 **Kinds of Marsupials**

Koalas sleep for about 18 hours each day. They eat eucalyptus leaves.

Young **kangaroos** that no longer live in their mother's pouch return to the pouch if there is any sign of danger.

When in danger, an **opossum** will lie perfectly still. It "plays dead" so predators will ignore it.

Endangered and Extinct Marsupials

The number of living marsupial species is decreasing. At least 22 of Australia's native mammal species have become extinct in the last 400 years. Many more are currently in danger. When Europeans came to Australia in the 18th and 19th centuries, they brought animals such as rabbits, cats, and foxes. Many of these species escaped into the wild. Some, such as rabbits, now compete with marsupials for food. Others, such as foxes, now prey on marsupials. The marsupials have no adaptations to protect themselves from these exotic species.

Exotic species are not the only threat to marsupials in Australia. Habitat destruction also threatens marsupials. And the Tasmanian tiger, shown in **Figure 5,** was hunted by people who saw it as a threat to their livestock. Today, conservation efforts across Australia are helping to protect the unique marsupials that live there.

Figure 5 *The Tasmanian tiger, a marsupial carnivore, is probably extinct. There have been no official sightings since 1936.*

SECTION Review

Summary

- Monotremes lay eggs instead of bearing live young. They produce milk but do not have nipples.
- The three living species of monotremes are two kinds of echidnas and the platypus.
- Marsupials give birth to live young, but the young are not fully developed when born. They finish developing in a mother's pouch.
- Many marsupials are endangered or extinct.

Using Key Terms

1. Use each of the following terms in a separate sentence: *monotreme* and *marsupial.*

Understanding Key Ideas

2. Which of the following characteristics is shared by monotremes and marsupials?
   - **a.** The young hatch from eggs.
   - **b.** Some species of both live in South America.
   - **c.** Females have no nipples.
   - **d.** Females produce milk.
3. What are the two kinds of monotremes?
4. Name three kinds of marsupials.
5. What has caused many marsupials in Australia to become endangered or extinct?
6. How are monotremes different from all other mammals? How are they similar?

Math Skills

7. What percentage of the approximately 5,000 known species of mammals are monotremes?

Critical Thinking

8. **Making Comparisons** How are monotremes similar to birds? How are they different?
9. **Making Inferences** Why do you think opossums play dead when they are in danger?

SCILINKS
NSTA
Developed and maintained by the National Science Teachers Association
For a variety of links related to this chapter, go to www.scilinks.org
Topic: Monotremes and Marsupials
SciLinks code: HSM0990

Using Scientific Methods

Model-Making Lab

What? No Dentist Bills?

When you and I eat, we must chew our food well. Chewing food into small bits is the first part of digestion. But birds don't have teeth. How do birds make big chunks of food small enough to begin digestion? In this activity, you will develop a hypothesis about how birds digest their food. Then, you will build a model of a bird's digestive system to test your hypothesis.

OBJECTIVES

Make a model of a bird's digestive system.

Test your model, using birdseed.

MATERIALS

- bags, plastic, sealable, various sizes (several)
- birdseed
- gravel, aquarium
- scissors (or other materials as needed)
- straw, plastic drinking
- string
- tape, transparent
- water

SAFETY

Ask a Question

1. Formulate a question about how a bird's digestive system can break down food even though the bird has no teeth. Your question may be something such as, "How are birds able to begin digestion without using teeth?"

Form a Hypothesis

2. Look at the diagram below of a bird's digestive system. Form a hypothesis about how birds digest their food without using teeth.

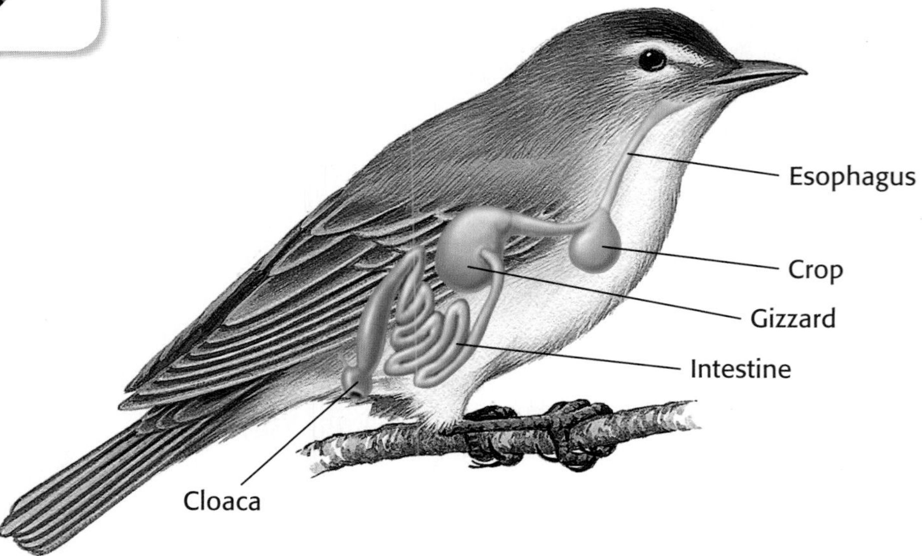

Test the Hypothesis

3. Design a model of a bird's digestive system. Include in your design as many of the following parts as possible: esophagus, crop, gizzard, intestine, and cloaca.
4. Obtain a plastic bag and the other materials you need from your teacher. Build your model.
5. Test your hypothesis by sending birdseed through your model digestive system.

Analyze the Results

1. **Describing Events** Did your model digestive system grind the birdseed? Describe what happened to the birdseed as it moved through the system.
2. **Analyzing Results** Which part of your model was most helpful in grinding? Which part of a real bird's digestive system is represented by this part of your model?
3. **Recognizing Patterns** Does the amount of material added to your model gizzard change the gizzard's ability to work effectively? Explain your answer.

Draw Conclusions

4. **Drawing Conclusions** Birds can break down food without using teeth. What conclusions can you draw about how they do this?
5. **Evaluating Results** Analyze the strengths and weaknesses of your hypothesis based on your results. Was your hypothesis correct? Explain your answer.
6. **Evaluating Models** What are some limitations of your model? How do you think you could improve it?

Applying Your Data

Did you know that scientists have found "gizzard stones" with fossilized dinosaur skeletons? Look in the library or on the Internet for information about the evolutionary relationship between dinosaurs and birds. List the similarities you find between the two types of animals.

Chapter Review

USING KEY TERMS

1. Use the following terms in the same sentence: *mammary gland, placental mammal, marsupial,* and *monotreme.*

Complete each of the following sentences by choosing the correct term from the word bank.

brooding	gestation period
contour feathers	lift
diaphragm	molting
down feathers	preening

2. The ___ is a muscle that helps animals breathe.
3. The embryos of placental mammals develop during a ___.
4. Birds grow new feathers as a part of the ___ process.
5. ___ help keep birds warm by trapping air near the body.
6. Birds use the ___ process to keep their eggs warm.
7. ___ form a streamlined surface that helps birds fly.

UNDERSTANDING KEY IDEAS

Multiple Choice

8. Both birds and reptiles
   - **a.** lay eggs.
   - **b.** brood their young.
   - **c.** have air sacs.
   - **d.** have feathers.

9. Only mammals
   - **a.** use internal fertilization.
   - **b.** nurse their young.
   - **c.** lay eggs.
   - **d.** have teeth.

10. Which of the following is NOT a primate?
    - **a.** a lemur
    - **b.** a human
    - **c.** a pika
    - **d.** a chimpanzee

11. Monotremes do NOT
    - **a.** have mammary glands.
    - **b.** care for their young.
    - **c.** give birth to live young.
    - **d.** have hair.

12. What is lift?
    - **a.** air that travels over the top of a wing
    - **b.** a force provided by a bird's air sacs
    - **c.** the upward force on a wing that keeps a bird in the air
    - **d.** a force created by pressure from the diaphragm

Short Answer

13. How are contour feathers and down feathers helpful to birds?

14. How do flightless birds, water birds, perching birds, and birds of prey differ from each other?

15. Which trait allowed early mammals to look for food at night?

16. Describe two ways that animals introduced to Australia threaten its native marsupials.

17. Which kind of marsupial lives in North America?

18. Which group of placental mammals includes the pinnipeds?

19. How is a bird's digestive system related to its ability to fly?

20. How can mammalian milks differ?

CRITICAL THINKING

21. **Concept Mapping** Use the following terms to create a concept map: *monotremes, endotherms, birds, mammals, mammary glands, placental mammals, marsupials, feathers,* and *hair.*

22. **Making Comparisons** The embryos of birds and monotremes get energy from the yolk of the egg. How do developing embryos of marsupials and placental mammals get the nutrition they need?

23. **Making Inferences** Most bats and cetaceans use echolocation. Why don't these mammals rely solely on sight to hunt and sense their surroundings?

24. **Applying Concepts** Suppose you are making a museum display of bird skeletons, but the skeletons have lost their labels. How can you separate the skeletons of flightless birds from those of birds that fly? Will you be able to tell which birds flew rapidly and which birds could soar? Explain your answer.

25. **Making Inferences** Suppose that you saw a bird flying above you. The bird has long, skinny legs and a long, sharp beak. To which group of birds do you think this bird probably belongs? Explain your answer.

INTERPRETING GRAPHICS

The illustrations below show three different kinds of bird feet. Use these illustrations to answer the questions that follow.

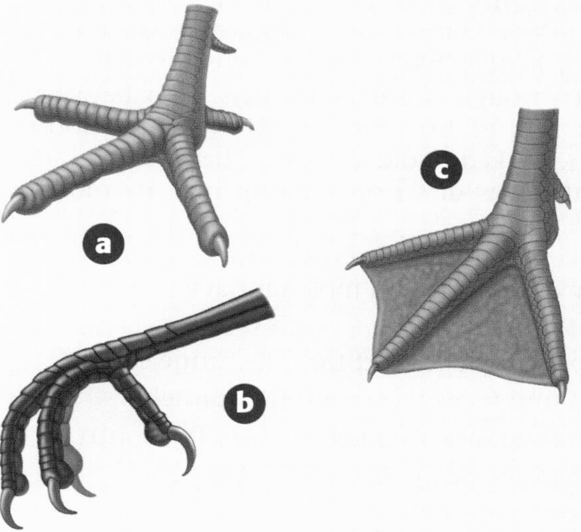

26. Which foot most likely belongs to a water bird? Explain your choice.

27. Which foot most likely belongs to a perching bird? Explain your choice.

28. To what kind of bird do you think the remaining foot could belong? Explain your answer.

Standardized Test Preparation

READING

Read each of the passages below. Then, answer the questions that follow the passage.

Passage 1 A naked mole rat is a rodent that looks like an overcooked hot dog. This nearly blind mammal is 7 cm long and lives in hot, dry regions of Kenya, Ethiopia, and Somalia. This animal has some strange characteristics. Its grayish pink skin hangs loosely on its body. The loose skin allows the naked mole rat to move easily through its home of narrow underground tunnels. At first glance, a naked mole rat appears to be hairless. Though the naked mole rat doesn't have fur, it does have hair. Its sensitive whiskers guide it through the dark tunnels. Hair between its toes acts as tiny brooms to sweep up loose dirt. The naked mole rat even has hair on its lips that keeps dirt from getting into its mouth while it digs.

1. Why does the naked mole rat have hair on its lips?

A to sweep loose dirt from its tunnels
B to find its way through the tunnels
C to keep dirt from getting into its mouth
D to move easily through its tunnels

2. Which of the following is a characteristic of naked mole rats?

F thick fur
G poor eyesight
H large toes
I hairless bodies

3. How do naked mole rats navigate through their tunnels?

A strong sense of hearing
B sensitive grayish pink skin
C tasting the dirt along their tunnel walls
D sensitive whiskers

Passage 2 For centuries, people have tried to imitate a spectacular feat that birds perfected millions of years ago—flight. The Wright brothers were not able to fly in a heavier-than-air flying machine until 1903. Their first flight lasted only 12 s, and they traveled only 37 m. Although modern airplanes are much more sophisticated, they still rely on the same principles of flight. The sleek body of a jet is shaped to battle drag, while the wings are shaped to battle Earth's gravity. In order to take off, airplanes must pull upward with a force greater than gravitational force. This upward force is called lift.

1. According to the passage, how are modern airplanes similar to the flying machine invented by the Wright brothers?

A Both look like birds.
B Both rely on the same principles of flight.
C Both are sophisticated.
D Both have sleek body shapes.

2. Which part of a jet's design works against Earth's gravity?

F the sleek shape
G the wings
H the heavier-than-air weight
I the tail

3. Based on the passage, which of the following statements is a fact?

A The Wright brothers were the first people to try building a flying machine.
B Modern airplanes can fly more easily than birds can fly.
C The Wright brothers' first flight lasted for only 12 s.
D Overcoming gravity with lift is the only force needed to fly an airplane.

INTERPRETING GRAPHICS

The graph below shows how many Calories a small dog uses while running at different speeds. Use this graph to answer the questions that follow.

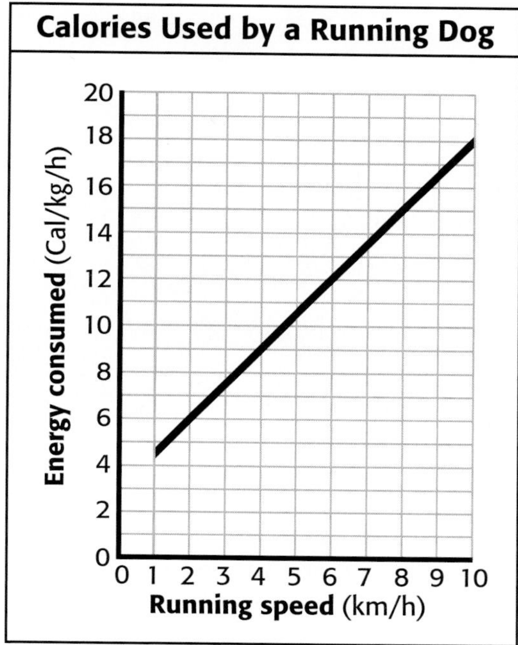

1. As the dog runs faster, how does the amount of energy it consumes per hour change?
   - **A** The energy consumed increases.
   - **B** The energy consumed decreases.
   - **C** The energy consumed remains the same.
   - **D** Changes in the energy consumed are not related to changes in the dog's speed.

2. How much energy per hour will this dog consume if it is running at 4 km/h?
   - **F** 1 Cal/kg/h
   - **G** 6 Cal/kg/h
   - **H** 9 Cal/kg/h
   - **I** 10 Cal/kg/h

3. How much energy per hour will this dog consume if it is running at 9 km/h?
   - **A** 4 Cal/kg/h
   - **B** 16 Cal/kg/h
   - **C** 16.5 Cal/kg/h
   - **D** 18 Cal/kg/h

4. Energy consumed is given in Calories per kilogram of body mass per hour. If the dog has a mass of 6 kg and is running at 7 km/h, how many Calories per hour will it use?
   - **F** 2.25 Cal/h
   - **G** 19.5 Cal/h
   - **H** 72 Cal/h
   - **I** 81 Cal/h

MATH

Read each question below, and choose the best answer.

1. A bird flying at 35 km/h consumes 60 Cal per gram of body mass per hour. If the bird has a mass of 50 g, how many Calories will it use if it flies for 30 min at this speed?
   - **A** 1,050 Cal
   - **B** 1,500 Cal
   - **C** 1,750 Cal
   - **D** 3,000 Cal

2. Cecilia's kitten weighed 2 lb when she got him. The kitten gained about 0.5 lb each month for the next 11 months. How much did the kitten weigh at the end of the 11 months?
   - **F** less than 6 lb
   - **G** between 6 lb and 7 lb
   - **H** between 7 lb and 8 lb
   - **I** more than 8 lb

3. Gina bought two birds for $31.96, a box of birdseed for $1.69, and some bird treats for $3.98. What is the best estimate of the total cost of Gina's purchase?
   - **A** between $35 and $36
   - **B** between $36 and $37
   - **C** between $37 and $38
   - **D** more than $38

4. On each of 5 days, Leo saw 5 rabbits. He saw 3 rabbits on each of 2 other days. How could you find *C*, the total number of rabbits he saw?
   - **F** $C = (5 \times 5) + (2 \times 3)$
   - **G** $C = (5 + 5) \times (2 + 3)$
   - **H** $C = 5 + 5 + 2 + 3$
   - **I** $C = (5 \times 5) - (2 \times 3)$

Science in Action

Science, Technology, and Society

Dolphins in the Navy

Did you know that some dolphins work for the Navy? One way that dolphins help the Navy's Marine Mammal Program is by detecting underwater mines, which are bombs that drift underwater. Most mines explode when a large object bumps into them. Dolphins can find mines safely by using a natural sonar system, called *echolocation,* which allows them to sense their surroundings even in murky waters. When dolphin finds a mine and alerts a person, experts can deactivate the mine.

Math Activity

Suppose that each dolphin in the Navy's program is trained for 5 years and each trained dolphin works for 25 years. If 10 dolphins began training each year for 10 years, how many would be working at the end of those 10 years? How many would still be in training?

Weird Science

Sounds of the Lyrebird

Imagine that you are hiking in an Australian forest. You hear many different bird calls, beaks snapping, and wings rustling. There must be many species of birds around, right? Not if a lyrebird is nearby—all those sounds could be coming from just one bird! The lyrebird imitates the songs of other birds. In fact, lyrebirds can imitate just about any sound they hear. Many Australians have heard lyrebirds singing the sounds of chainsaws, car engines, and dog barks. Supposedly, a lyrebird once confused timber-mill workers when it sang the sound of the mill's whistle, causing the workers to quit for the day.

Language Arts Activity

WRITING SKILL A lyrebird's ability to imitate noises could lead to a lot of humorous confusion for people who hear its songs. Think about how lyrebirds could mimic human-made sounds, causing confusion for the people nearby, and then write a short story about the situation.

People in Science

Irene Pepperberg

Bird Brains Dr. Irene Pepperberg studies bird brains. She works with a little African Grey parrot named Alex. Pepperberg began her work with Alex because she wanted to see if birds that could talk could also understand what they were saying.

Pepperberg developed a new kind of communication training, with Alex as her pupil. First, Alex was rewarded with the object that he identified—not with food. This reinforced that the word represented the object. Next, two trainers acted out a kind of play to teach Alex words. One trainer would ask a question, and the other would respond with the right or wrong answer. The first trainer would reward the second for a right answer but take the object away for a wrong answer. This training showed Alex what would happen when he gave an answer.

Pepperberg's experiment has been very successful. Not only can Alex say the names of objects but he can tell you what they are made of, what their shape is, and how one object is different from another. Pepperberg has shown that at least one parrot can pass intelligence tests at the same level as some nonhuman primates and marine mammals. She has discovered that with the right training, animals can teach us a lot about themselves.

Social Studies ACTIVITY

WRITING SKILL People train pets all the time. See if you can train your pet or a friend's pet to learn a simple behavior, such as following a command. Write up your results in a report.

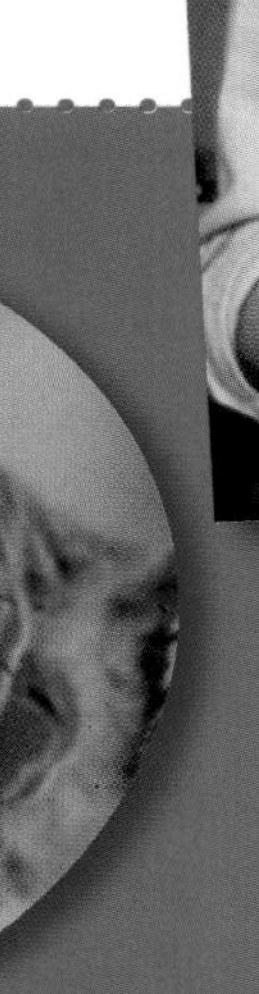

To learn more about these Science in Action topics, visit go.hrw.com and type in the keyword HL5VR2F.

Current Science

Check out Current Science® articles related to this chapter by visiting go.hrw.com. Just type in the keyword HL5CS17.

TIMELINE

Ecology

What did you have for breakfast this morning? Your breakfast was a result of living things working together. For example, milk comes from a cow. The cow eats plants to gain energy. Bacteria help the plants obtain nutrients from the soil. And the soil has nutrients because fungi break down dead trees.

All living things on Earth are interconnected. Our actions have an impact on our environment, and our environment has an impact on us. In this unit, you will study ecology, the interaction of living things. This timeline shows some of the ways that humans have studied and affected the Earth.

1661
John Evelyn publishes a book condemning air pollution in London, England.

1771
In his experiments with plants, Joseph Priestley finds that plants use carbon dioxide and release oxygen.

1933
The Civilian Conservation Corps is established. The corps plants trees, fights forest fires, and builds dams to control floods.

1990
To save dolphins from being caught in fishing nets, U.S. tuna processors announce that they will not accept tuna caught in nets that can kill dolphins.

1851

The United States imports sparrows from Germany to defend against crop-damaging caterpillars.

1854

Henry David Thoreau's *Walden* is published. In it, Thoreau asserts that people should live in harmony with nature.

1872

The first U.S. national park, Yellowstone, is established by Congress.

1962

Rachel Carson's book *Silent Spring,* which describes the wasteful use of pesticides and their destruction of the environment, is published.

1970

The Environmental Protection Agency (EPA) is formed to set and enforce pollution-control standards in the United States.

1973

The United States Congress passes the Endangered Species Act.

1993

Americans recycle 59.5 billion aluminum cans (two out of every three cans).

1996

The Glen Canyon Dam is opened, purposefully flooding the Grand Canyon. The flooding helps maintain the ecological balance by restoring beaches and sandbars and rejuvenating marshes.

2002

The U.S. Fish and Wildlife Service installs red neon lights along the Florida coast to replace lights that distract baby sea turtles from finding the ocean when they hatch.

Interactions of Living Things

About the PHOTO

A chameleon is about to grab an insect using its long tongue. A chameleon's body can change color to match its surroundings. Blending in helps the chameleon sneak up on its prey and also keeps the chameleon safe from animals that would like to make a snack out of a chameleon.

PRE-READING ACTIVITY

FOLDNOTES **Tri-Fold** Before you read the chapter, create the FoldNote entitled "Tri-Fold" described in the **Study Skills** section of the Appendix. Write what you know about the interactions of living things in the column labeled "Know." Then, write what you want to know in the column labeled "Want." As you read the chapter, write what you learn about the interactions of living things in the column labeled "Learn."

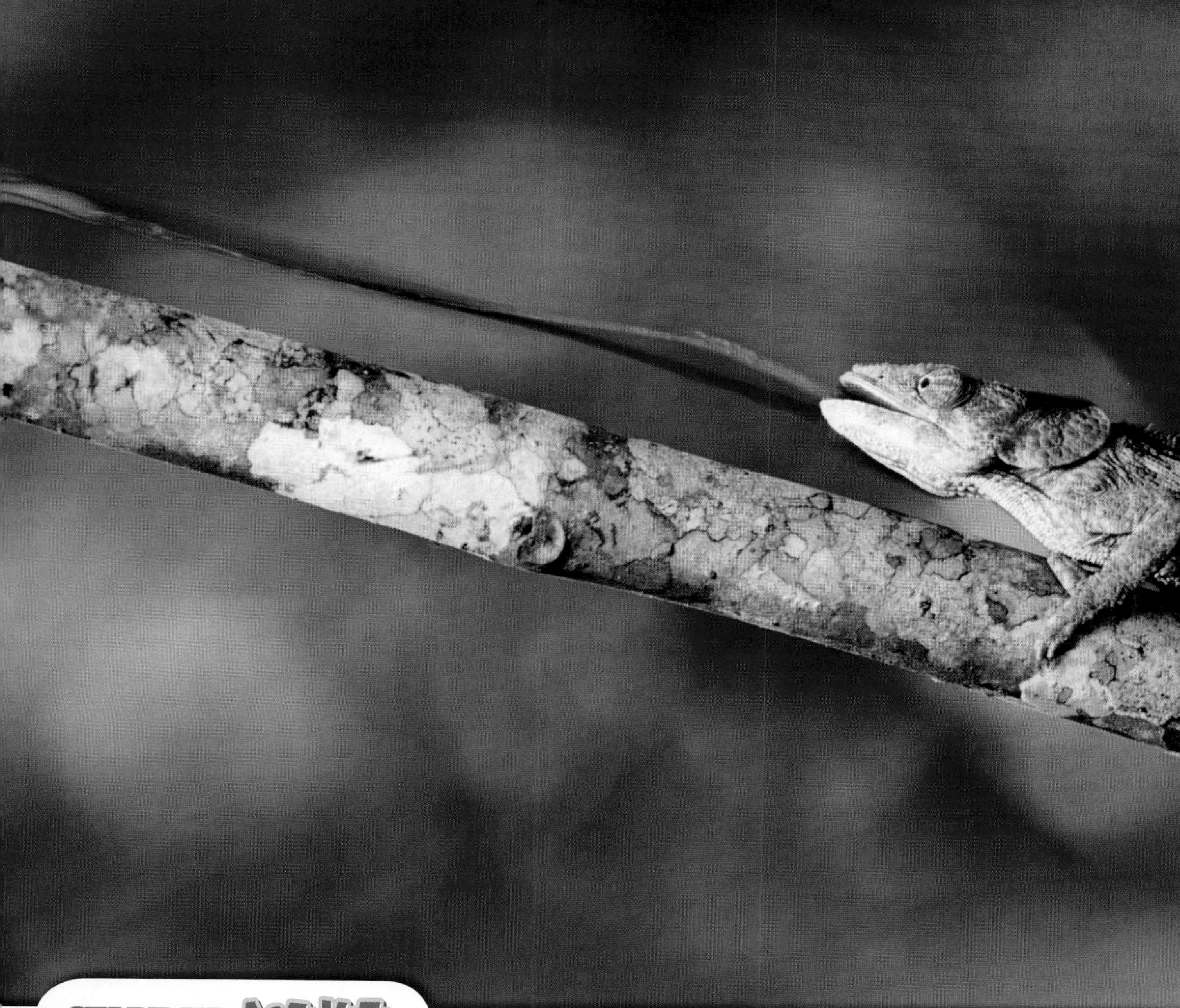

START-UP ACTIVITY

Who Eats Whom?

In this activity, you will learn how organisms interact when finding (or becoming) the next meal.

Procedure

1. On each of **five index cards,** print the name of one of the following organisms: killer whale, cod fish, krill shrimp, algae, and leopard seal.
2. On your desk, arrange the cards in a chain to show who eats whom.
3. Record the order of your cards.
4. In nature, would you expect to see more killer whales or cod? Arrange the cards in order of most individuals in an organism group to fewest.

Analysis

1. What might happen to the other organisms if algae were removed from this group? What might happen if the killer whales were removed?
2. Are there any organisms in this group that eat more than one kind of food? (Hint: What else might a seal, a fish, or a killer whale eat?) How could you change the order of your cards to show this information? How could you use pieces of string to show these relationships?

SECTION 1

Everything Is Connected

READING WARM-UP

Objectives

- Distinguish between the biotic and abiotic parts of the environment.
- Explain how populations and communities are related.
- Describe how the abiotic parts of the environment affect ecosystems.

Terms to Learn

ecology
biotic
abiotic
population
community
ecosystem
biosphere

READING STRATEGY

Reading Organizer As you read this section, create an outline of the section. Use the headings from the section in your outline.

An alligator drifts in a weedy Florida river, watching a long, thin fish called a gar. *The gar swims too close to the alligator. Then, in a rush of murky water, the alligator swallows the gar whole and slowly swims away.*

It is clear that two organisms have interacted when one eats the other. But organisms have many interactions other than simply "who eats whom." For example, alligators dig underwater holes to escape from the heat. After the alligators abandon these holes, fish and other aquatic organisms live in the holes during the winter dry period.

Studying the Web of Life

All living things are connected in a web of life. Scientists who study the web of life specialize in the science of ecology. **Ecology** is the study of the interactions of organisms with one another and with their environment.

The Two Parts of an Environment

An organism's environment consists of all the things that affect the organism. These things can be divided into two groups. All of the organisms that live together and interact with one another make up the **biotic** part of the environment. The **abiotic** part of the environment consists of the nonliving factors, such as water, soil, light, and temperature. How many biotic parts and abiotic parts do you see in **Figure 1?**

Figure 1 *The alligator affects, and is affected by, many organisms in its environment.*

Organization in the Environment

At first glance, the environment may seem disorganized. However, the environment can be arranged into different levels, as shown in **Figure 2.** The first level is made of an individual organism. The second level is larger and is made of similar organisms, which form a population. The third level is made of different populations, which form a community. The fourth level is made of a community and its abiotic environment, which form an ecosystem. The fifth and final level contains all ecosystems, which form the biosphere.

ecology the study of the interactions of living organisms with one another and with their environment

biotic describes living factors in the environment

abiotic describes the nonliving part of the environment, including water, rocks, light, and temperature

Figure 2 The Five Levels of Environmental Organization

Meeting the Neighbors

1. Explore two or three blocks of your neighborhood.
2. Draw a map of the area's biotic and abiotic features. For example, map the location of sidewalks, large rocks, trees, water features, and any animals you see. Remember to approach all plants and animals with caution. Use your map to answer the following questions.
3. How are the biotic factors affected by the abiotic factors?
4. How are the abiotic factors affected by the biotic factors?

population a group of organisms of the same species that live in a specific geographical area

community all the populations of species that live in the same habitat and interact with each other

Populations

A salt marsh, such as the one shown in **Figure 3,** is a coastal area where grasslike plants grow. Within the salt marsh are animals. Each animal is a part of a **population,** or a group of individuals of the same species that live together. For example, all of the seaside sparrows that live in the same salt marsh are members of a population. The individuals in the population often compete with one another for food, nesting space, and mates.

Communities

A **community** consists of all of the populations of species that live and interact in an area. The animals and plants you see in **Figure 3** form a salt-marsh community. The populations in a community depend on each other for food, shelter, and many other things.

Figure 3 *Examine the picture of a salt marsh. Try to find examples of each level of organization in this environment.*

Laughing gull
Egret
Cordgrass
Seaside sparrows eat insects, spiders, and small crabs. A male and his mate weave a nest out of cordgrass stalks.
Heron
Juvenile sea croaker
The little marsh crab eats cordgrass as well as tiny shrimp.
Jellyfish
Some animals eat cordgrass, along with the microscopic algae that grow on the surface of its leaves and stems.
The periwinkle snail eats the algae that grow on the cordgrass. The periwinkle snail also uses the cordgrass as a place to hide from predators.

Ecosystems

An **ecosystem** is made up of a community of organisms and the abiotic environment of the community. An ecologist studying the ecosystem could examine how organisms interact as well as how temperature, precipitation, and soil characteristics affect the organisms. For example, the rivers that empty into the salt marsh carry nutrients, such as nitrogen, from the land. These nutrients affect the growth of the cordgrass and algae.

ecosystem a community of organisms and their abiotic environment

biosphere the part of Earth where life exists

The Biosphere

The **biosphere** is the part of Earth where life exists. It extends from the deepest parts of the ocean to high in the air where plant spores drift. Ecologists study the biosphere to learn how organisms interact with the abiotic environment—Earth's atmosphere, water, soil, and rock. The water in the abiotic environment includes fresh water and salt water as well as water that is frozen in polar icecaps and glaciers.

For another activity related to this chapter, go to **go.hrw.com** and type in the keyword **HL5INTW.**

Reading Check **What is the biosphere?** (*See the Appendix for answers to Reading Checks.*)

SECTION Review

Summary

- All living things are connected in a web of life.
- The biotic part of an environment is made up of all of the living things found within it.
- The abiotic part of an environment is made up of all of the nonliving things found within it, such as water and light.
- An ecosystem is made up of a community of organisms and its abiotic environment.

Using Key Terms

1. In your own words, write a definition for the term *ecology*.
2. Use the following terms in the same sentence: *biotic* and *abiotic*.

Understanding Key Ideas

3. Which one of the following is the highest level of environmental organization?
   a. ecosystem
   b. community
   c. population
   d. organism
4. What makes up a community?
5. Give two examples of how abiotic factors can affect an ecosystem.

Math Skills

6. From sea level, the biosphere goes up about 9 km and down about 19 km. What is the thickness of the biosphere in meters?

Critical Thinking

7. **Analyzing Relationships** What would happen to the other organisms in the salt-marsh ecosystem if the cordgrass suddenly died?
8. **Identifying Relationships** Explain in your own words what people mean when they say that everything is connected.
9. **Analyzing Ideas** Do ecosystems have borders? Explain your answer.

For a variety of links related to this chapter, go to www.scilinks.org

Topic: Biotic and Abiotic Factors; Organization in the Environment

SciLinks code: HSM0164; HSM1079

SECTION 2

Living Things Need Energy

Do you think you could survive on only water and vitamins? Eating food satisfies your hunger because it provides something you cannot live without—energy.

READING WARM-UP

Objectives

- Describe the functions of producers, consumers, and decomposers in an ecosystem.
- Distinguish between a food chain and a food web.
- Explain how energy flows through a food web.
- Describe how the removal of one species affects the entire food web.

Terms to Learn

herbivore
carnivore
omnivore
food chain
food web
energy pyramid

READING STRATEGY

Reading Organizer As you read this section, make a table comparing producers, consumers, and decomposers.

Living things need energy to survive. For example, black-tailed prairie dogs, which live in the grasslands of North America, eat grass and seeds to get the energy they need. Everything a prairie dog does requires energy. The same is true for the plants that grow in the grasslands where the prairie dogs live.

The Energy Connection

Organisms, in a prairie or any community, can be divided into three groups based on how they get energy. These groups are producers, consumers, and decomposers. Examine **Figure 1** to see how energy passes through an ecosystem.

Producers

Organisms that use sunlight directly to make food are called *producers*. They do this by using a process called *photosynthesis*. Most producers are plants, but algae and some bacteria are also producers. Grasses are the main producers in a prairie ecosystem. Examples of producers in other ecosystems include cordgrass and algae in a salt marsh and trees in a forest. Algae are the main producers in the ocean.

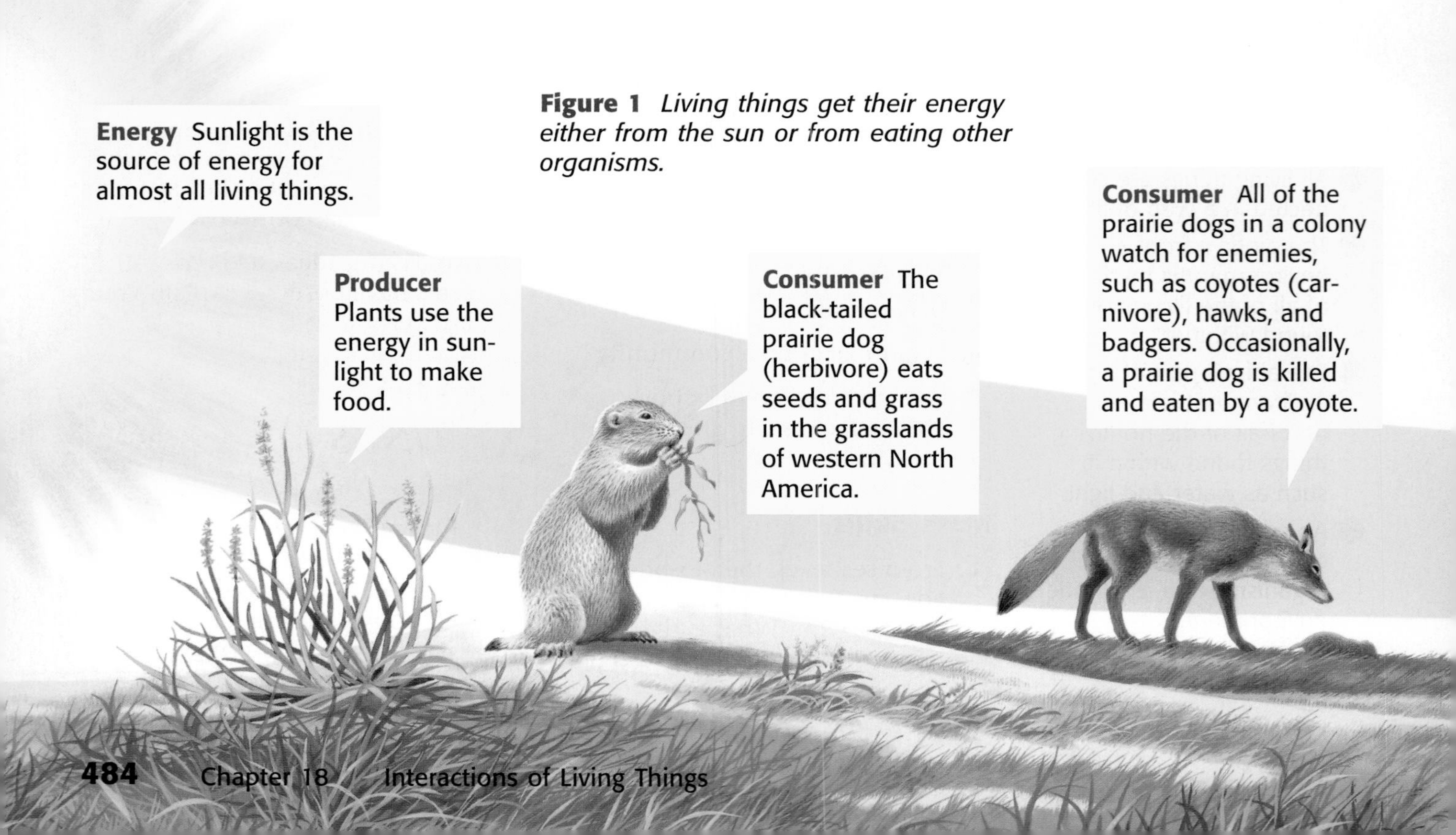

Figure 1 *Living things get their energy either from the sun or from eating other organisms.*

Energy Sunlight is the source of energy for almost all living things.

Producer Plants use the energy in sunlight to make food.

Consumer The black-tailed prairie dog (herbivore) eats seeds and grass in the grasslands of western North America.

Consumer All of the prairie dogs in a colony watch for enemies, such as coyotes (carnivore), hawks, and badgers. Occasionally, a prairie dog is killed and eaten by a coyote.

Consumers

Organisms that eat other organisms are called *consumers*. They cannot use the sun's energy to make food like producers can. Instead, consumers eat producers or other animals to obtain energy. There are several kinds of consumers. A consumer that eats only plants is called a **herbivore.** Herbivores found in the prairie include grasshoppers, prairie dogs, and bison. A **carnivore** is a consumer that eats animals. Carnivores in the prairie include coyotes, hawks, badgers, and owls. Consumers known as **omnivores** eat both plants and animals. The grasshopper mouse is an example of an omnivore. It eats insects, lizards, and grass seeds.

Scavengers are omnivores that eat dead plants and animals. The turkey vulture is a scavenger in the prairie. A vulture will eat what is left after a coyote has killed and eaten an animal. Scavengers also eat animals and plants that have died from natural causes.

Reading Check **What are organisms that eat other organisms called?** (*See the Appendix for answers to Reading Checks.*)

Decomposers

Organisms that get energy by breaking down dead organisms are called *decomposers*. Bacteria and fungi are decomposers. These organisms remove stored energy from dead organisms. They produce simple materials, such as water and carbon dioxide, which can be used by other living things. Decomposers are important because they are nature's recyclers.

herbivore an organism that eats only plants

carnivore an organism that eats animals

omnivore an organism that eats both plants and animals

A Chain Game

With the help of your parent, make a list of the foods you ate at your most recent meal. Trace the energy of each food back to the sun. Which foods on your list were consumers? How many were producers?

Consumer A turkey vulture (scavenger) may eat some of the coyote's leftovers. A scavenger can pick bones completely clean.

Decomposer Any prairie dog remains not eaten by the coyote or the turkey vulture are broken down by bacteria (decomposer) and fungi that live in the soil.

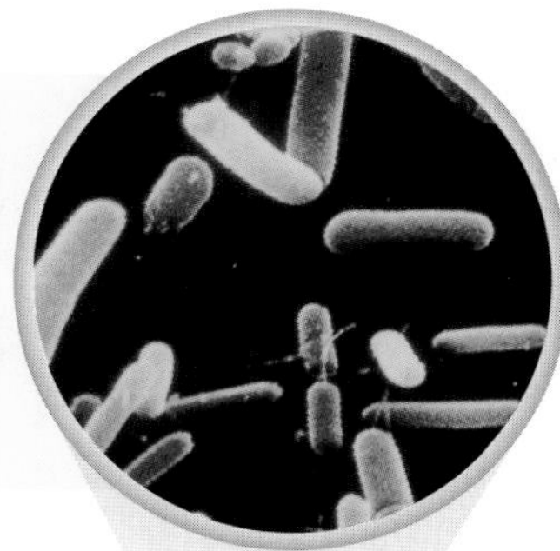

Food Chains and Food Webs

food chain the pathway of energy transfer through various stages as a result of the feeding patterns of a series of organisms

food web a diagram that shows the feeding relationships between organisms in an ecosystem

Figure 1 on the previous page, shows a food chain. A **food chain** is a diagram that shows how energy in food flows from one organism to another. Because few organisms eat just one kind of food, simple food chains are rare.

The energy connections in nature are more accurately shown by a food web than by a food chain. A **food web** is a diagram that shows the feeding relationships between organisms in an ecosystem. **Figure 2** shows a simple food web. Notice that an arrow goes from the prairie dog to the coyote, showing that the prairie dog is food for the coyote. The prairie dog is also food for the mountain lion. Energy moves from one organism to the next in a one-way direction, even in a food web. Any energy not immediately used by an organism is stored in its tissues. Only the energy stored in an organism's tissues can be used by the next consumer. There are two main food webs on Earth: a land food web and an aquatic food web.

Figure 2 *The green arrows show how energy moves when one organism eats another. Most consumers eat a variety of foods and can be eaten by a variety of other consumers.*

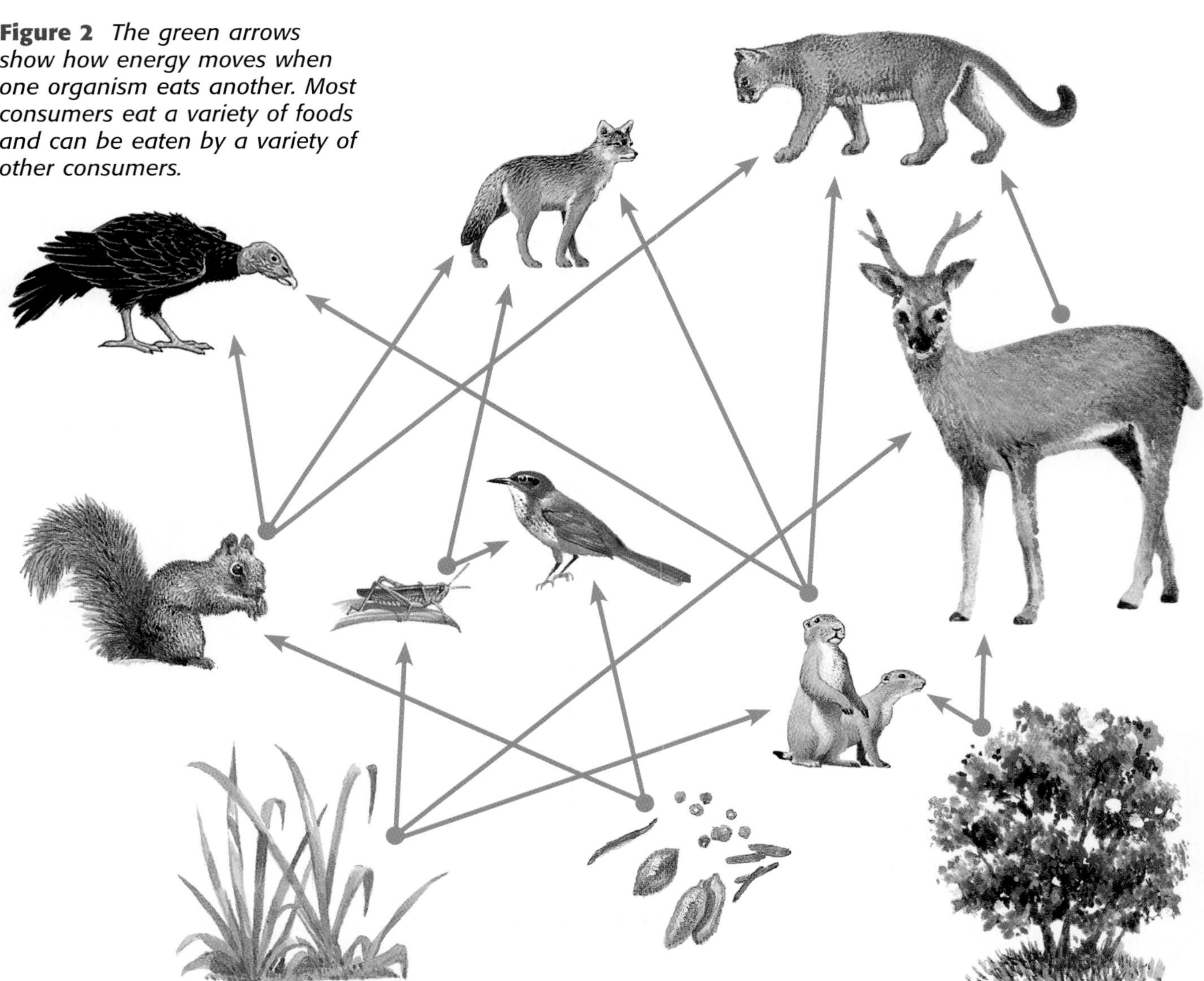

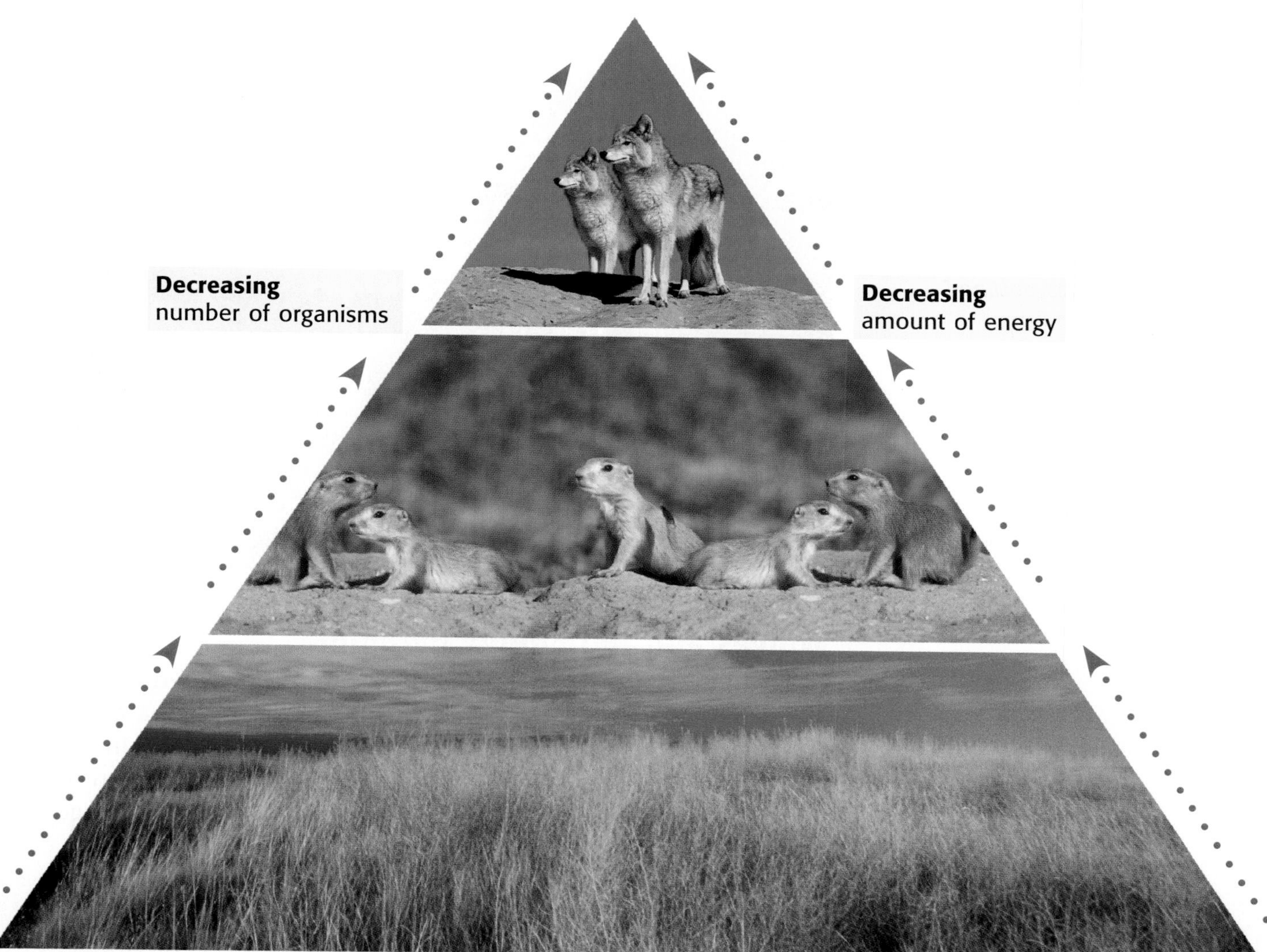

Figure 3 *The pyramid represents energy. As you can see, more energy is available at the base of the pyramid than at its top.*

Energy Pyramids

Grass uses most of the energy it gets from sunlight for its own life processes. But some of the energy is stored in the grass' tissues. This energy is used by the prairie dogs and other animals that eat the grass. Prairie dogs use most of the energy they get from eating grass and store only a little in their tissues. Therefore, a population of prairie dogs can support only a few coyotes. In the community, there must be more grass than prairie dogs and more prairie dogs than coyotes.

The energy at each level of the food chain can be seen in an energy pyramid. An **energy pyramid** is a diagram that shows an ecosystem's loss of energy. An example of an energy pyramid is shown in **Figure 3.** You can see that the energy pyramid has a large base and a small top. Less energy is available at higher levels because only energy stored in the tissues of an organism can be transferred to the next level.

energy pyramid a triangular diagram that shows an ecosystem's loss of energy, which results as energy passes through the ecosystem's food chain

Reading Check **What is an energy pyramid?**

Figure 4 *As the wilderness was settled, the gray wolf population in the United States declined.*

Wolves and the Energy Pyramid

One species can be very important to the flow of energy in an environment. Gray wolves, which are shown in **Figure 4,** are consumers that control the populations of many other animals. The diet of gray wolves can include anything from a lizard to an elk. Because gray wolves are predators that prey on large animals, their place is at the top of the food pyramid.

Once common throughout much of the United States, gray wolves were almost wiped out as the wilderness was settled. Without wolves, some species, such as elk, were no longer controlled. The overpopulation of elk in some areas led to overgrazing. The overgrazing left too little grass to support the elk and other populations who depended on the grass for food. Soon, almost all of the populations in the area were affected by the loss of the gray wolves.

Reading Check **How were other animals affected by the disappearance of the gray wolf?**

Gray Wolves and the Food Web

Gray wolves were brought back to Yellowstone National Park in 1995. The reintroduced wolves soon began to breed. **Figure 5** shows a wolf caring for pups. The U.S. Fish and Wildlife Service thinks the return of the wolves will restore the natural energy flow in the area, bring populations back into balance, and help restore the park's natural integrity.

Figure 5 *In small wolf packs, only one female has pups. They are cared for by all of the males and females in the pack.*

Not everyone approves, however. Ranchers near Yellowstone are concerned about the safety of their livestock. Cows and sheep are not the natural prey of wolves. However, the wolves will eat cows and sheep if they are given the chance.

Balance in Ecosystems

As wolves become reestablished in Yellowstone National Park, they kill the old, injured, and diseased elk. This process is reducing the number of elk. The smaller elk population is letting more plants grow. So, the numbers of animals that eat the plants, such as snowshoe hares, and the animals that eat the hares, such as foxes, are increasing.

All organisms in a food web are important for the health and balance of all other organisms in the food web. But the debate over the introduction of wolves to Yellowstone National Park will most likely continue for years to come.

Energy Pyramids

Draw an energy pyramid for a river ecosystem that contains four levels—aquatic plants, insect larvae, bluegill fish, and a largemouth bass. The plants obtain 10,000 units of energy from sunlight. If each level uses 90% of the energy it receives from the previous level, how many units of energy are available to the bass?

SECTION Review

Summary

- Producers use the energy in sunlight to make their own food.
- Consumers eat producers and other organisms to gain energy.
- Food chains represent how energy flows from one organism to another.
- All organisms are important to maintain the balance of energy in the food web.
- Energy pyramids show how energy is lost at each food chain level.

Using Key Terms

1. Use each of the following terms in a separate sentence: *herbivores, carnivores,* and *omnivores*.
2. In your own words, write a definition for each of the following terms: *food chain, food web,* and *energy pyramid*.

Understanding Key Ideas

3. Herbivores, carnivores, and scavengers are all examples of
   - **a.** producers.
   - **b.** decomposers.
   - **c.** consumers.
   - **d.** omnivores.
4. Explain the importance of decomposers in an ecosystem.
5. Describe how producers, consumers, and decomposers are linked in a food chain.
6. Describe how energy flows through a food web.

Math Skills

7. The plants in each square meter of an ecosystem obtained 20,810 Calories of energy from sunlight per year. The herbivores in that ecosystem ate all the plants but obtained only 3,370 Calories of energy. How much energy did the plants use?

Critical Thinking

8. **Identifying Relationships** Draw two food chains, and depict how they link together to form a food web.
9. **Applying Concepts** Are consumers found at the top or bottom of an energy pyramid? Explain your answer.
10. **Predicting Consequences** What would happen if a species disappeared from an ecosystem?

For a variety of links related to this chapter, go to www.scilinks.org

Topic: Food Chains and Food Webs
SciLinks code: HSM0594

SECTION 3

Types of Interactions

READING WARM-UP

Objectives

- Explain the relationship between carrying capacity and limiting factors.
- Describe the two types of competition.
- Distinguish between mutualism, commensalism, and parasitism. Give an example of coevolution.

Terms to Learn

carrying capacity	mutualism
prey	commensalism
predator	parasitism
symbiosis	coevolution

READING STRATEGY

Reading Organizer As you read this section, make a concept map by using the terms above.

Look at the seaweed forest shown in **Figure 1** *below. How many fish do you see? How many seaweed plants do you count? Why do you think there are more members of the seaweed population than members of the fish population?*

In natural communities, the sizes of populations of different organisms can vary greatly. This variation happens because everything in the environment affects every other thing. Populations also affect every other population.

Interactions with the Environment

Most living things produce more offspring than will survive. A female frog, for example, might lay hundreds of eggs in a small pond. In a few months, the population of frogs in that pond will be about the same as it was the year before. Why won't the pond become overrun with frogs? An organism, such as a frog, interacts with biotic and abiotic factors in its environment that can control the size of its population.

Limiting Factors

Populations cannot grow without stopping, because the environment contains a limited amount of food, water, living space, and other resources. A resource that is so scarce that it limits the size of a population is called a *limiting factor*. For example, food becomes a limiting factor when a population becomes too large for the amount of food available. Any single resource can be a limiting factor to a population's size.

Figure 1 *This seaweed forest is home to a large number of interacting species.*

Carrying Capacity

The largest population that an environment can support is known as the **carrying capacity.** When a population grows larger than its carrying capacity, limiting factors in the environment cause individuals to die off or leave. As individuals die or leave, the population decreases.

carrying capacity the largest population that an environment can support at any given time

For example, after a rainy season, plants may produce a large crop of leaves and seeds. This large amount of food may cause an herbivore population to grow. If the next year has less rainfall, there won't be enough food to support the large herbivore population. In this way, a population may become larger than the carrying capacity, but only for a little while. A limiting factor will cause the population to die back. The population will return to a size that the environment can support.

Interactions Between Organisms

Populations contain individuals of a single species that interact with one another, such as a group of rabbits feeding in the same area. Communities contain interacting populations, such as a coral reef with many species of corals trying to find living space. Ecologists have described four main ways that species and individuals affect each other: competition, predators and prey, symbiotic relationships, and coevolution.

Reading Check **What are four main ways organisms affect one another?** (*See the Appendix for answers to Reading Checks.*)

Competition

When two or more individuals or populations try to use the same resource, such as food, water, shelter, space, or sunlight, it is called *competition*. Because resources are in limited supply in the environment, their use by one individual or population decreases the amount available to other organisms.

Competition happens between individuals *within* a population. The elks in Yellowstone National Park are herbivores that compete with each other for the same food plants in the park. This competition is a big problem in winter when many plants die.

Competition also happens *between* populations. The different species of trees in **Figure 2** are competing with each other for sunlight and space.

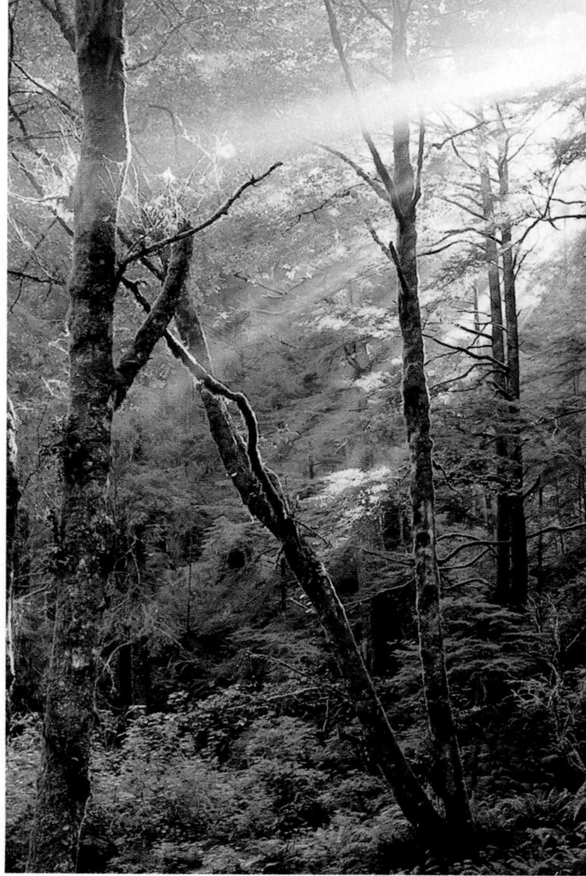

Figure 2 *Some of the trees in this forest grow tall to reach sunlight, which reduces the amount of sunlight available to shorter trees nearby.*

Predators and Prey

prey an organism that is killed and eaten by another organism

predator an organism that eats all or part of another organism

Many interactions between species consist of one organism eating another. The organism that is eaten is called the **prey.** The organism that eats the prey is called the **predator.** When a bird eats a worm, the worm is prey and the bird is the predator.

Predator Adaptations

To survive, predators must be able to catch their prey. Predators have a wide variety of methods and abilities for doing so. The cheetah, for example, is able to run very quickly to catch its prey. The cheetah's speed gives it an advantage over other predators competing for the same prey.

Other predators, such as the goldenrod spider, shown in **Figure 3,** ambush their prey. The goldenrod spider blends in so well with the goldenrod flower that all it has to do is wait for its next insect meal to arrive.

Figure 3 *The goldenrod spider is difficult for its insect prey to see. Can you see it?*

Prey Adaptations

Prey have their own methods and abilities to keep from being eaten. Prey are able to run away, stay in groups, or camouflage themselves. Some prey are poisonous. They may advertise their poison with bright colors to warn predators to stay away. The fire salamander, shown in **Figure 4,** sprays a poison that burns. Predators quickly learn to recognize its *warning coloration.*

Many animals run away from predators. Prairie dogs run to their underground burrows when a predator approaches. Many small fishes, such as anchovies, swim in groups called *schools.* Antelopes and buffaloes stay in herds. All the eyes, ears, and noses of the individuals in the group are watching, listening, and smelling for predators. This behavior increases the likelihood of spotting a potential predator.

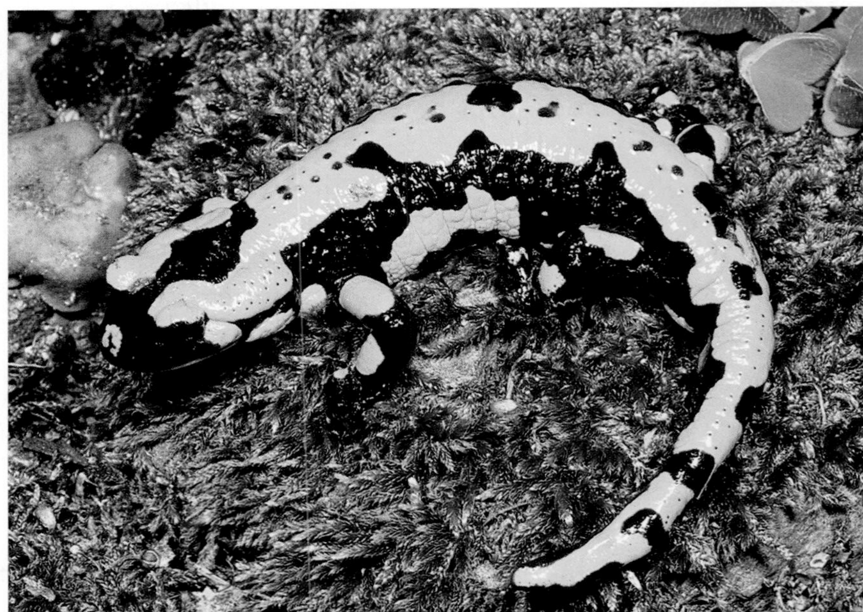

Figure 4 *Many predators know better than to eat the fire salamander! This colorful animal will make a predator very sick.*

Camouflage

One way animals avoid being eaten is by being hard to see. A rabbit often freezes so that its natural color blends into a background of shrubs or grass. Blending in with the background is called *camouflage*. Many animals mimic twigs, leaves, stones, bark, or other materials in their environment. One insect, called a walking stick, looks just like a twig. Some walking sticks even sway a bit, as though a breeze were blowing.

Reading Check **What is camouflage, and how does it prevent an animal from being eaten?**

CONNECTION TO Environmental Science

Pretenders Some animals are pretenders. They don't have defensive chemicals. But they use warning coloration to their advantage. The Scarlet king snake has colored stripes that make it look like the poisonous coral snake. Even though the Scarlet king snake is harmless, predators see its bright colors and leave it alone. What might happen if there were more pretenders than there were animals with real defensive chemicals?

Defensive Chemicals

The spines of a porcupine clearly signal trouble to a potential predator, but other defenses may not be as obvious. Some animals defend themselves with chemicals. The skunk and the bombardier beetle both spray predators with irritating chemicals. Bees, ants, and wasps inject a powerful acid into their attackers. The skin of both the poison arrow frog and a bird called the *hooded pitohui* contains a deadly toxin. Any predator that eats, or tries to eat, one of these animals will likely die.

Warning Coloration

Animals that have a chemical defense need a way to warn predators that they should look elsewhere for a meal. Their chemical weapons are often advertised by warning colors, as shown in **Figure 5.** Predators will avoid any animal that has the colors and patterns they associate with pain, illness, or unpleasant experiences. The most common warning colors are bright shades of red, yellow, orange, black, and white.

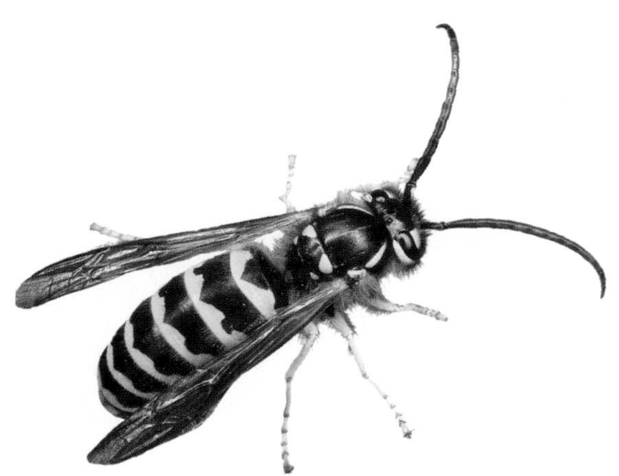

Figure 5 *The warning coloration of the yellow jacket (left) and the pitohui (above) warns predators that they are dangerous.*

Symbiosis

symbiosis a relationship in which two different organisms live in close association with each other

mutualism a relationship between two species in which both species benefit

commensalism a relationship between two organisms in which one organism benefits and the other is unaffected

Some species have very close interactions with other species. **Symbiosis** is a close, long-term association between two or more species. The individuals in a symbiotic relationship can benefit from, be unaffected by, or be harmed by the relationship. Often, one species lives in or on the other species. The thousands of symbiotic relationships in nature are often classified into three groups: mutualism, commensalism, and parasitism.

Mutualism

A symbiotic relationship in which both organisms benefit is called **mutualism** (MYOO choo uhl IZ uhm). For example, you and a species of bacteria that lives in your intestines benefit each other! The bacteria get food from you, and you get vitamins that the bacteria produce.

Another example of mutualism happens between corals and algae. Coral near the surface of the water provide a home for algae. The algae produce food for the coral by photosynthesis. When a coral dies, its skeleton is used by other corals. Over a long time, these skeletons build up large formations that lie under the surface of warm seas, as shown in **Figure 6.**

Figure 6 *In the smaller photo above, you can see the gold-colored algae inside the coral.*

Reading Check **Which organism benefits in mutualism?**

Commensalism

A symbiotic relationship in which one organism benefits and the other is unaffected is called **commensalism.** One example of commensalism is the relationship between sharks and smaller fish called *remoras.* **Figure 7** shows a shark with a remora attached to its body. Remoras "hitch a ride" and feed on scraps of food left by sharks. The remoras benefit from this relationship, while sharks are unaffected.

Figure 7 *The remora attached to the shark benefits from the relationship. The shark neither benefits from nor is harmed by the relationship.*

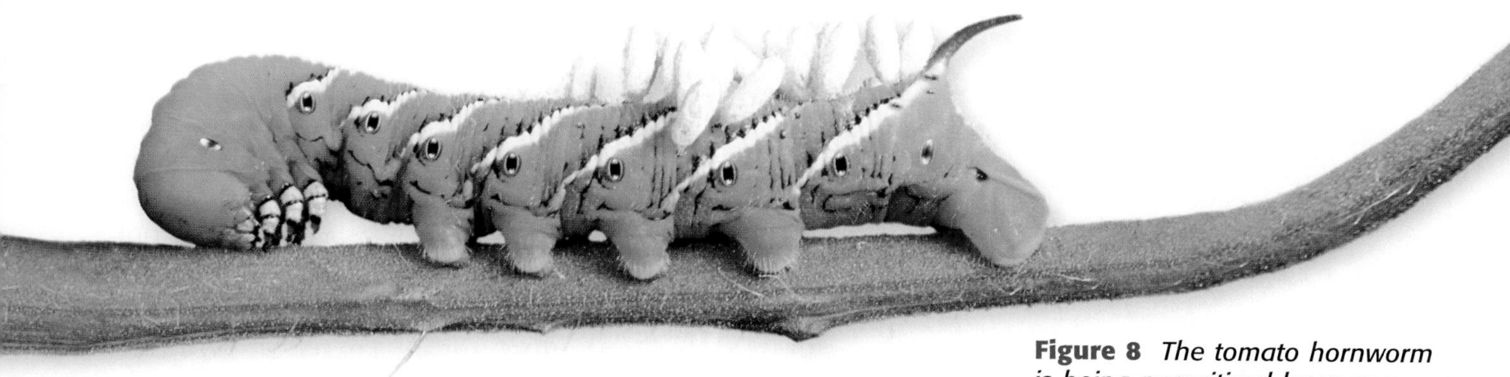

Figure 8 *The tomato hornworm is being parasitized by young wasps. Do you see their cocoons?*

Parasitism

A symbiotic association in which one organism benefits while the other is harmed is called **parasitism** (PAR uh SIT IZ uhm). The organism that benefits is called the *parasite.* The organism that is harmed is called the *host.* The parasite gets nourishment from its host while the host is weakened. Sometimes, a host dies. Parasites, such as ticks, live outside the host's body. Other parasites, such as tapeworms, live inside the host's body.

Figure 8 shows a bright green caterpillar called a *tomato hornworm.* A female wasp laid tiny eggs on the caterpillar. When the eggs hatch, each young wasp will burrow into the caterpillar's body. The young wasps will actually eat the caterpillar alive! In a short time, the caterpillar will be almost completely eaten and will die. When that happens, the adult wasps will fly away.

In this example of parasitism, the host dies. Most parasites, however, do not kill their hosts. Most parasites don't kill their hosts because parasites depend on their hosts. If a parasite were to kill its host, the parasite would have to find a new host.

parasitism a relationship between two species in which one species, the parasite, benefits from the other species, the host, which is harmed

coevolution the evolution of two species that is due to mutual influence, often in a way that makes the relationship more beneficial to both species

Coevolution

Relationships between organisms change over time. Interactions can also change the organisms themselves. When a long-term change takes place in two species because of their close interactions with one another, the change is called **coevolution.**

The ant and the acacia tree shown in **Figure 9** have a mutualistic relationship. The ants protect the tree by attacking other organisms that come near the tree. The tree has special structures that make food for the ants. The ants and the acacia tree may have coevolved through interactions between the two species. Coevolution can take place between any organisms that live close together. But changes happen over a very long period of time.

Figure 9 *Ants collect food made by the acacia tree and store the food in their shelter, which is also made by the tree.*

CONNECTION TO Social Studies

Rabbits in Australia In 1859, settlers released 12 rabbits in Australia. There was plenty of food and no natural predators for the rabbits. The rabbit population increased so fast that the country was soon overrun by rabbits. Then, the Australian government introduced a rabbit virus to control the population. The first time the virus was used, more than 99% of the rabbits died. The survivors reproduced, and the rabbit population grew large again. The second time the virus was used, about 90% of the rabbits died. Once again, the rabbit population increased. The third time the virus was used, only about 50% of the rabbits died. Suggest what changes might have occurred in the rabbits and the virus.

Coevolution and Flowers

A *pollinator* is an organism that carries pollen from one flower to another. Pollination is necessary for reproduction in most plants.

Flowers have changed over millions of years to attract pollinators. Pollinators such as bees, bats, and hummingbirds can be attracted to a flower because of its color, odor, or nectar. Flowers pollinated by hummingbirds make nectar with the right amount of sugar for the bird. Hummingbirds have long beaks, which help them drink the nectar.

Some bats, such as the one shown in **Figure 10,** changed over time to have long, thin tongues and noses to help them reach the nectar in flowers. As the bat feeds on the nectar, its nose becomes covered with pollen. The next flower it eats from will be pollinated with the pollen it is gathering from this flower. The long nose helps it to feed and also makes it a better pollinator.

Because flowers and their pollinators have interacted so closely over millions of years, there are many examples of coevolution between them.

Reading Check **Why do flowers need to attract pollinators?**

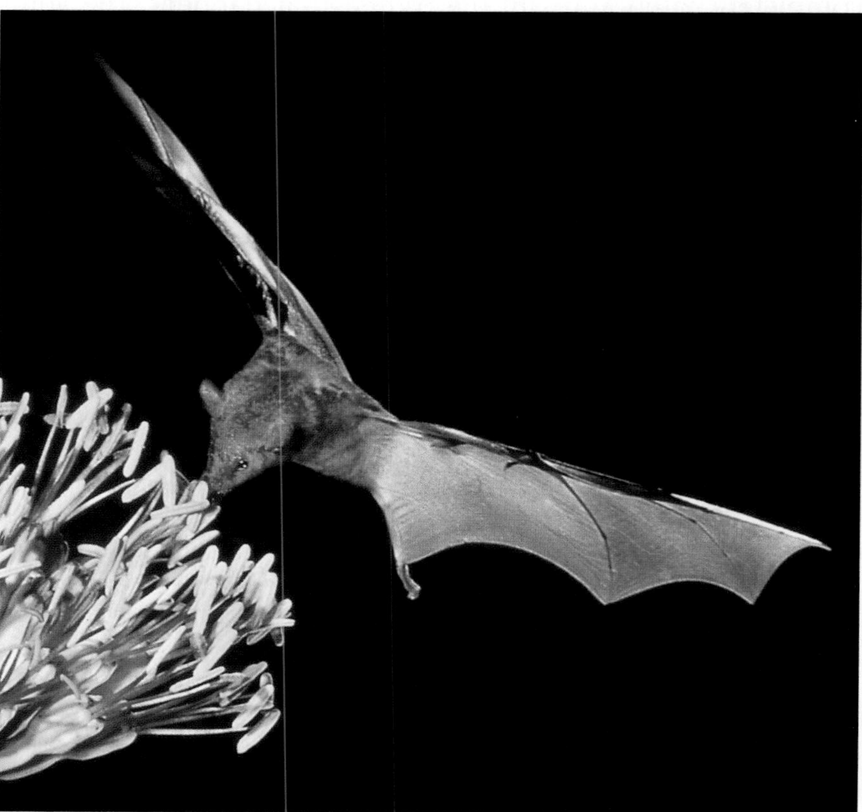

Figure 10 *This bat is drinking nectar with its long, skinny tongue. The bat has coevolved with the flower over millions of years.*

SECTION Review

- Limiting factors in the environment keep a population from growing without limit.
- Two or more individuals or populations trying to use the same resource is called *competition.*
- A predator is an organism that eats all or part of another organism. The organism that is eaten is called *prey.*
- Prey have developed features such as camouflage, chemical defenses, and warning coloration, to protect them from predators.
- Symbiosis occurs when two organisms form a very close relationship with one another over time.
- Close relationships over a very long time can result in coevolution. For example, flowers and their pollinators have evolved traits that benefit both.

Using Key Terms

1. In your own words, write a definition for the term *carrying capacity.*
2. Use each of the following terms in a separate sentence: *mutualism, commensalism,* and *parasitism.*

Understanding Key Ideas

3. Which of the following is NOT a prey adaptation?
   a. camouflage
   b. chemical defenses
   c. warning coloration
   d. parasitism
4. Identify two things organisms compete with one another for.
5. Briefly describe one example of a predator-prey relationship. Identify the predator and the prey.

Critical Thinking

6. **Making Comparisons** Compare coevolution with symbiosis.
7. **Identifying Relationships** Explain the probable relationship between the giant *Rafflesia* flower, which smells like rotting meat, and the carrion flies that buzz around it. (Hint: *Carrion* means "rotting flesh.")
8. **Predicting Consequences** Predict what might happen if all of the ants were removed from an acacia tree.

Interpreting Graphics

The population graph below shows the growth of a species of *Paramecium* (single-celled microorganism) over 18 days. Food was added to the test tube occasionally. Use this graph to answer the questions that follow.

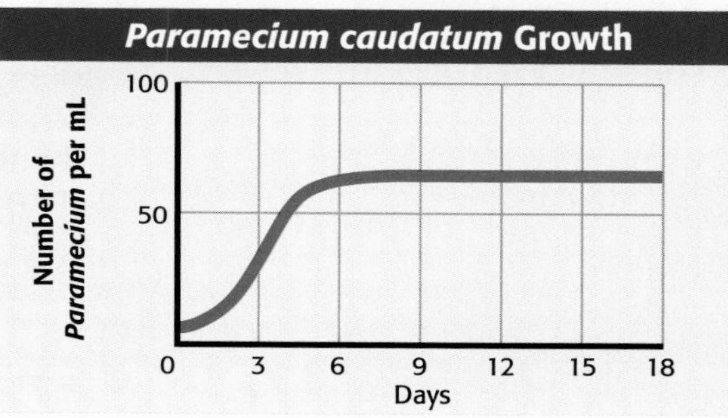

9. What is the carrying capacity of the test tube as long as food is added?
10. Predict what will happen if no more food is added?
11. What keeps the number of *Paramecium* at a steady level?

SCILINKS
NSTA
Developed and maintained by the National Science Teachers Association
For a variety of links related to this chapter, go to www.scilinks.org
Topic: Predator/Prey; Coevolution
SciLinks code: HSM1205; HSM0309

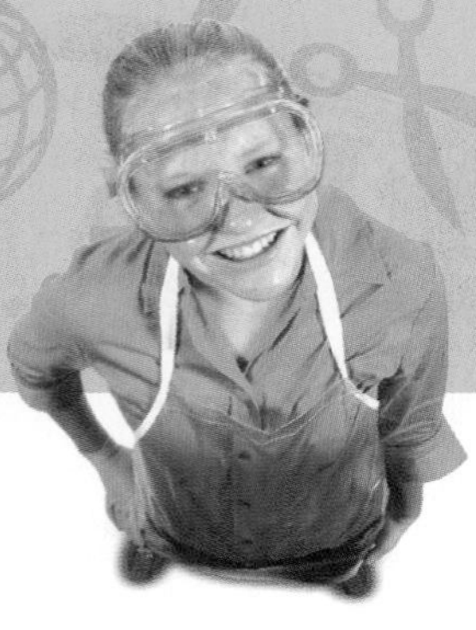

Skills Practice Lab

Capturing the Wild Bean

OBJECTIVES

Estimate the size of a "population" of beans.

Calculate the difference between your estimation and the actual number of beans.

MATERIALS

- bag, paper lunch, small
- beans, pinto
- calculator (optional)
- marker, permanent

When wildlife biologists study a group of organisms in an area, they need to know how many organisms live there. Sometimes, biologists worry that a certain organism is outgrowing the environment's carrying capacity. Other times, scientists need to know if an organism is becoming rare so that steps can be taken to protect it. However, animals can be difficult to count because they can move around and hide. Because of this challenge, biologists have developed methods to estimate the number of animals in a specific area. One of these counting methods is called the *mark-recapture method.*

In this activity, you will enter the territory of the wild pinto bean to estimate the number of beans that live in the paper-bag habitat.

Procedure

1. Prepare a data table like the one below.

Mark-Recapture Data Table				
Number of animals in first capture	Total number of animals in recapture	Number of marked animals in recapture	Calculated estimate of population	Actual total population
	DO NOT WRITE IN BOOK			

2. Your teacher will provide you with a paper bag containing an unknown number of beans. Carefully reach into the bag, and remove a handful of beans.

3. Count the number of beans you have "captured." Record this number in your data table under "Number of animals in first capture."
4. Use the permanent marker to carefully mark each bean that you have just counted. Allow the marks to dry completely. When all the marks are dry, place the marked beans back into the bag.
5. Gently mix the beans in the bag so that the marks won't rub off. Once again, reach into the bag. "Capture" and remove a handful of beans.
6. Count the number of beans in your "recapture." Record this number in your data table under "Total number of animals in recapture."
7. Count the beans in your recapture that have marks from the first capture. Record this number in your data table under "Number of marked animals in recapture."
8. Calculate your estimation of the total number of beans in the bag by using the following equation:

$$\frac{\text{number of beans in recapture} \times \text{number of beans marked}}{\text{number of marked beans in recapture}} = \text{calculated estimate of population}$$

   Enter this number in your data table under "Calculated estimate of population."
9. Place all the beans in the bag. Then empty the bag on your work table. Be careful that no beans escape! Count each bean as you place them one at a time back into the bag. Record the number in your data table under "Actual total population."

Analyze the Results

1. **Evaluating Results** How close was your estimate to the actual number of beans?

Draw Conclusions

2. **Evaluating Methods** If your estimate was not close to the actual number of beans, how might you change your mark-recapture procedure? If you did not recapture any marked beans, what might be the cause?

Applying Your Data

How could you use the mark-recapture method to estimate the population of turtles in a small pond? Explain your procedure.

Chapter Review

USING KEY TERMS

1. Use each of the following terms in a separate sentence: *symbiosis, mutualism, commensalism,* and *parasitism.*

Complete each of the following sentences by choosing the correct term from the word bank.

biotic	abiotic
ecosystem	community

2. The environment includes _____ factors including water, rocks, and light.
3. The environment also includes _____, or living, factors.
4. A community of organisms and their environment is called a(n) _____.

For each pair of terms, explain how the meanings of the terms differ.

5. *community* and *population*
6. *ecosystem* and *biosphere*
7. *producers* and *consumers*

UNDERSTANDING KEY IDEAS

Multiple Choice

8. A tick sucks blood from a dog. In this relationship, the tick is the _____ and the dog is the _____.
   - **a.** parasite, prey
   - **b.** predator, host
   - **c.** parasite, host
   - **d.** host, parasite

9. Resources such as water, food, or sunlight are likely to be limiting factors
   - **a.** when population size is decreasing.
   - **b.** when predators eat their prey.
   - **c.** when the population is small.
   - **d.** when a population is approaching the carrying capacity.

10. Nature's recyclers are
    - **a.** predators.
    - **b.** decomposers.
    - **c.** producers.
    - **d.** omnivores.

11. A beneficial association between coral and algae is an example of
    - **a.** commensalism.
    - **b.** parasitism.
    - **c.** mutualism.
    - **d.** predation.

12. The process by which energy moves through an ecosystem can be represented by
    - **a.** food chains.
    - **b.** energy pyramids.
    - **c.** food webs.
    - **d.** All of the above

13. Which organisms does the base of an energy pyramid represent?
    - **a.** producers
    - **b.** carnivores
    - **c.** herbivores
    - **d.** scavengers

14. Which of the following is the correct order in a food chain?
    - **a.** sun→producers→herbivores→scavengers→carnivores
    - **b.** sun→consumers→predators→parasites→hosts
    - **c.** sun→producers→decomposers→consumers→omnivores
    - **d.** sun→producers→herbivores→carnivores→scavengers

15 Remoras and sharks have a relationship that is best described as

a. mutualism.
b. commensalism.
c. predator and prey.
d. parasitism.

Short Answer

16 Describe how energy flows through a food web.

17 Explain how the food web changed when the gray wolf disappeared from Yellowstone National Park.

18 How are the competition between two trees of the same species and the competition between two different species of trees similiar?

19 How do limiting factors affect the carrying capacity of an environment?

20 What is coevolution?

CRITICAL THINKING

21 **Concept Mapping** Use the following terms to create a concept map: *herbivores, organisms, producers, populations, ecosystems, consumers, communities, carnivores,* and *biosphere.*

22 **Identifying Relationships** Could a balanced ecosystem contain producers and consumers but not decomposers? Why or why not?

23 **Predicting Consequences** Some biologists think that certain species, such as alligators and wolves, help maintain biological diversity in their ecosystems. Predict what might happen to other organisms, such as gar fish or herons, if alligators were to become extinct in the Florida Everglades.

24 **Expressing Opinions** Do you think there is a carrying capacity for humans? Why or why not?

INTERPRETING GRAPHICS

Use the energy pyramid below to answer the questions that follow.

25 According to the energy pyramid, are there more prairie dogs or plants?

26 What level has the most energy?

27 Would an energy pyramid such as this one exist in nature?

28 How could you change this pyramid to look like one representing a real ecosystem?

Standardized Test Preparation

READING

Read each of the passages below. Then, answer the questions that follow each passage.

Passage 1 Two or more individuals trying to use the same resource, such as food, water, shelter, space, or sunlight is called *competition*. Because resources are in limited supply in the environment, the use of them by one individual or population decreases the amount available to other organisms. Competition also occurs between individuals within a population. The elk in Yellowstone National Park are herbivores that compete with each other for the same food plants in the park.

1. According to the passage, competition occurs between which of the following?

- **A** individuals trying to use the same resource
- **B** elk and carnivores
- **C** food and shelter
- **D** individuals trying to use different resources

2. According to the passage, food, water, shelter, space, and sunlight are examples of

- **F** populations.
- **G** things found in Yellowstone National Park.
- **H** competition.
- **I** resources.

3. Based on the passage, which of the following statements is a fact?

- **A** Competition occurs only between individuals of different populations.
- **B** Competition occurs between individuals within a population and between individuals of different populations.
- **C** Competition increases the amount of resources available to individuals.
- **D** Because resources are abundant in the environment, competition rarely happens between individuals of different populations.

Passage 2 In the deserts of northern Africa and the Middle East, water is a scarce and valuable resource. In this area, no permanent streams flow except for the Nile. More than 1.6 million square kilometers of this region typically have no rainfall for years at a time. However, much of this area has large aquifers. The water that these aquifers contain dates back to much wetter times thousands of years ago. Occasionally, water reaches the surface to form an oasis. Wells supply the rest of the water used throughout the region. In some regions of Saudi Arabia and Kuwait, wells drilled for water more often strike oil.

1. According to the passage, an aquifer contains what resource?

- **A** oil
- **B** water
- **C** wells
- **D** oasis

2. Based on the passage, which of the following statements is a fact?

- **F** The Nile no longer flows through northern Africa and the Middle East.
- **G** The water found in aquifers is from recent rainfall.
- **H** Wells drilled in Saudi Arabia and Kuwait are more likely to strike oil than water.
- **I** The desert regions of northern Africa and the Middle East receive rainfall almost every day.

3. According to the passage, an oasis forms under what conditions?

- **A** when water stays beneath the surface
- **B** when water is drilled from a well
- **C** when it rains
- **D** when water reaches the surface

INTERPRETING GRAPHICS

The graphs below show the population growth for two populations. Use these graphs to answer the questions that follow.

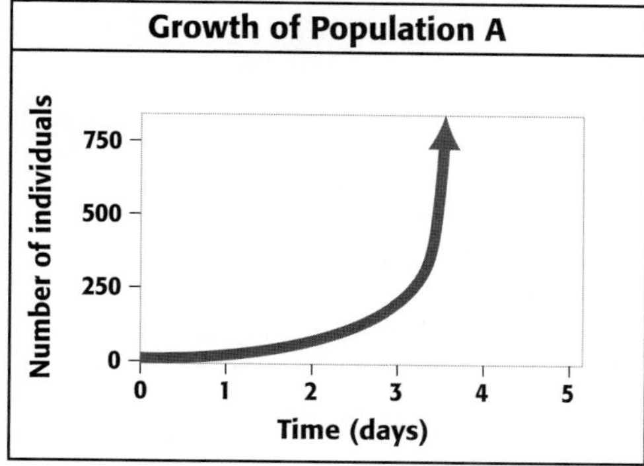

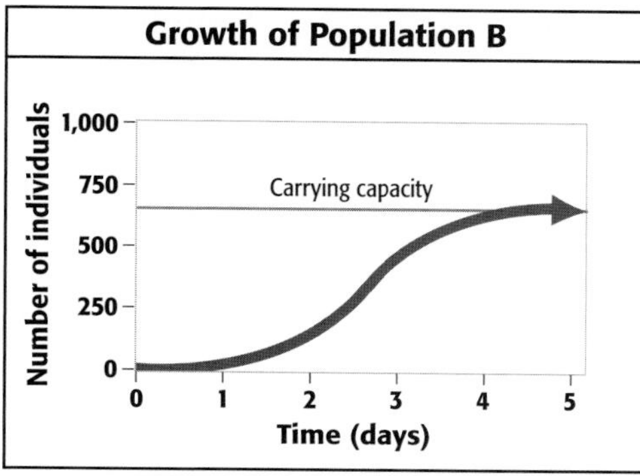

1. After 2 days, which population has more individuals?

A Population A has more individuals.
B Population B has more individuals.
C The populations are the same.
D There is not enough information to determine the answer.

2. After 5 days, which population has more individuals?

F Population A has more individuals.
G Population B has more individuals.
H The populations are the same.
I There is not enough information to determine the answer.

3. On day 10, which statement is probably true?

A Population B is larger than population A.
B Population A is the same as it was on day 5.
C Population A and B are the same.
D Population B is the same as it was on day 5.

MATH

Read each question below, and choose the best answer.

1. The figure below is a map of a forest ecosystem. What is the area of this ecosystem?

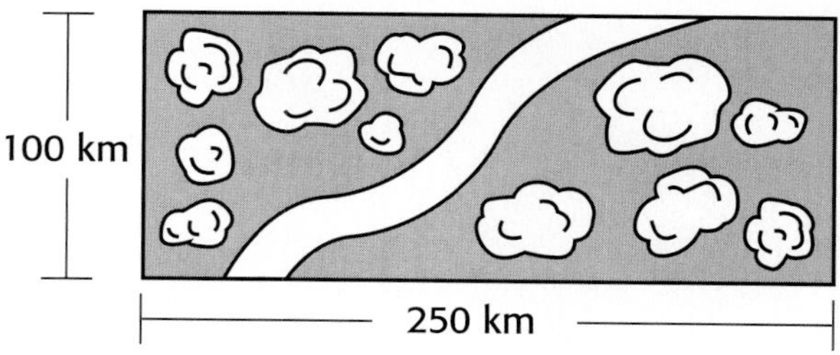

A 25,000 km^2
B 32,000 km
C 1,200 km^2
D 2,500 km

2. If an antelope eats 7 kg of vegetation in 2 days, how many kilograms of vegetation does it eat per day?

F 2/7 kg
G 3/5 kg
H 3 1/2 kg
I 7 1/2 kg

3. If $x = 3$ and $y = x + 2$, what is y?

A 2
B 4
C 5
D 8

4. If $x = 4$ and $y = x + 2$, what is y?

F 2
G 5
H 6
I 8

Science in Action

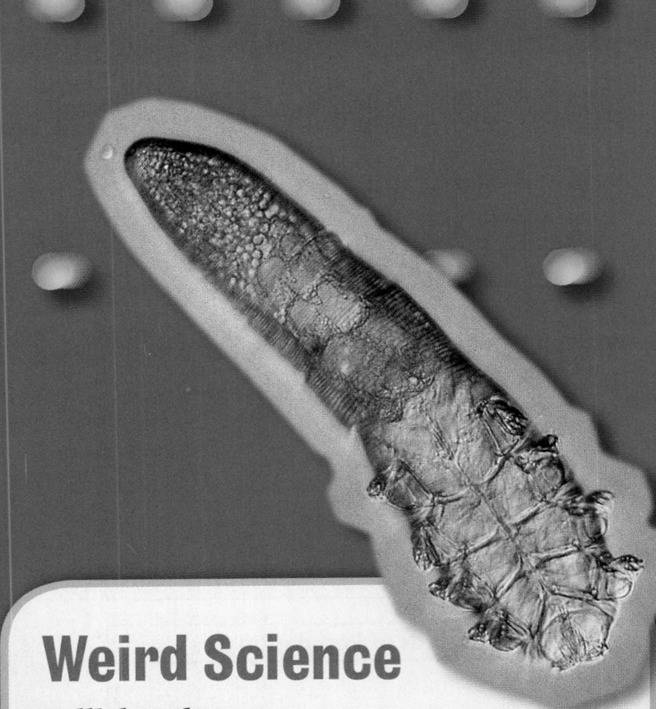

Scientific Debate

How Did Dogs Become Pets?

Did humans change dogs to be the social and helpful creatures they are today? Or were dogs naturally social? Did dogs start moving closer to our campfires long ago? Or did humans find dogs and bring them into our homes? The way in which dogs became our friends, companions, and helpers is still a question. Some scientists think humans and training are the reasons for many of our dogs' best features. Other scientists think dogs and humans have both changed over time to form their strong and unique bond.

Math Activity

Scientists have found fossils of dogs that are 15,000 years old. Generation time is the time between the birth of one generation and the next. If the generation time for dogs is 1.5 years, how many generations have there been in the last 15,000 years?

Weird Science

Follicle Mites

What has a tiny tubelike body and short stumpy legs and lives in your eyebrows and eyelashes? Would you believe a small animal lives there? It's called a follicle mite, and humans are its host. Studies show that more than 97% of adults have these mites. Except in rare cases, follicle mites are harmless.

Like all large animals, human beings are hosts to a variety of smaller creatures that live in or on our bodies and share our bodies' resources. Bacteria that live in our lower digestive tracks help to produce vitamins such as folic acid and vitamin K. Other bacteria may help maintain proper pH levels in our bodies.

Language Arts Activity

WRITING SKILL Imagine that you were shrunk to the size of a follicle mite. How would you get food? Where would you sleep? Write a short story describing one day in your new, tiny life.

Careers

Dalton Dockery

Horticulture Specialist Did you know that instead of using pesticides to get rid of insects that are eating the plants in your garden, you can use other insects? "It is a healthy way of growing vegetables without the use of chemicals and pesticides, and it reduces the harmful effects pesticides have on the environment," says Dalton Dockery, a horticulture specialist in North Carolina. Some insects, such as ladybugs and praying mantises, are natural predators of many insects that are harmful to plants. They will eat other bugs but leave your precious plants in peace. Using bugs to drive off pests is just one aspect of natural gardening. Natural gardening takes advantage of relationships that already exist in nature and uses these interactions to our benefit. For Dockery, the best parts about being a horticultural specialist are teaching people how to preserve the environment, getting to work outside regularly, and having the opportunity to help people on a daily basis.

Social Studies ACTIVITY

WRITING SKILL Research gardening or farming techniques in other cultures. Do other cultures use any of the same aspects of natural gardening as horticultural specialists? Write a short report describing your findings.

To learn more about these Science in Action topics, visit go.hrw.com and type in the keyword HL5INTF.

Current Science

Check out Current Science® articles related to this chapter by visiting go.hrw.com. Just type in the keyword HL5CS18.

Cycles in Nature

About the PHOTO

These penguins have a unique playground on this iceberg off the coast of Antarctica. Icebergs break off from glaciers and float out to sea. A glacier is a giant "river" of ice that slides slowly downhill. Glaciers are formed from snow piling up in mountains. Eventually, glaciers and icebergs melt and become liquid water. Water in oceans and lakes rises into the air and then falls down again as rain or snow. There is a lot of water on Earth, and most of it is constantly moving and changing form.

PRE-READING ACTIVITY

FOLDNOTES **Pyramid** Before you read the chapter, create the FoldNote entitled "Pyramid" described in the **Study Skills** section of the Appendix. Label the sides of the pyramid with "Water cycle," "Carbon cycle," and "Nitrogen cycle." As you read the chapter, define each cycle, and write the steps of each cycle on the appropriate pyramid side.

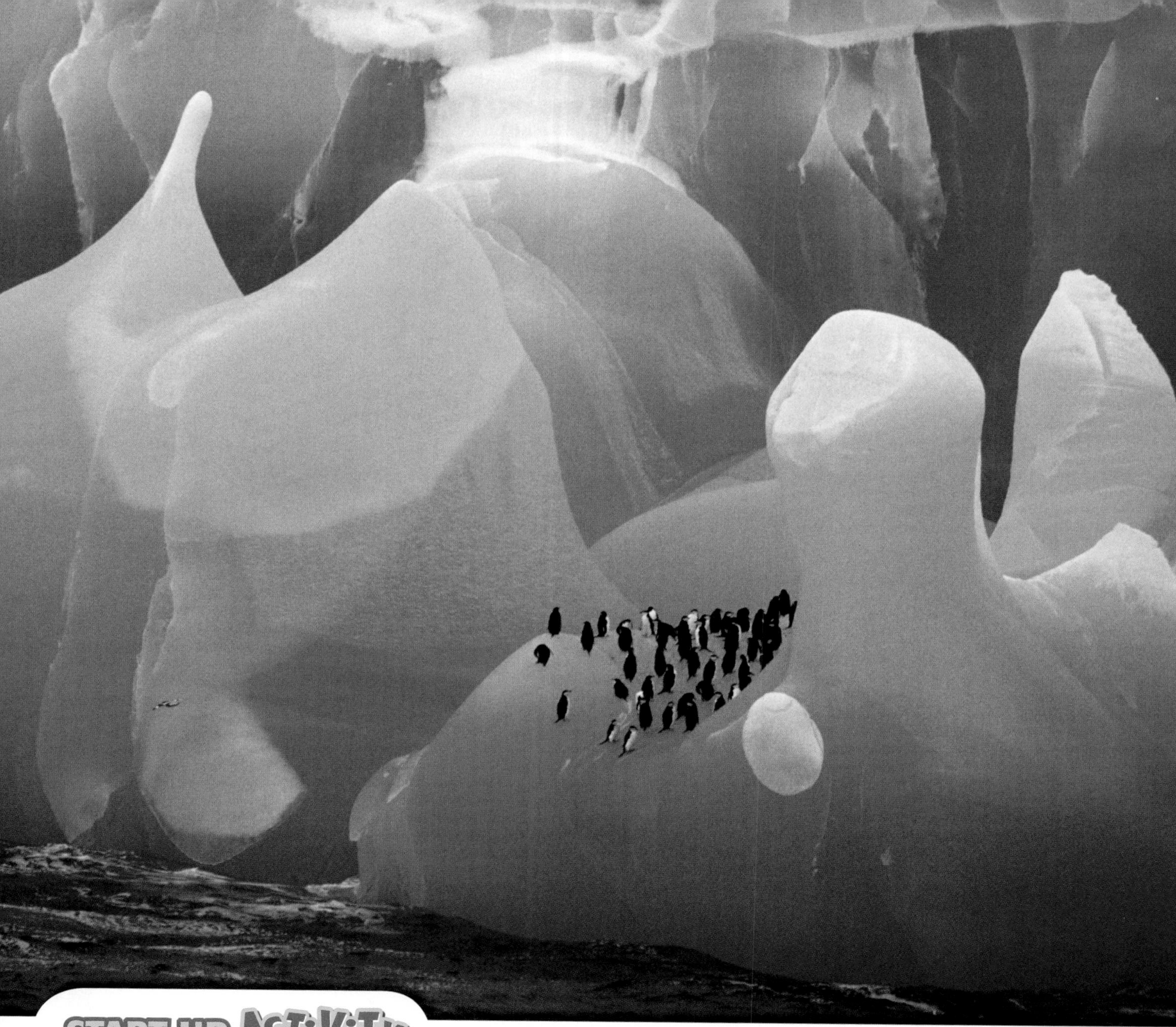

START-UP ACTIVITY

Making Rain

Do you have the power to make rain? Yes!—on a small scale. In this activity, you will cause water to change state in the same way that rain is formed. This process is one way that water is reused on Earth.

Procedure

1. Start with a **large, sealable, plastic freezer bag.** Be sure that the bag is clean and dry and has no leaks. Place a **small, dark-colored bowl** inside the bag. Position the bag with the opening at the top.
2. Fill the bowl halfway with water. Place a few drops of **red food coloring** in the water. Seal the bag.
3. Place the bowl and bag under a strong, warm **light source,** such as a lamp or direct sunlight.
4. Leave the bag in the light for as long as possible. Observe the bag at regular time intervals.

Analysis

1. Each time you observe the bag, describe what you see. Explain what you think is happening.
2. After observing the bag several times, carefully remove the bowl from the bag. Observe and describe any water that is now in the bag. Where did this water come from? How does it differ from the water in the bowl?

SECTION 1

The Cycles of Matter

The matter in your body has been on Earth since the planet formed billions of years ago!

READING WARM-UP

Objectives

- Diagram the water cycle, and explain its importance to living things.
- Diagram the carbon cycle, and explain its importance to living things.
- Diagram the nitrogen cycle, and explain its importance to living things.

Terms to Learn

evaporation
condensation
precipitation
decomposition
combustion

READING STRATEGY

Mnemonics As you read this section, create a mnemonic device to help you remember the parts of the water cycle.

Matter on Earth is limited, so the matter is used over and over again. Each kind of matter has its own cycle. In these cycles, matter moves between the environment and living things.

The Water Cycle

The movement of water between the oceans, atmosphere, land, and living things is known as the *water cycle*. The parts of the water cycle are shown in **Figure 1.**

How Water Moves

During **evaporation,** the sun's heat causes water to change from liquid to vapor. In the process of **condensation,** the water vapor cools and returns to a liquid state. The water that falls from the atmosphere to the land and oceans is **precipitation.** Rain, snow, sleet, and hail are forms of precipitation. Most precipitation falls into the ocean. Some of the precipitation that falls on land flows into streams, rivers, and lakes and is called *runoff*. Some precipitation seeps into the ground and is stored in spaces between or within rocks. This water, known as *groundwater,* will slowly flow back into the soil, streams, rivers, and oceans.

evaporation the change of a substance from a liquid to a gas

condensation the change of state from a gas to a liquid

precipitation any form of water that falls to the Earth's surface from the clouds

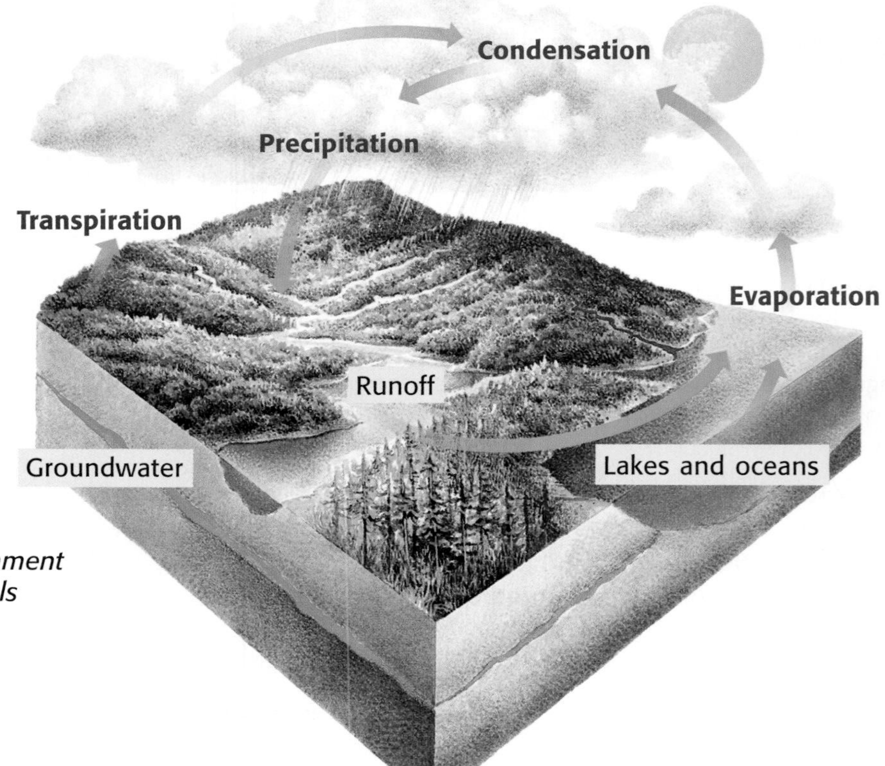

Figure 1 *Water from the environment moves through plants and animals and back to the environment.*

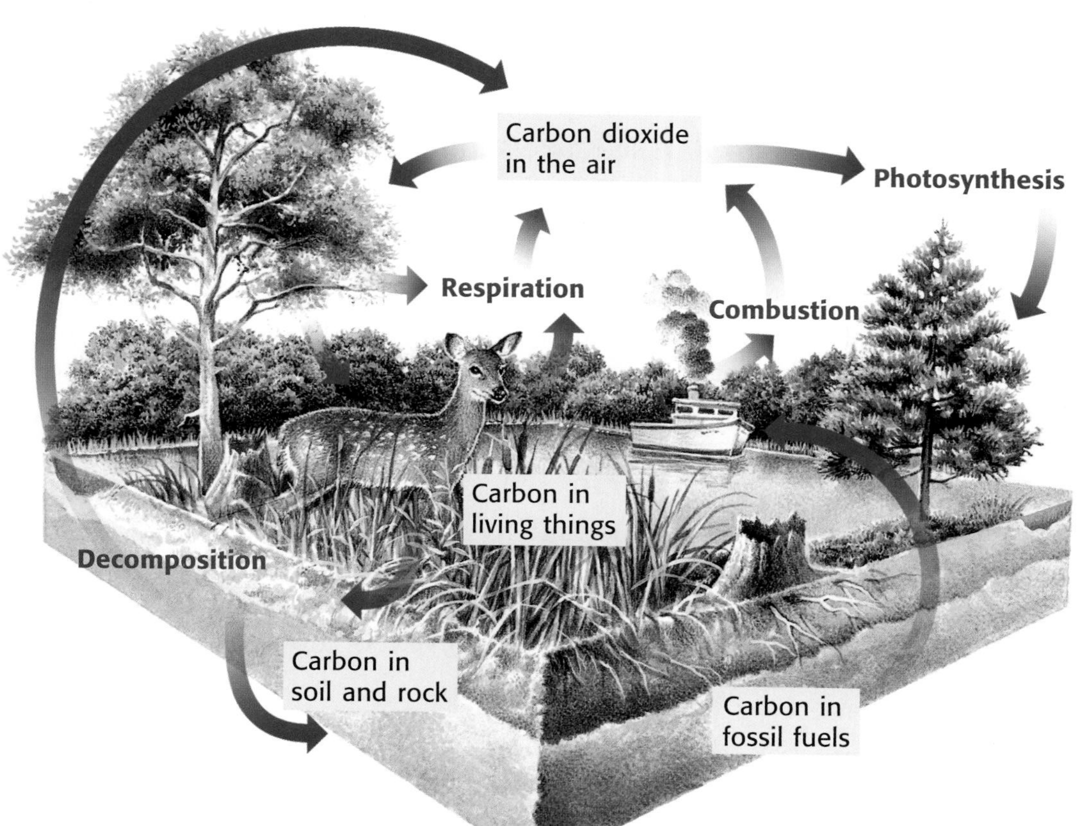

Figure 2 *Carbon may remain in the environment for millions of years before becoming available to living things.*

Water and Life

Without water, there would be no life on Earth. All organisms, from bacteria to animals and plants, are composed mostly of water. Water helps transport nutrients and wastes within an organism. Water also helps regulate temperature. For example, when you sweat, water evaporates from your skin and cools your body. Eventually, all the water taken in by organisms is returned to the environment. For example, plants release a large amount of water vapor in a process called *transpiration.*

Reading Check **Why is water important?** (*See the Appendix for answers to Reading Checks.*)

Where's the Water?

There are about 37.5 million cubic kilometers of fresh water on Earth. Of this fresh water, about 8.3 million cubic kilometers is groundwater. What percentage of Earth's fresh water is groundwater?

The Carbon Cycle

Besides water, the most common molecules in living things are *organic* molecules, or molecules that contain carbon. The exchange of carbon between the environment and living things is known as the *carbon cycle,* as shown in **Figure 2.**

Photosynthesis and Respiration

Photosynthesis is the basis of the carbon cycle. During photosynthesis, plants use carbon dioxide from air to make sugars. Most animals get the carbon and energy they need by eating plants. How does carbon return to the environment? It returns when sugar molecules are broken down to release energy. This process, called *respiration,* uses oxygen. Carbon dioxide and water are released as byproducts of respiration.

decomposition the breakdown of substances into simpler molecular substances

combustion the burning of a substance

Combustion

1. Place a **candle** on a **jar lid,** and secure the candle with **modeling clay.** Have your teacher light the candle.
2. Hold the jar near the candle flame. Do not cover the flame with the jar. Describe the jar. Where did the substance on the jar come from?
3. Now, place the jar over the candle. What is deposited inside the jar? Where did this substance come from?

Decomposition and Combustion

The breakdown of substances into simpler molecules is called **decomposition.** For example, when fungi and bacteria decompose organic matter, carbon dioxide and water are returned to the environment. You may have witnessed another way to break down organic matter—using fire. **Combustion** is the process of burning a substance, such as wood or fossil fuels. Like decomposition, combustion of organic matter releases carbon dioxide into the atmosphere.

The Nitrogen Cycle

Nitrogen is also important to living things. Organisms need nitrogen to build proteins and DNA for new cells. The movement of nitrogen between the environment and living things is called the *nitrogen cycle.* This cycle is shown in **Figure 3.**

Converting Nitrogen Gas

About 78% of the Earth's atmosphere is nitrogen gas. Most organisms cannot use nitrogen gas directly. However, bacteria in the soil are able to change nitrogen gas into forms that plants can use. This process is called *nitrogen fixation.* Other organisms may then get the nitrogen they need by eating plants or eating organisms that eat plants.

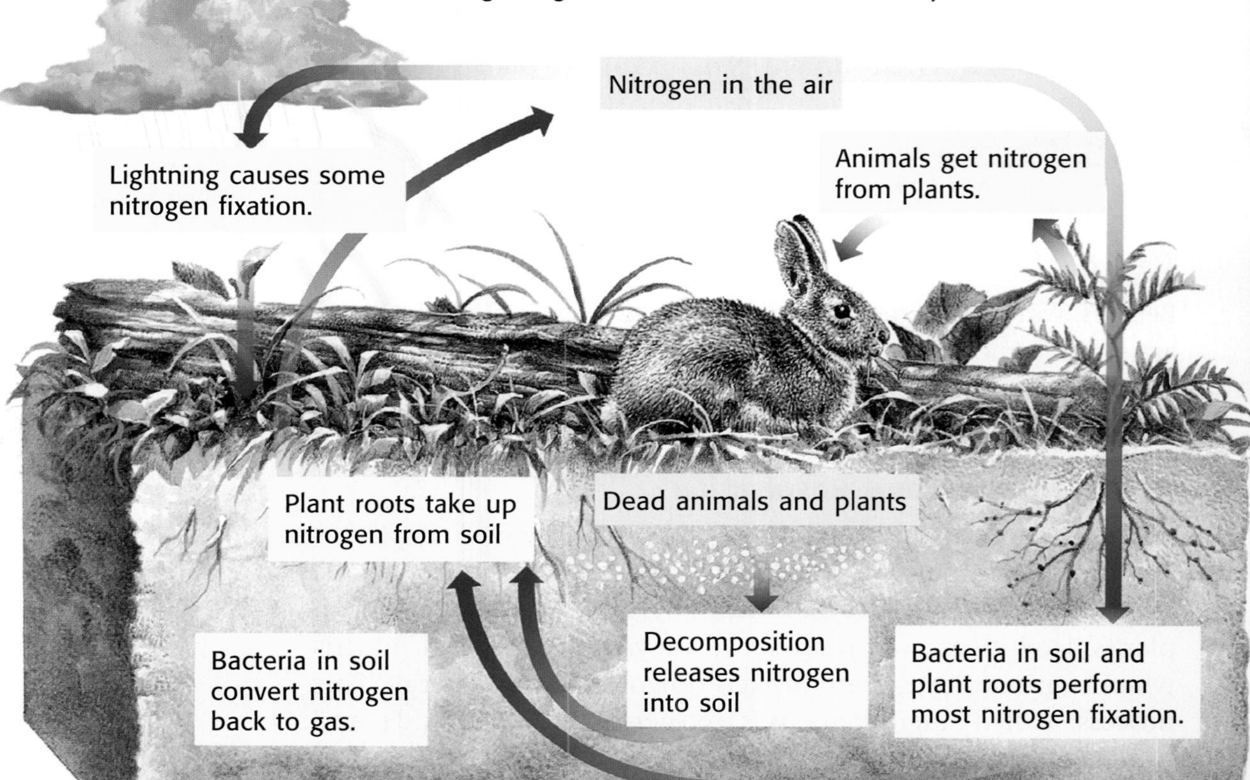
Nitrogen in the air
Lightning causes some nitrogen fixation.
Animals get nitrogen from plants.
Plant roots take up nitrogen from soil
Dead animals and plants
Bacteria in soil convert nitrogen back to gas.
Decomposition releases nitrogen into soil
Bacteria in soil and plant roots perform most nitrogen fixation.

Figure 3 *Without bacteria, nitrogen could not enter living things or be returned to the atmosphere.*

Passing It On

When organisms die, decomposers break down the remains. Decomposition releases a form of nitrogen into the soil that plants can use. Finally, certain types of bacteria in the soil convert nitrogen to a gas, which is returned to the atmosphere.

Many Cycles

Other forms of matter on Earth also pass through cycles. Many of the minerals that living cells need, such as calcium and phosphorous, are cycled through the environment. When an organism dies, every substance in its body is likely to be recycled or reused.

Each of the cycles is connected in many ways. For example, some forms of nitrogen and carbon are carried through the environment by water. Many nutrients pass from soil to plants to animals and back. Living organisms play a part in each of the cycles.

Reading Check **Give an example of a form of matter—other than carbon, water, or nitrogen—that is cycled through the environment.**

CONNECTION TO Environmental Science

Global Warming The quantity of carbon dioxide being released into the atmosphere is increasing. Carbon dioxide can cause the atmosphere to hold heat. A warmer atmosphere would cause the temperatures of the land and ocean to increase. Scientists think that this situation, known as *global warming,* may be happening. Research data on changes in average global temperature and carbon dioxide levels for the past 50 years, and summarize your findings.

SECTION Review

Summary

- Precipitation, evaporation, transpiration, and condensation are parts of the water cycle.
- Photosynthesis, respiration, decomposition, and combustion are parts of the carbon cycle.
- In the nitrogen cycle, nitrogen gas is converted into other forms and back to gas again.
- Many forms of matter on Earth pass through cycles. These cycles may be connected in many ways.

Using Key Terms

For each pair of terms, explain how the meanings of the terms differ.

1. *evaporation* and *condensation*
2. *decomposition* and *combustion*

Understanding Key Ideas

3. Nitrogen fixation
   a. is done only by plants.
   b. is done mostly by bacteria.
   c. is how animals make proteins.
   d. is a form of decomposition.
4. Describe the water cycle.
5. Describe the carbon cycle.

Math Skills

6. The average person in the United States uses about 78 gal of water each day. How many liters of water does this equal? How many liters of water will the average person use in a year?

Critical Thinking

7. **Analyzing Processes** Draw a simple diagram of each of the cycles discussed in this section. Draw lines between the cycles to show how parts of each cycle are related.
8. **Applying Concepts** Give an example of how the calcium in an animal's bones might be cycled back into the environment.

SCILINKS.
NSTA
Developed and maintained by the National Science Teachers Association
For a variety of links related to this chapter, go to www.scilinks.org
Topic: Cycles of Matter
SciLinks code: HSM0373

SECTION 2

Ecological Succession

Imagine you have a time machine that can take you back to the summer of 1988. If you had visited Yellowstone National Park during that year, you would have seen fires raging throughout the area.

By the end of that summer, large areas of the park were burned to the ground. When the fires were put out, a layer of gray ash blanketed the forest floor. Most of the trees were dead, although many of them were still standing.

READING WARM-UP

Objectives

- Describe the process of succession.
- Contrast primary and secondary succession.
- Explain how mature communities develop.

Terms to Learn

succession
pioneer species

READING STRATEGY

Reading Organizer As you read this section, make a table comparing primary succession and secondary succession.

Regrowth of a Forest

The following spring, the appearance of the "dead" forest began to change. **Figure 1** shows the changes after just one year. Some of the dead trees fell over, and small, green plants grew in large numbers. Within 10 years, scientists reported that many trees were growing and the forest community was coming back.

A gradual development of a community over time, such as the regrowth of the burned areas of Yellowstone National Park, is called **succession.** Succession takes place in all communities, not just those affected by disturbances such as forest fires.

succession the replacement of one type of community by another at a single place over a period of time

Reading Check **What happened after the Yellowstone fires?** (*See the Appendix for answers to Reading Checks.*)

Figure 1 *Huge areas of Yellowstone National Park were burned in 1988* (left). *By the spring of 1989, regrowth was evident in the burned parts of the park* (right).

Primary Succession

Sometimes, a small community starts to grow in an area where other organisms had not previously lived. There is no soil in this area. And usually, there is just bare rock. Over a very long time, a series of organisms live and die on the rock. The rock is slowly transformed into soil. This process is called *primary succession,* as shown in **Figure 2.** The first organisms to live in an area are called **pioneer species.**

pioneer species a species that colonizes an uninhabited area and that starts a process of succession

Figure 2 **An Example of Primary Succession**

1 A slowly retreating glacier exposes bare rock where nothing lives, and primary succession begins.

2 Most primary succession begins with lichens. Acids from the lichens begin breaking the rocks into small particles. These particles mix with the remains of dead lichens to start forming soil. Lichens are an example of a pioneer species.

3 After many years, there is enough soil for mosses to grow. The mosses eventually replace the lichens. Insects and other tiny organisms begin to live there. When they die, their remains add to the soil.

4 Over time, the soil deepens, and the mosses are replaced by ferns. The ferns may slowly be replaced by grasses and wildflowers. If there is enough soil, shrubs and small trees may grow.

5 After hundreds or even thousands of years, the soil may be deep and stable enough to support a forest.

For another activity related to this chapter, go to **go.hrw.com** and type in the keyword **HL5CYCW.**

Secondary Succession

Sometimes, an existing community is destroyed by a natural disaster, such as a fire or a flood. Sometimes, a community is affected by another type of disturbance. For example, a farmer might stop growing crops in an area that had been cleared. In either case, if soil is left intact, the original community may regrow through a series of stages called *secondary succession.* **Figure 3** shows an example of secondary succession.

Reading Check **How does secondary succession differ from primary succession?**

Figure 3 **An Example of Secondary Succession**

1 The first year after a farmer stops growing crops or the first year after some other major disturbance, weeds start to grow. In farming areas, crab grass is the weed that often grows first.

2 By the second year, new weeds appear. Their seeds may have been blown into the field by the wind, or insects may have carried them. Horseweed is common during the second year.

3 In 5 to 15 years, small conifer trees may start growing among the weeds. The trees continue to grow, and after about 100 years, a forest may form.

4 As older conifers die, they may be replaced by hardwoods, such as oak or maple trees, if the climate can support them.

Mature Communities and Biodiversity

In the early stages of succession, only a few species grow in an area. These species grow quickly and make many seeds that scatter easily. But all species are vulnerable to disease, disturbances, and competition. As a community matures, it may be dominated by well-adapted, slow-growing *climax species*.

Furthermore, as succession proceeds, more species may become established. The variety of species that are present in an area is referred to as *biodiversity*. Biodiversity is important to communities of organisms. For example, a forest that has a high degree of biodiversity is less likely to be destroyed by an invasion of insects. Most plant-damaging insects prefer to attack only one species of plants. The presence of a variety of plants will lessen the impact and spread of invading insects.

Keep in mind that a mature community may not always be a forest. A mature community simply has organisms that are well adapted to live together in the same area over time. For example, the plants of the Sonoran Desert, shown in **Figure 4,** are well-adapted to the desert's conditions.

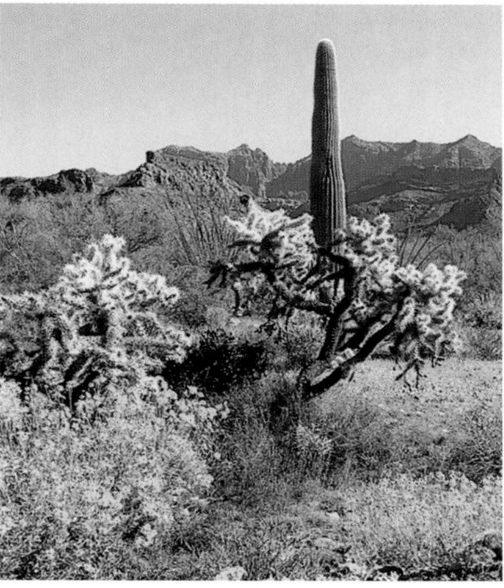

Figure 4 *This area of the Sonoran Desert in Arizona is a mature community.*

SECTION Review

Summary

- Ecological succession is the gradual development of communities over time. Often a series of stages is observed during succession.
- Primary succession occurs in an area that was not previously inhabited by living things; no soil is present.
- Secondary succession takes place in an area where an earlier community was disturbed by fire, landslides, floods, or plowing for crops and where soil is present.

Using Key Terms

1. In your own words, write a definition for the term *succession*.

Understanding Key Ideas

2. An area where a glacier has just melted away will begin the process of
   a. primary succession.
   b. secondary succession.
   c. stability.
   d. regrowth.
3. Describe succession that takes place in an abandoned field.
4. Describe a mature community. How does a mature community develop?

Math Skills

5. The fires in 1988 burned 739,000 of the 2.2 million acres that make up Yellowstone National Park. What percentage of the park was burned?

Critical Thinking

6. **Applying Concepts** Give an example of a community that has a high degree of biodiversity, and an example of one that has a low degree of biodiversity.
7. **Analyzing Ideas** Explain why soil formation is always the first stage of primary succession. Does soil formation ever stop? Explain your answer.

SCILINKS
NSTA
Developed and maintained by the National Science Teachers Association
For a variety of links related to this chapter, go to www.scilinks.org
Topic: Succession
SciLinks code: HSM1475

Skills Practice Lab

OBJECTIVES

Investigate the nitrogen cycle inside a closed system.

Discover how decomposers return nitrogen to the soil.

MATERIALS

- balance or scale
- beaker, 50 mL
- funnel
- gloves, protective
- graduated cylinder, 25 mL
- insects from home or schoolyard, large, dead (5)
- jar with lid, 1 pt (or 500 mL)
- paper, filter (2 pieces)
- pH paper
- soil, potting, commercially prepared without fertilizer
- water, distilled, 60 mL

SAFETY

Nitrogen Needs

The nitrogen cycle is one of several cycles that are vital to living organisms. Without nitrogen, living organisms cannot make amino acids, the building blocks of proteins. Animals obtain nitrogen by eating plants that contain nitrogen and by eating animals that eat those plants. When animals die, decomposers return the nitrogen to the soil in the form of a nitrogen-containing chemical called *ammonia*.

In this activity, you will investigate the nitrogen cycle inside a closed system to discover how decomposers return nitrogen to the soil.

Procedure

1. Fit a piece of filter paper into a funnel. Place the funnel inside a 50 mL beaker, and pour 5 g of soil into the funnel. Add 25 mL of distilled water to the soil.
2. Test the filtered water with pH paper, and record your observations.
3. Place some soil in a jar to cover the bottom with about 5 cm of soil. Add 10 mL of distilled water to the soil.
4. Place the dead insects in the jar, and seal the jar with the lid.
5. Check the jar each day for 5 days for an ammonia odor. (If you do not know what ammonia smells like, ask your teacher.) Record your observations. **Caution:** Your teacher will demonstrate how to check for a chemical odor by wafting. Notice how to gently wave the chemical fumes toward your nose with your hand. Do not put your nose in the jar and inhale!

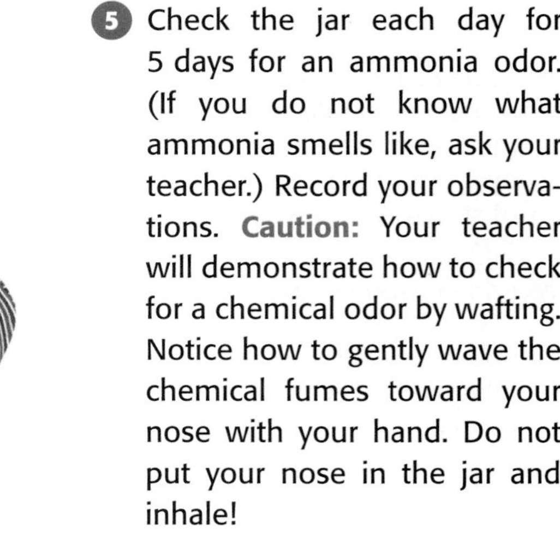

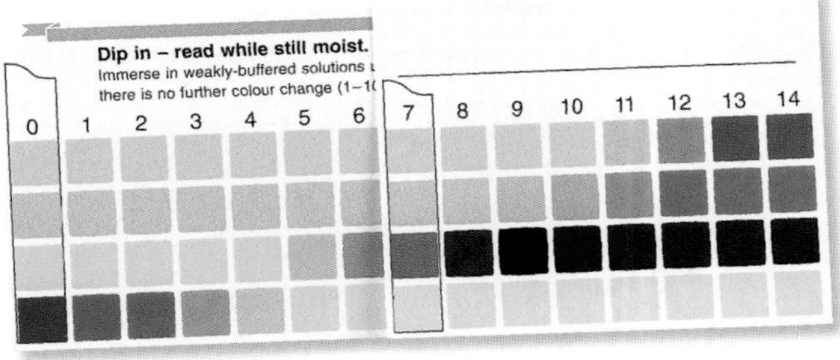

6. On the fifth day, place a second piece of filter paper into the funnel, and place the funnel inside a 50 mL beaker. Remove about 5 g of soil from the jar, and place it in the funnel. Add 25 mL of distilled water to the soil.

7. Once again, test the filtered water with pH paper, and record your observations.

Analyze the Results

1. **Examining Data** What was the pH of the water in the beaker in the first trial? A pH of 7 indicates that the water is neutral. A pH below 7 indicates that the water is acidic, and a pH above 7 indicates that the water is basic. Was the water in the beaker neutral, acidic, or basic?

2. **Analyzing Data** What was the pH of the water in the beaker in the second trial? Explain the difference, if any, between the results of the first trial and the results of the second trial.

Draw Conclusions

3. **Drawing Conclusions** Based on the results of your pH tests, do you think ammonia is acidic or basic?

4. **Evaluating Results** On which days in your investigation were you able to detect an ammonia odor? Explain what caused the odor.

5. **Applying Conclusions** Describe the importance of decomposers in the nitrogen cycle.

Applying Your Data

Test the importance of nitrogen to plants. Fill two 12 cm flowerpots with commercially prepared potting soil and water. Be sure to use soil that has had no fertilizer added. Obtain a dozen tomato or radish seeds. Plant six seeds in each pot. Water your seeds so that the soil is constantly damp but not soaked. Keep your pots in a sunny window. Use a nitrogen-rich liquid plant fertilizer to fertilize one of the pots once a week. Dilute or mix the fertilizer with water according to the directions on the container. Water the other pot once a week with plain tap water.

1. After the seedlings appear, use a metric ruler to measure the growth of the plants in both pots. Measure the plants once a week, and record your results.
2. You may plant other seeds of your choice, but do not use legume (bean) seeds. Research to find out why!

Chapter Review

USING KEY TERMS

Complete each of the following sentences by choosing the correct term from the word bank.

evaporation	condensation
precipitation	decomposition
combustion	succession

1. The breakdown of dead materials into carbon dioxide and water is called ___.

2. The gradual development of a community over time is called ___.

3. During ___, the heat causes water to change from liquid to vapor.

4. ___ is the process of burning a substance.

5. Water that falls from the atmosphere to the land and oceans is ___.

6. In the process of ___, water vapor cools and returns to a liquid state.

UNDERSTANDING KEY IDEAS

Multiple Choice

7. Clouds form in the atmosphere through the process of
   a. precipitation. **c.** condensation.
   b. respiration. **d.** decomposition.

8. Which of the following statements about groundwater is true?
   a. It stays underground for a few days.
   b. It is stored in underground caverns or porous rock.
   c. It is salty like ocean water.
   d. It never reenters the water cycle.

9. Burning gas in an automobile is a type of
   a. combustion. **c.** decomposition.
   b. respiration. **d.** photosynthesis.

10. Nitrogen in the form of a gas can be used directly by some kinds of
    a. plants. **c.** bacteria.
    b. animals. **d.** fungi.

11. Bacteria are most important in the process of
    a. combustion. **c.** nitrogen fixation.
    b. condensation. **d.** evaporation.

12. The pioneer species on bare rock are usually
    a. ferns. **c.** mosses.
    b. pine trees. **d.** lichens.

13. Which of the following is an example of primary succession?
    a. the recovery of Yellowstone National Park following the fires of 1988
    b. the appearance of lichens and mosses in an area where a glacier has recently melted away
    c. the growth of weeds in a field after a farmer stops using the field
    d. the growth of weeds in an empty lot that is no longer being mowed

14. One of the most common plants in a recently abandoned farm field is
    a. oak or maple trees.
    b. pine trees.
    c. mosses.
    d. crabgrass.

Short Answer

15. List four places where water can go after it falls as precipitation.

16. In what forms can water on Earth be found?

17. What role do animals have in the carbon cycle?

18. What roles do humans have in the carbon cycle?

19. Earth's atmosphere is mostly made up of what substance?

20. Compare and contrast the two forms of succession.

CRITICAL THINKING

21. **Concept Mapping** Use the following terms to create a concept map: *abandoned farmland, lichens, bare rock, soil formation, horseweed, succession, forest fire, primary succession, secondary succession,* and *pioneer species.*

22. **Identifying Relationships** Is snow a part of the water cycle? Why or why not?

23. **Analyzing Processes** Make a list of several places where water might be found on Earth. For each item on your list, state how it is part of the water cycle.

24. **Forming Hypotheses** Predict what would happen if the water on Earth suddenly stopped evaporating.

25. **Forming Hypotheses** Predict what would happen if all of the bacteria on Earth suddenly disappeared.

26. **Making Inferences** Describe why a lawn usually doesn't go through succession.

27. **Making Inferences** Can one scientist observe all of the stages of secondary succession on an abandoned field? Explain your answer.

INTERPRETING GRAPHICS

The graph below shows how water is used each day by an average household in the United States. Use the graph to answer the questions that follow.

Average Household Daily Water Use

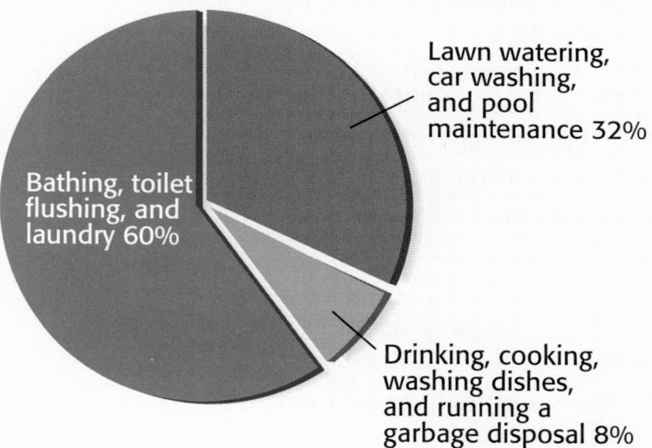

28. According to this graph, which of the following activities uses the greatest amount of water?
    a. bathing
    b. toilet flushing
    c. washing laundry
    d. There is not enough information to determine the answer.

29. An average family used 380 L of water per day, until they stopped washing their car, stopped watering their lawn, and stopped using their pool. Now, how much water per day do they use?

Standardized Test Preparation

READING

Read each of the passages below. Then, answer the questions that follow each passage.

Passage 1 The scientist woke up and jogged over to the rain forest. There she observed the water-recycling experiment. She took a swim in the ocean, and she walked through the aspen forest on her way home. At home, she ate lunch and then went to the computer lab. From the lab, she could monitor the sensors that would alert her if any part of the ecosystem failed to cycle properly. This monitoring was very important to the scientist and her research team because their lives depended on the health of their sealed environment. Several weeks ago, the sensors began to detect trouble.

1. In the passage, what does *aspen* mean?

A a type of experiment
B a type of tree
C beautiful
D ugly

2. Based on the passage, what can the reader conclude?

F The scientist lives in an artificial environment.
G The scientist lives by herself.
H The scientist and her research team are studying a newly discovered island.
I The scientist does not rely on the sensors to detect trouble.

3. Based on the passage, which of the following statements is a fact?

A The scientist is scared that her environment is being destroyed.
B The scientists depend on the sensors to alert them of trouble.
C The scientists live on an island.
D The scientist eats lunch at home every day.

Passage 2 Every summer, millions of fish are killed in an area in the Gulf of Mexico called a *hypoxia region*. Hypoxia is a condition that occurs when there is an unusually low level of oxygen in the water. The area is often referred to as the *dead zone* because almost every fish and crustacean in the area dies. In 1995, this zone covered more than 18,000 km^2, and almost 1 million fish were killed in a single week. Why does this happen? Can it be stopped?

1. Based on the passage, what is the **best** definition of a hypoxia region?

A a region where millions of fish are killed
B a region where there is a low level of oxygen
C a region that creates a "dead zone"
D a region that is 18,000 km^2

2. Why is the hypoxia region called a *dead zone*?

F because the oxygen in the region is dead
G because the region covers more area than fish can live in
H because the Gulf of Mexico is not a popular fishing zone anymore
I because almost every fish and crustacean in the area dies

3. What information would the paragraph following the passage provide?

A an explanation of the definition of hypoxia
B a description of how hypoxia occurs in other parts of the world
C a list all of the animals that died in the Gulf of Mexico in 1995
D an explanation of how the hypoxia region is formed in the Gulf of Mexico

INTERPRETING GRAPHICS

The illustration below shows what an area looked like when visited on several successive occasions. Use the illustration to answer the questions that follow.

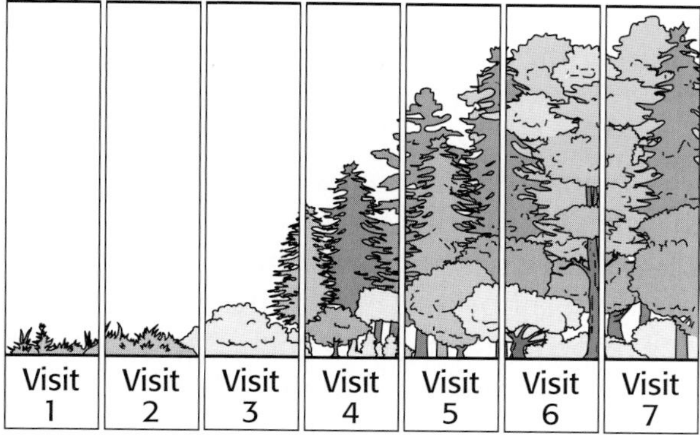

1. In the area illustrated, what process is evident over time?

A ecological succession
B combustion of fossil fuels
C pioneer speciation
D ecological organization

2. During which of the following visits would you see the **most** mature community?

F visit 1
G visit 3
H visit 5
I visit 7

3. Assume that a forest fire happened after the seventh visit. If the scientist were to visit again within 1 year after the fire, the area would most likely look like it did during which visit?

A visit 1
B visit 3
C visit 5
D visit 7

MATH

Read each question below, and choose the best answer.

1. Flushing the toilet accounts for almost half the water a person uses in a day. Some toilets use up to 6 gal per flush. More-efficient toilets use about 1.5 gal per flush. How many liters of water can you save each day by using a more-efficient toilet if you flush five times a day?

A 4.5 gal
B 20 gal
C 80 L
D 85 L

2. About 15 m of topsoil covers the eastern plains of the United States. If topsoil forms at the rate of 2.5 cm per 500 years, how long did it take for the 15 m of topsoil to form?

F 3,000 years
G 18,750 years
H 30,000 years
I 300,000 years

3. If $16 = 2x + 10$, what is x?

A 2
B 3
C 4
D 8

4. What is the area of the rectangle below?

F 22 m
G 22 m^2
H 105 m
I 105 m^2

Standardized Test Preparation

Science in Action

Science, Technology, and Society

Desalination

By the year 2025, it is estimated that almost a billion people on Earth will face water shortages. Only about 3% of the water on Earth is *fresh water*—the kind of water that we use for drinking and farming. And the human population is using and polluting Earth's fresh water too quickly. The other 97% of Earth's water is mostly in oceans and is much too salty for drinking or farming.

Until recently, it was very expensive and time-consuming to filter salt out of water, a process known as *desalination*. But new technologies are making desalination an affordable option for some areas.

Math Activity

You need to drink about 2 quarts of water each day. Imagine that you have a simple device that evaporates sea water and collects fresh, drinkable water at the rate of 6 mL/min. How long will it take your device to collect enough water each day?

Scientific Discoveries

The Dead Zone

Every summer, millions of fish are killed in an area in the Gulf of Mexico called a hypoxia region. *Hypoxia* (hy PAWK see UH) is a condition of water with unusually low levels of oxygen. The Gulf's hypoxia region is called a "dead zone" because a large number of organisms in the area die. Why does this happen? Scientists think that the region may be polluted with large amounts of nitrogen and phosphorus. These nutrients promote the growth of algae, which "bloom" and then die in huge numbers. When the algae is decomposed by bacteria, the bacteria use up oxygen in the water and hypoxia results. Scientists think that the polluting chemicals are washed into the Gulf by the Mississippi River. This river receives runoff from a large area that includes farms, housing, and cities. The scientists propose that adding wetlands to the Mississippi River watershed could reduce the chemicals reaching the Gulf.

Language Arts Activity

WRITING SKILL The Gulf of Mexico is not the only place where a hypoxia region exists. Research other bodies of water to find out how widespread the problem is. Write a short report telling what scientists are doing to reduce hypoxia in other places.

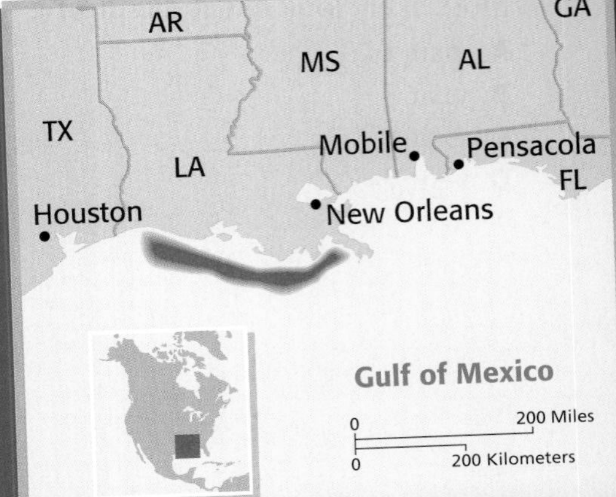

For several years after it was first noticed, the Gulf of Mexico hypoxia region became larger.

Careers

Michael Fan

Wastewater Manager If you are concerned about clean water and you like to work both in a laboratory and outdoors, you might like a career in wastewater management. The water cycle helps to keep water in nature pure enough for most organisms. But when humans use water in houses, factories, and farms, we create *wastewater*, often faster than natural processes can clean it up. To make the water safe again, we can imitate the ways water gets cleaned up in nature—and speed up the process.

Michael M. Fan is the Assistant Superintendent of wastewater operations at the Wastewater Treatment Plant at the University of California in Davis, California. This plant has one of the most advanced wastewater management systems in the country. Mr. Fan finds his job exciting. The plant operates 24 hours a day, and there are many tasks to manage. Running the plant requires skills in chemistry, physics, microbiology, and engineering. Many organisms in the Davis area are counting on Mr. Fan to make sure that the water used by the University campus is safely returned to nature.

Social Studies ACTIVITY

Research the ways that the ancient Romans managed their wastewater. Make a poster that illustrates some of their methods and technologies.

To learn more about these Science in Action topics, visit go.hrw.com and type in the keyword HL5CYCF

Current Science

Check out Current Science® articles related to this chapter by visiting go.hrw.com. Just type in the keyword HL5CS19.

20

The Earth's Ecosystems

About the PHOTO

Is this animal a movie monster? No! The thorny devil is a lizard that lives in the desert of Australia. The thorny devil's rough skin is an adaptation that helps it survive in the hot, dry desert. Grooves in the thorny devil's skin collect water that the lizard later drinks. Water lands on its back and runs along the tiny grooves to the thorny devil's mouth.

PRE-READING ACTIVITY

FOLDNOTES

Three-Panel Flip Chart

Before you read the chapter, create the FoldNote entitled "Three-Panel Flip Chart" described in the **Study Skills** section of the Appendix. Label the flaps of the three-panel flip chart with "Land biomes," "Marine ecosystems," and "Freshwater ecosystems." As you read the chapter, write information you learn about each category under the appropriate flap.

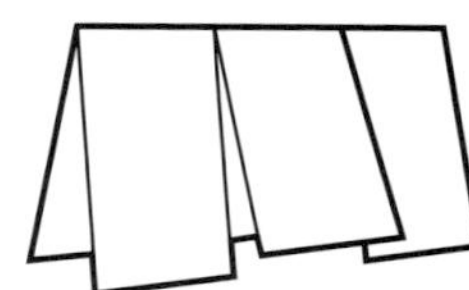

START-UP ACTIVITY

A Mini-Ecosystem

In this activity, you will build and observe a miniature ecosystem.

Procedure

1. Place a layer of **gravel** at the bottom of a **container,** such as a **large, wide-mouthed jar** or a **2 L soda bottle** with the top cut off. Then, add a layer of **soil.**
2. Add a variety of **plants** that need similar growing conditions. Choose small plants that will not grow too quickly.
3. Spray **water** inside the container to moisten the soil.
4. Loosely cover the container with a **lid** or **plastic wrap.** Place the container in indirect light.
5. Describe the appearance of your ecosystem.
6. Let your mini-ecosystem grow for 6 weeks. Add more water when the soil is dry.
7. Observe your mini-ecosystem every week. Record your observations.

Analysis

1. List the nonliving factors that make up the ecosystem that you built.
2. List the living factors that make up your ecosystem.
3. How is your mini-ecosystem similar to a real ecosystem? How is it different?

SECTION 1

Land Biomes

READING WARM-UP

Objectives

- Distinguish between abiotic factors and biotic factors in biomes.
- Identify seven land biomes on Earth.

Terms to Learn

biome
savanna
desert
tundra

READING STRATEGY

Reading Organizer As you read this section, create an outline of the section. Use the headings from the section in your outline.

What do you think of when you think of polar bears? You probably imagine them in a snow-covered setting. Why don't polar bears live in the desert?

Different ecosystems are home to different kinds of organisms. Polar bears don't live in the desert because they are adapted to very cold environments. Polar bears have thick fur. This fur keeps polar bears warm. It also hides them in the snow.

The Earth's Land Biomes

Imagine yourself in a hot, dry, dusty place. You see a cactus on your right. A lizard sits on a rock to your left. Where are you? You may not know exactly, but you probably think you are in a desert.

A desert is different from other places because of its abiotic (AY bie AHT ik) factors and biotic (bie AHT ik) factors. *Abiotic factors* are the nonliving parts of an environment. Soil, water, and climate are abiotic factors. Climate is the average weather conditions for an area over a long period of time. *Biotic factors* are the living parts of an environment. Plants and animals are biotic factors. Areas that have similar abiotic factors usually have similar biotic factors. A **biome** (BIE OHM) is a large area characterized by its climate and the plants and animals that live in the area. A biome contains related ecosystems. For example, a tropical rain forest biome contains treetop ecosystems and forest-floor ecosystems. The major land biomes on Earth are shown in **Figure 1.**

biome a large region characterized by a specific type of climate and certain types of plant and animal communities

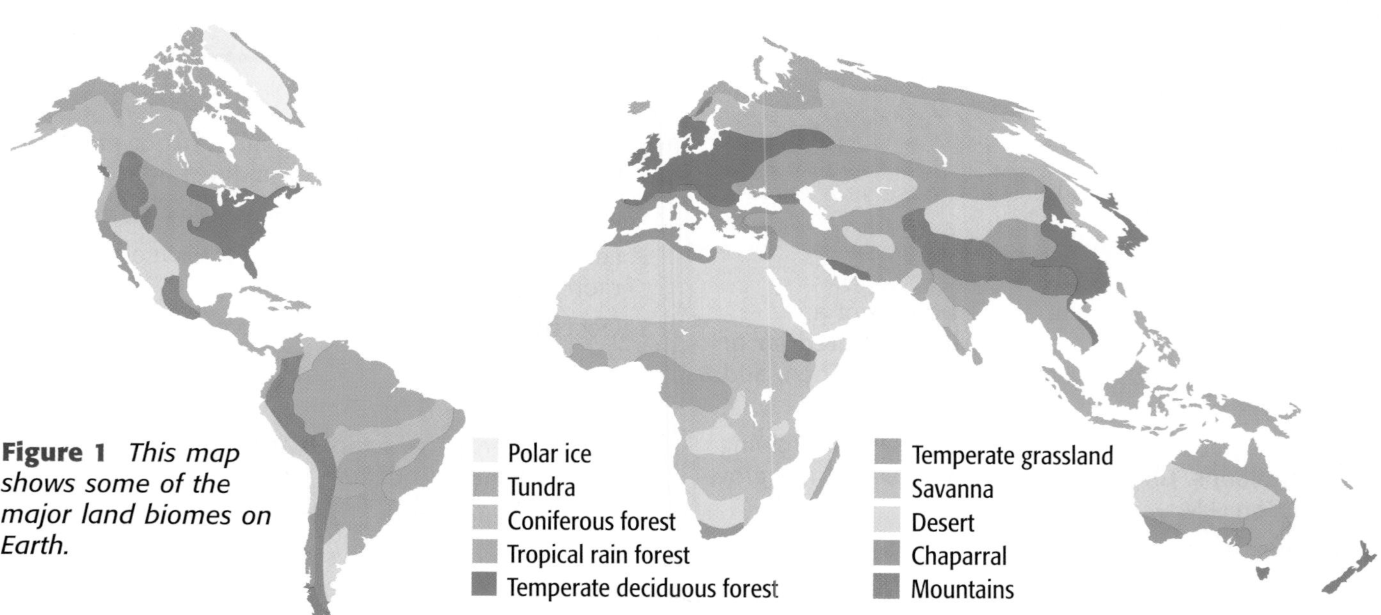

Figure 1 *This map shows some of the major land biomes on Earth.*

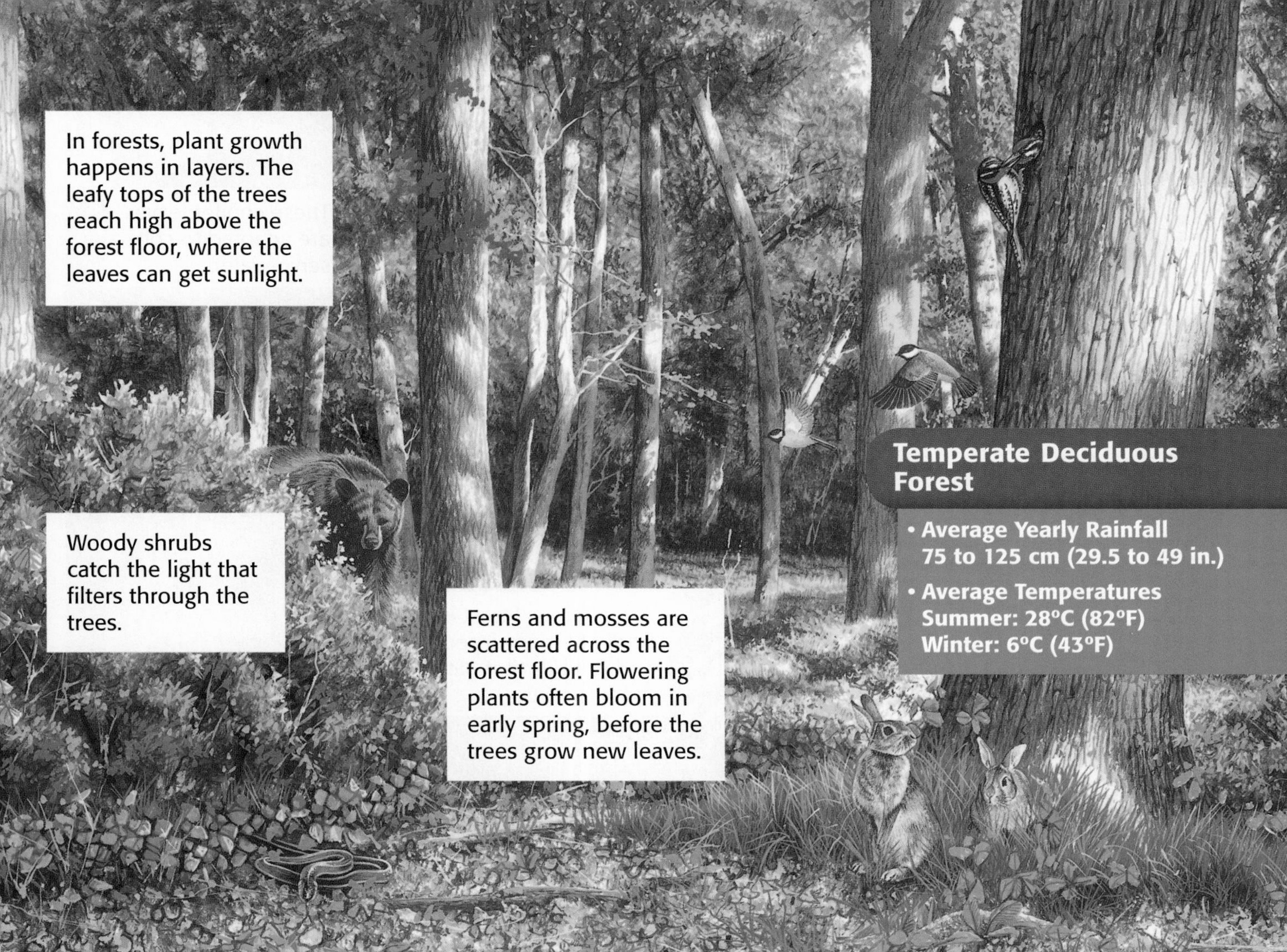

In forests, plant growth happens in layers. The leafy tops of the trees reach high above the forest floor, where the leaves can get sunlight.
Woody shrubs catch the light that filters through the trees.
Ferns and mosses are scattered across the forest floor. Flowering plants often bloom in early spring, before the trees grow new leaves.
Temperate Deciduous Forest
• Average Yearly Rainfall 75 to 125 cm (29.5 to 49 in.)
• Average Temperatures Summer: 28°C (82°F) Winter: 6°C (43°F)

Figure 2 *In a temperate deciduous forest, mammals, birds, and reptiles thrive on the many leaves, seeds, nuts, and insects.*

Forests

Forest biomes are often found in areas that have mild temperatures and plenty of rain. The kind of forest biome that develops depends on an area's temperatures and rainfall. Three forest biomes are temperate deciduous (dee SIJ oo uhs) forests, coniferous (koh NIF uhr uhs) forests, and tropical rain forests.

Temperate Deciduous Forests

Have you seen leaves change colors in the fall? Have you seen trees lose all of their leaves? If so, you have seen trees that are deciduous. The word *deciduous* comes from a Latin word that means "to fall off." Deciduous trees shed their leaves to save water during the winter or during the dry season. As shown in **Figure 2,** a variety of animals, such as bears, snakes, and woodpeckers, live in temperate deciduous forests.

Reading Check **How does the word *deciduous* describe temperate deciduous forests?** (*See the Appendix for answers to Reading Checks.*)

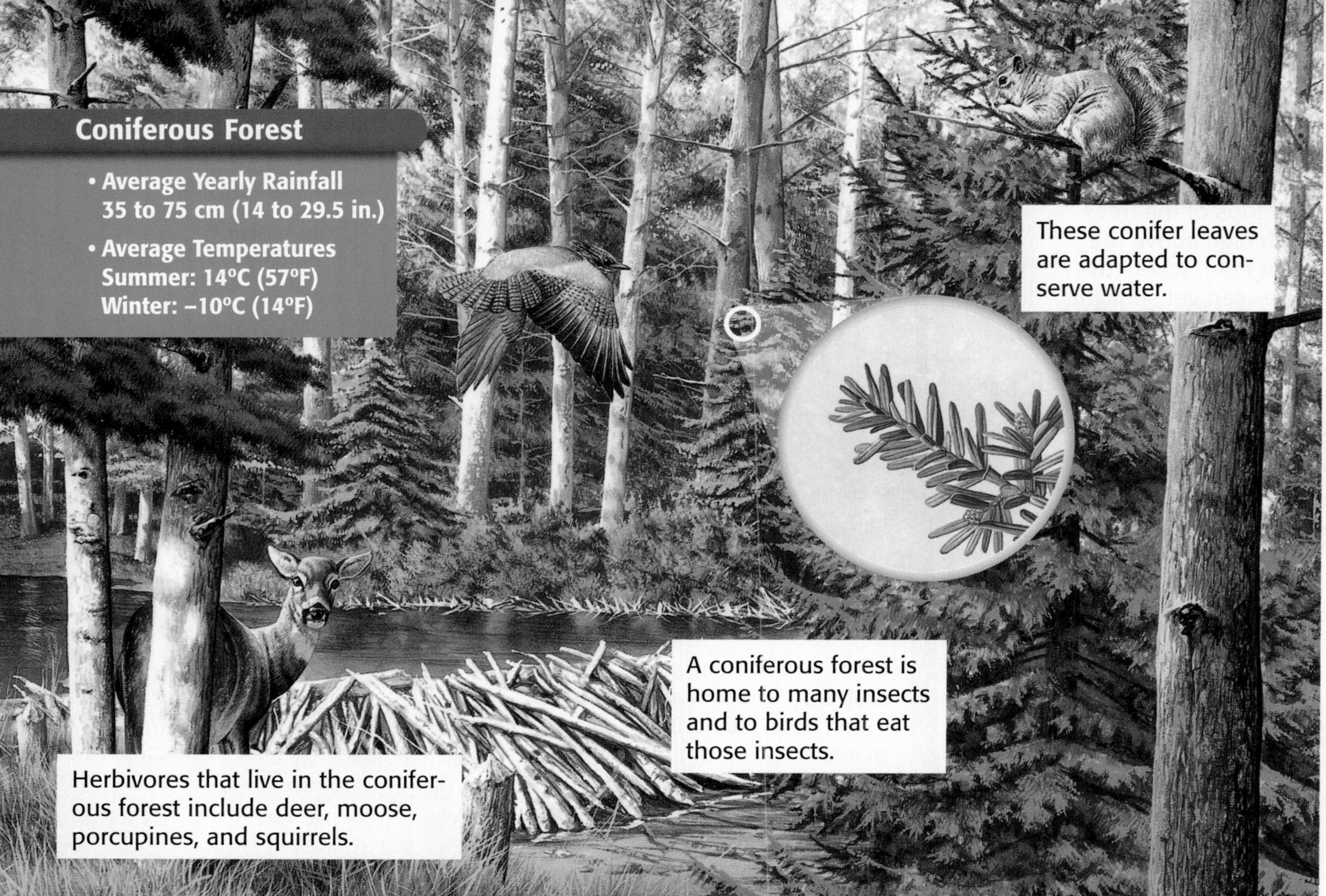

Coniferous Forest
• Average Yearly Rainfall
35 to 75 cm (14 to 29.5 in.)
• Average Temperatures
Summer: 14°C (57°F)
Winter: –10°C (14°F)
These conifer leaves are adapted to conserve water.
A coniferous forest is home to many insects and to birds that eat those insects.
Herbivores that live in the coniferous forest include deer, moose, porcupines, and squirrels.

Figure 3 *Many animals that live in a coniferous forest survive the harsh winters by hibernating or migrating to a warmer climate for the winter.*

Coniferous Forests

Most of the trees in a coniferous forest are called *conifers*. Conifers produce seeds in cones. Conifers also have special leaves that are shaped like needles. The leaves have a thick, waxy coating. This waxy coating has three functions. First, it helps keep conifer leaves from drying out. Second, the waxy coating protects needles from being damaged by cold winter temperatures. Finally, the waxy coating allows most conifers to keep many of their leaves year-round. So, most conifers do not change very much from summer to winter. Trees that stay green all year and do not lose all of their leaves at one time are known as *evergreen trees*.

Figure 3 shows a coniferous forest and some of the animals that live there. Squirrels and insects live in coniferous forests. Birds, such as finches, chickadees, and jays, are common in these forests. Herbivores, such as porcupines, elk, and moose, also live in coniferous forests. The ground beneath large conifers is often covered by a thick layer of needles. Also, very little light reaches the ground. So, few large plants can grow beneath these trees.

Reading Check **What is another name for most conifers? What are some animals that live in coniferous forests?**

Tropical Rain Forests

Tropical rain forests have more biological diversity than other places on Earth have. This means that rain forests have more kinds of plants and animals than any other land biome. For example, more than 100 different kinds of trees may grow in an area about one-fourth the size of a football field. Many animals live on the ground. But most animals live in the *canopy,* or the treetops. Many different animals live in the canopy. For example, nearly 1,400 species of birds live in the rain-forest canopy. **Figure 4** shows some of the diversity of the tropical rain forest.

Because of its diversity, the rain forest may seem as if it has nutrient-rich soil. But most of the nutrients in the tropical rain forest are found in the plants. The soil is actually very thin and poor in nutrients. Because the soil is so thin, many trees grow above-ground roots for extra support.

Figure 4 *Tropical rain forests have a greater variety of organisms than any other biome.*

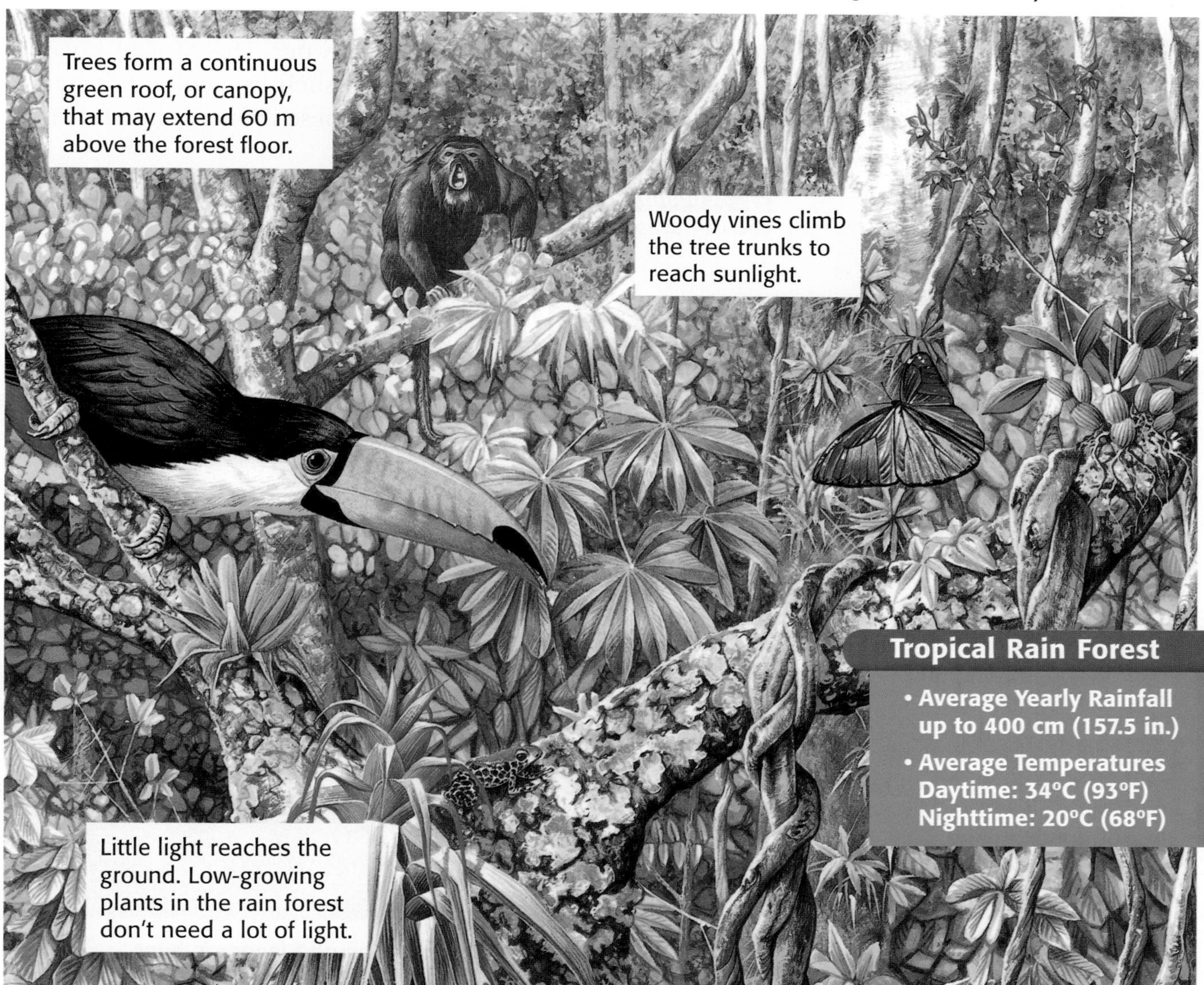

Trees form a continuous green roof, or canopy, that may extend 60 m above the forest floor.
Woody vines climb the tree trunks to reach sunlight.
Little light reaches the ground. Low-growing plants in the rain forest don't need a lot of light.
Tropical Rain Forest
• Average Yearly Rainfall up to 400 cm (157.5 in.)
• Average Temperatures Daytime: 34°C (93°F) Nighttime: 20°C (68°F)

Grasslands

Grasslands have many names, such as *steppes, prairies,* and *pampas*. Grasslands are found on every continent but Antarctica. They are often flat or have gently rolling hills.

Temperate Grasslands

Temperate grassland plants include grasses and other flowering plants. Temperate grasslands have few trees. Fires, drought, and grazing prevent the growth of trees and shrubs. Temperate grasslands support small seed-eating animals, such as prairie dogs and mice. Large grass eaters, such as the North American bison shown in **Figure 5,** also live in temperate grasslands.

Temperate Grassland

- Average Yearly Rainfall 25 to 75 cm (10 to 29.5 in.)
- Average Temperatures Summer: 30°C (86°F) Winter: 0°C (32°F)

Figure 5 *Bison once roamed North American temperate grasslands in great herds.*

Savannas

A grassland that has scattered clumps of trees and seasonal rains is called a **savanna.** Savannas are found in parts of Africa, India, and South America. During the dry season, savanna grasses dry out and turn yellow. But the grasses' deep roots survive for many months without water. The African savanna is home to many large herbivores, such as elephants, giraffes, zebras, and wildebeests. Some of these animals are shown in **Figure 6.**

Reading Check **What happens to grasses on a savanna during the dry season?**

savanna a grassland that often has scattered trees and that is found in tropical and subtropical areas where seasonal rains, fires, and drought happen

CONNECTION TO Environmental Science

WRITING SKILL **Mountains and Climate**

Mountains can affect the climate of the land around them. Research the ecosystems around a mountain range. In your **science journal,** write a report describing how the mountains affect the climate of the surrounding land.

Savanna
• Average Yearly Rainfall
150 cm (59 in.)
• Average Temperatures
Dry season: 34°C (93°F)
Wet season: 16°C (61°F)

Figure 6 *In the African savanna, lions and leopards hunt zebras and wildebeests.*

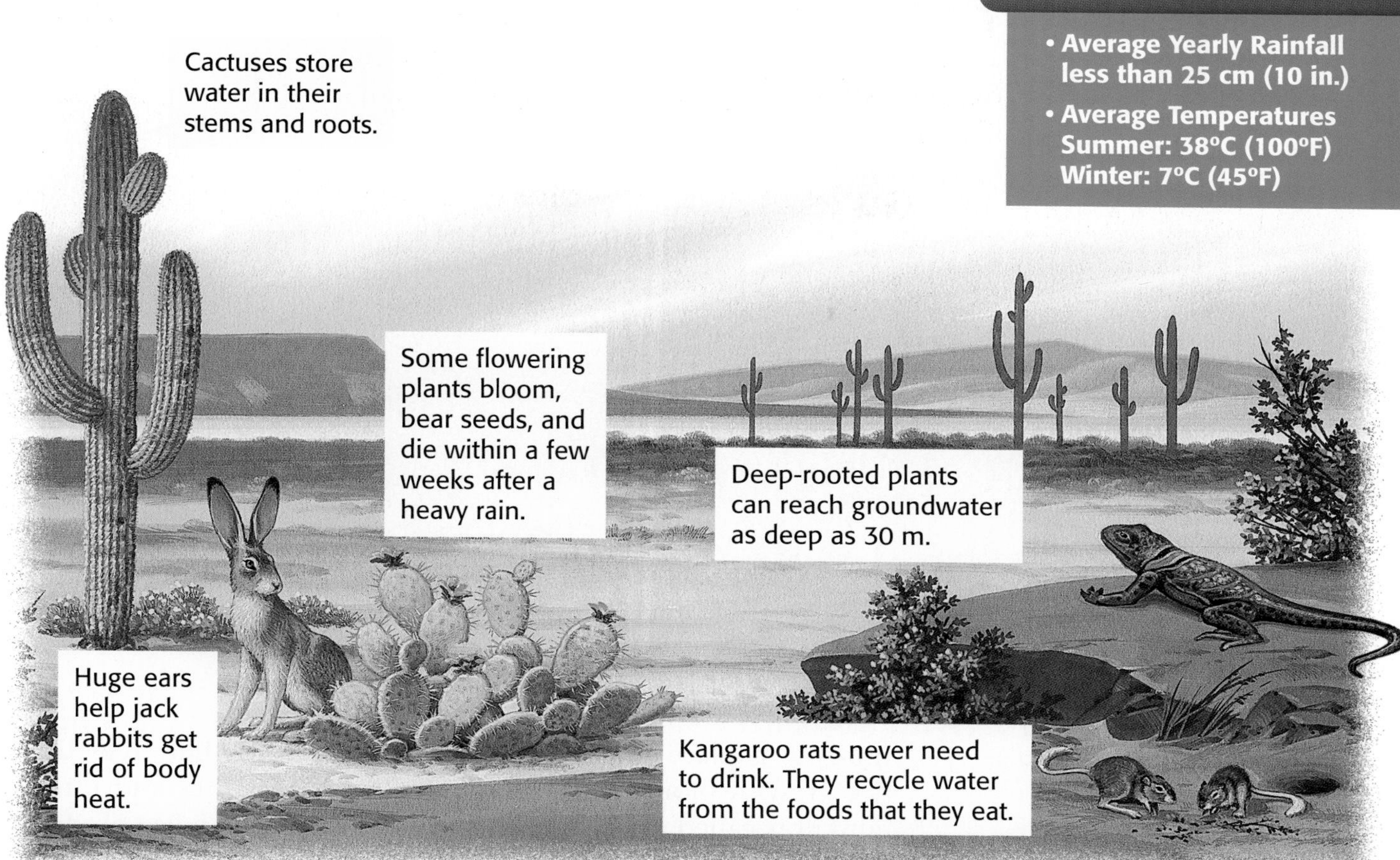

Desert
• Average Yearly Rainfall less than 25 cm (10 in.)
• Average Temperatures
Summer: 38°C (100°F)
Winter: 7°C (45°F)
Cactuses store water in their stems and roots.
Some flowering plants bloom, bear seeds, and die within a few weeks after a heavy rain.
Deep-rooted plants can reach groundwater as deep as 30 m.
Huge ears help jack rabbits get rid of body heat.
Kangaroo rats never need to drink. They recycle water from the foods that they eat.

Figure 7 *The residents of the desert biome have special adaptations to survive in a dry climate.*

Deserts

Biomes that are very dry and often very hot are called **deserts.** Many kinds of plants and animals are found only in deserts. These organisms have special adaptations to live in a hot, dry climate. For example, plants grow far apart so that the plants won't have to compete with each other for water. Some plants have shallow, widespread roots that grow just under the surface. These roots let plants take up water during a storm. Other desert plants, such as cactuses, have fleshy stems and leaves. These fleshy structures store water. The leaves of desert plants also have a waxy coating that helps prevent water loss.

desert a region that has little or no plant life, long periods without rain, and extreme temperatures; usually found in hot climates

Animals also have adaptations for living in the desert. Most desert animals are active only at night, when temperatures are cooler. Some animals, such as the spadefoot toad, bury themselves in the ground and are dormant during the dry season. Doing so helps these animals escape the heat of summer. Animals such as desert tortoises eat flowers or leaves and store the water under their shells. **Figure 7** shows how some desert plants and animals live in the heat with little water.

Reading Check What are some adaptations of desert plants?

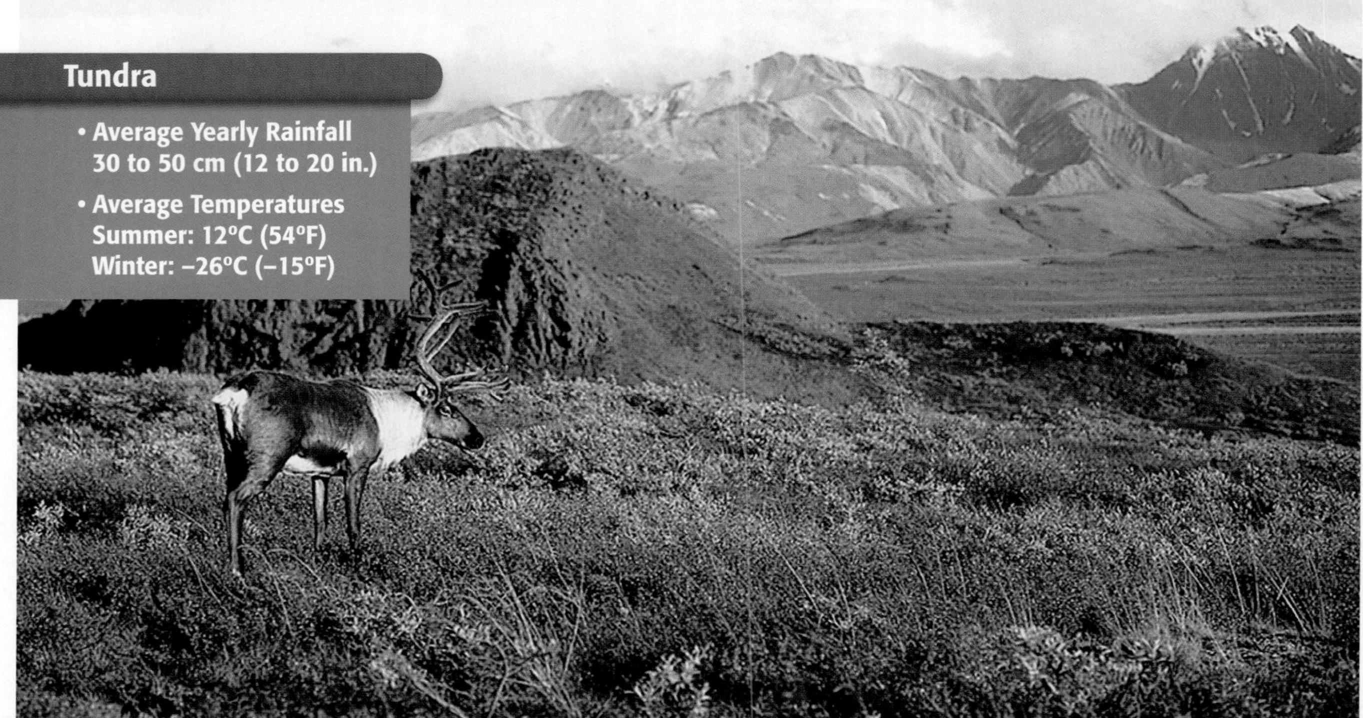

Figure 8 *During winters in the tundra, caribou migrate to grazing grounds that have a more-plentiful supply of food.*

Tundra

Imagine a place on Earth where it is so cold that trees do not grow. A biome that has very cold temperatures and little rainfall is called a **tundra.** Two types of tundra are polar tundra and alpine tundra.

tundra a treeless plain found in the Arctic, in the Antarctic, or on the tops of mountains that is characterized by very low winter temperatures and short, cool summers

Polar Tundra

Polar tundra is found near the North and South Poles. In polar tundra, the layer of soil beneath the surface soil stays frozen all the time. This layer is called *permafrost*. During the short, cool summers, only the surface soil thaws. The layer of thawed soil is too shallow for deep-rooted plants to live. So, shallow-rooted plants, such as grasses and small shrubs, are common. Mosses and lichens (LIE kuhnz) grow beneath these plants. The thawed soil above the permafrost becomes muddy. Insects, such as mosquitoes, lay eggs in the mud. Birds feed on these insects. Other tundra animals include musk oxen, wolves, and caribou, such as the one shown in **Figure 8.**

Local Ecosystems

WRITING SKILL With a parent, explore the ecosystems around your home. What kinds of plants and animals live in your area? In your **science journal,** write a short essay describing the plants and animals in the ecosystems near your home.

Alpine Tundra

Alpine tundra is similar to arctic tundra. Alpine tundra also has permafrost. But alpine tundra is found at the top of tall mountains. Above an elevation called the *tree line*, trees cannot grow on a mountain. Alpine tundra is found above the tree line. Alpine tundra gets plenty of sunlight and precipitation.

Reading Check What is alpine tundra?

SECTION Review

Summary

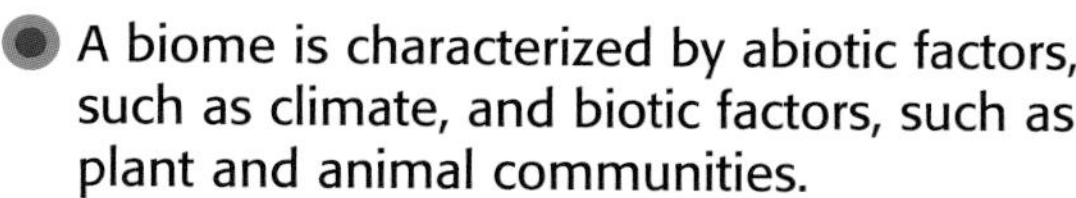

- A biome is characterized by abiotic factors, such as climate, and biotic factors, such as plant and animal communities.
- Three forest biomes are temperate deciduous forests, coniferous forests, and tropical rain forests.
- Grasslands are areas where grasses are the main plants. Temperate grasslands have hot summers and cold winters. Savannas have wet and dry seasons.
- Deserts are very dry and often very hot. Desert plants and animals competing for the limited water supply have special adaptations for survival.
- Tundras are cold areas that have very little rainfall. Permafrost, the layer of frozen soil below the surface of arctic tundra, determines the kinds of plants and animals that live on the tundra.

Using Key Terms

1. Use each of the following terms in a separate sentence: *biome* and *tundra*.
2. In your own words, write a definition for each of the following terms: *savanna* and *desert*.

Understanding Key Ideas

3. If you visited a savanna, you would most likely see
   - **a.** large herds of grazing animals, such as zebras, gazelles, and wildebeests.
   - **b.** dense forests stretching from horizon to horizon.
   - **c.** snow and ice throughout most of the year.
   - **d.** trees that form a continuous green roof, called the *canopy*.
4. Components of a desert ecosystem include
   - **a.** a hot, dry climate.
   - **b.** plants that grow far apart.
   - **c.** animals that are active mostly at night.
   - **d.** All of the above
5. List seven land biomes that are found on Earth.
6. What are two things that characterize a biome?

Critical Thinking

7. **Making Inferences** While excavating an area in the desert, a scientist discovers the fossils of very large trees and ferns. What might the scientist conclude about biomes in this area?
8. **Analyzing Ideas** Tundra receives very little rainfall. Could tundra accurately be called a *frozen desert*? Explain your answer.

Interpreting Graphics

Use the bar graph below to answer the questions that follow.

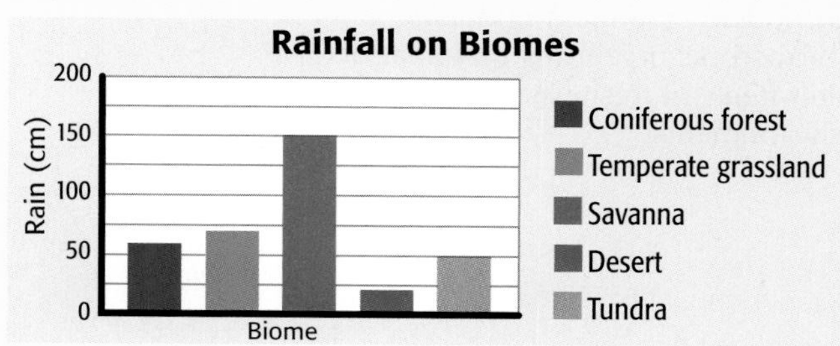

9. Which biomes receive 50 cm or more of rain each year?
10. Which biome receives the smallest amount of rain? the largest amount of rain?

SCILINKS
NSTA
Developed and maintained by the National Science Teachers Association
For a variety of links related to this chapter, go to www.scilinks.org
Topic: Forests
SciLinks code: HSM0609

SECTION 2

Marine Ecosystems

READING WARM-UP

Objectives

- List three abiotic factors that shape marine ecosystems.
- Describe four major ocean zones.
- Describe five marine ecosystems.

Terms to Learn

plankton
estuary

READING STRATEGY

Prediction Guide Before reading this section, write the title of each heading in this section. Next, under each heading, write what you think you will learn.

What covers almost three-fourths of Earth's surface? What holds both the largest animals and some of the smallest organisms on Earth?

If your answer to both questions is *oceans,* you are correct! Earth's oceans contain many different ecosystems. Scientists call ecosystems in the ocean *marine ecosystems.*

Life in the Ocean

Marine ecosystems are shaped by abiotic factors. These factors include water temperature, water depth, and the amount of sunlight that passes into the water. The animals and plants that live in the ocean come in all shapes and sizes. The largest animals on Earth, blue whales, live in the ocean. So do trillions of tiny plankton. **Plankton** are tiny organisms that float near the surface of the water. Many plankton are producers. They use photosynthesis to make their own food. Plankton form the base of the ocean's food chains. **Figure 1** shows plankton and an animal that relies on plankton for food.

Reading Check What are plankton? How are they important to marine ecosystems? (*See the Appendix for answers to Reading Checks.*)

plankton the mass of mostly microscopic organisms that float or drift freely in freshwater and marine environments

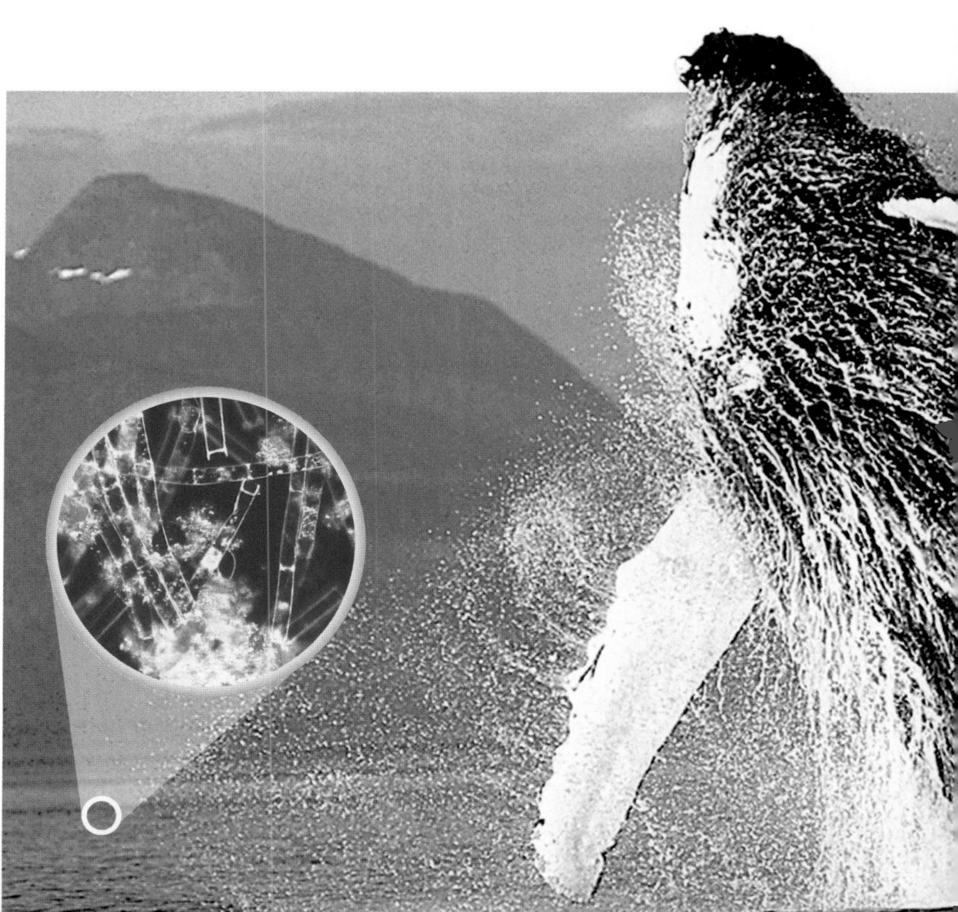

Figure 1 *Marine ecosystems support a broad diversity of life. Humpback whales rely on plankton for food.*

Temperature

The temperature of ocean water decreases as the depth of the water increases. However, the temperature change is not gradual. **Figure 2** shows the three temperature zones of ocean water. Notice that the temperature of the water in the surface zone is much warmer than in the rest of the ocean. Temperatures in the surface zone vary with latitude. Areas of the ocean along the equator are warmer than areas closer to the poles. Surface zone temperatures also vary with the time of year. During the summer, the Northern Hemisphere is tilted toward the sun. So, the surface zone is warmer than it is during the winter.

Temperature affects the animals that live in marine ecosystems. For example, fishes that live near the poles have adaptations to live in near-freezing water. In contrast, animals that live in coral reefs need warm water to live. Some animals, such as whales, migrate from cold areas to warm areas of the ocean to reproduce. Water temperature also affects whether some animals, such as barnacles, can eat. If the water is too hot or too cold, these animals may not be able to eat. A sudden change in temperature may cause these animals to die.

Reading Check **How does temperature affect marine animals?**

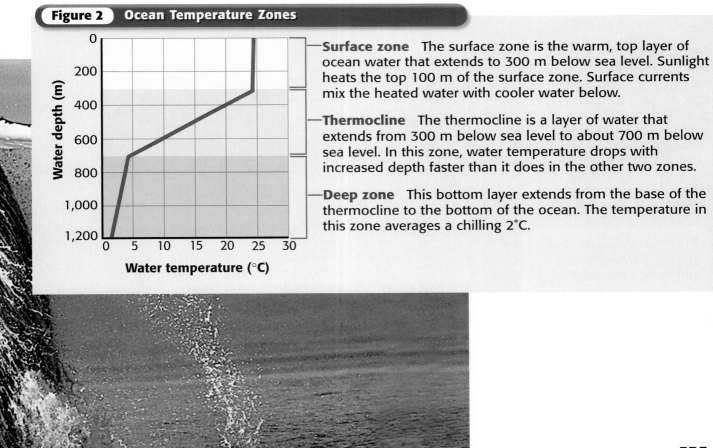

Figure 2 **Ocean Temperature Zones**

Surface zone The surface zone is the warm, top layer of ocean water that extends to 300 m below sea level. Sunlight heats the top 100 m of the surface zone. Surface currents mix the heated water with cooler water below.

Thermocline The thermocline is a layer of water that extends from 300 m below sea level to about 700 m below sea level. In this zone, water temperature drops with increased depth faster than it does in the other two zones.

Deep zone This bottom layer extends from the base of the thermocline to the bottom of the ocean. The temperature in this zone averages a chilling 2°C.

Depth and Sunlight

In addition to water temperature, life in the ocean is affected by water depth and the amount of sunlight that passes into the water. The major ocean zones are shown in **Figure 3.**

The Intertidal Zone

The intertidal zone is the place where the ocean meets the land. This area is exposed to the air for part of the day. Waves are always crashing on the rock and sand. The animals that live in the intertidal zone have adaptations to survive exposure to air and to keep from being washed away by the waves.

The Neritic Zone

As you move farther away from shore, into the neritic zone (nee RIT ik ZOHN), the water becomes deeper. The ocean floor starts to slope downward. The water is warm and receives a lot of sunlight. Many interesting plants and animals, such as corals, sea turtles, fishes, and dolphins, live in this zone.

Figure 3 *The life in a marine ecosystem depends on water temperature, water depth, and the amount of sunlight the area receives.*

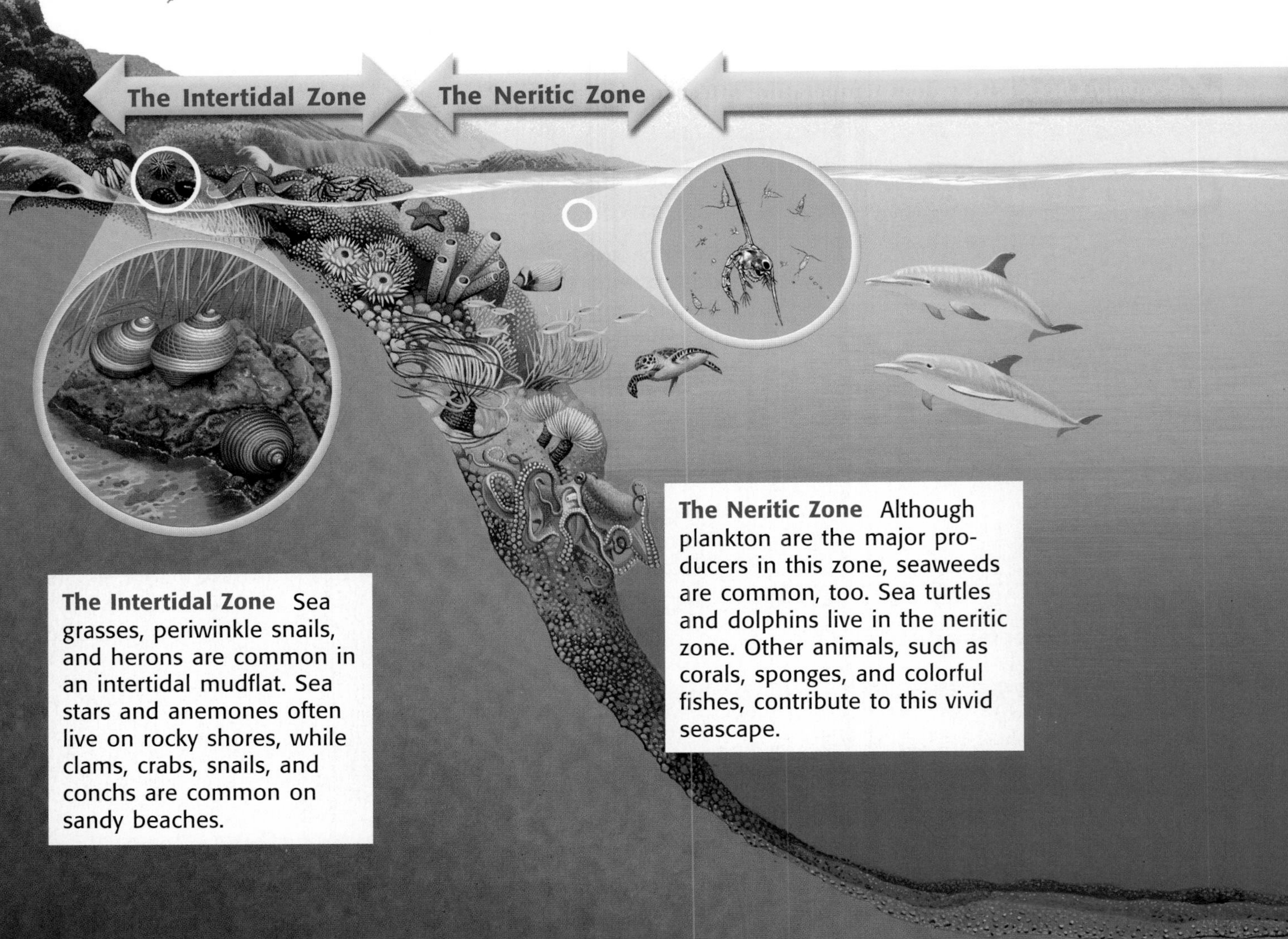

The Intertidal Zone Sea grasses, periwinkle snails, and herons are common in an intertidal mudflat. Sea stars and anemones often live on rocky shores, while clams, crabs, snails, and conchs are common on sandy beaches.

The Neritic Zone Although plankton are the major producers in this zone, seaweeds are common, too. Sea turtles and dolphins live in the neritic zone. Other animals, such as corals, sponges, and colorful fishes, contribute to this vivid seascape.

The Oceanic Zone

In the oceanic zone, the sea floor drops sharply. This zone contains the deep water of the open ocean. Plankton can be found near the water surface. Animals, such as fishes, whales, and sharks, are found in the oceanic zone. Some animals in this zone live in very deep water. These animals often get food from material that sinks down from the ocean surface.

The Benthic Zone

The benthic zone is the ocean floor. The deepest parts of the benthic zone do not get any sunlight. They are also very cold. Animals, such as fishes, worms, and crabs, have special adaptations to the deep, dark water. Many of these organisms get food by eating material that sinks from above. Some organisms, such as bacteria, get energy from chemicals that escape from thermal vents on the ocean floor. Thermal vents form at cracks in the Earth's crust.

Reading Check **How do animals in the benthic zone get food?**

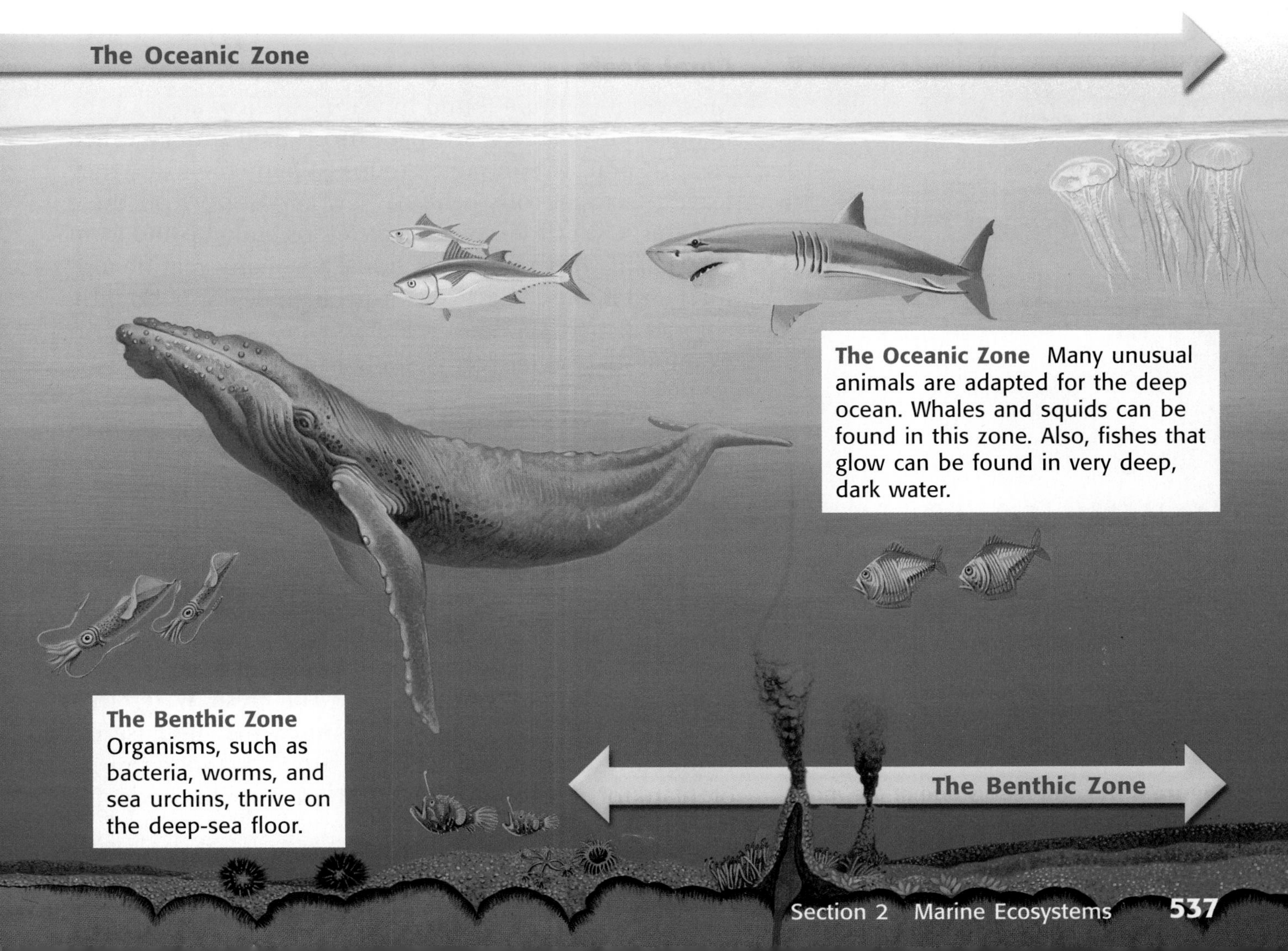

The Oceanic Zone Many unusual animals are adapted for the deep ocean. Whales and squids can be found in this zone. Also, fishes that glow can be found in very deep, dark water.

The Benthic Zone Organisms, such as bacteria, worms, and sea urchins, thrive on the deep-sea floor.

A Closer Look

Life on Earth depends on the ocean. Through evaporation, the ocean provides most of the water that makes up Earth's precipitation. Ocean temperatures and currents can affect world climates and wind patterns. Humans and many animals depend on the ocean for food.

Many ecosystems exist in the ocean. Some of these ecosystems are found on or near the shore. Other ecosystems are found in the middle of the ocean or near the poles.

Intertidal Areas

estuary an area where fresh water from rivers mixes with salt water from the ocean

Intertidal areas are found near the shore. These areas include mudflats, sandy beaches, and rocky shores. Intertidal organisms must be able to live both underwater and out of water. The organisms that live in mudflats include worms and crabs. Shorebirds feed on these animals. Organisms that live on sandy beaches include worms, clams, crabs, and plankton. On rocky shores, organisms have adaptations to keep from being swept away by crashing waves. Some organisms use rootlike structures called *holdfasts* to attach themselves to the rocks. Other organisms attach themselves to rocks by releasing a special glue.

Coral Reefs

Most coral reefs are found in warm, shallow areas of the neritic zone. The reefs are made up of small animals called *corals*. Corals live in large groups. When corals die, they leave their skeletons behind. New corals grow on these remains. Over time, layers of skeletons build up and form a reef. This reef provides a home for many marine animals and plants. These organisms include algae, brightly colored fishes, sponges, sea stars, and sea urchins. An example of a coral reef is shown in **Figure 4.**

Figure 4 *A coral reef is one of the most biologically diverse ecosystems on Earth.*

Reading Check How do coral reefs develop?

Estuaries

An area where fresh water from streams and rivers spills into the ocean is called an **estuary** (ES tyoo er ee). In estuaries, the fresh water from rivers and the salt water from the ocean are always mixing. Therefore, the amount of salt in the water is always changing. Plants and animals that live in estuaries must be able to survive the changing concentrations of salt. The fresh water that spills into an estuary is rich in nutrients. Because estuaries are so nutrient rich, they support large numbers of plankton. The plankton, in turn, provide food for many animals.

The Sargasso Sea

An ecosystem called the *Sargasso Sea* (sahr GAS oh SEE) is found in the middle of the Atlantic Ocean. This ecosystem contains floating rafts of algae called *sargassum* (sahr GAS uhm). Many of the animals that live in the Sargasso Sea are the same color as sargassum, which helps the animals hide from predators.

Polar Ice

The Arctic Ocean and the ocean around Antarctica make up another marine ecosystem. These icy waters are rich in nutrients, which support large numbers of plankton. Many fishes, birds, and mammals rely on the plankton for food. Animals, such as polar bears and penguins, live on the polar ice.

SECTION Review

Summary

- Abiotic factors that affect marine ecosystems are water temperature, water depth, and the amount of light that passes into the water.
- Plankton form the base of the ocean's food chains.
- Four ocean zones are the intertidal zone, the neritic zone, the oceanic zone, and the benthic zone.
- The ocean contains unique ecosystems, including intertidal areas, coral reefs, estuaries, the Sargasso Sea, and polar ice.

Using Key Terms

1. Use each of the following terms in a separate sentence: *plankton* and *estuary*.

Understanding Key Ideas

2. Water temperature
   a. has no effect on the animals in a marine ecosystem.
   b. affects the types of organisms that can live in a marine ecosystem.
   c. decreases gradually as water gets deeper.
   d. increases as water gets deeper.
3. What are three abiotic factors that affect marine ecosystems?
4. Describe four major ocean zones.
5. Describe five marine ecosystems. For each ecosystem, list an organism that lives there.

Math Skills

6. The ocean covers about 71% of the Earth's surface. If the total surface area of the Earth is about 510 million square kilometers, how many square kilometers are covered by the ocean?

Critical Thinking

7. **Making Inferences** Animals in the Sargasso Sea hide from predators by blending in with the sargassum. Color is only one way to blend in. What is another way that animals can blend in with sargassum?
8. **Identifying Relationships** Many fishes and other organisms that live in the deep ocean produce light. What are two ways in which this light might be useful?
9. **Applying Concepts** Imagine that you are studying animals that live in intertidal zones. You just discovered a new animal. Describe the animal and adaptations the animal has to survive in the intertidal zone.

SCiLINKS
NSTA
Developed and maintained by the National Science Teachers Association
For a variety of links related to this chapter, go to www.scilinks.org
Topic: Marine Ecosystems
SciLinks code: HSM0911

SECTION 3

Freshwater Ecosystems

A brook bubbles over rocks. A mighty river thunders through a canyon. A calm swamp echoes with the sounds of frogs and birds. What do these places have in common?

READING WARM-UP

Objectives

- Describe one abiotic factor that affects freshwater ecosystems.
- Describe the three zones of a lake.
- Describe two wetland ecosystems.
- Explain how a lake becomes a forest.

Terms to Learn

littoral zone
open-water zone
deep-water zone
wetland
marsh
swamp

READING STRATEGY

Paired Summarizing Read this section silently. In pairs, take turns summarizing the material. Stop to discuss ideas that seem confusing.

Brooks, rivers, and swamps are examples of freshwater ecosystems. The water in brooks and rivers is often fast moving. In swamps, water moves very slowly. Also, water in swamps is often found in standing pools.

Stream and River Ecosystems

The water in brooks, streams, and rivers may flow from melting ice or snow. Or the water may come from a spring. A spring is a place where water flows from underground to the Earth's surface. Each stream of water that joins a larger stream is called a *tributary* (TRIB yoo TER ee). As more tributaries join a stream, the stream contains more water. The stream becomes stronger and wider. A very strong, wide stream is called a *river*. **Figure 1** shows how a river develops.

Like other ecosystems, freshwater ecosystems are characterized by their abiotic factors. An important abiotic factor in freshwater ecosystems is how quickly water moves.

Streams and rivers are full of life. Plants line the edges of streams and rivers. Fish live in the open waters. And clams and snails live in the mud at the bottom of a stream or river. Organisms that live in fast-moving water have adaptations to keep from being washed away. Some producers, such as algae and moss, are attached to rocks. Consumers, such as tadpoles, use suction disks to hold themselves to rocks. Other consumers, such as insects, live under rocks.

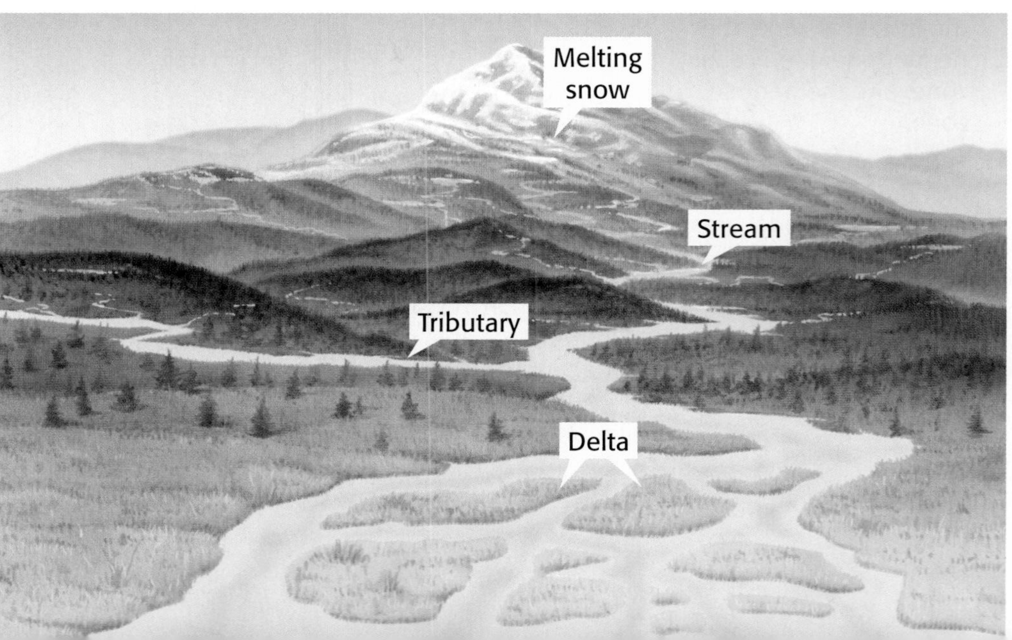

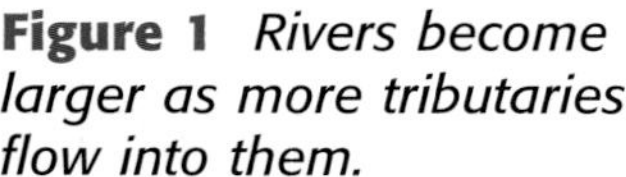

Figure 1 *Rivers become larger as more tributaries flow into them.*

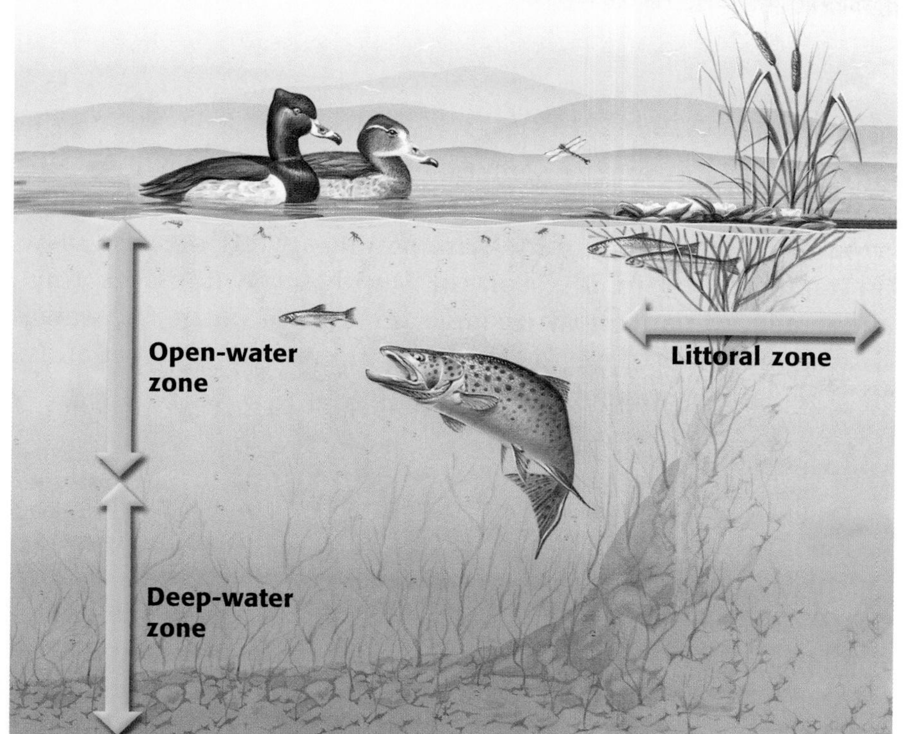

Figure 2 *Ponds and lakes can be divided into three zones. Each zone has different organisms and abiotic factors.*

Pond and Lake Ecosystems

Ponds and lakes have different ecosystems than streams and rivers do. **Figure 2** shows the zones of a typical lake.

Life near Shore

The area of water closest to the edge of a lake or pond is called the **littoral zone** (LIT uh ruhl ZOHN). Sunlight reaches the bottom of the littoral zone. This sunlight makes it possible for algae and plants to grow in the littoral zone. Algae grow beneath the surface of the water in the littoral zone. Plants that grow near the shore include cattails and rushes. Floating leaf plants, such as water lilies, grow farther from the shore. The plants of the littoral zone are home to small animals, such as snails and insects. Clams and worms bury themselves in the mud. Frogs, salamanders, turtles, fish, and snakes also live in this zone.

Life Away from Shore

The area of a lake or pond that extends from the littoral zone across the top of the water is called the **open-water zone.** The open-water zone goes as deep as sunlight can reach. This zone is home to bass, lake trout, and other fishes. Many photosynthetic plankton also live in this area. Beneath the open-water zone is the **deep-water zone,** where no sunlight reaches. Catfish, carp, worms, crustaceans, fungi, and bacteria live here. These organisms often feed on dead organisms that sink from above.

Reading Check **Describe the three zones of a lake.** *(See the Appendix for answers to Reading Checks.)*

Pond-Food Relationships

1. On **index cards,** write the names of some of the plants and animals that live in a typical freshwater pond or small lake. Write one type of organism on each card.
2. Use **yarn** or **string** to connect each organism to its food sources.
3. Describe the food relationships in a pond.

littoral zone the shallow zone of a lake or pond where light reaches the bottom and nurtures plants

open-water zone the zone of a pond or lake that extends from the littoral zone and that is only as deep as light can reach

deep-water zone the zone of a lake or pond below the open-water zone, where no light reaches

Figure 3 *This painted turtle suns itself on a log in a freshwater marsh.*

Wetland Ecosystems

An area of land that is sometimes underwater or whose soil contains a great deal of moisture is called a **wetland.** Wetlands support many different plants and animals. Wetlands also play an important role in flood control. During heavy rains or spring snow melt, wetlands soak up large amounts of water. The water in wetlands also moves deeper into the ground. So, wetlands help replenish underground water supplies.

Marshes

A treeless wetland ecosystem where plants, such as grasses, grow is called a **marsh.** A freshwater marsh is shown in **Figure 3.** Freshwater marshes are often found in shallow areas along the shores of lakes, ponds, rivers, and streams. The plants in a marsh vary depending on the depth of the water and the location of the marsh. Grasses, reeds, bulrushes, and wild rice are common marsh plants. Muskrats, turtles, frogs, and birds also live in marshes.

wetland an area of land that is periodically underwater or whose soil contains a great deal of moisture

marsh a treeless wetland ecosystem where plants such as grasses grow

swamp a wetland ecosystem in which shrubs and trees grow

Swamps

A wetland ecosystem in which trees and vines grow is called a **swamp.** Swamps, as shown in **Figure 4,** are found in low-lying areas and beside slow-moving rivers. Most swamps are flooded part of the year, depending on rainfall. Willows, bald cypresses, and oaks are common swamp trees. Vines, such as poison ivy, grow up tree trunks. Plants, such as orchids, may hang from tree branches. Water lilies and other plants grow in standing water. Many fishes, snakes, and birds also live in swamps.

Reading Check **What is a swamp?**

CONNECTION TO Language Arts

Compound Words A compound word is a word made up of two or more single words. In your **science journal,** define the two words that make up the word *wetland.* Then, define three more compound words.

Figure 4 *The trunks of these trees are adapted to give the trees more support in the wet, soft soil of a swamp.*

From a Lake to a Forest

Did you know that a lake or pond can disappear? How can this happen? Water entering a standing body of water usually carries nutrients and sediment. These materials settle to the bottom of the pond or lake. Dead leaves from overhanging trees and decaying plant and animal life also settle to the bottom. Then, bacteria decompose this material. This process uses oxygen in the water. The loss of oxygen affects the kinds of animals that can survive in the pond or lake. For example, many fishes would not be able to survive with less oxygen in the water.

Over time, the pond or lake is filled with sediment. Plants grow in the new soil. Shallow areas fill in first. So, plants slowly grow closer and closer to the center of the pond or lake. What is left of the lake or pond becomes a wetland, such as a marsh or swamp. Eventually, the wetland can become a forest.

Reading Check **What happens to some of the animals in a pond as the pond becomes a forest?**

For another activity related to this chapter, go to **go.hrw.com** and type in the keyword **HL5ECOW.**

SECTION Review

Summary

- An important abiotic factor in freshwater ecosystems is how quickly water moves.
- The three zones of a pond or lake are the littoral zone, the open-water zone, and the deep-water zone.
- Wetlands include marshes and swamps.
- Sediments and decaying plant and animal matter build up in a pond. Over time, the pond may fill completely and become a forest.

Using Key Terms

1. Use the following terms in the same sentence: *wetland, marsh,* and *swamp*.

Understanding Key Ideas

2. A major abiotic factor in freshwater ecosystems is the
   a. source of the water.
   b. speed of the water.
   c. width of the stream or river.
   d. None of the above
3. Describe the three zones of a lake.
4. Explain how a lake can become a forest over time.

Math Skills

5. Sunlight can penetrate a certain lake to a depth of 15 m. The lake is five and a half times deeper than the depth to which light can penetrate. In meters, how deep is the lake?

Critical Thinking

6. **Making Inferences** When bacteria decompose material in a pond, the oxygen in the water may be used up. So, fishes in the pond die. How might the absence of fish lead to a pond filling faster?
7. **Applying Concepts** Imagine a steep, rocky stream. What kinds of adaptations might animals living in this stream have? Explain your answer.

For a variety of links related to this chapter, go to www.scilinks.org

Topic: Freshwater Ecosystems
SciLinks code: HSM0621

Skills Practice Lab

Too Much of a Good Thing?

OBJECTIVES

Draw common pond-water organisms.

Observe the effect of fertilizer on pond-water organisms.

Describe how fertilizer affects the number and type of pond-water organisms over time.

MATERIALS

- beaker, 500 mL
- distilled water, 2.25 L
- eyedropper
- fertilizer
- gloves, protective
- graduated cylinder, 100 mL
- jars, 1 qt or 1 L (3)
- microscope
- microscope slides with coverslips
- pencil, wax
- plastic wrap
- pond water containing living organisms, 300 mL
- stirring rod

SAFETY

Plants need nutrients, such as phosphates and nitrates, to grow. Phosphates are often found in detergents. Nitrates are often found in animal wastes and fertilizers. When large amounts of these nutrients enter rivers and lakes, algae and plants grow rapidly and then die off. Microorganisms that decompose the dead matter use up oxygen in the water. Without oxygen, fish and other animals die. In this activity, you will observe the effect of fertilizers on organisms that live in pond water.

Procedure

1. Label one jar "Control," the second jar "Fertilizer," and the third jar "Excess fertilizer."
2. Pour 750 mL of distilled water into each jar. To the "Fertilizer" jar, add the amount of fertilizer recommended for 750 mL of water. To the "Excess fertilizer" jar, add 10 times the amount recommended for 750 mL of water. Stir the contents of each jar to dissolve the fertilizer.
3. Obtain a sample of pond water. Stir it gently to make sure that the organisms in it are evenly distributed. Pour 100 mL of pond water into each of the three jars.
4. Observe a drop of water from each jar under the microscope. Draw at least four of the organisms. Determine whether the organisms you see are producers, which are usually green, or consumers, which are usually able to move. Describe the number and type of organisms in the pond water.

Common Pond-Water Organisms

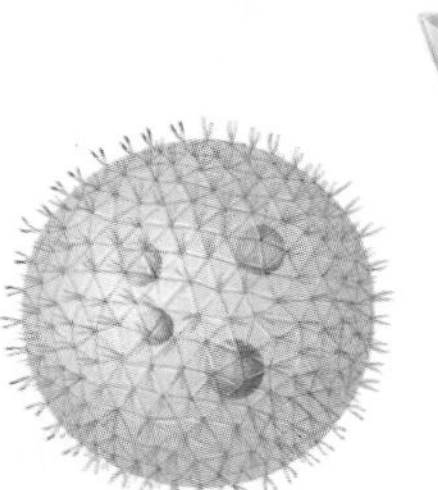

Volvox (producer)

Spirogyra (producer)

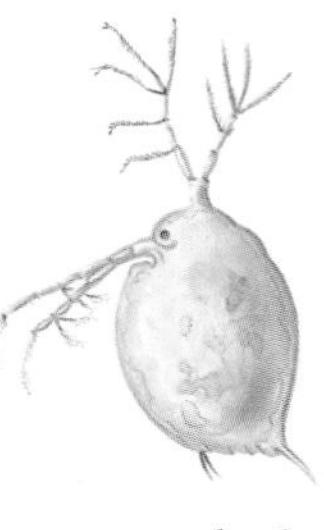

Daphnia (consumer)

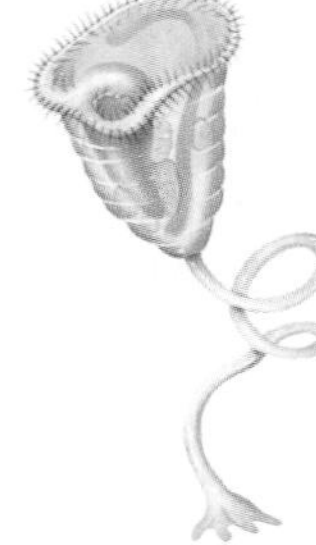

Vorticella (consumer)

5. Cover each jar loosely with plastic wrap. Place the jars near a sunny window but not in direct sunlight.
6. Make a prediction about how the pond organisms will grow in each of the three jars.
7. Make three data tables. Title one table "Control," as shown below. Title another table "Fertilizer," and title the third table "Excess fertilizer."

Control			
Date	Color	Odor	Other observations
	DO NOT WRITE IN BOOK		

8. Observe the jars when you first set them up and once every 3 days for the next 3 weeks. Note the color, the odor, and the presence of organisms. Record your observations.
9. When organisms become visible in the jars, use an eyedropper to remove a sample from each jar. Observe the sample under the microscope. How have the number and type of organisms changed since you first looked at the pond water?
10. At the end of the 3-week period, observe a sample from each jar under the microscope. Draw at least four of the most abundant organisms, and describe how the number and type of organisms have changed since your last microscope observation.

Analyze the Results

1. **Describing Events** After 3 weeks, which jar has the most abundant growth of algae?
2. **Analyzing Data** Did you observe any effects on organisms (other than algae) in the jar with the most abundant algal growth? Explain your answer.

Draw Conclusions

3. **Drawing Conclusions** What may have caused increased growth in the jars?
4. **Evaluating Results** Did your observations match your predictions? Explain your answer.
5. **Interpreting Information** Decaying plant and animal life contribute to the filling of lakes and ponds. How might the rapid filling of lakes and ponds be prevented or slowed?

Chapter Review

USING KEY TERMS

1. In your own words, write a definition for the following terms: *biome* and *tundra*.

2. Use each of the following terms in a separate sentence: *intertidal zone, neritic zone,* and *oceanic zone.*

For each pair of terms, explain how the meanings of the terms differ.

3. *savanna* and *desert*

4. *open-water zone* and *deep-water zone*

5. *marsh* and *swamp*

UNDERSTANDING KEY IDEAS

Multiple Choice

6. Trees that lose their leaves in the winter are called
   - **a.** evergreen trees.
   - **b.** coniferous trees.
   - **c.** deciduous trees.
   - **d.** None of the above

7. In which major ocean zone are plants and animals exposed to air for part of the day?
   - **a.** intertidal zone
   - **b.** neritic zone
   - **c.** oceanic zone
   - **d.** benthic zone

8. An abiotic factor that affects marine ecosystems is
   - **a.** the temperature of the water.
   - **b.** the depth of the water.
   - **c.** the amount of sunlight that passes through the water.
   - **d.** All of the above

9. _____ is a marine ecosystem that includes mudflats, sandy beaches, and rocky shores.
   - **a.** An intertidal area
   - **b.** Polar ice
   - **c.** A coral reef
   - **d.** The Sargasso Sea

Short Answer

10. What are seven land biomes?

11. Explain how a small lake can become a forest.

12. What are two factors that characterize biomes?

13. Describe the three zones of a lake.

14. How do rivers form?

15. What are three abiotic factors in land biomes? three abiotic factors in marine ecosystems? an abiotic factor in fresh-water ecosystems?

CRITICAL THINKING

16 **Concept Mapping** Use the following terms to create a concept map: *plants and animals, tropical rain forest, tundra, biomes, permafrost, canopy, desert,* and *abiotic factors.*

17 **Making Inferences** Plankton use photosynthesis to make their own food. They need sunlight for photosynthesis. Which of the four major ocean zones can support plankton growth? Explain your answer.

18 **Predicting Consequences** Wetlands, such as marshes and swamps, play an important role in flood control. Wetlands also help replenish underground water supplies. Predict what might happen if a wetland dries out.

19 **Analyzing Ideas** A scientist has a new hypothesis. He or she thinks that savannas and deserts are part of one biome rather than two separate biomes. Based on what you've learned, decide if the scientist's hypothesis is correct. Explain your answer.

20 **Applying Concepts** Imagine that you are a scientist. You are studying an area that gets about 100 cm of rain each year. The average summer temperatures are near 30°C. What biome are you in? What are some plants and animals you will likely encounter? If you stayed in this area for the winter, what kind of preparations might you need to make?

INTERPRETING GRAPHICS

Use the graphs below to answer the questions that follow.

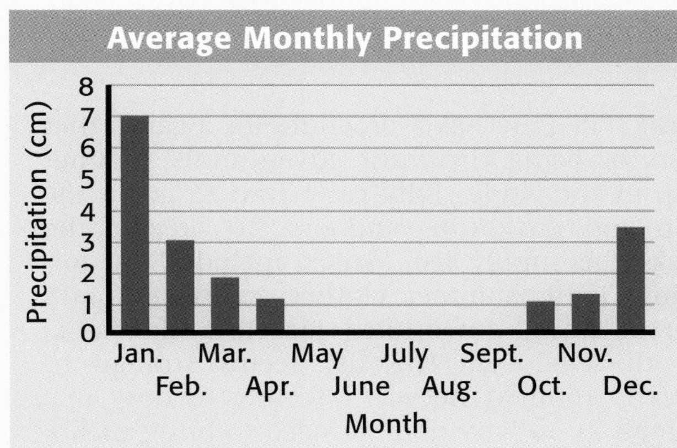

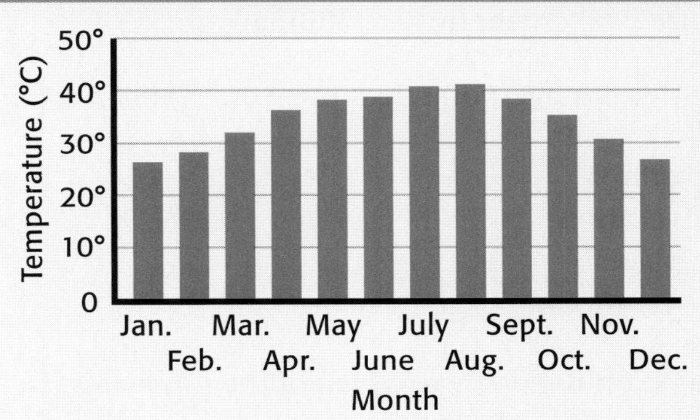

21 Which biome is most likely found in the region described by the graphs above? Explain your answer.

22 How many centimeters of rain fell in the region during the course of the year?

23 Which month is the hottest in the region? the coolest in the region?

24 What is the average monthly precipitation for the month that has the highest average high temperature?

Standardized Test Preparation

READING

Read each of the passages below. Then, answer the questions that follow each passage.

Passage 1 Billy has a brochure for a camp that boasts of being the most adventurous summer camp in the world. Billy can't wait to go to the camp and have fun outdoors. To prepare, he checks the supply list, which includes the following: light, summer clothes; sunscreen; rain gear; a heavy, down-filled jacket; a ski mask; and thick gloves. The list seems strange to Billy. He thought he was traveling to only one destination, so why does he need to bring such a wide variety of clothes? Billy rereads the brochure and learns that the campers will "climb the biomes of the world in just three days." The destination is Africa's tallest mountain, Kilimanjaro.

1. In this passage, what does the word *destination* likely mean?

A camp
B vacation
C place
D mountain

2. Based on the passage, which of the following statements is a fact?

F People ski on Kilimanjaro.
G Kilimanjaro is Africa's tallest mountain.
H It rains a lot on Kilimanjaro.
I The summers are cold on Kilimanjaro.

3. Why might Billy wonder if the brochure was advertising only one location?

A The brochure called the camp the most adventurous summer camp in the world.
B The brochure said that he would need light, summer clothes and sunscreen.
C The brochure said that he would need light, summer clothes and a heavy, down-filled jacket.
D The brochure said that the summers are cold on Kilimanjaro.

Passage 2 The layer of soil above the permafrost is too shallow for plants with deep roots to live. Grasses and shrubs can survive there because they have shallow roots. A sheet of mosses and lichens grows beneath these plants. When the soil above the permafrost thaws, the soil becomes muddy. Muddy soil is an excellent place for insects, such as mosquitoes, to lay eggs. Many birds spend the summer in the tundra to feed on these insects. Tundra animals include caribou, musk oxen, wolves, and other large mammals. Smaller animals, such as lemmings, shrews, and hares, also live in the tundra.

1. Based on the passage, what is one reason for the lack of trees on the tundra?

A Trees need more sunlight than is available.
B The roots of trees need more room than is available.
C The soil above the permafrost becomes too muddy for trees.
D Trees need more water than is available.

2. Based on the passage, which of the following statements about permafrost is true?

F It is a thawed layer of soil.
G It is always moist.
H It is always frozen.
I It is shallow.

3. Based on the passage, which of the following statements is a fact?

A Muddy soil is an excellent place for mosses and lichens to grow.
B Birds fly north to reach the tundra in the summer.
C Caribou and oxen are some of the large mammals that live in the tundra.
D The tundra is a beautiful biome that is home to diverse communities.

INTERPRETING GRAPHICS

The map below shows the biomes of Australia. Use the map to answer the questions that follow.

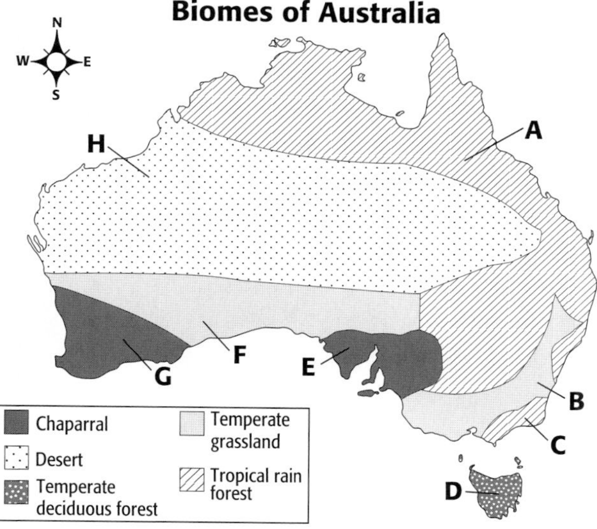

1. Which letters on the map correspond to areas that are chaparral?

A A and C
B B and F
C C and E
D E and G

2. If you lived in the area marked F, which biome would you live in?

F desert
G temperate grassland
H temperate deciduous forest
I tropical rain forest

3. If you wanted to live in a forest, which letters correspond to areas where you could live?

A A, B, and D
B A, C, and D
C B, C, and D
D C, D, and E

4. Which letter corresponds to desert?

F A
G D
H F
I H

MATH

Read each question below, and choose the best answer.

1. Larry wants to buy a glass tabletop for his science lab at home. The glass tabletop is 1 m wide and 2 m long. How many square meters is the surface of the glass tabletop?

A 2 m
B 2 m^2
C 3 m^2
D 6 m^2

2. A scuba diver was exploring a coral reef. She spent 1.5 h exploring on Friday and spent twice as many hours exploring on Saturday. Which equation could be used to find n, the total number of hours that the scuba diver spent exploring on Friday and Saturday?

F $n = 2 \div 1.5$
G $n = 1.5 + (2 \times 1.5)$
H $n = 1.5 + 1.5 + 2$
I $n = 2 \times 1.5$

3. How do you express $5 \times 5 \times 5 \times 5 \times 2 \times 2 \times 2$ in exponential notation?

A $(5 \times 4) + (2 \times 3)$
B $5^4 \times 2^3$
C $4^5 \times 3^2$
D $5^7 \times 2^7$

4. The tropical rain forest receives up to 400 cm of rain per year. The desert receives up to 25 cm of rain per year. Which of the following simplified fractions compares rainfall in the desert to rainfall in the rain forest?

F 1/400
G 1/25
H 1/16
I 16

Science in Action

Scientific Debate

Developing Wetlands

Wetlands are home to many flowering plants, birds, and turtles. Wetlands also play important roles in flood control and maintaining water quality. However, as more people need homes, grocery stores, and other facilities, some wetlands are being developed for construction. State governments often regulate the development of wetlands. Development is not allowed on many environmentally sensitive wetlands. But it is sometimes allowed on wetlands that are less sensitive. However, some people think that all wetlands should be protected, regardless of how sensitive an area is.

Language Arts ACTIVITY

WRITING SKILL Research wetland development on your own. Then, write a letter in which you describe your opinion about the development of wetlands.

Scientific Discoveries

Ocean Vents

Imagine the deepest parts of the ocean. There is no light at all, and it is very cold. Some of the animals that live here have found a unique place to live—vents on the ocean floor. Water seeps into the Earth between plates on the ocean floor. The water is heated and absorbs sulfuric gases. When the water blasts up through ocean vents, it raises the temperature of the ocean hundreds of degrees! Bacteria use the gases from the ocean vents to survive. In turn, mussels and clams feed on the bacteria. Without ocean vents, it would be much more difficult for these organisms to survive.

Math ACTIVITY

A thermal vent increases the temperature of the water around it to 360°C. If the temperature of the water was 2°C, what is the difference in temperature? By what percentage did the water temperature increase?

Careers

Alfonso Alonso-Mejía

Ecologist During the winter, ecologist Alfonso Alonso-Mejía visits sites in central Mexico where millions of monarch butterflies spend the winter. Unfortunately, the monarchs' winter habitat is threatened by human activity. Only nine of the monarchs' wintering sites remain. Five of the sites are set aside as sanctuaries for monarchs, but these sites are threatened by people who cut down fir trees for firewood or for commercial purposes.

Alonso-Mejía discovered that monarchs depend on understory vegetation, bushlike plants that grow beneath fir trees, to survive. When the temperature is low, monarchs can climb understory vegetation until they are at least 10 cm above the ground. This tiny difference in elevation can ensure that monarchs are warm enough to survive. Because of Alonso-Mejía's discovery, Mexican conservationists are working to protect understory vegetation and monarchs.

Social Studies ACTIVITY

Use your school library or the Internet to research the routes that monarchs use to migrate to Mexico. Draw a map illustrating your findings.

To learn more about these Science in Action topics, visit go.hrw.com and type in the keyword HL5ECOF.

Current Science

Check out Current Science® articles related to this chapter by visiting go.hrw.com. Just type in the keyword HL5CS20.

Environmental Problems and Solutions

About the PHOTO

After an oil spill, volunteers try to capture oil-covered penguins. The oil affects the penguins' ability to float. So, oil-covered penguins often won't go into the water to get food. The penguins may also swallow oil, harming their stomach, kidneys, and lungs. Once captured, the penguins are fed activated charcoal. The charcoal helps the penguins get rid of any oil they have swallowed. Then, the birds are washed to remove oil from their feathers.

PRE-READING ACTIVITY

FOLDNOTES

Two-Panel Flip Chart

Before you read the chapter, create the FoldNote entitled "Two-Panel Flip Chart" described in the **Study Skills** section of the Appendix. Label the flaps of the two-panel flip chart with "Environmental problems" and "Environmental solutions." As you read the chapter, write information you learn about each category under the appropriate flap.

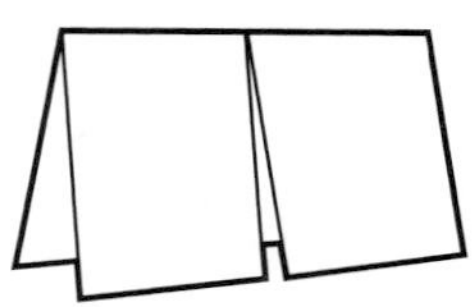

START-UP ACTIVITY

Recycling Paper

In this activity, you will be making paper without cutting down trees. You will be reusing paper that has already been made.

Procedure

1. Tear **two sheets of old newspaper** into small pieces, and put them in a **blender.** Add **1 L of water.** Cover and blend until the mixture is soupy.
2. Fill a **square pan** with **water** to a depth of 2 cm to 3 cm. Place a **wire screen** in the pan. Pour 250 mL of the paper mixture onto the screen, and spread the mixture evenly.
3. Lift the screen out of the water with the paper on it. Drain excess water into the pan.
4. Place the screen inside a **section of newspaper.** Close the newspaper, and turn it over so that the screen is on top of the paper mixture.
5. Cover the newspaper with a **flat board.** Press on the board to squeeze out excess water.
6. Open the newspaper, and let your paper mixture dry overnight. Use your recycled paper to write a note to a friend!

Analysis

1. How is your paper like regular paper? How is it different?
2. What could you do to improve your papermaking methods?

SECTION 1

Environmental Problems

Maybe you've heard warnings about dirty air, water, and soil. Or you've heard about the destruction of rain forests. Do these warnings mean our environment is in trouble?

READING WARM-UP

Objectives

- List five kinds of pollutants.
- Distinguish between renewable and nonrenewable resources.
- Describe the impact of exotic species.
- Explain why human population growth has increased.
- Describe how habitat destruction affects biodiversity.
- Give two examples of how pollution affects humans.

Terms to Learn

pollution
renewable resource
nonrenewable resource
overpopulation
biodiversity

READING STRATEGY

Reading Organizer As you read this section, make a concept map by using the terms above.

In the late 1700s, the Industrial Revolution began. People started to rely more and more on machines. As a result, more harmful substances entered the air, water, and soil.

Pollution

Today, machines don't produce as much pollution as they once did. But there are more sources of pollution today than there once were. **Pollution** is an unwanted change in the environment caused by substances, such as wastes, or forms of energy, such as radiation. Anything that causes pollution is called a *pollutant*. Some pollutants are produced by natural events, such as volcanic eruptions. Many pollutants are human-made. Pollutants may harm plants, animals, and humans.

pollution an unwanted change in the environment caused by substances or forms of energy

Garbage

The average American throws away more trash than the average person in any other nation—about 12 kg of trash a week. This trash often goes to a landfill like the one in **Figure 1.** Other landfills contain medical waste, lead paint, and other hazardous wastes. *Hazardous waste* includes wastes that can catch fire; corrode, or eat through metal; explode; or make people sick. Many industries, such as paper mills and oil refineries, produce hazardous wastes.

Reading Check What is hazardous waste? *(See the Appendix for answers to Reading Checks.)*

Figure 1 *Every year, Americans throw away about 200 million metric tons of garbage.*

Figure 2 *Fertilizer promotes the growth of algae. As dead algae decompose, oxygen in the water is used up. So, fish die because they cannot get oxygen.*

Chemicals

People need and use many chemicals. Some chemicals are used to treat diseases. Other chemicals are used in plastics and preserved foods. Sometimes, the same chemicals that help people may harm the environment. As shown in **Figure 2,** fertilizers and pesticides may pollute soil and water.

CFCs and PCBs are two groups of harmful chemicals. Ozone protects Earth from harmful ultraviolet light. CFCs destroy ozone. CFCs were used in aerosols, refrigerators, and plastics. The second group, PCBs, was once used in appliances and paints. PCBs are poisonous and may cause cancer. Today, the use of CFCs and PCBs is banned. But CFCs are still found in the atmosphere. And PCBs are still found in even the most remote areas on Earth.

CONNECTION TO Chemistry

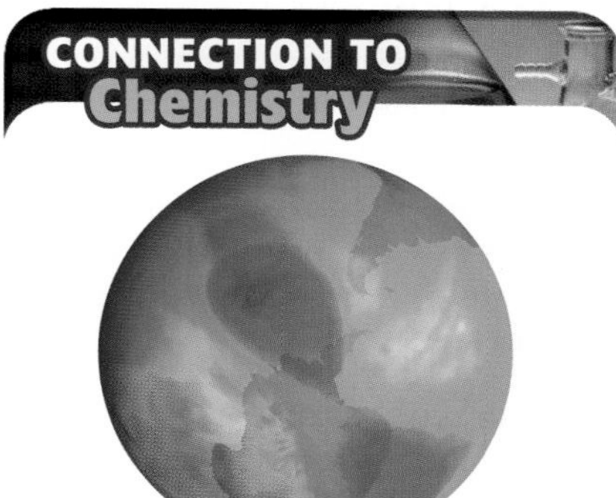

Ozone Holes This image of two holes in the ozone layer (the purple areas over Antarctica) was taken in 2002. Ozone in the stratosphere absorbs most of the ultraviolet light that comes from the sun. Ozone is destroyed by CFCs. Research how CFCs destroy ozone. Make a model demonstrating this process. Then, identify the effects of too much ultraviolet light.

ACTIVITY

High-Powered Wastes

Nuclear power plants provide electricity to many homes and businesses. The plants also produce radioactive wastes. *Radioactive wastes* are hazardous wastes that give off radiation. Some of these wastes take thousands of years to become harmless.

Gases

Earth's atmosphere is made up of a mixture of gases, including carbon dioxide. The atmosphere acts as a protective blanket. It keeps Earth warm enough for life to exist. Since the Industrial Revolution, however, the amount of carbon dioxide in the atmosphere has increased. Carbon dioxide and other air pollutants act like a greenhouse, trapping heat around the Earth. Many scientists think the increase in carbon dioxide has increased global temperatures. If temperatures continue to rise, the polar icecaps could melt. Then, the level of the world's oceans would rise. Coastal areas could flood as a result.

Water Depletion

In one day, millions of liters of water are removed from a water supply. Of this volume, 30 million liters cannot be replaced naturally. Today, the water supply has 60 billion liters of water. In years, how long would the water supply last if water continued to be removed at this rate? If water were removed at the same rate as it was replaced, how long would the water supply last?

Noise

Some pollutants affect the senses. These pollutants include loud noises. Too much noise is not just annoying. Noise pollution affects your ability to hear and think clearly. And it may damage your hearing. People who work in noisy environments, such as in construction zones, must protect their ears.

Resource Depletion

Some of Earth's resources are renewable. But other resources are nonrenewable. A **renewable resource** is one that can be used over and over or has an unlimited supply. Solar and wind energy are renewable resources, as are some kinds of trees. A **nonrenewable resource** is one that cannot be replaced or that can be replaced only over thousands or millions of years. Most minerals and fossil fuels, such as oil and coal, are nonrenewable resources.

renewable resource a natural resource that can be replaced at the same rate at which the resource is consumed

nonrenewable resource a resource that forms at a rate that is much slower than the rate at which it is consumed

Nonrenewable resources cannot last forever. These resources will become more expensive as they become harder to find. The removal of some materials from the Earth also carries a high price tag. This removal may lead to oil spills, loss of habitat, and damage from mining, as shown in **Figure 3.**

Renewable or Nonrenewable?

Some resources once thought to be renewable are becoming nonrenewable. For example, scientists used to think that fresh water was a renewable resource. However, in some areas, water supplies are being used faster than they are being replaced. Eventually, these areas may run out of fresh water. So, scientists are working on ways to keep these water supplies from being used up.

Figure 3 *This area has been mined for iron using a method called* strip mining.

Exotic Species

People are always on the move. Without knowing it, people carry other species with them. Plant seeds, animal eggs, and adult organisms are carried from one part of the world to another. An organism that makes a home for itself in a new place outside its native home is an *exotic species*. Exotic species often thrive in new places. One reason is that they are free from the predators found in their native homes.

Exotic species can become pests and compete with native species. In 2002, the northern snakehead fish was found in a Maryland pond. This fish, shown in **Figure 4,** is from Asia. Scientists are concerned because the northern snakehead eats other fish, amphibians, small birds, and some mammals. It can also move across land. The northern snakehead could invade more lakes and ponds.

Reading Check What are exotic species?

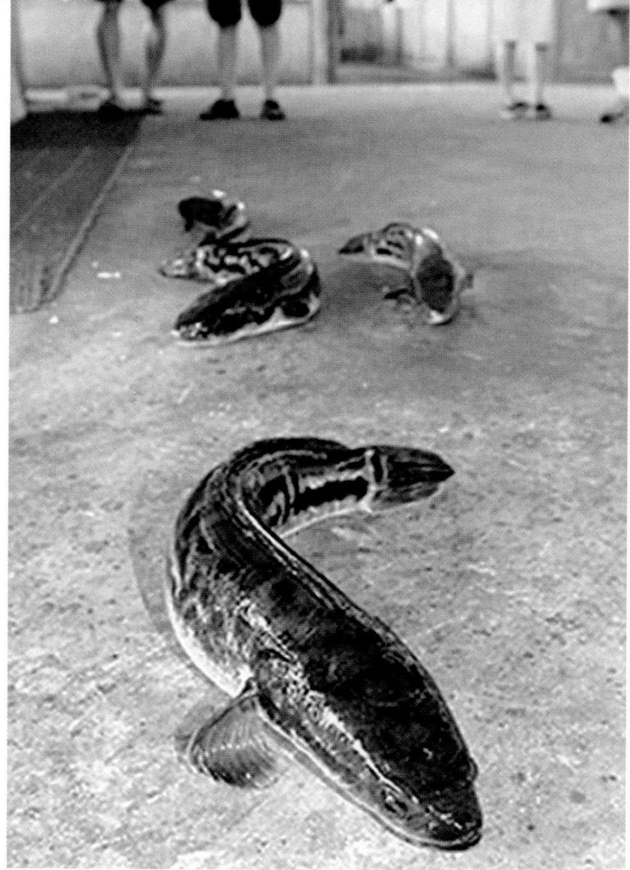

Figure 4 *Northern snakehead fish can move across land in search of water. These fish can survive out of water for up to four days!*

Human Population Growth

Look at **Figure 5.** In 1800, there were 1 billion people on Earth. By 2000, there were more than 6 billion people. Advances in medicine, such as immunizations, and advances in farming have made human population growth possible. Overall, these advances are beneficial. But some people argue that there may eventually be too many people on Earth. **Overpopulation** happens when the number of individuals becomes so large that the individuals can't get the resources they need to survive. However, many scientists think that human population growth will slow down or level off before it reaches that point.

overpopulation the presence of too many individuals in an area for the available resources

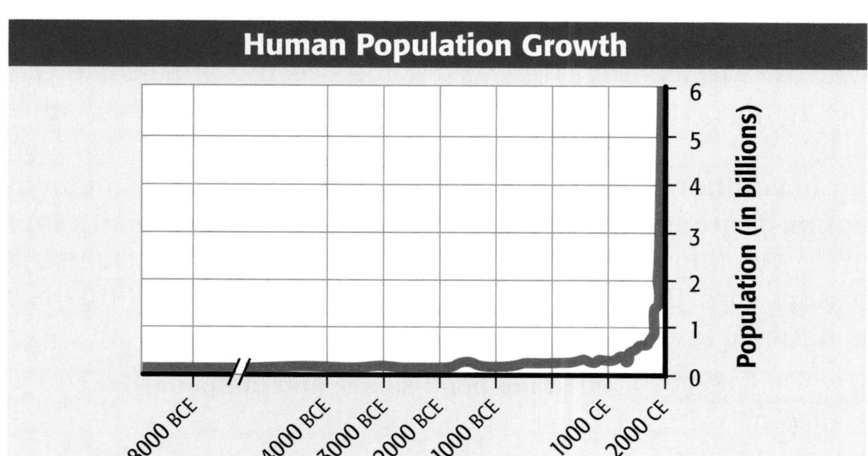

Figure 5 *Recently, the human population has been doubling every few decades.*

Figure 6 *Deforestation can leave soil exposed to erosion.*

Habitat Destruction

People need homes. People also need food and building materials. But when land is cleared for construction, crops, mines, or lumber, the topsoil may erode. Chemicals may pollute nearby streams and rivers. The organisms that were living in these areas may be left without food and shelter. These organisms may die.

An organism's *habitat* is where it lives. Every habitat has its own number and variety of organisms, or **biodiversity.** If a habitat is damaged or destroyed, biodiversity is lost.

biodiversity the number and variety of organisms in a given area during a specific period of time

Forest Habitats

Trees provide humans with oxygen, lumber, food, rubber, and paper. For some of these products, such as lumber and paper, trees must be cut down. *Deforestation* is the clearing of forest lands, as shown in **Figure 6.** At one time, many of these cleared forests were not replanted. Today, lumber companies often plant new trees to replace the trees that were cut down. However, some biodiversity is still lost.

Tropical rain forests, the most diverse habitats on Earth, are sometimes cleared for farmland, roads, and lumber. But after a tropical rain forest is cleared, the area cannot grow to be as diverse as it once was. Also, thin tropical soils are often badly damaged.

CONNECTION TO Social Studies

Wood Identify a country that is a major exporter of wood. List some of the ways this wood is used. Research the impact this exportation is having on that country's forests. Make a poster describing your findings.

ACTIVITY

Marine Habitats

Many people think of oil spills when they think of pollution in marine habitats. This is an example of *point-source pollution,* or pollution that comes from one source. Spilled oil pollutes both open waters and coastal habitats.

A second kind of water pollution is *nonpoint-source pollution.* This kind of pollution comes from many different sources. Nonpoint-source pollution often happens when chemicals on land are washed into rivers, lakes, and oceans. These chemicals can harm or kill many of the organisms that live in marine habitats.

In addition to oil and chemicals, plastics are also sometimes dumped into marine habitats. Animals may mistake plastics for food. Or animals may become tangled in plastics. Dumping plastics into the ocean is against the law. However, this law is difficult to enforce.

Reading Check **What are point-source and nonpoint-source pollution?**

Effects on Humans

Trees and marine life are not the only organisms affected by pollution and habitat destruction. Pollution and habitat destruction affect humans, too. Sometimes, the effect is immediate. Polluted air affects people with respiratory problems. If you drink polluted water, you may get sick. Sometimes, the damage is not apparent right away. Some chemicals cause cancers many years after a person is exposed to them. Over time, natural resources may be hard to find or used up. Your children or grandchildren may have to deal with these problems.

Anything that harms other organisms may eventually harm people, too. Caring for the environment means being aware of what is happening now and looking ahead to the future.

SECTION Review

- Pollutants include garbage, chemicals, high-energy wastes, gases, and noise.
- Renewable resources can be used over and over. Nonrenewable resources cannot be replaced or are replaced over thousands or millions of years.
- Exotic species can become pests and compete with native species.
- Overpopulation happens when a population is so large that it can't get what it needs to survive.
- Habitat destruction can lead to soil erosion, water pollution, and decreased biodiversity.
- In addition to harming the environment, pollution can harm humans.

Using Key Terms

The statements below are false. For each statement, replace the underlined term to make a true statement.

1. Coal is a <u>renewable resource</u>.
2. <u>Overpopulation</u> is the number and variety of organisms in an area.

Understanding Key Ideas

3. Which of the following can cause pollution?
   - **a.** noise
   - **b.** garbage
   - **c.** chemicals
   - **d.** All of the above
4. Pollution
   - **a.** does not affect humans.
   - **b.** can make humans sick.
   - **c.** makes humans sick only after many years.
   - **d.** None of the above
5. Compare renewable and nonrenewable resources.
6. Why has human population growth increased?
7. What is an exotic species?
8. How does habitat destruction affect biodiversity?

Math Skills

9. Jodi's family produces 48 kg of garbage each week. What is the percentage decrease if they reduce the amount of garbage to 40 kg per week?

Critical Thinking

10. **Applying Concepts** Explain how each of the following can help people but harm the environment: hospitals, old refrigerators, and road construction.
11. **Making Inferences** Explain how human population growth is related to pollution problems.
12. **Predicting Consequences** How can the pollution of marine habitats affect humans?

For a variety of links related to this chapter, go to www.scilinks.org

Topic: Air Pollution; Resource Depletion
SciLinks code: HSM0033; HSM1304

SECTION 2

Environmental Solutions

As the human population grows, it will need more resources. People will need food, healthcare, transportation, and waste disposal. What does this mean for the Earth?

All of these needs will have an impact on the Earth. If people don't use resources wisely, people will continue to pollute the air, soil, and water. More natural habitats could be lost. Many species could die out as a result. But there are many things people can do to protect the environment.

READING WARM-UP

Objectives

- Explain the importance of conservation.
- Describe the three Rs.
- Explain how biodiversity can be maintained.
- List five environmental strategies.

Terms to Learn

conservation
recycling

READING STRATEGY

Discussion Read this section silently. Write down questions that you have about this section. Discuss your questions in a small group.

Conservation

One way to care for the Earth is conservation (KAHN suhr VAY shuhn). **Conservation** is the preservation and wise use of natural resources. You can ride your bike to conserve fuel. At the same time, you prevent air pollution. You can use organic compost instead of chemical fertilizer in your garden. Doing so conserves the resources needed to make the fertilizer. Also, you may reduce soil and water pollution.

Practicing conservation means using fewer natural resources. Conservation helps reduce waste and pollution. Also, conservation can help prevent habitat destruction. The three Rs are shown in **Figure 1.** They describe three ways to conserve resources: Reduce, Reuse, and Recycle.

conservation the preservation and wise use of natural resources

Reading Check What are the three Rs? (*See the Appendix for answers to Reading Checks.*)

Figure 1 *By reducing, reusing, and recycling, these teens are conserving resources.*

Reduce

What is the best way to conserve the Earth's natural resources? Use less of them! Doing so also helps reduce pollution.

Reducing Waste and Pollution

As much as one-third of the waste produced by some countries is packaging material. Products can be wrapped in less paper and plastic to reduce waste. For example, fast-food restaurants used to serve sandwiches in large plastic containers. Today, sandwiches are usually wrapped in thin paper instead. This paper is more biodegradable than plastic. Something that is *biodegradable* can be broken down by living organisms, such as bacteria. Scientists, such as the ones in **Figure 2,** are working to make biodegradable plastics.

Figure 2 *These scientists are studying ways to make biodegradable plastics.*

Many people and companies are using less-hazardous materials in making their products. For example, some farmers don't use synthetic chemicals on their crops. Instead, they practice organic farming. They use mulch, compost, manure, and natural pest control. Agricultural specialists are also working on farming techniques that are better for the environment.

Reducing the Use of Nonrenewable Resources

Some scientists are looking for sources of energy that can replace fossil fuels. For example, solar energy can be used to power homes, such as the home shown in **Figure 3.** Scientists are studying power sources such as wind, tides, and falling water. Car companies have developed electric and hydrogen-fueled automobiles. Driving these cars uses fewer fossil fuels and produces less pollution than driving gas-fueled cars does.

Figure 3 *The people who live in this home use solar panels to get energy from the sun.*

Figure 4 *This home was built with reused tires and aluminum cans.*

Reuse

Do you get hand-me-down clothes from an older sibling? Do you try to fix broken sports equipment instead of throwing it away? If so, you are helping conserve resources by *reusing* products.

Reusing Products

Every time you reuse a plastic bag, one bag fewer needs to be made. Reusing the plastic bag at the grocery store is just one way to reuse the bag. Reusing products is an important way to conserve resources.

You might be surprised at how many materials can be reused. For example, building materials can be reused. Wood, bricks, and tiles can be used in new structures. Old tires can be reused, too. They can be reused for playground surfaces. As shown in **Figure 4,** some tires are even reused to build new homes!

Figure 5 *This golf course is being watered with reclaimed water.*

Reusing Water

About 100 billion liters of water are used each day in American homes. Most of this water goes down the drain. Many communities are experiencing water shortages. Some of these communities are experimenting with reusing, or reclaiming, wastewater.

One way to reclaim water is to use organisms to clean the water. These organisms include plants and filter-feeding animals, such as clams. Often, reclaimed water isn't pure enough to drink. But it can be used to water crops, lawns, and golf courses, such as the one shown in **Figure 5.** Sometimes, reclaimed water is returned to underground water supplies.

Reading Check Describe how water is reused.

Recycle

Another example of reuse is recycling. **Recycling** is the recovery of materials from waste. Sometimes, recyclable items, such as paper, are used to make the same kinds of products. Other recyclable items are made into different products. For example, yard clippings can be recycled into a natural fertilizer.

recycling the process of recovering valuable or useful materials from waste or scrap

Recycling Trash

Plastics, paper, aluminum, wood, glass, and cardboard are examples of materials that can be recycled. Every week, about half a million trees are used to make Sunday newspapers. Recycling newspapers could save millions of trees. Recycling aluminum saves 95% of the energy needed to change raw ore into aluminum. Glass can be recycled over and over again to make new bottles and jars.

Many communities make recycling easy. Some cities provide containers for glass, plastic, aluminum, and paper. People can leave these containers on the curb. Each week, the materials are picked up for recycling, as shown in **Figure 6.** Other cities have centers where people can take materials for recycling.

Figure 6 *In some communities, recyclable materials are picked up each week.*

Recycling Resources

Waste that can be burned can also be used to generate electricity. Electricity is generated in waste-to-energy plants, such as the one shown in **Figure 7.** Using garbage to make electricity is an example of *resource recovery.* Some companies are beginning to make electricity with their own waste. Doing so saves the companies money and conserves resources.

About 16% of the solid waste in the United States is burned in waste-to-energy plants. But some people are concerned that these plants pollute the air. Other people worry that the plants reduce recycling.

Figure 7 *A waste-to-energy plant can provide electricity to many homes and businesses.*

Figure 8 *What could happen if a fungus attacks a banana field? Biodiversity is low in fields of crops such as bananas.*

Maintaining Biodiversity

You know the three Rs. What else can you do to help the environment? You can help maintain biodiversity! So, how does biodiversity help the environment?

Imagine a forest with only one kind of tree. If a disease hit that species, the entire forest might die. Now, imagine a forest with 10 species of trees. If a disease hits one species, 9 other species will remain. Bananas, shown in **Figure 8,** are an important crop. But banana fields are not very diverse. Fungi threaten the survival of bananas. Farmers often use chemicals to control fungi. Growing other plants among the bananas, or increasing biodiversity, can also prevent the spread of fungi.

Biodiversity is also important because each species has a unique role in an ecosystem. Losing one species could disrupt an entire ecosystem. For example, if an important predator is lost, its prey will multiply. The prey might eat the plants in an area, keeping other animals from getting food. Eventually, even the prey won't have food. So, the prey will starve.

Figure 9 *Thanks to captive-breeding programs, the California condor population is increasing.*

Protecting Species

One way to maintain biodiversity is to protect individual species. In the United States, a law called the *Endangered Species Act* was designed to do just that. Endangered species are put on a special list. The law forbids activities that would harm a species on this list. The law also requires the development of recovery programs for each endangered species. Some endangered species, such as the California condor in **Figure 9,** are now increasing in number.

Anyone can ask the government to add a species to or remove a species from the endangered species list. This process can take years to complete. The government must study the species and its habitat before making a decision.

Protecting Habitats

Waiting until a species is almost extinct to begin protecting it is like waiting until your teeth are rotting to begin brushing them. Scientists want to prevent species from becoming endangered and from becoming extinct.

Plants, animals, and microorganisms depend on each other. Each organism is part of a huge, interconnected web of organisms. The entire web should be protected to protect these organisms. To protect the web, complete habitats, not just individual species, must be preserved. Nature preserves, such as the one shown in **Figure 10,** are one way to protect entire habitats.

Figure 10 *Setting aside public lands for wildlife is one way to protect habitats.*

Environmental Strategies

Laws have been passed to help protect the Earth's environment. By following those laws, people can help the environment. People can also use the following environmental strategies:

- **Reduce pollution.** Recycle as much as possible, and buy recycled products. Don't dump wastes on farmland, in forests, or into rivers, lakes, and oceans. Participate in a local cleanup project.
- **Reduce pesticide use.** Use only pesticides that are targeted specifically for harmful insects. Avoid pesticides that might harm beneficial insects, such as ladybugs or spiders. Use natural pesticides that interfere with how certain insects grow, develop, and reproduce.
- **Protect habitats.** Preserve entire habitats. Conserve wetlands. Reduce deforestation. Use resources at a rate that allows them to be replenished naturally.
- **Learn about local issues.** Attend local meetings about laws and projects that may affect your local environment. Research the impact of the project, and let people know about your concerns.
- **Develop alternative energy sources.** Increase the use of renewable energy, such as solar power and wind power.

The *Environmental Protection Agency* (EPA) is a government organization that helps protect the environment. The EPA works to help people have a clean environment in which to live, work, and play. The EPA keeps people informed about environmental issues and helps enforce environmental laws.

Reading Check What is the EPA?

For another activity related to this chapter, go to **go.hrw.com** and type in the keyword **HL5ENVW.**

What You Can Do

Reduce, reuse, and recycle. Protect the Earth. These are jobs for everyone. Children as well as adults can help clean up the Earth. By doing so, people can improve their environment. And they can improve their quality of life.

The list in **Figure 11** offers some suggestions for how *you* can help. How many of these things do you already do? What can you add to the list?

Figure 11 **How You Can Help the Environment**

1. Volunteer at a local preserve or nature center, and help other people learn about conservation.
2. Give away your old toys.
3. Use recycled paper.
4. Fill up both sides of a sheet of paper.
5. Start an environmental awareness club at your school or in your neighborhood.
6. Recycle glass, plastics, paper, aluminum, and batteries.
7. Don't buy any products made from an endangered plant or animal.
8. Turn off electrical devices when you are not using them.
9. Wear hand-me-downs.
10. Share books with friends, or use the library.
11. Walk, ride a bicycle, or use public transportation.
12. Carry a reusable cloth shopping bag to the store.
13. Use a lunch box, or reuse your paper lunch bags.
14. Turn off the water while you brush your teeth.
15. Buy products made from biodegradable and recycled materials.
16. Use cloth napkins and kitchen towels.
17. Buy things in packages that can be recycled.
18. Use rechargeable batteries.
19. Make a compost heap.

SECTION Review

Summary

- Conservation is the preservation and wise use of natural resources. Conservation helps reduce pollution, ensures that resources will be available in the future, and protects habitats.
- The three Rs are Reduce, Reuse, and Recycle. Reducing means using fewer resources. Reusing means using materials and products over and over. Recycling is the recovery of materials from waste.
- Biodiversity is vital for maintaining healthy ecosystems. A loss of one species can affect an entire ecosystem.
- Biodiversity can be preserved by protecting endangered species and entire habitats.
- Environmental strategies include reducing pollution, reducing pesticide use, protecting habitats, enforcing the Endangered Species Act, and developing alternative energy resources.

Using Key Terms

1. Use each of the following terms in a separate sentence: *conservation* and *recycling*.

Understanding Key Ideas

2. Which of the following is NOT a strategy to protect the environment?
   a. preserving entire habitats
   b. using pesticides that target all insects
   c. reducing deforestation
   d. increasing the use of solar power
3. Conservation
   a. has little effect on the environment.
   b. is the use of more natural resources.
   c. involves using more fossil fuels.
   d. can prevent pollution.
4. Describe the three Rs.
5. Describe why biodiversity is important. How can biodiversity be protected?

Critical Thinking

6. **Applying Concepts** Liza rode her bike to the store. She bought items that had little packaging and put her purchases into her backpack. Describe how Liza practiced conservation.
7. **Identifying Relationships** How does conservation of resources also reduce pollution and protect habitats?

Interpreting Graphics

Use the pie graph below to answer the questions that follow.

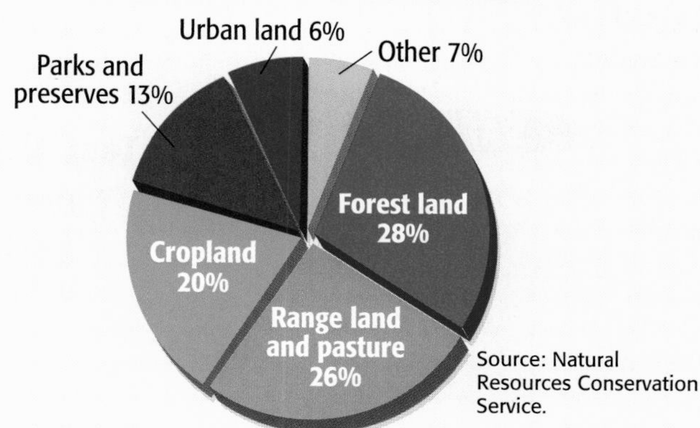

8. If half of the forest land were made into preserves, what percentage of total land would be parks and preserves?
9. If 10% of the cropland were not planted, what percentage of land would be used for crops?

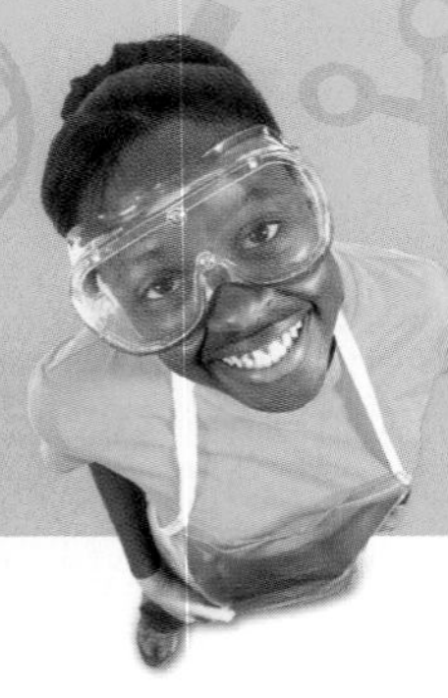

Using Scientific Methods

Inquiry Lab

Biodiversity—What a Disturbing Thought!

OBJECTIVES

Examine biodiversity in your community.

Identify which areas in your community have the greatest biodiversity.

MATERIALS

- items to be determined by the students and approved by the teacher (Possible field equipment includes a meterstick, binoculars, a magnifying lens, and forceps.)
- stakes (4)
- twine

SAFETY

Biodiversity is important for the stability of an ecosystem. Microorganisms, plants, and animals all have a role in an ecosystem. In this activity, you will investigate areas outside your school to determine which areas contain the greatest biodiversity.

Ask a Question

1. Based on your understanding of biodiversity, do you expect a forest or an area planted with crops to be more diverse?

Form a Hypothesis

2. Select an area that is highly disturbed (such as a yard) and an area that is relatively undisturbed (such as a vacant lot). Make a hypothesis about which area contains the greater biodiversity. Get your teacher's approval of your selected locations.

Test the Hypothesis

3. Design a procedure to determine which area contains the greater biodiversity. Have your plan approved by your teacher before you begin.

Prairie

Wheat Field

4. To discover smaller organisms, measure off a square meter, set stakes at the corners, and mark the area with twine. Use a magnifying lens to observe organisms. When you record your observations, refer to organisms in the following way: Ant A, Ant B, and so on. Make note of any visits by larger organisms.

5. Create any data tables that you might need for recording your data. If you observe your areas on more than one occasion, make data tables for each observation period. Organize your data into clear and understandable categories.

Analyze the Results

1. **Explaining Events** What factors did you consider before deciding which habitats were disturbed or undisturbed?

2. **Constructing Maps** Draw a map of the land around your school. Label areas of high biodiversity and those of lower biodiversity.

3. **Analyzing Data** What problems did you have while making observations and recording data for each habitat? How did you solve these problems?

Draw Conclusions

4. **Drawing Conclusions** Review your hypothesis. Did your data support your hypothesis? Explain your answer.

5. **Evaluating Methods** Describe possible errors in your investigation. What are ways you could improve your procedure to eliminate errors?

6. **Applying Conclusions** Do you think that the biodiversity around your school increased or decreased since the school was built? Explain your answer.

Applying Your Data

The photographs of the prairie and of the wheat field on this page are beautiful. One of these areas, however, is very low in biodiversity. Describe each photograph, and explain the difference in biodiversity.

Chapter Review

USING KEY TERMS

Complete each of the following sentences by choosing the correct term from the word bank.

conservation
pollution
recycling
biodiversity
overpopulation
renewable resource
nonrenewable resource

1. A(n) ___ is a resource that is replaced at a much slower rate than it is used.

2. The presence of too many individuals in a population for available resources is called ___.

3. ___ is an unwanted change in the environment caused by wastes.

4. The preservation and wise use of natural resources is called ___.

5. ___ is the number and variety of organisms in an area.

UNDERSTANDING KEY IDEAS

Multiple Choice

6. Preventing habitat destruction is important because
   - **a.** organisms do not live independently of each other.
   - **b.** protection of habitats is a way to promote biodiversity.
   - **c.** the balance of nature could be disrupted if habitats were destroyed.
   - **d.** All of the above

7. Exotic species
   - **a.** do not affect native species.
   - **b.** are species that make a home for themselves in a new place.
   - **c.** are not introduced by human activity.
   - **d.** do not take over an area.

8. A renewable resource
   - **a.** is a natural resource that can be replaced as quickly as it is used.
   - **b.** is a natural resource that takes thousands or millions of years to be replaced.
   - **c.** includes fossil fuels, such as coal or oil.
   - **d.** will eventually run out.

Short Answer

9. Describe how you can use the three Rs to conserve resources.

10. What are five kinds of pollutants?

11. Explain why human population growth has increased.

12. What are two things that can be done to maintain biodiversity?

13. List five environmental strategies.

CRITICAL THINKING

14 **Concept Mapping** Use the following terms to create a concept map: *pollution, radioactive wastes, gases, pollutants, CFCs, PCBs, hazardous wastes, chemicals, noise,* and *garbage.*

15 **Analyzing Ideas** How may deforestation have contributed to the extinction of some species?

16 **Predicting Consequences** Imagine that the supply of fossil fuels is going to run out in 50 years. What will happen if people are not prepared when the supply runs out? What might be done to prepare for such an event?

17 **Evaluating Conclusions** A scientist thinks that farms should be planted with many different kinds of crops instead of a single crop. Based on what you learned about biodiversity, evaluate the scientist's conclusion. What problems might this cause?

18 **Applying Concepts** Imagine that a new species has moved into a local habitat. The species feeds on some of the same plants that the native species do, but it has no natural predators. Describe what might happen to local habitats as a result.

19 **Making Inferences** Many scientists think that forests are nonrenewable resources. Explain why they might have this opinion.

INTERPRETING GRAPHICS

The line graph below shows the concentration of carbon dioxide in the atmosphere between 1958 and 1994. Use this graph to answer the questions that follow.

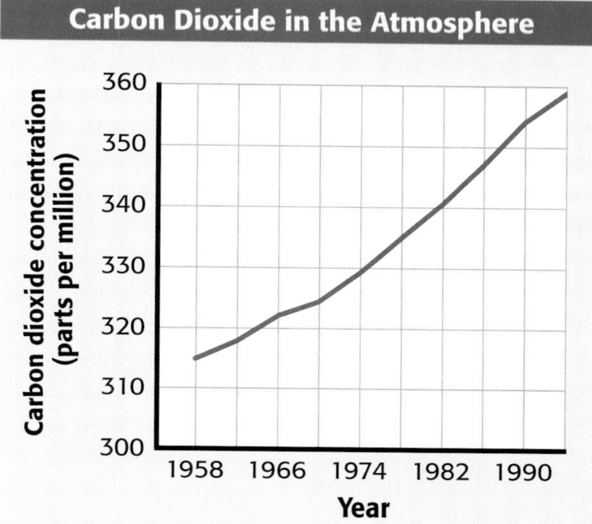

20 What was the concentration of carbon dioxide in parts per million in 1960? in 1994?

21 What is the average change in carbon dioxide concentration every 4 years?

22 If the concentration of carbon dioxide continues to change at the rate shown in the graph, what will the concentration be in 2010?

Standardized Test Preparation

READING

Read the passages below. Then, answer the questions that follow each passage.

Passage 1 The scientist woke up and jogged over to the rain forest. There she observed the water-recycling experiment. She took a swim in the ocean, after which she walked through a mangrove forest on her way home. At home, she ate lunch and went to the computer lab. From the lab, she could monitor the sensors that would alert her if any part of the ecosystem failed to cycle properly. This monitoring was very important to the scientist and her research team because their lives depended on the health of their sealed environment.

1. Based on the passage, the reader can conclude which of the following?

A The scientist lives in an artificial environment.
B The scientist lives by herself.
C The scientist and her research team are studying a newly discovered island.
D The scientist does not rely on the health of her environment.

2. Which of the following statements is a fact in the passage?

F The scientist is scared that her environment is being destroyed.
G The scientist depends on sensors to alert her to trouble.
H The scientist lives in an open environment.
I The scientist eats lunch at home every day.

3. Based on the passage, which of the following events happened first?

A The scientist walked through the mangrove forest.
B The scientist checked the water-recycling experiment.
C The scientist swam in the ocean.
D The scientist ate lunch.

Passage 2 All along the Gulf Coast, marine scientists and Earth scientists are trying to find methods to reduce or eliminate the dead zone. They have made models of the Mississippi River ecosystem that have accurately predicted the data that have since been collected. The scientists have changed the models to see what happens. For example, wetlands are one of nature's best filters. Wetlands take up a lot of the chemicals present in water. Scientists predict that adding wetlands to the Mississippi River watershed could reduce the chemicals reaching the Gulf of Mexico, possibly reducing the dead zone.

1. Based on the passage, what can you conclude about the dead zone?

A It is found in the Mississippi River.
B It may be prevented by adding wetlands to the Mississippi River watershed.
C It reduces the chemicals reaching the Gulf of Mexico.
D It is not caused by chemicals.

2. Based on the passage, which of the following statements about models is true?

F Models do not accurately predict data.
G Scientists do not change models.
H Scientists use models to make predictions.
I Models are always used for research.

3. Based on the passage, why did the scientists change their models?

A to predict the effects of adding wetlands to the Mississippi River watershed
B to find out why the dead zone happened
C to eliminate the dead zone
D to predict why there are a lot of chemicals in the Gulf of Mexico

INTERPRETING GRAPHICS

The table below shows the change in ozone levels between 1960 and 1990 above Halley Bay, Antarctica. Use the table to answer the questions that follow.

October Ozone Levels Above Halley Bay, Antarctica, in Dobson Units (DU)

Year	Ozone level (DU)
1960	300
1970	280
1980	235
1990	190

1. According to the table, which of the following is the most likely ozone level for October 2000?

A 120 DU
B 150 DU
C 235 DU
D 280 DU

2. According to the table, the ozone level above Halley Bay is doing which of the following?

F It steadily increased between 1960 and 1990.
G It fell by 37% between 1960 and 1990.
H It decreased by an average of 37 DU per year.
I It decreased by about 25% every 10 years.

3. What is the percent decrease in ozone level between 1980 and 1990?

A 16%
B 19%
C 24%
D 81%

4. What is the average loss of ozone level per year in DU?

F 4 DU
G 6 DU
H 37 DU
I 63 DU

MATH

Read each question below, and choose the best answer.

1. About 15 m of topsoil covers the western plains of the United States. If topsoil forms at the rate of 2.5 cm per 500 years, how long did it take for 15 m of topsoil to form?

A 3,000 years
B 7,500 years
C 18,750 years
D 300,000 years

2. The dimensions of a habitat are 16 km by 6 km. If these dimensions are decreased by 50%, what will the area of the habitat be?

F 22 km^2
G 24 km^2
H 48 km^2
I 96 km^2

3. If each person in a city of 500,000 people throws away 12 kg of trash each week, how many metric tons of trash does the city produce per year? (There are 1,000 kg in a metric ton.)

A 6,000 metric tons
B 26,000 metric tons
C 312,000 metric tons
D 312,000,000 metric tons

4. Producing one ton of new glass creates about 175 kg of mining waste. Using 50% recycled glass cuts this rate by 75%. Which of the following equations calculates *y*, the mass of mining waste produced using 50% recycled glass?

F $y = 175 \times 0.25$
G $y = 175 \times 0.75$
H $y = 175 \times 0.5$
I $y = 175 \div 0.75$

Science in Action

Scientific Debate

Where Should the Wolves Roam?

The U.S. Fish and Wildlife Service once listed the gray wolf as an endangered species and devised a plan to reintroduce the wolf to parts of the U.S. The goal was to establish a population of at least 100 wolves at each location. In April 2003, gray wolves were reclassified as a threatened species in much of the United States. Eventually, gray wolves may be removed from the endangered species list entirely. But some ranchers and hunters are uneasy about the reintroduction of gray wolves, and some environmentalists and wolf enthusiasts think the plan doesn't go far enough to protect wolves.

Math ACTIVITY

Scientists tried to establish a population of 100 wolves in Idaho. But the population grew to 285 wolves. By what percentage did the population exceed expectations?

Science, Technology, and Society

Hydrogen-Fueled Automobiles

Can you imagine a car that purrs quieter than a kitten and gives off water vapor instead of harmful pollutants? These cars may sound like science fiction. But such cars already exist! They run on one of the most common elements in the world—hydrogen. Some car companies are already speculating that one day all cars will run on hydrogen. The U.S. government has also taken notice. In 2003, President George W. Bush promised $1.2 billion to help research and develop hydrogen-fueled cars.

Language Arts ACTIVITY

WRITING SKILL Research hydrogen-fueled cars. Then, write a letter to a car company, your senator, or the President expressing your opinion about the development of hydrogen-fueled cars.

People in Science

Phil McCrory

Hairy Oil Spills Phil McCrory, a hairdresser in Huntsville, Alabama, asked a brilliant question when he saw an otter whose fur was drenched with oil from the *Exxon Valdez* oil spill. If the otter's fur soaked up all the oil, why wouldn't human hair do the same? McCrory gathered hair from the floor of his salon and took it home to perform his own experiments. He stuffed hair into a pair of his wife's pantyhose and tied the ankles together to form a bagel-shaped bundle. McCrory floated the bundle in his son's wading pool and poured used motor oil into the center of the ring. When he pulled the ring closed, not a drop of oil remained in the water!

McCrory approached the National Aeronautics and Space Administration (NASA) with his discovery. Based on tests performed by NASA, scientists estimated that 64 million kilograms of hair in reusable mesh pillows could have cleaned up all of the oil spilled by the *Exxon Valdez* within a week! Unfortunately, the $2 billion spent on the cleanup removed only about 12% of the oil.

Social Studies ACTIVITY

Make a map of an oil spill. Show the areas that were affected. Indicate some of the animal populations affected by the spill, such as penguins.

To learn more about these Science in Action topics, visit go.hrw.com and type in the keyword HL5ENVF.

Current Science

Check out Current Science® articles related to this chapter by visiting go.hrw.com. Just type in the keyword HL5CS21.

TIMELINE

Human Body Systems

Like a finely tuned machine, your body is made up of many systems that work together. Your lungs take in oxygen. Your brain reacts to things you see, hear, and smell and sends signals through your nervous system that cause you to react to those things. Your digestive system converts the food you eat into energy that the cells of your body can use. And those are just a few things that your body can do!

In this unit, you will study the systems of your body. You'll discover how the parts of your body work together.

Around 3000 BCE

Ancient Egyptian doctors are the first to study the human body scientifically.

1766

Albrecht von Haller determines that nerves control muscle movement and that all nerves are connected to the spinal cord or to the brain.

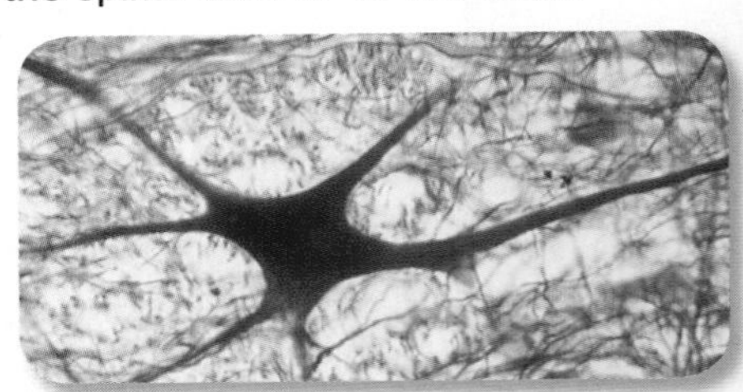

1824

Jean Louis Prevost and Jean Batiste Dumas prove that sperm is essential for fertilization.

1940

During World War II in Italy, Rita Levi-Montalcini is forced to leave her work at a medical school laboratory because she is Jewish. She sets up a laboratory in her bedroom and studies the development of the nervous system.

Around 500 BCE
Indian surgeon Susrata performs operations to remove cataracts.

1492
Christopher Columbus lands in the West Indies.

1543
Andreas Vesalius publishes the first complete description of the structure of the human body.

1616
William Harvey discovers that blood circulates and that the heart acts as a pump.

1893
Daniel Hale Williams, an African American surgeon, becomes the first person to repair a tear in the pericardium, the sac around the heart.

1922
Frederick Banting, Charles Best, and John McLeod discover insulin.

1930
Karl Landsteiner receives a Nobel Prize for his discovery of the four human blood types.

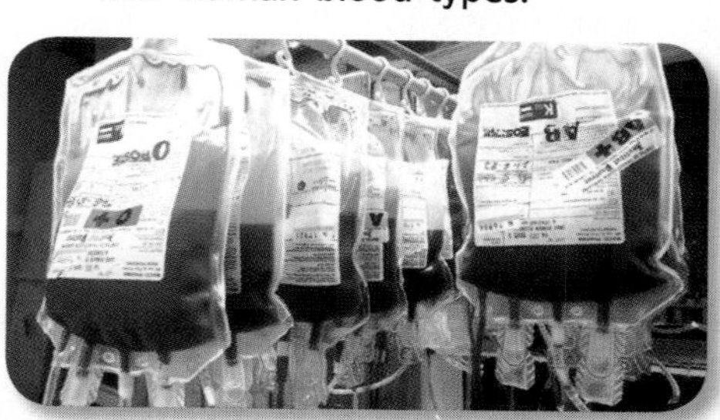

1982
Dr. William DeVries implants an artificial heart in Barney Clark.

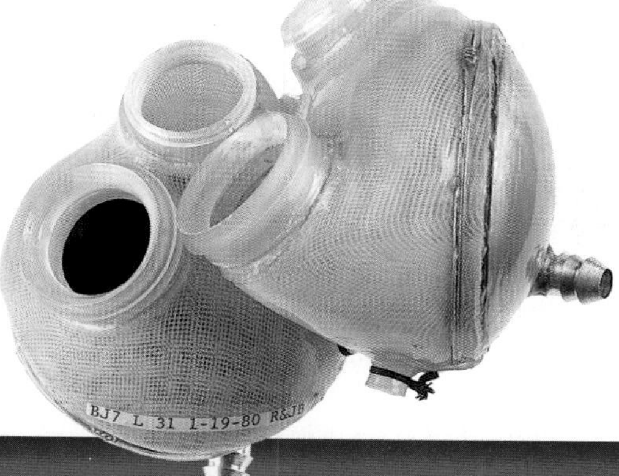

1998
The first sucessful hand transplant is performed in France.

2001
Drs. Laman A. Gray, Jr. and Robert D. Dowling at Jewish Hospital in Louisville, Kentucky, implant the first self-contained mechanical human heart.

Body Organization and Structure

Lance Armstrong has won the Tour de France several times. These victories are especially remarkable because he was diagnosed with cancer in 1996. But with medicine and hard work, he grew strong enough to win one of the toughest events in all of sports.

PRE-READING ACTIVITY

FOLDNOTES **Four-Corner Fold**

Before you read the chapter, create the FoldNote entitled "Four-Corner Fold" described in the **Study Skills** section of the Appendix. Label the flaps of the four-corner fold with "The skeletal system," "The muscular system," and "The integumentary system." Write what you know about each topic under the appropriate flap. As you read the chapter, add other information that you learn.

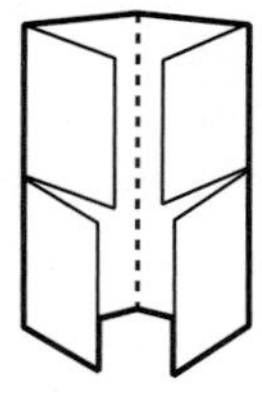

START-UP ACTIVITY

Too Cold for Comfort

Your nervous system sends you messages about your body. For example, if someone steps on your toe, your nervous system sends you a message. The pain you feel is a message that tells you to move your toe to safety. Try this exercise to watch your nervous system in action.

Procedure

1. Hold **a few pieces of ice** in one hand. Allow the melting water to drip into a **dish.** Hold the ice until the cold is uncomfortable. Then, release the ice into the dish.
2. Compare the hand that held the ice with your other hand. Describe the changes you see.

Analysis

1. What message did you receive from your nervous system while you held the ice?
2. How quickly did the cold hand return to normal?
3. What organ systems do you think helped restore your hand to normal?
4. Think of a time when your nervous system sent you a message, such as an uncomfortable feeling of heat, cold, or pain. How did your body react?

SECTION 1

Body Organization

Imagine jumping into a lake. At first, your body feels very cold. You may even shiver. But eventually you get used to the cold water. How?

READING WARM-UP

Objectives

- Describe how tissues, organs, and organ systems are related.
- List 12 organ systems.
- Identify how organ systems work together to maintain homeostasis.

Terms to Learn

homeostasis
organ
tissue

READING STRATEGY

Reading Organizer As you read this section, make a concept map by using the terms above.

Your body gets used to cold water because of homeostasis (HOH mee OH STAY sis). **Homeostasis** is the maintenance of a stable internal environment in the body. When you jump into a lake, homeostasis helps your body adapt to the cold water.

Cells, Tissues, and Organs

Maintaining homeostasis is not easy. Your internal environment is always changing. Your cells need nutrients and oxygen to survive. Your cells need wastes removed. If homeostasis is disrupted, cells may not get the materials they need. So, cells may be damaged or may die.

Your cells must do many jobs to maintain homeostasis. Fortunately, each of your cells does not have to do all of those jobs. Just as each person on a soccer team has a role during a game, each cell in your body has a job in maintaining homeostasis. Your cells are organized into groups. A group of similar cells working together forms a **tissue.** Your body has four main kinds of tissue. The four kinds of tissue are shown in **Figure 1.**

homeostasis the maintenance of a constant internal state in a changing environment

tissue a group of similar cells that perform a common function

Figure 1 Four Kinds of Tissue

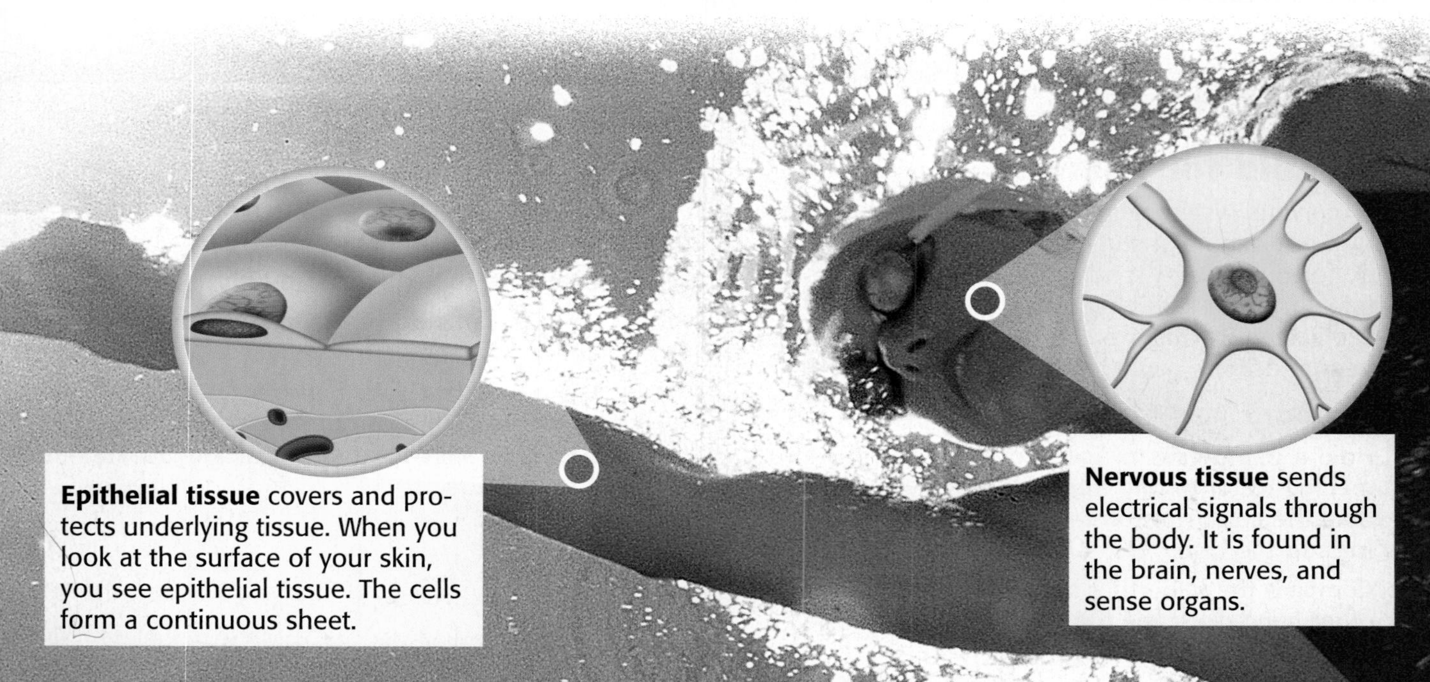

Epithelial tissue covers and protects underlying tissue. When you look at the surface of your skin, you see epithelial tissue. The cells form a continuous sheet.

Nervous tissue sends electrical signals through the body. It is found in the brain, nerves, and sense organs.

Figure 2 **Organization of the Stomach**

The stomach is an organ. The four kinds of tissue work together so that the stomach can carry out digestion.

Nervous tissue in the stomach partly controls the production of acids that aid in the digestion of food. Nervous tissue signals when the stomach is full.

Epithelial tissue lines the stomach.

Blood and another **connective tissue** called *collagen* are found in the wall of the stomach.

Layers of **muscle tissue** break up stomach contents.

Tissues Form Organs

One kind of tissue alone cannot do all of the things that several kinds of tissue working together can do. Two or more tissues working together form an **organ.** Your stomach, shown in **Figure 2,** uses all four kinds of tissue to carry out digestion.

organ a collection of tissues that carry out a specialized function of the body

Organs Form Systems

Your stomach does a lot to help you digest your food. But the stomach doesn't do it all. Your stomach works with other organs, such as the small and large intestines, to digest your food. Organs that work together make up an *organ system.*

Reading Check How is the stomach part of an organ system? (*See the Appendix for answers to Reading Checks.*)

Muscle tissue is made of cells that contract and relax to produce movement.
Connective tissue joins, supports, protects, insulates, nourishes, and cushions organs. It also keeps organs from falling apart.

Working Together

Organ systems work together to maintain homeostasis. Your body has 12 major organ systems, as shown in **Figure 3.** The circulatory and cardiovascular systems are shown together. The cardiovascular system includes your heart and blood vessels. Additionally, these organs are part of the circulatory system, which also includes blood. Together, these two systems deliver the materials your cells need to survive. This is just one example of how organ systems work together to keep you healthy.

Reading Check **Give an example of how organ systems work together in the body.**

Figure 3 Organ Systems

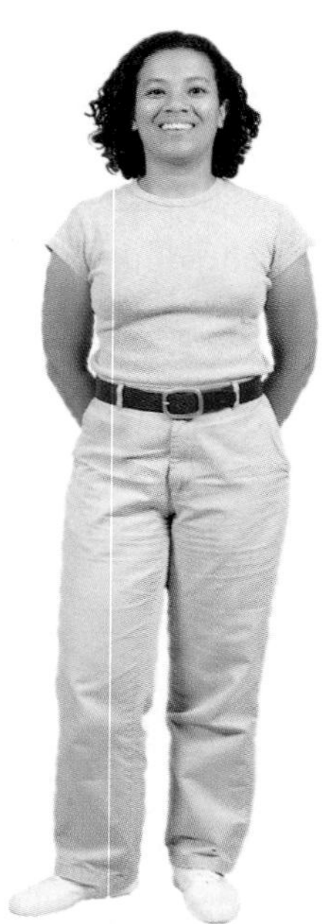

Integumentary System Your skin, hair, and nails protect the tissue that lies beneath them.

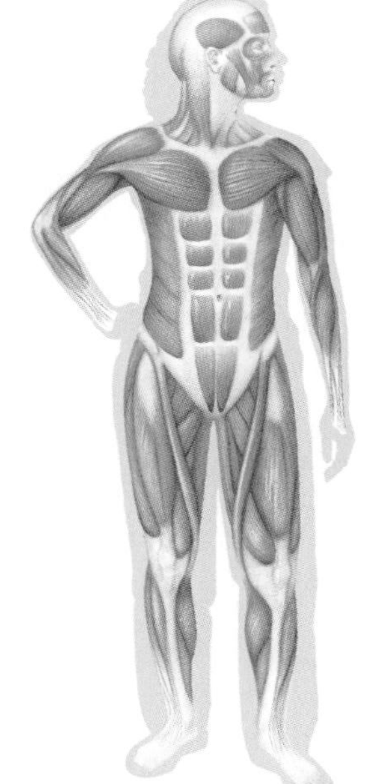

Muscular System Your muscular system works with the skeletal system to help you move.

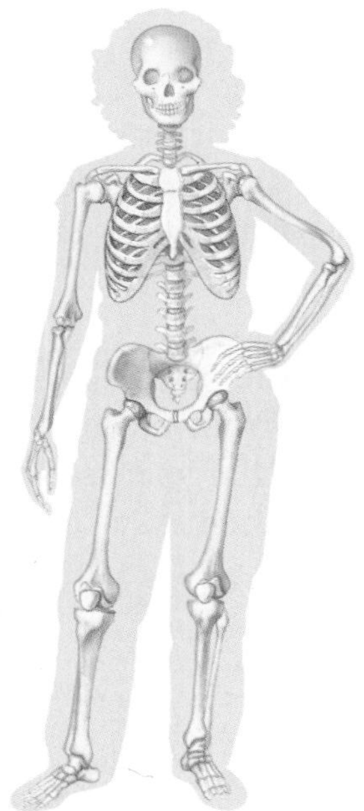

Skeletal System Your bones provide a frame to support and protect your body parts.

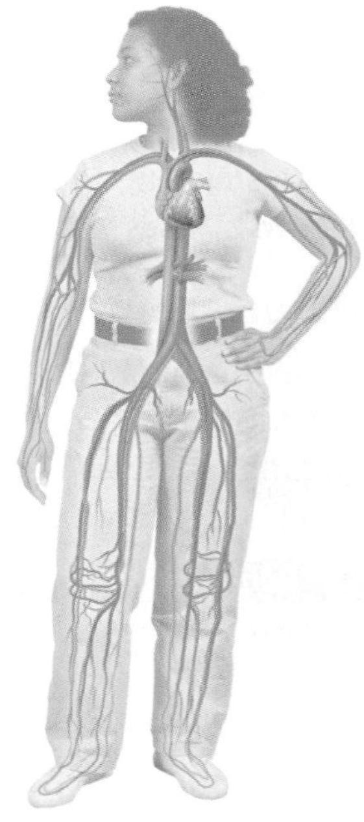

Cardiovascular and Circulatory Systems Your heart pumps blood through all of your blood vessels.

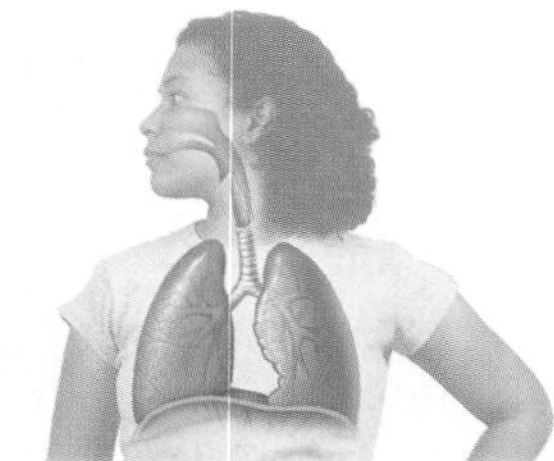

Respiratory System Your lungs absorb oxygen and release carbon dioxide.

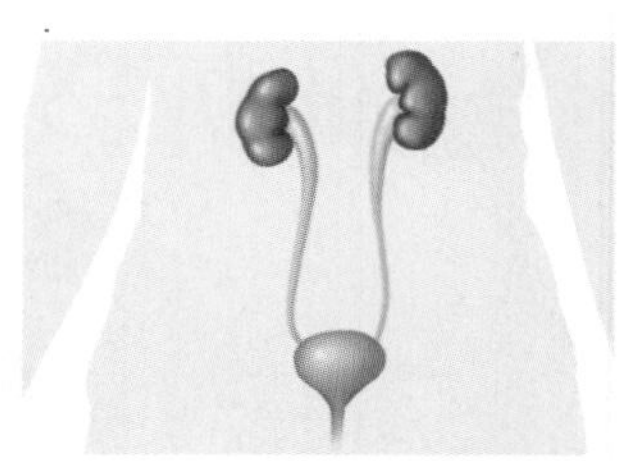

Urinary System Your urinary system removes wastes from the blood and regulates your body's fluids.

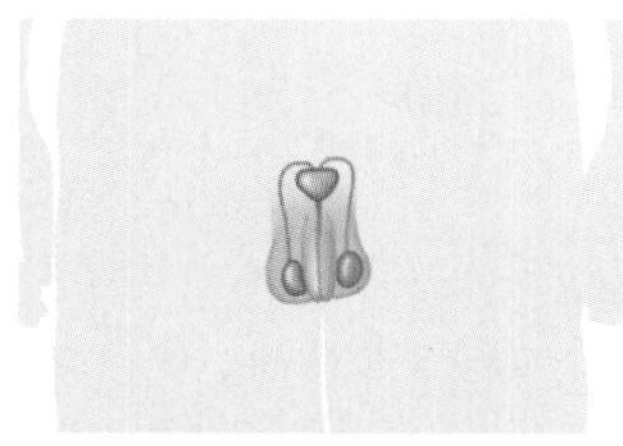

Male Reproductive System The male reproductive system produces and delivers sperm.

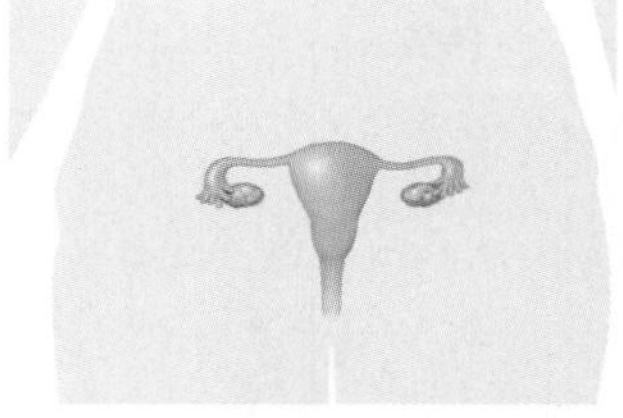

Female Reproductive System The female reproductive system produces eggs and nourishes and protects the fetus.

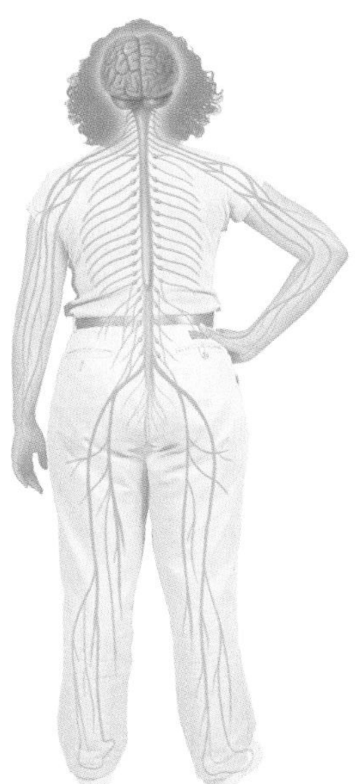

Nervous System Your nervous system receives and sends electrical messages throughout your body.

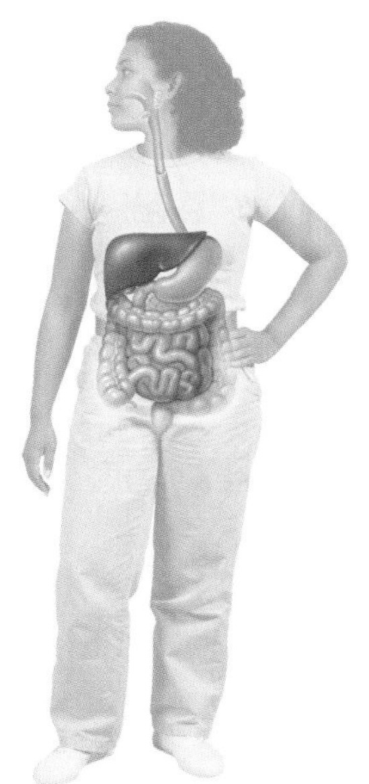

Digestive System Your digestive system breaks down the food you eat into nutrients that your body can absorb.

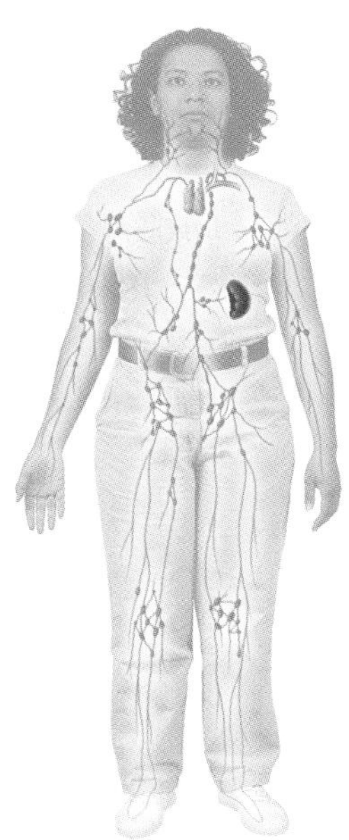

Lymphatic System The lymphatic system returns leaked fluids to blood vessels and helps get rid of bacteria and viruses.

Endocrine System Your glands send out chemical messages. Ovaries and testes are part of this system.

SECTION Review

Summary

- A group of cells that work together is a tissue. Tissues form organs. Organs that work together form organ systems.
- There are four kinds of tissue in the human body.
- There are 12 major organ systems in the human body.
- Organ systems work together to help the body maintain homeostasis.

Using Key Terms

1. Use the following terms in the same sentence: *homeostasis*, *tissue*, and *organ*.

Understanding Key Ideas

2. Which of the following statements describes how tissues, organs, and organ systems are related?
   a. Organs form tissues, which form organ systems.
   b. Organ systems form organs, which form tissues.
   c. Tissues form organs, which form organ systems.
   d. None of the above
3. List the 12 organ systems.

Math Skills

4. The human skeleton has 206 bones. The human skull has 22 bones. What percentage of human bones are skull bones?

Critical Thinking

5. **Applying Concepts** Tanya went to a restaurant and ate a hamburger. Describe how Tanya used five organ systems to eat and digest her hamburger.
6. **Predicting Consequences** Predict what might happen if the human body did not have specialized cells, tissues, organs, and organ systems to maintain homeostasis.

SCILINKS® NSTA Developed and maintained by the National Science Teachers Association

For a variety of links related to this chapter, go to www.scilinks.org

Topic: Tissues and Organs; Body Systems
SciLinks code: HSM1530; HSM0184

SECTION 2

The Skeletal System

When you hear the word skeleton, *you may think of the remains of something that has died. But your skeleton is not dead. It is very much alive.*

You may think your bones are dry and brittle. But they are alive and active. Bones, cartilage, and the connective tissue that holds bones together make up your **skeletal system.**

READING WARM-UP

Objectives

- Identify the major organs of the skeletal system.
- Describe four functions of bones.
- Describe three joints.
- List three injuries and two diseases that affect bones and joints.

Terms to Learn

skeletal system
joint

READING STRATEGY

Reading Organizer As you read this section, create an outline of the section. Use the headings from the section in your outline.

Bones

The average adult human skeleton has 206 bones. Bones help support and protect parts of your body. They work with your muscles so you can move. Bones also help your body maintain homeostasis by storing minerals and making blood cells. **Figure 1** shows the functions of your skeleton.

skeletal system the organ system whose primary function is to support and protect the body and to allow the body to move

Figure 1 The Skeleton

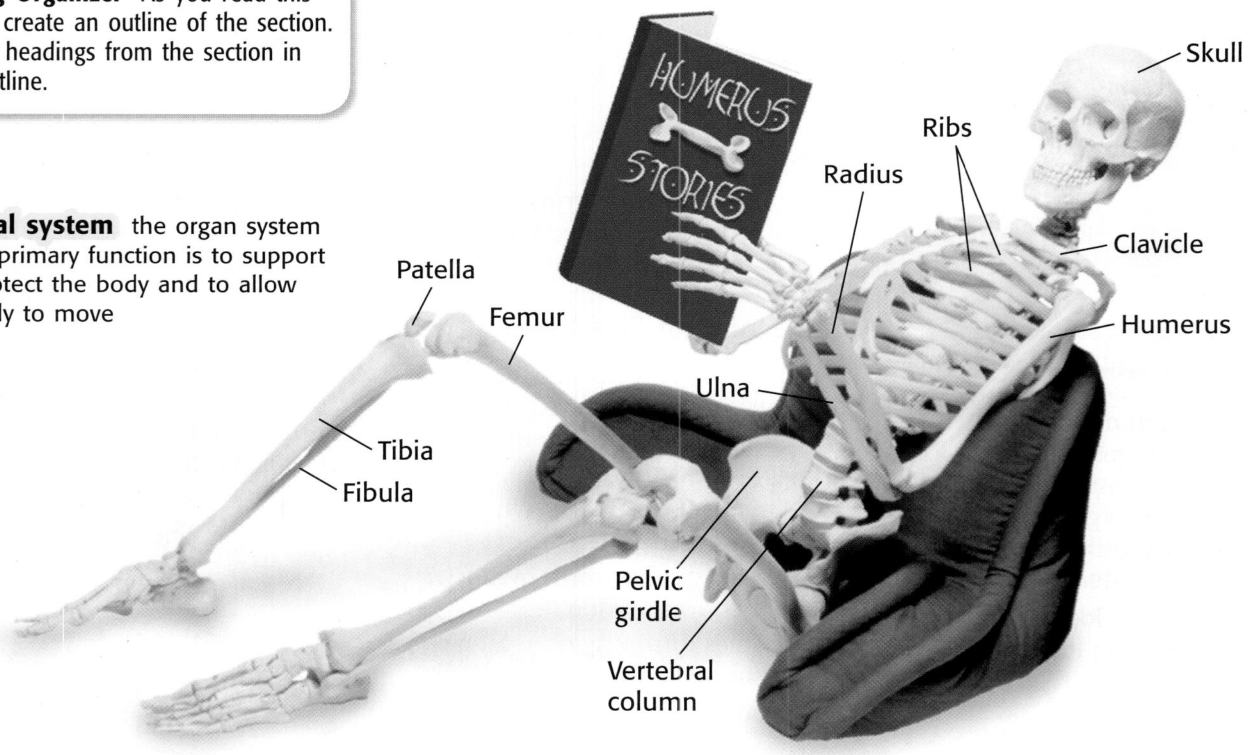

Protection Your heart and lungs are protected by ribs, your spinal cord is protected by vertebrae, and your brain is protected by the skull.

Storage Bones store minerals that help your nerves and muscles function properly. Long bones store fat that can be used for energy.

Movement Skeletal muscles pull on bones to produce movement. Without bones, you would not be able to sit, stand, walk, or run.

Blood Cell Formation Some of your bones are filled with a special material that makes blood cells. This material is called *marrow*.

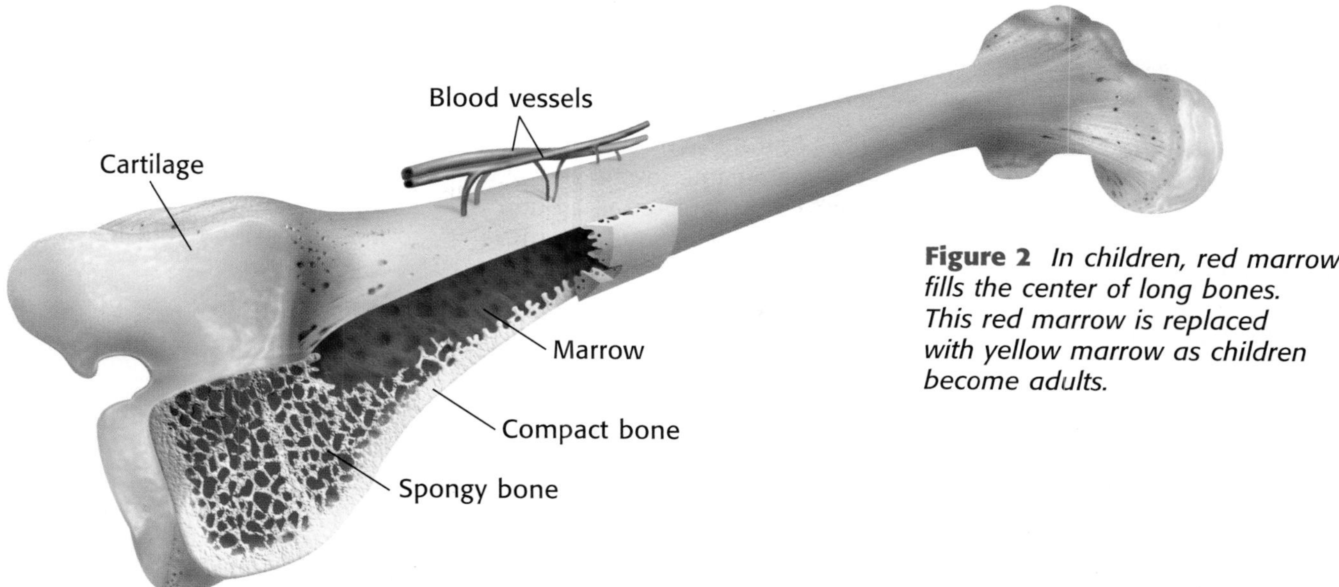

Figure 2 *In children, red marrow fills the center of long bones. This red marrow is replaced with yellow marrow as children become adults.*

Bone Structure

A bone may seem lifeless. But a bone is a living organ made of several different tissues. Bone is made of connective tissue and minerals. These minerals are deposited by living cells called *osteoblasts* (AHS tee oh BLASTS).

If you look inside a bone, you will notice two kinds of bone tissue. If the bone tissue does not have any visible open spaces, it is called *compact bone*. Compact bone is rigid and dense. Tiny canals within compact bone contain small blood vessels. Bone tissue that has many open spaces is called *spongy bone*. Spongy bone provides most of the strength and support for a bone.

Bones contain a soft tissue called *marrow*. There are two types of marrow. Red marrow produces both red and white blood cells. Yellow marrow, found in the central cavity of long bones, stores fat. **Figure 2** shows a cross section of a long bone, the femur.

Pickled Bones

1. Place a **clean chicken bone** in a **jar of vinegar.**
2. After 1 week, remove the bone and rinse it with **water.**
3. Describe the changes that you can see or feel.
4. How has the bone's strength changed?
5. What did the vinegar remove?

Bone Growth

Did you know that most of your skeleton used to be soft and rubbery? Most bones start out as a flexible tissue called *cartilage*. When you were born, you didn't have much true bone. But as you grew, most of the cartilage was replaced by bone. During childhood, most bones still have growth plates of cartilage. These growth plates provide a place for bones to continue to grow.

Feel the end of your nose. Or bend the top of your ear. These areas are two places where cartilage is never replaced by bone. These areas stay flexible.

Reading Check **How do bones grow?** (*See the Appendix for answers to Reading Checks.*)

Figure 3 Three Joints

Gliding Joint
Gliding joints allow bones in the hand and wrist to glide over one another and give some flexibility to the area.

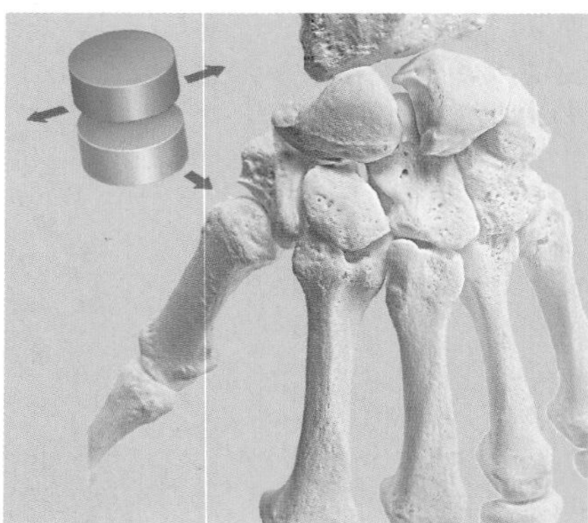

Ball-and-Socket Joint
As a video-game joystick lets you move your character all around, the shoulder lets your arm move freely in all directions.

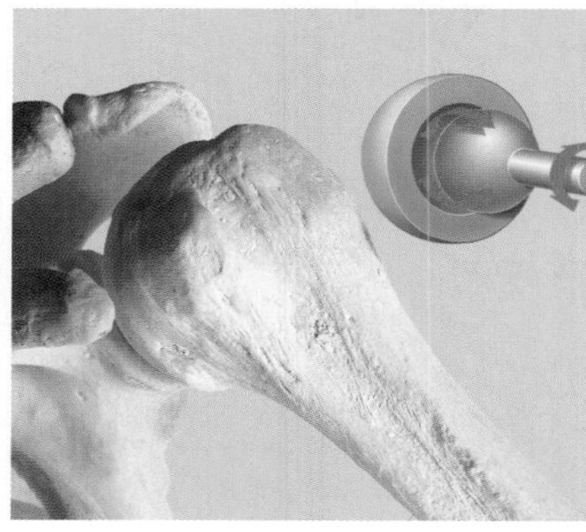

Hinge Joint
As a hinge allows a door to open and close, the knee enables you to flex and extend your lower leg.

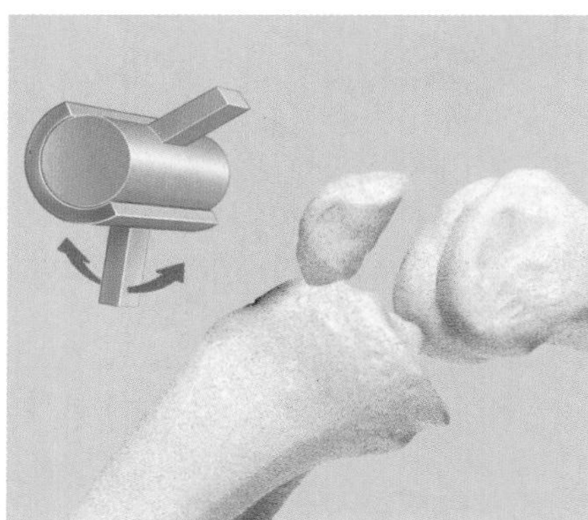

Joints

A place where two or more bones meet is called a **joint.** Your joints allow your body to move when your muscles contract. Some joints, such as fixed joints, allow little or no movement. Many of the joints in the skull are fixed joints. Other joints, such as your shoulder, allow a lot of movement. Joints can be classified based on how the bones in a joint move. For example, your shoulder is a ball-and-socket joint. Three joints are shown in **Figure 3.**

joint a place where two or more bones meet

Joints are held together by *ligaments* (LIG uh muhnts). Ligaments are strong elastic bands of connective tissue. They connect the bones in a joint. Also, cartilage covers the ends of many bones. Cartilage helps cushion the area in a joint where bones meet.

Reading Check Describe the basic structure of joints.

CONNECTION TO Environmental Science

WRITING SKILL **Bones from the Ocean** Sometimes, a bone or joint may become so damaged that it needs to be repaired or replaced with surgery. Often, replacement parts are made from a metal, such as titanium. However, some scientists have discovered that coral skeletons from coral reefs in the ocean can be used to replace human bone. Research bone surgery. Identify why doctors use metals such as titanium. Then, identify the advantages that coral may offer. Write a report discussing your findings.

Skeletal System Injuries and Diseases

Sometimes, parts of the skeletal system are injured. As shown in **Figure 4,** bones may be fractured, or broken. Joints can also be injured. A dislocated joint is a joint in which one or more bones have been moved out of place. Another joint injury, called a *sprain,* happens if a ligament is stretched too far or torn.

There are also diseases of the skeletal system. *Osteoporosis* (AHS tee OH puh ROH sis) is a disease that causes bones to become less dense. Bones become weak and break more easily. Age and poor eating habits can make it more likely for people to develop osteoporosis. Other bone diseases affect the marrow or make bones soft. A disease that affects the joints is called *arthritis* (ahr THRIET is). Arthritis is painful. Joints may swell or stiffen. As they get older, some people are more likely to have some types of arthritis.

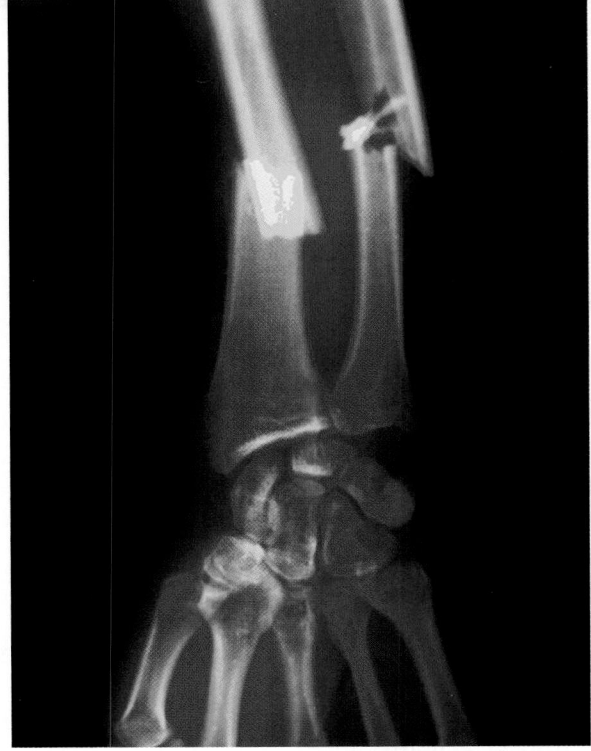

Figure 4 *This X ray shows that the two bones of the forearm have been fractured, or broken.*

SECTION Review

Summary

- The skeletal system includes bones, cartilage, and the connective tissue that connects bones.
- Bones protect the body, store minerals, allow movement, and make blood cells.
- Joints are places where two or more bones meet.
- Skeletal system injuries include fractures, dislocations, and sprains. Skeletal system diseases include osteoporosis and arthritis.

Using Key Terms

1. In your own words, write a definition for the term *skeletal system.*

Understanding Key Ideas

2. Which of the following is NOT an organ of the skeletal system?
   a. bone
   b. cartilage
   c. muscle
   d. None of the above
3. Describe four functions of bones.
4. What are three joints?
5. Describe two diseases that affect the skeletal system.

Math Skills

6. A broken bone usually heals in about six weeks. A mild sprain takes one-third as long to heal. In days, about how long does it take a mild sprain to heal?

Critical Thinking

7. **Identifying Relationships** Red bone marrow produces blood cells. Children have red bone marrow in their long bones, while adults have yellow bone marrow, which stores fat. Why might adults and children have different kinds of marrow?
8. **Predicting Consequences** What might happen if children's bones didn't have growth plates of cartilage?

SCiLINKS®
NSTA
Developed and maintained by the National Science Teachers Association
For a variety of links related to this chapter, go to www.scilinks.org
Topic: Skeletal System
SciLinks code: HSM1399

SECTION 3

The Muscular System

Have you ever tried to sit still, without moving any muscles at all, for one minute? It's impossible! Somewhere in your body, muscles are always working.

READING WARM-UP

Objectives

- List three kinds of muscle tissue.
- Describe how skeletal muscles move bones.
- Compare aerobic exercise with resistance exercise.
- Describe two muscular system injuries.

Terms to Learn

muscular system

READING STRATEGY

Discussion Read this section silently. Write down questions that you have about this section. Discuss your questions in a small group.

Your heart is a muscle. Muscles make you breathe. And muscles hold you upright. If all of your muscles rested at the same time, you would collapse. The **muscular system** is made up of the muscles that let you move.

Kinds of Muscle

Figure 1 shows the three kinds of muscle in your body. *Smooth muscle* is found in the digestive tract and in the walls of blood vessels. *Cardiac muscle* is found only in your heart. *Skeletal muscle* is attached to your bones for movement. Skeletal muscle also helps protect your inner organs.

Muscle action can be voluntary or involuntary. Muscle action that is under your control is *voluntary.* Muscle action that is not under your control is *involuntary.* Smooth muscle and cardiac muscle are involuntary muscles. Skeletal muscles can be both voluntary and involuntary muscles. For example, you can blink your eyes anytime you want to. But your eyes will also blink automatically.

Figure 1 Three Kinds of Muscle

Skeletal muscle enables bones to move.
Smooth muscle moves food through the digestive system.
Cardiac muscle pumps blood around the body.

Figure 2 **A Pair of Muscles in the Arm**

Skeletal muscles, such as the biceps and triceps muscles, work in pairs. When the biceps muscle contracts, the arm bends. When the triceps muscle contracts, the arm straightens.

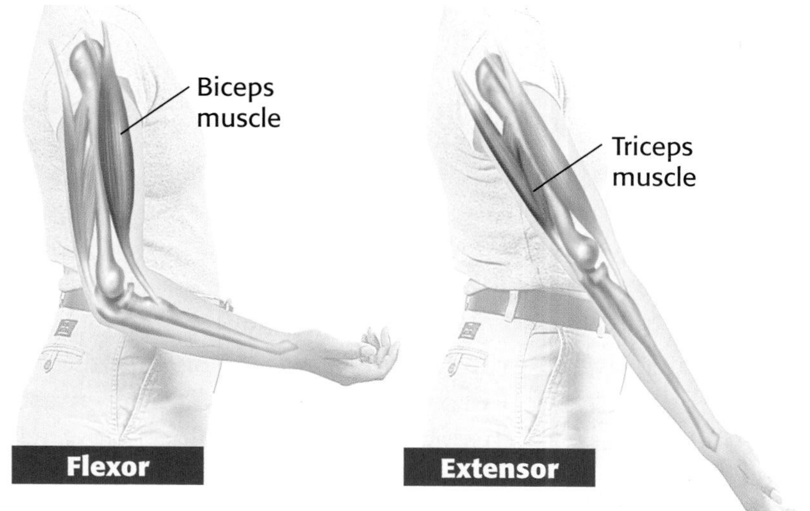

muscular system the organ system whose primary function is movement and flexibility

Movement

Skeletal muscles can make hundreds of movements. You can see many of these movements by watching a dancer, a swimmer, or even someone smiling or frowning. When you want to move, signals travel from your brain to your skeletal muscle cells. The muscle cells then contract, or get shorter.

Muscles Attach to Bones

Strands of tough connective tissue connect your skeletal muscles to your bones. These strands are called *tendons*. When a muscle that connects two bones gets shorter, the bones are pulled closer to each other. For example, tendons attach the biceps muscle to a bone in your shoulder and to a bone in your forearm. When the biceps muscle contracts, your forearm bends toward your shoulder.

Muscles Work in Pairs

Your skeletal muscles often work in pairs. Usually, one muscle in the pair bends part of the body. The other muscle straightens part of the body. A muscle that bends part of your body is called a *flexor* (FLEKS uhr). A muscle that straightens part of your body is an *extensor* (ek STEN suhr). As shown in **Figure 2,** the biceps muscle of the arm is a flexor. The triceps muscle of the arm is an extensor.

Reading Check **Describe how muscles work in pairs.** (*See the Appendix for answers to Reading Checks.*)

Power in Pairs

Ask a parent to sit in a chair and place a hand palm up under the edge of a table. Tell your parent to apply gentle upward pressure. Feel the front and back of your parent's upper arm. Next, ask your parent to push down on top of the table. Feel your parent's arm again. What did you notice about the muscles in your parent's arm when he or she was pressing up? pushing down?

ACTIVITY

Figure 3 *This girl is strengthening her heart and improving her endurance by doing aerobic exercise. This boy is doing resistance exercise to build strong muscles.*

Use It or Lose It

What happens when someone wears a cast for a broken arm? Skeletal muscles around the broken bone become smaller and weaker. The muscles weaken because they are not exercised. Exercised muscles are stronger and larger. Strong muscles can help other organs, too. For example, contracting muscles squeeze blood vessels. This action increases blood flow without needing more work from the heart.

Certain exercises can give muscles more strength and endurance. More endurance lets muscles work longer without getting tired. Two kinds of exercise can increase muscle strength and endurance. They are resistance exercise and aerobic exercise. You can see an example of each kind in **Figure 3.**

Resistance Exercise

Resistance exercise is a great way to strengthen skeletal muscles. During resistance exercise, people work against the resistance, or weight, of an object. Some resistance exercises, such as curl-ups, use your own weight for resistance.

Aerobic Exercise

Steady, moderately intense activity is called *aerobic exercise*. Jogging, cycling, skating, swimming, and walking are aerobic exercises. This kind of exercise can increase muscle strength. However, aerobic exercise mostly strengthens the heart and increases endurance.

Muscle Function Body chemistry is very important for healthy muscle function. Spasms or cramps happen if too much sweating, poor diet, or illness causes a chemical imbalance in muscles. Identify three chemicals that the body needs for muscles to work properly. Make a poster explaining how people can make sure that they have enough of each chemical.

ACTIVITY

Muscle Injury

Any exercise program should be started slowly. Starting slowly means you are less likely to get hurt. You should also warm up for exercise. A *strain* is an injury in which a muscle or tendon is overstretched or torn. Strains often happen because a muscle has not been warmed up. Strains also happen when muscles are worked too hard.

People who exercise too much can hurt their tendons. The body can't repair an injured tendon before the next exercise session. So, the tendon becomes inflamed. This condition is called *tendinitis*. Often, a long rest is needed for the injured tendon to heal.

Some people try to make their muscles stronger by taking drugs. These drugs are called *anabolic steroids* (A nuh BAH lik STER OIDZ). They can cause long-term health problems. Anabolic steroids can damage the heart, liver, and kidneys. They can also cause high blood pressure. If taken before the skeleton is mature, anabolic steroids can cause bones to stop growing.

Reading Check **What are the risks of using anabolic steroids?**

Runner's Time

Jan has decided to enter a 5 km road race. She now runs 5 km in 30 min. She would like to decrease her time by 15% before the race. What will her time be when she reaches her goal?

SECTION Review

Summary

- The three kinds of muscle tissue are smooth muscle, cardiac muscle, and skeletal muscle.
- Skeletal muscles work in pairs. Skeletal muscles contract to move bones.
- Resistance exercise improves muscle strength. Aerobic exercise improves heart strength and muscle endurance.
- Strains are injuries that affect muscles and tendons. Tendinitis affects tendons.

Using Key Terms

1. In your own words, write a definition for the term *muscular system*.

Understanding Key Ideas

2. Muscles

a. work in pairs.
b. move bones by relaxing.
c. get smaller when exercised.
d. All of the above

3. Describe three kinds of muscle.

4. List two kinds of exercise. Give an example of each.

5. Describe two muscular system injuries.

Math Skills

6. If Trey can do one curl-up every 2.5 s, about how long will it take him to do 35 curl-ups?

Critical Thinking

7. Applying Concepts Describe some of the muscle action needed to pick up a book. Include flexors and extensors in your description.

8. Predicting Consequences If aerobic exercise improves heart strength, what likely happens to heart rate as the heart gets stronger? Explain your answer.

For a variety of links related to this chapter, go to www.scilinks.org

Topic: Muscular System
SciLinks code: HSM1008

SECTION 4

The Integumentary System

What part of your body has to be partly dead to keep you alive? Here are some clues: It comes in many colors, it is the largest organ in the body, and it is showing right now!

READING WARM-UP

Objectives

- List four functions of skin.
- Describe the two layers of skin.
- Describe the structure and function of hair and nails.
- Describe two kinds of damage that can affect skin.

Terms to Learn

integumentary system
epidermis
dermis

READING STRATEGY

Paired Summarizing Read this section silently. In pairs, take turns summarizing the material. Stop to discuss ideas that seem confusing.

Did you guess your skin? If you did, you guessed correctly. Your skin, hair, and nails make up your **integumentary system** (in TEG yoo MEN tuhr ee SIS tuhm). The integumentary system covers your body and helps you maintain homeostasis.

integumentary system the organ system that forms a protective covering on the outside of the body

Functions of Skin

Why do you need skin? Here are four good reasons:

- Skin protects you by keeping water in your body and foreign particles out of your body.
- Skin keeps you in touch with the outside world. Nerve endings in your skin let you feel things around you.
- Skin helps regulate your body temperature. Small organs in the skin called *sweat glands* make sweat. Sweat is a salty liquid that flows to the surface of the skin. As sweat evaporates, the skin cools.
- Skin helps get rid of wastes. Several kinds of waste chemicals can be removed in sweat.

As shown in **Figure 1,** skin comes in many colors. Skin color is determined by a chemical called *melanin*. If a lot of melanin is present, skin is very dark. If little melanin is present, skin is very light. Melanin absorbs ultraviolet light from the sun. So, melanin reduces damage that can lead to skin cancer. However, all skin, even dark skin, is vulnerable to cancer. Skin should be protected from sunlight whenever possible.

Figure 1 *Variety in skin color is caused by the pigment melanin. The amount of melanin varies from person to person.*

Figure 2 **Structures of the Skin**

Beneath the surface, your skin is a complex organ made of blood vessels, nerves, glands, and muscles.

Blood vessels transport substances and help regulate body temperature.

Nerve fibers carry messages to and from the brain.

Hair follicles in the dermis make hair.

Muscle fibers attached to a hair follicle can contract and cause the hair to stand up.

Oil glands release oil that keeps hair flexible and waterproofs the epidermis.

Sweat glands release sweat to cool the body. Sweating is also a way to remove waste materials from the body.

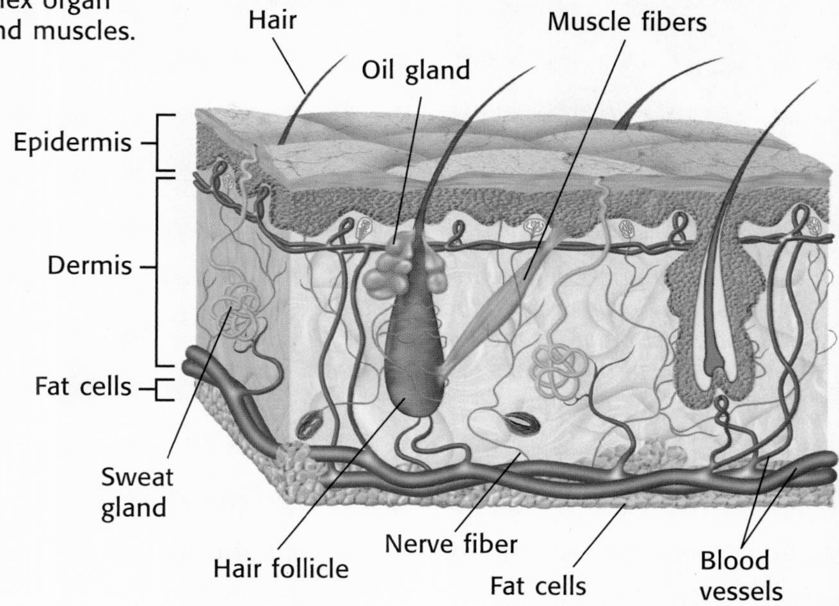

Layers of Skin

Skin is the largest organ of your body. In fact, the skin of an adult covers an area of about 2 m^2! However, there is more to skin than meets the eye. Skin has two main layers: the epidermis (EP uh DUHR mis) and the dermis. The **epidermis** is the outermost layer of skin. You see the epidermis when you look at your skin. The thicker layer of skin that lies beneath the epidermis is the **dermis.**

epidermis the surface layer of cells on a plant or animal

dermis the layer of skin below the epidermis

Epidermis

The epidermis is made of epithelial tissue. Even though the epidermis has many layers of cells, it is as thick as only two sheets of paper over most of the body. It is thicker on the palms of your hands and on the soles of your feet. Most cells in the epidermis are dead. These cells are filled with a protein called *keratin*. Keratin helps make the skin tough.

Dermis

The dermis lies beneath the epidermis. The dermis has many fibers made of a protein called *collagen*. These fibers provide strength. They also let skin bend without tearing. The dermis contains many small structures, as shown in **Figure 2.**

Reading Check **Describe the dermis. How does it differ from the epidermis?** (*See the Appendix for answers to Reading Checks.*)

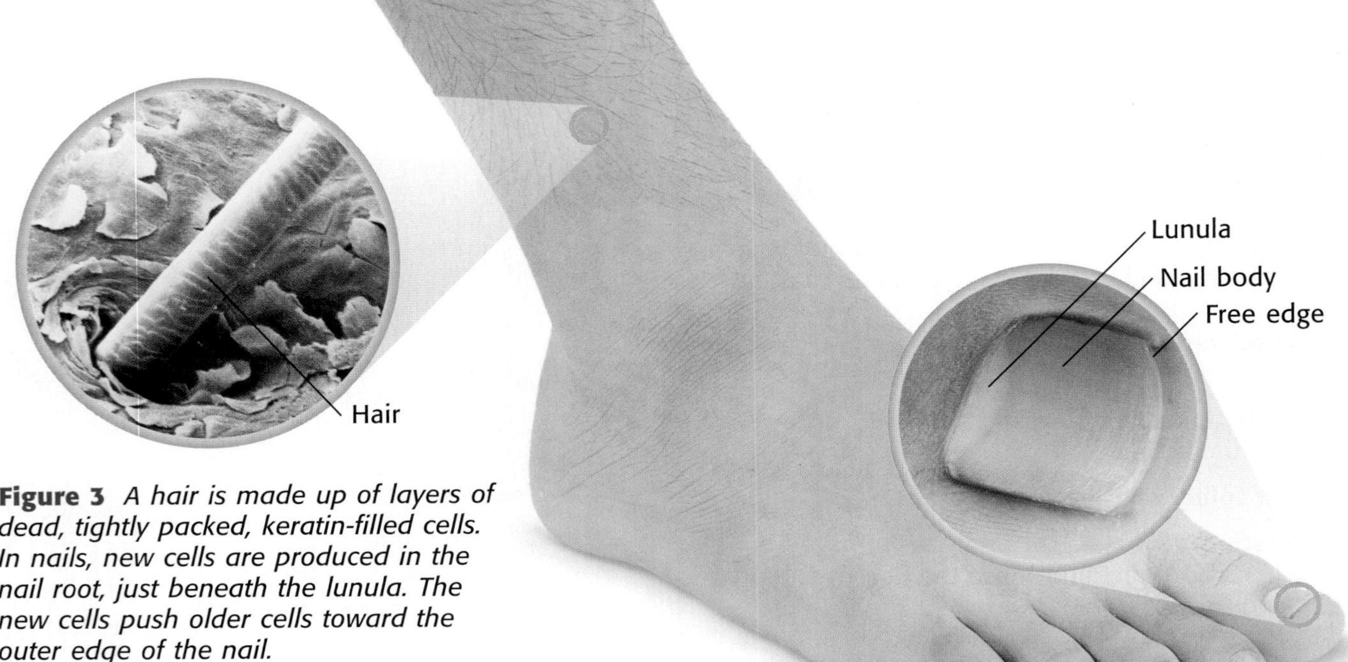

Figure 3 *A hair is made up of layers of dead, tightly packed, keratin-filled cells. In nails, new cells are produced in the nail root, just beneath the lunula. The new cells push older cells toward the outer edge of the nail.*

Hair and Nails

Hair and nails are important parts of the integumentary system. Like skin, hair and nails are made of living and dead cells. **Figure 3** shows hair and nails.

A hair forms at the bottom of a tiny sac called a *hair follicle.* The hair grows as new cells are added at the hair follicle. Older cells get pushed upward. The only living cells in a hair are in the hair follicle. Like skin, hair gets its color from melanin.

Hair helps protect skin from ultraviolet light. Hair also keeps particles, such as dust and insects, out of your eyes and nose. In most mammals, hair helps regulate body temperature. A tiny muscle attached to the hair follicle contracts. If the follicle contains a hair, the hair stands up. The lifted hairs work like a sweater. They trap warm air around the body.

A nail grows from living cells in the *nail root* at the base of the nail. As new cells form, the nail grows longer. Nails protect the tips of your fingers and toes. So, your fingers and toes can be soft and sensitive for a keen sense of touch.

Reading Check **Describe how nails grow.**

CONNECTION TO Social Studies

WRITING SKILL **Using Hair** Many traditional cultures use animal hair to make products, such as rugs and blankets. Identify a culture that uses animal hair. In your **science journal,** write a report describing how the culture uses animal hair.

Skin Injuries

Skin is often damaged. Fortunately, your skin can repair itself, as shown in **Figure 4.** Some damage to skin is very serious. Damage to the genetic material in skin cells can cause skin cancer. Skin may also be affected by hormones that cause oil glands in skin to make too much oil. This oil combines with dead skin cells and bacteria to clog hair follicles. The result is acne. Proper cleansing can help but often cannot prevent this problem.

Figure 4 **How Skin Heals**

1. A blood clot forms over a cut to stop bleeding and to keep bacteria from entering the wound. Bacteria-fighting cells then come to the area to kill bacteria.

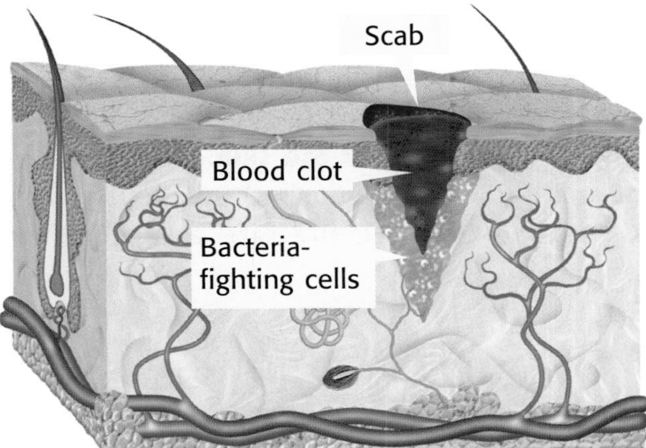

2. Damaged cells are replaced through cell division. Eventually, all that is left on the surface is a scar.

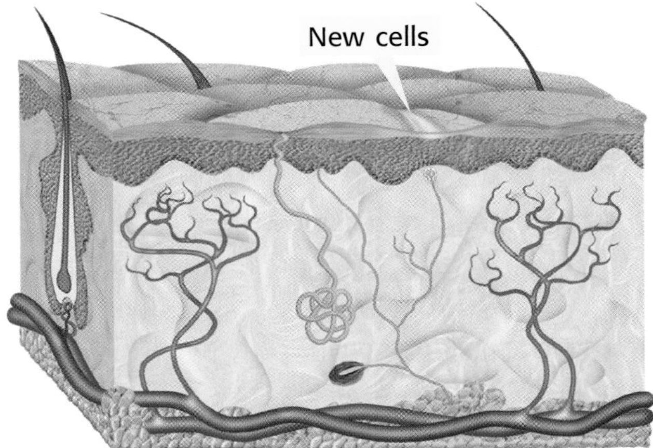

SECTION Review

Summary

- Skin keeps water in the body, keeps foreign particles out of the body, lets people feel things around them, regulates temperature, and removes wastes.
- The two layers of skin are the epidermis and the dermis.
- Hair grows from hair follicles. Nails grow from nail roots.
- Skin may develop skin cancer. Acne may develop if skin produces too much oil.

Using Key Terms

1. In your own words, write a definition for each of the following terms: *integumentary system*, *epidermis*, and *dermis*.

Understanding Key Ideas

2. Which of the following is NOT a function of skin?
   a. to regulate body temperature
   b. to keep water in the body
   c. to move your body
   d. to get rid of wastes
3. Describe the two layers of skin.
4. How do hair and nails develop?
5. Describe how a cut heals.

Math Skills

6. On average, hair grows 0.3 mm per day. How many millimeters does hair grow in 30 days? in a year?

Critical Thinking

7. **Making Inferences** Why do you feel pain when you pull on your hair or nails, but not when you cut them?
8. **Analyzing Ideas** The epidermis on the palms of your hands and on the soles of your feet is thicker than it is anywhere else on your body. Why might this skin need to be thicker?

SCILINKS.
NSTA
Developed and maintained by the National Science Teachers Association
For a variety of links related to this chapter, go to www.scilinks.org
Topic: Integumentary System
SciLinks code: HSM0803

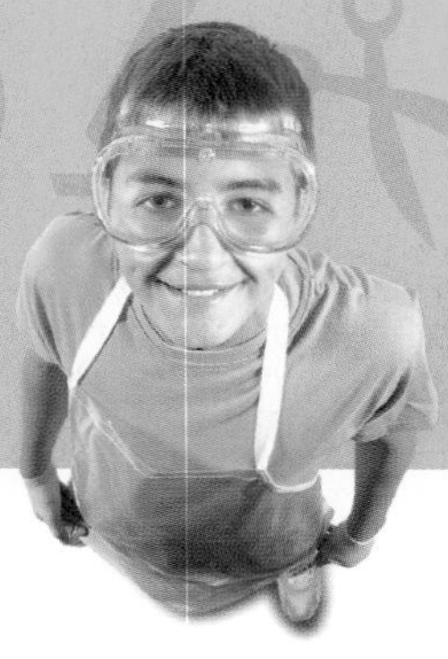

Skills Practice Lab

Seeing Is Believing

OBJECTIVES

Measure nail growth over time.

Draw a graph of nail growth.

MATERIALS

- graph paper (optional)
- metric ruler
- permanent marker

SAFETY

Like your hair and skin, fingernails are part of your body's integumentary system. Nails, shown in the figure below, are a modification of the outer layer of the skin. Nails grow from the nail bed and will grow continuously throughout your life. In this activity, you will measure the rate at which fingernails grow.

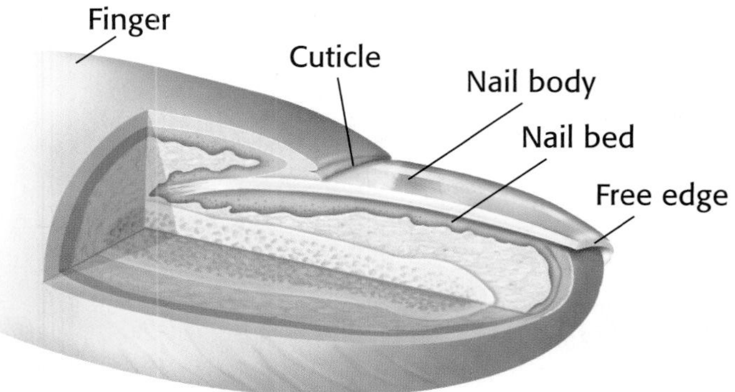

Procedure

1. Use a permanent marker to mark the center of the nail bed on your right index finger, as shown in the figure below. **Caution:** Do not get ink on your clothing.

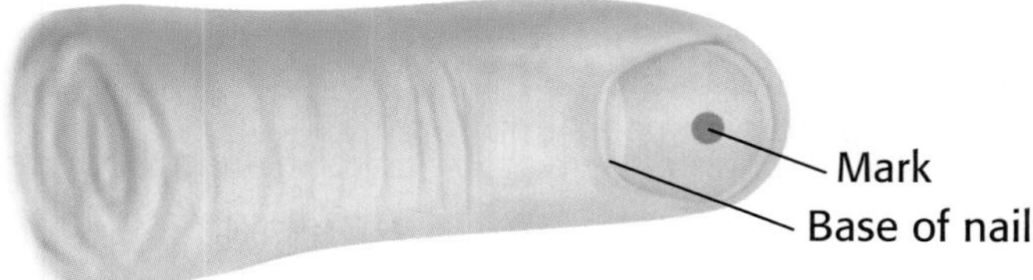

2. Measure from the mark to the base of your nail. Record the measurement, and label the measurement "Day 1."
3. Repeat steps 1 and 2 for your left index finger.
4. Let your fingernails grow for 2 days. Normal daily activity will not wash away the mark completely, but you may need to freshen the mark.
5. Measure the distance from the mark on your nail to the base of your nail. Record this distance, and label the measurement "Day 3."

6. Continue measuring and recording the growth of your nails every other day for 2 weeks. Refresh the mark as necessary. You may continue to file or trim your nails as usual throughout the course of the lab.
7. After you have completed your measurements, use them to create a graph similar to the graph below.

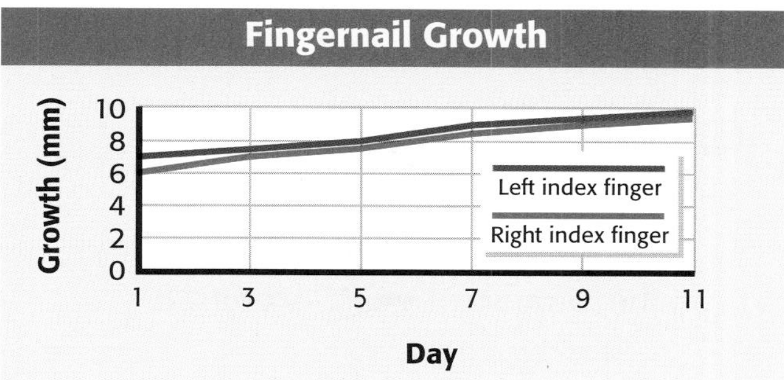

Analyze the Results

1. **Describing Events** Did the nail on one hand grow faster than the nail on the other hand?
2. **Examining Data** Did your nails grow at a constant rate, or did your nails grow more quickly at certain times?

Draw Conclusions

3. **Making Predictions** If one nail grew more quickly than the other nail, what might explain the difference in growth?
4. **Analyzing Graphs** Compare your graph with the graphs of your classmates. Do you notice any differences in the graphs based on gender or physical characteristics, such as height? If so, describe the difference.

Applying Your Data

Do additional research to find out how nails are important to you. Also, identify how nails can be used to indicate a person's health or nutrition. Based on what you learn, describe how your nail growth indicates your health or nutrition.

Chapter Review

USING KEY TERMS

Complete each of the following sentences by choosing the correct term from the word bank.

homeostasis	organ
joint	skeletal system
tissue	muscular system
epidermis	dermis
integumentary system	

1. A(n) ___ is a place where two or more bones meet.

2. ___ is the maintenance of a stable internal environment.

3. The outermost layer of skin is the ___.

4. The organ system that includes skin, hair, and nails is the ___.

5. A(n) ___ is made up of two or more tissues working together.

6. The ___ supports and protects the body, stores minerals, and allows movement.

UNDERSTANDING KEY IDEAS

Multiple Choice

7. Which of the following lists shows the way in which the body is organized?
   - **a.** cells, organs, organ systems, tissues
   - **b.** tissues, cells, organs, organ systems
   - **c.** cells, tissues, organs, organ systems
   - **d.** cells, tissues, organ systems, organs

8. Which muscle tissue can be both voluntary and involuntary?
   - **a.** smooth muscle
   - **b.** cardiac muscle
   - **c.** skeletal muscle
   - **d.** All of the above

9. The integumentary system
   - **a.** helps regulate body temperature.
   - **b.** helps the body move.
   - **c.** stores minerals.
   - **d.** None of the above

10. Muscles
    - **a.** work in pairs.
    - **b.** can be voluntary or involuntary.
    - **c.** become stronger if exercised.
    - **d.** All of the above

Short Answer

11. How do muscles move bones?

12. Describe the skeletal system, and list four functions of bones.

13. Give an example of how organ systems work together.

14. List three injuries and two diseases that affect the skeletal system.

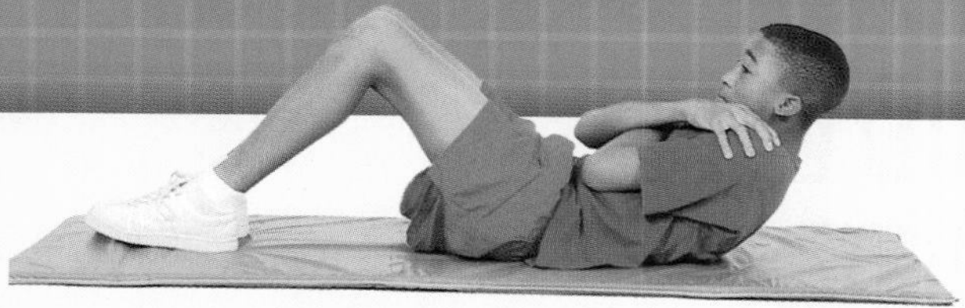

15. Compare aerobic exercise and resistance exercise.

16. What are two kinds of damage that may affect skin?

CRITICAL THINKING

17. **Concept Mapping** Use the following terms to create a concept map: *tissues, muscle tissue, connective tissue, cells, organ systems, organs, epithelial tissue,* and *nervous tissue.*

18. **Making Comparisons** Compare the shapes of the bones of the human skull with the shapes of the bones of the human leg. How do the shapes differ? Why are the shapes important?

19. **Making Inferences** Compare your elbows and fingertips in terms of the texture and sensitivity of the skin on these parts of your body. Why might the skin on these body parts differ?

20. **Making Inferences** Imagine that you are building a robot. Your robot will have a skeleton similar to a human skeleton. If the robot needs to be able to move a limb in all directions, what kind of joint would be needed? Explain your answer.

21. **Analyzing Ideas** Human bones are dense and are often filled with marrow. But many bones of birds are hollow. Why might birds have hollow bones?

22. **Identifying Relationships** Why might some muscles fail to work properly if a bone is broken?

INTERPRETING GRAPHICS

Use the cross section of skin below to answer the questions that follow.

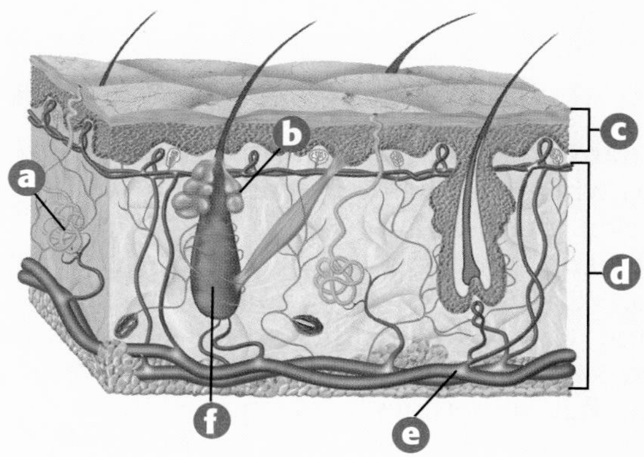

23. What is d called? What substance is most abundant in this layer?

24. What is the name and function of a?

25. What is the name and function of b?

26. Which letter corresponds to the part of the skin that is made up of epithelial tissue that contains dead cells?

27. Which letter corresponds to the part of the skin from which hair grows? What is this part called?

Standardized Test Preparation

READING

Read the passages below. Then, answer the questions that follow each passage.

Passage 1 Sometimes, doctors perform a skin graft to transfer some of a person's healthy skin to an area where skin has been damaged. Doctors perform skin grafts because skin is often the best "bandage" for a wound. Like cloth or plastic bandages, skin protects the wound. Skin allows the wound to breathe. Unlike cloth or plastic bandages, skin can regenerate itself as it covers a wound. But sometimes a person's skin is so severely damaged (by burns, for example) that the person doesn't have enough skin to spare.

1. Based on the passage, what can skin do that manufactured bandages can't do?

A Skin can protect a wound.
B Skin can stop more skin from being damaged.
C Skin can regenerate itself.
D Skin can prevent burns.

2. In the passage, what does the term *skin graft* most likely mean?

F a piece of skin transplanted from one part of the body to another
G a piece of skin made of plastic
H a piece of damaged skin that has been removed from the body
I burned skin

3. Based on the passage, why might a severe burn victim not receive a skin graft?

A Manufactured bandages are better.
B He or she doesn't have enough healthy skin.
C There isn't enough damaged skin to repair.
D Skin is the best bandage for a wound.

Passage 2 Making sure that your body maintains homeostasis is not an easy task. The task is difficult because your internal environment is always changing. Your body must do many different jobs to maintain homeostasis. Each cell in your body has a specific job in maintaining homeostasis. Your cells are organized into groups. A group of similar cells working together forms a tissue. Your body has four main kinds of tissue—epithelial tissue, connective tissue, muscle tissue, and nervous tissue. These tissues work together to form organs, which help maintain homeostasis.

1. Based on the passage, which of the following statements about tissues is true?

A Tissues do not help maintain homeostasis.
B Tissues form organ systems.
C Tissues are changing because the body's internal environment is always changing.
D There are four kinds of tissue.

2. According to the passage, which of the following statements about homeostasis is true?

F It is easy for the body to maintain homeostasis.
G The body must do different jobs to maintain homeostasis.
H Your internal environment rarely changes.
I Organs and organ systems do not help maintain homeostasis.

3. Which of the following statements about cells is false?

A Cells are organized into different groups.
B Cells form tissues.
C Cells work together.
D Cells don't maintain homeostasis.

INTERPRETING GRAPHICS

The line graph below shows hair growth over time. Use the graph to answer the questions that follow.

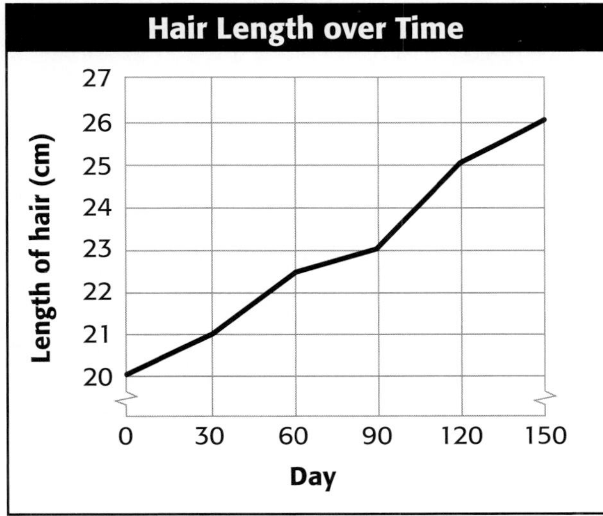

1. How long was the hair on day 60?
   A 20.0 cm
   B 21.0 cm
   C 22.5 cm
   D 23.0 cm

2. On which day was hair length 23 cm?
   F day 60
   G day 90
   H day 120
   I day 150

3. From day 0 to day 150, what is the average amount that hair grows every 30 days?
   A 0.5 cm
   B 1.2 cm
   C 1.5 cm
   D 2.0 cm

4. Based on the average amount of hair growth per 30-day period, how long would it take the hair to grow another 3.6 cm?
   F 30 days
   G 60 days
   H 90 days
   I 120 days

MATH

Read each question below, and choose the best answer.

1. About 40% of a person's mass is muscle tissue. If Max has a mass of 40 kg, about how much muscle tissue does he have?
   A 16 kg
   B 20 kg
   C 24 kg
   D 30 kg

2. When running, an adult inhales about 72 L of air per minute. That amount is 12 times the amount that an adult needs while resting. How much air does an adult inhale while resting?
   F 6 L/min
   G 12 L/min
   H 60 L/min
   I 64 L/min

3. Maggie likes to do bench presses, a resistance exercise. She bench presses 10 kg. If Maggie added 2 kg every 2 weeks, how long would it take her to reach 20 kg?
   A 4 weeks
   B 5 weeks
   C 10 weeks
   D 12 weeks

4. A box of 25 bandages costs $4.00. A roll of tape costs $1.50. Troy needs 125 bandages and 3 rolls of tape for a first-aid kit. Which of the following equations shows the cost of first-aid supplies, x?
   F $x = (125 \times 4.00) + (3 \times 1.50)$
   G $x = (25 \times 4.00) + (3 \times 1.50)$
   H $x = [(25 \times 4.00) \div 125] + (3 \times 1.50)$
   I $x = [(125 \div 25) \times 4.00] + (3 \times 1.50)$

5. Stephen wants to run a 10 K race. Right now, he can run 5 K. What is the percentage increase from 5 K to 10 K?
   A 50%
   B 100%
   C 200%
   D 500%

Science in Action

Weird Science

Engineered Skin

Your skin is your first line of defense against the outside world. Your skin keeps you safe from dehydration and infection, helps regulate body temperature, and helps remove some wastes. But what happens if a large portion of skin is damaged? Skin may not be able to function properly. For someone who has a serious burn, a doctor often uses skin from an undamaged part of the person's body to repair the damaged skin. But some burn victims don't have enough undamaged skin to spare. Doctors have discovered ways to engineer skin that can be used in place of human skin.

Math Activity

A doctor repaired 0.35 m^2 of an adult patient's skin with engineered skin. If an adult has about 2 m^2 of skin, what percentage of the patient's skin was repaired?

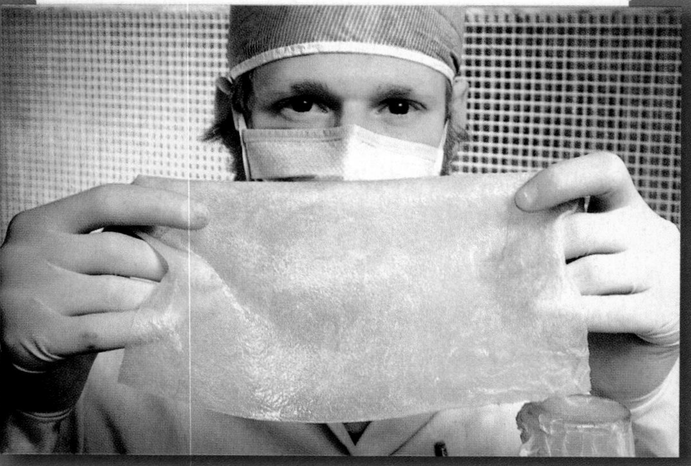

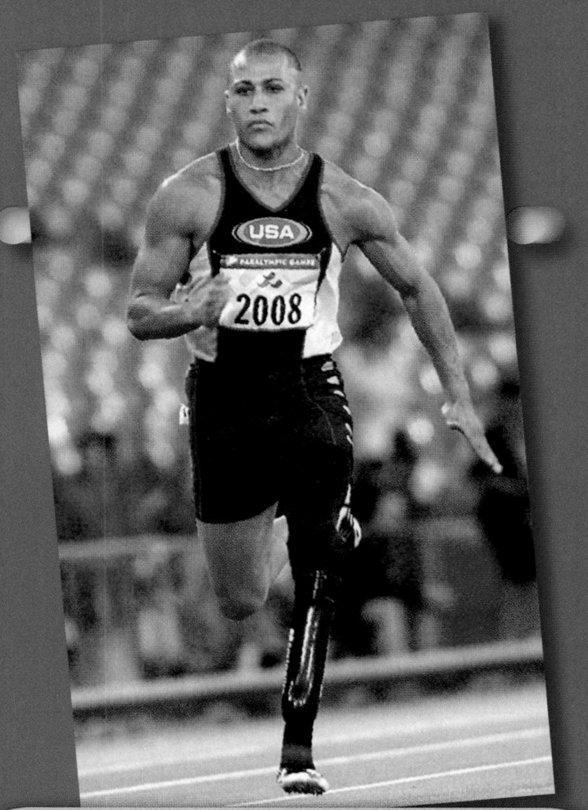

Science, Technology, and Society

Beating the Odds

Sometimes, people are born without limbs or lose limbs in accidents. Many of these people have prostheses (prahs THEE SEEZ), or human-made replacements for the body parts. Until recently, many of these prostheses made it more difficult for many people to participate in physical activities, such as sports. But new designs have led to lighter, more comfortable prostheses that move the way that a human limb does. These new designs have allowed athletes with physical disabilities to compete at higher levels.

Social Studies Activity

Research the use of prostheses throughout history. Create a timeline showing major advances in prosthesis use and design.

Careers

Zahra Beheshti

Physical Therapist A physical therapist is a licensed professional who helps people recover from injuries by using hands-on treatment instead of medicines. Dr. Zahra Beheshti is a physical therapist at the Princeton Physical Therapy Center in New Jersey. She often helps athletes who suffer from sports injuries.

After an injury, a person may go through a process called *rehabilitation* to regain the use of the injured body part. The most common mistake made by athletes is that they play sports before completely recovering from injuries. Dr. Beheshti explains, "Going back to their usual pre-injury routine could result in another injury."

Dr. Beheshti also teaches patients about preventing future sports injuries. "Most injuries happen when an individual engages in strenuous activities without a proper warm-up or cool-down period." Being a physical therapist is rewarding work. Dr. Beheshti says, "I get a lot of satisfaction when treating patients and see them regain their function and independence and return to their normal life."

Language Arts ACTIVITY

WRITING SKILL Interview a physical therapist who works in or near your community. Write a newspaper article about your interview.

To learn more about these Science in Action topics, visit go.hrw.com and type in the keyword HL5BD1F.

Current Science

Check out Current Science® articles related to this chapter by visiting go.hrw.com. Just type in the keyword HL5CS22.

Circulation and Respiration

About the PHOTO

Your circulatory system is made up of the heart, blood vessels, and blood. This picture is a colored scanning electron micrograph of red and white blood cells and cell fragments called *platelets.* Red blood cells are disk shaped, white blood cells are rounded, and platelets are the small green fragments. There are millions of blood cells in a drop of blood. Blood cells are so important that your body makes about 200 billion red blood cells every day.

PRE-READING ACTIVITY

FOLDNOTES

Four-Corner Fold

Before you read the chapter, create the FoldNote entitled "Four-Corner Fold" described in the **Study Skills** section of the Appendix. Label the flaps of the four-corner fold with the section titles "Cardiovascular system," "Blood," Lymphatic system," and "Respiratory system." Write what you know about each topic under the appropriate flap. As you read the chapter, add other information that you learn.

START-UP ACTIVITY

Exercise Your Heart

How does your heart respond to exercise? You can see this reaction by measuring your pulse.

Procedure

1. Take your pulse while remaining still. (Take your pulse by placing your fingers on the inside of your wrist just below your thumb.)
2. Using a **watch with a second hand,** count the number of heart beats in 15 s. Then, multiply this number by 4 to calculate the number of beats in 1 minute.
3. Do some moderate physical activity, such as jumping jacks or jogging in place, for 30 s.
4. Stop and calculate your heart rate again. **Caution:** Do not perform this exercise if you have difficulty breathing, if you have high blood pressure or asthma, or if you get dizzy easily.
5. Rest for 5 min.
6. Take your pulse again.

Analysis

1. How did exercise affect your heart rate? Why do you think this happened?
2. How does your heart rate affect the rate at which red blood cells travel throughout your body?
3. Did your heart rate return to normal (or almost normal) after you rested? Why or why not?

SECTION 1

The Cardiovascular System

READING WARM-UP

Objectives

- List four main parts of the cardiovascular system, and describe their functions.
- Describe the two types of circulation of blood in the body.
- List four cardiovascular problems.

Terms to Learn

cardiovascular system
artery
capillary
vein
pulmonary circulation
systemic circulation

READING STRATEGY

Paired Summarizing Read this section silently. In pairs, take turns summarizing the material. Stop to discuss ideas that seem confusing.

When you hear the word heart, *what do you think of first? Many people think of romance. Some people think of courage. But the heart is much more than a symbol of love or bravery. Your heart is an amazing pump.*

The heart is an organ that is part of your circulatory system. The *circulatory system* includes your heart; your blood; your veins, capillaries, and arteries; and your lymphatic system.

Your Cardiovascular System

Your heart creates pressure every time it beats. This pressure moves blood to every cell in your body through your cardiovascular system (KAR dee OH VAS kyoo luhr SIS tuhm). The **cardiovascular system** consists of the heart and the three types of blood vessels that carry blood throughout your body. The word *cardio* means "heart," and *vascular* means "blood vessel." The blood vessels—arteries, capillaries, and veins—carry blood pumped by the heart. **Figure 1** shows the major arteries and veins.

cardiovascular system a collection of organs that transport blood throughout the body

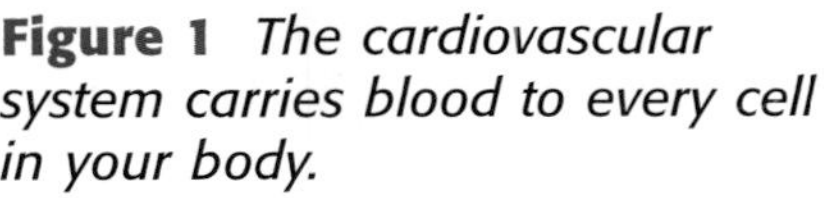

Reading Check What are the four main parts of the cardiovascular system? (*See the Appendix for answers to Reading Checks.*)

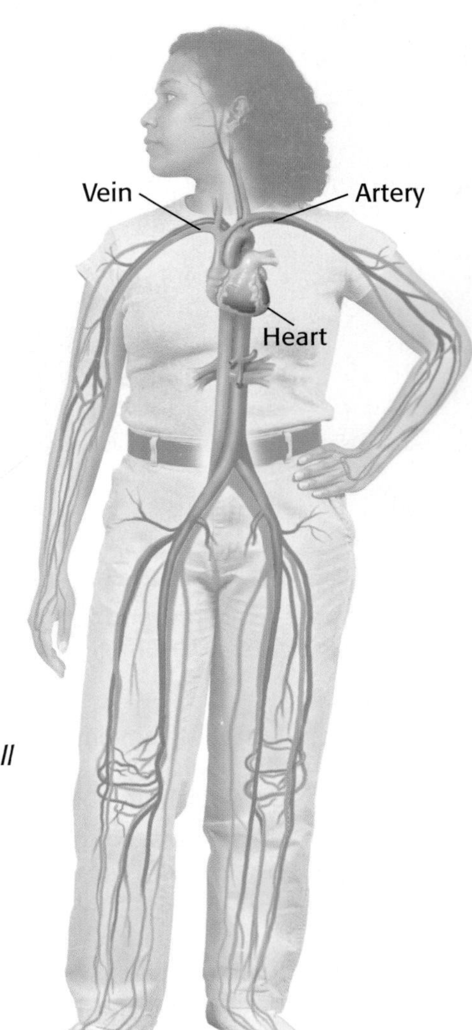

Figure 1 *The cardiovascular system carries blood to every cell in your body.*

The Heart

Your *heart* is an organ made mostly of cardiac muscle tissue. It is about the size of your fist and is almost in the center of your chest cavity. Like hearts of all mammals, your heart has a left side and a right side that are separated by a thick wall. The right side of the heart pumps oxygen-poor blood to the lungs. The left side pumps oxygen-rich blood to the body. As you can see in **Figure 2,** each side has an upper chamber and a lower chamber. Each upper chamber is called an *atrium* (plural, *atria*). Each lower chamber is called a *ventricle*.

Flaplike structures called *valves* are located between the atria and ventricles and in places where large arteries are attached to the heart. As blood moves through the heart, these valves close to prevent blood from going backward. The "lub-dub, lub-dub" sound of a beating heart is caused by the valves closing. **Figure 3** shows the flow of blood through the heart.

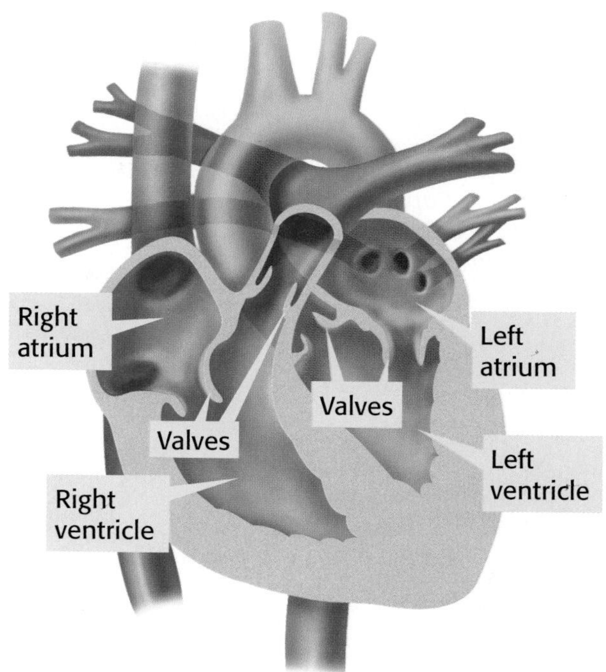

Figure 2 *The heart pumps blood through blood vessels. The vessels carrying oxygen-rich blood are shown in red. The vessels carrying oxygen-poor blood are shown in blue.*

Figure 3 **The Flow of Blood Through the Heart**

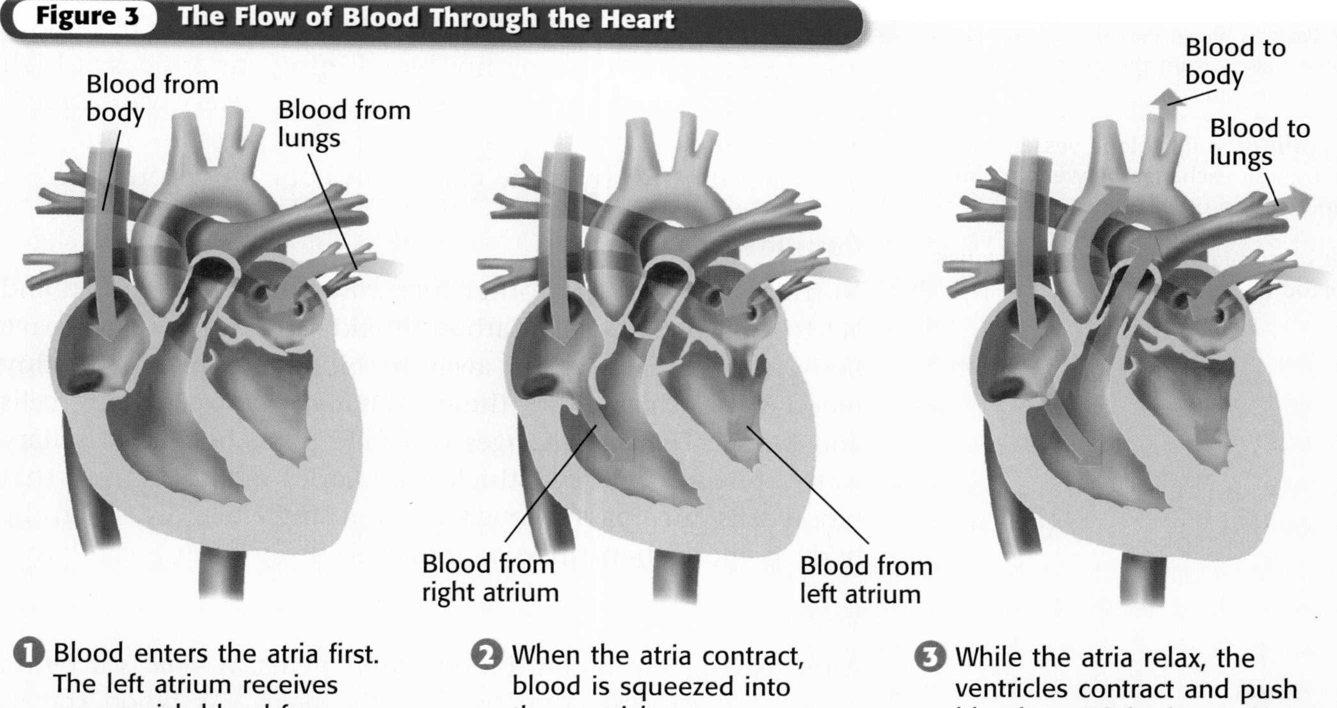

1. Blood enters the atria first. The left atrium receives oxygen-rich blood from the lungs. The right atrium receives oxygen-poor blood from the body.
2. When the atria contract, blood is squeezed into the ventricles.
3. While the atria relax, the ventricles contract and push blood out of the heart. Blood from the right ventricle goes to the lungs. Blood from the left ventricle goes to the rest of the body.

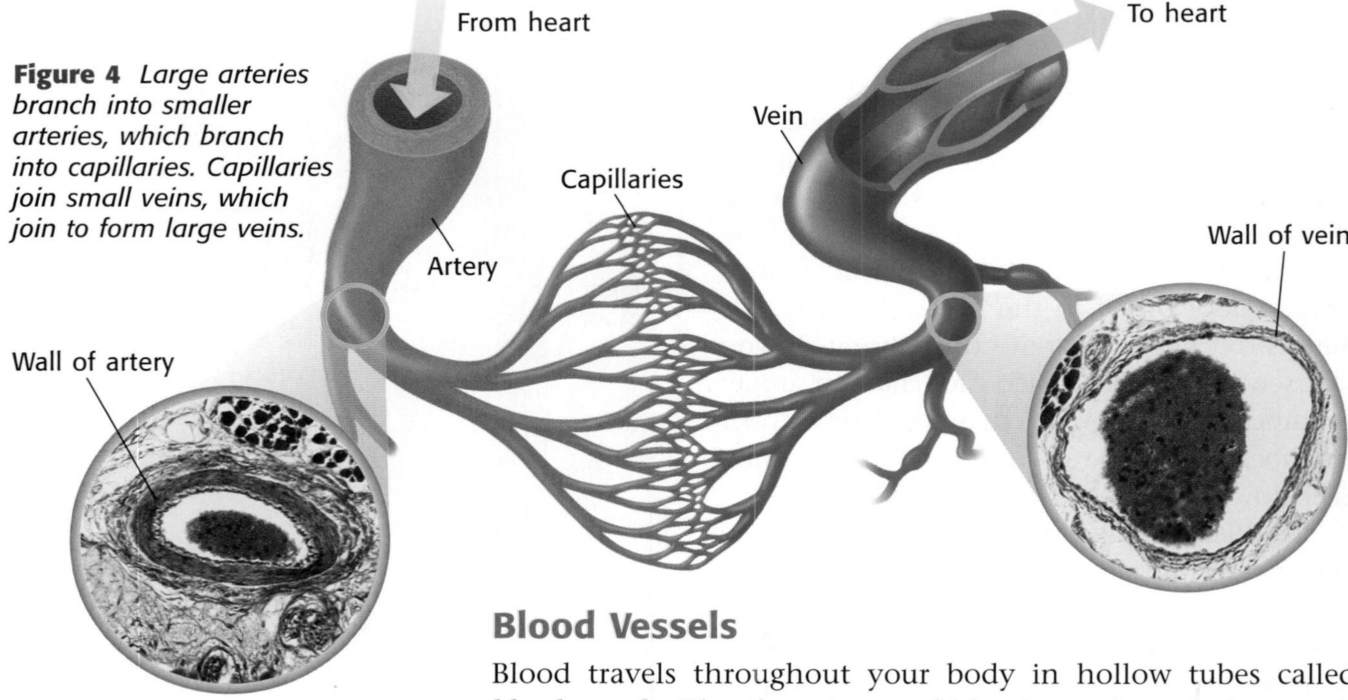

Figure 4 *Large arteries branch into smaller arteries, which branch into capillaries. Capillaries join small veins, which join to form large veins.*

Blood Vessels

Blood travels throughout your body in hollow tubes called *blood vessels.* The three types of blood vessels—arteries, capillaries, and veins—are shown in **Figure 4.**

Arteries

A blood vessel that carries blood away from the heart is an **artery.** Arteries have thick walls, which contain a layer of smooth muscle. Each heartbeat pumps blood into your arteries at high pressure. This pressure is your *blood pressure.* Artery walls stretch and are usually strong enough to stand the pressure. Your *pulse* is caused by the rhythmic change in your blood pressure.

artery a blood vessel that carries blood away from the heart to the body's organs

capillary a tiny blood vessel that allows an exchange between blood and cells in other tissue

vein in biology, a vessel that carries blood to the heart

Capillaries

Nutrients, oxygen, and other substances must leave blood and get to your body's cells. Carbon dioxide and other wastes leave body cells and are carried away by blood. A **capillary** is a tiny blood vessel that allows these exchanges between body cells and blood. These exchanges can take place because capillary walls are only one cell thick. Capillaries are so narrow that blood cells must pass through them in single file. No cell in the body is more than three or four cells away from a capillary.

Veins

After leaving capillaries, blood enters veins. A **vein** is a blood vessel that carries blood back to the heart. As blood travels through veins, valves in the veins keep the blood from flowing backward. When skeletal muscles contract, they squeeze nearby veins and help push blood toward the heart.

Reading Check Describe the three types of blood vessels.

Two Types of Circulation

Where does blood get the oxygen to deliver to your body? From your lungs! Your heart pumps blood to the lungs. In the lungs, carbon dioxide leaves the blood and oxygen enters the blood. The oxygen-rich blood then flows back to the heart. This circulation of blood between your heart and lungs is called **pulmonary circulation** (PUL muh NER ee SUHR kyoo LAY shuhn).

The oxygen-rich blood returning to the heart from the lungs is then pumped to the rest of the body. The circulation of blood between the heart and the rest of the body is called **systemic circulation** (sis TEM ik SUHR kyoo LAY shuhn). Both types of circulation are shown in **Figure 5.**

pulmonary circulation the flow of blood from the heart to the lungs and back to the heart through the pulmonary arteries, capillaries, and veins

systemic circulation the flow of blood from the heart to all parts of the body and back to the heart

Figure 5 **The Flow of Blood Through the Body**

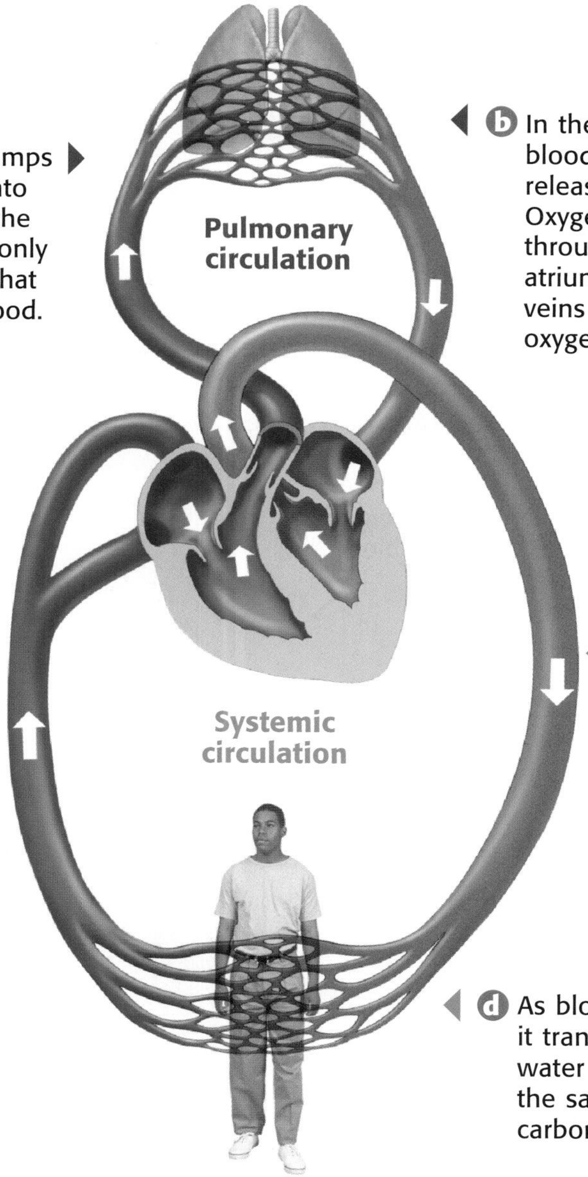

a The right ventricle pumps oxygen-poor blood into arteries that lead to the lungs. These are the only arteries in the body that carry oxygen-poor blood.

b In the capillaries of the lungs, blood takes up oxygen and releases carbon dioxide. Oxygen-rich blood travels through veins to the left atrium. These are the only veins in the body that carry oxygen-rich blood.

c The heart pumps oxygen-rich blood from the left ventricle into arteries and then into capillaries.

d As blood travels through capillaries, it transports oxygen, nutrients, and water to the cells of the body. At the same time, waste materials and carbon dioxide are carried away.

e Oxygen-poor blood travels back to the heart and is delivered into the right atrium by two large veins.

The Beat Goes On

A person's heart averages about 70 beats per minute.

1. Calculate how many times a heart beats in a day.
2. If a person lives for 75 years, how many times will his or her heart beat?
3. If an athlete's heart beats 50 times a minute, how many fewer times than an average heart will his or her heart beat in 30 days?

Cardiovascular Problems

More than just your heart and blood vessels are at risk if you have cardiovascular problems. Your whole body may be harmed. Cardiovascular problems can be caused by smoking, high levels of cholesterol in the blood, stress, physical inactivity, or heredity. Eating a healthy diet and getting plenty of exercise can reduce the risk of having cardiovascular problems.

Atherosclerosis

Heart diseases are the leading cause of death in the United States. A major cause of heart diseases is a cardiovascular disease called *atherosclerosis* (ATH uhr OH skluh ROH sis). Atherosclerosis happens when cholesterol (kuh LES tuhr AWL) builds up inside of blood vessels. This cholesterol buildup causes the blood vessels to become narrower and less elastic. **Figure 6** shows how clogged the pathway through a blood vessel can become. When an artery that supplies blood to the heart becomes blocked, the person may have a heart attack.

Reading Check Why is atherosclerosis dangerous?

High Blood Pressure

Atherosclerosis may be caused by hypertension. *Hypertension* is abnormally high blood pressure. The higher the blood pressure, the greater the risk of a heart attack, heart failure, kidney disease, and stroke. A *stroke* is when a blood vessel in the brain becomes clogged or ruptures. As a result, that part of the brain receives no oxygen. Without oxygen, brain cells die.

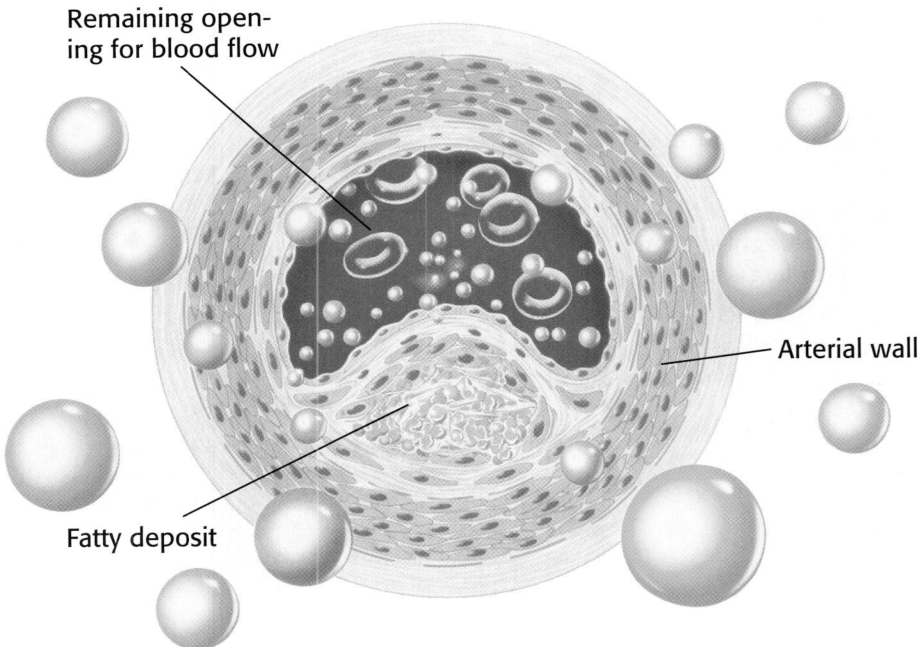

Figure 6 *This illustration shows the narrowing of an artery as the result of high levels of cholesterol in the blood. Lipid deposits (yellow) build up inside the blood vessel walls and block the flow of blood. Red blood cells and lipid particles (yellow balls) are shown escaping.*

Heart Attacks and Heart Failure

Two cardiovascular problems are heart attacks and heart failure. A *heart attack* happens when heart muscle cells die and part of the heart muscle is damaged. As shown in **Figure 7,** arteries that deliver oxygen to the heart may be blocked. Without oxygen, heart muscle cells die quickly. When enough heart muscle cells die, the heart may stop.

Heart failure is different. *Heart failure* happens when the heart cannot pump enough blood to meet the body's needs. Organs, such as the brain, lungs, and kidneys, may be damaged by lack of oxygen or nutrients, or by the buildup of fluids or wastes.

Figure 7 **Heart Attack**

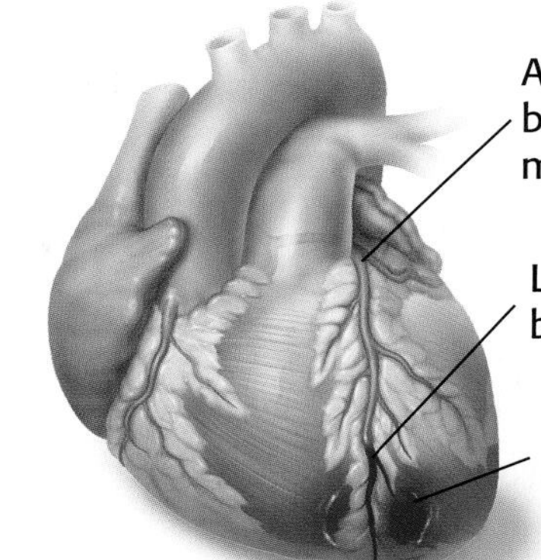

SECTION Review

Summary

- The cardiovascular system is made up of the heart and three types of blood vessels.
- The three types of blood vessels are arteries, veins, and capillaries.
- Oxygen-poor blood flows from the heart through the lungs, where it picks up oxygen.
- Oxygen-rich blood flows from the heart to the rest of the body.
- Cardiovascular problems include atherosclerosis, hypertension, heart attacks, and strokes.

Using Key Terms

For each pair of terms, explain how the meanings of the terms differ.

1. *artery* and *vein*
2. *systemic circulation* and *pulmonary circulation*

Understanding Key Ideas

3. Which of the following is true of blood in the pulmonary veins?
   a. The blood is going to the body.
   b. The blood is oxygen poor.
   c. The blood is going to the lungs.
   d. The blood is oxygen rich.
4. What are the four parts of the cardiovascular system? Describe the functions of each part.
5. What is the difference between a heart attack and heart failure?

Math Skills

6. An adult male's heart pumps about 2.8 million liters of blood a year. If his heart beats 70 times a minute, how much blood does his heart pump with each beat?

Critical Thinking

7. **Identifying Relationships** How is the structure of capillaries related to their function?
8. **Making Inferences** One of aspirin's effects is that it prevents platelets from being too "sticky." Why might doctors prescribe aspirin for patients who have had a heart attack?
9. **Analyzing Ideas** Veins and arteries are everywhere in your body. When a pulse is taken, it is usually taken at an artery in the neck or wrist. Explain why.
10. **Making Comparisons** Why is the structure of arteries different from the structure of capillaries?

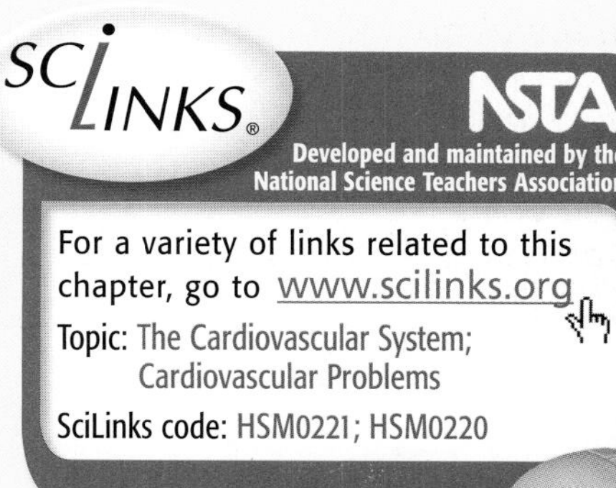

SCILINKS
NSTA
Developed and maintained by the National Science Teachers Association
For a variety of links related to this chapter, go to www.scilinks.org
Topic: The Cardiovascular System; Cardiovascular Problems
SciLinks code: HSM0221; HSM0220

SECTION 2

Blood

Blood is part of the circulatory system. It travels through miles and miles of blood vessels to reach every cell in your body. So, you must have a lot of blood, right?

Well, actually, an adult human body has about 5 L of blood. Your body probably has a little less than that. All the blood in your body would not fill two 3 L soda bottles.

READING WARM-UP

Objectives

- Identify the four main components of blood.
- Describe three functions of blood.
- Explain how blood pressure is measured.
- Explain what the ABO blood types are and why they are important.

Terms to Learn

blood
blood pressure

READING STRATEGY

Reading Organizer As you read this section, create an outline of the section. Use the headings from the section in your outline.

What Is Blood?

Your *circulatory system* is made up of your heart, your blood vessels, and blood. **Blood** is a connective tissue made up of plasma, red blood cells, platelets, and white blood cells. Blood carries oxygen and nutrients to all parts of your body.

blood the fluid that carries gases, nutrients, and wastes through the body and that is made up of plasma, red blood cells, platelets, and white blood cells

Reading Check What are the four main components of blood? (*See the Appendix for answers to Reading Checks.*)

Plasma

The fluid part of the blood is called plasma (PLAZ muh). *Plasma* is a mixture of water, minerals, nutrients, sugars, proteins, and other substances. Red blood cells, white blood cells, and platelets are found in plasma.

Red Blood Cells

Most blood cells are *red blood cells,* or RBCs. RBCs, such as the ones shown in **Figure 1,** take oxygen to every cell in your body. Cells need oxygen to carry out their functions. Each RBC has hemoglobin (HEE moh GLOH bin). *Hemoglobin* is an oxygen-carrying protein. Hemoglobin clings to the oxygen you inhale. RBCs can then transport oxygen throughout the body. Hemoglobin also gives RBCs their red color.

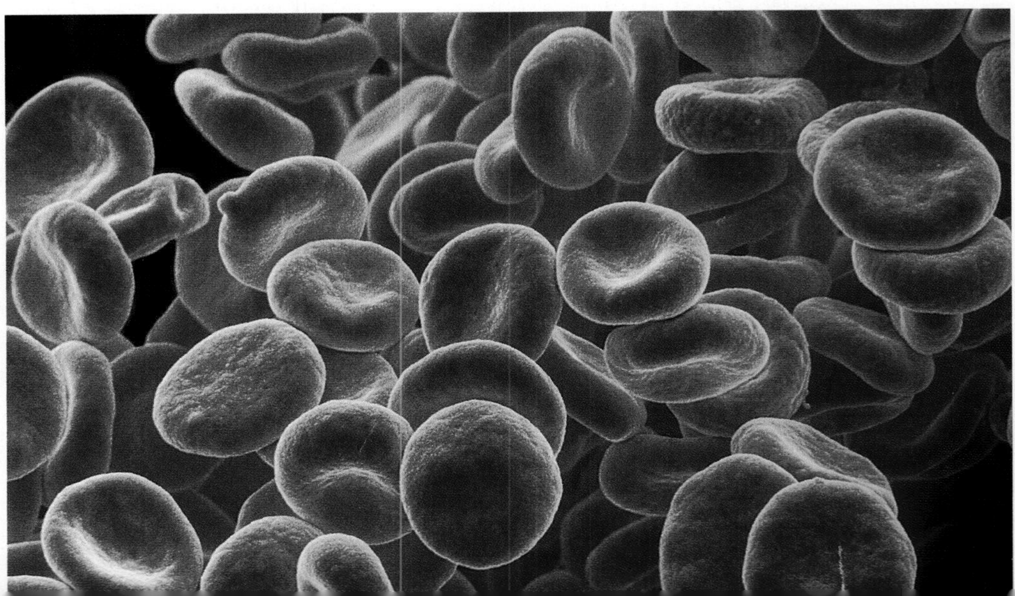

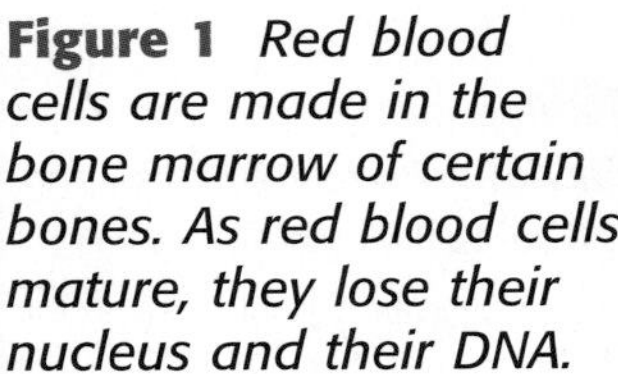

Figure 1 *Red blood cells are made in the bone marrow of certain bones. As red blood cells mature, they lose their nucleus and their DNA.*

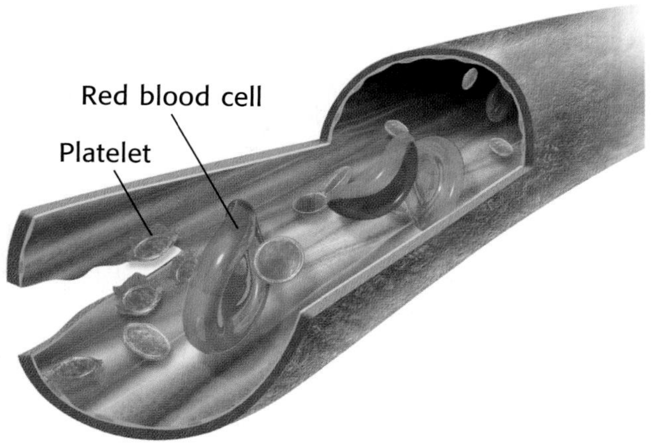

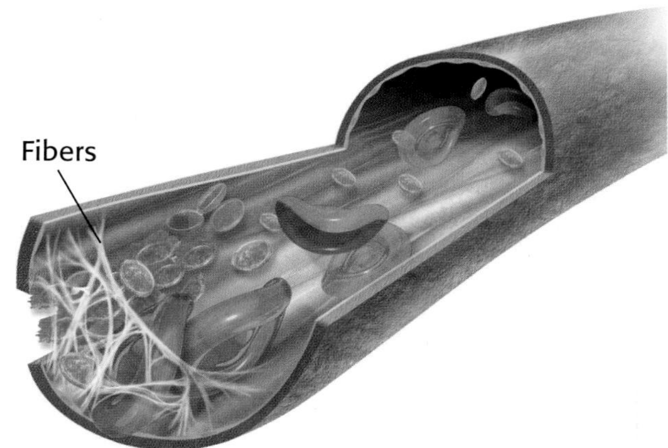

Figure 2 *Platelets release chemicals in damaged vessels and cause fibers to form. The fibers make a "net" that traps blood cells and stops bleeding.*

Platelets

Drifting among the blood cells are tiny particles called platelets. *Platelets* are pieces of larger cells found in bone marrow. These larger cells remain in the bone marrow, but fragments are pinched off and enter the bloodstream as platelets. Platelets last for only 5 to 10 days, but they are an important part of blood. When you cut or scrape your skin, you bleed because blood vessels have been opened. As soon as bleeding starts, platelets begin to clump together in the damaged area. They form a plug that helps reduce blood loss, as shown in **Figure 2.** Platelets also release chemicals that react with proteins in plasma. The reaction causes tiny fibers to form. The fibers help create a blood clot.

White Blood Cells

Sometimes *pathogens* (PATH uh juhnz)—bacteria, viruses, and other microscopic particles that can make you sick—enter your body. When they do, they often meet *white blood cells,* or WBCs. WBCs, shown in **Figure 3,** help keep you healthy by destroying pathogens. WBCs also help clean wounds.

WBCs fight pathogens in several ways. Some WBCs squeeze out of blood vessels and move around in tissues, searching for pathogens. When they find a pathogen, they destroy it. Other WBCs release antibodies. *Antibodies* are chemicals that identify or destroy pathogens. WBCs also keep you healthy by destroying body cells that have died or been damaged. Most WBCs are made in bone marrow. Some WBCs mature in the lymphatic system.

Reading Check **Why are WBCs important to your health?**

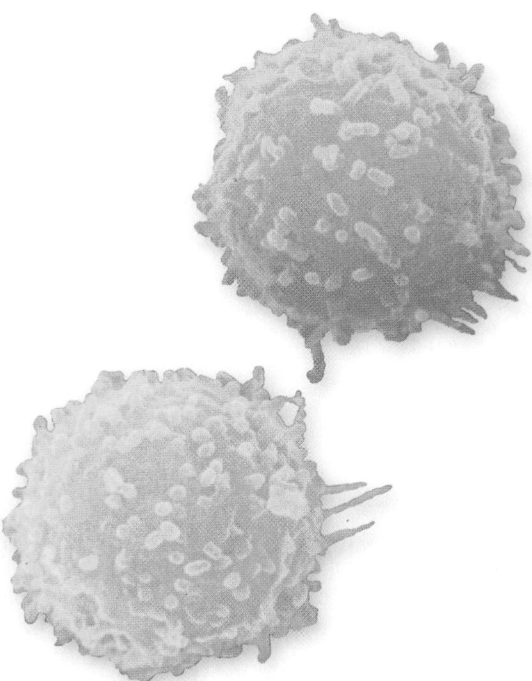

Figure 3 *White blood cells defend the body against pathogens. These white blood cells have been colored yellow to make their shape easier to see.*

Body Temperature Regulation

Your blood does more than supply your cells with oxygen and nutrients. It also helps regulate your body temperature. When your brain senses that your body temperature is rising, it signals blood vessels in your skin to enlarge. As the vessels enlarge, heat from your blood is transferred to your skin. This transfer helps lower your temperature. When your brain senses that your temperature is normal, it instructs your blood vessels to return to their normal size.

blood pressure the force that blood exerts on the walls of the arteries

Blood Pressure

Every time your heart beats, it pushes blood out of the heart and into your arteries. The force exerted by blood on the inside walls of arteries is called **blood pressure.**

Blood pressure is expressed in millimeters of mercury (mm Hg). For example, a blood pressure of 110 mm Hg means the pressure on the artery walls can push a narrow column of mercury to a height of 110 mm.

Blood pressure is usually given as two numbers, such as 110/70 mm Hg. Systolic (sis TAHL ik) pressure is the first number. *Systolic pressure* is the pressure inside large arteries when the ventricles contract. The surge of blood causes the arteries to bulge and produce a pulse. The second number, *diastolic* (DIE uh STAHL ik) *pressure,* is the pressure inside arteries when the ventricles relax. For adults, a blood pressure of 120/80 mm Hg or below is considered healthy. High blood pressure can cause heart or kidney damage.

Reading Check **What is the difference between systolic pressure and diastolic pressure?**

Blood Types

Every person has one of four blood types: A, B, AB, or O. Your blood type refers to the type of chemicals you have on the surface of your RBCs. These surface chemicals are called *antigens* (AN tuh juhnz). Type A blood has A antigens; type B has B antigens; and type AB has both A and B antigens. Type O blood has neither the A nor the B antigen.

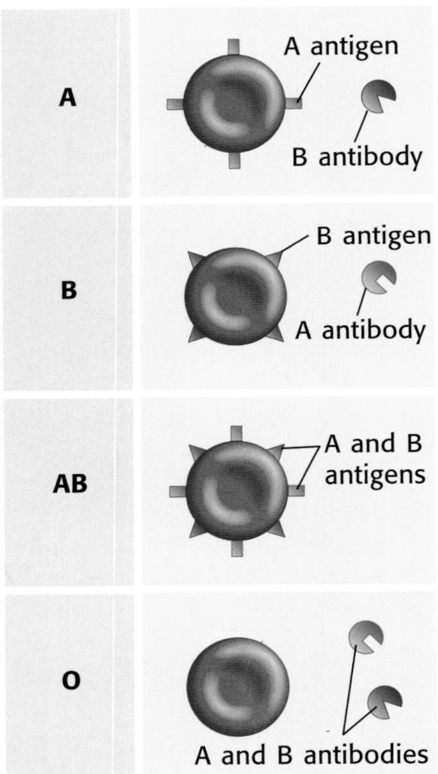

Figure 4 *This figure shows which antigens and antibodies may be present in each blood type.*

The different blood types have different antigens on their RBCs. They may also have different antibodies in the plasma. These antibodies react to antigens of other blood types as if the antigens were pathogens. As shown in **Figure 4,** type A blood has antibodies that react to type B blood. If a person with type A blood receives type B blood, the type B antibodies attach themselves to the type B RBCs. These RBCs begin to clump together, and the clumps may block blood vessels. A reaction to the wrong blood type may be fatal.

Blood Types and Transfusions

Sometimes, a person must be given a blood transfusion. A *transfusion* is the injection of blood or blood components into a person to replace blood that has been lost because of surgery or an injury. **Figure 5** shows bags of blood that may be given in a transfusion. The blood type is clearly marked. Because the ABO blood types have different antigen-antibody reactions, a person receiving blood cannot receive blood from just anyone. **Table 1** shows blood transfusion possibilities.

***Table 1* Blood Transfusion Possibilities**

Type	Can receive	Can donate to
A	A, O	A, AB
B	B, O	B, AB
AB	all	AB only
O	O	all

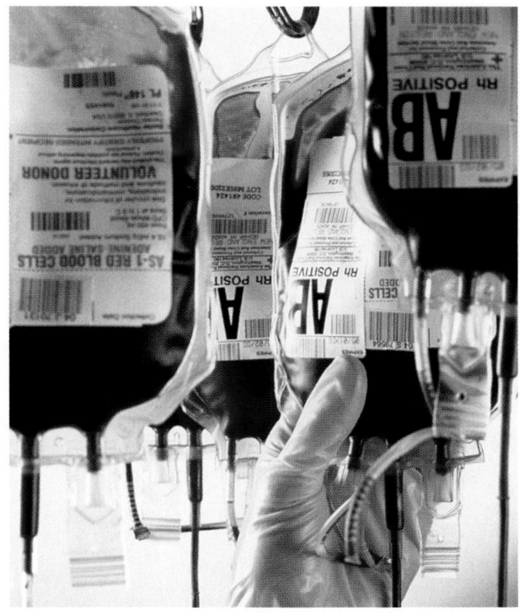

Figure 5 *The blood type must be clearly labeled on blood stored for transfusions.*

Reading Check **People with type O blood are sometimes called universal donors. Why might this be true?**

SECTION Review

Summary

- Blood's four main components are plasma, red blood cells, platelets, and white blood cells.
- Blood carries oxygen and nutrients to cells, helps protect against disease, and helps regulate body temperature.
- Blood pressure is the force blood exerts on the inside walls of arteries.
- Every person has one of four ABO blood types.
- Mixing blood types may be fatal.

Using Key Terms

1. Use each of the following terms in a separate sentence: *blood* and *blood pressure.*

Understanding Key Ideas

2. A person with type B blood can donate blood to people with which type(s) of blood?
   - **a.** B, AB
   - **b.** A, AB
   - **c.** AB only
   - **d.** All types
3. List the four main components of blood and tell what each component does.
4. Why is it important for a doctor to know a patient's blood type?

Math Skills

5. A person has a systolic pressure of 174 mm Hg. What percentage of normal (120 mm Hg) is this?

Critical Thinking

6. **Identifying Relationships** How does the body use blood and blood vessels to help maintain proper body temperature?
7. **Predicting Consequences** Some blood conditions and diseases affect the ability of red blood cells to deliver oxygen to cells of the body. Predict what might happen to a person with a disease of that type.

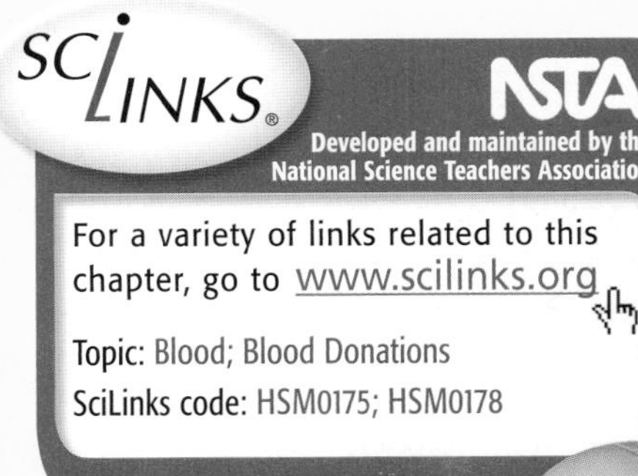

For a variety of links related to this chapter, go to www.scilinks.org

Topic: Blood; Blood Donations
SciLinks code: HSM0175; HSM0178

SECTION 3

The Lymphatic System

Every time your heart pumps, a little fluid is forced out of the thin walls of the capillaries. Some of this fluid collects in the spaces around your cells. What happens to this fluid?

READING WARM-UP

Objectives

- Describe the relationship between the lymphatic system and the circulatory system.
- Identify six parts of the lymphatic system, and describe their functions.

Terms to Learn

lymphatic system	thymus
lymph	spleen
lymph node	tonsils

READING STRATEGY

Prediction Guide Before reading this section, write the title of each heading in this section. Next, under each heading, write what you think you will learn.

Most of the fluid is reabsorbed through the capillaries into your blood. But some is not. Your body has a second circulatory system called the lymphatic (lim FAT ik) system.

The **lymphatic system** is the group of organs and tissues that collect the excess fluid and return it to your blood. The lymphatic system also helps your body fight pathogens.

lymphatic system a collection of organs whose primary function is to collect extracellular fluid and return it to the blood

lymph the fluid that is collected by the lymphatic vessels and nodes

Vessels of the Lymphatic System

The fluid collected by the lymphatic system is carried through vessels. The smallest vessels of the lymphatic system are *lymph capillaries.* Lymph capillaries absorb some of the fluid and particles from between the cells. These particles are too large to enter blood capillaries. Some of these particles are dead cells or pathogens. The fluid and particles absorbed into lymph capillaries are called **lymph.**

As shown in **Figure 1,** lymph capillaries carry lymph into larger vessels called *lymphatic vessels.* Skeletal muscles squeeze these vessels to force lymph through the lymphatic system. Valves inside lymphatic vessels stop backflow. Lymph drains into the large neck veins of the cardiovascular system.

Reading Check **How is the lymphatic system related to the cardiovascular system?** (*See the Appendix for answers to Reading Checks.*)

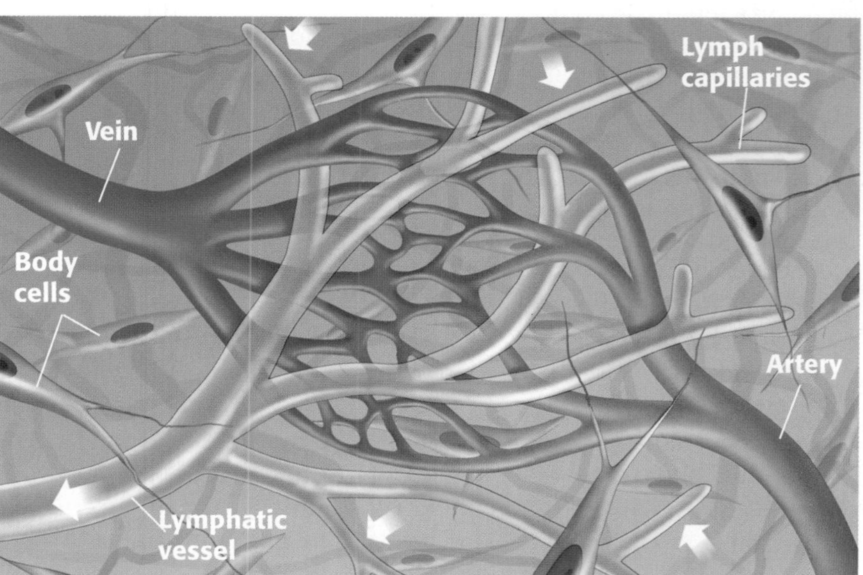

Figure 1 *The white arrows show the movement of lymph into lymph capillaries and through lymphatic vessels.*

Other Parts of the Lymphatic System

In addition to vessels and capillaries, several organs and tissues are part of the lymphatic system. These organs and tissues are shown in **Figure 2.** Bone marrow plays an important role in your lymphatic system. The other parts of the lymphatic system are the lymph nodes, the thymus gland, the spleen, and the tonsils.

lymph node an organ that filters lymph and that is found along the lymphatic vessels

thymus the main gland of the lymphatic system; it produces mature T lymphocytes

Bone Marrow

Bones—part of your skeletal system—are very important to your lymphatic system. *Bone marrow* is the soft tissue inside of bones. Bone marrow is where most red and white blood cells, including lymphocytes (LIM foh SIETS), are produced. *Lymphocytes* are a type of white blood cell that helps your body fight pathogens.

Lymph Nodes

As lymph travels through lymphatic vessels, it passes through lymph nodes. **Lymph nodes** are small, bean-shaped masses of tissue that remove pathogens and dead cells from the lymph. Lymph nodes are concentrated in the armpits, neck, and groin.

Lymph nodes contain lymphocytes. Some lymphocytes—called *killer T cells*—surround and destroy pathogens. Other lymphocytes—called *B cells*—produce antibodies that attach to pathogens. These marked pathogens clump together and are then destroyed by other cells.

When bacteria or other pathogens cause an infection, WBCs may multiply greatly. The lymph nodes fill with WBCs that are fighting the infection. As a result, some lymph nodes may become swollen and painful. Your doctor may feel these swollen lymph nodes to see if you have an infection. In fact, if your lymph nodes are swollen and sore, you or your parent can feel them, too. Swollen lymph nodes are sometimes an early clue that you have an infection.

Thymus

T cells develop from immature lymphocytes produced in the bone marrow. Before these cells are ready to fight infections, they develop further in the thymus. The **thymus** is the gland that produces T cells that are ready to fight infection. The thymus is located behind the breastbone, just above the heart. Mature lymphocytes from the thymus travel through the lymphatic system to other areas of your body.

Figure 2 The Lymphatic System

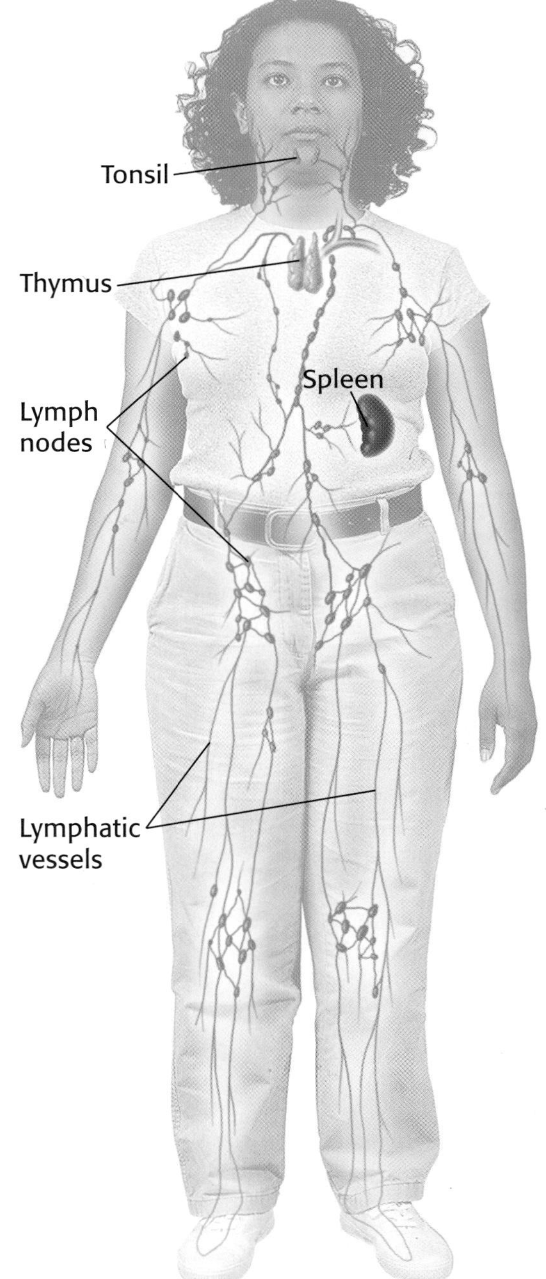

Spleen

spleen the largest lymphatic organ in the body

Your spleen is the largest lymphatic organ. The **spleen** stores and produces lymphocytes. It is a purplish organ about the size of your fist. Your spleen is soft and spongy. It is located in the upper left side of your abdomen. As blood flows through the spleen, lymphocytes attack or mark pathogens in the blood. If pathogens cause an infection, the spleen may also release lymphocytes into the bloodstream.

In addition to being part of the lymphatic system, the spleen produces, monitors, stores, and destroys blood cells. When red blood cells (RBCs) are squeezed through the spleen's capillaries, the older and more fragile cells burst. These damaged RBCs are then taken apart by some of the cells in the spleen. Some parts of these RBCs may be reused. For this reason, you can think of the spleen as the red-blood-cell recycling center.

The spleen has two important functions. The *white pulp,* shown in **Figure 3,** is part of the lymphatic system. It helps to fight infections. The *red pulp,* also shown in **Figure 3,** removes unwanted material, such as defective red blood cells, from the blood. However, it is possible to lead a healthy life without your spleen. If the spleen is damaged or removed, other organs in the body take over many of its functions.

Reading Check **What are two important functions of the spleen?**

CONNECTION TO Social Studies

WRITING SKILL **Vent Your Spleen** Why do we say that someone is "venting his spleen"? What does it mean? Conduct library or Internet research about this phrase. Write a report on what you have learned.

Figure 3 **White and Red Pulp in the Spleen**

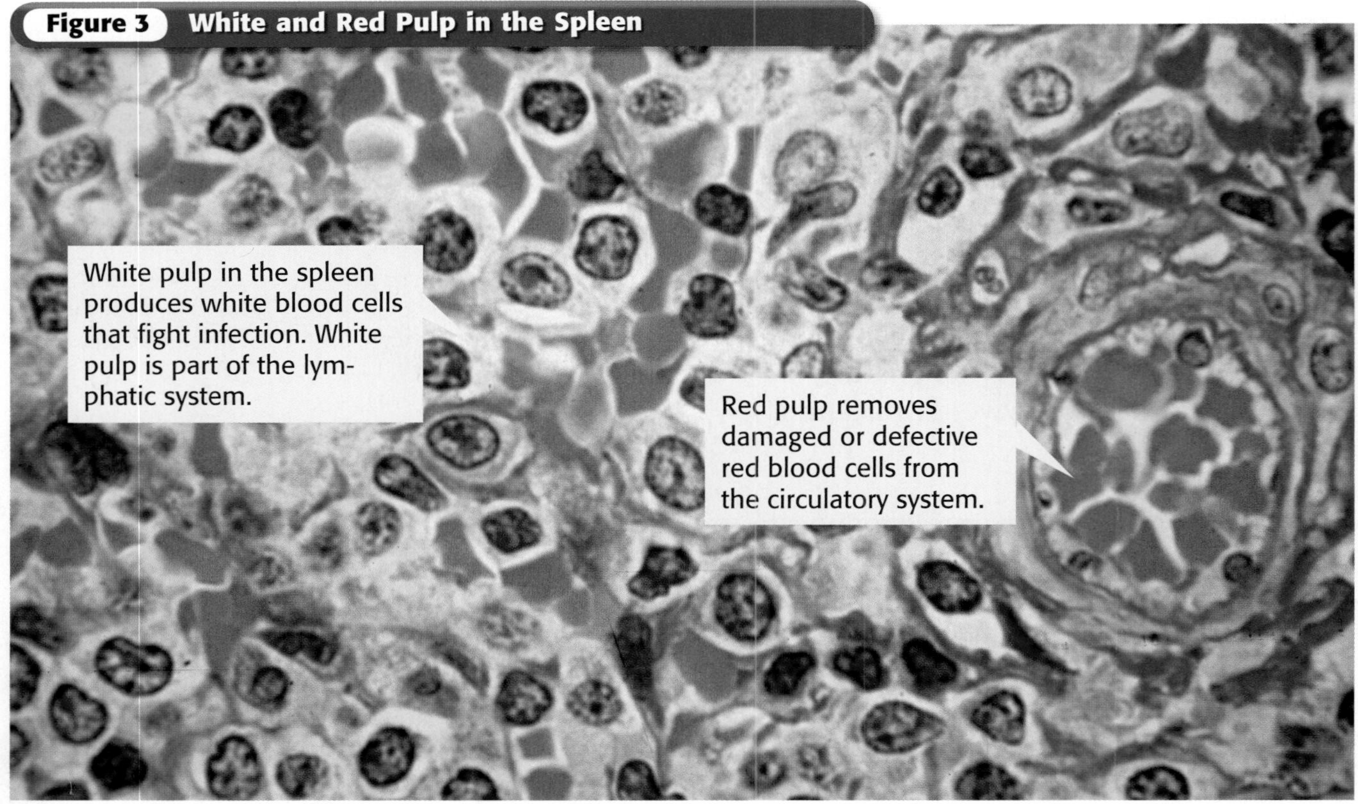

White pulp in the spleen produces white blood cells that fight infection. White pulp is part of the lymphatic system.
Red pulp removes damaged or defective red blood cells from the circulatory system.

Tonsils

The lymphatic system includes your tonsils. **Tonsils** are lymphatic tissue in the nasal cavity and at the back of the mouth on either side of the tongue. Each tonsil is about the size of a large olive.

Tonsils help defend the body against infection. Lymphocytes in the tonsils trap pathogens that enter the throat. Sometimes, tonsils become infected and are red, swollen, and very sore. Severely infected tonsils may be covered with patches of white, infected tissue. Sore, swollen tonsils, such as those in **Figure 4,** make swallowing difficult.

Sometimes, a doctor will suggest surgery to remove the tonsils. In the past, this surgery was frequently done in childhood. It is less common today. Surgery is now done only if a child has frequent, severe tonsil infections or if a child's tonsils are so enlarged that breathing is difficult.

tonsils small, rounded masses of lymphatic tissue located in the pharynx and in the passage from the mouth to the pharynx

Figure 4 *Tonsils help protect your throat and lungs from infection by trapping pathogens.*

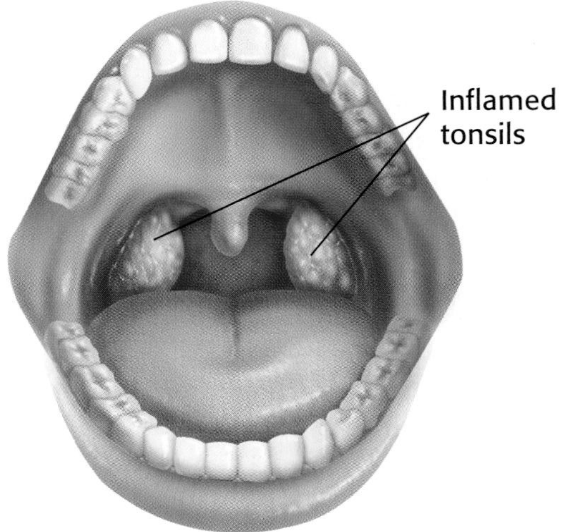

SECTION Review

Summary

- The lymphatic system collects fluid from between the cells and returns it to the blood.
- The lymphatic system contains cells that help the body fight disease.
- The lymphatic system consists of lymphatic vessels, lymph, and tissues and organs throughout the body.
- The thymus, spleen, and tonsils contain lymphocytes that help fight pathogens.

Using Key Terms

1. Use each of the following terms in a separate sentence: *lymph nodes, spleen,* and *tonsils.*

Understanding Key Ideas

2. Lymph
   a. is the same as blood.
   b. is fluid in the cells.
   c. drains into your muscles.
   d. is fluid collected by lymphatic vessels.
3. Name six parts of the lymphatic system. Tell what each part does.
4. How are your cardiovascular and lymphatic systems related?

Math Skills

5. One cubic millimeter of blood contains 5 million RBCs and 10,000 WBCs. How many times more RBCs are there than WBCs?

Critical Thinking

6. **Expressing Opinions** Some people have frequent, severe tonsil infections. These infections can be treated with medicine, and the infections usually go away after a few days. Do you think removing tonsils in such a case is a good idea? Explain.
7. **Analyzing Ideas** Why is it important that lymphatic tissue is spread throughout the body?

SCILINKS
NSTA
Developed and maintained by the National Science Teachers Association
For a variety of links related to this chapter, go to www.scilinks.org
Topic: The Lymphatic System
SciLinks code: HSM0891

SECTION 4

The Respiratory System

Breathing—you do it all the time. You're doing it right now. You hardly ever think about it, though, unless you suddenly can't breathe.

Then, it becomes very clear that you have to breathe in order to live. But why is breathing important? Your body needs oxygen in order to get energy from the foods you eat. Breathing makes this process possible.

READING WARM-UP

Objectives

- Describe the parts of the respiratory system and their functions.
- Explain how breathing happens.
- Discuss the relationship between the respiratory system and the cardiovascular system.
- Identify two respiratory disorders.

Terms to Learn

respiration	trachea
respiratory system	bronchus
pharynx	alveoli
larynx	

READING STRATEGY

Reading Organizer As you read this section, make a flowchart of the steps of the process of respiration.

Respiration and the Respiratory System

The words *breathing* and *respiration* are often used to mean the same thing. However, breathing is only one part of respiration. **Respiration** is the process by which a body gets and uses oxygen and releases carbon dioxide and water. Respiration is divided into two parts. The first part is breathing, which involves inhaling and exhaling. The second part is cellular respiration, which involves chemical reactions that release energy from food.

Breathing is made possible by your respiratory system. The **respiratory system** is the group of organs that take in oxygen and get rid of carbon dioxide. The nose, throat, lungs, and passageways that lead to the lungs make up the respiratory system. **Figure 1** shows the parts of the respiratory system.

respiration the exchange of oxygen and carbon dioxide between living cells and their environment; includes breathing and cellular respiration

respiratory system a collection of organs whose primary function is to take in oxygen and expel carbon dioxide

Figure 1 *Air moves into and out of the body through the respiratory system.*

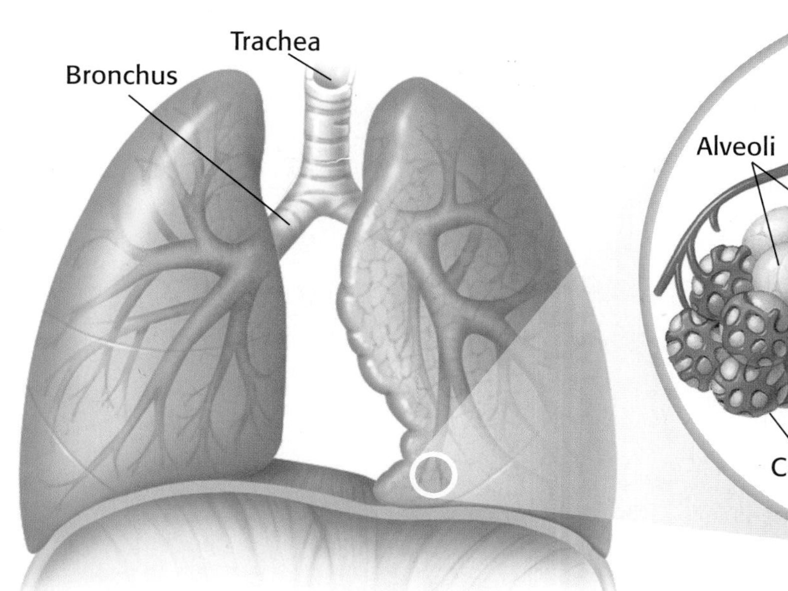

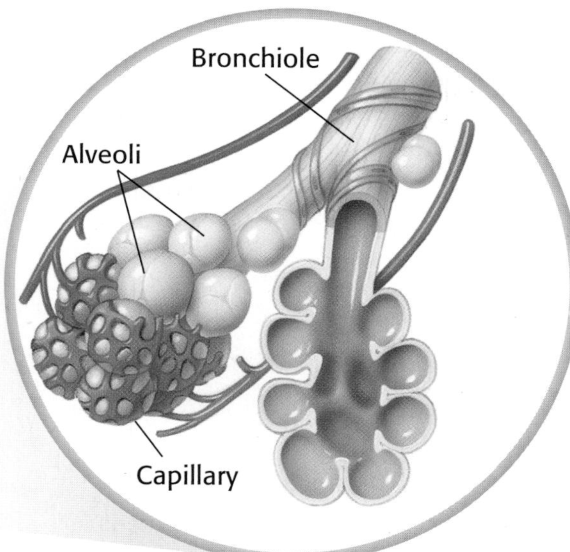

Figure 2 *Inside your lungs, the bronchi branch into bronchioles. The bronchioles lead to tiny sacs called alveoli.*

Nose, Pharynx, and Larynx

Your *nose* is the main passageway into and out of the respiratory system. Air can be breathed in through and out of the nose. Air can also enter and leave through the mouth.

From the nose, air flows into the **pharynx** (FAR ingks), or throat. Food and drink also travel through the pharynx on the way to the stomach. The pharynx branches into two tubes. One tube, the *esophagus,* leads to the stomach. The other tube is the larynx (LAR ingks). The larynx leads to the lungs.

The **larynx** is the part of the throat that contains the vocal cords. The *vocal cords* are a pair of elastic bands that stretch across the larynx. Muscles connected to the larynx control how much the vocal cords are stretched. When air flows between the vocal cords, the cords vibrate. These vibrations make sound.

pharynx the passage from the mouth to the larynx and esophagus

larynx the area of the throat that contains the vocal cords and produces vocal sounds

trachea the tube that connects the larynx to the lungs

bronchus one of the two tubes that connect the lungs with the trachea

alveoli any of the tiny air sacs of the lungs where oxygen and carbon dioxide are exchanged

Trachea

The larynx guards the entrance to a large tube called the **trachea** (TRAY kee uh), or windpipe. Your body has two large, spongelike lungs. The trachea, shown in **Figure 2,** is the passageway for air traveling from the larynx to the lungs.

Bronchi and Alveoli

The trachea splits into two branches called **bronchi** (BRAHNG KIE) (singular, *bronchus*). One bronchus connects to each lung. Each bronchus branches into smaller tubes that are called *bronchioles* (BRAHNG kee OHLZ). In the lungs, each bronchiole branches to form tiny sacs that are called **alveoli** (al VEE uh LIE) (singular, *alveolus*).

Reading Check **Describe the flow of air from your nose to your alveoli.** (*See the Appendix for answers to Reading Checks.*)

Figure 3 The Role of Blood in Respiration

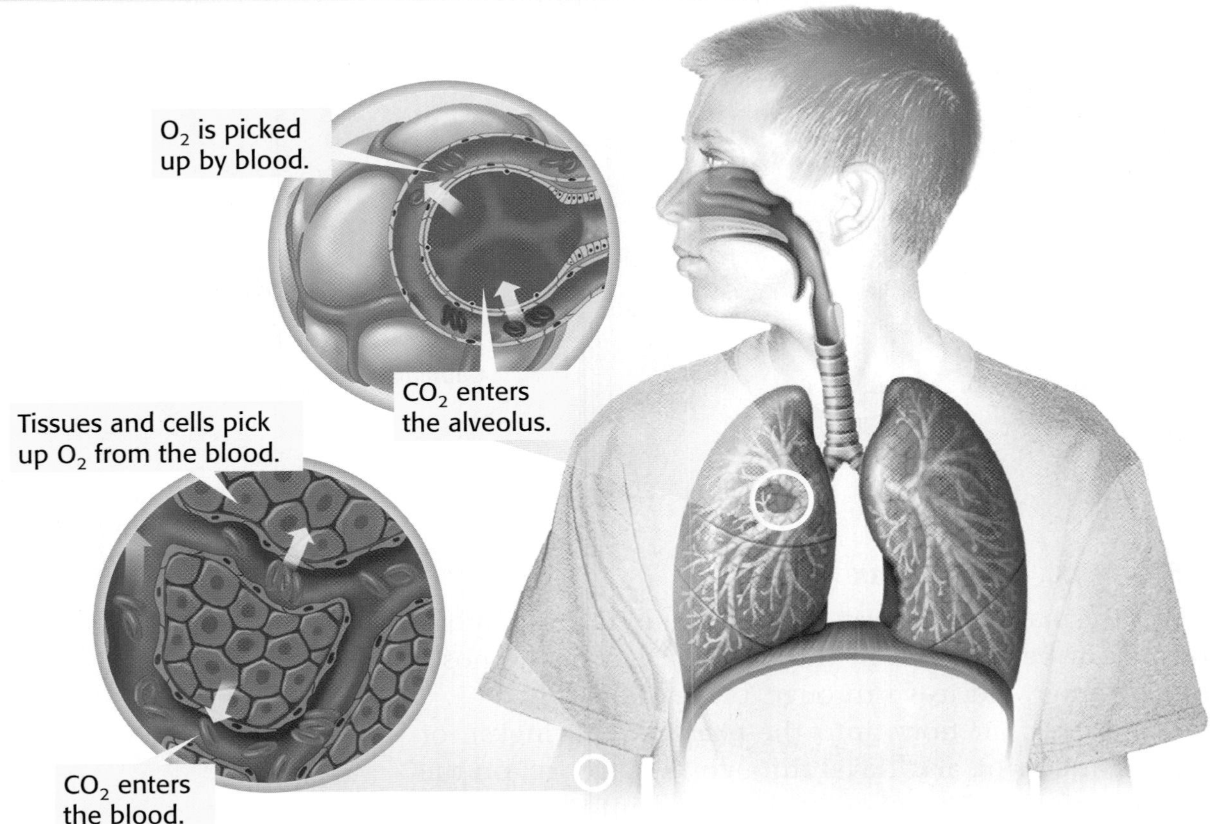
O_2 is picked up by blood.
CO_2 enters the alveolus.
Tissues and cells pick up O_2 from the blood.
CO_2 enters the blood.

Breathing

When you breathe, air is sucked into or forced out of your lungs. However, your lungs have no muscles of their own. Instead, breathing is done by the diaphragm (DIE uh FRAM) and rib muscles. The *diaphragm* is a dome-shaped muscle beneath the lungs. When you inhale, the diaphragm contracts and moves down. The chest cavity's volume increases. At the same time, some of your rib muscles contract and lift your rib cage. As a result, your chest cavity gets bigger and a vacuum is created. Air is sucked in. Exhaling is this process in reverse.

CONNECTION TO Chemistry

Oxygen and Blood When people who live at low elevations travel up into the mountains, they may find themselves breathing heavily even when they are not exerting themselves. Why might this happen?

Breathing and Cellular Respiration

In *cellular respiration,* oxygen is used by cells to release energy stored in molecules of glucose. Where does the oxygen come from? When you inhale, you take in oxygen. This oxygen diffuses into red blood cells and is carried to tissue cells. The oxygen then diffuses out of the red blood cells and into each cell. Cells use the oxygen to release chemical energy. During the process, carbon dioxide (CO_2) and water are produced. Carbon dioxide is exhaled from the lungs. **Figure 3** shows how breathing and blood circulation are related.

Reading Check What is cellular respiration?

Respiratory Disorders

Millions of people suffer from respiratory disorders. Respiratory disorders include asthma, emphysema, and severe acute respiratory syndrome (SARS). Asthma causes the bronchioles to narrow. A person who has asthma has difficulty breathing. An asthma attack may be triggered by irritants such as dust or pollen. SARS is caused by a virus. A person who has SARS may have a fever and difficulty breathing. Emphysema happens when the alveoli have been damaged. People who have emphysema have trouble getting the oxygen they need. **Figure 4** shows a lung damaged by emphysema.

Figure 4 *The photo on the left shows a healthy lung. The photo on the right shows the lung of a person who had emphysema.*

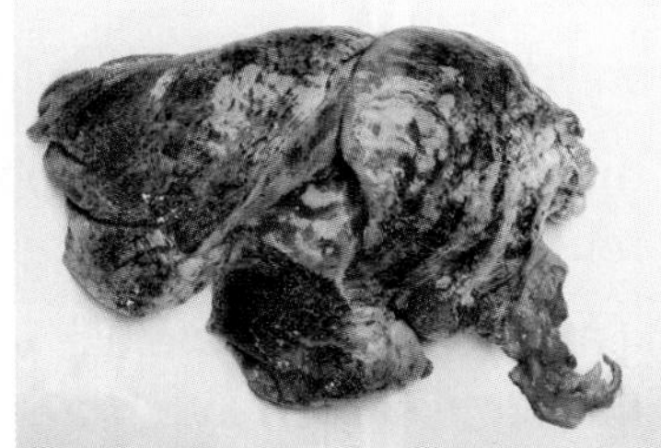

Quick Lab

Why Do People Snore?

1. Get a **15 cm² sheet of wax paper.**
2. Hum your favorite song.
3. Then, take the wax paper and press it against your lips. Hum the song again.
4. How was your humming different when wax paper was pressed to your mouth?
5. Use your observations to guess what might cause snoring.

SECTION Review

Summary

- Air travels to the lungs through the nose or mouth, pharynx, larynx, trachea, and bronchi.
- In the lungs, the bronchi branch into bronchioles, which branch into alveoli.
- Breathing involves lungs, muscles in the rib cage, and the diaphragm.
- Oxygen enters the blood through the alveoli in the lungs. Carbon dioxide leaves the blood and is exhaled.
- Respiratory disorders include asthma, SARS, and emphysema.

Using Key Terms

For each pair of terms, explain how the meanings of the terms differ.

1. *pharynx* and *larynx*

Understanding Key Ideas

2. Which of the following are respiratory disorders?
   a. SARS, alveoli, and asthma
   b. alveoli, emphysema, and SARS
   c. larynx, asthma, and SARS
   d. SARS, emphysema, and asthma
3. Explain how breathing happens.
4. Describe how your cardiovascular and respiratory systems work together.

Math Skills

5. Total lung capacity (TLC) is about 6 L. A person can exhale about 3.6 L. What percentage of TLC cannot be exhaled?

Critical Thinking

6. **Interpreting Statistics** About 6.3 million children in the United States have asthma. About 4 million of them had an asthma attack last year. What do these statistics tell you about the relationship between asthma and asthma attacks?
7. **Identifying Relationships** If a respiratory disorder causes lungs to fill with fluid, how might this affect a person's health?

For a variety of links related to this chapter, go to www.scilinks.org

Topic: The Respiratory System; Respiratory Disorders

SciLinks code: HSM1307; HSM1306

Skills Practice Lab

Carbon Dioxide Breath

OBJECTIVES

Detect the presence of carbon dioxide in your breath.

Compare the data for carbon dioxide in your breath with the data from your classmates.

MATERIALS

- calculator (optional)
- clock with a second hand, or a stopwatch
- Erlenmeyer flask, 150 mL
- eyedropper
- gloves, protective
- graduated cylinder, 150 mL
- paper towels
- phenol red indicator solution
- plastic drinking straw
- water, 100 mL

SAFETY

Carbon dioxide is important to both plants and animals. Plants take in carbon dioxide during photosynthesis and give off oxygen as a byproduct of the process. Animals—including you—take in oxygen during respiration and give off carbon dioxide as a byproduct of the process.

Procedure

1. Put on your gloves, safety goggles, and apron.
2. Use the graduated cylinder to pour 100 mL of water into a 150 mL flask.
3. Using an eyedropper, carefully place four drops of phenol red indicator solution into the water. The water should turn orange.
4. Place a plastic drinking straw into the solution of phenol red and water. Drape a paper towel over the flask to prevent splashing.
5. Carefully blow through the straw into the solution. **Caution:** Do not inhale through the straw. Do not drink the solution, and do not share a straw with anyone.

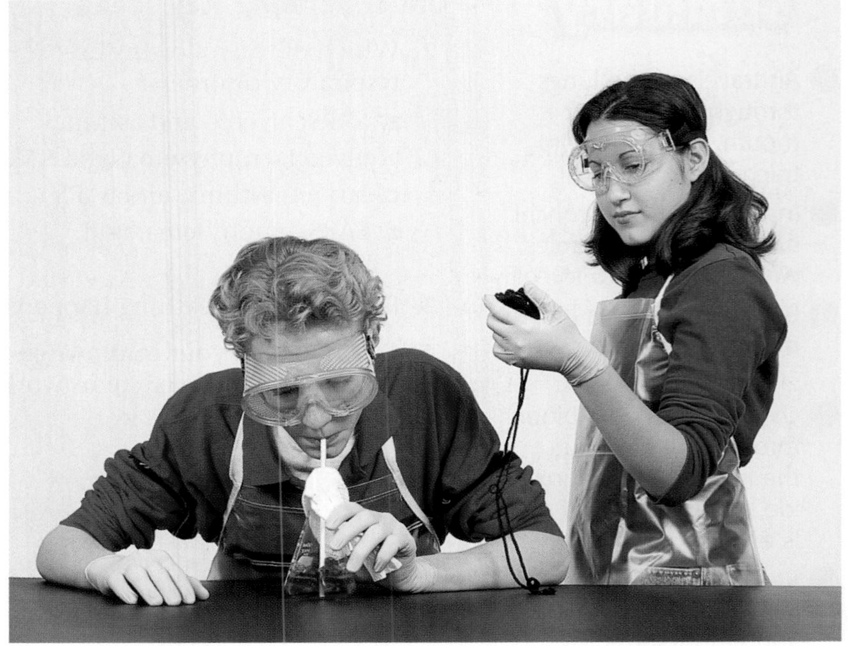

6. Your lab partner should begin keeping time as soon as you start to blow through the straw. Have your lab partner time how long the solution takes to change color. Record the time.

Analyze the Results

1. **Describing Events** Describe what happens to the indicator solution.
2. **Examining Data** Compare your data with those of your classmates. What was the longest length of time it took to see a color change? What was the shortest? How do you account for the difference?
3. **Constructing Graphs** Make a bar graph that compares your data with the data of your classmates.

Draw Conclusions

4. **Interpreting Information** Do you think that there is a relationship between the length of time the solution takes to change color and the person's physical characteristics, such as which gender the tester is or whether the tester has an athletic build? Explain your answer.
5. **Making Predictions** Predict how exercise might affect the results of your experiment. For example, would you predict that the level of carbon dioxide in the breath of someone who was exercising would be higher or lower than the carbon dioxide level in the breath of someone who was sitting quietly? Would you predict that the level of carbon dioxide in the breath would affect the timing of any color change in the phenol solution?

Applying Your Data

Do jumping jacks or sit-ups for 3 minutes, and then repeat the experiment. Did the phenol solution still change color? Did your exercising change the timing? Describe and explain any change.

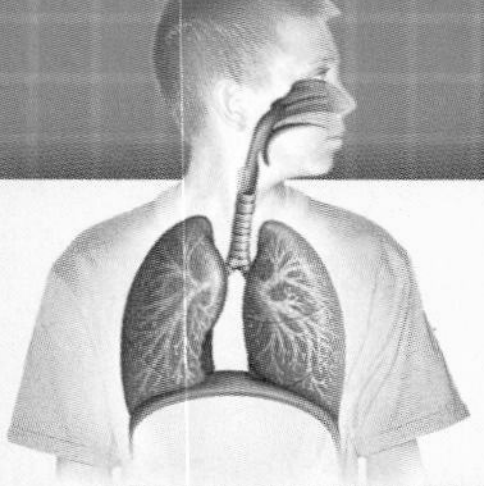

Chapter Review

USING KEY TERMS

Complete each of the following sentences by choosing the correct term from the word bank.

red blood cells	veins
white blood cells	arteries
lymphatic system	larynx
alveoli	bronchi
respiratory system	trachea

1. ___ deliver oxygen to the cells of the body.

2. ___ carry blood away from the heart.

3. The ___ helps the body fight pathogens.

4. The ___ contains the vocal cords.

5. The pathway of air through the respiratory system ends at the tiny sacs called ___.

UNDERSTANDING KEY IDEAS

Multiple Choice

6. Blood from the lungs enters the heart at the
   - **a.** left ventricle.
   - **b.** left atrium.
   - **c.** right atrium.
   - **d.** right ventricle.

7. Blood cells are made
   - **a.** in the heart.
   - **b.** from plasma.
   - **c.** from lymph.
   - **d.** in the bones.

8. Which of the following activities is a function of the lymphatic system?
   - **a.** returning excess fluid to the circulatory system
   - **b.** delivering nutrients to the cells
   - **c.** bringing oxygen to the blood
   - **d.** pumping blood to all parts of the body

9. Alveoli are surrounded by
   - **a.** veins.
   - **b.** muscles.
   - **c.** capillaries.
   - **d.** lymph nodes.

10. What prevents blood from flowing backward in veins?
    - **a.** platelets
    - **b.** valves
    - **c.** muscles
    - **d.** cartilage

11. Air moves into the lungs when the diaphragm muscle
    - **a.** contracts and moves down.
    - **b.** contracts and moves up.
    - **c.** relaxes and moves down.
    - **d.** relaxes and moves up.

Short Answer

12. What is the difference between pulmonary circulation and systemic circulation in the cardiovascular system?

13. Walton's blood pressure is 110/65. What do the two numbers mean?

14. What body process produces the carbon dioxide you exhale?

15. Describe how the circulatory system and the lymphatic system work together to keep your body healthy.

16. How is the spleen important to both the lymphatic system and the circulatory system?

17. Briefly describe the path that oxygen follows in your respiratory system and your circulatory system.

CRITICAL THINKING

18. **Concept Mapping** Use the following terms to create a concept map: *blood, oxygen, alveoli, capillaries,* and *carbon dioxide.*

19. **Making Comparisons** Compare and contrast the functions of the circulatory system and the lymphatic system.

20. **Identifying Relationships** Why do you think there are hairs in your nose?

21. **Applying Concepts** After a person donates blood, the blood is stored in one-pint bags until it is needed for a transfusion. A healthy person has about 5 million RBCs in each cubic millimeter (1 mm^3) of blood.

    a. How many RBCs are in 1 mL of blood? (One milliliter is equal to 1 cm^3 and to 1,000 mm^3.)

    b. How many RBCs are there in 1 pt? (One pint is equal to 473 mL.)

22. **Predicting Consequences** What would happen if all of the red blood cells in your blood disappeared?

23. **Identifying Relationships** When a person is not feeling well, a doctor may examine samples of the person's blood to see how many white blood cells are present. Why would this information be useful?

INTERPRETING GRAPHICS

The diagram below shows how the human heart would look in cross section. Use the diagram to answer the questions that follow.

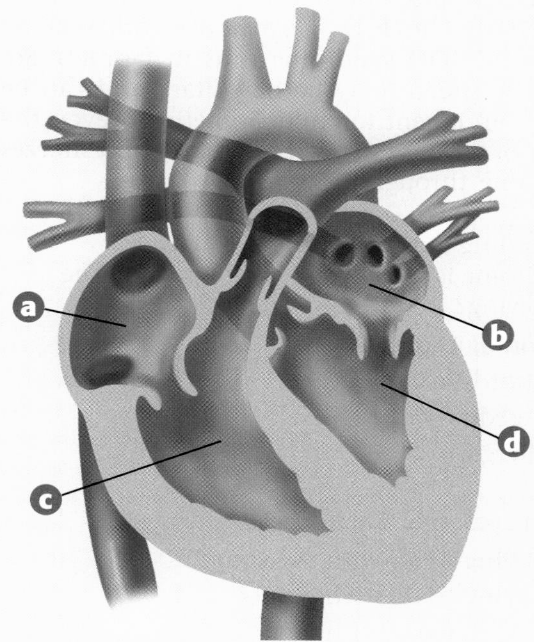

24. Which letter identifies the chamber that receives blood from systemic circulation? What is this chamber's name?

25. Which letter identifies the chamber that receives blood from the lungs? What is this chamber's name?

26. Which letter identifies the chamber that pumps blood to the lungs? What is this chamber's name?

Standardized Test Preparation

READING

Read each of the passages below. Then, answer the questions that follow each passage.

Passage 1 For some reason, about one in five people sneeze when they step from a dimly lit area into a brightly lit area. In fact, some may sneeze a dozen times or more! Fortunately, the sneezing usually stops relatively quickly. This sneeze reaction is called a photic sneeze reflex (FOHT ik SNEEZ REE FLEKS). No one knows for certain why it happens. A few years ago, some geneticists studied the photic sneeze reflex. They named it the *ACHOO syndrome*. Scientists know that the ACHOO syndrome runs in families. So, the photic sneeze may be hereditary and can be passed from parent to child. Sometimes, even the number of times in a row that each person sneezes is the same throughout a family.

1. According to the passage, the ACHOO syndrome is most likely to be which of the following?

A contagious
B photosynthetic
C hereditary
D allergic

2. In the passage, what does *photic* mean?

F having to do with sneezing
G having to do with plants
H having to do with genetics
I having to do with light

3. Which of the following statements is one clue that the photic sneeze reflex can be passed from parent to child?

A The reflex is triggered by bright light.
B Sneezing usually stops after a few sneezes.
C Family members even sneeze the same number of times.
D Scientists do not know what causes the ACHOO syndrome.

Passage 2 The two main functions of blood are transporting nutrients and oxygen from the lungs to cells and carrying carbon dioxide and other waste materials away from cells to the lungs or other organs. Blood also transfers body heat to the body surface and plays a role in defending the body against disease. The respiratory system transports gases to and from blood. The respiratory system and blood work together to carry out external respiration and internal respiration. External respiration is the exchange of gases between the atmosphere and blood. Internal respiration is the exchange of gases between blood and the cells of the body.

1. In the passage, what does *external respiration* mean?

A the exchange of gases outdoors
B the inhalation of gases as you breathe in
C the exchange of gases between blood and the atmosphere
D the exhalation of gases as you breathe out

2. Which of the following statements is a fact in the passage?

F The respiratory system transports oxygen to all the cells of the body.
G The respiratory system is part of the circulatory system.
H Blood is a kind of cardiac tissue.
I Blood transports oxygen to cells.

3. According to the passage, what are two of the roles blood plays in the human body?

A transferring body heat and defending against disease
B defending against disease and transporting gases to the circulatory system
C transporting carbon dioxide to body cells and transferring body heat
D external respiration and atmosphere

INTERPRETING GRAPHICS

Use the graph below to answer the questions that follow.

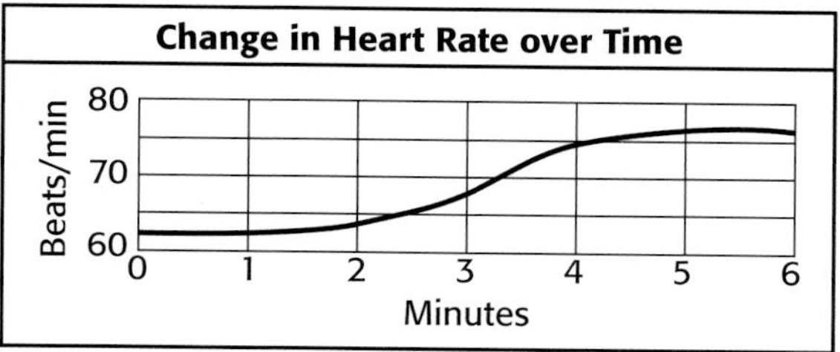

1. What is the most likely explanation for the change seen after the two-minute mark?
   A The person started exercising.
   B The person fell asleep.
   C The person inhaled.
   D The person sat down.

2. How much faster is the heart beating during minute 5 than during minute 2?
   F 10 beats per minute more
   G 12 beats per minute more
   H 15 beats per minute more
   I 17 beats per minute more

3. About how many minutes did it take for this person's heart rate to go from 65 beats per minute to 75 beats per minute?
   A 0.7 minute
   B 1.0 minute
   C 1.7 minutes
   D 4.0 minutes

4. After how many minutes does this person's heart rate return to its resting rate?
   F 1.0 minute
   G 2.0 minutes
   H 5.0 minutes
   I There is not enough information to determine the answer.

MATH

Read each question below, and choose the best answer.

1. If Jim's heart beats 73 times every minute, Jen's heart beats 68 times every minute, and Leigh's heart beats 81 times every minute, what is the average heart rate for these 3 people?
   A 73 beats per minute
   B 74 beats per minute
   C 141 beats per minute
   D 222 beats per minute

2. The Griffith family has 4 dogs. Each of the dogs eats between 0.9 kg and 1.3 kg of food every day. Which is a reasonable estimate of the total amount of food all 4 dogs eat every day?
   F 1 kg of food
   G 3 kg of food
   H 4 kg of food
   I 8 kg of food

3. Assume that the average person's resting heart rate is 70 beats per minute. The resting heart rate of a particular person is 10 beats per minute more than the average person's. If a person with the higher heart rate lives 75 years, about how many more times will his or her heart beat than the average person's heart in that time?
   A 3,942
   B 394,200
   C 3,942,000
   D 394,200,000

4. At rest, the cells of the human body use about 250 mL of oxygen per minute. At that rate, how much oxygen would the cells of the human body use every 24 hours?
   F about 36 L
   G about 360 L
   H about 36,000 L
   I about 360,000 L

Science in Action

Science, Technology, and Society

Artificial Blood

What happens when someone loses blood rapidly? Loss of blood can be fatal in a very short time, so lost blood must be replaced as quickly as possible. But what if enough blood, or blood of the right type, is not immediately available? Scientists are developing different types of artificial blood—including one based on cow hemoglobin—that may soon be used to save lives that would otherwise be lost.

Language Arts ACTIVITY

WRITING SKILL Imagine that you are a doctor and one of your patients needs surgery. Create a pamphlet or brochure that explains what artificial blood is and how it may be used in surgical procedures.

Weird Science

Circular Breathing and the Didgeridoo

Do you play a musical instrument such as a clarinet, flute, or tuba? How long can you blow into it before you have to take a breath? Can you blow into it for one minute? two minutes? And what happens when you stop to breathe? The Aboriginal people of Australia have a musical instrument called the *didgeridoo* (DIJ uh ree DOO). Didgeridoo players can play for hours without stopping to take a breath. They use a technique called *circular breathing* that lets them inhale and exhale at the same time. Circular breathing lets a musician play music without having to take breaths as often. With a little practice, maybe you can do it, too.

Social Studies ACTIVITY

WRITING SKILL Select a country from Africa or Asia. Research that country's traditional musical instruments or singing style. Write a description of how the instruments or singing style of that country differs from those of the United States. Illustrate your report.

People in Science

Anthony Roberts, Jr.

Leader in Training Anthony Roberts, Jr., has asthma. When he was in the 5th grade, his school counselor told him about a summer camp—The Boggy Creek Gang Camp—that was just being built. His counselor said that the camp was designed to serve kids who have asthma or other disabilities and diseases, such as AIDS, cancer, diabetes, epilepsy, hemophilia, heart disease, kidney disease, rheumatic diseases, and sickle cell anemia. Kids, in other words, who might otherwise never go to summer camp. Anthony jumped at the chance to go. Now, Anthony is too old to be a camper, and he is too young to be a regular counselor. But he can be a *Leader in Training* (LIT). Some camps have LIT programs that help young people make the transition from camper to counselor.

For Anthony, the chance to be an LIT fit perfectly with his love of camping and with his desire to work with kids with disabilities. Anthony remembers the fun he had and wants to help other kids have the same summer fun he did.

Math ACTIVITY

Research how many children under 17 years of age in the United States have asthma. Make a bar graph that shows how the number of children who have asthma has changed since 1981. What does this graph tell you about rates of asthma among children in the United States?

To learn more about these Science in Action topics, visit go.hrw.com and type in the keyword HL5BD2F.

Current Science

Check out Current Science® articles related to this chapter by visiting go.hrw.com. Just type in the keyword HL5CS23.

The Digestive and Urinary Systems

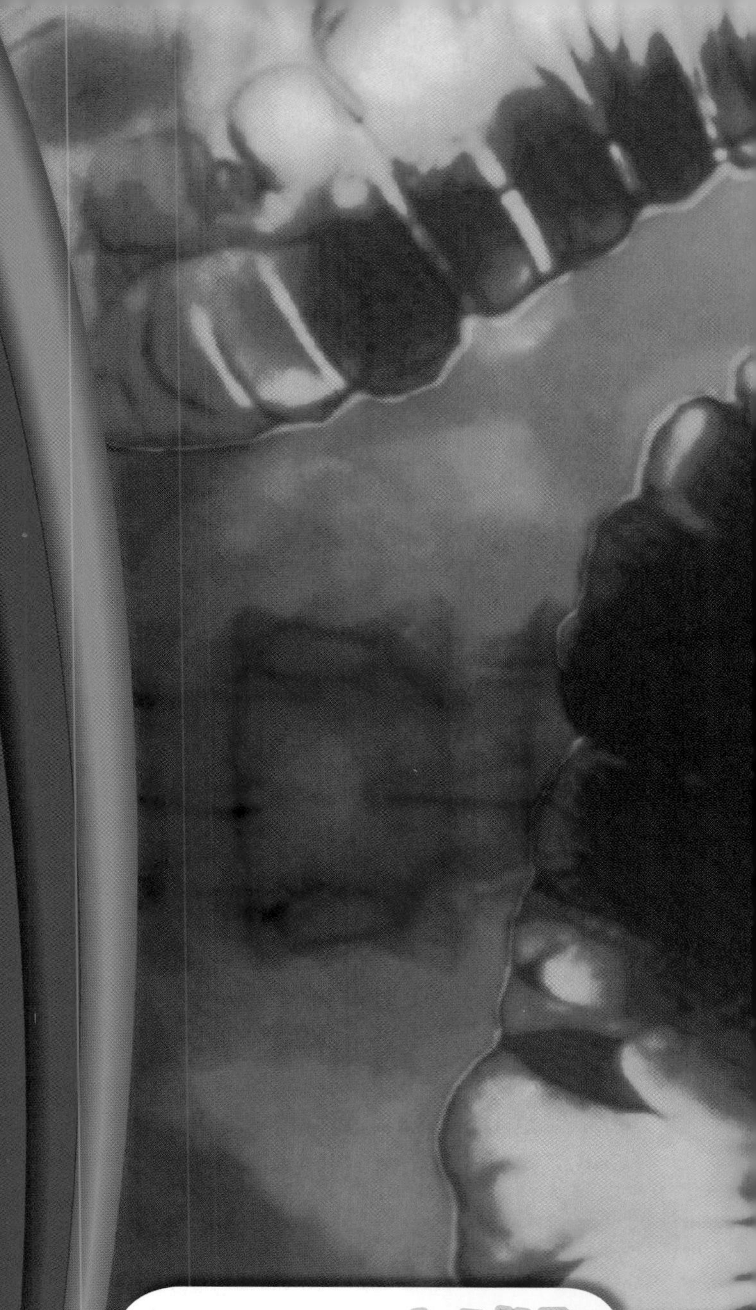

About the PHOTO

Is this a giant worm? No, it's an X ray of a healthy large intestine! Your large intestine helps your body preserve water. As mostly digested food passes through your large intestine, water is drawn out of the food. This water is returned to the bloodstream. The gray shadow behind the intestine is the spinal column. The areas that look empty are actually filled with organs. A special liquid helps this large intestine show up on the X ray.

PRE-READING ACTIVITY

Graphic Organizer

Chain-of-Events Chart Before you read the chapter, create the graphic organizer entitled "Chain-of-Events Chart" described in the **Study Skills** section of the Appendix. As you read the chapter, fill in the chart with details about each step of the processes that your body uses to digest food.

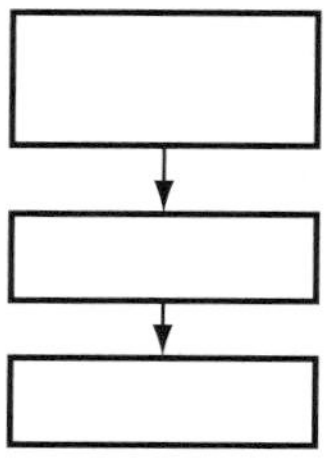

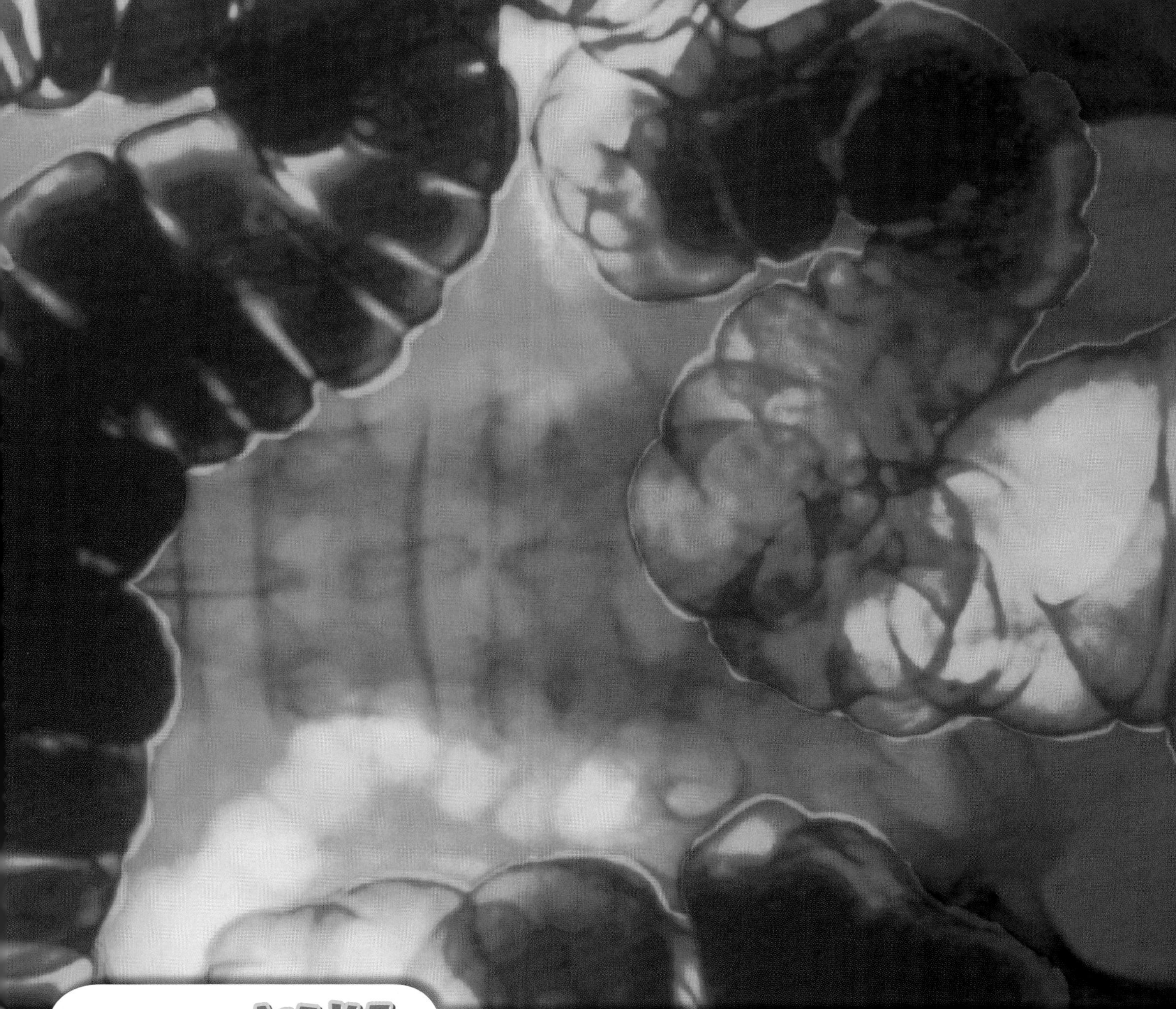

START-UP ACTIVITY

Changing Foods

The stomach breaks down food by, in part, squeezing the food. You can model the action of the stomach in the following activity.

Procedure

1. Add **200 mL of flour** and **100 mL of water** to a **resealable plastic bag.**
2. Mix **100 mL of vegetable oil** with the flour and water.
3. Seal the plastic bag.
4. Shake the bag until the flour, water, and oil are well mixed.
5. Remove as much air from the bag as you can, and reseal the bag carefully.
6. Knead the bag carefully with your hands for 5 min. Be careful to keep the bag sealed.

Analysis

1. Describe the mixture before and after you kneaded the bag.
2. How might the changes you saw in the mixture relate to how your stomach digests food?
3. Do you think this activity is a good model of how your stomach works? Explain your answer.

SECTION 1

The Digestive System

It's your last class before lunch, and you're starving! Finally, the bell rings, and you get to eat!

READING WARM-UP

Objectives

- Compare mechanical digestion with chemical digestion.
- Describe the parts and functions of the digestive system.

Terms to Learn

digestive system
esophagus
stomach
pancreas
small intestine
liver
gallbladder
large intestine

READING STRATEGY

Prediction Guide Before reading this section, write the title of each heading in this section. Next, under each heading, write what you think you will learn.

You feel hungry because your brain receives signals that your cells need energy. But eating is only the beginning of the story. Your body must change a meal into substances that you can use. Your **digestive system,** shown in **Figure 1,** is a group of organs that work together to digest food so that it can be used by the body.

digestive system the organs that break down food so that it can be used by the body

Digestive System at a Glance

The most obvious part of your digestive system is a series of tubelike organs called the *digestive tract.* Food passes through the digestive tract. The digestive tract includes your mouth, pharynx, esophagus, stomach, small intestine, large intestine, rectum, and anus. The human digestive tract can be more than 9 m long! The liver, gallbladder, pancreas, and salivary glands are also part of the digestive system. But food does not pass through these organs.

Figure 1 The Digestive System

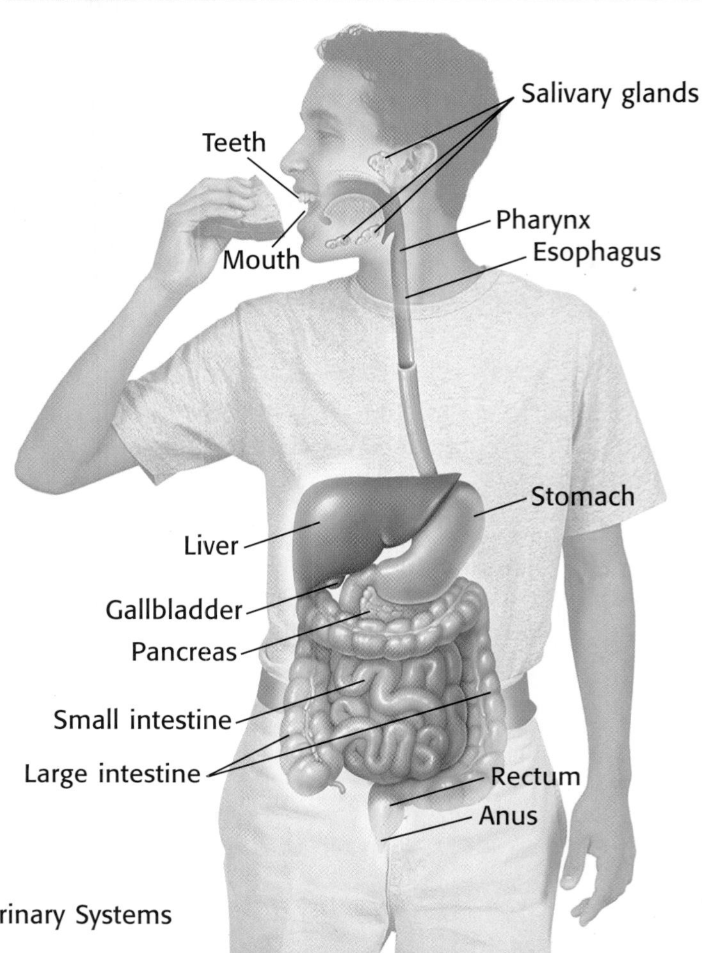

Breaking Down Food

Digestion is the process of breaking down food, such as a peanut butter and jelly sandwich, into a form that can pass from the digestive tract into the bloodstream. There are two types of digestion—mechanical and chemical. The breaking, crushing, and mashing of food is called *mechanical digestion*. In *chemical digestion,* large molecules are broken down into nutrients. Nutrients are substances in food that the body needs for normal growth, maintenance, and repair.

Three major types of nutrients—carbohydrates, proteins, and fats—make up most of the food you eat. In fact, a peanut butter and jelly sandwich contains all three of these nutrients. Substances called *enzymes* break some nutrients into smaller particles that the body can use. For example, proteins are chains of smaller molecules called *amino acids*. Proteins are too large to be absorbed into the bloodstream. So, enzymes cut up the chain of amino acids. The amino acids are small enough to pass into the bloodstream. This process is shown in **Figure 2.**

Reading Check How do enzymes help digestion? (*See the Appendix for answers to Reading Checks.*)

Quick Lab

Break It Up!

1. Drop **one piece of hard candy** into a **clear plastic cup of water.**
2. Wrap an **identical candy** in a **towel,** and crush the candy with a **hammer.** Drop the candy into a **second clear cup of water.**
3. The next day, examine both cups. What is different about the two candies?
4. What type of digestion is represented by breaking the hard candy?
5. How does chewing your food help the process of digestion?

Figure 2 **The Role of Enzymes in Protein Digestion**

1 Enzymes act as chemical scissors to cut the long chains of amino acids into small chains.

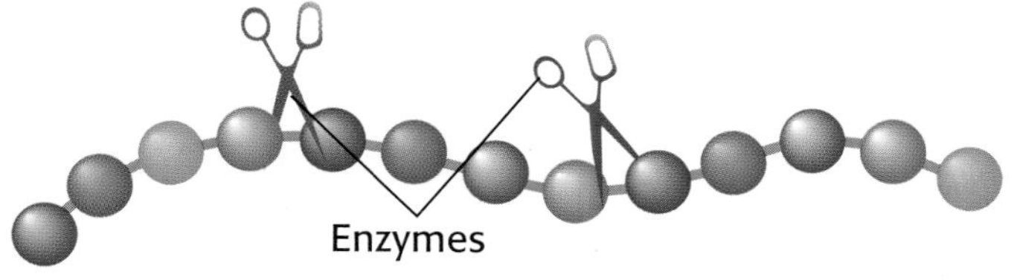

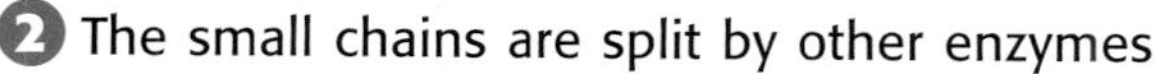

2 The small chains are split by other enzymes.

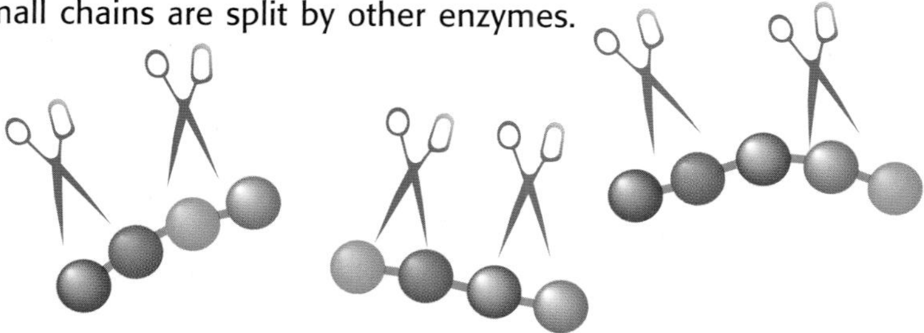

3 Individual amino acids are small enough to enter the bloodstream, where they can be used to make new proteins.

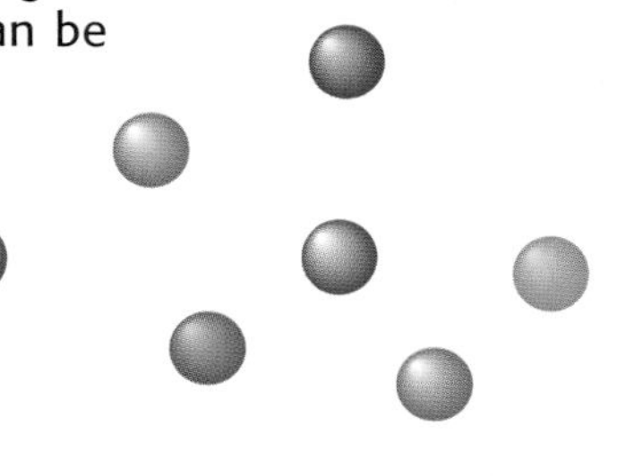

Digestion Begins in the Mouth

Chewing is important for two reasons. First, chewing creates small, slippery pieces of food that are easier to swallow than big, dry pieces are. Second, small pieces of food are easier to digest.

Teeth

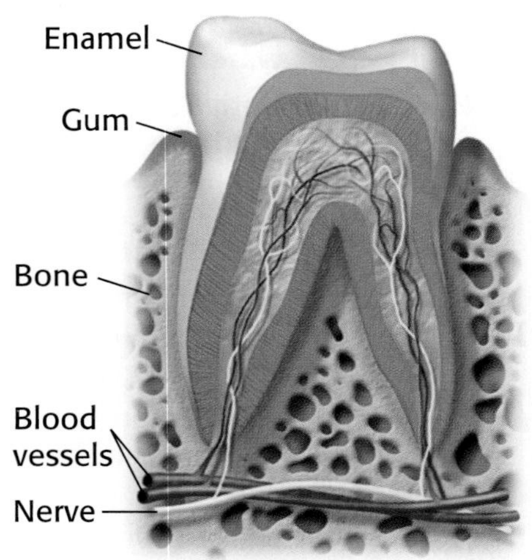

Figure 3 *A tooth, such as this molar, is made of many kinds of tissue.*

Teeth are very important organs for mechanical digestion. With the help of strong jaw muscles, teeth break and grind food. The outermost layer of a tooth, the *enamel,* is the hardest material in the body. Enamel protects nerves and softer material inside the tooth. **Figure 3** shows a cross section of a tooth.

Have you ever noticed that your teeth have different shapes? Look at **Figure 4** to locate the different kinds of teeth. The molars are well suited for grinding food. The *premolars* are perfect for mashing food. The sharp teeth at the front of your mouth, the *incisors* and *canines,* are for shredding food.

Saliva

As you chew, the food mixes with a liquid called *saliva*. Saliva is made in salivary glands located in the mouth. Saliva contains an enzyme that begins the chemical digestion of carbohydrates. Saliva changes complex carbohydrates into simple sugars.

Leaving the Mouth

esophagus a long, straight tube that connects the pharynx to the stomach

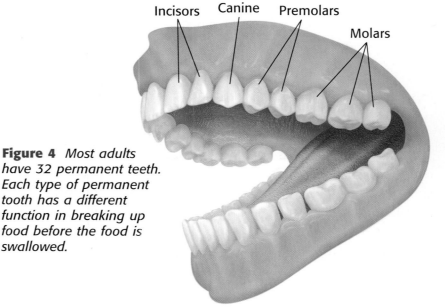

Once the food has been reduced to a soft mush, the tongue pushes it into the throat, which leads to a long, straight tube called the **esophagus** (i SAHF uh guhs). The esophagus squeezes the mass of food with rhythmic muscle contractions called *peristalsis* (PER uh STAL sis). Peristalsis forces the food into the stomach.

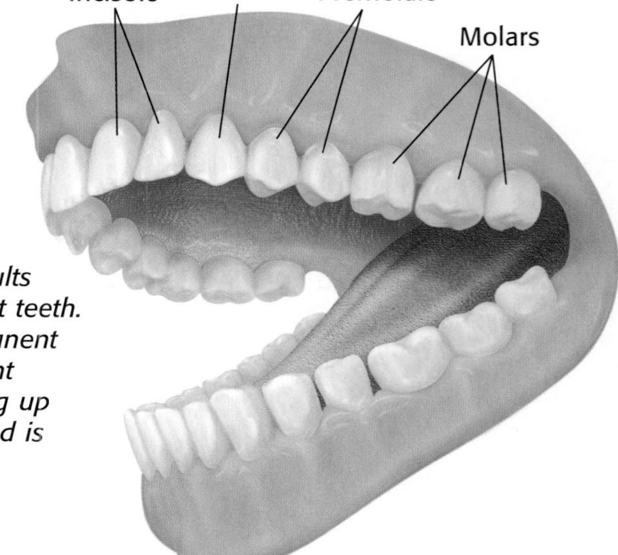

Figure 4 *Most adults have 32 permanent teeth. Each type of permanent tooth has a different function in breaking up food before the food is swallowed.*

Figure 5 **The Stomach**

The stomach squeezes and mixes food for hours before it releases the mixture into the small intestine.

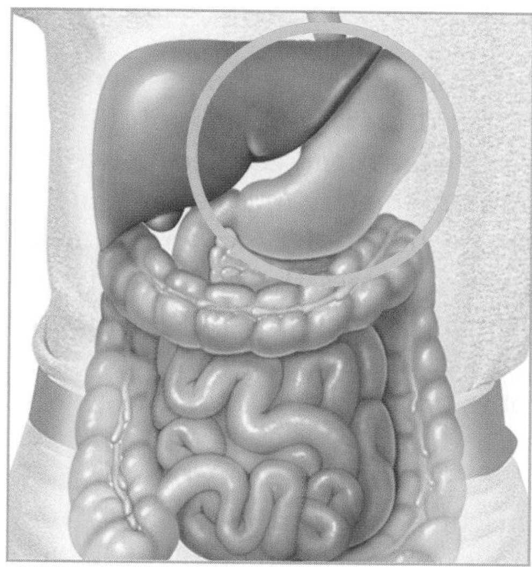

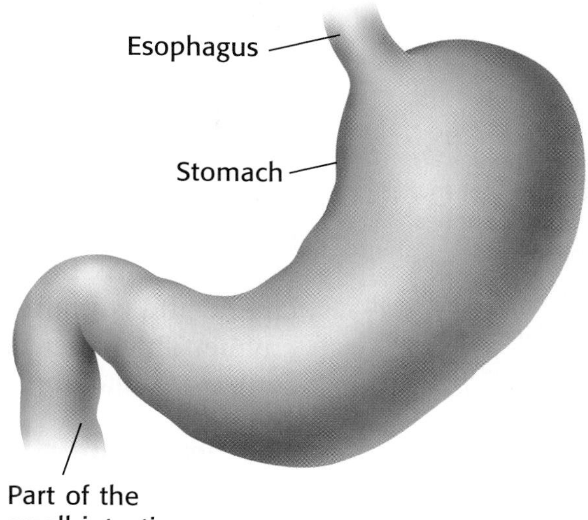

The Harsh Environment of the Stomach

The **stomach** is a muscular, saclike, digestive organ attached to the lower end of the esophagus. The stomach is shown in **Figure 5.** The stomach continues the mechanical digestion of your meal by squeezing the food with muscular contractions. While this squeezing is taking place, tiny glands in the stomach produce enzymes and acid. The enzymes and acid work together to break food into nutrients. Stomach acid also kills most bacteria that you might swallow with your food. After a few hours of combined mechanical and chemical digestion, your peanut butter and jelly sandwich has been reduced to a soupy mixture called *chyme* (KIEM).

stomach the saclike, digestive organ between the esophagus and the small intestine that breaks down food into a liquid by the action of muscles, enzymes, and acids

Reading Check What is chyme?

Leaving the Stomach

The stomach slowly releases the chyme into the small intestine through a small ring of muscle that works like a valve. This valve keeps food in the stomach until the food has been thoroughly mixed with digestive fluids. Each time the valve opens and closes, it lets a small amount of chyme into the small intestine. Because the stomach releases chyme slowly, the intestine has more time to mix the chyme with fluids from the liver and pancreas. These fluids help digest food and stop the harsh acids in chyme from hurting the small intestine.

Tooth Truth

Young children get a first set of 20 teeth called *baby teeth*. These teeth usually fall out and are replaced by 32 permanent teeth. How many more permanent teeth than baby teeth does a person have? What is the ratio of baby teeth to permanent teeth? Be sure to express the ratio in its most reduced form.

The Pancreas and Small Intestine

Most chemical digestion takes place after food leaves the stomach. Proteins, carbohydrates, and fats in the chyme are digested by the small intestine and fluids from the pancreas.

The Pancreas

When the chyme leaves the stomach, the chyme is very acidic. The pancreas makes fluids that protect the small intestine from the acid. The **pancreas** is an oval organ located between the stomach and small intestine. The chyme never enters the pancreas. Instead, the pancreatic fluid flows into the small intestine. This fluid contains enzymes that chemically digest chyme and contains bicarbonate, which neutralizes the acid in chyme. The pancreas also functions as a part of the endocrine system by making hormones that regulate blood sugar.

pancreas the organ that lies behind the stomach and that makes digestive enzymes and hormones that regulate sugar levels

small intestine the organ between the stomach and the large intestine where most of the breakdown of food happens and most of the nutrients from food are absorbed

The Small Intestine

The **small intestine** is a muscular tube that is about 2.5 cm in diameter. Other than having a small diameter, it is really not that small. In fact, if you stretched the small intestine out, it would be longer than you are tall—about 6 m! If you flattened out the surface of the small intestine, it would be larger than a tennis court! How is this possible? The inside wall of the small intestine is covered with fingerlike projections called *villi*, shown in **Figure 6.** The surface area of the small intestine is very large because of the villi. The villi are covered with tiny, nutrient-absorbing cells. Once the nutrients are absorbed, they enter the bloodstream.

CONNECTION TO Social Studies

WRITING SKILL **Parasites** Intestinal parasites are organisms, such as roundworms and hookworms, that infect people and live in their digestive tract. Worldwide, intestinal parasites infect more than 1 billion people. Some parasites can be deadly. Research intestinal parasites in a library or on the Internet. Then, write a report on a parasite, including how it spreads, what problems it causes, how many people have it, and what can be done to stop it.

Figure 6 **The Small Intestine and Villi**

The highly folded lining of the small intestine has many fingerlike projections called *villi*.

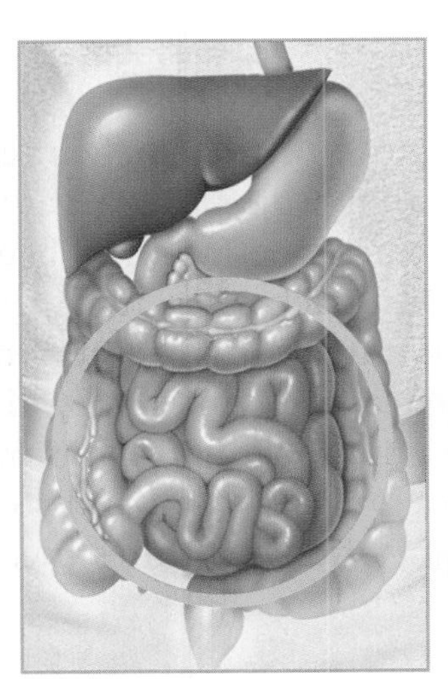

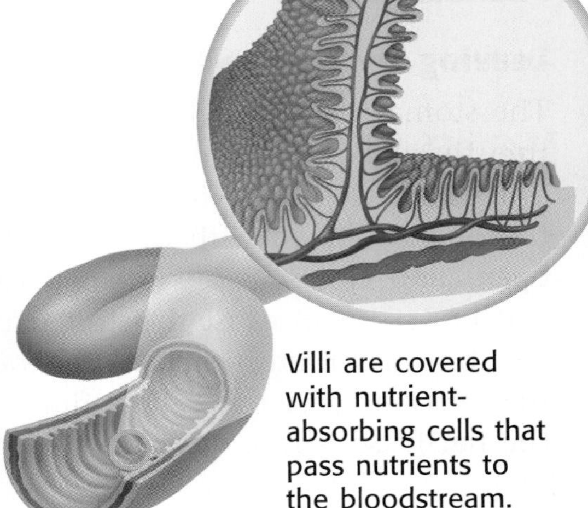

Villi are covered with nutrient-absorbing cells that pass nutrients to the bloodstream.

Figure 7 **The Liver and the Gallbladder**

Food does not move through the liver, gallbladder, and pancreas even though these organs are linked to the small intestine.

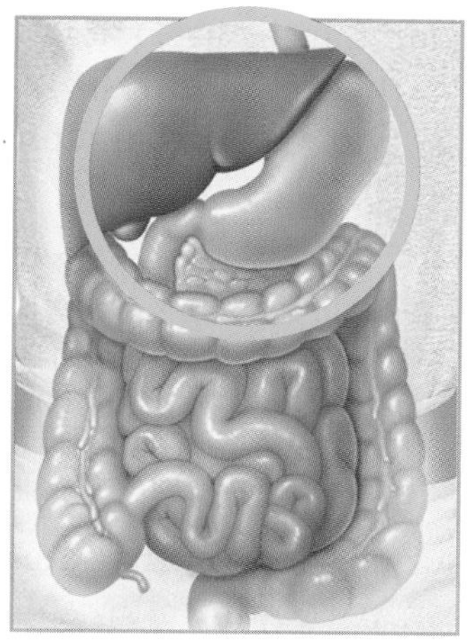

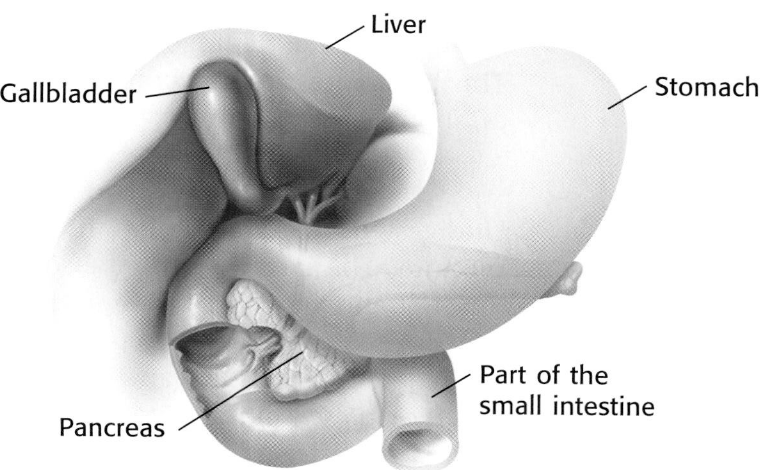

The Liver and Gallbladder

The **liver** is a large, reddish brown organ that helps with digestion. A human liver can be as large as a football. Your liver is located toward your right side, slightly higher than your stomach, as shown in **Figure 7.** The liver helps with digestion in the following ways:

- It makes bile to break up fat.
- It stores nutrients.
- It breaks down toxins.

liver the largest organ in the body; it makes bile, stores and filters blood, and stores excess sugars as glycogen

gallbladder a sac-shaped organ that stores bile produced by the liver

Breaking Up Fat

Although bile is made by the liver, bile is temporarily stored in a small, saclike organ called the **gallbladder,** shown in **Figure 7.** Bile is squeezed from the gallbladder into the small intestine, where the bile breaks large fat droplets into very small droplets. This mechanical process allows more fat molecules to be exposed to digestive enzymes.

Reading Check How does bile help digest fat?

Storing Nutrients and Protecting the Body

After nutrients are broken down, they are absorbed into the bloodstream and carried through the body. Nutrients that are not needed right away are stored in the liver. The liver then releases the stored nutrients into the bloodstream as needed. The liver also captures and detoxifies many chemicals in the body. For instance, the liver produces enzymes that break down alcohol and many other drugs.

Bile Model

You can model the way bile breaks down fat and oil by using dish soap. At home with a parent, put a small amount of water in a small jar. Then, add a few drops of vegetable oil to the water. Notice that the two liquids separate. Draw a picture of the jar and its contents. Next, add a few drops of dishwashing soap to the water, tighten the lid securely onto the jar, and shake the jar. What happened to the three liquids in the jar? Draw another picture of the jar and its contents.

The End of the Line

large intestine the wider and shorter portion of the intestine that removes water from mostly digested food and that turns the waste into semisolid feces, or stool

Material that can't be absorbed into the blood is pushed into the large intestine. The **large intestine** is the organ of the digestive system that stores, compacts, and then eliminates indigestible material from the body. The large intestine, shown in **Figure 8,** has a larger diameter than the small intestine. The large intestine is about 1.5 m long, and has a diameter of about 7.5 cm.

In the Large Intestine

Undigested material enters the large intestine as a soupy mixture. The large intestine absorbs most of the water in the mixture and changes the liquid into semisolid waste materials called *feces,* or *stool.*

Whole grains, fruits, and vegetables contain a carbohydrate, called *cellulose,* that humans cannot digest. We commonly refer to this material as *fiber*. Fiber keeps the stool soft and keeps material moving through the large intestine.

Reading Check How does eating fiber help digestion?

Leaving the Body

The *rectum* is the last part of the large intestine. The rectum stores feces until they can be expelled. Feces pass to the outside of the body through an opening called the *anus.* It has taken your sandwich about 24 hours to make this journey through your digestive system.

CONNECTION TO Environmental Science

Waste Away Feces and other human wastes contain microorganisms and other substances that can contaminate drinking water. Every time you flush a toilet, the water and wastes go through the sewer to a wastewater treatment plant. At the wastewater treatment plant, the disease-causing microorganisms are removed, and the clean water is released back to rivers, lakes, and streams. Find out where the wastewater treatment plants are in your area. Report to your class where their wastewater goes.

ACTIVITY

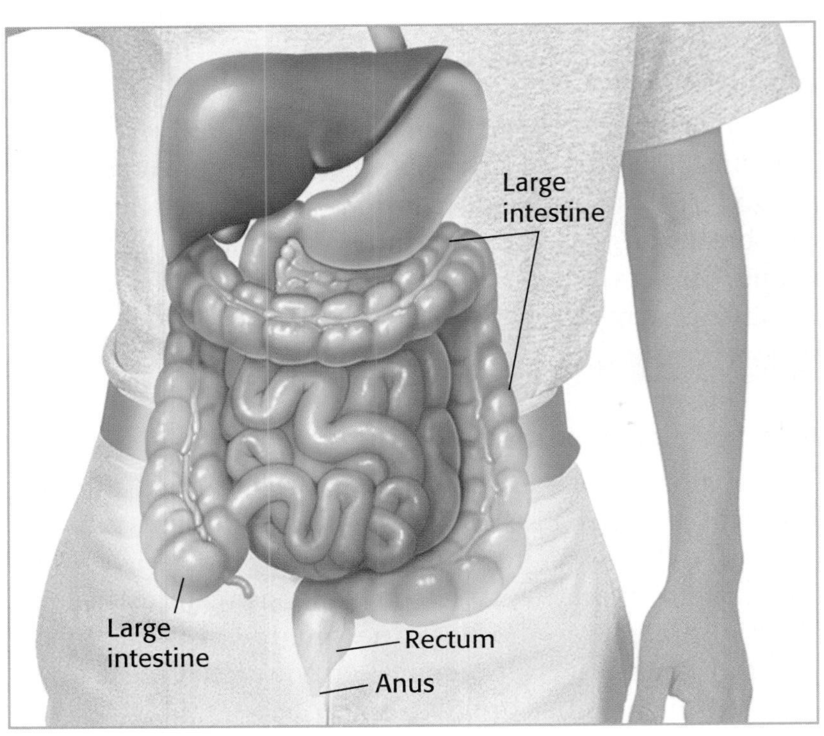

Figure 8 *The large intestine is the final organ of digestion.*

SECTION Review

Summary

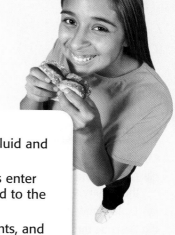

- Your digestive system is a group of organs that work together to digest food so that the nutrients from food can be used by the body.
- The breaking and mashing of food is called *mechanical digestion*. Chemical digestion is the process that breaks large food molecules into simpler molecules.
- The stomach mixes food with acid and enzymes that break down nutrients. The mixture is called *chyme.*
- In the small intestine, pancreatic fluid and bile are mixed with chyme.
- From the small intestine, nutrients enter the bloodstream and are circulated to the body's cells.
- The liver makes bile, stores nutrients, and breaks down toxins.
- The large intestine absorbs water, changing liquid waste into semisolid stool, or feces.

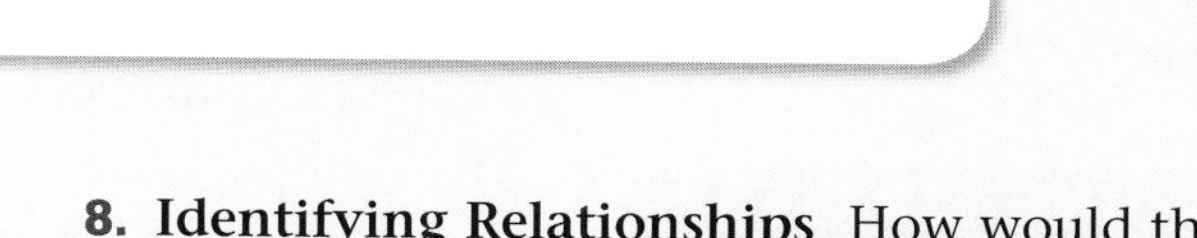

Using Key Terms

1. Use each of the following terms in a separate sentence: *digestive system, large intestine,* and *small intestine.*

Understanding Key Ideas

2. Which of the following is NOT a function of the liver?
   a. to secrete bile
   b. to store nutrients
   c. to detoxify chemicals
   d. to compact wastes
3. What is the difference between mechanical digestion and chemical digestion?
4. What happens to the food that you eat when it gets to your stomach?
5. Describe the role of the liver, gallbladder, and pancreas in digestion.
6. Put the following steps of digestion in order.
   a. Food is chewed by the teeth in the mouth.
   b. Water is absorbed by the large intestine.
   c. Food is reduced to chyme in the stomach.
   d. Food moves down the esophagus.
   e. Nutrients are absorbed by the small intestine.
   f. The pancreas releases enzymes.

Critical Thinking

7. **Evaluating Conclusions** Explain the following statement: "Digestion begins in the mouth."
8. **Identifying Relationships** How would the inability to make saliva affect digestion?

Interpreting Graphics

9. Label and describe the function of each of the organs in the diagram below.

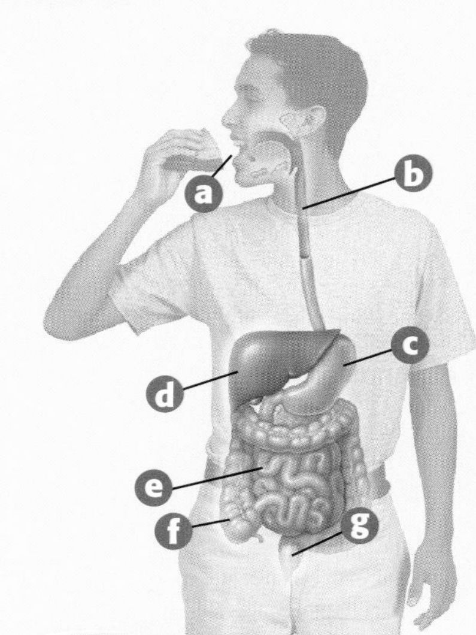

SCILINKS
NSTA
Developed and maintained by the National Science Teachers Association
For a variety of links related to this chapter, go to www.scilinks.org
Topic: The Digestive System
SciLinks code: HSM0409

SECTION 2

The Urinary System

As blood travels through the tissues, it picks up waste produced by the body's cells. Your blood is like a train that comes to town to drop off supplies and take away garbage. If the waste is not removed, your body can actually be poisoned.

READING WARM-UP

Objectives

- Describe the parts and functions of the urinary system.
- Explain how the kidneys filter blood.
- Describe three disorders of the urinary system.

Terms to Learn

urinary system
kidney
nephron

READING STRATEGY

Reading Organizer As you read this section, create an outline of the section. Use the headings from the section in your outline.

Excretion is the process of removing waste products from the body. Three of your body systems have a role in excretion. Your integumentary system releases waste products and water when you sweat. Your respiratory system releases carbon dioxide and water when you exhale. Finally, the **urinary system** contains the organs that remove waste products from your blood.

Cleaning the Blood

As your body performs the chemical activities that keep you alive, waste products, such as carbon dioxide and ammonia, are made. Your body has to get rid of these waste products to stay healthy. The urinary system, shown in **Figure 1,** removes these waste products from the blood.

urinary system the organs that produce, store, and eliminate urine

Figure 1 Urinary System

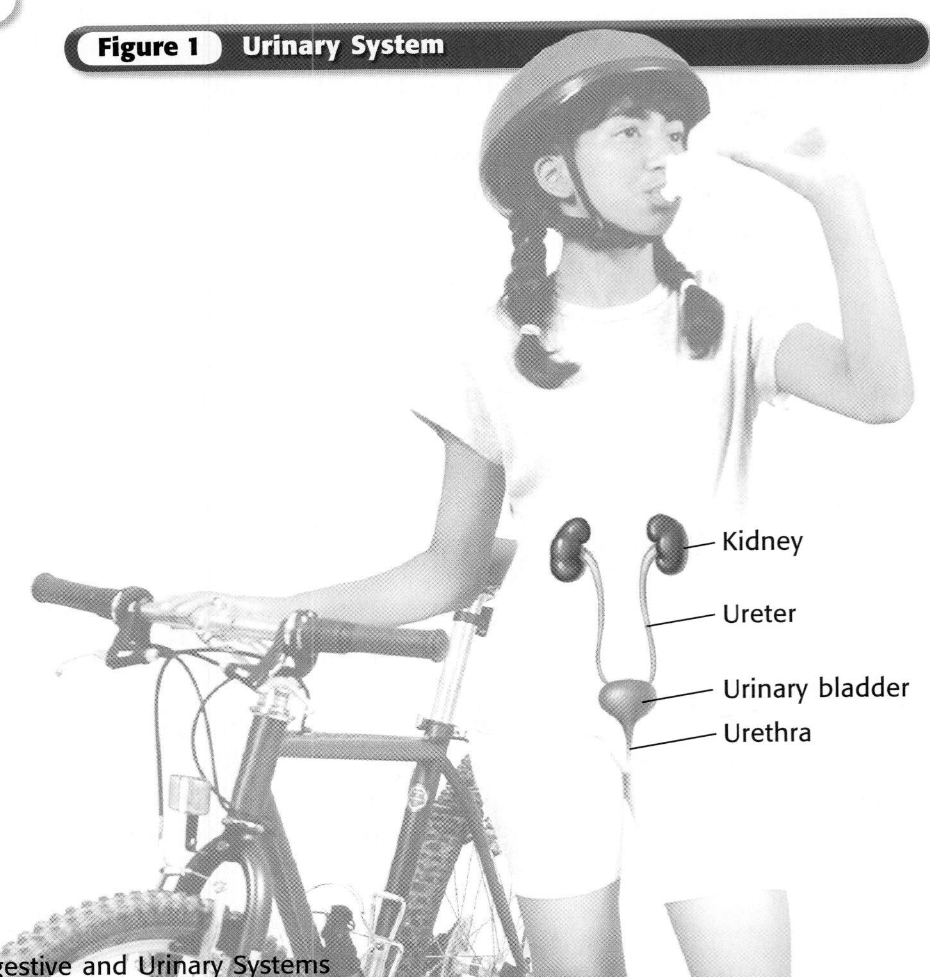

The Kidneys as Filters

The **kidneys** are a pair of organs that constantly clean the blood. Your kidneys filter about 2,000 L of blood each day. Your body holds only 5.6 L of blood, so your blood cycles through your kidneys about 350 times per day!

Inside each kidney, shown in **Figure 2,** are more than 1 million nephrons. **Nephrons** are microscopic filters in the kidney that remove wastes from the blood. Nephrons remove many harmful substances. One of the most important substances removed by nephrons is urea (yoo REE uh), which contains nitrogen and is formed when cells use protein for energy.

kidney one of the pair of organs that filter water and wastes from the blood and that excrete products as urine

nephron the unit in the kidney that filters blood

Reading Check **How are nephrons related to kidneys?** (*See the Appendix for answers to Reading Checks.*)

Figure 2 **How the Kidneys Filter Blood**

1. A large artery brings blood into each kidney.
2. Tiny blood vessels branch off the main artery and pass through part of each nephron.
3. Water and other small substances, such as glucose, salts, amino acids, and urea, are forced out of the blood vessels and into the nephrons.
4. As these substances flow through the nephrons, most of the water and some nutrients are moved back into blood vessels that wrap around the nephrons. A concentrated mixture of waste materials is left behind in the nephrons.
5. The cleaned blood, which has slightly less water and much less waste material, leaves each kidney in a large vein to recirculate in the body.
6. The yellow fluid that remains in the nephrons is called *urine.* Urine leaves each kidney through a slender tube called the *ureter* and flows into the *urinary bladder,* where urine is stored.
7. Urine leaves the body through another tube called the *urethra*. *Urination* is the process of expelling urine from the body.

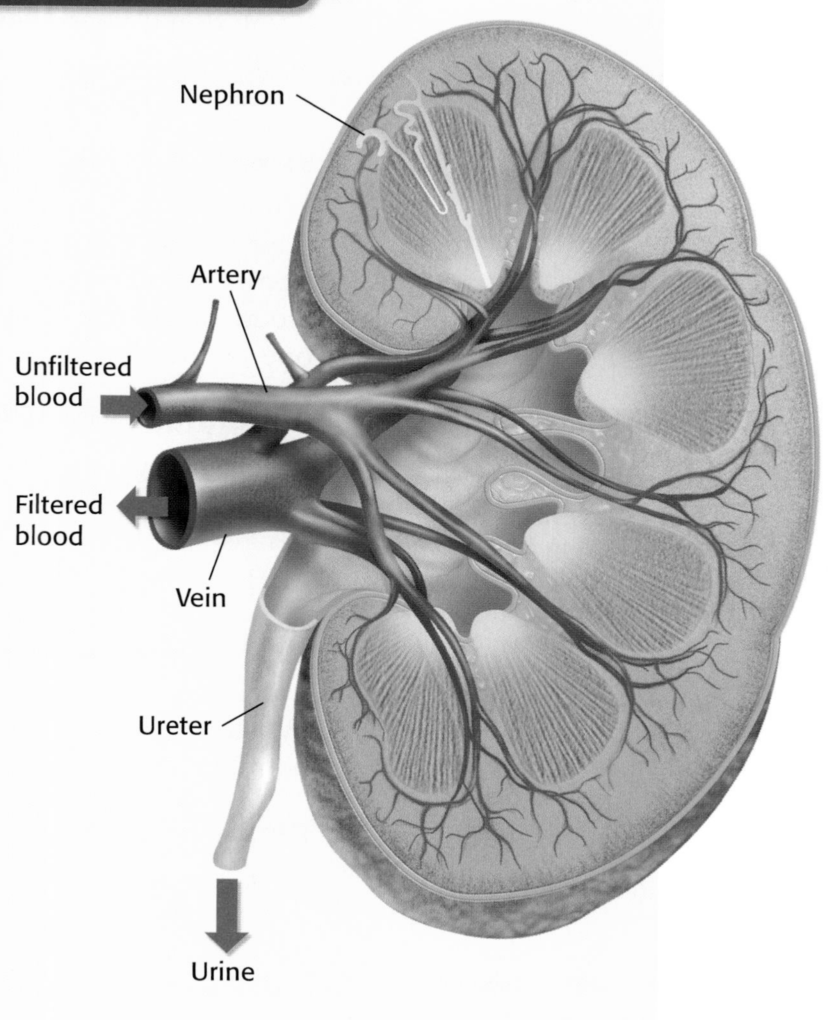

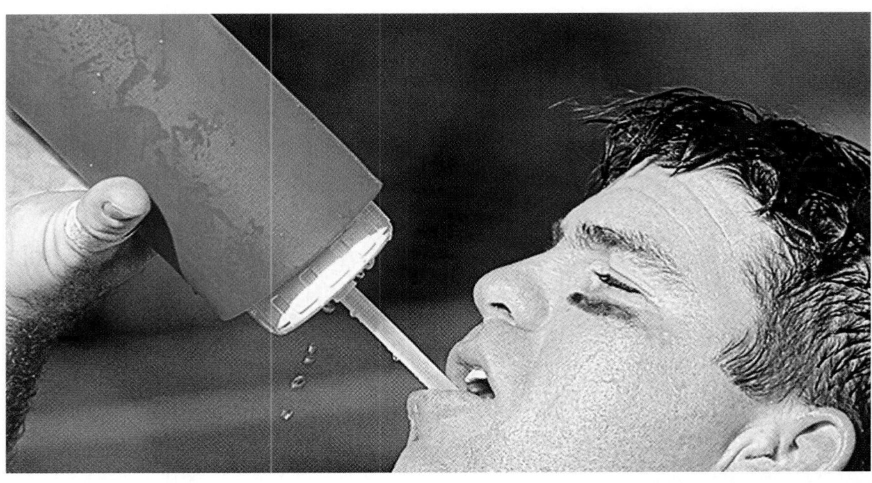

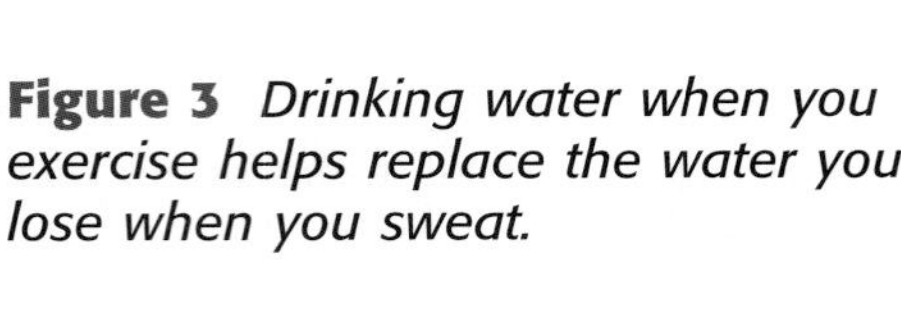

Figure 3 *Drinking water when you exercise helps replace the water you lose when you sweat.*

Water In, Water Out

You drink water every day. You lose water every day in sweat and urine. You need to get rid of as much water as you drink. If you don't, your body will swell up. So, how does your body keep the water levels in balance? The balance of fluids is controlled by chemical messengers in the body called *hormones*.

Sweat and Thirst

When you are too warm, as the boy in **Figure 3** is, you lose a lot of water in the form of sweat. The evaporation of water from your skin cools you down. As the water content of the blood drops, the salivary glands produce less saliva. This is one of the reasons you feel thirsty.

Antidiuretic Hormone

When you get thirsty, other parts of your body react to the water shortage, too. A hormone called *antidiuretic hormone* (AN tee DIE yoo RET ik HAWR MOHN), or ADH, is released. ADH signals the kidneys to take water from the nephrons. The nephrons return the water to the bloodstream. Thus, the kidneys make less urine. When your blood has too much water, small amounts of ADH are released. The kidneys react by allowing more water to stay in the nephrons and leave the body as urine.

Diuretics

Some beverages contain caffeine, which is a *diuretic* (DIE yoo RET ik). Diuretics cause the kidneys to make more urine, which decreases the amount of water in the blood. When you drink a beverage that contains water and caffeine, the caffeine increases fluid loss. So, your body gets to use less of the water from the caffeinated beverage than from a glass of water.

Reading Check **What are diuretics?**

WRITING SKILL **Beverage Ban** During football season, a football coach insists that all members of the team avoid caffeinated beverages. Many of the players are upset by the news. Pretend that you are the coach. Write a letter to the members of the team explaining why it is better for them to drink water than to drink beverages that contain caffeine. Read the letter aloud to members of your family. Ask them how you could make your letter more convincing.

Urinary System Problems

The urinary system regulates body fluids and removes wastes from the blood. Any problems with water regulation can become dangerous for your body. Some common urinary system problems are described below.

- **Bacterial Infections** Bacteria can get into the bladder and ureters through the urethra and cause painful infections. Infections should be treated early, before they spread to the kidneys. Infections in the kidneys can permanently damage the nephrons.
- **Kidney Stones** Sometimes, salts and other wastes collect inside the kidneys and form kidney stones like the one in **Figure 4.** Some kidney stones interfere with urine flow and cause pain. Most kidney stones pass naturally from the body, but sometimes they must be removed by a doctor.
- **Kidney Disease** Damage to nephrons can prevent normal kidney functioning and can lead to kidney disease. If a person's kidneys do not function properly, a kidney machine can be used to filter waste from the blood.

Figure 4 *This kidney stone had to be removed from a patient's urinary system.*

SECTION Review

Summary

- The urinary system removes liquid waste as urine. The filtering structures in the kidney are called *nephrons.*
- Most of the water in the blood is returned to the bloodstream. Urine passes through the ureter, into the bladder, and out of the body through the urethra.
- Disorders of the urinary system include infections, kidney stones, and kidney disease.

Using Key Terms

1. In your own words, write a definition for the term *urinary system.*

Understanding Key Ideas

2. Which event happens first?
   - **a.** Water is absorbed into blood.
   - **b.** A large artery brings blood into the kidney.
   - **c.** Water enters the nephrons.
   - **d.** The nephron separates water from wastes.
3. How do kidneys filter blood?
4. Describe three disorders of the urinary system.

Math Skills

5. A study has shown that 75% of teenage boys drink 34 oz of soda per day. How many 12 oz cans of soda would a boy drink in a week if he drank 34 oz per day?

Critical Thinking

6. **Applying Concepts** Which of the following contains more water: the blood going into the kidney or the blood leaving it?
7. **Predicting Consequences** When people have one kidney removed, their other kidney can often keep their blood clean. But the remaining kidney often changes. Predict how the remaining kidney may change to do the work of two kidneys.

SCILINKS
NSTA
Developed and maintained by the National Science Teachers Association
For a variety of links related to this chapter, go to www.scilinks.org
Topic: The Urinary System; Urinary System Ailments
SciLinks code: HSM1583; HSM1584

Using Scientific Methods

Skills Practice Lab

As the Stomach Churns

OBJECTIVES

Demonstrate chemical digestion in the stomach.

Investigate three forms of chemical digestion.

MATERIALS

- beef stew meat, 1 cm cubes (3)
- eyedropper
- gloves, protective
- graduated cylinder, 25 mL
- hydrochloric acid, very dilute, 0.1 M
- measuring spoon, 1/4 tsp
- meat tenderizer, commercially prepared, containing bromelain
- meat tenderizer, commercially prepared, containing papain
- tape, masking
- test tubes (4)
- test-tube marker
- test-tube rack
- water

SAFETY

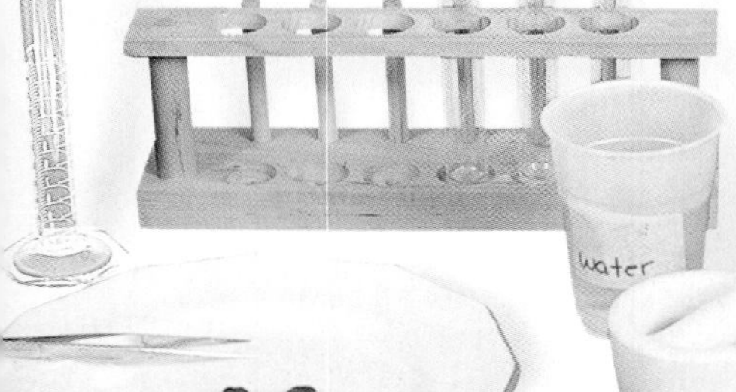

The stomach, as you know, performs not only mechanical digestion but also chemical digestion. As the stomach churns, which moves the food particles around, the digestive fluids—acid and enzymes—are added to begin protein digestion.

Commercially prepared meat tenderizers contain enzymes from plants that break down, or digest, proteins. Two types of meat tenderizer are commonly available at grocery stores. One type of tenderizer contains an enzyme called *papain,* from papaya. Another type of tenderizer contains an enzyme called *bromelain,* from pineapple. In this lab, you will test the effects of these two types of meat tenderizers on beef stew meat.

Ask a Question

1. Determine which question you will answer through your experiment. That question may be one of the following: Which meat tenderizer will work faster? Which one will make the meat more tender? Will the meat tenderizers change the color of the meat or water? What might these color changes, if any, indicate?

Form a Hypothesis

2. Form a hypothesis from the question you formed in step 1. **Caution:** Do not taste any of the materials in this activity.

Test the Hypothesis

3. Identify all variables and controls present in your experiment. In your notebook, make a data table that includes these variables and controls. Use this data table to record your observations and results.

4. Label one test tube with the name of one tenderizer, and label the other test tube with the name of the other tenderizer. Label the third test tube "Control." What will the test tube labeled "Control" contain?

5. Pour 20 mL of water into each test tube.
6. Use the eyedropper to add four drops of very dilute hydrochloric acid to each test tube. **Caution:** Hydrochloric acid can burn your skin. If any acid touches your skin, rinse the area with running water and tell your teacher immediately.
7. Use the measuring spoon to add 1/4 tsp of each meat tenderizer to its corresponding test tube.
8. Add one cube of beef to each test tube.
9. Record your observations for each test tube immediately, after 5 min, after 15 min, after 30 min, and after 24 h.

Analyze the Results

1. **Describing Events** Did you immediately notice any differences in the beef in the three test tubes? At what time interval did you notice a significant difference in the appearance of the beef in the test tubes? Explain the differences.
2. **Examining Data** Did one meat tenderizer perform better than the other? Explain how you determined which performed better.

Draw Conclusions

3. **Evaluating Results** Was your hypothesis supported? Explain your answer.
4. **Applying Conclusions** Many animals that sting have venom composed of proteins. Explain how applying meat tenderizer to the wound helps relieve the pain of such a sting.

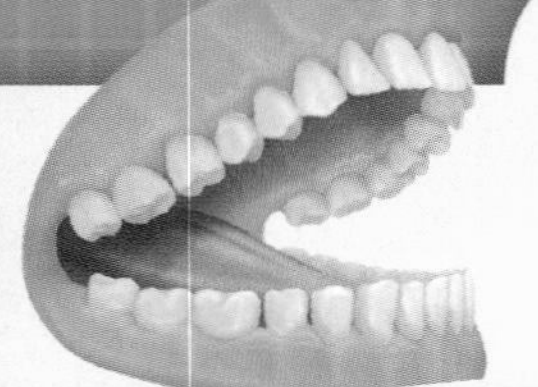

Chapter Review

USING KEY TERMS

Complete each of the following sentences by choosing the correct term from the word bank.

pancreas	digestive system
large intestine	stomach
kidney	small intestine
nephron	urinary system

1. The ____ secretes juices into the small intestine.

2. The saclike organ at the end of the esophagus is called the ____.

3. The ___ is an organ that contains millions of nephrons.

4. A group of organs that removes waste from the blood and excretes it from the body is called the ____.

5. The ____ is a group of organs that work together to break down food.

6. Indigestible material is formed into feces in the ____.

UNDERSTANDING KEY IDEAS

Multiple Choice

7. The hormone that signals the kidneys to make less urine is
   a. urea. **c.** ADH.
   b. caffeine. **d.** ATP.

8. Which of the following organs aids digestion by producing bile?
   a. stomach **c.** small intestine
   b. pancreas **d.** liver

9. The part of the kidney that filters the blood is the
   a. artery. **c.** nephron.
   b. ureter. **d.** urethra.

10. The fingerlike projections that line the small intestine are called
    a. emulsifiers.
    b. fats.
    c. amino acids.
    d. villi.

11. Which of the following is NOT part of the digestive tract?
    a. mouth **c.** stomach
    b. kidney **d.** rectum

12. The soupy mixture of food, enzymes, and acids in the stomach is called
    a. chyme. **c.** urea.
    b. villi. **d.** vitamins.

13. The stomach helps with
    a. storing food.
    b. chemical digestion.
    c. physical digestion.
    d. All of the above

14. The gall bladder stores
    a. food. **c.** bile.
    b. urine. **d.** villi.

15. The esophagus connects the
    a. pharynx to the stomach.
    b. stomach to the small intestine.
    c. kidneys to the nephrons.
    d. stomach to the large intestine.

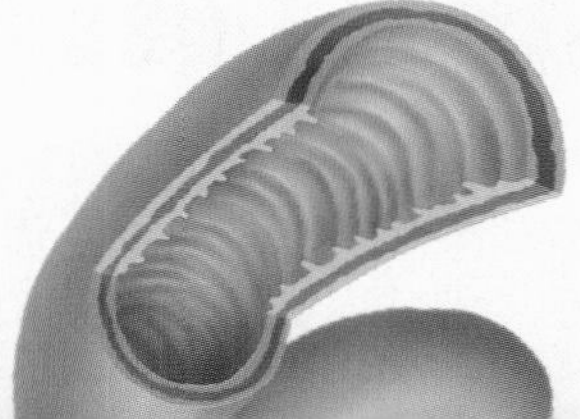

Short Answer

16 Why is it important for the pancreas to release bicarbonate into the small intestine?

17 How does the structure of the small intestine help the small intestine absorb nutrients?

18 What is a kidney stone?

CRITICAL THINKING

19 **Concept Mapping** Use the following terms to create a concept map: *teeth, stomach, digestion, bile, saliva, mechanical digestion, gallbladder,* and *chemical digestion.*

20 **Predicting Consequences** How would digestion be affected if the liver were damaged?

21 **Analyzing Processes** When you put a piece of carbohydrate-rich food, such as bread, a potato, or a cracker, into your mouth, the food tastes bland. But if this food sits on your tongue for a while, the food will begin to taste sweet. What digestive process causes this change in taste?

22 **Making Comparisons** The recycling process for one kind of plastic begins with breaking the plastic into small pieces. Next, chemicals are used to break the small pieces of plastic down to its building blocks. Then, those building blocks are used to make new plastic. How is this process both like and unlike human digestion?

INTERPRETING GRAPHICS

The bar graph below shows how long the average meal spends in each portion of your digestive tract. Use the graph below to answer the questions that follow.

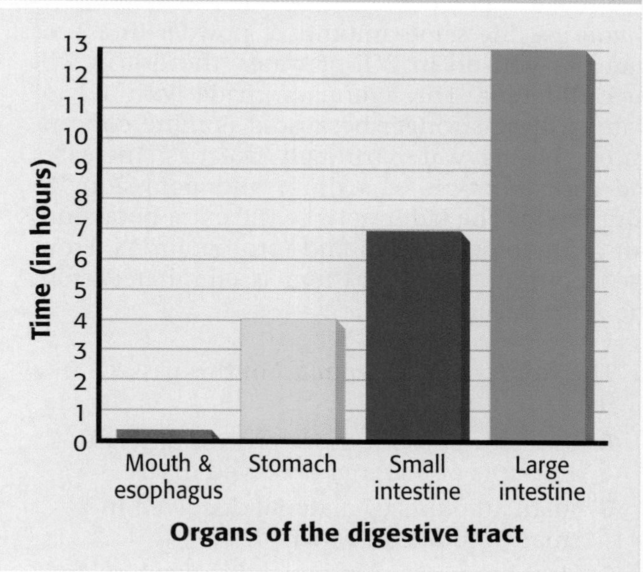

23 In which part of your digestive tract does the food spend the longest amount of time?

24 On average, how much longer does food stay in the small intestine than in the stomach?

25 Which organ mixes food with special substances to make chyme? Approximately how long does food remain in this organ?

26 Bile breaks large fat droplets into very small droplets. How long is the food in your body before it comes into contact with bile?

Standardized Test Preparation

READING

Read the passage below. Then, read each question that follows the passage. Decide which is the best answer to each question.

Passage 1 When you lose water, your blood becomes more concentrated. Think about how you make a powdered drink, such as lemonade. If you use the same amount of powder in 1 L of water as you do in 2 L of water, the drinks will taste different. The lemonade made with 1 L of water will be stronger because it is more concentrated. Losing water through sweating increases the concentration of sodium and potassium in your blood. The kidneys force the extra potassium out of the blood stream and into nephrons. From the nephrons, the potassium is eliminated from the body in urine.

1. The words *more concentrated* in this passage refer to
   - **A** the same amount of water with different amounts of material dissolved in it.
   - **B** small amounts of material dissolved in small amounts of water.
   - **C** large amounts of material dissolved in large amounts of water.
   - **D** a given amount of material dissolved in a smaller amount of water.

2. Which of the following statements is a fact from the passage?
   - **F** Blood contains both potassium and sodium.
   - **G** Losing too much sodium is dangerous.
   - **H** Potassium and sodium can be replaced by drinking an exercise drink.
   - **I** Tears contain sodium.

Passage 2 Three major types of nutrients—carbohydrates, proteins, and fats—make up most of the food you eat. Chemical substances called *enzymes* break these nutrients into smaller particles for the body to use. For example, proteins, which are chains of smaller molecules called *amino acids,* are too large to be absorbed into the bloodstream. So, enzymes cut the chain of amino acids. These amino acids are small enough to pass into the bloodstream to be used by the body.

1. According to the passage, what is a carbohydrate?
   - **A** an enzyme
   - **B** a substance made of amino acids
   - **C** a nutrient
   - **D** the only substance in a healthy diet

2. Which of the following statements is a fact from the passage?
   - **F** Carbohydrates, fats, and proteins are three major types of nutrients.
   - **G** Proteins are made of fats and carbohydrates.
   - **H** Some enzymes create chains of proteins.
   - **I** Fats are difficult to digest.

3. Which of the following can be inferred from the passage?
   - **A** To be useful to the body, nutrients must be small enough to enter the bloodstream.
   - **B** Carbohydrates are made of amino acids.
   - **C** Amino acids are made of proteins.
   - **D** Without enough protein, the body cannot grow.

INTERPRETING GRAPHICS

Use the figure below to answer the questions that follow.

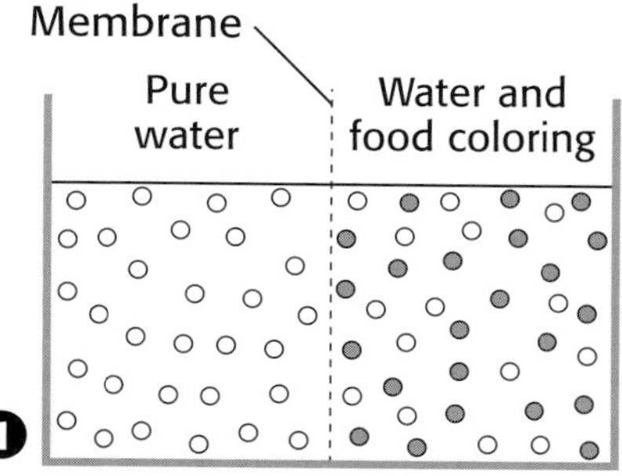

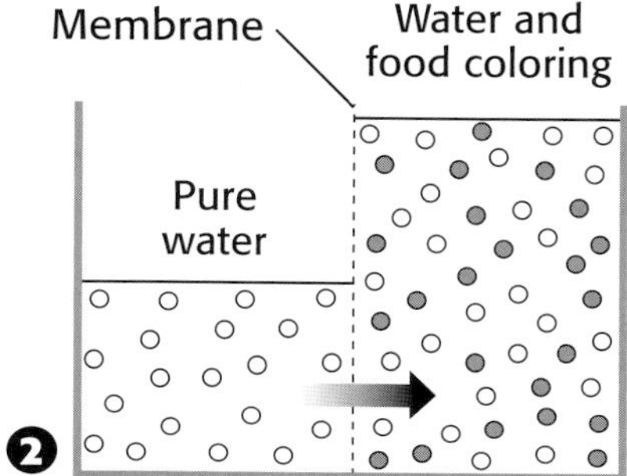

1. The container is divided by a membrane. What can you conclude from the diagram?
   - **A** Water molecules can pass through the membrane.
   - **B** Food-coloring molecules can pass through the membrane.
   - **C** Both water molecules and food-coloring molecules can pass through the membrane.
   - **D** Neither water molecules nor food-coloring molecules can pass through the membrane.

2. If the membrane has holes that separate molecules by size,
   - **F** food-coloring molecules are larger than water molecules.
   - **G** water molecules are larger than food-coloring molecules.
   - **H** water molecules and food-coloring molecules are the same size.
   - **I** the holes are smaller than both water molecules and food-coloring molecules.

3. The concentration of food-coloring molecules in the columns labeled "Water and food coloring"
   - **A** is greater in 2 than in 1.
   - **B** is greater in 1 than in 2.
   - **C** is the same in 1 and 2.
   - **D** cannot change.

MATH

Read each question below, and choose the best answer.

1. Cora is 1.5 m tall. Cora's small intestine is 6 m long. How many times longer is Cora's small intestine than her height?
   - **A** 3 times longer
   - **B** 4 times longer
   - **C** 5 times longer
   - **D** 6 times longer

2. During a water-balance study that was performed for one day, a woman drank 1,500 mL of water. The food she ate contained 750 mL of water, and her body produced 250 mL of water internally during normal body processes. She lost 900 mL of water in sweat, 1,500 mL in urine, and 100 mL in feces. Overall, how much water did she gain or lose during the day?
   - **F** She gained 1,500 mL of water.
   - **G** She lost 900 mL of water.
   - **H** She gained as much water as she lost.
   - **I** She lost twice as much water as she gained.

3. There are 6 blue marbles, 2 red marbles, and 4 green marbles in a bag. If someone selects 1 marble at random from the bag, what is the probability that the marble will be blue?
   - **A** 1/5
   - **B** 1/4
   - **C** 1/3
   - **D** 1/2

Science in Action

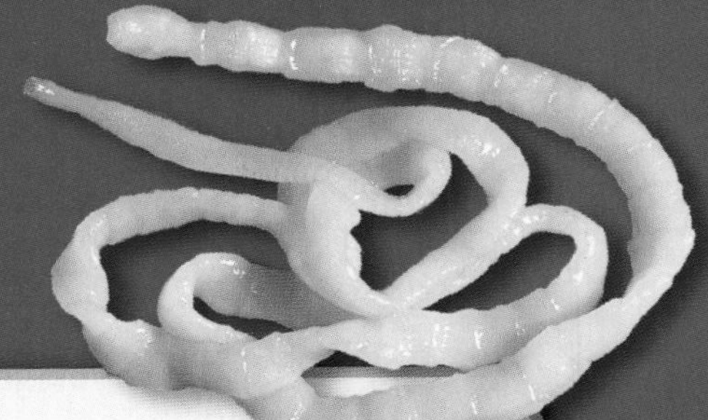

Weird Science

Tapeworms

What if you found out that you had a constant mealtime companion who didn't want just a bite but wanted it all? And what if that companion never asked for your permission? This mealtime companion might be a tapeworm. Tapeworms are invertebrate flatworms. These flatworms are parasites. A parasite is an organism that obtains its food by living in or on another organism. A tapeworm doesn't have a digestive tract of its own. Instead, a tapeworm absorbs the nutrients digested by the host. Some tape worms can grow to be over 10 m long. Cooking beef, pork, and fish properly can help prevent people from getting tapeworms. People or animals who get tapeworms can be treated with medicines.

Social Studies ACTIVITY

WRITING SKILL The World Health Organization and the Pan American Health Organization have made fighting intestinal parasites in children a high priority. Conduct library or Internet research on Worm Busters, which is a program for fighting parasites. Write a brief report of your findings.

Science, Technology, and Society

Pill Cameras

Open wide and say "Ahhhh." When you have a problem with your mouth or teeth, doctors can examine you pretty easily. But when people have problems that are further down their digestive tract, examination becomes more difficult. So, some doctors have recently created a tiny, disposable camera that patients can swallow. As the camera travels down the digestive tract, the camera takes pictures and sends them to a tiny recorder that patients wear on their belt. The camera takes about 57,000 images during its trip. Later, doctors can review the pictures and see the pictures of the patient's entire digestive tract.

Math ACTIVITY

If a pill camera takes 57,000 images while it travels through the digestive system and takes about two pictures per second, how many hours is the camera in the body?

Careers

Christy Krames

Medical Illustrator Christy Krames is a medical illustrator. For 19 years, she has created detailed illustrations of the inner workings of the human body. Medical illustrations allow doctors and surgeons to share concepts, theories, and techniques with colleagues and allow students to learn about the human body.

Medical illustrators often draw tiny structures or body processes that would be difficult or impossible to photograph. For example, a photograph of a small intestine can show the entire organ. But a medical illustrator can add to the photograph an enlarged drawing of the tiny villi inside the intestine. Adding details helps to better explain how small parts of organs work together so that the organs can function.

Medical illustration requires knowledge of both art and science. So, Christy Krames studied both art and medicine in college. Often, Krames must do research before she draws a subject. Her research may include reading books, observing surgical procedures, or even dissecting a pig's heart. This research results in accurate and educational drawings of the inner body.

Language Arts ACTIVITY

WRITING SKILL Pretend you are going to publish an atlas of the human body. Write a classified advertisement to hire medical illustrators. Describe the job, and describe the qualities that the best candidates will have. As you write the ad, remember you are trying to persuade the best illustrators to contact you.

To learn more about these Science in Action topics, visit go.hrw.com and type in the keyword **HL5BD3F.**

Current Science

Check out Current Science® articles related to this chapter by visiting go.hrw.com. Just type in the keyword HL5CS24.

Communication and Control

About the 

This picture may look like it shows a flower garden or a coral reef. But it really shows something much closer to home. It shows the human tongue (magnified thousands of times, of course). Those round bumps are taste buds. You use taste and other senses to gather information about your surroundings.

PRE-READING ACTIVITY

Graphic Organizer

Concept Map Before you read the chapter, create the graphic organizer entitled "Concept Map" described in the **Study Skills** section of the Appendix. As you read the chapter, fill in the concept map with details about each part or division of the nervous system. Include details about what each part or division does.

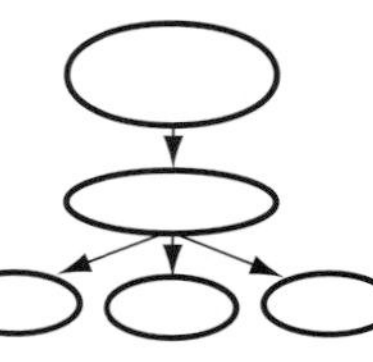

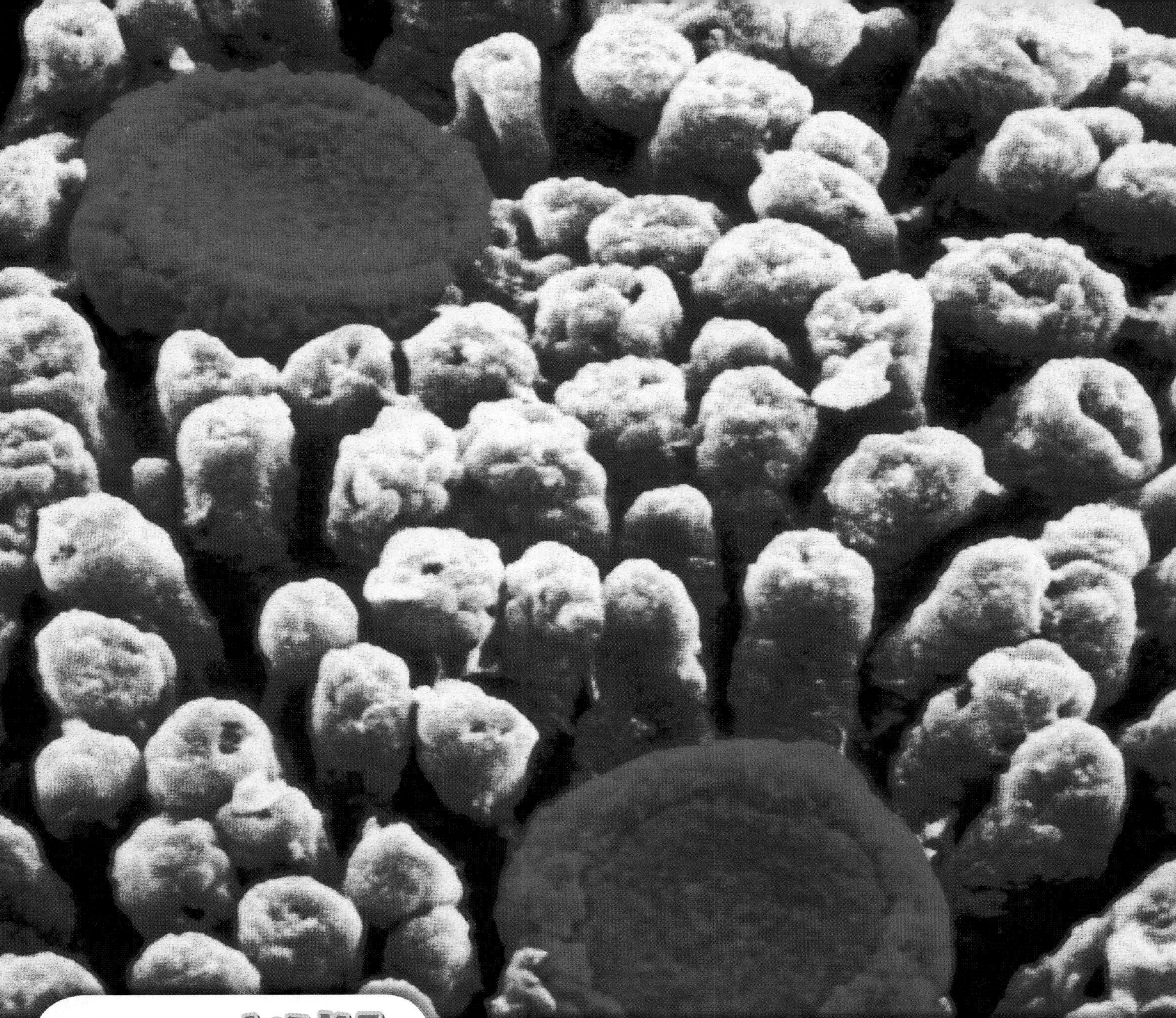

START-UP ACTIVITY

Act Fast!

If you want to catch an object, your brain sends a message to the muscles in your arm. In this exercise, you will see how long sending that message takes.

Procedure

1. Sit in a **chair** with one arm in a "handshake" position. Your partner should stand facing you, holding a **meterstick** vertically. The stick should be positioned so that it will fall between your thumb and fingers.
2. Tell your partner to let go of the meterstick without warning you. Catch the stick between your thumb and fingers. Your partner should catch the meterstick if it tips over.
3. Record the number of centimeters that the stick dropped before you caught it. That distance represents your reaction time.
4. Repeat steps 1–3 three times. Calculate the average distance.
5. Repeat steps 1–4 with your other hand.
6. Trade places with your partner, and repeat steps 1–5.

Analysis

1. Compare the reaction times of your own hands. Why might one hand react more quickly than the other?
2. Compare your results with your partner's. Why might one person react more quickly than another?

SECTION 1

The Nervous System

READING WARM-UP

Objectives

- Describe the relationship between the central nervous system and the peripheral nervous system.
- Compare the somatic nervous system with the autonomic nervous system.
- List one function of each part of the brain.

Terms to Learn

central nervous system
peripheral nervous system
neuron
nerve
brain

READING STRATEGY

Discussion Read this section silently. Write down questions that you have about this section. Discuss your questions in a small group.

Which of the following activities do NOT involve your nervous system: eating, playing a musical instrument, reading a book, running, or sleeping?

This is a trick question. All of these activities involve your nervous system. In fact, your nervous system controls almost everything you do.

Two Systems Within a System

The nervous system acts as the body's central command post. It has two basic functions. First, it gathers and interprets information. This information comes from inside your body and from the world outside your body. Then, the nervous system responds to that information as needed.

The nervous system has two parts: the central nervous system and the peripheral (puh RIF uhr uhl) nervous system. The **central nervous system** (CNS) is your brain and spinal cord. The CNS processes and responds to all messages coming from the peripheral nervous system. The **peripheral nervous system** (PNS) is all of the parts of the nervous system except for the brain and the spinal cord. The PNS connects all parts of the body to the CNS. The PNS uses specialized structures, called *nerves,* to carry information between your body and your CNS. **Figure 1** shows the major divisions of the nervous system.

Reading Check **Explain the difference between the CNS and the PNS.** (*See the Appendix for answers to Reading Checks.*)

central nervous system (CNS) the brain and the spinal cord

peripheral nervous system (PNS) all of the parts of the nervous system except for the brain and the spinal cord

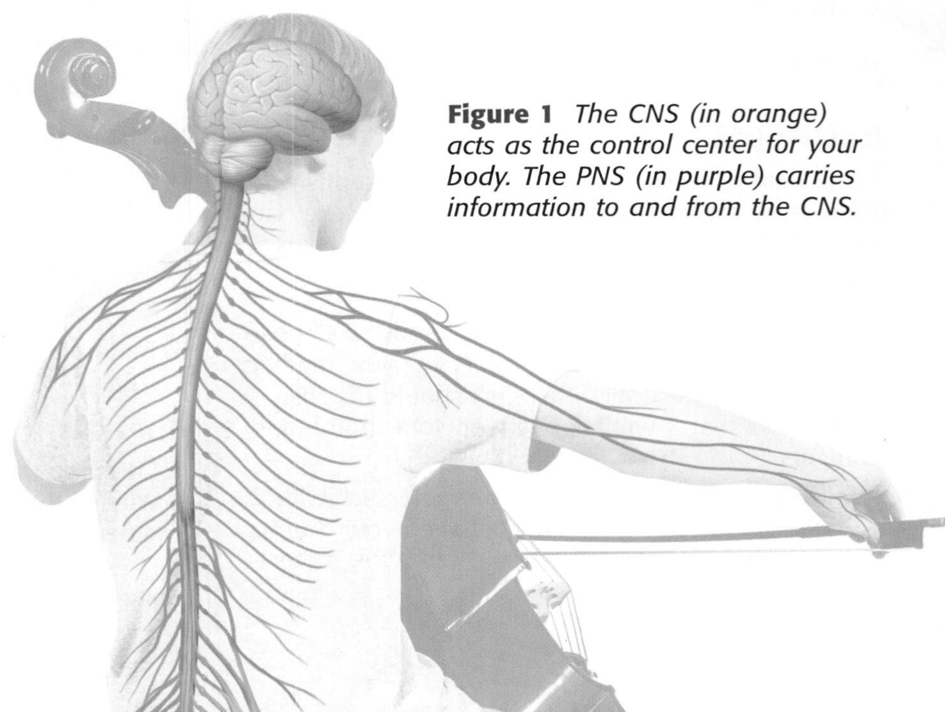

Figure 1 *The CNS (in orange) acts as the control center for your body. The PNS (in purple) carries information to and from the CNS.*

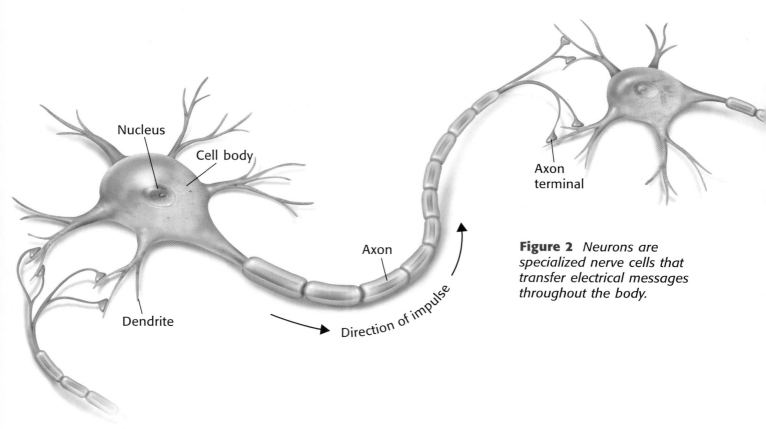

Figure 2 *Neurons are specialized nerve cells that transfer electrical messages throughout the body.*

The Peripheral Nervous System

Messages about your environment travel through the nervous system along neurons. A **neuron** (NOO RAHN) is a nerve cell that is specialized to transfer messages in the form of fast-moving electrical energy. These electrical messages are called *impulses*. Impulses may travel as fast as 150 m/s or as slow as 0.2 m/s. **Figure 2** shows a typical neuron transferring an impulse.

neuron a nerve cell that is specialized to receive and conduct electrical impulses

Neuron Structure

In many ways, a neuron is similar to other cells. A neuron has a large region in its center called the *cell body*. The cell body has a nucleus and cell organelles. But neurons also have special structures called dendrites and axons. *Dendrites* are usually short, branched extensions of the cell. Neurons receive information from other cells through their dendrites. A neuron may have many dendrites, which allows it to receive impulses from thousands of other cells.

Impulses are carried away from the cell body by axons. *Axons* are elongated extensions of a neuron. They can be very short or quite long. Some long axons extend almost 1 m from your lower back to your toes. The end of an axon often has branches that allow information to pass to other cells. The tip of each branch is called an *axon terminal*.

Reading Check **In your own words, describe a neuron.**

Time to Travel

To calculate how long an impulse takes to travel a certain distance, you can use the following equation:

$$time = \frac{distance}{speed}$$

If an impulse travels 100 m/s, about how long would it take an impulse to travel 10 m?

Information Collection

nerve a collection of nerve fibers (axons) through which impulses travel between the central nervous system and other parts of the body

Remember that neurons are a type of nerve cell that carries impulses. Some neurons are *sensory neurons.* These neurons gather information about what is happening in and around your body. They have specialized nerve endings called *receptors.* Receptors detect changes inside and outside the body. For example, receptors in your eyes detect light. Sensory neurons then send this information to the CNS for processing.

Delivering Orders

Neurons that send impulses from the brain and spinal cord to other systems are called *motor neurons.* When muscles get impulses from motor neurons, they respond by contracting. For example, motor neurons cause muscles around your eyes to contract when you are in bright light. These muscles make you squint. Squinting lets less light enter the eyes. Motor neurons also send messages to your glands, such as sweat glands. These messages tell sweat glands to start or stop making sweat.

Nerves

The central nervous system is connected to the rest of your body by nerves. A **nerve** is a collection of axons bundled together with blood vessels and connective tissue. Nerves are everywhere in your body. Most nerves have axons of both sensory neurons and motor neurons. Axons are parts of nerves, but nerves are more than just axons. **Figure 3** shows the structure of a nerve. The axon in this nerve transmits information from the spinal cord to muscle fibers.

Reading Check What is a nerve?

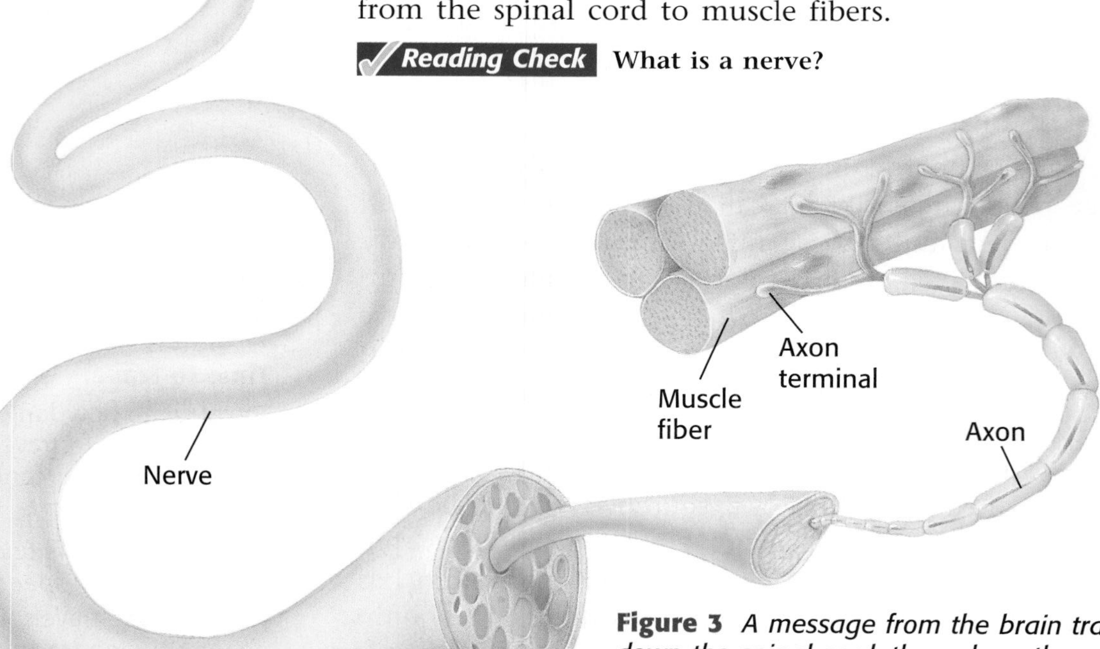

Figure 3 *A message from the brain travels down the spinal cord, then along the axon of a motor neuron inside a nerve to the muscle. The message makes the muscle contract.*

Somatic and Autonomic Nervous Systems

Remember, the PNS connects your CNS to the rest of your body. And the PNS has two main parts—the sensory part (sensory neurons) and the motor part (motor neurons). You know that sensory nerves collect information from your senses and send that information to the CNS. You also know that motor nerves carry out the CNS's responses to that sensory information. To carry those responses, the motor part of the PNS has two kinds of nerves: somatic nerves and autonomic nerves.

Somatic Nervous System

Most of the neurons that are part of the *somatic nervous system* are under your conscious control. These are the neurons that stimulate skeletal muscles. They control voluntary movements, such as writing, talking, smiling, or jumping.

Autonomic Nervous System

Autonomic nerves do not need your conscious control. These neurons are part of the autonomic nervous system. The *autonomic nervous system* controls body functions that you don't think about, such as digestion and heart rate (the number of times your heart beats per minute).

The main job of the autonomic nervous system is to keep all the body's functions in balance. Depending on the situation, the autonomic nervous system can speed up or slow down these functions. The autonomic nervous system has two divisions: the *sympathetic nervous system* and the *parasympathetic nervous system.* These two divisions work together to keep your internal environment stable. This is called *homeostasis.* Some of these functions are shown in **Table 1.**

Reading Check Describe three functions of the PNS.

CONNECTION TO Chemistry

Keeping Your Balance The autonomic nervous system has two parts—the sympathetic division and the parasympathetic division. These parts of your nervous system help keep all of your body systems in balance. Research these two parts of the nervous system, and make a poster showing how they keep your body healthy.

ACTIVITY

Table 1 Effects of the Autonomic Nervous System on the Body

Organ	Effect of sympathetic division	Effect of parasympathetic division
Eyes	pupils dilate (grow larger; makes it easier to see objects)	pupils constrict (vision normal)
Heart	heart rate increases (increases blood flow)	heart rate slows (blood flow slows)
Lungs	bronchioles dilate (grow larger; increases oxygen in blood)	bronchioles constrict
Blood vessels	blood vessels dilate (increases blood flow except to digestion)	little or no effect
Intestines	digestion slows (reduces blood flow to stomach and intestines)	digestion returns to normal

The Central Nervous System

The central nervous system receives information from the sensory neurons. Then it responds by sending messages to the body through motor neurons in the PNS.

The Control Center

brain the mass of nerve tissue that is the main control center of the nervous system

The largest organ in the nervous system is the brain. The **brain** is the main control center of the nervous system. Many processes that the brain controls happen automatically. These processes are called *involuntary.* For example, you couldn't stop digesting food even if you tried. On the other hand, some actions controlled by your brain are *voluntary.* When you want to move your arm, your brain sends signals along motor neurons to muscles in your arm. Then, the muscles contract, and your arm moves. The brain has three main parts—the cerebrum (suh REE bruhm), the cerebellum (SER uh BEL uhm), and the medulla (mi DUHL uh). Each part has its own job.

Reading Check **What is the difference between a voluntary action and an involuntary action?**

The Cerebrum

The largest part of your brain is called the *cerebrum.* It looks like a mushroom cap. This dome-shaped area is where you think and where most memories are stored. It controls voluntary movements and allows you to sense touch, light, sound, odors, taste, pain, heat, and cold.

The cerebrum has two halves, called *hemispheres.* The left hemisphere directs the right side of the body, and the right hemisphere directs the left side of the body. **Figure 4** shows some of the activities that each hemisphere controls. However, most brain activities use both hemispheres.

Figure 4 **The Cerebral Hemispheres**

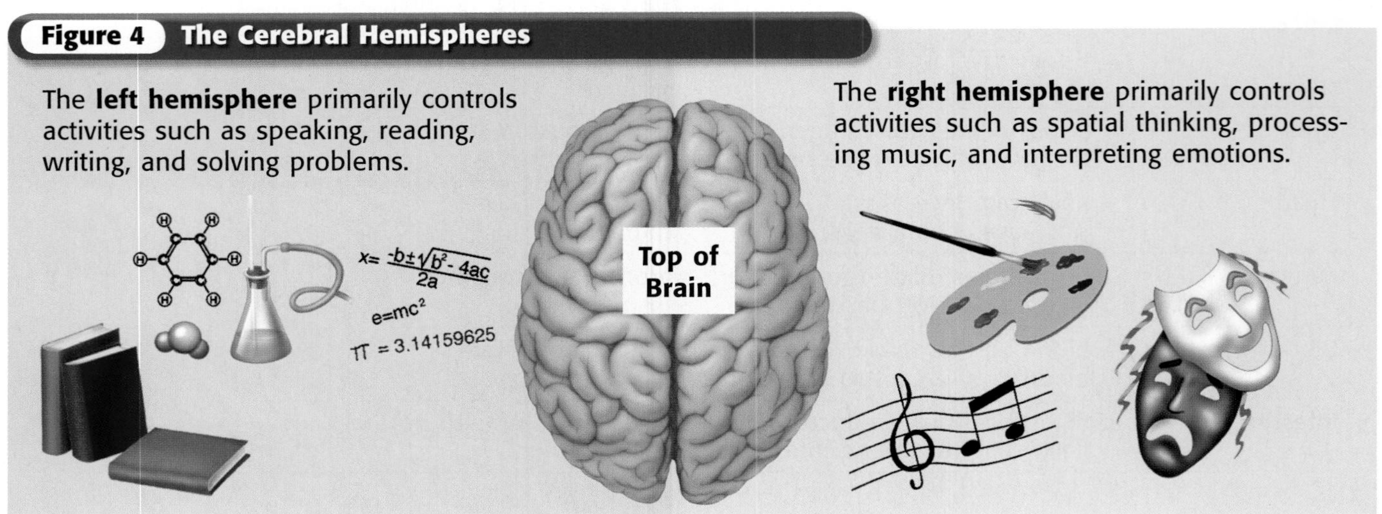

The **left hemisphere** primarily controls activities such as speaking, reading, writing, and solving problems.
$x = \frac{-b \pm \sqrt{b^2 - 4ac}}{2a}$
$e=mc^2$
$\pi = 3.14159625$
Top of Brain
The **right hemisphere** primarily controls activities such as spatial thinking, processing music, and interpreting emotions.

The Cerebellum

The second-largest part of your brain is the *cerebellum.* It lies beneath the back of the cerebrum. The cerebellum processes sensory information from your body, such as from skeletal muscles and joints. This allows the brain to keep track of your body's position. If you begin to lose your balance, the cerebellum sends impulses telling different skeletal muscles to contract. Those muscles shift a person's weight and keep a person, such as the girl in **Figure 5,** from losing her balance.

Figure 5 *Your cerebellum causes skeletal muscles to make adjustments so that you will stay upright.*

The Medulla

The *medulla* is the part of your brain that connects to your spinal cord. The medulla is about 3 cm long, and you can't live without it. The medulla controls involuntary processes, such as blood pressure, body temperature, heart rate, and involuntary breathing.

Your medulla constantly receives sensory impulses from receptors in your blood vessels. It uses this information to regulate your blood pressure. If your blood pressure gets too low, the medulla sends out impulses that tell blood vessels to tighten up. As a result, blood pressure rises. The medulla also sends impulses to the heart to make the heart beat faster or slower. **Figure 6** shows the location of the parts of the brain and some of the functions of each part.

Reading Check Explain why the medulla is important.

Figure 6 Areas of the Brain at Work

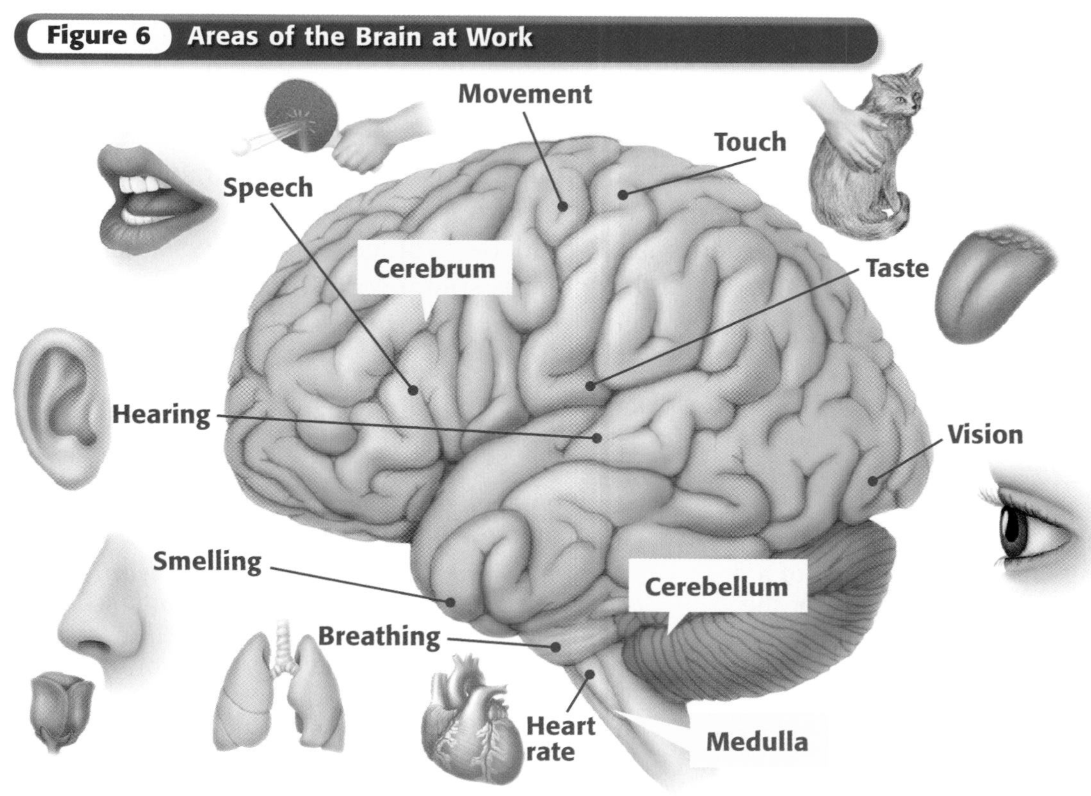

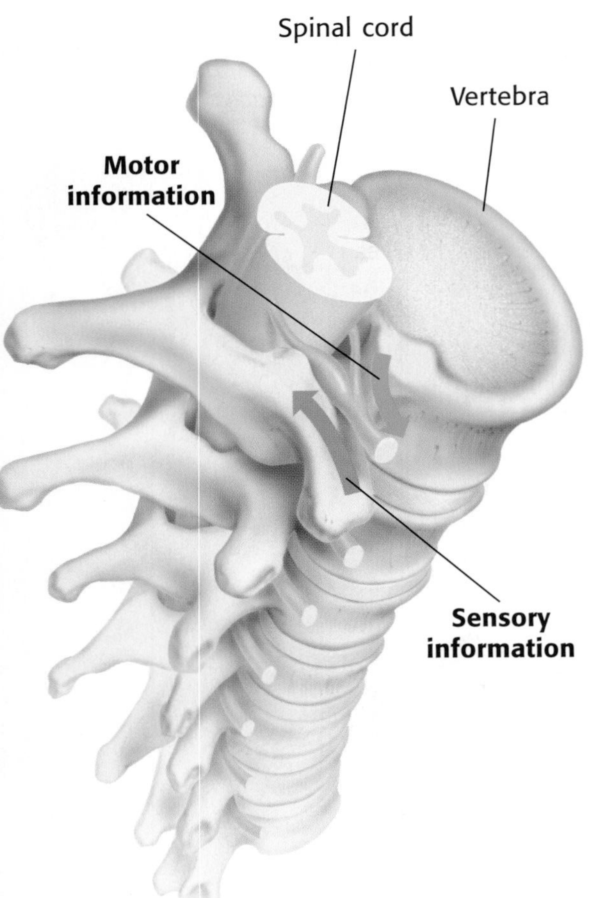

Figure 7 *The spinal cord carries information to and from the brain. Vertebrae protect the spinal cord.*

The Spinal Cord

Your spinal cord, which is part of your central nervous system, is about as big around as your thumb. The spinal cord is made of neurons and bundles of axons that pass impulses to and from the brain. As shown in **Figure 7,** the spinal cord is surrounded by protective bones called *vertebrae* (VUHR tuh BRAY).

The nerve fibers in your spinal cord allow your brain to communicate with your peripheral nervous system. Sensory neurons in your skin and muscles send impulses along their axons to your spinal cord. The spinal cord carries impulses to your brain. The brain interprets these impulses as pain, temperature, or other sensations. The brain then responds to the situation. Impulses moving from the brain down the spinal cord are relayed to motor neurons. Motor neurons carry the impulses along their axons to muscles and glands all over your body.

Reading Check **Describe the path of an impulse from the skin to the brain and the path of the response.**

Spinal Cord Injury

A spinal cord injury may block all information to and from the brain. Sensory information coming from below the injury may not get to the brain. For example, a spinal cord injury may block all sensory impulses from the feet and legs. People with such an injury would not be able to sense pain, touch, or temperature with their feet. And motor commands from the brain to the injured area may not reach the peripheral nerves. So, the person would not be able to move his or her legs.

Each year, thousands of people are paralyzed by spinal cord injuries. Many of these injuries happen in car accidents and could be avoided by wearing a seat belt. Among young people, spinal cord injuries are sometimes related to sports or other activities. These injuries might be prevented by wearing proper safety equipment.

Building a Neuron

1. Your teacher will provide at least four different colors of **modeling clay.** Build a model of a neuron by using different-colored clay for the various parts of the neuron.
2. Use **tape** to attach your model neuron to a **piece of plain white paper.**
3. On the paper, label each part of the neuron. Draw an arrow from the label to the part.
4. Using a **colored pencil, marker,** or **crayon,** draw arrows showing the path of an impulse traveling in your neuron. Tell whether the impulse is a sensory impulse or a motor impulse. Then, describe what will happen when the impulse reaches its destination.

SECTION Review

Summary

- The central nervous system (CNS) includes the brain and the spinal cord.
- The peripheral nervous system (PNS) is all the parts of the nervous system except the brain and spinal cord.
- The peripheral nervous system has nerves made up of axons of neurons.
- Sensory neurons have receptors that detect information about the body and its environment. Motor neurons carry messages from the brain and spinal cord to other parts of the body.
- The PNS has two types of motor nerves—somatic nerves and autonomic nerves.
- The cerebrum is the largest part of the brain and controls thinking, sensing, and voluntary movement.
- The cerebellum is the part of the brain that keeps track of the body's position and helps maintain balance.
- The medulla controls involuntary processes, such as heart rate, blood pressure, body temperature, and breathing.

Using Key Terms

1. In your own words, write a definition for each of the following terms: *neuron* and *nerve*.

2. Use the following terms in the same sentence: *brain* and *peripheral nervous system*.

Understanding Key Ideas

3. Someone touches your shoulder and you turn around. Which sequence do your impulses follow?

a. motor neuron, sensory neuron, CNS response
b. motor neuron, CNS response, sensory neuron
c. sensory neuron, motor neuron, CNS response
d. sensory neuron, CNS response, motor neuron

4. Describe one function of each part of the brain.

5. Compare the somatic nervous system with the autonomic nervous system.

6. Explain how a severe injury to the spinal cord can affect other parts of the body.

Critical Thinking

7. Applying Concepts Some medications slow a person's nervous system. These drugs are often labeled "May cause drowsiness." Explain why a person needs to know about this side effect.

8. Predicting Consequences Explain how your life would change if your autonomic nervous system suddenly stopped working.

Interpreting Graphics

Use the figure below to answer the questions that follow.

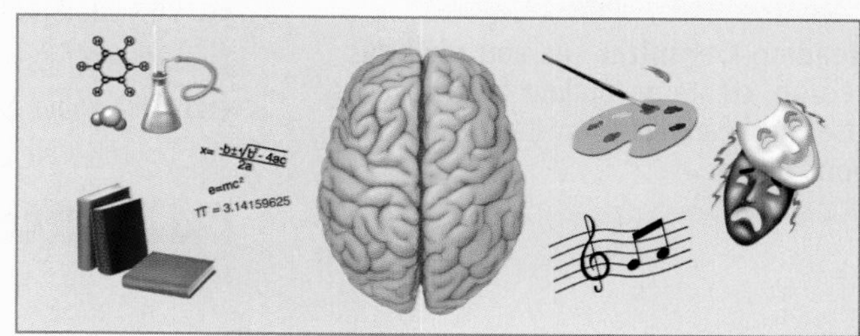

9. Which hemisphere of the brain recognizes and processes words, numbers, and letters? faces, places, and objects?

10. For a person whose left hemisphere is primarily in control, would it be easier to learn to play a new computer game by reading the rules and following instructions or by watching a friend play and imitating his actions?

SCILINKS.
NSTA
Developed and maintained by the National Science Teachers Association
For a variety of links related to this chapter, go to www.scilinks.org
Topic: Nervous System
SciLinks code: HSM1023

SECTION 2

Responding to the Environment

READING WARM-UP

Objectives

- List four sensations that are detected by receptors in the skin.
- Describe how a feedback mechanism works.
- Describe how light relates to sight.
- Describe how the senses of hearing, taste, and smell work.

Terms to Learn

integumentary system
reflex
feedback mechanism
retina
cochlea

READING STRATEGY

Reading Organizer As you read this section, create an outline of the section. Use the headings from the section in your outline.

You feel a tap on your shoulder. Who tapped you? You turn to look, hoping to see a friend. Your senses are on the job!

The tap produces impulses in sensory receptors on your shoulder. These impulses travel to your brain. Once the impulses reach your brain, they create an awareness called a *sensation*. In this case, the sensation is of your shoulder being touched. But you still do not know who tapped you. So, you turn around. The sensory receptors in your eyes send impulses to your brain. Now, your brain recognizes your best friend.

Sense of Touch

Touch is what you feel when sensory receptors in the skin are stimulated. It is the sensation you feel when you shake hands or feel a breeze. As shown in **Figure 1,** skin has different kinds of receptors. Each kind of receptor responds mainly to one kind of stimulus. For example, *thermoreceptors* respond to temperature change. Each kind of receptor produces a specific sensation of touch, such as pressure, temperature, pain, or vibration. Skin is part of the integumentary (in TEG yoo MEN tuhr ee) system. The **integumentary system** protects the body from damage. It includes hair, skin, and nails.

Reading Check List four sensations that your skin can detect. (*See the Appendix for answers to Reading Checks.*)

integumentary system the organ system that forms a protective covering on the outside of the body

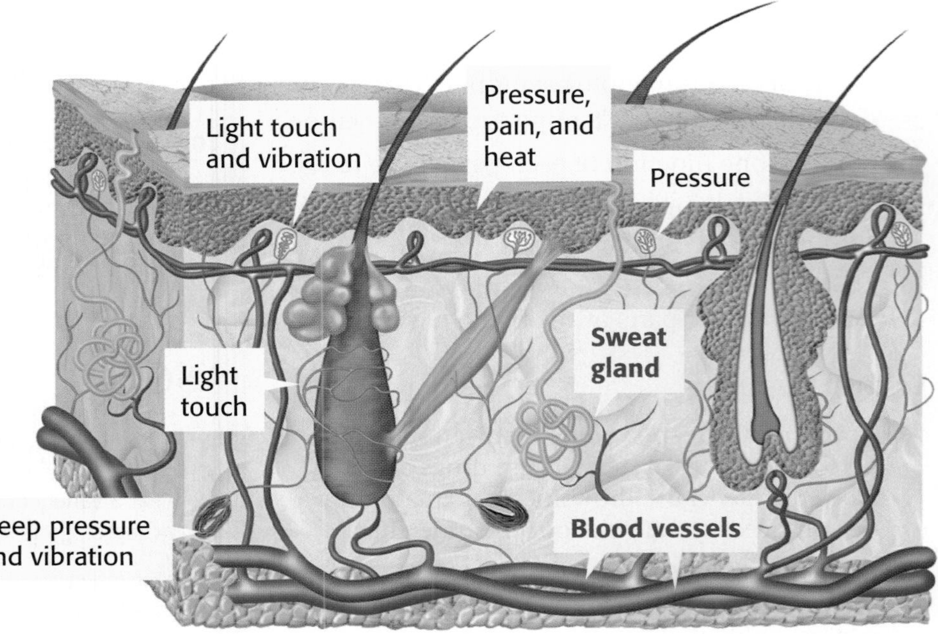

Figure 1 *Each type of receptor in your skin has its own structure and function.*

Responding to Sensory Messages

When you step on something sharp, as the man in **Figure 2** did, pain receptors in your foot or toe send impulses to your spinal cord. Almost immediately, a message to move your foot travels back to the muscles in your leg and foot. Without thinking, you quickly lift your foot. This immediate, involuntary action is called a **reflex.** Your brain isn't telling your leg to move. In fact, by the time the message reaches your brain, your leg and foot have already moved. If you had to wait for your brain to act, you toes might be seriously hurt!

reflex an involuntary and almost immediate movement in response to a stimulus

feedback mechanism a cycle of events in which information from one step controls or affects a previous step

Reading Check **Why are reflexes important?**

Feedback Mechanisms

Most of the time, the brain processes information from skin receptors. For example, on a hot day, heat receptors in your skin detect an increase in your temperature. The receptors send impulses to the brain. Your brain responds by sending messages to your sweat glands to make sweat. As sweat evaporates, it cools your body. Your brain also tells the blood vessels in your skin to dilate (open wider). Blood flow increases. Thermal energy from the blood in your skin moves to your surroundings. This also cools your body. As your body cools, it sends messages to your brain. The brain responds by sending messages to sweat glands and blood vessels to reduce their activity.

This cooling process is one of your body's feedback mechanisms. A **feedback mechanism** is a cycle of events in which information from one step controls or affects a previous step. The temperature-regulating feedback mechanism helps keep your body temperature within safe limits. This cooling mechanism works like a thermostat on an air conditioner. Once a room reaches the right temperature, the thermostat sends a message to the air conditioner to stop blowing cold air.

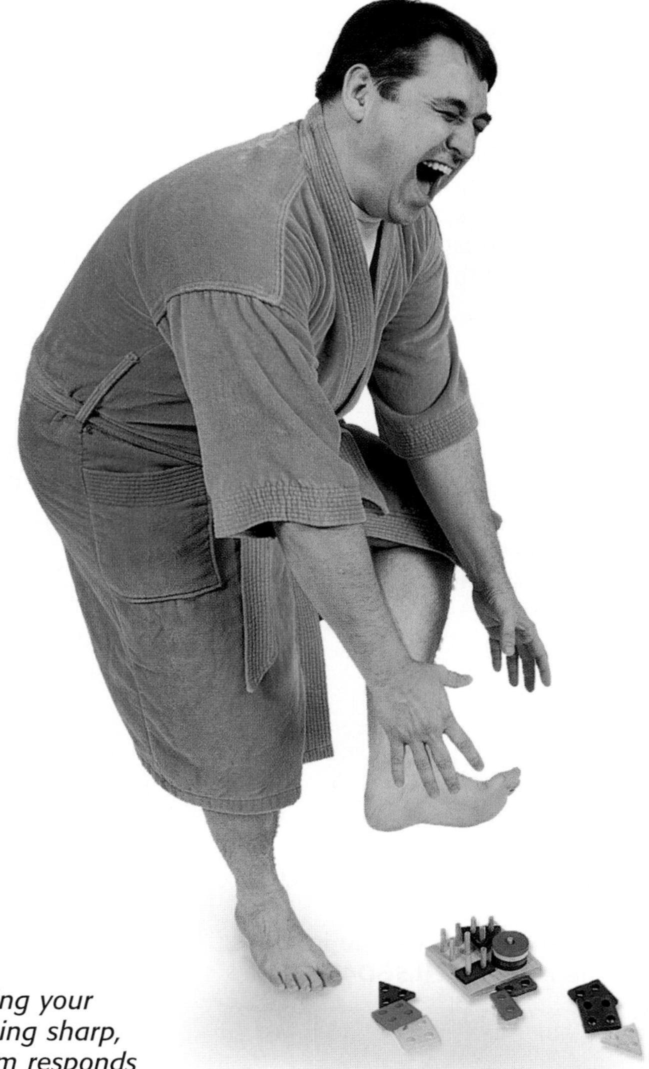

Figure 2 *A reflex, such as lifting your foot when you step on something sharp, is one way your nervous system responds to your environment.*

White light
Orange light
Cornea
Iris
Pupil
Lens
Retina
Optic nerve

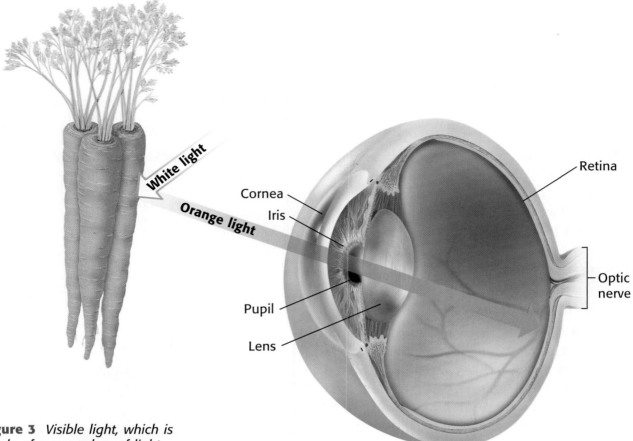

Figure 3 *Visible light, which is made of many colors of light, hits the carrots. Carrots look orange because they reflect orange light to your eyes.*

Sense of Sight

Sight is the sense that allows you to see the size, shape, motion, and color of objects around you. You see an object when it sends or reflects visible light toward your eyes. Your eyes detect this light, which enables your brain to form visual images.

Your eyes are complex sensory organs, as you can see in **Figure 3.** The front of the eye is covered by a clear membrane called the *cornea.* The cornea protects the eye but allows light to enter. Light from an object enters the front of your eye through an opening called the *pupil.* The light then travels through the lens to the back of the eye. There, the light strikes the **retina,** a layer of light-sensitive cells.

retina the light-sensitive inner layer of the eye; it receives images formed by the lens and transmits them through the optic nerve to the brain

The retina is packed with photoreceptors. A *photoreceptor* is a special neuron that changes light into electrical impulses. The retina has two kinds of photoreceptors: rods and cones. Rods are very sensitive to dim light. They are important for night vision. Impulses from rods are interpreted as black-and-white images. Cones are very sensitive to bright light. Impulses from cones allow you to see fine details and colors.

Impulses from the rods and cones travel along axons. The impulses leave the back of each eye through an optic nerve. The optic nerve carries the impulses to your brain, where the impulses are interpreted as the images that you see.

For another activity related to this chapter, go to **go.hrw.com** and type in the keyword **HL5BD4W.**

Reading Check **Describe how light and sight are related.**

Reacting to Light

Your pupil looks like a black dot in the center of your eye. In fact, it is an opening that lets light enter the eye. The pupil is surrounded by the *iris,* a ring of muscle. The iris controls the amount of light that enters the eye and gives the eye its color. In bright light, the iris contracts, which makes the pupil smaller. A smaller pupil reduces the amount of light entering the eye and passing onto the retina. In dim light, the iris opens the pupil and lets in more light.

Reading Check **How does your iris react to bright light?**

Focusing the Light

Light travels in straight lines until it passes through the cornea and the lens. The *lens* is an oval-shaped piece of clear, curved material behind the iris. Muscles in the eye change the shape of the lens in order to focus light onto the retina. When you look at objects close to the eye, the lens becomes more curved. When you look at objects far away, the lens gets flatter.

Figure 4 shows some common vision problems. In some eyes, the lens focuses the light in front of the retina, which results in nearsightedness. If the lens focuses the light just behind the retina, the result is farsightedness. Glasses, contact lenses, or surgery can usually correct these vision problems.

Where's the Dot?

1. Hold your **book** at arm's length, and close your right eye. Focus your left eye on the black dot below.

2. Slowly move the book toward your face until the white dot disappears. You may need to try a few times to get this result. The white dot doesn't always disappear for every person.
3. Describe your observations.
4. Use the library or the Internet to research the optic nerve and to find out why the white dot disappears.

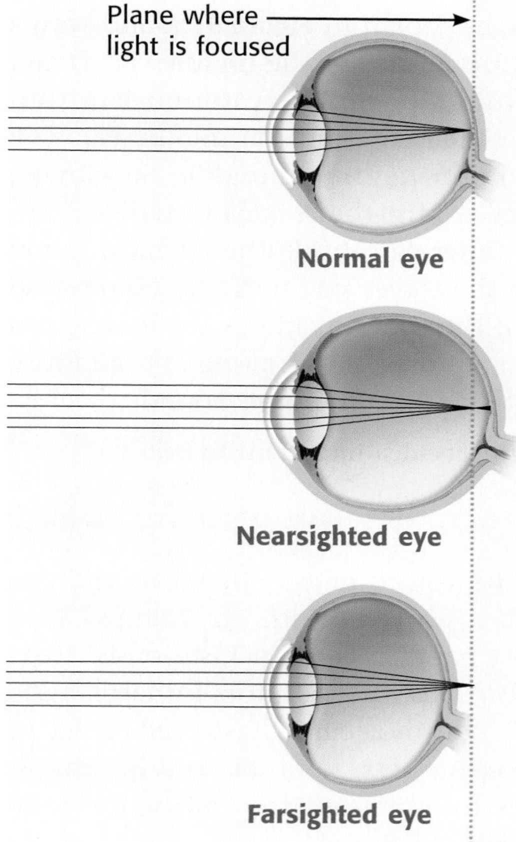

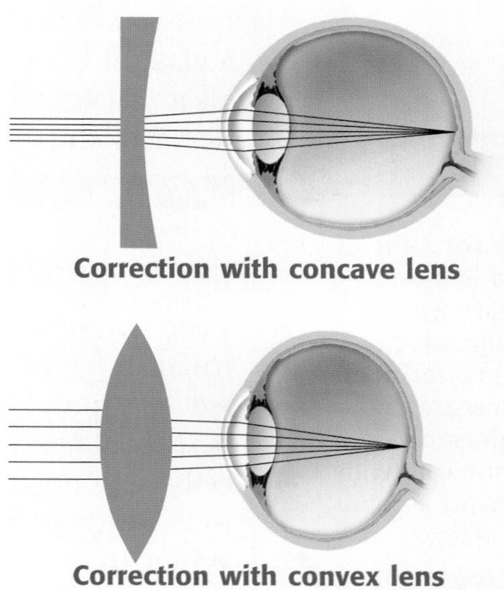

Figure 4 *A concave lens bends light rays outward to correct nearsightedness. A convex lens bends light rays inward to correct farsightedness.*

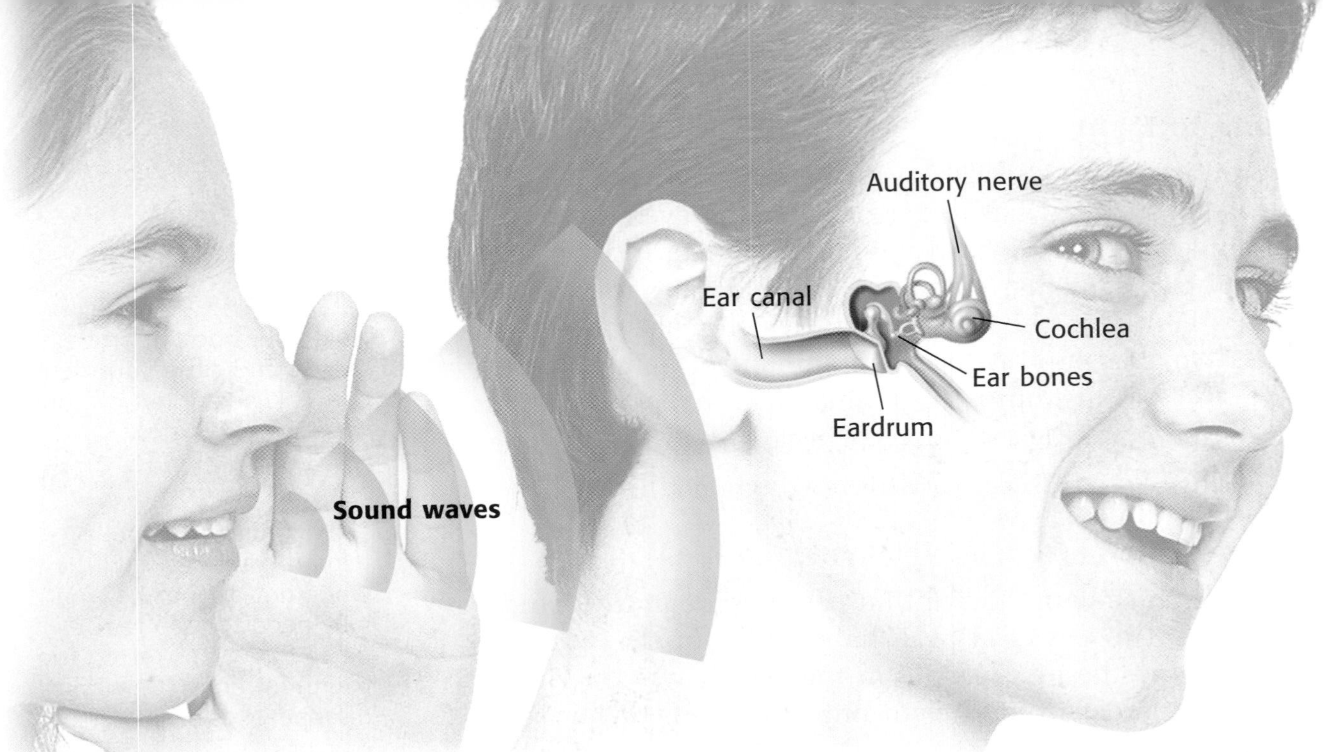

Figure 5 *A sound wave travels into the outer ear. It is converted into bone vibrations in the middle ear, then into liquid vibrations in the inner ear, and finally, into nerve impulses that travel to the brain.*

Sense of Hearing

Sound is produced when something, such as a drum, vibrates. Vibrations push on nearby air particles, which push on other air particles. The vibrations create waves of sound energy. Hearing is the sense that allows you to experience sound energy.

Ears are organs specialized for hearing. Each ear has an outer, middle, and inner portion, as shown in **Figure 5.** Sound waves reaching the outer ear are funneled into the middle ear. There, the waves make the eardrum vibrate. The eardrum is a thin membrane separating the outer ear from the middle ear. The vibrating eardrum makes tiny bones in the middle ear vibrate. One of these bones vibrates against the **cochlea** (KAHK lee uh), a fluid-filled organ of the inner ear. Inside the cochlea, vibrations make waves just like the waves you make by tapping on a glass of water. Neurons in the cochlea change the waves into electrical impulses. These impulses travel along the auditory nerve to the area of the brain that interprets sound.

cochlea a coiled tube that is found in the inner ear and that is essential to hearing

Reading Check **Why is the cochlea important to hearing?**

CONNECTION TO Physics

WRITING SKILL **Elephant Talk** Sound is produced by vibrating objects. Some sounds, called *infrasonic sounds*, are too low for human ears to detect. Research how elephants use infrasonic sounds to communicate with each other, and write a report about what you learn.

Sense of Taste

Taste is the sense that allows you to detect chemicals and distinguish flavors. Your tongue is covered with tiny bumps called *papillae* (puh PIL ee). Most papillae contain taste buds. Taste buds contain clusters of *taste cells,* the receptors for taste. Taste cells respond to dissolved food molecules. Taste cells react to four basic tastes: sweetness, sourness, saltiness, and bitterness. When the brain combines information from all of the taste buds, you taste a "combination" flavor.

Sense of Smell

As you can see in **Figure 6,** receptors for smell are located on *olfactory cells* in the upper part of your nasal cavity. An olfactory cell is a nerve cell that responds to chemical molecules in the air. You smell something when the receptors react to molecules that have been inhaled. The molecules dissolve in the moist lining of the nasal cavity and trigger an impulse. Olfactory cells send those impulses to the brain, which interprets the impulses as odors.

Taste buds and olfactory cells both detect dissolved molecules. Your brain combines information from both senses to give you sensations of flavor.

Figure 6 *Olfactory cells line the nasal cavity. These cells are sensory receptors that react to chemicals in the air.*

Brain

Olfactory cell

Nasal passage

SECTION Review

Summary

- Touch allows you to respond to temperature, pressure, pain, and vibration on the skin.
- Reflexes and feedback mechanisms help you respond to your environment.
- Sight allows you to respond to light energy.
- Hearing allows you to respond to sound energy.
- Taste allows you to distinguish flavors.
- Smell allows you to perceive different odors.

Using Key Terms

1. In your own words, write a definition for each of the following terms: *reflex* and *feedback mechanism.*
2. Use each of the following terms in a separate sentence: *retina* and *cochlea.*

Understanding Key Ideas

3. Three sensations that receptors in the skin detect are
   a. light, smell, and sound.
   b. touch, pain, and odors.
   c. temperature, pressure, and pain.
   d. pressure, sound, and touch.
4. Explain how light and sight are related.
5. Describe how your senses of hearing, taste, and smell work.
6. Explain why you might have trouble seeing bright colors at a candlelit dinner.
7. How is your sense of taste similar to your sense of smell, and how do these senses work together?
8. Describe how the feedback mechanism that regulates body temperature works.

Math Skills

9. Suppose a nerve impulse must travel 0.90 m from your toe to your central nervous system. If the impulse travels at 150 m/s, calculate how long it will take the impulse to arrive. If the impulse travels at 0.2 m/s, how long will it take the impulse to arrive?

Critical Thinking

10. **Making Inferences** Why is it important for the human body to have reflexes?
11. **Applying Concepts** Rods help you detect objects and shapes in dim light. Explain why it is important for human eyes to have both rods and cones.

SCILINKS
NSTA
Developed and maintained by the National Science Teachers Association
For a variety of links related to this chapter, go to www.scilinks.org
Topic: The Senses; The Eye
SciLinks code: HSM1378; HSM0560

SECTION 3

The Endocrine System

Have you ever heard of an epinephrine (EP uh NEPH rin) rush? You might have had one without realizing it. Exciting situations, such as riding a roller coaster or watching a scary movie, can cause your body to release epinephrine.

READING WARM-UP

Objectives

- Explain why the endocrine system is important to the body.
- Identify five glands of the endocrine system, and describe what their hormones do.
- Describe how feedback mechanisms stop and start hormone release.
- Name two hormone imbalances.

Terms to Learn

endocrine system
gland
hormone

READING STRATEGY

Discussion Read this section silently. Write down questions that you have about this section. Discuss your questions in a small group.

Epinephrine is one of the body's chemical messengers made by the endocrine system. Your endocrine system regulates body processes, such as fluid balance, growth, and development.

Hormones as Chemical Messengers

The **endocrine system** controls body functions by using chemicals that are made by the endocrine glands. A **gland** is a group of cells that make special chemicals for your body. Chemical messengers made by the endocrine glands are called hormones. A **hormone** is a chemical messenger made in one cell or tissue that causes a change in another cell or tissue in another part of the body. Hormones flow through the bloodstream to all parts of the body. Thus, an endocrine gland near your brain can control an organ that is somewhere else in your body.

Endocrine glands may affect many organs at one time. For example, in the situation shown in **Figure 1,** the adrenal glands release the hormone *epinephrine,* which is sometimes called *adrenaline.* Epinephrine increases your heartbeat and breathing rate. This response is called the "fight-or-flight" response. When you are frightened, angry, or excited, the "fight-or-flight" response prepares you to fight the danger or to run from it.

endocrine system a collection of glands and groups of cells that secrete hormones that regulate growth, development, and homeostasis

gland a group of cells that make special chemicals for the body

Figure 1 *When you have to move quickly to avoid danger, your adrenal glands make more blood glucose available for energy.*

More Endocrine Glands

Your body has several other endocrine glands. Some of these glands have many functions. For example, your pituitary gland stimulates skeletal growth and helps the thyroid gland work properly. It also regulates the amount of water in the blood. And the pituitary gland stimulates the birth process in women.

Your thyroid gland is very important during infancy and childhood. Thyroid hormones control the secretion of growth hormones for normal body growth. Thyroid hormones also control the development of the central nervous system. And they control your metabolism. *Metabolism* is the sum of all the chemical processes that take place in an organism.

Your thymus gland is important to your immune system. Cells called *killer T cells* grow and mature in the thymus gland. These T cells help destroy or neutralize cells or substances that invade your body. The names and some of the functions of endocrine glands are shown in **Figure 2.**

Reading Check **Name two endocrine glands, and explain why they are important to your body.** *(See the Appendix for answers to Reading Checks.)*

hormone a substance that is made in one cell or tissue and that causes a change in another cell or tissue in a different part of the body

CONNECTION TO Language Arts

WRITING SKILL **Fight or Flight?** Write a paragraph describing a time when you had a fight-or-flight experience. Include in your description the following terms: *hormones, fight-or-flight,* and *epinephrine.* If you cannot think of a personal experience, write a short story describing someone else's fight-or-flight experience.

Figure 2 **Endocrine Glands and Their Functions**

The **pituitary gland** secretes hormones that affect other glands and organs.

Your **thyroid gland** increases the rate at which you use energy.

The **parathyroid glands** (behind the thyroid) regulate calcium levels in the blood.

The **thymus gland** regulates the immune system, which helps your body fight disease.

The **adrenal glands** help the body respond to danger.

The **pancreas** regulates blood-glucose levels.

The **ovaries** (in females) produce hormones needed for reproduction.

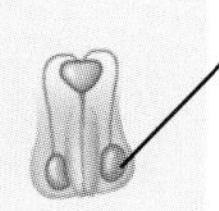

The **testes** (in males) produce hormones needed for reproduction.

Controlling the Endocrine Glands

Do you remember the feedback mechanisms at work in the nervous system? Endocrine glands control similar feedback mechanisms. For example, the pancreas has specialized cells that make two different hormones, *insulin* and *glucagon.* As shown in **Figure 3,** these two hormones control the level of glucose in the blood. Insulin lowers blood-glucose levels by telling the liver to convert glucose into glycogen and to store glycogen for future use. Glucagon has the opposite effect. It tells the liver to convert glycogen into glucose and to release the glucose into the blood.

Reading Check What does insulin do?

Figure 3 **Blood-Glucose Feedback Control**

1 Glucose is fuel for your body. Glucose is absorbed into the bloodstream from the small intestine.

2 When the glucose level in the blood is high, such as after a meal, the pancreas releases the hormone insulin into the blood.

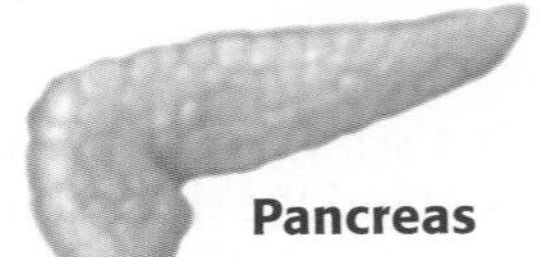

3 Insulin signals the liver to take in glucose from the blood, convert the glucose into glycogen, and to store glycogen for future energy needs.

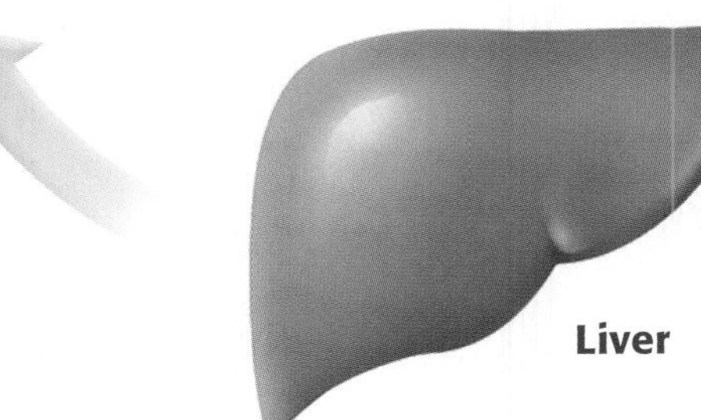

4 When the pancreas detects that your blood-glucose level has returned to normal, it stops releasing insulin.

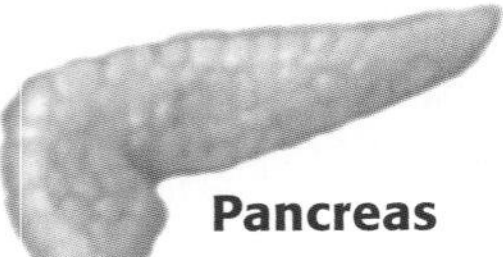

5a If your blood-glucose falls too far, glucagon tells the liver to break down glycogen and release the glucose into your blood.

5b Sometimes, to raise your blood-glucose level, you must eat something.

Hormone Imbalances

Occasionally, an endocrine gland makes too much or not enough of a hormone. For example, when a person's blood-glucose level rises, the pancreas secretes insulin. Insulin sends a message to the liver to convert glucose into glycogen. The liver stores glycogen for future use. But a person whose body does not use insulin properly or whose pancreas does not make enough insulin has a condition called *diabetes mellitus* (DIE uh BEET EEZ muh LIET uhs). A person who has diabetes may need daily injections of insulin to keep his or her blood-glucose levels within safe limits. Some patients, such as the woman in **Figure 4,** receive their insulin automatically from a small machine worn next to the body.

Another hormone imbalance is when a child's pituitary gland doesn't make enough growth hormone. As a result, the child's growth is stunted. Fortunately, if the problem is detected early, a doctor can prescribe growth hormone and monitor the child's growth. If the pituitary makes too much growth hormone, a child may grow taller than expected.

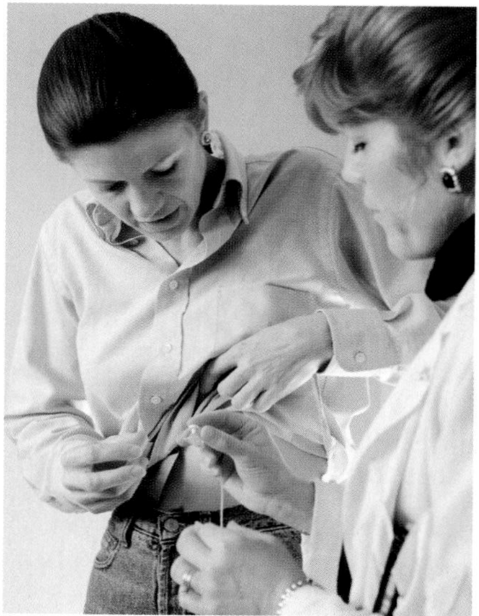

Figure 4 *This woman has diabetes and receives insulin from a device that monitors her blood-glucose level.*

SECTION Review

Summary

- Glands in the endocrine system use chemical messengers called *hormones*.
- Hormones regulate body functions by causing changes in cells or tissues.
- Feedback mechanisms tell endocrine glands when to turn hormones on and off.
- A hormone imbalance is when a gland releases too much or too little of a hormone.

Using Key Terms

1. Use the following terms in the same sentence: *endocrine system, glands,* and *hormone.*

Understanding Key Ideas

2. Identify five endocrine glands, and explain why their hormones are important to your body.
3. Hormone imbalances may cause
   a. feedback and insulin.
   b. diabetes and stunted growth.
   c. thyroid and pituitary.
   d. glucose and glycogen.
4. How do feedback mechanisms control hormone production?

Math Skills

5. One's bedtime blood-glucose level is normally 140 mg/dL. Ty's blood-glucose level is 189 mg/dL at bedtime. What percentage above 140 mg/dL is Ty's level?

Critical Thinking

6. **Making Inferences** Glucose is a source of energy. Epinephrine quickly increases the blood-glucose level. Why is epinephrine important in times of stress?
7. **Applying Concepts** The hormone glucagon is released when glucose levels fall below normal. Explain how the hormones glucagon and insulin work together to control blood-glucose levels.

SCILINKS
NSTA
Developed and maintained by the National Science Teachers Association
For a variety of links related to this chapter, go to www.scilinks.org
Topic: Hormones
SciLinks code: HSM0758

Skills Practice Lab

You've Gotta Lotta Nerve

OBJECTIVES

Locate areas on the skin that respond to certain stimuli.

Determine which areas on the skin are more sensitive to certain kinds of stimuli.

MATERIALS

- dissecting pin with a small piece of cork or a small rubber stopper covering the sharp end
- eyedropper, plastic
- paper, graphing
- pens or markers, washable, fine point
- ruler, metric
- tap water, hot
- water, very cold

SAFETY

Your skin has thousands of nerve receptors that detect sensations, such as temperature, pain, and pressure. Your brain is designed to filter out or ignore most of the input it receives from these skin receptors. If the brain did not filter input, simply wearing clothes would trigger so many responses that you couldn't function.

Some areas of the skin, such as the back of your hand, are more sensitive than others. In this activity, you will map the skin receptors for heat, cold, and pressure on the back of your hand.

Procedure

1. Form a group of three. One of you will volunteer the back of your hand for testing, one will do the testing, and the third will record the results.
2. Use a fine-point, washable marker or pen and a metric ruler to mark a 3 cm × 3 cm square on the back of one person's hand. Draw a grid within the area. Space the lines approximately 0.5 cm apart. You will have 36 squares in the grid when you are finished, as shown in the photograph below.
3. Mark off three 3 cm × 3 cm areas on a piece of graph paper. Make a grid in each area exactly as you did on the back of your partner's hand. Label one grid "Cold," another grid "Hot," and the third grid "Pressure."

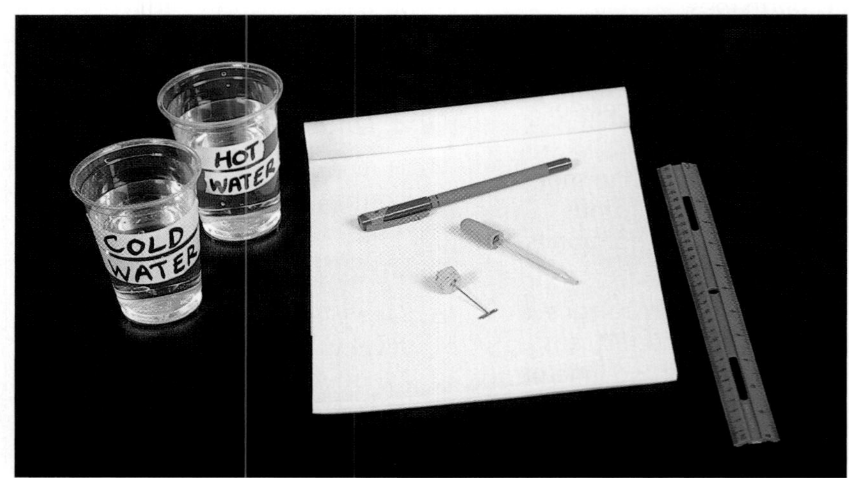

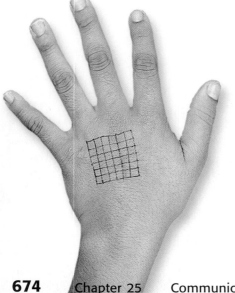

4. Use the eyedropper to apply one small droplet of cold water on each square in the grid on your partner's hand. Your partner should turn away while being tested. On your graph paper, mark an X on the "Cold" grid to show where your partner felt the cold droplet. Carefully blot the water off your partner's hand after several drops.

5. Repeat the test using hot-water droplets. The hot water should not be hot enough to hurt your partner. Mark an X on the "Hot" grid to indicate where your partner felt the hot droplet.

6. Repeat the test by using the head (not the point!) of the pin. Touch the skin to detect pressure receptors. Use a very light touch. On the graph paper, mark an X on the "Pressure" grid to indicate where your partner felt the pressure.

Analyze the Results

1. **Organizing Data** Count the number of Xs in each grid. How many heat receptor responses are there per 3 cm^2? How many cold receptor responses are there? How many pressure receptor responses are there?

2. **Explaining Events** Do you have areas on the back of your hand where the receptors overlap? Explain your answer.

3. **Recognizing Patterns** How do you think the results of this experiment would be similar or different if you mapped an area of your forearm? of the back of your neck? of the palm of your hand?

Draw Conclusions

4. **Interpreting Information** Prepare a written report that includes a description of your investigation and a discussion of your answers to items 1–3. What conclusions can you draw from your results?

Applying Your Data

Use the library or the Internet to research what happens if a receptor is continuously stimulated. Does the kind of receptor make a difference? Does the intensity or strength of the stimulus make a difference? Explain your answers.

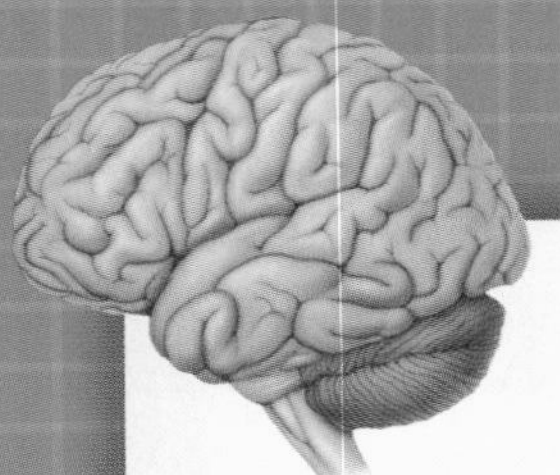

Chapter Review

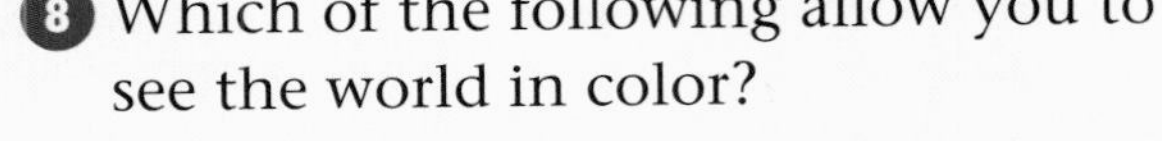

USING KEY TERMS

Complete each of the following sentences by choosing the correct term from the word bank.

insulin
hormone
retina
neuron
reflex
axon
nerve
central nervous system

1. The two parts of your _____ are your brain and spinal cord.

2. Sensory receptors in the _____ detect light.

3. Epinephrine is a(n) _____ that triggers the fight-or-flight response.

4. A(n) _____ is an involuntary and almost immediate movement in response to a stimulus.

5. One hormone that helps to regulate blood-glucose levels is _____ .

6. A(n) _____ is a specialized cell that receives and conducts electrical impulses.

UNDERSTANDING KEY IDEAS

Multiple Choice

7. Which of the following has receptors for smelling?
   a. cochlea cells
   b. thermoreceptors
   c. olfactory cells
   d. optic nerve

8. Which of the following allow you to see the world in color?
   a. cones
   b. rods
   c. lenses
   d. retinas

9. Which of the following glands makes insulin?
   a. adrenal gland
   b. pituitary gland
   c. thyroid gland
   d. pancreas

10. The peripheral nervous system does NOT include
   a. the spinal cord.
   b. axons.
   c. sensory receptors.
   d. motor neurons.

11. Which part of the brain regulates blood pressure?
   a. right cerebral hemisphere
   b. left cerebral hemisphere
   c. cerebellum
   d. medulla

12. The process in which the endocrine system, the digestive system, and the circulatory system control the level of blood glucose is an example of
   a. a reflex.
   b. an endocrine gland.
   c. the fight-or-flight response.
   d. a feedback mechanism.

Short Answer

13 What is the difference between the somatic nervous system and the autonomic nervous system? Why are both systems important to the body?

14 Why is the endocrine system important to your body?

15 What is the relationship between the CNS and the PNS?

16 What is the function of the bones in the middle ear?

17 Describe two interactions between the endocrine system and the body that happen when a person is frightened.

CRITICAL THINKING

18 **Concept Mapping** Use the following terms to create a concept map: *nervous system, spinal cord, medulla, peripheral nervous system, brain, cerebrum, central nervous system,* and *cerebellum.*

19 **Making Comparisons** Compare a feedback mechanism with a reflex.

20 **Analyzing Ideas** Why is it important to have a lens that can change shape inside the eye?

21 **Applying Concepts** Why it is important that reflexes happen without thinking about them?

22 **Predicting Consequences** What would happen if your autonomic nervous system stopped working?

23 **Making Comparisons** How are the nervous system and the endocrine system similar? How are they different?

INTERPRETING GRAPHICS

Use the diagram below to answer the questions that follow.

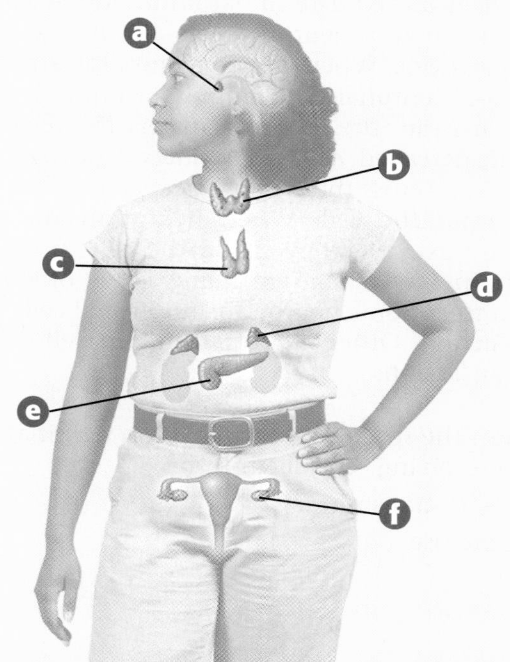

24 Which letter identifies the gland that regulates blood-glucose level?

25 Which letter identifies the gland that releases a hormone that stimulates the birth process?

26 Which letter identifies the gland that helps the body fight disease?

Standardized Test Preparation

READING

Read each of the passages below. Then, answer the questions that follow each passage.

Passage 1 The axon terminals of neurons usually do not touch the other cells. There is a small gap between an axon terminal and another cell. This space where a neuron meets another cell is called a *synapse*. When a nerve impulse arrives at an axon terminal, the impulse cannot cross the gap. Instead, the impulse triggers the release of chemicals called *neurotransmitters*. These neurotransmitters cross the synapse between the axon terminal and the cell. When neurotransmitters reach the next cell, they signal the cell to react in a certain way. There are many kinds of neurotransmitters. Some neurotransmitters tell cells to start an action. Other neurotransmitters tell cells to stop an action.

1. What is the space between a neuron terminal and a receiving cell called?

A a neurotransmitter
B a synapse
C an axon
D a nerve

2. Why are neurotransmitters necessary?

F They tell muscle cells to contract or relax.
G They create a gap that axons must cross.
H They carry messages across the synapse.
I They release chemical signals called *impulses*.

3. Which of the following statements is a fact in the passage?

A A synapse is an extension of a nerve cell.
B The space between an axon terminal and another cell is filled with neurons.
C Nerve impulses jump from an axon to another cell.
D There are many kinds of neurotransmitters.

Passage 2 Hormones are chemical messengers released by cells that regulate other cells in the body. Hormones regulate many body processes. Hormones control growth, direct the production and use of energy, keep body temperature within normal limits, and direct responses to stimuli outside the body. Hormones carry chemical messages that tell cells to change their activities. For example, one hormone tells the heart to beat faster. Another hormone tells certain cells to make proteins and stimulates bone and muscle growth. Each hormone communicates with specific cells. Each hormone is like a key that opens only one kind of lock. A hormone's message can be received only by cells that have the right kind of lock. Hormones control many important body functions, so their messages must be delivered properly.

1. According to the passage, which of the following statements about hormones is true?

A Hormones tell cells to change their activities.
B Hormones are electrical messengers.
C Hormones are like locks.
D Hormones are not important to your body.

2. What does the word *regulate* mean?

F to control or direct
G to beat faster
H to raise your temperature
I to reverse

3. According to the passage, what are two ways that one particular hormone affects the body?

A controls your temperature and heart rate
B responds to stimuli and makes proteins
C stimulates bone growth and makes proteins
D coordinates energy production and use and decreases temperature

INTERPRETING GRAPHICS

The diagram below shows a typical neuron. Use the diagram below to answer the questions that follow.

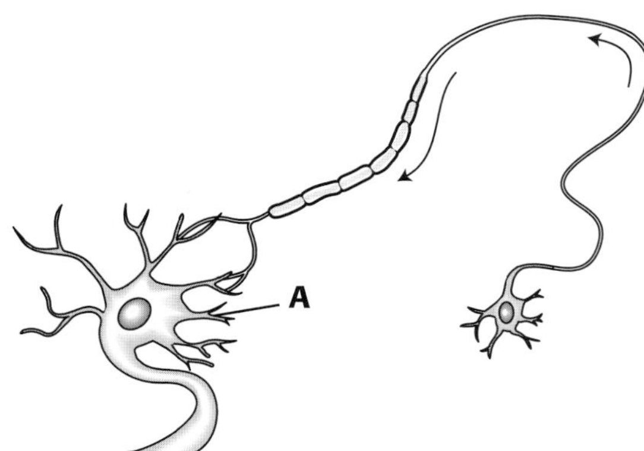

1. What does A represent?
   - **A** a cell body
   - **B** an axon
   - **C** a dendrite
   - **D** an axon terminal

2. Which of the following represents the path that an impulse in a neuron travels?
   - **F** dendrite, cell body, axon, axon terminal
   - **G** axon, axon terminal, cell body, dendrite
   - **H** dendrite, nucleus, cell body, axon
   - **I** nucleus, cell body, nucleus, axon

3. To where is an impulse that reaches an axon terminal transmitted?
   - **A** another axon terminal
   - **B** the brain
   - **C** a reflex
   - **D** dendrites of another neuron

4. What does having many dendrites allow a neuron to do?
   - **F** to be locked into place in the body
   - **G** to receive impulses from many other cells
   - **H** to send impulses to surrounding cells
   - **I** to get necessary nutrition

5. Which of the following statements about an axon is true?
   - **A** An axon is part of a gland.
   - **B** An axon connects the cell body to the axon terminal.
   - **C** An axon detects sights and sounds.
   - **D** An axon carries chemical messages.

MATH

Read each question below, and choose the best answer.

1. Sound travels about 335 m/s. How many kilometers would a sound travel in 1 min? (One kilometer is equal to 1,000 meters.)
   - **A** 335,000 km
   - **B** 20,100 km
   - **C** 20.1 km
   - **D** 0.335 km

2. Some axons send one impulse every 2.5 milliseconds. How many impulses could one of these axons send every second? (One second is equal to 1,000 milliseconds.)
   - **F** 4 impulses
   - **G** 40 impulses
   - **H** 400 impulses
   - **I** 4,000 impulses

3. The table below shows the results of Miguel's blood-glucose tests. Miguel ate lunch at 12:00 noon. His blood glucose was measured every hour after that time. What was the average hourly decrease in blood-glucose level?

Blood Glucose

Time tested	Blood-glucose level (mg/1,000 mL)
1:00 P.M.	178
2:00 P.M.	112
3:00 P.M.	100
4:00 P.M.	89

   - **A** approximately 160 mg/1,000 mL
   - **B** approximately 120 mg/1,000 mL
   - **C** approximately 30 mg/1,000 mL
   - **D** approximately 22 mg/1,000 mL

4. Your brain has about 1 billion neurons. How is 1 billion expressed in scientific notation?
   - **F** 1×10^3
   - **G** 1×10^6
   - **H** 1×10^9
   - **I** 1×10^{12}

Science in Action

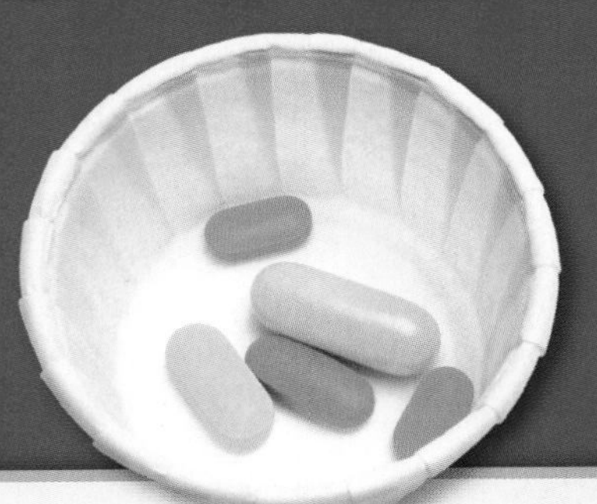

Scientific Discoveries

The Placebo Effect

A placebo (pluh SEE boh) is an inactive substance, such as a sugar pill, used in experimental drug trials. Some of the people who are test subjects are given a placebo as if it were the drug being tested. Usually, neither the doctor conducting the trial nor the test subjects know whether a person is taking a placebo or the test drug. In theory, any change in a subject's condition should be the result of the test drug. But for many years, scientists have known about the *placebo effect,* the effect of feeling better after taking the placebo pill. What makes someone who takes the placebo feel better? By studying brain activity, scientists are beginning to understand the placebo effect.

Social Studies 

Research the differences and similarities between ancient Chinese medical practices and traditional Western medical treatment. Both types of treatment rely in part on a patient's mental and emotional response to treatment. How might the placebo effect be part of both medical traditions? Create a poster showing the results of your research.

Science, Technology, and Society

Robotic Limbs

Cyborgs, or people that are part human and part robot, have been part of science fiction for many years and usually have super-human strength and X-ray vision. Meanwhile there are ordinary people on Earth who have lost the use of their arms and legs and could use some robot power. However, until recently, they have had to settle for clumsy mechanical limbs that were not a very good substitute for a real arm or hand. Today, thanks to advances in technology, scientists are developing artificial limbs—and eyes and ears—that can be wired directly into the nervous system and can be controlled by the brain. In the near future, artificial limbs and some artificial organs will be much more like the real thing.

Language Arts ACTIVITY

WRITING SKILL At the library or on the Internet, find examples of optical or visual illusions. Research how the brain processes visual information and how the brain "sees" and interprets these illusions. Write a report about why the brain seems to be fooled by visual tricks. How can understanding the brain's response to illusions help scientists create artificial vision?

People in Science

Bertha Madras

Studying Brain Activity The brain is an amazing organ. Sometimes, though, drugs or disease keep the brain from working properly. Bertha Madras is a biochemist who studies drug addiction. Dr. Madras studies brain activity to see how substances, such as cocaine, target cells or areas in the brain. Using a variety of brain scanning techniques, Dr. Madras can observe a brain on drugs. She can see how a drug affects the normal activity of the brain. During her research, Dr. Madras realized that some of her results could be applied to Parkinson's disease and to attention deficit hyperactivity disorder (ADHD) in adults. Her research has led to new treatments for both problems.

Math Activity

Using a search engine on a computer connected to the Internet, search the Internet for "reaction time experiment." Go to one of the Web sites and take the response-time experiment. Record the time that it took you to respond. Repeat the test nine more times, and record your response time for each trial. Then, make a line graph or a bar graph of your response times. Did your response times change? In what way did they change?

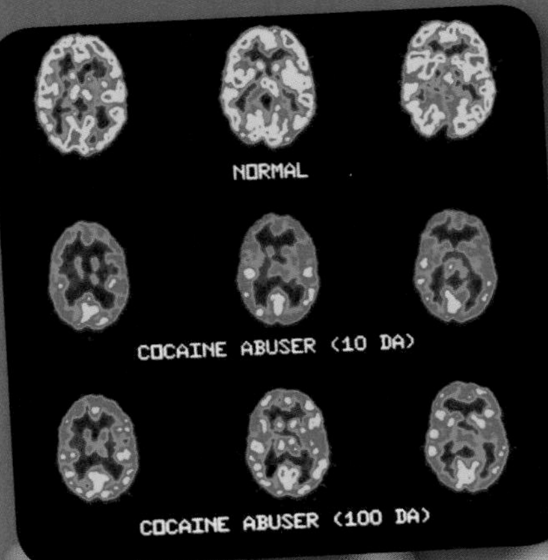

To learn more about these Science in Action topics, visit go.hrw.com and type in the keyword HL5BD4F.

Current Science

Check out Current Science® articles related to this chapter by visiting go.hrw.com. Just type in the keyword HL5CS25.

Reproduction and Development

About the PHOTO

If someone had taken your picture when your mother was about 13 weeks pregnant with you, that picture would have looked much like this photograph. You have changed a lot since then, haven't you? You started out as a single cell, and you became a complete person. And you haven't stopped growing and changing yet. In fact, you will continue to change for the rest of your life.

PRE-READING ACTIVITY

Graphic Organizer

Spider Map Before you read the chapter, create the graphic organizer entitled "Spider Map" described in the **Study Skills** section of the Appendix. Label the circle "Reproduction and Development." Create a leg for each section title. As you read the chapter, fill in the map with details about reproduction and development from each section.

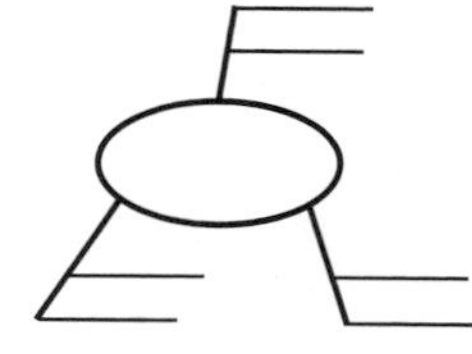

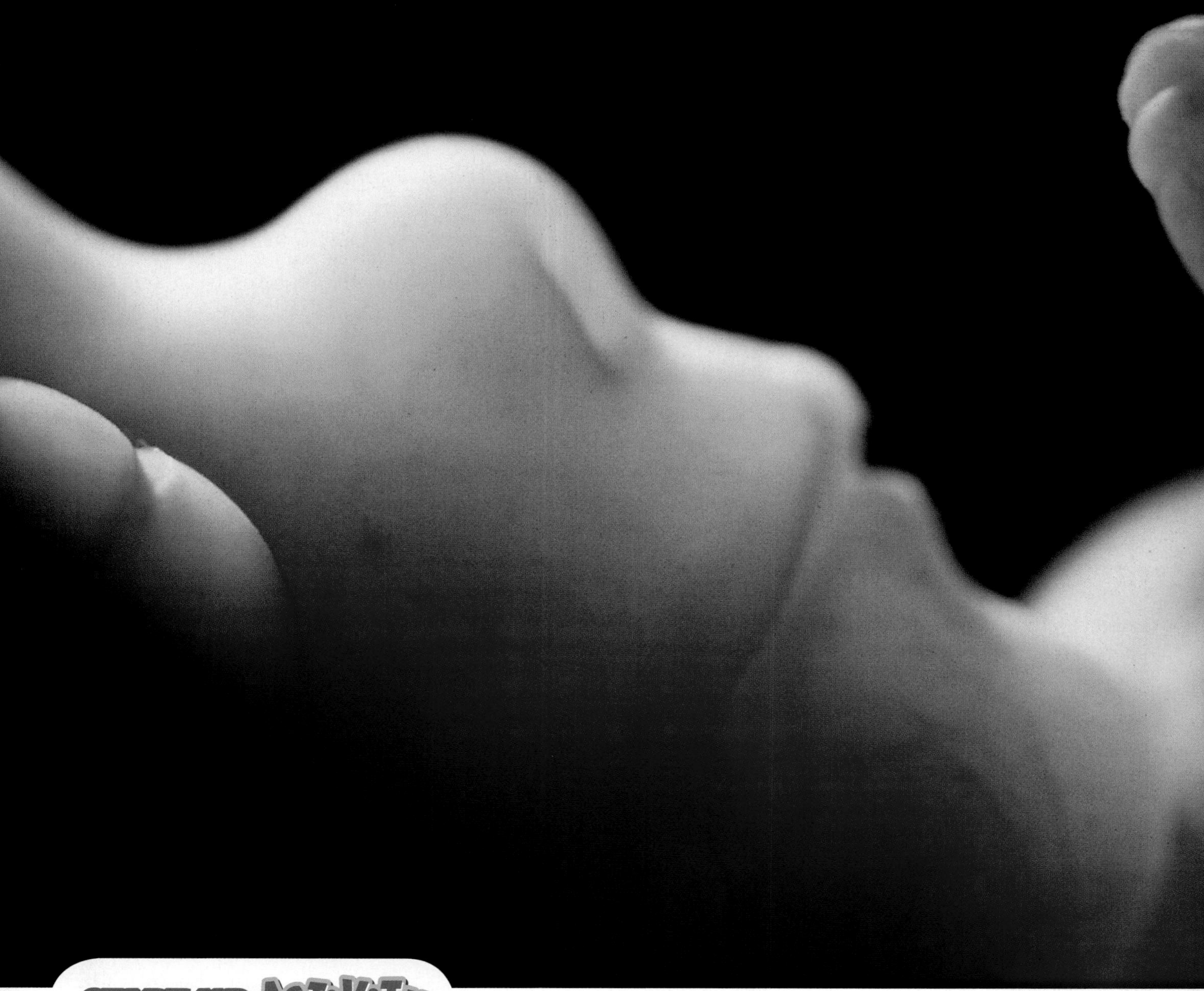

START-UP ACTIVITY

How Grows It?

As you read this paragraph, you are slowly aging. Your body is growing into the body of an adult. But does your body have the same proportions that an adult's body has? Complete this activity to find out.

Procedure

1. Have a classmate use a **tape measure** and **meterstick** to measure your total height, head height, and leg length. Your teacher will tell you how to take these measurements.
2. Use the following equations to calculate your head height–to–total body height proportion and your leg length–to–total body height proportion.

$$\text{head proportion} = \frac{\text{head height}}{\text{body height}} \times 100$$

$$\text{leg proportion} = \frac{\text{leg length}}{\text{body height}} \times 100$$

3. Your teacher will give you the head, body, and leg measurements of three adults. Calculate the head-body and leg-body proportions of each of the three adults. Record all of the measurements and calculations.

Analysis

1. Compare your proportions with the proportions of the three adults.

SECTION 1

Animal Reproduction

The life span of some living things is short compared with ours. For example, a fruit fly lives only about 40 days. Other organisms live much longer than we do. Some bristlecone pine trees, for example, are nearly 5,000 years old.

But all living things eventually die. If a species is to survive, its members must reproduce.

READING WARM-UP

Objectives

- Distinguish between asexual and sexual reproduction.
- Explain the difference between external and internal fertilization.
- Identify the three different types of mammalian reproduction.

Terms to Learn

asexual reproduction
sexual reproduction
egg
sperm
external fertilization
internal fertilization

READING STRATEGY

Prediction Guide Before reading this section, write the title of each heading in this section. Next, under each heading, write what you think you will learn.

Asexual Reproduction

Some animals, particularly simpler ones, reproduce asexually. In **asexual reproduction,** a single parent has offspring that are genetically identical to the parent.

One kind of asexual reproduction is called budding. *Budding* happens when a part of the parent organism pinches off and forms a new organism. The new organism separates from the parent and lives independently. The hydra, shown in **Figure 1,** reproduces by budding. The new hydra is genetically identical to its parent.

Fragmentation is a second kind of asexual reproduction. In *fragmentation,* parts of an organism break off and then develop into a new individual that is identical to the original one. Certain organisms, such as flatworms called *planaria,* reproduce by fragmentation. A third type of asexual reproduction, similar to fragmentation, is *regeneration.* When an organism capable of regeneration, such as the sea star in **Figure 2,** loses a body part, that part may develop into an entirely new organism.

asexual reproduction reproduction that does not involve the union of sex cells and in which a single parent produces offspring that are genetically identical to the parent

Figure 1 *The hydra bud will separate from its parent. Buds from other organisms, such as certain corals, remain attached to the parent.*

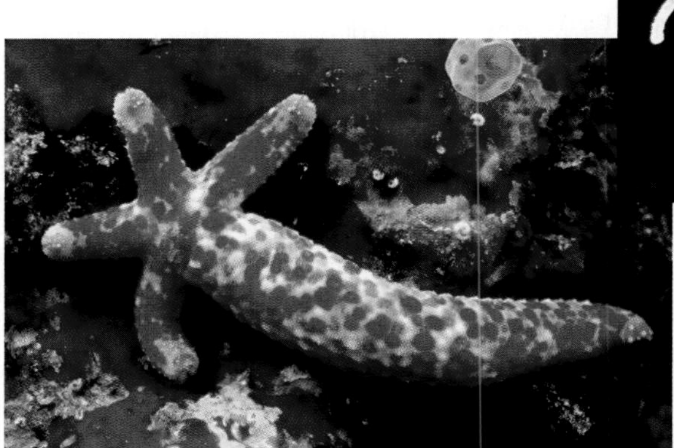

Figure 2 *The largest arm on this sea star was a fragment, from which a new sea star will regenerate. In time, all of the sea star's arms will grow to the same size.*

Sexual Reproduction

Most animals reproduce sexually. In **sexual reproduction,** offspring are formed when genetic information from more than one parent combines. Sexual reproduction in animals usually requires two parents—a male and a female. The female parent produces sex cells called **eggs.** The male parent produces sex cells called **sperm.** When an egg's nucleus and a sperm's nucleus join, a fertilized egg, called a *zygote* (ZIE GOHT), is created. This joining of an egg and sperm is known as *fertilization.*

Human cells—except eggs and sperm and mature red blood cells—contain 46 chromosomes. Eggs and sperm are formed by a process called *meiosis.* In humans, meiosis is the division of one cell that has 46 chromosomes into four cells that have 23 chromosomes each. When an egg and a sperm join to form a zygote, the original number of 46 chromosomes is restored.

Genetic information is found in *genes.* Genes are located on *chromosomes* (KROH muh SOHMZ) made of the cell's DNA. During fertilization, the egg and sperm each contribute chromosomes to the zygote. The combination of genes from the two parents results in a zygote that grows into a unique individual. **Figure 3** shows how genes mix through three generations.

Reading Check **What is sexual reproduction?** (*See the Appendix for answers to Reading Checks.*)

sexual reproduction reproduction in which sex cells from two parents unite to produce offspring that share traits from both parents

egg a sex cell produced by a female

sperm the male sex cell

Figure 3 **Inheriting Genes**

Eggs and sperm contain chromosomes. You inherit chromosomes—and the genes on them—from both of your parents. Your parents each inherited chromosomes from their parents.

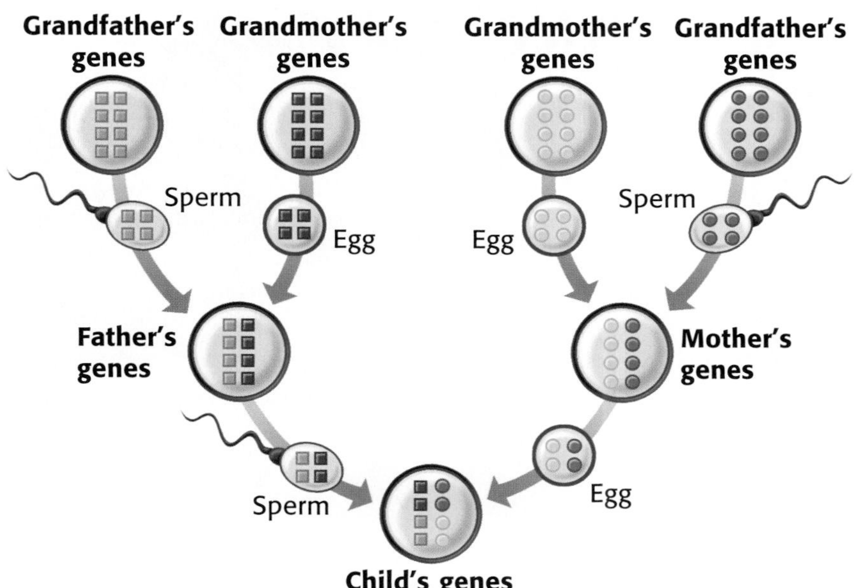

CONNECTION TO Language Arts

WRITING SKILL **Nature or Nurture?** Scientists debate whether genetics or upbringing is more important in shaping people. Use the Internet or library to research the issue of "nature versus nurture." Find information about identical twins who were raised apart. When you finish your research, write a persuasive essay supporting one side of the debate. Include evidence to support your argument.

Figure 4 *Some fish, such as these clownfish, fertilize their eggs externally. The eggs are the orange mass on the rock.*

Internal and External Fertilization

Fertilization can happen either outside or inside the female's body. When the sperm fertilizes the eggs outside the female's body, the process is called **external fertilization.** External fertilization must take place in a moist environment so that the delicate zygotes won't dry out. Some fishes, such as those in **Figure 4,** reproduce by external fertilization.

Many amphibians, such as frogs, use external fertilization. For example, the female frog releases her eggs. At the same time, the male frog releases his sperm over the eggs to fertilize them. Frogs usually leave the zygotes to develop on their own. In about two weeks, the fertilized eggs hatch into tadpoles.

Internal Fertilization

When the egg and sperm join inside the female's body, the process is called **internal fertilization**. Internal fertilization allows the female animal to protect the developing egg inside her body. Reptiles, birds, mammals, and some fishes reproduce by internal fertilization. Many animals that use internal fertilization can lay fertilized eggs. Female chickens, for example, usually lay one or two eggs after internal fertilization has taken place.

In most mammals, one or more fertilized eggs develop inside the mother's body. Many mammals give birth to young that are well developed. Young zebras, such as the one in **Figure 5,** can stand up and nurse almost immediately after birth.

external fertilization the union of sex cells outside the bodies of the parents

internal fertilization fertilization of an egg by sperm that occurs inside the body of a female

Reading Check **What is the difference between external and internal fertilization?**

Figure 5 *This zebra has just been born, but he is already able to stand. Within an hour, he will be able to run.*

Mammals

All mammals reproduce sexually. All mammals nurture their young with milk. And all mammals reproduce in one of the following three ways:

- **Monotreme** *Monotremes* (MAHN oh TREEMZ) are mammals that lay eggs. After the eggs are incubated and hatch, the young are nourished by milk that oozes from pores on the mother's belly. Echidnas and platypuses are monotremes.
- **Marsupial** Mammals that give birth to partially developed live young, such as the kangaroo in **Figure 6,** are *marsupials* (mahr SOO pee uhlz). Most marsupials have pouches where their young continue to develop after birth. Opossums, koalas, wombats, and Tasmanian devils are marsupials.
- **Placental Mammal** There are more than 4,000 species of placental mammals, including armadillos, humans, and bats. Placental mammals are nourished inside their mother's body before birth. Newborn placental mammals are more developed than newborn monotremes or marsupials are.

Reading Check Name two ways that all mammals are alike.

Figure 6 *The red kangaroo is a marsupial. A young kangaroo, such as this one in its mother's pouch, is called a* joey.

SECTION Review

Summary

- In asexual reproduction, a single parent produces offspring that are genetically identical to the parent.
- In sexual reproduction, an egg from one parent combines with a sperm from the other parent.
- Fertilization can be external or internal.
- All mammals reproduce sexually and nurture their young with milk.

Using Key Terms

For each pair of terms, explain how the meanings of the terms differ.

1. *internal fertilization* and *external fertilization*
2. *asexual reproduction* and *sexual reproduction*

Understanding Key Ideas

3. In humans, each egg and each sperm contain
   - **a.** 23 chromosomes.
   - **b.** 46 chromosomes.
   - **c.** 69 chromosomes.
   - **d.** 529 chromosomes.
4. List three types of asexual reproduction.
5. How do monotremes differ from marsupials?
6. Describe the process of meiosis.
7. Are humans placental mammals, monotremes, or marsupials? Explain.

Math Skills

8. Some bristlecone pine needles last 40 years. If a tree lives for 3,920 years, how many sets of needles might it grow?

Critical Thinking

9. **Making Inferences** Why is reproduction as important to a bristlecone pine as it is to a fruit fly?
10. **Applying Concepts** Describe one advantage of internal fertilization over external fertilization.

SCILINKS.
NSTA
Developed and maintained by the National Science Teachers Association
For a variety of links related to this chapter, go to www.scilinks.org
Topic: Reproduction
SciLinks code: HSM1293

SECTION 2

Human Reproduction

About nine months after a human sperm and egg combine, a mother gives birth to her baby. But how do humans make eggs and sperm?

READING WARM-UP

Objectives

- Identify the structures and functions of the male and female reproductive systems.
- Describe two reproductive system problems.

Terms to Learn

testes
penis
ovary
uterus
vagina

READING STRATEGY

Reading Organizer As you read this section, create an outline of the section. Use the headings from the section in your outline.

The Male Reproductive System

The male reproductive system, shown in **Figure 1,** produces sperm and delivers it to the female reproductive system. The **testes** (singular, *testis*) are a pair of organs that make sperm and testosterone (tes TAHS tuhr OHN). Testosterone is the main male sex hormone. It helps regulate the production of sperm and the development of male characteristics.

As sperm leave a testis, they are stored in a tube called an *epididymis* (EP uh DID i mis). Sperm mature in the epididymis. Another tube, called a *vas deferens* (vas DEF uh RENZ), passes from the epididymis into the body and through the *prostate gland*. The prostate gland surrounds the neck of the bladder. As sperm move through the vas deferens, they mix with fluids from several glands, including the prostate gland. This mixture of sperm and fluids is called *semen*.

To leave the body, semen passes through the vas deferens into the *urethra* (yoo REE thruh). The urethra is the tube that runs through the penis. The **penis** is the external organ that transfers semen into the female's body.

Reading Check **Describe the path that sperm take from the testes to the penis.** (*See the Appendix for answers to Reading Checks.*)

testes the primary male reproductive organs, which produce sperm and testosterone (singular, *testis*)

penis the male organ that transfers sperm to a female and that carries urine out of the body

Figure 1 **The Male Reproductive System**

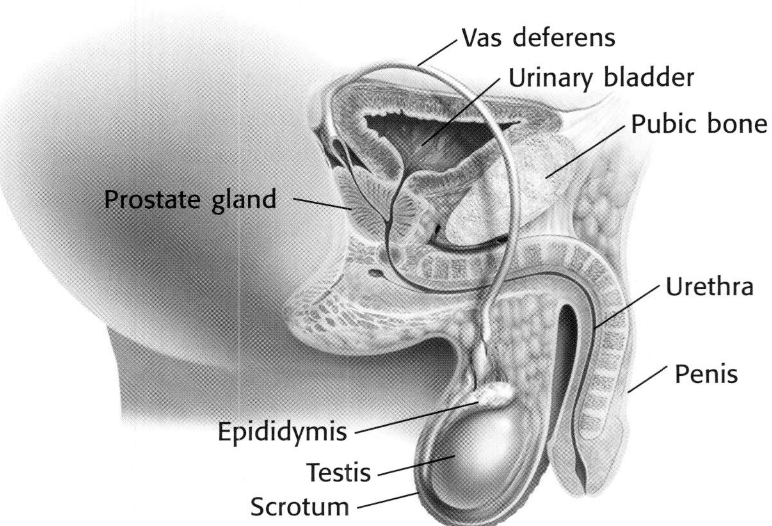

Figure 2 The Female Reproductive System

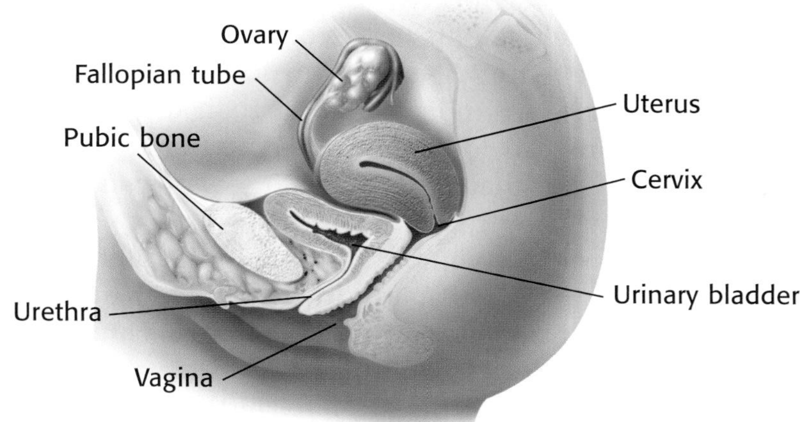

The Female Reproductive System

The female reproductive system, shown in **Figure 2,** produces eggs, nurtures fertilized eggs (zygotes), and gives birth. The two **ovaries** are the organs that make eggs. Ovaries also release estrogen (ES truh juhn) and progesterone (proh JES tuhr OHN), the main female sex hormones. These hormones regulate the release of eggs and development of female characteristics.

ovary in the female reproductive system of animals, an organ that produces eggs

uterus in female mammals, the hollow, muscular organ in which a fertilized egg is embedded and in which the embryo and fetus develop

vagina the female reproductive organ that connects the outside of the body to the uterus

The Egg's Journey

During *ovulation* (AHV yoo LAY shuhn), an egg is released from an ovary and passes into a *fallopian* (fuh LOH pee uhn) *tube.* A fallopian tube leads from each ovary to the uterus. The egg passes through the fallopian tube into the uterus. Fertilization usually happens in the fallopian tube. If the egg is fertilized, the resulting zygote enters the uterus. The zygote may become embedded in the thickened lining of the uterus. The **uterus** is the organ in which a zygote develops into a baby.

When a baby is born, he or she passes from the uterus through the vagina and emerges outside the body. The **vagina** is the canal between the outside of the body and the uterus.

Menstrual Cycle

From puberty through her late 40s or early 50s, a woman's reproductive system goes through monthly changes. These changes prepare the body for pregnancy and are called the *menstrual cycle* (MEN struhl SIE kuhl). The first day of *menstruation* (MEN STRAY shuhn), the monthly discharge of blood and tissue from the uterus, is counted as the first day of the cycle. Menstruation lasts about 5 days. When menstruation ends, the lining of the uterus thickens. Ovulation occurs on about the 14th day of the cycle. If the egg is not fertilized within a few days, menstruation begins and flushes the egg away. The cycle—which usually takes about 28 days—starts again.

Counting Eggs

1. The average woman ovulates each month from about age 12 to about age 50. How many mature eggs could she produce from age 18 to age 50?
2. A female's ovaries typically contain 2 million immature eggs. If she ovulates regularly from age 12 to age 50, what percentage of her eggs will mature?

Multiple Births

Figure 3 *Identical twins have genes that are exactly the same. Many identical twins who are raised apart have similar personalities and interests.*

Have you ever seen identical twins? Sometimes, they are so similar that even their parents have trouble telling them apart. The boys in **Figure 3** are identical twins. Fraternal twins, the other type of twins, are more common than identical twins are. Fraternal twins can look very different from each other. In every 1,000 births, there are about 30 sets of twins. About one-third of all twin births are identical twins.

Twins are the most common multiple births. But humans sometimes have triplets (3 babies). In the United States, there are about two sets of triplets in every 1,000 births. Humans also have quadruplets (4 babies), quintuplets (5 babies), and more. These types of multiple births are rare. Births of quintuplets or more happen only once in about 53,000 births.

Reading Check **What is the frequency of twin births?**

Reproductive System Problems

In most cases, the reproductive system functions flawlessly. But like any body system, the reproductive system sometimes has problems. These problems include disease and infertility.

STDs

Chlamydia, herpes, and hepatitis B are common sexually transmitted diseases. A *sexually transmitted disease,* or STD, is a disease that can pass from a person who is infected with the STD to an uninfected person during sexual contact. STDs are also called *sexually transmitted infections,* or STIs. These diseases affect many people each year, as shown in **Table 1.**

An STD you may have heard of is *acquired immune deficiency syndrome* (AIDS). AIDS is caused by *human immunodeficiency virus* (HIV). But you may not have heard of the STD *hepatitis B,* a liver disease also caused by a virus. This virus is spread in several ways, including sexual contact. In the United States, about 140,000 new cases of hepatitis B happen each year.

Twins and More

With a parent, discuss some challenges that are created by the birth of twins, triplets, quadruplets, or other multiples. Include financial, mental, emotional, and physical challenges.

Create a poster that shows these challenges and ways to meet them.

If twins or other multiples are in your family, discuss how the individuals differ and how they are alike.

Table 1 The Spread of STDs in the United States

STD	Approximate number of new cases each year
Chlamydia	3 to 10 million
Genital HPV (human papillomavirus)	5.5 million
Genital herpes	1 million
Gonorrhea	650,000
Syphilis	70,000
HIV/AIDS	40,000 to 50,000

Cancer

Sometimes, cancer happens in reproductive organs. *Cancer* is a disease in which cells grow at an uncontrolled rate. Cancer cells start out as normal cells. Then, something triggers uncontrolled cell growth. Different kinds of cancer have different triggers.

In men, the two most common reproductive system cancers are cancer of the testes and cancer of the prostate gland. In women, the two most common reproductive system cancers are breast cancer and cancer of the cervix. The *cervix* is the lower part, or neck, of the uterus. The cervix opens to the vagina.

Infertility

In the United States, about 15% of married couples have difficulty producing offspring. Many of these couples are *infertile*, or unable to have children. Men may be infertile if they do not produce enough healthy sperm. Women may be infertile if they do not ovulate normally.

Sexually transmitted diseases, such as gonorrhea and chlamydia, can lead to infertility in women. STD-related infertility occurs in men, but not as commonly as it does in women.

CONNECTION TO Social Studies

Understanding STDs Select one of the STDs in **Table 1.** Make a poster or brochure that identifies the cause of the disease, describes its symptoms, explains how it affects the body, and tells how it can be treated. Include a bar graph that shows the number of cases in different age groups.

ACTIVITY

SECTION Review

Summary

- The male reproductive system produces sperm and delivers it to the female reproductive system.
- The female reproductive system produces eggs, nurtures zygotes, and gives birth.
- Humans usually have one child per birth, but multiple births, such as those of twins or triplets, are possible.
- Human reproduction can be affected by cancer, infertility, and disease.

Using Key Terms

1. Use the following terms in the same sentence: *uterus* and *vagina.*

Understanding Key Ideas

2. Describe two problems of the reproductive system.
3. Identify the structures and functions of the male and female reproductive systems.
4. Identical twins happen once in 250 births. How many pairs of these twins might be at a school with 2,750 students?
   a. 1
   b. 11
   c. 22
   d. 250

Math Skills

5. In one country, 7 out of 1,000 infants die before their first birthday. Convert this figure to a percentage. Is your answer greater than or less than 1%?

Critical Thinking

6. **Making Inferences** What is the purpose of the menstrual cycle?
7. **Applying Concepts** Twins can happen when a zygote splits in two or when two eggs are fertilized. How can these two ways of twin formation explain how identical twins differ from fraternal twins?
8. **Predicting Consequences** How might cancer of the testes affect a man's ability to make sperm?

SCILINKS.
NSTA
Developed and maintained by the National Science Teachers Association
For a variety of links related to this chapter, go to www.scilinks.org
Topic: Reproduction System Irregularities or Disorders
SciLinks code: HSM1298

SECTION 3

Growth and Development

Every one of us started out as a single cell. How did that cell become a person made of trillions of cells?

A single cell divides many times and develops into a baby. But the development of a baby from a single cell is only the first stage of human development. Think about how you will change between now and when you become a grandparent!

READING WARM-UP

Objectives

- Summarize the processes of fertilization and implantation.
- Describe the development of the embryo and the fetus.
- Identify the stages of human development from birth to death.

Terms to Learn

embryo
placenta
umbilical cord
fetus

READING STRATEGY

Discussion Read this section silently. Write down questions that you have about this section. Discuss your questions in a small group.

From Fertilization to Embryo

Ordinarily, the process of human development starts when a man deposits millions of sperm into a woman's vagina. A few hundred sperm make it through the uterus into a fallopian tube. There, a few sperm cover the egg. Usually, only one sperm gets through the outer coating of the egg. When this happens, it triggers a response—a membrane forms around the egg to keep other sperm from entering. When the sperm's nucleus joins with the nucleus of the egg, the egg becomes fertilized.

The fertilized egg (zygote) travels down the fallopian tube toward the uterus. This journey takes 5 to 6 days. During the trip, the zygote undergoes cell division many times. Eleven to 12 days after fertilization, the zygote has become a tiny ball of cells called an **embryo.** The embryo implants itself in the uterus. *Implantation* happens when the zygote embeds itself in the thick, nutrient-rich lining of the uterus. Fertilization and implantation are outlined in **Figure 1.**

embryo a developing human, from fertilization through the first 8 weeks of development (the 10th week of pregnancy)

placenta the partly fetal and partly maternal organ by which materials are exchanged between fetus and mother

Reading Check **Describe the process of fertilization and implantation.** (*See the Appendix for answers to Reading Checks.*)

Figure 1 Fertilization and Implantation

b The egg is fertilized in the fallopian tube by a sperm.
a The egg is released from the ovary.
c The embryo implants itself in the uterus's wall.

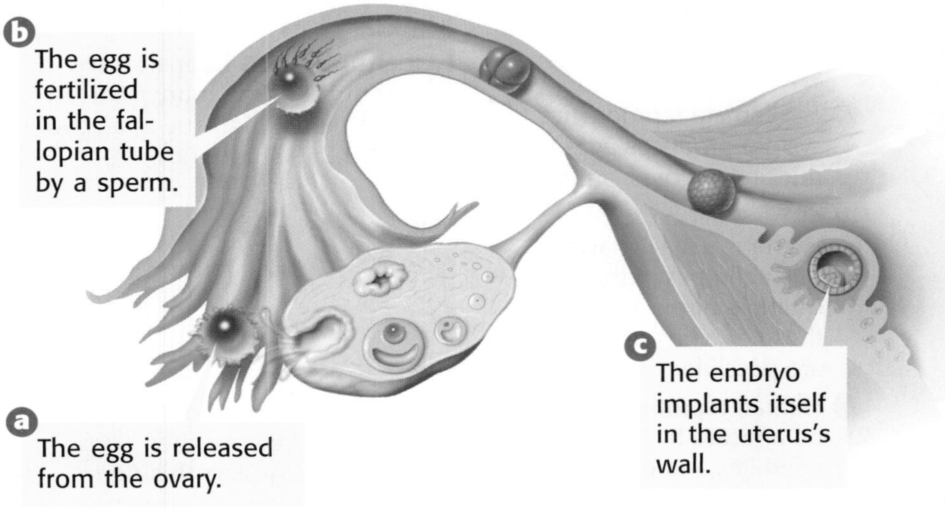

From Embryo to Fetus

After implantation, the placenta (pluh SEN tuh) begins to grow. The **placenta** is a special two-way exchange organ. It has a network of blood vessels that provides the embryo with oxygen and nutrients from the mother's blood. Wastes produced by the embryo are removed in the placenta. They are carried by the mother's blood so that her body can excrete them. The embryo's blood and the mother's blood flow very near each other in the placenta, but they normally do not mix.

Reading Check **Why is the placenta important?**

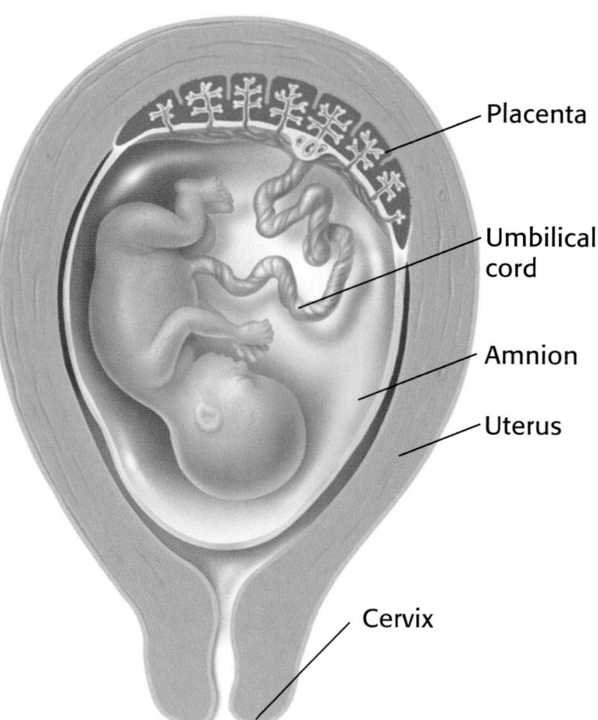

Figure 2 *The placenta, amnion, and umbilical cord are the life support system for the fetus. This fetus is about 20 to 22 weeks old.*

Weeks 1 and 2

Doctors commonly count the time of a woman's pregnancy as starting from the first day of her last menstrual period. Even though fertilization has not yet taken place, that day is a convenient date from which to start counting. A normal pregnancy lasts about 280 days, or 40 weeks, from that day.

Weeks 3 and 4

Fertilization takes place at about the end of week 2. In week 3, after fertilization, the zygote moves to the uterus. As the zygote travels, it divides many times. It becomes a ball of cells that implants itself in the wall of the uterus. The zygote is now called an *embryo*. At the end of week 4, implantation is complete and the woman is pregnant. The embryo's blood cells begin to form. At this point, the embryo is about 0.2 mm long.

umbilical cord the structure that connects the fetus to the placenta

Weeks 5 to 8

Weeks 5 to 8 of pregnancy are weeks 3 to 6 of embryonic development. In this stage, the embryo becomes surrounded by a thin membrane called the *amnion* (AM nee AHN). The amnion is filled with amniotic fluid and protects the growing embryo from bumps and injury. During week 5, the umbilical cord forms. The **umbilical cord** (uhm BIL i kuhl KAWRD) is a cord that connects the embryo to the placenta. **Figure 2** shows the umbilical cord, amnion, and placenta.

In this stage, the heart, brain, other organs, and blood vessels start to form. They grow quickly. In weeks 5 and 6, eyes and ears take shape. The spinal cord begins to develop. In week 6, tiny limb buds appear. These buds will become arms and legs. In week 8, muscles start developing. Nerves grow into the shoulders and upper arms. Fingers and toes start to form. The embryo, now about 16 mm long, can swallow and blink.

Growing Up

With a parent, discuss the physical and mental changes that you went through between your birth and your first day of school. Make a poster illustrating those changes.

ACTIVITY

fetus a developing human from seven or eight weeks after fertilization until birth

Weeks 9 to 16

At week 9, the fetus may begin to make tiny movements. After week 10, the embryo is called a **fetus** (FEET uhs). In about week 13, the fetus's face begins to look more human. During this stage, fetal muscles grow stronger. As a result, the fetus can make a fist and begins to move. The fetus grows rapidly during this stage. It doubles, and then triples, its size within a month. For example, in week 10, the fetus is about 36 mm long. A little later, at week 16, the fetus is about 108 mm to 116 mm long. Use **Figure 3** to follow some of the changes that take place in the fetus as it develops.

Reading Check **Describe three changes the fetus undergoes during weeks 9 to 16.**

Weeks 17 to 24

By week 17, the fetus can make faces. Usually, in week 18, the fetus starts to make movements that the mother can feel. By week 18, the fetus can hear sounds through the mother's uterus. It may even jump at loud noises. By week 23, the fetus's movements may be quite vigorous! If the fetus were born after week 24, it might survive. But babies born at 24 weeks require a lot of help. In weeks 17 to 24, the fetus grows to between 25 cm and 30 cm in length.

CONNECTION TO Physics

Using Ultrasound Doctors often use ultrasound to view a fetus in the uterus. Research how an ultrasound machine works, and make a poster explaining how sound waves can show what is happening inside a human body.

ACTIVITY

Weeks 25 to 36

At about 25 or 26 weeks, the fetus's lungs are well developed but not fully mature. The fetus still gets oxygen from its mother through the placenta. The fetus will not take its first breath of air until it is born. By the 32nd week, the fetus's eyes can open and close. Studies of fetal heart rate and brain activity show that fetuses respond to light. Some scientists have observed brain activity and eye movements in sleeping fetuses that resemble those activities in sleeping children or adults. These scientists think that a sleeping fetus may dream. After 36 weeks, the fetus is almost ready to be born.

Birth

At 37 to 38 weeks, the fetus is fully developed. A full-term pregnancy usually lasts about 40 weeks. Typically, as birth begins, the mother's uterus begins a series of muscular contractions called *labor.* Usually, these contractions push the fetus through the mother's vagina, and the baby is born. The newborn is still connected to the placenta by its umbilical cord, which is tied and cut. All that will remain of the point where the umbilical cord was attached is the baby's navel. Soon, the mother expels the placenta, and labor is complete.

Figure 3 **Pregnancy Timeline**

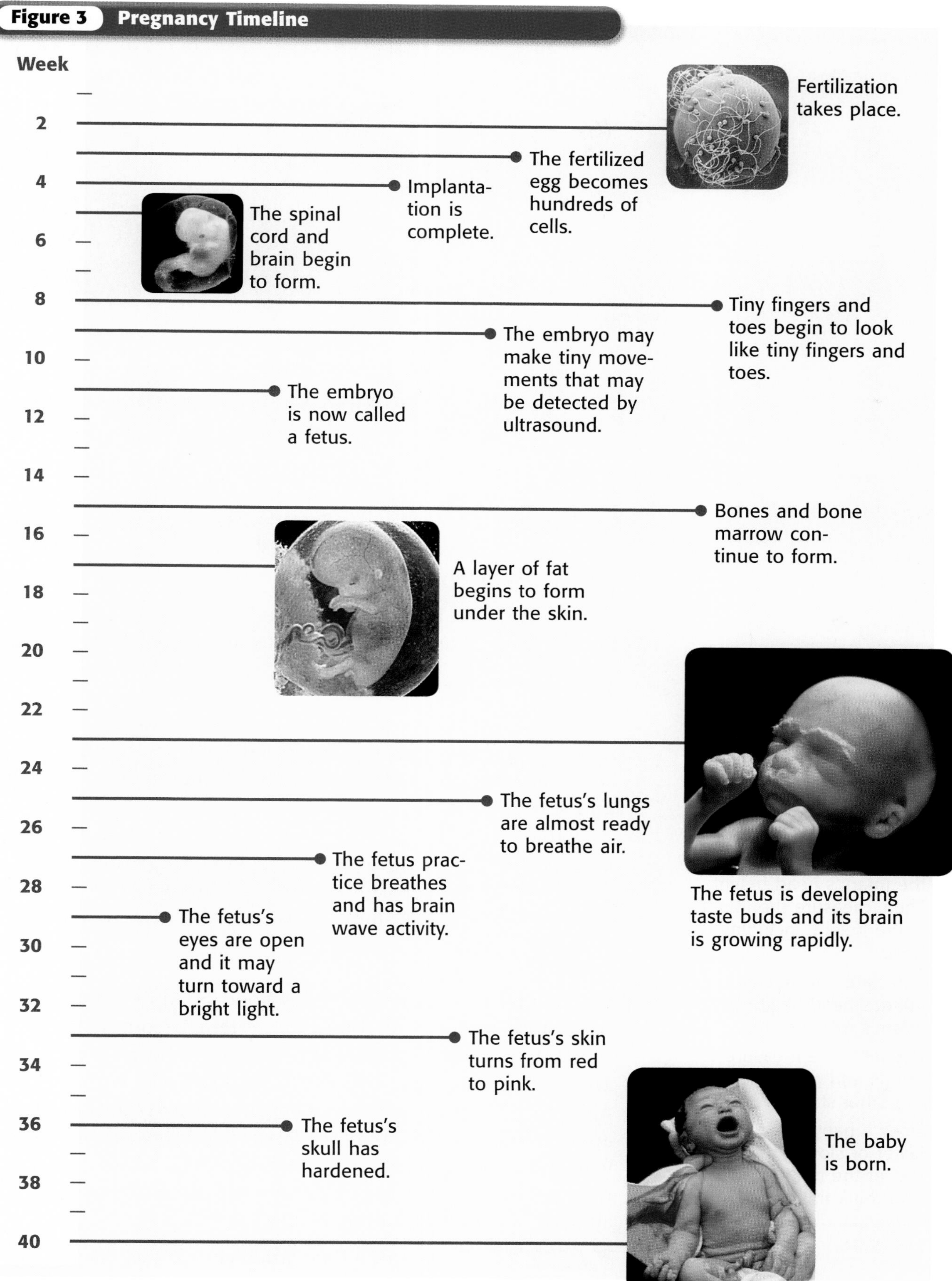
Week
2
4
6
8
10
12
14
16
18
20
22
24
26
28
30
32
34
36
38
40
Fertilization takes place.
The fertilized egg becomes hundreds of cells.
Implantation is complete.
The spinal cord and brain begin to form.
Tiny fingers and toes begin to look like tiny fingers and toes.
The embryo may make tiny movements that may be detected by ultrasound.
The embryo is now called a fetus.
Bones and bone marrow continue to form.
A layer of fat begins to form under the skin.
The fetus is developing taste buds and its brain is growing rapidly.
The fetus's lungs are almost ready to breathe air.
The fetus practice breathes and has brain wave activity.
The fetus's eyes are open and it may turn toward a bright light.
The fetus's skin turns from red to pink.
The fetus's skull has hardened.
The baby is born.

Figure 4 Stages of Human Development

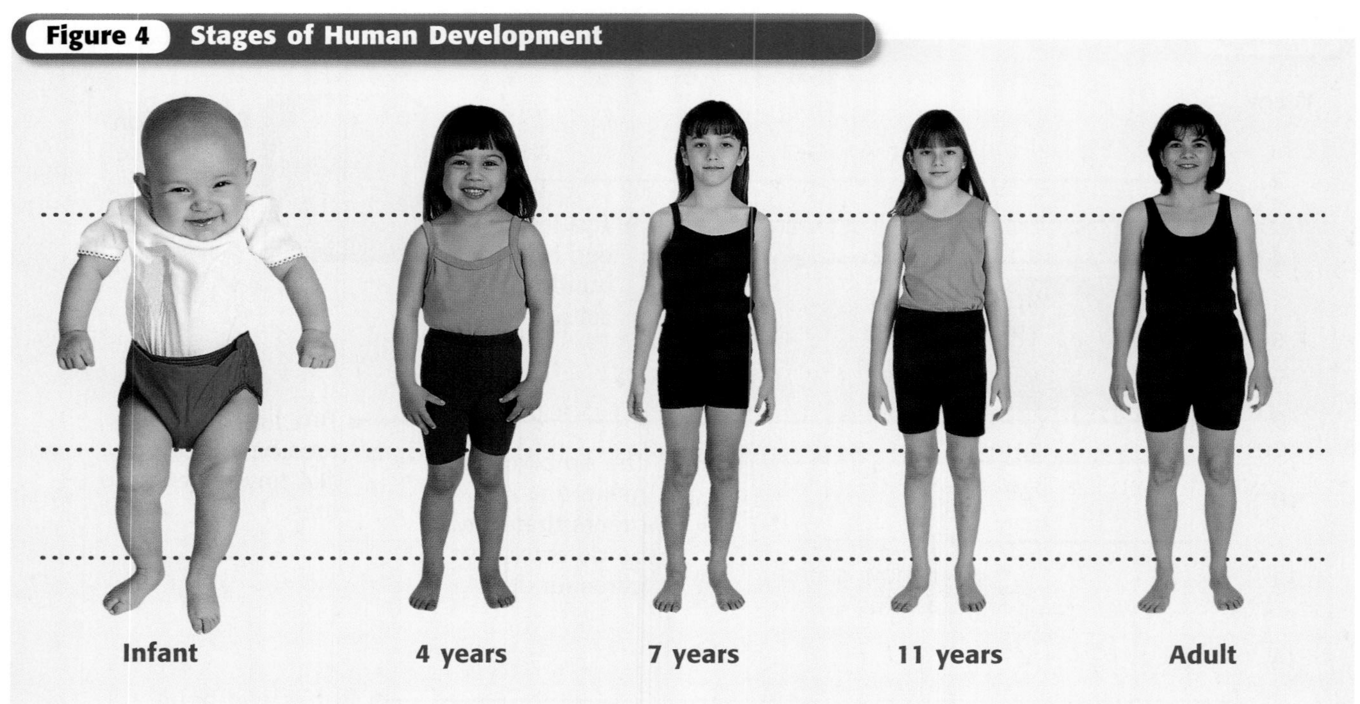

From Birth to Death

After birth, the human body goes through several stages of development. Some of those stages are shown in **Figure 4.**

Life Grows On

Use **Figure 4** to complete this activity.

1. Use a **ruler** to measure the infant's head height. Then, measure the infant's entire height, including the head.
2. Calculate the ratio of the infant's head height to the infant's total height.
3. Repeat these measurements and calculations for the other stages.
4. Does a baby's head grow faster or slower than the rest of the body? Why do you think this is so?

Infancy and Childhood

Generally, infancy is the stage from birth to age 2. During infancy, you grew quickly and your baby teeth appeared. As your nervous system developed, you became more coordinated and started to walk.

Childhood—another period of fast growth—lasts from age 2 to puberty. Your baby teeth were replaced by permanent teeth. And your muscles became more coordinated, which allowed you to ride a bicycle, jump rope, and do other activities.

Adolescence

The stage from puberty to adulthood is adolescence. During puberty, a person's reproductive system becomes mature. In most boys, puberty takes place between the ages of 11 and 16. During this time, the young male's body becomes more muscular, his voice becomes deeper, and body and facial hair appear. In most girls, puberty takes place between the ages of 9 and 14. During puberty in females, the amount of fat in the hips and thighs increases, the breasts enlarge, body hair appears, and menstruation begins.

Reading Check **Name an important change that takes place during adolescence.**

Adulthood

From about age 20 to age 40, you will be a young adult. You will be at the peak of your physical development. Beginning around age 30, changes associated with aging begin. These changes are gradual and different for everyone. Some early signs of aging include loss of flexibility in muscles, deterioration of eyesight, increase in body fat, and some loss of hair.

The aging process continues in middle age (between 40 and 65 years old). During this time, hair may turn gray, athletic abilities will decline, and skin may wrinkle. A person who is more than 65 years old is considered an older adult. Although the aging process continues, many older adults lead very active lives, as is shown in **Figure 5.**

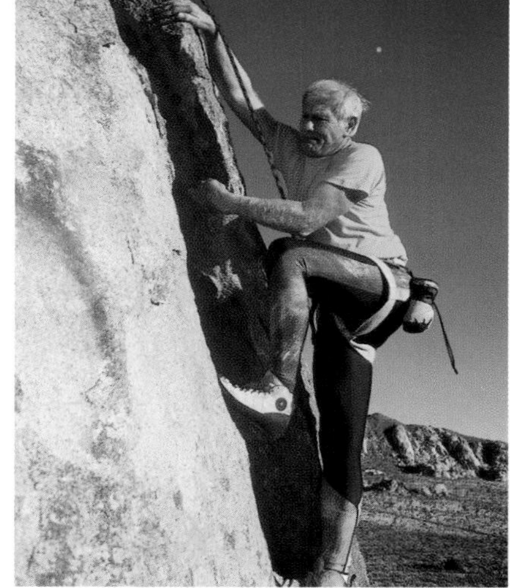

Figure 5 *Older adults can still enjoy activities that they enjoyed when they were younger.*

SECTION Review

Summary

- Fertilization occurs when a sperm from the male joins with an egg from the female.
- The embryo and fetus undergo many changes between implantation and birth.
- The first stage of human development lasts from fertilization to birth.
- After birth, a human goes through four more stages of growth and development.

Using Key Terms

1. In your own words, write a definition for the term *umbilical cord.*
2. Use the following terms in the same sentence: *embryo* and *fetus.*

Understanding Key Ideas

3. After birth, the two periods of most rapid growth are
   - **a.** infancy and adolescence.
   - **b.** childhood and adulthood.
   - **c.** infancy and childhood.
   - **d.** adolescence and adulthood.
4. After birth, which stage of human development is the longest?
   - **a.** infancy
   - **b.** childhood
   - **c.** adolescence
   - **d.** adulthood
5. Describe the development of the embryo and the fetus.
6. What is the function of the placenta?
7. Summarize the processes of fertilization and implantation.
8. What are five stages of human development?

Math Skills

9. Suppose a person is 80 years old and that puberty took place when he or she was 12 years old.
   - **a.** Calculate the percentage of the person's life that he or she spent in each of the four stages of development that follow birth.
   - **b.** Make a bar graph showing the percentage for each stage.

Critical Thinking

10. **Applying Concepts** Why does the egg's covering change after a sperm has entered the egg?
11. **Analyzing Ideas** Do you think any one stage of development is more important than other stages? Explain your answer.

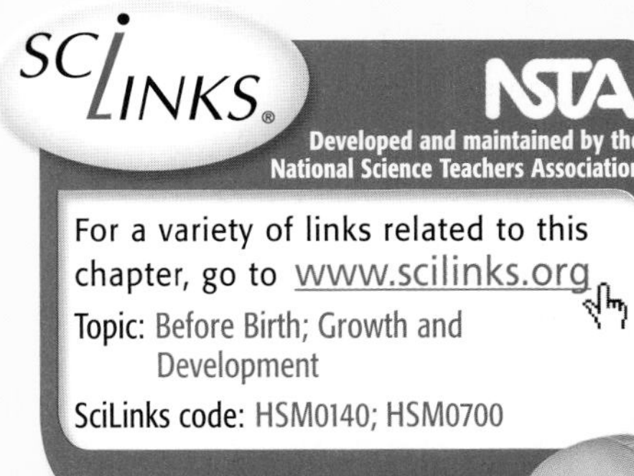

SCILINKS
NSTA
Developed and maintained by the National Science Teachers Association
For a variety of links related to this chapter, go to www.scilinks.org
Topic: Before Birth; Growth and Development
SciLinks code: HSM0140; HSM0700

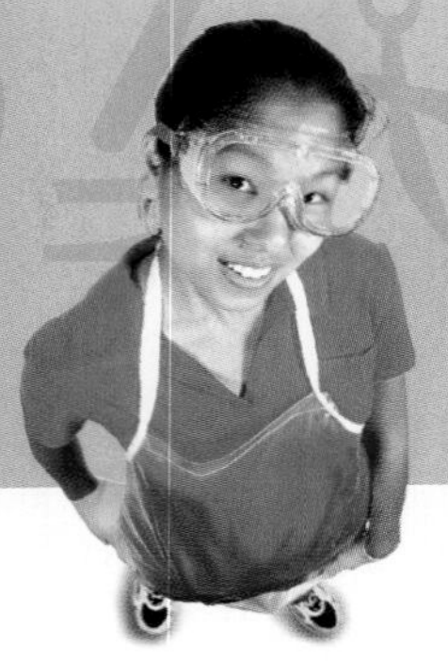

Using Scientific Methods

Skills Practice Lab

It's a Comfy, Safe World!

OBJECTIVES

Construct a model of a human uterus protecting a fetus.

Compare the protection that a bird's egg gives a developing baby bird with the protection that a human uterus gives a fetus.

MATERIALS

- computer (optional)
- cotton, soft fabric, or other soft materials
- eggs, soft-boiled and in the shell (2 to 4)
- eggs, soft-boiled and peeled (3 or 4)
- gloves, protective
- mineral oil, cooking oil, syrup, or other thick liquid
- plastic bags, sealable
- water

SAFETY

Before birth, baby birds live inside a hard, protective shell until the baby has used up all the food supply. Most mammal babies develop within their mother's uterus, in which they are surrounded by fluid and connected to a placenta, before they are born. Before human babies are born, they lead a comfy life. By the seventh month, they lie around sucking their thumb, blinking their eyes, and perhaps even dreaming.

Ask a Question

1. Inside which structure is a developing organism better protected from bumps and blows: the uterus of a placental mammal or the egg of a bird?

Form a Hypothesis

2. A placental mammal's uterus protects a developing organism from bumps and blows better than a bird's egg does.

Test the Hypothesis

3. Brainstorm several ideas about how you will construct and test your model of a mammalian uterus. Then, use the materials provided by your teacher to build your model. A peeled, soft-boiled egg will represent the fetus inside your model uterus.
4. Make a data table similar to **Table 1** below. Test your model, examine the egg for damage, and record your results.

***Table 1* First Model Test**

Original model	Modified model
DO NOT	WRITE
IN B	OOK

5. Modify your model as necessary; test this modified model using another peeled, soft-boiled egg; and record your results.

6. When you are satisfied with the design of your model, obtain another peeled, soft-boiled egg and an egg in the shell. The egg in the shell represents the baby bird inside the egg.

7. Make a data table similar to **Table 2** below. Test your new eggs, examine them for damage, and record your results in your data table.

Table 2 **Final Model Test**	
	Test Results
Model	DO NOT WRITE IN BOOK
Egg in shell	

Analyze the Results

1. **Explaining Events** Explain any differences in the test results for the model and the egg in a shell.

2. **Analyzing Results** What modification to your model was the most effective in protecting the fetus?

Draw Conclusions

3. **Evaluating Data** Review your hypothesis. Did your data support your hypothesis? Why or why not?

4. **Evaluating Models** What modifications to your model might make it more like a uterus?

Applying Your Data

Use the Internet or the library to find information about the development of monotremes, such as the echidna or the platypus, and marsupials, such as the koala or the kangaroo. Then, using what you have learned in this lab, compare the development of placental mammals with that of marsupials and monotremes.

Chapter Review

USING KEY TERMS

For each pair of terms, explain how the meanings of the terms differ.

1. *internal fertilization* and *external fertilization*
2. *testes* and *ovaries*
3. *asexual reproduction* and *sexual reproduction*
4. *fertilization* and *implantation*
5. *umbilical cord* and *placenta*

UNDERSTANDING KEY IDEAS

Multiple Choice

6. The sea star reproduces asexually by
   - a. fragmentation.
   - b. budding.
   - c. external fertilization.
   - d. internal fertilization.

7. Which list shows in order sperm's path through the male reproductive system?
   - a. testes, epididymis, urethra, vas deferens
   - b. epididymis, urethra, testes, vas deferens
   - c. testes, vas deferens, epididymis, urethra
   - d. testes, epididymis, vas deferens, urethra

8. Identical twins are the result of
   - a. a fertilized egg splitting in two.
   - b. two separate eggs being fertilized.
   - c. budding in the uterus.
   - d. external fertilization.

9. If the onset of menstruation is counted as the first day of the menstrual cycle, on what day of the cycle does ovulation typically occur?
   - a. 2nd day
   - b. 5th day
   - c. 14th day
   - d. 28th day

10. How do monotremes differ from placental mammals?
    - a. Monotremes are not mammals.
    - b. Monotremes have hair.
    - c. Monotremes nurture their young with milk.
    - d. Monotremes lay eggs.

11. All of the following are sexually transmitted diseases EXCEPT
    - a. chlamydia.
    - b. AIDS.
    - c. infertility.
    - d. genital herpes.

12. Where do fertilization and implantation, respectively, take place?
    - a. uterus, fallopian tube
    - b. fallopian tube, vagina
    - c. uterus, vagina
    - d. fallopian tube, uterus

Short Answer

13. Which human reproductive organs produce sperm? produce eggs?

14. Explain how the fetus gets oxygen and nutrients and how it gets rid of waste.

15. What are four stages of human life following birth?

16 Name three problems that can affect the human reproductive system, and explain why each is a problem.

17 Draw a diagram showing the structures of the male and female reproductive systems. Label each structure, and explain how each structure contributes to fertilization and implantation.

CRITICAL THINKING

18 **Concept Mapping** Use the following terms to create a concept map: *asexual reproduction, budding, external fertilization, fragmentation, reproduction, internal fertilization,* and *sexual reproduction.*

19 **Identifying Relationships** The environment in which organisms live may change over time. For example, a wet, swampy area may gradually become a grassy area with a small pond. Explain how sexual reproduction may give species that live in a changing environment a survival advantage.

20 **Applying Concepts** What is the function of the uterus? How is this function related to the menstrual cycle?

21 **Making Inferences** In most human body cells, the 46 chromosomes are duplicated during cell division so that each new cell receives 46 chromosomes. Cells that make eggs and sperm also split and duplicate their 46 chromosomes. But then, in the process of meiosis, the two cells split again to form four cells (egg or sperm) that each have 23 chromosomes. Why is meiosis important to human reproduction and to the human species?

INTERPRETING GRAPHICS

The following graph illustrates the cycles of the female hormone estrogen and the male hormone testosterone. The blue line shows the estrogen level in a female over 28 days. The red line shows the testosterone level in a male over the same amount of time. Use the graph below to answer the questions that follow.

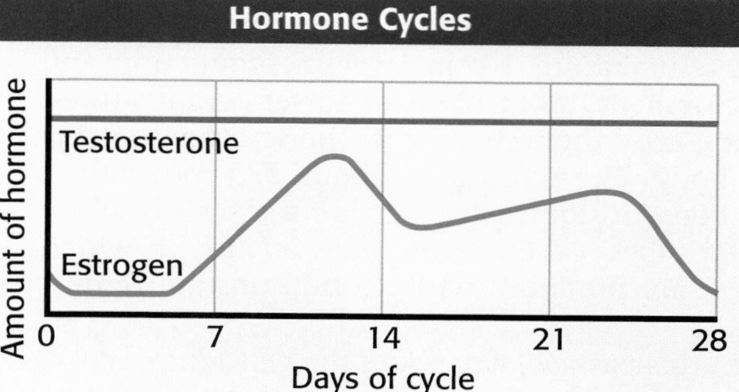

22 What is the major difference between the levels of the two hormones over the 28 days?

23 What cycle do you think estrogen affects?

24 Why might the level of testosterone stay the same?

25 Do you think that the above estrogen cycle would change in a pregnant woman? Explain your answer.

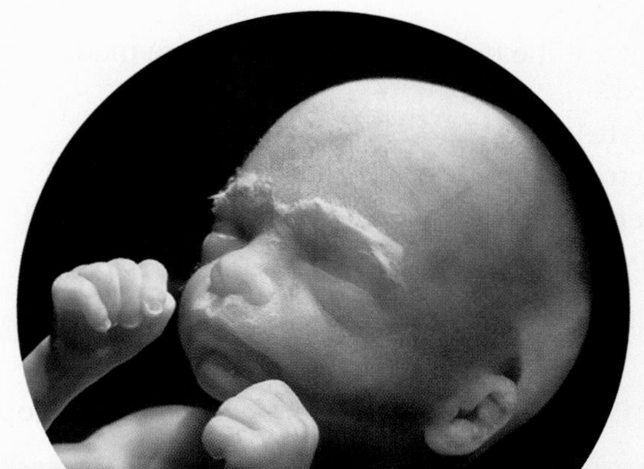

Standardized Test Preparation

READING

Read each of the passages below. Then, answer the questions that follow each passage.

Passage 1 The male reproductive system is made up of internal and external organs. The external organs of this system are the penis and the scrotum. The scrotum is a skin-covered sac that hangs outside the body. Normal human body temperature is about 37°C. Normal sperm production and development cannot take place at that temperature. Normal sperm production and development takes place at lower temperatures. That is why the testes rest in the scrotum, outside the body. The scrotum is about 2°C cooler than the body. Inside each testis are masses of tightly coiled tubes, called *seminiferous tubules,* in which sperm are produced when conditions are right.

1. In this passage, what does the word *external* mean?

- **A** not part of the body
- **B** outside the body
- **C** inside the body
- **D** lasting a long time

2. Which of the following statements is a fact according to the passage?

- **F** The temperature in the scrotum is higher than body temperature.
- **G** Testes are internal organs of the male reproductive system.
- **H** Normal sperm production cannot take place at normal body temperature.
- **I** Normal human body temperature is about 37°F.

3. What are the tubes in which sperm are made called?

- **A** testes
- **B** scrotum
- **C** seminiferous tubules
- **D** external organs

Passage 2 In a normal pregnancy, the fertilized egg travels to the uterus and implants itself in the uterus's wall. But, in about 7 out of 1,000 pregnancies in the United States, a woman has an ectopic pregnancy. The term *ectopic* is from two Greek words meaning "out of place." In an ectopic pregnancy, the fertilized egg implants itself in an ovary, a fallopian tube, or another area of the female reproductive system that is not the lining of the uterus. Because the zygote cannot develop properly outside of the uterus, an ectopic pregnancy can be very dangerous for both the mother and zygote. As the zygote grows, it causes the mother pain and bleeding. For example, an ectopic pregnancy in a fallopian tube can rupture the tube and cause abdominal bleeding. If an ectopic pregnancy is not treated quickly enough, the mother may die.

1. In the passage, what does the term *ectopic pregnancy* probably mean?

- **A** a pregnancy that takes place at the wrong time
- **B** a type of pregnancy that happens about 7 out of 100 times in the United States
- **C** a type of pregnancy caused by a problem with a fallopian tube
- **D** a pregnancy in which the zygote implants itself in the wrong place

2. Which of the following statements is a fact according to the passage?

- **F** Ectopic pregnancies take place in about 7% of all pregnancies.
- **G** The ectopic pregnancy rate in the United States is less than 1%.
- **H** Ectopic pregnancies take place in the uterus.
- **I** An ectopic pregnancy is harmless.

INTERPRETING GRAPHICS

Use the diagrams below to answer the questions that follow.

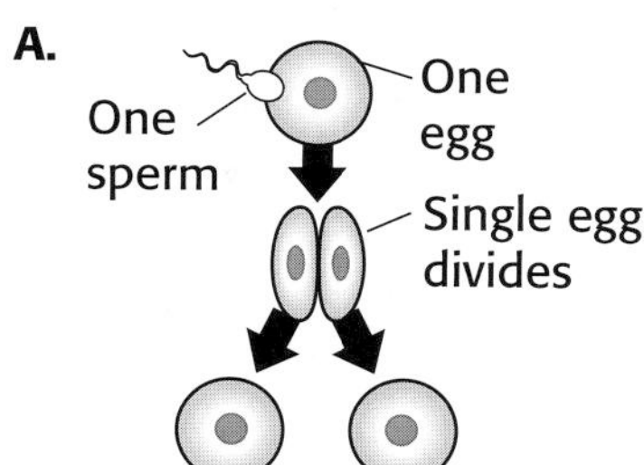

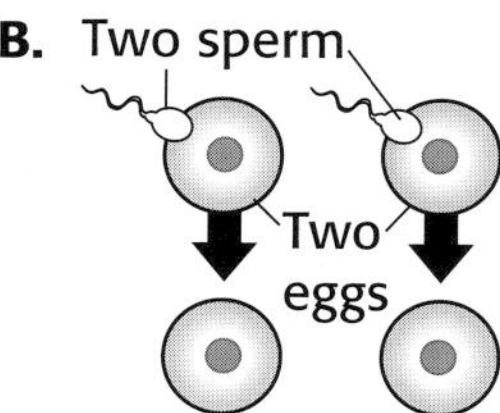

1. Which diagram of cell division would produce identical twins: A or B?

A diagram B, because each egg is fertilized by a separate sperm cell
B both diagram A and diagram B, because twins result in both cases
C diagram A, because a single fertilized egg separates into two halves
D diagram B, because two eggs are released by an ovary

2. Which of the following could describe fraternal twins?

F both boys
G both girls
H one girl and one boy
I any of these combinations

3. Which diagram of cell division could explain triplets, two of whom are identical and one of whom is fraternal?

A diagram A
B diagram B
C either diagram A or diagram B
D neither diagram A or diagram B

MATH

Read each question below, and choose the best answer.

1. Identify the group that contains equivalent fractions, decimals, and percents.

A 7/10, 0.7, 7%
B 1/2, 0.5, 50%
C 3/8, 0.38, 38%
D 3/100, 0.3, 33%

2. A geologist was exploring a cave. She spent 2.7 h exploring on Saturday and twice as many hours exploring on Sunday. Which equation could be used to find *n,* the total number of hours the geologist spent exploring the cave on those 2 days?

F $n = 2 \div 2.7$
G $n = 2.7 + (2 \times 2.7)$
H $n = 2.7 + 2.7 + 2$
I $n = 2 \times 2.7$

3. Which of the following story problems can be solved by the equation below?

$$(60 + 70 + 68 + 80 + x) \div 5 = 70$$

A The heights of four buildings in South Braintree are 60 ft, 70 ft, 68 ft, and 80 ft. Find *x,* the average height of the buildings.
B The weights of four dogs Jason is raising are 60 lb, 70 lb, 68 lb, and 80 lb. Find *x,* the sum of the weights of the four dogs.
C Kayla's first four handmade bracelets sold for \$60, \$70, \$68, and \$80. Find *x,* the amount for which Kayla needs to sell her fifth bracelet to have an average selling price of \$70.
D The times it took Taylor to complete each of four 100 m practice swims were 60 s, 70 s, 68 s, and 80 s. Find *x,* the average time it took Taylor to complete his practice swims.

Science in Action

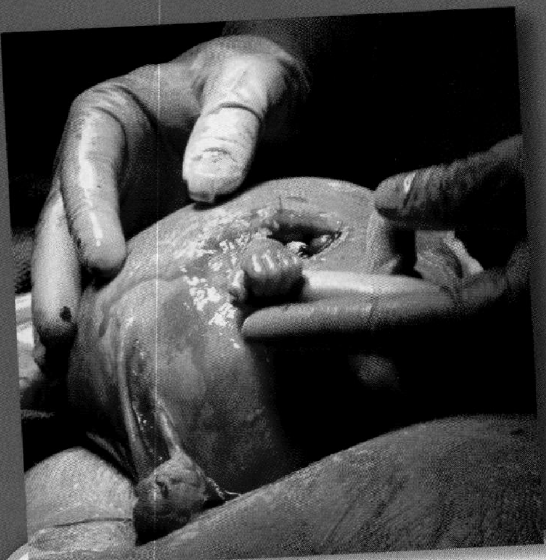

Doctors operated on a fetus, whose hand is visible in this photo, to correct spina bifida.

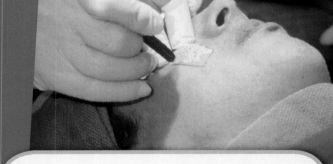

Science, Technology, and Society

Fetal Surgery

Sometimes, a developing fetus has a serious medical problem. In many cases, surgery after birth can correct the problem. But some problems can be treated while the fetus is still in the uterus. For example, fetal surgery may be used to correct spina bifida (part of the spinal cord is exposed because the backbone doesn't form properly). Doctors now can fix several types of problems before a baby is born.

Social Studies 

WRITING SKILL Research the causes of spina bifida. Write a brochure telling expectant mothers what precautions they can take to prevent spina bifida.

Scientific Discoveries

Lasers and Acne

Many people think that acne affects only teenagers, but acne can strike at any age. Some acne is mild, but some is severe. Now, for some severe cases of acne, lasers may provide relief. That's right—lasers can be used to treat acne! Surgeons who specialize in the health and diseases of the skin use laser light to treat the skin disease known as *acne*.

In addition, laser treatments may stimulate the skin cells that produce collagen. Collagen is a protein found in connective tissue. Increased production of collagen in the skin improves the skin's texture and helps smooth out acne scars.

Language Arts ACTIVITY

WRITING SKILL Write a story about how severe acne affects a teen's life. Tell what happens when a doctor refers the teen to a specialist for laser treatment and how the successful treatment changes the teen's life.

Careers

Reva Curry

Diagnostic Medical Sonographer Sounds are everywhere in our world. But only some of those sounds—such as your favorite music playing on the stereo or the dog barking next door—are sounds that we can hear. There are sound waves whose frequency is too high for us to hear. These high-pitched sounds are called *ultrasound*. Some animals, such as bats, use ultrasound to hunt and to avoid midair collisions.

Humans use ultrasound, too. Ultrasound machines can peer inside the human body to look at hearts, blood vessels, and fetuses. Diagnostic medical sonographers are people who use sonography equipment to diagnose medical problems and to follow the growth and development of a fetus before it is born. One of the leading professionals in the field of diagnostic medical sonography is Dr. Reva Curry. Dr. Curry spent many years as a sonographer. Her primary job was to use high-tech instruments to create ultrasound images of parts of the body and interpret the results for other medical professionals. Today, Dr. Curry works with students as the dean of a community college.

Math Activity

At 20°C, the speed of sound in water is 1,482 m/s and in steel is 5,200 m/s. How long would it take a sound to travel 815.1 m in water? In that same length of time, how far would a sound travel in a steel beam?

To learn more about these Science in Action topics, visit go.hrw.com and type in the keyword HL5BD5F.

Current Science

Check out Current Science® articles related to this chapter by visiting go.hrw.com. Just type in the keyword HL5CS26.

TIMELINE

Human Health

In many ways, living in the 21st century is good for your health. Many deadly diseases that plagued our ancestors now have cures. Some diseases, such as smallpox, have been wiped out entirely. And others can be prevented by vaccines and other methods. Many researchers, including the people on this timeline, have worked to understand diseases and to find cures.

But people still get sick, and many diseases have no cure. In this unit, you will learn how your body protects itself and fights illness. You will also learn about ways to keep yourself healthy so that your body can operate in top form.

1403
The first quarantine is imposed in Venice, Italy, to stop the spread of the plague, or Black Death.

1717
Lady Mary Wortley Montague introduces a smallpox vaccine in England.

1854
Nurse Florence Nightingale introduces hygienic standards into military hospitals during the Crimean War.

1895
X rays are discovered by Wilhelm Roentgen.

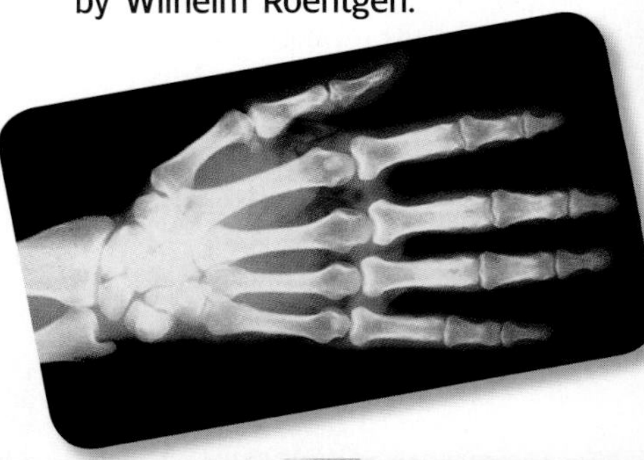

1953
Cigarette smoking is linked to lung cancer.

1816

R. T. Laënnec invents the stethoscope.

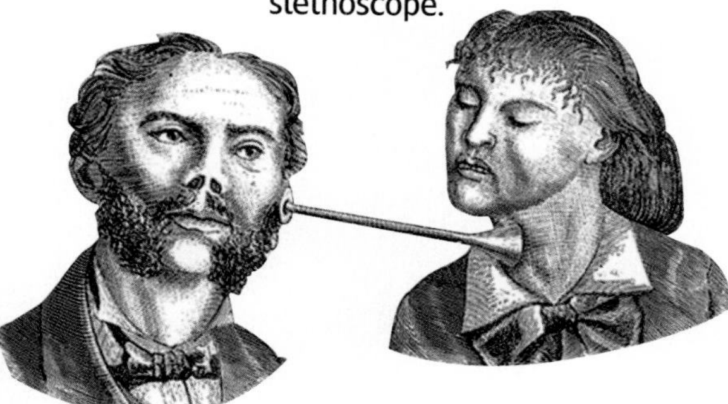

1853

Charles Gerhardt synthesizes aspirin for the first time.

1900

Walter Reed discovers that yellow fever is carried by mosquitoes.

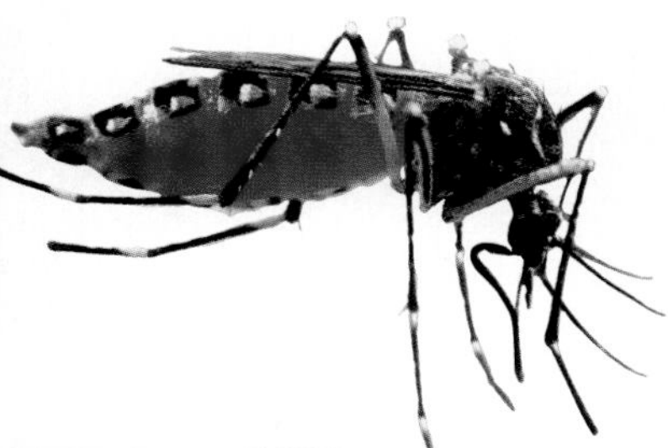

1906

Upton Sinclair writes *The Jungle*, which describes unsanitary conditions in the Chicago stockyards and leads to the creation of the Pure Food and Drug Act.

1921

A tuberculosis vaccine is produced.

1979

Smallpox is eradicated.

1997

Researchers discover that high doses of alcohol in early pregnancy switch off a gene that controls brain, heart, limb, and skull development in the fetus.

2003

More than 8,000 people are infected with severe acute respiratory syndrome (SARS), which is caused by a newly discovered virus.

Body Defenses and Disease

About the PHOTO

No, this photo is not from a sci-fi movie. It is not an alien insect soldier. This is, in fact, a greatly enlarged image of a house dust mite that is tinier than the dot of an *i.* Huge numbers of these creatures live in carpets, beds, and sofas in every home. Dust mites often cause problems for people who have asthma or allergies. The body's immune system fights diseases and alien factors, such as dust mites, that cause allergies.

PRE-READING ACTIVITY

FOLDNOTES **Tri-Fold** Before you read the chapter, create the FoldNote entitled "Tri-Fold" described in the **Study Skills** section of the Appendix. Write what you know about the body's defenses in the column labeled "Know." Then, write what you want to know in the column labeled "Want." As you read the chapter, write what you learn about the body's defenses in the column labeled "Learn."

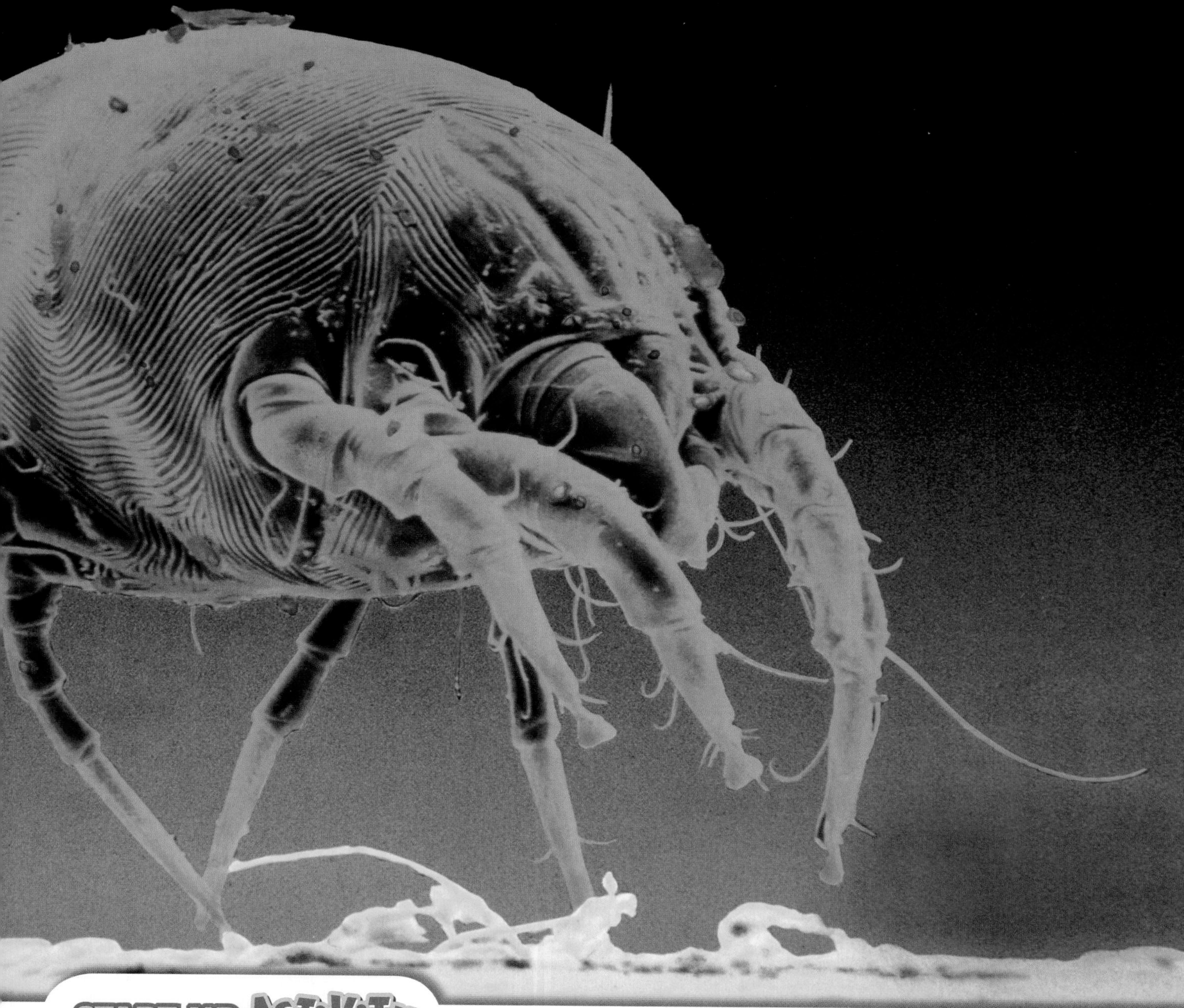

START-UP ACTIVITY

Invisible Invaders

In this activity, you will see tiny organisms grow.

Procedure

1. Obtain **two Petri dishes containing nutrient agar.** Label them "Washed" and "Unwashed."
2. Rub **two marbles** between the palms of your hands. Observe the appearance of the marbles.
3. Roll one marble in the Petri dish labeled "Unwashed."
4. Put on a pair of **disposable gloves.** Wash the other marble with **soap** and **warm water** for 4 min.
5. Roll the washed marble in the Petri dish labeled "Washed."
6. Secure the lids of the Petri dishes with **transparent tape.** Place the dishes in a warm, dark place. Do not open the Petri dishes after they are sealed.
7. Record changes in the Petri dishes for 1 week.

Analysis

1. How did the washed and unwashed marbles compare? How did the Petri dishes differ after several days?
2. Why is it important to wash your hands before eating?

SECTION 1

Disease

You've probably heard it before: "Cover your mouth when you sneeze!" "Wash your hands!" "Don't put that in your mouth!"

What is all the fuss about? When people say these things to you, they are concerned about the spread of disease.

READING WARM-UP

Objectives

- Explain the difference between infectious diseases and noninfectious diseases.
- Identify five ways that you might come into contact with a pathogen.
- Discuss four methods that have helped reduce the spread of disease.

Terms to Learn

noninfectious disease
infectious disease
pathogen
immunity

READING STRATEGY

Paired Summarizing Read this section silently. In pairs, take turns summarizing the material. Stop to discuss ideas that seem confusing.

Causes of Disease

When you have a *disease,* your normal body functions are disrupted. Some diseases, such as most cancers and heart disease, are not spread from one person to another. They are called **noninfectious diseases.**

Noninfectious diseases can be caused by a variety of factors. For example, a genetic disorder causes the disease hemophilia (HEE moh FIL ee uh), in which a person's blood does not clot properly. Smoking, lack of physical activity, and a high-fat diet can greatly increase a person's chances of getting certain noninfectious diseases. Avoiding harmful habits may help you avoid noninfectious diseases.

A disease that can be passed from one living thing to another is an **infectious disease.** Infectious diseases are caused by agents called **pathogens.** Viruses and some bacteria, fungi, protists, and worms may all cause diseases. **Figure 1** shows some enlarged images of common pathogens.

noninfectious disease a disease that cannot spread from one individual to another

infectious disease a disease that is caused by a pathogen and that can be spread from one individual to another

pathogen a virus, microorganism, or other organism that causes disease

Figure 1 Pathogens

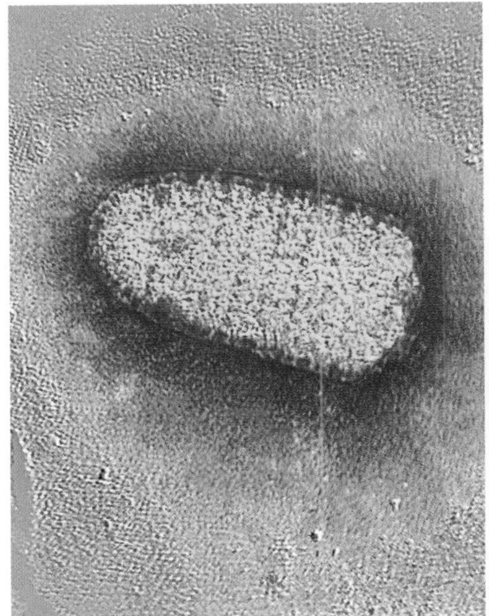

▲ This virus causes rabies.

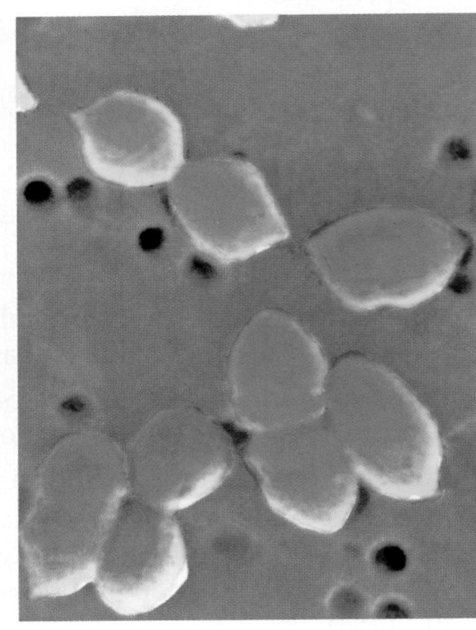

▲ *Streptococcus* bacteria can cause strep throat.

Pathways to Pathogens

There are many ways pathogens can be passed from one person to another. Being aware of them can help you stay healthy.

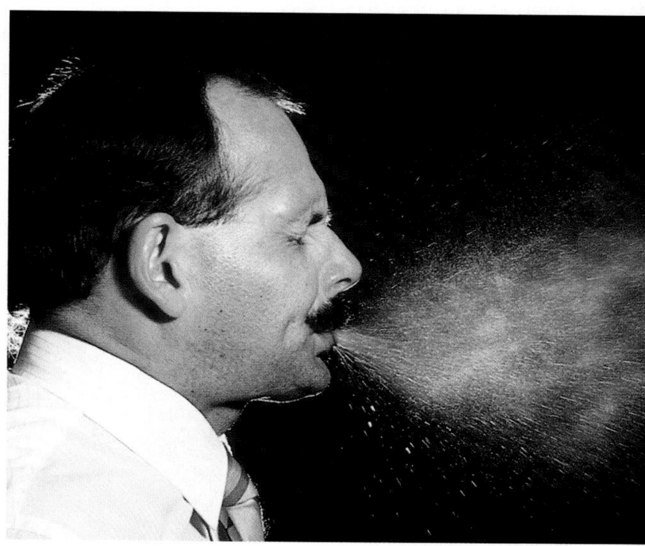

Figure 2 *A sneeze can force thousands of pathogen-carrying droplets out of your body at up to 160 km/h.*

Air

Some pathogens travel through the air. For example, a single sneeze, such as the one shown in **Figure 2,** releases thousands of tiny droplets of moisture that can carry pathogens.

Contaminated Objects

You may already know that if you drink from a glass that an infected person has just used, you could become infected with a pathogen. A person who is sick may leave bacteria or viruses on many other objects, too. For example, contaminated doorknobs, keyboards, combs, and towels can pass pathogens.

Person to Person

Some pathogens are spread by direct person-to-person contact. You can become infected with some illnesses by kissing, shaking hands, or touching the sores of an infected person.

Animals

Some pathogens are carried by animals. For example, humans can get a fungus called *ringworm* from handling an infected dog or cat. Also, ticks may carry bacteria that cause Lyme disease or Rocky Mountain spotted fever.

Food and Water

Drinking water in the United States is generally safe. But water lines can break, or treatment plants can become flooded. These problems may allow microorganisms to enter the public water supply. Bacteria growing in foods and beverages can cause illness, too. For example, meat, fish, and eggs that are not cooked enough can still contain dangerous bacteria or parasites. Even leaving food out at room temperature can give bacteria such as salmonella the chance to grow and produce toxins in the food. Refrigerating foods can slow the growth of many of these pathogens. Because bacteria grow in food, washing all used cooking surfaces and tools is also important.

Reading Check **Why must you cook meat and eggs thoroughly?** (*See the Appendix for answers to Reading Checks.*)

CONNECTION TO Social Studies

Disease and History Many diseases have shaped history. For example, yellow fever, which is caused by a virus that is spread by mosquitoes, was one of the obstacles in building the Panama Canal. Only after people learned how to prevent the spread of the yellow fever virus could the canal be completed.

Use information from Internet and library research to create a poster describing how one infectious disease affected history.

ACTIVITY

Putting Pathogens in Their Place

Until the twentieth century, surgery patients often died of bacterial infections. But doctors learned that simple cleanliness could help prevent the spread of some diseases. Today, hospitals and clinics use a variety of technologies to prevent the spread of pathogens. For example, ultraviolet radiation, boiling water, and chemicals are used to kill pathogens in health facilities.

SCHOOL to HOME

Label Check

At home or in a local store, find a product that has been pasteurized. In your **science journal,** write down other safety information you find on the label, including the product's refrigeration needs. Why do you think most products that require pasteurization also require refrigeration?

ACTIVITY

Pasteurization

During the mid-1800s, Louis Pasteur, a French scientist, discovered that microorganisms caused wine to spoil. The uninvited microorganisms were bacteria. Pasteur devised a method of using heat to kill most of the bacteria in the wine. This method is called *pasteurization* (PAS tuhr i ZAY shuhn), and it is still used today. The milk that the girl in **Figure 3** is drinking has been pasteurized.

immunity the ability to resist or to recover from an infectious disease

Vaccines and Immunity

In the late 1700s, no one knew what a pathogen was. During this time, Edward Jenner studied a disease called *smallpox*. He observed that people who had been infected with cowpox seemed to have protection against smallpox. These people had a resistance to the disease. The ability to resist or recover from an infectious disease is called **immunity.** Jenner's work led to the first modern vaccine. A *vaccine* is a substance that helps your body develop immunity to a disease.

Today, vaccines are used all over the world to prevent many serious diseases. Modern vaccines contain pathogens that are killed or specially treated so that they can't make you very sick. The vaccine is enough like the pathogen to allow your body to develop a defense against the disease.

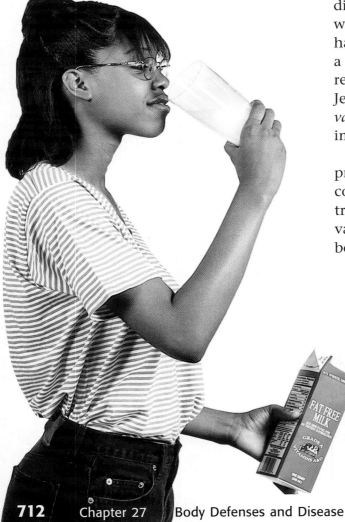

Figure 3 *Today, pasteurization is used to kill pathogens in many different types of food, including dairy products, shellfish, and juices.*

Antibiotics

Have you ever had strep throat? If so, you have had a bacterial infection. Bacterial infections can be a serious threat to your health. Fortunately, doctors can usually treat these kinds of infections with antibiotics. An *antibiotic* is a substance that can kill bacteria or slow the growth of bacteria. Antibiotics may also be used to treat infections caused by other microorganisms, such as fungi. You may take an antibiotic when you are sick. Always take antibiotics according to your doctor's instructions to ensure that all the pathogens are killed.

Viruses, such as those that cause colds, are not affected by antibiotics. Antibiotics can kill only living things, and viruses are not alive. The only way to destroy viruses in your body is to locate and kill the cells they have invaded.

Reading Check **Frank caught a bad cold just before the opening night of a school play. He visited his doctor and asked her to prescribe antibiotics for his cold. The doctor politely refused and advised Frank to stay home and get plenty of rest. Why do you think the doctor refused to give Frank antibiotics?**

Epidemic!

You catch a cold and return to your school while sick. Your friends don't have immunity to your cold. On the first day, you expose five friends to your cold. The next day, each of those friends passes the virus to five more people. If this pattern continues for 5 more days, how many people will be exposed to the virus?

SECTION Review

Summary

- Noninfectious diseases cannot be spread from one person to another.
- Infectious diseases are caused by pathogens that are passed from one living thing to another.
- Pathogens can travel through the air or can be spread by contact with other people, contaminated objects, animals, food, or water.
- Cleanliness, pasteurization, vaccines, and antibiotics help control the spread of pathogens.

Using Key Terms

1. In your own words, write a definition for each of the following terms: *infectious disease, noninfectious disease,* and *immunity.*

Understanding Key Ideas

2. Vaccines contain
   a. treated pathogens.
   b. heat.
   c. antibiotics.
   d. pasteurization.
3. List five ways that you might come into contact with a pathogen.
4. Name four ways to help keep safe from pathogens.

Math Skills

5. If 10 people with the virus each expose 25 more people to the virus, how many people will be exposed to the virus?

Critical Thinking

6. **Identifying Relationships** Why might the risk of infectious disease be high in a community that has no water treatment facility?
7. **Analyzing Methods** Explain what might happen if a doctor did not wear gloves when treating patients.
8. **Applying Concepts** Why do vaccines for diseases in animals help prevent some illnesses in people?

For a variety of links related to this chapter, go to www.scilinks.org

Topic: Pathogens; What Causes Diseases?
SciLinks code: HSM1118; HSM1653

SECTION 2

Your Body's Defenses

Bacteria and viruses can be in the air, in the water, and on all the surfaces around you.

READING WARM-UP

Objectives

- Describe how your body keeps out pathogens.
- Explain how the immune system fights infections.
- Describe four challenges to the immune system.

Terms to Learn

immune system
macrophage
T cell
B cell
antibody
memory B cell
allergy
autoimmune disease
cancer

READING STRATEGY

Reading Organizer As you read this section, make a flowchart of the steps of how your body responds to a virus.

Your body must constantly protect itself against pathogens that are trying to invade it. But how does your body do that? Luckily, your body has its own built-in defense system.

First Lines of Defense

For a pathogen to harm you, it must attack a part of your body. Usually, though, very few of the pathogens around you make it past your first lines of defense.

Many organisms that try to enter your eyes or mouth are destroyed by special enzymes. Pathogens that enter your nose are washed down the back of your throat by mucus. The mucus carries the pathogens to your stomach, where most are quickly digested.

Your skin is made of many layers of flat cells. The outermost layers are dead. As a result, many pathogens that land on your skin have difficulty finding a live cell to infect. As **Figure 1** shows, the dead skin cells are constantly dropping off your body as new skin cells grow from beneath. As the dead skin cells flake off, they carry away viruses, bacteria, and other microorganisms. In addition, glands secrete oil onto your skin's surface. The oil contains chemicals that kill many pathogens.

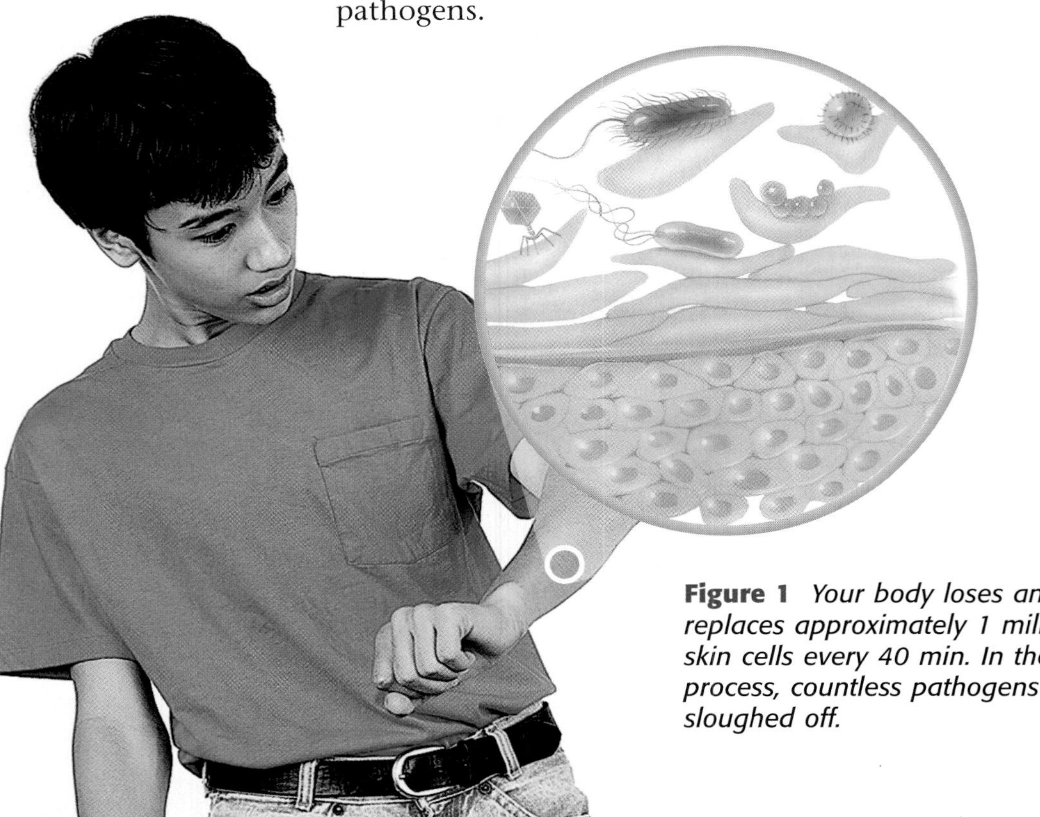

Figure 1 *Your body loses and replaces approximately 1 million skin cells every 40 min. In the process, countless pathogens are sloughed off.*

Failure of First Lines

Sometimes, skin is cut or punctured and pathogens can enter the body. The body acts quickly to keep out as many pathogens as possible. Blood flow to the injured area increases. Cell parts in the blood called *platelets* help seal the open wound so that no more pathogens can enter.

The increased blood flow also brings cells that belong to the **immune system,** the body system that fights pathogens. The immune system is not localized in any one place in your body. It is not controlled by any one organ, such as the brain. Instead, it is a team of individual cells, tissues, and organs that work together to keep you safe from invading pathogens.

immune system the cells and tissues that recognize and attack foreign substances in the body

macrophage an immune system cell that engulfs pathogens and other materials

T cell an immune system cell that coordinates the immune system and attacks many infected cells

B cell a white blood cell that makes antibodies

antibody a protein made by B cells that binds to a specific antigen

Cells of the Immune System

The immune system consists mainly of three kinds of cells. One kind is the macrophage (MAK roh FAYJ). **Macrophages** engulf and digest many microorganisms or viruses that enter your body. If only a few microorganisms or viruses have entered a wound, the macrophages can easily stop them.

The other two main kinds of immune-system cells are T cells and B cells. **T cells** coordinate the immune system and attack many infected cells. **B cells** are immune-system cells that make antibodies. **Antibodies** are proteins that attach to specific antigens. *Antigens* are substances that stimulate an immune response. Your body is capable of making billions of different antibodies. Each antibody usually attaches to only one kind of antigen, as illustrated in **Figure 2.**

Reading Check How do macrophages help fight disease? *(See the Appendix for answers to Reading Checks.)*

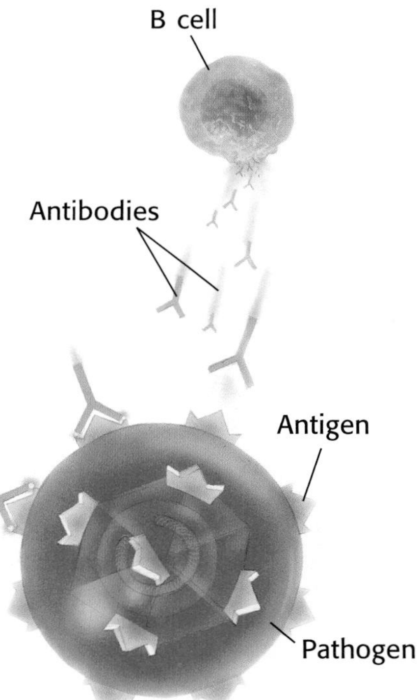

Figure 2 *An antibody's shape is very specialized. It matches an antigen like a key fits a lock.*

Only Skin Deep

1. Cut an **apple** in half.
2. Place **plastic wrap** over each half. The plastic wrap will act as skin.
3. Use **scissors** to cut the plastic wrap on one of the apple halves, and then use an **eyedropper** to drip **food coloring** on each apple half. The food coloring represents pathogens coming into contact with your body.
4. What happened to each apple half?
5. How is the plastic wrap similar to skin?
6. How is the plastic wrap different from skin?

For another activity related to this chapter, go to **go.hrw.com** and type in the keyword **HL5BD6W.**

Responding to a Virus

If virus particles enter your body, some of the particles may pass into body cells and begin to replicate. Other virus particles will be engulfed and broken up by macrophages. This is just the beginning of the immune response. The process your immune system uses to fight an invading virus is summarized in the figure below.

Reading Check **What are two things that can happen to virus particles when they enter the body?**

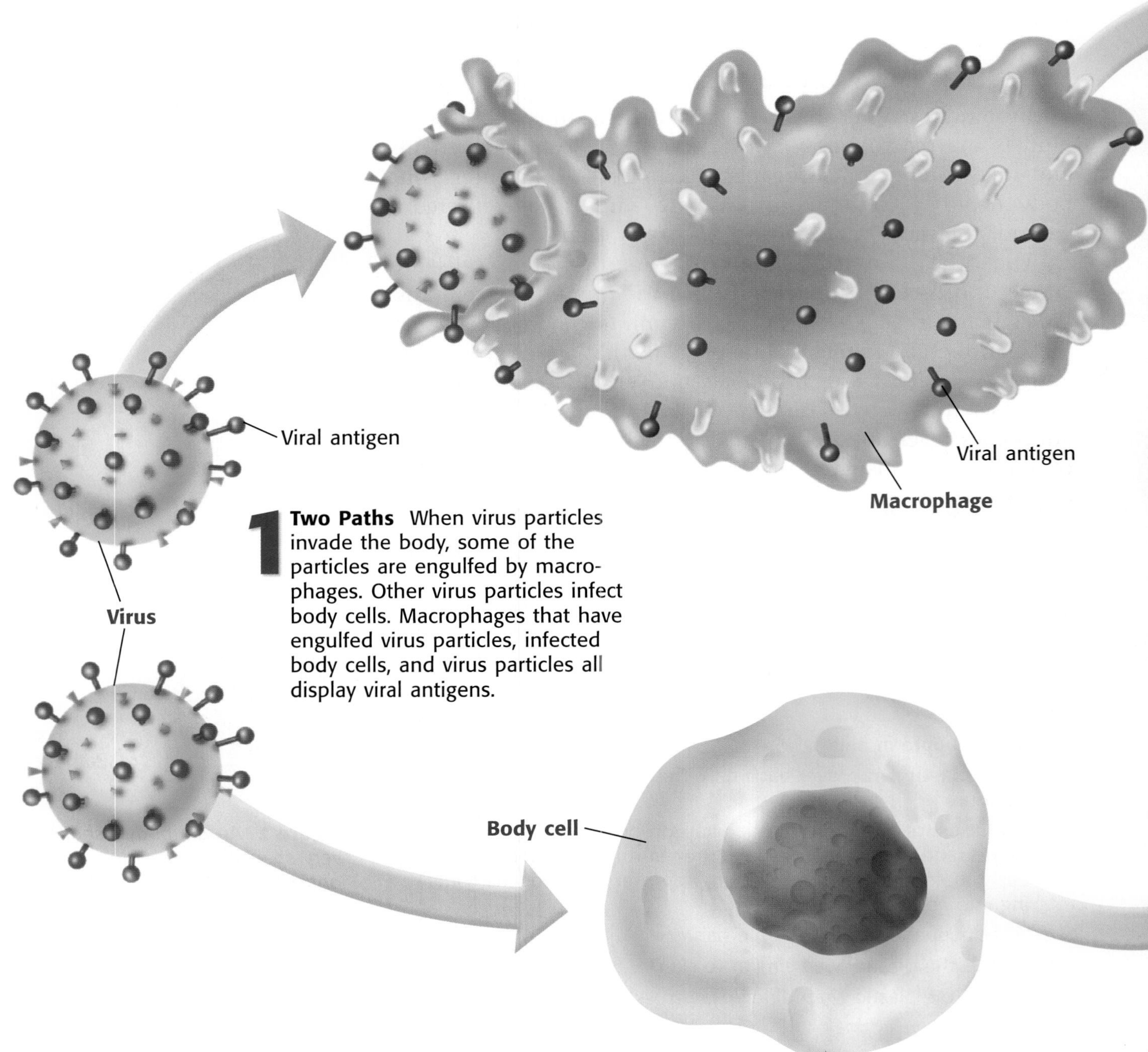

1 Two Paths When virus particles invade the body, some of the particles are engulfed by macrophages. Other virus particles infect body cells. Macrophages that have engulfed virus particles, infected body cells, and virus particles all display viral antigens.

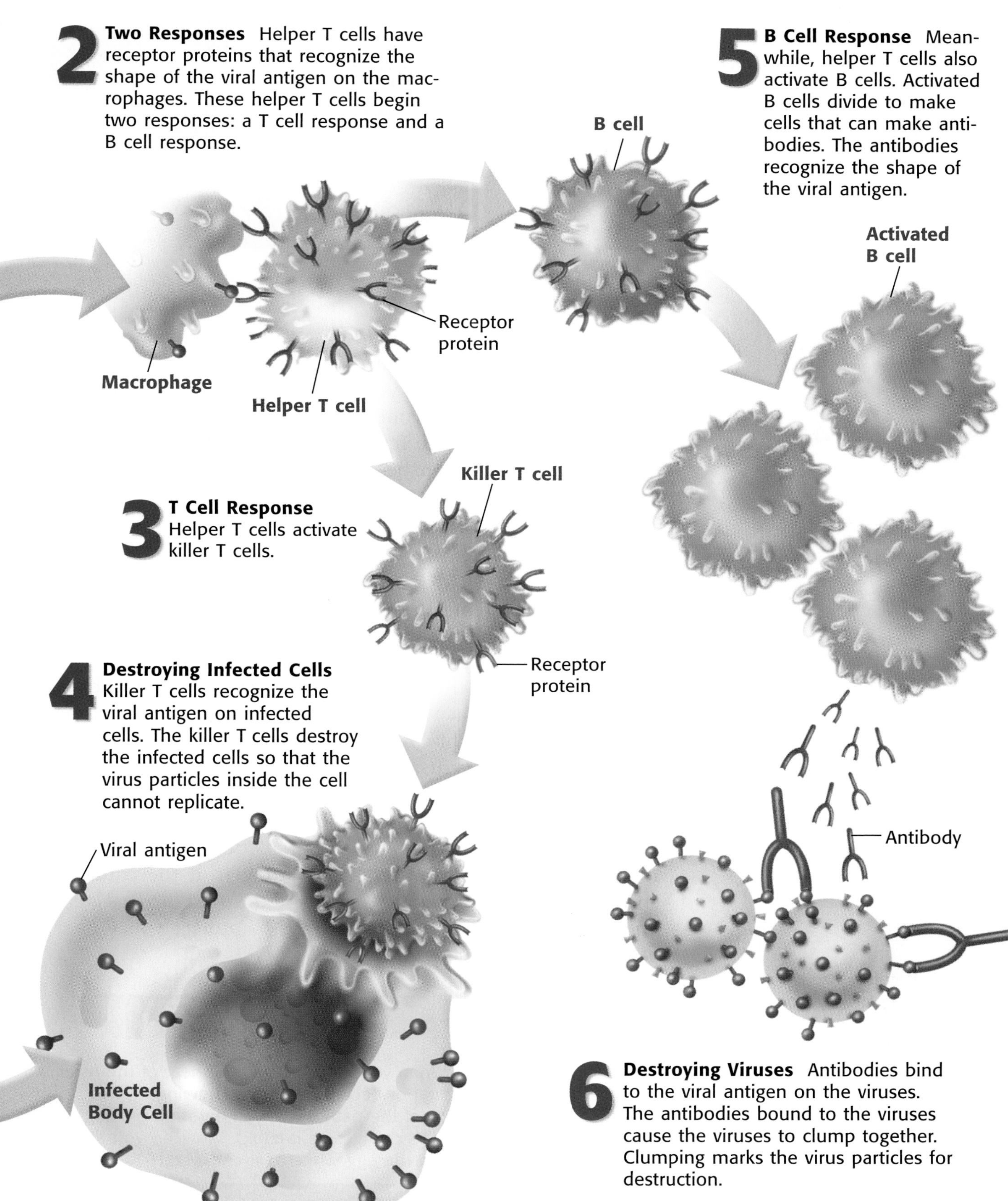
2
Two Responses Helper T cells have receptor proteins that recognize the shape of the viral antigen on the macrophages. These helper T cells begin two responses: a T cell response and a B cell response.
Macrophage
Helper T cell
Receptor protein
5
B Cell Response Meanwhile, helper T cells also activate B cells. Activated B cells divide to make cells that can make antibodies. The antibodies recognize the shape of the viral antigen.
B cell
Activated B cell
3
T Cell Response
Helper T cells activate killer T cells.
Killer T cell
Receptor protein
4
Destroying Infected Cells
Killer T cells recognize the viral antigen on infected cells. The killer T cells destroy the infected cells so that the virus particles inside the cell cannot replicate.
Viral antigen
Infected Body Cell
Antibody
6
Destroying Viruses Antibodies bind to the viral antigen on the viruses. The antibodies bound to the viruses cause the viruses to clump together. Clumping marks the virus particles for destruction.

Figure 3 *You may not feel well when you have a fever. But a fever is one way that your body fights infections.*

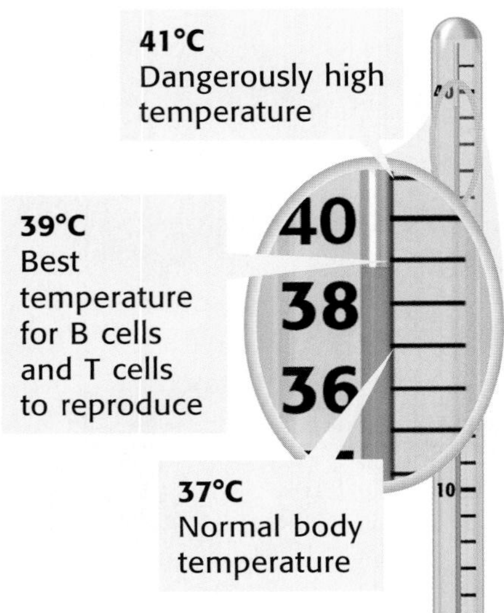

Figure 4 *A slight fever helps immune cells reproduce. But a fever of more than a few degrees can become dangerous.*

Fevers

The man in **Figure 3** is sick and has a fever. What is a fever? When macrophages activate the helper T cells, they send a chemical signal that tells your brain to turn up the thermostat. In a few minutes, your body's temperature can rise several degrees. A moderate fever of one or two degrees actually helps you get well faster because it slows the growth of some pathogens. As shown in **Figure 4,** a fever also helps B cells and T cells multiply faster.

Memory Cells

Your immune system can respond to a second encounter faster than it can respond the first time. B cells must have had previous contact with a pathogen before they can make the correct antibodies. During the first encounter with a new pathogen, specialized B cells make antibodies that are effective against that particular invader. This process takes about 2 weeks, which is far too long to prevent an infection. Therefore, the first time you are infected, you usually get sick.

A few of the B cells become memory B cells. **Memory B cells** are cells in your immune system that "remember" how to make an antibody for a particular pathogen. If the pathogen shows up again, the memory B cells produce B cells that make enough antibodies in just 3 or 4 days to protect you.

memory B cell a B cell that responds to an antigen more strongly when the body is reinfected with an antigen than it does during its first encounter with the antigen

CONNECTION TO Chemistry

Bent out of Shape When you have a fever, the heat of the fever changes the shape of viral or bacterial proteins, slowing or preventing the reproduction of the pathogen. With an adult present, observe how an egg white changes as it cooks. What do you think happens to the protein in the egg white as it cooks?

ACTIVITY

Challenges to the Immune System

The immune system is a very effective body-defense system, but it is not perfect. The immune system is unable to deal with some diseases. There are also conditions in which the immune system does not work properly.

allergy a reaction to a harmless or common substance by the body's immune system

autoimmune disease a disease in which the immune system attacks the organism's own cells

Allergies

Sometimes, the immune system overreacts to antigens that are not dangerous to the body. This inappropriate reaction is called an **allergy.** Allergies may be caused by many things, including certain foods and medicines. Many people have allergic reactions to pollen, shown in **Figure 5.** Symptoms of allergic reactions range from a runny nose and itchy eyes to more serious conditions, such as asthma.

Doctors are not sure why the immune system overreacts in some people. Scientists think allergies might be useful because the mucus draining from your nose carries away pollen, dust, and microorganisms.

Figure 5 *Pollen is one substance that can cause allergic reactions.*

Autoimmune Diseases

A disease in which the immune system attacks the body's own cells is called an **autoimmune disease.** In an autoimmune disease, immune-system cells mistake body cells for pathogens. One autoimmune disease is rheumatoid arthritis (ROO muh TOYD ahr THRIET IS), in which the immune system attacks the joints. A common location for rheumatoid arthritis is the joints of the hands, as shown in **Figure 6.** Other autoimmune diseases include type 1 diabetes, multiple sclerosis, and lupus.

Reading Check Name four autoimmune diseases.

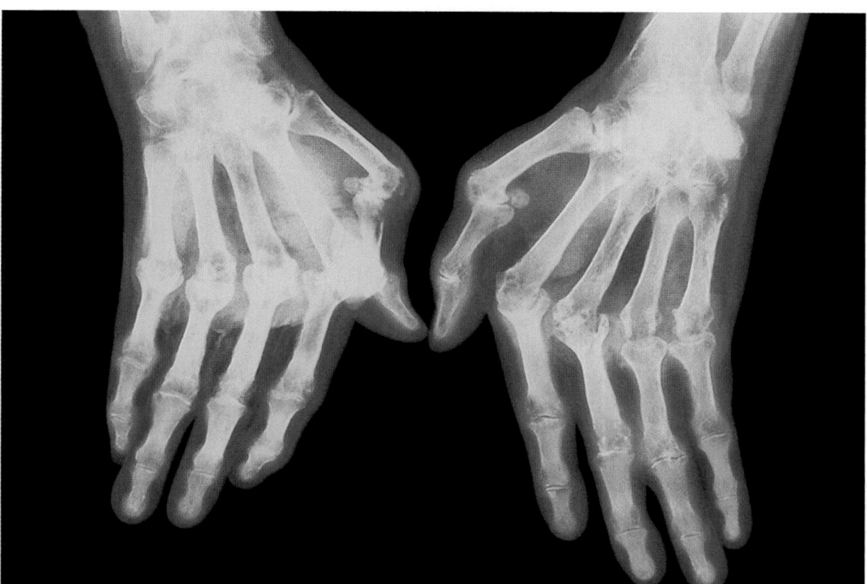

Figure 6 *In rheumatoid arthritis, immune-system cells cause joint-tissue swelling, which can lead to joint deformities.*

Figure 7 **Immune Cells Fighting Cancer**

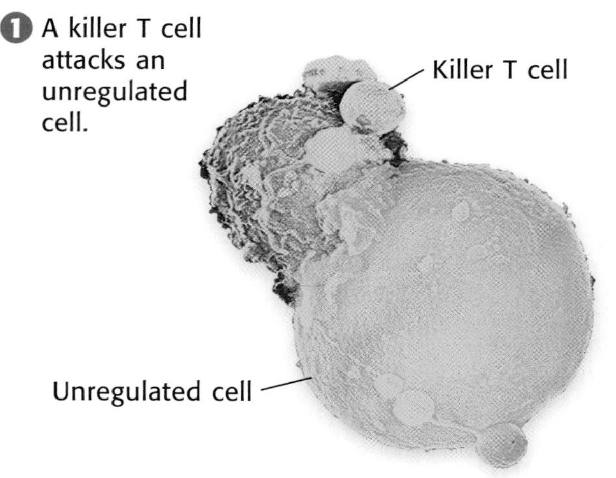

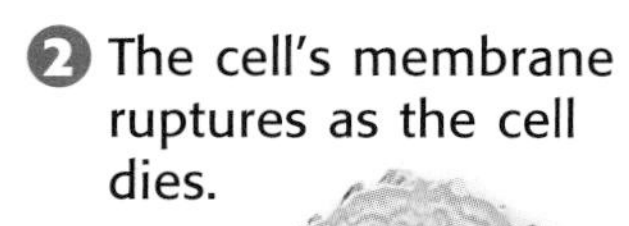

1 A killer T cell attacks an unregulated cell.

Unregulated cell

2 The cell's membrane ruptures as the cell dies.

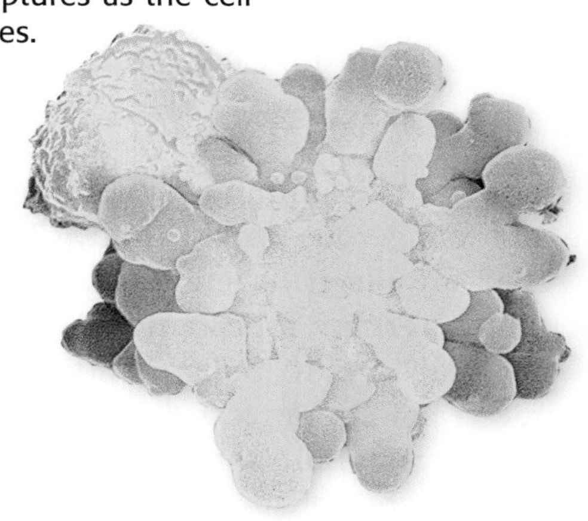

Cancer

cancer a disease in which the cells begin dividing at an uncontrolled rate and become invasive

Healthy cells divide at a carefully regulated rate. Occasionally, a cell doesn't respond to the body's regulation and begins dividing at an uncontrolled rate. As can be seen in **Figure 7,** killer T cells destroy this type of cell. Sometimes, the immune system cannot control the division of these cells. **Cancer** is the condition in which cells divide at an uncontrolled rate.

Many cancers will invade nearby tissues. They can also enter the cardiovascular system or lymphatic system. Cancers can then be transported to other places in the body. Cancers disrupt the normal activities of the organs they have invaded, sometimes leading to death. Today, though, there are many treatments for cancer. Surgery, radiation, and certain drugs can be used to remove or kill cancer cells or slow their division.

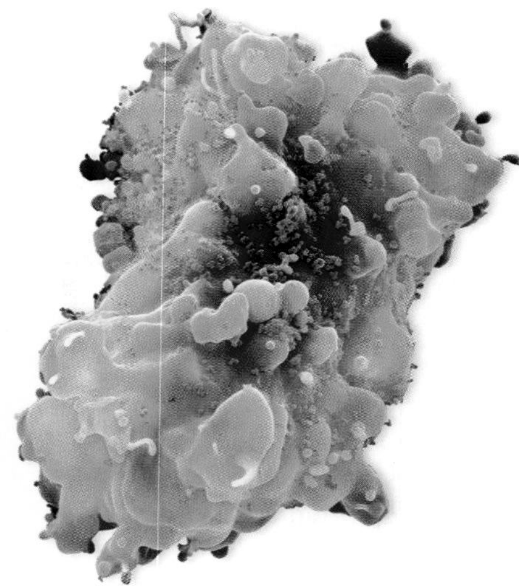

Figure 8 *The blue particles on this helper T cell are human immunodeficiency viruses. They replicated inside the T cell.*

AIDS

The human immunodeficiency virus (HIV) causes acquired immune deficiency syndrome (AIDS). Most viruses infect cells in the nose, mouth, lungs, or intestines, but HIV is different. HIV infects the immune system itself, using helper T cells as factories to produce more viruses. You can see HIV particles in **Figure 8.** The helper T cells are destroyed in the process. Remember that the helper T cells put the B cells and killer T cells to work.

People with AIDS have very few helper T cells, so nothing activates the B cells and killer T cells. Therefore, the immune system cannot attack HIV or any other pathogen. People with AIDS don't usually die of AIDS itself. They die of other diseases that they are unable to fight off.

Reading Check What virus causes AIDS?

SECTION Review

Summary

- Macrophages engulf pathogens, display antigens on their surface, and activate helper T cells. The helper T cells put the killer T cells and B cells to work.
- Killer T cells kill infected cells. B cells make antibodies.
- Fever helps speed immune-cell growth and slow pathogen growth.
- Memory B cells remember how to make an antibody for a pathogen that the body has previously fought.
- An allergy is the overreaction of the immune system to a harmless antigen.
- Autoimmune diseases are responses in which the immune system attacks healthy tissue.
- Cancer cells are cells that undergo uncontrolled division.
- AIDS is a disease that results when the human immunodeficiency virus kills helper T cells.

Using Key Terms

For each pair of terms, explain how the meanings of the terms differ.

1. *B cell* and *T cell*
2. *autoimmune disease* and *allergy*

Understanding Key Ideas

3. Your body's first line of defense against pathogens includes
   a. skin.
   b. macrophages.
   c. T cells.
   d. B cells.
4. List three ways your body defends itself against pathogens.
5. Name three different cells in the immune system, and describe how they respond to pathogens.
6. Describe four challenges to the immune system.
7. What characterizes a cancer cell?

Critical Thinking

8. **Identifying Relationships** Can your body make antibodies for pathogens that you have never been in contact with? Why or why not?
9. **Applying Concepts** If you had chickenpox at age 7, what might prevent you from getting chickenpox again at age 8?

Interpreting Graphics

10. Look at the graph below. Over time, people with AIDS become very sick and are unable to fight off infection. Use the information in the graph below to explain why this occurs.

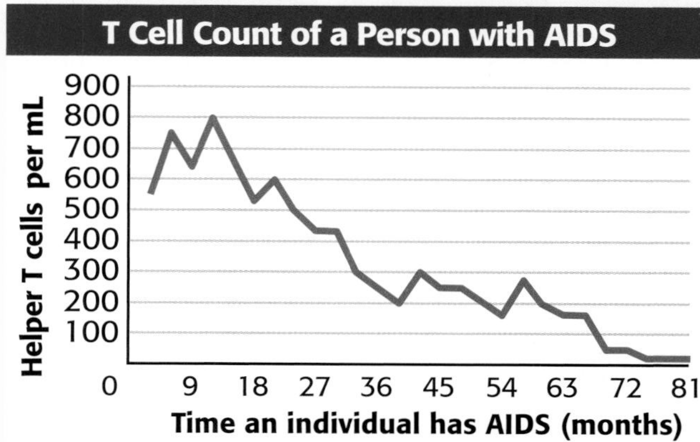

SCILINKS
NSTA
Developed and maintained by the National Science Teachers Association
For a variety of links related to this chapter, go to www.scilinks.org
Topic: Body Defenses; Allergies
SciLinks code: HSM0181; HSM0048

Using Scientific Methods

Skills Practice Lab

Passing the Cold

OBJECTIVES

Investigate how diseases spread.

Analyze data about how diseases spread.

MATERIALS

- beaker or a cup, 200 mL
- eyedropper
- gloves, protective
- solution, unknown, 50 mL

SAFETY

There are more than 100 viruses that cause the symptoms of the common cold. Any of the viruses can be passed from person to person—through the air or through direct contact. In this activity, you will track the progress of an outbreak in your class.

Ask a Question

1. With other members of your group, form a question about the spread of disease. For example "How are cold viruses passed from person to person?" or "How can the progress of an outbreak be modeled?"

Form a Hypothesis

2. Form a hypothesis based on the question you asked.

Test the Hypothesis

3. Obtain an empty cup or beaker, an eyedropper, and 50 mL of one of the solutions from your teacher. Only one student will have the "cold virus" solution. You will see a change in your solution when you have become "infected."
4. Your teacher will divide the class into two equal groups. If there is an extra student, that person will record data on the board. Otherwise, the teacher will act as the recorder.
5. The two groups should form straight lines, facing each other.
6. Each time your teacher says the word *mix,* fill your eyedropper with your solution, and place 10 drops of your solution in the beaker of the person in the line opposite you without touching your eyedropper to the other liquid.
7. Gently stir the liquid in your cup with your eyedropper. Do not put your eyedropper in anyone else's solution.
8. If your solution changes color, raise your hand so that the recorder can record the number of students who have been "infected."
9. Your teacher will instruct one line to move one person to the right. Then, the person at the end of the line without a partner should go to the other end of the line.

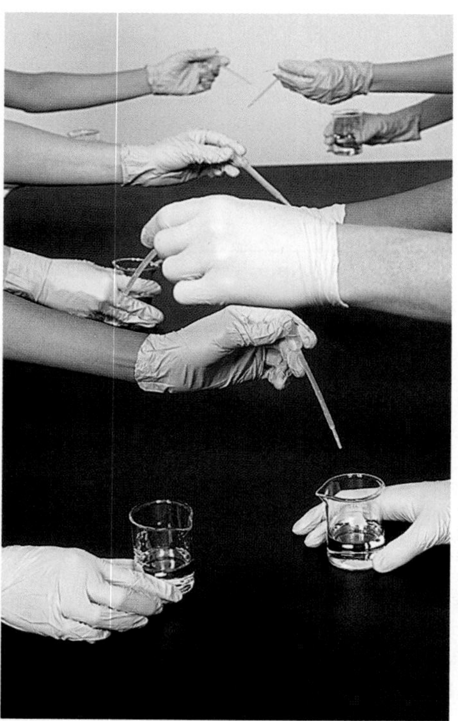

Results of Experiment			
Trial	Number of infected people	Total number of people	Percentage of infected people
1			
2			
3			
4			
5			
6			
7			
8			
9			
10			

10. Repeat steps 5–9 nine more times for a total of 10 trials.

11. Return to your desk, and create a data table in your notebook similar to the table above. The column with the title "Total number of people" will remain the same in every row. Enter the data from the board into your data table.

12. Find the percentage of infected people for the last column by dividing the number of infected people by the total number of people and multiplying by 100 in each line.

Analyze the Results

1. **Describing Events** Did you become infected? If so, during which trial did you become infected?

2. **Examining Data** Did everyone eventually become infected? If so, how many trials were necessary to infect everyone?

Draw Conclusions

3. **Interpreting Information** Explain at least one reason why this simulation may underestimate the number of people who might have been infected in real life.

4. **Applying Conclusions** Use your results to make a line graph showing the change in the infection percentage per trial.

Applying Your Data

Do research in the library or on the Internet to find out some of the factors that contribute to the spread of a cold virus. What is the best and easiest way to reduce your chances of catching a cold? Explain your answer.

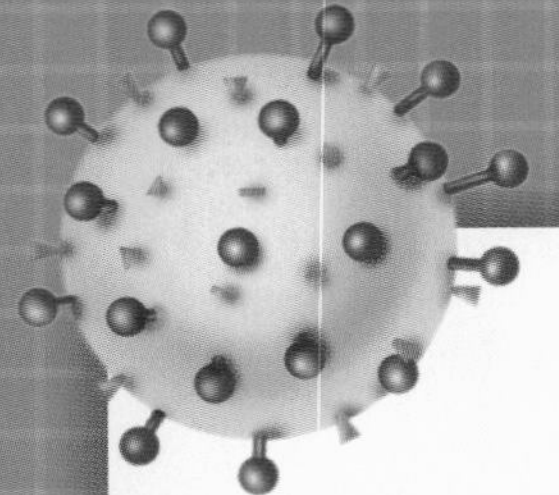

Chapter Review

USING KEY TERMS

Complete each of the following sentences by choosing the correct term from the word bank.

antibody	cancer
infectious disease	B cell
noninfectious disease	T cell
pathogen	allergy

1. A(n) ____ is caused by a pathogen.
2. Antibiotics can be used to kill a(n) ____.
3. Macrophages attract helper ____.
4. A(n) ____ binds to an antigen.
5. An immune-system overreaction to a harmless substance is a(n) ____.
6. ____ is the unregulated growth of cells.

UNDERSTANDING KEY IDEAS

Multiple Choice

7. Pathogens are
   - **a.** all viruses and microorganisms.
   - **b.** viruses and microorganisms that cause disease.
   - **c.** noninfectious organisms.
   - **d.** all bacteria that live in water.
8. Which of the following is an infectious disease?
   - **a.** allergies
   - **b.** rheumatoid arthritis
   - **c.** asthma
   - **d.** a common cold
9. The skin keeps pathogens out by
   - **a.** staying warm enough to kill pathogens.
   - **b.** releasing killer T cells onto the surface.
   - **c.** shedding dead cells and secreting oils.
   - **d.** All of the above
10. Memory B cells
    - **a.** kill pathogens.
    - **b.** activate killer T cells.
    - **c.** activate killer B cells.
    - **d.** produce B cells that make antibodies.
11. A fever
    - **a.** slows pathogen growth.
    - **b.** helps B cells multiply faster.
    - **c.** helps T cells multiply faster.
    - **d.** All of the above
12. Macrophages
    - **a.** make antibodies.
    - **b.** release helper T cells.
    - **c.** live in the gut.
    - **d.** engulf pathogens.

Short Answer

13. Explain how macrophages start an immune response.
14. Describe the role of helper T cells in responding to an infection.
15. Name two ways that you come into contact with pathogens.

CRITICAL THINKING

16 **Concept Mapping** Use the following terms to create a concept map: *macrophages, helper T cells, B cells, antibodies, antigens, killer T cells,* and *memory B cells.*

17 **Identifying Relationships** Why does the disappearance of helper T cells in AIDS patients damage the immune system?

18 **Predicting Consequences** Many people take fever-reducing drugs as soon as their temperature exceeds 37°C. Why might it not be a good idea to reduce a fever immediately with drugs?

19 **Evaluating Data** The risk of dying from a whooping cough vaccine is about one in 1 million. In contrast, the risk of dying from whooping cough is about one in 500. Discuss the pros and cons of this vaccination.

INTERPRETING GRAPHICS

The graph below compares the concentration of antibodies in the blood the first time you are exposed to a pathogen with the concentration of antibodies the next time you are exposed to the pathogen. Use the graph below to answer the questions that follow.

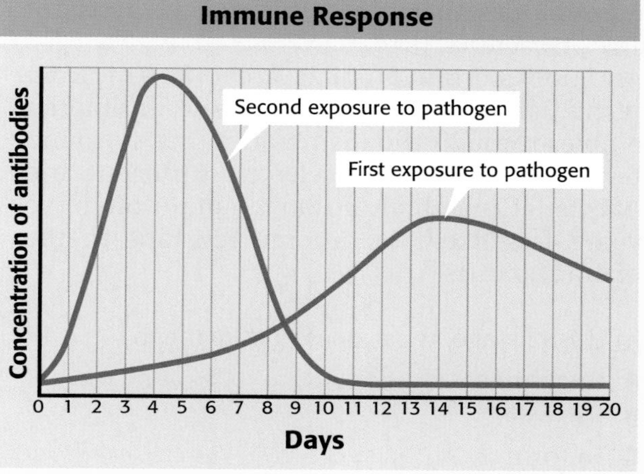

20 Are there more antibodies present during the first week of the first exposure or the first week of the second exposure? Why do you think this is so?

21 What is the difference in recovery time between the first exposure and second exposure? Why?

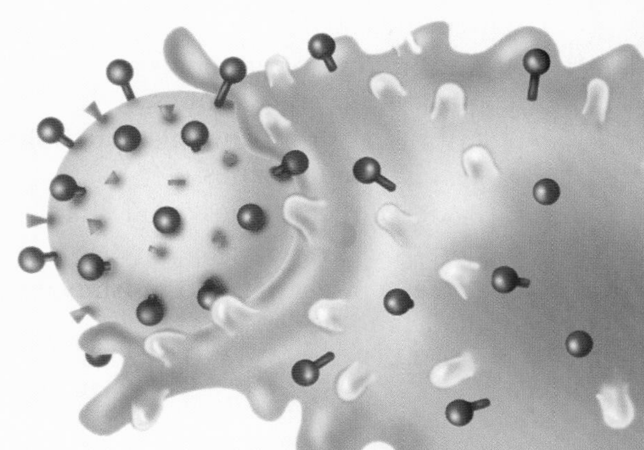

Standardized Test Preparation

READING

Read each of the passages below. Then, answer the questions that follow each passage.

Passage 1 Bacteria are becoming resistant to many human-made antibiotics, which means that the drugs no longer affect the bacteria. Scientists now face the challenge of developing new antibiotics that can overcome the resistant strains of bacteria.

Antibiotics from animals are different from some human-made antibiotics. These antibiotics bore holes through the membranes that surround bacterial cells, causing the cells to disintegrate and die. Bacterial membranes don't <u>mutate</u> often, so they are less likely to become resistant to the animal antibiotics.

1. In this passage, what does *mutate* mean?
- **A** to change
- **B** to grow
- **C** to form
- **D** to degrade

2. Based on the passage, which of the following statements is a fact?
- **F** Bacterial membranes are on the inside of the bacterial cell.
- **G** Bacterial membranes are on the outside of the bacterial cell.
- **H** All strains of bacteria mutate.
- **I** Bacterial membranes never change.

3. Based on the passage, which of the following sentences is false?
- **A** Antibiotics from animals are different from human-made antibiotics.
- **B** Antibiotics from animals bore holes in bacterial membranes.
- **C** Bacterial membranes don't change very often.
- **D** Bacteria rarely develop resistance to human-made antibiotics.

Passage 2 Drinking water in the United States is generally safe, but water lines can break, or treatment plants can become flooded, allowing microorganisms to enter the public water supply. Bacteria growing in foods and beverages can cause illness, too. Refrigerating foods can slow the growth of many of these <u>pathogens</u>, but meat, fish, and eggs that are not cooked enough can still contain dangerous bacteria or parasites. Leaving food out at room temperature can give bacteria such as *salmonella* time to grow and produce toxins in the food. For these reasons, it is important to wash all used cooking tools.

1. Which of the following statements can you infer from this passage?
- **A** Treatment plants help keep drinking water safe.
- **B** Treatment plants never become flooded.
- **C** Eliminating treatment plants would help keep water safe.
- **D** New treatment plants are better than old ones.

2. Which of the following statements can you infer from the passage?
- **F** Bacteria that live in food produce more toxins than molds produce.
- **G** Cooking food thoroughly kills bacteria living in the food.
- **H** Some bacteria are helpful to humans.
- **I** Illnesses caused by bacteria living in food are seldom serious.

3. According to this passage, what do pathogens cause?
- **A** disease
- **B** flooding
- **C** water-line breaks
- **D** water supplies

INTERPRETING GRAPHICS

The graph below shows the reported number of people living with HIV/AIDS. Use the graph to answer the questions that follow.

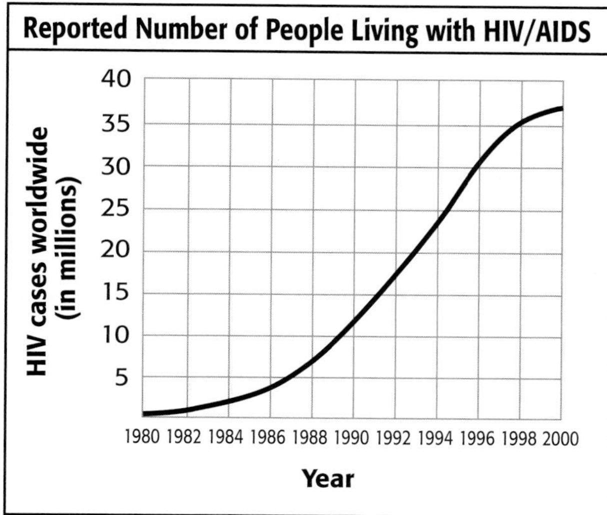

Source: Joint United Nations Program on HIV/AIDS

1. When did the number of people living with HIV/AIDS reach 5 million?

A 1985
B 1986
C 1987
D 1988

2. When did the number of people living with HIV/AIDS reach 30 million?

F 1996
G 1997
H 1998
I 1999

3. When was the rate of increase of people with HIV/AIDS the **greatest**?

A from 1980 to 1982
B from 1984 to 1986
C from 1988 to 1990
D from 1998 to 2000

4. What percentage of the people who are infected with HIV do not yet have AIDS?

F 10%
G 24%
H 75%
I There is not enough information to determine the answer.

5. If the virus continued to spread as the graph indicates, in the year 2002, about how many people would be infected with HIV?

A 30 million
B 35 million
C 39 million
D 60 million

6. Which part of the graph indicates the rate of infection?

F *x*-axis
G *y*-axis
H slope of the line being graphed
I number of years in the sample

MATH

Read each question below, and choose the best answer.

1. Suppose you have 50,000 flu viruses on your fingers and you rub your eyes. Only 20,000 viruses enter your eyes, 10,000 dissolve in chemicals, and 10,000 are washed down into your nose. Of those, you sneeze out 2,000. How many viruses are left to wash down the back of your throat and possibly start an infection?

A 50,000
B 10,000
C 8,000
D 5,000

2. In which of the following lists are the numbers in order from smallest to greatest?

F 0.027, 0.072, 0.270, 0.720
G 0.270, 0.072, 0.720, 0.270
H 0.072, 0.027, 0.270, 0.720
I 0.720, 0.270, 0.072, 0.027

Science in Action

Weird Science

Frogs in the Medicine Cabinet?

Frog skin, mouse intestines, cow lungs, and shark stomachs are all being tested to make more effective medicines to combat harmful bacteria. In 1896, a biologist named Michael Zasloff was studying African clawed frogs. He noticed that cuts in the frogs' skin healed quickly and never became infected. Zasloff decided to investigate further. He found that when a frog was cut, its skin released a liquid antibiotic that killed invading bacteria. Furthermore, sand sharks, moths, pigs, mice, and cows also contain chemicals that kill bacteria and other microorganisms. These useful antibiotics are even found in the small intestines of humans!

Social Studies 

Many medicines were discovered in plants or animals by people living near those plants or animals. Research the origin of one or two common medicines discovered this way. Make a poster showing a world map and the location of the medicines that you researched.

Scientific Discoveries

Medicine for Peanut Allergies

Scientists estimate that 1.5 million people in the United States suffer from peanut allergies. Every year 50 to 100 people in the United States die from an allergic reaction to peanuts. Peanuts and peanut oil are used to make many foods. People who have a peanut allergy sometimes mistakenly eat these foods and suffer severe reactions. A new drug has been discovered to help people control severe reactions. The drug is called TNX-901. The drug is actually an antibody that binds to the antibodies that the body makes during the allergic reaction to the peanuts. By binding these antibodies, the drug controls the allergic response.

Math ACTIVITY

During the testing of the new drug, 84 people were given four injections over the course of 4 months. One-fourth of the people participating received injections of a control that had no medicine in it. The rest of the people participating received different doses of the drug. How many people received the control? How many people received medicine? How many shots containing medicine were administered during the 4-month test?

Careers

Terrel Shepherd III

Nurse Terrel Shepherd III is a registered nurse (RN) at Texas Children's Hospital in Houston, Texas. RNs have many responsibilities. These responsibilities include giving patients their medications, assessing patients' health, and establishing intravenous access. Nurses also serve as a go-between for the patient and the doctor. Although most nurses work in hospitals or clinics, some nurses work for corporations. Pediatric nurses such as Shepherd work specifically with infants, children, and adolescents. The field of nursing offers a wide variety of job opportunities including home-care nurses, traveling nurses, and flight nurses. The hospital alone has many areas of expertise for nurses, including geriatrics (working with the elderly), intensive care, administration, and surgery. Traditionally, nursing has been considered to be a woman's career. However, since nursing began as a profession, men and women have practiced nursing. A career in nursing is possible for anyone who does well in science, enjoys people, and wants to make a difference in people's lives.

Language Arts ACTIVITY

WRITING SKILL Create a brochure that persuades people to consider a career in nursing. Describe nursing as a career, the benefits of becoming a nurse, and the education needed to be a nurse. Illustrate the brochure with pictures of nurses from the Internet or from magazines.

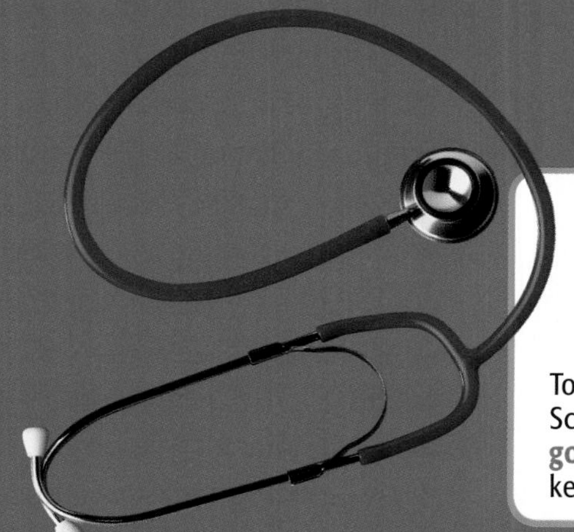

To learn more about these Science in Action topics, visit go.hrw.com and type in the keyword HL5BD6F.

Current Science

Check out Current Science® articles related to this chapter by visiting go.hrw.com. Just type in the keyword HL5CS27.

28

Staying Healthy

About the PHOTO

What do you see in this photo? Sure, you can see five students facing the camera, but what else does the picture tell you? The bright eyes, happy smiles, and shiny hair show radiant health. Having a clear mind and a long, active life depend on having a healthy body. Keeping your body healthy depends on eating well; avoiding drugs, cigarettes, and alcohol; and staying safe.

PRE-READING ACTIVITY

FOLDNOTES **Booklet** Before you read the chapter, create the FoldNote entitled "Booklet" described in the **Study Skills** section of the Appendix. Label each page of the booklet with a main idea from the chapter. As you read the chapter, write what you learn about each main idea on the appropriate page of the booklet.

START-UP ACTIVITY

Conduct a Survey

How healthy are the habits of your classmates? Find out for yourself.

Procedure

1. Copy and answer yes or no to each of the five questions at right. Do not put your name on the survey.

Analysis

1. As a class, record the data from the completed surveys in a chart. For each question, calculate the percentage of your class that answered yes.
2. What good and bad habits do your classmates have?

1. Do you exercise at least three times a week?
2. Do you wear a seat belt every time you ride in a car?
3. Do you eat five or more servings of fruits and vegetables every day?
4. Do you use sunscreen to protect your skin when you are outdoors?
5. Do you eat a lot of high-fat foods?

SECTION 1

Good Nutrition

Does the saying "You are what you eat" mean that you are pizza? No, but substances in pizza help build your body.

Protein in the cheese may become part of your hair. Carbohydrates in the crust can give you energy for your next race.

READING WARM-UP

Objectives

- Identify the six groups of nutrients, and explain their importance to good health.
- Describe the Food Guide Pyramid.
- Understand how to read Nutrition Facts labels.
- Explain the dangers of various nutritional disorders.

Terms to Learn

nutrient
carbohydrate
protein
fat
mineral
vitamin
malnutrition

READING STRATEGY

Reading Organizer As you read this section, create an outline of the section. Use the headings from the section in your outline.

Nutrients

Are you more likely to have potato chips or broccoli for a snack? If you eat many foods that are high in fat, such as potato chips, your food choices probably are not as healthy as they could be. Broccoli is a healthier food than potato chips. But eating only broccoli, as the person in **Figure 1** is doing, does not give you a balanced diet.

To stay healthy, you need to take in **nutrients,** or substances that provide the materials needed for life processes. Nutrients are grouped into six classes: *carbohydrates, proteins, fats, water, vitamins,* and *minerals*. Carbohydrates, proteins, and fats provide energy for the body in units called *Calories* (Cal).

Carbohydrates

Carbohydrates are your body's main source of energy. A **carbohydrate** is a chemical composed of simple sugars. There are two types of carbohydrates: simple and complex. *Simple carbohydrates* are sugars. They are easily digested and give you quick energy. *Complex carbohydrates* are made up of many sugar molecules linked together. They are digested slowly and give you long-lasting energy. Some complex carbohydrates are good sources of fiber. Fiber is a part of a healthy diet and is found in whole-grain foods, such as brown rice and whole-wheat bread. Many fruits and vegetables also contain fiber.

nutrient a substance in food that provides energy or helps form body tissues and that is necessary for life and growth

carbohydrate a class of energy-giving nutrients that includes sugars, starches, and fiber

Figure 1 *Eating only one food, even a healthy food, will not give you all the substances your body needs.*

Protein

Proteins are found in body fluids, muscle, bone, and skin. **Proteins** are nutrients used to build and repair your body. Your body makes the proteins it needs, but it must have the necessary building blocks, called *amino acids*. Your digestive system breaks down protein into individual amino acids that are then used to make new proteins. Some foods, such as poultry, fish, milk, and eggs, provide all of the amino acids your body needs. Foods that contain all of these essential amino acids are called *complete proteins*. *Incomplete proteins* contain only some of the essential amino acids. Most plant foods contain incomplete protein, but eating a variety of plant foods will provide all of the amino acids your body needs.

Figure 2 *This sample meal provides many of the nutrients a growing teenager needs.*

Reading Check What is an incomplete protein? (*See the Appendix for answers to Reading Checks.*)

Fats

Another class of nutrients that is important to a healthy meal, such as the meal shown in **Figure 2,** is fat. **Fats** are energy-storage nutrients. Fats are needed to store and transport vitamins, produce hormones, keep skin healthy, and provide insulation. Fats also provide more energy than either proteins or carbohydrates. There are two types of fats: saturated and unsaturated. *Saturated fats* are found in meat, dairy products, coconut oil, and palm oil. Saturated fats raise blood cholesterol levels. Although *cholesterol* is a fat-like substance found naturally in the body, high levels can increase the risk of heart disease. *Unsaturated fats* and foods high in fiber may help reduce blood cholesterol levels. Your body cannot make unsaturated fats. They must come from vegetable oils and fish in your diet. The body needs both kinds of fats.

protein a molecule that is made up of amino acids and that is needed to build and repair body structures and to regulate processes in the body

fat an energy-storage nutrient that helps the body store some vitamins

Water

You cannot survive for more than a few days without water. Your body is about 70% water. Water is in every cell of your body. The main functions of water are to transport substances, regulate body temperature, and provide lubrication. Some scientists think you should drink at least eight glasses of water a day. When you exercise you need more water, as shown in **Figure 3.** You also get water from other liquids you drink and the foods you eat. Fresh fruits and vegetables, juices, soups, and milk are good sources of water.

Figure 3 *When you exercise, you need to drink more water.*

Table 1 Some Essential Vitamins

Vitamin	What it does	Where you get it
A	keeps skin and eyes healthy; builds strong bones and teeth	yellow and orange fruits and vegetables, leafy greens, meats, and milk
B (various forms)	helps body use carbohydrates; helps blood, nerves, and heart function	meats, whole grains, beans, peas, nuts, and seafood
C	strengthens tissues; helps the body absorb iron, fight disease	citrus fruits, leafy greens, broccoli, peppers, and cabbage
D	builds strong bones and teeth; helps the body use calcium and phosphorus	sunlight, enriched milk, eggs, and fish
E	protects red blood cells from destruction; keeps skin healthy	oils, fats, eggs, whole grains, wheat germ, liver, and leafy greens
K	assists with blood clotting	leafy greens, tomatoes, and potatoes

Minerals

If you eat a balanced diet, you should get all of the vitamins and minerals you need. **Minerals** are elements that are essential for good health. You need six minerals in large amounts: calcium, chloride, magnesium, phosphorus, potassium, and sodium. There are at least 12 minerals that are required in very small amounts. These include fluorine, iodine, iron, and zinc. Calcium is necessary for strong bones and teeth. Magnesium and sodium help the body use proteins. Potassium is needed to regulate your heartbeat and produce muscle movement, and iron is necessary for red blood cell production.

mineral a class of nutrients that are chemical elements that are needed for certain body processes

vitamin a class of nutrients that contain carbon and that are needed in small amounts to maintain health and allow growth

Vitamins

Vitamins are another class of nutrients. **Vitamins** are compounds that control many body functions. Only vitamin D can be made by the body, so you have to get most vitamins from food. **Table 1** provides information about six essential vitamins.

CONNECTION TO Oceanography

Nutritious Seaweed Kelp, a type of seaweed, is a good source of iodine. This nutritious food is grown on special farms off the coasts of China and Japan. What other nutritious foods come from the sea?

Eating for Good Health

Now you have learned which nutrients you need for good health. But how can you be sure to get all the important nutrients in the right amounts? To begin, keep in mind that most teenage girls need about 2,200 Cal per day, and most boys need about 2,800 Cal. Because different foods contain different nutrients, *where* you get your Calories is as important as *how many* you get. The Food Guide Pyramid, shown in **Figure 4,** can help you make good food choices.

Reading Check **Using the Food Guide Pyramid below, design a healthy lunch that includes one food from each food group.**

Brown Bag Test

1. Cut a **brown paper bag** into squares.
2. Gather a variety of **foods.** Place a piece of each food on a different square and leave overnight.
3. What do you see when you remove the food?
4. Which food had the most oil? Which food had the least?

Figure 4 **The Food Guide Pyramid**

The U.S. Department of Agriculture and the Department of Health and Human Services developed the Food Guide Pyramid to help Americans make healthy food choices. The Food Guide Pyramid divides foods into six groups. It shows how many servings you need daily from each group and gives examples of foods for each. This pyramid also provides sample serving sizes for each group. Within each group, the food choices are up to you.

Fats, oils, and sweets
Use sparingly.

Milk, yogurt, and cheese
2 to 3 servings
- 1 cup of milk or yogurt
- 1 1/2 oz of natural cheese
- 2 oz of processed cheese

Meat, poultry, fish, beans, eggs, and nuts 2 to 3 servings
- 2 to 3 oz of cooked poultry, fish, or lean meat
- 1/2 cup of cooked dried beans
- 1 egg

Vegetables 3 to 5 servings
- 1/2 cup of chopped vegetables
- 1 cup of raw, leafy vegetables
- 3/4 cup of cooked vegetables

Fruits 2 to 4 servings
- 1 medium apple, banana, or orange
- 1/2 cup of chopped, cooked, or canned fruit
- 3/4 cup of fruit juice

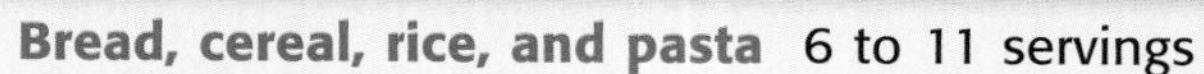

Bread, cereal, rice, and pasta 6 to 11 servings
- 1 slice of bread
- 1 oz of ready-to-eat cereal
- 1/2 cup of rice or pasta
- 1/2 cup of cooked cereal

Nutrition Facts

Serving Size 1/2 cup (120 ml) ← **Serving information**
Servings per Container 2.5

Amount per Serving	Prepared
Calories	70 ← **Number of Calories per serving**
Calories from Fat	25
	% Daily Value
Total Fat 2.5 g	4%
Saturated Fat 1 g	5%
Cholesterol 15 mg	5%
Sodium 960 mg	40%
Total Carbohydrate 8 g	3%
Dietary Fiber less than 1 g	4%
Sugars 1 g	
Protein 3 g	
Vitamin A	15%
Vitamin C	0%
Calcium	0%
Iron	4%

Percentage of daily values

*Percent Daily Values are based on a 2,000 Calorie diet. Your daily values may be higher or lower depending on your Calorie needs:

	Calories	2,000	2,500
Total Fat	Less than	65g	80g
Sat Fat	Less than	20g	25g
Cholesterol	Less than	300mg	300mg
Sodium	Less than	2,400mg	2,400mg
Total Carbohydrate		300g	375g
Dietary Fiber		25g	30g
Protein		50g	60g

Figure 5 *Nutrition Facts labels provide a lot of information.*

Reading Food Labels

Packaged foods must have Nutrition Facts labels. **Figure 5** shows a Nutrition Facts label for chicken noodle soup. Nutrition Facts labels show what amount of each nutrient is in one serving of the food. You can tell whether a food is high or low in a nutrient by looking at its daily value. Reading food labels can help you make healthy eating choices. The percentage of daily values shown is based on a diet that consists of 2,000 Cal per day. Most teenagers need more than 2,000 Cal per day. The number of Calories needed depends on factors such as height, weight, age, and level of activity. Playing sports and exercising use up Calories that need to be replaced for you to grow.

✓ Reading Check **For what nutrients does chicken noodle soup provide more than 10% of the daily value?**

Nutritional Disorders

Unhealthy eating habits can cause nutritional disorders. **Malnutrition** occurs when someone does not eat enough of the nutrients needed by the body. Malnutrition can result from eating too few or too many Calories or not taking in enough of the right nutrients. Malnutrition affects how one looks and how quickly one's body can repair damage and fight illness.

malnutrition a disorder of nutrition that results when a person does not consume enough of each of the nutrients that are needed by the human body

Anorexia Nervosa and Bulimia Nervosa

Anorexia nervosa (AN uh REKS ee uh nuhr VOH suh) is an eating disorder characterized by self-starvation and an intense fear of gaining weight. Anorexia nervosa can lead to severe malnutrition.

Bulimia nervosa (boo LEE mee uh nuhr VOH suh) is a disorder characterized by binge eating followed by induced vomiting. Sometimes, people suffering from bulimia nervosa use laxatives or diuretics to rid their bodies of food and water. Bulimia nervosa can damage teeth and the digestive system and can lead to kidney and heart failure.

Both anorexia and bulimia can cause weak bones, low blood pressure, and heart problems. These eating disorders can be fatal if not treated. If you are worried that you or someone you know may have an eating disorder, talk to an adult.

What Percentage?

Use the Nutrition Facts label above to answer the following question. The recommended daily value of fat is 72 g for teenage girls and 90 g for teenage boys. What percentage of the daily recommended fat value is provided in one cup of soup?

Obesity

Eating too much food that is high in fat and low in other nutrients, such as junk food and fast food, can lead to malnutrition. *Obesity* (oh BEE suh tee) is having an extremely high percentage of body fat. People suffering from obesity may not be eating a variety of foods that provide them with the correct balance of essential nutrients. Having an inactive lifestyle can also contribute to obesity.

Obesity increases the risk of high blood pressure, heart disease, and diabetes. Eating a more balanced diet and exercising regularly can help reduce obesity. Obesity may also be caused by other factors. Scientists are studying the links between obesity and heredity.

SECTION Review

Summary

- A healthy diet has a balance of carbohydrates, proteins, fats, water, vitamins, and minerals.
- The Food Guide Pyramid is a good guide for healthy eating.
- Nutrition Facts labels provide information needed to plan a healthy diet.
- Anorexia nervosa and bulimia nervosa cause malnutrition and damage to many body systems.
- Obesity can lead to heart disease and diabetes.

Using Key Terms

1. In your own words, write a definition for each of the following terms: *nutrient, mineral,* and *vitamin.*

Understanding Key Ideas

2. Malnutrition can be caused by
   a. obesity.
   b. bulimia nervosa.
   c. anorexia nervosa.
   d. All of the above
3. What information is found on a Nutrition Facts label?
4. Give an example of a carbohydrate, a protein, and a fat.
5. If vitamins and minerals do not supply energy, why are they important to a healthy diet?
6. How do anorexia nervosa and bulimia nervosa differ?
7. How can someone who is obese suffer from malnutrition?

Math Skills

8. If you eat 2,500 Cal per day and 20% are from fat, 30% are from protein, and 50% are from carbohydrates, how many Calories of each nutrient do you eat?

Critical Thinking

9. **Applying Concepts** Name some of the nutrients that can be found in a glass of milk.
10. **Identifying Relationships** Explain how eating a variety of foods can help ensure good nutrition.
11. **Predicting Consequences** How would your growth be affected if your diet consistently lacked important nutrients?
12. **Applying Concepts** Explain how you can use the Nutrition Facts label to choose food that is high in calcium.

SCILINKS.
NSTA
Developed and maintained by the National Science Teachers Association
For a variety of links related to this chapter, go to www.scilinks.org
Topic: Food Pyramids; Nutritional Disorders
SciLinks code: HSM0598; HSM1057

SECTION 2

Risks of Alcohol and Other Drugs

READING WARM-UP

Objectives

- Describe the difference between psychological and physical dependence.
- Explain the hazards of tobacco, alcohol, and illegal drugs.
- Distinguish between the positive and negative uses of drugs.

Terms to Learn

drug
addiction
nicotine
alcoholism
narcotic

READING STRATEGY

Reading Organizer As you read this section, make a table comparing the positive and negative uses of drugs.

You see them in movies and on television and read about them in magazines. But what are drugs?

You are exposed to information, and misinformation, about drugs every day. So, how can you make the best decisions?

What Is a Drug?

Any chemical substance that causes a physical or psychological change is called a **drug.** Drugs come in many forms, as shown in **Figure 1.** Some drugs enter the body through the skin. Other drugs are swallowed, inhaled, or injected. Drugs are classified by their effects. *Analgesics* (AN'l JEE ziks) relieve pain. *Antibiotics* (AN tie bie AHT iks) fight bacterial infections, and *antihistamines* (AN tie HIS tuh MEENZ) control cold and allergy symptoms. *Stimulants* speed up the central nervous system, and *depressants* slow it down. When used correctly, legal drugs can help your body heal. When used illegally or improperly, however, drugs can do great harm.

Dependence and Addiction

The body can develop *tolerance* to a drug. Tolerance means that larger and larger doses of the drug are needed to get the same effect. The body can also form a *physical dependence* or need for a drug. If the body doesn't receive a drug that it is physically dependent on, withdrawal symptoms occur. Withdrawal symptoms include nausea, vomiting, pain, and tremors.

Addiction is the loss of control of drug-taking behavior. Once addicted, a person finds it very hard to stop taking a drug. Sometimes, the need for a drug is not due only to physical dependence. Some people also form *psychological dependence* on a drug, which means that they feel powerful cravings for the drug.

Figure 1 *All of these products contain drugs.*

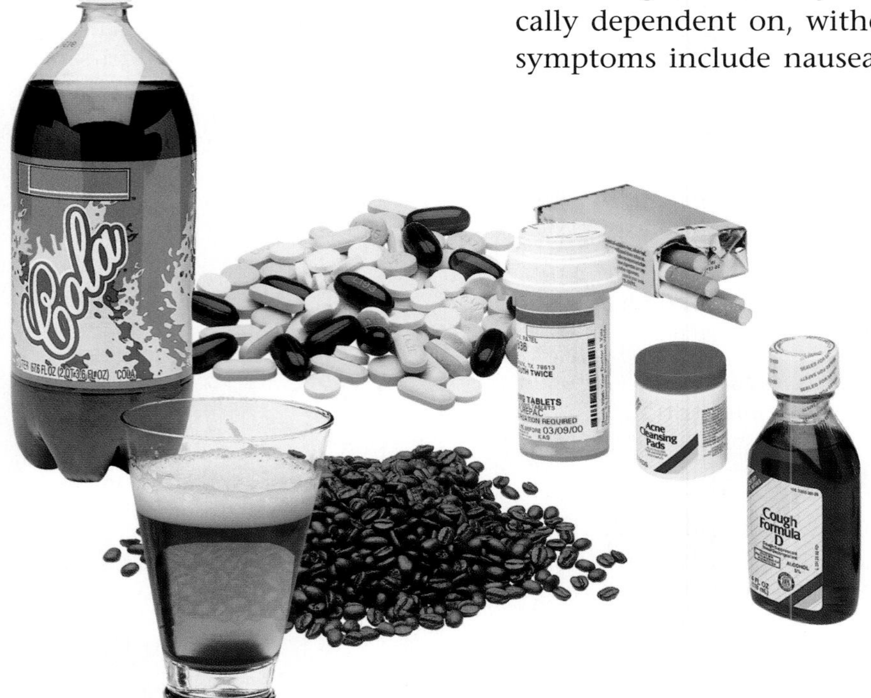

Types of Drugs

There are many kinds of drugs. Some drugs are made from plants, and some are made in a lab. You can buy some drugs at the grocery store, while others can be prescribed only by a doctor. Some drugs are illegal to buy, sell, or possess.

drug any substance that causes a change in a person's physical or psychological state

addiction a dependence on a substance, such as alcohol or another drug

Herbal Medicines

Information about herbal medicines has been handed down for centuries, and some herbs contain chemicals with important healing properties. The tea in **Figure 2** contains chamomile and is made from a plant. Chamomile has chemicals in it that can help you sleep. However, herbs are drugs and should be used carefully. The Federal Drug Administration does not regulate herbal medicines or teas and cannot guarantee their safety.

Figure 2 *Some herbs can be purchased in health-food stores. Medicinal herbs should always be used with care.*

Over-the-Counter and Prescription Drugs

Over-the-counter drugs can be bought without a prescription. A prescription is written by a doctor and describes the drug, directions for use, and the amount of the drug to be taken.

Many over-the-counter and prescription drugs are powerful healing agents. However, some drugs also produce unwanted side effects. *Side effects* are uncomfortable symptoms, such as nausea, headaches, drowsiness, or more serious problems.

Whether purchased with or without a prescription, all drugs must be used with care. Information on proper use can be found on the label. **Figure 3** shows some general drug safety tips.

Reading Check **What is the difference between an over-the-counter drug and a prescription drug?** (*See the Appendix for answers to Reading Checks.*)

Figure 3 **Drug Safety Tips**

- *Never take another person's prescription medicine.*
- *Read the label before each use. Always follow the instructions on the label and those provided by your doctor or pharmacist.*
- *Do not take more or less medication than prescribed.*
- *Consult a doctor if you have any side effects.*
- *Throw away leftover and out-of-date medicines.*

Figure 4 **Effects of Smoking**

Healthy lung tissue of a nonsmoker

Damaged lung tissue of a smoker

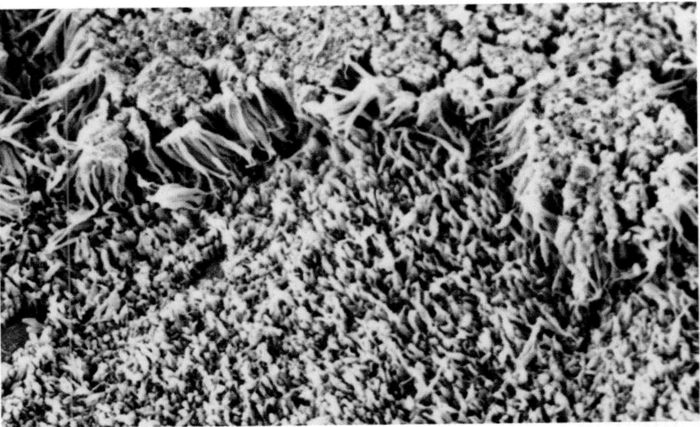

nicotine a toxic, addictive chemical that is found in tobacco and that is one of the major contributors to the harmful effects of smoking

alcoholism a disorder in which a person repeatedly drinks alcoholic beverages in an amount that interferes with the person's health and activities

Tobacco

Cigarettes are addictive, and smoking has serious health effects. **Nicotine** (NIK uh TEEN) is a chemical in tobacco that increases heart rate and blood pressure and is extremely addictive. Smokers experience a decrease in physical endurance. **Figure 4** shows the effects of smoking on the cilia of your lungs. Cilia clean the air you breathe and prevent debris from entering your lungs. Smoking increases the chances of lung cancer, and it has been linked to other cancers, emphysema, chronic bronchitis, and heart disease. Experts estimate that there are more than 430,000 deaths related to smoking each year in the United States. Secondhand smoke also poses significant health risks.

Like cigarettes, smokeless, or chewing, tobacco is addictive and can cause health problems. Nicotine is absorbed through the lining of the mouth. Smokeless tobacco increases the risk of several cancers, including mouth and throat cancer. It also causes gum disease and yellowing of the teeth.

Alcohol

It is illegal in most of the United States for people under the age of 21 to use alcohol. Alcohol slows down the central nervous system and can cause memory loss. Excessive use of alcohol can damage the liver, pancreas, brain, nerves, and cardiovascular system. In very large quantities, alcohol can cause death. Alcohol is a factor in more than half of all suicides, murders, and accidental deaths. **Figure 5** shows the results of one alcohol-related accident. Alcohol also affects decision making and can lead you to take unhealthy risks.

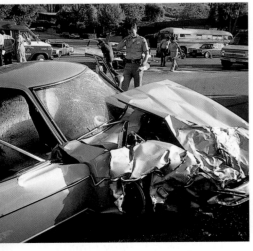

Figure 5 *This car was in an accident involving a drunk driver.*

People can suffer from **alcoholism,** which means that they are physically and psychologically dependent on alcohol. Alcoholism is considered a disease, and genetic factors are thought to influence the development of alcoholism in some people.

Figure 6 *Smoking marijuana can make your health and dreams go up in smoke.*

Marijuana

Marijuana is an illegal drug that comes from the Indian hemp plant. Marijuana affects different people in different ways. It may increase anxiety or cause feelings of paranoia. Marijuana slows reaction time, impairs thinking, and causes a loss of coordination. Regular use of marijuana can affect many areas of your life, as described in **Figure 6.**

narcotic a drug that is derived from opium and that relieves pain and induces sleep

Cocaine

Cocaine and its more purified form, crack, are made from the coca plant. Both drugs are illegal and highly addictive. Users can become addicted to them in a very short time. Cocaine can produce feelings of intense excitement followed by anxiety and depression. Both drugs increase heart rate and blood pressure and can cause heart attacks, even among first-time users.

Reading Check What are two dangers to users of cocaine?

Narcotics and Designer Drugs

Drugs made from the opium plant are called **narcotics.** Some narcotics are used to treat severe pain. Narcotics are illegal unless prescribed by a doctor. Some narcotics are never legal. For example, heroin is one of the most addictive narcotics and is always illegal. Heroin is usually injected, and users often share needles. Therefore, heroin users have a high risk of becoming infected with diseases such as hepatitis and AIDS. Heroin users can also die of an overdose of the drug.

Other illegal drugs include inhalants, barbiturates (bahr BICH uhr itz), amphetamines (am FET uh MEENZ), and *designer drugs*. Designer drugs are made by making small changes to existing drugs. Ecstasy, or "X," is a designer drug that causes feelings of well-being. Over time, the drug causes lesions (LEE zhuhnz), or holes, in a user's brain, as shown in **Figure 7.** Ecstasy users are also more likely to develop depression.

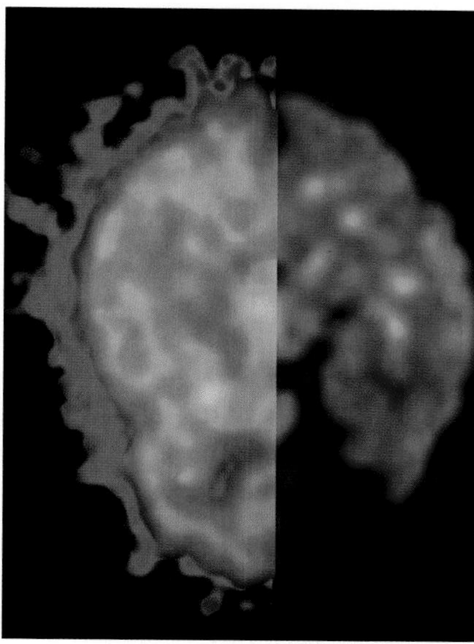

Figure 7 *The brain scan on the left shows a healthy brain. The scan on the right is from a teenager who has regularly used Ecstasy.*

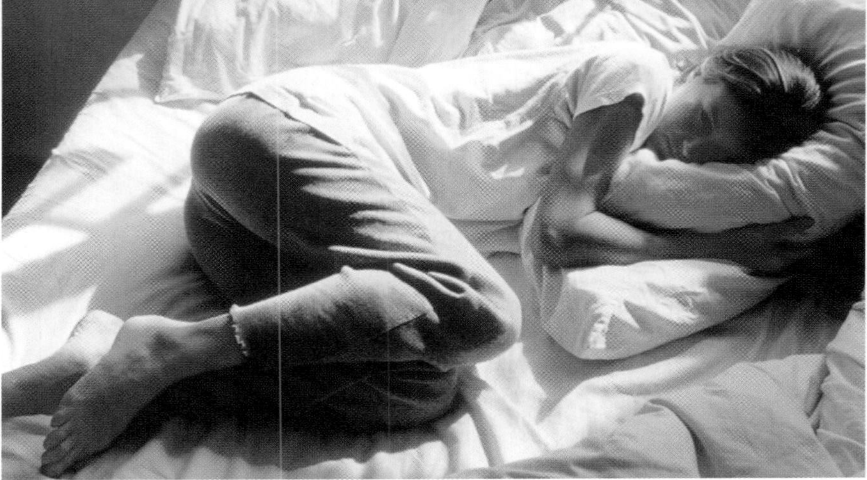

Figure 8 *Drug abuse can leave you depressed and feeling alone.*

Figure 9 Drug Myths

Myth ***"It's only alcohol, not drugs."***

Reality Alcohol is a mood-altering and mind-altering drug. It affects the central nervous system and is addictive.

Myth ***"I won't get hooked on one or two cigarettes a day."***

Reality Addiction is not related to the amount of a drug used. Some people become addicted after using a drug once or twice.

Myth ***"I can quit any time I want."***

Reality Addicts may quit and return to drug usage many times. Their inability to stay drug-free shows how powerful the addiction is.

Good Reasons

WRITING SKILL Discuss with your parent the possible effects of drug abuse on your family. Then, write yourself a letter giving reasons why you should stay drug-free. Put your letter in a safe place. If you ever find yourself thinking about using drugs, take out your letter and read it.

ACTIVITY

Hallucinogens

Hallucinogens (huh LOO si nuh juhnz) distort the senses and cause mood changes. Users have hallucinations, which means that they see and hear things that are not real. LSD and PCP are powerful, illegal hallucinogens. Sniffing glue or solvents can also cause hallucinations and serious brain damage.

Drug Abuse

A drug user takes a drug to prevent or improve a medical condition. The drug user obtains the drug legally and uses the drug properly. A drug abuser does not take a drug to relieve a medical condition. An abuser may take drugs for the temporary good feelings they produce, to escape from problems, or to belong to a group. The drug is often obtained illegally, and it is often taken without knowledge of the drug's dangers.

Reading Check **What is the difference between drug use and drug abuse?**

How Drug Abuse Starts

Nicotine, alcohol, and marijuana are sometimes called *gateway drugs* because they are often the first drugs a person abuses. The abuse of other, more dangerous drugs may follow the abuse of gateway drugs. Peer pressure is often the reason that young people begin to use drugs. Teenagers may drink, smoke, or try marijuana to make friends or avoid being teased. Because drug abusers often stand out, it can sometimes be hard to see that many teenagers do not abuse drugs.

Many teenagers begin using illegal drugs to feel part of a group, but drug abuse has many serious consequences. Drug abuse can lead to problems with friends, family, school, and handling money. These problems often lead to depression and social isolation, as shown in **Figure 8.**

Many people who start using drugs do not recognize the dangers. Misinformation about drugs is everywhere. Several common drug myths are discussed in **Figure 9.**

Getting Off Drugs

People who abuse drugs undergo emotional and physical changes. Teenagers who had few problems often begin to have problems with school, family, and money when they start to use drugs.

The first step to quitting drugs is to admit to abusing drugs and to decide to stop. It is important for the addicted person to get the proper medical treatment. There are drug treatment centers, like the one shown in **Figure 10,** available to help. Getting off drugs can be extremely difficult. Withdrawal symptoms are often painful, and powerful cravings for a drug can continue long after a person quits. But people who stop abusing drugs lead happier and healthier lives.

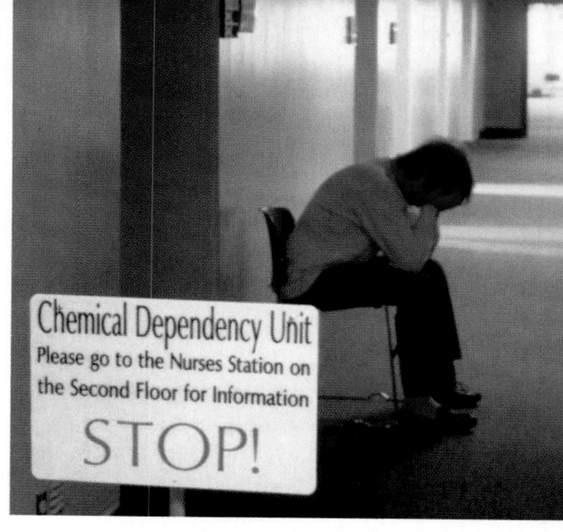

Figure 10 *Drug treatment centers help people get off drugs and back on track to healthier, happier lives.*

SECTION Review

Summary

- Physical dependence causes withdrawal symptoms when a person stops using a drug. Psychological dependence causes powerful cravings.
- There are many types of drugs, including over-the-counter, prescription, and herbal medicines.
- Tobacco contains the highly addictive chemical nicotine.
- Abuse of alcohol can lead to alcoholism.
- Illegal drugs include marijuana, cocaine, hallucinogens, designer drugs, and many narcotics.
- Getting off drugs requires proper medical treatment.

Using Key Terms

1. In your own words, write a definition for the terms *drug, addiction,* and *narcotic.*

Understanding Key Ideas

2. Which of the following products does NOT contain a drug?
   a. cola
   b. fruit juice
   c. herbal tea
   d. cough syrup
3. Describe the difference between physical and psychological dependence.
4. What is the difference between drug use and drug abuse?
5. How does addiction occur, and what are two consequences of drug addiction?
6. Name two different kinds of illegal drugs, and give examples of each.

Math Skills

7. If 2,200 people between the ages of 16 and 20 die every year in alcohol-related car crashes, how many die every day?

Critical Thinking

8. **Analyzing Relationships** How are nicotine, alcohol, heroin, and cocaine similar? How are they different?
9. **Analyzing Ideas** What are two ways that a person who abuses drugs can get in trouble with the law?
10. **Predicting Consequences** How can drug abuse damage family relationships?
11. **Making Inferences** Driving a car while under the influence of drugs can put others in danger. Describe another situation in which one person's drug abuse could put other people in danger.

SCILINKS®
NSTA
Developed and maintained by the National Science Teachers Association
For a variety of links related to this chapter, go to www.scilinks.org
Topic: Drug and Alcohol Abuse
SciLinks code: HSM0428

SECTION 3

Healthy Habits

Do you like playing sports or acting in plays? How does your health affect your favorite activities?

Whatever you do, the better your health is, the better you can perform. Keeping yourself healthy is a daily responsibility.

READING WARM-UP

Objectives

- Describe three important aspects of good hygiene.
- Explain why exercise and sleep are important to good health.
- Describe methods of handling stress.
- List three ways to stay safe at home, on the road, and outdoors.
- Plan what you would do in the case of an accident.

Terms to Learn

hygiene
aerobic exercise
stress

READING STRATEGY

Prediction Guide Before reading this section, write the title of each heading in this section. Next, under each heading, write what you think you will learn.

Taking Care of Your Body

The science of preserving and protecting your health is known as **hygiene.** It sounds simple, but washing your hands is the best way to prevent the spread of disease and infection. You should always wash your hands after using the bathroom and before and after handling food. Taking care of your skin, hair, and teeth is important for good hygiene. Good hygiene includes regularly using sunscreen, shampooing your hair, and brushing and flossing your teeth daily.

hygiene the science of health and ways to preserve health

Good Posture

Posture is also important to health. Good posture helps you look and feel your best. Bad posture strains your muscles and ligaments and makes breathing difficult. To have good posture, imagine a vertical line passing through your ear, shoulder, hip, knee, and ankle when you stand, as shown in **Figure 1.** When working at a desk, you should maintain good posture by pulling your chair forward and planting your feet firmly on the floor.

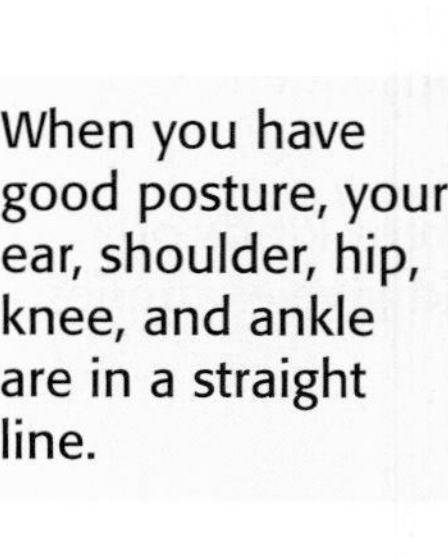
When you have good posture, your ear, shoulder, hip, knee, and ankle are in a straight line.

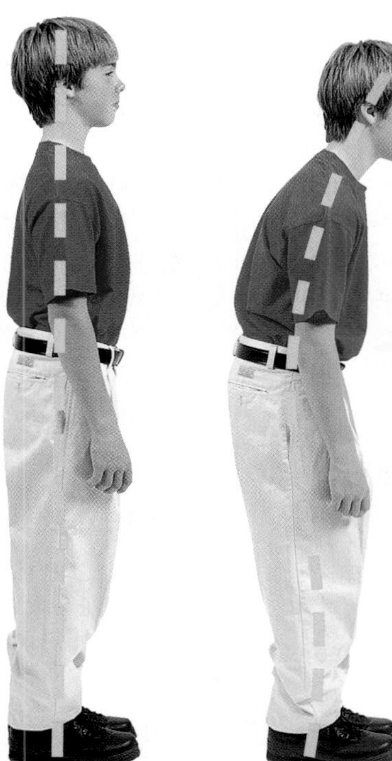
Bad posture strains your muscles and ligaments and can make breathing difficult.

Figure 1 *A slumped posture strains your lower back.*

Exercise

Aerobic exercise at least three times a week is essential to good health. **Aerobic exercise** is vigorous, constant exercise of the whole body for 20 minutes or more. Walking, running, swimming, and biking are all examples of aerobic exercise. **Figure 2** shows another popular aerobic exercise—basketball.

Aerobic exercise increases the heart rate. As a result, more oxygen is taken in and distributed throughout the body. Over time, aerobic exercise strengthens the heart, lungs, and bones. It burns Calories, helps your body conserve some nutrients, and aids digestion. It also gives you more energy and stamina. Aerobic exercise protects your physical and mental health.

Figure 2 *Aerobic exercise can be fun if you choose an activity you enjoy.*

Reading Check **What are two benefits of regular exercise?** (*See the Appendix for answers to Reading Checks.*)

Sleep

Believe it or not, teenagers actually need more sleep than younger children. Do you ever fall asleep in class, like the girl in **Figure 3,** or feel tired in the middle of the afternoon? If so, you may not be getting enough sleep. Scientists say that teenagers need about 9.5 hours of sleep each night.

At night, the body goes through several cycles of progressively deeper sleep, with periods of lighter sleep in between. If you do not sleep long enough, you will not enter the deepest, most restful period of sleep.

aerobic exercise physical exercise intended to increase the activity of the heart and lungs to promote the body's use of oxygen

Figure 3 *If you fall asleep easily during the day, you are probably not getting enough sleep.*

CONNECTION TO Language Arts

Dreamy Poetry

You are not wrong, who deem
That my days have been a dream;
Yet if hope has flown away
In a night, or in a day,
In a vision, or in none,
Is it therefore the less gone?
All that we see or seem
Is but a dream within a dream.

(Edgar Allan Poe,
"A Dream Within a Dream")

What do you think Poe means by "a dream within a dream?" Why do you think there are many poems written about dreams or sleep?

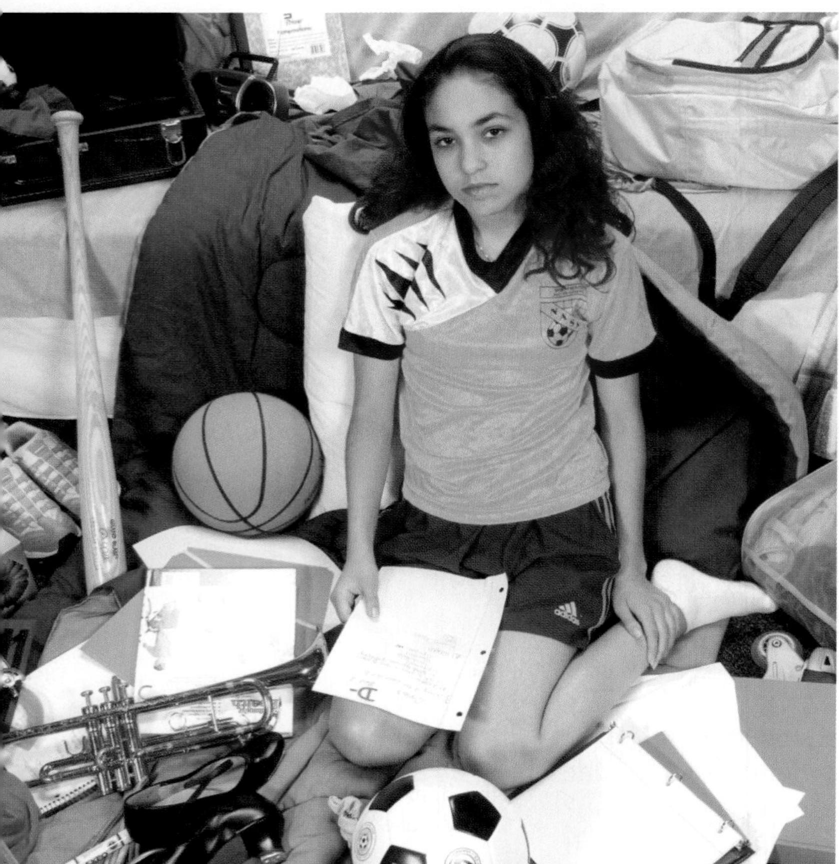

Figure 4 *Can you identify all of the things in this picture that could cause stress?*

Coping with Stress

You have a big soccer game tomorrow. Are you excited and ready for action? You got a low grade on your English paper. Are you upset or angry? The game and the test are causing you stress. **Stress** is the physical and mental response to pressure.

Some stress is a normal part of life. Stress stimulates your body to prepare for difficult or dangerous situations. However, sometimes you may have no outlet for the stress, and it builds up. Many things are causing stress for the girl shown in **Figure 4.** Excess stress is harmful to your health and can decrease your ability to carry out your daily activities.

You may not even realize you are stressed until your body reacts. Perhaps you get a headache, have an upset stomach, or lie awake at night. You might feel tired all the time or begin an old nervous habit, such as nail-biting. You may become irritable or resentful. All of these things can be signs of too much stress.

Dealing with Stress

stress a physical or mental response to pressure

Different people are stressed by different things. Once you identify the source of the stress, you can find ways to deal with it. If you cannot remove the cause of stress, here are some ideas for handling stress.

- Share your problems. Talk things over with someone you trust, such as a parent, friend, teacher, or school counselor.
- Make a list of all the things you would like to get done, and rank the things in order of importance. Do the most important things first.
- Exercise regularly, and get enough sleep.
- Pet a friendly animal.
- Spend some quiet time alone, or practice deep breathing or other relaxation techniques.

For another activity related to this chapter, go to **go.hrw.com** and type in the keyword **HL5BD7W.**

Injury Prevention

Have you ever fallen off your bike or sprained your ankle? Accidents happen, and they can cause injury and even death. It is impossible to prevent all accidents, but you can decrease your risk by using your common sense and following basic safety rules.

Safety Outdoors

Always dress appropriately for the weather and for the activity. Never hike or camp alone. Tell someone where you are going and when you expect to return. If you do not bring water from home, be sure to purify any water you drink in the wilderness.

Learn how to swim. It could save your life! Never swim alone, and do not dive into shallow water or water of unknown depth. When in a boat, wear a life jacket. If a storm threatens, get out of the water and seek shelter.

Reading Check Name three safety tips for the outdoors.

Safety at Home

Many accidents can be avoided. **Figure 5** shows tips for safety around the house.

Figure 5 Home Safety Tips

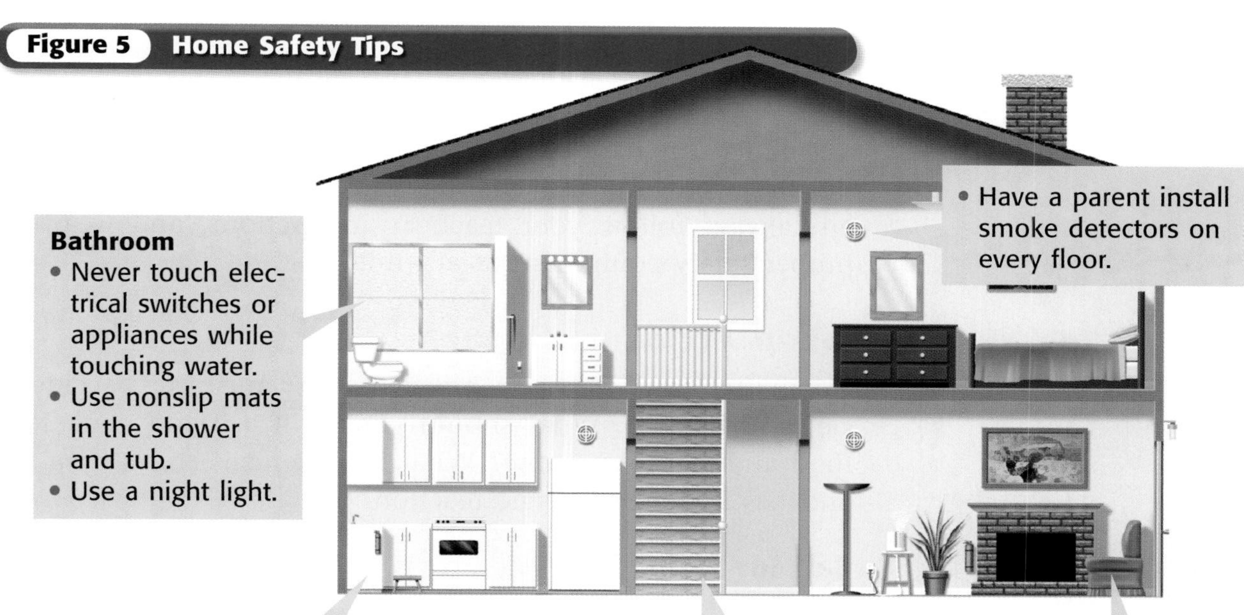

Bathroom
• Never touch electrical switches or appliances while touching water.
• Use nonslip mats in the shower and tub.
• Use a night light.
• Have a parent install smoke detectors on every floor.
Kitchen
• Clean up spills quickly.
• Do not allow pot handles to extend over the edge of the stove.
• Use a stool to reach high shelves.
• Keep grease and drippings away from open flames.
Entrance and Stairs
• Use a railing.
• Never leave objects on stairs.
Living Room
• Keep electrical cords out of walkways.
• Do not plug too many electrical devices into one outlet.

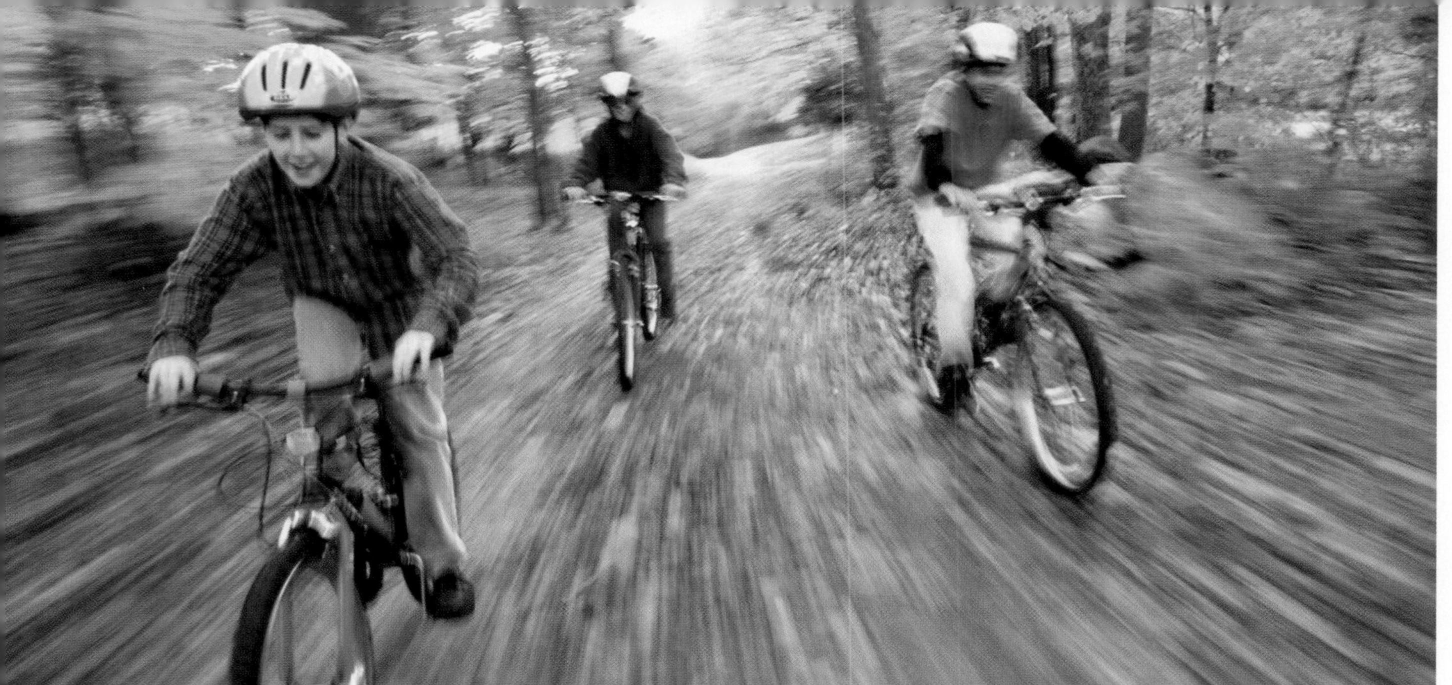

Figure 6 *It is always important to use the appropriate safety equipment.*

Safety on the Road

In the car, always wear a seat belt, even if you are traveling only a short distance. Never ride in a car with someone who has been drinking. Safety equipment and common sense are your best defense against injury. When riding a bicycle, always wear a helmet like those shown in **Figure 6.** Ride with traffic, and obey all traffic rules. Be sure to signal when stopping or turning.

Safety in Class

Accidents can happen in school, especially in a lab class or during woodworking class. To avoid hurting yourself and others, always follow your teacher's instructions, and wear the proper safety equipment at all times.

When Accidents Happen

No matter how well you practice safety measures, accidents can still happen. What should you do if a friend chokes on food and cannot breathe? What if a friend is stung by a bee and has a violent allergic reaction?

Call for Help

Figure 7 *When calling 911, stay calm and listen carefully to what the dispatcher tells you.*

Once you've checked for other dangers, call for medical help immediately, as the person shown in **Figure 7** is doing. In most communities, you can dial 911. Speak slowly and clearly. Give the complete address and a description of the location. Describe the accident, the number of people injured, and the types of injuries. Ask what to do, and listen carefully to the instructions. Let the other person hang up first to be sure there are no more questions or instructions for you.

Learn First Aid

If you want to learn more about what to do in an emergency, you can take a first-aid or CPR course, such as the one shown in **Figure 8.** *CPR* can revive a person who is not breathing and has no heartbeat. If you are over 12 years old, you can become certified in both CPR and first aid. Some baby-sitting classes also provide information on first aid. The American Red Cross, community organizations, and local hospitals offer these classes. However, you should not attempt any lifesaving procedure unless you have been trained.

Reading Check What is CPR, and how can you learn it?

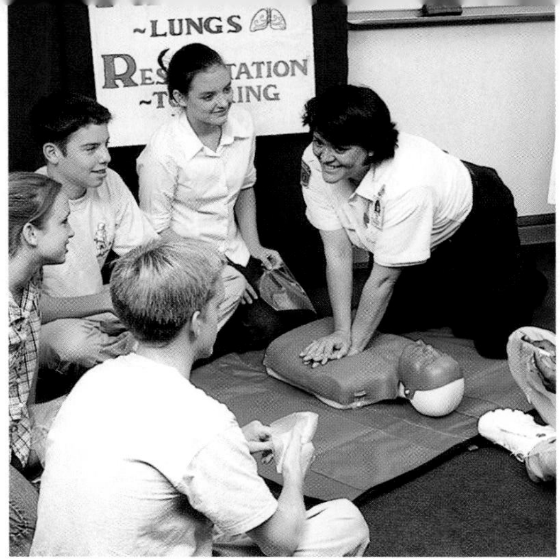

Figure 8 *These teenagers are taking a CPR course to prepare themselves for emergency situations.*

SECTION Review

Summary

- Good hygiene includes taking care of your skin, hair, and teeth.
- Good posture is important to health.
- Exercise keeps your heart, lungs, and bones healthy.
- Teenagers need more than 9 hours of sleep to stay rested and healthy.
- Coping with stress is an important part of staying physically and emotionally healthy.
- It is important to be aware of the possible hazards around your home, outdoors, and at school. Using the appropriate safety equipment can also help keep you safe.

Using Key Terms

Complete each of the following sentences by choosing the correct term from the word bank.

hygiene, aerobic exercise, sleep, stress

1. The science of protecting your health is called ___.
2. ___ strengthens your heart, lungs, and bones.
3. ___ is the physical and mental response to pressure.

Understanding Key Ideas

4. Which of the following is important for good health?
   a. irregular exercise
   b. getting your hair cut
   c. taking care of your teeth
   d. getting plenty of sun
5. List two things you should do when calling for help in a medical emergency.
6. List three ways to stay safe when you are outside, and three ways to stay safe at home.
7. How do seat belts and safety equipment protect you?

Math Skills

8. It is estimated that only 65% of adults wear their seat belts. If there are 10,000 people driving in your area right now, how many of them are wearing their seat belts?

Critical Thinking

9. **Applying Concepts** What situations cause you stress? What can you do to help relieve the stress you are feeling?
10. **Making Inferences** According to the newspaper, the temperature outside is 61°F right now. Later, it will be 90°F outside. If you and your friends want to play soccer in the park, what should you wear? What should you bring with you?

SCILINKS
NSTA
Developed and maintained by the National Science Teachers Association
For a variety of links related to this chapter, go to www.scilinks.org
Topic: Safety
SciLinks code: HSM1339

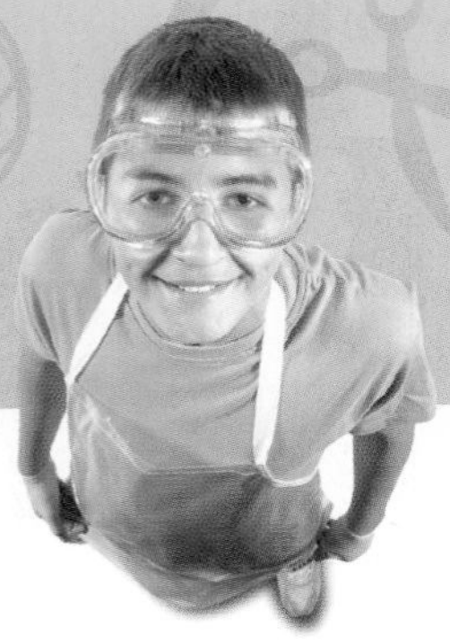

Skills Practice Lab

Keep It Clean

One of the best ways to prevent the spread of bacterial and viral infections is to frequently wash your hands with soap and water. Many companies advertise that their soap ingredients can destroy bacteria normally found on the body. In this activity, you will investigate how effective antibacterial soaps are at killing bacteria.

OBJECTIVES

Investigate how well antibacterial soap works.

Practice counting bacterial colonies.

MATERIALS

- incubator
- pencil, wax
- Petri dishes, nutrient agar–filled, sterile (3)
- scrub brush, new
- soap, liquid antibacterial
- stopwatch
- tape, transparent

SAFETY

Procedure

1. Keeping the agar plates closed at all times, use the wax pencil to label the bottoms of three agar plates. Label one plate "Control," one plate "No soap," and one plate "Soap."
2. Without washing your hands, carefully press several surfaces of your hands on the agar plate marked "Control." Have your partner immediately put the cover back on the plate. After you touch the agar, do not touch anything with either hand.
3. Hold your right hand under running water for 2 min. Ask your partner to scrub all surfaces of your right hand with the scrub brush throughout these 2 min. Be sure that he or she scrubs under your fingernails. After scrubbing, your partner should turn off the water and open the plate marked "No soap." Touching only the agar, carefully press on the "No soap" plate with the same surfaces of your right hand that you used to press on the "Control" plate.

4. Repeat step 3, but use your left hand instead of your right. This time, ask your partner to scrub your left hand with liquid antibacterial soap and the scrub brush. Use the plate marked "Soap" instead of the plate marked "No soap."

5. Secure the lid of each plate to its bottom half with transparent tape. Place the plates upside down in the incubator. Incubate all three plates overnight at 37°C.

6. Remove the plates from the incubator, and turn them right side up. Check each plate for the presence of bacterial colonies, and count the number of colonies present on each plate. Record this information. **Caution:** Do not remove the lids on any of the plates.

Analyze the Results

1. **Examining Data** Compare the bacterial growth on the plates. Which plate contained the most growth? Which contained the least?

Draw Conclusions

2. **Drawing Conclusions** Does water alone effectively kill bacteria? Explain.

Applying Your Data

Repeat this experiment, but scrub with regular, not antibacterial, liquid soap. Describe how the results of the two experiments differ.

Chapter Review

USING KEY TERMS

Complete each of the following sentences by choosing the correct term from the word bank.

nutrients	Food Guide Pyramid
addiction	drug
malnutrition	

1. Carbohydrates, proteins, fats, vitamins, minerals, and water are the six categories of ___.

2. The ___ divides foods into six groups and gives a recommended number of servings for each group.

3. Both bulimia nervosa and anorexia nervosa cause ___.

4. A physical or psychological dependence on a drug can lead to ___.

5. A(n) ___ is any substance that causes a change in a person's physical or psychological state.

UNDERSTANDING KEY IDEAS

Multiple Choice

6. Which of the following statements about drugs is true?
   - **a.** A child cannot become addicted to drugs.
   - **b.** Smoking just one or two cigarettes is safe for anyone.
   - **c.** Alcohol is not a drug.
   - **d.** Withdrawal symptoms may be painful.

7. What does alcohol do to the central nervous system (CNS)?
   - **a.** It speeds the CNS up.
   - **b.** It slows the CNS down.
   - **c.** It keeps the CNS regulated.
   - **d.** It has no effect on the CNS.

8. To keep your teeth healthy,
   - **a.** brush your teeth as hard as you can.
   - **b.** use a toothbrush until it is worn out.
   - **c.** brush at least twice a day.
   - **d.** floss at least once a week.

9. According to the Food Guide Pyramid, what foods should you eat most?
   - **a.** meats
   - **b.** milk, yogurt, and cheese
   - **c.** fruits and vegetables
   - **d.** bread, cereal, rice, and pasta

10. Which of the following can help you deal with stress?
    - **a.** ignoring your homework
    - **b.** drinking a caffeinated drink
    - **c.** talking to a friend
    - **d.** watching television

11. Tobacco use increases the risk of
    - **a.** lung cancer.
    - **b.** car accidents.
    - **c.** liver damage.
    - **d.** depression.

Short Answer

12 Are all narcotics illegal? Explain.

13 What are three dangers of tobacco and alcohol use?

14 What are the three types of nutrients that provide energy in Calories, and what is the main function of each type in the body?

15 Name two conditions that can lead to malnutrition.

16 Explain why you should always wear safety equipment when you ride your bicycle.

CRITICAL THINKING

17 **Concept Mapping** Use the following terms to create a concept map: *carbohydrates, water, proteins, nutrients, fats, vitamins, minerals, saturated fats,* and *unsaturated fats.*

18 **Applying Concepts** You have recently become a vegetarian, and you worry that you are not getting enough protein. Name two foods that you could eat to get more protein.

19 **Analyzing Ideas** Your two-year-old cousin will be staying with your family. Name three things that you can do to make sure that the house is safe for a young child.

INTERPRETING GRAPHICS

Look at the photos below. The people in the photos are not practicing safe habits. List the unsafe habits shown in these photos. For each unsafe habit, tell what the corresponding safe habit is.

20

21

Standardized Test Preparation

READING

Read each of the passages below. Then, answer the questions that follow each passage.

Passage 1 A chronic disease is a disease that, once developed, is always present and will not go away. Chronic bronchitis is a disease that causes the airways in the lungs to become swollen. This irritation causes a lot of mucus to form in the lungs. As a result, a person who has chronic bronchitis coughs a lot. Another chronic condition is emphysema. Emphysema destroys the tiny air sacs and the walls in the lungs. The holes in the air sacs cannot heal. Eventually, the lung tissue dies, and the lungs can no longer work. Cigarette smoking causes more than 80% of all cases of chronic bronchitis and emphysema.

1. In the passage, what does the word *chronic* mean?

A disappearing
B temporary
C always present
D mucus filled

2. According to the passage, what disease destroys the tiny air sacs and walls of the lungs?

F chronic bronchitis
G emphysema
H chronic cough
I cigarette smoking

3. Which of the following is a true statement according to the passage?

A Holes in the air sacs of lungs heal very quickly.
B Cigarette smoking causes more than 80% of all cases of chronic bronchitis and emphysema.
C Cigarette smoking does not cause chronic bronchitis or emphysema.
D Chronic bronchitis will go away after a person stops smoking cigarettes.

Passage 2 Each body reacts differently to alcohol. Several factors affect how a body reacts to alcohol. A person who has several drinks in a short time is likely to be affected more than a person who has a single drink in the same amount of time. Food in a drinker's stomach can also slow alcohol absorption into the blood. Finally, the way that women absorb and process alcohol differs from the way that men do. If a man and a woman drink the same amount of alcohol, the woman's blood alcohol content (BAC) will be higher than the man's. As BAC increases, mental and physical abilities decline. Muscle coordination, which is especially important for walking and driving, decreases. Vision becomes blurred. Speech and memory are impaired. A high BAC can cause a person to pass out or even die.

1. According to the passage, what does *BAC* stand for?

A blood alcohol content
B blood alcohol contaminant
C blurred alcohol capacity
D blood alcoholic coordination

2. According to the passage, which of the following factors can affect BAC?

F time of day
G food in the stomach
H age
I physical activity

3. Which of the following is a fact according to the passage?

A Alcohol does not affect mood or mental abilities.
B Men absorb alcohol in the same way that women do.
C Alcohol decreases muscle coordination.
D Everybody reacts to alcohol in the same way.

INTERPRETING GRAPHICS

The figure below shows a sample prescription drug label. Use this figure to answer the questions that follow.

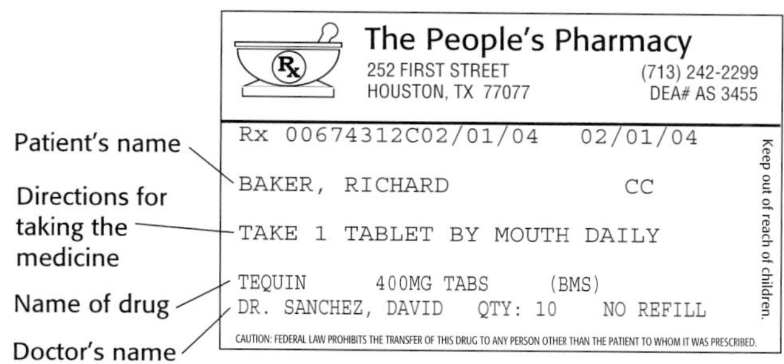

The People's Pharmacy
252 FIRST STREET
HOUSTON, TX 77077
(713) 242-2299
DEA# AS 3455
Rx 00674312C02/01/04 02/01/04
BAKER, RICHARD CC
TAKE 1 TABLET BY MOUTH DAILY
TEQUIN 400MG TABS (BMS)
DR. SANCHEZ, DAVID QTY: 10 NO REFILL
CAUTION: FEDERAL LAW PROHIBITS THE TRANSFER OF THIS DRUG TO ANY PERSON OTHER THAN THE PATIENT TO WHOM IT WAS PRESCRIBED.
Keep out of reach of children.
Patient's name
Directions for taking the medicine
Name of drug
Doctor's name

1. According to the label, what is the patient's name?

A Richard Baker
B Baker Richard
C David Sanchez
D James Beard

2. According to the label, how often should the medication be taken?

F once a day
G twice a day
H three times a day
I once a week

3. According to the label, how many refills remain on the prescription?

A 0
B 1
C 2
D 3

4. If this patient follows the directions exactly, how long will he need to take this medicine?

F 1 day
G 5 days
H 10 days
I There is not enough data to determine the answer.

MATH

Read each question below, and choose the best answer.

1. Which of the following ratios is equal to 2/4?

A 1/2
B 17/18
C 5/2
D 7/2

2. If 1 gal = 3.79 L, how many liters are in 3 gal?

F 3.79 L
G 7.58 L
H 11.37 L
I 15.16 L

3. Approximately how many liters are in 5 gal?

A 5 L
B 10 L
C 20 L
D 30 L

4. Ada has just built a car for a Pinewood Derby. She wants to find the average speed of her new car. During her first test run, she goes 5 mi/h. During her second run, she goes 4 mi/h, and in her third run, she goes 6 mi/h. What is her average speed?

F 4 mi/h
G 5 mi/h
H 6 mi/h
I 7 mi/h

5. Which of the following numbers is largest?

A 1×10^2
B 1×10^5
C 3×10^5
D 5×10^4

6. On Saturday, Mae won a goldfish at the school carnival. On the way home, Mae and her mother bought a fishbowl for $10.25, a container of fish food for $3.75, and a plastic coral for $8.15. How much money did Mae and her mother spend?

F $11.90
G $18.40
H $22.15
I $30.30

Science in Action

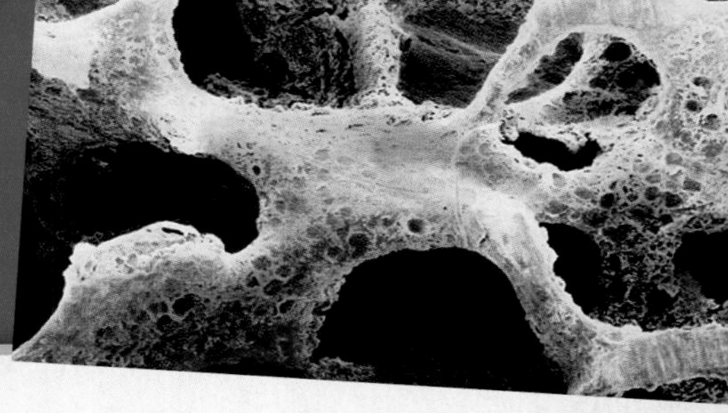

Bones can become severely weakened by the female athlete triad.

Science, Technology, and Society

Meatless Munching

Recent studies suggest that a vegetarian diet may reduce the risk of heart disease, adult-onset diabetes, and some forms of cancer. However, a vegetarian diet takes careful planning. Vegetarians must ensure that they get the proper balance of protein and vitamins in their diet. New foods that can help vegetarians remain healthy are being developed constantly. Meat substitutes are now made from soybeans, textured vegetable protein, and tofu. One new food, which is shown above, is made of a fungus that is a relative of mushrooms and truffles.

Social Studies ACTIVITY

WRITING SKILL Research a culture that has a mostly vegetarian diet, such as Hindu or Buddhist. What kinds of food do the people eat? Why don't they eat animals? Write a short report on your findings.

Scientific Discoveries

Female Athlete Triad

Getting enough exercise is an important part of staying healthy. But in 1992, doctors learned that too much exercise can be harmful for women. When a girl or woman exercises too much, three things can happen. She may lose too much weight. She may stop having her period. And her bones may become very weak. These three symptoms form the female athlete triad. To prevent this condition, female athletes need to take in enough Calories. Women who exercise heavily and try to lose weight may have a reduction in estrogen. Estrogen is the hormone that helps regulate the menstrual cycle. Low levels of estrogen and inadequate nutrition can cause bones to become weak and brittle. The photo above shows bone that has been weakened greatly.

Math ACTIVITY

Some scientists recommend that teenagers get 1,200 to 1,500 mg of calcium every day. A cup of milk has 300 mg of calcium, and a serving of yogurt has 400 mg of calcium. Calculate two combinations of milk and yogurt that would give you the recommended 1,500 mg of calcium.

Careers

Russell Selger

Guidance Counselor Guidance counselors help students think about their future by helping them discover their interests. After focusing their interests, a guidance counselor helps students plan a good academic schedule. A guidance counselor might talk to you about taking an art or computer science class that may help you discover a hidden talent. Many skills are vital to being a good guidance counselor. The job requires empathy, which is the ability to understand and sympathize with another person's feelings. Counselors also need patience, good listening skills, and a love of helping young people. Russell Selger, a guidance counselor at Timberlane Middle School, has a great respect for middle school students. "The kids are just alive. They want to learn. There's something about the spark that they have, and it's so much fun to guide them through all of this stuff," he explains.

WRITING SKILL Visit the guidance counselor's office at your school. What services does your guidance counselor offer? Conduct an interview with a guidance counselor. Ask why he or she became a counselor. Write an article for the school paper about your findings.

To learn more about these Science in Action topics, visit go.hrw.com and type in the keyword HL5BD7F.

Current Science

Check out Current Science® articles related to this chapter by visiting go.hrw.com. Just type in the keyword HL5CS28.

LabBook

Contents

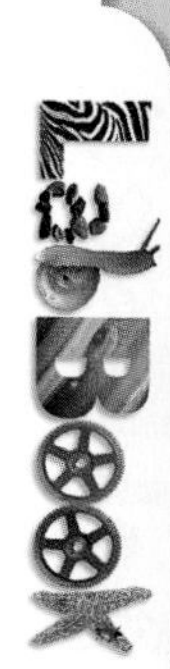

Skills Practice Lab

Graphing Data

When performing an experiment, you usually need to collect data. To understand the data, you can often organize them into a graph. Graphs can show trends and patterns that you might not notice in a table or list. In this exercise, you will practice collecting data and organizing the data into a graph.

MATERIALS

- beaker, 400 mL
- clock (or watch) with a second hand
- gloves, heat-resistant
- hot plate
- ice
- paper, graph
- thermometer, Celsius, with a clip
- water, 200 mL

SAFETY

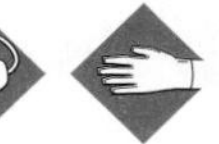

Procedure

1. Pour 200 mL of water into a 400 mL beaker. Add ice to the beaker until the waterline is at the 400 mL mark.
2. Place a Celsius thermometer into the beaker. Use a thermometer clip to prevent the thermometer from touching the bottom of the beaker. Record the temperature of the ice water.
3. Place the beaker and thermometer on a hot plate. Turn the hot plate on medium heat, and record the temperature every minute until the water temperature reaches 100°C.
4. Using heat-resistant gloves, remove the beaker from the hot plate. Continue to record the temperature of the water each minute for 10 more minutes. **Caution:** Don't forget to turn off the hot plate.
5. On a piece of graph paper, create a graph similar to the one below. Label the horizontal axis (the *x*-axis) "Time (min)," and mark the axis in increments of 1 min as shown. Label the vertical axis (the *y*-axis) "Temperature (°C)," and mark the axis in increments of 10° as shown.
6. Find the 1 min mark on the *x*-axis, and move up the graph to the temperature you recorded at 1 min. Place a dot on the graph at that point. Plot each temperature in the same way. When you have plotted all of your data, connect the dots with a smooth line.

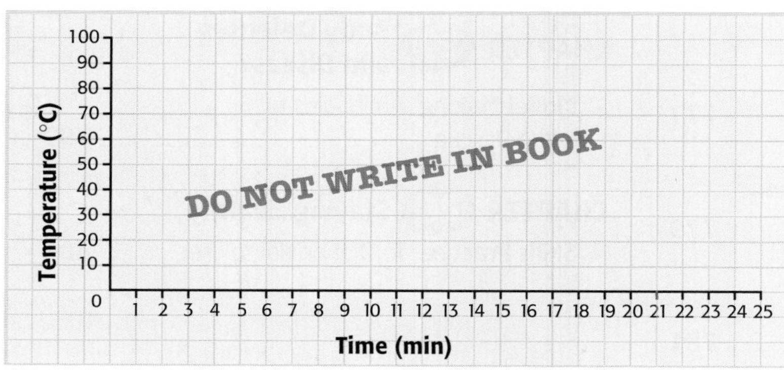

Analyze the Results

1. Examine your graph. Do you think the water heated faster than it cooled? Explain.
2. Estimate what the temperature of the water was 2.5 min after you placed the beaker on the hot plate. Explain how you can make a good estimate of temperature between those you recorded.

Draw Conclusions

3. Explain how a graph may give more information than the same data in a table.

Model-Making Lab

A Window to a Hidden World

Have you ever noticed that objects underwater appear closer than they really are? The reason is that light waves change speed when they travel from air into water. Anton van Leeuwenhoek, a pioneer of microscopy in the late 17th century, used a drop of water to magnify objects. That drop of water brought a hidden world closer into view. How did Leeuwenhoek's microscope work? In this investigation, you will build a model of it to find out.

MATERIALS

- eyedropper
- hole punch
- newspaper
- plastic wrap, clear
- poster board, 3 cm × 10 cm
- tape, transparent
- water

Procedure

1. Punch a hole in the center of the poster board with a hole punch, as shown in (a) at right.
2. Tape a small piece of clear plastic wrap over the hole, as shown in (b) at right. Be sure the plastic wrap is large enough so that the tape you use to secure it does not cover the hole.
3. Use an eyedropper to put one drop of water over the hole. Check to be sure your drop of water is dome-shaped (convex), as shown in (c) at right.
4. Hold the microscope close to your eye and look through the drop. Be careful not to disturb the water drop.
5. Hold the microscope over a piece of newspaper, and observe the image.

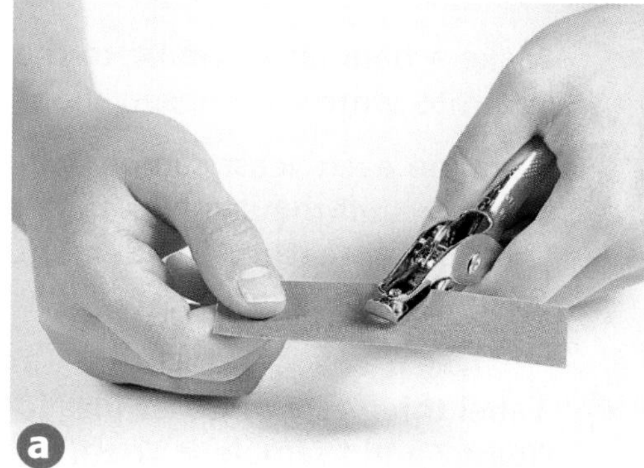
a

b

c

Analyze the Results

1. Describe and draw the image you see. Is the image larger than or the same size as it is without the microscope? Is the image clear or blurred? Is the shape of the image distorted?

Draw Conclusions

2. How do you think your model could be improved?

Applying Your Data

Robert Hooke and Zacharias Janssen contributed much to the field of microscopy. Research one of them, and write a paragraph about his contributions.

Skills Practice Lab

The Best-Bread Bakery Dilemma

The chief baker at the Best-Bread Bakery thinks that the yeast the bakery received may be dead. Yeast is a central ingredient in bread. Yeast is a living organism, a member of the kingdom Fungi, and it undergoes the same life processes as other living organisms. When yeast grows in the presence of oxygen and other nutrients, yeast produces carbon dioxide. The gas forms bubbles that cause bread dough to rise. Thousands of dollars may be lost if the yeast is dead.

The Best-Bread Bakery has requested that you test the yeast. The bakery has furnished samples of live yeast and some samples of the yeast in question.

MATERIALS

- beaker, 250 mL
- flour
- gloves, heat-resistant
- graduated cylinder
- hot plate
- magnifying lens
- scoopula (or small spoon)
- stirring sticks, wooden (3)
- sugar
- test-tube rack
- test tubes (3) (or clear plastic cups)
- thermometer, Celsius, with clip
- water, 125 mL
- yeast samples (live, A, and B)

SAFETY

Procedure

1. Make a data table similar to the one below. Leave plenty of room to write your observations.
2. Examine each yeast sample with a magnifying lens. You may want to sniff the samples to determine the presence of an odor. (Your teacher will demonstrate the appropriate way to detect odors in this lab.) Record your observations in the data table.
3. Label three test tubes or plastic cups "Live Yeast," "Sample A Yeast," and "Sample B Yeast."
4. Fill a beaker with 125 mL of water, and place the beaker on a hot plate. Use a thermometer to be sure the water does not get warmer than 32°C. Attach the thermometer to the side of the beaker with a clip so the thermometer doesn't touch the bottom of the beaker. Turn off the hot plate when the water temperature reaches 32°C.

Yeast sample	Observations	0 min	5 min	10 min	15 min	20 min	25 min	Dead or alive?
Live								
Sample A								
Sample B								

5. Add a small scoop (about 1/2 tsp) of each yeast sample to the correctly labeled container. Add a small scoop of sugar to each container.
6. Add 10 mL of the warm water to each container, and stir.
7. Add a small scoop of flour to each container, and stir again. The flour will help make the process more visible but is not necessary as food for the yeast.
8. Observe the samples carefully. Look for bubbles. Make observations at 5 min intervals. Write your observations in the data table.
9. In the last column of the data table, write "alive" or "dead" based on your observations during the experiment.

Analyze the Results

1. Describe any differences in the yeast samples before the experiment.
2. Describe the appearance of the yeast samples at the conclusion of the experiment.
3. Why was a sample of live yeast included in the experiment?
4. Why was sugar added to the samples?
5. Based on your observations, is either Sample A or Sample B alive?

Draw Conclusions

6. Write a letter to the Best-Bread Bakery stating your recommendation to use or not use the yeast samples. Give reasons for your recommendation.

Applying Your Data

Based on your observations of the nutrient requirements of yeast, design an experiment to determine the ideal combination of nutrients. Vary the amount of nutrients, or examine different energy sources.

Skills Practice Lab

Cells Alive!

You have probably used a microscope to look at single-celled organisms such as those shown below. They can be found in pond water. In the following exercise, you will look at *Protococcus*—algae that form a greenish stain on tree trunks, wooden fences, flowerpots, and buildings.

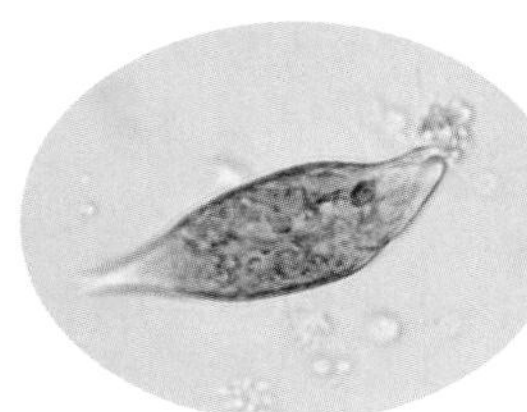

Euglena

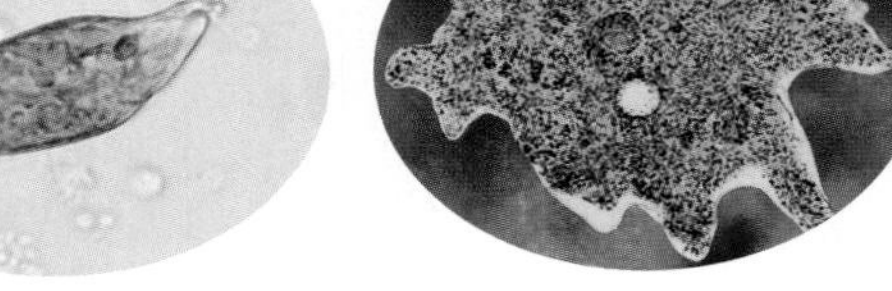

Amoeba

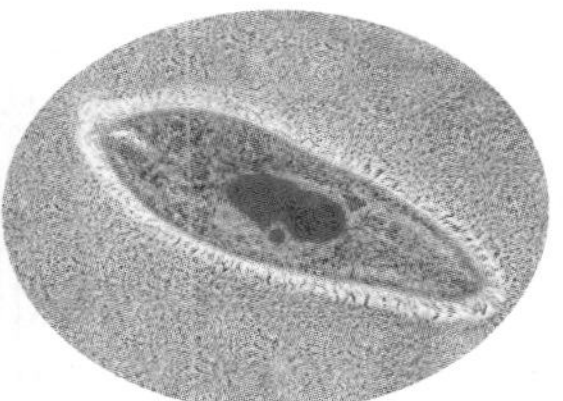

Paramecium

MATERIALS

- eyedropper
- microscope
- microscope slide and coverslip
- *Protococcus* (or other algae)
- water

Procedure

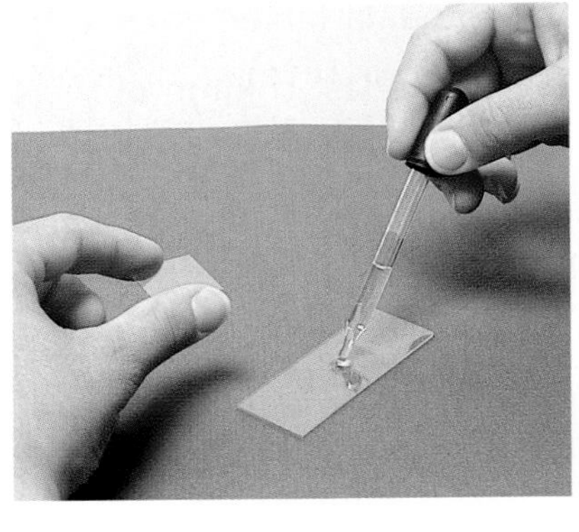

1. Locate some *Protococcus*. Scrape a small sample into a container. Bring the sample to the classroom, and make a wet mount of it as directed by your teacher. If you can't find *Protococcus* outdoors, look for algae on the glass in an aquarium. Such algae may not be *Protococcus,* but it will be a very good substitute.
2. Set the microscope on low power to examine the algae. On a separate sheet of paper, draw the cells that you see.
3. Switch to high power to examine a single cell. Draw the cell.
4. You will probably notice that each cell contains several chloroplasts. Label a chloroplast on your drawing. What is the function of the chloroplast?
5. Another structure that should be clearly visible in all the algae cells is the nucleus. Find the nucleus in one of your cells, and label it on your drawing. What is the function of the nucleus?
6. What does the cytoplasm look like? Describe any movement you see inside the cells.

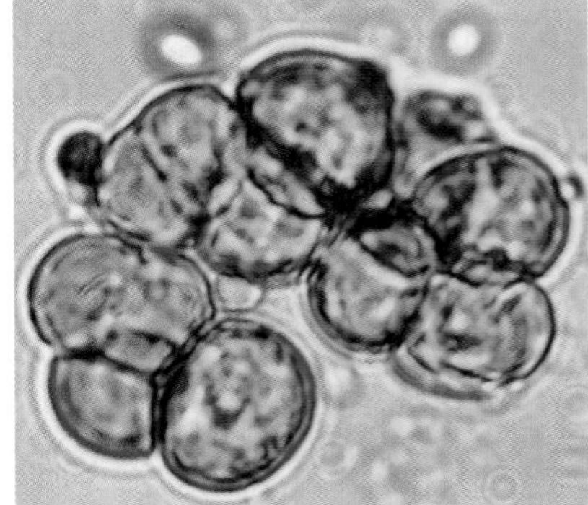

Protococcus

Analyze the Results

1. Are *Protococcus* single-celled organisms or multicellular organisms?
2. How are *Protococcus* different from amoebas?

Skills Practice Lab

Stayin' Alive!

Every second of your life, your body's trillions of cells take in, use, and store energy. They repair themselves, reproduce, and get rid of waste. Together, these processes are called *metabolism.* Your cells use the food that you eat to provide the energy you need to stay alive.

Your Basal Metabolic Rate (BMR) is a measurement of the energy that your body needs to carry out all the basic life processes while you are at rest. These processes include breathing, keeping your heart beating, and keeping your body's temperature stable. Your BMR is influenced by your gender, your age, and many other things. Your BMR may be different from everyone else's, but it is normal for you. In this activity, you will find the amount of energy, measured in Calories, you need every day in order to stay alive.

MATERIALS

- bathroom scale
- tape measure

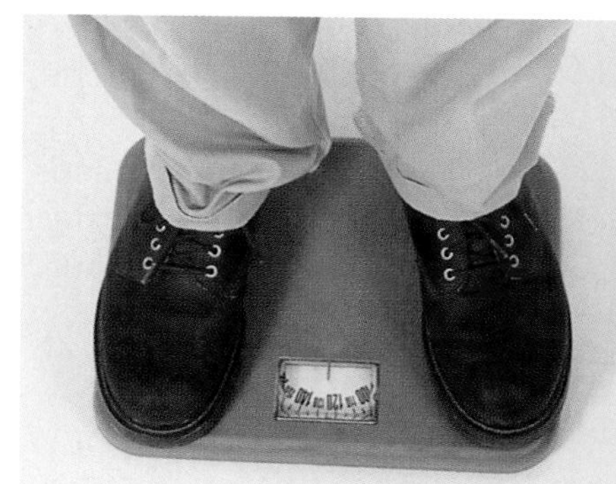

Procedure

1. Find your weight on a bathroom scale. If the scale measures in pounds, you must convert your weight in pounds to your mass in kilograms. To convert your weight in pounds (lb) to mass in kilograms (kg), multiply the number of pounds by 0.454.

Example: If Carlos weighs 125 lb, his mass in kilograms is:

$$\begin{array}{r} 125 \text{ lb} \\ \times\ \underline{0.454} \\ 56.75 \text{ kg} \end{array}$$

2. Use a tape measure to find your height. If the tape measures in inches, convert your height in inches to height in centimeters. To convert your height in inches (in.) to your height in centimeters (cm), multiply the number of inches by 2.54.

If Carlos is 62 in. tall, his height in centimeters is:

$$\begin{array}{r} 62 \text{ in.} \\ \times\ \underline{2.54} \\ 157.48 \text{ cm} \end{array}$$

3. Now that you know your height and mass, use the appropriate formula below to get a close estimate of your BMR. Your answer will give you an estimate of the number of Calories your body needs each day just to stay alive.

Calculating Your BMR	
Females	**Males**
65 + (10 × your mass in kilograms)	66 + (13.5 × your mass in kilograms)
+ (1.8 × your height in centimeters)	+ (5 × your height in centimeters)
− (4.7 × your age in years)	− (6.8 × your age in years)

4. Your metabolism is also influenced by how active you are. Talking, walking, and playing games all take more energy than being at rest. To get an idea of how many Calories your body needs each day to stay healthy, select the lifestyle that best describes yours from the table at right. Then multiply your BMR by the activity factor.

Activity Factors	
Activity lifestyle	**Activity factor**
Moderately inactive (normal, everyday activities)	1.3
Moderately active (exercise 3 to 4 times a week)	1.4
Very active (exercise 4 to 6 times a week)	1.6
Extremely active (exercise 6 to 7 times a week)	1.8

Analyze the Results

1. In what way could you compare your whole body to a single cell? Explain.
2. Does an increase in activity increase your BMR? Does an increase in activity increase your need for Calories? Explain your answers.

Draw Conclusions

3. If you are moderately inactive, how many more Calories would you need if you began to exercise every day?

Applying Your Data

The best energy sources are those that supply the correct amount of Calories for your lifestyle and also provide the nutrients you need. Research in the library or on the Internet to find out which kinds of foods are the best energy sources for you. How does your list of best energy sources compare with your diet?

List everything you eat and drink in 1 day. Find out how many Calories are in each item, and find the total number of Calories you have consumed. How does this number of Calories compare with the number of Calories you need each day for all your activities?

Inquiry Lab

Tracing Traits

Have you ever wondered about the traits you inherited from your parents? Do you have a trait that neither of your parents has? In this project, you will develop a family tree, or pedigree, similar to the one shown in the diagram below. You will trace an inherited trait through a family to determine how it has passed from generation to generation.

Procedure

1. The diagram at right shows a family history. On a separate piece of paper, draw a similar diagram of the family you have chosen. Include as many family members as possible, such as grandparents, parents, children, and grandchildren. Use circles to represent females and squares to represent males. You may include other information, such as the family member's name, birth date, or picture.

2. Draw a table similar to the one on the next page. Survey each of the family members shown in your family tree. Ask them if they have hair on the middle segment of their fingers. Write each person's name in the appropriate square. Explain to each person that it is normal to have either trait. The presence of hair on the middle segment is the dominant form of this trait.

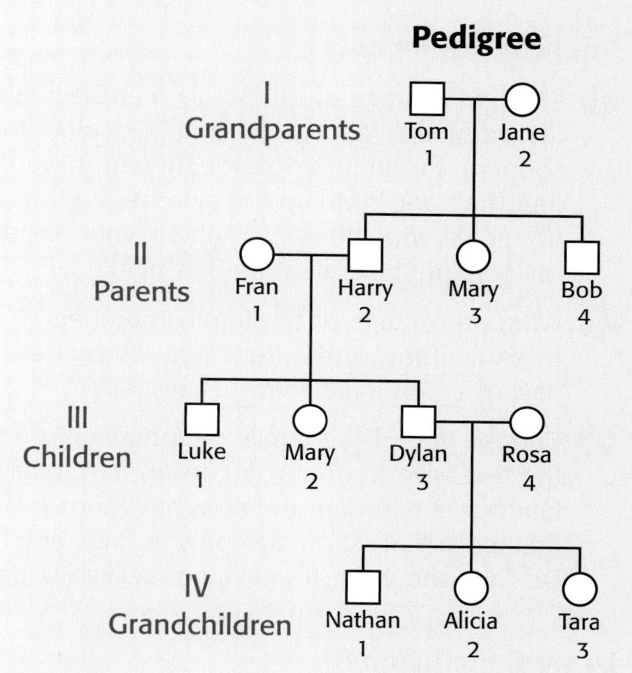

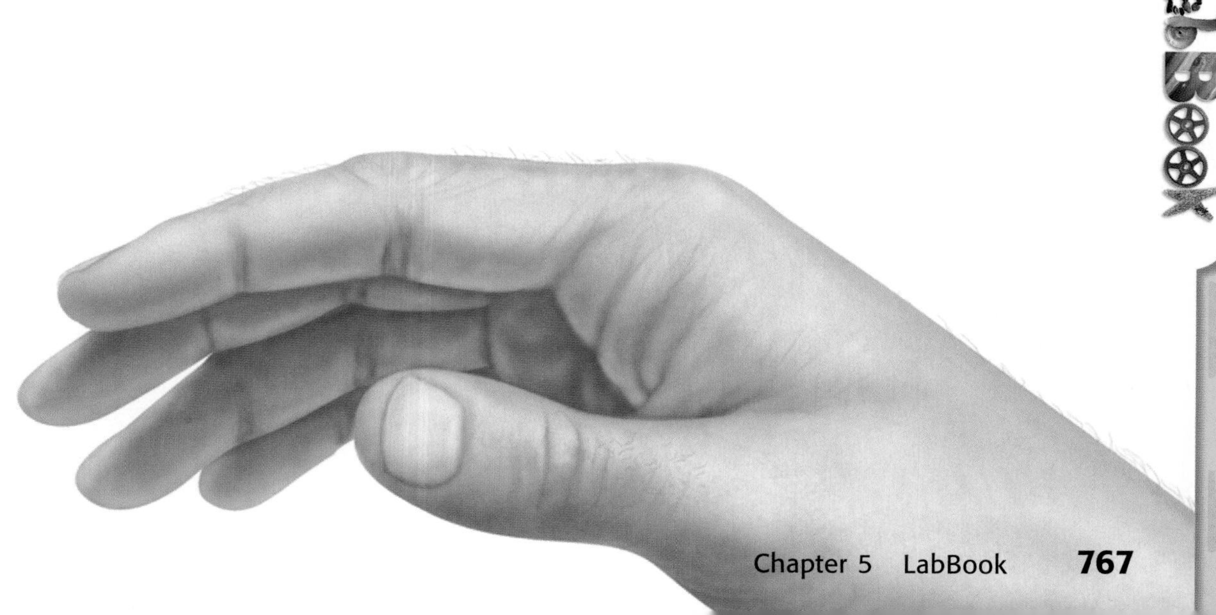

Dominant trait	Recessive trait	Family members with the dominant trait	Family members with the recessive trait
Hair present on the middle segment of fingers (*H*)	Hair absent on the middle segment of fingers (*h*)		

3. Trace this trait throughout the family tree you diagrammed in step 1. Shade or color the symbols of the family members who demonstrate the dominant form of this trait.

Analyze the Results

1. What percentage of the family members demonstrate the dominant form of the trait? Calculate this by counting the number of people who have the dominant trait and dividing this number by the total number of people you surveyed. Multiply your answer by 100. An example has been done at right.

Example: Calculating percentage

$$\frac{\text{10 people with trait}}{\text{20 people surveyed}} = \frac{1}{2}$$

$$\frac{1}{2} = 0.50 \times 100 = 50\%$$

2. What percentage of the family members demonstrate the recessive form of the trait? Why doesn't every family member have the dominant form of the trait?

3. Choose one of the family members who demonstrates the recessive form of the chosen trait. What is this person's genotype? What are the possible genotypes for the parents of this individual? Does this person have any brothers or sisters? Do they show the dominant or recessive trait?

Draw Conclusions

4. Draw a Punnett square like the one at right. Use this to determine the genotypes of the parents of the person you chose in step 3. Write this person's genotype in the bottom right-hand corner of your Punnett square. **Hint:** There may be more than one possible genotype for the parents. Don't forget to consider the genotypes of the person's brothers and sisters.

	?	?
Mother ?		
?		

Skills Practice Lab

The Half-life of Pennies

Carbon-14 is a special unstable element used in the absolute dating of material that was once alive, such as fossil bones. Every 5,730 years, half of the carbon-14 in a fossil specimen decays or breaks down into a more stable element. In the following experiment you will see how pennies can show the same kind of "decay."

MATERIALS

- container with a cover, large
- pennies (100)

Procedure

1. Place 100 pennies in a large, covered container. Shake the container several times, and remove the cover. Carefully empty the container on a flat surface making sure the pennies don't roll away.

2. Remove all the coins that have the "head" side of the coin turned upward. Record the number of pennies removed and the number of pennies remaining in a data table similar to the one at right.

Shake number	Number of coins remaining	Number of coins removed
1		
2	DO NOT WRITE IN BOOK	
3		

3. Repeat the process until no pennies are left in the container. Remember to remove only the coins showing "heads."

4. Draw a graph similar to the one at right. Label the *x*-axis "Number of shakes," and label the *y*-axis "Pennies remaining." Using data from your data table, plot the number of coins remaining at each shake on your graph.

Analyze the Results

1. Examine the Half-life of Carbon-14 graph at right. Compare the graph you have made for pennies with the one for carbon-14. Explain any similarities that you see.

2. Recall that the probability of landing "heads" in a coin toss is 1/2. Use this information to explain why the remaining number of pennies is reduced by about half each time they are shaken and tossed.

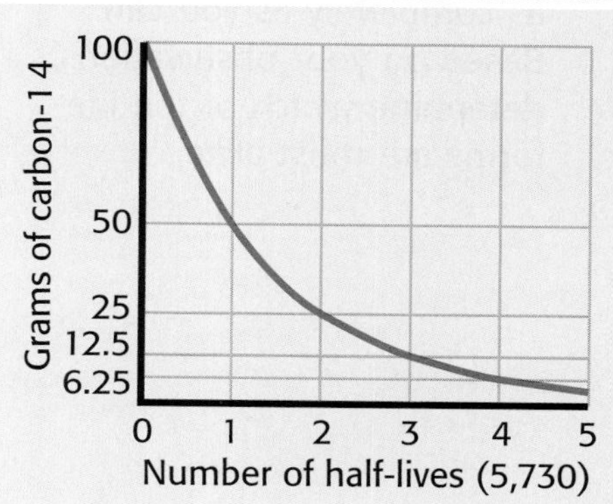

Skills Practice Lab

Voyage of the USS *Adventure*

You are a crew member on the USS *Adventure*. The *Adventure* has been on a 5-year mission to collect life-forms from outside the solar system. On the voyage back to Earth, your ship went through a meteor shower, which ruined several of the compartments containing the extraterrestrial life-forms. Now it is necessary to put more than one life-form in the same compartment.

You have only three undamaged compartments in your starship. You and your crewmates must stay in one compartment, and that compartment should be used for extraterrestrial life-forms only if absolutely necessary. You and your crewmates must decide which of the life-forms could be placed together. It is thought that similar life-forms will have similar needs. You can use only observable characteristics to group the life-forms.

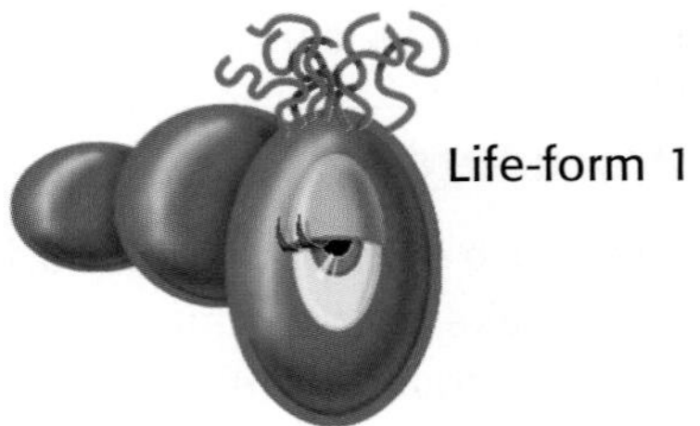

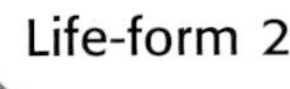

Procedure

1. Make a data table similar to the one below. Label each column with as many characteristics of the various life-forms as possible. Leave enough space in each square to write your observations. The life-forms are pictured on this page.

Life-form Characteristics				
	Color	**Shape**	**Legs**	**Eyes**
Life-form 1				
Life-form 2				
Life-form 3				
Life-form 4				

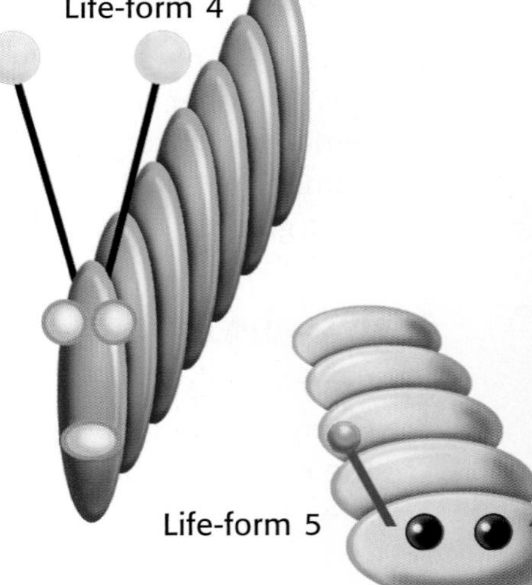

2. Describe each characteristic as completely as you can. Based on your observations, determine which of the life-forms are most alike.

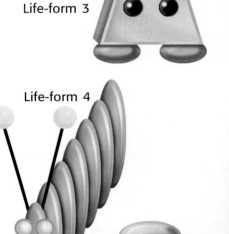

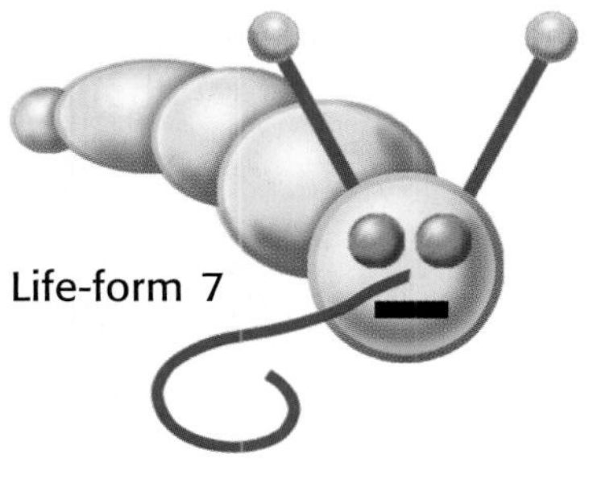

3. Make a data table like the one below. Fill in the table according to the decisions you made in step 2. State your reasons for the way you have grouped your life-forms.

Life-form Room Assignments		
Compartment	**Life-forms**	**Reasons**
1		
2		
3		DO NOT WRITE IN BOOK

4. The USS *Adventure* has to make one more stop before returning home. On planet X437 you discover the most interesting life-form ever found outside of Earth—the CC9, shown at right. Make a decision, based on your previous grouping of life-forms, about whether you can safely include CC9 in one of the compartments for the trip to Earth.

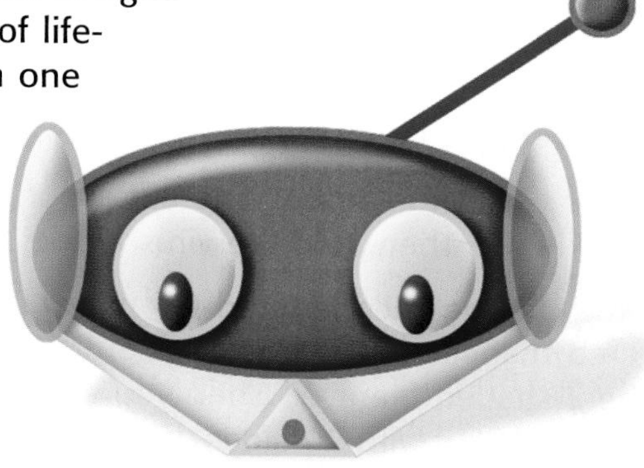

CC9

Analyze the Results

1. Describe the life-forms in compartment 1. How are they similar? How are they different?
2. Describe the life-forms in compartment 2. How are they similar? How do they differ from the life-forms in compartment 1?
3. Are there any life-forms in compartment 3? If so, describe their similarities. In which compartment will you and your crewmates remain for the journey home?

Draw Conclusions

4. Are you able to transport life-form CC9 safely back to Earth? If so, in which compartment will it be placed? How did you decide?

Applying Your Data

In 1831, Charles Darwin sailed from England on a ship called the HMS *Beagle*. You have studied the finches that Darwin observed on the Galápagos Islands. What were some of the other unusual organisms he found there? For example, find out about the Galápagos tortoise.

LabBook

Model-Making Lab

Viral Decorations

Although viruses are made of only protein and nucleic acids, their structures have many different shapes that help them attach to and invade living cells. One viral shape can be constructed from the template provided by your teacher. In this activity, you will construct and modify a model of a virus.

MATERIALS

- glue (or tape)
- markers, colored
- paper, construction
- pipe cleaners, twist ties, buttons, string, plastic wrap, and other scrap materials for making variations of the virus
- scissors
- virus model template

SAFETY

Procedure

1. Obtain a virus model template from your teacher. Carefully copy the template on a piece of construction paper. You may make the virus model as large as your teacher allows.
2. Plan how you will modify your virus. For example, you might want to add the tail and tail fibers of a bacteriophage or wrap the model in plastic to represent the envelope that surrounds the protein coat in HIV.
3. Color your virus model, and cut it out by cutting on the solid black lines. Then, fold the virus model along the dotted lines.
4. Glue or tape each lettered tab under the corresponding lettered triangle. For example, glue or tape the large *Z* tab under the *Z*-shaded triangle. When you are finished, you should have a closed box with 20 sides.
5. Apply the modifications that you planned. Give your virus a name, and write it on the model. Decorate your classroom with your virus and those of your classmates.

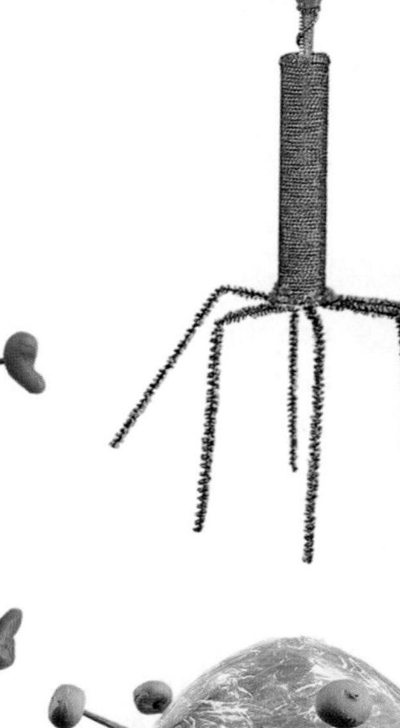

Analyze the Results

1. Describe the modifications you made to your virus model, and explain how the virus might use them.
2. If your virus causes disease, explain what disease it causes, how it reproduces, and how the virus is spread.

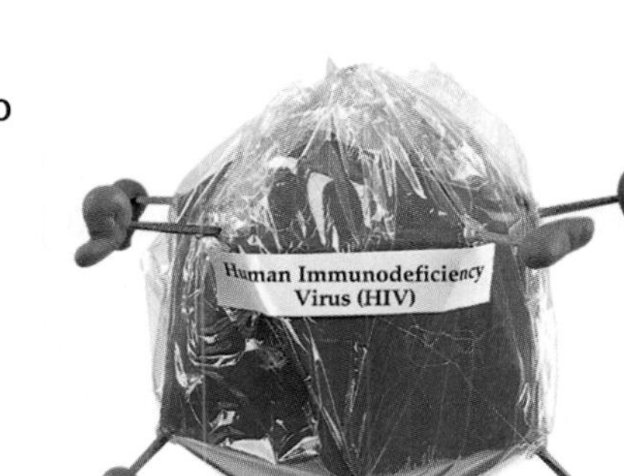

Influenza

Communicating Your Data

Research in the library or on the Internet an unusual virus that causes an illness, such as the influenza virus, HIV, or Ebola virus. Write a paragraph explaining what is unusual about the virus, what illness it causes, and how it might be avoided.

Model-Making Lab

Making a Protist Mobile

You have studied many of the diverse species of organisms within the kingdom Protista. This may be the first time you have ever seen many of these single-celled eukaryotes. In this activity, you will have an opportunity to express a bit of creativity by using what you have learned about these interesting organisms.

MATERIALS

- clothes hanger, wire
- markers, colored
- paper (heavyweight construction paper or poster board)
- recycled material of your choice
- scissors
- string, yarn, lightweight wire, or fishing line
- tape, transparent (or glue)

SAFETY

Procedure

1. Research the different kinds of protists you have studied. You may cut out pictures of them from magazines, or you may find examples of protists on the Internet. You may want to investigate *Plasmodium, Euglena,* amoebas, slime molds, *Radiolaria, Paramecium, Foraminifera,* various other protozoans, or even algae.
2. Using the paper and recycled materials, make a model of each protist you want to include on your mobile. Be sure to include the special features of each protist, such as vacuoles, pseudopods, shells, cilia, or flagella.
3. Use tape or glue to attach special features to give your protists a three-dimensional look.
4. Provide labels for your protist models. For each protist, provide its name, classification, method of movement (if any), method for obtaining food, and any other interesting facts you have learned about it.
5. Attach your protist models to the wire hanger with wire or string. Use tape or glue to attach your labels to each model.

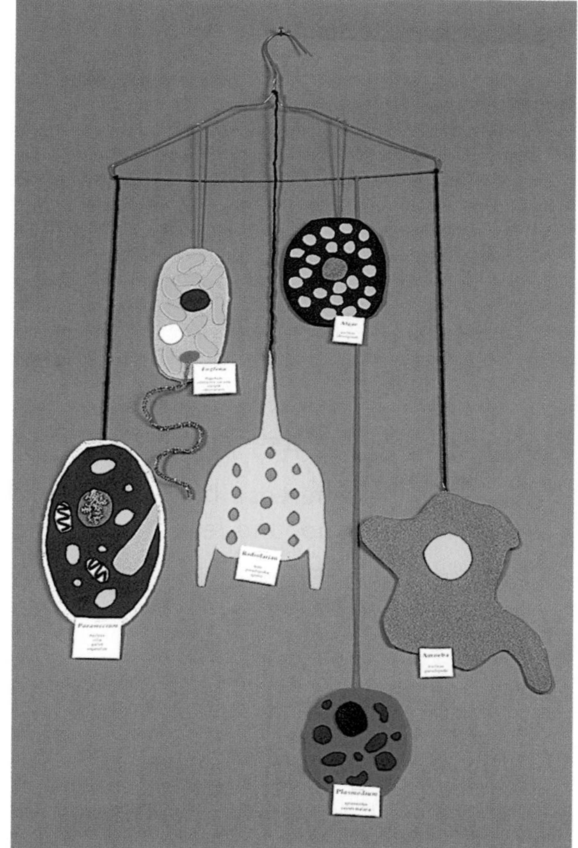

Analyze the Results

1. What have you learned about the diversity of protists? Include at least three habitats where protists may be found.

Communicating Your Data

Choose a disease-causing protist. Write a report describing the disease, its effect on people or the environment, and the efforts being made to control it.

Skills Practice Lab

Leaf Me Alone!

Imagine you are a naturalist all alone on an expedition in a rain forest. You have found several plants that you think have never been seen before. You must contact a botanist, a scientist who studies plants, to confirm your suspicion. Because there is no mail service in the rain forest, you must describe these species completely and accurately by radio. The botanist must be able to draw the leaves of the plants from your description. In this activity, you will carefully describe five plant specimens by using the examples and vocabulary lists in this lab.

MATERIALS

- gloves, protective
- leaf specimens (5)
- plant guidebook (optional)

SAFETY

Procedure

1. Examine the leaf characteristics illustrated on the next page. These examples can be found on the following page. You will notice that more than one term is needed to completely describe a leaf. The leaf shown at right has been labeled for you using the examples and vocabulary lists found in this lab.
2. On a sheet of paper, draw a diagram of a leaf from each plant specimen.
3. Next to each drawing, carefully describe the leaf. Include general characteristics, such as relative size and color. For each plant, identify the following: leaf shape, stem type, leaf arrangement, leaf edge, vein arrangement, and leaf-base shape. Use the terms and vocabulary lists provided to describe each leaf as accurately as possible and to label your drawings.

Compound Leaf

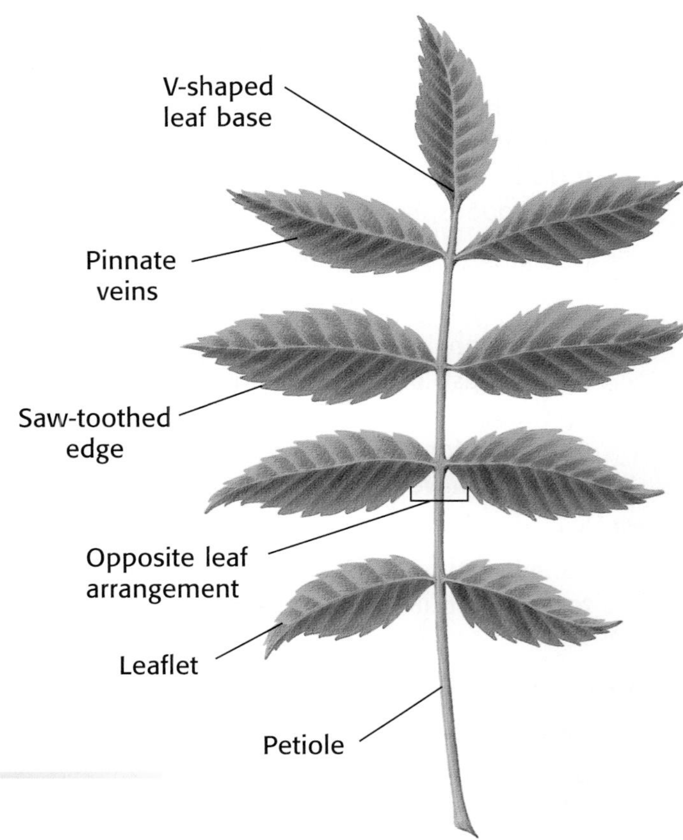

Analyze the Results

1. What is the difference between a simple leaf and a compound leaf?
2. Describe two different vein arrangements in leaves.
3. Based on what you know about adaptation, explain why there are so many different leaf variations.

Communicating Your Data

Choose a partner. Using the keys and vocabulary in this lab, describe a leaf, and see if your partner can draw the leaf from your description. Switch roles, and see if you can draw a leaf from your partner's description.

Leaf Shapes Vocabulary List

cordate—heart shaped
lanceolate—sword shaped
lobate—lobed
oblong—rounded at the tip
orbicular—disk shaped
ovate—oval shaped, widest at base of leaf
peltate—shield shaped
reniform—kidney shaped
sagittate—arrow shaped

Stems Vocabulary List

herbaceous—green, nonwoody stems
woody—bark or barklike covering on stem

Leaf Arrangements Vocabulary List

alternate—alternating leaves or leaflets along stem or petiole
compound—leaf divided into segments, or several leaflets on a petiole
opposite—compound leaf with several leaflets arranged oppositely along a petiole
palmate—single leaf with veins arranged around a center point
palmate compound—several leaflets arranged around a center point
petiole—leaf stalk
pinnate—single leaf with veins arranged along a center vein
pinnate compound—several leaflets on either side of a petiole
simple—single leaf attached to stem by a petiole

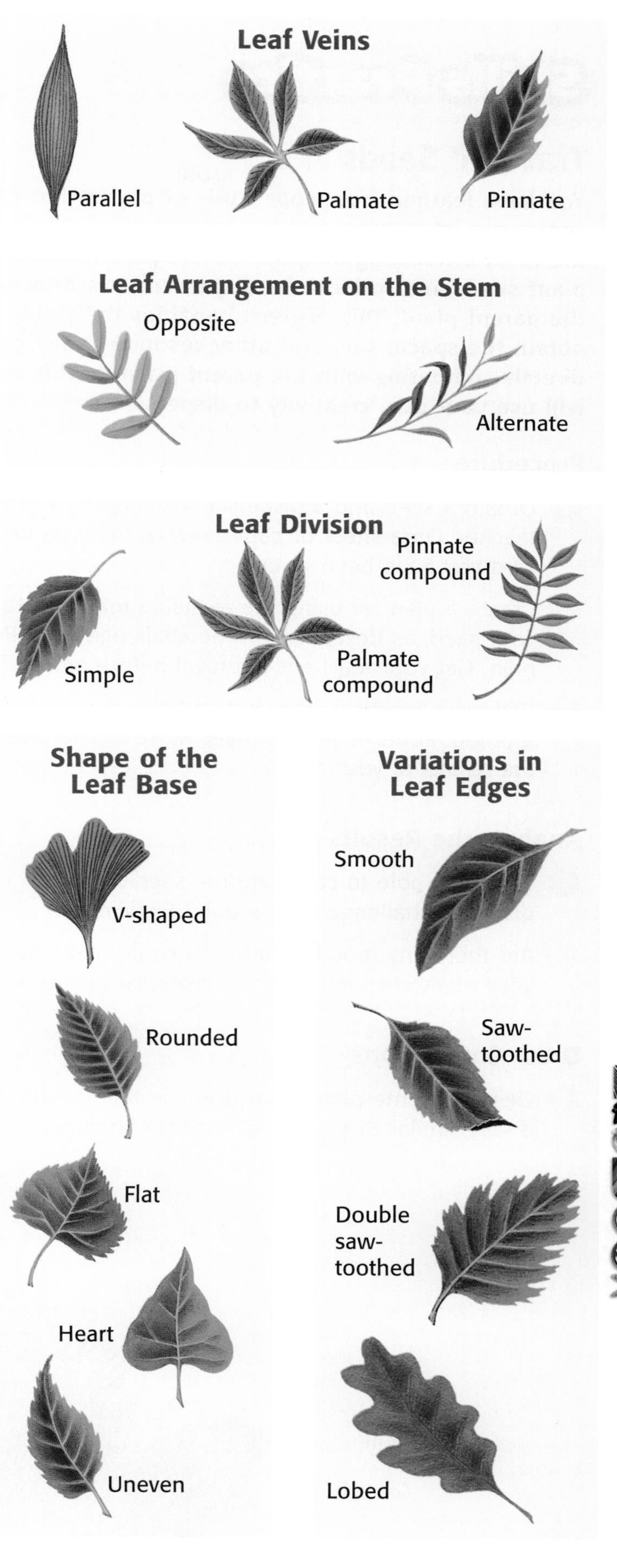

Skills Practice Lab

Travelin' Seeds

You have learned from your study of plants that there are some very interesting and unusual plant adaptations. Some of the most interesting adaptations are modifications that allow plant seeds and fruits to be dispersed, or scattered, away from the parent plant. This dispersal enables the young seedlings to obtain the space, sun, and other resources they need without directly competing with the parent plant. In this activity, you will use your own creativity to disperse a seed.

MATERIALS

- bean seed
- seed-dispersal challenge card
- various household or recycled materials (examples: glue, tape, paper, paper clips, rubber bands, cloth, paper cups and plates, paper towels, and cardboard)

Procedure

1. Obtain a seed and a dispersal challenge card from your teacher. On a sheet of paper, record the type of challenge card you have been given.
2. Create a plan for using the available materials to disperse your seed, as described on the challenge card. Record your plan. Get your teacher's approval before proceeding.
3. With your teacher's permission, test your seed-dispersal method. Perform several trials. Make a data table, and record the results of your trials.

Analyze the Results

1. Were you able to complete the seed-dispersal challenge successfully? Explain.
2. Are there any modifications you could make to your method to improve the dispersal of your seed?

Draw Conclusions

3. Describe some plants that disperse their seeds in a way similar to your seed-dispersal method.

◀ Mangrove seed

◀ Cottonwood

Wild berry ▶

Grass bur ▶

Skills Practice Lab

Weepy Weeds

You are trying to find a way to drain an area that is flooded with water polluted with fertilizer. You know that a plant releases water through the stomata in its leaves. As water evaporates from the leaves, more water is pulled up from the roots through the stem and into the leaves. By this process, called *transpiration,* water and nutrients are pulled into the plant from the soil. About 90% of the water a plant takes up through its roots is released into the atmosphere as water vapor through transpiration. Your idea is to add plants to the flooded area that will transpire the water and take up the fertilizer in their roots.

How much water can a plant take up and release in a certain period of time? In this activity, you will observe transpiration and determine one stem's rate of transpiration.

MATERIALS

- clock
- coleus or other plant stem cutting
- glass-marking pen
- metric ruler
- paper, graph
- test tube (2)
- test-tube rack
- water

SAFETY

Procedure

1. Make a data table similar to the one below for recording your measurements.

Height of Water in Test Tubes

Time	Test tube with plant	Test tube without plant
Initial		
After 10 min		
After 20 min	DO NOT WRITE IN BOOK	
After 30 min		
After 40 min		
Overnight		

2. Fill each test tube approximately three-fourths full of water. Place both test tubes in a test-tube rack.
3. Place the plant stem so that it stands upright in one of the test tubes. Your test tubes should look like the ones in the photograph at right.
4. Use the glass-marking pen to mark the water level in each of the test tubes. Be sure you have the plant stem in place in its test tube before you mark the water level. Why is this necessary?

5. Measure the height of the water in each test tube. Be sure to hold the test tube level, and measure from the waterline to the bottom of the curve at the bottom of the test tube. Record these measurements on the row labeled "Initial."
6. Wait 10 min, and measure the height of the water in each test tube again. Record these measurements in your data table.
7. Repeat step 6 three more times. Record your measurements each time.
8. Wait 24 hours, and measure the height of the water in each test tube. Record these measurements in your data table.
9. Construct a graph similar to the one below. Plot the data from your data table. Draw a line for each test tube. Use a different color for each line, and make a key below your graph.
10. Calculate the rate of transpiration for your plant by using the following operations:

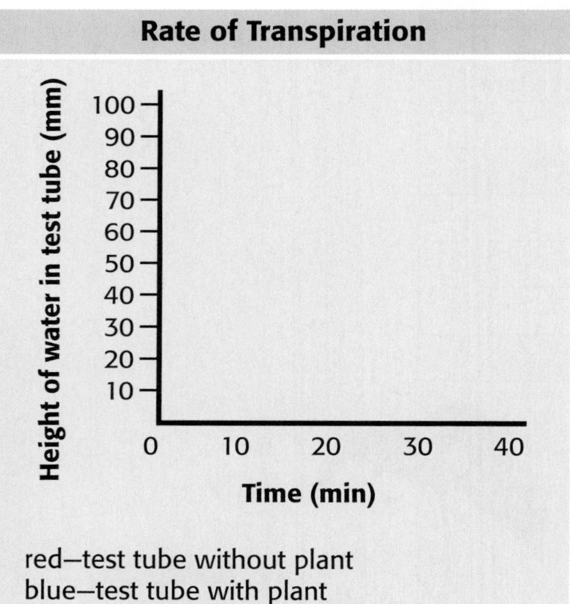

Test tube with plant:
Initial height
− Overnight height
Difference in height of water **(A)**

Test tube without plant:
Initial height
− Overnight height
Difference in height of water **(B)**

Water height difference due to transpiration:
Difference **A**
− Difference **B**
Water lost due to transpiration (in millimeters) in 24 hours

Analyze the Results

1. What was the purpose of the test tube that held only water?
2. What caused the water to go down in the test tube containing the plant stem? Did the same thing happen in the test tube with water only? Explain your answer.
3. What was the calculated rate of transpiration per day?
4. Using your graph, compare the rate of transpiration with the rate of evaporation alone.
5. Prepare a presentation of your experiment for your class. Use your data tables, graphs, and calculations as visual aids.

Applying Your Data

How many leaves did your plant sprigs have? Use this number to estimate what the rate of transpiration might be for a plant with 200 leaves. When you have your answer in millimeters of height in a test tube, pour this amount into a graduated cylinder to measure it in milliliters.

Skills Practice Lab

Wet, Wiggly Worms!

Earthworms have been digging in the Earth for more than 100 million years! Earthworms fertilize the soil with their waste and loosen the soil when they tunnel through the moist dirt of a garden or lawn. Worms are food for many animals, such as birds, frogs, snakes, rodents, and fish. Some say they are good food for people, too!

In this activity, you will observe the behavior of a live earthworm. Remember that earthworms are living animals that deserve to be handled gently. Be sure to keep your earthworm moist during this activity. The skin of the earthworm must stay moist so that the worm can get oxygen. If the earthworm's skin dries out, the worm will suffocate and die. Use a spray bottle to moisten the earthworm with water.

MATERIALS

- celery leaves
- clock
- dissecting pan
- earthworm, live
- flashlight
- paper towels
- probe
- ruler, metric
- shoe box, with lid
- soil
- spray bottle
- water

SAFETY

Procedure

1. Place a wet paper towel in the bottom of a dissecting pan. Put a live earthworm on the paper towel, and observe how the earthworm moves. Record your observations.
2. Use the probe to carefully touch the anterior end (head) of the worm. Gently touch other areas of the worm's body with the probe. Record the kinds of responses you observe.
3. Place celery leaves at one end of the pan. Record how the earthworm responds to the presence of food.
4. Shine a flashlight on the anterior end of the earthworm. Record the earthworm's reaction to the light.
5. Line the bottom of the shoe box with a damp paper towel. Cover half of the shoe box with the box top.
6. Place the worm on the uncovered side of the shoe box in the light. Record your observations of the worm's behavior for 3 min.

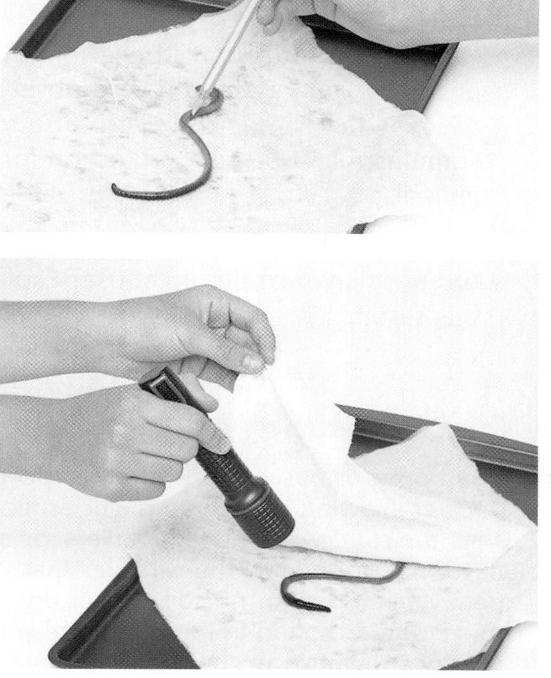

7. Place the worm in the covered side of the box. Record your observations for 3 min.
8. Repeat steps 6–7 three times.
9. Spread some loose soil evenly in the bottom of the shoe box so that the soil is about 4 cm deep. Place the earthworm on top of the soil. Observe and record the earthworm's behavior for 3 min.
10. Dampen the soil on one side of the box, and leave the other side dry. Place the earthworm in the center of the box between the wet and dry soil. Cover the box, and wait 3 min. Uncover the box, and record your observations. Repeat this procedure three times. (You may need to search for the worm!)

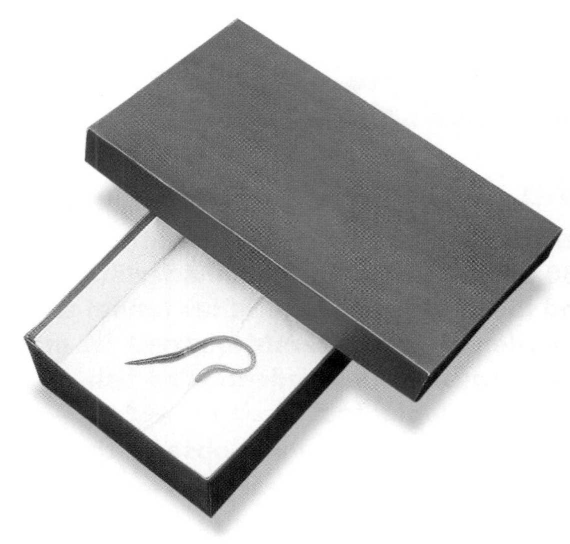

Analyze the Results

1. How did the earthworm respond to being touched? Were some areas more sensitive than others?
2. How did the earthworm respond to the presence of food?

Draw Conclusions

3. How is the earthworm's behavior influenced by light? Based on your observations, describe how an animal's response to a stimulus might provide protection for the animal.
4. When the worm was given a choice of wet or dry soil, which did it choose? Explain this result.

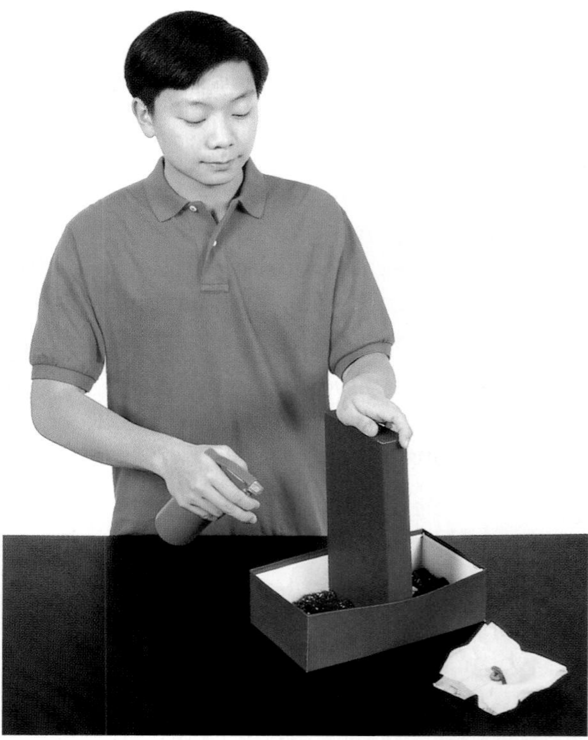

Communicating Your Data

Based on your observations of an earthworm's behavior, prepare a poster showing where you might expect to find earthworms. Draw a picture with colored markers, or cut out pictures from magazines. Include all the variables that you used in your experiment, such as soil or no soil, wet or dry soil, light or dark, and food. Write a caption at the bottom of your poster describing where earthworms might be found in nature.

Skills Practice Lab

The Cricket Caper

Insects are a special class of invertebrates with more than 750,000 known species. Insects may be the most successful group of animals on Earth. In this activity you will observe a cricket's structure and the simple adaptive behaviors that help make it so successful. Remember, you will be handling a living animal that deserves to be treated with care.

MATERIALS

- aluminum foil
- apple
- bags, plastic, sealable (2)
- beaker, 600 mL (2)
- cricket (2)
- hand lens (optional)
- ice, crushed
- lamp
- plastic wrap
- tape, masking
- water, tap, hot

SAFETY

Procedure

1. Place a cricket in a clean 600 mL beaker, and quickly cover the beaker with plastic wrap. The supply of oxygen in the container is enough for the cricket to breathe while you complete your work.
2. While the cricket is getting used to the container, make a data table similar to the one below. Be sure to allow enough space to write your descriptions.

Cricket Body Structures	
Number	**Description**
Body segments	
Antennae	
Eyes	
Wings	

3. Without making much movement, begin to examine the cricket. Fill in your data table with your observations of the cricket's structure.
4. Place a small piece of apple in the beaker. Set the beaker on a table. Sit quietly for several minutes and observe the cricket. Any movement may cause the cricket to stop what it is doing. Record your observations.
5. Remove the plastic wrap from the beaker, remove the apple, and quickly attach a second beaker. Join the two beakers together at the mouths with masking tape. Handle the beakers carefully. Remember, there is a living animal inside.

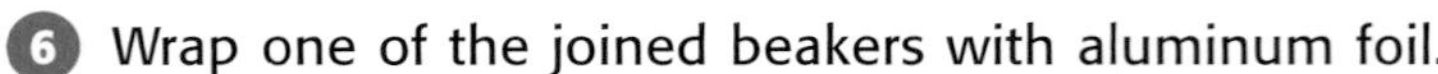

6. Wrap one of the joined beakers with aluminum foil.

7. If the cricket is hiding under the aluminum foil, gently tap the sides of the beaker until the cricket is exposed. Lay the joined beakers on their sides, and shine a lamp on the uncovered side. Record the cricket's location.

8. Record the cricket's location after 5 min. Without disturbing the cricket, carefully move the aluminum foil to the other beaker. After 5 min, record the cricket's location. Repeat this process one more time to see if you get the same result.

9. Fill a sealable plastic bag halfway with crushed ice. Fill another bag halfway with hot tap water. Seal each bag, and arrange them side by side on the table.

10. Remove the aluminum foil from the beakers. Gently rock the joined beakers from side to side until the cricket is in the center. Place the beakers on the plastic bags, as shown below.

11. Observe the cricket's behavior for 5 min. Record your observations.

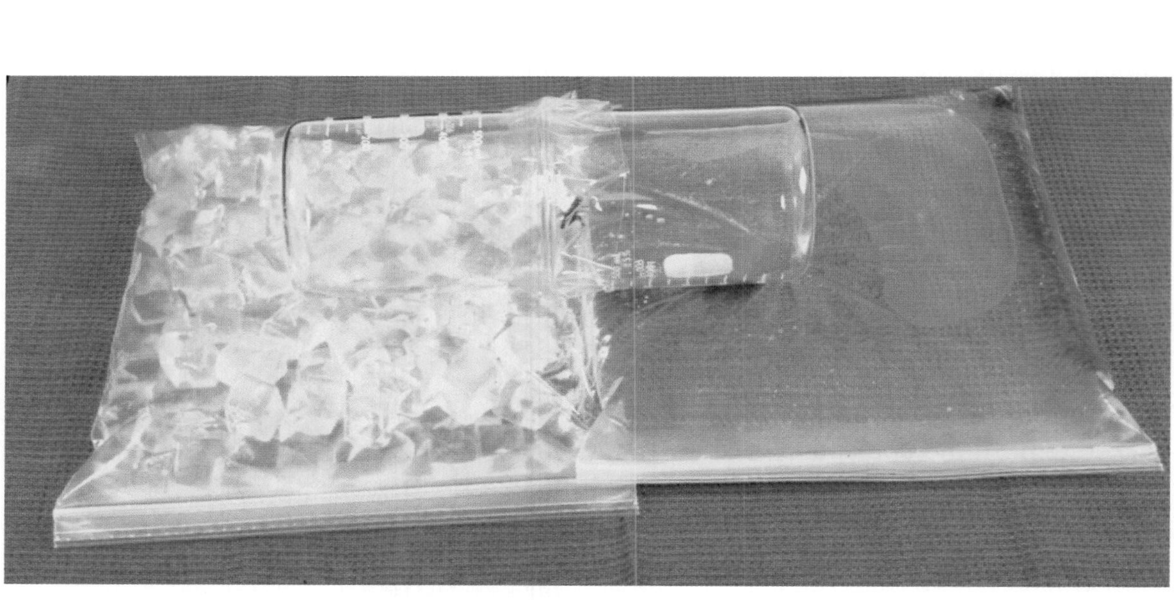

12. Set the beakers on one end for several minutes to allow them to return to room temperature. Repeat steps 10–12 three times. (Why do you think it is necessary to allow the beakers to return to room temperature each time?)
13. Set the beakers on one end. Carefully remove the masking tape, and separate the beakers. Quickly replace the plastic wrap over the beaker containing the cricket. Allow your cricket to rest while you make two data tables similar to those at right.
14. Observe the cricket's movement in the beaker every 15 seconds for 3 min. Fill in the Cricket (alone) data table using the following codes: 0 = no movement, 1 = slight movement, and 2 = rapid movement.
15. Obtain a second cricket from your teacher, and place this cricket in the container with the first cricket. Every 15 seconds, record the movement of each cricket in the Cricket A and Cricket B data table using the codes given in step 14.

Cricket (alone)	
15 s	
30 s	
45 s	
60 s	
75 s	
90 s	DO NOT WRITE IN BOOK
105 s	
120 s	
135 s	
150 s	
165 s	
180 s	

Cricket A and Cricket B		
	A	B
15 s		
30 s		
45 s		
60 s		
75 s		
90 s	DO NOT WRITE IN BOOK	
105 s		
120 s		
135 s		
150 s		
165 s		
180 s		

Analyze the Results

1. Describe crickets' feeding behavior. Are they lappers, suckers, or chewers?
2. Do crickets prefer light or darkness? Explain.
3. From your observations, what can you infer about a cricket's temperature preferences?

Draw Conclusions

4. Based on your observations of Cricket A and Cricket B, what general statements can you make about the social behavior of crickets?

Applying Your Data

Make a third data table titled "Cricket and Another Species of Insect." Introduce another insect, such as a grasshopper, into the beaker. Record your observations for 3 min. Write a short summary of the cricket's reaction to another species.

Skills Practice Lab

A Prince of a Frog

Imagine that you are a scientist interested in amphibians. You have heard in the news about amphibians disappearing all over the world. What a great loss it will be to the environment if all amphibians become extinct! Your job is to learn as much as possible about how frogs normally behave so that you can act as a resource for other scientists who are studying the problem. In this activity, you will observe a normal frog in a dry container and in water.

MATERIALS

- beaker, 600 mL
- container half-filled with dechlorinated water
- crickets, live
- frog, live, in a dry container
- gloves, protective
- rock, large (optional)

SAFETY

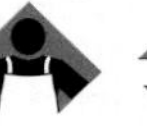

Procedure

1. Make a table similar to the one below to note all of your observations of the frog in this investigation.

Observations of a Live Frog	
Characteristic	**Observation**
Breathing	
Eyes	
Legs	
Response to food	DO NOT WRITE IN BOOK
Skin texture	
Swimming behavior	
Skin coloration	

2. Observe a live frog in a dry container. Draw a picture of the frog. Label the eyes, nostrils, front legs, and hind legs.
3. Watch the frog's movements as it breathes air with its lungs. Write a description of the frog's breathing.
4. Look closely at the frog's eyes, and note their location. Examine the upper and lower eyelids as well as the transparent third eyelid. Which of these three eyelids actually moves over the eye?
5. Study the frog's legs. Note in your data table the difference between the front and hind legs

6. Place a live insect, such as a cricket, in the container. Observe and record how the frog reacts.
7. Carefully pick up the frog, and examine its skin. How does it feel?
   Caution: Remember that a frog is a living thing and deserves to be handled gently and with respect.
8. Place a 600 mL beaker in the container. Place the frog in the beaker. Cover the beaker with your hand, and carry it to a container of dechlorinated water. Tilt the beaker and gently submerge it in the water until the frog swims out of the beaker.
9. Watch the frog float and swim in the water. How does the frog use its legs to swim? Notice the position of the frog's head.
10. As the frog swims, bend down and look up into the water so that you can see the underside of the frog. Then look down on the frog from above. Compare the color on the top and the underneath sides of the frog. Record your observations in your data table.

Analyze the Results

1. From the position of the frog's eyes, what can you infer about the frog's field of vision? How might the position of the frog's eyes benefit the frog while it is swimming?
2. How can a frog "breathe" while it is swimming in water?
3. How are the hind legs of a frog adapted for life on land and in water?
4. What differences did you notice in coloration on the frog's top side and its underneath side? What advantage might these color differences provide?
5. How does the frog eat? What senses are involved in helping the frog catch its prey?

Applying Your Data

Observe another type of amphibian, such as a salamander. How do the adaptations of other types of amphibians compare with those of the frog you observed in this investigation?

Model-Making Lab

Adaptation: It's a Way of Life

Since the beginning of life on Earth, species have had special characteristics called *adaptations* that have helped them survive changes in environmental conditions. Changes in a species' environment include climate changes, habitat destruction, or the extinction of prey. These things can cause a species to die out unless the species has a characteristic that helps it survive. For example, a species of bird may have an adaptation for eating sunflower seeds and ants. If the ant population dies out, the bird can still eat seeds and can therefore survive.

In this activity, you will explore several adaptations and design an organism with adaptations you choose. Then, you will describe how these adaptations help the organism survive.

MATERIALS

- arts-and-crafts materials, various
- markers, colored
- magazines for cutouts
- poster board
- scissors

SAFETY

Procedure

1. Study the chart below. Choose one adaptation from each column. For example, an organism might be a scavenger that burrows underground and has spikes on its tail!

Adaptations		
Diet	**Type of transportation**	**Special adaptation**
carnivore	flies	uses sensors to detect heat
herbivore	glides through the air	is active only at night and has excellent night vision
omnivore	burrows underground	changes colors to match its surroundings
scavenger	runs fast	has armor
decomposer	swims	has horns
	hops	can withstand extreme temperature changes
	walks	secretes a terrible and sickening scent
	climbs	has poison glands
	floats	has specialized front teeth
	slithers	has tail spikes
		stores oxygen in its cells so it does not have to breathe continuously
		one of your own invention

2. Design an organism that has the three adaptations you have chosen. Use poster board, colored markers, picture cutouts, or craft materials of your choosing to create your organism.
3. Write a caption on your poster describing your organism. Describe its appearance, its habitat, its niche, and the way its adaptations help it survive. Give your organism a two-part "scientific" name that is based on its characteristics.
4. Display your creation in your classroom. Share with classmates how you chose the adaptations for your organism.

Analyze the Results

1. What does your imaginary organism eat?
2. In what environment or habitat would your organism be most likely to survive—in the desert, tropical rain forest, plains, icecaps, mountains, or ocean? Explain your answer.
3. Is your creature a mammal, a reptile, an amphibian, a bird, or a fish? What modern organism (on Earth today) or ancient organism (extinct) is your imaginary organism most like? Explain the similarities between the two organisms. Do some research outside the lab, if necessary, to find out about a real organism that may be similar to your imaginary organism.

Draw Conclusions

4. If there were a sudden climate change, such as daily downpours of rain in a desert, would your imaginary organism survive? What adaptations for surviving such a change does it have?

Applying Your Data

Call or write to an agency such as the U.S. Fish and Wildlife Service to get a list of endangered species in your area. Choose an organism on that list. Describe the organism's niche and any special adaptations it has that help it survive. Find out why it is endangered and what is being done to protect it. Examine the illustration of the animal at right. Based on its physical characteristics, describe its habitat and niche. Is this a real animal?

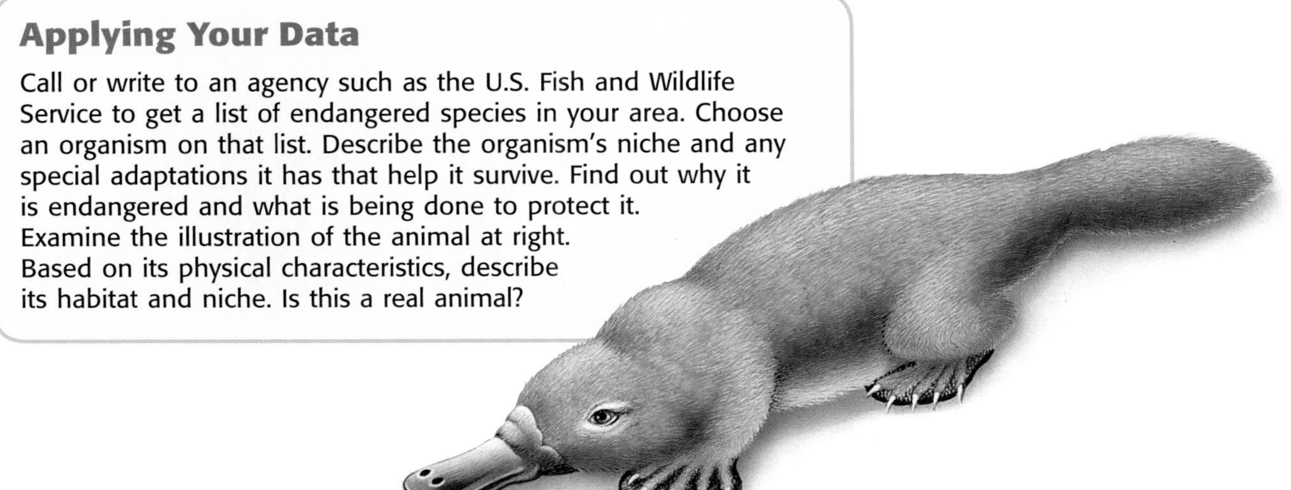

Model-Making Lab

A Passel o' Pioneers

Succession is the natural process of the introduction and development of living things in an area. The area could be one that has never supported life before and has no soil, such as a recently cooled lava flow from a volcano. In an area where there is no soil, the process is called *primary succession.* In an area where soil already exists, such as an abandoned field or a forest after a fire, the process is called *secondary succession.*

In this investigation, you will build a model of secondary succession using natural soil.

MATERIALS

- balance
- graduated cylinder, 250 mL
- large fishbowl
- plastic wrap
- protective gloves
- soil from home or schoolyard, 500 g
- water, 250 mL

SAFETY

Procedure

1. Place the natural soil you brought from home or the schoolyard into the fishbowl, and dampen the soil with 250 mL of water. Cover the top of the fishbowl with plastic wrap, and place the fishbowl in a sunny window.
   Caution: Do not touch your face, eyes, or mouth during this activity. Wash your hands thoroughly when you are finished.
2. For 2 weeks, observe the fishbowl for any new growth. Describe and draw any new organisms you observe. Record these and all other observations.
3. Identify and record the names of as many of these new organisms as you can.

Analyze the Results

1. What kinds of plants sprouted in your model of secondary succession? Were they tree seedlings, grasses, or weeds?

2. Were the plants that sprouted in the fishbowl unusual or common for your area?

Draw Conclusions

3. Explain how the plants that grew in your model of secondary succession can be called pioneer species.

Applying Your Data

Examine each of the photographs on this page. Determine whether each area, if abandoned forever, would undergo primary or secondary succession. You may decide that an area will not undergo succession at all. Explain your reasoning.

Bulldozed land

Eutrophic pond

Mount St. Helens volcano

Shipping port parking lot

Using Scientific Methods

Inquiry Lab

Life in the Desert

Organisms that live in the desert have some unusual methods for conserving water. Conserving water is a special challenge for animals that live in the desert. In this activity you will invent a water-conserving "adaptation" for a desert animal, represented by a piece of sponge. You will protect your wet desert sponge so it will dry out as little as possible over a 24 h period.

MATERIALS

- balance
- sponge, dry, 8 cm × 8 cm × 2 cm (2 pieces)
- water
- other materials as needed

Ask a Question

1. How can an animal conserve water in the desert?

Form a Hypothesis

2. Plan a method for keeping your "desert animal" from drying out. Your "animal" must be in the open for at least 4 h during the 24 h period. Real desert animals expose themselves to the dry desert heat to search for food. Write your plan and predictions about the outcome of your experiment.
3. Design and draw data tables, if necessary. Have your teacher approve your plan before you begin.

Test the Hypothesis

4. Soak two pieces of sponge in water until they begin to drip. Place each piece on a balance, and record its mass.
5. Immediately protect one sponge according to your plan. Place both pieces in an area where they will not be disturbed. You should take your protected "animal" out for feeding for a total of at least 4 h.
6. At the end of 24 h, place each piece of sponge on the balance again, and record its mass.

Analyze the Results

1. Describe the adaptation you used to help your "animal" survive. Was it effective? Explain.
2. What was the purpose of leaving one of the sponges unprotected? How did the water loss in each of your sponges compare?

Communicating Your Data

Conduct a class discussion about other adaptations and results. How can you relate these invented adaptations to adaptations for desert survival among real organisms?

Using Scientific Methods

Inquiry Lab

Discovering Mini-Ecosystems

In your study of ecosystems, you learned that a biome is a very large ecosystem that includes a set of smaller, related ecosystems. For example, a coniferous forest biome may include a river ecosystem, a wetland ecosystem, and a lake ecosystem. Each of those ecosystems may include several other smaller, related ecosystems. Even cities have mini-ecosystems! You may find a mini-ecosystem on a patch of sidewalk, in a puddle of rainwater, under a leaky faucet, in a shady area, or under a rock. In this activity, you will design a method for comparing two different mini-ecosystems found near your school.

MATERIALS

- items to be determined by the students and approved by the teacher

SAFETY

Ask a Question

1. Examine the grounds around your school, and select two different areas you wish to investigate. Decide what you want to learn about your mini-ecosystems. For example, you may want to know what kind of living things each area contains. Be sure to get your teacher's approval before you begin.

Form a Hypothesis

2. For each mini-ecosystem, make data tables for recording your observations.

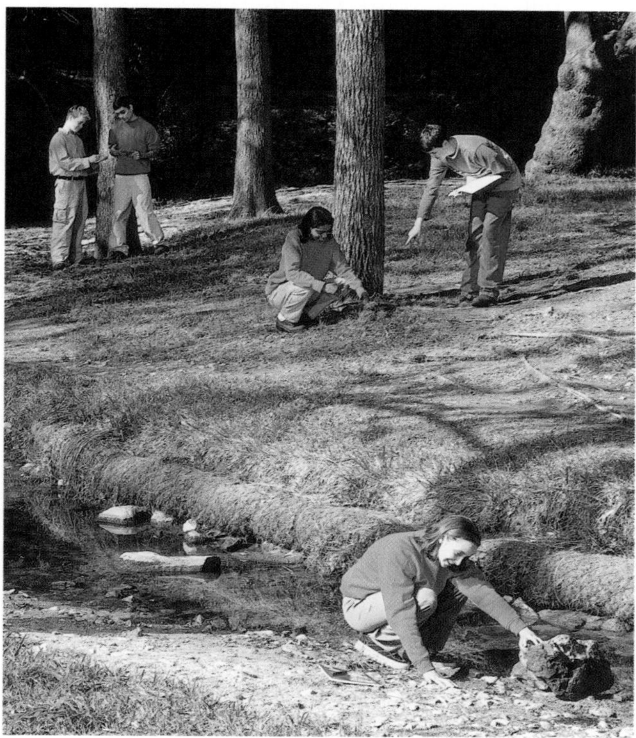

Test the Hypothesis

3. Observe your mini-ecosystem according to your plan at several different time points throughout the day. Record your observations.
4. Wait 24 h and observe your mini-ecosystem again at the same times that you observed it the day before. Record your observations.
5. Wait 1 week, and observe your mini-ecosystem again at the same times. Record your observations.

Analyze the Results

1. What factors determine the differences between your mini-ecosystems? Identify the factors that set each mini-ecosystem apart from its surrounding area.
2. How do the populations of your mini-ecosystems compare?
3. Identify some of the adaptations that the organisms living in your two mini-ecosystems have. Describe how the adaptations help the organisms survive in their environment.

Draw Conclusions

4. Write a report describing and comparing your mini-ecosystems with those of your classmates.

Skills Practice Lab

Deciding About Environmental Issues

You make hundreds of decisions every day. Some of them are complicated, but many of them are very simple, such as what to wear or what to eat for lunch. Deciding what to do about an environmental issue can be very difficult. There are many different factors that must be considered. How will a certain solution affect people's lives? How much will it cost? Is it ethically right?

In this activity, you will analyze an issue in four steps to help you make a decision about it. Find out about environmental issues that are being discussed in your area. Examine newspapers, magazines, and other publications to find out what the issues are. Choose one local issue to evaluate. For example, you could evaluate whether the city should spend the money to provide recycling bins and special trucks for picking up recyclable trash.

MATERIALS

- newspapers, magazines, and other publications containing information about environmental issues

A Four-Step Decision-Making Model

Gather Information

Consider Values

Explore Consequences

Make a Decision

Procedure

1. Write a statement about an environmental issue.
2. Read about your issue in several publications. On a separate sheet of paper, summarize important facts.
3. The values of an issue are the things that you consider important. Examine the diagram below. Several values are given. Which values do you think apply most to the environmental issue you are considering? Are there other values that you believe will help you make a decision about the issue? Consider at least four values in making your decision.

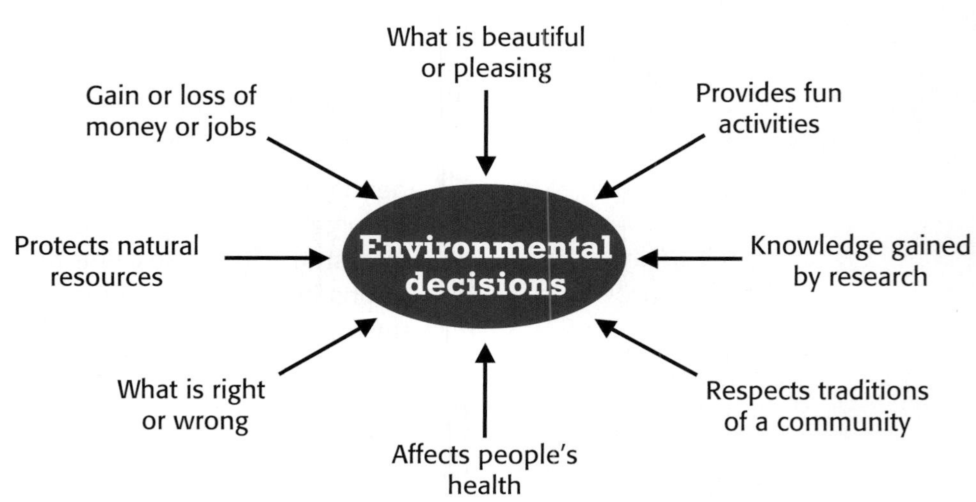

4. Consequences are the things that result from a certain course of action. Create a table similar to the one below. Use your table to organize your thoughts about consequences related to your environmental issue. List your values at the top. Fill in each space with the consequences for each value.

Consequences Table				
	Values			
Consequences				
Positive short-term consequences				
Negative short-term consequences				
Positive long-term consequences				
Negative long-term consequences				

5. Thoroughly consider all of the consequences you have recorded in your table. Evaluate how important each consequence is. Make a decision about what course of action you would choose on the issue.

Analyze the Results

1. In your evaluation, did you consider short-term consequences or long-term consequences to be more important? Why?

2. Which value or values had the greatest influence on your final decision? Explain your reasoning.

Communicating Your Data

Compare your table with your classmates' tables. Did you all make the same decision about a similar issue? If not, form teams, and organize a formal classroom debate of a specific environmental issue.

Using Scientific Methods

Inquiry Lab

Muscles at Work

Have you ever exercised outside on a cold fall day wearing only a thin warm-up suit or shorts? How did you stay warm? The answer is that your muscle cells contracted, and when contraction takes place, some energy is used to do work, and the rest is converted to thermal energy. This process helps your body maintain a constant temperature in cold conditions. In this activity, you will learn how the release of energy can cause a change in your body temperature.

MATERIALS

- clock (or watch) with a second hand
- thermometer, small, hand held
- other materials as approved by your teacher

Ask a Question

1. Write a question that you can test about how activity affects body temperature.

Form a Hypothesis

2. Form a group of four students. In your group, discuss several exercises that can produce a change in body temperature. Write a hypothesis that could answer the question you asked.

Test the Hypothesis

3. Develop an experimental procedure that includes the steps necessary to test your hypothesis. Be sure to get your teacher's approval before you begin.
4. Assign tasks to individuals in the group, such as note taking, data recording, and timing. What observations and data will you be recording? Design your data tables accordingly.
5. Perform your experiment as planned by your group. Be sure to record all observations in your data tables.

Analyze the Results

1. How did you determine if muscle contractions cause the release of thermal energy? Was your hypothesis supported by your data? Explain your results in a written report. Describe how you could improve your experimental method.

Applying Your Data

Why do humans shiver in the cold? Do all animals shiver? Find out why shivering is one of the first signs that your body is becoming too cold.

Model-Making Lab

Build a Lung

When you breathe, you actually pull air into your lungs because your diaphragm muscle causes your chest to expand. You can see this is true by placing your hands on your ribs and inhaling slowly. Did you feel your chest expand?

In this activity, you will build a model of a lung by using some common materials. You will see how the diaphragm muscle works to inflate your lungs. Refer to the diagrams at right as you construct your model.

MATERIALS

- bag, trash, small plastic
- balloon, small
- bottle, top half, 2 L
- clay, golf-ball-sized piece
- rubber bands (2)
- ruler, metric
- straw, plastic
- tape, transparent

Procedure

1. Attach the balloon to the end of the straw with a rubber band. Make a hole through the clay, and insert the other end of the straw through the hole. Be sure at least 8 cm of the straw extends beyond the clay. Squeeze the ball of clay gently to seal the clay around the straw.
2. Insert the balloon end of the straw into the neck of the bottle. Use the ball of clay to seal the straw and balloon into the bottle.
3. Turn the bottle gently on its side. Place the trash bag over the cut end of the bottle. Expand a rubber band around the bottom of the bottle to secure the bag. You may wish to reinforce the seal with tape. Before the plastic is completely sealed, gather the excess material of the bag into your hand, and press toward the inside of the bottle slightly. (You may need to tie a knot about halfway up from the bottom of the bag to take up excess material.) Use tape to finish sealing the bag to the bottle with the bag in this position. The excess air will be pushed out of the bottle.

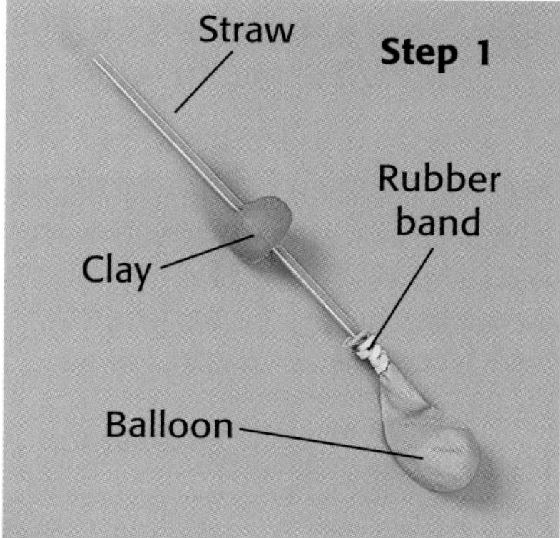

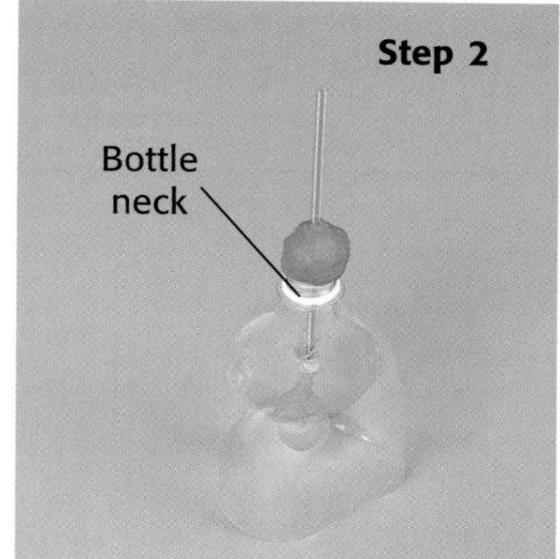

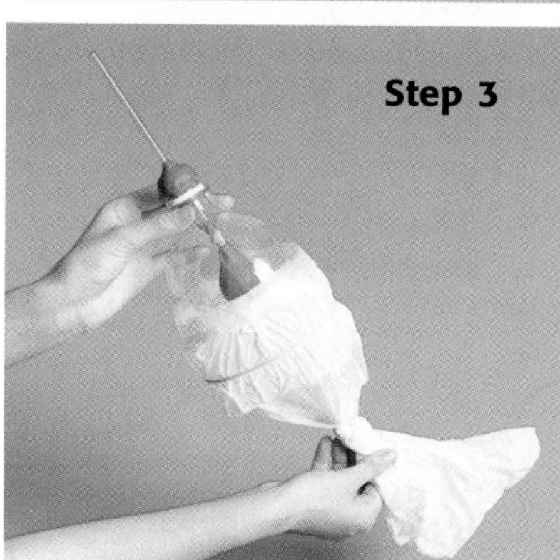

Analyze the Results

1. What can you do with your model to make the "lung" inflate?
2. What do the balloon, the plastic wrap, and the straw represent in your model?
3. Using your model, demonstrate to the class how air enters the lung and how air exits the lung.

Applying Your Data

Do some research to find out what an "iron lung" is and why it was used in the past. Research and write a report about what is used today to help people who have difficulty breathing.

Skills Practice Lab

Enzymes in Action

You know how important enzymes are in the process of digestion. This lab will help you see enzymes at work. Hydrogen peroxide is continuously produced by your cells. If it is not quickly broken down, hydrogen peroxide will kill your cells. Luckily, your cells contain an enzyme that converts hydrogen peroxide into two nonpoisonous substances. This enzyme is also present in the cells of beef liver. In this lab, you will observe the action of this enzyme on hydrogen peroxide.

MATERIALS

- beef liver, 1 cm cubes (3)
- gloves, protective
- graduated cylinder, 10 mL
- hydrogen peroxide, fresh (4 mL)
- mortar and pestle (or fork and watch glass)
- plate, small
- spatula
- test tube (3)
- test-tube rack
- tweezers
- water

SAFETY

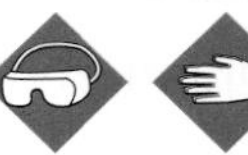

Procedure

1. Draw a data table similar to the one below. Be sure to leave enough space to write your observations.

Data Table		
Size and condition of liver	**Experimental liquid**	**Observations**
1 cm cube beef liver	2 mL water	
1 cm cube beef liver	2 mL hydrogen peroxide	
1 cm cube beef liver (mashed)	2 mL hydrogen peroxide	

2. Get three equal-sized pieces of beef liver from your teacher, and use your forceps to place them on your plate.

3. Pour 2 mL of water into a test tube labeled "Water and liver."

4. Using the tweezers, carefully place one piece of liver in the test tube. Record your observations in your data table.

5. Pour 2 mL of hydrogen peroxide into a second test tube labeled "Liver and hydrogen peroxide."
Caution: Do not splash hydrogen peroxide on your skin. If you do get hydrogen peroxide on your skin, rinse the affected area with running water immediately, and tell your teacher.

6. Using the tweezers, carefully place one piece of liver in the test tube. Record your observations of the second test tube in your data table.

7. Pour another 2 mL of hydrogen peroxide into a third test tube labeled "Ground liver and hydrogen peroxide."

8. Using a mortar and pestle (or fork and watch glass), carefully grind the third piece of liver.

9. Using the spatula, scrape the ground liver into the third test tube. Record your observations of the third test tube in your data table.

Analyze the Results

1. What was the purpose of putting the first piece of liver in water? Why was this a necessary step?

2. Describe the difference you observed between the liver and the ground liver when each was placed in the hydrogen peroxide. How can you account for this difference?

Applying Your Data

Do plant cells contain enzymes that break down hydrogen peroxide? Try this experiment using potato cubes instead of liver to find out.

Skills Practice Lab

My, How You've Grown!

In humans, the process of development that takes place between fertilization and birth lasts about 266 days. In 4 weeks, the new individual grows from a single fertilized cell to an embryo whose heart is beating and pumping blood. All of the organ systems and body parts are completely formed by the end of the seventh month. During the last 2 months before birth, the baby grows, and its organ systems mature. At birth, the average mass of a baby is about 33,000 times as much as that of an embryo at 2 weeks of development! In this activity, you will discover just how fast a fetus grows.

MATERIALS

- paper, graph
- pencils, colored

Procedure

1. Using graph paper, make two graphs—one entitled "Length" and one entitled "Mass." On the length graph, use intervals of 25 mm on the *y*-axis. Extend the *y*-axis to 500 mm. On the mass graph, use intervals of 100 g on the *y*-axis. Extend this *y*-axis to 3,300 g. Use 2-week intervals for time on the *x*-axes for both graphs. Both *x*-axes should extend to 40 weeks.
2. Examine the data table at right. Plot the data in the table on your graphs. Use a colored pencil to draw the curved line that joins the points on each graph.

Increase of Mass and Length of Average Human Fetus

Time (weeks)	Mass (g)	Length (mm)
2	0.1	1.5
3	0.3	2.3
4	0.5	5.0
5	0.6	10.0
6	0.8	15.0
8	1.0	30.0
13	15.0	90.0
17	115.0	140.0
21	300.0	250.0
26	950.0	320.0
30	1,500.0	400.0
35	2,300.0	450.0
40	3,300.0	500.0

Analyze the Results

1. Describe the change in mass of a developing fetus. How can you explain this change?
2. Describe the change in length of a developing fetus. How does the change in mass compare to the change in length?

Applying Your Data

Using the information in your graphs, estimate how tall a child would be at age 3 if he or she continued to grow at the same average rate that a fetus grows.

Model-Making Lab

Antibodies to the Rescue

Some cells of the immune system, called *B cells,* make antibodies that attack and kill invading viruses and microorganisms. These antibodies help make you immune to disease. Have you ever had chickenpox? If you have, your body has built up antibodies that can recognize that particular virus. Antibodies will attach themselves to the virus, tagging it for destruction. If you are exposed to the same disease again, the antibodies remember that virus. They will attack the virus even quicker and in greater number than they did the first time. This is the reason that you will probably never have chickenpox more than once.

In this activity, you will construct simple models of viruses and their antibodies. You will see how antibodies are specific for a particular virus.

MATERIALS

- craft materials, such as buttons, fabric scraps, pipe cleaners, and recycled materials
- paper, colored
- scissors
- tape (or glue)

Procedure

1. Draw the virus patterns shown on this page on a separate piece of paper, or design your own virus models from the craft supplies. Remember to design different receptors on each of your virus models.
2. Write a few sentences describing how your viruses are different.
3. Cut out the viruses, and attach them to a piece of colored paper with tape or glue.

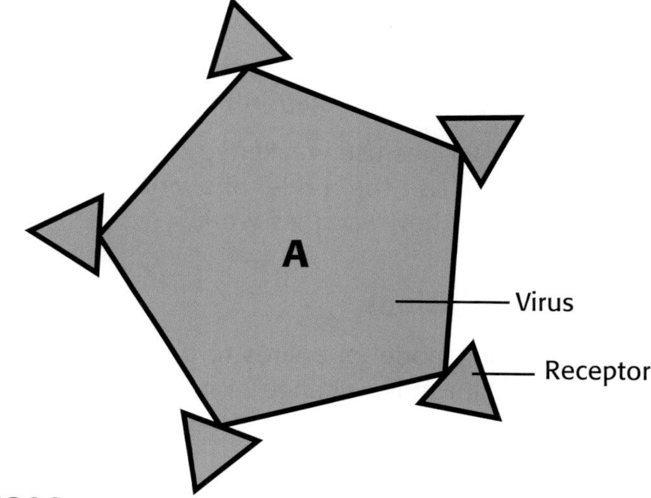

Viruses

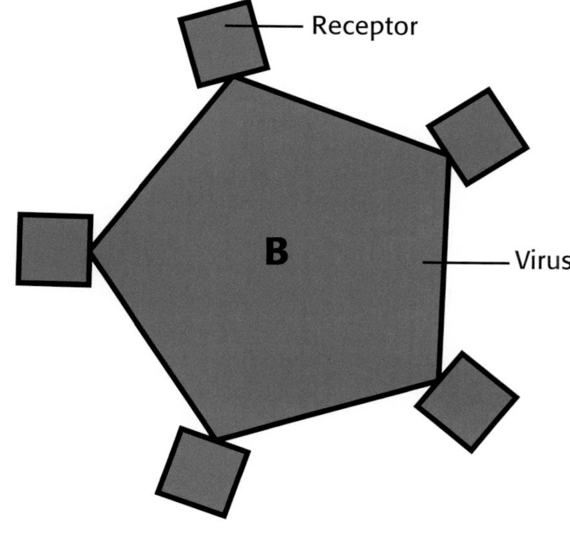

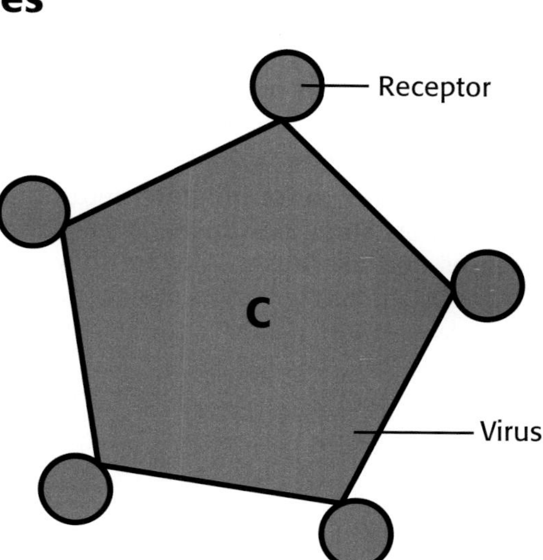

4. Select the antibodies drawn below, or design your own antibodies that will exactly fit on the receptors on your virus models. Draw or create each antibody enough times to attach one to each receptor site on the virus.

Antibodies

5. Cut out the antibodies you have drawn. Arrange the antibodies so that they bind to the virus at the appropriate receptor. Attach them to the virus with tape or glue.

Analyze the Results

1. Explain how an antibody "recognizes" a particular virus.
2. After the attachment of antibodies to the receptors, what would be the next step in the immune response?
3. Many vaccines use weakened copies of the virus to protect the body. Use the model of a virus and its specific antibody to explain how vaccines work.

Draw Conclusions

4. Use your model of a virus to demonstrate to the class how a receptor might change or mutate so that a vaccine would no longer be effective.

Applying Your Data

Research in the library or on the Internet to find information about the discovery of the Salk vaccine for polio. Include information on how polio affects people today.

Research in the library or on the Internet to find information and write a report about filoviruses. What do they look like? What diseases do they cause? Why are they especially dangerous? Is there an effective vaccine against any filovirus? Explain.

Skills Practice Lab

To Diet or Not to Diet

There are six main classes of foods that we need in order to keep our bodies functioning properly: water, vitamins, minerals, carbohydrates, fats, and proteins. In this activity you will investigate the importance of a well-balanced diet in maintaining a healthy body. Then you will create a poster or picture that illustrates the importance of one of the three energy-producing nutrients—carbohydrates, fats, and proteins.

MATERIALS

- crayons (or markers), assorted colors
- diet books
- menus, fast-food (optional)
- nutrition reference books
- paper, white unlined

Procedure

1. Draw a table like the one below. Research in the library, on nutrition labels, in nutrition or diet books, or on the Internet to find the information you need to fill out the chart.

Nutrition Data Table

	Fats	Carbohydrates	Proteins
Found in which foods			
Functions in the body		DO NOT WRITE IN BOOK	
Consequences of deficiency			

2. Choose one of the foods you have learned about in your research, and create a poster or picture that describes its importance in a well-balanced diet.

Analyze the Results

1. Based on what you have learned in this lab, how might you change your eating habits to have a well-balanced diet? Does the nutritional value of foods concern you? Why or why not? Write down your answers, and explain your reasoning.

Communicating Your Data

Write a paragraph explaining why water is a nutrient. Analyze a typical fast-food meal, and determine its overall nutritional value.

Contents

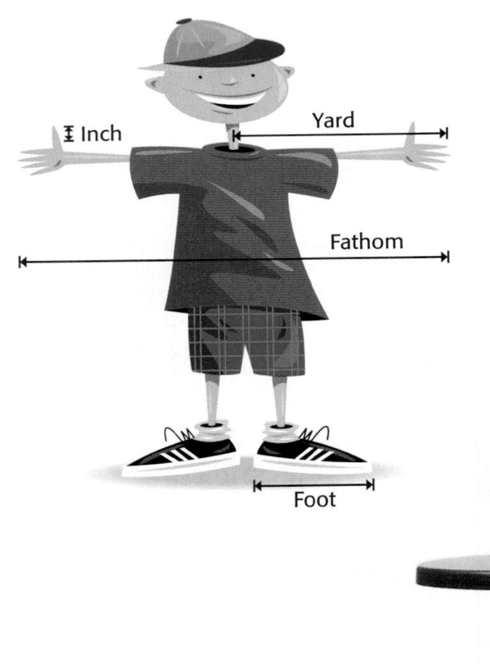

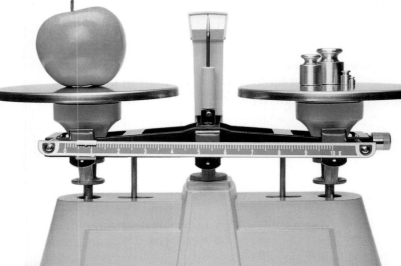

Reading Check Answers

Chapter 1 The World of Life Science

Section 1

Page 6: the study of living things

Page 9: Sample answer: ocean pollution that harms mammals, birds, and fish.

Section 2

Page 10: a series of steps used by scientists to solve problems

Page 12: the possibility that an experiment can be designed to test the hypothesis

Page 14: only one

Page 16: because the scientist has learned something

Section 3

Page 19: a mathematical model

Page 20: to explain a broad range of observations, facts, and tested hypotheses, to predict what might happen, and to organize scientific thinking

Section 4

Page 23: SEMs produce three-dimensional images, and TEMs produce flat images.

Page 25: square units, such as square meters (m^2) and square centimeters (cm^2)

Page 26: how hot or cold it is or how much energy it has

Chapter 2 It's Alive!! Or Is It?

Section 1

Page 39: Sample answer: They control their body temperature by moving from one environment to another. If they get too warm, they move to the shade. If they get too cool, they move out into the sunlight.

Page 40: making food, breaking down food, moving materials into and out of cells, and building cells

Section 2

Page 42: photosynthesis

Page 45: Simple carbohydrates are made of one sugar molecule. Complex carbohydrates are made of many sugar molecules linked together.

Page 46: Most fats are solid, and most oils are liquid.

Chapter 3 Cells: The Basic Units of Life

Section 1

Page 61: Sample answer: All organisms are made of one or more cells, the cell is the basic unit of all living things, and all cells come from existing cells.

Page 62: If a cell's volume gets too large, the cell's surface area will not be able to take in enough nutrients or get rid of wastes fast enough to keep the cell alive.

Page 63: Organelles are structures within a cell that perform specific functions for the cell.

Page 65: One difference between eubacteria and archaea is that bacterial ribosomes are different from archaebacterial ribosomes.

Page 66: The main difference between prokaryotes and eukaryotes is that eukaryotic cells have a nucleus and membrane-bound organelles and prokaryotic cells do not.

Section 2

Page 68: Plant, algae, and fungi cells have cell walls.

Page 69 A cell membrane encloses the cell and separates and protects the cell's contents from the cell's environment. The cell wall also controls the movement of materials into and out of the cell.

Page 70: The cytoskeleton is a web of proteins in the cytoplasm. It gives the cell support and structure.

Page 72: Most of a cell's ATP is made in the cell's mitochondria.

Page 74: Lysosomes destroy worn-out organelles, attack foreign invaders, and get rid of waste material from inside the cell.

Section 3

Page 76: Sample answer: larger size, longer life, and cell specialization

Page 77: An organ is a structure of two or more tissues working together to perform a specific function in the body.

Page 78: cell, tissue, organ, organ system

Chapter 4 The Cell in Action

Section 1

Page 91: Red blood cells would burst in pure water because water particles move from outside, where particles were dense, to inside the cell, where particles were less dense. This movement of water would cause red blood cells to fill up and burst.

Page 93: Exocytosis is the process by which a cell moves large particles to the outside of the cell.

Section 2

Page 95: Cellular respiration is a chemical process by which cells produce energy from food. Breathing supplies oxygen for cellular respiration and removes the carbon dioxide produced by cellular respiration.

Page 97: One kind of fermentation produces CO_2, and the other kind produces lactic acid.

Section 3

Page 99: No, the number of chromosomes is not always related to the complexity of organisms.

Page 100: During cytokinesis in plant cells, a cell plate is formed. During cytokinesis in animal cells, a cell plate does not form.

Chapter 5 Heredity

Section 1

Page 114: the passing of traits from parents to offspring

Page 117: During his second set of experiments, Mendel allowed the first-generation plants, which resulted from his first set of experiments, to self-pollinate.

Page 118: A ratio is a relationship between two different numbers that is often expressed as a fraction.

Section 2

Page 120: A gene contains the instructions for an inherited trait. The different versions of a gene are called *alleles*.

Page 122: Probability is the mathematical chance that something will happen.

Page 124: In incomplete dominance, one trait is not completely dominant over another.

Section 3

Page 127: 23 chromosomes

Page 128: During meiosis, one parent cell makes four new cells.

Chapter 6 Genes and DNA

Section 1

Page 145: Guanine and cytosine are always found in DNA in equal amounts, as are adenine and thymine.

Page 147: every time a cell divides

Section 2

Page 148: a string of nucleotides that give the cell information about how to make a specific trait

Page 151: They transfer amino acids to the ribosome.

Page 152: a physical or chemical agent that can cause a mutation in DNA

Page 153: Sickle cell disease is caused by a mutation in a single nucleotide of DNA, which then causes a different amino acid to be assembled in a protein used in blood cells.

Page 154: a near-identical copy of another organism, created with the original organism's genes

Chapter 7 The Evolution of Living Things

Section 1

Page 166: if they mate with each other and produce more of the same type of organism

Page 168: by their estimated ages and physical similarities

Page 170: a four-legged land mammal

Page 172: that they have common ancestry

Section 2

Page 175: 965 km (600 mi) west of Ecuador

Page 177: that Earth had been formed by natural processes over a long period of time

Page 178: *On the Origin of Species by Means of Natural Selection*

Section 3

Page 181: because they often produce many offspring and have short generation times

Page 182: Sample answer: A newly formed canyon, mountain range, or lake could divide the members of a population.

Chapter 8 The History of Life on Earth

Section 1

Page 195: absolute dating

Page 197: periods of sudden extinction of many species

Page 198: the idea that the Earth's continents once formed a single landmass surrounded by ocean

Section 2

Page 200: The early Earth was very different from today—there were violent events and a harsh atmosphere.

Page 203: a mass extinction

Page 204: "recent life"

Section 3

Page 207: the hominid family

Page 208: Africa

Page 211: Paleontologists will review their ideas about the evolution of hominids.

Chapter 9 Classification

Section 1

Page 222: **Sample answer:** How many known species are there? What are the defining characteristics of each species? and What are the relationships between these species?

Page 225: genus and species

Page 226: A dichotomous key is an identification aid that uses a series of descriptive statements.

Section 2

Page 229: *Escherichia coli*

Page 231: Sample answer: Plants make energy through photosynthesis. Some members of the kingdoms Fungi, Protista, and Eubacteria consume plants. When these organisms digest the plant material, they get energy and nutrients made by the plants.

Page 233: Sponges don't have sense organs, and they usually can't move around.

Chapter 10 Bacteria and Viruses

Section 1

Page 246: Bacteria make up the kingdoms Eubacteria and Archaebacteria.

Page 248: Binary fission is a process of cell division in which one cell splits into two. All bacteria reproduce by binary fission.

Section 2

Page 252: Nitrogen fixing is the process by which nitrogen gas in the air is transformed into a form that plants can use.

Page 254: In genetic engineering, scientists change the genes of bacteria or other living things.

Section 3

Page 257: Viruses can be classified by shape or by the type of genetic material that they contain. Other possible answers are that viruses can be classified by life cycle or by the kind of disease that they cause.

Page 258: when a virus attacks living cells and turns them into virus factories

Chapter 11 Protists and Fungi

Section 1

Page 271: Protist producers make their own food through photosynthesis.

Page 272: binary fission and multiple fission

Section 2

Page 275: Red algae also have a red pigment in their cells that gives the algae a red color.

Page 276: salt water, fresh water, and snow

Page 278: radiolarians and foraminiferans

Page 280: as decomposers or as parasites

Section 3

Page 283: hyphae breaking apart so that each piece becomes a new fungus or fungi producing spores

Page 284: asexually by releasing spores from sporangia or sexually by different individuals growing together into specialized sporangia

Page 286: the spore-forming structures, called *basidia*

Page 288: Lichens make acids that break down rocks, which causes cracks.

Chapter 12 Introduction to Plants

Section 1

Page 301: In the sporophyte stage, plants make spores, which grow into gametophytes. The gametophytes produce eggs and sperm. A sperm fertilizes an egg. The fertilized egg grows into a sporophyte.

Page 302: nonvascular plants, seedless vascular plants, gymnosperms, and angiosperms

Page 303: Sample answer: Green algae and plant cells have the same kind of chlorophyll, have similar cell walls, and make their own food through photosynthesis. Both store energy in the form of starch and have a two-stage life cycle.

Section 2

Page 305: Sample answer: Nonvascular plants are usually the first plants to live in a new environment. They form a thin layer of soil, where new plants can grow. Nonvascular plants also prevent erosion.

Page 307: Sample answer: Seedless vascular plants prevent erosion. They can grow in new soil and add to the soil's depth.

Section 3

Page 308: Sample answer: Seed plants produce seeds. The gametophytes of seed plants do not live independently of the sporophyte. The sperm of seed plants don't need water to fertilize eggs.

Page 309: Sample answer: Seeds have stored food to nourish a young plant, while spores do not. Seeds can be spread by animals, while spores are spread by wind. Animals spread seeds more efficiently than the wind does.

Page 311: Sample answer: Sperm from the male cone fertilize the eggs of the female cone. A fertilized egg develops into a young sporophyte surrounded by a seed within the female cone. Eventually, seeds are released from the cone.

Page 312: Sample answer: Flowers help angiosperms reproduce. Fruits surround and protect the seeds. Some fruits attract animals, which spread the seeds.

Page 313: Sample answer: Major food crops are flowering plants. Flowering plants provide building material, are used to make clothing and rope, and are used to make medicines, rubber, and perfume oils.

Section 4

Page 315: taproot systems and fibrous root systems

Page 316: Sample answer: Herbaceous stems are soft, thin, and flexible. Poppies have herbaceous stems.

Page 318: epidermis, palisade layer, and spongy layer

Page 320: Sample answer: Stamens, which have filaments topped by anthers, are the male reproductive parts of flowers. A pistil is the female part of a flower. A pistil has a stigma, style, and ovary.

Chapter 13 Plant Processes

Section 1

Page 332: Sample answer: Plants are green because the chlorophyll reflects most wavelengths of green light.

Page 335: Sample answer: Photosynthesis provides the oxygen that organisms need for cellular respiration. Photosynthetic organisms form the base of nearly all food chains on Earth.

Section 2

Page 337: Sample answer: Animals may eat fruits and discard the seeds away from the parent plant. Other fruits, such as burrs, get caught in an animal's fur. Some fruits are carried by the wind.

Page 338: plantlets, tubers, and runners

Section 3

Page 340: Sample answer: The shoot tips will probably bend toward the light.

Page 341: Sample answer: Plants respond to the change in the length of day.

Page 342: Sample answer: Evergreen trees always have some leaves on them. Deciduous trees lose all of their leaves around the same time each year.

Chapter 14 Animals and Behavior

Section 1

Page 357: vertebrates

Page 358: heart, lung, and kidneys

Section 2

Page 361: A predator hunts prey as its food.

Page 362: A rabbit can "freeze" to hide from predators, or it can try to outrun predators.

Page 364: mice, squirrels, and skunks

Section 3

Page 366: defend a territory, find food, warn others of danger, identify family, frighten predators, and find mates

Page 368: They use body language to communicate where to find food sources.

Chapter 15 Invertebrates

Section 1

Page 381: The coelom is the space in the body that surrounds the gut.

Page 382: Water enters a sponge's body through pores.

Page 385: planarians, flukes, and tapeworms

Page 386: pinworms, hookworms, and *Trichinella spiralis*

Section 2

Page 389: An open circulatory system has a heart that pumps blood through blood vessels that empty into sinuses. A closed circulatory system has a heart that pumps blood through a closed loop of blood vessels.

Page 391: Doctors use leeches to prevent swelling and to prevent and break down blood clots.

Section 3

Page 393: Both an exoskeleton and an internal skeleton support an animal's body and allow the animal to move.

Page 395: Spiders are helpful because they catch small insects that are pests to humans.

Page 397: egg, nymph, and adult

Section 4

Page 399: Radial nerves control the movements of a sea star's arms.

Page 401: A sea lily's body is at the end of a long stalk, while a feather star does not have a stalk.

Chapter 16 Fishes, Amphibians, and Reptiles

Section 1

Page 413: cartilage

Page 414: Because most fishes are ectotherms, the body temperature of most fishes would increase as the temperature of their environment increased.

Page 416: Hagfish eat dead fishes on the ocean floor. Lampreys suck other animals' blood and flesh through a toothed suction cup–like mouth.

Page 418: Bony fishes have skeletons made of bone, have bodies covered in bony scales, and can rest in one place without swimming.

Section 2

Page 420: Most amphibians get oxygen through lungs.

Page 423: Most salamanders lose gills and grow lungs but do not go through a tadpole stage.

Page 424: Frogs use vocal sacs to sing, which helps frogs mark territories and attract mates.

Section 3

Page 427: Reptile eggs have a shell that keeps the embryo from drying out on land.

Page 428: turtles and tortoises, crocodiles and alligators, lizards and snakes, and tuataras

Page 431: Tuataras are most active at low temperatures, and they have no visible ear openings on the outside of the body.

Chapter 17 Birds and Mammals

Section 1

Page 443: Down feathers help birds stay warm.

Page 444: The heart beats rapidly so that it can pump enough blood to power the flight muscles.

Page 446: A bird's body heat warms the eggs.

Section 2

Page 449: rounded, flat beaks and long, sharp beaks

Page 450: The perching bird's feet will remain closed around the branch.

Section 3

Page 453: water, protein, fat, and sugar

Page 455: until the young mammal is grown

Section 4

Page 457: They gnaw and chew.

Page 458: Rabbits have two sets of sharp front teeth in their upper jaw, and they have a short tail.

Page 461: all of their time

Page 462: large brains, grasping hands and feet, flexible shoulder joints, and forward-facing eyes

Section 5

Page 465: A platypus uses its bill to dig for food and dig tunnels in the riverbanks where it can lay its eggs.

Page 466: as small as a bumblebee

Chapter 18 Interactions of Living Things

Section 1

Page 483: The biosphere is the part of Earth where life exists.

Section 2

Page 485: Organisms that eat other organisms are called *consumers*.

Page 487: An energy pyramid is a diagram that shows an ecosystem's loss of energy.

Page 488: Other animals in Yellowstone National Park were affected by the disappearance of the gray wolf because the food web was interrupted. The animals that would normally be prey for the gray wolf were more plentiful. These larger populations ate more vegetation.

Section 3

Page 491: The main ways that organisms affect each other are through competition, predator and prey relationships, symbiotic relationships, and coevolution.

Page 493: Camouflage helps an organism blend in with its surroundings because of its coloring. It is harder for a predator to find a camouflaged prey.

Page 494: In a mutualistic relationship, both organisms benefit from the relationship.

Page 496: Flowers need to attract pollinators to help the flowers reproduce with other members of their species.

Chapter 19 Cycles in Nature

Section 1

Page 509: Without water, there would be no life on Earth.

Page 511: Sample answer: calcium

Section 2

Page 512: Plants grew back, and the area is recovering.

Page 514: Primary succession happens in an area where organisms did not previously exist; secondary succession happens where organisms already exist.

Chapter 20 The Earth's Ecosystems

Section 1

Page 527: Sample answer: *Deciduous* comes from a Latin word that means "to fall off." In temperate deciduous forests, the trees lose their leaves in the fall.

Page 528: evergreen trees; squirrels, insects, finches, chickadees, jays, porcupines, elk, and moose

Page 530: During the dry season, grasses on the savanna dry out and turn yellow. But their deep roots survive for many months without water.

Page 531: Sample answer: Desert plants grow far apart. Some plants have shallow, widespread roots to take up water after a storm. Some desert plants have fleshy stems and leaves to store water. They also have waxy coatings to prevent water loss.

Page 532: Sample answer: Alpine tundra is tundra found at the top of tall mountains, above the tree line.

Section 2

Page 534: Sample answer: Plankton are tiny organisms that float near the surface of the water. They form the base of the ocean's feeding relationships.

Page 535: Sample answer: Fishes that live near the poles have adaptations for the near-freezing water. Animals in coral reefs need warm water to live. Some animals migrate to warmer waters to reproduce. Water temperature affects whether some animals can eat.

Page 537: Sample answer: Some animals get food from material that sinks to the bottom from the surface. Other animals get energy from chemicals released by thermal vents.

Page 538: Sample answer: When corals die, they leave behind their skeletons. Other corals grow on these remains. Over time, the layers build up to form a coral reef.

Section 3

Page 541: Sample answer: The littoral zone is the zone closest to shore in which light reaches the lake bottom. The open zone extends from the littoral zone and goes as deep as sunlight can reach. The deep-water zone lies beneath the open-water zone.

Page 542: A swamp is a wetland ecosystem in which trees and vines grow.

Page 543: Sample answer: Many fishes will die as the pond fills in because bacteria that decompose material in the pond use up the oxygen in the water.

Chapter 21 Environmental Problems and Solutions

Section 1

Page 554: Sample answer: Hazardous waste is waste that can catch fire, wear through metal, explode, or make people sick.

Page 557: Sample answer: Exotic species are organisms that make a home for themselves in a new place.

Page 558: Point-source pollution is pollution that comes from one place. Nonpoint-source pollution is pollution that comes from many places.

Section 2

Page 560: reduce, reuse, and recycle

Page 562: Sample answer: Water is reclaimed with plants or filter-feeding animals. Then, it can be used to water crops, parks, lawns, and golf courses.

Page 565: Sample answer: The EPA is a government organization that helps protect the environment.

Chapter 22 Body Organization and Structure

Section 1

Page 581: The stomach works with other organs, such as the small and large intestines, to digest food.

Page 582: Sample answer: The cardiovascular system includes the heart and blood vessels. These organs are also part of the circulatory system, which includes blood. Together, these systems deliver the materials cells need to survive.

Section 2

Page 585: Sample answer: As people grow, most of the cartilage that they start out with is replaced with bone.

Page 586: Sample answer: Joints are held together by ligaments. Cartilage cushions the area in a joint where bones meet.

Section 3

Page 589: Sample answer: One muscle, the flexor, bends part of the body. Another muscle, the extensor, straightens part of the body.

Page 591: Sample answer: Anabolic steroids can damage the heart, liver, and kidneys. They can also cause high blood pressure. Anabolic steroids can cause bones to stop growing.

Section 4

Page 593: The dermis is the layer of skin that lies beneath the epidermis. It is composed of a protein called *collagen,* while the epidermis contains keratin.

Page 594: Sample answer: A nail grows from living cells in the nail root at the base of the nail. As new cells form, the nail grows longer.

Chapter 23 Circulation and Respiration

Section 1

Page 606: The four main parts of the cardiovascular system are the heart and the arteries, capillaries, and veins.

Page 608: Arteries have thick, stretchy walls and carry blood away from the heart. Capillaries are tiny blood vessels that allow the exchange of oxygen, carbon dioxide, and nutrients between cells and blood. Veins are blood vessels that carry blood back to the heart.

Page 610: Atherosclerosis is dangerous because it is the buildup of material inside an artery. When the artery becomes blocked, blood can't flow and can't reach the cells. In some cases, a person can have a heart attack from a blocked artery.

Section 2

Page 612: plasma, red blood cells, white blood cells, and platelets

Page 613: White blood cells identify and attack pathogens that may make you sick.

Page 614: Systolic pressure is the pressure inside arteries when the ventricles contract. Diastolic pressure is the pressure inside the arteries when the ventricles are relaxed.

Page 615: The red blood cells of a person who has type O blood have no A or B antigens. The A or B antibodies in another person's blood will not react to the type O cells. It is safe for anyone to receive type O blood.

Section 3

Page 616: The lymphatic system is a secondary circulatory system in the body. The lymphatic system collects fluid and particles from between the cells and returns them to the cardiovascular system.

Page 618: The white pulp of the spleen is part of the lymphatic system. It helps fight infections by storing and producing lymphocytes. The red pulp of the spleen removes unwanted material, such as defective red blood cells, from the circulatory system.

Section 4

Page 621: nose, pharynx, larynx, trachea, bronchi, bronchioles, alveoli

Page 622: Cellular respiration is the process inside a cell in which oxygen is used to release energy stored in molecules of glucose. During the process, carbon dioxide (CO_2) and water are released.

Chapter 24 The Digestive and Urinary Systems

Section 1

Page 635 Enzymes cut proteins into amino acids that the body can use.

Page 637 Chyme is a soupy mixture of partially digested food in the stomach.

Page 639 Bile breaks large fat droplets into very small droplets. This process allows more fat molecules to be exposed to digestive enzymes.

Page 640 Fiber keeps the stool soft and keeps material moving through the large intestine.

Section 2

Page 643 Nephrons are microscopic filters inside the kidneys.

Page 644 Diuretics are chemicals that cause the kidneys to make more urine.

Chapter 25 Communication and Control

Section 1

Page 656: The CNS is the brain and the spinal cord. The PNS is all of the parts of the nervous system except the brain and the spinal cord.

Page 657: A neuron is a cell that has a cell body and a nucleus. A neuron also has dendrites that receive signals from other neurons and axons that send signals to other neurons.

Page 658: A nerve is a collection of nerve fibers, or axons, bundled together with blood vessels through which impulses travel between the central nervous system and other parts of the body.

Page 659: The PNS connects your CNS to the rest of your body, controls voluntary movements, and keeps your body's functions in balance.

Page 660: A voluntary action is an action over which you have conscious control. Voluntary activities include throwing a ball, playing a video game, talking to your friends, taking a bite of food, and raising your hand to answer a question in class. An involuntary action is an action that happens automatically. It is an action or process over which you do not have conscious control.

Page 661: The medulla is important because it controls your heart rate, blood pressure, and ordinary breathing.

Page 662: When someone touches your skin, an impulse that travels along a sensory neuron to your spinal cord and then to your brain is created. The response travels back from your brain to your spinal cord and then along a motor neuron to a muscle.

Section 2

Page 664: Skin can detect pressure, temperature, pain, and vibration.

Page 665: Reflexes are important because they can protect you from injury.

Page 666: Light strikes cells on the retina and triggers impulses in those cells. The impulses are carried to the brain, which interprets the impulses as images that you "see."

Page 667: In bright light, your iris contracts and reduces the amount of light entering the eye.

Page 668: Neurons in the cochlea convert waves into electrical impulses that the brain interprets as sound.

Section 3

Page 671: Sample answer: The thyroid gland increases the rate at which the body uses energy. The thymus gland regulates the immune system, which helps your body fight disease.

Page 672: Insulin helps regulate the amount of glucose in the blood.

Chapter 26 Reproduction and Development

Section 1

Page 685: Sexual reproduction is reproduction in which the sex cells (egg and sperm) of two parents unite to form a new individual.

Page 686: External fertilization happens when the sex cells unite outside of the female's body. Internal fertilization happens when the sex cells unite inside the female's body.

Page 687: All mammals reproduce sexually and nurture their young with milk.

Section 2

Page 688: testes, epididymis, vas deferens, urethra, penis

Page 690: Twins happen about 30 times in every 1,000 births.

Section 3

Page 692: Fertilization happens when the nucleus of a sperm unites with the nucleus of an egg. Implantation happens after the fertilized egg travels down the fallopian tube to the uterus and embeds itself in the wall of the uterus.

Page 693: The placenta is important because it provides the embryo with oxygen and nutrients from the mother's blood. Wastes from the embryo also travel to the placenta, where they are carried to the mother so that she can excrete them.

Page 694: The embryo is now called a *fetus.* The fetus's face begins to look more human, and the fetus can swallow, grows rapidly (triples in size), and begins to make movements that the mother can feel.

Page 696: A person's reproductive system becomes mature.

Chapter 27 Body Defenses and Disease

Section 1

Page 711: Cooking kills dangerous bacteria or parasites living in meat, fish, and eggs.

Page 713: Frank's doctor did not prescribe antibiotics because Frank had a cold. Colds are caused by viruses. Antibiotics can't stop viruses.

Section 2

Page 715: Macrophages engulf, or eat, any microorganisms or viruses that enter your body.

Page 716: If a virus particle enters the body, it may pass into body cells and begin to replicate. Or it may be engulfed and broken up by macrophages.

Page 719: rheumatoid arthritis, diabetes, multiple sclerosis, and lupus

Page 720: HIV causes AIDS.

Chapter 28 Staying Healthy

Section 1

Page 733: An incomplete protein does not contain all of the essential amino acids.

Page 735: Sample answer: a peanut butter sandwich, a glass of milk, and fresh fruit and vegetable slices

Page 736: One serving of chicken noodle soup provides more than 10% of the daily recommended allowance of vitamin A and sodium.

Section 2

Page 739: Over-the-counter drugs can be bought without a prescription. Prescription drugs can be bought only with a prescription from a doctor or other medical professional.

Page 741: First-time use of cocaine can cause a heart attack or can cause a person to become addicted.

Page 742: Drug use is the proper use of a legal drug. Drug abuse is either the use of an illegal drug or the improper use of a legal drug.

Section 3

Page 745: Aerobic exercise strengthens the heart, lungs, and bones and reduces stress. Regular exercise also burns Calories and can give you more energy.

Page 747: Sample answers: Never hike or camp alone, dress for the weather, learn how to swim, wear a life jacket, and never drink unpurified water.

Page 749: CPR is a way to revive someone whose heart has stopped beating. CPR classes are available in many places in the community.

Study Skills

FoldNote Instructions

Have you ever tried to study for a test or quiz but didn't know where to start? Or have you read a chapter and found that you can remember only a few ideas? Well, FoldNotes are a fun and exciting way to help you learn and remember the ideas you encounter as you learn science!

FoldNotes are tools that you can use to organize concepts. By focusing on a few main concepts, FoldNotes help you learn and remember how the concepts fit together. They can help you see the "big picture." Below you will find instructions for building 10 different FoldNotes.

Pyramid

1. Place a sheet of paper in front of you. Fold the lower left-hand corner of the paper diagonally to the opposite edge of the paper.
2. Cut off the tab of paper created by the fold (at the top).
3. Open the paper so that it is a square. Fold the lower right-hand corner of the paper diagonally to the opposite corner to form a triangle.
4. Open the paper. The creases of the two folds will have created an X.
5. Using scissors, cut along one of the creases. Start from any corner, and stop at the center point to create two flaps. Use tape or glue to attach one of the flaps on top of the other flap.

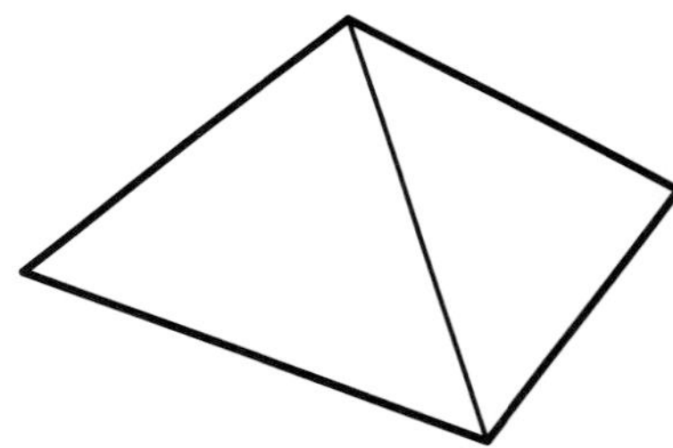

Double Door

1. Fold a sheet of paper in half from the top to the bottom. Then, unfold the paper.
2. Fold the top and bottom edges of the paper to the crease.

Appendix

Booklet

1. Fold a sheet of paper in half from left to right. Then, unfold the paper.
2. Fold the sheet of paper in half again from the top to the bottom. Then, unfold the paper.
3. Refold the sheet of paper in half from left to right.
4. Fold the top and bottom edges to the center crease.
5. Completely unfold the paper.
6. Refold the paper from top to bottom.
7. Using scissors, cut a slit along the center crease of the sheet from the folded edge to the creases made in step 4. Do not cut the entire sheet in half.
8. Fold the sheet of paper in half from left to right. While holding the bottom and top edges of the paper, push the bottom and top edges together so that the center collapses at the center slit. Fold the four flaps to form a four-page book.

Layered Book

1. Lay one sheet of paper on top of another sheet. Slide the top sheet up so that 2 cm of the bottom sheet is showing.
2. Hold the two sheets together, fold down the top of the two sheets so that you see four 2 cm tabs along the bottom.
3. Using a stapler, staple the top of the FoldNote.

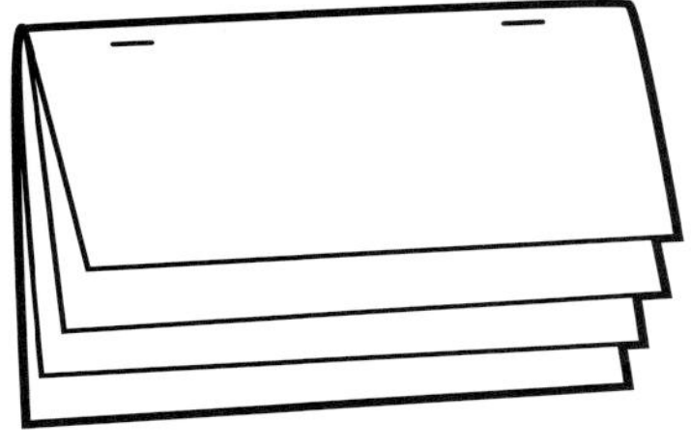

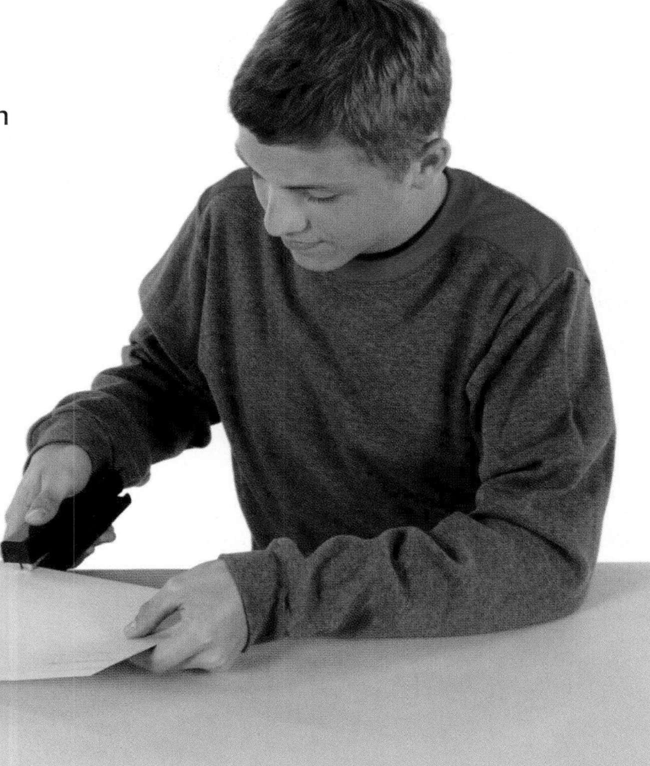

Key-Term Fold

1. Fold a sheet of lined notebook paper in half from left to right.
2. Using scissors, cut along every third line from the right edge of the paper to the center fold to make tabs.

Four-Corner Fold

1. Fold a sheet of paper in half from left to right. Then, unfold the paper.
2. Fold each side of the paper to the crease in the center of the paper.
3. Fold the paper in half from the top to the bottom. Then, unfold the paper.
4. Using scissors, cut the top flap creases made in step 3 to form four flaps.

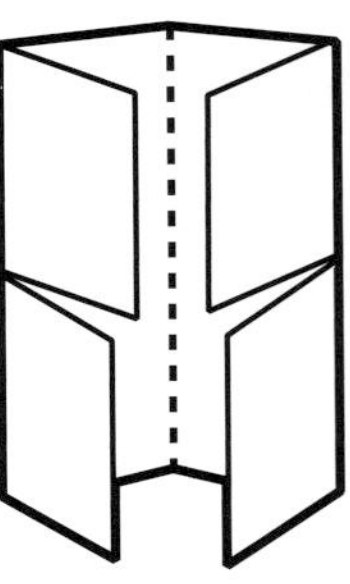

Three-Panel Flip Chart

1. Fold a piece of paper in half from the top to the bottom.
2. Fold the paper in thirds from side to side. Then, unfold the paper so that you can see the three sections.
3. From the top of the paper, cut along each of the vertical fold lines to the fold in the middle of the paper. You will now have three flaps.

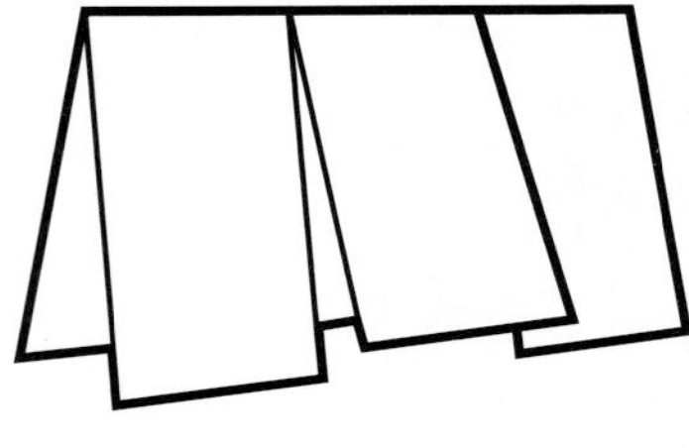

Table Fold

1. Fold a piece of paper in half from the top to the bottom. Then, fold the paper in half again.
2. Fold the paper in thirds from side to side.
3. Unfold the paper completely. Carefully trace the fold lines by using a pen or pencil.

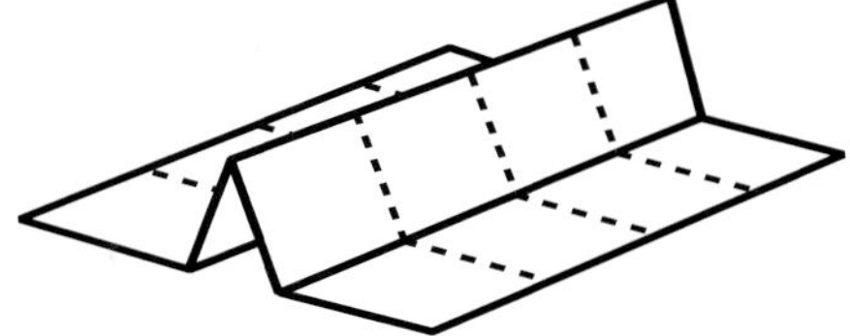

Two-Panel Flip Chart

1. Fold a piece of paper in half from the top to the bottom.
2. Fold the paper in half from side to side. Then, unfold the paper so that you can see the two sections.
3. From the top of the paper, cut along the vertical fold line to the fold in the middle of the paper. You will now have two flaps.

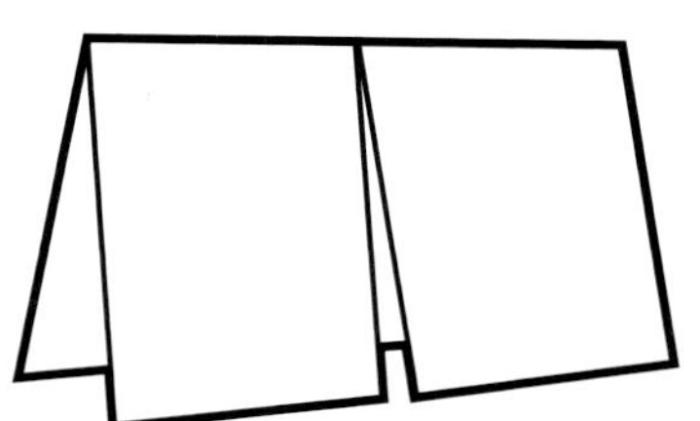

Tri-Fold

1. Fold a piece a paper in thirds from the top to the bottom.
2. Unfold the paper so that you can see the three sections. Then, turn the paper sideways so that the three sections form vertical columns.
3. Trace the fold lines by using a pen or pencil. Label the columns "Know," "Want," and "Learn."

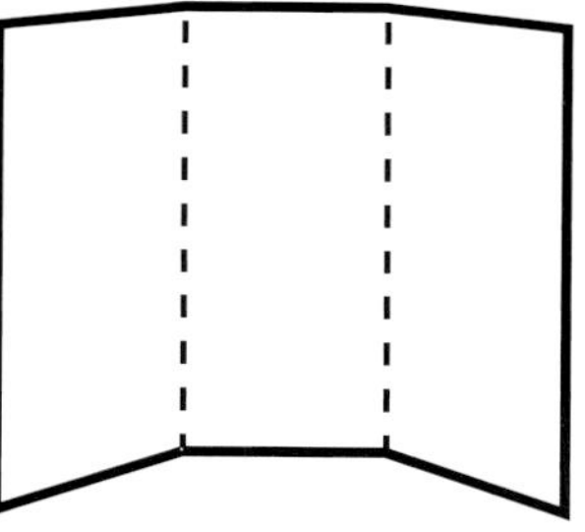

Graphic Organizer Instructions

Have you ever wished that you could "draw out" the many concepts you learn in your science class? Sometimes, being able to *see* how concepts are related really helps you remember what you've learned. Graphic Organizers do just that! They give you a way to draw or map out concepts.

All you need to make a Graphic Organizer is a piece of paper and a pencil. Below you will find instructions for four different Graphic Organizers designed to help you organize the concepts you'll learn in this book.

Spider Map

1. Draw a diagram like the one shown. In the circle, write the main topic.
2. From the circle, draw legs to represent different categories of the main topic. You can have as many categories as you want.
3. From the category legs, draw horizontal lines. As you read the chapter, write details about each category on the horizontal lines.

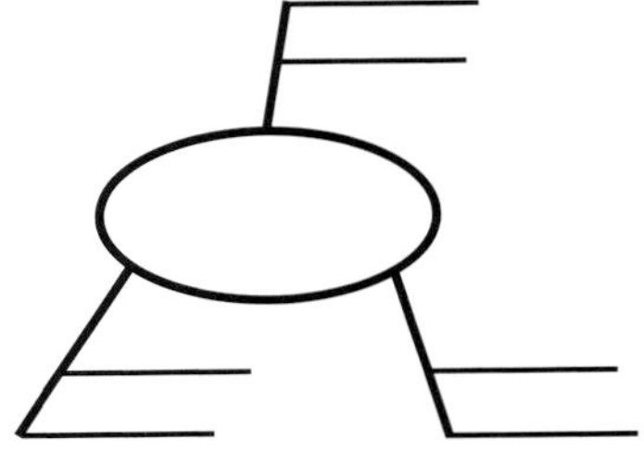

Comparison Table

1. Draw a chart like the one shown. Your chart can have as many columns and rows as you want.
2. In the top row, write the topics that you want to compare.
3. In the left column, write characteristics of the topics that you want to compare. As you read the chapter, fill in the characteristics for each topic in the appropriate boxes.

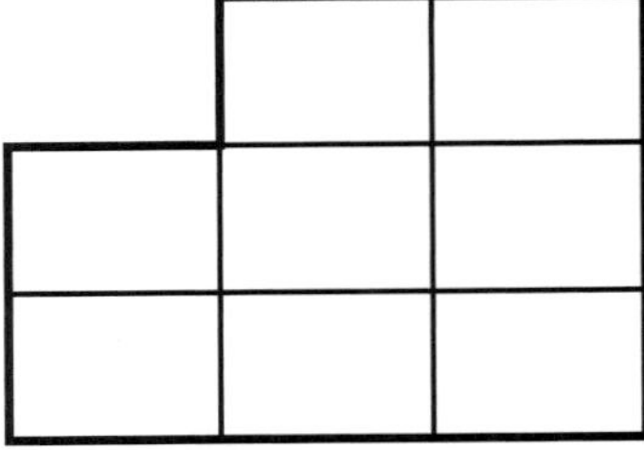

Appendix

Chain-of-Events-Chart

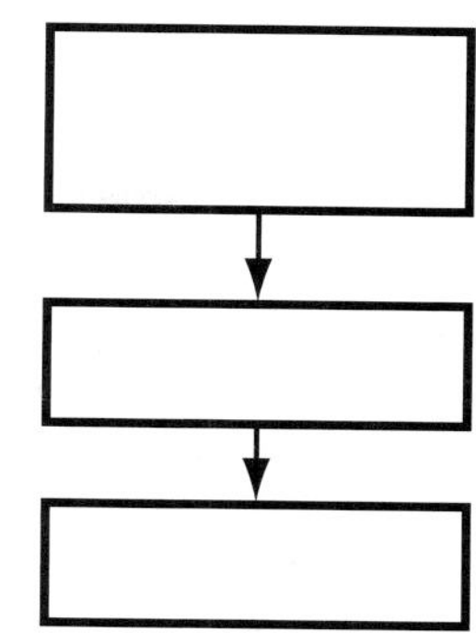

1. Draw a box. In the box, write the first step of a process or the first event of a timeline.
2. Under the box, draw another box, and use an arrow to connect the two boxes. In the second box, write the next step of the process or the next event in the timeline.
3. Continue adding boxes until the process or timeline is finished.

Concept Map

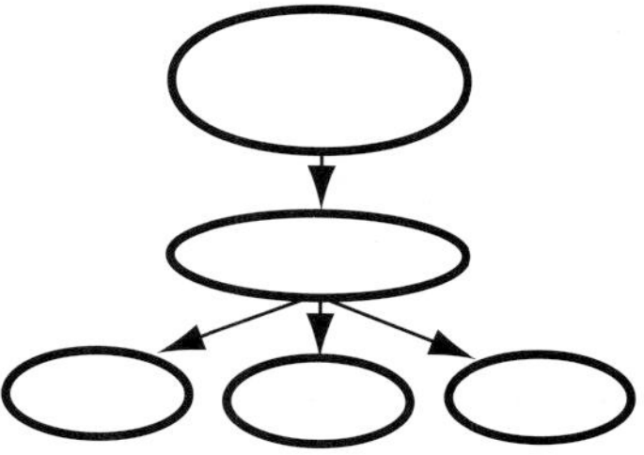

1. Draw a circle in the center of a piece of paper. Write the main idea of the chapter in the center of the circle.
2. From the circle, draw other circles. In those circles, write characteristics of the main idea. Draw arrows from the center circle to the circles that contain the characteristics.
3. From each circle that contains a characteristic, draw other circles. In those circles, write specific details about the characteristic. Draw arrows from each circle that contains a characteristic to the circles that contain specific details. You may draw as many circles as you want.

SI Measurement

The International System of Units, or SI, is the standard system of measurement used by many scientists. Using the same standards of measurement makes it easier for scientists to communicate with one another.

SI works by combining prefixes and base units. Each base unit can be used with different prefixes to define smaller and larger quantities. The table below lists common SI prefixes.

SI Prefixes

Prefix	Symbol	Factor	Example
kilo-	k	1,000	kilogram, 1 kg = 1,000 g
hecto-	h	100	hectoliter, 1 hL = 100 L
deka-	da	10	dekameter, 1 dam = 10 m
		1	meter, liter, gram
deci-	d	0.1	decigram, 1 dg = 0.1 g
centi-	c	0.01	centimeter, 1 cm = 0.01 m
milli-	m	0.001	milliliter, 1 mL = 0.001 L
micro-	μ	0.000 001	micrometer, 1 μm = 0.000 001 m

SI Conversion Table

SI units	From SI to English	From English to SI
Length		
kilometer (km) = 1,000 m	1 km = 0.621 mi	1 mi = 1.609 km
meter (m) = 100 cm	1 m = 3.281 ft	1 ft = 0.305 m
centimeter (cm) = 0.01 m	1 cm = 0.394 in.	1 in. = 2.540 cm
millimeter (mm) = 0.001 m	1 mm = 0.039 in.	
micrometer (μm) = 0.000 001 m		
nanometer (nm) = 0.000 000 001 m		
Area		
square kilometer (km^2) = 100 hectares	1 km^2 = 0.386 mi^2	1 mi^2 = 2.590 km^2
hectare (ha) = 10,000 m^2	1 ha = 2.471 acres	1 acre = 0.405 ha
square meter (m^2) = 10,000 cm^2	1 m^2 = 10.764 ft^2	1 ft^2 = 0.093 m^2
square centimeter (cm^2) = 100 mm^2	1 cm^2 = 0.155 in.^{2}	1 in.^{2} = 6.452 cm^2
Volume		
liter (L) = 1,000 mL = 1 dm^3	1 L = 1.057 fl qt	1 fl qt = 0.946 L
milliliter (mL) = 0.001 L = 1 cm^3	1 mL = 0.034 fl oz	1 fl oz = 29.574 mL
microliter (μL) = 0.000 001 L		
Mass		
kilogram (kg) = 1,000 g	1 kg = 2.205 lb	1 lb = 0.454 kg
gram (g) = 1,000 mg	1 g = 0.035 oz	1 oz = 28.350 g
milligram (mg) = 0.001 g		
microgram (μg) = 0.000 001 g		

Measuring Skills

Using a Graduated Cylinder

When using a graduated cylinder to measure volume, keep the following procedures in mind:

1. Place the cylinder on a flat, level surface before measuring liquid.
2. Move your head so that your eye is level with the surface of the liquid.
3. Read the mark closest to the liquid level. On glass graduated cylinders, read the mark closest to the center of the curve in the liquid's surface.

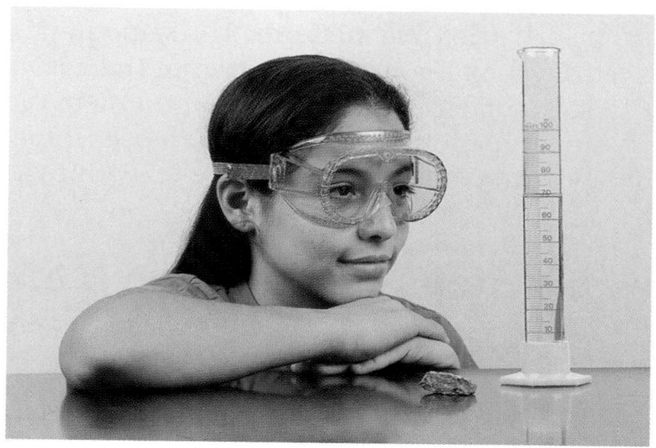

Using a Meterstick or Metric Ruler

When using a meterstick or metric ruler to measure length, keep the following procedures in mind:

1. Place the ruler firmly against the object that you are measuring.
2. Align one edge of the object exactly with the 0 end of the ruler.
3. Look at the other edge of the object to see which of the marks on the ruler is closest to that edge. (Note: Each small slash between the centimeters represents a millimeter, which is one-tenth of a centimeter.)

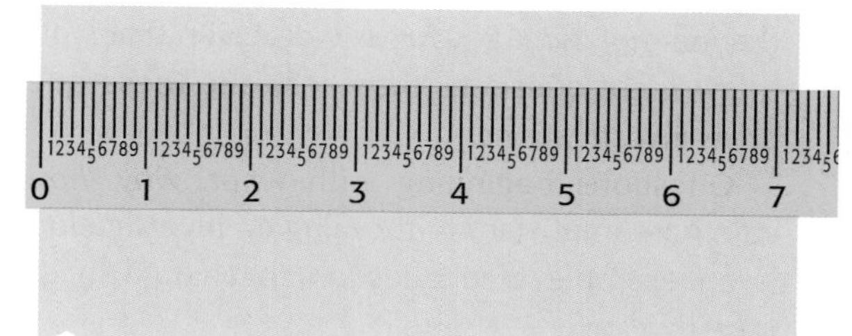

Using a Triple-Beam Balance

When using a triple-beam balance to measure mass, keep the following procedures in mind:

1. Make sure the balance is on a level surface.
2. Place all of the countermasses at 0. Adjust the balancing knob until the pointer rests at 0.
3. Place the object you wish to measure on the pan. **Caution:** Do not place hot objects or chemicals directly on the balance pan.
4. Move the largest countermass along the beam to the right until it is at the last notch that does not tip the balance. Follow the same procedure with the next-largest countermass. Then, move the smallest countermass until the pointer rests at 0.
5. Add the readings from the three beams together to determine the mass of the object.
6. When determining the mass of crystals or powders, first find the mass of a piece of filter paper. Then, add the crystals or powder to the paper, and remeasure. The actual mass of the crystals or powder is the total mass minus the mass of the paper. When finding the mass of liquids, first find the mass of the empty container. Then, find the combined mass of the liquid and container. The mass of the liquid is the total mass minus the mass of the container.

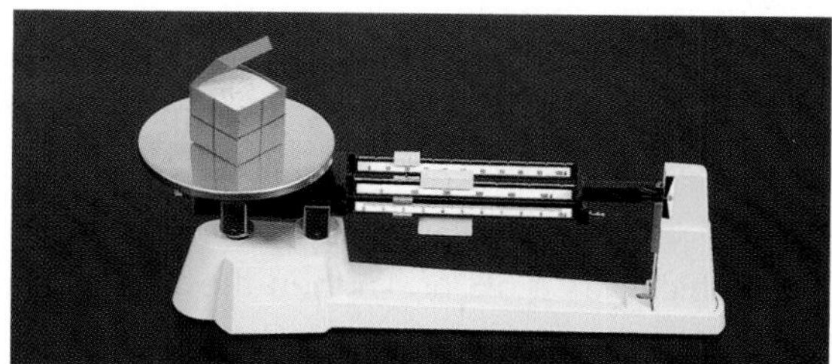

Scientific Methods

The ways in which scientists answer questions and solve problems are called **scientific methods.** The same steps are often used by scientists as they look for answers. However, there is more than one way to use these steps. Scientists may use all of the steps or just some of the steps during an investigation. They may even repeat some of the steps. The goal of using scientific methods is to come up with reliable answers and solutions.

Six Steps of Scientific Methods

Good questions come from careful **observations.** You make observations by using your senses to gather information. Sometimes, you may use instruments, such as microscopes and telescopes, to extend the range of your senses. As you observe the natural world, you will discover that you have many more questions than answers. These questions drive investigations.

Questions beginning with *what, why, how,* and *when* are important in focusing an investigation. Here is an example of a question that could lead to an investigation.

Question: How does acid rain affect plant growth?

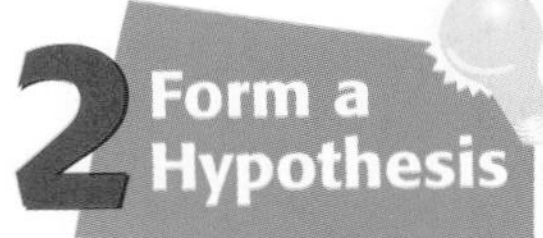

After you ask a question, you need to form a **hypothesis.** A hypothesis is a clear statement of what you expect the answer to your question to be. Your hypothesis will represent your best "educated guess" based on what you have observed and what you already know. A good hypothesis is testable. Otherwise, the investigation can go no further. Here is a hypothesis based on the question, "How does acid rain affect plant growth?"

Hypothesis: Acid rain slows plant growth.

The hypothesis can lead to predictions. A prediction is what you think the outcome of your experiment or data collection will be. Predictions are usually stated in an if-then format. Here is a sample prediction for the hypothesis that acid rain slows plant growth.

Prediction: If a plant is watered with only acid rain (which has a pH of 4), then the plant will grow at half its normal rate.

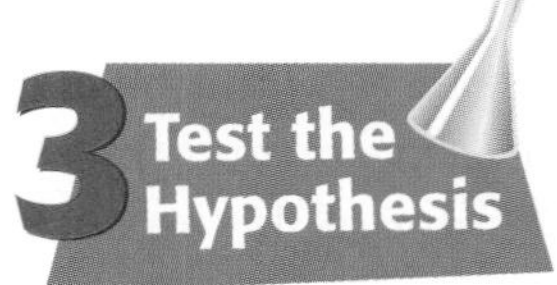

After you have formed a hypothesis and made a prediction, your hypothesis should be tested. One way to test a hypothesis is with a controlled experiment. A **controlled experiment** tests only one factor at a time. In an experiment to test the effect of acid rain on plant growth, the **control group** would be watered with normal rain water. The **experimental group** would be watered with acid rain. All of the plants should receive the same amount of sunlight and water each day. The air temperature should be the same for all groups. However, the acidity of the water will be a variable. In fact, any factor that is different from one group to another is a **variable.** If your hypothesis is correct, then the acidity of the water and plant growth are *dependant variables.* The amount a plant grows is dependent on the acidity of the water. However, the amount of water each plant receives and the amount of sunlight each plant receives are *independent variables.* Either of these factors could change without affecting the other factor.

Sometimes, the nature of an investigation makes a controlled experiment impossible. For example, the Earth's core is surrounded by thousands of meters of rock. Under such circumstances, a hypothesis may be tested by making detailed observations.

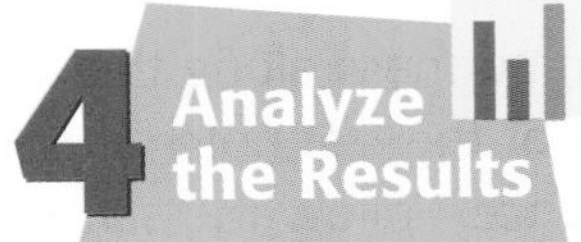

After you have completed your experiments, made your observations, and collected your data, you must analyze all the information you have gathered. Tables and graphs are often used in this step to organize the data.

After analyzing your data, you can determine if your results support your hypothesis. If your hypothesis is supported, you (or others) might want to repeat the observations or experiments to verify your results. If your hypothesis is not supported by the data, you may have to check your procedure for errors. You may even have to reject your hypothesis and make a new one. If you cannot draw a conclusion from your results, you may have to try the investigation again or carry out further observations or experiments.

After any scientific investigation, you should report your results. By preparing a written or oral report, you let others know what you have learned. They may repeat your investigation to see if they get the same results. Your report may even lead to another question and then to another investigation.

Scientific Methods in Action

Scientific methods contain loops in which several steps may be repeated over and over again. In some cases, certain steps are unnecessary. Thus, there is not a "straight line" of steps. For example, sometimes scientists find that testing one hypothesis raises new questions and new hypotheses to be tested. And sometimes, testing the hypothesis leads directly to a conclusion. Furthermore, the steps in scientific methods are not always used in the same order. Follow the steps in the diagram, and see how many different directions scientific methods can take you.

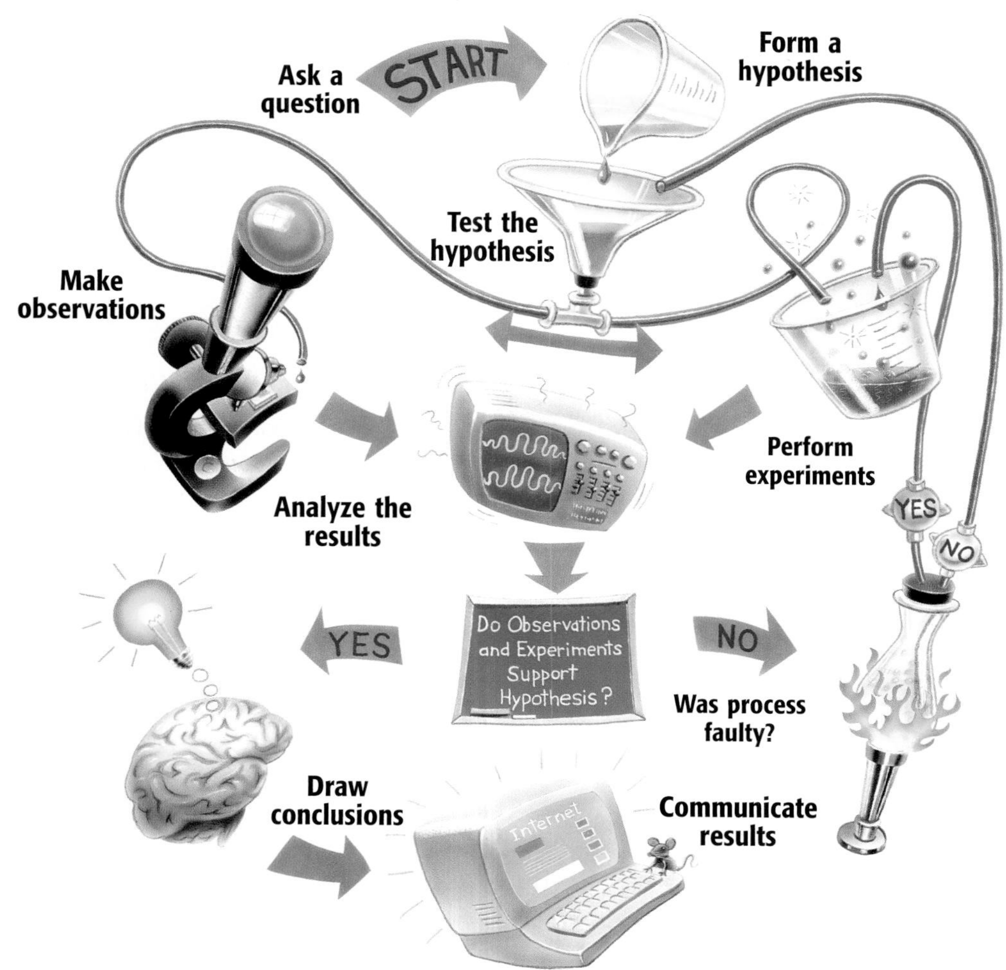

Temperature Scales

Temperature can be expressed by using three different scales: Fahrenheit, Celsius, and Kelvin. The SI unit for temperature is the kelvin (K). Although 0 K is much colder than 0°C, a change of 1 K is equal to a change of 1°C.

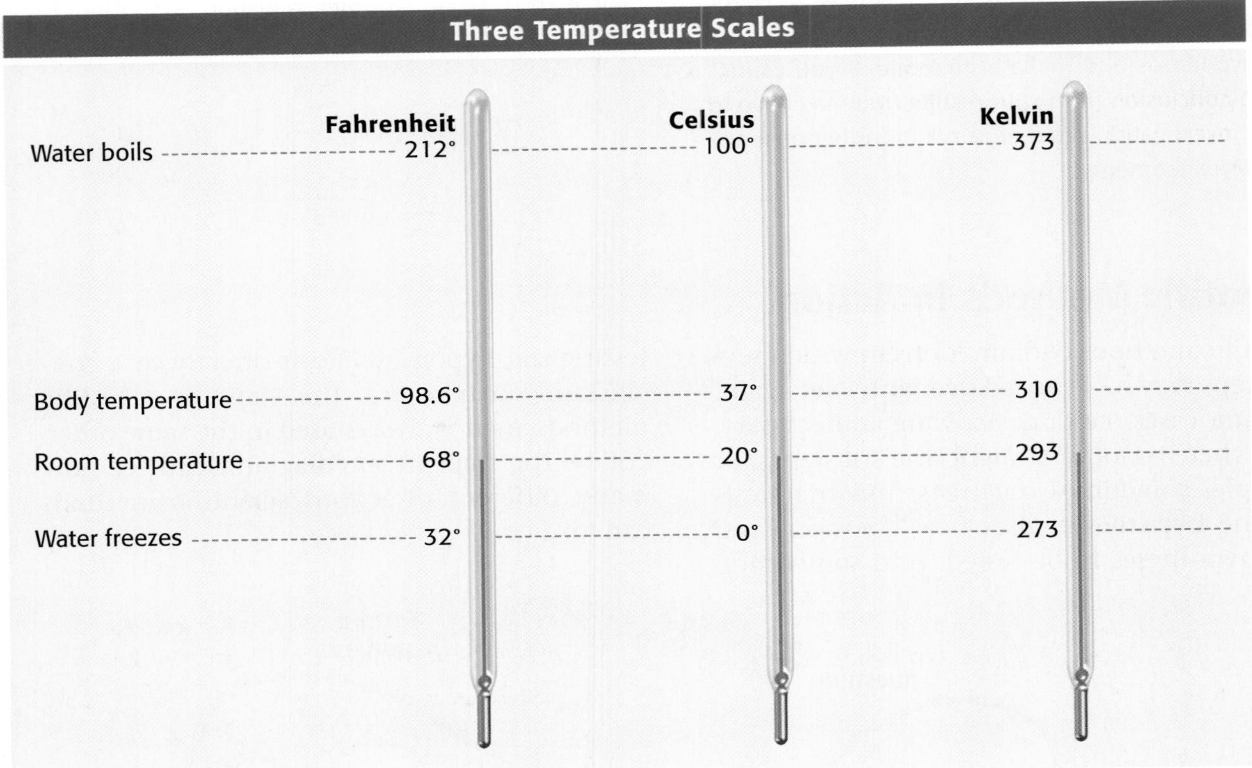

Temperature Conversions Table

To convert	Use this equation:	Example
Celsius to Fahrenheit °C → °F	$°F = \left(\frac{9}{5} \times °C\right) + 32$	Convert 45°C to °F. $°F = \left(\frac{9}{5} \times 45°C\right) + 32 = 113°F$
Fahrenheit to Celsius °F → °C	$°C = \frac{5}{9} \times (°F - 32)$	Convert 68°F to °C. $°C = \frac{5}{9} \times (68°F - 32) = 20°C$
Celsius to Kelvin °C → K	$K = °C + 273$	Convert 45°C to K. $K = 45°C + 273 = 318\ K$
Kelvin to Celsius K → °C	$°C = K - 273$	Convert 32 K to °C. $°C = 32K - 273 = -241°C$

Appendix

Making Charts and Graphs

Pie Charts

A pie chart shows how each group of data relates to all of the data. Each part of the circle forming the chart represents a category of the data. The entire circle represents all of the data. For example, a biologist studying a hardwood forest in Wisconsin found that there were five different types of trees. The data table at right summarizes the biologist's findings.

Wisconsin Hardwood Trees	
Type of tree	**Number found**
Oak	600
Maple	750
Beech	300
Birch	1,200
Hickory	150
Total	3,000

How to Make a Pie Chart

1. To make a pie chart of these data, first find the percentage of each type of tree. Divide the number of trees of each type by the total number of trees, and multiply by 100.

$$\frac{600 \text{ oak}}{3{,}000 \text{ trees}} \times 100 = 20\%$$

$$\frac{750 \text{ maple}}{3{,}000 \text{ trees}} \times 100 = 25\%$$

$$\frac{300 \text{ beech}}{3{,}000 \text{ trees}} \times 100 = 10\%$$

$$\frac{1{,}200 \text{ birch}}{3{,}000 \text{ trees}} \times 100 = 40\%$$

$$\frac{150 \text{ hickory}}{3{,}000 \text{ trees}} \times 100 = 5\%$$

2. Now, determine the size of the wedges that make up the pie chart. Multiply each percentage by 360°. Remember that a circle contains 360°.

$20\% \times 360° = 72°$ $\quad 25\% \times 360° = 90°$

$10\% \times 360° = 36°$ $\quad 40\% \times 360° = 144°$

$5\% \times 360° = 18°$

3. Check that the sum of the percentages is 100 and the sum of the degrees is 360.

$20\% + 25\% + 10\% + 40\% + 5\% = 100\%$

$72° + 90° + 36° + 144° + 18° = 360°$

4. Use a compass to draw a circle and mark the center of the circle.
5. Then, use a protractor to draw angles of 72°, 90°, 36°, 144°, and 18° in the circle.
6. Finally, label each part of the chart, and choose an appropriate title.

A Community of Wisconsin Hardwood Trees

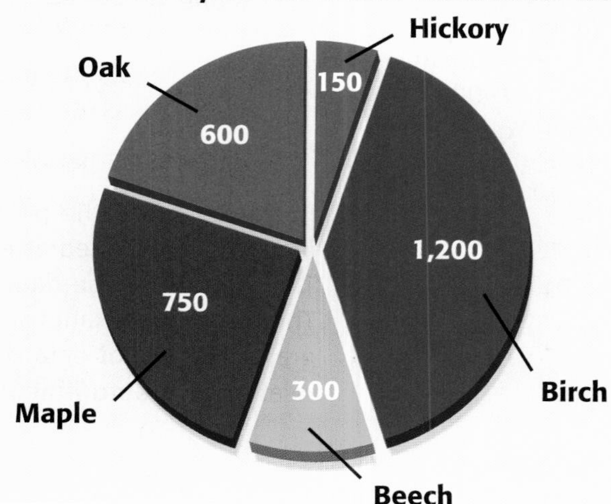

Appendix

Line Graphs

Line graphs are most often used to demonstrate continuous change. For example, Mr. Smith's students analyzed the population records for their hometown, Appleton, between 1900 and 2000. Examine the data at right.

Because the year and the population change, they are the *variables*. The population is determined by, or dependent on, the year. Therefore, the population is called the **dependent variable,** and the year is called the **independent variable.** Each set of data is called a **data pair.** To prepare a line graph, you must first organize data pairs into a table like the one at right.

Population of Appleton, 1900–2000

Year	Population
1900	1,800
1920	2,500
1940	3,200
1960	3,900
1980	4,600
2000	5,300

How to Make a Line Graph

1. Place the independent variable along the horizontal (x) axis. Place the dependent variable along the vertical (y) axis.
2. Label the x-axis "Year" and the y-axis "Population." Look at your largest and smallest values for the population. For the y-axis, determine a scale that will provide enough space to show these values. You must use the same scale for the entire length of the axis. Next, find an appropriate scale for the x-axis.
3. Choose reasonable starting points for each axis.
4. Plot the data pairs as accurately as possible.
5. Choose a title that accurately represents the data.

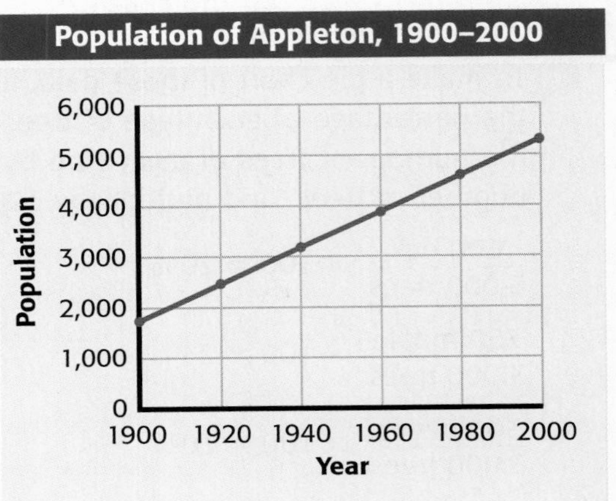

How to Determine Slope

Slope is the ratio of the change in the y-value to the change in the x-value, or "rise over run."

1. Choose two points on the line graph. For example, the population of Appleton in 2000 was 5,300 people. Therefore, you can define point a as (2000, 5,300). In 1900, the population was 1,800 people. You can define point b as (1900, 1,800).
2. Find the change in the y-value. (y at point a) − (y at point b) = 5,300 people − 1,800 people = 3,500 people
3. Find the change in the x-value. (x at point a) − (x at point b) = 2000 − 1900 = 100 years
4. Calculate the slope of the graph by dividing the change in y by the change in x.

$$slope = \frac{change\ in\ y}{change\ in\ x}$$

$$slope = \frac{3{,}500\ \text{people}}{100\ \text{years}}$$

$$slope = 35\ \text{people per year}$$

In this example, the population in Appleton increased by a fixed amount each year. The graph of these data is a straight line. Therefore, the relationship is **linear.** When the graph of a set of data is not a straight line, the relationship is **nonlinear.**

Using Algebra to Determine Slope

The equation in step 4 may also be arranged to be

$$y = kx$$

where y represents the change in the y-value, k represents the slope, and x represents the change in the x-value.

$$slope = \frac{change\ in\ y}{change\ in\ x}$$

$$k = \frac{y}{x}$$

$$k \times x = \frac{y \times x}{x}$$

$$kx = y$$

Bar Graphs

Bar graphs are used to demonstrate change that is not continuous. These graphs can be used to indicate trends when the data cover a long period of time. A meteorologist gathered the precipitation data shown here for Hartford, Connecticut, for April 1–15, 1996, and used a bar graph to represent the data.

Precipitation in Hartford, Connecticut April 1–15, 1996

Date	Precipitation (cm)	Date	Precipitation (cm)
April 1	0.5	April 9	0.25
April 2	1.25	April 10	0.0
April 3	0.0	April 11	1.0
April 4	0.0	April 12	0.0
April 5	0.0	April 13	0.25
April 6	0.0	April 14	0.0
April 7	0.0	April 15	6.50
April 8	1.75		

How to Make a Bar Graph

1. Use an appropriate scale and a reasonable starting point for each axis.
2. Label the axes, and plot the data.
3. Choose a title that accurately represents the data.

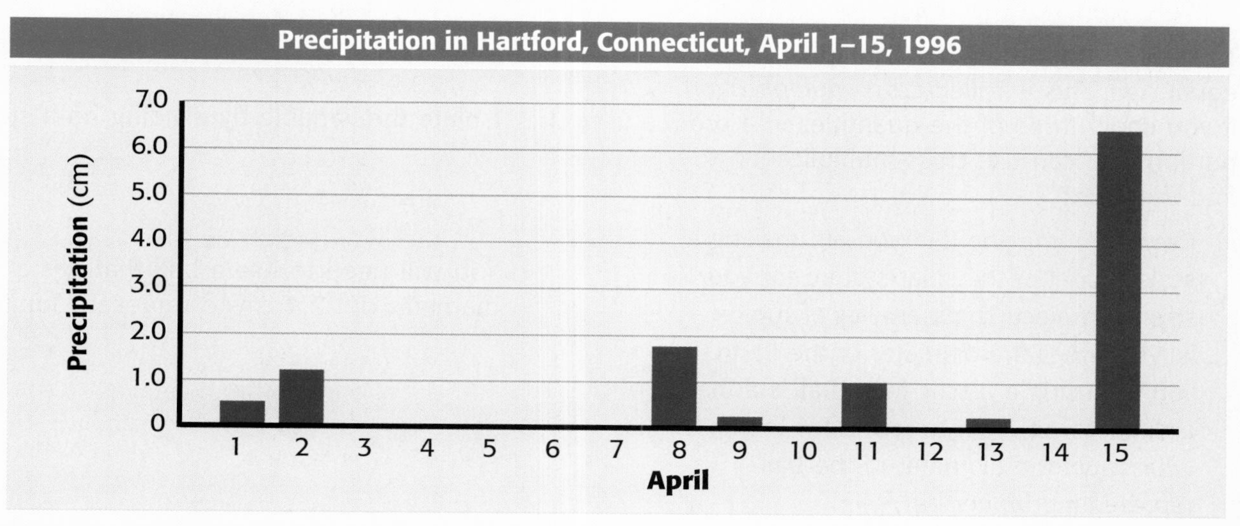

Appendix

Math Refresher

Science requires an understanding of many math concepts. The following pages will help you review some important math skills.

Averages

An **average,** or **mean,** simplifies a set of numbers into a single number that *approximates* the value of the set.

Example: Find the average of the following set of numbers: 5, 4, 7, and 8.

Step 1: Find the sum.

$$5 + 4 + 7 + 8 = 24$$

Step 2: Divide the sum by the number of numbers in your set. Because there are four numbers in this example, divide the sum by 4.

$$\frac{24}{4} = 6$$

The average, or mean, is **6.**

Ratios

A **ratio** is a comparison between numbers, and it is usually written as a fraction.

Example: Find the ratio of thermometers to students if you have 36 thermometers and 48 students in your class.

Step 1: Make the ratio.

$$\frac{36 \text{ thermometers}}{48 \text{ students}}$$

Step 2: Reduce the fraction to its simplest form.

$$\frac{36}{48} = \frac{36 \div 12}{48 \div 12} = \frac{3}{4}$$

The ratio of thermometers to students is **3 to 4,** or $\frac{3}{4}$. The ratio may also be written in the form 3:4.

Proportions

A **proportion** is an equation that states that two ratios are equal.

$$\frac{3}{1} = \frac{12}{4}$$

To solve a proportion, first multiply across the equal sign. This is called *cross-multiplication*. If you know three of the quantities in a proportion, you can use cross-multiplication to find the fourth.

Example: Imagine that you are making a scale model of the solar system for your science project. The diameter of Jupiter is 11.2 times the diameter of the Earth. If you are using a plastic-foam ball that has a diameter of 2 cm to represent the Earth, what must the diameter of the ball representing Jupiter be?

$$\frac{11.2}{1} = \frac{x}{2 \text{ cm}}$$

Step 1: Cross-multiply.

$$\frac{11.2}{1} \times \frac{x}{2}$$

$$11.2 \times 2 = x \times 1$$

Step 2: Multiply.

$$22.4 = x \times 1$$

Step 3: Isolate the variable by dividing both sides by 1.

$$x = \frac{22.4}{1}$$

$$x = 22.4 \text{ cm}$$

You will need to use a ball that has a diameter of **22.4** cm to represent Jupiter.

Appendix

Percentages

A **percentage** is a ratio of a given number to 100.

Example: What is 85% of 40?

Step 1: Rewrite the percentage by moving the decimal point two places to the left.

0.85

Step 2: Multiply the decimal by the number that you are calculating the percentage of.

$0.85 \times 40 = 34$

85% of 40 is **34.**

Decimals

To **add** or **subtract decimals,** line up the digits vertically so that the decimal points line up. Then, add or subtract the columns from right to left. Carry or borrow numbers as necessary.

Example: Add the following numbers: 3.1415 and 2.96.

Step 1: Line up the digits vertically so that the decimal points line up.

$$\begin{array}{r} 3.1415 \\ +\ 2.96 \\ \hline \end{array}$$

Step 2: Add the columns from right to left, and carry when necessary.

$$\begin{array}{r} {\scriptstyle 1\ 1} \\ 3.1415 \\ +\ 2.96 \\ \hline 6.1015 \end{array}$$

The sum is **6.1015.**

Fractions

Numbers tell you how many; **fractions** tell you *how much of a whole.*

Example: Your class has 24 plants. Your teacher instructs you to put 5 plants in a shady spot. What fraction of the plants in your class will you put in a shady spot?

Step 1: In the denominator, write the total number of parts in the whole.

$$\frac{?}{24}$$

Step 2: In the numerator, write the number of parts of the whole that are being considered.

$$\frac{5}{24}$$

So, $\mathbf{\frac{5}{24}}$ of the plants will be in the shade.

Reducing Fractions

It is usually best to express a fraction in its simplest form. Expressing a fraction in its simplest form is called *reducing* a fraction.

Example: Reduce the fraction $\frac{30}{45}$ to its simplest form.

Step 1: Find the largest whole number that will divide evenly into both the numerator and denominator. This number is called the *greatest common factor* (GCF).

Factors of the numerator 30:

1, 2, 3, 5, 6, 10, **15,** 30

Factors of the denominator 45:

1, 3, 5, 9, **15,** 45

Step 2: Divide both the numerator and the denominator by the GCF, which in this case is 15.

$$\frac{30}{45} = \frac{30 \div 15}{45 \div 15} = \frac{2}{3}$$

Thus, $\frac{30}{45}$ reduced to its simplest form is $\mathbf{\frac{2}{3}}$.

Appendix

Adding and Subtracting Fractions

To **add** or **subtract fractions** that have the **same denominator,** simply add or subtract the numerators.

Examples:

$$\frac{3}{5} + \frac{1}{5} = ? \text{ and } \frac{3}{4} - \frac{1}{4} = ?$$

Step 1: Add or subtract the numerators.

$$\frac{3}{5} + \frac{1}{5} = \frac{4}{} \text{ and } \frac{3}{4} - \frac{1}{4} = \frac{2}{}$$

Step 2: Write the sum or difference over the denominator.

$$\frac{3}{5} + \frac{1}{5} = \frac{4}{5} \text{ and } \frac{3}{4} - \frac{1}{4} = \frac{2}{4}$$

Step 3: If necessary, reduce the fraction to its simplest form.

$\mathbf{\frac{4}{5}}$ cannot be reduced, and $\frac{2}{4} = \mathbf{\frac{1}{2}}$.

To **add** or **subtract fractions** that have **different denominators,** first find the least common denominator (LCD).

Examples:

$$\frac{1}{2} + \frac{1}{6} = ? \text{ and } \frac{3}{4} - \frac{2}{3} = ?$$

Step 1: Write the equivalent fractions that have a common denominator.

$$\frac{3}{6} + \frac{1}{6} = ? \text{ and } \frac{9}{12} - \frac{8}{12} = ?$$

Step 2: Add or subtract the fractions.

$$\frac{3}{6} + \frac{1}{6} = \frac{4}{6} \text{ and } \frac{9}{12} - \frac{8}{12} = \frac{1}{12}$$

Step 3: If necessary, reduce the fraction to its simplest form.

The fraction $\frac{4}{6} = \mathbf{\frac{2}{3}}$, and $\mathbf{\frac{1}{12}}$ cannot be reduced.

Multiplying Fractions

To **multiply fractions,** multiply the numerators and the denominators together, and then reduce the fraction to its simplest form.

Example:

$$\frac{5}{9} \times \frac{7}{10} = ?$$

Step 1: Multiply the numerators and denominators.

$$\frac{5}{9} \times \frac{7}{10} = \frac{5 \times 7}{9 \times 10} = \frac{35}{90}$$

Step 2: Reduce the fraction.

$$\frac{35}{90} = \frac{35 \div 5}{90 \div 5} = \mathbf{\frac{7}{18}}$$

Dividing Fractions

To **divide fractions,** first rewrite the divisor (the number you divide by) upside down. This number is called the *reciprocal* of the divisor. Then multiply and reduce if necessary.

Example:

$$\frac{5}{8} \div \frac{3}{2} = ?$$

Step 1: Rewrite the divisor as its reciprocal.

$$\frac{3}{2} \rightarrow \frac{2}{3}$$

Step 2: Multiply the fractions.

$$\frac{5}{8} \times \frac{2}{3} = \frac{5 \times 2}{8 \times 3} = \frac{10}{24}$$

Step 3: Reduce the fraction.

$$\frac{10}{24} = \frac{10 \div 2}{24 \div 2} = \mathbf{\frac{5}{12}}$$

Appendix

Scientific Notation

Scientific notation is a short way of representing very large and very small numbers without writing all of the place-holding zeros.

Example: Write 653,000,000 in scientific notation.

Step 1: Write the number without the place-holding zeros.

653

Step 2: Place the decimal point after the first digit.

6.53

Step 3: Find the exponent by counting the number of places that you moved the decimal point.

6.53000000

The decimal point was moved eight places to the left. Therefore, the exponent of 10 is positive 8. If you had moved the decimal point to the right, the exponent would be negative.

Step 4: Write the number in scientific notation.

$\mathbf{6.53 \times 10^{8}}$

Area

Area is the number of square units needed to cover the surface of an object.

Formulas:

area of a square = *side* × *side*
area of a rectangle = *length* × *width*
area of a triangle = $\frac{1}{2}$ × *base* × *height*

Examples: Find the areas.

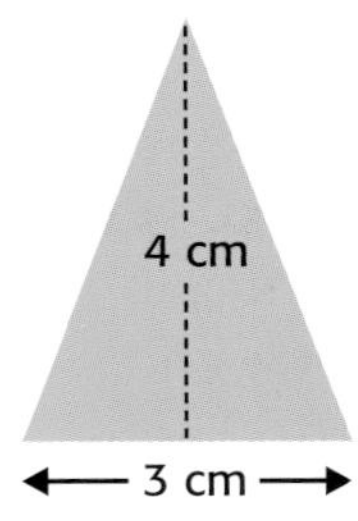

Triangle

area = $\frac{1}{2}$ × *base* × *height*

area = $\frac{1}{2}$ × 3 cm × 4 cm

area = **6 cm²**

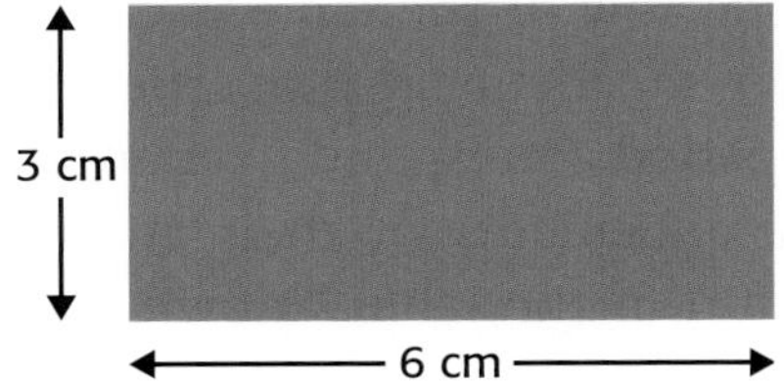

Rectangle

area = *length* × *width*
area = 6 cm × 3 cm
area = $\mathbf{18\ cm^2}$

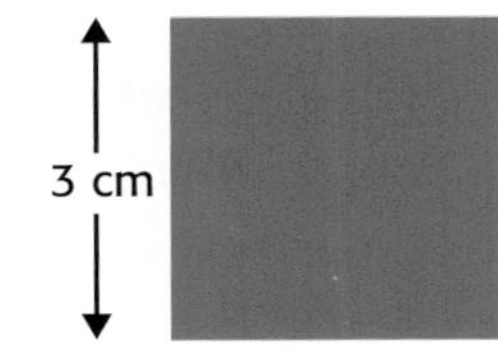

Square

area = *side* × *side*
area = 3 cm × 3 cm
area = $\mathbf{9\ cm^2}$

Volume

Volume is the amount of space that something occupies.

Formulas:

volume of a cube = *side* × *side* × *side*

volume of a prism = *area of base* × *height*

Examples:

Find the volume of the solids.

Cube

volume = *side* × *side* × *side*
volume = 4 cm × 4 cm × 4 cm
volume = $\mathbf{64\ cm^3}$

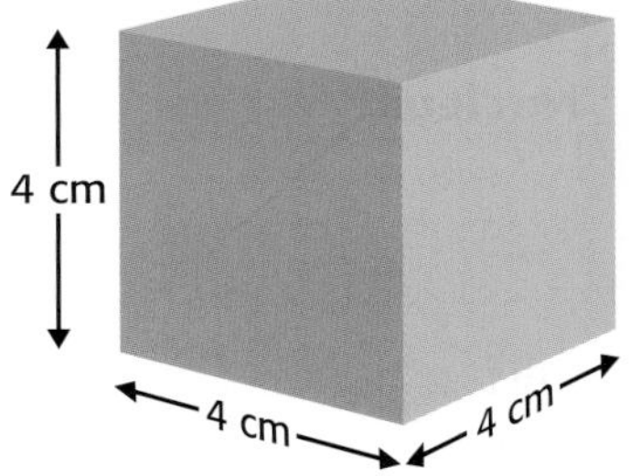

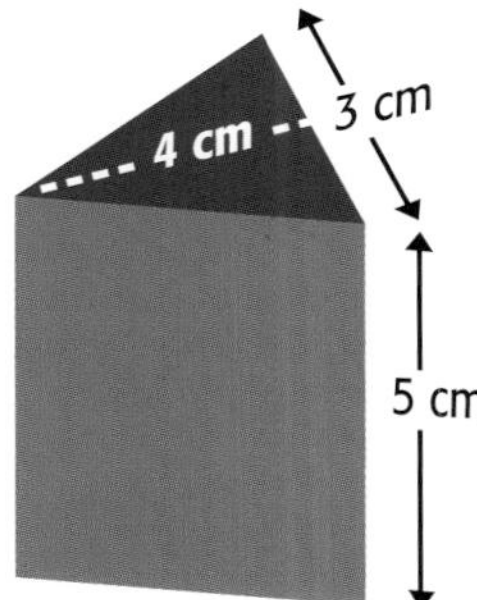

Prism

volume = *area of base* × *height*
volume = (*area of triangle*) × *height*
volume = ($\frac{1}{2}$ × 3 cm × 4 cm) × 5 cm
volume = 6 cm^2 × 5 cm
volume = $\mathbf{30\ cm^3}$

Appendix

Physical Science Refresher

Atoms and Elements

Every object in the universe is made up of particles of some kind of matter. **Matter** is anything that takes up space and has mass. All matter is made up of elements. An **element** is a substance that cannot be separated into simpler components by ordinary chemical means. This is because each element consists of only one kind of atom. An **atom** is the smallest unit of an element that has all of the properties of that element.

Atomic Structure

Atoms are made up of small particles called subatomic particles. The three major types of subatomic particles are **electrons, protons,** and **neutrons.** Electrons have a negative electric charge, protons have a positive charge, and neutrons have no electric charge. The protons and neutrons are packed close to one another to form the **nucleus.** The protons give the nucleus a positive charge. Electrons are most likely to be found in regions around the nucleus called **electron clouds.** The negatively charged electrons are attracted to the positively charged nucleus. An atom may have several energy levels in which electrons are located.

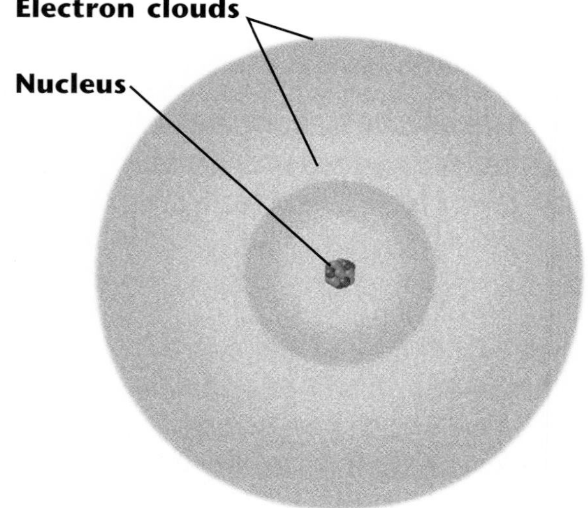

Atomic Number

To help in the identification of elements, scientists have assigned an **atomic number** to each kind of atom. The atomic number is the number of protons in the atom. Atoms with the same number of protons are all the same kind of element. In an uncharged, or electrically neutral, atom there are an equal number of protons and electrons. Therefore, the atomic number equals the number of electrons in an uncharged atom. The number of neutrons, however, can vary for a given element. Atoms of the same element that have different numbers of neutrons are called **isotopes.**

Periodic Table of the Elements

In the periodic table, the elements are arranged from left to right in order of increasing atomic number. Each element in the table is in a separate box. An uncharged atom of each element has one more electron and one more proton than an uncharged atom of the element to its left. Each horizontal row of the table is called a **period.** Changes in chemical properties of elements across a period correspond to changes in the electron arrangements of their atoms. Each vertical column of the table, known as a **group,** lists elements with similar properties. The elements in a group have similar chemical properties because their atoms have the same number of electrons in their outer energy level. For example, the elements helium, neon, argon, krypton, xenon, and radon all have similar properties and are known as the noble gases.

Molecules and Compounds

When two or more elements are joined chemically, the resulting substance is called a **compound.** A compound is a new substance with properties different from those of the elements that compose it. For example, water, H_2O, is a compound formed when hydrogen (H) and oxygen (O) combine. The smallest complete unit of a compound that has the properties of that compound is called a **molecule.** A chemical formula indicates the elements in a compound. It also indicates the relative number of atoms of each element present. The chemical formula for water is H_2O, which indicates that each water molecule consists of two atoms of hydrogen and one atom of oxygen. The subscript number after the symbol for an element indicates how many atoms of that element are in a single molecule of the compound.

Acids, Bases, and pH

An ion is an atom or group of atoms that has an electric charge because it has lost or gained one or more electrons. When an acid, such as hydrochloric acid, HCl, is mixed with water, it separates into ions. An **acid** is a compound that produces hydrogen ions, H+, in water. The hydrogen ions then combine with a water molecule to form a hydronium ion, H_3O^+. A **base,** on the other hand, is a substance that produces hydroxide ions, OH^-, in water.

To determine whether a solution is acidic or basic, scientists use pH. The **pH** is a measure of the hydronium ion concentration in a solution. The pH scale ranges from 0 to 14. The middle point, pH = 7, is neutral, neither acidic nor basic. Acids have a pH less than 7; bases have a pH greater than 7. The lower the number is, the more acidic the solution. The higher the number is, the more basic the solution.

Chemical Equations

A chemical reaction occurs when a chemical change takes place. (In a chemical change, new substances with new properties are formed.) A chemical equation is a useful way of describing a chemical reaction by means of chemical formulas. The equation indicates what substances react and what the products are. For example, when carbon and oxygen combine, they can form carbon dioxide. The equation for the reaction is as follows: $C + O_2 \rightarrow CO_2$.

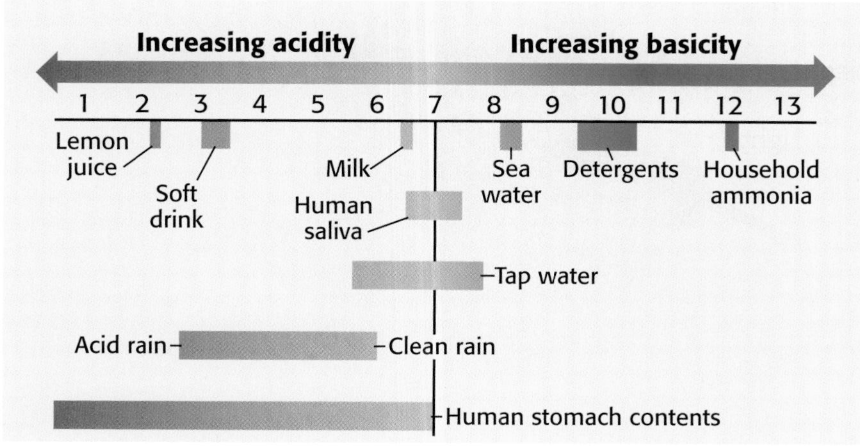

Using the Microscope

Parts of the Compound Light Microscope

- The **ocular lens** magnifies the image 10×.
- The **low-power objective** magnifies the image 10×.
- The **high-power objective** magnifies the image either 40× or 43×.
- The **revolving nosepiece** holds the objectives and can be turned to change from one magnification to the other.
- The **body tube** maintains the correct distance between the ocular lens and objectives.
- The **coarse-adjustment knob** moves the body tube up and down to allow focusing of the image.
- The **fine-adjustment knob** moves the body tube slightly to bring the image into sharper focus.
- The **stage** supports a slide.
- **Stage clips** hold the slide in place for viewing.
- The **diaphragm** controls the amount of light coming through the stage.
- The light source provides a **light** for viewing the slide.
- The **arm** supports the body tube.
- The **base** supports the microscope.

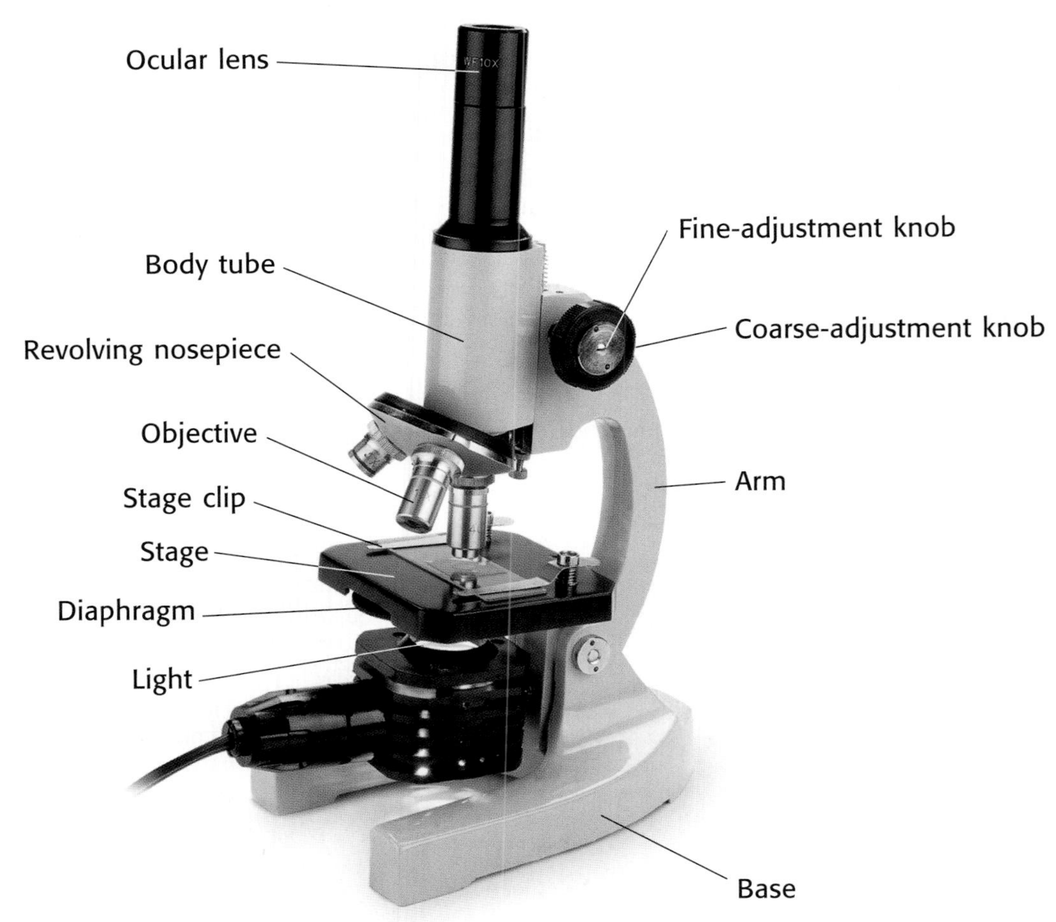

Appendix

Proper Use of the Compound Light Microscope

1. Use both hands to carry the microscope to your lab table. Place one hand beneath the base, and use the other hand to hold the arm of the microscope. Hold the microscope close to your body while carrying it to your lab table.
2. Place the microscope on the lab table at least 5 cm from the edge of the table.
3. Check to see what type of light source is used by your microscope. If the microscope has a lamp, plug it in and make sure that the cord is out of the way. If the microscope has a mirror, adjust the mirror to reflect light through the hole in the stage. **Caution:** If your microscope has a mirror, do not use direct sunlight as a light source. Direct sunlight can damage your eyes.
4. Always begin work with the low-power objective in line with the body tube. Adjust the revolving nosepiece.
5. Place a prepared slide over the hole in the stage. Secure the slide with the stage clips.
6. Look through the ocular lens. Move the diaphragm to adjust the amount of light coming through the stage.
7. Look at the stage from eye level. Slowly turn the coarse adjustment to lower the objective until the objective almost touches the slide. Do not allow the objective to touch the slide.
8. Look through the ocular lens. Turn the coarse adjustment to raise the low-power objective until the image is in focus. Always focus by raising the objective away from the slide. Never focus the objective downward. Use the fine adjustment to sharpen the focus. Keep both eyes open while viewing a slide.
9. Make sure that the image is exactly in the center of your field of vision. Then, switch to the high-power objective. Focus the image by using only the fine adjustment. Never use the coarse adjustment at high power.
10. When you are finished using the microscope, remove the slide. Clean the ocular lens and objectives with lens paper. Return the microscope to its storage area. Remember to use both hands when carrying the microscope.

Making a Wet Mount

1. Use lens paper to clean a glass slide and a coverslip.
2. Place the specimen that you wish to observe in the center of the slide.
3. Using a medicine dropper, place one drop of water on the specimen.
4. Hold the coverslip at the edge of the water and at a 45° angle to the slide. Make sure that the water runs along the edge of the coverslip.
5. Lower the coverslip slowly to avoid trapping air bubbles.
6. Water might evaporate from the slide as you work. Add more water to keep the specimen fresh. Place the tip of the medicine dropper next to the edge of the coverslip. Add a drop of water. (You can also use this method to add stain or solutions to a wet mount.) Remove excess water from the slide by using the corner of a paper towel as a blotter. Do not lift the coverslip to add or remove water.

Glossary

A

abiotic describes the nonliving part of the environment, including water, rocks, light, and temperature (480)

absolute dating any method of measuring the age of an event or object in years (195)

active transport the movement of substances across the cell membrane that requires the cell to use energy (92)

adaptation a characteristic that improves an individual's ability to survive and reproduce in a particular environment (166)

addiction a dependence on a substance, such as alcohol or drugs (739)

aerobic exercise physical exercise intended to increase the activity of the heart and lungs to promote the body's use of oxygen (745)

alcoholism a disorder in which a person repeatedly drinks alcoholic beverages in an amount that interferes with the person's health and activities (740)

algae (AL JEE) eukaryotic organisms that convert the sun's energy into food through photosynthesis but that do not have roots, stems, or leaves (singular, *alga*) (274)

allele (uh LEEL) one of the alternative forms of a gene that governs a characteristic, such as hair color (120)

allergy a reaction to a harmless or common substance by the body's immune system (719)

alveoli (al VEE uh LIE) any of the tiny air sacs of the lungs where oxygen and carbon dioxide are exchanged (621)

amniotic egg (AM nee AHT ik EG) a type of egg that is surrounded by a membrane, the amnion, and that in reptiles, birds, and egg-laying mammals contains a large amount of yolk and is surrounded by a shell (427)

angiosperm (AN jee oh SPUHRM) a flowering plant that produces seeds within a fruit (302)

Animalia a kingdom made up of complex, multicellular organisms that lack cell walls, can usually move around, and quickly respond to their environment (232)

antenna a feeler that is on the head of an invertebrate, such as a crustacean or an insect, and that senses touch, taste, or smell (394)

antibiotic medicine used to kill bacteria and other microorganisms (254)

antibody a protein made by B cells that binds to a specific antigen (715)

Archaebacteria (AHR kee bak TEER ee uh) a kingdom made up of bacteria that live in extreme environments (229)

area a measure of the size of a surface or a region (25)

artery a blood vessel that carries blood away from the heart to the body's organs (608)

asexual reproduction reproduction that does not involve the union of sex cells and in which one parent produces offspring that are genetically identical to the parent (40, 684)

ATP **a**denosine **t**ri**p**hosphate, a molecule that acts as the main energy source for cell processes (46)

autoimmune disease a disease in which the immune system attacks the organism's own cells (719)

B

B cell a white blood cell that makes antibodies (715)

binary fission (BIE nuh ree FISH uhn) a form of asexual reproduction in single-celled organisms by which one cell divides into two cells of the same size (248)

biodiversity the number and variety of organisms in a given area during a specific period of time (558)

biome (BIE OHM) a large region characterized by a specific type of climate and certain types of plant and animal communities (526)

bioremediation (BIE oh ri MEE dee AY shuhn) the biological treatment of hazardous waste by living organisms (253)

biosphere the part of Earth where life exists (483)

biotic describes living factors in the environment (480)

bird of prey a bird that hunts and eats other animals (451)

blood the fluid that carries gases, nutrients, and wastes through the body and that is made up of platelets, white blood cells, red blood cells, and plasma (612)

blood pressure the force that blood exerts on the walls of the arteries (614)

brain the mass of nerve tissue that is the main control center of the nervous system (660)

bronchus (BRAHNG kuhs) one of the two tubes that connect the lungs with the trachea (621)

brooding to sit on and cover eggs to keep them warm until they hatch; to incubate (446)

C

cancer a tumor in which the cells begin dividing at an uncontrolled rate and become invasive (720)

capillary a tiny blood vessel that allows an exchange between blood and cells in tissue (608)

carbohydrate a class of energy-giving nutrients that includes sugars, starches, and fiber; contains carbon, hydrogen, and oxygen (45, 732)

cardiovascular system a collection of organs that transport blood throughout the body (606)

carnivore an organism that eats animals (485)

carrying capacity the largest population that an environment can support at any given time (491)

cell in biology, the smallest unit that can perform all life processes; cells are covered by a membrane and contain DNA and cytoplasm (38, 60)

cell cycle the life cycle of a cell (98)

cell membrane a phospholipid layer that covers a cell's surface and acts as a barrier between the inside of a cell and the cell's environment (63)

cellular respiration the process by which cells use oxygen to produce energy from food (95, 333)

cell wall a rigid structure that surrounds the cell membrane and provides support to the cell (68)

Cenozoic era (SEN uh ZOH ik ER uh) the most recent geologic era, beginning 65 million years ago; also called the *Age of Mammals* (204)

central nervous system the brain and the spinal cord; its main function is to control the flow of information in the body (656)

chlorophyll (KLAWR uh FIL) a green pigment that captures light energy for photosynthesis (332)

chromosome in a eukaryotic cell, one of the structures in the nucleus that are made up of DNA and protein; in a prokaryotic cell, the main ring of DNA (98)

circadian rhythm a biological daily cycle (364)

classification the division of organisms into groups, or classes, based on specific characteristics (222)

closed circulatory system a circulatory system in which the heart circulates blood through a network of vessels that form a closed loop; the blood does not leave the blood vessels, and materials diffuse across the walls of the vessels (389)

cochlea (KAHK lee uh) a coiled tube that is found in the inner ear and that is essential to hearing (668)

coelom (SEE luhm) a body cavity that contains the internal organs (381)

coevolution the evolution of two species that is due to mutual influence, often in a way that makes the relationship more beneficial to both species (495)

combustion the burning of a substance (510)

commensalism a relationship between two organisms in which one organism benefits and the other is unaffected (494)

communication a transfer of a signal or message from one animal to another that results in some type of response (366)

community all of the populations of species that live in the same habitat and interact with each other (482)

compound eye an eye composed of many light detectors (393)

compound light microscope an instrument that magnifies small objects so that they can be seen easily by using two or more lenses (23)

condensation the change of state from a gas to a liquid (508)

conservation (KAHN suhr VAY shuhn) the preservation and wise use of natural resources (560)

consumer an organism that eats other organisms or organic matter (43, 359)

contour feather one of the most external feathers that cover a bird and that help determine its shape (443)

controlled experiment an experiment that tests only one factor at a time by using a comparison of a control group with an experimental group (14)

cytokinesis the division of the cytoplasm of a cell (100)

D

decomposer an organism that gets energy by breaking down the remains of dead organisms or animal wastes and consuming or absorbing the nutrients (43)

decomposition the breakdown of substances into simpler molecular substances (510)

deep-water zone the zone of a lake or pond below the open-water zone, where no light reaches (541)

dermis the layer of skin below the epidermis (593)

desert an area that has little or no plant life, long periods without rain, and extreme temperatures; usually found in hot climates (531)

diaphragm (DIE uh FRAM) a dome-shaped muscle that is attached to the lower ribs and that functions as the main muscle in respiration (453)

dichotomous key (die KAHT uh muhs KEE) an aid that is used to identify organisms and that consists of the answers to a series of questions (226)

diffusion (di FYOO zhuhn) the movement of particles from regions of higher density to regions of lower density (90)

digestive system the organs that break down food so that it can be used by the body (634)

DNA **d**eoxyribo**n**ucleic **a**cid, a molecule that is present in all living cells and that contains the information that determines the traits that a living thing inherits and needs to live (144)

dominant trait the trait observed in the first generation when parents that have different traits are bred (117)

dormant describes the inactive state of a seed or other plant part when conditions are unfavorable to growth (338)

down feather a soft feather that covers the body of young birds and provides insulation to adult birds (443)

drug any substance that causes a change in a person's physical or psychological state (738)

E

ecology the study of the interactions of living organisms with one another and with their environment (480)

ecosystem a community of organisms and their abiotic, or nonliving, environment (483)

ectotherm (EK toh thuhrm) an organism that needs sources of heat outside of itself (414)

egg a sex cell produced by a female (685)

electron microscope a microscope that focuses a beam of electrons to magnify objects (23)

embryo (EM bree OH) a plant or an animal in an early stage of development (358); a developing human, from fertilization through the first 8 weeks of development (the 10th week of pregnancy) (692)

endocrine system a collection of glands and groups of cells that secrete hormones that regulate growth, development, and homeostasis; includes the pituitary, thyroid, parathyroid, and adrenal glands, the hypothalamus, the pineal body, and the gonads (670)

endocytosis (EN doh sie TOH sis) the process by which a cell membrane surrounds a particle and encloses the particle in a vesicle to bring the particle into the cell (92)

endoplasmic reticulum (EN doh PLAZ mik ri TIK yuh luhm) a system of membranes that is found in a cell's cytoplasm and that assists in the production, processing, and transport of proteins and in the production of lipids (71)

endoskeleton (EN doh SKEL uh tuhn) an internal skeleton made of bone and cartilage (398)

endospore (EN doh SPAWR) a thick-walled protective spore that forms inside a bacterial cell and resists harsh conditions (249)

endotherm (EN doh THUHRM) an animal that can use body heat from chemical reactions in the body's cells to maintain a constant body temperature (414)

energy pyramid a triangular diagram that shows an ecosystem's loss of energy, which results as energy passes through the ecosystem's food chain (487)

epidermis (EP uh DUHR mis) the surface layer of cells on a plant or animal (593)

esophagus (i SAHF uh guhs) a long, straight tube that connects the pharynx to the stomach (636)

estivation a period of inactivity and lowered body temperature that some animals undergo in summer as a protection against hot weather and lack of food (364)

estuary (ES tyoo er ee) an area where fresh water from rivers mixes with salt water from the ocean (538)

Eubacteria (YOO bak TEER ee uh) a kingdom that contains all prokaryotes except archaebacteria (229)

eukaryote an organism made up of cells that have a nucleus enclosed by a membrane; eukaryotes include animals, plants, and fungi but not archaebacteria or eubacteria (66)

evaporation the change of a substance from a liquid to a gas (508)

evolution the process in which inherited characteristics within a population change over generations such that new species sometimes arise (167)

exocytosis (EK soh sie TOH sis) the process in which a cell releases a particle by enclosing the particle in a vesicle that then moves to the cell surface and fuses with the cell membrane (93)

exoskeleton a hard, external, supporting structure (393)

external fertilization the union of sex cells outside the bodies of the parents (686)

extinct describes a species that has died out completely (197)

F

fat an energy-storage nutrient that helps the body store some vitamins (733)

feedback mechanism a cycle of events in which information from one step controls or affects a previous step (665)

fermentation the breakdown of food without the use of oxygen (95)

fetus (FEET uhs) a developing human from seven or eight weeks after fertilization until birth (694)

food chain the pathway of energy transfer through various stages as a result of the feeding patterns of a series of organisms (486)

food web a diagram that shows the feeding relationships between organisms in an ecosystem (486)

fossil the remains or physical evidence of an organism preserved by geological processes (168, 194)

fossil record a historical sequence of life indicated by fossils found in layers of the Earth's crust (168)

function the special, normal, or proper activity of an organ or part (79)

Fungi (FUHN JIE) a kingdom made up of nongreen, eukaryotic organisms that have no means of movement, reproduce by using spores, and get food by breaking down substances in their surroundings and absorbing the nutrients (230)

fungus an organism whose cells have nuclei, rigid cell walls, and no chlorophyll and that belongs to the kingdom Fungi (282)

G

gallbladder a sac-shaped organ that stores bile produced by the liver (639)

ganglion (GANG glee uhn) a mass of nerve cells (381)

gene one set of instructions for an inherited trait (120)

generation time the period between the birth of one generation and the birth of the next generation (181)

genotype the entire genetic makeup of an organism; also the combination of genes for one or more specific traits (121)

geologic time scale the standard method used to divide the Earth's long natural history into manageable parts (196)

gestation period (jes TAY shuhn PIR ee uhd) in mammals, the length of time between fertilization and birth (456)

gill a respiratory organ in which oxygen from the water is exchanged with carbon dioxide from the blood (415)

gland a group of cells that make special chemicals for the body (670)

Golgi complex (GOHL jee KAHM PLEKS) cell organelle that helps make and package materials to be transported out of the cell (73)

gut the digestive tract (381)

gymnosperm (JIM noh SPUHRM) a woody, vascular seed plant whose seeds are not enclosed by an ovary or fruit (302)

H

herbivore an organism that eats only plants (485)

heredity the passing of genetic traits from parent to offspring (40, 114)

heterotroph (HET uhr oh TROHF) an organism that gets food by eating other organisms or their byproducts and that cannot make organic compounds from inorganic materials (271)

hibernation a period of inactivity and lowered body temperature that some animals undergo in winter as a protection against cold weather and lack of food (364)

homeostasis (HOH mee OH STAY sis) the maintenance of a constant internal state in a changing environment (39, 580)

hominid a type of primate characterized by bipedalism, relatively long lower limbs, and lack of a tail; examples include humans and their ancestors (207)

homologous chromosomes (hoh MAHL uh guhs KROH muh SOHMZ) chromosomes that have the same sequence of genes and the same structure (99, 126)

Homo sapiens (HOH moh SAY pee UHNZ) the species of hominids that includes modern humans and their closest ancestors and that first appeared about 100,000 to 150,000 years ago (210)

hormone a substance that is made in one cell or tissue and that causes a change in another cell or tissue in a different part of the body (670)

host an organism from which a parasite takes food or shelter (256, 271)

hygiene the science of health and ways to preserve health (744)

hypha (HIE fuh) a nonreproductive filament of a fungus (283)

hypothesis (hie PAHTH uh sis) an explanation that is based on prior scientific research or observations and that can be tested (12)

I

immune system the cells and tissues that recognize and attack foreign substances in the body (715)

immunity the ability to resist or recover from an infectious disease (712)

infectious disease a disease that is caused by a pathogen and that can be spread from one individual to another (710)

innate behavior an inherited behavior that does not depend on the environment or experience (360)

integumentary system (in TEG yoo MEN tuhr ee SIS tuhm) the organ system that forms a protective covering on the outside of the body (592, 664)

internal fertilization fertilization of an egg by sperm that occurs inside the body of a female (686)

invertebrate (in VUHR tuh brit) an animal that does not have a backbone (380)

J

joint a place where two or more bones meet (586)

K

kidney one of the pair of organs that filter water and wastes from the blood and that excrete products as urine (643)

L

large intestine the wider and shorter portion of the intestine that removes water from mostly digested food and that turns the waste into semisolid feces, or stool (640)

larynx (LAR ingks) the area of the throat that contains the vocal cords and produces vocal sounds (621)

lateral line a faint line visible on both sides of a fish's body that runs the length of the body and marks the location of sense organs that detect vibrations in water (415)

law a summary of many experimental results and observations; a law tells how things work (20)

learned behavior a behavior that has been learned from experience (360)

lichen (LIE kuhn) a mass of fungal and algal cells that grow together in a symbiotic relationship and that are usually found on rocks or trees (288)

life science the study of living things (6)

lift an upward force on an object that moves in a fluid (446)

lipid a type of biochemical that does not dissolve in water; fats and steroids are lipids (46)

littoral zone (LIT uh ruhl ZOHN) the shallow zone of a lake or pond where light reaches the bottom and nurtures plants (541)

liver the largest organ in the body; it makes bile, stores and filters blood, and stores excess sugars as glycogen (639)

lung a respiratory organ in which oxygen from the air is exchanged with carbon dioxide from the blood (420)

lymph the fluid that is collected by the lymphatic vessels and nodes (616)

lymphatic system (lim FAT ik SIS tuhm) a collection of organs whose primary function is to collect extracellular fluid and return it to the blood; the organs in this system include the lymph nodes and the lymphatic vessels (616)

lymph node an organ that filters lymph and that is found along the lymphatic vessels (617)

lysosome (LIE suh SOHM) a cell organelle that contains digestive enzymes (74)

M

macrophage (MAK roh FAYJ) an immune system cell that engulfs pathogens and other materials (715)

malnutrition a disorder of nutrition that results when a person does not consume enough of each of the nutrients that are needed by the human body (736)

mammary gland in a female mammal, a gland that secretes milk (453)

marsh a treeless wetland ecosystem where plants such as grasses grow (542)

marsupial (mahr SOO pee uhl) a mammal that carries and nourishes its young in a pouch (465)

mass a measure of the amount of matter in an object (26)

meiosis (mie OH sis) a process in cell division during which the number of chromosomes decreases to half the original number by two divisions of the nucleus, which results in the production of sex cells (gametes or spores) (126)

memory B cell a B cell that responds to an antigen more strongly when the body is reinfected with an antigen than it does during its first encounter with the antigen (718)

Mesozoic era (MES oh ZOH ik ER uh) the geologic era that lasted from 248 million to 65 million years ago; also called the *Age of Reptiles* (203)

metabolism (muh TAB uh LIZ uhm) the sum of all chemical processes that occur in an organism (40)

metamorphosis (MET uh MAWR fuh sis) a phase in the life cycle of many animals during which a rapid change from the immature form of an organism to the adult form takes place (396, 422)

mineral a class of nutrients that are chemical elements that are needed for certain body processes (734)

mitochondrion (MIET oh KAHN dree uhn) in eukaryotic cells, the cell organelle that is surrounded by two membranes and that is the site of cellular respiration (72)

mitosis in eukaryotic cells, a process of cell division that forms two new nuclei, each of which has the same number of chromosomes (99)

model a pattern, plan, representation, or description designed to show the structure or workings of an object, system, or concept (18)

mold in biology, a fungus that looks like wool or cotton (284)

molting the shedding of an exoskeleton, skin, feathers, or hair to be replaced by new parts (442)

monotreme (MAHN oh TREEM) a mammal that lays eggs (464)

muscular system the organ system whose primary function is movement and flexibility (588)

mutation a change in the nucleotide-base sequence of a gene or DNA molecule (152)

mutualism (MYOO choo uhl IZ uhm) a relationship between two species in which both species benefit (494)

mycelium (mie SEE lee uhm) the mass of fungal filaments, or hyphae, that forms the body of a fungus (283)

N

narcotic a drug that is derived from opium and that relieves pain and induces sleep; examples include heroine, morphine, and codeine (741)

natural selection the process by which individuals that are better adapted to their environment survive and reproduce more successfully than less well adapted individuals do; a theory to explain the mechanism of evolution (178)

nephron the unit in the kidney that filters blood (643)

nerve a collection of nerve fibers through which impulses travel between the central nervous system and other parts of the body (658)

neuron (NOO RAHN) a nerve cell that is specialized to receive and conduct electrical impulses (657)

nicotine (NIK uh TEEN) a toxic, addictive chemical that is found in tobacco and that is one of the major contributors to the harmful effects of smoking (740)

noninfectious disease a disease that cannot spread from one individual to another (710)

nonrenewable resource a resource that forms at a rate that is much slower than the rate at which it is consumed (556)

nonvascular plant the three groups of plants (liverworts, hornworts, and mosses) that lack specialized conducting tissues and true roots, stems, and leaves (302)

nucleic acid a molecule made up of subunits called *nucleotides* (47)

nucleotide in a nucleic-acid chain, a subunit that consists of a sugar, a phosphate, and a nitrogenous base (144)

nucleus in a eukaryotic cell, a membrane-bound organelle that contains the cell's DNA and that has a role in processes such as growth, metabolism, and reproduction (63)

nutrient a substance in food that provides energy or helps form body tissues and that is necessary for life and growth (732)

O

omnivore an organism that eats both plants and animals (485)

open circulatory system a circulatory system in which the circulatory fluid is not contained entirely within vessels; a heart pumps fluid through vessels that empty into spaces called *sinuses* (389)

open-water zone the zone of a pond or lake that extends from the littoral zone and that is only as deep as light can reach (541)

organ a collection of tissues that carry out a specialized function of the body (77, 581)

organelle one of the small bodies in a cell's cytoplasm that are specialized to perform a specific function (63)

organism a living thing; anything that can carry out life processes independently (78)

organ system a group of organs that work together to perform body functions (78)

osmosis (ahs MOH sis) the diffusion of water through a semipermeable membrane (91)

ovary in flowering plants, the lower part of a pistil that produces eggs in ovules (320); in the female reproductive system of animals, an organ that produces eggs (689)

overpopulation the presence of too many individuals in an area for the available resources (557)

P

Paleozoic era (PAY lee OH ZOH ik ER uh) the geologic era that followed Precambrian time and that lasted from 543 million to 248 million years ago (202)

pancreas the organ that lies behind the stomach and that makes digestive enzymes and hormones that regulate sugar levels (638)

parasite an organism that feeds on an organism of another species (the host) and that usually harms the host; the host never benefits from the presence of the parasite (271)

parasitism (PAR uh SIET IZ uhm) a relationship between two species in which one species, the parasite, benefits from the other species, the host, which is harmed (495)

passive transport the movement of substances across a cell membrane without the use of energy by the cell (92)

pathogen a virus, microorganism, or other organism that causes disease (710)

pathogenic bacteria (PATH uh JEN ik bak TIR ee uh) bacteria that cause disease (254)

pedigree a diagram that shows the occurrence of a genetic trait in several generations of a family (132)

penis the male organ that transfers sperm to a female and that carries urine out of the body (688)

peripheral nervous system (puh RIF uhr uhl NUHR vuhs SIS tuhm) all of the parts of the nervous system except for the brain and the spinal cord (656)

petal one of the usually brightly colored, leaf-shaped parts that make up one of the rings of a flower (319)

pharynx (FAR ingks) in flatworms, the muscular tube that leads from the mouth to the gastrovascular cavity; in animals with a digestive tract, the passage from the mouth to the larynx and esophagus (621)

phenotype (FEE noh TIEP) an organism's appearance or other detectable characteristic (120)

pheromone (FER uh MOHN) a substance that is released by the body and that causes another individual of the same species to react in a predictable way (367)

phloem (FLOH EM) the tissue that conducts food in vascular plants (314)

phospholipid (FAHS foh LIP id) a lipid that contains phosphorus and that is a structural component in cell membranes (46)

photosynthesis (FOHT oh SIN thuh sis) the process by which plants, algae, and some bacteria use sunlight, carbon dioxide, and water to make food (94, 332)

phytoplankton (FIET oh PLANGK tuhn) the microscopic, photosynthetic organisms that float near the surface of marine or fresh water (274)

pioneer species a species that colonizes an uninhabited area and that starts a process of succession (513)

pistil the female reproductive part of a flower that produces seeds and consists of an ovary, style, and stigma (320)

placenta (pluh SEN tuh) the structure that attaches a developing fetus to the uterus and that enables the exchange of nutrients, wastes, and gases between the mother and the fetus (693)

placental mammal a mammal that nourishes its unborn offspring through a placenta inside its uterus (456)

plankton the mass of mostly microscopic organisms that float or drift freely in freshwater and marine environments (534)

Plantae a kingdom made up of complex, multicellular organisms that are usually green, have cell walls made of cellulose, cannot move around, and use the sun's energy to make sugar by photosynthesis (231)

plate tectonics the theory that explains how large pieces of the Earth's outermost layer, called *tectonic plates,* move and change shape (198)

pollen the tiny granules that contain the male gametophyte of seed plants (308)

pollination the transfer of pollen from the male reproductive structures to the female structures of seed plants (311)

pollution an unwanted change in the environment caused by substances or forms of energy (554)

population a group of organisms of the same species that live in a specific geographical area (482)

Precambrian time (pree KAM bree uhn TIEM) the period in the geologic time scale from the formation of the Earth to the beginning of the Paleozoic era, from about 4.6 billion to 543 million years ago (200)

precipitation any form of water that falls to the Earth's surface from the clouds (508)

predator an organism that eats all or part of another organism (492)

preening in birds, the act of grooming and maintaining their feathers (442)

prey an organism that is killed and eaten by another organism (492)

primate a type of mammal characterized by opposable thumbs and binocular vision (206)

probability the likelihood that a possible future event will occur in any given instance of the event (122)

producer an organism that can make its own food by using energy from its surroundings (43)

prokaryote (pro KAR ee OHT) an organism that consists of a single cell that does not have a nucleus (64, 247)

protein a molecule that is made up of amino acids and that is needed to build and repair body structures and to regulate processes in the body (44, 733)

protist an organism that belongs to the kingdom Protista (270)

Protista (proh TIST uh) a kingdom of mostly one-celled eukaryotic organisms that are different from plants, animals, bacteria, and fungi (230)

pulmonary circulation (PUL muh NER ee SUHR kyoo LAY shuhn) the flow of blood from the heart to the lungs and back to the heart through the pulmonary arteries, capillaries, and veins (609)

R

recessive trait a trait that is apparent only when two recessive alleles for the same characteristic are inherited (117)

recycling the process of recovering valuable or useful materials from waste or scrap; the process of reusing some items (563)

reflex an involuntary and almost immediate movement in response to a stimulus (665)

relative dating any method of determining whether an event or object is older or younger than other events or objects (195)

renewable resource a natural resource that can be replaced at the same rate at which the resource is consumed (556)

respiration in biology, the exchange of oxygen and carbon dioxide between living cells and their environment; includes breathing and cellular respiration (620)

respiratory system a collection of organs whose primary function is to take in oxygen and expel carbon dioxide; the organs of this system include the lungs, the throat, and the passageways that lead to the lungs (620)

retina the light-sensitive inner layer of the eye, which receives images formed by the lens and transmits them through the optic nerve to the brain (666)

rhizoid (RIE ZOYD) a rootlike structure in nonvascular plants that holds the plants in place and helps plants get water and nutrients (304)

rhizome a horizontal, underground stem that produces new leaves, shoots, and roots (306)

ribosome a cell organelle composed of RNA and protein; the site of protein synthesis (71, 151)

RNA **r**ibo**n**ucleic **a**cid, a molecule that is present in all living cells and that plays a role in protein production (150)

S

savanna a grassland that often has scattered trees and that is found in tropical and subtropical areas where seasonal rains, fires, and drought happen (530)

scientific methods a series of steps followed to solve problems (10)

segment any part of a larger structure, such as the body of an organism, that is set off by natural or arbitrary boundaries (390)

selective breeding the human practice of breeding animals or plants that have certain desired characteristics (176)

sepal in a flower, one of the outermost rings of modified leaves that protect the flower bud (319)

sex chromosome one of the pair of chromosomes that determine the sex of an individual (131)

sexual reproduction reproduction in which the sex cells from two parents unite to produce offspring that share traits from both parents (40, 685)

skeletal system the organ system whose primary function is to support and protect the body and to allow the body to move (584)

small intestine the organ between the stomach and the large intestine where most of the breakdown of food happens and most of the nutrients from food are absorbed (638)

social behavior the interaction between animals of the same species (366)

speciation (SPEE shee AY shuhn) the formation of new species as a result of evolution (182)

species a group of organisms that are closely related and can mate to produce fertile offspring (166)

sperm the male sex cell (685)

spleen the largest lymphatic organ in the body; serves as a blood reservoir, disintegrates old red blood cells, and produces lymphocytes and plasmids (618)

spore a reproductive cell or multicellular structure that is resistant to stressful environmental conditions and that can develop into an adult without fusing with another cell (283)

stamen the male reproductive structure of a flower that produces pollen and consists of an anther at the tip of a filament (320)

stimulus anything that causes a reaction or change in an organism or any part of an organism (39)

stoma one of many openings in a leaf or a stem of a plant that enable gas exchange to occur (plural, *stomata*) (334)

stomach the saclike, digestive organ between the esophagus and the small intestine that breaks down food by the action of muscles, enzymes, and acids (637)

stress a physical or mental response to pressure (746)

structure the arrangement of parts in an organism (79)

succession the replacement of one type of community by another at a single location over a period of time (512)

swamp a wetland ecosystem in which shrubs and trees grow (542)

swim bladder in bony fishes, a gas-filled sac that is used to control buoyancy; also known as a *gas bladder* (418)

symbiosis a relationship in which two different organisms live in close association with each other (494)

systemic circulation (sis TEM ik SUHR kyoo LAY shuhn) the flow of blood from the heart to all parts of the body and back to the heart (609)

T

tadpole the aquatic, fish-shaped larva of a frog or toad (422)

taxonomy (taks AHN uh mee) the science of describing, naming, and classifying organisms (223)

T cell an immune system cell that coordinates the immune system and attacks many infected cells (715)

technology the application of science for practical purposes; the use of tools, machines, materials, and processes to meet human needs (22)

temperature a measure of how hot (or cold) something is; specifically, a measure of the average kinetic energy of the particles in an object (26)

territory an area that is occupied by one animal or a group of animals that do not allow other members of the species to enter (361)

testes the primary male reproductive organs, which produce sperm cells and testosterone (singular, *testis*) (688)

theory an explanation that ties together many hypotheses and observations (20)

thymus the main gland of the lymphatic system; it releases mature T lymphocytes (617)

tissue a group of similar cells that perform a common function (77, 580)

tonsils small, rounded masses of lymphatic tissue located in the pharynx and in the passage from the mouth to the pharynx (619)

trachea (TRAY kee uh) in insects, myriapods, and spiders, one of a network of air tubes; in vertebrates, the tube that connects the larynx to the lungs (621)

trait a genetically determined characteristic (176)

transpiration the process by which plants release water vapor into the air through stomata; *also* the release of water vapor into the air by other organisms (334)

tropism (TROH PIZ uhm) growth of all or part of an organism in response to an external stimulus, such as light (340)

tundra a treeless plain found in the Arctic, in the Antarctic, or on the tops of mountains that is characterized by very low winter temperatures and short, cool summers (532)

U

umbilical cord (uhm BIL i kuhl KAWRD) the structure that connects an embryo and then the fetus to the placenta and through which blood vessels pass (693)

urinary system the organs that make, store, and eliminate urine (642)

uterus in female mammals, the hollow, muscular organ in which a fertilized egg is embedded and in which the embryo and fetus develop (689)

V

vagina the female reproductive organ that connects the outside of the body to the uterus (689)

variable a factor that changes in an experiment in order to test a hypothesis (14)

vascular plant a plant that has specialized tissues that conduct materials from one part of the plant to another (302)

vein in biology, a vessel that carries blood to the heart (608)

vertebrate (VUHR tuh brit) an animal that has a backbone (412)

vesicle (VES i kuhl) a small cavity or sac that contains materials in a eukaryotic cell; forms when part of the cell membrane surrounds the materials to be taken into the cell or transported within the cell (73)

virus a microscopic particle that gets inside a cell and often destroys the cell (256)

vitamin a class of nutrients that contain carbon and that are needed in small amounts to maintain health and allow growth (734)

volume a measure of the size of a body or region in three-dimensional space (25)

W

waterfowl an aquatic bird, such as a duck, goose, or swan (449)

water vascular system a system of canals filled with a watery fluid that circulates throughout the body of an echinoderm (399)

wetland an area of land that is periodically underwater or whose soil contains a great deal of moisture (542)

X

xylem (ZIE luhm) the type of tissue in vascular plants that provides support and conducts water and nutrients from the roots (314)

Spanish Glossary

A

abiotic/abiótico término que describe la parte sin vida del ambiente, incluyendo el agua, las rocas, la luz y la temperatura (480)

absolute dating/datación absoluta cualquier método que sirve para determinar la edad de un suceso u objeto en años (195)

active transport/transporte activo el movimiento de substancias a través de la membrana celular que requiere que la célula gaste energía (92)

adaptation/adaptación una característica que mejora la capacidad de un individuo para sobrevivir y reproducirse en un determinado ambiente (166)

addiction/adicción una dependencia de una substancia, tal como el alcohol o las drogas (739)

aerobic exercise/ejercicio aeróbico ejercicio físico cuyo objetivo es aumentar la actividad del corazón y los pulmones para hacer que el cuerpo use más oxígeno (745)

alcoholism/alcoholismo un trastorno en el cual una persona consume bebidas alcohólicas repetidamente en una cantidad tal que interfiere con su salud y sus actividades (740)

algae/algas organismos eucarióticos que transforman la energía del Sol en alimento por medio de la fotosíntesis, pero que no tienen raíces, tallos ni hojas (274)

allele/alelo una de las formas alternativas de un gene que rige un carácter, como por ejemplo, el color del cabello (120)

allergy/alergia una reacción del sistema inmunológico del cuerpo a una substancia inofensiva o común (719)

alveoli/alveolo cualquiera de las diminutas bolsas de aire de los pulmones, en donde ocurre el intercambio de oxígeno y dióxido de carbono (621)

amniotic egg/huevo amniótico un tipo de huevo que está rodeado por una membrana, el amnios, y que en los reptiles, las aves y los mamíferos que ponen huevos contiene una gran cantidad de yema y está rodeado por una cáscara (427)

angiosperm/angiosperma una planta que da flores y que produce semillas dentro de la fruta (302)

Animalia/Animalia un reino formado por organismos pluricelulares complejos que no tienen pared celular, normalmente son capaces de moverse y reaccionan rápidamente a su ambiente (232)

antenna/antena una estructura ubicada en la cabeza de un invertebrado, como por ejemplo, un crustáceo o un insecto, que percibe sensaciones de tacto, gusto u olor (394)

antibiotic/antibiótico medicina utilizada para matar bacterias y otros microorganismos (254)

antibody/anticuerpo una proteína producida por las células B que se une a un antígeno específico (715)

Archaebacteria/arqueobacteria un reino formado por bacterias que viven en ambientes extremos (229)

area/área una medida del tamaño de una superficie o región (25)

artery/arteria un vaso sanguíneo que transporta sangre del corazón a los órganos del cuerpo (608)

asexual reproduction/reproducción asexual reproducción que no involucra la unión de células sexuales, en la que un solo progenitor produce descendencia que es genéticamente igual al progenitor (40, 684)

ATP/ATP adenosín trifosfato, una molécula orgánica que funciona como la fuente principal de energía para los procesos celulares (46)

autoimmune disease/enfermedad autoinmune una enfermedad en la que el sistema inmunológico ataca las células del propio organismo (719)

B

B cell/célula B un glóbulo blanco de la sangre que fabrica anticuerpos (715)

binary fission/fisión binaria una forma de reproducción asexual de los organismos unicelulares, por medio de la cual la célula se divide en dos células del mismo tamaño (248)

biodiversity/biodiversidad el número y la variedad de organismos que se encuentran en un área determinada durante un período específico de tiempo (558)

biome/bioma una región extensa caracterizada por un tipo de clima específico y ciertos tipos de comunidades de plantas y animales (526)

bioremediation/bioremediación el tratamiento biológico de desechos peligrosos por medio de organismos vivos (253)

biosphere/biosfera la parte de la Tierra donde existe la vida (483)

biotic/biótico término que describe los factores vivientes del ambiente (480)

bird of prey/ave de presa un ave que caza y se alimenta de otros animales (451)

blood/sangre el líquido que lleva gases, nutrientes y desechos por el cuerpo y que está formado por plaquetas, glóbulos blancos, glóbulos rojos y plasma (612)

blood pressure/presión sanguínea la fuerza que la sangre ejerce en las paredes de las arterias (614)

brain/encéfalo la masa de tejido nervioso que es el centro principal de control del sistema nervioso (660)

bronchus/bronquio uno de los dos tubos que conectan los pulmones con la tráquea (621)

brooding/empollar sentarse y cubrir los huevos para mantenerlos calientes hasta que las crías salgan del cascarón; incubar (446)

C

cancer/cáncer un tumor en el cual las células comienzan a dividirse a una tasa incontrolable y se vuelven invasivas (720)

capillary/capilar diminuto vaso sanguíneo que permite el intercambio entre la sangre y las células de los tejidos (608)

carbohydrate/carbohidrato una clase de nutrientes que proporcionan energía; incluye los azúcares, los almidones y las fibras; contiene carbono, hidrógeno y oxígeno (45, 732)

cardiovascular system/aparato cardiovascular un conjunto de órganos que transportan la sangre a través del cuerpo (606)

carnivore/carnívoro un organismo que se alimenta de animales (485)

carrying capacity/capacidad de carga la población más grande que un ambiente puede sostener en cualquier momento dado (491)

cell/célula en biología, la unidad más pequeña que puede realizar todos los procesos vitales; las células están cubiertas por una membrana y tienen ADN y citoplasma (38, 60)

cell cycle/ciclo celular el ciclo de vida de una célula (98)

cell membrane/membrana celular una capa de fosfolípidos que cubre la superficie de la célula y funciona como una barrera entre el interior de la célula y el ambiente de la célula (63)

cellular respiration/respiración celular el proceso por medio del cual las células utilizan oxígeno para producir energía a partir de los alimentos (95, 333)

cell wall/pared celular una estructura rígida que rodea la membrana celular y le brinda soporte a la célula (68)

Cenozoic era/era Cenozoica la era geológica más reciente, que comenzó hace 65 millones de años; también llamada *Edad de los Mamíferos* (204)

central nervous system/sistema nervioso central el cerebro y la médula espinal; su principal función es controlar el flujo de información en el cuerpo (656)

chlorophyll/clorofila un pigmento verde que capta la energía luminosa para la fotosíntesis (332)

chromosome/cromosoma en una célula eucariótica, una de las estructuras del núcleo que está hecha de ADN y proteína; en una célula procariótica, el anillo principal de ADN (98)

circadian rhythm/ritmo circadiano un ciclo biológico diario (364)

classification/clasificación la división de organismos en grupos, o clases, en función de características específicas (222)

closed circulatory system/aparato circulatorio cerrado un aparato circulatorio en el que el corazón hace que la sangre circule a través de una red de vasos que forman un circuito cerrado; la sangre no sale de los vasos sanguíneos y los materiales pasan a través de las paredes de los vasos por difusión (389)

cochlea/cóclea un tubo enrollado que se encuentra en el oído interno y es esencial para poder oír (668)

coelom/celoma una cavidad del cuerpo que contiene los órganos internos (381)

coevolution/coevolución la evolución de dos especies que se debe a su influencia mutua, a menudo de un modo que hace que la relación sea más beneficiosa para ambas (495)

combustion/combustión fenómeno que ocurre cuando una substancia se quema (510)

commensalism/comensalismo una relación entre dos organismos en la que uno se beneficia y el otro no es afectado (494)

communication/comunicación la transferencia de una señal o mensaje de un animal a otro, la cual resulta en algún tipo de respuesta (366)

community/comunidad todas las poblaciones de especies que viven en el mismo hábitat e interactúan entre sí (482)

compound eye/ojo compuesto un ojo compuesto por muchos detectores de luz (393)

compound light microscope/microcopio óptico compuesto un instrumento que magnifica objetos pequeños de modo que se puedan ver fácilmente usando dos o más lentes (23)

condensation/condensación el cambio de estado de gas a líquido (508)

conservation/conservación la preservación y el uso inteligente de los recursos naturales (560)

consumer/consumidor un organismo que se alimenta de otros organismos o de materia orgánica (43, 359)

contour feather/pluma de contorno una las plumas más externas que cubren a un ave y que sirven para determinar su forma (443)

controlled experiment/experimento controlado un experimento que prueba sólo un factor a la vez, comparando un grupo de control con un grupo experimental (14)

cytokinesis/citoquinesis la división del citoplasma de una célula (100)

D

decomposer/descomponedor un organismo que, para obtener energía, desintegra los restos de organismos muertos o los desechos de animales y consume o absorbe los nutrientes (43)

decomposition/descomposición la desintegración de substancias en substancias moleculares más simples (510)

deep-water zone/zona de aguas profundas la zona de un lago o laguna debajo de la zona de aguas abiertas, a donde no llega la luz (541)

dermis/dermis la capa de piel que está debajo de la epidermis (593)

desert/desierto una región con poca vegetación o sin vegetación, largos períodos sin lluvia y temperaturas extremas; generalmente se ubica en climas calientes (531)

diaphragm/diafragma un músculo en forma de cúpula que está unido a las costillas inferiores y que es el músculo principal de la respiración (453)

dichotomous key/clave dicotómica una ayuda para identificar organismos, que consiste en las respuestas a una serie de preguntas (226)

diffusion/difusión el movimiento de partículas de regiones de mayor densidad a regiones de menor densidad (90)

digestive system/aparato digestivo los órganos que descomponen la comida de modo que el cuerpo la pueda usar (634)

DNA/ADN **á**cido **d**esoxirribo**n**ucleico, una molécula que está presente en todas las células vivas y que contiene la información que determina los caracteres que un ser vivo hereda y necesita para vivir (144)

dominant trait/carácter dominante el carácter que se observa en la primera generación cuando se cruzan progenitores que tienen caracteres diferentes (117)

dormant/aletargado término que describe el estado inactivo de una semilla u otra parte de las plantas cuando las condiciones son desfavorables para el crecimiento (338)

down feather/plumón una pluma suave que cubre el cuerpo de las crías de las aves y sirve como aislante en las aves adultas (443)

drug/droga cualquier substancia que produce un cambio en el estado físico o psicológico de una persona (738)

E

ecology/ecología el estudio de las interacciones de los seres vivos entre sí mismos y entre sí mismos y su ambiente (480)

ecosystem/ecosistema una comunidad de organismos y su ambiente abiótico o no vivo (483)

ectotherm/ectotermo un organismo que necesita fuentes de calor fuera de sí mismo (414)

egg/óvulo una célula sexual producida por una hembra (685)

electron microscope/microscopio electrónico microscopio que enfoca un haz de electrones para aumentar la imagen de los objetos (23)

embryo/embrión una planta o un animal en una de las primeras etapas de su desarrollo (358); un ser humano desde la fecundación hasta las primeras 8 semanas de desarrollo (décima semana del embarazo) (692)

endocrine system/sistema endocrino un conjunto de glándulas y grupos de células que secretan hormonas que regulan el crecimiento, el desarrollo y la homeostasis; incluye las glándulas pituitaria, tiroides, paratiroides y suprarrenal, el hipotálamo, el cuerpo pineal y las gónadas (670)

endocytosis/endocitosis el proceso por medio del cual la membrana celular rodea una partícula y la encierra en una vesícula para llevarla al interior de la célula (92)

endoplasmic reticulum/retículo endoplásmico un sistema de membranas que se encuentra en el citoplasma de la célula y que tiene una función en la producción, procesamiento y transporte de proteínas y en la producción de lípidos (71)

endoskeleton/endoesqueleto un esqueleto interno hecho de hueso y cartílago (398)

endospore/endospora una espora protectiva que tiene una pared gruesa, se forma dentro de una célula bacteriana y resiste condiciones adversas (249)

endotherm/endotermo un animal que puede utilizar el calor del cuerpo producido por las reacciones químicas de sus células para mantener una temperatura corporal constante (414)

energy pyramid/pirámide de energía un diagrama triangular que muestra la pérdida de energía en un ecosistema, producida a medida que la energía pasa a través de la cadena alimenticia del ecosistema (487)

epidermis/epidermis la superficie externa de las células de una planta o animal (593)

esophagus/esófago un conducto largo y recto que conecta la faringe con el estómago (636)

estivation/estivación un período de inactividad y menor temperatura corporal por el que pasan algunos animales durante el verano para protegerse del calor y la falta de alimento (364)

estuary/estuario un área donde el agua dulce de los ríos se mezcla con el agua salada del océano (538)

Eubacteria/Eubacteria un reino que agrupa a todos los procariotes, excepto a las arqueobacterias (229)

eukaryote/eucariote un organismo cuyas células tienen un núcleo rodeado por una membrana; entre los eucariotes se encuentran los animales, las plantas y los hongos, pero no las arqueobacterias (66)

evaporation/evaporación el cambio de una substancia de líquido a gas (508)

evolution/evolución el proceso por medio del cual las características heredadas dentro de una población cambian con el transcurso de las generaciones de manera tal que a veces surgen nuevas especies (167)

exocytosis/exocitosis el proceso por medio del cual una célula libera una partícula encerrándola en una vesícula que luego se traslada a la superficie de la célula y se fusiona con la membrana celular (93)

exoskeleton/exoesqueleto una estructura de soporte, dura y externa (393)

external fertilization/fecundación externa la unión de células sexuales fuera del cuerpo de los progenitores (686)

extinct/extinto término que describe a una especie que ha desaparecido por completo (197)

F

fat/grasa un nutriente que almacena energía y ayuda al cuerpo a almacenar algunas vitaminas (733)

feedback mechanism/mecanismo de retroalimentación un ciclo de sucesos en el que la información de una etapa controla o afecta a una etapa anterior (665)

fermentation/fermentación la descomposición de los alimentos sin utilizar oxígeno (95)

fetus/feto un ser humano en desarrollo de las semanas siete a ocho después de la fecundación hasta el nacimiento (694)

food chain/cadena alimenticia la vía de transferencia de energía través de varias etapas, que ocurre como resultado de los patrones de alimentación de una serie de organismos (486)

food web/red alimenticia un diagrama que muestra las relaciones de alimentación entre los organismos de un ecosistema (486)

fossil/fósil los restos o las pruebas físicas de un organismo preservados por los procesos geológicos (168, 194)

fossil record/registro fósil una secuencia histórica de la vida indicada por fósiles que se han encontrado en las capas de la corteza terrestre (168)

function/función la actividad especial, normal o adecuada de un órgano o parte (79)

Fungi/Fungi un reino formado por organismos eucarióticos no verdes que no tienen capacidad de movimiento, se reproducen por esporas y obtienen alimento al descomponer substancias de su entorno y absorber los nutrientes (230)

fungus/hongo un organismo que tiene células con núcleos y pared celular rígida, pero carece de clorofila, perteneciente al reino Fungi (282)

G

gallbladder/vesícula biliar un órgano que tiene la forma de una bolsa y que almacena la bilis producida por el hígado (639)

ganglion/ganglio una masa de células nerviosas (381)

gene/gene un conjunto de instrucciones para un carácter heredado (120)

generation time/tiempo de generación el período entre el nacimiento de una generación y el nacimiento de la siguiente generación (181)

genotype/genotipo la constitución genética completa de un organismo; *también* la combinación genes para uno o más caracteres específicos (121)

geologic time scale/escala de tiempo geológico el método estándar que se usa para dividir la larga historia natural de la Tierra en partes razonables (196)

gestation period/período de gestación en los mamíferos, el tiempo que transcurre entre la fecundación y el nacimiento (456)

gill/branquiaen un órgano respiratorio en el que el oxígeno del agua se intercambia con el dióxido de carbono de la sangre (415)

gland/glándula un grupo de células que elaboran ciertas substancias químicas para el cuerpo (670)

Golgi complex/aparato de Golgi un organelo celular que ayuda a hacer y a empacar los materiales que serán transportados al exterior de la célula (73)

gut/tripa el tracto digestivo (381)

gymnosperm/gimnosperma una planta leñosa vascular que produce semillas que no están contenidas en un ovario o fruto (302)

H

herbivore/herbívoro un organismo que sólo come plantas (485)

heredity/herencia la transmisión de caracteres genéticos de padres a hijos (40, 114)

heterotroph/heterótrofo un organismo que se alimenta comiendo otros organismos o sus productos secundarios y que no puede producir compuestos orgánicos a partir de materiales inorgánicos (271)

hibernation/hibernación un período de inactividad y disminución de la temperatura del cuerpo que algunos animales experimentan en invierno como protección contra el tiempo frío y la escasez de comida (364)

homeostasis/homeostasis la capacidad de mantener un estado interno constante en un ambiente en cambio (39, 580)

hominid/homínido un tipo de primate caracterizado por ser bípedo, tener extremidades inferiores relativamente largas y no tener cola; incluye a los seres humanos y sus ancestros (207)

homologous chromosomes/cromosomas homólogos cromosomas con la misma secuencia de genes y la misma estructura (99, 126)

Homo sapiens/Homo sapiens la especie de homínidos que incluye a los seres humanos modernos y a sus ancestros más cercanos; apareció hace entre 100,000 y 150,000 años (210)

hormone/hormona una substancia que es producida en una célula o tejido, la cual causa un cambio en otra célula o tejido ubicado en una parte diferente del cuerpo (670)

host/huésped el organismo del cual un parásito obtiene alimento y refugio (256, 271)

hygiene/higiene la ciencia de la salud y las formas de preservar la salud (744)

hypha/hifa un filamento no-reproductor de un hongo (283)

hypothesis/hipótesis una explicación que se basa en observaciones o investigaciones científicas previas y que se puede probar (12)

I

immune system/sistema inmunológico las células y tejidos que reconocen y atacan substancias extrañas en el cuerpo (715)

immunity/inmunidad la capacidad de resistir una enfermedad infecciosa o recuperarse de ella (712)

infectious disease/enfermedad infecciosa una enfermedad que es causada por un patógeno y que puede transmitirse de un individuo a otro (710)

innate behavior/conducta innata una conducta heredada que no depende del ambiente ni de la experiencia (360)

integumentary system/sistema integumentario el sistema de órganos que forma una cubierta de protección en la parte exterior del cuerpo (592, 664)

internal fertilization/fecundación interna fecundación de un óvulo por un espermatozoide, la cual ocurre dentro del cuerpo de la hembra (686)

invertebrate/invertebrado un animal que no tiene columna vertebral (380)

J

joint/articulación un lugar donde se unen dos o más huesos (586)

K

kidney/riñón uno de los dos órganos que filtran el agua y los desechos de la sangre y excretan productos en fomra de orina (643)

L

large intestine/intestino grueso la porción más ancha y más corta del intestino, que elimina el agua de los alimentos casi totalmente digeridos y convierte los desechos en heces semisólidas o excremento (640)

larynx/laringe el área de la garganta que contiene las cuerdas vocales y que produce sonidos vocales (621)

lateral line/línea lateral una línea apenas visible que se encuentra a ambos lados del cuerpo de unpez y que recorre la longitud del cuerpo, marcando la ubicación de los órganos de los sentidos que detectan vibraciones en el agua (415)

law/ley un resumen de muchos resultados y observaciones experimentales; una ley dice cómo funcionan las cosas (20)

learned behavior/conducta aprendida una conducta que se ha aprendido por experiencia (360)

lichen/liquen una masa de células de hongos y de algas que crecen juntas en una relación simbiótica y que normalmente se encuentran en rocas o árboles (288)

life science/ciencias de la vida el estudio de los seres vivos (6)

lift/propulsión una fuerza hacia arriba en un objeto que se mueve en un fluido (446)

lipid/lípido un tipo de substancia bioquímica que no se disuelve en agua; las grasas y los esteroides son lípidos (46)

littoral zone/zona litoral la zona poco profunda de un lago o una laguna donde la luz llega al fondo y nutre a las plantas (541)

liver/hígado el órgano más grande del cuerpo; produce bilis, almacena y filtra la sangre, y almacena el exceso de azúcares en forma de glucógeno (639)

lung/pulmón un órgano respiratorio en el que el oxígeno del aire se intercambia con el dióxido de carbono de la sangre (420)

lymph/linfa el fluido que es recolectado por los vasos y nodos linfáticos (616)

lymphatic system/sistema linfático un conjunto de órganos cuya función principal es recolectar el fluido extracelular y regresarlo a la sangre; los órganos de este sistema incluyen los nodos linfáticos y los vasos linfáticos (616)

lymph nodes/nodos linfáticos masas ovaladas de tejido linfático que se encuentran en los vasos linfáticos y filtran la linfa (617)

lysosome/lisosoma un organelo celular que contiene enzimas digestivas (74)

M

macrophage/macrófago una célula del sistema inmunológico que envuelve a los patógenos y otros materiales (715)

malnutrition/desnutrición un trastorno de nutrición que resulta cuando una persona no consume una cantidad suficiente de cada nutriente que el cuerpo humano necesita (736)

mammary gland/glándula mamaria en los mamíferos hembra, una glándula que secreta leche (453)

marsh/pantano un ecosistema pantanoso sin árboles, donde crecen plantas tales como el pasto (542)

marsupial/marsupial un mamífero que lleva y alimenta a sus crías en una bolsa (465)

mass/masa una medida de la cantidad de materia que tiene un objeto (26)

meiosis/meiosis un proceso de división celular durante el cual el número de cromosomas disminuye a la mitad del número original por medio de dos divisiones del núcleo, lo cual resulta en la producción de células sexuales (gametos o esporas) (126)

memory B cell/célula B de memoria una célula B que responde con mayor eficacia a un antígeno cuando el cuerpo vuelve a infectarse con él que cuando lo encuentra por primera vez (718)

Mesozoic era/era Mesozoica la era geológica que comenzó hace 248 millones de años y terminó hace 65 millones de años; también llamada *Edad de los Reptiles* (203)

metabolism/metabolismo la suma de todos los procesos químicos que ocurren en un organismo (40)

metamorphosis/metamorfosis una fase del ciclo de vida de muchos animales durante la cual ocurre un cambio rápido de la forma inmadura del organismo a la adulta (396, 422)

mineral/mineral una clase de nutrientes que son elementos químicos necesarios para ciertos procesos del cuerpo (734)

mitochondrion/mitocondria en las células eucarióticas, el organelo celular rodeado por dos membranas que es el lugar donde se lleva a cabo la respiración celular (72)

mitosis/mitosis en las células eucarióticas, un proceso de división celular que forma dos núcleos nuevos, cada uno de los cuales posee el mismo número de cromosomas (99)

model/modelo un diseño, plan, representación o descripción cuyo objetivo es mostrar la estructura o funcionamiento de un objeto, sistema o concepto (18)

mold/moho en biología, un hongo que tiene la apariencia de lana o algodón (284)

molting/pelechar la muda de un exoesqueleto, piel, plumas o pelo, los cuales son reemplazados por partes nuevas (442)

monotreme/monotrema un mamífero que pone-huevos (464)

muscular system/sistema muscular el sistema de órganos cuya función principal es permitir el movimiento y la flexibilidad (588)

mutation/mutación un cambio en la secuencia de la base de nucleótidos de un gene o de una molécula de ADN (152)

mutualism/mutualismo una relación entre dos especies en la que ambas se benefician (494)

mycelium/micelio una masa de filamentos de hongos, o hifas, que forma el cuerpo de un hongo (283)

N

narcotic/narcótico una droga que proviene del opio, la cual alivia el dolor e induce el sueño; entre los ejemplos se encuentran la heroína, morfina y codeína (741)

natural selection/selección natural el proceso por medio del cual los individuos que están mejor adaptados a su ambiente sobreviven y se reproducen con más éxito que los individuos menos adaptados; una teoría que explica el mecanismo de la evolución (178)

nephron/nefrona la unidad del riñón que filtra la sangre (643)

nerve/nervio un conjunto de fibras nerviosas a través de las cuales se desplazan los impulsos entre el sistema nervioso central y otras partes del cuerpo (658)

neuron/neurona una célula nerviosa que está especializada en recibir y transmitir impulsos eléctricos (657)

nicotine/nicotina una substancia química tóxica y adictiva que se encuentra en el tabaco y que es una de las principales causas de los efectos dañinos de fumar (740)

noninfectious disease/enfermedad no infecciosa una enfermedad que no se contagia de una persona a otra (710)

nonrenewable resource/recurso no renovable un recurso que se forma a una tasa que es mucho más lenta que la tasa a la que se consume (556)

nonvascular plant/planta no vascular los tres tipos de plantas (hepáticas, milhojas y musgos) que carecen de tejidos transportadores y de raíces, tallos y hojas verdaderas (302)

nucleic acid/ácido nucleico una molécula formada por subunidades llamadas *nucleótidos* (47)

nucleotide/nucleótido en una cadena de ácidos nucleicos, una subunidad formada por un azúcar, un fosfato y una base nitrogenada (144)

nucleus/núcleo en una célula eucariótica, un organelo cubierto por una membrana, el cual contiene el ADN de la célula y participa en procesos tales como el crecimiento, metabolismo y reproducción (63)

nutrient/nutriente una substancia de los alimentos que proporciona energía o ayuda a formar tejidos corporales y que es necesaria para la vida y el crecimiento (732)

O

omnivore/omnívoro un organismo que come tanto plantas como animales (485)

open circulatory system/aparato circulatorio abierto un aparato circulatorio en el que el fluido circulatorio no está totalmente contenido en los vasos sanguíneos; un corazón bombea fluido por los vasos sanguíneos, los cuales se vacían en espacios llamados *senos* (389)

open-water zone/zona de aguas superiores la zona de un lago o una laguna que se extiende desde la zona litoral y cuya profundidad sólo alcanza hasta donde penetra la luz (541)

organ/órgano un conjunto de tejidos que desempeñan una función especializada en el cuerpo (77, 581)

organelle/organelo uno de los cuerpos pequeños del citoplasma de una célula que están especializados para llevar a cabo una función específica (63)

organism/organismo un ser vivo; cualquier cosa que pueda llevar a cabo procesos vitales independientemente (78)

organ system/aparato (o sistema) de órganos un grupo de órganos que trabajan en conjunto para desempeñar funciones corporales (78)

osmosis/ósmosis la difusión del agua a través de una membrana semipermeable (91)

ovary/ovario en las plantas con flores, la parte inferior del pistilo que produce óvulos (320); en el aparato reproductor femenino de los animales, un órgano que produce óvulos (689)

overpopulation/sobrepoblación la presencia de demasiados individuos en un área para los recursos disponibles (557)

P

Paleozoic era/era Paleozoica la era geológica que vino después del período Precámbrico; comenzó hace 543 millones de años y terminó hace 248 millones de años (202)

pancreas/páncreas el órgano que se encuentra detrás del estómago y que produce las enzimas digestivas y las hormonas que regulan los niveles de azúcar (638)

parasite/parásito un organismo que se alimenta de un organismo de otra especie (el huésped) y que normalmente lo daña; el huésped nunca se beneficia de la presencia del parásito (271)

parasitism/parasitismo una relación entre dos especies en la que una, el parásito, se beneficia de la otra, el huésped, que resulta perjudicada (495)

passive transport/transporte pasivo el movimiento de substancias a través de una membrana celular sin que la célula tenga que usar energía (92)

pathogen/patógeno un virus, microorganismo u otra substancia que causa enfermedades (710)

pathogenic bacteria/bacteria patogénica bacteria que causa una enfermedad (254)

pedigree/pedigrí un diagrama que muestra la incidencia de un carácter genético en varias generaciones de una familia (132)

penis/pene el órgano masculino que transfiere espermatozoides a una hembra y que lleva la orina hacia el exterior del cuerpo (688)

peripheral nervous system/sistema nervioso periférico todas las partes del sistema nervioso, excepto el encéfalo y la médula espinal (656)

petal/pétalo una de las partes de una flor que normalmente tienen colores brillantes y forma de hoja, las cuales forman uno de los anillos de una flor (319)

pharynx/faringe en los gusanos planos, el tubo muscular que va de la boca a la cavidad gastrovascular; en los animales que tienen tracto digestivo, el conducto que va de la boca a la laringe y al esófago (621)

phenotype/fenotipo la apariencia de un organismo u otra característica perceptible (120)

pheromone/feromona una substancia que el cuerpo libera y que hace que otro individuo de la misma especia reaccione de un modo predecible (367)

phloem/floema el tejido que transporta alimento en las plantas vasculares (314)

phospholipid/fosfolípido un lípido que contiene fósforo y que es un componente estructural de la membrana celular (46)

photosynthesis/fotosíntesis el proceso por medio del cual las plantas, las algas y algunas bacterias utilizan la luz solar, el dióxido de carbono y el agua para producir alimento (94, 332)

phytoplankton/fitoplancton los organismos microscópicos fotosintéticos que flotan cerca de la superficie del agua dulce o marina (274)

pioneer species/especie pionera una especie que coloniza un área deshabitada y empieza un proceso de sucesión (513)

pistil/pistilo la parte reproductora femenina de una flor, la cual produce semillas y está formada por el ovario, estilo y estigma (320)

placenta/placenta la estructura que une al feto en desarrollo con el útero y que permite el intercambio de nutrientes, desechos y gases entre la madre y el feto (693)

placental mammal/mamífero placentario un mamífero que nutre a sus crías aún no nacidas a través de una placenta que se encuentra dentro de su útero (456)

plankton/plancton la masa de organismos en su mayoría microscópicos que flotan o se encuentran a la deriva en ambientes de agua dulce o marina (534)

Plantae/Plantae un reino formado por organismos pluricelulares complejos que normalmente son verdes, tienen una pared celular de celulosa, no tienen capacidad de movimiento y utilizan la energía del Sol para producir azúcar mediante la fotosíntesis (231)

plate tectonics/tectónica de placas la teoría que explica cómo se mueven y cambian de forma las placas tectónicas, que son grandes porciones de la capa más externa de la Tierra (198)

pollen/polen los gránulos diminutos que contienen el gametofito masculino en las plantas con semilla (308)

pollination/polinización la transferencia de polen de las estructuras reproductoras masculinas a las estructuras femeninas de las plantas con semillas (311)

pollution/contaminación un cambio indeseable en el ambiente producido por substancias dañinas, desechos, gases, ruidos o radiación (554)

population/población un grupo de organismos de la misma especie que viven en un área geográfica específica (482)

Precambrian time/tiempo Precámbrico el período en la escala de tiempo geológico que abarca desde la formación de la Tierra hasta el comienzo de la era Paleozoica; comenzó hace aproximadamente 4.6 mil millones de años y terminó hace 543 millones de años (200)

precipitation/precipitación cualquier forma deagua que cae de las nubes a la superficie de la Tierra (508)

predator/depredador un organismo que se alimenta de otro organismo o de parte de él (492)

preening/acicalamiento en las aves, el acto de limpiar y mantener saludables las plumas (442)

prey/presa un organismo al que otro organismo mata para alimentarse de él (492)

primate/primate un tipo de mamífero caracterizado por tener pulgares oponibles y visión binocular (206)

probability/probabilidad la probabilidad de que ocurra un posible suceso futuro en cualquier caso dado del suceso (122)

producer/productor un organismo que puede elaborar sus propios alimentos utilizando la energía de su entorno (43)

prokaryote/procariote un organismo que está formado por una sola célula y que no tiene núcleo (64, 247)

protein/proteína una molécula formada por aminoácidos que es necesaria para construir y reparar estructuras corporales y para regular procesos del cuerpo (44, 733)

protist/protista un organismo que pertenece al reino Protista (270)

Protista/Protista un reino compuesto principalmente por organismo eucarióticos unicelulares que son diferentes de las plantas, animales, bacterias y hongos (230)

pulmonary circulation/circulación pulmonar el flujo de sangre del corazón a los pulmones y de vuelta al corazón a través de las arterias, los capilares y las venas pulmonares (609)

R

recessive trait/carácter recesivo un carácter que se hace aparente sólo cuando se heredan dos alelos recesivos de la misma característica (117)

recycling/reciclar el proceso de recuperar materiales valiosos o útiles de los desechos o de la basura; el proceso de reutilizar algunas cosas (563)

reflex/reflejo un movimiento involuntario y prácticamente inmediato en respuesta a un estímulo (665)

relative dating/datación relativa cualquier método que se utiliza para determinar si un acontecimiento u objeto es más viejo o más joven que otros acontecimientos u objetos (195)

renewable resource/recurso renovable un recurso natural que puede reemplazarse a la misma tasa a la que se consume (556)

respiration/respiración en biología, el intercambio de oxígeno y dióxido de carbono entre células vivas y su ambiente; incluye la respiración y la respiración celular (620)

respiratory system/aparato respiratorio un conjunto de órganos cuya función principal es tomar oxígeno y expulsar dióxido de carbono; los órganos de este aparato incluyen a los pulmones, la garganta y las vías que llevan a los pulmones (620)

retina/retina la capa interna del ojo, sensible a la luz, que recibe imágenes formadas por el lente ocular y las transmite al cerebro por medio del nervio óptico (666)

rhizoid/rizoide una estructura parecida a una raíz que se encuentra en las plantas no vasculares; mantiene a las plantas en su lugar y las ayuda a obtener agua y nutrientes (304)

rhizome/rizoma un tallo horizontal subterráneo que produce nuevas hojas, brotes y raíces (306)

ribosome/ribosoma un organelo celular compuesto de ARN y proteína; el sitio donde ocurre la síntesis de proteínas (71, 151)

RNA/ARN **á**cido **r**ibo**n**ucleico, una molécula que está presente en todas las células vivas y que juega un papel en la producción de proteínas (150)

S

savanna/sabana una región de pastizales que, a menudo, tiene árboles dispersos; se encuentra en áreas tropicales y subtropicales donde se producen lluvias, incendios y sequías estacionales (530)

scientific methods/métodos científicos una serie de pasos que se siguen para solucionar problemas (10)

segment/segmento cualquier parte de una estructura más grande, como el cuerpo de un organismo, que se determina por límites naturales o arbitrarios (390)

selective breeding/reproducción selectiva la práctica humana de cruzar animales o plantas que tienen ciertas características deseadas (176)

sepal/sépalo en una flor, uno de los anillos más externos de hojas modificadas que protegen el capullo de la flor (319)

sex chromosome/cromosoma sexual uno de los dos cromosomas que determinan el sexo de un individuo (131)

sexual reproduction/reproducción sexual reproducción en la que se unen las células sexuales de los dos progenitores para producir descendencia que comparte caracteres de ambos progenitores (40, 685)

skeletal system/sistema esquelético el sistema de órganos cuya función principal es sostener y proteger el cuerpo y permitir que se mueva (584)

small intestine/intestino delgado el órgano que se encuentra entre el estómago y el intestino grueso en el cual se produce la mayor parte de la descomposición de los alimentos y se absorben la mayoría de los nutrientes (638)

social behavior/comportamiento social la interacción entre animales de la misma especie (366)

speciation/especiación la formación de especies nuevas como resultado de la evolución (182)

species/especie un grupo de organismos que tienen un parentesco cercano y que pueden aparearse para producir descendencia fértil (166)

sperm/espermatozoide la célula sexual masculina (685)

spleen/bazo el órgano linfático más grande del cuerpo; funciona como depósito para la sangre, desintegra los glóbulos rojos viejos y produce linfocitos y plásmidos (618)

spore/espora una célula reproductora o estructura pluricelular que resiste las condiciones ambientales adversas y que se puede desarrollar hasta convertirse en un adulto sin necesidad de fusionarse con otra célula (283)

stamen/estambre la estructura reproductora masculina de una flor, que produce polen y está formada por una antera ubicada en la punta del filamento (320)

stimulus/estímulo cualquier cosa que causa una reacción o cambio en un organismo o cualquier parte de un organismo (39)

stoma/estoma una de las muchas aberturas de una hoja o de un tallo de una planta, la cual permite que se lleve a cabo el intercambio de gases (334)

stomach/estómago el órgano digestivo con forma de bolsa ubicado entre el esófago y el intestino delgado, que descompone los alimentos por la acción de músculos, enzimas y ácidos (637)

stress/estrés una respuesta física o mental a la presión (746)

structure/estructura el orden y distribución de las partes de un organismo (79)

succession/sucesión el reemplazo de un tipo de comunidad por otro en un mismo lugar a lo largo de un período de tiempo (512)

swamp/ciénaga un ecosistema de pantano en el que crecen arbustos y árboles (542)

swim bladder/vejiga natatoria en los peces óseos, una bolsa llena de gas que se usa para controlar la flotabilidad; también se llama *vejiga de aire* (418)

symbiosis/simbiosis una relación en la que dos organismos diferentes viven estrechamente asociados uno con el otro (494)

systemic circulation/circulación sistémica el flujo de sangre del corazón a todas las partes del cuerpo y de vuelta al corazón (609)

T

tadpole/renacuajo la larva acuática, parecida a un pez, de una rana o sapo (422)

taxonomy/taxonomía la ciencia de describir, nombrar y clasificar organismos (223)

T cell/célula T una célula del sistema inmunológico que coordina el sistema inmunológico y ataca a muchas células infectadas (715)

technology/tecnología la aplicación de la ciencia con fines prácticos; el uso de herramientas, máquinas, materiales y procesos para satisfacer las necesidades de los seres humanos (22)

temperature/temperatura una medida de qué tan caliente (o frío) está algo; específicamente, una medida de la energía cinética promedio de las partículas de un objeto (26)

territory/territorio un área que está ocupada por un animal o por un grupo de animales que no permiten que entren otros miembros de la especie (361)

testes/testículos los principales órganos reproductores masculinos, los cuales producen espermatozoides y testosterona (688)

theory/teoría una explicación que relaciona muchas hipótesis y observaciones (20)

thymus/timo la glándula principal del sistema linfático; libera linfocitos T maduros (617)

tissue/tejido un grupo de células similares que llevan a cabo una función común (77, 580)

tonsils/amígdalas masas pequeñas y redondas de tejido linfático, ubicadas en la faringe y en el paso de la boca a la faringe (619)

trachea/tráquea en los insectos, miriápodos y arañas, uno de los conductos de una red de conductos de aire; en los vertebrados, el conducto que une la laringe con los pulmones (621)

trait/carácter una característica determinada genéticamente (176)

transpiration/transpiración el proceso por medio del cual las plantas liberan vapor de agua al aire por medio de los estomas; *también,* la liberación de vapor de agua al aire por otros organismos (334)

tropism/tropismo el movimiento de un organismo o de una parte de él en respuesta a un estímulo externo, como por ejemplo, la luz (340)

tundra/tundra una llanura sin árboles situada en la región ártica o antártica o en la cumbre de las montañas; se caracteriza por temperaturas muy bajas en el invierno y veranos cortos y frescos (532)

U

umbilical cord/cordón umbilical la estructura que une al embrión y después al feto con la placenta, a través de la cual pasan vasos sanguíneos (693)

urinary system/sistema urinario los órganos que producen, almacenan y eliminan la orina (642)

uterus/útero en los mamíferos hembras, el órgano hueco y muscular en el que se incrusta el óvulo fecundado y en el que se desarrollan el embrión y el feto (689)

V

vagina/vagina el órgano reproductivo femenino que conecta la parte exterior del cuerpo con el útero (689)

variable/variable un factor que se modifica en un experimento con el fin de probar una hipótesis (14)

vascular plant/planta vascular una planta que tiene tejidos especializados que transportan materiales de una parte de la planta a otra (302)

vein/vena en biología, un vaso que lleva sangre al corazón (608)

vertebrate/vertebrado un animal que tiene columna vertebral (412)

vesicle/vesícula una cavidad o bolsa pequeña que contiene materiales en una célula eucariótica; se forma cuando parte de la membrana celular rodea los materiales que van a ser llevados al interior la célula o transportados dentro de ella (73)

virus/virus una partícula microscópica que se introduce en una célula y a menudo la destruye (256)

vitamin/vitamina una clase de nutrientes que contiene carbono y que es necesaria en pequeñas cantidades para mantener la salud y permitir el crecimiento (734)

volume/volumen una medida del tamaño de un cuerpo o región en un espacio de tres dimensiones (25)

W

waterfowl/aves acuáticas pájaros acuáticos, como por ejemplo, un pato, un ganso o un cisne (449)

water vascular system/sistema vascular acuoso un sistema de canales que están llenos de un fluido acuoso que circula por todo el cuerpo de los equinodermos (399)

wetland/pantano un área de tierra que está periódicamente bajo el agua o cuyo suelo contiene una gran cantidad de humedad (542)

X

xylem/xilema el tipo de tejido que se encuentra en las plantas vasculares, el cual provee soporte y transporta el agua y los nutrientes desde las raíces (314)

Index

Boldface page numbers refer to illustrative material, such as figures, tables, margin elements, photographs, and illustrations.

B

C

Index

D

Index

E

Index

G

Index

H

I

J

K

L

M

P

Q

R

S

T

U

V

W

X

Y

Z

Acknowledgments
continued from page ii

Eva Oberdoerster, Ph.D.
Lecturer
Department of Biology
Southern Methodist University
Dallas, Texas

Michael H. Renfroe, Ph.D.
Professor of Biology
Department of Biology
James Madison University
Harrisonburg, Virginia

Laurie Santos, Ph.D.
Assistant Professor
Department of Psychology
Yale University
New Haven, Connecticut

Patrick K. Schoff, Ph.D.
Research Associate
Natural Resources Research Institute
University of Minnesota—Duluth
Duluth, Minnesota

Richard P. Vari, Ph.D.
Research Scientist and Curator
Division of Fishes
National Museum of Natural History
Washington, D.C.

Teacher Reviewers

Diedre S. Adams
Physical Science Instructor
West Vigo Middle School
West Terre Haute, Indiana

Barbara Gavin Akre
Teacher of Biology, Anatomy-Physiology, and Life Science
Duluth Independent School District
Duluth, Minnesota

Sarah Carver
Science Teacher
Jackson Creek Middle School
Bloomington, Indiana

Hilary Cochran
Science Teacher
Indian Crest Junior High School
Souderton, Pennsylvania

Karen Dietrich, S.S.J., Ph.D.
Principal and Biology Instructor
Mount Saint Joseph Academy
Flourtown, Pennsylvania

Debra S. Kogelman, MAed.
Science Teacher
University of Chicago Laboratory Schools
Chicago, Illinois

Augie Maldonado
Science Teacher
Grisham Middle School
Round Rock, Texas

Jean Pletchette
Health Educator
Winterset Community Schools
Winterset, Iowa

Elizabeth Rustad
Science Teacher
Higley School District
Gilbert, Arizona

Helen P. Schiller
Instructional Coach
The School District of Greenville County
Greenville, South Carolina

Stephanie Snowden
Science Teacher
Canyon Vista Middle School
Austin, Texas

Florence Vaughan
Science Teacher
University of Chicago Laboratory Schools
Chicago, Illinois

Larry A. Weber, M.S.
Science Teacher
Marshall School
Duluth, Minnesota

Angie Williams
Teacher
Riversprings Middle School
Crawfordville, Florida

Lab Development

Diana Scheidle Bartos
Research Associate
School of Mines
Golden, Colorado

Carl Benson
General Science Teacher
Plains High School
Plains, Montana

Charlotte Blassingame
Technology Coordinator
White Station Middle School
Memphis, Tennessee

Marsha Carver
Science Teacher and Department Chair
McLean County High School
Calhoun, Kentucky

Kenneth E. Creese
Science Teacher
White Mountain Junior High School
Rock Springs, Wyoming

Linda Culp
Science Teacher and Department Chair
Thorndale High School
Thorndale, Texas

James Deaver
Science Teacher and Department Chair
West Point High School
West Point, Nebraska

Frank McKinney, Ph.D.
Professor of Geology
Appalachian State University
Boone, North Carolina

Alyson Mike
Science Teacher
East Valley Middle School
East Helena, Montana

C. Ford Morishita
Biology Teacher
Clackamas High School
Milwaukie, Oregon

Patricia D. Morrell, Ph.D.
Associate Professor
School of Education
University of Portland
Portland, Oregon

Hilary C. Olson, Ph.D.
Research Associate
Institute for Geophysics
The University of Texas at Austin
Austin, Texas

James B. Pulley
Science Editor and Former Science Teacher
North Kansas City, Missouri

Denice Lee Sandefur
Science Chairperson
Nucla High School
Nucla, Colorado

Patti Soderberg
Science Writer
The BioQUEST Curriculum Consortium
Biology Department
Beloit College
Beloit, Wisconsin

Phillip Vavala
Science Teacher and Department Chair
Salesianum School
Wilmington, Delaware

Albert C. Wartski, M.A.T.
Biology Teacher
Chapel Hill High School
Chapel Hill, North Carolina

Lynn Marie Wartski
Science Writer and Former Science Teacher
Hillsborough, North Carolina

Ivora D. Washington
Science Teacher and Department Chair
Hyattsville Middle School
Washington, D.C.

Lab Testing

Barry L. Bishop
Science Teacher and Department Chair
San Rafael Junior High School
Ferron, Utah

Yvonne Brannum
Science Teacher and Department Chair
Hine Junior High School
Washington, D.C.

Gladys Cherniak
Science Teacher
St. Paul's Episcopal School
Mobile, Alabama

James Chin
Science Teacher
Frank A. Day Middle School
Newtonville, Massachusetts

Randy Christian
Science Teacher
Stovall Junior High School
Houston, Texas

Georgiann Delgadillo
Science Teacher
East Valley Continuous Curriculum School
Spokane, Washington

Alonda Droege
Biology Teacher
Evergreen High School
Seattle, Washington

Susan Gorman
Science Teacher
North Ridge Middle School
North Richland Hills, Texas

Karma Houston-Hughes
Science Mentor
Kyrene Middle School
Tempe, Arizona

Kerry A. Johnson
Science Teacher
Isbell Middle School
Santa Paula, California

M. R. Penny Kisiah
Science Teacher and Department Chair
Fairview Middle School
Tallahassee, Florida

Kathy LaRoe
Science Teacher
East Valley Middle School
East Helena, Montana

Jane M. Lemons
Science Teacher
Western Rockingham Middle School
Madison, North Carolina

Maurine O. Marchani
Science Teacher and Department Chair
Raymond Park Middle School
Indianapolis, Indiana

Jason P. Marsh
Biology Teacher
Montevideo High School and Montevideo Country School
Montevideo, Minnesota

Edith C. McAlanis
Science Teacher and Department Chair
Socorro Middle School
El Paso, Texas

Kevin McCurdy, Ph.D.
Science Teacher
Elmwood Junior High School
Rogers, Arkansas

Terry J. Rakes
Science Teacher
Elmwood Junior High School
Rogers, Arkansas

Elizabeth Rustad
Science Teacher
Crane Middle School
Yuma, Arizona

Debra A. Sampson
Science Teacher
Booker T. Washington Middle School
Elgin, Texas

David M. Sparks
Science Teacher
Redwater Junior High School
Redwater, Texas

Ivora Washington
Science Teacher and Department Chair
Hyattsville Middle School
Washington, D.C.

Christopher Wood
Science Teacher
Western Rockingham Middle School
Madison, North Carolina

Feature Development

Hatim Belyamani
John A. Benner
David Bradford
Jennifer Childers
Mickey Coakley
Susan Feldkamp
Jane Gardner
Erik Hahn
Christopher Hess
Deena Kalai
Charlotte W. Luongo, MSc
Michael May
Persis Mehta, Ph.D.
Eileen Nehme, MPH
Catherine Podeszwa
Dennis Rathnaw
Daniel B. Sharp
April Smith West
John M. Stokes
Molly F. Wetterschneider

Answer Checking

Hatim Belyamani
Austin, Texas

Staff Credits

Editorial

Robert Todd, *Vice President, Editorial Science*
Debbie Starr, *Managing Editor*
Kelly Rizk, *Senior Editor*

Editorial Development Team

Karin Akre
Amy Fry
Frieda Gress
Betsy Roll
Marjorie Roueché
Kenneth Shepardson
David Westerberg

Copyeditors

Dawn Marie Spinozza, *Copyediting Manager*
Anne-Marie De Witt
Jane A. Kirschman
Kira J. Watkins

Editorial Support Staff

Mary Anderson
Suzanne Krejci
Shannon Oehler

Online Products

Bob Tucek, *Executive Editor*
Wesley M. Bain

Design

Book Design

Kay Selke, *Director of Book Design*
Sonya Mendeke, *Designer*
Holly Whittaker, *Project Administrator*

Media Design

Richard Metzger, *Design Director*
Chris Smith, *Senior Designer*

Image Acquisitions

Curtis Riker, *Director*
Jeannie Taylor, *Photo Research Manager*
Terry Janecek, *Photo Researcher*
Elaine Tate, *Art Buyer Supervisor*
Angela Boehm, *Senior Art Buyer*

Design New Media

Ed Blake, *Director*
Kimberly Cammerata, *Design Manager*
Michael Rinella, *Senior Designer*

Cover Design

Bill Smith Studio

Publishing Services

Carol Martin, *Director*

Graphic Services

Bruce Bond, *Director*
Jeff Bowers, *Graphic Services Manager*
JoAnn Stringer, *Senior Graphics Specialist II*
Cathy Murphy, *Senior Graphics Specialist*
Nanda Patel, *Graphics Specialist*
Katrina Gnader, *Graphics Specialist*

Technology Services

Laura Likon, *Director*
Juan Baquera, *Technology Services Manager*
Lana Kaupp, *Senior Technology Services Analyst*
Margaret Sanchez, *Senior Technology Services Analyst*
Sara Buller, *Technology Services Analyst*
Patty Zepeda, *Technology Services Analyst*
Jeff Robinson, *Ancillary Design Manager*

New Media

Armin Gutzmer, *Director*
Melanie Baccus, *New Media Coordinator*
Lydia Doty, *Senior Project Manager*
Cathy Kuhles, *Technical Assistant*
Marsh Flournoy, *Quality Assurance Analyst*
Tara F. Ross, *Senior Project Manager*

Production

Eddie Dawson, *Production Manager*
Sherry Sprague, *Senior Production Coordinator*
Suzanne Brooks, *Production Coordinator*

Teacher Edition

Alicia Sullivan
David Hernandez
April Litz

Manufacturing and Inventory

Ivania Quant Lee
Wilonda Ieans

Ancillary Development and Production

General Learning Communications, Northbrook, Illinois

Credits

Abbreviations used: (t) top, (c) center, (b) bottom, (l) left, (r) right, (bkgd) background

PHOTOGRAPHY

Front Cover (tr), Corbis; (bl), JH Pete Carmichael/Getty Images; (tl), Dennis Kunkel/Phototake; (br), Victor Englebert; (owl), Kim Taylor/Bruce Coleman

Skills Practice Lab Teens Sam Dudgeon/HRW

Connection to Astrology Corbis Images; **Connection to Biology** David M. Phillips/Visuals Unlimited; **Connection to Chemistry** Digital Image copyright © 2005 PhotoDisc; **Connection to Environment** Digital Image copyright © 2005 PhotoDisc; **Connection to Geology** Letraset Phototone; **Connection to Language** Arts Digital Image copyright © 2005 PhotoDisc; **Connection to Meteorology** Digital Image copyright © 2005 PhotoDisc; **Connection to Oceanography** © ICONOTEC; **Connection to Physics** Digital Image copyright © 2005 PhotoDisc

Table of Contents iii (t), Peter Van Steen/HRW; iii (b), Uniphoto; iv (t), Chip Simmons/Discover Channel; iv (b), Wolfgang Bayer; vi (t), Ned M. Seidler/National Geographic Society Image Collection; vi (b), Sam Dudgeon/HRW; vii (tl), James Beveridge/Visuals Unlimited; vii (tr), © Gail Shumway/Getty Images/FPG International; viii (t), © G. Randall/Getty Images/FPG International; viii (b), CNRI/Science Photo Library/Photo Researchers; viii-ix (t), © Stan Osolinski/Getty Images/FPG International; ix (c), SuperStock; ix (b), Digital Image copyright © 2005 PhotoDisc; x (t), Breck P. Kent/Animals Animals/Earth Scenes; x (b), Ron Kimball; xi (t), © Jeffrey L. Rotman/CORBIS; xi (c), © Kevin Schafer/CORBIS; xi (b), Kenneth Fink/Bruce Coleman, Inc.; xii (t), Sylvain Cordier/Photo Researchers; xiii (t), Kim Heacox/DRK Photo; xiii (bl), © Jeff Hunter/Getty Images/The Image Bank; xiv (tl), © Sindre Ellingsen/Alamy Photos; xiv (b), Sam Dudgeon/HRW; xiv-xv (tc), © Nih/Science Source/Photo Researchers, Inc.; xvi (t), Sam Dudgeon/HRW; xvi (b), Photo Lennart Nilsson/Albert Bonniers Forlag AB, A Child Is Born, Dell Publishing Company; xvii (b), © Rob Van Petten/Getty Images/The Image Bank; xviii-xxxiii (all), Sam Dudgeon/HRW

Unit One 2 (tl), O.S.F./Animals Animals; 2 (cl), Hulton Archive/Getty Images; 2 (bl), Digital Image copyright © 2005 PhotoDisc; 2-3 (br & bl), Peter Veit/DRK Photo; 3 (cl), University of Pennsylvania/Hulton Getty; 3 (t), National Portrait Gallery, Smithsonian Institution/Art Resource; 3 (br), © National Geographic Image Collection/O. Louis Mazzatenta; 3 (cr), Digital Image copyright © 2005 PhotoDisc

Chapter One 4-5 Craig Line/AP/Wide World Photos; 6 (b), Peter Van Steen/HRW; 7 (l), NASA; 7 (c), Gerry Gropp; 7 (r), Chip Simmons/Discover Channel; 8 (t), Hank Morgan/Photo Researchers, Inc.; 8 (b), Mark Lennihan/AP/Wide World Photos; 9 © National Geographic Image Collection/Dale Miquelle; 11 (tr), Peter Van Steen/HRW; 11 (b), Sam Dudgeon/HRW; 12 Sam Dudgeon/HRW; 14 John Mitchell/Photo Researchers; 16 (b), Sam Dudgeon/HRW; 17 John Mitchell/Photo Researchers; 18 © Royalty-Free/CORBIS; 20 Art by Christopher Sloan/Photograph by Mark Thiessen both National Geographic Image Collection/© National Geographic Image Collection; 22 (bl), Alfred Pasieka/Photo Researchers; 22 (bl), Howard Sochurek/The Stock Market; 23 (tl), CENCO; 23 (bl), Robert Brons/Biological Photo Service; 23 (tc), Sinclair Stammers/Science Photo Library/Photo Researchers; 23 (tr), RJ Lee Instruments Limited; 23 (bc), Microworks/Phototake; 23 (br), Visuals Unlimited/Karl Aufderheide; 24 (t), Victoria Smith/HRW; 24 (bc), Victoria Smith/HRW; 24 (b), Victoria Smith/HRW; 24 (tc), Sam Dudgeon/HRW; 25 (bl), Peter Van Steen/HRW; 25 (br), Peter Van Steen/HRW; 27 (b), Dr. Jeremy Burgess/Science Photo Library/Photo Reseachers, Inc.; 28 Sam Dudgeon/HRW; 29 Sam Dudgeon/HRW; 30 (b), Peter Van Steen/HRW; 30 (t), John Mitchell/Photo Researchers; 34 (l), Craig Fugii/©1988 The Seattle Times; 35 (r), NASA; 35 (l), NASA

Chapter Two 36-37 (t), Rick Friedman/Blackstar Publishing/Picture Quest; 38 (r), Visuals Unlimited/Science Visuals Unlimited; 38 (l), Wolfgang Kaehler Photography; 39 (l), David M. Dennis/Tom Stack and Associates; 39 (r), David M. Dennis/Tom Stack and Associates; 40 (l), Visuals Unlimited/Stanley Flegler; 40 (r), James M. McCann/Photo Researchers, Inc. ; 42 (b), Wolfgang Bayer; 43 (t), Visuals Unlimited/Rob Simpson ; 43 (b), © Alex Kerstitch/Visuals Unlimited, Inc.; 44 (l), William J. Hebert/Stone; 44 (c), SuperStock; 44 (r), Kevin Schafer/Peter Arnold, Inc.; 45 Peter Dean/Grant Heilman Photography; 49 Peter Van Steen/HRW; 50 David M. Dennis/Tom Stack and Associates; 51 (tc), Victoria Smith/HRW; 51 (c), Victoria Smith/HRW; 51 (bc), Victoria Smith/HRW; 51 (t), © Wolfgang Kaehler/Liaison International/Getty News Images; 51 (b), © Alex Kerstitch/Visuals Unlimited, Inc.; 54 (b), Chip East/Reuters/NewsCom; 55 (r), Courtesy Janis Davis-Street/NASA; 55 (l), NASA

Unit Two 56 (c), The National Archives/Corbis; 56 (b), Cold Spring Harbor Laboratory; 56 (t), © Burstein Collection/CORBIS; 57 (t), Ed Reschke/Peter Arnold; 57 (tcr), Keith Porter/Photo Researchers; 57 (bcl), Ed Reschke/Peter Arnold, Inc.; 57 (br), © Dr. Ian Wilmut/Liaison/Getty News Images; 57 (bl), Dan McCoy/Rainbow; 57 (bcr), © Glen Allison/Getty Images/Stone; 57 (tcl), © Bettmann/CORBIS

Chapter Three 58-59, Dennis Kunkel/Phototake; 60 (l), Visuals Unlimited/Kevin Collins; 60 (r), Leonard Lessin/Peter Arnold; 61 (r), T.E. Adams/Visuals Unlimited; 61 (cl), Roland Birke/Peter Arnold, Inc.; 61 (bkgd), Jerome Wexler/Photo Researchers, Inc.; 61 (cr), Biophoto Associates/Photo Researchers, Inc.; 61 (l), M.I. Walker/Photo Researchers, Inc.; 62 Photodisc, Inc.; 63 (t), William Dentler/BPS/Stone; 63 (b), Dr. Gopal Murti/Science Photo Library/Photo Researchers, Inc.; 65 Wolfgang Baumeister/Science Photo Library/Photo Researchers, Inc.; 66 (l), Biophoto Associates/Photo Researchers, Inc.; 70 (bl), Don Fawcett/Visuals Unlimited; 70 (t), Dr. Peter Dawson/Science Photo Library/Photo Researchers, Inc.; 71 (r), R. Bolender-D. Fawcett/Visuals Unlimited; 72 (cl), Don Fawcett/Visuals Unlimited; 72 (bl), Newcomb & Wergin/BPS/Tony Stone Images; 73 (br), Garry T Cole/BPS/Stone; 74 (tl), Dr. Gopal Murti/Science Photo Library/Photo Researchers, Inc.; 74 (cl), Dr. Jeremy Burgess/Science PhotoLibrary/Science Source/Photo Researchers; 76 Quest/Science Photo Library/Photo Researchers, Inc.; 77 Manfred Kage/Peter Arnold, Inc. ; 80 (b), Sam Dudgeon/HRW; 86 (r), Photo Researchers, Inc.; 86 (l), Science Photo Library/Photo Researchers, Inc.; 87 (b), Digital Image copyright © 2005 Artville; 87 (t), Courtesy Caroline Schooley

Chapter Four 88-89 © Michael & Patricia Fogden/CORBIS; 90 Sam Dudgeon/HRW; 92 (br), Photo Researchers; 93 (tr), Birgit H. Satir; 94 (l), Runk/Schoenberger/Grant Heilman; 95 (r), John Langford/HRW Photo; 97 Corbis Images; 98 CNRI/Science Photo Library/Photo Researchers, Inc. ; 99 (t), L. Willatt, East Anglian Regional Genetics Service/Science Photo Library/Photo Researchers, Inc. ; 99 (b), Biophoto Associates/Photo Researchers; 100 (b), Visuals Unlimited/R. Calentine; 100 (cl), Ed Reschke/Peter Arnold, Inc.; 100 (c), Ed Reschke/Peter Arnold, Inc.; 100 (cr), Ed Reschke/Peter Arnold, Inc.; 101 (cl), Ed Reschke/Peter Arnold, Inc.; 101 (c), Biology Media/Photo Researchers, Inc.; 101 (cr), Biology Media/Photo Researchers, Inc.; 102 Sam Dudgeon/HRW; 103 Sam Dudgeon/HRW; 104 (l), Runk/Schoenberger/Grant Heilman; 105 (cl), Biophoto Associates/Science Source/Photo Researchers; 105 (cr), Biophoto Associates/Science Source/Photo Researchers; 105 (br), John Langford/HRW Photo; 108 (l), Lee D. Simons/Science Souce/Photo Researchers; 109 (tr), Courtesy Dr. Jarrel Yakel; 109 (tr), David McCarthy/SPL/Photo Researchers, Inc.

Unit Three 110 (t), Library of Congress/Corbis; 110 (c), MBL/WHOI Library; 110 (b), NASA; 111 (cr), John Reader/Science Photo Library/Photo Researchers, Inc.; 111 (bl), John Reader/Science Photo Library/Photo Researchers, Inc.; 111 (br), Ted Thai/Time Magzine; 111 (cl), © Ken Eward/Bio Grafx/Photo Researchers, Inc.; 111 (tl), © John Conrad/CORBIS

Chapter Five 112-113 © Maximilian Weinzierl/Alamy Photos; 114 Ned M. Seidler/National Geographic Society Image Collection; 119 © Andrew Brookes/CORBIS; 120 © Joe McDonald/Visuals Unlimited; 121 (b), Sam Dudgeon/HRW; 123 Digital Image copyright © 2005 PhotoDisc; 124 (b), © Mervyn Rees/Alamy Photos; 125 (b), Image Copyright ©2001 Photodisc, Inc.; 125 (tl), Sam Dudgeon/HRW; 125 (tr), Sam Dudgeon/HRW; 126 (br), Biophoto Associates/Photo Researchers, Inc.; 126 (b), Phototake/CNRI/Phototake NYC; 131 (b), © Rob vanNostrand; 132 (b), © ImageState; 133 © ImageState; 134 (b), Sam Dudgeon/HRW; 135 (b), Sam Dudgeon/HRW; 137 (r), © Mervyn Rees/Alamy Photos; 137 (l), © Rob vanNostrand; 140 (c), Dr. F. R. Turner, Biology Dept., Indiana University; 140 (r), Dr. F. R. Turner, Biology Dept., Indiana University; 140 (l), Hank Morgan/Rainbow; 141, Courtesy of Stacey Wong

Chapter Six 142-143 US Department of Energy/Science Photo Library/Photo Researchers, Inc.; 145 (r), Science Photo Library/Photo Researchers, Inc.; 145 (l), Hulton Archive/Getty Images; 148 (l), Sam Dudgeon/HRW; 148 (l), Sam Dudgeon/HRW; 149 (bl), David M. Phillips/Visuals Unlimited; 149 (cl), J.R. Paulson & U.K. Laemmli/University of Geneva; 153 (br), Jackie Lewin/Royal Free Hospital/Science Photo Library/Photo Researchers, Inc.; 153 (tr), Jackie Lewin/Royal Free Hospital/Science Photo Library/Photo Researchers, Inc.; 154 (t), Visuals Unlimited/Science Visuals Unlimited/Keith Wood ; 154 (b), Volker Steger/Peter Arnold; 155 Sam Dudgeon/HRW; 157 Victoria Smith/HRW; 162 (l), Robert Brook/Science Photo Library/Photo Researchers, Inc.; 163 (r), Photo courtesy of the Whitehead Institute for Biomedical Research at MIT; 163 (l), Garry Watson/Science Photo Library/Photo Researchers, Inc.

Chapter Seven 164-165 (t), © Stuart Westmorland/CORBIS; 166 (bl), James Beveridge/Visuals Unlimited; 166 (tc), © Gail Shumway/Getty Images/FPG International; 166 (br), Doug Wechsler/Animals Animals; 168 (l), Ken Lucas; 168 (r), John Cancalosi/Tom Stack & Associates; 169 (cl), © SuperStock; 169 (bl), © Martin Ruegner/Alamy Photos; 169 (br), © James D. Watt/Stephen Frink Collection/Alamy Photos; 169 (tl), © Ron Kimball/Ron Kimball Stock; 169 (tr), © Carl & Ann Purcell/CORBIS; 169 (cr), © Martin B. Withers; Frank Lane Picture Agency/CORBIS; 170 (tr), Illustration by Carl Buell, and taken from http://www.neoucom.edu/Depts/Anat/Pakicetid.html. ; 170 (tl), Courtesy of Research Casting International; 170 (b), Courtesy of Research Casting International; 171 (t), © 1998 Philip Gingerich/Courtesy of the Museum of Paleontology, The University of Michigan; 171 (c), Courtesy of Betsy Webb, Pratt Museum, Homer, Alaska; 171 (b), Courtesy of Betsy Webb, Pratt Museum, Homer, Alaska; 173 (b), Visuals Unlimited/H.W. Robison; 173 (t), James Beveridge/Visuals Unlimited; 174 (l), Christopher Ralling; 174 (r), © William E. Ferguson; 176 (b), Carolyn A. McKeone/Photo Researchers, Inc. ; 180 (b), Getty Images/Stone; 183 (r), Zig Leszczynski/Animals Animals/Earth Scenes; 183 (l), Gary Mezaros/Visuals Unlimited; 185 Victoria Smith/HRW; 186 (t), James Beveridge/Visuals Unlimited; 187 Courtesy of Betsy Webb, Pratt Museum, Homer, Alaska; 190 (l), Doug Wilson/Westlight; 191 (r), Wally Emerson/Courtesy of Raymond Pierotti; 191 (l), George D. Lepp/Photo Researchers, Inc.

Chapter Eight 192-193 © Reuters NewMedia Inc./CORBIS; 206 (r), © Daniel J. Cox/Getty Images/Stone; 208 (b), John Reader/Science Photo Library/Photo Researchers; 208 (t), © Partick Robert/CORBIS; 209 John Gurche; 210 (tr), John Reader/Science Photo Library/Photo Researchers; 210 (tl & tc), E.R. Degginger/Bruce Coleman; 210 (bl), Neanderthal Museum; 210 (br), Volker Steger/Nordstar-4 Million Years, of Man/Science Photo Library/Photo Researchers, Inc.; 218 (r), Rikki Larma/AP/Wide World Photos; 218 (l), Copyright M. Ponce de León and Christoph Zollikofer, Zurich; 219 (r), © Robert Campbell/CORBIS; 219 (l), John Reader/Science Photo Library/Photo Researchers, Inc.

Chapter Nine 220-221 Frans Lanting/Minden Pictures; 222 Gerry Ellis/ENP Images; 228 Biophoto Associates/Photo Researchers; 229 (t), Sherrie Jones/Photo Researchers; 229 (br), Dr. Tony Brian & David Parker/Science Photo Library/Photo Researchers; 229 (inset), Dr. Tony Brian & David Parker/Science Photo Library/Photo Researchers; 230 (t), Visuals Unlimited/Stanley Flegler; 230 (b), © Phil A. Dotson/Photo Researchers, Inc.; 231 (l), © Royalty-free/CORBIS; 231 (r), David R. Frazier/Photo Researchers, Inc.; 232 (tl), SuperStock; 232 (tr), © G. Randall/Getty Images/FPG International; 232 (bl), SuperStock; 233, Corbis Images; 233 Dr. Tony Brian & David Parker/Science Photo Library/Photo Researchers; 236 (b), Dr. Tony Brian & David Parker/Science Photo Library/Photo Researchers; 237 (b), SuperStock; 240 (r), Piotr Naskrecki/Conservation International; 241 (r), © National Geographic Image Collection/Michael Nichols; 241 (l), © National Geographic Image Collection/Michael Fay

Unit Four 242 (t), David L. Brown/Tom Stack; 242 (c), Frederick Warne & Co./Courtesy of the National Trust; 242 (b), Charles O'Rear/Westlight; 243 (tl), Dr. Tony Brian & David Parker/Science Photo Library/Photo Researchers, Inc.; 243 (tr), Larry Ulrich/DRK Photo; 243 (cl), Oliver Meches/MPI-Tubingen/Photo Researchers; 243 (bl), Gelderblom/Photo Researchers; 243 (cr), National Library of Medicine/Science Photo Library/Photo Researchers, Inc.; 243 (br), Dr. Tony Brain/Science Photo Library/Photo Researchers, Inc.

Chapter Ten 244 (t), Digital Image copyright © 2005 PhotoDisc Green; 244-245 (t), CAMR/A.B. Dowsett/Science Photo Library/Photo Researchers, Inc.; 246 (b), Robert Yin/Corbis; 246 (inset), Dr. Norman R. Pace and Dr. Esther R. Angert; 247 (c), Visuals Unlimited/David M. Phillips; 247 (l), Fran Heyl Associates; 247 (r), CNRI/Science Photo Library/Photo Researchers; 248 (b), Institut Pasteur/CNRI/Phototake; 249 (t), Heather Angel; 249 (bl), SuperStock; 249 (bc), SuperStock; 249 (br), © David M. Phillips/Visuals Unlimited; 250 (br), SuperStock; 250 (bl), Dr. Kari Lounatmaa/Science Photo Library/Photo Researchers, Inc.; 251 (t), Robert Yin/Corbis; 253 (tr), Bio-Logic Remediation LTD; 253 (b), Peter Van Steen/HRW; 254 (b), © Aaron Haupt/Photo Researchers, Inc.; 254 (t), © Carmela Leszczynski/Animals Animals/Earth Scenes; 255 (t), Visuals Unlimited/Sherman Thomson; 256 (b), E.O.S./Gelderblom/Photo Researchers; 257 (tl), Visuals Unlimited/Hans Gelderblom; 257 (tr), Visuals Unlimited/K. G. Murti; 257 (bl), Dr. O. Bradfute/Peter Arnold; 257 (br), Oliver Meckes/MPI-Tubingen/Photo Researchers; 259 (tr), Omni Photo Communications, Inc./Index Stock Imagery, Inc.; 260 (b), Victoria Smith/HRW; 262 (t), © Carmela Leszczynski/Animals Animals/Earth Scenes; 263 (b), Digital Image copyright © 2005 PhotoDisc Green; 266 (l), HRW Photo composite; 266 (r), ©CORBIS; 267 Courtesy of Annie O'Neal, Laytonville Middle School

Chapter Eleven 268-269 (t), Bassot Jean-Marie/Photo Researchers, Inc.; 270 (tl), Visuals Unlimited/David Phillips; 270 (tr), Matt Meadows/Peter Arnold; 270 (bl), Breck P. Kent; 270 (br), Michael Abbey/Photo Researchers; 271 David M. Dennis/Tom Stack & Associates; 272 (t), Dr. Hilda Canter-Lund; 272 (b), Eric Grave/Science Source/Photo Researchers; 274 Dr. E. R. Degginger; 275 (b), Manfred Kage/Peter Arnold; 275 (t), Runk/Schoenberger/Grant Heilman Photography; 276 (t), Robert Brons/Biological Photo Service; 276 (br), David M. Phillips/Science Source/Photo Researchers, Inc.; 277 (b), P. Parks/OSF/Animals Animals; 278 (t), Manfred Kage/Peter Arnold; 278 (b), Eric Grave/Photo Researchers, Inc.; 279 (r), Michael Abbey/Photo Researchers, Inc.; 280 (b), Matt Meadows/Peter Arnold; 280 (t), Fred Rhoades/Mycena Consulting; 281 (b), Dr. Hossler/Custom Medical Stock Photo; 281 (t), Manfred Kage/Peter Arnold; 282 (l), Runk/Schoenberger/Grant Heilman; 282 (c), Visuals Unlimited/Stan Flegler; 282 (r), David M. Dennis/Tom Stack; 283 (b), A. Davies/Bruce Coleman; 284 (t), Ralph Eague/Photo Researchers; 284 (b), Andrew Syred/Science Photo Library/Photo Researchers; 285 (c), J. Forsdyke/Gene Cox/Science Photo Library/Photo Researchers; 285 (b), Laurie Campbell/NHPA; 285 (t), Bill Beatty/Minden Pictures; 286 (t), Visuals Unlimited/Wally Eberhart; 286 (br), Michael P. Gadomski/Photo Researchers, Inc.; 286 (bl), Hoang Cong Minh/Photo Researchers, Inc.; 287 (t), Michael Fogden/DRK; 287 (c), Visuals Unlimited/Inga Spence; 287 (b), Walter H. Hodge/Peter Arnold; 288 (tl), Stephen & Sylvia Duran Sharnoff/National Geographic Society Image Collection; 288 (tr), Stephen & Sylvia Duran Sharnoff/National Geographic Society Image Collection; 288 (b), © Stan Osolinski/Getty Images/FPG International; 289 (b), Dr. E. R. Degginger; 289 (t), David M. Dennis/Tom Stack; 291 Sam Dudgeon/HRW; 292 (t), Visuals Unlimited/David Phillips; 293 (tl), Omikron/Photo Researchers, Inc.; 293 (tr), Omikron/Photo Researchers, Inc.; 293 (cl), Omikron/Photo Researchers, Inc.; 293 (cr), Omikron/Photo Researchers, Inc.; 293 (b), David M. Dennis/Tom Stack; 296 (l), Victoria Smith/HRW; 296 (tr), © Richard Rowan/Photo Researchers, Inc.; 296 (inset), © Dr. Paul A. Zahl/Photo Researchers, Inc.; 297 (r), © 2003 MSUCOM, Michigan State University College of Osteopathic Medicine; 297 (b), Barclay Graham/Corbis Sygma

Chapter Twelve 298-299 © Gary Braasch/CORBIS; 300 © Paul Harris/Getty Images/Stone; 303 (r), Runk/Schoenberger/Grant Heilman; 303 (l), Bruce Coleman, Inc.; 305 (r), Ed Reschke/Peter Arnold; 305 (l), Runk/Schoenberger/Grant Heilman; 308 © T. Branch/Photo Researchers, Inc.; 310 (tl), Tom Bean; 310 (tr), Jim Strawser/Grant Heilman; 310 (br), Visuals Unlimited/John D. Cunningham; 310 (bl), Walter H. Hodge/Peter Arnold; 312 (t), William E. Ferguson; 314 (bc), Runk/Schoenberger/Grant Heilman; 314 (br), Nigel Cattlin/Holt Studios International/Photo Researchers; 314 (bl), Dwight R. Kuhn; 315 (r), Ed Reschke/Peter Arnold, Inc.; 315 (l), Runk/Rannels/Grant Heilman Photography; 316 (tl), Larry Ulrich/DRK Photo; 316 (br), Stephen J. Krasemann/Photo Researchers; 317 (tr), Tom Bean; 317 (b), © Everett Johnson/Index Stock Imagery/PictureQuest ; 319 Digital Image copyright © 2005 PhotoDisc; 320 (l), George Bernard/Science Photo Library/Photo Researchers; 321, SuperStock; 323 (c), © Pixtal/SuperStock; 323 (b), © Richard Cummins/CORBIS; 323 (t), SuperStock; 324 © T. Branch/Photo Researchers, Inc.; 328 (l), © Roderick Chen/SuperStock; 328 (r), Jeff Lepore/Photo Researchers, Inc.; 328 (cl), Digital Image copyright © 2005 PhotoDisc; 329 (r), Mark Philbrick/Brigham Young University; 329 (l), Phillip-Lorca DiCorcia

Chapter Thirteen 330-331 Breck P. Kent/Animals Animals/Earth Scenes; 334 (l), Dr. Jeremy Burgess/Science Photo Library/Photo Researchers; 337 (b), Visuals Unlimited/W. Ormerod; 339 (c), Paul Hein/Unicorn; 339 (l), Jerome Wexler/Photo Researchers; 339 (r), George Bernard/Earth Scenes; 340 (b), © Cathlyn Melloan/Getty Images/Stone; 341 (l), R. F. Evert; 341 (r), R. F. Evert; 342 (l), Dick Keen/Unicorn; 342 (r), Visuals Unlimited/E. Webber; 343 (l), Visuals Unlimited/Bill Beatty; 343 (r), Visuals Unlimited/Bill Beatty; 344 Sam Dudgeon/HRW; 346 Jerome Wexler/Photo Researchers; 347 (t), Dr. Jeremy Burgess/Science Photo Library/Photo Researchers; 350 (l), © AFP/CORBIS; 350 (r), © Robert Landau/CORBIS; 351 (r), International Canopy Network/Evergreen State College; 351 (l), International Canopy Network/Evergreen State College

Unit Five 352 (t), Runk/Schoenberger/Grant Heilman; 352 (c), John James Audobon/Collection of the New York Historical Society; 352 (b), © Art Wolfe/Getty Images/Stone; 353 (tl), Johnny Johnson/DRK Photo; 353 (tr), © Gail Shumway/Getty Images/FPG International; 353 (cl), © M. Corsetti/Getty Images/FPG International; 353 (c), Grant Heilman; 353 (cr), M. Gunther/BIOS/Peter Arnold; 353 (bl), Susan Erstgaard; 353 (br), Gene Dalton/The Roanoke Times/Corbis Sygma

Chapter Fourteen 354-355 Bruce Coleman, Ltd./Natural Selection; 356 © David B. Fleetham/Getty Images/FPG International; 357 (bc), Digital Image copyright © 2005 Artville; 357 (bl), Digital Image copyright © 2005 Artville; 357 (br), Digital Image copyright © 2005 Artville; 357 (tl), Digital Image copyright © 2005 Artville; 357 (tr), Digital Image copyright © 2005 Artville; 358 (t), Visuals Unlimited/Fred Hossler ; 359 (t), © Keren Su/Getty Images/Stone; 359 (b), Digital Image copyright © 2005 Artville; 360 © Michael & Patricia Fogden/CORBIS; 361 © Tim Davis/Getty Images/Stone; 362 (r), Fernandez & Peck/Adventure Photo & Film; 362 (l), © Tom Brakefield/CORBIS; 363 (t), Gerard Lacz/Peter Arnold; 363 (b), © George D. Lepp/Getty Images/Stone; 364 © Ralph A. Clevenger/CORBIS; 365 Brian Kenney; 366 Peter Weimann/Animals Animals; 367 (t), Johnny Johnson/Animals Animals; 367 (b), Kenneth G. Ross; 368 (b), Ron Kimball; 369 Richard R. Hansen/Photo Researchers, Inc.; 372 (t), Digital Image copyright © 2005 Artville; 372 (b), Richard R. Hansen/Photo Researchers, Inc.; 376 (r), Todd Sumlin/© The Charlotte Observer; 376 (l), © National Geographic Image Collection/Michael K. Nichols; 377 Photo courtesy The International Crane Foundation

Chapter Fifteen 378-379 W. Gregory Brown/Animals Animals; 381 (b), © Keith Philpott/Getty Images/The Image Bank; 383 (tr), Jeffrey L. Rotman/Peter Arnold, Inc.; 383 (cr), © Jeffrey L. Rotman/CORBIS; 384 (br), Randy Morse/Tom Stack & Associates; 384 (cl), Biophoto Associates/Science Source/Photo Researchers; 384 (bc), © Lee Foster/Getty Images/FPG International; 384 (bl), David B. Fleetham/ Visuals Unlimited; 385 (t), Visuals Unlimited/T. E. Adams; 385 (b), CNRI/Science Photo Library/Photo Researchers; 386 (t), Visuals Unlimited/R. Calentine; 386 (b), Visuals Unlimited/A. M. Siegelman; 387 (t), Randy Morse/Tom Stack & Associates; 388 (l), Nigel Cattlin/Holt Studios International/Photo Researchers; 388 (r), Visuals Unlimited/David M. Phillips; 389 (t), © David Fleetham/Getty Images/FPG International; 390 (t), Milton Rand/Tom Stack & Associates; 390 (b), Mary Beth Angelo/Photo Researchers; 391 (t), St. Bartholomew's Hospital/Science Photo Library/Photo Researchers; 392 Leroy Simon/Visuals Unlimited; 393 (b), CNRI/ Science Photo Library/Photo Researchers; 393 (t), © M. H. Sharp/Photo Researchers, Inc.; 394 (tl), Visuals Unlimited/A. Kerstitch; 394 (cl), Dr. E.R. Degginger, FPSA; 394 (b), Daniel Gotshall/Visuals Unlimited; 394 (inset), © M. i. Walker/Photo Researchers, Inc.; 395 (brc), Uniphoto; 395 (tc), Stephen Dalton/NHPA; 395 (bl), © Gail Shumway/Getty Images/FPG International; 396 (t), Leroy Simon/Visuals Unlimited; 398 (br), © Paul McCormick/Getty Images/The Image Bank; 398 (bl), Visuals Unlimited/Cabisco; 400 (br), Visuals Unlimited/Marty Snyderman; 400 (tl), Andrew J. Martinez/Photo Researchers; 400 (tr), Robert Dunne/Photo Researchers; 400 (bl), Flip Nicklin/Minden Pictures; 401 (l), Visuals Unlimited/Daniel W. Gotshall; 401 (r), Chesher/Photo Researchers; 402 (c), Digital imagery® copyright 2002 PhotoDisc, Inc.; 403 Victoria Smith/HRW; 404 (b), © David Fleetham/Getty Images/FPG International; 405 (b), Leroy Simon/Visuals Unlimited; 405 (t), © Paul McCormick/ Getty Images/The Image Bank; 408 (r), © Tim Rock/Lonely Planet Images; 408 (l), © Bill Beatty/Visuals Unlimited; 409 (r), Ed Seibel ©2000 MBARI; 409 (b), © 2005 Norbert Wu/www.norbertwu.com

Chapter Sixteen 410-411 (t), MARTIN WENDLER/NHPA; 412 (tr), Randy Morse/Tom Stack; 412 (bl), Brian Parker/Tom Stack; 412 (br), G.I. Bernard OSF/Animals Animals; 413 (b), Grant Heilman; 414 (t), ©James Watt/Animals Animals/Earth Scenes; 416 (r), Hans Reinhard/Bruce Coleman; 416 (l), Steinhart Aquarium/Photo Researchers, Inc.; 417 (b), Index Stock; 417 (tr), © Martin Barraud/Getty Images/Stone; 417 (tl), ©2000 Norbert Wu/www.norbertwu.com; 418 (br), Bruce Coleman; 418 (bl), Steinhart Aquarium/Tom McHugh/Photo Researchers; 418 (bc), Ron & Valerie Taylor/ Bruce Coleman, Inc.; 419 Doug Perrine/DRK Photo; 420 (l), Michael Fogden/DRK Photo; 420 (r), Visuals Unlimited/Nathan W. Cohen; 421 (t), David M. Dennis/Tom Stack & Associates; 421 (b), C.K. Lorenz/Photo Researchers; 422 (b), Michael and Patricia Fogden; 423 (t), M.P.L. Fogden/Bruce Coleman; 423 (br), Stephen Dalton/ NHPA; 423 (bl), Richard Thom/Visuals Unlimited; 424 (tl), Leonard Lee Rue/Photo Researchers; 424 (tr), Breck P. Kent; 424 (b), Telegraph Color Library/Getty Images/ FPG International; 425 ©Michael & Patricia Fogden/Minden Pictures; 426 (bl), Visuals Unlimited; 426 (br), Kenneth Fink/Bruce Coleman, Inc.; 426 (t), Danilo B. Donadoni/ Bruce Coleman, Inc.; 427 (t), © Gail Shumway/Getty Images/FPG International; 427 (bl), Stanley Breeden/DRK Photo; 427 (br), Visuals Unlimited/Joe McDonald; 428 (b), Visuals Unlimited/Rob & Ann Simpson; 429 (tl), © Mike Severns/Getty Images/Stone; 429 (br), Kevin Schafer/Peter Arnold; 429 (bl), Wayne Lynch/DRK Photo; 429 (tr), Carl Ernst; 430 (bl), C. E. Schmida/F.P./Bruce Coleman, Inc.; 430 (tl), E. R. Degginger/ Bruce Coleman, Inc.; 430 (br), © Uhlenhut, Klaus/Animals Animals/Earth Scenes; 430 (tr), © Unknown PhotographerAnimals Animals/Earth Scenes; 431 © Kevin Schafer/ CORBIS; 432 Peter Van Steen/HRW; 434 (b), Steinhart Aquarium/Tom McHugh/ Photo Researchers; 434 (t), Visuals Unlimited/Rob & Ann Simpson; 435 (t), Brian Parker/Tom Stack; 435 (b), Leonard Lee Rue/Photo Researchers; 438 (r), Rick Bowmer/AP/Wide World Photos; 438 (tl), Victoria Smith/HRW; 439 (t), Karen M. Allen; 439 (b), Karen Allen

Chapter Seventeen 440-441 Bianca Lavies/National Geographic Society Image Collection; 442 (tr), © Stan Osolinski; 442 (br), © Gail Shumway/Getty Images/FPG International; 442 (l), G.C. Kelley/Photo Researchers; 446 (b), D. Cavagnaro/DRK Photo; 447 Hal H. Harrison/Grant Heilman; 448 (c), © Gavriel Jecan/Getty Images/ Stone; 448 (r), APL/J. Carnemolla/Westlight; 448 (l), © Kevin Schafer/Getty Images/ Stone; 449 (tl), Tui De Roy/Minden Pictures; 449 (b), Wayne Lankinen/Bruce Coleman; 449 (tr), S. Nielsen/DRK Photo; 450 (t), Stephen J. Krasemann/DRK Photo; 450 (b), Visuals Unlimited/S. Maslowski; 450 (cl), Frans Lanting/Minden Pictures; 451 (l), © Greg Vaughn/Getty Images/Stone; 451 (r), Fritz Polking/Bruce Coleman; 452 (l), Gerard Lacz/Animals Animals; 452 (r), Tim Davis/Photo Researchers; 452 (c), Nigel Dennis/Photo Researchers; 453 Hans Reinhard/Bruce Coleman; 454 (t), © David E. Myers/Getty Images/Stone; 454 (bl), © Tom Tietz/Getty Images/Stone; 454 (br), Sylvain Cordier/Photo Researchers; 455 © Kathy Bushue/Getty Images/Stone; 456 (l), Wayne Lynch/DRK Photo; 456 (r), John D. Cunningham/Visuals Unlimited; 457 (tr), © Gail Shumway/Getty Images/FPG International; 457 (tl), D. R. Kuhn/Bruce Coleman; 457 (br), Frans Lanting/Minden Pictures; 457 (bl), Gerry Ellis/Minden Pictures; 458 (tl), David Cavagnaro/Peter Arnold; 458 (tr), John Cancalosi; 458 (bl), Art Wolfe/Stone; 458 (br), Merlin D. Tuttle/Bat Conservation International; 459 (tl), © Gail Shumway/Getty Images/FPG International; 459 (tr), Arthur C. Smith III/Grant Heilman; 459 (bl), © Art Wolfe/Getty Images/Stone; 459 (br), Manoi Shah/Stone; 460 (br), © Scott Daniel Peterson/Liaison/Getty News Images; 460 (tl), © Gail Shumway/Getty Images/FPG International; 460 (bl), Roberto Arakaki/International Stock; 461 (tl), Flip Nicklin/Minden Pictures; 461 (b), Tom & Therisa Stack; 461 (tr), Pete Atkinson/NHPA; 462 (c), J. & P. Wegner/Animals Animals; 462 (bl), Inga Spence/Tom Stack; 462 (br), Martin Harvey/NHPA; 463 (b), Joe McDonald/Bruce Coleman; 463 (t), © Scott Daniel Peterson/Liaison/Getty News Images; 464 (r), Edwin & Peggy Bauer/Bruce Coleman; 464 (l), © Pavel German/NHPA; 465 Dave Watts/Nature Picture Library; 466 (bc), Jean-Paul Ferrero/AUSCAPE; 466 (br), Hans Reinhard/Bruce Coleman; 466 (bl), © Art Wolfe/Getty Images/Stone; 466 (t), © Mitsuaki Iwago/Minden Pictures; 467 (t), © Photo Researchers, Inc.; 469 (b), Sam Dudgeon/HRW; 470 (t), Tui De Roy/Minden Pictures; 470 (b), Merlin D. Tuttle/Bat Conservation International; 471 (t), © Stan Osolinski/Getty Images/FPG International; 474 (l), U.S. Navy, Brien Aho, HO/AP/Wide World Photos; 474 (r), Dave Watts/Nature Picture Library; 475 (r), William Munoz; 475 (l), William Munoz

Unit Six 476 (t), Carr Clifton/Minden Pictures; 476 (c), Getty Images/FPG International; 476 (b), Tom Brakefield/Corbis; 477 (tr), Photo Researchers; 477 (cr), SuperStock; 477 (bl), © David Young Wolff/Getty Images/Stone; 477 (cl), Alfred Eisenstaedt/Life Magazine © Time Inc.; 477 (br), © James Watt/Visuals Unlimited; 477 (tl), © Tony Hamblin/CORBIS

Chapter Eighteen 478-479 © Roine Magnusson/Getty Images/The Image Bank; 485 (r), © David M. Phillips/Visuals Unlimited; 487 (t), © George H. H. Huey/CORBIS; 487 (c), © D. Robert & Lorri Franz/CORBIS; 487 (b), © Jason Brindel Photography/ Alamy Photos; 488 (t), Laguna Photo/Liaison International/Getty News Images; 488 (b), Jeff Lepore/Photo Researchers; 490 Jeff Foott/AUSCAPE; 491 © Ross Hamilton/ Getty Images/Stone; 492 (l), Visuals Unlimited/Gerald & Buff Corsi; 492 (cr), Hans Pfletschinger/Peter Arnold; 493 (r), W. Peckover/Academy of Natural Sciences Philadelphia/VIREO; 493 (l), Leroy Simon/Visuals Unlimited; 494 (b), Ed Robinson/ Tom Stack & Associates; 494 (tl), © Telegraph Color Library/Getty Images/FPG International; 494 (tr), OSF/Peter Parks/Animals Animals Earth Scenes; 495 (t), © Gay Bumgarner/Getty Images/Stone; 495 (b), Carol Hughes/Bruce Coleman; 496 (tl), CSIRO Wildlife & Ecology; 496 (r), © Rick & Nora Bowers/Visuals Unlimited; 497 Leroy Simon/Visuals Unlimited; 498 Sam Dudgeon/HRW; 499 Sam Dudgeon/HRW; 499 Sam Dudgeon/HRW; 500 Leroy Simon/Visuals Unlimited; 504 (r), © National Geographic Image Collection/Darlyne Murawski; 504 (l), Digital Image copyright © 2005 PhotoDisc; 505 (r), Photo from the Dept. of Communication Services, North Carolina State University; 505 (l), Digital Image copyright © 2005 Artville

Chapter Nineteen 506-507 © Bryan and Cherry Alexander Photography; 512 (l), Diana L. Stratton/Tom Stack & Associates; 512 (r), © Stan Osolinski; 515 Kim Heacox/DRK Photo; 516 Sam Dudgeon/HRW; 517 (br), Sam Dudgeon/HRW; 517 (bl), Sam Dudgeon/HRW; 517 (t), Sam Dudgeon/HRW; 522 (t), Reed Saxon/AP/Wide World Photos; 523 (t), Neil Michel/Axiom; 523 (b), Neil Michel/Axiom

Chapter Twenty 524-525 © Studio Carlo Dani/Animals Animals/Earth Scenes; 530 (t), Grant Heilman; 530 (b), Tom Brakefield/Bruce Coleman; 532 (t), © Kathy Bushue/Getty Images/Stone; 534-535 (b), Stuart Westmorland/Getty Images/Stone; 534 (inset), Manfred Kage/Peter Arnold; 538 (b), © Jeff Hunter/Getty Images/The Image Bank; 542 (t), Dwight Kuhn; 542 (b), Hardie Truesdale/International Stock; 545 Sam Dudgeon/HRW; 550 (r), Dr. Verena Tunnicliffe; 550 (l), © Raymond Gehman/CORBIS; 551 (t), Lincoln P. Brower; 551 (b), © Royalty-Free/CORBIS

Chapter Twenty One 552-553 Martin Harvey/NHPA; 554 Larry Lefever/Grant Heilman Photography; 555 (t), J. Roche/Peter Arnold, Inc.; 555 (b), NASA; 556 (b), © Jacques Jangoux/Getty Images/Stone; 557 REUTERS/Jonathan Searle/NewsCom; 558 © Rex Ziak/Getty Images/Stone; 559 REUTERS/Jonathan Searle/NewsCom; 560 (l), Peter Van Steen/HRW; 560 (c), Peter Van Steen/HRW; 560 (r), Peter Van Steen/HRW; 561 (t), Argonne National Laboratory; 561 (b), Digital Image copyright © 2005 PhotoDisc; 562 (b), PhotoEdit; 562 (t), Kay Park-Rec Corp.; 563 (t), Peter Van Steen/HRW; 563 (b), Martin Bond/Science Photo Library/Photo Researchers; 564 (b), K. W. Fink/Bruce Coleman; 564 (t), © Sindre Ellingsen/Alamy Photos; 565 Stephen J. Krasemann/DRK Photo; 566 (bl), Sam Dudgeon/HRW; 566 (t), © Will & Deni McIntyre/Getty Images/Stone; 566 (br), Stephen J. Krasemann/DRK Photo; 567 (t), K. W. Fink/Bruce Coleman; 568 Peter Van Steen/HRW; 569 (tl), Tom Bean/DRK Photo; 569 (tr), Darrell Gulin/DRK Photo; 570 (l), Peter Van Steen/HRW; 570 (r), Peter Van Steen/HRW; 571 Larry Lefever/Grant Heilman Photography; 574 (l), Art Wolfe; 574 (r), © Toru Yamanaka/AFP/CORBIS; 575 (b), Gamma-Liaison/Getty News Images; 575 (t), Huntsville Times

Unit Seven 576 (t), Geoffrey Clifford/Woodfin Camp; 576 (c), J & L Weber/Peter Arnold; 576 (b), AP/Wide World Photos; 577 (cl), Brown Brothers; 577 (cr), SuperStock; 577 (tl), Gamma-Liaison/Getty News Images; 577 (bl), Enrico Ferorelli; 577 (tr), Sheila Terry/Science Photo Library/Photo Researchers, Inc.; 577 (br), © CORBIS

Chapter Twenty Two 578-579 AFP/CORBIS; 580-581 (b-bkgd), © David Madison/Getty Images/Stone; 582 Sam Dudgeon/HRW; 584 Sam Dudgeon/HRW; 586 (c), HRW Photo by Sergio Purtell/FOCA; 586 (r), HRW Photo by Sergio Purtell/FOCA; 586 (l), SP/FOCA/HRW Photo; 587 Scott Camazine/Photo Researchers, Inc.; 588 (bkgd), © Bob Torrez/Getty Images/Stone; 588 (bl-inset), Dr. E.R. Degginger; 588 (r-inset), Manfred Kage/Peter Arnold, Inc. ; 588 (tl-inset), © G.W. Willis/Biological Photo Service; 590 (r), Sam Dudgeon/HRW; 590 (l), Chris Hamilton; 592 Sam Dudgeon/HRW; 594 (bkgd), Peter Van Steen/HRW; 594 (l), Dr. Robert Becker/Custom Medical Stock Photo; 594 (r), Peter Van Steen/HRW; 597 Sam Dudgeon/HRW; 598 Sam Dudgeon/HRW; 599 (t), Sam Dudgeon/HRW; 599 (b), Peter Van Steen/HRW; 602 (l), © Dan McCoy/Rainbow; 602 (r), Reuters/David Gray/NewsCom; 603 (t), Photo courtesy of Dr. Zahra Beheshti; 603 (b), Creatas/PictureQuest

Chapter Twenty Three 604-605 © Nih/Science Source/Photo Researchers, Inc.; 608 (l), O. Meckes/Nicole Ottawa/Photo Researchers; 608 (r), O. Meckes/Nicole Ottawa/Photo Researchers; 610 © John Bavosi/Photo Researchers, Inc.; 612 Susumu Nishinaga/Science Photo Library/Photo Researchers, Inc.; 613 (b), Don Fawcett/Photo Researchers; 615 © Getty Images/The Image Bank; 618 © Collection CNRI/Phototake Inc./Alamy Photos; 623 (l), Matt Meadows/Peter Arnold, Inc.; 623 (r), Matt Meadows/Peter Arnold, Inc.; 624 (b), Sam Dudgeon/HRW; 630 (l), Richard T. Nowitz/Phototake; 630 (r), © Paul A. Souders/CORBIS; 631 Courtesy of the Boggy Creek Gang Camp

Chapter Twenty Four 632-633 © ISM/Phototake; 641 (t), Victoria Smith/HRW; 644 Getty Images/The Image Bank; 645 Stephen J. Krasemann/DRK Photo; 646 (b), Sam Dudgeon/HRW; 652 (l), J.H. Robinson/Photo Researchers; 652 (r), REUTERS/David Gray/NewsCom; 653 (t), Peter Van Steen/HRW

Chapter Twenty Five 654-655 Omikron/Photo Researchers, Inc.; 661 (t), Sam Dudgeon/HRW; 665 Sam Dudgeon/HRW; 672 (c), Sam Dudgeon/HRW; 673 Will & Deni McIntyre/Photo Researchers; 674 (r), Sam Dudgeon/HRW; 674 (l), Sam Dudgeon/HRW; 675 Sam Dudgeon/HRW; 677 (t), Sam Dudgeon/HRW; 680 (l), Victoria Smith/HRW; 680 (r), Mike Derer/AP/Wide World Photos; 681 (t), Photo courtesy of Dr. Bertha Madras; 681 (b), SPL/Photo Researchers, Inc.

Chapter Twenty Six 682-683 Photo Lennart Nilsson/Albert Bonniers Forlag AB, A Child Is Born, Dell Publishing Company; 684 (r), Visuals Unlimited/Cabisco; 684 (l), Innerspace Visions; 686 (b), Photo Researchers; 686 (t), Digital Image copyright © 2005 PhotoDisc Green; 687 © Charles Phillip/CORBIS; 690 Chip Henderson; 695 (tl), Petit Format/Nestle/Science Source/Photo Researchers, Inc.; 695 (cl), Photo Lennart Nilsson/Albert Bonniers Forlag AB, A Child Is Born, Dell Publishing Company; 695 (cr), Photo Lennart Nilsson/Albert Bonniers Forlag AB, A Child Is Born, Dell Publishing Company; 695 (br), Keith/Custom Medical Stock Photo; 695 (tr), David M. Phillips/Photo Researchers, Inc.; 696 (l), Peter Van Steen/HRW; 696 (cl), Peter Van Steen/HRW; 696 (c), Peter Van Steen/HRW; 696 (cr), Peter Van Steen/HRW; 696 (r), Peter Van Steen/HRW; 697 © Mark Harmel/Getty Images/FPG International; 699 Digital Image copyright © 2005 PhotoDisc; 700 Peter Van Steen/HRW; 701 Photo Lennart Nilsson/Albert Bonniers Forlag AB, A Child Is Born, Dell Publishing Company; 704 (r), Jim Tunell/Zuma Press/NewsCom; 704 (l), © Michael Clancy; 705 (l), ZEPHYR/Science Photo Library/Photo Researchers, Inc.; 705 (r), Salem Community College

Unit Eight 706 (c), Erich Schrempp/Photo Researchers, Inc.; 706 (t), Gervase Spencer/E.T. Archive; 707 (tl), Mary Evans Picture Library; 707 (tr), Wayne Floyd/Unicorn Stock Photos; 707 (cl), © LSHTM/Getty Images/Stone; 707 (cr), UPI/Corbis-Bettmann; 707 (b), Wang Haiyan/China Features/CORBIS

Chapter Twenty Seven 708-709 (t), © K. Kjeldsen/Photo Researchers, Inc.; 710 (br), CNRI/Science Photo Library/Photo Researchers; 710 (bl), Tektoff-RM/CNRI/Science Photo Library/Photo Researchers; 711 (t), Kent Wood/Photo Researchers; 712 (b), Peter Van Steen/HRW ; 714 (b), Peter Van Steen/HRW; 718 (t), John Langford/HRW Photo; 719 (b), Clinical Radiology Dept., Salisbury District Hospital/Science Photo Library/Photo Researchers; 719 (t), SuperStock; 720 (b), Photo Lennart Nilsson/Albert Bonniers Forlag AB; 720 (tl), Dr. A. Liepins/Science Photo Library/Photo Researchers; 720 (tr), Dr. A. Liepins/Science Photo Library/Photo Researchers; 722 Sam Dudgeon/HRW; 725 (t), Peter Van Steen/HRW ; 728 (l), E. R. Degginger/Bruce Coleman; 728 (r), Chris Rogers/Index Stock Imagery, Inc.; 729 (t), Peter Van Steen/HRW; 729 (b), Corbis

Chapter Twenty Eight 730-731 © Arthur Tilley/Getty Images/Taxi; 732 Peter Van Steen/HRW; 733 (b), Peter Van Steen/HRW; 733 (t), Sam Dudgeon/HRW; 734 (c), Image Copyright ©2004 PhotoDisc, Inc./HRW; 734 (t), Image Copyright ©2004 PhotoDisc, Inc./HRW; 734 (bl), CORBIS Images/HRW; 734 (br), CORBIS Images/HRW; 735 © John Kelly/Getty Images/Stone; 736 John Burwell/FoodPix; 737 Peter Van Steen/HRW; 738 Peter Van Steen/HRW; 739 (b), Peter Van Steen/HRW; 739 (t), ©1999 Steven Foster; 740 (tl), E. Dirksen/Photo Researchers; 740 (b), Spencer Grant/Photo Researchers, Inc.; 740 (tr), Dr. Andrew P. Evans/Indiana University; 742 Jeff Greenberg/PhotoEdit; 743 Mike Siluk/The Image Works; 744 Sam Dudgeon/HRW; 745 (t), © Rob Van Petten/Getty Images/The Image Bank; 745 (b), Peter Van Steen/HRW; 746 Sam Dudgeon/HRW; 748 (b), Peter Van Steen/HRW; 748 (t), © Mug Shots/CORBIS; 749 Peter Van Steen/HRW; 750 Digital Image copyright © 2005 PhotoDisc; 752 (t), © John Kelly/Getty Images/Stone; 752 (b), Peter Van Steen/HRW; 753 (t), Peter Van Steen/HRW; 753 (b), Peter Van Steen/HRW; 756 (l), Brian Hagiwara/FoodPix; 757 (r), Courtesy Russell Selger; 757 (l), © Eyebyte/Alamy Photos

Lab Book/Appendix "LabBook Header", "L", Corbis Images; "a", Letraset Phototone; "b", and "B", HRW; "o", and "k", images ©2006 PhotoDisc/HRW; 758 (l, tr, br), Sam Dudgeon/HRW; 758 (c), Scott Van Osdol/HRW; 761 (t), Sam Dudgeon/HRW; 761 (c), Sam Dudgeon/HRW; 761 (b), Sam Dudgeon/HRW; 763 Sam Dudgeon/HRW; 764 (tl), Runk/Schoenberger/Grant Heilman; 764 (tc), Runk/Schoenberger/Grant Heilman; 764 (tr), Michael Abbey/Photo Researchers, Inc.; 764 (tr), Sam Dudgeon/HRW; 764 (br), Runk/Schoenberger/Grant Heilman; 765 (b), Sam Dudgeon/HRW; 765 (c), Sam Dudgeon/HRW; 766 Sam Dudgeon/HRW; 769 (all), Sam Dudgeon/HRW; 772 (tr), Peter Van Steen/HRW; 772 (c), Peter Van Steen/HRW; 772 (br), Peter Van Steen/HRW; 773 Sam Dudgeon/HRW; 776 (b), Breck P. Kent; 776 (br), Stephen J. Krasemann/Photo Researchers; 776 (c), Visuals Unlimited/R. Calentine; 776 (t), Runk/Schoenberger/Grant Heilman; 777 Sam Dudgeon/HRW; 779 (t), John Langford/HRW Photo; 779 (b), John Langford/HRW Photo; 780 (t), Sam Dudgeon/HRW; 780 (c), Sam Dudgeon/HRW; 782 (t), Sam Dudgeon/HRW; 782 (b), Sam Dudgeon/HRW; 784 Rod Planck/Photo Researchers; 785 Peter Van Steen/HRW; 788 Peter Van Steen/HRW; 789 (tr), © Kenneth Gabrielsen; 789 (cl), Visuals Unlimited/Doug Sokell; 789 (br), Larry Nielsen/Peter Arnold; 789 (bl), Phil Degginger; 791 Peter Van Steen/HRW; 793 Peter Van Steen/HRW; 794 Sam Dudgeon/HRW; 795 (t), Sam Dudgeon/HRW; 795 (c), Sam Dudgeon/HRW; 795 (b), Sam Dudgeon/HRW; 796 Sam Dudgeon/HRW; 797 Sam Dudgeon/HRW; 801 Peter Van Steen/HRW; 802 (t), Sam Dudgeon/HRW; 802 (b), Sam Dudgeon/HRW; 811 Sam Dudgeon/HRW; 812 Sam Dudgeon/HRW; 817 (t), Peter Van Steen/HRW; 817 (b), Sam Dudgeon/HRW; 830 CENCO